INTERNATIONAL ENCYCLOPEDIA OF DANCE

INTERNATIONAL ENCYCLOPEDIA OF

DANCE

A project of Dance Perspectives Foundation, Inc.

FOUNDING EDITOR

Selma Jeanne Cohen

AREA EDITORS

George Dorris   Nancy Goldner   Beate Gordon
Nancy Reynolds   David Vaughan
Suzanne Youngerman

CONSULTANTS

Thomas F. Kelly   Horst Koegler   Richard Ralph
Elizabeth Souritz

VOLUME 2

OXFORD UNIVERSITY PRESS

New York   1998   Oxford

OXFORD UNIVERSITY PRESS

Oxford   New York
Athens   Auckland   Bangkok   Bogotá   Bombay
Buenos Aires   Calcutta   Cape Town   Dar es Salaam
Delhi   Florence   Hong Kong   Istanbul   Karachi
Kuala Lumpur   Madras   Madrid   Melbourne
Mexico City   Nairobi   Paris   Singapore
Taipei   Tokyo   Toronto   Warsaw
and associated companies in
Berlin   Ibadan

Copyright © 1998 by Oxford University Press, Inc.

Published by Oxford University Press, Inc.,
198 Madison Avenue, New York, New York 10016

Oxford is a registered trademark of Oxford University Press

This work was initiated with funds granted by the
National Endowment for the Humanities,
a federal agency

Library of Congress Cataloging-in-Publication Data
International encyclopedia of dance : a project of Dance
Perspectives Foundation, Inc. / founding editor, Selma Jeanne Cohen;
area editors, George Dorris et al.; consultants, Thomas F. Kelly et al.
p.   cm.
Includes bibliographical references and index.
1. Dance—Encyclopedias. 2. Ballet—Encyclopedias. I. Cohen,
Selma Jeanne, 1920-. II. Dance Perspectives Foundation.
GV1585.I586   1998   97-36562   792.6′2′03—dc21   CIP
ISBN 0-19-509462-X (set)
ISBN 0-19-512306-9 (vol. 2)

Printing (last digit): 9 8 7 6 5 4 3 2

Printed in the United States of America
on acid-free paper

BRUCE, CHRISTOPHER (born 3 October 1945 in Leicester), British dancer and choreographer. Bruce studied at the Rambert School and joined the Ballet Rambert as a dancer in 1963. In 1967 his performance of the title role in Glen Tetley's *Pierrot Lunaire* established him as one of the finest British male dancers of his generation. He has choreographed regularly for Ballet Rambert since 1969 (his first work was *George Frideric*) and was appointed associate director in 1975. In 1974 he was awarded the London *Evening Standard*'s first dance award. From 1979 to 1987, Bruce was associate choreographer of the Ballet Rambert, from 1986 to 1991 associate choreographer of English National Ballet (then known as the London Festival Ballet), and was appointed resident choreographer with the Houston Ballet in 1989. Since the 1980s, he has revived and created works for companies throughout Europe and in Israel and Australia; he prefers to work with companies with whom he can build a relationship and personally supervise the staging and revival of his dances. He has choreographed for operas and musicals, including *Joseph and the Amazing Technicolor Dreamcoat* (1972) and *Mutiny* (1985), and has also worked in straight theater with the Royal Shakespeare Company.

In most of his works, Bruce endeavors to confront universal problems. In *Wings* (1971), he treated the theme of human conflict and isolation, drawing on images of birds; in *Weekend* (1974), he dealt with impermanent relationships. Other pieces have more specific frames of reference: *for these who die as cattle* (1972) is about the horrors of war (the title is from a poem by Wilfred Owen); *Ghost Dances* (1981) and *Silence Is the End of Our Song* (1983, for the Royal Danish Ballet) are compassionate statements about iniquitous political systems in South America; and *Land* (1985, for the London Festival Ballet; revived for Rambert Dance Company in 1993) deals with invasion and its victors and victims. *Swansong* (1987, for London Festival Ballet) is about liberation of the soul from physical imprisonment and is inspired by the book *A Man* by Oriana Fallaci as well as Bruce's support for Amnesty International. *Waiting* (1993, for London Contemporary Dance Theatre), set in a South African Township, utilizes a stark decor by Marian Bruce and suggests a corrugated iron prison or stockade. Errolyn Wallen's music, written to celebrate Nelson Mandela's release, displays the dramatic intensity and physical weight characteristic of Bruce's choreographic style. The full-length *Cruel Garden* (1977), a collaboration with mime artist Lindsay Kemp, is a panorama of the life and work of Federico García Lorca, embracing prewar Spain's traditions, feudalism, poverty, and ultimate capitulation to fascism. Bruce has also created dances about children emerging into adolescence—*Ancient Voices of Children* (1975) and *Preludes and Songs* (1980)—and pieces with light or humorous content, such as *Night with Waning Moon* (1979), in which he introduces *commedia dell'arte* characters. *Sergeant Early's Dream* (1984) depicts a sturdy folk community facing the tragedy of separation but also showing the high spirited anticipation of life in the New World.

Bruce's early work was greatly influenced by Tetley, in a style that derived from both Martha Graham and ballet. Since 1981, Bruce has incorporated into his vocabulary movements loosely based on folk dance, introducing a new intricacy of footwork and a greater rhythmic variety and connection with musical structure. Some recent dances have drawn upon popular music and its themes and have incorporated social dance steps, such as *The Dream Is Over* (1986, for the Cullberg Ballet) to music by John Lennon; *Rooster* (1991, for the Geneva Ballet, revived for the London Contemporary Dance Theatre in 1992) to music by the Rolling Stones; *Moonshine* (1993, for Netherlands Dance Theater 3) to music by Bob Dylan; and *Swansong*, which includes protracted tap dance routines for the interrogators. Fluid, free torso movement and an earthy feeling of gravity have remained characteristic of his work.

Many of his dances are cast in suite form—series of short dances featuring different combinations of performers. In the early 1970s, he commissioned scores (three from Brian Hodgson) to fit his existing conception of a structure. Since 1974 he has favored existing music, often as his creative starting point—notably five scores by George Crumb (*Ancient Voices of Children* and *Black Angels*, 1976; *Echoes of a Night Sky*, 1977; *Night with Waning Moon*, 1979; and *Song*, 1988); and two works in collaboration with the composer Philip Chambon (*Swansong* and *Nature Dances*). Recent work for Rambert Dance Company has seen the use of scores by the contemporary composers Michael Nyman (*Meeting Point*, 1995; *Quicksilver*, 1996) and Henryk Górecki (*Crossing*, 1994). Bruce has

BRUCE. Matz Skoog, Koen Onzia, and Kevin Richmond, the original cast, in Bruce's *Swansong* (1987), presented by the London Festival Ballet. (Photograph by Bill Cooper; used by permission.)

worked frequently with designers Nadine Baylis, Pamela Marre, and Walter Nobbe.

In April 1994 he renewed his close association with Rambert Dance Company with his appointment as artistic director. He has embarked upon a highly ambitious new project which so far has included enlarging the company from seventeen to twenty-five dancers with the intention of training an ensemble capable of bridging the gap between classical ballet and contemporary dance, and has commissioned new works for the company by internationally renowned choreographers such as Jiří Kylián. In March 1993 Bruce received the International Theatre Institute Award for excellence in international dance.

BIBLIOGRAPHY

Austin, Richard. *Birth of a Ballet*. London, 1976.
Brinson, Peter, and Clement Crisp. *The Pan Book of Ballet and Dance*. Rev. ed. London, 1981.
Gow, Gordon. "Christopher Bruce, Dancer and Choreographer." *The Dancing Times* (March 1973): 304–305.
Kane, Angela. "Christopher Bruce's Choreography: Inroads or Retracing Old Steps?" *The Dancing Times* 82 (October 1991): 44–53.
Nugent, Ann. "Waiting with Certainty." *Dance Now* 2 (Autumn 1993): 18–21.

STEPHANIE JORDAN and BONNIE ROWELL

BRUHN, ERIK (Erik Belton Evers Bruhn; born 3 October 1928 in Copenhagen, died 1 April 1986 in Toronto), Danish dancer, choreographer, and company director.

Erik Bruhn is considered one of the finest dancers ever produced by the Royal Danish Ballet School and is generally acknowledged as one of the foremost ballet artists of the twentieth century.

Bruhn began his dance training when he was six years old at a local ballet school in the village of Gentofte, a few miles from Copenhagen. He entered the ballet school of the Royal Theater in Copenhagen in 1937, when he was nine, and pursued his studies there—in academic subjects as well as dancing—for the next ten years. The ballet teacher of greatest importance to him as a youth was Harald Lander. In 1942, at age fourteen, Bruhn appeared as a principal dancer in a student production of August Bournonville's *Napoli* and displayed in public for the first time the purity of his line, the lightness of his jump, the cleanness of his footwork, and his exceptional facility for the Bournonville technique. He would later pursue his studies with Vera Volkova, who came to Copenhagen in 1951, and with Stanislas Idzikowski in London.

Soon after joining the Royal Danish Ballet in 1947, Bruhn was granted the unusual privilege of a six-month leave of absence that permitted him to accept an engagement as a guest artist with the London-based Metropolitan Ballet. In his first season with this company he danced leading roles in the Petipa classics *Swan Lake* and *The Sleeping Beauty* and in Michel Fokine's *Les Sylphides* and *Le Spectre de la Rose*. He also danced the first role created especially for him, in Frank Staff's *The Lovers' Gallery*

(1947). Upon returning to Copenhagen and joining the Royal Danish Ballet in the spring of 1948, Bruhn was almost immediately cast in leading roles in ballets that Léonide Massine was mounting for the company, *Le Beau Danube* and *Symphonie Fantastique*. In these and other works Bruhn dazzled the Danish audiences and critics with his astonishing technical abilities. He returned to the Metropolitan Ballet for the summer season in 1948, creating roles in *Designs with Strings* (1948) by John Taras—in which he was paired with the youthful Svetlana Beriosova—and *The Pilgrim's Progress* (1948) by Andrée Howard.

In June 1949 Bruhn and Margrethe Schanne appeared in excerpts from act 2 of Bournonville's *La Sylphide* at a gala performance at the Royal Theater in Copenhagen. In the audience were Hans Beck, of the Royal Danish Ballet School, and an official of Ballet Theatre Foundation from New York. Both men were impressed by Bruhn's prodigious performance as James, and he was consequently invited to join Ballet Theatre as a guest. The management of the Royal Danish Ballet was once again indulgent: not only was Bruhn promoted to *solodanser* ("soloist," or "principal dancer") in the company and cast in leading roles in the repertory but he was once again granted a leave of absence that allowed him to accept an attractive engagement overseas.

Bruhn's first season with Ballet Theatre in New York was the beginning of what would prove to be a truly extraordinary international career. He danced both in the United States and in Denmark from 1949 to 1956, when he finally severed his official connection with the Royal Danish Ballet. In the following three decades, he appeared as guest artist with numerous companies, including the New York City Ballet, the Royal Ballet (London), the Paris Opera Ballet, the Stuttgart Ballet, the Australian Ballet, La Scala Ballet (Milan), the Rome Opera Ballet, the Harkness Ballet, the National Ballet of Canada, and, frequently, the Royal Danish Ballet. His longest associations were with Ballet Theatre, later called American Ballet Theatre (1955–1958, 1960–1961, 1968–1969), and the National Ballet of Canada (1973–1981). From 1967 to 1971 he served as artistic director of the Royal Swedish Ballet, and from 1983 until his death in the spring of 1986 he was artistic director of the National Ballet of Canada.

In the first part of his career, Bruhn was the epitome of the classical dancer—*le danseur noble et sérieux*—and one of the most elegant performers in the world. With his pale Nordic beauty, immaculate technique, innate musicality, and strong dramatic sense, he was perfectly suited to dance all the princes in the classical repertory—*Swan Lake, The Sleeping Beauty, The Nutcracker*—as well as the heroes of the Bournonville repertory. Among the latter, James in *La Sylphide* was one of Bruhn's most beautiful and touching portrayals. His range extended from the poetic youth in *Les Sylphides* to the mischievous Franz in *Coppélia* to one of the virtuoso roles in Lander's *Études*, which he first danced in 1951 and later memorably repeated on Danish television in 1969.

The early part of Bruhn's performing career reached a climax on 1 May 1955, when he first danced Albrecht in *Giselle*, partnering the legendary English ballerina Alicia Markova, in a matinee performance with Ballet Theatre at the Metropolitan Opera House in New York. John Martin, dance critic for the *New York Times*, commented:

> It may well be a date to write down in the history books, for it was as if the greatest Giselle of today were handing over a sacred trust to what is probably the greatest Albrecht of tomorrow. . . . In the second act, Mr. Bruhn really came into his own. His dancing was like velvet, and his support of Miss Markova was easy, gracious, and totally in accord with her, in both mood and technique. . . . The final parting, when at dawn Giselle must return to the grave, was as deeply moving a scene as one has ever encountered in the ballet.
>
> (Quoted in Gruen, 1979, p. 67)

This single performance brought Bruhn enormous critical acclaim, won him a promotion to first soloist with Ballet Theatre, and made him famous as one of the world's greatest classical dancers.

Renowned for his partnering skills as well as his solo execution, Bruhn danced with many of the leading ballerinas of his generation, including Sonia Arova, Nora Kaye, Alicia Alonso, Lupe Serrano, Mona Vangsaae, Kirstin Simone, Maria Tallchief, Violette Verdy, Yvette Chauviré, Cynthia Gregory, Carla Fracci, and Natalia Makarova. He formed especially memorable partnerships with Arova, Tallchief, Fracci, and Makarova. It is characteristic of Bruhn that he continued to work on the challenging role of Albrecht, studying it thoroughly before he danced it on film in 1968 with Fracci, who became his most frequent partner in *Giselle* during the later years of his dancing career.

From the mid-1950s onward, Bruhn continued to grow as a dancer, adding a rich range of feelings to his superb technique and natural authority on stage. He strove especially to bring the princes of the classical repertory to full-blooded life and to present them as real men facing real, although fantastic problems. In the modern repertory, he made a seamless transition from the quintessential *danseur noble* to a mature and powerful character dancer. Two roles still bear his indelible stamp: in 1958 he portrayed a polished, obsequious, yet brutal Jean in Birgit Cullberg's *Miss Julie*, and in 1960 he danced for the first time his stunning interpretation of Don José in Roland Petit's *Carmen*, creating a brooding figure of rare pride and violent passion.

During the 1960s Bruhn's career as an international guest artist continued to flourish. Early in the decade he

BRUHN. An immaculate technician and *premier danseur par excellence,* Bruhn appears here in one of his signature roles, James in August Bournonville's *La Sylphide.* (Photograph © 1961 by Rigmor Mydtskov; used by permission.)

met Rudolf Nureyev, the young Russian superstar who had just defected from the Soviet Union, and the two men formed a friendship that lasted throughout their lives. With the ballerina Sonia Arova, they also formed a small touring group, which lasted only a short time. For this company, Bruhn choreographed two works in 1962, *Fantasie,* set to traditional Spanish music, and *Toccata and Fugue,* to the music of J. S. Bach. That same year he made *Serenade,* set to music by Ole Olsen, for the Bavarian State Opera Ballet in Munich, and in 1965 he created *Scottish Fantasy,* to music by George Crumb, for the Harkness Ballet. None of these works revealed that he possessed any significant talent as a choreographer.

As a stage director, however, Bruhn proved to be wonderfully adept at mounting the classics. From the Bournonville repertory, he staged the famous pas de six from *Napoli* for the Royal Ballet (London), the equally well-known pas de deux from *Flower Festival in Genzano* for several major ballet companies, and the rarely seen pas de trois from *La Ventana* for American Ballet Theatre,

where he danced it with Cynthia Gregory and Rudolf Nureyev. He mounted full-length productions of *La Sylphide* for the National Ballet of Canada, the Rome Opera Ballet, the Royal Swedish Ballet, American Ballet Theatre, and the Australian Ballet. He also mounted *Giselle* for the Royal Danish Ballet and the Royal Swedish Ballet, *Coppélia* for the National Ballet of Canada, and *Swan Lake* for the Rome Opera Ballet and, twice, for the National Ballet of Canada, first in 1967 and again in 1979. In all these works he combined his eminent sense of style with his understanding that an artist must have a personal relationship to these old ballets if they are to be made interesting to modern audiences.

Bruhn continued to perform almost to the end of his life. Among his new roles in the 1970s were a pas de deux created for him and Makarova in Alvin Ailey's *The River* (1971), the title role in Ulf Gadd's *The Miraculous Mandarin,* and Claudius in John Neumeier's *Hamlet—Connotations.* He also undertook the title roles in Fokine's *Petrouchka,* in José Limón's *The Moor's Pavane,* and in James Clouser's *Rasputin, the Holy Devil* (1978) as well as the character parts of Doctor Coppélius in *Coppélia* and Madge, the Witch, in *La Sylphide.*

In recognition of his talents and accomplishments, Bruhn was the recipient of numerous honors and awards. In 1963 he was named a knight of the Order of Dannebrog by King Frederick IX of Denmark, and in Paris he was presented with the Nijinsky Prize, awarded by the Polish Ministry of Culture for significant contribution to the world of dance. He was elected to the Roll of Honor of the Students' Association of Denmark in 1965, and in New York he was given a *Dance Magazine* Award in 1968. He received a Diplôme d'Honneur from the Canadian Conference of the Arts in 1974 and a Litteris et Artibus Medal from the Swedish government in 1980.

[*See also* American Ballet Theatre; National Ballet of Canada; Royal Swedish Ballet.]

BIBLIOGRAPHY

Aschengreen, Erik. "Bruhn, Erik." In *Dansk biografisk leksikon.* 3d ed. Copenhagen, 1979–.

Bland, Alexander, and John Percival. *Men Dancing: Performers and Performances.* New York, 1984.

Bruhn, Erik. "Beyond Technique." *Dance Perspectives* 36 (1968). A short monograph that includes Bruhn's description of his manner of preparing his major roles.

Bruhn, Erik, and Lillian Moore. *Bournonville and Ballet Technique: Studies and Comments on August Bournonville's "Études choréographiques."* London and New York, 1961.

Gruen, John. *Erik Bruhn, Danseur Noble.* New York, 1979. Includes a chronology of roles and productions, a filmography, and a selected bibliography.

Gruen, John. "Erik Bruhn." In Gruen's *People Who Dance: Twenty-Two Dancers Tell Their Own Stories.* Princeton, N.J., 1988.

Kragh-Jacobsen, Svend. *Æreskunstenren Erik Bruhn.* Copenhagen, 1965.

Lidova, Irène. "Erik Bruhn." *Saisons de la danse,* no. 17 (October 1969): 18–21.

Neufeld, James. *Power to Rise: The Story of the National Ballet of Canada.* Toronto, 1996.
Stuart, Otis. *Perpetual Motion: The Public and Private Lives of Rudolf Nureyev.* New York, 1995.

ERIK ASCHENGREEN

BUBBLES, JOHN W. (John Sublett; born 19 February 1902 in Louisville, Kentucky, died 18 May 1986 in Los Angeles), American tap dancer and singer. Nicknamed "Bubber," Bubbles is best known for his original portrayal of Sportin' Life in George Gershwin's *Porgy and Bess* (1935) and as one half of the famous singing-and-dancing comedy act of Buck and Bubbles. The act, which began when the ten-year-old Bubbles teamed with six-year-old Ford Lee ("Buck") Washington, lasted almost fifty years. The two were featured in the *Ziegfeld Follies of 1931* and were the first black artists to appear at New York's Radio City Music Hall.

Known as "the father of rhythm," Bubbles influenced an entire generation of dancers during tap dancing's innovative period of the 1920s and 1930s. He made tap a jazz

BUBBLES. A 1935 portrait of Bubbles as Sportin' Life in George Gershwin's *Porgy and Bess*. (Photograph by Carl Van Vechten; used by permission of the Estate of Carl Van Vechten.)

form when he created new accents by the drop of his heels, introducing gradations of tone and complex syncopations. Tap dancers previously had tended to stay on their toes; when Bubbles experimented with turns and heel drops, he changed the accenting and timing.

Tap dancers traveled from around the country to watch Bubbles work out at the Hoofers Club in Harlem and appear in three shows a day in vaudeville theaters. Because of all the attention, he changed his routine with every show in order to prevent dancers from stealing his steps; however, he was amused when someone was able to unravel his material.

Bubbles appeared in films such as *Varsity Show* (1937), *Cabin in the Sky* (1943), and *A Song Is Born* (1948). In 1967, while performing with Judy Garland at the Palace Theater in New York, he suffered a stroke that left him paralyzed on the left side. Nevertheless he continued to perform for several years as a singer, passing on his unique rhythmic sensibility from a wheelchair. George Wein flew Bubbles from his Los Angeles home to appear at the Newport Jazz Festival and in the show *Black Broadway* (1979–1980). In 1980 he also received the American Guild of Variety Artists (AGVA) Life Achievement Award.

[*See also* Tap Dance.]

BIBLIOGRAPHY
Frank, Rusty E. *Tap! The Greatest Tap Dance Stars and Their Stories, 1900–1955.* Rev. ed. New York, 1994.
Horosko, Marian. "Tap, Tapping, and Tappers." *Dance Magazine* (October 1971): 32–37.
Smith, Bill. *The Vaudevillians.* New York, 1976.
Stearns, Marshall, and Jean Stearns. *Jazz Dance.* Rev. ed. New York, 1994.

FILM.   Stephan Chodorov, *Honi Coles: The Class Act of Tap* (1993).

JANE GOLDBERG

BUGAKU. Imperial Japanese court dances are subsumed under the generic term *bugaku.* Purely instrumental performances *(kangen)* combined with *bugaku* dances are known as *gagaku,* which encompasses the entire tradition of Japanese court music and dance. Of continental Asian origin, *bugaku* first came to Japan via the Korean peninsula in the sixth century CE and by the eighth century was established in Japanese court life. In the ninth century the diverse forms of music and dance then existing in Japan were collected and divided into two repertories, *tōgaku* (pieces from China, Southeast Asia, and India) and *komagaku* (music from Korea and Manchuria). Some of the music was adapted to Japanese styles, and new pieces were composed. Murasaki Shikibu's eleventh-century novel of courtly life, *The Tale of Genji,* describes courtiers performing such music and dances, some of which survive. The twelfth-century *Shinzei kogaku zu* scroll shows how viable and varied were the dance, music, and entertainment of the Heian period (794–1185).

Bugaku traditions declined after the beginning of the Kamakura period (1185–1333), but they were maintained by modest imperial support, incorporation into Buddhist services, and use at Shintō shrines. The dances were also kept alive by private preservation groups. The Meiji Restoration, a period of modernization that began in 1868, included a movement to restore Japanese traditions. Accordingly, the history, theory, and practice of *bugaku* became a focus of both university and religious-study programs. The social and financial status of *bugaku* began to improve in the 1950s. The form has also influenced and been influenced by contemporary international dance.

Following Confucian theory, *tōgaku* dances are considered "left" and emphasize red in their costumes, while *komagaku* are "right" and use green. *Tōgaku* dances are accompanied by wind and percussion instruments, including the *ryūteki* (a flute), the *hichiriki* (a small double-reed instrument), and the *shō* (a small mouth organ). *Komagaku* dances are accompanied by the *hichiriki*, the *komabue* (a flute that differs from the *ryūteki*), and three percussion instruments. "Left" dances are said to be stronger and "right" to be more fluid, but each repertory has a variety of dances. *Bun no mai* dances, which constitute the largest portion of the repertory, depict courtiers of the Heian period. *Bu no mai* are military-style dances

BUGAKU. Dancer at Iwashimizu-Hachimangu Shrine near Kyoto, Japan. (Photograph © 1985 by Jack Vartoogian; used by permission.)

of the same period. *Hashiri-mai* are vigorous solo dances with costumes, masks, and movements unique to the genre. Outside the palace children perform *dobu* dances, which are divided into *karyōbin* (named after the bird that danced when Buddha attained enlightenment) and *kochō* (a butterfly dance).

A full *bugaku* program usually begins with a short *embu* purification dance, first in a left form and then in a right. Sometimes they are performed together, in which case two kinds of music combine. The next section, called *tsugaimono*, contains left and right dances that are carefully paired in both number of pieces and number of performers. *Hashiri mai* follows. A program closes with *chōgeishi* music accompanying the exits of the last dancers. The entire program and each dance are guided by a fundamental aesthetic principle called *jo ha kyū*, or "introduction, scattering, and rushing toward the end." This principle was first noted in *bugaku* and has remained basic to explanations of all Japanese music and dance for more than a thousand years.

About sixty-two pieces are known in the *bugaku* repertory; in addition six Shintō-related dances are accompanied by song. The titles of pieces reflect the civilizations of ancient Asia. Southeast Asian influence is seen in *Bato*, in which a boy hunts a tiger that killed his father; *Soriko* is the name of a Korean winemaker; and *Tagyūraku* is an abstraction of an ancient polo game. *Karyōbin* dancers, who represent a mythical bird whose origin is India, wear wings and strike cymbals.

All *bugaku* dances tend to be slow, stylized, and symmetrical in their patterns. The dramatic and narrative aspects of the original dances have long since been abstracted into a set formalism. All movements made by the feet, head, and body during a *bugaku* dance have specific names, and their combinations are highly conventional. There are subtle differences between left and right renderings of some of the movements, for example the sliding of the feet. Thus a technical appreciation of *bugaku* requires an awareness and concentration equal to that found in the tea ceremony or the viewing of ink drawings. Even without such training, one can appreciate the serious, slow pace and abstract, symmetrical design of these dances. They are distant but beautiful remnants of one of the most refined and colorful periods in world dance history.

[See also Asian Dance Traditions, *overview article;* Gagaku; *and* Japan, *overview article.*]

BIBLIOGRAPHY

Bugaku: Treasures from the Kasuga Shrine. Nara, 1984.
Harich-Schneider, Eta. *A History of Japanese Music.* London, 1973.
Malm, Joyce Rutherford. "The Legacy of Nihon Buyō." *Dance Research Journal* 9 (Spring–Summer 1977): 12–24.
Wolz, Carl. *Bugaku: Japanese Court Dance.* Providence, R.I., 1971.

VIDEOTAPE. *Gagaku,* produced by Eugene Enrico for the Early Music Television Series, University of Oklahoma (1990).

WILLIAM P. MALM

BULGARIA. [*To survey traditional and theatrical dance in Bulgaria, this entry comprises two articles: the first article discusses folk and traditional dance; the second traces the history of theatrical dance.*]

Folk and Traditional Dance

Bulgaria's known dance heritage dates to the ancient Thracian tribes that inhabited the Balkan Peninsula in the third millennium BCE. Their cult of the god Dionysos, which later became an element of ancient Greek theater, assigned a prominent place to music and dance. From the sixth century BCE to the sixth century CE, when Bulgaria was colonized successively by the ancient Greek city-states, by Macedon, and by Rome, dance was included in theatrical spectacles. The gladiatorial fights of the Roman era were often accompanied by pantomime and dance interludes. During the Middle Ages, after the foundation of the Bulgarian state (679–681), the *skomrachs* (descendants of the ancient mimes and dancers) appeared; they were wandering actors, singers, dancers, and acrobats, similar to the troubadours of medieval Europe.

Folk Dance. Bulgaria's professional musical culture was suppressed by Ottoman domination (1394–1878). As a result, folk dance and music assumed the sociocultural functions of professional music and dance, and autonomous institutions were established for their maintenance. This trend was reinforced by an ethnic self-consciousness that surfaced toward the end of the Ottoman period, which was manifested in a renaissance of folklore.

Bulgaria's dances, which are closely involved with its complex history, still exhibit the characteristics and styles of past historical periods. Many dances were performed in conjunction with special occasions in the Bulgarian folk calendar, which associates life's most prominent events (birth, premarital initiation, marriage, and death) with the change of seasons and the agricultural year. Ritual, practical, and artistic activities centered around these key events.

For the Bulgarian peasant, autumn and winter were a period of light work. This became the time for male initiations and premarital rites—including singing, dancing, masquerades, and games. During the winter, large festive dances called *horos* (or *khoros*) were performed by both sexes in the village square on Christian occasions—on Saint Nicholas's Day, Christmas Day, and Epiphany. In addition to the *horo*-leading songs sung by the women, these dances were accompanied by bagpipes *(gayda)*, flutes *(kaval)*, drums, and other folk instruments. Bachelors who had gone through the male initiation rites could display their skill by leading these dances, demonstrating their manliness and readiness for marriage. The *horo* dances allowed young men and women to meet and fall in love, and often led to a ritual abduction of marriageable maidens.

Winter was also the time for weddings. Ritual songs and dances of purification, mainly for women, alternated with impetuous bacchanals and handkerchief dances, mainly for men. This was also a time for indoor festivities and working bees, which often included small *horo* dances or dance solos and duets. On Midwives' Day dur-

BULGARIA: Folk and Traditional Dance. Women of the Bulgarian National Ensemble in a theatrical presentation of a folkloric dance. Traditionally, dances for Bulgarian women are more closely related to ritual traditions, while the men's dances tend to be more purely recreational. (Photograph from the Dance Collection, New York Public Library for the Performing Arts.)

ing this season, women had the unique opportunity to hold a female bacchanalia that allowed them to drink wine, dance, lead the *horo*, joke, and engage in other typically male amusements.

For Christians, the culmination of the yearly cycle was the first Sunday of Lent, when winter rituals and dances gave way to those of spring. On that day, long mixed-sex *horos* were danced, perhaps to enhance fertility: the men's movements included kneeling and stamping to awaken and "fertilize" the earth. All members of the community were required to take part in this round dance, lending their energy and force to make the earth fertile.

During Lent mixed *horos* with instrumental music were banned, but this was a time for premarital initiation rites for girls—for Buenets, Kumichene, trekking, singing in the woods, and such. Major Christian holidays, such as Easter or Saint George's Day, were celebrated with slow round dances accompanied by singing, some secular and others with a ceremonial character. In the ritual Easter and Saint George's Day *horos*, the newly initiated girls and those married in the past winter "took the pardon"; ritual bans were dropped, and mixed *horo* dances to instrumental music were resumed. The newly initiated girls proclaimed their new social status by taking part in the *horo* dances.

The hard agricultural labor of the late spring and summer precluded much dancing, but during the harvest small *horo* dances were organized in the evenings for relaxation. On major holidays, such as the Virgin Mary's Day, large village fairs were held at which the *horo* was danced all day long.

Some rites were associated with specific regions. In southeastern Bulgaria, rituals for unmarried women involving fortune-telling and curing took place on Midsum-

mer's Day. Northern and southwestern Bulgaria were the site of *rusali* and *kalushari* dances, male curative rituals involving trance techniques and well-developed dances; these rituals were once connected with the Week of Rusali Maids but were later shifted to winter. The Nestinal fire dance of the southeast (related to the Anastenaria in Greece), which closed the festival of Saint Constantine and Saint Helena on 2 and 3 June, was associated with fortune-telling, preventive charms, and accompaniment by the *gayda* and drums.

The difference between women's and men's dances is related to their differing roles in the agricultural community. Because the men have more contact with music and dance outside the folk tradition, their dances have been affected by the incorporation of an almost professional level of musical accompaniment and tend to have an artistic or recreational focus. The women's dances have been more closely tied to folklore and ritual tradition. This sexual division has helped to perpetuate ritual dancing as a distinct system. In some areas (especially in northwestern Bulgaria, where female ritual dance has practically disappeared), male and female dancing become unified, with men and women dancing together in the holiday *horo* dances.

There are also regional styles. In northern Bulgaria light and fast *horos* performed to *kaval* pipes or bagpipes are characteristic. The steps are small and rapid and change directions quickly, usually employing mirror symmetry. These mixed *horos* emphasize body oscillation, especially of the shoulders. Characteristic *horos* are the *sitna, vurteshka, gankino, torlachka*, and many other diversified *ruchenitsas* performed in a chain.

The *horos* of the Dobrudja region (*opas, sborenka, ruka,*

ruchenik, and others) are complicated, with diversified steps done to instrumental accompaniment. They are mixed dances performed in a circle. Occasionally men separate from the group to execute complex figures, often in a kneeling position. The basic features of this style are shoulder-shaking (a heavier and slower movement than in northern Bulgaria) along with frequent foot-thumping, "knocking" feet, and sliding steps, which occur in practically all Dobrudja dances.

The Thracian *horos* (*pravo, trite puti, muzhko na pojas, vodena* kerchief dances, and others) are long in duration, and their predominantly smooth and quiet character is diversified by the insertion of slightly faster steps. They are danced in a long, open chain that winds into a spiral or meanders through different figures on the village square. Some *horos* are limited to men, allowing them to show off their skill. The women perform quiet *horos* to their own rich repertory of *horo*-leading songs.

The dances of midwestern Bulgaria are characterized by varying rhythms and dynamics, virtuosic performance, and quick, jerky steps—the so-called shaking step of the Shop or Graovo region, in which the body and shoulder react to specific footwork. The *horos* are danced in a circle or in a chain whose two ends wind about in response to its leaders. Singing or instrumental music accompany these dances. The better-known *horos* are the *selsko, chetvorno, sitno,* and *na mesto.*

Horos accompanied by singing are well preserved in southwestern Bulgaria, where they are also performed to instrumental music, usually bagpipes. Here the rich rhythms of western Bulgaria meet the quiet, calm, smooth dancing, accompanied by songs, typical of the whole of southern Bulgaria. As in Thrace, there are also men's *horos* that move in winding forms. The most prominent *horos* are the *chetvorno, stareshkoto, tezhkoto, chorbadjiiskoto;* these and many others bear the names of the songs to which they are danced.

The festive Sunday *horo*, danced in the village square, has come to occupy an important place in the Bulgarian system of folk rituals. Although this *horo* is similar throughout Bulgaria, it has been affected by the changes of the twentieth century, in the relationships among social groups—men and women, young and old, married and unmarried. The changing norms of behavior are reflected in the *horo*'s appearance, the arrangement of dancers, the ways dancers hold each other, and the performance style and demeanor. Many of the regional differences in the *horo* have developed incrementally in recent years. Thus, in southeastern Bulgaria (Thrace), the *horo* commences with maidens' songs; only later, after shouts and ritual laughter, do the bachelors enter with the instrumentalist. They break up the circle of the women's *horo* and lead it into a large, open-ended, meandering chain. The arrangement of the dancers by hierarchy—old men, young men, brides,

maidens, and so on—has been kept until recently in the Thracian dances.

In northern Bulgaria the *horo* proceeds in the opposite way: first the band (bagpipes, flutes, or other instruments) plays and the men begin the *horo* dance, then the women break up the chain. In this case, priority belongs to the most skillful, and the best dancers are the first in the line.

In most of the *horos* in southern Bulgaria, the close proximity of the dancers, who hold each other tightly at the belt, creates a well-knit *horo* line with the feeling of a single unit. In northern Bulgaria the dancers usually hold hands, allowing them greater freedom to shake their shoulders, to react with their whole bodies to the quickly changing movements, and to release their hands at crucial moments.

In southern Bulgaria the same *horo* is often danced for hours, but in northern Bulgaria the musicians usually form several *horo* lines simultaneously and perform suites of dances. They may start with the *pravo horo* in a 2/4 beat, then go to the *daichovo horo* in 9/16, with the *paidushko, elenino,* and other *horos* quickly following in sequence.

In the development of the Bulgarian festive *horo*, the leading creative role formerly exercised by women is being transferred to men; that is, the somber *horo* dance associated with women's ritual activity has evolved into the festive mixed and men's *horos*. The men have also introduced new *horos* accompanied by instrumental music,

BULGARIA: Folk and Traditional Dance. Women of the Bulgarian National Ensemble in a spinning dance. (Photograph from the Dance Collection, New York Public Library for the Performing Arts.)

which have gradually replaced the women's *horos* accompanied by singing, particularly in northern Bulgaria.

Bulgarian festive *horos* can thus be divided into two basic groups: *horos* of ritual origin, which have not been altered in village practice into mixed or men's dances; and *horos* of later origin created for artistic purposes. To the former belong the basic types: *pravo horo* (2/4), *ruchenichino* horo (7/16), *chetvorno* (with alternatives in 2/4, 7/16, 3/8, and 7/16), and *krivo (povurnato) horo* (9/16 or 11/16). These dances have many variants. Although stages and degrees of historical development are evident, they have preserved their ritual formula. The *pravo horo* is found throughout the Balkan Peninsula but is seen in its greatest variety in Bulgaria.

In the second group of *horos* the artistic impulse manifests itself in ornamental and complex combinations of different types of steps, jerks, and other dance movements. These *horos* have a rich dance lexicon. Among them are the popular *paidushko* (5/16), *daichovo* (9/16), *elenino* (7/8), *trite puti* (2/4), *trikorka* (2/4), *gruncharka* (9/16), and *tropanka* (2/4).

Bulgarian dances are generally characterized by the richness and diversity of their forms, rhythms, holds, step combinations, footwork, and ornamental character. Gestures and movements that express emotions are absent. Bulgarian folk dances are mainly group dances of the *horo*-leading type, performed either in an open line or in a closed circle, with the dancers using different hand grips. The more complex virtuosic *horos* are performed by a smaller number of dancers (usually fewer than sixteen), in either a crooked or a straight line.

With the exception of some ritual dances, solos and duets are less frequent in Bulgarian dance. The most characteristic of these are the *peshachka*, *posenitsa*, and *tsonina* of western Bulgaria; the *kasumska* of Thrace; and the *treperushka* of northern Bulgaria. The *ruchenitsa* (kerchief dance), the most popular of Bulgarian solo dances, may be found all over the country in many variants.

Some characteristic orgiastic and symbolic movements of the hands or body have been kept and stylized in the *kapanska* (male nuptial kerchief dance) of north Bulgaria, although this dance has been developed into an artistic type. In midwestern and northwestern Bulgaria, the kerchief dance has developed small, quick, virtuosic steps. Farther north it approaches a virtuosic dance, while in the Shop area, something of the primary erotic quality of this dance has been preserved, though in a rather artistic and humorous style. The Dobrudjanski *ruchenik* mixes elements of the kerchief dance and male nuptial dances, but these have been reduced to symbolic farming movements (sowing, mowing, sheaf-carrying, and so on). The kerchief dance in Thrace developed into a male dance of subtle plastic movements of the hands and body.

Today there are many new kinds of dance in Bulgaria, enabling the rich folk heritage to develop into an artistic genre. Amateur dance companies are the main contexts in which dances with a folk basis are created and developed. With the growth of these amateur groups and of state-sponsored song and dance ensembles, Bulgarian folk dance has begun to develop as a separate type of art, with its own specific rules and problems. Aside from the change in its place of performance (from the village square to the stage), the dance has undergone major changes in its system of classification. Dances are now characterized not by their social function but by their choreographic features. Thus scholars refer to solo, chamber, and mass dances; or dances of ideas, subjects, or themes. They also refer to stylized, arranged, restored, or authentic folk dances. Regional styles (Thracian, Shop, and so on), stylized and generalized, have also found their way onto the stage.

In their short history of theatrical adaptation, folk dance performances have evolved from the simplest stage *horo* presentation (the mechanical linkage of dances into suites) to elementary choreographic arrangements and finally complex choreographic and narrative works. The growth of folk dance performances has, in turn, stimulated the desire to discover and preserve Bulgarian folk traditions.

BIBLIOGRAPHY

Ilieva, Anna. *Bulgarian Dance Folklore.* Translated by Thomas Roncevic. Pittsburgh, 1977.

Ilieva, Anna. *Narodni tantsi ot Srednogorieto.* Sofia, 1978.

Ilieva, Anna. "On Changes of Style in the Bulgarian Dance Folklore." *Dance Studies* 7 (1983): 57–72.

Katzarova-Kukudova, Raina. *Hora i igri ot Severozapadna Bulgaria.* Sofia, 1956.

Katzarova-Kukudova, Raina. *Narodni hora i igri ot selo Hlevene.* Sofia, 1966.

Katzarova-Kukudova, Raina, and Kiril Djenev. *Bulgarian Folk Dances.* Translated by Nevena Geliazkova and Marguerite Alexieva. Cambridge, Mass., 1976.

Kerr, Kathleen A. "Differentiation of Ethnic Culture Regions Using Laban Movement Analysis: A Study of Bulgarian Dance." Ph.D. diss., Texas Woman's University, 1991.

ANNA ILIEVA

Theatrical Dance

There was no theatrical dance in Bulgaria until rule by the Ottoman Empire ended in 1878. The country's first opera company, the Bulgarian Opera Society, was founded in Sofia in 1908 and was renamed the Sofia National Opera in 1922. The post of ballet master was consecutively filled by Aleksandŭr Dimitrov (1911–1912), Pešo Radoev (1912–1926, with some interruptions), and R. Koleva, all choreographers and folklorists. Radoev's many activities included the 1919 establishment of a children's ballet school, which existed until 1927. He also staged dances in drama and opera productions, worked as a journalist, and strove to popularize theatrical dance. In 1928 he attempted to found a dance magazine.

During the early 1920s, the Russian ballet dancers who performed in Sofia and in smaller towns after the 1917 Russian Revolution indirectly encouraged the development of professional ballet in Bulgaria. Among the Russian dancers were such well-known figures as Maria Yurieva, Margarita Froman, Elizabeth Anderson-Ivantzova (partnered by Aleksandr Kochetovsky), Viktorina Kriger, Boris Kniaseff (who created a short-lived Bulgarian-Russian group in 1921), and Tamara Karsavina. As a result of their tours a number of Bulgarian ballet dancers were inspired to complete their training with Russian teachers in schools in Paris and Berlin.

After Bulgaria's fascist coup of 1923, the artistic interests of the Bulgarian ruling class drew closer to those of Germany, so German dance and plastique exerted increasing influence. Among the German dancers who visited at this time were the three Wiesenthal sisters, Gertrud Bodenwieser, and W. Kratina. A Czech group led by M. Majorowa also toured, and two Bulgarian dancers, S. Georgieva and L. Vâlkova-Beševič, went to study in Germany.

In 1927 Anastas Petrov, dancer, teacher, and ballet master at the Sofia National Opera, established a ballet school that trained many of the company's future soloists. His staging of *Coppélia* in 1928 is considered to mark the beginning of professional Bulgarian ballet. In 1937 he created the first Bulgarian ballet, *The Dragon and Jana*, based on popular legends and folktales and danced to a score by Emanuil Manolov. He often used folk dance to impart new vigor to classical technique. [*See the entry on Petrov.*]

From 1936 to 1938 the Russian dancer and ballet master Maksimilijan Froman worked at the Sofia National Opera; his staging of the Russian classic *The Sleeping Beauty* strengthened the company's classical repertory. In 1939 Petrov staged another Russian classic, *Raymonda*. A disciple of the German modern dancers Rudolf Laban and Mary Wigman, Maria Dimova, gave performances in the 1930s. Her dance drama entitled *The Fire Dancer* (1942), produced at the Sofia National Opera to music by Marin Goleminov, successfully reflected the Bulgarian popular world view.

After the 1944 establishment of a communist state in Bulgaria, the conditions for the development of Bulgarian ballet changed radically. The government founded opera and ballet theaters in Stara Zagora, Varna, Ruse, and Plovdiv. In 1951 the State School of Choreography was established in Sofia, the capital. Creative bonds grew with Russian teachers and ballet masters, and a number of Bulgarian dancers studied and danced at Soviet schools and theaters. In 1945 the Russian ballerina Nina Anisimova staged Boris Asafiev's *The Fountain of Bakhchisarai* at the Sofia National Opera. The Soviet ballet master

Nikolai Kholfin also worked there from 1949 to 1953, staging ballets such as *The Rivals* (his own version of *La Fille Mal Gardée*), *Doctor Aibolit*, and *The Red Poppy*, as well as the Bulgarian heroic ballet *A Haidouk Song*, to music by Aleksandŭr Raičev. F. I. Balabanova's 1959 staging of *The Sleeping Beauty* launched the careers of a number of major Bulgarian dancers, among them Vera Kirova, Krasimira Koldamova, Kalina Bogoeva, A. Stoinov, A. Samev, and I. Doičinov.

During the 1950s and 1960s Petrov staged such classics as *Swan Lake*, *Esmeralda*, and *Giselle*, as well as the national ballet *Orpheus and Rhodope* (1961), composed by C. Cvetanov.

In the 1960s a new generation of choreographers emerged, many of whom created symphonic ballets or used scores by contemporary composers. Notable works have included Bogdanov Kovačev's *Daphnis and Chloe* and *Petrouchka*, and P. Lukanov's *Apollon Musagète*, *Agon*, and *Classical Symphony*. *Romeo and Juliet* was choreographed in 1963 by G. and S. Jordanov, and in 1971 by the Russian choreographer Oleg Vinogradov. Scores by Bulgarian composers accompanied ballets such as Anisimova's *The Legend of the Lake* (1962), Jiří Němeček's *Madara Horseman* (1965), Witold Borkowski's *Pope Joan* (1969), Lukanov's *Kalojan's Daughter* (1973) and *The Goat Horn* (1981), and M. Arnaudova's *The Shadow* (1983). Other noteworthy productions have included D. Horonzo's *The Wooden Prince*, Yuri Grigorovich's *The Stone Flower*, and Leonid Lavrovsky's restaging of *Giselle*.

A number of ballerinas rose to prominence at the Sofia National Opera, such as Nadežda (Nina) Kiradžieva, who studied in Moscow with Rostislav Zakharov and entered the company in 1929. She served as a ballerina, ballet mistress, teacher, and artistic director. Among the ballets she staged are *The Fire Dancer*, *The Three-Cornered Hat*, and *The Sleeping Beauty*. Liljana (Lili) Beron began her training with Radoev and Petrov, then studied with Lubov Egorova in Paris and at the Leningrad Choreographic Institute. From 1937 to 1939 she toured with the Ballet Youth group in Paris. A member of the Sofia National Opera since 1934, she was named an honored artist in 1965. Beron's pupil Kalina Bogoeva also studied at the Moscow Choreographic Institute with Elisaveta Gerdt. In addition to being a dancer, she became a prominent teacher and an artistic director of Bulgaria's State Choreographic Institute. Another pupil of Beron, Krasimira Koldamova, worked in France and with Pavel Gerdt in Moscow. She was acclaimed in the role of Juliet. Vera Kirova joined the Sofia National Opera in 1958, upon her graduation from the State Choreographic Institute, and became a *prima ballerina* in 1967.

The experimental ballet group Arabesk, founded in Sofia in 1967, has staged mainly one-act works to music by both Bulgarian and other composers; M. Arnaudova became its artistic director in 1974, enriching its repertory with Bulgarian works such as *The Fire Dancer* (1978) and *Midsummer Day Eve* (1981), as well as new versions of *The Rite of Spring* and *The Firebird*. Other major productions include Alberto Alonso's *Carmen Suite*, Françoise Adret's *The Four Temperaments*, H. Kareli's *Carmina Burana*, and A. Leclair's *Ritus Paganus*.

In the repertory of the Stara Zagora Opera are T. Stičeva's Bulgarian ballet *Kârdzali* (1959), Kiradžieva's *The Fire Dancer*, and Arnaudova's stagings of *The Fountain of Bakhchisarai* and Petrov's *The Creation of the World*. The company has also danced such classics as *The Nutcracker* and *Don Quixote*.

The Varna ballet group performed the Bulgarian comic ballet *The Silver Shoes* (1962) and *A Haidouk Song* (1978), in addition to classics such as *Chopiniana*, *Giselle*, *Le Corsaire*, and *Cinderella*.

The Ruse People's Opera presented contemporary works such as *The Miraculous Mandarin*, Lukanov's *The Prodigal Son*, and Kovačev's *A Fair in Sofia* (1973), a modern grotesque work. A. Manolov and A. Gavrilov staged classics such as *Giselle* and *The Fountain of Bakhchisarai*.

Kovačev also staged a number of works for the Plovdiv Opera, notably *A Fair in Sofia* (1969) and *The Silver Shoes* (1970), a ballet full of folk humor, to Paraslikev Hadžiev's music. *Medea* and *Coppélia* have been staged by F. Bakalov.

BIBLIOGRAPHY
Aleksandrova, Ana. *S krilete na Terpsikhora*. Sofia, 1972.
Konsulova, Violetta. *Anastas Petrov i bulgarskiiat balet*. Sofia, 1976.
Konsulova, Violetta. *Iz istoriiata bulgarskiia balet*. Sofia, 1981.
Popov, Teodor, and Eliana Mitova. *Sreshti s baletni deitsi*. Sofia, 1987.
Popov, Teodor. *Baletut v profil i anfas*. Sofia, 1992.
Popov, Teodor. *Za baleta*. Sofia, 1993.
Popov, Teodor. *Zvezdi na bulgarskiia balet*. Sofia, 1993.
Sagaev, Liubomir. *Bulgarskogo operno tvorchestvo*. Sofia, 1958.

VIOLETTA KONSULOVA

BUNRAKU, the classical puppet theater of Japan, whose plays, costumes, and styles of movement have influenced *kabuki* dance drama. *Bunraku* is also known by such terms as *ningyō jōruri* (from *ningyō*, "puppet," and *jōruri*, a musical narrative technique used to accompany the plays), *ningyō shibai* (literally, "puppet theater"), *gidayū* (a style of chanting), and other names. Although the form itself was established in the late sixteenth century, the term *bunraku* derives from the name of a producer, Uemura Bunrakuken (1747–1810).

The Form of Bunraku. *Bunraku* is notable for being a tripartite art form: it combines the chanting of onstage narrators, who perform all the dialogue, with the musical accompaniment of the three-stringed *shamisen* and the manipulation of three-quarter life-sized puppets by three-man teams.

Puppets and puppeteers. The chief manipulator (*omozukai*) manages the puppet's head and right arm; his first assistant (*hidarizukai*) handles the left arm; and the second assistant (*ashizukai*) moves the legs. The three-man arrangement is required because the puppets are heavy and well articulated—often having movable eyes, eyebrows, mouths, hands, and wrists and other joints. The puppets are manipulated according to classical conventions for specific roles and role-types. Their movements are often highly realistic, and they can perform such delicate tasks as smoking, writing, and playing musical instruments.

Puppet manipulators are never hidden; the *omozukai* usually wears colorful garments while his aides dress in black robes with mesh hoods covering their faces (though in many cases their faces are uncovered). The high sandals worn by the *omozukai* raise him well above the other men and assist him in controlling the puppet's movements. Once one has accepted the convention of the puppeteers' visible presence, the manipulators barely distract from the puppets and their drama.

Narration and accompaniment. The narrator, or *tayū*, sits on a platform at stage left, the *shamisen* accompanist at his left side, and chants all the characters' dialogue as well as the descriptive and lyrical passages. His has always been the most important position in *bunraku*, and many people go to the puppet theater to listen to the highly charged narrative and musical accompaniment more than to watch the puppets. (In some instances, a group of narrators appears, each assigned a separate character.) The narrator changes his delivery for each character, using a falsetto for females. He sits before an ornate reading stand holding his script, but he has actually memorized the entire play. Just as the narrator is responsible for establishing the tone of the play, so is the *shamisen* player necessary for heightening the atmosphere, accentuating the narrative, and providing various sound effects.

Playhouses. The plays are performed in proscenium theaters that resemble scaled-down versions of *kabuki* playhouses. The main *bunraku* theater is in Osaka, but one of the two theaters at Tokyo's National Theater also houses *bunraku* productions. The manipulators work on a stage divided by various panels that run parallel to the front of the stage; these panels hide the lower halves of the puppeteers' bodies, and their top edges serve to suggest the ground or floor on which the puppets stand or sit. Settings—for example, whether the characters are inside or out of doors—are suggested by a variety of conventions. Although it is not a traditional part of *bunraku*, the raised auditorium passageway of the *kabuki* theater, the *hanamichi*, has been added to the modern *bunraku* playhouse.

BUNRAKU. It takes three people to manipulate the three-quarter life-sized *bunraku* puppets. The *omozukai* (left) controls the puppet's head and right arm in a performance of the drama *Ichinotani Futaba Gunki* (Chronicle of the Battle of Ichinotani). (Photograph © 1983 by Jack Vartoogian; used by permission.)

Characters. As in the *kabuki* theater, which shares many of the same plays in slightly different versions, the characters belong to specific categories, which are indicated by the types of puppet heads used. The heads—made of wood—are detachable, and most are used for a variety of roles. They are combined with different torsos, costumes, and wigs to create different characters. The articulation of the heads differs depending on the importance of the characters: most principal-characters' heads can move at least one facial feature (usually the eyes), but those of lesser characters who appear only as "extras" are comparatively crude and are limited to a single expression. Female heads often have a tiny pin near the lips so that the puppet may deliberately snag a piece of cloth there to suggest that the character is fighting tears by biting on the cloth. The important heads, beautifully carved and painted, are significant artworks.

Historical Antecedents. Japan has a long tradition of puppetry, going back to ancient times, when puppets were used in Shintō religious ceremonies. In the seventh century, Korean puppeteers migrated to Japan, and bands of these outcasts wandered throughout the country, performing with small puppets manipulated in boxes hanging from their necks.

By the late sixteenth century, puppet performances had been combined with the recitation of a narrative romance about Princess Jōruri and Ushiwakamaru (the early name of the shogun Minamoto Yoshitsune). The narrative was called *jōruri* and was accompanied by a lutelike instrument called the *biwa*. When the *biwa* was replaced by the *shamisen*, imported from Okinawa, the essential elements of *bunraku* were in place.

Evolution of Bunraku. During the seventeenth century, the new art form slowly evolved. From its beginnings in the Osaka-Kyoto region, it spread to the Kanto area, where Edo (now Tokyo) is situated. Edo favored a violent form of puppet theater called *kinpira jōruri*, in which the narrator often destroyed one or more of the puppets in a fit of emotion.

Several outstanding and original narrators worked in Kyoto, but it was in Osaka that *bunraku* advanced, when the great narrator Takemoto Gidayū (1615–1724) opened his Takemoto-Za in 1684. Working with the master playwright Chikamatsu Monzaemon (1653–1724) and the puppeteer Hachirobei Tatsumatsu (died 1734), Gidayū established a golden age for the art. So powerful was Gidayū's influence that his name was given to the narrative style that has since remained preeminent in Japan's puppet theater.

Chikamatsu turned to the writing of puppet plays—and revolutionized the genre—after becoming dissatisfied with the vagaries of the *kabuki* actors for whom he had been writing. He wrote both *jidaimono*, period plays, and *sewamono*, realistic dramas of everyday life, but *sewamono* were the more radical and sensational. Often they depicted tragic events—especially double suicides—that had occurred only a few weeks prior to a play's first production.

Development and Decline. In the eighteenth century, many advances occurred in *bunraku*, including the enlargement of the dolls and their mechanical elaboration.

Whereas puppets in Chikamatsu's period were each handled by a single manipulator, now three men to a puppet became the style. The puppet theater rose to its height of popularity, and *kabuki* began the wholesale borrowing of its repertory and techniques; this eventually led to *kabuki*'s becoming the dominant form of urban theatrical entertainment.

By the late 1760s, *bunraku* had a serious decline. Toward the end of the eighteenth century, Uemura Bunrakuken helped spur a mild resurgence of the art, and his successors in the nineteenth century struggled to keep it from dying out. During the second half of the nineteenth century, a renewed interest emerged in *bunraku*, as many significant artists appeared and advanced the art.

Ultimately, however, popular interest in *bunraku* faded, and only one company survives, in Osaka. Its theater, the Bunraku Theater, was destroyed in a 1945 air raid; a new playhouse, the Asahi Theater, was constructed for the company in 1955, but it in turn was replaced by the National Bunraku Theater, opened in 1984. The postwar period witnessed attempts to generate renewed interest in *bunraku* with puppet plays based on Western models, such as *Hamlet* and *Madama Butterfly*, and with *bunraku* adaptations of *kabuki* dance plays. These, however, have failed to supplant in audiences' favor the great pieces of the traditional repertory.

Bunraku survives today through a combination of private and government subsidies. Various professional and semiprofessional troupes exist, most notably the professional troupe of Awaji Island, which, like some other companies, has toured outside Japan.

[*See also* Asian Dance Traditions, *article on* Influence of Puppetry, *and* Kabuki Theater.]

BIBLIOGRAPHY

Adachi, Barbara. *The Voices and Hands of Bunraku.* Tokyo, 1978.
Keene, Donald. *Bunraku.* Tokyo, 1965.
Shūzaburō Hironaga. *Bunraku: Japan's Unique Puppet Theatre.* Rev. ed. Tokyo, 1964.
Tsuruo Ando. *Bunraku: The Puppet Theatre.* Translated by Don Kenny. Tokyo, 1970.
Yoshinobu Inoura and Toshio Kawatake. *The Traditional Theater of Japan.* New York, 1981.

SAMUEL L. LEITER

BURGMÜLLER, FRIEDRICH (Johann Friedrich Franz Burgmüller; born 4 December 1806 in Ratisbon [Regensburg], Germany, died 13 February 1874 in Beaulieu, France), German pianist and composer. Burgmüller was the son of the composer and musical director Johann August Franz Burgmüller and the brother of the composer Norbert Burgmüller. After receiving his initial musical training in Ratisbon, he studied composition with Louis Spohr in Kassel. In 1832 he went to Paris, where he became piano teacher to the children of King Louis Philippe and also composed a number of piano pieces for Parisian salons. His music, while lacking the exuberance and virtuosity of works by Sigismund Thalberg, Liszt, and Chopin, was nevertheless notable for its refined sensibility, melodic charm, and elegance of expression. Burgmüller often based his piano works on melodies from operas, and he composed many popular quadrilles, waltzes, gallops, polonaises, and polkas. He published a great many *fiori musicali*, and his études are still played by aspiring pianists.

In the 1840s Burgmüller composed for the stage, beginning with the "Pas de Deux des Jeunes Paysans" (peasant pas de deux), a piece originally known as "Souvenirs de Ratisbon," inserted in act 1 of Adolphe Adam's *Giselle*. He wrote the music for Théophile Gautier and Jean Coralli's *La Péri*, performed at the Paris Opera on 7 July 1843, his most notable work. [*See* Péri, La.] Besides a dance for the Opera ("Polka dansé à l'Opéra par Marie et Eugène Coralli," 1844), he participated, in collaboration with Friedrich von Flotow and Édouard Deldevez, in the ballet-pantomime *Lady Henriette, ou La Servante de Greenwich* (1844). After 1844 he withdrew almost completely from active participation in the artistic life of Paris and devoted most of his time to teaching, although he still published some new compositions.

The score of *La Péri* is traditionally structured as a series of dance pieces. The many dances are especially elegant and full of melodic motifs that imprint themselves on the memory, as does Burgmüller's waltz from *Giselle*. The music of the tableaux ("Le Rêve" and "La Prison") is somewhat simple, but the music for the dances "calls the steps forth." Especially notable is his "Pas de l'Abeille" (Dance of the Bee), a harem dance. Burgmüller's music is clearly influenced by Gioacchino Rossini, Daniel Auber, and especially Adam, and it evokes the ballet world of the 1840s.

BIBLIOGRAPHY

Gautier, Théophile. *Histoire de l'art dramatique en France depuis vingt-cinq ans.* Vol. 3. Leipzig, 1859.
Gautier, Théophile. *Gautier on Dance.* Translated and edited by Ivor Guest. London, 1986.
Guest, Ivor. *The Romantic Ballet in Paris.* 2d rev. ed. London, 1980.
Obituary. *Revue et gazette musical de Paris* (22 February 1874).
Schumann, Robert. *Gesammelte Schriften über Musik und Musiker.* 3d ed. Leipzig, 1883.

OLE NØRLYNG

BURMA. *See* Myanmar.

BURMEISTER, VLADIMIR (Vladimir Pavlovich Burmeister, also spelled Bourmeister; born 2 [15] July 1904 in Vitebsk, Belorussia [now Belarus], died 6 March 1971 in Moscow), dancer and choreographer. As a student at the Moscow Drama Studio (where he studied with Sofia Khalyutina and Maria Zhdanova, actresses of the Moscow Art Theater), Vladimir Burmeister never thought of becoming a ballet dancer but rather envisioned acting in classical Russian drama. Frequently, however, he was given roles in touring theaters' dance recitals and in variety shows, and before long dancing became an important part of his life. He eventually left the dramatic stage and entered the Lunacharsky Theater Technicum (1925–1929), where training conformed with the strictest standards and classes were conducted by prominent Moscow dancers and teachers. While still a student, Burmeister took part in variety shows, performing Spanish and Hungarian dances. He also appeared with the company of the Dramatic Ballet Workshop, directed by Nina Gremina. In 1930 he joined the Moscow Art Ballet, then directed by Viktorina Kriger. In 1933 the company merged with the Nemirovich-Danchenko Musical Theater (after 1941 the Stanislavsky and Nemirovich-Danchenko Musical Theater).

Burmeister was a gifted actor who chose his roles with discrimination. He was not inspired by abstract classical roles or by those of the dreamy and melancholic Romantic ballets but was drawn instead to sharply delineated character roles. His favorites were realistic: the dramatic Aleko in Nikolai Kholfin's *The Gypsies* or the dexterous knave and glutton Sir John Falstaff in *The Merry Wives of Windsor,* choreographed by Burmeister himself with Ivan Kurilov. Burmeister's definition and plasticity of line, in addition to his pantomimic technique, greatly helped him in creating characters such as the Corregidor in Kholfin's *The Three-Cornered Hat* and Kum in *Christmas Eve,* choreographed by Burmeister and Fedor Lopukhov. Other notable roles were those of the Polish Nobleman and the Tatar Nur-Ali in Rostislav Zakharov's *The Fountain of Bakhchisarai* and Niqueuse in Kholfin's *The Rivals.* Spanish dances—his favorites—were performed by Burmeister in a strict and reserved manner based on Andalusian dance, noted for its contained but manly style.

Burmeister's career as a choreographer began in 1933, first for the ballet company directed by Kriger and subsequently for the Musical Theater itself. There his choreographic and directorial talents blossomed under the influence of its director, Vasily Nemirovich-Danchenko, and the originality of his style came to fruition. He made his debut staging dances in the Offenbach operettas *La Belle Hélène* (1938) and *La Périchole* (1940). His collaboration with Lopukhov on the ballet *Christmas Eve* premiered in 1938. From 1941 to 1960 and again from 1963 to 1971, Burmeister was the chief choreographer of the Stanislavsky and Nemirovich-Danchenko Musical Theater. The theater was the cradle of a whole set of new ideas about the art of dance. It had an original repertory, its own traditions of artistic expressiveness, and an un-

matched performance style. Its ballets fostered the talents of Eleonora Vlasova, Violetta Bovt, Mirra Redina, Lubov Yukunina, Aleksandr Klein, and Ivan Kurilov.

As a choreographer Burmeister always sought to base dances firmly in the realities of life but at the same time to transform and illuminate those realities with artistic imagination. It was important to him to have the actions onstage be psychologically sound and convincing. The choreography in his best productions was always subordinated to dramatic action, to the theme of the ballet and its characterizations.

Burmeister created ballets in a wide variety of genres—comic, dramatic, epic—and forms. His full-length works include Oransky's *The Merry Wives of Windsor* (1942, with Kurilov), *La Esmeralda* (1950), and Eugen Kapp's *Kalevipoeg* (1961). He also created the one-act ballets *Straussiana* (1941), *Schéhérazade* (1944), *Le Carnaval* (1946), Aleksandr Krein's *Tatiana* (1947, for the Kirov Ballet), Ravel's *Boléro* (1964), Beethoven's *Appassionata* (1970), and *The Snow Maiden,* to music by Tchaikovsky (1961, for London's Festival Ballet; the Musical Theater, 1963). In 1953 Burmeister created his own version of *Swan Lake,* retaining only the second act of the traditional production, choreographed by Lev Ivanov. Burmeister restored the cuts in the music and the original sequence of the numbers, gave the character of the magician Rothbart a larger role, and shifted the suite of character dances to a new place. This production, brought to the Paris Opera in 1960, added a new and important chapter to the stage history of *Swan Lake.* Here again Burmeister displayed his gift for providing a sound psychological and dramaturgical basis for the choreography of even a classical ballet.

Burmeister defined his overriding theme as the ideals of heroic struggle and courage as manifested by men and women of high-minded impulses and daring actions. In the dance *Spanish Grenadiers,* set to folk tunes, he created a poetic image of Spain at war and paid tribute to the fiery spirit of her people. The heroic theme rings out as well in *Lola* (1943), *Tatiana* (1947), *The Coast of Happiness* (1948), and *Jeanne d'Arc* (1957).

Lola, to music by Sergei Vasilenko and based on Napoleon's invasion of Spain, was created during World War II. The ballet evoked vivid and topical associations with world events of the early 1940s. Its appeal sprang from its grimness and realistic presentation and from the powerful portrayal of its principal characters. The heroism of the people rising up against the invaders of their homeland was expressed through dances full of fiery dynamism and impetuous movement. All the dances in *Lola* were conceived as a well-integrated suite whose parts, rather like the flame of a torch in a strong wind, surged up and then subsided, only to flare again.

The Coast of Happiness, to music by Antonio Spadavecchia and on which Kurilov collaborated, was dedicated by

Burmeister to the heroes of World War II. Life itself inspired this choreographed poem, whose theme was the heroism of Soviet youth. We are introduced to the heroes when, still in their teens, they enjoy life on the shores of the Crimea. Later the audience sees them undergoing arduous trials. In the battle scenes combat is expressed purely through dance movements.

In *Jeanne d'Arc*, to music by Nikolai Peiko, Burmeister continued his search for a convincing presentation of the heroic theme, choosing an epoch of cruel wars and upheavals. Joan of Arc's dances are strict and noble, their form and line restrained and pure, contrasting sharply with the stiff and sensuous court dances. The heavy tread of the British soldiers in armor is set against the free, joyful, and sparkling dances of the French peasants. There were no conventional patterns in the ballet; everything was made as realistic as possible to convey an authentic period atmosphere as well as the character of the nations involved.

Perforce a practitioner of socialist realism, Burmeister nevertheless found ways to bring immediacy to its larger-than-life themes and characters and diversity within its strictures. His rich output defined and ensured the endurance of the Stanislavsky and Nemirovich-Danchenko Musical Theater.

BUTLER. Lawrence Rhodes and Alba Calzada in the Pennsylvania Ballet's revival of Butler's *After Eden*, originally created for the Harkness Ballet in 1967. (Photograph © 1976 by Max Waldman; used by permission.)

BIBLIOGRAPHY
Elyash, Nikolai I. "Vlast' odnoi dumy." *Teatralnaia Zhizn* 13 (1964).
Roslavleva, Natalia. *Era of the Russian Ballet* (1966). New York, 1979.
Sheremetyevskaya, Natalia. *Molodye baletnye teatry.* Moscow, 1976.
Swift, Mary Grace. *The Art of the Dance in the U.S.S.R.* Notre Dame, 1968.

NIKOLAI I. ELYASH
Translated from Russian

BUTLER, JOHN (John Nielson Butler; born 29 September 1920 in Memphis, Tennessee, died 11 September 1993 in New York City), American dancer and choreographer. Often noted for the dramatic-erotic content of his style, which is equally compatible with ballet and modern dance, Butler produced works for dance and opera companies, television, and the theater. His ballets have been included in the repertories of American Ballet Theatre, the Joffrey Ballet, the Dance Theatre of Harlem, the Pennsylvania Ballet, the Paris Opera Ballet, the Australian Ballet, the Alvin Ailey American Dance Theater, the Metropolitan Opera, the New York City Opera, and La Scala Ballet, Milan, to name but a few. He served as director of his own company, the John Butler Dance Theatre, and was dance director of the Spoleto (Italy) Festival in 1958 and 1959.

Raised in Greenwood, Mississippi, Butler began his major training in New York City during the 1940s when he was on scholarship concurrently at the School of American Ballet and the Martha Graham School. In 1943 he joined Graham's company, where he stayed for ten years while also choreographing on his own. In 1947 Butler commenced his long association with the composer Gian-Carlo Menotti for *The Consul* (1949). Butler later choreographed Menotti's *Amahl and the Night Visitors* (1951), *The Unicorn, the Gorgon, and the Manticore* (1956), later taken into the New York City Ballet's repertory, and *Sebastian* (1963). Butler has said, "My parents, so to speak, were really Menotti and Graham. They brought me up, you know. They came to every premiere. And they were very strict parents; they would let me have it straight across the teeth if they didn't like it."

Butler left Graham to form his own company in 1955. By then he had established himself as a choreographer of note, working with the New York City Opera and on television shows, such as *Lamp unto My Feet* and *Camera Three*. Running a company was not to his liking, however, so he became a freelance choreographer, working throughout the United States and in Europe. In 1964 he received the *Dance Magazine* Award.

Although Butler worked with classical music and opera, he was primarily stimulated by modern composers and used music by George Crumb, Luciano Berio, Krzysztof Penderecki, Edgard Varèse, and Carl Orff, among others. Butler's best-known works include *Carmina Burana*

(1959), to the music of Orff; *Portrait of Billie* (1961), to music by Billie Holiday; *Catulli Carmina* (1964), to music by Orff; *After Eden* (1967), to music by Lee Hoiby; and *Medea* (1975), to music by Samuel Barber. Based in New York, Butler set ballets all over the world. In April 1987, for example, *Dance Magazine* reported that he was working in Princeton, New Jersey, Warsaw, Poland, and with the soloist Margie Gillis in Toronto, Canada. That year he also created a twenty-five-minute concert version of *Lulu*, the opera by Alban Berg, with Carla Fracci at the Teatro alla Scala in Milan, Italy; it was his fifth collaboration with the ballerina.

BIBLIOGRAPHY

Butler, John. "Confessions of a Choreographer." In *The Dance Experience*, edited by Myron H. Nadel and Constance G. Nadel. New York, 1970.

Loney, Glenn. "All the Strange Things: John Butler on Opera Choreography among Other Kinds of Dance." *Dance Magazine* (August 1971): 22–27.

Loney, Glenn. "Busy John Butler Reports on Roving Choreography." *Dance Magazine* (January 1974):44–50.

Victor, Thomas, ed. *The Making of a Dance: Mikhail Baryshnikov and Carla Fracci in Medea Choreographed by John Butler*. New York, 1976.

KITTY CUNNINGHAM

BUTŌ. Contemporary Japanese dance comprises a wide variety of styles, from folk dances and traditional dance-drama genres such as *nō* and *kabuki* to imported forms such as ballet, modern and postmodern dance, and performance-art forms that incorporate dance. *Butō*, which began to develop in the 1950s, is a contemporary form that draws on both Western and indigenous Japanese sources. According to Dance Research Tokyo, fifty-five *butō* choreographers and companies were active as of late 1994.

The term *butō* (from *bu*, "dance," and *tō*, "step" or "stomp") was used during Japan's Meiji era to mean the Western-style ballroom dancing then being introduced into the country. (The term was also used in ancient Japan to designate ritual dance.) By the mid-twentieth century, however, the word had fallen into disuse, until revived—and given a new meaning—by choreographer Hijikata Tatsumi.

Contemporary *butō* has its origin in the new dance movements presented in the late 1950s, in the works of Hijikata, Ōno Kazuo, and Kasai Akira—all of whom opposed contemporary Japanese modern dance's strict adherence to Western styles. The first *butō* dance, Hijikata's *Kinjiki*, was performed in 1959 and again soon afterward as part of *Hijikata Tatsumi 650 Dance Experience no Kai*. (The title refers to the 650 seats of the theater in which the performance took place—and to Hijikata's contention that the "experience" was participated in by all 650 specta-

BUTŌ. Ōno Kazuo, one of the pioneers of *butō*, an expressionist dance genre that developed in post–World War II Japan. He is seen here in "Vienna Waltz" from his work *The Dead Sea*. (Photograph © 1985 by Linda Vartoogian; used by permission.)

tors.) This violent, improvisation-based performance, however, was very different from *butō* as it later developed.

Butō has gone through several stylistic phases. Hijikata's first style, which he named *ankoku butō* (or, originally, *ankoku buyō*, "dance of darkness"), exhibited the influences of German *Neuer Tanz* and American "happenings." The *ankoku butō* fad came to an end in 1968, with Hijikata's solo performance *Hijikata Tatsumi to Nihon-jin—Nikutai no Hanran* (Hijikata Tatsumi and the Japanese—Revolt of the Flesh).

In 1970, some ten years after he had begun *butō* with *Kinjiki*, Hijikata inaugurated a new kind of *butō* with his work *Shiki no Tameno 27 Ban* (27 Nights for Four Seasons), performed on twenty-seven consecutive evenings in an old movie theater in the Shinjuku district of Tokyo. Elements of this work—the distorted, emaciated bodies and shaved heads of the dancers, their white-plastered faces (to erase their humanness), and the costumes made from old kimonos—established the style known as *Hijikata butō*, which continues to influence contemporary *butō*, especially the work of Ōno but also that of the Dai Raku-

BUTŌ. Sankai Juku, the company founded by Amagatsu Ushio, in *Kinkan Shonen* (The Kumquat Seed), performed in 1984 at the City Center of Music and Drama, New York. (Photograph © 1984 by Jack Vartoogian; used by permission.)

Not yet four decades old, *butō* has not developed a well-defined style. Nudity, shaved heads, white-plaster make-up, and transvestism are often considered essential elements of *butō* because they have so often been used by Hijikata and Ōno Kazuo. Nevertheless, Hijikata, the creator of *butō*, himself believed that the soul of *butō* consisted in imposing a peculiarly Japanese quality on physical action and in emphasizing the spiritual climate of Asia and especially Japan. Therefore, elements like those listed do not necessarily define *butō* style.

Besides the dancers already named, others belonging to the evolving *butō* tradition include Nakajima Natsu of Muteki-sha, Ishii Mitsutaka, Takai Tomiko, and Kazukuri Yukio of Kozensha, all of whom studied with Hijikata; Fukuhara Tetsuro and Oomori Masahide, both of whom studied with Kasai; Amagatsu Ushio of Dai Rakudakan and Sankai Juku; Yoshimoto Daisuke, who studied *butō* independently; and Goi Teru. Outside Tokyo, *butō* performers include Katsura Kan in Kyoto and Mori Shigeya in Yamagata.

[*For further discussion, see* Costume in Asian Traditions *and* Japan, *article on* Modern Dance. *See also entries on the principal figures mentioned herein. For related information, see* Amagatsu Ushio, Eiko and Koma, Kasai Akira, Maro Akaji, Tanaka Min, *and* Yamada Setsuko.]

BIBLIOGRAPHY

Durland, Steven. "Contemporary Art in Japan." *High Performance* (Summer 1990): 22–31.

Garafola, Lynn. "Variations on a Theme of Butoh." *Dance Magazine* (April 1989): 66–68.

Hamera, Judith. "Derevo, Butoh, and Imagining the Real." *High Performance* (Spring 1990): 36–39.

Holborn, Mark. *Butoh: Dance of the Dark Soul.* New York, 1987.

Klein, Susan B. *Ankoku Butō: The Premodern and Postmodern Influences on the Dance of Utter Darkness.* Ithaca, N.Y., 1988.

Mikami Kayo. *Utsuwa to shite no shintai: Hijikata Tatsumi ankoku butō gihō e no apurōchi.* Tokyo, 1993.

Miyabi Ichikawa. "Butoh: The Denial of the Body." *Ballett International* 12 (September 1989): 14–19.

Paszkowska, Alexandra. *Butō-Tanz: Ushio Amagatsu und die Sankai Juku Gruppe.* Munich, 1983.

Tanemura Suehiro et al. *Hijikata Tatsumi butō taiken.* Tokyo, 1993.

Viala, Jean, and Nourit Masson-Sekine. *Butoh: Shades of Darkness.* Tokyo, 1988.

FILM.   Michael Blackwood, *Butoh: Body on the Edge of Crisis* (1990).

HASEGAWA ROKU
Translated from Japanese

dakan, Byakkosha (dissolved 1994), and Hakutobo companies.

While Hijikata investigated the "shape" of dance through bodily distortion, Kasai has used *butō* to express the invisible, interior world of human thought as well as cosmology and the spiritual world. Kasai's excellence as a performer is matched by his exceptional teaching ability; a number of noted *butō* dancers, including Yamada Setsuko, received training at his studio, Tenshi-kan. In the late 1970s, Kasai became interested in Rudolf Steiner's anthroposophy and in the movement theory known as eurhythmics, which he traveled to Germany to study. He eventually returned to the *butō* style, giving his first *butō* performance in fifteen years in January 1994; Kasai's later style incorporates elements from both his earlier, improvisational *butō* and eurhythmics.

Butō has been well received outside Japan. Among performers who have moved abroad are Ikeda Carlotta of Ariadone no Kai, based in France; Murobushi Ko of Butoh-ha Sebi (formerly of Dai Rakudakan) and Furukawa Anzu of Dance Butter, both in Germany; and Tamano Koichi, director of Haru-pin Ha in San Francisco.

BUTSOVA, HILDA (Hilda Boot; born 11 July 1896 in Nottingham, England, died 21 March 1976 in White Plains, New York), dancer. One of the first English dancers to make a career in a Russian ballet troupe, Butsova toured with Anna Pavlova's company for nearly fourteen years, achieving a rank second only to Pavlova and serving as her understudy. Born Hilda Boot into a nontheatrical family, she first studied dance in her native Nottingham. In 1909 she began training at the Stedman Academy in London, performing in Christmas pantomimes and school productions. She later studied with Enrico Cecchetti and Alexandre Volinine.

In 1911 she danced in Serge Diaghilev's Ballets Russes in its first London season. In 1912, Pavlova, who had seen the young English dancer perform in a short school demonstration, invited Butsova to join her company midway through its British tour. Butsova performed with Pavlova's troupe until 1925 and again in 1927–1928, rising through the ranks until she became a soloist. Her stamina, versatility, and good memory served her well during the Pavlova company's long and grueling tours; her charming, even-tempered personality helped her to win Pavlova's trust and friendship.

Butsova was with Pavlova on her final trip to Russia in 1914. She also appeared in New York City in 1915–1916 and toured with Pavlova's troupe in the United States, Europe, South America, and Asia. She danced leading roles in such works as *The Sleeping Beauty, Coppélia, A Polish Wedding, Chopiniana, The Magic Flute,* and *La Fille Mal Gardée.*

In 1925 Butsova married Harry Mills, then the Pavlova company's manager, and retired briefly in the United States to give birth to their son. She then performed with Mikhail Mordkin's company in the United States in 1926–1927 and joined Anton Dolin in a 1929 concert tour of Great Britain. She settled in the United States in 1930, performing in live prologues to films shown at the Capitol Theater in New York City. A successful teacher, Butsova had her own school in Brooklyn, New York, and also taught at the schools of Chester Hale (1931–1945) and Thalia Mara (1945–1960).

BIBLIOGRAPHY

Butsova, Hilda. "My Days with Pavlova." *Dance Magazine* (May 1926): 13–15, 56–57.
Horosko, Marian. "In the Shadow of Russian Tradition: Hilda Butsova." *Dance Magazine* (November 1972): 64–69.
Marsh, Lucile. "An Interview with Hilda Butsova." *Dance Magazine* (April 1943): 4–5; 33.
Money, Keith. *Anna Pavlova: Her Life and Art.* New York, 1982.

INTERVIEW.   Hilda Butsova, by Elizabeth B. Kendall (1975), Dance Collection, New York Public Library for the Performing Arts.

KATY MATHESON

BYRD, DONALD (born 21 July 1949 in New London, North Carolina), American dancer and choreographer. As a youth, Donald Byrd became interested in the performing arts. In high school he played classical flute, and during his years at Yale and Tufts universities, he studied acting. However, at sixteen, he had seen a performance by George Balanchine's New York City Ballet, and it made a strong impression on him. An overwhelming response to a performance by Alvin Ailey's dance company led the young African-American man to make his own career in dance. Initially, dance classes only supplemented his theater studies; eventually, additional ballet and contemporary dance classes followed, both in the United States and in England, as did concentrated study at Ailey's dance school in New York City. Admiration for Ailey and Balanchine, coupled with the experience of working with Gus Solomons, Jr., Twyla Tharp, and Karole Armitage all helped shape Byrd's development from dancer to dancemaker.

Byrd founded his own company of dancers, Donald Byrd / The Group, in Los Angeles in 1978 and moved it to New York City in 1983. Because he wanted "to get people's attention," Byrd chose punk music for the intermix of ballet, modern, and street-dance elements in his earliest work. He subsequently dropped the punk strain and adopted, with some regularity, subject matter concerned with issues of African-American culture and of racism. Beyond early works with titles such as *Low Down Dirty Rag* (1983), when Byrd the choreographer was also performing in dances by the so-called punk priestess, Armitage, he moved on to create a social-comment dance that provoked some controversy and gained him some recognition: *The Minstrel Show.* Created in 1991 and variously revived thereafter, the two-hour work takes elements of American minstrelsy—variety acts, folk costumes, scripted and ad-libbed jokes, popular music, and

BYRD. Leonora Stapelton and Michael Blake in *Bristle* (1993), Byrd's interpretation of Maurice Ravel's *La Valse,* at the Brooklyn Academy of Music, New York. (Photograph © 1994 by Johan Elbers; used by permission.)

dances—and recycles them into an event that both re-creates and rethinks the source. Byrd's *Minstrel Show* direction included participation by the audience and usually stirred heated responses. Jennifer Dunning of the *New York Times* characterized Byrd's dances with racial and social-issue themes as works of "intense evocation" rather than "overt protest." Intense kinetic images have consistently characterized Byrd's dancemaking. Extreme physical accentuation, such as split-leg postures for moments of held balance or for partnered couplings, have become a Byrd hallmark. In his ways with such inventions, Byrd blends the cool formalities of ballet academicism with the burning extroverted individuality of modern dance.

A 1987 commission from Sylvia Waters, to create a work for the Alvin Ailey Repertory Ensemble, brought Byrd to Ailey's attention. In 1988, the choreographer, whose work had so inspired Byrd, commissioned him to create a dance for his world-renowned troupe. After *Shards* (1988), Byrd continued to create for the Ailey company, even after Ailey died in 1989: *Dance at the Gym* (1991) and *Folkdance* (1992). Several iconographic works of dance history have inspired Byrd to remake them according to his own whim: *Prodigal* (1991) looks askance at Balanchine's *Prodigal Son; Bristle* (1993) looks into Maurice Ravel's *La Valse; Life Situations* (1994) reshapes *Giselle;* and *The Harlem Nutcracker* (1994–1996) reconsiders an American Christmas tradition. After his punk-music phase, Byrd collaborated almost exclusively with electronic composer Mio Morales. His original music and/or reworkings of "sacred-cow" scores provide Byrd with sounds that are more atmospheric for than organic to his dances.

BIBLIOGRAPHY

Anderson, Jack. "Donald Byrd: An Unabashed Eclectic." *New York Times* (14 August 1994).

Dunning, Jennifer. "Creating a 'Folk Dance' for Friends of Long Standing." *New York Times* (13 December 1992).

Fanger, Iris M. "Prodigal Talent." *Dance Magazine* (July 1993): 42–45.

Pasles, Christopher. "Donald Byrd's Dance of Reality." *Los Angeles Times* (25 April 1993).

ROBERT GRESKOVIC

C

CACHUCHA, LA. *See* Diable Boiteux, Le. *See also the entries on Jean Coralli and the Elssler sisters.*

CAGE, JOHN (born 5 September 1912 in Los Angeles, died 12 August 1992 in New York City), American composer, author, artist, and philosopher. For nearly fifty years, Cage was at the forefront of the American avant-garde. His long association with choreographer Merce Cunningham, with whom he worked steadily from 1942, was one of the significant partnerships in the annals of dance.

Cage's contribution to music, and to the performing arts in general, was to free them from the constraints of convention. Over a five decade career he systematically stripped his music of elements long deemed essential to the form, substituting noise for pitched tones, silence for sound, and the workings of chance for self-expression. He originated the concept that a performance should be not the re-creation of a previous artistic experience but a process that creates a new one. After 1958 most of his compositions were to some degree "indeterminate"—sufficiently open-ended, that is, to ensure a range of equally acceptable possibilities at every performance.

The son of an inventor, Cage spent most of his childhood in Los Angeles. Among his first music teachers was Fannie Charles Dillon, under whose tutelage he became a competent pianist and developed an adolescent passion for the music of Edvard Grieg. An exceptionally bright, self-motivated student, at age fifteen he graduated from Los Angeles High School as class valedictorian. After two years at Pomona College in Claremont, California, he traveled to Europe, where he desultorily pursued music, painting, dance, and architecture. Upon returning to California in late 1932, he resumed his musical education, studying composition and theory with Richard Buhlig, Henry Cowell, Adolph Weiss, and Arnold Schoenberg. Of these, Cowell exerted the greatest influence. He introduced Cage to the thriving new music communities in San Francisco and New York, exposed him to Eastern music, and served as both friend and mentor. Schoenberg, with whom Cage studied harmony and counterpoint from 1935 to 1937, offered no encouragement, though some

years later he characterized his former student as an "inventor of genius." Cage's earliest extant works date from this period and include *Sonata for Clarinet* (1933) and *Quartet* (1935) and *Trio* (1936) for percussion.

In 1938 Cage was hired as accompanist by Bonnie Bird, head of the dance department at the Cornish School in Seattle. There he met Cunningham, a second-year student majoring in dance. Soon after his arrival Cage organized a small percussion orchestra, the first standing ensemble of its kind. Its nucleus was Cage, his wife Xenia, and two members of the Cornish faculty; various students, Cunningham among them, performed with it as extras from time to time. Cage composed several works for the orchestra and persuaded other composers to do likewise. As a consequence, the percussion literature swelled from about six pieces to more than seventy-five in less than five years.

Schoenberg had emphasized the importance of harmony as a structural element in composition. Rejecting this dictum, in 1939 Cage devised a novel structure based on proportional rhythmic patterns. This structure, first applied to *First Construction (in Metal)*, was to have a far-reaching impact on the traditional relationship between music and dance, in that it eliminated the need to make either subservient to the other. Simply by agreeing in advance to a common rhythmic structure, a composer and a choreographer could work independently, uniting their separate contributions only when both were finished. Cage and Cunningham followed this procedure throughout the 1940s. Subsequently they went even further: in the early 1950s their collaborations were typified by total independence of music and movement, the two having nothing in common with each other beyond the circumstance of their being performed simultaneously.

In 1938, for a solo dance choreographed by Syvilla Fort, another of Bird's students, Cage invented the "prepared piano" and composed his first work for it, *Bacchanale*. To prepare the piano, Cage inserted screws, bolts (with or without nuts), coins, pencil erasers, and strips of rubber, leather, felt, and other materials between the strings of a concert grand, thereby muting and otherwise transforming its sound into an unexpectedly beautiful collection of pings and thuds. In essence a one-player percussion band, the prepared piano became Cage's most famous invention. Between 1940 and the mid-1950s he composed more than a dozen works for it, many to accompany dances by Cunningham. His most famous piece, however, is a concert work, *Sonatas and Interludes* (1946–1948), a seventy-minute solo intended to express the nine permanent emotions of Indian thought.

In 1947, after two years in Seattle, one in San Francisco, and one in Chicago (where he taught "sound experiments" at László Moholy-Nagy's School of Design), Cage moved to New York, where a percussion concert at the Museum of Modern Art made him overnight a force on the city's new music scene.

In New York he formed a working alliance with Cunningham, who had preceded him east in 1939 as a member of Martha Graham's company. It was largely due to his encouragement that Cunningham left Graham in 1945 to concentrate on a solo career. During the 1940s Cage and Cunningham gave frequent joint recitals, usually to small, sometimes hostile, audiences. Cage composed and performed most of the music for their concerts. He also worked sporadically with other dancers, among them Jean Erdman, Pearl Primus, and Hanya Holm.

In 1947 Cunningham and Cage were commissioned by Lincoln Kirstein to create a work for Ballet Society. The result was *The Seasons*, Cunningham's first dance for a ballet troupe and Cage's first composition for orchestra. *The Seasons* was sufficiently well-received to be revived in the two following years, lending new prestige to the Cage-Cunningham partnership.

1951 marked the turning point in Cage's creative life. For several years, inspired by the Eastern idea that music's proper function is to quiet the mind, thereby rendering it open to divine influences, he had sought to purge his music of the distracting effect of his own tastes. In his *String Quartet in Four Parts* (1949–1950), *Sixteen Dances* (1951), and *Concerto for Prepared Piano and Chamber Orchestra* (1951), he had used charts resembling magic squares to determine the note-by-note process of composition. The breakthrough was his discovery of the *I Ching*, an ancient Chinese book of divination that contains a simple but reliable method—the tossing of three coins six times—for randomly generating numbers from one to sixty-four. Cage realized that he could employ this system to make the decisions he had formerly been obligated to make for himself—the pitch, volume, and timbre of every sound, and the duration of every sound and silence.

The first major composition in which Cage used chance operations exclusively was *Music of Changes* (1951–1952), a monumental forty-three minute piano solo composed for David Tudor, who subsequently became the foremost interpreter of Cage's keyboard works and a charter member of the musical ensemble that regularly performed with Cunningham's troupe. *Music of Changes* was but one in a series of extraordinary works that included *Imaginary*

Landscape No. 4 (1951), for twelve radios and twenty-four performers, a highly unpredictable piece whose sounds are determined by what is being broadcast at the time of its performance; *Williams Mix* (1952), a 192-page score designed as a pattern for splicing together a magnetic tape collage; the celebrated *4'33"* (1952), with the pianist sitting motionless for four minutes and thirty-three seconds of ambient sounds; and *Music for Piano 1* (1952), in which the placement of notes was determined by imperfections in the paper on which the composition was written.

His decision to substitute chance for self-expression set Cage irrevocably outside the mainstream of modern music. It was a factor in the withering of his close friendships with composers Lou Harrison and Virgil Thomson, among others, and it has contributed to widespread misunderstanding about his methods and aims. It proved no obstacle, however, to Cunningham, who had himself employed chance, though to a more limited extent, in many of his dances.

When Cunningham formed his own company in 1953, Cage assumed the position of music director, a title he retained until the mid-1970s. In truth he was considerably more than that. For more than a decade he functioned as the troupe's de facto manager, especially on tour. Long after the company had hired a full-time manager, Cage remained its chief fund-raiser. *Notations* (1969, with Alison Knowles), his book of musical manuscripts donated by some 270 modern composers, began as a scheme to generate revenue for the dance company. Cage was also largely responsible for Cunningham's long-standing policy of engaging distinguished artists—such as Robert Rauschenberg, Jasper Johns, and Frank Stella—to design decor and costumes.

By the late 1960s the company was firmly established as one of America's leading modern dance ensembles, and young choreographers everywhere were familiar with Cunningham's concept of dance as process—the corollary of Cage's position with respect to music. More than fifty Cage scores were performed in conjunction with Cunningham dances, and although many were composed for specific dances (e.g., *Telephones and Birds* for *Travelogue*, 1977), Cage never hesitated to borrow pieces written for the concert hall for use in the theater.

It would be difficult to overstate Cage's value to Cunningham as a friend, collaborator, and source of inspiration. No other choreographer of note has been so closely identified with one composer for so long a period, and few composers, if any, have played so intimate and influential a role in the life of a dance troupe.

In 1954 Cage joined a newly formed artists' cooperative in Stony Point, New York, where he became interested in flora generally and mushrooms particularly. Immersing himself in their study, he swiftly mastered the fine points of mushroom identification and became a respected amateur mycologist. (While visiting Milan in 1959, he won the grand prize on an Italian television quiz show by answering increasingly recondite questions about edible fungi over a five-week span. He used his winnings, about $6,000, to buy a new van for the Cunningham company.)

1958 marked the twenty-fifth anniversary of the beginning of Cage's career. The occasion was celebrated with a major retrospective concert at Town Hall, New York, for which Cage composed *Concert for Piano and Orchestra,* a work employing eighty-four different compositional techniques in the piano part alone, which Cunningham "conducted." Similar events occurred with increasing frequency after 1962, the year of Cage's fiftieth birthday. In 1982, when he turned seventy, there were observances in many cities and a national new music festival, held in Chicago in July, was dedicated to him.

Cage's position as dean of the American avant-garde was solidified in 1961 by the publication of *Silence,* a collection of his lectures, essays, anecdotes, and other literary items. It has become a classic in its field and is frequently assigned as required reading in college music courses. In *Silence* and its sequels—*A Year from Monday* (1967), *M* (1972), and *Empty Words* (1979)—Cage repeatedly returned to those themes which interested him most deeply: music and the organization of sound, social engineering, nature, Eastern thought (Cage was a dedicated Zen Buddhist), language and communication, mushrooms, chess, and the ideas of other artists and thinkers who have influenced him: Marcel Duchamp, Buckminster Fuller, Marshall McLuhan, Erik Satic, Henry David Thoreau, and James Joyce. True to form, he devised ingenious ways to apply his musical principles to the printed page, letting chance operations decide various questions of typography, layout, and even, at times, content: he selected the title of *M,* for instance, by subjecting the twenty-six letters of the alphabet to the impartial wisdom of the *I Ching.*

The 1960s and 1970s witnessed no diminution of Cage's creative energy. Major compositions of the 1960s included *Atlas Eclipticalis* (1961–1962), an orchestral work wherein note placement was determined by star charts; a series of highly indeterminate pieces named *Variations;* and *HPSCHD* (1967–1969), an immense multi-media pageant for seven amplified harpsichords, fifty-two tape players, eight film projectors, and sixty-four slide projectors. Works of the 1970s included *Etudes Australes* (1974–1975), a suite of thirty-two increasingly complex piano solos; *Renga* with *Apartment House 1776* (1976), for four vocal soloists and large orchestra; and *Roaratorio* (1979), a radio play consisting of sounds recorded in locales mentioned in *Finnegans Wake.* He also completed two substantial literary works, *Writing through Finnegans Wake* (1978) and *Empty Words* (1979), the former in five distinct versions.

Both reflected his growing interest in purging language of meaning, thereby distilling it to its essence: sounds.

In 1978 Cage embarked on a second career as a graphic artist, producing a series of etchings created by subjecting various images to *I Ching* chance operations. This was appropriate, in that he was the first composer to treat the printed score as a work of art.

That Cage has been one of the most influential artists of modern times is beyond argument. Despite the hostility of many critics and much of the concert-going public, his ideas have taken root and continue to flourish.

[*See also* Music for Dance, *article on* Western Music since 1900; *and the entry on Cunningham.*]

BIBLIOGRAPHY

Adam, Judy, ed. *Dancers on a Plane: Cage, Cunningham, Johns.* New York, 1990.
Ballet Review 13 (Fall 1985): 23–40. Panel discussion entitled "The Forming of an Aesthetic: Merce Cunningham and John Cage."
Cage, John. *Silence.* Middletown, Conn., 1961.
Cage, John. *A Year from Monday.* Middletown, Conn., 1967.
Cage, John. *M.* Middletown, Conn., 1972.
Cage, John. *For the Birds.* Boston, 1981.
Cage, John. *X.* Middletown, Conn., 1983.
Hamm, Charles. "Cage, John." In *The New Grove Dictionary of Music and Musicians.* London, 1980.
Kostelanetz, Richard, ed. *John Cage.* New York, 1970.
Nyman, Michael. *Experimental Music: Cage and Beyond.* New York, 1981.
Tomkins, Calvin. *The Bride and the Bachelors.* New York, 1965.
Vaughan, David. "Duet." *Ballet News* 4 (March 1983): 20–22.
Vaughan, David. "Cunningham, Cage, and Joyce: 'this longawaited messiagh of roaratorios." *Choreography and Dance* 1.4 (1992): 79–89.
Yates, Peter. *Twentieth-Century Music.* New York, 1967.

ROY M. CLOSE

CAJUN DANCE TRADITIONS comprise a group of dances known in southern Louisiana and southeastern Texas among the people called Cajun and Creole. The name *Cajun* is a corruption of *acadien,* and designates a person from the Acadiana region of Louisiana. The term *Creole,* which signifies people of European ancestry born in the New World, was used in this region for the descendants of the original French and Spanish settlers of Louisiana (as distinguished from the Cajuns), but it has come to mean also a person of mixed Creole and black (Afro-Caribbean) ancestry. The term *Creole,* however, is used mainly in and around New Orleans; people of mixed Afro-Caribbean and Cajun ancestry in Cajun country call themselves "black Cajuns," or simply "Cajuns."

A permanent French colony was first established within the modern boundaries of Louisiana in 1714. The first black slaves (mainly Afro-Caribbeans) were brought to the region at about the same time; large numbers arrived after 1719. Spanish settlers first came in 1762. The Acadiana region (mainly the parishes of Saint Mary, Vermilion, and Acadia in the Attakapas country, the bayous west of New Orleans) was settled in the mid-1760s by several hundred French-speaking refugees expelled from Nova Scotia (formerly part of the French colony of Acadie, or "Acadia" in English) by the British in 1755 and 1758, because they refused to take an oath of loyalty to the British sovereign during the Seven Years' War. Other immigrants came from central and southern Europe and the Middle East. Over the years, Cajuns, Creoles, and the other groups have intermarried to a considerable extent; the ethnic mix is reflected in the variety of their social dances.

Dancing can be found at practically any Cajun social occasion, and many restaurants and beer halls also have dance floors. The most popular occasion for dancing has been for many years the *fais do-do* ("go to sleep" in nursery slang). Entire families attend; the babies are put on the floor in a side room, called the *parc au petits* (lit., "playpen"), to sleep. In the days before the telephone invitations would arrive by horseback: the rider would simply gallop through the yards and fields, yelling at the top of his voice, "*Fais do-do* tonight!" followed by the location.

Cajun dances, done by couples in facing position, include a one-step swing dance and several variations of the two-step and waltz. Older dances include the mazurka, polka, schottische, and several forms of country-style circle and contradance (often spelled *contra dance* in the United States). The music for the one-step and two-step dances is all played in duple meter. To do the one-step swing, known as the Cajun Jitterbug or Jig, partners face each other, hold hands at arm's length, and execute a variety of arm-twisting figures. The steps are fast-paced, four to a measure, stepping on the ball of one foot and flat on the other.

One of the older, but still common, styles of the two-step is more relaxed. Partners hold one another in ballroom-dance position, facing each other with one arm on or around the partner's shoulder while the other arm is slightly extended, holding the partner's free hand. The dancers go from side to side with a step-close-step-pause sequence in each measure, often turning as they move about the floor. Sometimes in this style the dancers step up on the balls of the feet on the first step of each side-to-side sequence. Another common style of the two-step dance is similar in rhythm to the dance of Cuban origin known as the rumba. Couples hold each other in the same ballroom position, but the step rhythm is step-pause-step-step in each measure. The last step is most often backward, causing the dancers to feel as if they are pulling away from each other. The dancers turn and travel around the floor, but do not move from side to side. It is this style that is also known as Zydeco when danced to the rock-and-roll version of Cajun two-step music of the same name. Zydeco dancers also move their hips more and use fancy footwork. The word *Zydeco* is a corruption of the ti-

tle of the song "Les Haricots," which was made popular by musician Clifton Chenier. The Cowboy Two-Step, popular in country-western dance halls throughout the United States, is occasionally done in Acadiana to Cajun two-step music, but it is entirely different from the Cajun Two-Step and is not considered to be a Cajun dance.

In Cajun (southeastern) Texas, another version of rumba-style two-step also goes by the name Cajun Jitterbug. It incorporates arm figures and twisting foot movements. Sometimes there is a kick slightly forward with the free foot on each pause, which means that the man may kick between the woman's legs as she kicks to the left of his legs on the first step of the first measure; this motif is reversed on the first step of the second measure. This is similar to, and may be a version of, the *cumbia* (a variant of the mambo), a social dance of Latin America.

The waltz in Cajun country is most unusual. Partners hold each other in the ballroom-style facing position, and while some dance in the usual European three-count method with one big step followed by two short steps, others merely travel the same distance with each step and call it the "one-step waltz." Others take the big step on count two, and still others take the big step on count three. Other unusual syncopated dances are also done to waltz music and are thus called waltzes. One variation involves a step on count one, a pause for the second count and a half, followed by two more steps, which results in a catch step just before count three. The other syncopated waltzes are variations on a sequence of four steps taken over six counts of music (two measures). This involves two slow (two-count) steps and two quick (one-count) steps. The dancers usually travel around the floor, the man going forward, his partner backward, with an occasional half turn that allows the woman to go forward. When the dancers stay in one place for a while they do a gentle rocking motion in the same rhythm. Another "waltz" is actually a mazurka, in which the dancers step on the first two beats and add a weightless touch on count three. Still another variant is actually a schottische, but done to waltz music rather than to four-count schottische music. Although the dance step is four counts long, which does not fit waltz music, the dancers do not seem to notice.

Some dances that were popular in the past are rarely seen anymore, though they are remembered by older dancers and/or are mentioned at various places in the literature. These include couple dances and forms of square and circle dances properly included among early American dances rather than Cajun dances. Among these obsolete couple dances are a Mexican one-step (a varient of the merengue), the mazurka, and the Jilliling (a corruption of "Jenny Lind," an old-time square dance). The once-popular *contredanse* was not a contradance in the current sense, with two opposing lines of partners.

Rather, it was more like the early American big circle dance for an unspecified number of couples, which begins and ends in a circle formation, breaking during the course of the dance into small groups of two or more couples that perform figures around each other, as in square dancing. Other dances, such as the Lancers, were done with four or eight couples facing in square, or quadrille, formation. Similar to both of these were the singing dances, which were done in both circle and square formations.

BIBLIOGRAPHY
Carbine, Elizabeth. "They Dance the Fait[*sic*]-do-do." *Evangeline Parish* magazine supplement to the *New Orleans Times-Picayune* (15 August 1926).
Duke, Jerry C. *Dances of the Cajuns.* San Francisco, 1990.
Keys, Frances Parkinson. *All This is Louisiana.* New York, 1950.
Ramsey, Carolyn. *Cajuns on the Bayous.* New York, 1957.

JERRY C. DUKE

CAKEWALK. Originated by enslaved Africans living on Caribbean and North American plantations, the cakewalk was a festive dance for which the best executor received a cake as the prize. Dances were witnessed and judged by plantation owners, and slaves were taken from plantation to plantation to compete in the contests. The dance consisted of "a kind of shuffling movement which evolved into a smooth walking step with the body held erect. The backward sway was added, and as the dance became more of a satire on the dance of the white plantation owners, the movement became a prancing strut" (Emery, 1972).

Because of its theatricality, the cakewalk lent itself to the stage. As an all-male, noncouple dance, it was a regular feature in the minstrel show finale and remained a staple of the popular stage thereafter. By the 1890s it was introduced into productions of *Uncle Tom's Cabin* to enliven the hackneyed format.

Even as minstrelsy declined, the cakewalk thrived. In 1899 *The Creole Show* (an African-American, New York production) featured Dora Dean and Charles Johnson in a cakewalk. By omitting blackface makeup and using female performers, it was purportedly the first African-American show to break the minstrel format. Johnson and Dean thereafter became a famous cakewalk act. With the addition of female performers, the dance returned to its original, heterosexual format and the potential for improvisation was expanded.

Like many theatrical dances that followed, the cakewalk moved from the pre-vaudeville stage to the ballroom floor and was performed by blacks and whites, both nationwide and abroad. It was the first African-American dance to become popular in the white world; it launched the ballroom "dance fever" and was followed by such fad dances as the Turkey Trot, Ballin' the Jack, the Black Bottom, and the Charleston, all African-American in origin.

CAKEWALK. An embellished photograph of cakewalk dancers, which probably appeared on the cover of sheet music in the nineteenth century. (Photograph from the Dance Collection, New York Public Library for the Performing Arts.)

One of the ironies of American racial discrimination is highlighted in the evolution of the cakewalk. As a plantation form, the strutting exhibitionism of the African-American cakewalkers was an imitation of the pompous manners of the plantation owners performing the Grand March at their balls. By the turn of the century, however, whites had become the imitators as they attempted to capture the African-American style of the dance.

In 1898 the cakewalk was introduced to the legitimate stage in the African-American musical *Clorindy, or The Origin of the Cakewalk.* Bert Williams and George Walker were significant in the dissemination of the dance, and it became their trademark and was danced in the many turn-of-the-century operettas that they wrote, produced, and starred in; their *In Dahomey* (1903) played abroad and popularized the dance in England and France. In the same era, stars such as Florence Mills began their careers as winners of amateur cakewalk contests, while Ida Forsyne made the dance a mainstay of her act.

By the second decade of the twentieth century the cakewalk had been replaced by new ballroom dances. However, African-American concert dance was in its inception. The Hampton Institute Creative Dance Group arranged the cakewalk and other historical African-American dances for concert stage presentation. Katherine Dunham included the dance in her suite of *Plantation Dances* (1943), and it was featured in Ruthanna Boris's *Cakewalk* ballet (1951).

Along with blackface minstrelsy, the cakewalk was part of fraternity celebrations at several American colleges until the 1960s, when such performances were outlawed due to their racial stereotyping.

[*See also* United States of America, *article on* African-American Dance Traditions.]

BIBLIOGRAPHY

Emery, Lynne Fauley. *Black Dance in the United States from 1619 to 1970*. Palo Alto, Calif., 1972. Rev. ed. Princeton, 1988.

Sampson, Henry T. *Blacks in Blackface: A Source Book on Early Black Musical Shows*. Metuchen, N.J., 1980.

RECORDING. *I'll Dance Till De Sun Breaks Through* (Saydisc Records, 1983), with early recordings of ragtime, cakewalk, and stomps.

BRENDA DIXON GOTTSCHILD

CALLOT, JACQUES (born 1592 in Nancy, Duchy of Lorraine, died 1635 in Nancy), French printmaker and master of etching technique. Many of Callot's images doc-

ument early seventeenth-century courtly festivities and theatrical traditions. Following an apprenticeship to an engraver in Rome, Callot settled in Florence, where in 1614 he secured the patronage of the Medici grand ducal court and achieved considerable fame. When Grand Duke Cosimo II de' Medici died in 1621, Callot left Florence and returned to his native Nancy, where the remainder of his career was centered.

Callot's artistic output was prodigious. He produced more than fourteen hundred prints, for which a large body of preparatory drawings survives. His technical innovations—the use of hard varnish and repeated bitings of the plates—enabled him to achieve etching effects with engravings, producing prints characterized by rich tonal contrasts and varied qualities of line. Callot was both an acute observer of his world and a lover of exaggeration and elegant stylization; his most characteristic works combine a powerful sense of reality with formal grace and fantasy. His vast range of subject matter includes religious themes, warfare and its effects, landscape, portraiture, the

CALLOT. Etching of a scene from the fête *Le Combat à la Barrière* (1627). A bird with extended wings supports a group of musicians; several warriors with plumed helmets ride a giant reptile; and three floats are pulled by a winged man, a monster, and dogs. (Dance Collection, New York Public Library for the Performing Arts.)

various classes of society (as isolated figures or in social contexts), and theatrical works, many commissioned to illustrate festival books published in conjunction with spectacles organized by the Medici court.

The chief organizer and designer of these innovative spectacles was Giulio Parigi, under whose guidance Callot began to make his festival prints. Two groups of etchings of 1616, *The War of Love* and *The War of Beauty*, depict court-sponsored festivities held in the Piazza Santa Croce. Each spectacle consisted of an opening procession of elaborate floats and costumed participants, mock combat, and a concluding equestrian ballet, the last being a new mode of performance that would spread from Italy throughout Europe during the seventeenth century. *The Fan* (1619) illustrates a mock combat between weavers and dyers staged on the Arno River and concluded by a fireworks display.

In three etchings of 1617 entitled the *Intermezzi*, Callot depicted a Medici court entertainment *(veglia)* that combined scenic representation onstage with a courtly ballet in the auditorium. The *First Intermezzo*, the only visual record of the great court stage of 1585/86 built in the Uffizi Theater, shows the dancers moving from the stage along curving ramps into the auditorium, where the grand duke and archduchess joined the ballet. Callot also produced five etchings to illustrate the first edition of Prospero Bonarelli's tragedy, *Il Solimano,* published in Florence in 1620. Callot's last festival prints were made in Nancy in 1627 to record *Le Combat à la Barrière* a Carnival entertainment staged in the ducal palace. Callot's images present the floats, the participants, and the great hall of the palace—with the entire court observing or participating in mock combat.

Callot produced a number of prints animated by the spirit of the *commedia dell'arte*. *Three Italian Comedians* (c.1618–1620) illustrates famous stock characters (Pantalone, Il Capitano, Arlecchino) against backdrops of staged comic performances. The *Balli di Sfessania* (c.1622), among Callot's most famous and widely imitated works, seems most directly inspired by the impromptu street entertainment that abounded in Italian cities, especially during Carnival season. The foreground of each original image shows a pair of comic performers who dance, mime, play musical instruments, and perform acrobatic feats.

BIBLIOGRAPHY

Choné, Paulette, Daniel Ternois, Jean-Marc Dupluvrez, and Brigette Heckel. *Jacques Callot: 1592–1635.* Paris, 1992.
Lieure, Jules. *Jacques Callot.* 8 vols. Paris, 1924–1927.
Nagler, A. M. *Theatre Festivals of the Medici, 1539–1637.* New Haven, 1964.
Russell, H. Diane, and Jeffrey Blanchard. *Jacques Callot: Prints and Related Drawings.* Washington, D.C., 1975.
Ternois, Daniel. *Jacques Callot.* Paris, 1962.

JEFFREY BLANCHARD

CAMARGO, MARIE (Marie-Anne de Cupis de Camargo; born 15 April 1710 in Brussels, died 28 April 1770 in Paris), French dancer. The name of Mademoiselle Camargo is so gloriously prominent in the history of Western dance that it has come to symbolize the whole eighteenth century to which she so fittingly belonged. From the outset, she was a "star," and the scandals, gossip, and vicarious interest that her extravagant and unconventional life generated filled up the social chronicles of her time. What marks a performer for such attention is almost always elusive and inexplicable. Choreographer Jean-Georges Noverre, who had seen her dance, noted that

> Mademoiselle Camargo was neither pretty, nor tall, nor well formed . . . but her mind was good . . . and it prompted her to select a style [of dancing] suitable to her physique . . . a lively and vivacious style which left no time for the spectators to detect the faults in her anatomy. Her dancing was quick, light, full of gaiety and brilliancy. She could perform with extreme facility *jetés battus*, the royale, cleanly cut *entrechats*, all those steps now removed from the dance catalogue but which were seductively brilliant. She only danced to lively music, and such fast tempi does not permit the display of grace. For this, she substituted ease, speed, and gaiety.   (Noverre, 1804)

As none of Camargo's dances was ever notated in the Feuillet system, we must defer to Noverre's critical observations. However, if one may judge by Mademoiselle Guyot's solos of similar character and recorded thirty years earlier, Camargo's technique could have indeed been that of a virtuoso. Nevertheless, there is no evidence to support the legend that she was the first female dancer to shorten her skirts in order to display her technique.

During her career of twenty-five years, she was featured twenty-seven times as a shepherdess, twenty-one times as a sailor, seven times as a bacchante, five times as Terpsichore, twice as a Sylphide, and only once as a Grace. In person, she was typed as a southern beauty—Bohemian, Egyptian, Ethiopian, Greek, Israelite, Moorish, Provençal—and was cast often as a demon or a huntress.

There is no better résumé of the dancer's life and career than the obituaries that appeared in 1771 in the *Nécrologe des hommes célèbres* and the *Almanach des spectacles de Paris.* On her father's side, Camargo's family was Roman and had produced a few cardinals attached to the house of Austria. Her grandfather, Monsieur Cuppi, had settled in Flanders, where he married a Spaniard from the noble family of Camargo. He died early, leaving a son, Ferdinand-François de Cupis (alias "Camargo"), who, because of financial misfortune, had to earn his living from the teaching of dance and music. Camargo's training was thus first given by her father.

Camargo's progress was such that by the age of ten or twelve she was sent to Paris to further her studies with

CAMARGO. A well-known image of Camargo. The engraving is by Laurent Car after Nicolas Lancret's painting from the 1730s, now in the Musée des Beaux-Arts, Nantes. (Courtesy of Madison U. Sowell and Debra H. Sowell, Brigham Young University, Provo, Utah.)

the famous Françoise Prévost. Her sponsors were the Princess de Lignes and other wealthy ladies of the Brussels court. On her return from Paris, Camargo received a lucrative engagement at the Rouen Opera and finally the coveted honor to join the Paris Opera. She made her debut there on 5 May 1726 in a piece choreographed by Prévost, *Les Caractères de la Danse*, which she performed

> with all the liveliness and intelligence that could possibly be expected from a young person aged fifteen to sixteen . . . her cabrioles and *entrechats* were effortless, and, although she has still many perfections to acquire before she can venture comparison with her illustrious teacher, she is considered to be one of the most brilliant dancers to be seen, in particular for her sensitive ear for music, her airiness, and her strength.
>
> (*Mercure*, 1726)

The public, however, immediately fell for the young dancer, regardless of her immaturity, or perhaps on account of it.

Prévost thought otherwise and returned the dancer to the corps. At this point, says the *Nécrologe*, "A happy set of circumstances . . . rekindled a fame which jealousy had attempted to suppress." In a ballet where Dumoulin was to make a solo entrance but was nowhere to be seen, Camargo made her final leap to stardom by improvising the part of the absentee dancer, under showers of applause. This last incident ended forever the relationship between teacher and pupil, and Prévost refused to go on with her lessons. None other than Guillaume-Louis Pecour and Michel Blondy offered to replace her.

> It is thanks to the second of these masters, that Camargo disciplined the fire of her execution and added grace, lightness, and this seductive gaiety which she always displayed onstage . . . but this spark of joy which lighted the dancer's eyes and her every movement was lost the moment she regained the wings.
>
> (*Nécrologe*, 1771)

Camargo had a lovely voice and sang in tune, a facility that she displayed in *Les Fêtes d'Hébé, ou Les Talents Lyriques*. Her eulogy in the *Almanach des spectacles* also recalled a pas de trois with Blondy and David Dumoulin and

> an admirable pas de six, which amply justified the verses that accompanied her portrait by Lancret:

> > Fidèle aux lois de la cadence,
> > Je forme au gré de l'art, les pas les plus haradis,
> > Originale danse ma danse,
> > Je peux le disputer aux Ballons et aux Blondis.

Camargo retired from the Paris Opera in 1734 at the height of her career but returned in 1740, "without a visible trace of her six years absence." She had sought the advice of Louis Dupré and "brought more variety to her dances than ever before." From her teachers, Prévost, Pecour, Blondy, and Dupré, she had developed her own style, "which owed to theirs but was in no way their copy" (*Nécrologe*, 1771). Camargo retired a second time from the Paris Opera in 1751, with the largest pension given to a dancer, fifteen hundred livres. She died in 1770 a wealthy woman, surrounded by her many cats, dogs, parrots, pigeons, and budgerigars. The inventory of her belongings lists her fortune at sixteen thousand livres, as opposed to Marie Sallé's three thousand. Her cellar alone, which contained some five hundred bottles of the finest wines, disproves the rumors that the dancer had been reduced to penury in her last years.

BIBLIOGRAPHY

Almanach des spectacles de Paris, ou Calendrier historique et chronologique des théâtres. Paris, 1771.

Aubry, Pierre, and Émile Dacier. *Les caractères de la danse.* Paris, 1905.

Beaumont, Cyril W. *Three French Dancers of the Eighteenth Century: Camargo, Sallé, Guimard.* London, 1934.

Daniels, Diana P. "The First Ballerina?" *Dance Magazine* (January 1960): 52–53.

Dorat, Claude Charles. *La danse.* Paris, 1767.

Letainturier-Fradin, Gabriel. *La Camargo* (1908). Geneva, 1973.

Migel, Parmenia. *The Ballerinas: From the Court of Louis XIV to Pavlova.* New York, 1972.

Moore, Lillian. "Marie Camargo." In Moore's *Artists of the Dance.* New York, 1938.

Noverre, Jean-Georges. *Lettres sur la danse, sur les ballets et les arts.* 4 vols. St. Petersburg, 1803–1804.

Poinsinet de Sivry, J., et al. *Le nécrologe des hommes célèbres de France, par une société de gens de lettres.* Paris, 1767–.

Prudhommeau, Germaine. "Camargo-Sallé: Duel au pied levé." *Danser* (March 1986): 78–81.

Schneider, Marcel. "Camargo-Sallé: L'art d'être rivales." *Danser* (May 1993): 44–46.

Winter, Marian Hannah. *The Pre-Romantic Ballet.* London, 1974.

RÉGINE ASTIER

CAMBODIA. In its early history, Cambodia received Hindu influence from India; Buddhism spread to it in the seventh century. The Khmer Empire developed and flourished there from about the fourth to the fifteenth century, when it ruled the entire Mekong valley and had tributary states. From the thirteenth century, it was attacked by the Siamese to the north and the Annamese to the east; it had become a vassal to Siam (now Thailand) when France colonized Indochina in the nineteenth century. The kingdom of Cambodia became independent in 1953 but was increasingly involved in the conflict in Vietnam, a traditional enemy. The country fell to an anticommunist military coup in 1970, and both U.S. and South Vietnamese troops fought against communist strongholds (including the Khmer Rouge) in Cambodia. The Khmer Rouge grew stronger in the 1970s, culminating in the 1975 reign of terror. In 1979, Vietnam invaded and installed a communist government; the Khmer Rouge regime fell, but resistance from them and from the monarchists remains. In 1991, a peace treaty was signed by all the factions and the United Nations assumed governmental responsibilities, working with Cambodia's factions until elections were held in November 1993.

The Khmer dance styles of Cambodia are rooted in three major sources. First are the dances of the indigenous Austroasiatic inhabitants of the region. Next, sacred dance styles developed during the period of Hindu and Buddhist influence from India. Finally, there is the classical concert dance of the modern period, which developed under the patronage of the court.

Folk Dance. Although no evidence for dance during earliest times exists, the tribal and folk dances performed today in the remote regions of the country most probably preserve some elements from prehistoric times. Modern concert versions of the same dances have been choreographed for folkloric ensembles, such as that established by the University of Fine Arts in the capital, Phnom Penh, in the 1950s. Among these dances are "Leng Trott" (Dance of the Stag)—probably originally a hunting ritual—and "Sneng Tonsong" (Dance of the Wild Oxen). Village humor prevails in the *chha-yam*, in which masked dancers with gongs and drums precede religious processions, their antics accompanied by the singing of comic verses. These and other village dances are often performed at Khmer new year festivals in Cambodia and occasionally in the West.

Ritual Temple Dance. Most dances of the Khmer Kingdom of Angkor (802–1431) consisted of huge ensembles of female dancers dedicated to the temple, performing ritual temple dances. The substance of these dances has been lost over the intervening centuries, but carvings of dancing *apsara* (the name later given to the carved celestial nymphs) at the temple of Angkor Wat preserve

CAMBODIA. *(left)* Devi Yim in an outdoor performance of the Cambodian court dance *Monosanhchetana*. *(right)* A scene from the dance drama *Muni Mekhala*, in which Mekhala, the Water Goddess, flees her adversary Ream Eyso, the Storm Spirit. The performance was produced by a company of Cambodian refugees at Jacob's Pillow, Becket, Massachusetts. (Left photograph © 1994 by Linda Vartoogian; right photograph © 1981 by Jack Vartoogian; both used by permission.)

some of the characteristic dance positions, particularly the extreme second-position *plié* with diagonally tilted pelvis and the sole of one foot flat against the opposite upper thigh, heel-to-crotch, elbows raised and fingers flexed back nearly to the wrist. The costumes depicted consist primarily of ornaments, including hip-girdles, wristlets, anklets, shoulder-bracelets, pendulous earrings on elongated earlobes, flowing scarves, floral garlands, and elaborate headdresses. So-called *devatas* ("goddesses") are depicted not in dancing position but standing in repose; however, their hands are often held in symbolic gestures (*mudrās*), and their costumes are similar to those of the *apsara*, but with a calf-length skirt *(sampot)* folded in front in various modes.

The Khmer kingdom seems to have ended abruptly in 1431 with the defeat and destruction of Angkor by the Siamese, who carried off hundreds of the temple dancers to their own court. It is believed that Thai classical dance is based on Khmer artistry imported at this time.

Classical Dance in the Modern Period. During the reign of King Ang Duong, who ruled from 1846 to 1860, a dance renaissance took place in Cambodia, marking the beginning of the present period of court and concert dance. In this phase, costumes and movements of the Khmer-based Thai dance taught by dancers from the Siamese court were combined with Khmer features, either retained from an earlier period or inspired by temple carvings.

In 1931, dancers who had left the king's private dance troupe traveled to Europe to perform. Subsequent international tours were frequent, as were public performances for tourists in Cambodia. The traditional palace school, which continued until 1975, trained more than thirty female dancers at a time, and some 160 pupils studied there. Using teachers from the palace, the University of Fine Arts has also been training classical dancers since the 1950s.

Most Khmer educational and cultural institutions were destroyed during the Khmer Rouge takeover in 1975, and many dancers and musicians were executed or otherwise died. Some artists have resettled in France and the United States and attempt to continue their traditions abroad. There has also been a resurgence of government-sponsored patronage for the dance in Cambodia since 1979, and numerous tours have taken place. Ritual elements have been retained in Buongsuong danced rituals as well as the Manimekhala sequence for bringing rain.

Elements of Dance. The essential elements of traditional Cambodian dance style are suppleness and grace. At about the age of five, girls begin learning exercises designed to stretch the joints, such as bending back the fingers to touch the forearm, pressing the elbow against the knee, twisting and arching the waist, and lying prone with legs crossed in full lotus position; each position must be held for long periods. By about age ten, girls begin to learn the *chha banhchos*—the basic vocabulary of abstract and meaningful gestures, movements, and poses. Only after completing this stage of training are they taught the repertory of nonnarrative group dances.

The classical repertory consists of two types of dance, nonnarrative group dances *(robam)* and narrative dance dramas *(roeung)*. Most prominent in the first group is the *apsara* dance, depicting celestial nymphs who visit a garden on Earth. Its costumes recall those of carved *devatas* at Angkor.

Narrative dance dramas depict stories from Khmer Hindu–Buddhist mythology as well as from indigenous legends. Helmet masks are worn by the gods and demons, traditionally depicted by women, who may also perform the principal roles of certain group dances. Until recently, male dancers performed only comic and simian roles, but men have now begun to dance the masked and male characters as well. One of the most popular dance dramas is the *Reamker,* based on the Indian *Rāmāyana* epic. This story has acquired new significance for Khmer refugees in the West, for whom it symbolizes their escape from a war-torn country, their exile, and the desire for family reunification.

Like many other aspects of Khmer dance, the costumes display similarities to Thai and Laotian forms, but there are differences—for example, the bare right shoulder of the female Khmer dancer. A feature shared by all three is the use of a raised platform *(tiang)*, which serves as a low table for all seated or reclining scenes and as a pedestal during martial scenes.

The *pin peat* ensemble of xylophones, tuned gongs, oboes, and drums is the traditional dance orchestra, with cognates in Thailand and Laos. Seated with the musicians is the *chamrieng* ("chorus"), which sings the Khmer poetic texts essential to many of the dances. Most of the ensemble dancing in narrative dance drama—depicting battles, journeys, and chases—occurs in the intervals between these songs and is accompanied by the orchestra. During lyrical scenes, such as amorous duets or sad moments, the *chamrieng* sings accompanied only by a pair of small

CAMBODIA. Cambodian refugees performing "Peacock of Dursad," a theatrical version of a folk dance, at Jacob's Pillow, Becket, Massachusetts. (Photograph © 1981 by Jack Vartoogian; used by permission.)

hand cymbals to alternating open and closed strokes.

The Khmer are continuing to preserve their dance traditions both in Cambodia and abroad. The former star of the Royal Palace Ballet, Princess Bopha Devi, now advises a classical troupe in France. In Paris, the Centre de Documentation et de Recherche sur la Civilisation Khmère publishes a wide variety of materials. In the United States, the trance dancers and musicians and the Asian Arts Ensemble in Washington, D.C., administers a professional performing group. Another professional troupe, TYRANA, is based in Minnesota. Sophiline Shapiro, former faculty member at the University of Fine Arts, Phom Penh, performs and directs a professional troupe in Los Angeles, called Danse Celeste. In addition, many Cambodian émigré communities support dance teachers who train young girls and folkloric ensembles to perform for the new year and ancestral celebrations annually.

[*See also* Costume in Asian Traditions.]

BIBLIOGRAPHY

Brandon, James R. *Theatre in Southeast Asia.* Cambridge, Mass., 1967.

Catlin, Amy. "Apsaras and Other Goddesses in Khmer Music, Dance, and Ritual." In *Apsara: The Feminine in Cambodian Art,* edited by Amy Catlin. Los Angeles, 1987.

Catlin, Amy. *Khmer Classical Dance Songbook.* Van Nuys, Calif., 1992.

Cravath, Paul. "Earth in Flower: An Historical and Descriptive Study of the Classical Dance Drama of Cambodia." 2 vols. Ph.D. diss., University of Hawaii, 1985.

Cravath, Paul. "The Ritual Origins of the Classical Drama of Cambodia." *Asian Theatre Journal* 3 (Fall 1986): 179–200.

Cuisinier, Jeanne. "The Gestures in the Cambodian Ballet: Their Traditional and Symbolic Significance." *Indian Arts and Letters* 1.2 (1927): 92–103.

Groslier, George. *Danseuses cambodgiennes, anciennes et modernes.* Paris, 1913.

Sam, Chan Moly. *Khmer Court Dance.* Newington, Conn., 1987.

Sam, Sam-Ang, and Chan Moly Sam. *Khmer Folk Dance.* Newington, Conn., 1987.

Shapiro, Toni. "Dance and the Spirit of Cambodia." Ph.D. diss., Cornell University, Ithaca, N.Y., 1995.

Thiounn, Samdach Chaufea. *Danses cambodgiennes.* 2d ed. Pnom Penh, 1956.

Zarina, Xenia. *Classic Dances of the Orient.* New York, 1967.

AMY CATLIN

CAMEROON. Often described as "Africa in miniature," the United Republic of Cameroon is a multicultural society with a population of twelve million people, representing some two hundred fifty ethnic groups. Dance is a basic cultural activity in all these groups; all rituals and festivals include dance as a means of providing a link between the physical and spiritual worlds. Many dances, however, are secular and exist purely for entertainment. Cameroonian dance is marked by its spontaneity and abandon, but traditional dance patterns practiced from childhood underlie a dancer's improvisations.

Music defines the nature of the movement and mood of Cameroonian dance. Often the tempos encourage a heightened psychological state (a trance), in which the personality and spirit are thought to become one. The Cameroonian orchestra includes drums of all shapes and sizes, tambourines, xylophones, rattles, clappers, zithers, horns, gongs, trumpets, and lithophones.

Costumes and masks, simple or elaborate, visually establish the dance situation. Baggy gowns or shirts made of raffia, batik, tree bark, animal skins, feathers, and beads add color and sparkle. Masks can be classified by structure or material (basket, face, helmet, woven, leaf, or sculptured masks) or by their iconography (spiritual, animal, or anthropomorphic).

There are dances honoring births, deaths, betrothals, and naming ceremonies. Certain trade societies, cults, and occupational groups have their own dances, and there are dances exclusive to one sex or age group. Each dance has its own costumes and masks. Dances may be composed of simple individualized movements or of complex acrobatic group choreographies. There is also a contemporary dance culture resulting from the influence of modern popular music on traditional dances.

Five main subgroups can be identified in Cameroonian society: the Douala group in the southwestern and littoral provinces, who occupy the forest and coastal area; the Tikar people of the mountainous grassland regions; the Adamawa group, who occupy the Sahel zone to the north; the Pygmies and the Eastern Betis of the remote equatorial regions; and the major Beti group of the south, which is covered by dense equatorial forest. Geography seems to play a large part in the nature and signification of dances.

The Douala region has had the most exposure to Western traditions, and here contemporary dances are perhaps more visible than traditional ones. Surviving traditional dances include the *joki,* a graceful female ceremonial dance, and the *male,* the elephant dance, reserved exclusively for male adults. At the Molimi or Ngondo festivals in this region, masquerades include the *male, ekopangomo, wutame, ekpanga tete,* and *mekongo.* Each masquerade is specially costumed and has a dance particular to it. Many cult dances also exist, including the *obasinjom* (also found in Nigeria), the *ambgu,* and the *mantchong.* Dances from this region that have gained national popularity and are now part of the popular culture include the *ambas bay, assiko, bolo bolo,* and the *makossa;* the last is undoubtedly Cameroon's most popular dance.

Many of the dances from the forest region are characterized by eroticism and concentrate on the torso, with limited head and leg movements.

The northwest and west of Cameroon remain the most traditional regions. The dances here are energetic and acrobatic. Many are associated with the royal court; the most elegant is the Bamileke *tso,* with its conical head-gear, leopardskin cloaks, and blue batik gowns with red trimmings. Other dances include the *mewoup, bamend-jou, mbansie, kwa-kwa, njang, banji, moka, ekale-mbo, nkurung, assamba, lela, menang, lanka, mfou, kom, ngang,* and *mbangalum.* Costumes are very rich and often made of raffia or feathers. Dancers wear rattles to accentuate their movements.

Tikar dances are often beautifully choreographed, expansive, and vigorous. They involve much stamping, jumps, lifts, and acrobatics.

The Adamawa group in the north are predominantly Muslim. Their dances tend to have a sensuality which belies their religious affiliation. In many, young girls dance while shaking their bare breasts; in others, the buttocks are shaken wildly. Male dances tend to be more solemn. The popular dances of this region include the *laka, kege, yerwa, douroue, gangakouka, madai, guaemere, mbororo, za, labi, man,* and *patengue.*

A highly developed tradition of dance drama is found among the Pygmies of the eastern region. One such drama, the *maindo,* has been popularized by the National Dance Ensemble. It is a ritual describing the encounter between human and divine. Villagers stand in a semicircle around the dancers, led by three magicians. One magician dances off and returns with a masquerader in a raffia costume, holding a lance. Strong drumbeats and a song begin, to which both actors and spectators dance. A masquerader representing the divine appears suddenly in their midst, seemingly injured, and is chased from the scene by the leader of the dancers. The masquerader returns and is killed, but as the music rises to a crescendo, he is revived and begins to dance with a gyrating movement, rising from a fetal crouch to a great height. The helpless humans recognize the perpetual triumph of the divine and begin a dance of supplication as the dancer representing the deity disappears into the forest.

The *ozilla* is another ritual dance, expressing a myth of creation and eternal return and symbolically portraying aging, work, and everyday life. The dancers and musicians seem to hold a dialogue in music and movement, both danced and mimed. Other eastern dances include the *mbondele, mekum, modjadja, bekoe,* and *mbol.*

The most famous dance tradition among the Beti group is the *mvet,* which is actually a folk performance combining song, chanting, narrative, and dance. It is named after a harp-zither. Pure dance can be seen in this region in the *bikutsi*—now as popular as the *makossa*—the *mengan, mbali, assiko, elak, ekokombo, mendjang, mbime, keng-keng, keneng, akuma-mba, java,* and *manga.* Most of these dances are quite erotic, with emphasis on the torso and buttocks. The costumes are often of raffia and animal skin.

In 1963, to help preserve the dances of Cameroon's regions, the National Dance Ensemble was formed. The troupe toured extensively in Europe and America and represented Cameroon in the African cultural festivals. Independent dance troupes, which exploit traditional material but are strongly influenced by Western modern dance, include Les Ballets Bantou, Les Ballets Bafia, Les Miniyakan, and Les Ballets Camerounais. During national cultural festivals, many of these troupes are featured and dance occupies a preeminent place. The best-known choreographers include Bebey Black, Adolph Nkake, Doual'a Mouteng, Liza Ngwa, Alice Nyonga, Bantongha, and Paul Kengmo. Working within the tradition of "total theater," which exploits both dialogue and dance, the Yaounde University Theatre is noted for its experimental work.

[*See also* Sub-Saharan Africa *and* West Africa.]

BIBLIOGRAPHY

Abéga, Séverin Cécile. *L'esana chez les Beti.* Yaoundé, 1987.
Bebey, Francis. *Musique de l'Afrique.* Paris, 1969.
de Graff, J. C. "Roots in African Theatre." *African Literature Today* 8 (1976).
Gebauer, Paul. "Dances of Cameroon." *African Arts* 4 (1971).
Huet, Michel. *The Dance, Art, and Ritual of Africa.* New York, 1978.
Huet, Michel, and Claude Savary. *Africa Dances.* London, 1995.
Keita, Fodeba. "La danse africaine et la scène." *Presence africaine* 14–15 (1957).

HANSEL NDUMBE EYOH

CAMPANINI, BARBARA. *See* Barbarina, La.

CAMPRA, ANDRÉ (baptized 4 December 1660 in Aix-en-Provence, died 29 June 1744 in Versailles), French composer and director. The son of a Piedmont surgeon, Campra began his musical education at the age of fourteen in his native city, under the direction of Guillaume Poitevin. At first (until 1697), he seems to have devoted himself to religious music. In 1681 he was appointed chapel master at Sainte-Trophime in Arles; in 1683 he became music master at Saint-Étienne in Toulouse; and in 1694 he assumed that post at Notre-Dame de Paris. In 1697 the success of his first opera, *L'Europe Galante,* encouraged Campra to compose more operas. He was obliged in 1700 to resign from his position at Notre-Dame, since at that time it was not considered proper for cathedral masters to write for the secular stage, where the level of morality was not always very high.

Early in the eighteenth century Campra became the orchestra director of the Paris Opera, which paid him a generous salary. Thanks to his growing fame, he was commissioned to teach composition to the duke of Chartres, the future regent; after the death of Louis XIV in 1715, his position provided him with additional advantages. In 1718 Campra began receiving annual royalties from the performances and balls at the Paris Opera. In 1722, with Michel-Richard Delalande, Charles-Hubert Gervais, and Nicolas Bernier, he was appointed to one of the four posts at the Royal Chapel in Versailles. These new positions, in addition to his 1721 posting at the Jesuit Collège Louis-le-Grande, gave him the opportunity to compose thirty works of religious music.

Campra had not given up the art that had made him famous. He reworked several of his operas and, five years after he was appointed *inspecteur de l'Opéra* in 1730, his new *tragédie lyrique* was performed, *Achille et Deidamie* (1735). Circumstances also enabled him to create other nonreligious works. In 1722, as music director for the Prince de Conti, he wrote *La Feste de l'Isle-Adam*, a *divertissement*. Two years later he composed *Le Lis et la Rose* for the marriage of the regent's son, a work that he included in his last book of cantatas in 1728. Despite the honors bestowed on him and his fame among various wealthy patrons and the Paris public, Campra spent the last years of his life in a modest lodging in Versailles, where he died at the age of eighty-three.

Campra's creations for the dance are to be found in the works he composed for the Paris Opera. His *tragédies lyriques* (*Hésione*, 1700; *Tancrède*, 1702; *Alcine*, 1705; *Hippodamie*, 1708; *Idoménée*, 1712; *Télèphe*, 1713; *Camille, Reine des Volsques*, 1717; and *Achille et Deidamie*, 1735), like those of Jean-Baptiste Lully, contain in each act a *divertissement* combining several ballet airs. Some are constructed according to an existing structure, bearing the specific names of *bourrée, sarabande, gigue, menuet*, and *passepied*. Others follow in the tradition of Lully, endeavoring to describe the nature of a character or a dramatic situation, such as the airs for the Winds and the Pleasures or the triumphal marches.

Campra was particularly adept at using these various dances in his "ballets." Several of these spectacles, *Le Carnaval de Venise* (1699), *Aréthuse, ou La Vengeance de l'Amour* (1701), and *Les Amours de Mars et de Vénus* (1712) offered a continuous action, while others provided an independent action for each act (also called an *entrée*), thereby presenting a series of tableaux connected only by a general theme, for example, the various ages of human life. Thus they met the strict definition that was to be applied later to the *opéra-ballet*. Campra was not the creator of the genre, but he contributed greatly to its development. In his *L'Europe Galante*, which is set in France, Spain, Italy, and Turkey, the principal characters were not taken from mythology, as in the *tragédies lyriques*, but from a more realistic universe that empha-

sized a certain preference for local color. Campra's principal merit was that he was able to describe the charm of the subjects suggested to him, and to do this he borrowed from the music of other countries. For example, in *Les Fêtes Vénitiennes* (1710), in order to capture the atmosphere in the city of the doges, he introduced a cantata, a supremely Italian genre, at three places in the work. He was also the first to compose for the Paris lyric theater a *forlana*, a Venetian dance, that he used to increase the authenticity of the tableau "L'Italie," which constituted the *entrée* for *L'Europe Galante*. Campra's fondness for local color, which contributed to the great success of *L'Europe Galante* and *Les Fêtes Vénitiennes*, was not confined to the *opéra-ballet*, as is demonstrated by his ballets offering a continuous action, such as *Le Carnaval de Venise*. Some of Campra's *opéra-ballets* even featured characters taken from Greco-Roman antiquity. One example is *Les Muses* (1703), which marked the first time that a *contredanse* was performed on the stage of the Paris Opera. Including *Les Ages* (1718), the composer left four *opéra-ballets* with a total of 123 dances, among which *passepieds, menuets*, and marches (which often introduced the *divertissements*) play an important role. He ultimately produced fifteen "ballets" and *tragédies lyriques*, some of which (including *Hésione, Tancrède*, and *Les Fêtes Vénitiennes*) were revived several times during his life.

Campra's ballet airs were performed by universally admired dancers, who helped to popularize the works of this Provençal musician. Several choreographies created by Guillaume-Louis Pecour were even published on the occasion of the performances, and valuable information on the steps assigned to the dancers at the time of the creation of *L'Europe Galante, Hésione, Aréthuse, Tancrède*, and *Les Fêtes Vénitiennes* has survived, enabling Campra's operas to be performed with greater attention to authenticity.

[*For related discussion, see* Opéra-Ballet and Tragédie Lyrique.]

BIBLIOGRAPHY

Anthony, James R. "The Opera-Ballets of André Campra." Ph.D. diss., University of Southern California, 1964.

Anthony, James R. "Some Uses of the Dance in the French Opera-Ballet." *Recherches sur la Musique Française Classique* 9 (1969).

Barthélemy, Maurice. *André Campra*. Paris, 1957.

Barthélemy, Maurice. *André Campra: Étude biographique et musicologique*. Arles, 1995.

Beaussant, Philippe, and Jean Lionnet, eds. *André Campra à Versailles*. Versailles, 1993.

Brown, Leslie E. "The 'Tragedie Lyrique' of André Campra and His Contemporaries." Ph.D. diss., University of North Carolina, 1978.

Smith, Christine D. "André Campra's *Idoménée*." Ph.D. diss., University of Kentucky, 1988.

JÉRÔME DE LA GORCE
Translated from French

CANADA. [*To survey the dance traditions of Canada, this entry comprises five articles:*

    Folk and Traditional Dance in French Canada
    Theatrical Dance
    Contemporary Theatrical Dance
    Dance Education
    Dance Research and Publication

For discussion of the dance traditions of indigenous peoples, see Native American Dance. *For further discussion of theatrical dance, see entries on individual companies, choreographers, and dancers.*]

Folk and Traditional Dance in French Canada

Canada's history reflects the struggle between France and England as they expanded their overseas empires during the sixteenth to nineteenth centuries. After the Seven Years' War (1756–1763, called the French and Indian War in North America), France lost all its Canadian colonies to England by the Treaty of Paris. During and after the American Revolution (1775–1783), Canada—mainly Quebec, Nova Scotia, and Prince Edward Island—absorbed thousands of British Loyalist refugees; Canada also received French colonists from the Louisiana territory after Napoleon sold it to the United States in 1803.

French immigrants to Canada in the seventeenth and eighteenth centuries came from all parts of France, but mostly from the regions of Normandy, Île-de-France, and Poitou. Although nothing is written about the dances of these settlers, we know they danced because of denunciations by their clergy. The French upper classes (members of the governing body and *seigneurs*) danced the contemporary fashionable dances of France, including the *branle, menuet, cotillon,* and English longways *(contredanse)*. Dancing among the French lower classes *(habitants)* was similar, since boundaries between *habitant* and *seigneur* were more flexible in Canada than were those between serf and master under the feudal system in France.

With the English conquest of Canada and the 1763 Treaty of Paris, the dancing activities of the Canadian *habitants* came under the influence of British Isles' traditions. Already familiar was the *contredanse;* soon the Scottish reel, Irish jig *(gigue)*, Sword Dance, and French quadrilles became part of the social dance repertory. (Also recorded is a *"danse du barbier,"* a mimed *gigue* dance with a death-and-resurrection theme.)

In the mid-nineteenth century, when a number of French Canadians worked in industries in New England, the American "called" square dance *(danse carrée)* was introduced to Canada. Sometimes the calls were the only English words the Francophone dancers knew. In the late twentieth-century, as a result of renewed national pride, especially in the separatist province of Quebec, most calls have been translated into French.

Present-day social dancing in Quebec—in community centers, barns, and church halls—includes elaborate quadrilles, *cotillons,* simple *danses carrées, contredanses,* sung-circle dances *(ronds),* and the *gigue*. Quadrilles have evolved so that they might have six or seven parts, assume a longways formation (partners stand side by side facing another couple with whom they interact and no progression occurs), or they expand to include six, eight, twelve, or sixteen couples. The *danses carrées* are similar to those in the northeastern United States, where each couple takes a turn being active, dancing a pattern with each of the other couples. Often, elaborate finales close the dance, doubling their length. In *contredanse* progressions, the top couple usually descends to the bottom, at the end of a repetition of the dance. An old favorite like "Le Brandy" (a variant of "Strip the Willow") is an example of this type. *Ronds* have generally passed into the children's repertory.

Probably the most characteristic dance form of Quebec is the *gigue*. Traditionally a solo dance for men, it can take place in the context of a friendly competition, as a step in the figure dances to get from place to place, as part of a figure in the dance, or to fill in time while waiting. Performance style is recognizably unique. With the body upright in a relaxed but held stance, the legs and feet move rapidly, mostly from the knees down. This upright, held style is also found in figure dancing. Arms are relaxed by the sides, but occasionally one is lifted to the side in response to an inner musical feeling. Feet are extremely close to the floor and use almost exclusively close-range space; heel and toe create the rhythmic, percussive sound. Traditionally, metallic taps, which limit subtlety and variation of sound, are not worn, but some contemporary *gigueurs* use them because of the increased volume they produce.

Whether French Canadians dance or not depends not so much on age or area of domicile but on whether one comes from a dancing family or community. Places where dancing is an integral part of social life continue to pass down dances and style. Opportunities to dance include *veillées* ("home parties"), *noces* ("weddings"), and secular holidays such as the New Year. In some areas, weekly dances are held, especially in summer and tourist season.

An active revival movement provides several avenues for new dancers. In Montreal, the Fédération des Loisirs-danse du Québec not only hosts activities such as *soirées* and weekend workshops but also encourages research and houses archival material. Les Danseries in Quebec City provides weekly classes in pedagogy, calling for dances, and traditional fiddle and accordion playing.

The popularity of folk dance–inspired troupes is well established, and there is enthusiastic audience support.

From the *soirées* sponsored by folklorists Marius Barbeau and Édouard-Zotique Massicotte in 1919 to Les Folkloristes du Québec in the 1950s, Les Feux Follets and Les Gens de Mon Pays in the 1960s and 1970s, and the current Les Sortilèges, these performances have grown from casual presentations to highly theatricalized spectacles.

Research is conducted through the Université Laval's folklore department, where faculty members Simonne Voyer and Madeleine Doyon-Ferland have spent considerable time in the field. Others working in this field include Jean Trudel, Robert-Lionel Séguin, and Ellen Shifrin.

[*See also* Step Dancing, *article on* Step Dancing on Cape Breton.]

BIBLIOGRAPHY

Barbeau, Charles-Marius, and Édouard-Zotique Massicotte. *Veillées du bon vieux temps à la Bibliothèque Saint-Sulpice à Montréal.* Montreal, 1920.

Doyon-Ferland, Madeleine. *Jeux, rythmes et divertissements traditionnels.* Montreal, 1980.

Massicotte, Édouard-Zotique. "Les danses mimées du Canada française." *Bulletin des recherches historiques* 34 (1928).

Séguin, Robert-Lionel. *Les divertissements en Nouvelle-France.* Ottawa, 1968.

Séguin, Robert-Lionel. *La danse traditionnelle au Québec.* Sillery, Quebec, 1986.

Shifrin, Ellen. "Traditional French-Canadian Dance: An Analysis of Selected Iconography." Master's thesis, York University, 1982.

Shifrin, Ellen. "Traditional French-Canadian Dance Iconography: A Methodology for Analysis." *Canadian Folklore Canadien* 6 (1984).

Trudel, Jean. "La danse traditionnelle au Québec." *Forces*, no. 32 (1975).

Voyer, Simonne. "Danses de folklore." In *Le congrès de la refrancisation*, vol. 3. Quebec, 1959.

Voyer, Simonne. *La danse traditionnelle dans l'est du Canada: Quadrilles et cotillons.* Quebec, 1986.

ELLEN SHIFRIN

Theatrical Dance

Professional theatrical dancing has existed in Canada for more than three hundred years, having been imported from France and England in the sixteenth and seventeenth centuries. While its development was initially impeded by a repressive and conservative church, the massive immigrations to Canada in the mid-nineteenth and early twentieth centuries and the growing influence of developments in dance in the United States in the twentieth century did much to stimulate interest and activity in the art.

A masque, probably containing dance, was presented in the harbor at Port Royal (now Annapolis Royal, Nova Scotia) in 1606, and it was the colonizing French who presented the first recorded ballet performance—"a kind of ballet, to wit, five soldiers," according to the diaries of the Jesuit fathers—at a wedding in Quebec City in 1646. The following February another ballet performance was recorded, at the warehouse of the Company of One Hundred Associates. Despite the view of the French church that dancing was an abomination, enthusiasm for dance was always widespread; when British rule was imposed in 1763, public performance of dance, usually as an accompaniment to plays, became frequent.

By the end of the eighteenth century, itinerant foreign artists were touring Canada. One of the earliest visitors was America's first professional dancer, John Durang. In 1797 and 1798 he paid a year-long visit to Montreal and Quebec City with the Ricketts Circus of Philadelphia. A performance of *La Fille Mal Gardée* was given in Quebec City in 1816, and the famous French dancer Madame Céleste (Céleste Keppler) danced to great acclaim in Quebec in 1829 and 1835. Soon, cities farther west, like

CANADA: Theatrical Dance. Olivia Wyatt (center) and members of the Royal Winnipeg Ballet in Gweneth Lloyd's *Romance* (1949), set to music by Aleksandr Glazunov. Clockwise from top right, the seated dancers are Kit Copping, Sheila Mackinnon, Naomi Kimura, Rachel Browne, and Beverly Barkley. (Photograph courtesy of the Royal Winnipeg Ballet.)

CANADA: Theatrical Dance. Members of the National Ballet of Canada in Antony Tudor's *Dark Elegies*, acquired by the company in 1955. (Photograph by Ken Bell; used by permission of the National Ballet of Canada.)

Toronto and Kingston, were hosting touring companies such as the Danseuses Viennoises, a troupe of forty-eight children who visited Canada and the United States in 1847 and 1848.

The earliest evidence of a Canadian dancer performing internationally is found in this period. Miss S. Aspinall, an Englishwoman who claimed to have been taught by Auguste Vestris, gave several solo performances in the mid-1820s in Quebec City (where she had settled in 1820), then embarked on a series of annual presentations in New York.

By the late nineteenth century, the influences on theatrical dance in Canada were almost entirely American. After the phenomenal success of *The Black Crook* (1866),

which ran for several decades in New York and on tour, spectacle-extravaganzas became the measuring stick, followed by skirt dancing and vaudeville. Loie Fuller did her *Fire Dance* in Vancouver in 1896; Anna Pavlova made the first of several tours in 1910; Ruth St. Denis and Ted Shawn displayed their oriental exotica on the vaudeville circuits of Canada between 1914 and 1924.

Touring by foreign companies intensified in the early part of the twentieth century. Diaghilev's Ballets Russes made its only Canadian appearance in Vancouver in 1917; later, appearances by the companies of Martha Graham, Doris Humphrey, Mary Wigman, Harald Kreutzberg, and Kurt Jooss provided Canada with intensive exposure to modern dance in both its North American and European incarnations. When Sol Hurok inaugurated his "dance decade" in 1933, with the importation of Colonel de Basil's Ballets Russes de Monte Carlo, he found that Canada could sustain a string of engagements.

CANADA: Theatrical Dance. Eric Hyrst (on floor) and members of Les Ballets Chiriaeff in *Petrouchka*, staged by Ludmilla Chiriaeff and Joy McPherson, after Fokine, in 1957. Hyrst, formerly a principal dancer with the Sadler's Wells Theatre Ballet, worked closely with Chiriaeff during the early years of Les Grands Ballets Canadiens. (Photograph by Varkony; from the archives of Les Grands Ballets Canadiens, courtesy of Ludmilla Chiriaeff.)

The arrival of the touring Russian companies did two things: it created a taste for teaching in the Russian style, and it accentuated the drain of Canadian dancing talent to other lands. By far the most significant of the numerous Russian émigré teachers to make their way to Canada in those years was Boris Volkoff. He settled in Toronto in 1930, probably illegally, after a career as a character dancer in Russia, China, and San Francisco. In 1936, Volkoff took a group of his students to represent Canada in the dance section of the Berlin Olympics, where they were favorably received.

Meanwhile, twenty-six hundred miles away in Vancouver, June Roper, from Rosebud, Texas, was having an important influence on both the Canadian and international dance scene. Trained in Los Angeles by Ernest Belcher, she had a brilliant career in the United States and Europe in supported adagio before arriving in Vancouver in 1934. Inspired by the touring de Basil company, she devoted herself to producing dancers in the vivid Russian style of that era. In the five years between 1934 and 1939 she trained so many dancers for the world's companies (more than seventy, eight of them for the Ballets Russes alone) that *Dance Magazine* later described her as "North America's greatest star-maker."

Roper was not the first of Canada's immigrant teachers to send Canadian dancers to the international companies. In the early 1930s Boston-born Gwendolyn Osborne sent her pupil Nesta Toumine to London and later to the Ballet Russe de Monte Carlo. She also sent two sisters for further study in the United States; Nora White later danced with Colonel W. de Basil's Ballets Russes, and Patricia Wilde eventually became one of the best-known principal dancers of the New York City Ballet. Teachers in cities as far apart as Montreal, Quebec, and Victoria, British Columbia (which produced Ian Gibson for Sergei Denham's Ballet Russe de Monte Carlo) managed similar feats.

By the end of the 1930s, it was becoming possible for Canadian dancers with serious ambitions as performers to find work at home. In 1939, Volkoff launched the Volkoff Canadian Ballet, Canada's first company, predating by a matter of weeks the launching of what was to become the Royal Winnipeg Ballet. Although Volkoff trained many fine dancers, among them Toronto-born Melissa Hayden, and mounted an ambitious repertory, his company was short-lived.

The Winnipeg company grew from a ballet club founded by teachers Gweneth Lloyd and Betty Farrally, who had moved to the prairie city from England in 1938. One of its first members was David Adams, later to become a principal dancer with the National Ballet of Canada (1951–1960). For its first decade the company's repertory consisted of light, accessible works by Lloyd, aimed at a broad and unsophisticated audience. In 1958, after a series of artistic and administrative upheavals (during which it was briefly under the artistic control first of Ruthanna Boris, then of Benjamin Harkarvy), the company was taken over by Arnold Spohr, a former principal dancer. It was Spohr who guided the company's rise to international acclaim in the late 1960s, keeping its size around a conveniently portable twenty-five. He built an eclectic repertory with wide popular appeal, introducing large-scale productions of *Giselle, Romeo and Juliet,* and *Swan Lake* but also emphasizing modern ballets by choreographers such as Oscar Araiz, John Neumeier, Rudi van Dantzig, Vicente Nebrada, Hans van Manen, and the Canadians Brian Macdonald and Norbert Vesak. [*See* Royal Winnipeg Ballet.]

The end of the 1940s was a period of ferment in the arts in Canada. Emerging from the conservatism of the 1930s and the postwar years, the country developed a new willingness to embrace values that extended beyond the material. Pressure for federal government recognition of the arts mounted steadily. In 1949 a Royal Commission was called on national development in the arts, letters, and sciences; its report led to the creation in 1956 of the Canada Council, a federal support agency that was to play a crucial role in Canada's cultural development.

It was in this period of ferment, from the late 1940s to the mid-1950s, that Canada's far-flung dance pioneers began to realize that they were not alone, that dance activity—albeit much of it of an amateur kind—was blossoming across the land. In 1948 the Canadian Ballet Festival movement was launched. The first festival, held in Winnipeg, brought together the Winnipeg and Volkoff groups and a Montreal-based modern group headed by a Polish immigrant, Ruth Sorel. Thereafter, ballet festivals were held annually until 1954 and became an important proving ground for new talent. The movement drew international attention. The founder-editor of *Dance News,* Anatole Chujoy, became so enthusiastic about the concept that he urged its adoption in the United States. This advocacy led to the founding of the regional ballet movement. [*See* United States of America, *article on* Regional Ballet Companies.]

If a thrust for a new national awareness was at the heart of the success of the first ballet festival, a very different assertion of cultural nationalism was being voiced in Montreal the same year. It was heard most clearly in *Le refus global,* the artistic manifesto of Les Automatistes, a group of surrealist artists influenced by André Breton and led by a Montreal painter, Paul-Émile Borduas. *Le refus global* was a cry of rebellion against the social and political restrictions imposed on art in the province of Quebec by the administration of premier Maurice Duplessis. Three pioneers of Quebec modern dance, Françoise Sullivan, Jeanne Renaud, and Françoise Riopelle, were involved with Les Automatistes, and the spirit of irreverence, exploration, and free inquiry that permeated the manifesto was increasingly evident in their work.

It was at the second ballet festival, held in Toronto in 1949, that the seeds of the National Ballet of Canada were sown. Fired by their enthusiasm for the first Canadian performances that year of the Sadler's Wells Ballet and reluctant to allow the highly acclaimed Winnipeg company to take supremacy in the field of ballet in Canada, a group of Toronto dance enthusiasts invited Celia Franca, a former Wells principal, to form a national company in Toronto. Launching the company in the fall of 1951, Franca aimed from the start to make it the country's chief showcase of ballet classicism, with a repertory rooted firmly in the standard works of the late nineteenth and early twentieth centuries. In its early years it also presented major works by Antony Tudor and its resident Canadian choreographer, Grant Strate. The addition of John Cranko's *Romeo and Juliet* in 1964 signaled the start of a long period of growth for the company. [*See* National Ballet of Canada.]

Canada's third major ballet company, Les Grands Ballets Canadiens, grew from a small troupe created for television work by the Russian dancer and choreographer Ludmilla Chiriaeff shortly after her arrival in Montreal in 1952. The company was officially launched in 1958, dancing a repertory chiefly of Chiriaeff ballets. It developed into a modern-ballet company with a repertory covering a broad range of styles, from Fernand Nault's setting of the rock opera *Tommy* to works of George Balanchine, John Butler, Ronald Hynd, Maurice Béjart, and a number of Canadian choreographers, principal among them Brian Macdonald and James Kudelka. [*See* Grands Ballets Canadiens, Les.]

Modern dance in Canada evolved more slowly than ballet. Much of the early activity was in Montreal, centered around the Wigman-influenced Ruth Sorel, Elizabeth

CANADA: Theatrical Dance. Madeleine Bouchard and Attila Ficzere in *The Shining People of Leonard Cohen* (1970), created by Brian Macdonald for the Royal Winnipeg Ballet. The ballet was danced to a reading of Cohen's poems and an electronic sound montage composed by Harry Freedman. (Photograph by Jerry Kopelow; courtesy of the Royal Winnipeg Ballet.)

CANADA: Theatrical Dance. Frank Augustyn and Karen Kain, stars of the National Ballet of Canada during the 1970s, in Frederick Ashton's *La Fille Mal Gardée*. Television broadcasts made Augustyn and Kain widely known across Canada. (Photograph from the Dance Collection, New York Public Library for the Performing Arts.)

Leese (a former member of the Trudi Schoop company), and Les Automatistes. Françoise Sullivan had her own modern group in Montreal in the late 1940s and revived it in the late 1970s after a hiatus of many years. Jeanne Renaud and Françoise Riopelle were to form another company; in 1967, under the direction of Renaud and former U.S. dancer Peter Boneham, it became Le Groupe de la Place Royale, one of the country's boldest experimenters. Many of Canada's most innovative and influential modern dancers have passed through the company. When it moved to Ottawa in 1977 its role as modern dance crucible in Montreal was assumed by Le Groupe Nouvelle Aire, founded in 1968 as a center for contemporary dance research by Martine Époque. Le Groupe Nouvelle Aire was the incubator for many of the independent dancers and choreographers who came to dominate the Montreal dance scene in the early 1980s.

Modern dance did not win a footing in English Canada until some years after a series of modern dance festivals in Toronto in the early 1960s. Patricia Beatty, a Torontonian who had studied in the United States with Martha Graham and danced with Pearl Lang, returned to Toronto in 1967 to establish the New Dance Group of Toronto with the aim of spreading the word about the Graham style.

The following year her company was absorbed into the newly formed Toronto Dance Theatre, headed by two more Graham disciples, the Canadian David Earle and Brooklyn-born Peter Randazzo, a former Graham principal; the three dancer-choreographers directed the company jointly until 1963, when company alumnus Christopher House joined them as resident choeogorapher and Kenny Pearl became artistic director. In the late 1960s and early 1970s, modern dance groups were also being formed in Winnipeg, Regina, and Vancouver.

The great bulk of early Canadian modern dance was imitative, not innovative. The impetus of revolution, so important in the development of modern dance in the United States, was not felt in Canada. Compromise, cooperation, and the smooth absorption of influences have been the Canadian characteristics.

In the decade that followed the Canadian centennial celebrations of 1967 and the mounting of Expo 67 in Montreal, a renewed sense of national identity emerged. The government recognized the value of the arts in helping the country shape a national identity in the face of long-term cultural colonization. This was also a period of social and intellectual liberalization throughout the West. In Canada, funding for arts was significantly increased; art of all forms flourished; and new dance companies sprang up from coast to coast. Prominent among them were the Anna Wyman Dance Theatre in Vancouver and the Danny Grossman Dance Company in Toronto, both built around innovative and highly individual modern choreographers. By the mid-1970s, however, economic cutbacks meant that the Canada Council was unable to fully support the growth it had fostered. Some companies died; the rest split into two camps—those with adequate federal funds and those without—both of which were represented by national lobbying organizations.

A strong thrust toward independent activity evolved under a complex of pressures: financial necessity, an increased desire on the part of individuals to create outside formal companies, an increased willingness on the part of government grant agencies to support individual experiment rather than new large-company ventures, and the influence of New York's postmodernists. Some artists (such as Margie Gillis, Linda Rabin, Judith Marcuse, and Jennifer Mascall) made their way alone; others formed loose, exploratory ensembles, such as Terminal City Dance in Vancouver and Toronto Independent Dance Enterprise. The independents' work often had an imaginative vitality that compensated for a lack of formal technique. In Quebec (which in the 1960s and 1970s underwent its own, quite separate political-cultural revolution) the work of audacious independents like Jean-Pierre Perreault, Paul-André Fortier, Édouard Lock, Daniel Leveillé, and Marie Chouinard was by far the most stimulating element of the Montreal dance scene in the early 1980s. [*See the following article on* Contemporary Dance Theater.]

The athletic, risk-taking style that evolved in Montreal in those years became internationally celebrated, and spawned a new generation of theatrical experimenters; the work done in the country's two other principal centers of dance creation, Toronto and Vancouver, tended to have a cooler, more conservative feel, although Vancouver choreographers, influenced by Karen Jamieson and the Kokoro duo of Jay Hirabayashi and Barbara Bourget, have increasingly explored Pacific Rim and Native peoples' materials as themes for their work.

The financial pressures of the international economic slowdown of the late 1980s and the early 1990s made it difficult for new dance companies to become established in Canada. In eastern Canada, one victim of that process was the Ottawa Ballet. Directed by Frank Augustyn, a former principal of the National Ballet of Canada, this company was the successor to the Ottawa-based Theatre Ballet of Canada, which itself evolved in 1981 from two earlier companies, Entre-Six, founded in 1975 in Montreal by Lawrence Gradus and his wife Jacqueline Lemieux, and Ballet Ys, a Toronto-based dance troupe founded by Gloria Grant in 1971. Gradus, formerly a

CANADA: Theatrical Dance. Vincent Warren (center) and members of the male ensemble of Les Grands Ballets Canadiens in Fernand Nault's *Cérémonie* (1972), set to music by Pierre Henry and Gary Wright. (Photograph by Ian Westbury; from the archives of Les Grands Ballets Canadiens, courtesy of Ludmilla Chiriaeff.)

soloist with Les Grands Ballets Canadiens, directed the Theatre Ballet of Canada until 1989, when he was succeeded by Augustyn, who renamed the company the Ottawa Ballet. After five years, it collapsed under financial pressure in 1994.

In western Canada, however, two ballet companies—the well-established Alberta Ballet and the newly founded Ballet British Columbia—managed to weather the economic decline of the late 1980s. The Edmonton-based Alberta Ballet had originated as a small amateur ensemble founded by former Volkoff dancer Ruth Carse in 1955. It had turned professional in 1966, and when Brydon Paige, a Vancouver native, became artistic director in 1976 he began to build an all-purpose touring repertory including works by Balanchine as well as works by himself, Norbert Vesak, and Lambros Lambrou, a Greek-Canadian who was resident choreographer for a decade. Paige was succeeded in 1988 by Ali Pourfarrokh, who continued to develop the company as a popular and mobile troupe featuring classical-contemporary programming by choreographers including himself, John Butler, Peter Pucci, and the Canadians Mark Godden and Crystal Pite.

Ballet British Columbia was launched in Vancouver in 1985 after two decades of unsuccessful attempts to establish a ballet troupe in the city. B.C.-born Reid Anderson returned from a performing career in Germany to become artistic director in 1987, and he established the beginnings of a distinctive European-modern identity for the company with works by such choreographers as John

CANADA: Theatrical Dance. *(left above)* Members of the Royal Winnipeg Ballet in Lambros Lambrou's *Sundances*, made for the Alberta Ballet in 1979. *(right)* Charie Evans and Gaetan Massen in Renald Rabu's *The Creation of Eve*, made for Pacific Ballet Theatre in 1981. *(bottom left)* Andrea Boardman and Derek Reid in Nacho Duato's *Rassemblement*, acquired by Les Grands Ballets Canadiens in the early 1990s. (Photographs by Ed Ellis, Rodney Polden, and David Cooper [used by permission]; courtesy of the Royal Winnipeg Ballet, Pacific Ballet Theatre, and Les Grands Ballets Canadiens.)

Cranko. Patricia Neary, who succeeded Anderson when he left Vancouver to head the National Ballet of Canada in 1989, brought works from the repertory of her alma mater, the New York City Ballet, but it was not until John Alleyne became artistic director in 1990 that the company took on the dynamic, modernist character for which it has become internationally known.

Alleyne, an alumnus of the National Ballet School, and a former principal dancer with the Stuttgart Ballet, has built a repertory in which his own ballets are augmented by works by such European modernists as William Forsythe and Jiří Kylián and by such Canadian choreographers as Serge Bennathan, Jean Grand-Maître, James Kudelka, Mark Godden, and Crystal Pite. Regarded as one of the strongest new choreographic voices in Canada, Alleyne has twice been part of the New York City Ballet's Diamond Project, which was established expressly to encourage the creation of new dance works.

Canada's three main ballet companies continue to flourish. Arnold Spohr retired as artistic director of the Royal Winnipeg Ballet in 1988 and was succeeded by Henny Jurriens (1988–1989), André Lewis (1989), John Meehan (1990–1993), and William Whitener (1993–1995). Former principal dancer André Lewis became permanent artistic director in 1996. The National Ballet of Canada, after the retirement of Celia Franca in 1974, was ably directed by Alexander Grant (1976–1983), Erik Bruhn (1983–1986), Valerie Wilder, Lynn Wallis, and Glen Tetley (1986–1988), and Reid Anderson (1989–1996). James Kudelka, who had been appointed artist in residence in 1992, became artistic director in 1996. In Montreal, Les Grands Ballets Canadiens prospered under the direction of Ludmilla Chiriaeff and Fernand Nault until 1974, when they were succeeded by Brian Macdonald (1974–1977), Linda Stearns, Daniel Jackson, Colin McIntyre, and Jeanne Renaud (variously, 1977–1989), and Lawrence Rhodes (1989 to the present).

During the 1990s a number of modern dance troupes also found new life under new directors, among them Toronto's Dancemakers and Winnipeg's Contemporary Dancers. In Montreal, always a vital source of experimentation in dance and performance art, a new generation of modernist choreographers—among them Ginette Laurin, Danielle Desnoyers, and Sylvain Emard—emerged into the national and international spotlight. Stimulated by the activities of established companies, by national choreographic awards, and by government grants for choreographic experiment, new work is currently being done in Canada in the broadest conceivable range of dance forms.

[*See also the entries on the principal figures mentioned herein.*]

BIBLIOGRAPHY
Bell, Ken, and Celia Franca. *The National Ballet of Canada: A Celebration.* Toronto, 1978.
Crabb, Michael, ed. *Visions: Ballet and the Future.* Toronto, 1978.
Geddes, Murray, et al., eds. *The Canadian Dancers' Survival Manual.* Toronto, 1980.
Guilmette, Pierre. *Bibliographie de la danse théâtrale au Canada.* Ottawa, 1970.
Jackson, Graham. *Dance as Dance: Selected Reviews and Essays.* Scarborough, Ont., 1978.
Lorrain, Roland. *Les Grands Ballets Canadiens, ou, Cette femme qui nous fit danser.* Montreal, 1973.
Neufeld, James. *Power to Rise.* Toronto, 1996.
Oxenham, Andrew, and Michael Crabb. *Dance Today in Canada.* Toronto, 1977.
Taplin, Diana Theodores, ed. *New Directions in Dance.* Toronto, 1979.
Whittaker, Herbert. *Canada's National Ballet.* Toronto, 1967.
Wyman, Max. *The Royal Winnipeg Ballet: The First Forty Years.* Toronto, 1978.
Wyman, Max. *Dance Canada: An Illustrated History.* Vancouver, 1989.
MAX WYMAN

Contemporary Theatrical Dance

Canadian modern dance began to acquire official status in several parts of the country by the end of the 1960s, even though many choreographers had been steadily working in isolation since 1930. Ballet had had its first nationwide exposure with the annual Canadian Ballet Festival, held in various provincial capitals from 1948 to 1954 and featuring troupes from across the country. Canadian theatergoers and dance artists were thus able to take stock of budding choreographic talent; this helped integrate and promote this art form as part of the national culture. Later, the Dance in Canada Association, founded in 1973, wished to revive this idea by holding annual conferences and showcases.

The first Canadian modern dance festival was held in Toronto in 1960, and subsequent festivals slowly established a venue for dance experimentation. The country's sturdiest survivors among dance experimentalists are three pioneering companies that remain active to this day under new leadership and represent Canada's modern dance establishment. First came Rachel Browne (born 1934), an American-born former soloist with the Royal Winnipeg Ballet, who in 1964 launched the Contemporary Dancers of Winnipeg (later renamed Contemporary Dancers, Canada). This oldest modern dance institution aimed to display European and North American contemporary choreography. In the 1980s, when Tedd Robinson and later Tom Stroud took over the directorship, the emphasis was on creation of Canadian choreography rather than presentation of an international repertory.

Browne was closely followed by Jeanne Renaud (born 1928), who in 1966 founded Le Groupe de la Place Royale in Montreal, relocated to Ottawa in 1977 under the directorship of Peter Boneham (born 1934). Renaud had been linked since the late 1940s to Quebec's artistic vanguard, Les Automatistes, a group of visual artists who discarded traditional art and encouraged spontaneous expression and abstract creation. Her dance company continued work previously done in conjunction with the choreographers Françoise Riopelle (born 1927) and Françoise Sullivan (born 1925), who were among the signatories of the 1948 Automatiste manifesto, *Le refus global*. These choreographers are the founding mothers of French Canadian modern dance. Their homegrown talents championed an

CANADA: Contemporary Theatrical Dance. Jeanne Renaud in *Densité*, a solo she created in 1963. Founder of Le Groupe de la Place Royale in 1966, Renaud was the recipient of the Governor General's Award in 1995 for her services to the performing arts in Canada. (Photograph courtesy of Vincent Warren.)

art form based on individuality, freedom of expression, and abstraction. When Boneham took over the helm of Place Royale, he adhered to the company's mandate of encouraging individual expression and strengthening the ties between the fine arts and the performing arts. However, assisted by dancer-choreographer and co–artistic director Jean-Pierre Perreault, Boneham also wished to create an integrated performance style requiring the dancers to sing, talk, and act as well as dance. By the end of the 1980s the company, now run by Boneham alone, decided to promote intensive workshops on the creative process to help young choreographers hone their craft. To this day it is the only professional company serving the community in that manner.

Third came the founding of Toronto Dance Theatre in 1968, the result of collaboration by three independent dancer-teacher-choreographers, Patricia Beatty (born 1936), David Earle (born 1939), and Peter Randazzo (born 1943). The choreography and training were Graham-based; indeed, this was Canada's closest link with Martha Graham's aesthetic. Stylistically and thematically, these choreographers reflected humanistic concerns; their work showed poetic, philosophical, and spiritual dimensions. With the arrival of Christopher House (born 1955) as resident choreographer and co–artistic director, the

company retained its well-crafted look but became more pluralistic in its style and inspiration.

In general, modern dance in Canada shows the combined influences of German *Ausdruckstanz* and American modern dance. After World War II, European dancemakers had been attracted to Canada by a recent immigration law which gave artists the same status as specialized laborers, and many of these immigrants opened schools in various Canadian provinces. Ruth Abramowitz Sorel (1907–1974) had danced with Mary Wigman and won first prize at the Warsaw International Choreography competition in 1933. The Montreal school and troupe that she directed, taught, and performed with for ten years from the mid-1940s included ballet as well as German expressionist dance. Of Danish-German ancestry, Elizabeth Leese (1916–1962) trained with Rudolf Laban and Kurt Jooss and danced with Trudi Schoop; she finally settled in Montreal in 1944 after working in Toronto and Ottawa. These respected choreographers were featured in the Canadian Ballet Festivals, proving their versatility by being both modernists and classicists. Dancer-choreographers Yone Kvietys, Nancy Lima Dent, and Bianca Rogge also came from eastern Europe after World War II, opened schools, gave concerts, and organized modern dance festivals in Toronto. Much later, Laban student Anna Wyman (born

CANADA: Contemporary Theatrical Dance. Members of the Toronto Dance Theatre in David Earle's *Sacra Conversazione* (1984), set to parts of Mozart's *Requiem*. Created for the Banff Festival of the Arts, it was mounted for the Toronto Dance Theatre in 1988, for the company's twentieth-anniversary season. Under Earle's directorship, the Toronto Dance Theatre achieved widespread recognition in the late 1980s, giving as many performances across the country as the National Ballet of Canada. Of the company's three founders, Earle works in a style most closely related to that of Martha Graham. The expansive gesture seen here, which infuses his essentially narrative approach with lyricism, is typical of his work. (Photograph by John Lauener; courtesy of Toronto Dance Theatre.)

1928) came to Canada in 1967 from Austria; she founded the Anna Wyman Dance Theatre in Vancouver (1972–1990) and added a ballet emphasis and a formalist concern to her choreography.

By 1971, York University offered the first dance degrees in Canadian higher education, and modern dance gained further respectability. Dancemakers, a dynamic repertory company of new works, was founded by York graduates, among them Andrea Ciel Smith, Carol Anderson, and Pat Fraser. Eventually these dancer-choreographers branched out to pursue their own careers, and Dancemakers is now run by French-born Serge Bennathan. Earlier, the Université de Montréal in 1968 offered an unlikely venue for what was to become the breeding ground of much dance innovation in the years to come. Le Groupe Nouvelle Aire (1968–1982) was a modernist dance troupe originally consisting of young students and faculty members of the physical education department. Its main leader was Martine Epoque (born 1942), who had recently emigrated from France to teach a Dalcroze rhythm course at the university. In time Nouvelle Aire lost its physical-education roots, and Epoque strove to forge an original gestural language that would reflect a Québécois sensibility. Nouvelle Aire also nurtured such choreographers as Paul-André Fortier (born 1948), Daniel Léveillé (born 1952), Ginette Laurin (born 1955), and Édouard Lock (born 1954), who became responsible for creating Quebec's idiosyncratic theatrical dance styles.

In the late 1970s Montreal's burgeoning choreographic activity spawned many independent dancemakers bent on renewing the creative possibilities of dance. This centered round iconoclastic works such as Fortier's *Violence* (1980) and *Fin* (1980) as well as Léveillé's *Voyeurisme* (1979), *Fleurs de Peau* (1979), and *L'inceste* (1980). These creators consciously acted as *agents provocateurs* and shunned dance conventions. The new form displayed much theatricality and social criticism, drawing its inspiration from Pina Bausch's type of dance theater. Sexuality, alienation, anonymity, and lack of communication were recurring themes choreographically treated with provocation. In time, Léveillé and Fortier moved away from such theatricality to embrace a more visual approach. By contrast, Ginette Laurin and her company O Vertigo (founded in 1984) and Édouard Lock through La La La Human Steps (founded in 1982) are more intent on honing an innovative, high-energy, gravity-defying dance vocabulary than on dealing overtly with existential themes. Their fast-paced, acrobatic dances are acclaimed internationally as stretching the boundaries of the art.

Chamber companies reflecting the unique and personal aesthetics of their director-choreographers abound in Canada. Danny Grossman (born 1942), an American expatriate who had danced with Paul Taylor, founded his own Toronto troupe in 1975 to illustrate his inventive,

CANADA: Contemporary Theatrical Dance. Maria Formolo and Keith Urban in *Renaissance*, a suite of duets created by Urban in 1980 for Regina Modern Dance Works. (Photograph by Frank Richards; reprinted from Wyman, 1989, p. 192.)

technically demanding personal style. *Higher* (1975) is a jazzy duet romp on a ladder; *Curious School of Theatrical Dancing* (1977) is an athletic, comic but difficult solo; while *Endangered Species* (1981), a group piece, reveals humanistic concerns. Fellow Torontonian Robert Desrosiers (born 1953) studied at the National Ballet of Canada but chose experimentation, founding Desrosiers Dance Theatre in Toronto in 1980. His *Blue Snake* (1989), commissioned by the National Ballet, is a fitting example of the audacious large-scale pieces he devises, inspired by Lindsay Kemp's theater and incorporating magician's tricks, acrobatics, mime, ballet, and modern dance.

Jean-Pierre Perreault (born 1947), working in Montreal, also creates monumental works, though of a radically different kind. Associated with Le Groupe de la Place Royale practically since its inception, Perreault moved back to Montreal in the 1980s. His epoch-making *Joe* (1983) crystallized his previous choreographic experimentation and signature style. *Joe* captured Everyman's squalid existence, with two dozen men and women wearing uniform bowler hats, raincoats, and army boots as they stampeded in anonymous unison. Perreault's dancers provide their own music as they stamp, tap, and swish through their repetitive phrases to portray an urban, depersonalized universe. As master builder of carefully crafted pieces, Perreault creates impressive scenography, uses drab ready-made costumes, and com-

CANADA: Contemporary Theatrical Dance. One of the most successful companies to emerge from Montreal's experimental dance scene in the 1980s is Édouard Lock's La La La Human Steps, known for its frenzied, risky movement style. Raw-edged early works like *Lily Marlene in the Jungle*, pictured here in a 1980 performance at The Kitchen, New York, paved the way for the violent theatrical spectacles that made Lock's reputation in the mid-1980s. (Photograph © 1980 by Johan Elbers; used by permission.)

poses the body's musical accompaniment as well as the choreography.

Vancouver choreographers Judith Marcuse (born 1947) and Karen Jamieson (born 1946) each head their own companies. Marcuse, a Montrealer by birth, danced with Ballet Rambert and Les Grands Ballets Canadiens before settling in Vancouver in the 1980s. Her troupe features a contemporary repertory which mostly, but not solely, performs her own slick, classically influenced works. Jamieson's originality lies in creating choreography that has primal, archetypal roots. She approaches choreography as an anthropologist; her company, formed in 1983, has been commissioned for site-specific works at the National Gallery in Ottawa and at Vancouver's Museum of Anthropology. *Sisyphus* (1985), a strong, dramatic group piece, explores the existential dilemma with hurling bodies crashing on back walls, then tumbling to the floor.

Several solo performers have also gained international recognition. Margie Gillis (born 1953) is the most widely known. Hailed as the new Isadora Duncan for her freestyle, expressive dancing, the Montreal-based Gillis tours a great deal, performing her emotional compositions to capacity crowds. Her popularity, like that of the ballet-jazz that swept Quebec in the 1970s and early 1980s, helped audiences bridge the gap between classical frills and hermetic, more intellectual experimentation. Gillis's dancing, like ballet-jazz (the hybrid brainchild of Eva von Gencsy), had immediate popular appeal; both created cult followings, by allowing the public to em-

pathize with extroverted expressions they could easily grasp.

At the other end of the spectrum, Marie Chouinard (born 1955), also a highly individualistic soloist, gained her reputation as the *enfant terrible* of Montreal dance. Her provocative, controversial one-woman shows depicted sexual themes and intimate actions with a certain primitivism in portraying basic sensual or bodily pleasures. Recently Chouinard tackled group choreography still relying on vocals, individual gestures, and a primitive movement vocabulary. Among her most sensational pieces are personal rereadings of *L'Après-midi d'un Faune* (1987) and *Le Sacre du Printemps* (1993).

Canadian dance experimentation is stronger, better organized, and well publicized in the 1990s, partly owing to events such as the biennial Festival International de Nouvelle Danse (created in Montreal in 1985), which offer important recurring showcases for national and international avant-garde choreography.

BIBLIOGRAPHY

Tembeck, Iro Valaskakis. *Dancing in Montreal: Seeds of a Choreographic History.* Studies in Dance History, vol. 5.2. Madison, Wis., 1994. Includes an extensive bibliography.

Wyman, Max. *Dance Canada: An Illustrated History.* Vancouver, 1989.

IRO VALASKAKIS TEMBECK

Dance Education

Dance education in Canada dates from the seventeenth-century settlements in New France, where dance and etiquette were taught in seminaries and ladies' schools. By the late eighteenth century, dancing masters were opening schools in Quebec: both Louis Dulongpré and Antoine Rod gave instruction in Montreal, while a Miss Aspinall taught in Quebec City. In the 1840s theatrical dancers, such as Anne Hill, sometimes combined teaching dance with performing in resident theater companies. As settlers moved westward, dancing masters followed. By the mid-nineteenth century, itinerant dance instructors, such as Thomas McIndoe, taught on a circuit that included several towns in central Canada.

Dancing masters gradually settled in major cities across Canada. Among the most notable teachers, in the late nineteenth century, were Toronto's Augustin Noverre, grandnephew of Jean-Georges Noverre, and John Freeman Davis, author of *The Modern Dance Tutor: or, Society Dancing* (1878) and numerous pieces of sheet music. Davis was founding president of the Western Association Normal School Masters of Dancing in 1894. Montreal-born Frank Norman had a substantial Anglophone and Francophone clientele. He wrote a technical manual and was vice-president of the Western Association Normal School Masters of Dancing in 1897.

In the early twentieth century, several teacher training schools were established. The most famous was the Margaret Eaton School opened in 1901, under the direction of Emma Scott Raff, to offer classes in literature, expression, and physical education, including creative movement, aesthetic and folk dancing, and Dalcroze eurhythmics. The school merged with the Department of Physical Education at the University of Toronto in 1942. Toronto teacher Amy Sternberg began a three-year teacher training course in 1910 to prepare students for private studio teaching. In Montreal, Barnjum's Gymnasium offered teacher training in physical culture, until the gymnasium was assimilated into McGill University. By the end of World War II, there were gifted teachers in many cities. A wide range of dance forms were taught, including ballet, ballroom, tap, and acrobatics. Teachers preparing students for professional careers concentrated on ballet instruction. In Montreal, Gérald Crevier taught ballet and introduced the Royal Academy of Dancing syllabus; Elizabeth Leese taught both modern dance and ballet, and introduced the Cecchetti syllabus in Quebec. Toronto's Boris Volkoff launched the Boris Volkoff Ballet Company in 1939. He provided several dancers for the debut season of the Canadian National Ballet in 1951. One of his most gifted dancers, Melissa Hayden, became a ballerina with the New York City Ballet. Ottawa's Gwendolyn Osborne trained New York City Ballet dancer Patricia Wilde. Another Osborne student, Nesta Toumine, danced both with René Blum's Ballets de Monte Carlo and with de Basil's Ballets Russes before establishing her own school and the Ottawa Ballet Company in 1947. In Winnipeg, Gweneth

Lloyd and Betty Farrally founded a school in 1938 to provide dancers for their Winnipeg Ballet Club. Vancouver teacher June Roper trained several dancers who toured with the Ballet Russe de Monte Carlo and Ballet Theatre. Other influential teachers were Mara McBirney and, in Victoria, Dorothy Wilson.

Today, each of Canada's three major ballet companies has a professional school that receives government funding. The National Ballet School, founded in 1959 by Celia Franca and Betty Oliphant, is a residential day school for students in grades five to twelve; it offers a teacher training program as well. The professional division of the Royal Winnipeg Ballet provides advanced training for talented students who have left secondary school. In 1958 Ludmilla Chiriaeff established a professional school affiliated with Les Grands Ballets Canadiens, and in 1966 a second school, the École Supérieure de Danse du Québec, was founded by Chiriaeff. The 1958 school was for older adolescents who had left school; the École Supérieure taught children as well as adults training as professionals. [*See the entry on Chiriaeff.*]

The promotion of dance education has been facilitated by two organizations. The Canadian Dance Teachers' Association, established in 1950, brought together studio teachers to improve teaching standards. The Canadian Association for Health, Physical Education and Recreation (CAPHER) was founded in the 1920s and a dance committee was created in 1965. This organization has lobbied strenuously for the inclusion of dance in the school curriculum. In 1978, CAPHER sponsored the first Dance and the Child International Conference in Edmonton.

Modern dance was included in physical education courses in some Canadian universities prior to 1970 with the content often based on Rudolf Laban's theories. In 1929, McGill University was the first institution of higher learning to offer credit courses in creative dance through the Physical Education Department. Under Thelma Wagner, a former student of Hanya Holm and Doris Humphrey, a dance concentration within physical education was begun in 1938. Until Wagner's retirement in 1967, she trained many Montreal teachers and dancers, including Elsie Salomons and Nina Caiserman. Several modern dance teachers settled in Toronto in the 1950s, including Nancy Lima Dent, and European-trained Yone Kvietys, Biroute Nagys, and Bianca Rogge. In the 1960s, Kvietys taught at the University of Toronto where she established a modern dance group. Intensive modern training was not available until Patricia Beatty, David Earle, and Peter Randazzo founded the Toronto Dance Theatre in 1966 and began a school to subsidize their company. The school, based on the Graham technique, was formally established in 1974 and began receiving government funding in 1977. The School of Contemporary Dancers began in 1972 as an apprenticeship program to Winnipeg's Contemporary Dancers under the direction of Rachel Browne. Currently the program offers a B.A. degree through the University of Winnipeg. An innovative program is run by Les Ateliers de Danse Moderne de Montréal. Founded in 1985, the program concentrates primarily on Limón technique. In 1991, the school was recognized by the province of Quebec as a college-level vocational school, and Quebec residents accepted into the school now receive free tuition. Vancouver's Main Dance Performance Training Program, begun in 1987, is recognized as a post-secondary school. The two-year program provides training in Limón technique and ballet.

Currently five universities offer a dance major. The York University Department of Dance in Toronto was established in 1970 by Grant Strate. It is the most comprehensive university dance program in Canada, with training in both ballet and modern as well as courses in history, criticism, notation, ethnology, and education. The master's degree program was the first in the world to offer study in history and criticism, and it has been expanded to include ethnology and movement analysis. In British Columbia, Simon Fraser University began giving noncredit dance courses in 1965 and established a dance degree in 1980. The program has a strong focus on contemporary dance and interdisciplinary study. In Quebec, Concordia University concentrates on choreography, while the Université du Québec à Montréal, begun in 1979, has three streams: teaching, performance, and choreography. Recently the master's degree was introduced. The University of Calgary has offered a dance minor for more than twenty years, and in 1996 introduced a dance major as a cooperative program between the faculties of kinesiology and fine arts. In Ontario, the University of Waterloo dance program, established in 1972, gave a B.A. degree until the university terminated the program in 1994. Ryerson Polytechnic University offers a three-year diploma with emphasis on performance and training teachers in the Royal Academy of Dancing (RAD) method. It anticipates offering a degree in the future. There are several community colleges across Canada that offer diploma courses in dance. Among the best known are Grant MacEwan in Edmonton, Cambrian Dance Arts Program in Sudbury, and the School of Classical and Contemporary Dance run by Ballet Jörgen in partnership with George Brown College in Toronto.

Although Laban-based movement education has been taught in many Canadian schools by generalist teachers since the 1950s, the move toward training and certification of dance teachers for the school system has been recent. An innovative approach has developed in Saskatchewan, where all students in grades one through nine are exposed to dance, with specialized courses available in grades ten through twelve. Since 1982, at the University of Regina in Saskatchewan, arts educators are given basic training in five arts education areas (dance, drama, literature, music, and visual art) and receive specialized training in two art forms. In Ontario, dance became a credited subject in 1991. At the elementary level, all students are expected to receive some dance instruction and students may continue dance at the secondary level if available in their school. The curriculum exposes students to a minimum of three forms selected from ballet, modern, jazz, ethno-cultural, or social dance. Since 1993, York University has offered teacher certification in dance. British Columbia teaches dance to all students in grades one through seven, and offers optional courses through to grade twelve. The province is developing dance teacher certification courses. In Quebec, students are taught three out of four arts disciplines. Teachers must have a dance degree to teach the dance courses. In the other provinces dance is offered only as a component of physical education.

With the inclusion of dance in the school system in several provinces, many in the field anticipate that the need for recreational and professional dance teachers will increase as more qualified young dancers apply to professional training schools and university dance programs.

BIBLIOGRAPHY

Arts and Education Advisory Committee of the Canadian Conference of the Arts. *Backgrounder: A Look at the State of Arts Education in Canada in 1993/1994*. Ottawa, 1994.

Byl, John. "The Margaret Eaton School, 1901–1942: Women's Education in Elocution, Drama and Physical Education." Ph.D. diss., State University of New York at Buffalo, 1992.

Crabb, Michael. "Dance in the Ivory Tower . . . But with Feet Firmly on the Ground." *Dance in Canada* 27 (Spring 1981): 6–12.

Kaiser, Pat. "New Myths Die Harder: The School of the Toronto Dance Theatre Steps from Graham's Shadow." *Dance in Canada* 29 (Fall 1981): 9–10.

Littler, William. "Celebration: The National Ballet School Marks Its 25th Anniversary." *Dance in Canada* 41 (Fall 1984): 4–8.

Oliphant, Betty. *Miss O: My Life in Dance*. Winnipeg, 1996.

Pickard, Garth. "Making Dance Education a Reality: A Unique Approach to Teacher Training in Arts Education." *Dance in Canada* 42 (Winter 1985): 26–27.

Strate, Grant. "Dance Education." In *The Canadian Encyclopedia*. Edmonton, 1985.

Strate, Grant. *The Guide to Career Training in the Dance Arts*. Toronto, 1995.

Tembeck, Iro. *Dancing in Montreal: Seeds of a Choreographic History*. Studies in Dance History, vol. 5.2. Madison, Wis., 1994.

Warner, MaryJane. *Toronto Dance Teachers: 1825–1925*. Toronto, 1995.

Warner, MaryJane. "York University, Toronto, Canada." In *World Ballet and Dance*, vol. 3, edited by Bent Schønberg. London, 1991–1992.

Wyman, Max. *Dance Canada: An Illustrated History*. Vancouver, 1989.

MARYJANE WARNER

Dance Research and Publication

The same factors that have affected the history of dance in Canada—sparse population, linguistic division, native and European ethnic diversity, and proximity to the United States—have also helped to determine the current state of dance scholarship. Although never entirely the domain of the universities, dance research in Canada has received major impetus from programs there. The first dance department was established at York University in 1970. During the 1970s, programs developed at the University of Waterloo, Ontario; at Simon Fraser University in British Columbia; at the University of Calgary, Alberta; and at three institutions in Montreal. The undergraduate program at York includes theoretical courses, and that at Waterloo has a strong emphasis on research. A master's degree program in dance history inaugurated at York in the mid-1970s awarded more than thirty graduate degrees in dance and related interdisciplinary topics in its first thirteen years. Several other universities foster research by dance faculty in physical education departments.

Coincident with the development of university programs was the creation of Dance in Canada, a national umbrella organization that has held conferences involving both scholars and performers. It also sponsors the journal *Dance in Canada, Danse au Canada* (1973–), which, though not scholarly in focus, has provided an essential record of Canadian dance.

Since the day of Nathan Cohen, a number of perceptive dance critics have written for newspapers and journals. In addition to *Dance in Canada*, more than thirty periodicals have recorded aspects of dance, from Montreal's avant-garde *Parachute* to the *Manitoba Square-dancer*. The unfortunately short-lived *York Dance Review* (1972–1978) was the only scholarly journal in Canada devoted to dance.

The general interest in Canadian culture that has grown in both French and English Canada has led to increasing interest in Canadian dance history, pursued both inside and outside the universities. This has resulted in several independent courses and has led to the development of basic research tools, historical studies, and reconstruction. The groundwork for Canadian dance research was laid by Pierre Guilmette's *Bibliographie de la danse théâtrale au Canada* (1970) and his bilingual collaboration with Cliff Collier, *Dance Resources in Canadian Libraries* (1982), which lists important archives. Another major research tool, the *Dictionary of Canadian Dance*, is being developed by Jillian Officer at Waterloo. Cliff Collier's *Index* (1988) increases the usefulness of *Dance in Canada* for the study of recent dance history.

Historical studies of Canadian dance are not plentiful. The first book-length treatment was Max Wyman's *Dance Canada: An Illustrated History* (1989); a condensed history by Michael Crabb appeared in Andrew Oxenham's *Dance Today in Canada* (1977). More specific studies include two works on the National Ballet of Canada, one by Ken Bell and Celia Franca (1978) and one by Herbert Whittaker (1967), as well as histories of the Royal Winnipeg Ballet by Max Wyman (1978) and Les Grands Ballets Canadiens by Roland Lorrain (1973). Reconstruction, another means of recapturing the national dance history, is the object of Encore! Encore!, an ongoing project under the direction of Lawrence and Miriam Adams that aims to investigate and document some of the nearly lost, post-1940s theatrical dance repertory.

Scholars in Quebec have given special attention to dance within Francophone culture. Iro Tembeck's ongoing studies of the history of modern dance in Quebec, as well as the efforts of Michèle Febvre, have attempted to place the recent extraordinary flowering of dance in Montreal within a wider contemporary context. Reconstruction has been important here too, as exemplified by the remounting of a 1948 dance recital to mark the fortieth anniversary of *Le refus global*, artistic Montreal's declaration of independence from the conservative regime of the day. Traditional social dancing has received much attention in French Canada. Responding to a desire for cultural continuity, scholars, teachers, and performing groups—supported by such institutions as the Centre d'Études sur la Langue, les Arts, et les Traditions Populaires of Université Laval—have tried to keep traditions alive. Noteworthy are Robert-Lionel Séguin's *La danse traditionelle au Québec* (1986) and Simonne Voyer's *La danse traditionelle dans l'est du Canada: Quadrilles et cotillons* (1986), which records rural dances and studies their evolution.

Although dance ethnography is taught at York and Waterloo, study of the dances of native peoples has gone on in relative isolation from the dance community, despite the fact that Canadian choreographers have often used native themes. Scholarly work on native Canadian dance by Gertrude Prokosch Kurath and many others is listed in Edward Buller's *Indigenous Performing and Ceremonial Arts in Canada: A Bibliography* (1981).

Much of the dance research in Canada does not have a specifically national focus. Canada's proximity to the United States has meant that many Canadians have participated in U.S. dance research organizations.

Despite their small number, Canadian scholars have a broad range of research interests. Selma Odom, Dianne Woodruff, Francis Sparshott, and William Littler have made notable contributions. York faculty members are interested in dance therapy and in the historical, stylistic, and pedagogical implications of the ways dance is taught. Researchers at Simon Fraser focus on interdisciplinary approaches to dance theory. Research on dance medicine takes place at the University of Western Ontario. Thomas Calvert and his associates at Simon Fraser are developing a computer-based human-movement language, including a graphics system with potential as a choreographic tool; at Waterloo, Rhonda Ryman is completing a computerized version of Benesh notation for choreological use. Dance in education receives attention in at least ten universities across the country and is given focus by the Dance Committee of the Canadian Association for Health, Physical Education, and Recreation.

Scholars working outside dance departments have also made significant contributions. Most notable is Francis Sparshott's work in dance aesthetics, especially *Off the Ground* (1988). John Chapman's detailed studies of Romantic ballet, Frank Hoff's work on Japanese dance, and Felix Cherniavsky's biography of dancer Maud Allan also deserve mention. Some significant collections of scholarly essays from Canada include Diana Taplin's *New Directions in Dance* (1979) and *Dance Spectrum* (1982). Although Canadians are fortunate to have a sympathetic funding agency in the Social Sciences and Humanities Research Council, there are relatively few indigenous publishing opportunities for the small but vibrant dance research community.

EVAN ALDERSON

CANARY. The term *canary* (It., Sp., *canario;* Fr., *canarie*) denotes two types of dances. The first is a *villancico* from the Canary Islands, called a *negrilla* when it represents in music and dance the islands' blacks, descendants of the Africans brought there by the Spanish slave trade. It is a leaping dance in the syncopated meter (with shifting accents) of *villancicos* (sesquialtera, 6/8 and 3/4), often with a narrative text in dialect.

In European dance history, *canary* denotes a sixteenth- to eighteenth-century dance in fast triple (or compound duple, 6/8) meter. It first appeared in Fabritio Caroso's *Il ballarino* (1581) and other dance manuals of the late sixteenth century as a fiery wooing dance, marked by rapid heel-and-toe stamps (resembling the current Mexican *zapateado*), by noisy sliding steps with which the partners alternately advance and retreat, and by distinctive music. By the eighteenth century these characteristics are almost gone, but the charm and spirited affect remained.

No concrete choreographic proof exists of the canary's provenance. It was thought either to have come to Spain from the Canary Islands and thence to Europe (Covarrubias Horozco, in *Tesoro de la lengua castellana o espanola* [1611], terms it a *saltarello gracioso*), or to have been invented for a spectacle (cf. Thoinot Arbeau, 1588). The first known references are Spanish (e.g., Diego Sanchez de Badajoz, 1554), and Spanish sources from the mid-sixteenth century onward continue to mention it (Miguel de Cervantes, Lope de Vega). Other references, however (e.g., Shakespeare, *Love's Labour's Lost*, act 3, scene 1: "canary to it with your feet"; *All's Well That Ends Well*, act 2, scene 1: "and make you dance canary / With spritely fire and motion"), and many musical sources from western Europe and England attest to its universal popularity. John Florio (1598, 1611) refers to castanets as "little shels used of those that dance the canaries to clacke or snap with their fingers." Whatever its real origins, then, its title and "Spanish" character place it with many other "exotic" dances typically borrowed or invented throughout the ages to reinvigorate "civilized" social dance.

The major sixteenth-century choreographic sources of the canary are Italian (Caroso, 1581, 1600; Livio Lupi, 1600, 1607; and Cesare Negri, 1602, 1604). (See Example 1.) They give discrete canary choreographies, each containing numerous variations, which presumably were intended as a pool of ideas from which dancers could extract choreographed variations for their "improvised" canaries. (Livio Lupi provides more than one hundred variations and *passeggi*.) Caroso and Cesare Negri place a canary movement at the end of fourteen *balletto* suites.

From France comes a brief description and only two variations; they are similar to the Italian canaries in movement and music, though in simple duple meter (Arbeau). Theatrical canaries appear in two *balli* by Emilio de' Cavalieri (in the sixth *intermedio* of the Florentine spectacles of 1589 and in *La rappresentazione di anima et di corpo*, 1600); these are specified for men only, and there are no choreographies. Cavalieri's canary music is neither distinctive nor typical; in fact, in his *La rappresentazione*, a *galliard*, a *canario*, and a *corrente (courante)* are danced successively to the same music. None of the sixteenth-century choreographic sources mentions the use of castanets; there is no way of knowing whether this was deliberate, whether the castanets or finger snapping were simply assumed, or whether the Italians omitted them as unsuitable for aristocratic dancers.

The typical sixteenth-century ballroom canary consists of alternating male and female variations framed and interspersed with passages danced together—a pattern similar to that of the *passo e mezzo, galliard,* or *tordiglione* (tordion). More specific to the canary, however, are the pantomimic courting elements: the challenging approach to and retreat from the partner *(retirata)*, often with strong flanking movements, and the complex and percussive alternating footwork. Indeed, a number of canaries in *balletto* suites contain such a quick alternation of rhythmic footwork between the partners as to suggest a rapid-fire dialogue (termed *pedalogue* and defined by Caroso) that enhances the flirtatious mock fury of the dance. Canary steps in the Italian manuals are always so named when used in other dance types and are always in rapid triple meter (e.g., the *seguito battuto del canario* in "Allegrezza d'Amore," a *cascarda* in both of Caroso's books).

Canary music in the Renaissance manuals (and in a number of musical collections, e.g., Michael Praetorius's *Terpsichore* [1612]) is instantly recognizable, based on one of several closely related and short bass ostinatos with re-

CANARY. Example 1. The music for the Canary section found in the *balletto Laura Suave*. Instructions for the dance are found in Fabritio Caroso's *Nobiltà di dame* (1600).

iterated chordal schemes and on similarly related short melodies of narrow range with repeated (usually) dotted rhythms and melodic motives. Phrase lengths are regular, and the short length of most tunes (four, eight, or twelve bars) means that they are repeated often to accompany a complete dance variation. Such insistent repetitions of internally repetitious music, when combined with footwork that joins the dancers to the musical ensemble, indeed produces a colorful effect. (The earliest musical source of a canary is Diego Pisador's *Endechas de canario* for *vihuela,* from 1552, a lament apparently unrelated to other canaries.)

The absence of precise canary choreographies from about 1620 to 1700 makes it impossible to know how its style changed in the seventeenth century. Nevertheless, there is ample evidence of the canary's continuing popularity. Marin Mersenne, in 1636–1637 described it as virtuosic, with *batteries de pieds* (three, six, or twelve), half capers, and turns on the ground or in the air; he gave a standard tune. Juan de Esquivel Navarro mentioned it in 1642 among the dances taught at dancing schools in Spain, but without details. After 1650, many opera and ballet types include canaries (Jean-Baptiste Lully has fifteen) but without choreographies.

The earliest choreographed examples of Baroque canaries appear in Raoul-Auger Feuillet's publications of 1700 and 1704; the music to some of his notations dates from before 1700, so those choreographies may also be earlier: for example, Guillaume-Louis Pecour's "Canarie pour Deux Hommes" in the 1704 collection is from Henri Desmarets's opera *Didon*, from 1693. By then the canary was considerably different from earlier ones; although still either a discrete dance or part of a suite, and still both social and theatrical, it became less distinctive and its pantomimic aspects were gone. As in other Baroque dances, partners danced simultaneously on mirrored paths; even in social settings, the dance might then have been a solo or may have had partners of the same sex. Steps were also mirrored, the step vocabulary (e.g., con-

tretemps, pas glissés) typical of lively and showy dances like the *gigue* (with which the canary is sometimes identified at this time), and the music lost its pervasive ostinatos. Nevertheless, the Baroque canary was still seen as a Spanish dance from the Canary Islands (Samuel Rudolph Behr, 1713). Some of its steps were associated with other "Spanish" dances of different tempo and affect (e.g., *chaconne, sarabande*), especially a beaten step (see also Kellom Tomlinson, 1735). In Spain, however, a stamped step still existed, termed *passo de canario* and described by Bartolomé Ferriol y Boxeraus (1745).

The canary continued to be danced through much of the eighteenth century, gradually losing popularity; Jean-Jacques Rousseau wrote in 1768 that it was no longer in use. It survives as a folk song in Spain, however.

BIBLIOGRAPHY: SOURCES

Arbeau, Thoinot. *Orchésographie et traicte en forme de dialogve, par leqvel tovtes personnes pevvent facilement apprendre & practiquer l'honneste exercice des dances.* Langres, 1588, 1589. Facsimile reprint, Langres, 1988. Reprinted with expanded title as *Orchésographie, metode, et teorie en forme de discovrs et tablatvre povr apprendre a dancer, battre le Tambour en toute sorte & diuersité de bateries, Iouët du fifre & arigot, tirer des armes & escrimer, auec autres honnestes exercices fort conuenables à la Ieunesse.* Langres, 1596. Facsimile reprint, Geneva, 1972.

Arbeau, Thoinot. *Orchesography.* 1589. Translated into English by Mary Stewart Evans. New York, 1948. Reprint with corrections, a new introduction, and notes by Julia Sutton, and representative steps and dances in Labanotation by Mireille Backer. New York, 1967.

Behr, Samuel Rudolph. *L'art de bien danser, oder, Die Kunst wohl zu Tantzen.* Leipzig, 1713.

Caroso, Fabritio. *Il ballarino* (1581). Facsimile reprint, New York, 1967.

Caroso, Fabritio. *Nobiltà di dame.* Venice, 1600, 1605. Facsimile reprint, Bologna, 1970. Reissued with order of illustrations changed as *Raccolta di varij balli.* Rome, 1630. Translated into English with eight introductory chapters by Julia Sutton, the music transcribed by F. Marian Walker. Oxford, 1986. Reprint with a step manual in Labanotation by Rachelle Palnick Tsachor and Julia Sutton, New York, 1995.

Cavalieri, Emilio de'. "Intermedio VI." In Cristofano Malvezzi's *Intermedii et concerti, fatti per la Commedia rappresentata in Firenze nelle Nozze del Serenissimo Don Ferdinando Medici et Madama Christiana di Loreno, Granduchi di Toscana.* Venice, 1591. Translated and edited by D. P. Walker as *Les Fêtes de Florence: Musique des intermèdes de "La Pellegrina."* Paris, 1963.

Cavalieri, Emilio de'. *La rappresentazione di anima e di corpo* (1600). Facsimile reprint, Bologna, 1967.

Esquivel Navarro, Juan de. *Discursos sobre el arte del dancado* (1642). Facsimile reprint, Madrid, 1947.

Ferriol y Boxeraus, Bartolomé. *Reglas utiles para los aficionados a danzar.* Capua, 1745.

Feuillet, Raoul-Auger. *Chorégraphie, ou L'art de décrire la dance, par caractères, figures et signes démonstratifs, avec lesquels on apprend facilement de soy-même toutes sortes de dances.* Paris, 1700. 2d ed. 1709, 1713. Facsimile reprint, New York, 1968; also Hildesheim and New York 1979.

Feuillet, Raoul-Auger. *Recucil de danses composées par M. Feuillet.* Paris, 1700. Facsimile reprint, New York, 1968.

Feuillet, Raoul-Auger. *Recueil de dances: Entrées de ballet de M. Pecour.* Paris, 1704.

Florio, John. *A World of Wordes.* London, 1598. Facsimile reprint, Hildesheim, 1972. 2d ed., *Queen Anna's New World of Words.* London, 1611. Facsimile reprint of 1611 ed., Menston, England, 1973.

Gaudrau, Michel. *Nouveau recueil de dances de bal et celle de ballet, contenant un très grand nombres des meillieures entrées di ballet de la composition de Mr. Pécour.* Paris, 1713.

Isaac, Mister. *The Royal Gailliarde.* London, 1710.

Jacobilli, Ludovico. *Modo di ballare.* Circa 1615. Manuscript located in Foligno, Biblioteca Jacobilli, AIII.19,ff.102–104.

L'Abbé, Anthony. *The Canary: A New Dance for the Year 1724.* London, 1724.

L'Abbé, Anthony. *A New Collection of Dances.* London, 1725. Edited by Carol G. Marsh. London, 1991.

Lupi, Livio. *Libro di gagliarde, tordiglione, passo e mezzo, canari e passeggi.* Palermo, 1600. Rev. ed., Palermo, 1607.

Mersenne, Marin. *Harmonie universelle* (1636–1637). Facsimile reprint, Paris, 1963. English translation of Book 2 by J. B. Egan. Ph.D. diss., Indiana University, 1962.

Negri, Cesare, *Le gratie d'amore.* Milan, 1602. Reissued as *Nuove invenzione di balli.* Milan, 1604. Translated into Spanish by Don Balthasar Carlos for Señor Condé, Duke of Sanlucar, 1630. Manuscript located in Madrid, Biblioteca Nacional, MS 14085. Facsimile reprint of 1602, New York and Bologna, 1969. Literal translation into English and musical transcription by Yvonne Kendall. D.M.A. diss., Stanford University, 1985.

Pecour, Louis. *Les canaries de madame la dauphine.* Paris, c.1712. Manuscript located in Paris, Bibliothèque du Musée et de l'Opéra, Res.841 (16bis).

Rossi, Bastiano de'. *Descrizione del magnificentissimo Apparato rappresentata nella felicissime Nozze degli Illustrissimi Don Ferdinando Medici, e Madama Christina di Lorena, Gran Duchi di Toscana.* Florence, 1589.

Rousseau, Jean-Jacques. *Dictionnaire de musique.* Paris, 1768. Facsimile reprint, 1969. Translated by William Waring. 2d ed. London, 1779.

Sánchez de Badajoz, Diego. *Farsa da Sancta Barbara.* Seville, 1554.

Tomlinson, Kellom. *A Work Book by Kellom Tomlinson: Commonplace Book of an Eighteenth-Century English Dancing Master* (c.1708–1722). Edited by Jennifer Shennan. Stuyvesant, N.Y., 1992.

Tomlinson, Kellom. *The Art of Dancing Explained by Reading and Figures.* 2 vols. London, 1735. Facsimile reprint, London and New York, 1970.

BIBLIOGRAPHY: OTHER STUDIES

Chilesotti, Oscar, ed. *Biblioteca di rarità musicali,* vol. 1, *Danze del secolo XVI trascritte in notazione moderne dalle opere: "Nobiltà di dame" del Sig. F. Caroso da Sermoneta; "Le gratie d'amore" di C. Negri, Milanese, detto il Trombone.* Milan, 1884.

Collins, Michael B. "The Performance of Coloration, Sesquialtera, and Hemiolia, 1450–1750." Ph.D. diss., Stanford University, 1963.

Collins, Michael B. "The Performance of Sesquialtera and Hemiolia in the Sixteenth Century." *Journal of the American Musicological Society* 17 (Spring 1964): 5–28.

Cotarelo y Mori, Emilio. *Colección de entremeses, loas, bailes, jácaras, y mojigangas.* Madrid, 1911.

Esses, Maurice. *Dance and Instrumental Diferencias in Spain during the Seventeenth and Early Eighteenth Centuries.* Stuyvesant, N.Y., 1992.

García Matos, Manuel. "Viejas canciones y melodias en la musica instrumental popular de las danzas procesionales," in *Miscelànea en homenajea Monseñor Higinio Angles.* Barcelona, 1958.

Hilton, Wendy. *Dance of Court and Theatre: The French Noble Style, 1690–1725.* Princeton, 1981.

Hudson, Richard. "Canary." In *The New Grove Dictionary of Music and Musicians.* London, 1980.

Jones, Pamela. "The Relation between Music and Dance in Cesare Negri's 'Le gratie d'amore' (1602)." 2 vols. Ph.D. diss., University of London, 1988.

Little, Meredith Ellis, and Carol G. Marsh. *La Danse Noble: An Inventory of Dances and Sources.* Williamstown, Mass., 1992.

Matteo (Vittucci, Matteo Marcellus) with Carola Goya. *The Language of Spanish Dance.* Norman, Okla., 1990.

Moe Lawrence H. "Dance Music in Printed Italian Lute Tablatures from 1507 to 1611." Ph.D. diss., Harvard University, 1956.

Querol Gavaldá, Miguel. *La música en las obras de Cervantes.* Barcelona, 1948.

Sasportes, José. "Feasts and Folias: The Dance in Portugal." *Dance Perspectives* 42 (1970).

Stanford, E. Thomas. "Negrilla." In *The New Grove Dictionary of Music and Musicians.* London, 1980.

Sutton, Julia. *Renaissance Revisited: Twelve Dances Reconstructed [in Labanotation] from the Originals of Thoinot Arbeau, Fabritio Caroso, and Cesare Negri.* New York, 1972.

Sutton, Julia. "Canario." In *Die Musik in Geschichte und Gegenwart.* 2d ed., vol. 2, 1995. Kassel, 1994–.

Tani, Gino. "Canario." In *Enciclopedio dello spettacolo.* 9 vols. Rome, 1954–1968.

VIDEOTAPE.   Julia Sutton, *Il Ballarino (The Dancing Master),* a teaching videotape featuring a glossary of steps and three sixteenth-century Italian dances by Caroso and Negri (Pennington, N.J., 1991).

JULIA SUTTON
with Pamela Jones

CAN-CAN. This French dance first appeared during the 1840s. At the time, dance writers compared it with the *chahut,* a rowdy dance performed in Paris at public ballrooms—such as the Prado, Mabille, and Grande Chaumière—by students, working girls, and young clerks.

An acrobatic form of the quadrille, the can-can is characterized by its freedom from propriety and its imaginativeness. This dance requires great flexibility, a good sense of rhythm, and remarkable vivacity. It has no set steps and permits the most audacious improvisations. Originally it was performed by couples, who abandoned themselves to invention, leaping and kicking their legs as high as possi-

CAN-CAN. A wood engraving by Winslow Homer of dancers at the Mabille ballroom in Paris, c.1867. Holding her foot and hopping on one leg, the woman in the center demonstrates one of the can-can's most characteristic steps. (Metropolitan Museum of Art, New York; Harris Brisbane Dick Fund, 1936 [no. 36.13.12]; photograph used by permission.)

ble. The women flung up their flaring petticoats, which were edged with lace or embellished with embroidered ribbons—a gesture that charmed the audience, excited their partners, and shocked prudes at a time when an excessive display of ankle was considered dissolute. According to Desrat, the can-can was "far from crude and licentious"; initially it seemed to be "marked by an originality that could be called spiritual."

The popularity of the can-can began to wane in the mid-nineteenth century, but professional dancers sensed its potential as an audience-pleaser. Since the 1880s it has been a popular feature in French music halls and cabarets, including the Casino de Paris and the Moulin Rouge. One of the few men to dance the can-can professionally was Valentin le Désossé ("the Boneless"), a popular Moulin Rouge performer of the 1890s. The can-can is a complicated and technically demanding dance. Its most spectacular step is a pirouette on one foot, with the other foot grasped around the ankle and raised to eye level; other steps include high kicks, cartwheels, rapid runs, and wide splits. The can-can has inspired several choreographers, particularly Léonide Massine and Maurice Béjart. Massine used it as a climax in his ballets *La Boutique Fantasque* and *Gaîté Parisienne*. It was the subject of the 1953 Broadway hit *Can-Can*, featuring Cole Porter's music and Gwen Verdon's dancing, and of Jean Renoir's 1955 film *French Cancan*.

[*See also* Music Hall, *article on* French Traditions.]

BIBLIOGRAPHY

Desrat, G. *Dictionnaire de la danse*. Paris, 1895.
Gribble, Francis. "The Origin of the Can-Can" (1933). *The Dancing Times* (October 1990): 53–54.
Guest, Ivor. "Queens of the Cancan." *Dance and Dancers* (December 1952): 14.
Pessis, Jacques, and Jacques Crépineau. *The Moulin Rouge*. New York, 1990.
Price, David. "The Cancan: Misconceptions and Misrepresentations." *The Dancing Times* (August 1993): 1073–1075.
Souvais, Michel. *Les Cancans de La Goulue*. Paris, 1992.

MARIE-FRANÇOISE CHRISTOUT
Translated from French

CANDOMBLÉ. *See* Brazil, *article on* Popular and Ritual Dance.

CANFIELD. Choreography: Merce Cunningham. Music: Pauline Oliveros; *In Memoriam NIKOLA TESLA, Cosmic Engineer*. Scenery: Robert Morris. Costumes: (uncredited) Jasper Johns. First performance: 4 March 1969 (without decor), Nazareth College, Rochester, New York; 15 April 1969 (in silence), Brooklyn Academy of Music, Merce Cunningham Dance Company. Dancers: Merce Cunningham, Carolyn Brown, Sandra Neels, Valda Setterfield, Meg Harper, Susana Hayman-Chaffey, Jeff Slayton, Chase Robinson, Mel Wong.

Canfield is the quintessential example of the John Cage–Merce Cunningham collaborative aesthetic, in which choreographer, composer, and designer work separately, with the final results not assembled until performance. The title refers to a game of solitaire named after Richard A. Canfield, an American gambling house proprietor. The choreography for nine dancers has twenty-six sections—thirteen "hands" and thirteen "deals"—that may appear in any order. Only when all twenty-six sections are performed is *Canfield* presented as an evening-length work. More often it is given in a shorter version. Cunningham managed with only nine dancers to create a sense of mass, of architectural sculpture, an impression of molecular structures fulfilling their inevitable destinies.

The music, derived from Nikola Tesla's experiment with mechanical resonance, bears no relationship to Cunningham's schemata derived from Canfield's game of solitaire, but it too is different in each performance. Pauline Oliveros's score requires the musicians to discuss the acoustical environment of the theatre over the public address system, to test the environment in order to find its resonant frequency, to record the process, and finally to play the information back to the audience along with a long, slow crescendo (from inaudibility to extremely loud) produced by two or more audio generators. In *Canfield*'s first New York performance, the work was presented in silence due to a labor dispute.

Robert Morris's set for the first New York performance was a motorized vertical column furnished with intensely brilliant aircraft landing lights. Slowly and continuously it traversed back and forth across the front of the stage, transfixing everything before it in searing illumination. Sprayed with light-reflective paint, both the cyclorama and the costumes (tights and leotard in shades of gray) were intended to glow a phosphorescent white when the traversing light beams were in the direct line of each individual audience member's vision. However, the device seldom worked as intended. Apparently what was needed was for members of the audience to have their own hand-held aircraft landing lights.

With or without the music and decor, and despite the fact that every performance of *Canfield* was inevitably a new experience, the essence of the work—its classical and awesome severity—prevailed.

BIBLIOGRAPHY
Cunningham, Merce, in conversation with Jacqueline Lesschaeve. *The Dancer and the Dance.* New York, 1985.
Mazo, Joseph H. *Prime Movers: The Makers of Modern Dance in America.* New York, 1977.

CAROLYN BROWN

CANNABICH, CHRISTIAN (Johann Christian Innocenz Bonaventura Cannabich; born December 1731 in Mannheim, died 20 January 1798 in Frankfurt-am-Main), German composer, violinist, and conductor. Cannabich was a member of a family of musicians at the courts of Mannheim and Munich. As a pupil of Johann Stamitz he entered the famous Mannheim orchestra at the age of twelve. Around 1750 the culture-loving elector Carl Theodor granted him a scholarship to study with Niccolò Jommelli in Rome, where he stayed until 1753; then, together with Jommelli, he went to the court orchestra in Stuttgart. By 1758 he had succeeded Stamitz in Mannheim, where he appeared as composer of the ballet *Arlichino Fortunato nell'Amore* (1758) and as concert master. In 1764 and 1766 Cannabich visited Paris, making contact with various Parisian publishers; from this time onward most of his works were published in Paris.

In 1775, Cannabich was nominated as director of instrumental music, conductor, and trainer of the Mannheim court orchestra, and in 1778 he moved with the court to Munich, where his presence stimulated middle-class musical life. As an orchestra leader he was admired for his cultivation of the new dimension of varying instrumental color and a new concept of dynamic shading. Cannabich was very well known and had innumerable contacts among important musicians; most famous is his connection with Leopold and Wolfgang Amadeus Mozart.

Cannabich is important as a composer of around ninety symphonies and a great amount of other instrumental music. He also composed for the stage. In about 1758 he began a collaboration with the newly appointed court ballet master Étienne Lauchery, which brought about a flowering of dramatic ballet in Mannheim. Cannabich created scores for more than thirty-five ballets, among them *Les Fêtes du Sérail, Renaud et Armide,* and *Roland Furieux* (all 1768), *Les Mariages des Samnites* (1772), *Admète et Alceste* and *Médor et Angélique* (both 1770), and *Médée et Jason* (1772).

Cannabich touched upon a world of sound more akin to romanticism than to classicism. At the same time, he belongs to the early days of classicism, when symmetry and simplicity of form were reestablished. His ballet scores are rich in vivid expression. He built his movements upon simple melodic motifs, often of no more than two bars. He had a great sense of sound and color, derived from a fine understanding of differentiated instrumentation. His use of the gradual crescendo and other dynamic effects are typical of the Mannheim style.

BIBLIOGRAPHY
Burney, Charles. *The Present State of Music in Germany, the Netherlands, and United Provinces.* 2 vols. London, 1773.
Kloiber, Rudolf. "Die dramatischen Ballette von Christian Cannabich." Ph.D. diss., University of Munich, 1928.
Komma, Karl M. "Cannabich." In *Die Musik in Geschichte und Gegenwart.* Kassel, 1949–.
Scholes, Percy, ed. *Dr. Burney's Musical Tours in Europe.* 2 vols. London, 1959.
Walter, Friedrich. *Geschichte des Theaters und der Musik am kurpfälzischen Hofe.* Leipzig, 1898.
Würtz, Roland. "Cannabich." In *The New Grove Dictionary of Music and Musicians.* London, 1980.

OLE NØRLYNG

CANZIANI, GIUSEPPE (*fl.* 1771–1793), Italian dancer, choreographer, and teacher. Although the exact dates and places of Canziani's birth and death are not known, it is known that his first marriage was to Maria Casassi, a ballerina active in the 1770s at the Teatro San Benedetto in Venice; that his second marriage was to Caterina Bonafini; and that his career was blessed with good fortune. The records of Canziani's professional life span twenty years, between the 1770s and 1790s, when he worked in northern Italy (Venice, Padua, Turin, Bologna, Milan) and abroad (Munich, Saint Petersburg). These were the active years of Jean-Georges Noverre, Gaspero Angiolini, Claude Legrand, and Charles Le Picq, with whom Canziani sometimes collaborated.

A prolific choreographer, Canziani's first known works were made at the Hoftheater of Munich from 1771 to 1774, when he created "The Judgment of Paris" for the opera *Zenobia* by Antonio Tozzi in 1773. In the subsequent four years, Canziani worked in Turin, Padua, and Venice, where he presented many ballets with tragic or pastoral subjects and heroic pantomimes. Thus, there appeared *Ines di Castro* and *Il Volubile* (The Fickle One) in 1775; *Linceo*, *Le Reclute del Villeggio* (The Village Recruit), *Porzia*, and *Amor Non Puó Celors* (Love Cannot Be Hidden) in 1776; *Coriolanos* and *L'Amante Generosa* (The Generous Lover) in 1777; and *Cleopatra*, *Li Selveggi del Kamtchadal* (The Wild Men of Kamtchadal), *L'Arrivo di Venere nell'Isola di Cipro* (The Arrival of Venus on the Island of Cyprus), *L'Americana* (The American), and *L'Amante Travestito* (The Disguised Lover) in 1778.

In 1778 Canziani worked as *primo ballerino* and choreographer in Bologna, where he created the intermezzi for a production of Christoph Willibald Gluck's opera *Alceste*, which had first been given in Vienna in 1767. On the occasion of the Bologna production, the intellectual circles connected with Raniero de Calzabigi, the librettist for *Alceste*, criticized Canziani for creating two ballets completely independent of the opera, disregarding the principles of Gluck's reform stated in his preface to the published score. Canziani also worked at the Teatro alla Scala in Milan, where he staged, for its inauguration in 1778, *Apollo Placato*, with music by Louis de Baillou, and other ballets. Also at La Scala, in the Carnival season 1778/79, he presented the ballets *Porzia* and *L'Arrivo di Venere nell'Isola di Cipro*, set to music by Felice Alessandri. In 1779 he succeeded Angiolini as court choreographer in Saint Petersburg, where he created the ballets for operas by Giovanni Paisiello, who at that time enjoyed the favor of Catherine the Great. In 1780 he composed the dances for the *fête théâtrale* entitled *The Temple of Universal Happiness*, and in 1781 he composed the ballet *Admetus and Alcestis*.

Canziani returned to Venice in 1783, where he again presented some of his ballets, including *Cupido Trionfa-*tore, o sia Apollo e Dafne, set to music by Carlo Canobbio, and *La Maggior Impresa d'Ercole, o sia Admeto e Alceste*. In 1784, he returned to Saint Petersburg, where he worked for several more years as a teacher in the Imperial Theater School, with the task of "forming Russian dancers able of replacing foreign ones" (Mooser, 1951). One of his pupils, Ivan Valberkh, was to become the first great Russian teacher and choreographer.

As the decade of the 1780s drew to a close, Canziani enjoyed the first of several notable successes in Russia. In 1789, his *Bacchus and Ariadne*, with music by Canobbio, was presented in Saint Petersburg, and in 1790 some of Canziani and Le Picq's *divertissements* were inserted in the spectacular opera *The Early Reign of Oleg*. Given at the Hermitage Theater on 15 October 1790, this work had a libretto by Catherine the Great herself and was set to music by Giuseppe Sarti, Canobbio, and Vasily Pashkevich. During this period Canziani presented *Ines di Castro* in Count Dmitri Shcheremetev's theater at Kuskovo, and in Saint Petersburg he created *La Sourde Supposée* (1790) and *Pyramus and Thisbe* (1791), to music by Canobbio.

When his contract with the Imperial Theaters expired in 1792, Canziani accepted his pension of five hundred rubles and established himself at Venice's Teatro San Samuele, where, in 1793, he composed and presented his last ballets: *Il Tradimento Punito*, *Il Giudizio di Paride*, and *La Pastorella Fedele*. No work of his dated later than 1793 is known.

BIBLIOGRAPHY

Hansell, Kathleen Kuzmick. *Il ballo teatrale e l'opera italiana*. In *Storia dell'opera italiana*, vol. 5, pp. 175–306. Turin, 1987.

Lawson, Joan. "Pages from the History of Russian Ballet" (parts 1–6). *The Dancing Times* (December 1940–May 1941).

Lo Iacono, Concetta. "Il balletto in Russia." In *Musica in scena: Storia dello spettacolo musicale*, edited by Alberto Basso, vol. 5, pp. 297–390. Turin, 1995.

Massaro, Maria Nevilla. "Il ballo pantomimo al Teatro Nuovo di Padova, 1751–1830." *Acta musicologica* 57.2 (1985): 215–275.

Massaro, Maria Nevilla. "Balli e ballerini fra Padova e Venezia." *La danza italiana* 5–6 (Autumn 1987): 77–88.

Mooser, R. Aloys. *Annales de la musique et des musiciens en Russie au XVIIIeme siècle*. Geneva, 1951.

Pasi, Mario, ed. *Il balletto: Repertorio del teatro di danza dal 1581*. Milan, 1979.

Roslavleva, Natalia. *Era of the Russian Ballet*. London, 1966.

Winter, Marian Hannah. *The Pre-Romantic Ballet*. London, 1974.

CLAUDIA CELI
Translated from Italian

CAPAB BALLET. Cape Town has the longest tradition of dance in South Africa, dating back to 1802. It also has the oldest and most stable ballet company, which has performed continuously for more than sixty years. In 1934 Dr. Dulcie Howes founded the University of Cape Town

CAPAB BALLET. The final scene from *The Rain Queen* (1973), David Poole's ballet based on a South African legend. Carol Kinsey, held aloft, portrays the Rain Queen; the Four Ancestors in front support Johan Jooste as Thana. (Photograph by Pat Bromilow-Downing; used by permission.)

(UCT) Ballet, which in 1963 became the basis for the professional, government-subsidized company established under the aegis of the Cape Performing Arts Board (CAPAB). Until that time, the UCT Ballet was the only South African ballet company to tour extensively in South Africa, the Rhodesias (now Zambia and Zimbabwe), South West Africa (now Namibia), and Mozambique. In 1963, when the South African government decided to subsidize the arts and gave grants to all four provinces to fund ballet companies, the Cape was the only province that had an existing company with experienced personnel on which to build.

Fully funded by government, provincial, and municipal grants, the newly created CAPAB Ballet was headed by a trio of experienced personnel: Dulcie Howes was, of course, the artistic director; David Poole was named ballet master; and Frank Staff was appointed as resident choreographer. Both Poole and Staff also performed in the company's productions and greatly enriched them by their artistry and mastery of theatrical skills. Through an agreement with the Dulcie Howes Trust Fund, rights to the UCT Ballet repertory, costumes, stage settings, and music scores were transferred to the new company.

At first the company retained a dual name, performing in Cape Town as the UCT/CAPAB Ballet and on tour as CAPAB Ballet. The Cape Performing Arts Board had adopted a racially restrictive policy regarding audiences, and by performing as the UCT Ballet Howes was able to maintain her policy of performing to multiracial audiences, at least in Cape Town. For this joint company Staff mounted his stunning production of *Romeo and Juliet*, set to Prokofiev's score, in November 1964. The principal dancers were Phyllis Spira and Gary Burne, with Poole and Staff in supporting character parts. Other notable productions of the late 1960s included Richard Glasstone's mounting of Ninette de Valois's *The Rake's Progress* and his own original work entitled *Mandoline* (1967), set to music by Vivaldi. Howes retired in 1967, handing over the artistic direction of the company to Poole. Thereafter, Burne was to be ballet master for a brief period, when Poole resigned in 1969 to go overseas. On his return in

1970, he resumed the post of artistic director, with Burne as resident choreographer. Howes steered the company through the difficult transition stages in the 1960s, and in the 1970s Poole led it firmly into professional status. Their inspiring leadership provided the strong foundation on which the present company is built.

In 1971 CAPAB Ballet opened the new Nico Malan Opera House in Cape Town, which was to become the company's permanent home and where performances are accompanied by the resident CAPAB Orchestra, conducted for more than a decade (1971–1982) by David Tidboald. To inaugurate the company's new home, three original works were mounted for the 1971 season: Richard Glasstone created *Ritual*, set to a symphonic poem entitled *Primavera* by South African composer Arnold van Wyk; Gary Burne gave the company his inventively choreographed, abstract ballet *Variations within Space*, set to music by Bach played on a synthesizer; and Marina Keet created *Misa Flamenca*, to music by Torregrosa, for four local Spanish dancers who joined the company as guest artists: Hazel Acosta, Mavis Becker, Deanna Blacher, and Cynthia Rowe.

Over the years, Poole was to produce many ballets in the classical repertory for the company. Among others, he mounted *Giselle*, *Coppélia*, and *Firebird* in 1965, *Swan Lake* in 1967, *The Sleeping Beauty* in 1968, *Le Carnaval* in 1971, and *The Nutcracker* in 1972, when he also reconstructed Fokine's choreography for the *Polovtsian Dances* from *Prince Igor*. Productions of most of these works remain in the active repertory, periodically revised to keep them fresh. Poole also staged Frederick Ashton's *Les Rendezvous* in 1963 and John Cranko's *The Lady and the Fool* in 1965 and *Pineapple Poll* in 1977, as well as enriching

the repertory with numerous original works of his own. He created *The Snow Queen* to a Tchaikovsky score in 1966 and *A Midsummer Night's Dream*, set to music by Handel, in 1970. In 1973 the company took into its repertory his dramatic social comment on oppression, *Le Cirque*, set to music by Bach, which he had originally made for the UCT Ballet.

That same year Poole rechoreographed Frank Staff's ballet *The Rain Queen*, based on an African legend and set to a score by Graham Newcater, which was performed in homage to Staff, who died before he could stage it. In 1976 Poole created *Kami*, another notable ballet with a South African theme. Choreographed to a score by Michael Tuffin and based on a play by C. Louis Leipoldt that is set in Cape Town and Java, the ballet tells the story of a former governor of the Cape colony.

In 1971 Veronica Paeper, a former dancer and Frank Staff's widow, mounted for the company a memorable production of her late husband's ballet *Transfigured Night*, set to Schoenberg's haunting score. In 1974 Paeper was appointed resident choreographer of CAPAB Ballet, and she again seized the opportunity to present a major work by Staff, restaging his *Romeo and Juliet* in a beautiful new production. In the years that followed she created many original works of her own, including *Still Life with Moonbeams* (1981), to music by Peter Klatzow; a full-length *Don Quixote* (1981), to the lively Minkus score; *Drie Diere* (Three Animals; 1982), again to music by Klatzow; and *A Christmas Carol* (1983), to music by several composers arranged by David Tidboald. Particularly successful was her 1982 production of *Orpheus in the Underworld*. Set to Offenbach's irresistible music, arranged by Tuffin, and

CAPAB BALLET. Mandy Stober as Eurydice, Jeremy Hodges at the wheel as Pluto, and the "Mafia" in a 1993 performance of Veronica Paeper's *Orpheus in the Underworld* (1982). One of the company's most popular works, this ballet sets the Greek myth in the 1920s. (Photograph by Pat Bromilow-Downing; used by permission.)

with sumptuous decor by Peter Cazalet, it broke all box-offices records for ballet performances.

Several visiting choreographers have enriched the CAPAB Ballet repertory. One of the company's most successful productions was Attilio Labis's staging of *Swan Lake* (1971), in which he danced with guest ballerina Margot Fonteyn. Alfred Rodrigues staged three ballets in 1976—*Souvenir*, to music by Tchaikovsky; *A Time of Parting*, to music by Ginastera; and *Judith*, to music by Isiköslü—and in 1977 mounted a production of *Raymonda*. In 1973 Petrus Bosman produced and danced the title role in *Petrouchka*, his farewell performance as a dancer. He returned in 1975 to stage dances from August Bournonville's *Napoli*, which shared the program with Anna Markard's staging of Kurt Jooss's masterful *The Green Table*. In 1980 Norman Furber restaged *Raymonda*, and in 1983 André Prokovsky staged his *Zhivago*. Most of the main productions of CAPAB Ballet have been designed by Peter Cazalet, who, with Stephen de Villers, has played an important role in the company's fortunes by setting high artistic standards for decor and costumes.

Throughout its history, CAPAB Ballet has been a notably stable company, with many of its original members remaining in its service for long periods. The ballerina roles in the repertory have been danced by Phyllis Spira, formerly of the Royal Ballet and the National Ballet of Canada; Elizabeth Triegaardt, the company's principal ballet mistress; and Olga Twell. Sharing the leading male roles with Eduard Greyling have been Keith Mackintosh, Keith Maidwell, John Simons, Owen Murray, and Norman Furber, all of whom have been equally adept at character roles.

In 1988, the company's *prima ballerina assoluta*, Phyllis Spira, retired and became its ballet mistress. In the same year CAPAB celebrated its twenty-fifth anniversary by honoring the first director, Dulcie Howes, and other dancers and teachers. Eduard Greyling, the principal male dancer, retired in 1989. David Poole retired in 1990 and was succeeded as director by Veronica Paeper in 1991. Poole devoted his time until his death on 27 August 1991 to establishing a ballet fund for assisting the training of black dancers. Howes died at the age of eighty-four on 7 October 1993.

Both these pioneers of ballet in Cape Town lived to feel the winds of change begin to blow in South Africa. By the mid-1980s, the dance scene in the Cape Province was vibrant with activity by various performing groups, and by the early 1990s, political events, which would lead to great social and cultural change in South Africa, had begun to have a direct effect on CAPAB Ballet. In 1994, the company, billed as The Cape Ballet, appeared in London for a short season at Sadler's Wells Theatre, thus bringing to an end years of geographical and cultural isolation. The season in London was notable for the personal success won by ballerina Carol Kinsey.

Pursuant to the election of a new government under the leadership of Nelson Mandela in 1994, South Africa's provincial structure was reorganized, and new measures of government funding of the arts were proposed. By terms of a 1996 White Paper on the Arts, ballet and opera companies subsidized by the former provincial arts councils will face diminishing funding from the national government and be forced to seek support from the private and corporate sector. Reflecting the division of the former Cape Province into three new provinces—Eastern Cape, Western Cape, and Northern Cape—CAPAB Ballet officially changed its name to Cape Town City Ballet in April 1997.

[*See also* South Africa, *article on* Ballet; *and the entries on Paeper, Poole, and Staff. For related discussion, see* PACT Ballet.]

BIBLIOGRAPHY

Beukes, Alec. *CAPAB Ballet: Twenty-One Years, 1963–1984*. Cape Town, 1984.

Borland, Eve. "CAPAB and PACT Ballet South Africa." *Dance Gazette* (March 1985): 29–32.

Botha, Amanda. *Phyllis Spira: A Tribute*. Cape Town, 1988.

Clarke, Mary, and David Vaughan, eds. *The Encyclopedia of Dance and Ballet*. New York, 1977.

Glasstone, Richard. "The Cape Ballet." *The Dancing Times* (September 1994): 1153–1157.

Grut, Marina. *The History of Ballet in South Africa*. Cape Town, 1981.

Merrett, Sue. "Plans and Productions." *The Dancing Times* (January 1990): 319–320.

Cooper, Montgomery, and Jane Allyn. *Dance for Life: Ballet in South Africa*. Cape Town, 1980.

MARINA GRUT
Amended by Claude Conyers

CAPOEIRA is a stylized fight dance of Brazil that combines elements of dance, music, song, ritual, and myth. The exact origins of *capoeira* are unknown, although it is believed to have been developed by African slaves on Brazilian plantations and used as a means to practice for escape. To hide its true nature, *capoeira* was practiced to music and disguised as a dance. In the eighteenth century, *capoeira* became urbanized; by the mid-nineteenth century, *capoeiristas* ("fighters") were a social menace, fighting among themselves, assaulting citizens, and terrorizing street festivals in their quest for social power.

Capoeiristas were often hired by political bosses and plantation owners to settle vendettas and enforce the owner's rule. Laws were specifically enacted to prosecute *capoeiristas*, and repression reached its peak in the late 1800s. Localized in three of Brazil's major urban centers—Rio de Janeiro, Salvador in Bahia, and Recife—*capoeira* did not begin to win social acceptance until the 1940s when Mestre Bimba, a *capoeirista* in Bahia, developed a new style that he named "regional." It was a synthesis of the traditional (now known as *capoeira angola*), jujitsu, *savate*, and another Brazilian fight dance called *batuque*. Bimba opened the first registered *academia de capoeira* and taught it as a sport and physical-fitness program.

CAPOEIRA. Two dancers from Jelon Vieira's New York-based company DanceBrazil demonstrate acrobatic *capoeira* moves. (Photograph by Cylla von Tiedemann; used by permission.)

Today, *capoeira* is practiced as a sport in schools, clubs, and tournaments, and performed in folkloric shows, in the streets, and in festivals—the last primarily in Bahia, a state on the northeastern coast of Brazil. Both regional and traditional *capoeiras* are performed in a circle that consists of musicians, contestants, and observers. A match starts when two adversaries enter the circle and crouch by the musicians for an opening song. Subsequent pairs of fighters may, but need not, repeat this opening ritual. The *capoeira* is done principally with the feet. *Golpes*, striking moves, are usually performed consecutively. For each *golpe* there is a *saída*, or counterpart defensive move. A two-step movement, the *ginga*, keeps the contestant in time with the music between *golpes* and *saídas*. The resultant jumps, falls, parrying attacks, and defenses produce a graceful but dangerous simulated fight. Dances continue until one of the contestants drops out from exhaustion.

Each *capoeira* has a master, who is the lead singer and musician. The accompanying musical instruments are the *berimbau* (single-string musical bow with a resonance box), the *pandeiro* (tambourine), the *agogô* (twin metal cowbells struck with a rod), the *atabaque* (African drum), and the *reco reco* (corrugated wooden scraper). The last two are seldom seen outside folkloric shows. The *berimbau* symbolizes *capoeira* and leads the other instruments. *Capoeira* songs are performed in a traditional African format, with a chorus following a lead singer. Usually short, the songs are characterized by rhyme and repetition, and they cover topics such as slavery, plantation life, rebellion, Catholic saints, African deities, and the adventures of famous *capoeiristas*. Once restricted to blacks, males, and the lower classes, *capoeira* is increasingly practiced by whites, women, and the middle and upper classes in most regions of Brazil. It has been designated a national sport in Brazil and, today, is also taught and practiced in the United States and elsewhere.

[*See also* Brazil, *article on* Ritual and Popular Dance. *For related discussion, see* Asian Martial Arts.]

BIBLIOGRAPHY

Almeida, Bira. *Capoeira: A Brazilian Art Form.* Richmond, Calif., 1981.

d'Aquino, Iria. "Capoeira: Strategies for Status, Power, and Identity." Ph.D. diss., University of Illinois, Urbana-Champaign, 1983.

Rego, Waldeloir. *Capoeira Angola.* Rio de Janeiro, 1968.

IRIA D'AQUINO

CARACTÈRES DE LA DANSE, LES. Solo *divertissement*. Choreography: Françoise Prévost. Music: Jean-Féry Rebel. First performance: c.1715, Théâtre National de l'Opéra, Paris. Dancer: Françoise Prévost.

The score of *Les Caractères de la Danse*, composed especially for Prévost, was published in 1715. This *divertissement* is constructed around a suite of dances that illustrates scenes on the general theme of love. A succession of *courantes, menuets, bourrées, chaconnes, sarabandes, gigues, rigaudons, passepieds, gavottes*, bagpipes, and *musettes* introduces an interesting variety of characters. The *courante* depicts the blunders of an elderly lover; the *gigue* inspires a young fool; a deceived lover dances a grave *sarabande;* a gracious young girl does the *menuet;* an abandoned lover mourns her lost happiness with a *gavotte;* and a happy lover renders thanks in the form of a *musette*. Françoise Prévost—an elegant, sensitive dancer whom Pierre Rameau describes in *Le maître à danser* (1725) as characterized by "grace, correctness, lightness, and precision" and the rare power to use "all forms at will"—gave life to these brilliant and varied steps.

On 5 May 1726, the sixteen-year-old Marie Camargo made her debut in *Les Caractères. Le Mercure* praised her sprightliness and vivacity and marveled at her leaps and *entrechats*. Her dancing was charming, but it also departed from the subtle interpretation of her predecessor. The intelligent, refined execution of Marie Sallé, who replaced Prévost on 14 September 1727, was closer to Prévost's own style. *Le Mercure* reported major innovations when, on 17 February 1729, Sallé danced *Les Caractères* with her partner Antoine Bandieri de Laval, "both in street clothes and without masks." Her performance at the theater of Lincoln's Inn Fields in London in 1731 was a triumph. The popularity of this ballet remained undiminished throughout the eighteenth century.

[*See also the entries on Camargo and Prévost.*]

BIBLIOGRAPHY

Aubry, Pierre, and Émile Dacier. *Les Caractères de la Danse.* Paris, 1905.

Rameau, Pierre. *Le maître à danser*. Paris, 1725. Translated by Cyril W. Beaumont as *The Dancing Master* (London, 1931).

Ranum, Patricia. "Les 'Caractères' des danses françaises." *Recherches sur la musique française classique* 23 (1985): 45–70.

Semmens, Richard T. "Terpsichore Reborn: The French Noble Style and Drama." In *Proceedings of the Tenth Annual Conference, Society of Dance History Scholars, University of California, Irvine, 13–15 February 1987*, compiled by Christena L. Schlundt. Riverside, Calif., 1987.

JEANNINE DORVANE
Translated from French

CAREY FAMILY, three generations of dancers and choreographers. Individually and collectively, the peripatetic Carey family ranged over much of Europe in the nineteenth century, with the consequence that the family name was variously spelled as *Carey, Carré, Carrey,* and *Carrez*. Notable members were the father, **Isidore Carey** (André Isidore Carey; born in 1790 in Paris), and his two sons, **Édouard Carey** (called Édouard the elder; born c.1816 in Stockholm [?]) and **Gustave Carey** (Isidore Camille Gustave [also Gustavo] Carey; born c.1818 in Stockholm [?], died 16 October 1881 in Copenhagen). In the third generation were Édouard's son, **Édouard Carey** (called Édouard the younger; born 1841/2, died 1908), and Gustave's daughters, **Fanny Carey** (born after 1845) and **Léontine Carey** (born after 1845). Although at present only a smattering is known about the Careys' movements and activities, they were evidently part of the international community of dancers that helped disseminate the art of ballet.

The family was apparently of French origin: Isidore, the head of the clan, was born in Paris and studied with Auguste Vestris. From 1815 to 1823 he danced at the Royal Theater in Stockholm. There he married the ballerina Joséphine Sainte-Claire (born 1785), who had formerly danced in Saint Petersburg. Also a choreographer, she produced *Det Nye Narcis* (The New Narcissus) at the Royal Theater in Copenhagen in 1820.

The Careys' two sons, Édouard and Gustave, were brought up to the trade. The great Danish choreographer August Bournonville, who described Isidore as "an old friend and artistic colleague," taught the two boys at the ages of eleven and eight, while their parents worked in cities such as Warsaw and Berlin. Both boys began performing at an early age. Édouard was still a minor in 1834, when he made his debut at the Paris Opera. Gustave danced with his father in Italy in the early 1830s and appeared in 1834 in Louis Henry's *Chao-Kang* at the Théâtre Nautique in Paris. As dancers, both were known for their strength and virtuosity.

The Carey couple and their sons took part in Léon's ballet-pantomime *Les Amours de Faublas* at the Théâtre de la Porte-Saint-Martin in Paris in 1835; later that year the three men danced in Amsterdam. A certain amount of confusion sets in after they began to pursue separate careers, because the playbills, programs, and reviews of the time often listed them by surname only.

In 1843, Isidore staged ballets at the Teatro São Carlos in Lisbon for the American ballerina Augusta Maywood. His later career is unknown.

From April 1838 to February 1839, Édouard was in Moscow, where he choreographed and danced in the *divertissement* called *Zéphyr et l'Amour*. His strong physique and virtuosic style earned him the nickname "Hercules of the North" during his brief stay at the Paris Opera in 1841. He and Bournonville both danced in Naples later that year, and he remained in Italy during most of the 1840s, though he danced at London's Theatre Royal, Drury Lane, in 1843. Little is known about him until 1874, when Bournonville observed his class in Paris.

Gustave's career, the best documented of the family, was mainly divided among Vienna, Italy, and Copenhagen. During his first Viennese engagement (1838–1845), he partnered Marie Taglioni, Fanny Elssler, Fanny Cerrito, and Augusta Maywood in Romantic staples such as *La Sylphide* and *Giselle*. He again danced in Vienna from 1850 to 1854 and played Mephistopheles in Elssler's farewell performance of Jules Perrot's *Faust* in 1851. In the late 1840s and from the mid-1850s to the early 1860s, he danced in Italian cities such as Milan, Venice, Naples, and Genoa; he was named a *primo ballerino serio* at Milan's prestigious Teatro alla Scala, where he danced in Domenico Ronzani's restagings of Perrot's *Odetta* and *Esmeralda*. In Naples he and Salvatore Taglioni collaborated on restagings of Giovanni Casati's *Shakespeare* (1855) and Perrot's *La Filleule des Fées*, renamed *Isaura* (1856).

Gustave staged two pas de deux (one from *Giselle*) in Copenhagen in 1854, returning in 1861 to fill the post of ballet master, temporarily vacated by Bournonville. He then mounted the Royal Theater's first production of *Giselle* and danced in his own ballet *The Nymph and the Faun*. Though this appointment ended in 1863, he returned to Copenhagen in the late 1860s, after engagements in Kassel and Barcelona, and choreographed dances for the debuts of his daughters Fanny and Léontine at the Tivoli Gardens' Pantomime Theater in 1868 and the ballet *Aladdin* for the Casino. In 1871 he went to Paris to create the insect ballet in Jacques Offenbach's satirical operetta *Le Roi Carotte* (1872). He then returned to Copenhagen, where the Danish dancer Hans Beck studied with him from 1878 to 1879. His *divertissement* called *Les Guirlandes* was choreographed for Tivoli in 1881.

To date very little is known about the careers of the younger Édouard, named after his father, and Gustave's daughters Fanny and Léontine. Édouard danced in Paris in 1873, and the two women performed for several years at the Pantomime Theater in Tivoli.

BIBLIOGRAPHY
Lillian Moore's manuscript, "The Carey Family of Dancers and Ballet Masters: A Chronology," is held in the Dance Collection, New York Public Library for the Performing Arts. See as well Ivor Guest's *The Romantic Ballet in Paris*, 2d rev. ed. (London, 1980), and Tom Veale's "Bournonville Preserved," *Dance Magazine* (August 1965).

SUSAN AU

CARIBBEAN REGION. The vivid and diverse dances of the Caribbean are both influential and popular in the Americas, Europe, and Africa. Caribbean countries and island territories sustaining strong, viable dance in the twentieth century include Haiti, the Dominican Republic, Martinique, Cuba, Puerto Rico, Trinidad, the Bahamas, and Jamaica, as well as the coastal regions of such Caribbean-rim nations as Colombia, Venezuela, Belize, Guatemala, Honduras, Nicaragua, Panama, and the United States.

The study of dance in the region is inseparable from the issue of migration. European colonizers entered the Caribbean at the end of the fifteenth century; at that time Native American peoples had lived on the islands and along the coasts for thousands of years. After missionizing, colonizing, and losing most of them to overwork and epidemics, African slaves were forcibly transported to the Caribbean by European slave traders until the nineteenth century. Slaves escaping island conditions immigrated to the coastal mainland of Mesoamerica, North America, and South America. Under postcolonial laws, Caribbean citizens were granted rights to immigrate to the countries of their European colonizers—Spain, France, Britain, the Netherlands, and after the Spanish-American War of 1898, the United States.

Caribbean migration to the United States expanded greatly after World War II. Children with one Caribbean and one mainland parent, or U.S.-born with two Caribbean parents, frequently migrate between the two cultures. On a smaller scale, tourists visit and stay in the region, or they maintain lifelong connections—scholars make the region a focus of their work, and people of the African diaspora visit extensively to research its manifestations of pan-African culture. All have brought with them forms of dance and have diffused versions of the dances they found.

In the Caribbean are many races, many social classes, and many expressions of dance—sacred or profane, ritual or entertaining, purely African or purely European, and some in between. Dance was repressed by authorities, was hidden, transformed, expressed freely, and performed for tourists. The dynamism of continual migration is reflected in the dynamic heterogeneity of pan-Caribbean dance, both historically and in the present.

Controversy surrounds this evolution, as it surrounds any emerging art form. For example, in 1855 in the Dominican Republic, the merengue, a couples dance, replaced the *tumba* (a polyrhythmic African dance also popular in Dutch Curaçao and in Belize, where it was a solo exhibition dance) as the most popular dance. Its violence incited controversy in the press at the time, yet it survived into the 1880s, when the accordion replaced the guitars that normally accompanied it. Controversy had also surrounded a dance called the *puertorrico* when it reached

CARIBBEAN REGION. The long-drum dance *(baile de palos)* from the south-central region of the Dominican Republic, where the rhythms *palo abajo* and *paloarriba* are associated with the dead. Elements of this dance include a balancing step, seen here, and a ritual pursuit in alternating directions. In other regions the same dance is faster, livelier, and more virtuosic. This performance, at Villa Mella, Los Morenos, the enclave of a family with Haitian origins, is in honor of the death of the late patriarch of the family, Don Alejandro Mercedes. (Photograph by Martha Ellen Davis; used by permission.)

Lima, Peru, in 1598—in this case because of its libidinous character.

Dynamism in intercultural dance is apparent even in language. *Areito* is a word originating in the sixteenth-century Antilles, perhaps in an African-Spanish creole. In a document of 1524 it meant "to dance" or "everybody dance in a ring." By the 1850s it had come to denote a call-and-response dance song unique to Hispaniola but, according to the observer, having characteristics common to leader-follower dances in Spain and Flanders. In documents dating as early as 1650, "dance" is used interchangeably for "music," "song," or "musical piece." Music and dance are inseparable in Africa, and traditionally in Europe—no dance existed without its accompanying music. The Cuban composer Ignacio Cervantes Kawanag (1847–1905) published five collections of *danzas*, most with a specifically Cuban theme. The *danza* evolved from the Spanish contradance and the habanera, brought to Puerto Rico from Cuba in 1844. *Danza* was a social couples dance; the rhythm a triplet; and *danza* titles often reflected and encouraged the growth of Puerto Rican nationalism. In the twentieth century, words such as *mambo* or *merengue* imply both movement and music.

A complex example of Caribbean dance syncretism is seen in the Garifuna, a black-Carib dance culture. These people are descended from African slaves who escaped to Saint Vincent, intermarried with the indigenous Carib population, and were later removed to the island of Roatan off Honduras, whence they made their way to Belize. [*See* Garifuna Dance.] Their dances include the *punta*, borrowed from the Ladinos of Honduras; the *wanaragua*, clearly related to the African-derived Jamaican Jonkonnu festival dance [*see* Jonkonnu Festival]; and the *hunguhungu*, a sacred dance of indigenous origin.

The ways in which Caribbean dance is preserved are sometimes surprising. In the Dominican Republic, dictator Rafael Trujillo invited scholar Jacob Coopersmith to survey the traditional music and dance of the country. Trinidadian dance has been preserved in Labanotation, a written symbolic system for notating dance that was developed by Rudolf Laban. A dissertation and related research by Lisa Lekis at the University of Florida, Gainesville, surveyed dances of the extinct Native American peoples, the Africans in many Caribbean locales, and the Europeans who colonized the Caribbean.

The interplay among diverse influences is also seen on the island of Hispaniola. In its western portion in the 1780s (today's Haiti), some slaves, even when freed, chose to dance in exact imitation of the slaveowners, performing the *menuet, contradanse, allemande,* and *anglais.* Others, however, preferred purely African dances brought from their homelands in West Africa—Senegal, Ghana, or the Congo. There were also differences among the colonists: the island's English danced less than the French

or Spanish, and all three less than *mestizos* or Creoles (islanders of mixed ancestry—European, African, and/or Carib). Dances that in Africa might have lasted all night were restricted to *redoutes*, held in the early evening, so that fieldworkers could rise early the next morning. African women were excluded from mixed-race dances, so they created balls to which they invited only European men. A document from Cuba in 1790 records restrictions on the times when slaves could dance but reports that women and men were free to dance together.

Music and dance appeared in novel combinations. Africa-derived drums accompany a dance featuring a heel-first step characteristic of an English dance. The *Don Pedre* dance was created by "a Spanish Negro from Petit-Gouave" as one element of a cult, based on his own supernatural powers, intoxication, singing, and trance-dance. The *chica*, a dance from the Congo, spread throughout the Windward Islands, evolved into the better-known fandango, and became popular in Spain.

Dances performed as part of the Shango cult brought from Nigeria to Trinidad were nearly identical to their original forms. The dancers moved back and forth within a short range, rapidly bending and straightening the knees, circling in a single file with a bouncing step, and swaying, awaiting possession, upon which the dancing became more animated. A document from 1790 describes the principal Jamaican festival as a burial. Offerings of food and liquor, a decorated casket, songs, and howling, were a prelude to the dancing that followed the burial, allowing the day to end in cheerfulness.

Dance in the Caribbean cannot be separated from the history of colonialism in the area. The original contact made by Christopher Columbus in 1492 began the process of extermination of indigenous Arawak, Carib, Lucayan, Siboney, Taíno, and other peoples. In one of the first contacts in 1498, while approaching Trinidad, Columbus ordered a pipe-and-tabor player to perform a sailors' dance for about twenty-five approaching Arawaks, to attract them to the fleet. The dancing and pipe music were, however, taken by them as a sign of war. Guacanagari, a Taíno who received Columbus, arranged a dance with castanets performed by girls, who danced to the sound of snailshells (on strings worn around arms, hips, calves, and heels), maracas, rattling bones, and the beat of a drum similar to one used by the Aztec of Mexico.

British, French, Dutch, and other European colonizers developed the sugar plantation culture that became sustained by slaves from Africa; especially in Haiti do we see their dance evolution. Haiti had been colonized by Spain, had been ceded to France, and had become independent in 1804, after rebellions forced French planters to flee. Those who went to Cuba in the 1790s added the gavotte and *passepied* to the contradance already popular there. As late as 1900 in Haiti, countryside dances were accom-

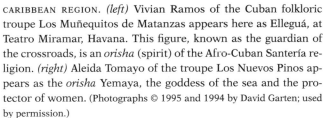

CARIBBEAN REGION. *(left)* Vivian Ramos of the Cuban folkloric troupe Los Muñequitos de Matanzas appears here as Elleguá, at Teatro Miramar, Havana. This figure, known as the guardian of the crossroads, is an *orisha* (spirit) of the Afro-Cuban Santería religion. *(right)* Aleida Tomayo of the troupe Los Nuevos Pinos appears as the *orisha* Yemaya, the goddess of the sea and the protector of women. (Photographs © 1995 and 1994 by David Garten; used by permission.)

panied by the *banza*, a stringed instrument; from 1915 to 1934, Haiti was occupied by U.S. peacekeeping forces who brought recorded music, which then widely replaced minuets played on violins.

Existing traditional or folkloric Caribbean dance is thus a mix of European and African styles; some dances are more African and some more European in movement, style, meaning, or costume. The closest fusion may be seen in set dances, such as the quadrille, the Lancers, the polka, waltz, and schottische. Originating as peasant dances, in nineteenth-century Europe they became social dances for the courts and ballrooms, crossed the ocean to become popular among Caribbean masters and slaves, and assumed a new life as African-inspired Caribbean dances.

Dance is inseparable from music, and the history of music in the Caribbean cannot be studied without also studying dance. Calypso, often considered a product of Trinidad, is really an outgrowth of *habanera* (from Havana) rhythm, as are *danzon, son, danza, rhumba* (rumba), *bamboula, merengue,* and others; yet it took its present form in the Virgin Islands of Saint Thomas, Saint John, and Saint Croix. In Trinidad, calypso may be played on tuned steel oil drums to accompany the "jump-off" street dancing during Carnival. When played or danced in a ballroom, it is similar to a fast rumba. Some form of calypso is sung, played, and danced in Trinidad at all seasons except during Lent.

On Curaçao in the Netherlands Antilles, Jan Gerard Palm (1831–1906) founded a dynasty of local musicians known for their fast Antillean waltzes, *danzas,* mazurkas, and marches. These were played for generations on Curaçao by dance orchestras consisting of violin, flute, guitars, *wiri,* triangle, *matrimoniaal* (a stick from which pieces of tin dangled), various sizes of drums, clarinet, and Italian barrel organ.

In Haiti in 1784, a production of the opera *Orphée et Eurydice* (by Christoph Willibald Gluck) was staged with "decorations, machines, ballets"; and a certain Haller composed "ballets" there, produced in 1765, 1766, and 1767. *Inkle and Yarico, a Historical Ballet* was an opera written and produced by British and German composers in various versions from 1772 to 1807; based on the true story of a mainland Indian, Yarico, sold into slavery by her English lover, Inkle, one version describes how they become acquainted with each other by demonstrating their native dances; the native people admit the superiority of the British dances and in their delight at learning them admit Inkle to the tribe, only to be betrayed when he sells Yarico into slavery in Barbados.

Another example of the integral relationship of music and dance is a Puerto Rican dance called the *borinqueña*, described as having been written in Mayaguez by Félix Astol in 1867. How and when the dance was added to the composition has not yet been traced.

In the Virgin Islands, typical dances that originated on the plantations of Saint Croix in the nineteenth century were the *curaçao* and *mackshun;* on Saint Thomas, the *curaçao* and *bamboula.* There, the contradance and the merengue were outgrowths of these drum-based dances, to which were added guitar, triangle, flute, accordion, and *guiro.* Also closely tied to the drum was the dance of Saint Lucia, nearly always accompanied by drumming. Unique to Saint Croix plantations was the masquerade dance, popular until about 1900. This dance was an opportunity to settle disputes. One dancer made a complaint in rhymed verse and called for music, to which he danced. A second dancer responded, following the same format. A chorus sang the verdict. Another example of how dance, music, and utilitarian function were combined comes from Martinique.

In 1698 it was recorded that in Martinique and Guadeloupe, a "belly dance" from Guinea, West Africa, accompanied by two drums, was danced. The dancers lined up in two rows, men on one side and women on the other; spectators formed a ring. The lasciviousness of the movements caused the prohibition of the dance. Africans from the Congo region danced in the round, not moving from their spot but kicking high in the air and then stamping on the ground, accompanied by violin and banjo. A French observer in the eighteenth century noted that the Africans of Martinique sang while they worked, with their entire bodies moving in unison to the beat. Observations by Europeans of African dance in the colonial period are useful but sometimes suspect.

In Surinam in 1667, an Englishman reported that Carib funeral rites were followed by a "drunken Feast and confused Dancing (in which they are . . . excessive)." In Surinam in 1788, it was reported that African Surinamese had produced no musicians because the study of notes was too tedious for them, whereas dance interested them longer. The African Surinamese, however, while dancing and singing at great length (up to thirty-six hours without a break), copied European balls, the men in Dutch-style trousers, the women in petticoats, the women spinning, the men performing intricate dance steps. Some partnered their shadows projected on a wall. Also in Surinam, one of the Africans' two major song forms, the *banja* (the other being the *doe*), has dance elements, namely, a woman "tripping" back and forth in front of the musicians and keeping time with their song by waving two scarves. The *banja* was recorded in 1935, by which time the purely sung version had died out, approximately twenty-five years earlier. Recorded with the *banja* was the *sousa*, a song as well as a dance. Both men and boys danced the *sousa*, characterized by foot movements closely tied to the hand clapping of bystanders. Large cultural differences existed between Africans unmixed with European or other ancestry and Creoles (the mixed races). "Town Negroes" were generally mixed and "Bush Negroes" generally not. In 1940 it was recorded in Surinam that rural peoples danced possession rituals, or "Winti dances," whenever the spirit moved them; in the towns this so-called orgiastic dance was performed only four times a year. Four distinctively shaped drums accompanied the Winti dances.

Dance in Cuba in the 1850s showed the effects of class divisions. The *zapateo* and the contradance from Europe were the most popular dances. Compositions for the latter by Cubans of African descent were more popular among the Creole class and with foreigners than were those of purely European origin. Dance in Puerto Rico around the middle of the nineteenth century also has been characterized by socioeconomic class. The upper classes favored the contradance and waltz and, to a lesser extent, the *rigaudon, galop,* mazurka, *cotillon,* and polka. The middle class (Ladinos or *mestizos*) favored the *cadenas* ("chains"), *fandanguillo* ("little fandango," a variation of the *chica* dance from Congo), *son duro* ("hard sound"), *matatoros* ("bullfighter"), *caballo* ("horse"), and especially the *seis* ("six"). The working classes performed dances from Africa and Curaçao; one of these, the *bomba*, was both a dance and a song, accompanied by drums, maracas, and a female singer.

In rare cases, precolonial Caribbean dance was documented or has even survived. The first European to record this culture was Bartolomé de Las Casas, who described the dances, festivals, and songs of present-day Nicaragua and Honduras and the surrounding areas. There, the Carib people were described in the seventeenth century as performing a dance to restore the moon during an eclipse. Young and old, men and women, danced all night with intermittent howling, hopping with their feet together, one hand on their head and the other on their buttocks. The rattling of a pebble-filled gourd, howling, and a general uproar, but no singing, accompanied this dance. In 1658, Carib dance in Saint Vincent was described as limited to solemn occasions and to performances in the *carbet* ("public house"); dance was subordinate to music, which was played on drums and pipes. Another Carib dance was described in Saint Vincent in 1789. In this, a couple dancing nude extended their arms forward and pulled them back repeatedly, a movement unchanging over the course of two hours, accompanying themselves with "croaking in monotonous and lugubrious sounds." In Surinam, an indigenous bird dance was recorded in the nineteenth century, in which women imitated bird calls and men replied with animal cries. Native American peoples of French Guiana were described as dancing in a circle, without holding hands, a dance primarily focused on unison movement to the beat of small drums, flutes, and horns. Their so-called orgiastic dances were those described as accompanying the rituals in which parts of the bodies of prisoners of war were cut up and roasted for eating.

In the nineteenth and twentieth centuries independence from colonial powers and the increasing ease of international travel gave rise to a pan-Caribbean desire for nationalistic expression in dance. National dance schools and companies studied the African roots of many dances in a quest for authenticity. The goal of professionalization, so that Caribbean dance companies could compete on world stages, led to the incorporation of European and U.S.-based dance training for performers. This process of investigation, professionalization, and internationalism resulted in dance companies oriented less toward folklore and more toward international styles, though still rooted in regional traditions, conditions, and history.

Caribbean migration, largely to the United States, has been a dominant force in the development of contemporary dance there. Noted U.S. dance artists such as Katherine Dunham and Lavinia Williams established careers based largely on the continual interchange of U.S. and Caribbean dance elements; such great Caribbean dance artists as Rex Nettleford and Garth Fagan developed their companies, careers, and styles on free adaptations of dance methods learned in the United States.

Uniting the Caribbean are such cultural traits as the Jonkonnu festival, which had been celebrated in West Africa long before the slave trade and in the Caribbean since the sixteenth century. It is now supported in part as a nationalistic and touristic promotional tool. Calypso is another music-dance form that unites islands, including Haiti, Carriacou, Bequia, and Trinidad. In Trinidad, calypso is believed to have derived from *kalinda*, the stick-fighting rituals with elements of dance; the fighting was stylized, brightly colored costumes were worn, and the fights were interspersed with dance-song performed by women. When *kalinda* was suppressed in 1881, *cariso*, the women's activity, persisted. Late twentieth-century dance artists such as Merián Soto, Gabri Christa, and Alice Farley have freely adapted Caribbean legends, dance styles, and sociopolitical history to create choreography both emergent from and freed of Caribbean traditions. The vitality of Caribbean dance is exemplified by the case of Lavinia Williams. In a contest promoted by the Bahamian Ministry of Tourism, she choreographed a dance in which

CARIBBEAN REGION. Female members of the National Dance Theatre Company of Jamaica in *Celebration*, a tribute to traditional Jamaican and pan-Caribbean music and dance. Drawing on folk, modern, and classical styles, the company's diverse repertory includes staged rituals, dance dramas, and abstract works. (Photograph from the archives of the National Dance Theatre Company of Jamaica, Kingston; courtesy of Rex Nettleford.)

two narrators, Brer Buky and Brer Rabby (drawn from the Spider tales of Africa) tell the history of the Bahamas to an African-American family visiting the Caribbean in search of their cultural heritage. The dance is as new as 1978, when Williams won the competition, yet as old as the timeless legends of Africa.

Pan-Caribbean dance genres not specifically influenced by the African diaspora are classical ballet and modern dance. Classical ballet was performed in Cuba as early as 1800. Beginning with visits to Cuba by Anna Pavlova's ballet company in 1915–1918 and Les Ballets Jooss (of Germany and England), in the 1940s, both ballet and modern expressive dance have taken root around the region. In countries with large urban areas and large European-descended populations, ballet companies modeled on those of Europe have been founded. In the latter half of the twentieth century, such U.S. institutions as the Jacob's Pillow Dance Festival, American Dance Festival, and the Fulbright Scholars program have promoted Caribbean dance with exchanges of dancers, teachers, choreographers, and writers. Unlike American modern dance, which tends to be abstract and psychological in its artistic expression, Caribbean modern dance seeks cultural identity. It asks questions about colonial history, racial mixture, the uniqueness of Caribbean culture, so-called underdevelopment, dance as a source of individual and national pride, and the Caribbean's place in the world.

[*For related discussion, see* Cuba; Dominican Republic; Haiti; Jamaica; *and* Puerto Rico.]

BIBLIOGRAPHY

Adams, Alton J. "Whence Came the Calypso?" *The Caribbean* (Port of Spain) 8 (May 1955): 218–220.

Ahye, Molly. *The Dance in Trinidad and Tobago.* Petit Valley, Trinidad and Tobago, 1978.

Ahye, Molly. *Cradle of Caribbean Dance: Beryl McBurnie and the Little Carib Theatre.* Petit Valley, Trinidad and Tobago, 1983.

Alonso (Pacheco), Manuel A. "Bailes de Puerto Rico." *Revista del Instituto de Cultura Puertorriqueña* 16 (July–September 1962): 47–50.

Baxter, Ivy. *The Arts of an Island: The Development of the Culture and of the Folk and Creative Arts in Jamaica, 1494–1962 (Independence).* Metuchen, N.J., 1970.

Beckford, William. *A Descriptive Account of the Island of Jamaica.* 2 vols. London, 1790. See volume 1, pages 215–218, and volume 2, pages 387–389.

Benoît, Pierre-Jacques. *Voyage à Suriname, description des possessions neerlandaises dans la Guyane.* Brussels, 1839.

Bettelheim, Judith. "The Afro-Jamaican Jonkonnu Festival." Ph.D. diss., Yale University, 1979.

Biet, Antoine. *Voyage de la France Eqvinoxiale en l'Isle de Cayenne, entrepris par les François en l'année M.DC.LII.* Paris, 1664.

Boskaljon, Rudolf Frederik Willem. "Het muziekleen." In *Oranje en de zes Caraibische parelen: Officieel gedenkboek.* Amsterdam, 1948.

Boskaljon, Rudolf Frederik Willem. *Honderd jaar muziekleven op Curacao.* Assen, 1958.

Bravo, Juan S. "Estampas Precolombinianas: La danza." *Puerto Rico Ilustrado* 25 (27 January 1934): 16.

Brown, Ernest D. "Carnival, Calypso, and Steel Band in Trinidad." *Black Perspective in Music* 18.1–2 (1990): 84–100.

Casas, Bartolomé de las. *Historia de las Indias.* Edited by Juan Pérez de Tudela Bueso. Madrid, 1957.

Casas, Bartolomé de las. *Apologética historia.* Edited by Juan Pérez de Tudela Bueso. Madrid, 1958.

Cervantes, Ignacio. *40 danzas.* Havana, 1959.

Chanvalon, Jean-Baptiste Thibault de. *Voyage à la Martinique.* Paris, 1763.

Coll y Toste, Cayetano. "Rectificaciones históricas: Donde, cuando y por quien se escribió la Borinqueña?" *Boletín Histórico de Puerto Rico* 9.5 (1922): 266–269.

Comvalius, Theodoor A. C. "Het Surinaamse negerlied: De Banja en de Doe." *West-Indische Gids* 17 (November 1935): 213–220.

Coopersmith, J. M. "Music and Musicians of the Dominican Republic: A Survey." *Musical Quarterly* 31 (January 1945): 71–88; 31 (April 1945): 212–226.

Cowley, John. *Carnival, Canboulay, and Calypso: Traditions in the Making.* Cambridge, 1996.

Crowley, Daniel J. "Song and Dance in St. Lucia." *Ethnomusicology Newsletter,* no. 9 (January 1957): 4–14.

Crowley, Daniel J. "Trinidad Carnival Songs and Dances." *Dance Notation Record* 9 (Summer 1958): 3–7.

Crowley, Daniel J. "Toward a Definition of 'Calypso.'" *Ethnomusicology* 3 (May 1959): 57–66; 3 (September 1959): 117–124.

Daniel, Yvonne P. "Dancing Down the River: A Presentation on the Dance in Suriname." *Journal of the Association of Graduate Dance Ethnologists* 7 (Spring 1983): 25–32.

Du Tertre, Jean-Baptiste. *Histoire générale des Antilles habitées by les François.* 2 vols. Paris, 1667–1671. See volume 2, pages 526–527.

Elder, Jacob Delworth. "*Kalinda:* Song of the Battling Troubadours of Trinidad." *Journal of the Folklore Institute* (Bloomington) 3 (August 1966): 192–203.

Emery, Lynne Fauley. *Black Dance from 1619 to Today.* 2d rev. ed. Princeton, 1988.

Fernández de Oviedo y Valdés, Gonzalo. *Historia general y natural de las Indias* (1851–1855). 5 vols. Edited by Juan Pérez de Tudela Bueso. Madrid, 1959.

Figueroa Berríos, Edwin. "Los sones de la bomba en la tradición popular de la costa sur de Puerto Rico." *Revista del Instituto de Cultura Puertorriqueña* 6 (October–December 1963): 46–48.

Focke, Hendrik Charles. *West-Indie: Bijdragen tot de bevordering van de kennis der nederlandsch west-indische kolonien.* 2 vols. Haarlem, 1855–1858.

Fouchard, Jean. *Les marrons du syllabaire.* Port-au-Prince, 1953.

Fouchard, Jean. *Artistes et répertoire des scènes de Saint-Domingue.* Port-au-Prince, 1955.

Fuentes (Matons), Laureano. *Las artes en Santiago de Cuba: Apuntes históricos.* Santiago, 1893.

Gilbert, Will G. *Ken en ander over de negroide muziek an Suriname.* Amsterdam, 1940.

Goines, Margaretta B. "African Retentions in the Dance of the Americas." *Dance Research Monograph One.* New York, 1973.

González, Jorge Antonio. "Apuntes para la historia del ballet en Cuba." *Revista de Música* 2 (October 1961): 228–248.

Hadel, Richard E. "Carib Dance Music and Dance." *National Studies* (Belize) 1 (November 1973): 4–11.

Herskovits, Melville J., and Frances S. Herskovits. *Suriname Folk-Lore with Transcriptions of Suriname Songs and Musicological Analysis by Dr. Mieczyslaw Kolinski.* New York, 1936.

Hurston, Zora Neale. *Voodoo Gods: An Inquiry into Native Myths and Magic in Jamaica and Haiti.* London, 1939.

Labat, Jean-Baptiste. *Nouveau voyage aux islees de l'Amérique.* 6 vols. Paris, 1722. See vol. 4, pp. 154–157.

Lekis, Lisa. "The Dance as an Expression of Caribbean Folklore." In *The Caribbean: Its Culture*, edited by A. Curtis Wilgus. Gainesville, Fla., 1955.

Lekis, Lisa. "The Origin and Development of Ethnic Caribbean Dance and Music." Ph.D. diss., University of Florida, 1956.

Lovén, Sven. *Origins of the Tainan Culture, West Indies*. Gothenburg, 1935.

Moreau de St.-Méry, Médéric L. E. *De la danse*. Parma, 1803.

Motolinía, Toribio. *Memoriales* (1569). Edited by Edmundo O'Gorman. 2d ed. Mexico City, 1971.

Muñoz, María Luisa. *La música en Puerto Rico: Panorama histórico-cultural*. Sharon, Conn., 1966.

Nettleford, Rex. "Cultural Resistance in Caribbean Society: Dance and Survival." In Nettleford's *Inward Stretch, Outward Reach*. London, 1993.

Nunley, John W., and Judith Bettelheim. *Caribbean Festival Arts*. Saint Louis, 1988.

Ortiz Fernández, Fernando. *La africanía de la música folklórica de Cuba*. Havana, 1950.

Pedreira, Antonio S. *Bibliografía puertorriqueña, 1493–1930*. Madrid, 1932.

Price, Lawrence Marsden. *Inkel and Yarico Album*. Berkeley, 1937.

Powles, Louis D. *The Land of the Pink Pearl, or, Recollections of Life in the Bahamas*. London, 1888.

Quiñones, Samuel R. "Otra versión sobre el orígen de la danza puertorriqueña." *Revista del Instituto de Cultura Puertorriqueña* 9 (January–March 1966): 5–6.

Regents of the Surinamese Sephardim. *Essai historique sur la Colonie de Surinam*. Paramaribo, 1788. Translated by Simon Cohen as *Historical Essay on the Colony of Surinam, 1788*. Cincinnati, 1974.

"Respuesta firmada por varios hacendados cubanos a una Real Cédula dada por el Rey con fecha de 31 de mayo de 1789." Archivo General de Indias (Seville), Indiferente General, Legajo 802. Published in Francisco Morales Padrón, "La vida cotidiana en una hacienda de esclavos," *Revista del Instituto de Cultura Puertorriqueña* 4 (January–March 1961): 26–33.

Rochefort, Charles de. *Histoire naturelle et morale des Iles Antilles de l'Amérique . . . avec un vocabulaire Caraibe*. Rotterdam, 1658. Translated by John Davies as *The History of the Caribby-Islands*. London, 1666.

Rodríguez, Augusto A. "Historia de la danza puertorriqueña." *Isla* (November 1939): 13–15.

Rodríguez Demorizi, Emilio. *Música y baile en Santo Domingo*. Santo Domingo, 1971.

Rosas de Oquendo, Mateo. "Cartapacio de diferentes versos á diversos asuntos." Edited by A. Paz y Melia from MS 19387 at the Biblioteca Nacional, Madrid ("Satira hecha por Mateo Rosas de Oquendo a las cosas que pasan en el Piru, año de 1598"), *Bulletin Hispanique* 8.2–3 (1906).

Sánchez de Fuentes (y Peláez), Eduardo. *Folklorismo*. Havana, 1928.

Sargant, William Walters. *The Mind Possessed*. New York, 1973.

Shedd, Margaret. "Carib Dance Patterns." *Theatre Arts* 17 (January 1933): 65–77.

Simpson, George E. *The Shango Cult in Trinidad*. Rio Piedras, 1965.

Stedman, John Gabriel. *Narrative of a Five Years' Expedition against the Revolted Negroes of Surinam in Guiana, on the Wild Coast of South America, from the Year 1772 to 1777*. 2 vols. London, 1796.

Stevenson, Robert. *A Guide to Caribbean Music History*. Lima, 1975.

Szwed, John F., and Morton Marks. "The Afro-American Transformation of European Set Dances and Dance Suites." *Dance Research Journal* 20 (Summer 1988): 29–36.

Torre, José María de la. *Lo que fuimos y lo que somos o la Habana antiqua y moderna*. Havana, 1857.

Trinidad Carnival. Port of Spain, 1988.

Vecilla de las Heras, Delfín. "La evolución religiosa de la Diócesis de Puerto Rico." Ph.D. diss., University of Madrid, 1966.

Veray, Amaury. "La misión social de la danza de Juan Morel Campos." *Revista del Instituto de Cultural Puertorriqueña* 2 (October–December 1959): 35–38.

Walle, J. van de. *De Nederlandse Antillen*. Baarn, 1954.

Walle, J. van de. "Walsen, danza's en tuma's der Antillen." *Oost en West* 47 (1954): 11–12.

Warren, George. *An Impartial Description of Surinam upon the Continent of Guiana in America*. London, 1667.

Whipple, Emory Clark. "Music of the Black Caribs of British Honduras." Master's thesis, University of Texas, Austin, 1971.

Williams, Lavinia. *Dances of the Bahamas and Haiti*. New York, 1980.

Zaretsky, Irving I., and Cynthia Shambaugh. *Spirit Possession and Spirit Mediumship in Africa and Afro-America: An Annotated Bibliography*. New York, 1978.

JAN MICHAEL HANVIK

CARICATURE AND COMIC ART. Both of these art forms perform the much-needed service of giving us a fresh perspective on dance. They make us laugh at the antics of performers, choreographers, teachers, and students, all of whom are sometimes inclined to take themselves too seriously. They exaggerate the absurdities of social dance and puncture the pretensions of dance intended as art. Because they are not meant to flatter, they are often more truthful—sometimes brutally so—than pictures whose aim is to please.

Dance caricatures have been produced by such luminaries as William Hogarth, William Makepeace Thackeray, Pablo Picasso, and Jean Cocteau, as well as a host of lesser-known painters and draftsmen. Other caricatures have come from set and costume designers, who are in a particularly good position to observe the dance world, and from dancers themselves. Even dance critics occasionally draw instead of write their opinions; an example is Richard Buckle (born 1916), whose caricatures have appeared under the pseudonym Fitzpyx.

A *caricature* is defined as an exaggerated likeness, distorted to create a grotesque or comical effect. Anatomical and physiognomical exaggerations, common to caricature in general, may appear in dance caricatures along with exaggerated or contorted representations of dance positions. The trappings of dance—costumes, scenery, hairdos, headdresses, and makeup—may also come under fire.

Because a caricature makes its point by referring to a recognizable subject, most caricatures are topical, depicting well-known personalities, dance forms, and theatrical works of the day. They are closely linked to their period and can provide valuable insights; however, difficulties arise if the allusions grow obscure with the passage of the years.

The word *cartoon* originally signified a preparatory drawing or painting. It acquired its present-day meaning,

CARICATURE AND COMIC ART. An engraving by Philibert Debucourt (1755–1832) entitled *La Manie de la Danse* (The Dance Mania), depicting overenthusiastic dancers at a ball. (Metropolitan Museum of Art, New York; Harris Brisbane Dick Fund, 1935 [no. 35.100.25]; photograph used by permission.)

that of a satirical drawing, in 1843, when John Leech (1817–1864) created parodies of the cartoons submitted to a fresco competition for the new Houses of Parliament. Sometimes defined as a satire with topical or political allusions and sometimes used interchangeably with caricature, cartoon is frequently used today to signify any humorous picture.

With dance art, sometimes it is difficult to tell whether the exaggerated or humorous elements were imposed upon it by the artist (making it a true satire) or whether they were an inherent and accepted part of the dance. Our own cultural conditioning influences our perceptions; something that seems risible to us may have been perfectly serious to an audience of the period. A case in point is John Boydell's (1719–1804) engraving of Jean-Georges Noverre's *Médée et Jason* (1782), which is often called a caricature and yet is also used to illustrate the exagger-

ated acting style of Noverre's period. Since there is no comic text or dialogue on the print and no gross anatomical or physiognomical distortion, it seems highly probable that this was actually a straightforward representation—many pictures of actors at that time reveal similar poses and facial expressions.

Dance caricatures and cartoons may appear in a number of media and formats. They have not been limited to images on paper; the ancient Egyptians, Greeks, and Romans often included dance caricatures on wall paintings, vase paintings, and sculptures. Medieval European artists used them on the decorative parts of illuminated manuscripts, architectural sculpture, and furniture.

The bulk of dance caricatures appear as prints. Printing is a reproductive medium, resulting in multiple copies that can be widely disseminated. Woodcuts, the first type of prints to be developed, were circulated as cheap broadsheets. Engraved and etched caricatures from metal plates enjoyed a heyday in the eighteenth century, when artists such as James Gillray (1757–1815) and Thomas Rowlandson (1756–1827) were active. These caricatures were sold separately or in series; in the 1790s they were collected in folios and rented out for an evening. Caricatures of this period are often accompanied by captions, poems, songs, or dialogue, issuing in balloons from the figures' mouths.

In the nineteenth century, wood engraving and lithography were developed, which superseded the earlier techniques. They were widely used for book and periodical illustrations as well as for independent prints, and caricatures appeared in all three formats. Several satirical journals had been started by midcentury, notably *Punch* in England and *Le charivari* and *La caricature* in France, all of which published dance caricatures and cartoons.

In the twentieth century, dance caricatures and cartoons are most frequently found in newspapers and magazines. Collections of them sometimes appear in books, among them Alex Gard's *Ballet Laughs* (1941) and Peter Revitt's *Ballet Guyed* (1949). The strip cartoon is sometimes used, such as Jules Feiffer's cartoons that began in 1957 for the *Village Voice*.

Although entertainment is the primary function of most dance caricatures and cartoons, they can also be adapted for other uses. The artist may wish to make a point about or draw a comparison to a subject that has nothing to do with dance, such as political events. Caricatures and cartoons can also be used to lend visual appeal to written materials on the dance. They are an eye-catching and appealing way to publicize performances. Gard's caricatures provided amusing previews of the season in the *New York Herald Tribune* in the 1940s, and Remy Charlip's cartoons have appeared since the 1960s on posters for the dance companies of Dan Wagoner, Merce Cunningham, and others.

Throughout history, dance caricatures and cartoons have found many different targets. Foremost among them are dancers, both real and imaginary, particularly those who have achieved fame and fortune. In the eighteenth century, Gäetan and Auguste Vestris were favorite targets. A play on Auguste's name led to many puns on the word *goose*, including *A Vestrician Dish, or Caper Sauce for a Goose Pye* (1781) by F. Assen and J. Jones, in which the fox-headed dancer performs before a goose-headed audience.

During the nineteenth century, Fanny Elssler was often portrayed riding in carriages drawn by her male admirers or hefting moneybags from one country to another; and the many conquests of the notorious Lola Montez are commemorated in caricatures such as the undated *Lola Coming! Europe Farewell! America I Come*.

Caricaturists sometimes commented cruelly on a dancer's physical shortcomings. Louise Fitzjames, who was thin in a period when slenderness was not admired, was depicted by Caboche Grégoire as an asparagus in an imaginary vegetable ballet (c.1837).

Among the dancers who caricatured their fellows are the brothers Sergei Legat (1875–1905) and Nikolai Legat (1869–1937), whose drawings, published in the album *Russkii balet v karikatura* (Russian Ballet in Caricature; 1902–1905), feature Marius Petipa, Matilda Kshessinska, Michel Fokine, Anna Pavlova, and other members of the Imperial Russian Ballet. Modern dancer Mary Wigman (1886–1973) drew caricatures of Hanya Holm, Meta Menz, Erika Thimey, and other German dancers.

Imaginary dancers may be depicted simply as dancers or as metaphors for qualities commonly associated with

CARICATURE AND COMIC ART. A tiny, misshapen girl receives instruction from a man twice her size while two amused boys look on; plate 3 of *The Dancing Lesson* (1835), George Cruikshank's four-part series satirizing dance instruction. (Metropolitan Museum of Art, New York; Harris Brisbane Dick Fund, 1917 [no. 17.3.888-170]; photograph used by permission.)

CARICATURE AND COMIC ART. This cartoon, captioned "Serge Diaghilev Dispatches His Company Abroad," was printed in a Russian newspaper in 1909. Along with umbrella and pack, Diaghilev carries two cages with his star "birds," Anna Pavlova and Vaslav Nijinsky. (Photograph from the State Museum of Theatrical and Musical Arts, Saint Petersburg.)

the dance. Because of the nature of caricature, the list is unflattering: vanity, frivolity, worldliness, artfulness, sensuality, and so on. However, there are exceptions. The modern dancer who appears in Feiffer's cartoons in the *Village Voice* is an appealing personality. Idealistic, optimistic, quixotic, she reaffirms her faith in the human spirit in the face of alarming political and social trends. Her recurring theme—"A dance to . . ."—celebrates new seasons and new years in terms of movement as well as words.

Nondancers who are active in the dance world also come in for their share of barbs. The most prominent figure in this category is the Russian impresario of the Ballets Russes, Serge Diaghilev, who was caricatured by associates such as author Jean Cocteau (1889–1963) and dancer Mikhail Larionov (1881–1964).

People who are neither dancers nor attached to the dance world are sometimes depicted as dancers for satirical effect. Politicians are especially liable to be caricatured in this way. Although they most frequently are pictured in the tutu and toe shoes that symbolize ballet to the general public, social dances, modern dance, and musical comedy dancing also are represented. The Duke of Wellington was a popular target in nineteenth-century England; he appears in A. Ducoté's *The Rival Artistes* (1832) and in two versions of *The Political Pas de Quatre*, published in *Punch* and *Joe Miller the Younger* in 1845; the latter was based on an actual ballet, Jules Perrot's *Pas de Quatre* (1845).

The Romantic ballet was so popular in London that many political cartoons were based either directly on ballets or on prints of the ballets. *The Pas d'Extase, or Ministerial Fascination* (published in *Punch*, 1845) depicts Sir Robert Peel and Daniel O'Connell in a pose already made famous by John Brandard's (1812–1863) lithograph of Perrot's *Éoline, ou La Dryade* (1845).

Political cartoonists often personify nations as dancers in order to comment on situations that require balance, control, adroitness, and caution. Sometimes the dance image signifies clumsiness, a false step, or a mismatched couple. Russia and its leaders are often personified as ballet dancers because of that country's long tradition of classical ballet. China is also personified as a ballet dancer, perhaps because of the highly political content of ballets such as *The Red Detachment of Women* (1964) and *The White-Haired Girl* (1964).

The changing fads in social dances and the efforts of the public to learn them are always rich sources of material. All classes and dance forms are represented, from the humble folk in Rowlandson's *A Tailors Wedding [sic]* (1814) to the more refined company in George Cruikshank's *Moulinet—Elegancies of Quadrille Dancing* (1817). The craze for the waltz in the early 1800s sparked many caricatures; later targets were the polka, the tango, and the Charleston, to name only a few. The dancing masters who taught social dances were often caricatured in the eighteenth century, along with their hapless pupils. An example is *Grown Gentlemen Taught to Dance* (1768), an engraving after a drawing by John Collett (1725–1780).

Caricaturists frequently capture a side of dance instruction that seldom appears in more idealized depictions. The various contraptions used to force the turned-out position of the feet in those not sufficiently gifted by nature are recorded in Cruikshank's four-part series *The Dancing Lesson* (1835) and Édouard de Beaumont's (1821–1888) series *L'Opéra au XIXe siècle* (published in *Le charivari*, 1844–1845).

Dance technique is frequently lampooned. In *The Charmers of the Age* (1741), William Hogarth portrayed La Barberina (who was Barbara Campanini) and Philip Desnoyer onstage, with "prickt lines shewing the rising Height" of their jumps. Grandville (pseudonym of Jean-Ignace-Isidore Gérard, 1803–1847) depicted the gradual transformation of a ballerina into a spinning top and a *danseur* into a disembodied leg in his book *Un autre monde* (1844). The nineteenth-century ballerina Sofia Fuoco, who was nicknamed "La Pointue," balances precariously on impossibly long, thin, pointed feet in the undated *Une Danseuse à Pointes*. In the twentieth century, the dancer Iva Kitchell pointed out eight common faults in the May 1949 issue of *Dance Magazine*, among them "too coy," "too rigid," and "holding arabesques indefinitely." Aline Fruhauf observed Martha Graham and her pupils at the Bennington School of the Dance in 1936. Amphibian dancers demonstrate steps in Donald Elliott's *Frogs and the Ballet* (1979).

The more ludicrous aspects of actual theatrical works seldom escape attack. In *Modern Grace* (1796), Gillray portrays Charles Didelot and his partners in a vertiginous moment from Giacomo Onorati's *Alonzo e Cora* (1796). Alfred Edward Chalon, known to dance lovers for his delicate lithographs of Marie Taglioni, furnished Louis-François Gosselin with a chin as sharp as his nose in a caricature of a pose from *Le Carnaval de Venise* (1830). A revival of Didelot's *Flore et Zéphire* inspired William Makepeace Thackeray's 1836 series of the same title, which was lithographed by Edward Morton. *Grise-aile*, published in *La revue philipon* in 1842, was Alcide Joseph Lorentz's (born 1813) answer to *Giselle*. Cham (pseudonym of Amédée de Noé, 1818–1879) recorded Carlotta Grisi's leap from a six-foot height in *La Péri* (1843) by showing her feet at the top of the page while Lucien Petipa waits below with outstretched arms.

In the twentieth century, Pablo Picasso drew *Les Sylphides* as danced by somewhat bulbous sylphs (1919). Nerman interprets in Art Deco style *Le Train Bleu* and *The Prodigal Son*, as published in the *Tatler* in 1924 and 1929, respectively. Edward Gorey, who, in *The Lavender Leotard* (1973), concentrates on the repertory of New York City Ballet, pokes fun at the angular arm movements of the second theme of *The Four Temperaments*.

Glimpses of the dancer's life backstage and offstage are provided by de Beaumont's *L'Opéra au XIXᵉ siècle*, which shows the dancers chatting with colleagues, peeping at the audience, discussing finances, doing laundry, and spending a holiday fishing. In *L'Amour et Sa Mère* (1853), Honoré Daumier (1808–1879) depicts the ubiquitous stage mother and her child. In *The Gilded Bat* (1966), Gorey describes the life of a dancer who becomes a star in a ballet called *La Chauvre-Souris Dorée*.

Because caricatures are seldom concerned with preserving the theatrical illusion, they are often frank and informative about theatrical devices and machines and soon dispel any illusions about flying sylphs and vanishing demons. The practical realities of the theater are revealed—Cocteau, about 1911, shows how Vaslav Nijinsky was revived after his famous leap in *Le Spectre de la Rose*—one helper supports his chair while another flaps a towel in his face and Diaghilev watches in concern.

The relationships between female dancers and their male patrons have always been relished by caricaturists and the adoring public. The Duke of Queensbury admired Mademoiselle Parisot in *A Peep at the Parisot with Q in the Corner* (1796). In the 1820s, favorite targets were Lise Noblet and Maria Mercandotti and their wealthy admirers Lord Fife and Edward Hughes Ball-Hughes, or "Golden Ball." Céline Céleste works her wiles on U.S. president Andrew Jackson and his staff in Henry R. Robinson's *The Celeste-al Cabinet* (1836). Gustave Doré's *Rats (d'Opéra)*, published in *La ménagerie parisienne* (1854), shows the corps de ballet unashamedly returning the ogles of the audience. During the nineteenth century, scenes of dancers with their patrons in the wings or in their dressing rooms

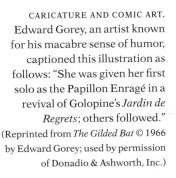

CARICATURE AND COMIC ART. Edward Gorey, an artist known for his macabre sense of humor, captioned this illustration as follows: "She was given her first solo as the Papillon Enragé in a revival of Golopine's *Jardin de Regrets*; others followed." (Reprinted from *The Gilded Bat* © 1966 by Edward Gorey; used by permission of Donadio & Ashworth, Inc.)

proliferated and seemingly exerted a strong erotic appeal. Constantin Guys (1808–1892) and Paul Gavarni (pseudonym of Sulpice Guillaume Chevalier, 1804–1866) are among the many artists who worked in this genre. Philippe Jullian (1920–1977) carried on this tradition in *Les Coulisses Scandaleuses* (published in *Ballet*, May 1947).

In the twentieth century, caricaturists have frequently drawn comparisons between sports and dance. After viewing Nijinsky's ballet *Jeux* (1913), Ernest Howard Shepard (1879–1976), the illustrator of *Winnie-the-Pooh*, cast cricket players and others in imaginary sports ballets. Football players are often caricatured as ballet dancers, perhaps because some of them actually take ballet lessons to improve their precision and coordination.

Grandville, whose favorite theme was animals engaged in human pursuits, depicted a pas de trois of crabs, insects, and mice in *Un autre monde*. Political cartoonists sometimes personify Russia as a dancing bear. Charlip's delightful *Kitty Tango* (1977) shows feline dancers in action. The frogs in Elliott's *Frogs and the Ballet* are tricked out in the tutus, tights, jerkins, tiaras, and false eyelashes of human ballet dancers.

Since turnabout is fair play, it should be noted that at least one ballet has been inspired by a dance caricature: Ninette de Valois's *The Prospect before Us* (1940), based on Rowlandson's print of the same title (1791).

[*See also* Artists and the Dance *and* Prints and Drawings.]

BIBLIOGRAPHY

Beaumont, Cyril W. "Gaetano and Auguste Vestris in English Caricature." *Ballet* 5 (March 1948): 19–29.

Feaver, William, and Ann Gould. *Masters of Caricature: From Hogarth and Gillray to Scarfe and Levine.* New York, 1981.

Guest, Ivor. "Chalon at the Ballet: Caricatures." *Ballet* (November 1951).

Guest, Ivor. "Thackeray and the Ballet." *Dancing Times* 62 (January 1972): 188–190.

Jackson, Barry. "Being Funny about Ballet." *Dance and Dancers* (July–August 1986): 19–23.

Klingender, F. D., ed. *Hogarth and the English Caricature.* London, 1944.

Lucie-Smith, Edward. *The Art of Caricature.* London, 1981.

Moore, Lillian. "200 Years of Theatrical Dance in Caricature." *Dance Magazine* 24 (September 1950): 14–19.

Moore, Lillian. "La Belle Assemblée." *Dance Magazine* 25 (April 1951): 20–21.

SUSAN AU

CARMAGNOLE, LA. A circle dance and the song accompanying it, both called "La Carmagnole," became famous during the French Revolution at the end of the eighteenth century. The name originally denoted a narrow jacket with a large collar, short tails, and several rows of metal buttons; this was adopted first by the revolutionary *fédérés* of Marseille and later by the rebels of Paris, who combined it with black woolen trousers, a red, white, and blue vest, and the floppy Phrygian cap that symbolized liberty.

The song's melody was borrowed from an old Provençal air. Its words, by an unknown author, incited the people against King Louis XVI and Queen Marie Antoinette (whom the song called Monsieur and Madame Veto), the aristocracy, and the Swiss Guards.

The dance is believed to be related to folk fertility dances of great antiquity. It was performed by a circle or chain of dancers who wound around the "tree of liberty" during festivals, or around the guillotine at executions, especially during the Reign of Terror. Napoleon Bonaparte banned "La Carmagnole" in 1799, but its refrain persists in popular memory:

> Dansons la Carmagnole,
> Vive le son, vive le son,
> Dansons la Carmagnole,
> Vive le son du canon.
>
> (Let's dance the Carmagnole,
> Long live the sound, long live the sound,
> Let's dance the Carmagnole,
> Long live the sound of the cannon.)

Boris Asafiev included the song in the score of his ballet *The Flames of Paris*, staged in Leningrad (Saint Petersburg) in 1932.

BIBLIOGRAPHY

Alford, Violet. *The Traditional Dance.* London, 1935.

Bertaud, Jean-Paul. *La vie quotidienne au temps de la Révolution.* Paris, 1983.

Conté, Pierre. *Danses anciennes de cour et de théâtre en France.* Paris, 1974.

JEANNINE DORVANE
Translated from French

CARNAVAL, LE. Ballet in one act. Choreography and libretto: Michel Fokine. Music: Robert Schumann. Scenery and costumes: Léon Bakst. First performance: 20 February [5 March] 1910, Pavlov Hall, Saint Petersburg. Principals: Tamara Karsavina (Columbine), Leonid Leontiev (Harlequin), Vaslav Nijinsky (Florestan), Ludmilla Schollar (Estrella), Aleksandr Shiriaev (Eusebius), Bronislava Nijinska (Papillon), Alfred Bekefi (Pantalon), Vsevolod Meyerhold (Pierrot).

Le Carnaval, set to Robert Schumann's piano suite *Carnaval: Scènes Mignonnes sur Quatre Notes*, premiered at a charity ball sponsored by *Satyrikon* magazine. In this first version the ballet flowed out among the ball guests during the main action, but all later productions were confined to the stage. The original cast was Maryinsky dancers, masked for anonymity because of contract restrictions.

The ballet was restaged for Diaghilev's Ballets Russes with the score orchestrated by Nikolai Rimsky-Korsakov, Aleksandr Glazunov, Anatol Liadov, and Nikolai Tcherepnin. The first stage version opened on 20 May 1910 at the Theater des Westens, Berlin, with Lydia Lopokova as Columbine, Leonid Leontiev as Harlequin, Aleksei Bulgakov as Pierrot, and Enrico Cecchetti as Pantalon. Léon Bakst's decor set the ballet in the Viennese Biedermeier period around 1840. With a new Bakst setting, it premiered at the Maryinsky Theater in Saint Petersburg on 6 February 1911, with Michel Fokine as Harlequin, Tamara Karsavina as Columbine, Bronislava Nijinska as Papillon, and Adolph Bolm as Pierrot.

The ballet's action, a stream of flirtations and character vignettes, was based on Schumann's notion of his dual personality (personified in Florestan and Eusebius) and on the titles in his musical score. It is a matter of disagreement whether the dancers represent *commedia dell'arte* figures or people masquerading as these characters.

Harlequin's solo, which Vaslav Nijinsky began to perform in 1911, is an astonishing series of cabrioles, *entrechats dix*, and pirouettes, finishing with a *grande pirouette à la seconde* that gradually sinks to the ground. Richard Buckle (1971) called this "the most uncanny and least human of all Nijinsky's creations."

The appealing Romantic flavor of the ballet assured its popularity, and it was performed throughout the Diaghilev company's existence. Subsequent productions were staged by Fokine for the Royal Swedish Ballet, the Ballet Russe de Monte Carlo, the Original Ballet Russe, and Ballet Theatre. A Labanotation score was made in 1962. David Vaughan (1978–1979) termed *Le Carnaval* the "most exquisite and most elusive" of Fokine's extant works.

[*See also the entries on the principal figures mentioned herein.*]

BIBLIOGRAPHY

Baer, Nancy Van Norman. *The Art of Enchantment: Diaghilev's Ballets Russes, 1909–1929.* San Francisco, 1988.

Buckle, Richard. *Nijinsky.* London, 1971.

Garafola, Lynn. *Diaghilev's Ballets Russes.* New York, 1989.

Levinson, André. *Ballet Old and New.* Translated by Susan Cook Summer. New York, 1982.

Nijinska, Bronislava. *Early Memoirs.* Translated and edited by Irina Nijinska and Jean Rawlinson. New York, 1981.

Vaughan, David. "Fokine in the Contemporary Repertory." *Ballet Review* 7.2–3 (1978–1979): 19–27.

SUZANNE CARBONNEAU

CAROSO, FABRITIO (Fabritio Caroso da Sermoneta; born between 1526 and 1535 in Sermoneta, Italy, died after 1605, place unknown), prominent Italian dancing master and author. Caroso published two large and significant manuals of court dance, *Il ballarino* (1581) and *Nobiltà di dame* (1600; 1605), that give rules for dance style, steps, figures, and etiquette and include specific choreographies with music (in mensural notation and Italian lute tablature) for more than one hundred different dances. These manuals, along with *Le gratie d'amore* by Cesare Negri (1602; 1604), are the chief sources of the late Renaissance social dance repertory of the Italian nobility.

According to oral history in Sermoneta, Caroso was of peasant extraction and was sponsored by the Caetani, the powerful ducal family of Sermoneta and Rome. Other evidence of Roman connections is the preponderant number in both books of specific dance dedications to ladies of the Caetani and other prominent Roman families (e.g., the Orsini, Farnese, and Aldobrandini); Torquato Tasso's laudatory poem to Caroso in *Nobiltà*, presumably written when the poet was in Rome (1592–1594); and the reissue in Rome of *Nobiltà* as *Raccolta di varij balli* (1630), doubtless after Caroso's death. Caroso gives no further autobiographical information, and little other evidence of his life has yet been found. Whether he traveled beyond Rome is unknown. However, his dedications to queens, princesses, and duchesses of the Medici, Gonzaga, Este, and other non-Roman families of high rank and his prescriptive rules for court etiquette in *Nobiltà* (e.g., how a bride should behave when a princess calls on her) indicate that he taught in princely circles, perhaps in various cities of northern Italy. Both his books were sumptuously printed in Venice, capital of the Italian publishing world, to which Caroso may have journeyed briefly to oversee publication. His place and date of death are unknown: Felippo degli Alessandri (1620) refers to him as no longer alive and no longer in style, yet mentions nine of his dances.

Caroso's professional ties may be represented by the contributors of specific dances whom he acknowledges in *Il ballarino* (e.g., "Contentezza d'Amore, Balletto di M[aestro] Battistino"), but he tells nothing about them. In *Nobiltà* he credits all the choreographies to himself, even those to which he had ascribed another author in the earlier book. What is clearer is that Caroso was a contemporary of the authors of the other well-known manuals of the time—Thoinot Arbeau, Cesare Negri, Livio Lupi, and Prospero Lutii. Negri and Lupi appear, in fact, to have quoted directly from *Il ballarino*; there is no direct evidence, however, that either of them studied with Caroso. The breadth of geographic influence of Caroso's dances is indicated by the ownership of his manuals by distant libraries, such as the royal libraries of England. The reissue of *Nobiltà* in 1630 and the translation of Negri's book at the same time into Spanish suggest that Caroso's style had a wider geographic spread than Italy and continued through the first third of the seventeenth century.

Caroso's manuals, like those of his contemporaries, represent the mainstream of Italy's social-dance tradition; in addition, however, concordances of dance types, floor patterns, and step patterns, between his manuals and Thoinot Arbeau's *Orchésographie* (1588, the only contemporary French source), suggest that there was a basic western European dance style, probably with regional or national differences: Caroso's basic galliard pattern is identical to Arbeau's second galliard variation in its changes of weight; Caroso's kicks are straight-legged, however, while Arbeau's are bent.

Il ballarino is the first known comprehensive Italian dance manual after Guglielmo Ebreo da Pesaro's treatise of 1463. (Lutio Compasso's 1560 publication explains very few of the step names it includes and gives no music, and the five mid-century dances published by Gino Corti (1977) give no step explanations.) Caroso's manual is thus highly significant, for it includes the first complete and precise directions, with music, for many late Renaissance dance types whose names hark back to the fifteenth century *(ballo, balletto, bassa, alta, tordiglione)* and the first examples of some sixteenth-century dance types that became popular (pavan, *pavaniglia, passo e mezzo,* canary). *Il ballarino* and *Nobiltà di dame* together also provide the only precise directions anywhere for some dance types mentioned but not described in other sixteenth-century sources *(saltarello, contrapasso, chiaranzana,* spagnoletta, "Ballo del Fiore"), and many examples of a fast triple-dance type called *cascarda* only by Caroso and closely resembling his *saltarello* movements in *balletto* suites.

Deriving clear definitions of all these dance types from Caroso's manuals is problematic, however. Like the other Renaissance treatises, Caroso's seem to mingle traditional materials and new ideas indiscriminately: old dance types (such as the *bassa* [*bassadanza?*]) are modified and modernized; new dance types are added to old (e.g., canary movements are almost all appended to *balletto* suites); and further obfuscation undoubtedly results from Caroso's adhering to the pervasive late Renaissance practices of improvisation, ornamentation, and variation on well-known models. It is difficult therefore to discern the underlying models, especially of those types more than fifty years old (such as the *passo e mezzo*). Thus, Caroso's dances present perhaps insoluble mysteries of provenance and probably equally indecipherable layers of variation.

Although *Il ballarino*, with eighty dances and fifty-four rules for step patterns, may be the better known of Caroso's books, *Nobiltà di dame*, with forty-nine dances and sixty-eight rules for steps, may be the more valuable to scholars. It redefines and corrects much of the terminology and many of the choreographies of the first book; its terms for and definitions of step patterns incorporate and explain time values more precisely (e.g., one *seguito breve* equals one musical breve); its musical notation is more careful; and the punctuation in the choreographic text is more systematically employed to coincide with musical phrasing

and repetition. Caroso calls *Nobiltà* the second edition of *Il ballarino*, but its far greater clarity may well improve what is understood of all the sixteenth-century manuals, even of the smaller manuscripts with more cryptic texts. *Nobiltà* also contains new step patterns and choreographies and a lengthy new section on etiquette for both sexes, with emphasis on manners at a ball.

All of Caroso's choreographies are social dances for aristocrats. Indeed, most are for the basic unit of one couple, most plausibly even for one couple at a time. Of dances for more participants, most call for a small number of dancers (three or six most commonly); unusual numbers are required only rarely (as in *Nobiltà*'s "Ballo del Fiore," a mixer for five). Only one dance is in longways formation for any number of couples ("Chiaranzana," in *Il ballarino*); there are no two-couple dances (one of Negri's favorite formations); nor are there dances for any number of couples in a circle, as in Arbeau's branles. Furthermore, there are no dances specifically for the lower classes (such as Arbeau's "Morisque"), or openly imitating them (such as Arbeau's "Branle des Lavandières"); nor are there any hints of the clearly theatrical dances that appear in other sources (e.g., Arbeau's "Mattachins" or Negri's "Austria Felice"). The fact that Caroso's step vocabulary was also employed in contemporary Italian theatrical choreographies by Negri and Emilio de'Cavalieri, however, validates his specific teachings for dance style in various kinds of late Renaissance spectacle.

The dances Caroso describes are courtly but flirtatious, charming but vigorous, elegant but skillful, playful but sophisticated. They are the dances of young gentlemen who recognized dance as a manly art demonstrating as much skill as fencing or riding; of young ladies who saw dance as an opportunity to display their charms with grace and energy; and of young aristocrats who sought always to enjoy themselves while ornamenting their surroundings and pleasing their observers. All the dances are flirtatious, but few are programmatic; those few mime aspects of the tournament, a common metaphor in Renaissance art for romantic interplay (such as "Torneo Amoroso" in *Il ballarino* and all versions of "Il Barriera" in both books).

The paths of the dancers are always related both to their partners and the dancing space. One popular couple-dance type consists of opening honors; a lead-in figure that traverses the ballroom (to attract attention and to acknowledge the onlookers); the giving of right hands round, left hands round, and both hands round; a reverse S-shaped figure in which the partners exchange places; and a leading-out figure with honors (e.g., "Rosa Felice" in *Nobiltà*; note the striking similarity here to eighteenth-century dance figures, especially those in the minuet). Another scheme has figures danced at the same time alternating with those in which the partners dance to each other in

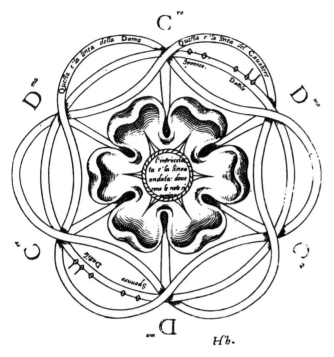

DELLA NOBILTA DI DAME LIB. II.   241

IL CONTRAPASSO FATTO CON VERA MATHEMATICA
sopra   i; uersi   d' Ouidio

CAROSO. This illustration accompanies Caroso's "Contrapasso Nuovo," a dance for three men and three women created according to a mathematical formula based on Ovid's verse. The top left path is the path of the lady; the top right is the path of the gentleman. The dance is described in Caroso's 1600 treatise *Nobiltà di dame*. (Dance Collection, New York Public Library for the Performing Arts.)

dling all this paraphernalia are found in *Nobiltà*'s notes on etiquette. Posture remains ever erect, with the arms gracefully quiet at the sides; pride of bearing is accentuated by an elegant strutting *(pavoneggiare)* that sways the cape or skirt; flirtation is abetted by playful flanking and pivoting movements toward and away from partners *(fiancheggiare)*, as in fencing; only the feet, of course, touch the floor. Step patterns require vigorous, complex, and rapid footwork demanding endurance and elevation, and all are accomplished with flexed ankle, straight legs, and slight *pliés*. Turnout is precisely forbidden ("Keep your toes parallel, not . . . one toe pointing east, the other west," Caroso instructs); hands take or clap partner's hands or hold the hilt of a sword or a handkerchief; arms are rarely raised above the head and have no purely ornamental gestures.

Minor differences in style exist between the sexes in Caroso, reflecting the social mores of the time. Only the gentlemen, for example, undertake the most difficult feats, such as multiple capers or turns in the air. In such technical demands Caroso is moderate, certainly more sophisticated and demanding than Arbeau, but he does not approach the brilliant male virtuosity Negri and others (e.g., Compasso, Lutii, and Lupi) describe in great detail.

All the masters agree that dancers should be able to improvise appropriately on accepted models, but Caroso is the only one to insist, especially in *Nobiltà*, that in so doing one must follow the *vera Regola* ("true rule") of absolute symmetry, to ensure that all step patterns and figures are in harmony with the late Renaissance neo-Platonic aesthetic. Aside from this *vera Regola*, however, the dominant formal principle of Caroso's choreographies is that of variation. His separate dances, as well as individual movements within his *balletto* suites, always involve varied figures and step patterns to music that is repeated as often as needed (as in "Celeste Giglio" in *Nobiltà*). The complex forms that can result when the principle of variation is applied in different ways, sometimes even combining strophic with rondo or ternary forms in the dance, in the music, or in both, reveal real sophistication and a mastery of variation techniques.

The music in Caroso's manuals is anonymous "music for use" and varies greatly in quality. Most of those pieces notated in lute tablature only are really skeletal chord progressions, probably intended for the expert players who worked for the noble families to elaborate on by improvising variations. The music is simple and homophonic; it is also thoroughly formulaic and sometimes has rubrics to guide the correlation between it and the text. Each piece is made up of from one to three four-bar—or multiples of four-bar—strains in the same key. In fact, many dance pieces apparently consist of small melodic and harmonic units used and reused for their temporal durations rather

turn (e.g., "Passo e Mezzo," in both books). Yet a third pattern has the couple traversing the floor side by side, dancing simultaneously throughout (as in "Amorosina Grimana, Pavaniglia," in *Nobiltà*). Still another has a refrain of steps and/or paths at the end of each figure (as in "Alta Regina" in both books). Dances for more than one couple often include the same figures, with additional circles and various kinds of heys (as in "Contrapasso Nuovo," in both books).

Caroso's dance style is essentially identical for both sexes and well suited to the garb and social status of noble youth. The gentlemen wear hats and gloves, with capes and swords; the ladies wear high *pianelle* (Fr., *chopines*; Eng., *pantofles*) and short-trained skirts over farthingales and layers of petticoats; they hold handkerchiefs, gloves, or muffs, or toy with their jewelry. Strict rules for han-

than their aesthetic qualities. They are otherwise built on well-known ostinato basses, chord schemes, or melodies with basses (such as the *passo e mezzo*), which were common throughout sixteenth-century Europe. The age and sources of the music, just as the dances, cannot be determined precisely, for Caroso's manuals present different notational styles that seem to span a century of change and development. As with the dances, so too the music may have been revised and modified according to Caroso's needs and the prevailing fashion. The many problems of correlating text and music are beginning to yield to study, however, thus permitting more systematic reconstruction and enabling dances of the time of Elizabeth I of England and Philip II of Spain, William Shakespeare and Miguel de Cervantes, John Dowland and Claudio Monteverdi, to take their rightful place among the social arts of late Renaissance courtly life.

[*See also* Ballo and Balletto; *and the entries on the principal dance types mentioned herein. For related discussion see the entry on Negri.*]

BIBLIOGRAPHY: SOURCES

Alessandri, Filippo degli. *Discorso sopra il ballo.* Terni, 1620.

Arbeau, Thoinot. *Orchésographie et traicte en forme de dialogve, par leqvel tovtes personnes pevvent facilement apprendre & practiquer l'honneste exercice des dances.* Langres, 1588, 1589. Facsimile reprint, Langres, 1988. Reprinted with expanded title as *Orchésographie, metode, et teorie en forme de discovrs et tablatvre povr apprendre a dancer, battre le Tambour en toute sorte & diuersité de bateries, Iouët du fifre & arigot, tirer des armes & escrimer, auec autres honnestes exercices fort conuenables à la Ieunesse.* Langres, 1596. Facsimile reprint, Geneva, 1972

Arbeau, Thoinot. *Orchesography.* 1589. Translated into English by Mary Stewart Evans. New York, 1948. Reprint with corrections, a new introduction, and notes by Julia Sutton, and representative steps and dances in Labanotation by Mireille Backer, New York, 1967.

Caroso, Fabritio. *Il ballarino.* (1581). Facsimile reprint, New York, 1967.

Caroso, Fabritio. *Nobiltà di dame.* Venice, 1600, 1605. Facsimile reprint, Bologna, 1970. Reissued with order of illustrations changed as *Raccolta di varij balli.* Rome, 1630. Translated into English with eight introductory chapters by Julia Sutton, the music transcribed by F. Marian Walker. Oxford 1986. Reprint with step manual in Labanotation by Rachelle Palnick Tsachor and Julia Sutton, New York, 1995.

Cavalieri, Emilio de'. "Intermedio VI." In Cristofano Malvezzi's *Intermedii et concerti, fatti per la Commedia rappresentata in Firenze nelle Nozze del Serenissimo Don Ferdinando Medici et Madama Christiana di Loreno, Granduchi di Toscana.* Venice, 1591. Translated and edited by D. P. Walker as *Les Fête de Florence: Musique des intermèdes de "La Pellegrina."* Paris, 1963.

Cavalier, Emilio de'. *La rappresentazione di anima e di corpo* (1600). Facsimile reprint, Bologna, 1967.

Compasso, Lutio. *Ballo della gagliarda.* Florence, 1560. Facsimile reprint with introduction by Barbara Sparti, Freiburg, 1995.

Corso, Rinaldo. *Dialogo del ballo.* Venice, 1559. Facsimile reprint, Bologna, 1969.

Corti, Gino. "Cinque balli toscani del cinquecento." *Rivista Italiana di Musicologia* 12 (1977): 73–75.

Della Casa, Giovanni. *Galateo.* Milan, 1559.

Esquivel Navarro, Juan de. *Discursos sobre el arte del dancado* (1642). Facsimile reprint, Madrid, 1947.

Florio, John. *A World of Wordes.* London 1598. Facsimile reprint, Hildesheim, 1972. 2d ed., *Queen Anna's New World of Words.* London, 1611. Facsimile reprint of 1611 ed., Menston, England, 1973.

Jacobilli, Ludovico. *Modo di ballare.* Circa 1615. Manuscript located in Foligno, Biblioteca Jacobilli, AIII.19,ff.102–104.

Lauze, F[rançois] de. *Apologie de la danse, 1623.* Translated by Joan Wildeblood, and with original text, as *A Treatise of Instruction in Dancing and Deportment.* London, 1952.

Lupi, Livio. *Libro di gagliarde, tordiglione, passo e mezzo, canari e passeggi.* Palermo, 1600. Rev. ed., Palermo, 1607.

Lutii, Prospero. *Opera bellissima nella quale si contengono molte partite, et passeggi di gagliarda.* Perugia, 1589.

Mancini, Giulio. *Del origine et nobiltà del ballo* (c.1623–1630). Facsimile with introduction by Barbara Sparti, Freiburg, 1996.

Negri, Cesare. *Le gratie d'amore.* Milan, 1602. Reissued as *Nuove invenzione di balli.* Milan, 1604. Translated into Spanish by Don Balthasar Carlos for Señor Condé, Duke of Sanlucar, 1630. Manuscript located in Madrid, Biblioteca Nacional, MS 14085. Facsimile reprint of 1602, New York and Bologna, 1969. Literal translation into English and musical transcription by Yvonne Kendall. D.M.A. diss., Stanford University, 1985.

Rossi, Bastiano de'. *Descrizione del magnificentissimo Apparato rappresentata nella felicissime Nozze degli Illustrissimi Don Ferdinando Medici, e Madama Christina di Lorena, Gran Duchi di Toscana.* Florence, 1589.

Zuccolo da Cologna, Simeon. *La pazzia del ballo* (1549). Facsimile reprint, Bologna, 1969.

BIBLIOGRAPHY: OTHER STUDIES

Aldrich, Putnam. *Rhythm in Seventeenth-Century Italian Monody.* New York, 1966.

Bank, J. A. *Tactus, Tempo, and Notation in Mensural Music from the Thirteenth to the Seventeenth Century.* Amsterdam, 1972.

Brooks, Lynn Matluck. *The Dances of the Processions of Seville in Spain's Golden Age.* Kassel, 1988.

Chew, Geoffrey. "Notation: III, 4. Mensural Notation from 1500." In *The New Grove Dictionary of Music and Musicians.* London, 1980.

Chilesotti, Oscar, ed. *Biblioteca di rarità musicali,* vol. 1, *Danze del secolo XVI trascritte in notazione moderne dalle opere: "Nobiltà di dame" del Sig. F. Caroso da Sermoneta; "Le gratie d'amore" di C. Negri, Milanese, detto il Trombone.* Milan, 1884.

Collins, Michael B. "The Performance of Sesquialtera and Hemiolia in the Sixteenth Century." *Journal of the American Musicological Society* 17 (Spring 1964): 5–28.

Commune di Roma Assessorato alla Cultura. *La danza tradizionale in Italia, mostra documentaria.* Rome, 1981.

Dalhaus, Carl. "Zur Theorie des Tactus im 16. Jahrhundert." *Archiv für Musikwissenschaft* 17 (1960): 22–39.

Esses, Maurice. *Dance and Instrumental Diferencias in Spain during the Seventeenth and Early Eighteenth Centuries.* Stuyvesant, N.Y., 1992.

Fenlon, Iain. "Music and Spectacle at the Gonzaga Court, c.1580–1600." *Proceedings of the Royal Musical Association* 103 (1976–1977): 90–105.

Feves. Angene. "Caroso's Patronesses." In *Proceedings of the Ninth Annual Conference, Society of Dance History Scholars, City College of the City University of New York, 14–17 February 1986,* compiled by Christena L. Schlundt. Riverside, Calif., 1986.

Feves Angene. "Fabritio Caroso and the Changing Shape of the Dance, 1550–1600." *Dance Chronicle* 14 (1991): 159–174.

Gelernter, Judith. "Mannerist Aesthetics in the Court Dance of Fabritio Caroso." In *Proceedings of the Seventeenth Annual Conference, Society of Dance History Scholars, Brigham Young University, 10–13*

February 1994, compiled by Linda J. Tomko. Riverside, Calif., 1994.

Ghisi, Federico. *Feste musicali della Firenze Medicea, 1480–1589*. Florence, 1939.

Hudson, Richard, and Suzanne G. Cusick. "Balletto." In *The New Grove Dictionary of Music and Musicians*. London, 1980.

Hudson Richard. "Canary," "Passamezzo," Pavaniglia." In *The New Grove Dictionary of Music and Musicians*. London, 1980.

Jones, Pamela. "The Relation between Music and Dance in Cesare Negri's 'Le gratie d'amore' (1602)." 2 vols. Ph.D. Diss., University of London, 1988.

Kendall, Yvonne. "Rhythm, Meter, and *Tactus* in Sixteenth-Century Italian Court Dance: Reconstruction from a Theoretical Base." *Dance Research* (Spring 1990): 3–27.

Little, Meredith Ellis. "Saltarello." In *The New Grove Dictionary of Music and Musicians*. London, 1980.

Matteo (Vittucci, Matteo Marcellus) with Carola Goya. *The Language of Spanish Dance*. Norman, Okla., 1990.

Meyer, Ernst Hermann. "Ballo" and "Galliarde." In *Die Musik in Geschichte und Gegenwart*. 1st ed., vol. 1, 1949–1951; vol. 4, 1955. Kassel, 1949–1979.

Moe, Lawrence H. "Dance Music in Printed Italian Lute Tablatures from 1507 to 1611." Ph.D. diss., Harvard University, 1956.

Mönkemeyer, Helmut, ed. *Fabritio Caroso: "Il ballarino."* 2 vols. Rodenkirchen, 1971. Music.

Pirrotta, Nino, and Elena Povoledo. *Music and Theatre from Poliziano to Monteverdi*. Translated by Karen Eales. Cambridge, 1982.

Poulton, Diana. "Notes on the Spanish Pavan." *Lute Society Journal* 3 (1961): 5–16.

"Proportions." In *The New Grove Dictionary of Music and Musicians*. London, 1980.

Solerti, Angelo. *Musica, ballo e drammatica alla corte medicea dal 1600 al 1637*. Florence, 1905.

Sphor, Helga. "Studien zur italienischen Tanzcomposition um 1600." Ph.D. diss., University of Freiburg, 1956.

Sutton, Julia. "Reconstruction of Sixteenth-Century Dance." In *Dance History Research: Perspectives from Related Arts and Disciplines*, edited by Joann W. Kealiinohomoku. New York, 1970.

Sutton, Julia, and Charles P. Coldwell. Review of Helmut Mönkemeyer's *Fabritio Caroso: "Il ballarino." Notes* 30 (1973): 357–359.

Sutton, Julia. "Caroso, Fabritio" and "Negri, Cesare." In *The New Grove Dictionary of Music and Musicians*. London, 1980.

Sutton, Julia. "Triple Pavans: Clues to Some Mysteries in Sixteenth-Century Dance." *Early Music* 14.2 (1986): 174–181.

Sutton, Julia. "Musical Forms and Dance Forms in the Dance Manuals of Sixteenth-Century Italy: Plato and the Varieties of Variation." In *The Marriage of Music and Dance: Papers from a Conference Held at the Guildhall School of Music and Drama, London, 9th–11th August 1991*. Cambridge, 1992.

Sutton, Julia, and Sibylle Dahms. "Ballo, Balletto." In *Die Musik in Geschichte und Gegenwart*, 2d ed., vol. 1, 1994. Kassel, 1994–.

Sutton, Julia. "Canario." In *Die Musik in Geschichte und Gegenwart*, 2d ed., vol. 2, 1995. Kassel, 1994–.

Tani, Gino. "Canario." In *Enciclopedio dello spettacolo*. 9 vols. Rome, 1954–1968.

Walker, D. P. "Musical Humanism in the Sixteenth and Early Seventeenth Centuries" (parts 1–5). *Music Review* 2.1–3.1 (1941–1942).

Ward, John M. "Passamezzo." In *Die Musik in Geschichte und Gegenwart*, 1st ed., vol. 10, 1962. Kassel, 1949–1979.

VIDEOTAPE.   Julia Sutton, *Il Ballarino (The Dancing Master)*, a teaching videotape featuring a glossary of steps and three sixteenth-century Italian dances by Caroso and Negri (Pennington, N.J., 1991).

JULIA SUTTON

CASCARDA. The *cascarda* was an Italian social dance of the late sixteenth and early seventeenth centuries for one couple or, more rarely, a trio or two couples. It is recorded in the dancing manuals of Fabritio Caroso, who lists twenty-one *cascarde* in *Il ballarino* (1581) and eleven in *Nobiltà di dame* (1600), designating a discrete, quick dance in triple meter (i.e., compound duple) and of playfully flirtatious character. The only other source for the term is Livio Lupi's dance manual (1607), which has a similar dance termed *cascarda*, but in duple.

As a type, the *cascarda* appears to be close choreographically and musically to the quick after-dances *(sciolte)* called *saltarelli* in Caroso's *balletto* suites. Some *cascarde* have the same music as some *saltarello* movements (e.g., "Allegrezza d'Amore," a *cascarda*, is musically identical to the *saltarello* in "Alta Vittoria"). The choreographic differences between the *cascarda* and the *saltarello* appear to lie chiefly in the number of figures; the former is a complete dance, with as many as ten figures, performed by partners either simultaneously or alternately, and with formal openings and closings; the latter may be as short as one figure (usually done simultaneously), chosen to fit the choreographic needs of the entire *balletto* suite. The light and graceful affect is the same in both *cascarde* and *saltarelli*, and the step vocabulary belongs to all quick triple dances as well as duple dances in which time values are subdivided into quick steps (e.g., *seguito spezzato, Saffice*).

The origin of the term *cascarda* is unknown. The term may come from *cascare* ("to fall," "to collapse," and, by derivation, "to break into pieces") and is perhaps akin in meaning to terms Caroso applies to the after-dances in *balletto* suites that alter (that is, break up) the original duple music into triple in mathematical proportion: *sciolta* (from *sciolto*, "loose, nimble, quick"), and *rotta* ("a break," "a fracture"). Hence *cascarda*, like the other terms, may connote simultaneously mensuration, tempo, and character.

BIBLIOGRAPHY: SOURCES

Caroso, Fabritio. *Il ballarino* (1581). Facsimile reprint, New York, 1967.

Caroso, Fabritio. *Nobiltà di dame*. Venice, 1600, 1605. Facsimile reprint, Bologna, 1970. Reissued with order of illustrations changed as *Raccolta di varij balli*. Rome, 1630. Translated into English with eight introductory chapters by Julia Sutton, the music transcribed by F. Marian Walker. Oxford, 1986. Reprint with a step manual in Labanotation by Rachelle Palnick Tsachor and Julia Sutton, New York, 1995.

Lupi, Livio. *Libro di gagliarde, tordiglione, passo e mezzo, canari e passeggi*. Palermo, 1600. Rev. ed., Palermo, 1607.

BIBLIOGRAPHY: OTHER STUDIES

Sutton, Julia. "Cascarda." In *The New Grove Dictionary of Music and Musicians*. London, 1980.

Tani, Gino. "Cascards." In *Enciclopedio dello spettacolo*. 9 vols. Rome, 1954–1968.

JULIA SUTTON
with David Hahn

CASSE-NOISETTE. *See* Nutcracker, The.

CASTANETS. A percussion instrument, castanets consist of two shell-shaped pieces of hardwood or synthetic material that are joined in pairs, one castanet for each hand; each hand can then manipulate its castanet separately to create a rhythmic accompaniment to dance. Contrary to general belief, castanets are neither indigenous nor unique to Spain. Their beginnings have been traced to ancient Egypt, to about 3000 BCE, as a development of the throw stick, a weapon similar to the boomerang. From at least the sixth century BCE, Greek iconographic representations show dancing women wielding *krotala*, long wooden clacks.

Castanets or their idiophonic counterparts exist in many diverse forms, among which are the Turkish *kásik*, Japanese *yotsudake*, Indian *kartali*, Swiss *chefeli*, and the Chinese *cha pan*, which are manipulated by the dancer or used as a time-marking device in dance-drama orchestras.

There are two major styles for playing Spanish castanets *(castañuelas),* classic and folkloric. Castanets held in the right hand *(hembra,* "female") are of higher pitch than those held in the left *(macho,* "male"). In the classic style, castanets are tied to the thumbs, thereby allowing the fingers of the right hand to strum successively on the outer shell to produce *carretillas* (rolls and trills) as the left-hand pair marks the rhythm with *golpes* (single strokes). Manuscripts of the Baroque era (c.1600–1750) give specific directions and diagrams for rolling both castanets simultaneously. In folkloric dances, castanets are usually larger, have a lower pitch, and are strung on one or more fingers. With a flicking action of the wrist the two halves are thrown against the palm, producing a loud staccato sound that is quite different from the sound produced when castanets are played in the classical manner.

Solo and group Spanish dance sequences in which castanets are used have appeared in classical ballets since the seventeenth century. Contemporary ballets have made comparatively little use of castanets because few dancers have mastered these deceptively difficult instruments. In addition, the artist must compose his or her own score and render an effortless appearance while coordinating playing with movement.

The most far-reaching and lasting contribution toward the refinement of castanets and the art of playing them was made by La Argentina (Antonia Mercé y Luque), the Spanish dancer who made several world tours at the beginning of the twentieth century. The first dancer to perform as a castanetist with large symphony orchestras was the American dancer Carola Goya, whose first such appearance was in 1955.

Castanet concerts, including duets, quartets, and sextets become increasingly successful—this largely due to the method of preserving and making available castanet compositions by means of two notation systems, the Emma Maleras system of Europe and the Matteo Casta-notation system of the Americas.

BIBLIOGRAPHY

Arriaza, Aurora. *Spanish Castanette Playing.* New York, 1924.

Chadima, Helen Gower. "The Use of Castanets in Baroque Dance." In *Proceedings of the Sixth Annual Conference, Society of Dance History Scholars, the Ohio State University, 11P13 February 1983,* edited by Christena L. Schlundt. Milwaukee, 1983.

Horosko, Marian. "Spanish Dance! Where." *Dance Magazine* (April, 1986).

Ivanova, Anna. *The Dance in Spain.* New York, 1970.

Matteo. "Woods That Dance." *Dance Perspectives,* no. 33 (Spring 1968).

Matteo. *The Language of Spanish Dance.* Norman, Okla., 1990.

Meri, La [Russell Meriwether Hughes]. *Spanish Dancing* (1948). Pittsfield, Mass., 1967.

Posticeo (1990–). Newsletter, issued three times a year, in German and English, by the Internationale Gesellschaft für Kunstlerisches Kastagnettenspiel (International Association for the Artistic Playing of Castanets), Cologne.

Schneider, Ria. "Matteo." *Posticeo* (March, 1995).

Udaeta, Jose de. *La castañuela española: Origen y evolución.* Barcelona, 1989.

MATTEO

CASTLE, IRENE AND VERNON, American dancers and teachers, a married couple who gave social dancing a substantial boost during an acclaimed public career together from 1912 to 1916. With the help of their music arranger, Ford T. Dabney, an African American, the Castles eschewed nineteenth-century rhythms and set their routines to lively jazz and ragtime beats, thus spreading the influence of black music. By their good manners, decorum, and respectability as a married couple, the Castles made otherwise suggestive body contacts and a great deal of improvisation acceptable to a wide audience. In addition, Irene Castle set a new style for American women, who copied her bobbed hairstyle, headband, little Dutch bonnet, and light, floating "Castle frocks."

Among the dances popularized by the Castles between 1912 and 1916 were the one-step, the maxixe, the Castle Polka, the tango, the Hesitation Waltz, and the Castle Walk. The fox trot was introduced later in their career. Vernon choreographed their dances, but the charm and grace of his wife and their extraordinary sharing of movement enlivened with a "sense of humor" (Castle, 1958, p. 87) contributed to their appeal.

Vernon Castle (Vernon William Blythe; born 2 May 1887 in Norwich, England, died 15 February 1918 at Fort Benbrook, Texas), as the youngest child in a family with four older sisters, developed an early interest in magic tricks; by the age of twenty, he was appearing in magic shows at clubs and at private parties. After graduating from Birmingham University with a degree in engineering, he went to New York City with his sister Coralie and her husband Lawrence Grossmith, both of them actors. By March 1907, Vernon was appearing in New York and on tour in various Lew Fields productions, including

About Town (1906), *The Girl behind the Counter* (1907), *Old Dutch* and *The Midnight Sons* (both 1909), *The Summer Widowers* (1910), and *The Hen-Pecks* (1911). He took the stage name Castle because his sister performed under the family name. Castle was known as an eccentric comedian, whose angular figure—he weighed 118 pounds and was five feet, eleven inches tall—accentuated his performance in vaudeville sketches. He was the dancing partner of Lotta Faust and Topsy Siegrist in several shows.

Irene Castle (Irene Foote; born 7 April 1893 in New Rochelle, New York, died 25 January 1969 in Eureka Springs, Arkansas) was the second daughter of Dr. Hubert Townsend Foote and Annie Elroy (Thomas) Foote. As a child, Irene studied skirt dancing with Rosetta O'Neill. At age seven, Irene was sent to Saint Mary's Episcopal Convent in Peekskill, New York, and later to National Park Seminary, near Washington, D.C., but she did not finish high school. By age sixteen, Irene was appearing in amateur theatricals, often imitating Bessie McCoy in the number "Yama Yama Man" from *The Three Twins* (1908). In later years, Irene attributed features of her own dancing to McCoy's style, including the so-called Castle mannerisms of the high shoulder, the way she held her hands, and as she said in an interview, "whatever looked good about my dancing."

In 1910, after meeting Vernon Castle at the Rowing Club in New Rochelle, Irene obtained an audition with Lew Fields, who engaged her as a dancer replacement for *The Summer Widowers*. Vernon and Irene became engaged in March 1911 and were married on 28 May 1911 in New Rochelle. After a brief honeymoon in England to meet Vernon's family, they returned to New York City for the August 1911 reopening of Vernon's show *The Hen-Pecks*. Irene joined the cast.

In March 1912, the Castles appeared in *Enfin . . . Une Revue* (Théâtre Olympia, Paris), which included a dance number by the Castles to Irving Berlin's song "Alexander's Ragtime Band." It was their first public appearance as a dance team. In May 1912, they tried out a dance act at the Café de Paris and were an instant hit because, according to Irene, "We were young, clean, married, and well-mannered" (Castle, 1919, p. 41). After six months of performing in Paris and London, the couple returned to New York City, where they had continued success, performing at Louis Martin's Café de l'Opéra and at private parties.

The Castles joined the cast of Charles Dillingham's *The Lady of the Slipper* (music by Victor Herbert) in 1912 but soon left the show, Irene during the rehearsal period, Vernon after the New York opening. Their next show was Charles Frohman's *The Sunshine Girl* (premiered February 1913 at the Knickerbocker). Elizabeth Marbury, who had become their agent, arranged for society patrons to support Castle House, the couple's dancing school across from the Ritz Hotel. They also opened Sans Souci, a supper club, and later Castles in the Air, on the roof of the Forty-fourth Street Theater. The Castles were the first white performers to use black musicians. James Reese Europe and Ford Dabney's orchestra provided the music both at the Castles' clubs and on their nationwide Whirlwind Tour (1914), playing thirty-two cities in twenty-eight days.

The Castles opened in Dillingham's *Watch Your Step* (music by Irving Berlin) on 8 December 1914 at the New Amsterdam Theater in New York City. The show, permeated with dancing, celebrated the Castles at the height of their popularity. [*See* United States of America, *article on* Musical Theater.]

Vernon left the tour of *Watch Your Step* to join the British Royal Air Force (RAF). Before he sailed for England, the Castles gave two farewell performances at the New York Hippodrome. Irene continued in *Watch Your Step* until 1916, then played an heiress in *Patria*, a fifteen-

CASTLE. A studio portrait taken in Chicago in 1913. The Castles created a sensation in the 1910s with their elegant and lively ballroom dancing. (Photograph by Moffett, Chicago; from the Dance Collection, New York Public Library for the Performing Arts.)

part silent film serial for Pathé. She appeared in sixteen more films by 1923, for Astra Corporation, Paramount-Artcraft, and Hol-Tre Productions. Irene was also in the Broadway flop *Miss 1917*, produced by Dillingham and Florenz Ziegfeld in 1917.

During World War I, Vernon became an aerial photographer for Britain's Royal Air Force (1916–1917) and was awarded the Croix de Guerre for bravery. He was then sent to Canada to train student pilots. Transferred to Texas with his squadron, Vernon died in a plane crash while on an instructional flight.

Irene Castle married three more times, to Robert E. Treman, Frederick McLaughlin, and George Enzinger. With McLaughlin she had two children, Barbara Irene and William. According to letters in the McLaughlin-Castle family archive, Vernon and Irene Castle had been estranged before his death, but this fact was not made public. In 1919, Irene published a book of her first husband's letters, heavily edited, entitled *My Husband*.

After Vernon's death, Irene appeared in vaudeville with dance partner William Reardon (1921–1922), acted as adviser to the 1939 Fred Astaire–Ginger Rogers film *The Story of Vernon and Irene Castle*, ran a wholesale millinery company, taught children's dance classes, wrote a fashion column, and appeared several times in summer stock. Her chief interest, however, was animal rescue work. At her death, she was buried next to Vernon at Woodlawn Cemetery in the Bronx, New York.

BIBLIOGRAPHY

Brock, Alan. "Irene Castle: Dancing on Air." *Dance Pages* 10 (Summer 1992): 24–29.
Castle, Irene, and Vernon Castle. *Modern Dancing*. New York, 1914.
Castle, Irene. *My Husband*. New York, 1919.
Castle, Irene. *Castles in the Air*. Garden City, N.Y., 1958.
Erenberg, Lewis A. "Everybody's Doin' It: The Pre–World War I Dance Craze, the Castles, and the Modern American Girl." *Feminist Studies* (Fall 1975).
Lasser, Michael. "'My Wife Is Dancing Mad': Irene Castle and the Dance Craze." *Attitude* 11 (Spring 1995): 3–9.

FILMS. *Mr. and Mrs. Vernon Castle before the Camera* (1914). *The Whirl of Life* (1915).

ARCHIVES. Irene and Vernon Castle scrapbooks, Billy Rose Collection, New York Public Library for the Performing Arts. Irene Castle dance dresses, Costume Institute Collection, Metropolitan Museum of Art, New York, and Theatre and Music Collection, Museum of the City of New York (which also has several pieces belonging to Vernon Castle).

IRIS M. FANGER

CATALUÑA. *See* Sardana.

CATARINA. Full title: *Catarina, ou la Fille du Bandit*. Also known as *Caterina, ovvero La Figlia del Bandito* and *Katerina, Doch'razboinika*. Ballet in three acts and five scenes. Choreography: Jules Perrot. Music: Cesare Pugni. Libretto: Jules Perrot. Scenery: Charles Marshall. First performance: 3 March 1846, Her Majesty's Theatre, London. Principals: Lucile Grahn (Catarina), Louis Gosselin (Salvator Rosa), Jules Perrot (Diavolino).

The independence and unconventionality of bandit life inspired many works of art in the nineteenth century. Jules Perrot derived the plot of *Catarina* partly from a comic opera, Daniel Auber's *Les Diamants de la Couronne* (1841), and partly from Lady Morgan's popular biography (1824) of the seventeenth-century Italian painter Salvator Rosa. Its costumes were based on the bandit paintings of Louis Léopold Robert and others.

The ballet depicts an apocryphal episode in the life of Salvator Rosa, who was famed for his bandit paintings. While on a sketching expedition he is waylaid by bandits but freed by their chief, Catarina. When the bandits' outpost is attacked, Catarina flees with her lieutenant, Diavolino, who secretly loves her, to Salvator's studio in Rome. She is caught and imprisoned, then rescued by Diavolino. At the Carnival in Rome she is killed by a sword thrust aimed at Salvator by the jealous Diavolino.

The choreographic high point of the ballet was the *pas stratégique*, in which Catarina and the female corps de ballet executed military maneuvers with muskets. Perrot revived the ballet for Fanny Elssler, who had great success with it in Milan in 1847 and Saint Petersburg in 1849.

BIBLIOGRAPHY

Au, Susan. "The Bandit Ballerina: Some Sources of Jules Perrot's *Catarina*." *Dance Research Journal* 10 (Spring-Summer 1978): 2–5.
Beaumont, Cyril W. *Complete Book of Ballets*. London, 1937.
Guest, Ivor. *Fanny Elssler*. London, 1970.
Guest, Ivor. *The Romantic Ballet in England*. London, 1972.
Guest, Ivor. *Jules Perrot: Master of the Romantic Ballet*. London, 1984.

SUSAN AU

CAVERLEY, THOMAS (born 1651?, died October 1745 in London), dancing master and writer. Caverley's origins are obscure, but he may have been the Thomas Caverley, son of William and Jane Caverley, whose baptism was recorded on 11 June 1651 at Saint James, Clerkenwell. By 1700 he was well established as a dancing master and in the early eighteenth century he was regarded as the leader of the dancing profession in London. With his sister he ran an admired boarding school for girls, first at Bedford Street and, beginning in 1721, at the Two Golden Lamps, Queen's Square, Holborn. He was also an important teacher of dancing masters; Kellom Tomlinson, who was apprenticed to him from 1707 to 1714, referred to the admirable instruction in theory that he received.

Caverley engaged the affection and respect of a whole professional generation that looked to him for an example of correct practice. John Weaver wrote in his historical apology and manifesto for dance, *An Essay towards an History of Dancing* (1712), that Caverley had made "singular and curious improvements" to the "art of dancing."

It was Caverley's practical grasp of what Weaver termed "certain Rules of the Art" that particularly impressed his younger colleagues. He taught in accordance with his own method, and it was through observation of the method's success that Weaver was prompted to marvel in his *Anatomical and Mechanical Lectures upon Dancing* (1721) that

> the Art of Dancing, by due Study and Application, was Capable of Such Improvements, which in Process of Time, would not only make it Valuable, . . . but render it worthy of Regard and Consideration, as well as Reflexion, of the learned World; since so many Arts and Sciences, are conducive to its Perfection.

Caverley became Weaver's main patron after 1707, encouraging him to continue the promotion and improvement of dancing begun with Weaver's translation of Raoul-Auger Feuillet's *Chorégraphie*, which appeared in 1706. Weaver's *Essay towards an History of Dancing* and *Anatomical and Mechanical Lectures upon Dancing* were both dedicated to Caverley, whose good social connections helped to advance Weaver's career. One of Caverley's friends, Sir Richard Steele, shared Weaver's interest in the reformation and advocacy of dance and gave him important opportunities as a writer and theatrical dancing master.

Caverley's character and his educational philosophy emerge clearly from Weaver's two dedications and from the first chapter of his *Essay towards an History of Dancing*. Caverley paid careful attention to the full development of the individual and prepared the young for an accomplished and responsible social and domestic life. Caverley was married twice and was survived by three sons and three daughters. According to his will, his estate was considerable and was left in trust for his daughters.

Two of Caverley's dances survive in notation, a figured minuet for five ladies in Edmund Pemberton's *Essay for the Further Improvement of Dancing* (1711), a work dedicated to Caverley; and the *Slow Minuet*, which survives in two versions, one of which was notated by Kellom Tomlinson.

BIBLIOGRAPHY
Goff, Moira. "Dancing-Masters in Early Eighteenth-Century London." *Historical Dance* 3.3 (1994): 17–23.
Ralph, Richard. *The Life and Works of John Weaver.* London, 1985.
RICHARD RALPH
with Moira Goff

CÉBRON, JEAN (born 29 April 1927 in Paris), French ballet dancer and teacher. Cébron studied first with his mother, Mauricette Cébron, a dancer at the Paris Opera (1911–1936) and later a ballet mistress at its school (1934–1956). He went to London in 1947 to study ballet at the Sigurd Leeder school and to learn various styles of East Asian dance. Within a year Cébron was performing publicly. Leeder, a collaborator of Kurt Jooss, invited Cébron to tour Chile in 1948 as a soloist in *The Green Table* and *The Big City*.

In 1949 Cébron returned to Leeder's school in London and debuted with his own group in 1956. He then danced for three years with the Stockholm Opera Festival Ballet. Ted Shawn saw him there and invited Cébron to join the faculty at Jacob's Pillow, home of a summer dance festival in Beckett, Massachusetts. There Cébron taught classes and performed dances he arranged himself. He later went to New York to teach master classes at the Juilliard School while continuing to teach at Jacob's Pillow. In 1976 Cébron began teaching at the Folkwang Schule in Essen, also dancing with the Folkwang Ballet and as a guest with Lotte Goslar's troupe.

Although Cébron has choreographed some avant-garde dances for the Hamburg State Opera Ballet, he has concentrated mainly on teaching, holding courses at the Palucca summer academy in Dresden, the London Contemporary Dance School, the Accademia Nazionale di Danza in Rome, and the Wuppertal Dance Theater. He also has worked closely with the José Limón company. Cébron is now resident ballet master of Pina Bausch's Tanztheater Wuppertal.

BIBLIOGRAPHY
Servos, Norbert. *Pine Bausch Wuppertal Dance Theater.* Translated by Patricia Stadié. Cologne, 1984.
Tegeder, Ulrich. "That There Is Never Any Ultimate Goal in Our Art." *Ballett International* 8 (March 1985).
HORST KOEGLER

CECCHETTI, ENRICO (born 21 June 1850 in Rome, died 13 November 1928 in Milan), Italian dancer, choreographer, and teacher. The son of Serafina Casagli, a dancer, and Cesare Cecchetti, a dancer and choreographer, Enrico Cecchetti was born in a dressing room at the Teatro di Apollo in Rome. He was only five years old when he made his debut, as a fairy, in Giuseppe Rota's *Il Giuocatore* in Genoa. At seven, he also appeared in some American productions with his parents, who were on tour with the company of Domenico Ronzani.

Cecchetti's father tried to interest his son in law, but Enrico had set his mind on a career in ballet. His parents finally acceded to his wishes and entrusted him to the care of the ballet master Giovanni Lepri, who had been a pupil of Carlo Blasis and who had a school in Florence. While under Lepri's guidance, Cecchetti participated in performances organized by his own family and in 1866 took part in his father's *L'Eroina della Siberia* at the Teatro Pagliano in Florence, partnering his sister Pia.

On 31 December 1870, Cecchetti appeared at the Teatro alla Scala in Milan as *primo ballerino* in Pasquale Borri's *La Dea del Valhalla* and was much admired for his virtuosic technique. He subsequently made a long tour abroad, dancing in Denmark, Norway, the Netherlands, Germany, and Austria before appearing in Russia in 1874. In 1878 he married dancer Giuseppina de Maria, who had also studied at Lepri's school in Florence.

As a principal dancer at La Scala from 1885 to 1887, Cecchetti participated in all the major creations of Luigi Manzotti. In the English revival of *Excelsior*, Cecchetti performed at Her Majesty's Theatre in London in 1885 with Giovannina Limido. At La Scala he performed leading roles in *Amor* in 1886 and in *Rolla* and *Narenta* in 1887.

In the summer of 1887, with Limido as *prima ballerina* and his wife, Giuseppina, as principal mime, Cecchetti founded his own company, with which he returned to Russia. At the Arcadia Theater in Saint Petersburg he presented two ballets by Manzotti—*Sieba* and a shortened version of *Excelsior* (which, being unauthorized, provoked a lawsuit by the original choreographer)—along with a work of his own, *Le Pouvoir de l'Amour* (The Power of Love). At the end of the season, Ivan Vsevolozhsky, director of the Imperial Russian Ballet, offered Cecchetti a post as principal dancer and second ballet master at the side of the great Marius Petipa.

Cecchetti's debut at the Maryinsky Theater took place in 1887, in Lev Ivanov's *The Tulip of Haarlem*. From then until 1902, Cecchetti worked regularly for the Maryinsky Theater, staging numerous revivals, including Jules Perrot's *Catarina, ou La Fille du Bandit* (1889) and a new version of Arthur Saint-Léon's *Coppélia* (1894). He also collaborated with Ivanov on dances for Nikolai Rimsky-Korsakov's opera-ballet *Mlada* (1892) and with Petipa and Ivanov on a sumptuous production of *Cinderella* (1893), featuring Pierina Legnani. In 1890, Cecchetti danced in the first complete performance of Petipa's *The Sleeping Beauty* and gave ample proof of his versatile talent, appearing both as Carabosse and as the Bluebird. From 1892 to 1902 he also taught at the Imperial Theater School. In 1888, 1891, and 1892, he was invited to the Empire Theatre in London, where he danced in choreographies by Katti Lanner.

Following difficulties with the new management of the Maryinsky Theater, Cecchetti moved to Poland in 1902, becoming ballet master at the Imperial Theater of Warsaw. In that capacity, he invited as guests such Russian artists as Vera Trefilova, Anna Pavlova, Matilda Kshessinska, and Olga Preobrajenska. The Russian Revolution of 1905 forced Cecchetti to return for a time to Italy, after which he went back to Russia, where he opened his own ballet school in Saint Petersburg. Anna Pavlova seized this opportunity to submit to the judgment of the great

CECCHETTI. Enrico Cecchetti as the evil enchanter Kastchei in the original production of *The Firebird* (1910). Aleksandr Golovin designed the scenery and collaborated with Léon Bakst on the elaborate costumes. (Photograph from the Dance Collection, New York Public Library for the Performing Arts.)

master, who agreed to be her teacher. She later wrote as an homage to him:

> When you finished your brilliant career as the first dancer of your day, you devoted your life to the difficult art of teaching others; with what proud satisfaction you can now look round, for in every part of the world nearly all who have made a name for themselves in choreography at the present time have passed through your hands.   (Quoted in Racster, 1922)

In 1910, Cecchetti joined the Ballets Russes de Serge Diaghilev as teacher and mime—a position he held until

1918, except for a short period in 1913 when he accompanied Pavlova on an American tour. For Diaghilev, Cecchetti created several memorable mime roles in ballets by Michel Fokine and Léonide Massine. A frequent observer wrote:

> How well one remembers his Grand Eunuch in *Schéhérazade* [1910] . . . a doddering old man who waddled to and fro, his plump, pendulous cheeks creased in a fatuous smile. Do you remember the rapacious joy with which he fondled the mass of jewels which was the price of his releasing the negro slaves; then his terror at the return of the Shah, the rolling eyeballs, the horrible writhings of his body as four of the eunuchs choked out his life?   (Beaumont, 1929)

And in *Petrouchka* (1911), Cecchetti was the

> half-magician, half-showman, who caused three puppets to dance to the strains of his flute. Do you recall how cruel he was to Petrouchka, and how, when Petrouchka was killed by the Moor, he dispelled the growing suspicion of the crowd that murder had been done, by reducing the prostrate figure to a thing of wood and sawdust?   (Ibid.)

Cecchetti also created memorable roles in other Fokine works, including Kastchei in *The Firebird* (1910) and the Astrologer in *Le Coq d'Or* (1914), and in three major works by Massine: he appeared as the Marquis di Luca in *Les*

Femmes de Bonne Humeur (1917), as the Shopkeeper in *La Boutique Fantasque* (1919), and as the Doctor in *Pulcinella* (1920). In these interpretations for the Ballets Russes, Cecchetti was able to harmonize the heritage of gestures and mimic conventions deriving from the Italian school with the new requirements of modern ballet.

In 1918, Cecchetti settled in London and opened his Academy of Dancing, where he taught until 1923. During his years in Russia and Poland, he had developed his own ways of teaching, and during his time in England he formalized them into a codified method. The Cecchetti method is based on a weekly plan for the gradual and systematic learning of the technique of academic dance. It provides a graduated work program based on a logical progression of technical difficulties and muscular effort, following a rigorous training schedule. Besides basic structures for practice at the *barre*, the method includes *enchaînements* and study patterns that cover every aspect of the art of dancing: formal, dynamic, rhythmic, and performative. In the course of time, the method, in the lessons of the *maestro* himself, acquired a certain ductility, becoming less rigid and providing for compositional variants based on the same models. On this example, Cecchetti's followers developed programs for beginner courses.

While in London, Cecchetti and Stanislas Idzikowski worked with the balletomane, author, and bookseller Cyril W. Beaumont on composing *A Manual of the Theory and Practice of Classical Theatrical Dancing*, which was pub-

CECCHETTI. The master teacher (right) and his wife, Giuseppina (far left), with the company of the Ballets Russes de Serge Diaghilev, Monte Carlo, c.1925. (Photograph from the Dance Collection, New York Public Library for the Performing Arts.)

lished in 1922. That same year, Beaumont, together with Margaret Craske, Friderica Derra de Moroda, Ninette de Valois, Jane Forestier, Molly Lake, and Marie Rambert, founded the Cecchetti Society. Under the leadership of Cecchetti and his wife, this organization was devoted to disseminating the Cecchetti method. In 1924 the organization was incorporated into the Imperial Society of Teachers of Dancing.

In 1925, at the age of seventy-five, Cecchetti was invited by Arturo Toscanini, then principal conductor and artistic director of the Teatro alla Scala, to direct the ballet school of the theater. Despite his age, two years later he appeared as the Charlatan in a production of *Petrouchka* choreographed by Giovanni Pratesi. Also in 1927 Cecchetti choreographed "The Dance of the Hours" in Amilcare Ponchielli's opera *La Gioconda*, with, as *prima ballerina*, his pupil Cia Fornaroli, to whom before his death in 1928 he left the direction of La Scala's school.

Many among the dancers who studied with Cecchetti transmitted in their turn his teaching to their pupils. The influence of Cecchetti was particularly evident in the training of dancers in England, also on the choreographies by de Valois, Rambert, Frederick Ashton, and Antony Tudor. In France the master's legacy was handed down by Olga Preobrajenska and Matilda Kshessinska; Preobrajenska in Russia had also taught Agrippina Vaganova, who would include in her method several of Cecchetti's principles. George Balanchine and Adolph Bolm trained with Cecchetti when they were dancers with the Ballets Russes, and both later transmitted his influence in the United States, where also Luigi Albertieri and Cia Fornaroli formed many pupils.

Manuals of the Cecchetti method have been translated into Italian and published in Italy only recently (Pappacena, 1984; Hamlyn Bencini, 1989). Also recently discovered and published was a manuscript written between 1946 and 1956 by Enrico's son Grazioso (1892–1965), who was trained by his parents and who taught in Turin. Grazioso's two-volume handbook (G. Cecchetti, 1995, 1997), which includes musical examples and original drawings, together with Enrico's writings (E. Cecchetti, 1997) represent a direct testimony of Cecchetti's method and offer at the same time a precious insight about the "Italian school." In 1939 the Cecchetti Council of America was established to train teachers in the master's method.

[*See also* Ballet Technique, *article on* Major Schools, *and entries on the principal figures, works, and companies mentioned herein.*]

BIBLIOGRAPHY

Bailey, Sally, ed. "Letters from the Maestro: Enrico Cecchetti to Gisella Caccialanza." Translated by Gisella Caccialanza. *Dance Perspectives*, no. 45 (Spring 1971).

Beaumont, Cyril W., and Stanislas Idzikowski. *A Manual of the Theory and Practice of Classical Theatrical Dancing: Cecchetti Method* (1922). Rev. ed. London, 1940. Reprint, New York, 1975.

Beaumont, Cyril W. *Enrico Cecchetti: A Memoir*. London, 1929.

Beaumont, Cyril W. "Cecchetti's Legacy to the Dance." *Ballet Annual* 2 (1948): 59–70.

Brillarelli, Livia. *I Cecchetti: Una dinastia di ballerini*. Civitanova Marche, 1992. Translated into English as *Cecchetti: A Ballet Dynasty* (Toronto, 1995).

Cecchetti, Enrico. *Inediti teorico-tecnici*. Monographic issue of *Chorégraphie: Studi e ricerche sulla danza*. Rome, 1997.

Cecchetti, Grazioso. *Manuale completo di danza classica: Metodo Enrico Cecchetti*. 2 vols. Edited by Flavia Pappacena. Rome, 1995, 1997.

Celli, Vincenzo. "Enrico Cecchetti." *Dance Index* 7 (July 1946): 159–179.

Craske, Margaret, and Cyril W. Beaumont. *The Theory and Practice of Allegro in Classical Ballet: Cecchetti Method*. London, 1930.

Craske, Margaret, and Friderica Derra de Moroda. *The Theory and Practice of Advanced Allegro in Classical Ballet: Cecchetti Method*. London, 1956.

Foresi, Andrea, ed. *Enrico Cecchetti, maestro di danza nel mondo*. Proceedings of an international congress, Civitanova Marche, 4–5 December 1992. Civitanova Marche, 1993.

Garafola, Lynn. *Diaghilev's Ballets Russes*. New York and Oxford, 1989.

Glasstone, Richard. "Ashton, Cecchetti, and the English School." *Dance Theatre Journal* 2.3 (Autumn 1984): 13–14.

Gregory, John. *The Legat Saga*. 2d ed. London, 1993.

Greskovic, Robert. "Ballet, Barre and Center, on the Bookshelf." *Ballet Review* 6.2 (1977–1978): 1–56.

Guest, Ivor. *Ballet in Leicester Square*. London, 1992.

Hamlyn Bencini, Brenda, ed. *Theoria e pratica della danza classica: Metodo Enrico Cecchetti*, vol. 2, *Allegro*. Translated from English by Francesca Falcone. Rome, 1989.

Karsavina, Tamara. *Theatre Street: The Reminiscences of Tamara Karsavina* (1930). Rev. and enl. ed. London, 1948.

Krasovskaya, Vera. *Russkii baletnyi teatr vtoroi poloviny deviatnadtsatogo veka*. Leningrad, 1963.

Moore, Lillian. "Enrico Cecchetti." In Moore's *Artists of the Dance*. New York, 1938.

Moore, Lillian. "Enrico Cecchetti" (parts 1–2). *Dance Magazine* (September–October 1953).

Page, Ruth. "Classwork: Enrico Cecchetti." In Page's *Class: Notes on Dance Classes around the World, 1915–1980*. Princeton, N.J., 1984.

Pappacena, Flavia, ed. *Teoria e pratica della danza classica: Metodo di Enrico Cecchetti*. Translated from English by Luciano Jorio. Rome, 1984.

Poesio, Giannandrea. "Maestro's Early Years." *The Dancing Times* (September 1992): 1125–1127.

Poesio, Giannandrea. "Enrico Cecchetti: The Influence of Tradition." In *Dance History: An Introduction*, 2d ed., rev., edited by Janet Adshead-Lansdale and June Layson, pp. 117–131. London, 1994.

Racster, Olga. *The Master of the Russian Ballet: The Memoirs of Cav. Enrico Cecchetti*. London, 1922. Reprint, New York, 1978.

Rossi, Luigi. *Enrico Cecchetti, il maestro dei maestri*. Vercelli, 1978.

Rozanova, Olga. "Enriko Chekketi i russkii balet." In *Permskii ezhegodnik – 95: Khoreographiia*. Perm, 1995.

Van Schoor, Diane. "The Living Tradition." *Ballet International / Tanz Aktuell* 4 (April 1995): 50–52.

Veroli, Patrizia. "Un grade maestro ritorna alla Scala: Lettere inedite di Enrico Cecchetti a Cia Fornaroli." *La danza italiana*, n.s. 1 (1996).

Willoughby, Athol. "Master of Method." *Dance Australia* (December 1994–January 1995): 34–47.

Winslow, Liz. "Cecchetti and His Method." *Dance Teacher Now* 17 (October 1995): 38–45.

ARCHIVE.   Cecchetti's "Manuel des exercises de danse théâtrale" (Saint Petersburg, 1894) is held in the Dance Collection, New York Public Library for the Performing Arts. The text of this manual is given in Cecchetti's *Inediti teorico-tecnici* (Rome, 1997).

CLAUDIA CELI
Translated from Italian

CELEBES ISLANDS. *See* Indonesia, *article on* Dance Traditions of the Outlying Islands.

CÉLESTE, MADAME (Anastasie Céleste des Rousselles; born 6 August 1810 in Marcilly-la-Campagne, France, died 18 February 1882 in Paris), French dancer, actress, and theater manager. Although Céleste, known as Mademoiselle or Madame Céleste, continued to dance until almost the end of her long career, her great popularity rested mainly on her eloquent performances in melodrama, in which she was particularly noted for her command of gesture.

While studying at the Académie de Musique, Paris, Céleste performed children's roles at the Opera; by adolescence she was either in the corps de ballet or a *figurante* there. On 27 June 1827 she made her American debut, dancing at the Bowery Theater, New York, in a *pas seul* from *Les Pages du Duc de Vendôme*, and within three months she had appeared in a pas de trois in Boston with the established performers Francisque Hutin and Joseph Barbiere. In 1828 she married Baltimore businessman Henry Elliott but left him before his death in 1842.

During the early 1830s in Europe, Céleste first attempted several works that ultimately would be important to her career, including, in 1830, Daniel-François Auber's opera *Masaniello, or The Dumb Girl of Portici* (which attracted Anna Pavlova and Marie Taglioni—a personal friend of Céleste—as well) and, in 1833, his *opéra-ballet Le Dieu et la Bayadère*; the role of Zoloë, the dancing *bayadère*, was her favorite. In 1831, she first appeared in her most successful vehicle, *The French Spy*, which became one of the best-known melodramas of the nineteenth century. Céleste's roles, without dialogue, were those of a refined French lady, a dashing cadet of the Lancers (the spy of the title), and an Arab boy, whose "wild dance" was always considered a highlight and was heavily advertised. Her predilection for trouser parts and for playing several characters, some of exotic background and all mute, also found expression in the melodramas *The Dumb Brigand, The Spirit Bridge,* and *The Green Bushes,* among others.

From 1834 to 1837 Céleste again toured America; her excerpts from *Le Dieu et la Bayadère* in 1834 and *La Sylphide* in 1835 in New York may well have been American premieres of these well-known works. In 1836 she was presented to President Andrew Jackson in Washington, D.C., an incident recorded in a satirical lithograph entitled *The Celeste-al Cabinet*. Ecstatic reviews praised her vivacity, muscular attack, and speed in various roles. Indeed, in America her popularity was surpassed only by that of Fanny Elssler—whose fees she rivaled as well. Noah M. Ludlow, actor, author, and energetic frontier town manager, wrote that she was "the most gifted lady, in her peculiar line of stage performances, that to this day has been in these United States" (Ludlow, 1880).

Returning to Europe, Céleste commissioned several pieces for herself, including James Robinson Planché's *Child of the Wreck* and the most famous spectacle of her later years, *The Green Bushes, or A Hundred Years Ago,* in which she played a French noblewoman and a Mississippi Indian princess. Here, in the judgment of a London critic,

> her touching devotion to her husband, her doubts of his fidelity towards her, her remorse and mental agony after his murder, and the final breaking of her crushed heart and flight of her wounded spirit even while fondling the child of her faithless husband, are painfully true to nature.

Of another melodrama in which she achieved great success, Walt Whitman wrote, "I remember well the Frenchwoman Celeste, a splendid pantomimist, and her emotional *Wept of Wish-ton-Wish.*"

Céleste performed a great variety of national dances, including the *cachucha* of Andalusia (made famous by Elssler), the tarantella, and the *cracovienne*; her 1837 performance of the "Danse Normande" from the melodrama *Saint Mary's Eve,* in which she was often pictured, was particularly celebrated. She also danced the lead in Charles Selby's 1847 "new burlesque version" of *Giselle,* called *The Phantom Dancers,* and, in 1856, the title role, *en travesti,* in *Harlequin à la Watteau.* Her farewell tour of America took place in 1865–1866; she retired in 1874 after her final London performance of *The Green Bushes.*

Céleste became a theater manager in 1843 at the Theatre Royal, Liverpool, with the English dancer Benjamin Webster and soon moved with him to the Adelphi in London, where they remained for fourteen years. She then managed the Lyceum in London until 1863.

Although clearly a commanding stage presence, Celeste may have had spotty technique: despite advertising "her wonderful treble pirouette of thirty revolutions" and being described as pirouetting in "the true French style," she was refused employment at the Paris Opera in 1837 on the grounds that she had been "found wanting." Pictorial evidence does not make it certain that she danced on pointe.

In her tireless pursuit of a career, Céleste traveled to many parts of North America (including sparsely settled areas in the United States and Canada), to Europe, and even to Australia.

BIBLIOGRAPHY

Chaffee, George. "A Chart to the American Souvenir Lithographs of the Romantic Ballet, 1825–1870." *Dance Index* 1 (February 1942): 20–35.

Chaffee, George. "The Romantic Ballet in London, 1821–1858." *Dance Index* 2 (September–December 1943): 120–199.

Durang, Charles. *History of the Philadelphia Stage between the Years 1749 and 1855.* 7 vols. Philadelphia, 1868.

Kendall, John Smith. *The Golden Age of the New Orleans Theater.* Baton Rouge, 1932.

Ludlow, Noah M. *Dramatic Life as I Found It* (1880). Reprint, New York, 1966.

"Madame Celeste." *The Players* (1 June and 8 June 1861).

Moore, Lillian. "Prints on Pushcarts: The Dance Lithographs of Currier and Ives." *Dance Perspectives*, no. 15 (1962).

Odell, George C. D. *Annals of the New York Stage.* 15 vols. New York, 1927–1949.

Swift, Mary Grace. *Belles and Beaux on Their Toes: Dancing Stars in Young America.* Washington, D.C., 1980.

NANCY REYNOLDS

CENTRAL AND EAST AFRICA. The Manyanani Dancers from Nyanga, a port town in Gabon, perform a variety of traditional dances, including the gumboot dance seen here. Zulus in South Africa developed *isicathulo* ("boot dance") on the docks of Durban by exploiting the percussive possibilities of large rubber Wellington boots. (Photograph by Doug Pithey; used by permission of the Cape Newspaper Picture Service.)

CENDRILLON. *See* Cinderella.

CENTRAL AND EAST AFRICA. It is not easy to delineate precise boundaries for the dance cultures of Central and East Africa, because the political boundaries reflect the European colonial partition of Africa, not its sociocultural realities. Many peoples have territories that straddle political boundaries. For example, the Kongo people live in Angola and Congo (formerly Zaïre), and Congo Republic; the Lunda and Chokwe in Angola, Zambia, and Congo; the Zande, in Congo and Sudan; and the Yao in Tanzania, Malawi, and Mozambique.

Central and East Africa stretches roughly from the South Atlantic in the west to the Indian Ocean in the east; from the Central African Republic in the north to Angola and Zambia in the south. The countries in this region are Gabon, Congo, the Central African Republic, the southern part of Sudan, Ethiopia, Congo Republic, Rwanda, Burundi, Uganda, Kenya, Tanzania, Angola, and Zambia.

Although Central and East African dance literature is abundant, little has been written by trained observers of movement, and little has been free of ethnocentrism. The sheer size of the area under investigation and the inadequacy of documentation make it difficult to do justice to the richness and variety of the indigenous choreographic traditions. Dance styles and genres vary both regionally and ethnically. Nevertheless, some generalizations can be made. Similarities are found among many dance traditions in the easternmost region of southern Sudan, Uganda, Rwanda, Burundi, Kenya, and Tanzania. The most striking feature is the use of high leaps, usually with the feet together, the hands held down against the body, and the torso held straight, as if the dancer were standing to attention in midair, sometimes reaching astonishing heights. Such leaps are performed, for example, among the Gikuyu (Kikuyu) of Kenya, the Tutsi (Watutsi) of Rwanda, the Acholi, Masaba (Bagesu and Basabei), and the Nyankole (Ankole) of Uganda, and the Zande of Sudan and Congo. Some dancers vary the leap: the Dilu of Sudan whirl their arms backward like a windmill; the Kare (Toposa) and Lu'dayati of Sudan, jump with their feet well apart. The Lango of Uganda fling their legs sideways while leaping, or turn around before landing. The Elgeyo of Kenya use sticks to boost themselves. These leaps are usually reserved for male dancing, but the women of the Elmolo of Kenya and the Lotuko (Otuho) of Sudan also perform them.

Among the pastoralists of the region—such as the Nuer, Shilluk, and Dinka of Sudan, the Turkana of Kenya, and the Karamojong of Uganda—the dances show a deep sense of involvement with the cattle herds. In some Dinka dances, the arms are held up and wide apart, imitating the shape of cattle horns; the Karamojong leap and frisk in imitation of young cattle, shaking their heads or staring like bulls.

Similarities can also be seen among the competition dances found from the eastern coast of Kenya down to Tanzania, Malawi, and Zambia. Most villages traditionally had a number of dance associations, which also served for socializing. Usually, they also had a strong interest in mutual aid. Each club had its own name, and male and female teams were separate. Any person was free to join, but in practice the main body of dancers consisted of young people.

Since the mid-twentieth century most dance associations in East Africa have been structured along quasi-military lines. They are based on a continuing tradition of communal competitions expressed through dance, processions, and mock combat. The performances are taken seriously, and the dancing teams and bands practice frequently to improve their technique. Well-organized systems of musical and dance contests usually take place on weekends. Two rival societies, villages, football teams, or sections of towns may compete. The dancing and participation are emphasized more than the results of the competition; little fuss is made over winning teams. The dancers usually wear some sort of military uniform. The dance consists of two major sections, a procession and the dance proper. The latter consists of a number of drill-like dance steps performed either in circular formation or in lines, with occasional pantomimes and acrobatics. The attentive onlookers study the dancers and praise or criticize their dancing, singing, and the quality of the accompanying band.

The dance style of the Central African peoples formerly known as "Pygmies" is very different from the styles of neighboring peoples. These small-statured peoples are hunters and gathers of several distinct ethnolinguistic groups, among them the Baka (Aka), Mbuti, and Efe, all of whom inhabit the equatorial forests of central Africa in Cameroon, the Central African Republic, Gabon, Congo Republic, and Congo. Throughout the area they are perceived by their neighbors as expert musicians and dancers; often, however, they adopt the choreographic and musical styles of their neighbors. Those who live close to Bantu villages use drums, while the forest-dwellers tend to accompany their dancing with singing and with hand- or stick-clapping. Near the villages they often dance in a circle of men and women, who turn toward one another as couples to make approaches that are accepted or rejected. In the forest, the circles tend to be segregated, with men and women dancing separately, but there are some solo dances for each.

The style of dancing is very soft, composed of shuffles, twists, and turns, with the arms held loosely along the body, hands on the head or at the waist. The dance style

CENTRAL AND EAST AFRICA. Young Banda women perform *gaza*, a group female initiation rite, in the Central African Republic. (Photograph by Michel Huet; used by permission.)

contains both introverted and extroverted elements, and surprise effects are important in the choreography; for example, a solo dancer who is stepping toward the audience may abruptly move away, or the music may suddenly stop and the dancers stand quite still, staring up at the sky with their heads and necks trembling. Dances are very short and rarely last more than two or three minutes, starting again after a break of indefinite length. Animals are common themes of the dances, which are often intended to bring success in the hunt.

Like East Africa, southern Central Africa displays some similar dance traditions. Throughout Zambia and into Angola, Congo, Congo Republic, Burundi, and Uganda, kings once had royal song-dance bands, which accompanied and represented them. Because the dancers in these bands were symbols of power and prestige, their dances were great spectacles, involving many dancers—sometimes hundreds—all young and fit, often carrying shields and spears, performing in unison, leaping into the air as one, and beating their shields.

Throughout Zambia and Angola, the dances of the *makishi* masks were performed by solo dancers. These masks were used among the Mbunda-Lubala and related Bantu peoples, primarily during the circumcision ceremonies of boys but also in some areas at social occasions, when they were sponsored by wealthy patrons. For the boys' initiation, dancers patrolled the vicinity of the ceremonial lodge to ward off intruders, walked the roads, and danced at doorsteps for gifts of cash. They appeared at organized dances held between the time the initiates' wounds healed and their return home. The great moments came approximately one week before the emergence of the youths from confinement, when ancestors and nature spirits were called up, and also on the day before the youths emerged, when a ritual of presentation and final dedication was held. Many *makishi* masks were then present, representing typical characters, not heroes or gods. The masks were presented to the initiates and used as teaching devices to explain to the youths the significance of the ancestors' institutions. Each category of mask had its own dancing style, performed to fast drum rhythms and songs. The female masks danced with shoulder movements, like Mbunda women, while most of the male *makishi* danced with hip movements. The dances were enjoyed by non-initiates as entertainment, and women were also allowed to join in the dance.

In most of Africa, the Western distinction between music and dance is irrelevant; both are seen as parts of a single phenomenon. The structures of choreography and music mirror each other and are inseparable. The dancers often provide part or all of their own musical accompaniment so that there is great congruence between the motional patterns of the music and the dance. According to Gerhard Kubik (1979), "Frequently such patterns are named, for instance by means of syllabic or verbal formula, which are used as a means of communication between teachers and pupils in dance instruction."

Dance in Africa was completely integrated into social life and associated with the most important events and life crises—birth and mourning rituals, weddings, the installation of rulers, work, and recreation. The contexts in which dance is used most vary from one society to another. Dance is always an integral part of boys' and girls' initiation ceremonies. These may include some physical modification, such as circumcision or scarification. Generally, ceremonies consist of three distinct sections: the separation, when the youths are taken away from their families; a period of seclusion, in which they learn about their new roles and status; and some sort of coming-out ceremony, in which they are reintegrated into society with new status.

CENTRAL AND EAST AFRICA. Mangbetu women dance in a horseshoe formation in the Belgian Congo (present-day Congo), 1910. This particular dance was characterized by small advancing steps and half-turns done in place. (Photograph by Herbert Lang; from the Department of Library Services, American Museum of Natural History, New York [no. 224588]; used by permission.)

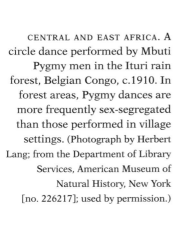

CENTRAL AND EAST AFRICA. A circle dance performed by Mbuti Pygmy men in the Ituri rain forest, Belgian Congo, c.1910. In forest areas, Pygmy dances are more frequently sex-segregated than those performed in village settings. (Photograph by Herbert Lang; from the Department of Library Services, American Museum of Natural History, New York [no. 226217]; used by permission.)

The initiation dances are performed at different stages in different societies. Among the Kamba of Kenya, as soon as parents announce that their son is ready for circumcision, the youths of the village publicize the event with songs and dances, moving from house to house and gathering dancers until they arrive at the boy's home.

The actual learning of dances may be one of the major aspects of initiation. Among the Chokwe of Angola, Zambia, and Congo, virtuoso dancers and drummers are assigned the task of teaching the esoteric songs and dances of circumcision to the male or female initiates. Among the Lunda of Zambia, female novices spend much of their seclusion period learning and perfecting many dance steps, preparing themselves to dance before several hundred people at the coming-out ritual. Among the Kaonde of Zambia, in the *chisungu* initiation ceremony, the initiates dance to show off their beauty and decorations, to greet their husbands-to-be, and to collect presents. Dance is often used to show the strength of the initiates, as among the Yao of southern Tanzania, where the boys perform exhausting dances as a test of physical stamina. At the end of the seclusion period, the initiates often prove through the energy they display in dance that they have passed their ordeal and that initiation has given them strength, as among the Gbaya, Banda, and Ngbaka of the Central African Republic.

Throughout Central and East Africa the most common dance formations are symmetrical lines, circles, and horseshoe patterns. The formation of two lines facing each other, men on one side and women on the other, is found almost everywhere in the region. There are many types of circles: a single circle of dancers of one sex, who either remain stationary or move counterclockwise; a single circle of dancers of both sexes, each sex making up half of the circle; two concentric circles that move in opposite directions, usually with the women in the inner circle and the men in the outer; a circle of couples; or a circle several dancers deep.

Most of these dances feature a solo section. Soloists perform in the middle of the circle or horseshoe; couples perform between the lines, either moving toward one another and returning to their places, or moving up and down between the lines. It is usually considered acceptable to try to take center stage and call attention to the excellence of one's own performance, each dancer trying to outdo the others. The circle formations tend to involve the whole community, while the two-line formation tends to be used by the unmarried age groups, especially children and young people, as a means of allowing them to meet one another. Among the Samburu of Kenya, for example, young unmarried men and women are permitted almost no other type of communication, and casual familiarity between the sexes seems to occur only during or after a dance.

Throughout the region, extreme suppleness of the whole body, especially of the hips, abdomen, and shoul-

CENTRAL AND EAST AFRICA. Chosen for their exceptional height, these Watusi dancers were part of an elite group of professionals who performed at the Burundi court before the monarchy was abolished in 1966. Their costumes were fashioned from leopard skins; the headdresses from colobus monkey fur. (Photograph from a private collection.)

trifugal motion and leaping, and kicking. A performance of King Munza of northern Congo, was described thus by a European observer:

> His dancing was furious. His arms dashed themselves in every direction though always making the time of the music, whilst his legs exhibited all the contorsions of an acrobat's, being at one moment stretched out horizontally to the ground and the next upwards and elevated in the air.   (Thompson, 1947, p. 38)

In communal dancing, the energy level tends to remain fairly constant, with sporadic bursts especially at the end of the performance. In contrast, dances that involve solo or small-group exhibitionistic dancing change in intensity with each soloist or group working up to a climax, then returning to the basic level before surrendering the dance floor to the next performer. When men and women dance together, they may be spatially separated, as in the circles mentioned above, or fairly close, as in the line dances where lines can be as close as one arm's length away, or as much as thirty to forty feet (10 to 13 meters) apart. In some dances men and women embrace, holding each other by the waist and shoulders. Generally speaking, in traveling the central region from west to east and coming closer to the Indian Ocean, more dances of mixed gender are encountered and there is closer bodily contact between partners.

ders, is displayed in many dances. The feet are usually kept apart to lend more flexibility to the hips. All the joints are loose and the knees always flexed, allowing the dancers to perform wavelike movements. Body parts are often used in isolation, either throughout the repertory or more often as a stylistic characteristic of a specific dance. Ethiopian dances emphasize shaking the shoulders and upper body; shoulders are featured among the Kongo of Congo, hips among the Lugbara of Uganda, and breasts and hips among the Acholi of Uganda; the Nyoro women of Uganda move the hips while keeping the torso still.

Often the distinctive feature of a particular dance is communicated by the aid of costumes and props. Among the Lozi of Zambia, dancers in some dances wear high-rising furred shoulder bands to emphasize the twitching of their shoulders; among the Kaondé of Zambia, women wrap bundles of cloth tightly around their hips to emphasize their rapid vibrations. Young Ngombe girls of Congo balance a hoop lightly on the hips to exaggerate their supple movements of hips and abdomen. Royal Tutsi dancers in Rwanda wear headdresses made of colobus monkey fur or of banana fibers, in imitation of a lion's mane, to emphasize head movements.

Many dance styles of the region feature explosive, enlarged body movements, flinging limbs up and out, cen-

CENTRAL AND EAST AFRICA. A young Okiek couple in a jumping dance at a ceremonial gathering in the Narok District, Kenya. This dance is simply referred to as *ketwaal*, the Okiek verb meaning "to jump." (Photograph © 1974 by Corinne A. Kratz; used by permission.)

CENTRAL AND EAST AFRICA. A line of male dancers from the Tanzanian state-sponsored KIUBATA (Tanga Port Authority Cultural Troupe). Presented as part of a Mei Mosi (May Day celebration), this performance of a Makonde initiation dance called *mbuji* was accompanied by a song with newly composed Swahili lyrics praising the government. (Photograph © 1993 by Kelly M. Askew; used by permission.)

Dances are usually accompanied by singing with a solo and chorus; the lead singer is often the lead dancer as well. The majority of the dancers provide the chorus and are supported by a number of musical instruments, although dances unaccompanied by instruments can also be found. Drums are used, but they do not have as dominant a role as in West Africa. Rhythmic accompaniment is often provided by other instruments, such as xylophones, rattles, or lamellaphones.

Masks, worn primarily by men, are used throughout the region, especially in Central Africa south into Angola and Zambia and southeast into southern Tanzania and Mozambique. They appear in a number of contexts. Among the Phende of Congo they were used during fertility rituals, and among the Lunda during mortuary rituals. Most often, they were employed in initiation ceremonies, such as the *makishi* masks mentioned above. Masks serve the dual functions of transfiguration and heightened realism. They often symbolize ancestors, spirits, or deities. Usually the dancer who dons a mask is viewed as becoming a supernatural being. There is a great variety in masks. Some are made of wood and are very elaborate and sculptural; these are found especially in western Central Africa (Gabon and Congo) and are related to the masks of West Africa. Other masks, made of sisal or other fibers, may extend to cover the body. The evil-spirit mask found among the Yao, Makua, and Makonde peoples of southern Tanzania and Mozambique is made of a series of many bamboo coils covered with rags and linked in such a way that they can be made to expand and contract when manipulated by the dancer; the structure looks like a huge caterpillar struggling to climb into the air on a windy day. In East Africa masks become less common and give way to elaborate facial and body makeup, often masklike in character, as among the Turu of Tanzania.

Animal mime dances are popular throughout Central and East Africa. The animals may be represented by a whole group of dancers, as among the Turkana of Kenya, where a double column moves along a zig-zag course, and the dancers sway their bodies to suggest the neck movements of the giraffe. Dances about elephants have the dancers stamping their feet, waving their heads, and swaying an outstretched arm to imitate the trunk; in those about crocodiles, dancers jump as if into water and bend their bodies, opening their mouths wide to snatch at fish; and in those about baboons, dancers scratch themselves and imitate these monkeys in eating and nursing. Other dances imitate birds such as the crane, sparrowhawk, or vulture. Animal dances may be simply mimetic, in that the dancers imitate an animal objectively, by observing its behavior and reproducing it; in other cases, the dancers imitate animals subjectively, "becoming" the animals and assuming their point of view.

Another regional genre comprises curative songs and dances. These therapy rituals vary, but because the primary purpose of the dance is to achieve an altered state of consciousness (such as a trance) to help solve the problem at hand, with enjoyment by the audience secondary, there are many constant elements. This is usually a solo dance, although several dancers may perform idiosyncratic movements simultaneously. Muscular trembling, shaking, and apparent convulsions are typical of these therapeutic dances, in which people surrender to a kind of abstract ecstasy or hypnotic state. Usually the dances begin slowly and then gather momentum, often becoming quite violent as performers work themselves into a frenzy. Among the Zande of Sudan, the curative dances involved leaping and whirling with remarkable agility and force; they were spirited and violent, while other Zande dances were slow, calm, and restrained.

Despite these observations, caution must be exercised in generalizing about the dance of Central and East Africa. Until more ethnochoreologists (researchers of traditional dance) do extensive fieldwork in this region and provide detailed information about specific dance traditions, where they still exist, our knowledge will remain superficial.

[*See also* Cameroon; Digo Dance; Ethiopia; Giriama Dance; Mbuti Dance; Nuba Dance; Pokot Dance; *and* Samburu Dance. *For general discussion, see* Sub-Saharan Africa.]

BIBLIOGRAPHY

Anley, V. R. "Some Dances (Ancient and Modern) of the Bakonde Tribe of Northern Rhodesia." *NADA* (Salisbury) 4 (1926): 83–85.

Baker, Richard St. Barbe. "Dancing on the Equator." *The Dancing Times* (February 1924): 482–485.

Ballif, Noël. *Dancers of God.* Translated by James Cameron. London, 1955.

Bantje, Han. *Kaonde Song and Ritual.* Tervuren, 1978.

Bebey, Francis. *Musique de l'Afrique.* Paris, 1969.

Bere, R. M. "Acholi Dances (Myel)." *Uganda Journal* 1 (1934): 64–65.

Bourgeois, René. *Banyarwanda et Burundi: Religion et magie.* Brussels, 1956.

Bourgeois, René. *Banyarwanda et Burundi: Ethnographie.* Brussels, 1957.

Bouveigne, O. de. "La musique indigène au Congo Belge." In *Les arts au Congo Belge et au Ruanda-Urundi.* Brussels, 1950.

Brandel, Rose. *The Music of Central Africa.* The Hague, 1961.

Brelsford, W. V. *African Dances of Northern Rhodesia.* Livingstone, 1948.

Cagnolo, Costanzo. *The Akikuyu: Their Customs, Traditions, and Folklore.* Nyeri, 1933.

Clark, D. "Memorial Service for an Ox in Karamoja." *Uganda Journal* 16.1 (1952): 69–71.

Comhaire-Sylvain, Jean. "Les danses Nkundu du territoire d'Oshwe au Congo Belge." *African Studies* 6.3 (1947): 124–130.

Driberg, J. H. *The Lango: A Nilotic Tribe of Uganda.* London, 1923.

Edel, May. *The Chiga of Western Uganda.* New York, 1957.

Evans-Pritchard, E. E. "The Dance." *Africa* 1.4 (1928): 446–462.

Evans-Pritchard, E. E. "The Zande Corporations of Witchdoctors." *Journal of the Royal Anthropological Institute* 62 (1932): 291–336.

Fourche, J. A. Tiarko. "La danse de Tshishimbi chez les Lulua du Kasai." *Institut Royal Colonial* 8 (1937): 395–429.

Gluckman, Max. "Notes on the Social Background of Barotse Music." In *African Music in Northern Rhodesia and Some Other Places,* edited by A. M. Jones. Livingstone, 1949.

Grau, Andrée. *Ugandan Dances.* London, 1976.

Gulliver, P. H. "Dancing Clubs of the Nyasa." *Tanganyika Notes and Records,* no. 41 (1955): 58–59.

Haller, S., and Manfred Kremser. "Danse et théâtre thérapeutique chez les Azande." *Bulletin of the International Committee on Urgent Anthropological and Ethnological Research* 17 (1975): 65–78.

Hambly, Wilfrid D. *Tribal Dancing and Social Development.* London, 1926.

Hanna, Judith Lynne, and William John Hanna. "Heart Beat of Uganda." *African Arts* 1.3 (1968): 42–43.

Hillaby, John D. *Journey to the Jade Sea.* London, 1964.

Hobley, C. W. *Bantu Beliefs and Magic.* London, 1922.

Huet, Michel. *The Dance, Art, and Ritual of Africa.* New York, 1978.

Iyandza-Lopoloko, Joseph. *Bobongo danse renommée des Ekonda.* Tervuren, 1961.

Johnson, E. V. "African Harvest Dance." *Tanganyika Notes and Records,* no. 37 (1954): 138–142.

Jones, A. M. "African Music: The Mganda Dance." *African Studies* 4 (1945): 180–188.

Jones, A. M. *The Icila Dance Old Style.* Roodeport, 1952.

Kavyu, Paul N. *An Introduction to Kamba Music.* Kampala, 1977.

Kenyatta, Jomo. *Facing Mount Kenya: The Tribal Life of the Gikuyu.* London, 1961.

Kubik, Gerhard. "Pattern Perception and Recognition in Dance Music." In *The Performing Arts: Music and Dance,* edited by John Blacking and Joann W. Kealiinohomoku. The Hague, 1979.

Martin, György. "Dance Types in Ethiopia." *Journal of the International Folk Music Council* 19 (1967): 23–27.

Massam, J. A. *The Cliff Dwellers of Kenya.* London, 1927.

Mensah, A. A. "Performing Arts in Zambia: Music and Dance." *Bulletin of the International Committee on Urgent Anthropological and Ethnological Research* 13 (1971a): 67–82.

Mensah, A. A. *Music and Dance in Zambia.* Ndola, 1971b.

Merriam, Alan P. *African Music in Perspective.* New York, 1982.

Mitchell, J. Clyde. *The Kalela Dance: Aspects of Social Relationship among Urban Africans in Northern Rhodesia.* Livingstone, 1956.

Mubitana, Kafungulwa. "Wiko Masquerades." *African Arts* 4.3 (1971): 58–62.

Njungu, A. "Music of My People: Dances in Barotseland." *African Music* 2.4 (1961): 77–80.

Nourrit, Chantal, ed. *Musique traditionnelle de l'Afrique noire: Zaire.* Paris, 1978–.

Orde-Browne, Granville St.-John. *The Vanishing Tribes of Kenya.* London, 1925.

pa'Lukobo, O. "Acholi Dance and Dance-Songs." *Ugandan Journal* 35.1 (1971): 55–61.

Philippart de Foy, Guy. *Les Pygmées d'Afrique centrale.* Roquevaire, France, 1984.

Primus, P. "Views of Dance around the World: Africa." *Dance Magazine* (March 1958): 43–49, 90–91.

Ranger, T. O. *Dance and Society in Eastern Africa, 1890–1970: The Beni Ngoma.* London, 1975.

Robbins, L. H., and Martha E. Robbins. "A Note on Turkana Dancing." *Ethnomusicology* 15.2 (1971): 231–235.

Roscoe, John. *The Bagesu.* Cambridge, 1923a.

Roscoe, John. *The Banyankole.* Cambridge, 1923b.

Sasson, Jack M. "Two African Dances." *Geographical Magazine* 25 (1952–1953): 242–247.

Schebesta, Paul. *Among Congo Pygmies.* London, 1933.

Sousberghe, Léon de. *Les danses rituelles mungonge et kela des baPende (Congo belge).* Académie Royale des Sciences Coloniales, Brussels, Classe des Sciences Morales et Politiques, vol. 9.1. Brussels, 1956.

Spencer, Paul. *The Samburu: A Study of Gerontocracy in a Nomadic Tribe.* London, 1965.

Thompson, Robert Farris. *African Art in Motion.* 2d ed. Los Angeles, 1979.

Timmermans, P. "Les Lwala." *Africa Tervuren* 13.3–4 (1967): 73–90.

Tucker, A. N. *Tribal Music and Dancing in the Southern Sudan.* London, 1931.

Turner, Victor. *Lunda Rites and Ceremonies.* Livingstone, 1953.

Turner, Victor. *The Drums of Affliction.* Oxford, 1968.

Vadasy, Tibor. "Ethiopian Folk Dance I." *Journal of Ethiopian Studies* 8.2 (1970): 119–146.

Vadasy, Tibor. "Ethiopian Folk Dance II: Tegré and Guragé." *Journal of Ethiopian Studies* 9.2 (1971): 191–218.

Vadasy, Tibor. "Ethiopian Folk Dance III: Wällo and Galla." *Journal of Ethiopian Studies* 11.1 (1973): 213–231.

Vrydagh, P. Andre. "Makisi of Zambia." *African Arts* 10.4 (1977): 12–19.

Wembah-Rashid, J. A. R. "Isinyago and Midimu: Masked Dancers of Tanzania and Mozambique." *African Arts* 4.2 (1971): 38–44.

Werner, Alice. *The Natives of British Central Africa.* London, 1906.

Wiesauer, E. "Swahili and Bajuni Traditional Dances." *Bulletin of the International Committee on Urgent Anthropological and Ethnological Research* 16 (1974): 19–21.

Wing, Joseph van. "Les danses Bakongo." *Congo: Revue Générale de la Colonie Belge* 18.2 (1937): 121–131.

Wolfe, Alvin W. *In the Ngombe Tradition: Continuity and Change in the Congo.* Evanston, Ill., 1961.

Zebila, Lucky. *Méthode Lucky Zébila: La danse africaine, ou, L'intelligence du corps.* Paris, 1982.

ANDRÉE GRAU

CERRITO, FANNY (Francesca Teresa Giuseppa Raffaela Cerrito; born 11 May 1817 in Naples, died 6 May 1909 in Paris), Italian ballerina and choreographer. Fanny Cerrito is one of the great names of the Romantic ballet, a period known for its great ballerinas. As a dancer she was famed for her technical facility, particularly in steps of elevation; her lightness and *ballon* were celebrated. Although she excelled in rapid movements, she could also move with grace in adagio, and the French critic Théophile Gautier likened her arms to "the pink draperies that flutter about the nymphs in the dark background of the frescoes of Herculaneum." She was small in stature and had a tendency toward plumpness, particularly in later life, but her feminine charm made her an ideal exponent of the bewitching heroines of *Alma* (1842) and *Ondine* (1843). Cerrito was a choreographer as well as a dancer; she made her first essay at choreography at an early age and ultimately was honored as one of the few women to create a ballet at the Paris Opera.

The daughter of an army veteran, Cerrito began dancing lessons as part of the normal education for a girl of her social class. When her talent became evident, she entered the ballet school of the Teatro Regio in Naples. She was given the rank of principal ballerina without having to work her way through the company, and she made her debut on 28 July 1832 in a pas de deux from Giovanni Galzerani's ballet *L'Oroscopo.* Her success was immediate and, in the following years, she was invited to dance in several Italian cities.

In 1836 she made her first appearance at the Kärntnertor Theater in Vienna, where she met and worked with Jules Perrot, who greatly improved her style. Her first choreographic effort, a pas de cinq, was presented on 8 April 1837 as part of Pietro Campilli's *Die Wohltaetige Fee.*

Cerrito returned to Italy in 1838 to make her debut at the Teatro alla Scala, Milan. While dancing there she took private lessons with Carlo Blasis. She did not remain there long, however, although she danced the title roles of the theater's first productions of *La Sylphide* and *Giselle,* staged in 1841 and 1843, respectively, by Antonio Cortesi. Her last appearance at La Scala was on 22 March 1843.

Much more of her career was spent in London, where she first danced in 1840 at Her Majesty's Theatre, the site of her greatest English triumphs. Although her first scheduled performance was aborted by the notorious "Tamburini row" (patrons who instigated a riot because the tenor Antonio Tamburini had not been reengaged), she was rapturously greeted on 2 May in Antonio Guerra's *Une Nuit de Bal.* In July she choreographed a pas de trois that was performed as part of a *divertissement* from Filippo Taglioni's *La Gitana.*

In Vienna in 1841 she first performed with Arthur Saint-Léon, who was to become her husband. Her first full-length ballet, *Amors Zögling,* was given on 11 December at the Kärntnertor Theater. A character pas de deux that she choreographed at the same time was later developed into *La Vivandière,* a *divertissement.*

CERRITO. An engraving by J. Bouvier showing Fanny Cerrito waving a tambourine in the *pas de fascination* from *Alma* (1842). (Dance Collection, New York Public Library for the Performing Arts.)

CERRITO. The Shadow Dance (pas de l'ombre) from Jules Perrot's Ondine, ou La Naïade (1843) was one of Cerrito's most memorable creations. Ivor Guest, Cerrito's biographer, says that "In no other pas, and in no other ballet, did Fanny's magic weave such a spell. . . . It was a spell that lingered long after the curtain had fallen, like the aftermath of a dream . . . in which there had glided and glistened in a world of moonlight, roses, and crystal" a creature combining the lovableness of a woman with the airiness of a fairy. (Lithograph by Nathaniel Currier, New York, 1846. Courtesy of Madison U. Sowell and Debra H. Sowell, Brigham Young University, Provo, Utah.)

In 1842, Cerrito collaborated with Perrot and André Deshayes on *Alma, ou La Fille de Feu*, presented at Her Majesty's Theatre on 23 May; she contributed a pas de trois, a *pas de femmes*, and a *pas espagnol d'Andalousie*. Cerrito was greatly acclaimed for her performance of the title role of Alma, a statue that comes to life. [*See* Alma.] The success of this ballet led to Perrot's engagement as ballet master of Her Majesty's, a position that he occupied until 1848. Cerrito danced leading roles in many of the ballets he created there, including *Ondine* (1843), *Pas de Quatre* (1845), *Lalla Rookh* (1846), and *Le Jugement de Pâris* (1846).

In 1843, Cerrito was to find herself pitted against the two lodestars of the Romantic ballet, Marie Taglioni and Fanny Elssler. Early in that year, she and Taglioni appeared at La Scala, sometimes on the same evening, giving rise to rival bands of *Cerritisti* and *Taglionisti*. During that summer, she danced a pas de deux with Elssler at Her Majesty's Theatre; Perrot's choreography allowed both dancers to display their special qualities, Elssler her quickness and precision in *taqueté* steps and Cerrito her *ballon* and elevation.

On 22 June 1843 Cerrito created one of her most famous roles, the love-stricken water sprite in Perrot's *Ondine*, presented at Her Majesty's Theatre. Perhaps the most memorable part of the ballet was Ondine's *pas de l'ombre* (shadow dance), in which she celebrates her acquisition of both human substance and a shadow. Images of this dance were reproduced in many prints of the period, including a political cartoon. Cerrito choreographed a pas de six in the ballet's dream scene, which she danced with Saint-Léon.

Triumphant seasons in Rome and Brussels followed in that year, with *La Vivandière*, attributed to Saint-Léon, presented in Rome in November. When it was given its first London performance in 1844, it was credited to Cerrito. This short ballet consisted of three principal dances—a *pas de la vivandière*, a pas de quatre, and a redowa, a type of polka—all linked by a slender story. Cerrito and Saint-Léon were much applauded for their lively, witty performance of the redowa, then in vogue as a ballroom dance.

On 17 April 1845 Cerrito and Saint-Léon were married in the Église des Batignolles, Paris. On 29 May the first performance of Cerrito's *Rosida, ou Les Mines de Syracuse* was presented at Her Majesty's Theatre, with the newlyweds in the leading roles. The ballet, a romantic tale of temptation and redemption, contained some felicitous dances, particularly the opening *pas sicilienne*, but was given only six performances. [*See the entry on Saint-Léon.*] On 12 July 1845 Cerrito took part in one of the most famous ballets of the Romantic period, Perrot's *Pas de Quatre*, performed at Her Majesty's Theatre. Four of the greatest ballerinas of the day—Taglioni, Cerrito, Carlotta Grisi, and Lucile Grahn—made up the cast. Cerrito danced a pas de deux with Grisi, then performed a variation filled with her celebrated leaps. All four dancers joined in the coda. [*See* Pas de Quatre.] This ballet was so enthusiastically received that Perrot repeated the formula in each of the next three years, presenting various combinations of major ballerinas in ballets with minimal narrative content and a thinly disguised flavor of competition. Cerrito danced in all of them: she was a goddess in *Le Jugement de*

Pâris (1846), Air in *Les Éléments* (1847), and Spring in *Les Quatre Saisons* (1848).

In 1847, Cerrito was given the opportunity of dancing the title role of *La Esmeralda* in Berlin. This ballet, which was considered Perrot's masterpiece, had been created in London in 1844 for Grisi. Saint-Léon, who had played the role of Phoebus in that production, was responsible for the Berlin staging. Although Cerrito was not so convincing an actress as Grisi or Elssler, who had also danced the role, she was well received by the Berlin audiences.

Cerrito realized a long-cherished ambition in the same year, when she and Saint-Léon were engaged to dance at the Paris Opera. For their debut on 20 October, Saint-Léon mounted a new version of *Alma*, retitled *La Fille de Marbre*. Although the ballet was not a success, both dancers were greeted with approval. Cerrito performed at the Paris Opera, between engagements in London and other European capitals, until 1855. Her major creations there included four of Saint-Léon's works: an expanded version of *La Vivandière* (1848), *Le Violon du Diable* (1849), *Stella* (1850), and *Pâquerette* (1851).

In 1851, the couple went to Madrid, where they danced at the Teatro Real. They decided to separate in June of that year, and in October they made their last appearance together onstage in Paris. Cerrito's official return to the Paris Opera was marked by the ballet *Orfa* on 29 December 1852, choreographed for her by Joseph Mazilier. After an engagement in Vienna, she went into temporary retirement and on 6 October 1853 gave birth to a daughter, Matilde. The child's father was a Spanish nobleman, the Marqués de Bedmar y de Escaluna, whom Cerrito had met in Madrid.

Upon her return to the Paris Opera, Cerrito began to prepare a new ballet, *Gemma*, to music by Count Niccolò Gabrielli. The scenario was by Théophile Gautier, who had previously written scenarios for *Giselle*, *La Péri*, and *Pâquerette*. A ballet produced by a woman was a rare event at the male-dominated Paris Opera; previously only Thérèse Elssler had done so with *La Volière* in 1838. Despite problems with the unruly corps de ballet and a difficult principal dancer who had to be replaced, Cerrito presented the ballet on 31 May 1854. She herself danced the title role of a young girl, Gemma, hypnotized by the wicked Marquis (danced by Louis Mérante) who hopes to marry her for her fortune. Her lover, the painter Massimo (danced by Lucien Petipa), goes mad at her loss, but Gemma restores him to sanity by removing her portrait from its frame and taking its place. Massimo and the Marquis ultimately fight a duel above a raging mountain torrent, into which the Marquis falls after receiving Massimo's fatal blow.

Cerrito unashamedly borrowed special effects from earlier ballets by fellow choreographers: for example, a leap out of the window came from Perrot's *Ondine* and the por-trait scene from his *La Délire d'un Peintre* (1843). Critics also discerned references to Saint-Léon's *La Fille de Marbre* and *Stella*. Particularly striking was a "mirror dance" for Gemma and her ladies-in-waiting; this was not a new effect, but had seldom been attempted on so large a scale.

Plans for an American tour in the following year were never realized, and Cerrito went instead to Saint Petersburg, where Perrot was working as ballet master of the Bolshoi Theater. He created a new ballet, *Armida*, for her Russian debut on 20 November 1855. The ballet, loosely based on Torquato Tasso's epic poem about the Crusades, lasted some four-and-a-half hours. Cerrito was rather coolly received in this and other ballets because of the public's preference for native Russian dancers, such as Marfa Muravieva. However, Cerrito remained in Russia until the end of the 1855/56 season, then returned in autumn 1856 at the command of Tsar Alexander II to dance in his coronation celebrations in Moscow.

Cerrito's last season as a dancer took place in 1857 at the Lyceum Theatre in London. Her final appearance on the stage was on 18 June 1857, in the minuet of Mozart's opera *Don Giovanni* (1787). She went into retirement in Paris, where she died in obscurity on 6 May 1909, only twelve days before Serge Diaghilev's Ballets Russes opened in the West, bringing new life and vigor to theatrical ballet. Her death was unremarked in the Paris press.

BIBLIOGRAPHY

Beaumont, Cyril W. *Complete Book of Ballets*. London, 1937.

Binney, Edwin, 3d. *Les ballets de Théophile Gautier*. Paris, 1965.

Celi, Claudia. "L'arivamento de la gran maravija der ballo ossia il ballo a Roma dal 1845 al 1854." *La danza italiana* 8–9 (Winter 1990): 73–107.

Gautier, Théophile. *The Romantic Ballet*. Translated and edited by Cyril W. Beaumont. Rev. ed. London, 1947.

Guest, Ivor. *The Romantic Ballet in England*. London, 1972.

Guest, Ivor. *The Ballet of the Second Empire*. London, 1974.

Guest, Ivor. *Fanny Cerrito*. 2d rev. ed. London, 1974.

Guest, Ivor. *Jules Perrot: Master of the Romantic Ballet*. London, 1984.

Moore, Lillian. "Fanny Cerrito and Arthur Saint-Léon." In Moore's *Artists of the Dance*. New York, 1938.

Murphy, Anne. "Age of Enchantment." *Ballet News* 3 (March 1982): 10–14.

Saint-Léon, Arthur. *Letters from a Ballet Master: The Correspondence of Arthur Saint-Léon*. Edited by Ivor Guest. New York, 1981.

ARCHIVE.   Walter Toscanini Collection of Research Materials in Dance, New York Public Library for the Performing Arts.

SUSAN AU

CHABUKIANI, VAKHTANG (Vakhtang Mikhailovich Chabukiani; born 27 February [12 March] 1910 in Tbilisi, Georgian Soviet Socialist Republic, died 6 April 1992 in Tbilisi), dancer, choreographer, and teacher. Chabukiani studied at Maria Perrini's ballet studio as a scholarship student from 1922 to 1924, then spent the next two years performing Georgian national dances at the Opera Theater in Tbilisi, leaving when he was sixteen to study at the Leningrad Choreographic Institute. He was placed in an evening course for "overage" but promising applicants, but he soon transferred to the regular daytime school, where he studied with Viktor Semenov, Vladimir Ponomarev, and Aleksandr Shiriaev. Remarkably talented, he covered the entire syllabus of academic and professional education in just three years. He made his debut in the ballet company of the State Academic Theater of Opera and Ballet (later renamed Kirov) in 1929, performing in two concert pieces of his own creation, *Fire Dance* and *The Overthrow of Slavery*. Between 1931 and 1941 Chabukiani was a leading soloist of the Kirov Ballet, during which time he and his Leningrad and Moscow colleagues, including Aleksei Yermolayev and Asaf Messerer, moved to inject new spirit and vigor into the major roles of the classical repertory. Chabukiani, who possessed a solid technique and a riveting personality, established a new heroic style of male dancing. His numerous additions and changes to the choreography of the princes in *Swan*

CHABUKIANI. A portrait of Vakhtang Chabukiani, a dancer admired for his athletic technique and heroic presence. (Photograph from the Dance Collection, New York Public Library for the Performing Arts.)

Lake and *The Sleeping Beauty*, Basil in *Don Quixote*, Solor in *La Bayadère*, and the Slave in the pas de deux from *Le Corsaire* entered the standard ballet repertory, leading the Japanese dancer and choreographer Hideteru Kitahara to remark in 1982 that, without realizing it, many dancers around the world dance like Chabukiani.

Chabukiani created leading roles in a number of landmark Soviet ballets: the Sportsman in Vasily Vainonen's *The Golden Age* (1930) and Jérome in his *The Flames of Paris* (1932); Vatslav in Rostislav Zakharov's *The Fountain of Bakhchisarai* (1934) and the Premier Danseur in his *Lost Illusions* (1936); Kerim in Vainonen's *Partisan Days* (1937). It was his own ballet productions, however, that allowed Chabukiani to give free rein to his imagination. His first important work, *Heart of the Hills*, presented in his native Tbilisi as *Mzechabuki* in 1937 and restaged at the Kirov in 1938, was a blend of classical ballet and Georgian folk dance steps set to music by Andrei Balanchivadze. *Laurencia* (1939), to music by Aleksandr Krein and based on Lope de Vega's *Fuente Ovejuna*, concerned a peasant uprising in Castile. In it Chabukiani created sharply defined characters whose emotions and thoughts were vividly expressed through dance. In another departure from tradition, he placed the corps de ballet on a par with the soloists by weaving it into the dramatic fabric of the action; it did not function simply as a *divertissement*. [*See* Laurencia.]

Soon after the establishment of diplomatic relations between the United States and the Soviet Union in 1934, Chabukiani and Tatiana Vecheslova became the first Soviet dancers to tour the United States. During some thirty performances Chabukiani dazzled audiences with his soaring elevation, lightning-quick turns, and athletic energy. When the Soviet Union entered World War II in 1941, Chabukiani returned to Tbilisi, where he became principal dancer, chief choreographer, and teacher at the Paliashvili Theater of Opera and Ballet. Starting with a small nucleus of administrators, dancers, and students, he formed a polished, highly trained ballet troupe. Drawing first on the classical repertory and eventually on a predominantly national one, the company ultimately developed its own style and creative identity. Chabukiani expanded the ballet studio at the Paliashvili Theater into a full-scale ballet school, which he headed until 1973; he also worked as a teacher and ballet adviser throughout the world. He taught at ballet schools in Moscow, Leningrad, Kiev, Novosibirsk, and Kuibyshev (now Samara), and served as guest teacher in Paris, Vienna, Teheran, Tokyo, Buenos Aires, Sofia, and Manila.

Chabukiani retired from dancing in 1968. Until then he had taken the leading role in every ballet he produced. His creations for the Tbilisi company include *Sinatle* (1947), *Gorda* (1950), and *Othello* (1957), all to scores by Georgian composers. He then fashioned a new ballet genre, the

CHABUKIANI. *A scene from act 2 of Chabukiani's* Laurencia *with Nadezhda Kapustina in the center. Created for the Kirov Ballet in 1939, this ballet, set in fifteenth-century Spain, remained in the company's repertory for more than thirty-five years. (Photograph reprinted from Hélène Bellew,* Ballet in Moscow Today, *Greenwich, Conn., p. 144.)*

romantic ballet-poem with a philosophical message, the first of which was *The Demon* (1961), again to a Georgian score and based on Mikhail Lermontov's eponymous poem. In *Poem-Ballet* (1963), to the music of Franz Liszt and George Gershwin, Chabukiani combined a tragic story and a romantic-philosophical poem. He also produced *Dawn* (1967), *The Unconquered* (1970), *Hamlet* (1971), and *Appassionata* (1980). *Hamlet* represents a synthesis of his achievements in that it convincingly blended tender lyricism and devastating sarcasm. Chabukiani produced new versions of many classical ballets as well as reviving his own works—*Laurencia* in 1978 and the second act of *Heart of the Hills* in 1982—for the Paliashvili Theater.

Chabukiani directed and danced the leading roles in the films *Masters of the Georgian Ballet* (1955) and *Othello* (1961). He also appeared in the movie *Stars of the Russian Ballet* (1946), dancing the leading role in *The Flames of Paris*. The winner of three state prizes, in 1941, 1947, and 1949, Chabukiani was named a People's Artist of the USSR in 1950. His other awards include the Lenin Prize (1957) for *Othello*, the Grand Prix of the Académie Royale de Danse (1966) for *Gorda* and *Othello*, and the gold medal of the Milan Gallery of Arts. He was also named Hero of Socialist Labor in 1990.

BIBLIOGRAPHY
Andronnikov, I. "Demon ostayetsya nepokornym." *Ogonek* 24 (1961).
Dumbadze, Éteri, and Georgii Margvelashvili. *Iskusstvo slova, slovo ob iskusstve.* Tbilisi, 1979.
"Four Russian Dancers of Today." *The Dancing Times* (October 1941): 12–14.
Krasovskaya, Vera. *Vakhtang Chabukiani* (in Russian). 2d ed. Leningrad, 1960.
Mamontov, George. "Two Dancers: Alexei Yermolayev and Vakhtang Chabukiani." In *The Soviet Ballet,* by Yuri Slonimsky et al. New York, 1947.
Parker, Henry Taylor. *Motion Arrested: Dance Reviews of H. T. Parker.* Edited by Olive Holmes. Middletown, Conn., 1982.
Roslavleva, Natalia. *Era of the Russian Ballet* (1966). New York, 1979.
Smakov, Gennady. *The Great Russian Dancers.* New York, 1984.
Swift, Mary Grace. *The Art of the Dance in the U.S.S.R.* Notre Dame, 1968.

ÉTERI A. DUMBADZE
Translated from Russian

CHA-CHA. *See* Ballroom Dance Competition.

CHACONNE AND PASSACAILLE. The *chaconne* (Sp., *chacona;* It., *ciaccona;* Eng., chacoon) and *passacaille* (Sp., *pasacalle, passacalle;* It., *passacaglia, passacaglio*) were two dances in triple meter that developed independently in the early seventeenth century but that both evolved into extended compositions based on continuous variation over a ground, or *ostinato*. As dances, both reached the height of their development in French operas of the late seventeenth and early eighteenth centuries. Of the two, the *chaconne* has a longer history as a dance, spanning two hundred years, from the late sixteenth to the late eighteenth century, whereas the *passacaille* developed later and declined in popularity sooner. As performed in France, both were primarily, if not exclusively, theatrical dances and were among the most difficult of their period because of the virtuosic technique required of the dancers and the stamina needed for these longest of Baroque dances.

The earliest references to the *chacona* are found in Spanish literary sources starting from 1598, which reveal that at this time the *chacona* was a wild, erotic dance of popular character. It probably originated in the New World, as both the writings about the *chacona* and the texts sung to *chacona* music suggest. There has been considerable speculation about the origin of the name of the dance, with various theories ascribing its derivation to proper nouns (such as the Indians of Chaco, Argentina), to words meaning "beautiful" or "country song," to verbal imitations of castanets, or to the Italian word for a blind man *(cieco)*, but none has been substantiated.

The *chacona* texts, of which fifteen survive in Spanish, exude a spirit of humor, irreverence, and sensuality. Most of the refrains refer to the good life *(la vida bona)*. The lascivious character of the *chacona*, which it held in common with the *zarabanda* (in the earliest literary references the two dances are generally mentioned together), led to its being banned from the theater in 1615. The ban seems to have had little effect, as references to the *chacona* continue for the next several decades. However, by 1635 it was being referred to as an old dance.

Nothing specific is known about the choreography of the *chacona* beyond its openly sexual character. A description from Miguel de Cervantes suggests that it was open to any number of couples. The *chacona* was both a social and a theatrical dance, and was performed to the accompaniment of a sung text, a guitar, and percussion instruments such as castanets and the tambourine.

The *chacona* was introduced very early in the seventeenth century from Spain into Italy, where once again it was condemned for its lascivious movements and its corrupting influence. The first musical examples of the *ciaccona* and the *passacaglio*, as the names were written in Italian, may be found in Girolamo Montesardo's *Nuova inventione d'intavolatura, per sonare li balletti sopra la chitarra spagniuola* of 1606, an Italian adaptation of Spanish guitar technique. In this work the *ciaccona* was classified as a *balletto*, whereas the *passacaglio* was not a dance at all, but rather a *ritornello*, or little interlude to be played between the stanzas of a song or to introduce a dance. In the numerous guitar books published in both Italy and Spain during the first half of the seventeenth century, and in books of keyboard music starting with Girolamo Frescobaldi's *Secondo libro di toccate* of 1627, both the *ciaccona* and *passacaglio* consisted musically of short harmonic formulas, usually four measures long, which were strung together to create pieces of the desired length, with variations above the formulas presumably improvised by the performer. Very little is known about the actual uses made of the *ciaccona* as a dance beyond the fact that it did appear in theatrical productions from the first half of the

century. Richard Hudson has suggested that the dance may have been incorporated into the *commedia dell'arte* as early as 1622, thus beginning a tradition that is in evidence in eighteenth-century *chaconne* choreographies. It is possible that both the Spanish *passacalle* and the Italian *passacaglio* were not danced at all during this period.

The turning point in the history of both dance forms came with their introduction into France in the first decades of the seventeenth century. A *passacalle* by Henri de Bailly, used as an instrumental introduction to a vocal piece with a Spanish text, may be found in *Airs de différents auteurs, Cinquiesme livre* (1614), and the earliest French instrumental *chaconne* is one by lutenist Nicolas Vallet in his *Secret des Muses* of 1615. During the following years both *chaconnes* and *passacailles* began to appear in lute and keyboard suites by composers such as Ennemond and Denis Gaultier, Jacques Champion de Chambonnières, and Louis Couperin. The earliest known use of the *chaconne* as a dance in France is the "Entrée des Chaconistes Espagnols" from *Le Ballet des Fées de la Forêt de Saint-Germain* (1625), in which both men and women, costumed in the Spanish manner, danced to the music of a guitar.

When the *passacaille* was first used as a dance is not known, but it may not have been until 1682, when Jean-Baptiste Lully composed his first *passacaille* for the stage, for the opera *Persée*. It was, in fact, the Florentine-born Lully (1632–1687) who was responsible for developing both dance types into standard components of French operas. Starting with one of his early ballets in 1658, chaconnes appeared in a growing proportion of his stage works, and a *chaconne* or a *passacaille* held a prominent position in each of his last nine operas. In all, Lully wrote seventeen *chaconnes* and four *passacaille* for the stage, all of which were danced.

As seen in Lully's mature works and in the works of other French composers of the period, both the *chaconnes* and *passacailles* were through-composed pieces in triple meter of substantial length (in comparison to the much shorter two-reprise dance types such as the *menuet* and *sarabande*) and were built on a series of continuous variations over an eight-measure harmonic or melodic pattern. Each eight-bar phrase was further broken into two repeated four-measure units. The two dances were differentiated from each other in that the *passacailles* were often in minor keys, usually started on the downbeat of the measure, and, according to numerous French theorists, had a slower tempo. The *chaconnes* were generally in major keys, often started on the second beat of the measure, and had a livelier tempo. Lully often used either a *chaconne* or a *passacaille* as part of the finale of an act, either as the very last number or as part of a closing complex of pieces that frequently included a chorus built on the same musical material. Indications in the scores and librettos of Lully's works show that *chaconnes* and *passacailles* were generally performed by a substantial number of dancers, but reports of operatic performances indicate that, at least on some occasions, soloists alternated with the group as a whole. The roles represented by dancers of *chaconnes* and *passacailles* ranged from the noble to the comic, with characters as diverse as heroes and heroines from classical antiquity, the peoples of Cathay, Harlequins, and dancing giants.

There are fourteen *chaconne* and six *passacaille* choreographies in Feuillet notation dating from the early part of the eighteenth century, some of English origin. Fifteen of the twenty are for a single dancer; the remaining five are for a couple. All the solo *passacaille* choreographies are for a woman, and nine of the eleven solo *chaconne* choreographies are for a man; whether this differentiation in the notations was reflected in actual practice in the eighteenth century is unknown. A special kind of technical ability is demanded by the three choreographed *chaconnes* for Harlequin, which make use of false foot positions and include instructions for gestures with the head, arms, and hat. Although *chaconnes* and *passacailles* were primarily the province of professional dancers, they were occasionally danced by nobles of outstanding balletic ability at court balls.

French composers of stage music after Lully, such as André Campra and Jean-Philippe Rameau, followed their predecessor's practice of using a *passacaille* or, more frequently, a *chaconne* to end an act or even an entire work, particularly in their serious operas. This tradition continued until the last quarter of the eighteenth century, as seen in the fact that three of the operas composed by Christoph Willibald Gluck for Paris in the 1770s end with *chaconnes*. Even Wolfgang Amadeus Mozart wrote both a *chaconne* and a *passacaille* in the ballet music for his *opera seria, Idomeneo,* of 1781. However, it was clear by this time that both dances were decidedly old-fashioned, and they did not survive the century.

[*For related discussion, see* Ballet Technique, History of, *article on* French Court Dance.]

BIBLIOGRAPHY

Fischer, Kurt von. "Passacaglia." In *Die Musik in Geschichte und Gegenwart* (1962). Kassel, 1949–.

Harris-Warrick, Rebecca. "Interpreting Pendulum Markings for French Baroque Dances." *Historical Performance* 6.1 (1993): 9–22.

Hudson, Richard. "Further Remarks on the Passacaglia and Ciaccona." *Journal of the American Musicological Society* 23 (1970).

Hudson, Richard. "Chaconne." In *The New Grove Dictionary of Music and Musicians.* London, 1980.

Hudson, Richard. "Passacaglia." In *The New Grove Dictionary of Music and Musicians.* London, 1980.

Hudson, Richard. *Passacaglia and Ciaccona: From Guitar Music to Italian Keyboard Variations in the Seventeenth Century.* Ann Arbor, Mich., 1981.

Little, Meredith Ellis (Helen Meredith Ellis). "The Dances of J. B. Lully." Ph.D. diss., Stanford University, 1967.

Little, Meredith Ellis, and Carol G. Marsh. *La Danse Noble: An Inventory of Dances and Sources.* Williamstown, Mass., 1992.

Machabey, Armand. "Les origines de la chaconne et de la passacaille." *Revue de Musicologie* 28 (1946): 1–21.

Reichert, George. "Chaconne." In *Die Musik in Geschichte und Gegenwart* (1952). Kassel, 1949–.

Walker, Thomas. "Ciaccona and Passacaglia: Remarks on Their Origin and Early History." *Journal of the American Musicological Society* 21 (1968).

REBECCA HARRIS-WARRICK

CHAIN AND ROUND DANCES. Most of the European chain and round dances still in living tradition are found in eastern and southeastern Europe. These are the regions of Europe that account for the largest variety of basic floor patterns and their derivations. In central, northern, and northeastern Europe chain dances vanished toward the end of the nineteenth century, with the exception of relatively few that were danced until World War II and a very small number that still can be seen in Poland's Mazowsze region, north of Warsaw. In northwestern Europe the Faeroe Islands form a remarkable exception to this trend, as they continue to have a strong song-dance tradition. Dances of these types have also vanished more slowly in France than in other places in western Europe. The people of Brittany, the Pays Basque, Provence, Languedoc, and Roussillon kept their dance traditions until the 1950s. In southwestern and southern Europe chain and round dances are rare. They can, however, still be seen on Italy's island of Sardinia and, on special occasions, in the northern provinces of Spain.

Analyses and comparisons based on the floor patterns of European chain and round dances show that most

CHAIN AND ROUND DANCES. Male dancers of the Koutev Bulgarian National Ensemble hook arms in a straight line dance. (Photograph from the Dance Collection, New York Public Library for the Performing Arts.)

CHAIN AND ROUND DANCES. *Syrtós*, the general term for a variety of regional Greek line dances that form open circles, implies a pulling or shuffling action. These men and women perform a *syrtós* from Messogheia, a plain near Athens. The women's costumes from this region are embroidered with gold thread and are traditionally the most elaborate in Greece. (Photograph courtesy of Alkis Raftis, Greek Dances Theater, Athens.)

dances fall within one of a limited number of main categories, with subcategories to match, that seem to be generally in use among various European groups. Dances of the same pattern may be distinguished from one another by their local names, their music (including meter, tempo, melody), possible song words, and contexts of which the dances form a part. In addition, the type of accompaniment (vocal, or vocal/instrumental, and accompanying instruments), the style of dress, the dance site, and the dancers' mood influence the way, and the style, in which a particular dance is performed.

In song dances, in which the pattern often is very simple and the words are of special importance, the dance itself may assume the character of a rhythmic-kinetic ostinato (a short melodic motif persistently repeated) accompaniment to the singing. This can be witnessed in the Faeroe Islands, where a "good dance" may be two hundred stanzas long. In other regions, this same dance pattern can hold the germ for a multiplicity of variations and individual improvisations, depending on local traditions and the momentary state of mind of each dancer.

An uncomplicated dance based on a simple pattern can function as a means of locomotion for a group of people passing from place to place. This can be seen in many of the dances connected with the various festivals of New Year, Carnival, and spring, where groups go from house to house and perform whatever dance has been prepared for that particular occasion. That same dance pattern, however, when performed in another context, can bring the very same people into a state of ecstasy, as can be witnessed at the Anastenaria (fire-walking ritual) in northern Greece.

Most basic patterns have a progressing as well as a reversed version, although both versions may not necessarily be practiced in the same village or region. In dances of the progressing type, the dancers move mainly in one direction; in dances based on the principle of reversion, they move back and forth in a kind of pendulum movement.

Probably the simplest dance pattern within European tradition is made up of nothing but walking or running steps. These steps will be referred to generically as traveling steps. Dances in this category include *angaliastós* (eastern Crete), *na Lazar* (central Bulgaria), *širo kolo* (Slavonia), *karikázo* (Hungary), *kolo* (Moravia and southern Bohemia), and *karička* (Slovakia). Traveling steps can be performed in various directions, some of which transform the natural walking or running steps into a more artificial movement; moving sideways, for example, results in a series of step-closes or various crossover-steps, or, possibly, in combinations of both. Dances in which such variations occur include *hora mare* (Transylvania), *koleso* (Slovakia), *kerekecskézés* (southern Hungary), *žita* (Slavonia), and *velikdensko horo* (central Bulgaria). In other dances—the *tráta* (Attica), *mésa éxo* (Epirus), and *kolo* (Moravia)—traveling steps are done in augmented form; this leaves time to bring the unsupported foot up to the weight-bearing foot before the next traveling step is performed and the weight is transferred, thus creating a kind of rocking movement. (This pattern could, in some cases, be analyzed as a series of progressive hesitation steps.)

Most dances of this category are, however, based on one of several derivations of the traveling step as, for example, skipping steps in the *farandole* (southern France) and the *na Bojan* (central Bulgaria). In other dances the traveling steps are substituted by even step-hops or hop-steps. Other common derivations of the traveling steps are doubling of either the odd or the even steps, thus creating composites of quick-quick-slow or slow-quick-quick steps, respectively. Dances based on the quick-quick-slow pattern are the *vodena răčenica* (Bulgaria), *orijent* (Serbia), *zălulţa* (Transylvania), and *koleso* (Slovakia); examples of slow-quick-quick dances are the *sta dío* (Epirus), *syrtós* (Greek islands), and *kolo* (Moravia). Dances based on traveling steps in chain formation often include various figurations, such as the winding and unwinding of spirals, going through gates, and threading the needle. It is also worth noting that the traveling step is the most common step in children's song-and-dance games.

Many dances include hesitation steps, which function as pauses or hesitations to break the monotony of the progression of a series of traveling steps. The simplest form of the hesitation step is made up of any one of the compositional elements step-hold, step-close, or step-swing followed by its symmetrical repetition; in this way the second half of the hesitation step counterbalances the first. By adding a pair of hesitation steps to two traveling steps an altogether different dance pattern appears; an example of this is the basic dance of the Faeroe Islands. This pattern is exceedingly widespread among the chain and round dances of eastern and southeastern Europe, and it also seems to have been very common in places where dances of these types have disappeared. Generally speaking, in western Europe dances based on this pattern move left or clockwise, whereas in eastern and southeastern Europe they move right or counterclockwise.

In Greece, where the dance tradition is still very much alive, numerous names are applied to this pattern, according to when, where, why, and by whom the dance is used. In some cases the name hints at the style in which the dance is performed, for example, the *koutsós chorós* ("limping dance") of Macedonia, the *soústa* ("spring," referring to the bouncing style) of the Dodecanese, the *sighanós chorós* ("calm dance") of Crete, and the *peidhiktós chorós* ("leaping dance") of Epirus. This way of naming dances was common all over Europe and remains so in areas with a living dance tradition. Dances may also be named after an outstanding local dancer, a particular dance tune, the performing musician, or some of the words to the song accompanying the dance. Dance names describing a certain style of dancing may refer to any basic pattern; however, the name *sta tría* ("three steps"), common especially in the northern part of Greece, always refers to the pattern created by adding a pair of hesitation steps to two traveling steps.

In Bulgaria, this dance pattern is known almost everywhere as the *pravo horo* ("straight dance"), but there are also local names for it, such as *krivata* ("the winding one"), *dălgo horo* ("long dance"), *starčeskoto* ("that of the old men"), and *skoklivo* ("leaping"). This pattern is found in the southern Balkan states, where the common names in Macedonia are *pravoto* ("the straight one") and *lesnoto* ("the light one"); other names are *maško oro* ("men's dance"), *se napred* ("forward"), and *šiptarsko* ("Albanian"). Among Albanians living in Macedonia, dances of this pattern are seen in the women's song-dance repertory. In Romania this pattern forms the basis of the popular dance *sîrba* but also has local names, such as *coconiţa* ("little lady"), *bumbacul* ("cotton"), *chindia* ("sunset"), and *mocăneasca* ("shepherdlike"). In Slovakia this pattern appears in the dance suites *karička* and *koleso*, and in Hungary it is found in the vocal round dances of the women, the *karikázo* and *körtánc*. In the Faeroe Islands, if at all named, this dance is known as *foeroyskur dansur* (as opposed to *engelskur dansur,* which generally covers all dances that do not belong to the local dance repertory and to couple dances in particular). The dance is known in Brittany as *laridés* or *ridées*, in Spain as *sardana*, and on Sardinia as *ballu tundu*.

The following dances are based on the reversed pattern, consisting of two traveling steps and one-half or one-and-one-half hesitation steps followed by the reverse of the pattern: *zervó-dexió* (Dodecanese), *kokonešta* (Bulgaria), *moravsko kolo* (Serbia), *hora mare* (Romania), *karikázo* (Hungary), *karička* (Slovakia), and *demi-danse* (Brittany). A different pattern, consisting of four traveling steps and two hesitation steps, forms the basis of two very popular Greek dances, the *kalamatianós* and the mainland *syrtós*. In Greece, this pattern almost always appears as a doubling of every second traveling step, with the hesitation

CHAIN AND ROUND DANCES. In this Romanian *hora*, men and women form a circle facing outward. (Photograph courtesy of the Romanian Center for the International Theatre Institute.)

steps performed a slow-quick-quick (each first step slow, each second step doubled). The progressing form of this pattern seems to be rare in the traditional dance material outside Greece, whereas dances based on the reversed form are found in relatively great variety in Bulgaria and in the former Yugoslavia.

Dances based on a pattern made up of six traveling steps and two hesitation steps are rare, but dances of the reversed type based on six traveling steps and a half hesitation step are relatively common. This is especially the case in multipart dances, in which this pattern may represent the traveling part, forming a contrast to other parts based on different patterns. The pattern is also used because it often coincides with the melodic phrase of the accompanying dance tune.

In Hungary and in the Czech and the Slovakian republics there is a tradition of organizing chain and round dances either in dance suites or according to the rondo form. Additionally, dances based on extending certain patterns, for example, doubling each step of the basic pattern and thus creating a proportional extension in time and space, are commonly used in some parts of Greece, Bulgaria, and the former Yugoslavia. Finally, it should be pointed out that patterns other than those discussed in this article exist, although they are less widespread.

European chain and round dances are vanishing; this results from improved communications and the impact of modern lifestyles on even the most remote villages. In addition, the decrease in village populations—where young people leave for towns and cities—has hindered the passing on of traditions. The resulting decline in the number of traditional occasions for dance leads to a continual reduction of the dance repertory, even in places where chain and round dances are still practiced. In some areas these dances are rarely performed but are still remembered, yet there are areas where they have disappeared and been forgotten.

In many countries, however, expatriate populations or local people with a special interest in dance have begun a wave of revivals, giving new life to the traditional dances, even if the contexts in which the dances are performed is altered. Thus both the function and significance of chain and round dances continue to evolve.

[*For related discussion, see* European Traditional Dance.]

BIBLIOGRAPHY

Dąbrowska, Grażyna, *Taniec ludowy na Mazowszu*. Cracow, 1980.
Dąbrowska, Grażyna, and Kurt Petermann, eds. *Analyse und Klassifikation von Volkstänzen*. Cracow, 1983.
Guilcher, Jean-Michel. *La tradition populaire de danse en Basse-Bretagne*. Paris, 1963.
Guilcher, Yves. "Dance as a Reflection of Society." *Choreography and Dance* 2.1 (1992): 77–107.
Giurchescu, Anca, and Sunni Bloland. *Romanian Traditional Dance: A Contextual and Structural Approach*. Mill Valley, Calif., 1995.
Ilieva, Anna. *Narodni tanci ot Srednogorieto*. Sofia, 1978.
Martin, György. *A magyar körtánc és Európai rokonsága*. Budapest, 1979.
Nemcová, Melánia. *Chorovody a dievčenské tance z východného slovenska*. 2d ed. Kosice, 1992.
Pajtondziev, Gančo. *Makedonski narodni ora*. Skopje, 1973.
Petrides, Ted. *Folk Dances and Related Folklore of the Province of Attica*. Unpublished manuscript.
Torp, Lisbet. *Chain and Round Dance Patterns: A Method for Structural Analysis and Its Application to European Material*. 3 vols. Copenhagen, 1990.

FILMS.   Centre National de la Recherche Scientifique (CNRS), Ivry. Institut für den Wissenschaftlichen Film, Göttingen.

LISBET TORP

CHAINÉ TURNS. *See* Ballet Technique, *article on* Turning Movements.

CHAKI-SIRCAR, MANJUSRI (born in Behrampur, West Bengal), Indian dancer and choreographer. Chaki-Sircar was inspired in her youth by the works of the Nobel Prize–winning poet Rabindranath Tagore, which led her to develop a style and methodology outside the boundaries of classical Indian dance. She was trained in *bharata nāṭyam* by Maruthappa Pillai and in *kathak* by Prahlad Das in Calcutta; she also studied Manipuri and Oḍissi dance. She performed as a soloist in both classical and innovative styles in theaters and universities in many parts of the world.

Chaki-Sircar spent about two decades abroad in Nigeria and the United States. She taught dance at Vassar College and the State University of New York. During this period she also performed in North America, Great Britain, and Germany.

In 1981 Chaki-Sircar returned to India and established her own company, Dancers' Guild. In collaboration with her daughter, Ranjabati Sircar, she developed a style which she calls *navanṛtya* ("new dance"), using eight groups of movements derived from classical Indian dance to create a new vocabulary for contemporary dance. In works such as *Tomari Matir Kanya*, based on Tagore's dance drama *Chandalika*, she reinterpreted older material for contemporary relevance. *Aranya Amrita* deals with threats to the environment; *Drums of the War* emphasizes the horrors of war. Chaki-Sircar prefers themes of social repression and the subjugation of women, working to create awareness of women's issues. She has also choreographed abstract pieces that reinterpret the *rāga*s of Hindustani classical music and the associated traditional iconography.

A scholar as well as a performer, Chaki-Sircar has a master's degree in Bengali literature from the University of Calcutta and a Ph.D. in anthropology from Columbia University in New York. Her research has focused on religion, ritual, the performing arts, and the gender roles of women. She is the author of two books, *Feminism in a Traditional Society: An Analysis of Lai Haraoba Dance Ritual of Manipur,* and *Women and Children in a Bengal Village;* the latter is a socioreligious interpretation of ritual life.

Chaki-Sircar has participated in many national and international festivals, including some in the United States and China. She now lives in Calcutta and heads Dancers' Guild, training young dancers in her technique and choreographing new works. Her daughter assists her in choreography, gives solo performances, and creates works of her own. For her creative contributions to dance, Chaki-Sircar has received the Central Sangeet Natak Akademi award as well as numerous honors from cultural institutions in West Bengal.

BIBLIOGRAPHY

Chaki-Sircar, Manjusri. *Feminism in a Traditional Society: Women of the Manipur Valley.* New Delhi, 1984.
Crowder, Tinsley. "Manjusri in *Shyama.*" *Dance Magazine* (June 1972): 82–83.
Dove, Simon. "'Navanritya': New Dance." *Ballett International* 13 (November 1990): 24–27.
Kothari, Sunil, ed. *Bharata Natyam: Indian Classical Dance Art.* Bombay, 1979.
Venkataraman, Leela. "Sangeet Natak Akademi." *Sruti* (Madras), no. 35 (August 1987): 16–21.

SUNIL KOTHARI

CHALON. A famous Romantic-era print by Chalon, depicting (from left to right) Carlotta Grisi, Marie Taglioni, Lucile Grahn, and Fanny Cerrito in a tableau from Jules Perrot's *Pas de Quatre* (1845). This ballet was created specifically to showcase the talents of these four celebrated ballerinas. (Courtesy of Madison U. Sowell and Debra H. Sowell, Brigham Young University, Provo, Utah.)

CHALON, ALFRED (Alfred Edward Chalon; born 15 February 1780 in Geneva, died 3 October 1860 in London), painter and lithographer. Chalon's lithographs of the Romantic-era ballet are eerily evocative of the period. Their delicate textures, curving lines, and insubstantial forms seem to embody the spirit of the era. Chalon's prints enshrine the greatest ballerina of the period, Marie Taglioni, and two of its seminal ballets, Filippo Taglioni's *La Sylphide* (1832) and Jules Perrot's *Pas de Quatre* (1845). Moreover, the sheer aesthetic beauty of Chalon's lithographs is prized by dance lovers and fine arts connoisseurs.

Chalon was born into a Swiss family that moved to England in 1789. He became a student at the Royal Academy in London in 1797, attaining the rank of an associate in 1812 and full membership in 1816. His facility in watercolor painting soon made him London's most fashionable watercolor portraitist, and in 1838 he was appointed official portrait painter to England's Queen Victoria.

Most of his work was small in scale, his watercolor portraits measuring between ten to fifteen inches in height. He also painted miniatures on ivory. Many of his portraits of opera singers and dancers were reproduced as prints, a tribute to their popularity. Chalon himself did not execute his drawings on the lithographic stone, but entrusted this phase of the printmaking process to artists such as Richard James Lane (1800–1872), who executed many of his ballet lithographs.

Although Chalon worked chiefly in watercolors, he also made large-scale oil paintings. Some were on historical or religious themes, such as *John Knox Reproving the Ladies of Queen Mary's Court* (1837), but he also treated romantic or genre subjects, such as *Hunt the Slipper* (1831).

He was an accomplished musician, and his early interest in opera and ballet is testified by his caricatures of dancers at the King's Theatre in the 1820s. His best-known ballet prints date from the 1830s and 1840s. In 1831, the year before Marie Taglioni's epoch-making appearance in *La Sylphide,* Chalon published *Six Sketches of Mademoiselle Taglioni,* depicting her in roles such as Flora and the Bayadère. Toward the close of her career, he published another six-print series, *La Sylphide: Souvenir d'Adieu de Marie Taglioni* (1845).

Chalon's print of Perrot's *Pas de Quatre* immortalized a single pose from this ballet; depicting Taglioni, Fanny

Cerrito, Lucile Grahn, and Carlotta Grisi, it has often reappeared in the works of later choreographers, ranging from Anton Dolin's reconstruction of the *Pas de Quatre* (1941) to Maurice Béjart's *Wien, Wien, Nur du Allein* (1981).

Chalon's works are often used as source material by dance historians, dancers, and costume designers. Tamara Karsavina, for example, copied her first-act costume for *Giselle* (Diaghilev's Ballets Russes revival, 1910) from his steel-engraved portrait of Grisi in *Les beautés de l'Opéra* (1845).

[*See also* Prints and Drawings.]

BIBLIOGRAPHY. Chalon's life and career are discussed in Richard and Samuel Redgrave, *A Century of British Painters* (1866), new edition by Ruthven Todd (London, 1947), as well as Samuel Redgrave, *A Dictionary of Artists of the English School* (1878; new ed., Amsterdam, 1970). Ivor Guest, "Chalon at the Ballet: Caricatures," *Ballet* (November 1951), reveals an amusing and less well-known aspect of Chalon's work.

SUSAN AU

CHANDRALEKHA (born 6 December 1929 in Nadiad, Gujarat), Indian dancer, choreographer, writer, and designer. One of the most important voices of the Indian avant-garde, Chandralekha was trained in classical *bharata nāṭyam* by Elappa Pillai of Kanchipuram in southern India. She rose to fame as a soloist with a style noted for its musicality and the intensity of its *abhinaya* (expressive technique). After a decade-long performing career in the late 1950s and early 1960s, when she was one of the most noted dancers of her time, she left the classical dance scene, rejecting what she perceived as its degradation into commercial entertainment. In subsequent years she wrote poetry and fiction, designed posters and books, worked on multimedia projects, and was involved in the movements for women's rights and human rights.

In 1985 Chandralekha returned to the stage, taking the dance world by storm with her production of *Angika*, which explored the relationships of dance and other traditional physical disciplines of India and postulated a new kind of content for dance. Since then she has annually choreographed and presented original multidisciplinary productions. Her earlier works, such as *Devadasi*, *Navagraha*, and *Primal Energy*, revealed her new approach to Indian dance. Other landmarks of the contemporary Indian dance movement include *Namaskar*, choreographed for the opening ceremony of the Festival of India in Moscow; *Request Concert*, combining dance and theater; *Lilavati*, based on a tenth-century Sanskrit mathematics text by Bhaskaracharya; *Prana*, based on the movement of breath and the relation between yoga and dance; and *Sri*, reflecting her concepts on the empowerment and enslavement of women. *Yantra* (1994) was created on the occasion of an Indian tour by Pina Bausch and Tanztheater Wuppertal, and *Mahakala* was choreographed in 1995.

Chandralekha and her company have toured widely in India and abroad, participating in several major national and international festivals. She had successful appearances at the Jacob's Pillow Dance Festival and in New York in 1994.

Continuing to write as well as dance, Chandralekha has published a short novel, *The Street*, and a collection of poems. She developed and designed an exhibition on Indian women, *Stree*, for the Festival of India in Moscow, expressing historical Indian concepts of empowered women and their harsh condition today. In 1969 she developed an exhibition on Mahatma Gandhi for the National Institute of Design.

In recognition of her creative contributions to dance, Chandralekha has received the Central Sangeet Natak Akademi award (1992) and the Time Out/Dance Umbrella award (United Kingdom, 1993). She was given the Gaia Award for Cultural Ecology in Italy in 1991. *Chandralekha*, a book on her life, dance, art, and politics, was written by Rustom Bharucha. Chandralekha lives in Madras.

BIBLIOGRAPHY

Arudra. "Chandralekha's *Angika*." *Sruti* (Madras), no. 20 (December 1985): 51–54.

Bharucha, Rustom. *Chandralekha: Woman, Dance, Resistance.* New Delhi, 1995.

Kolmes, Jacqueline. "Chandralekha Forges Feminist Abstractions." *Dance Magazine* (December 1994): 34–36.

Kothari, Sunil, ed. *Bharata Natyam: Indian Classical Dance Art.* Bombay, 1979.

Rubidge, Sarah. "Modern Movement and Traditional Tales." *Dance Theatre Journal* 10 (Spring–Summer 1993): 32–37.

Witzeling, Klaus. "Clearing a Path Towards a Deeper Significance of Tradition." *Ballett International/Tanz Aktuell* (August–September 1995): 26–31.

SUNIL KOTHARI

CHANDRASHEKHAR, C. V. (born 22 May 1935 in Simla, Himachal Pradesh), Indian dancer and choreographer. C. V. Chandrashekhar was trained as a classical Karnatic vocalist in childhood; the great dancer Rukmini Devi recognized his potential as a dancer and trained him in *bharata nāṭyam* at her institute, Kalakshetra. There were few male dancers studying this art at the time. Chandrashekhar received thorough training in solo performance and took part in dance dramas choreographed by Rukmini Devi at Kalakshetra, acquiring a sound knowledge of music, dance, and choreography. At the suggestion of Rukmini Devi, Chandrashekhar moved to Varanasi to teach music and *bharata nāṭyam* at the women's college there. He also studied Hindustani classical music and choreographed dances to it, with lyrics in Hindi.

In 1980 Chandrashekhar became a professor and head of the dance department at the M. S. University in Baroda. Working with his wife Jaya and their daughters Chitra and Manjari, all *bharata nāṭyam* dancers, he choreographed several dance dramas and presented them with success in India and abroad. The outstanding features of his works are the music and the arresting line. Austere, dignified, and compact, his dances are imbued with the spirit of Rukmini Devi and the Kalakshetra tradition. *Meghasandesh* and *Ritu Samhara*, based on the Sanskrit poems of Kalidasa, as well as *Shakti* and the recent *Panchamahabhuta*, reveal Chandrashekhar's virtuosity and imagination in choreographing group works.

For his contributions to dance, Chandrashekhar received the Central Sangeet Natak Akademi award and the Nṛtya Choodamani award as well as other honors. He traveled extensively both in India and abroad, taking part in several national and international dance conferences. He continued to teach in Baroda after his retirement from the university as well as choreographing and conducting master classes at various locations. He now lives in Madras.

BIBLIOGRAPHY
Kothari, Sunil, ed. *Bharata Natyam: Indian Classical Dance Art.* Bombay, 1979.
Sarada, S. *Kalakshetra-Rukmini Devi: Reminiscences.* Madras, 1985.
SUNIL KOTHARI

CHAPPELL, WILLIAM (born 27 September 1908 in Wolverhampton, Staffordshire, died 1 January 1994), English dancer, designer, director, and producer. While still a student at the Chelsea School of Art, William Chappell was introduced to Marie Rambert with the idea that he should become one of her pupils. At that time she had several female pupils but only one male—Frederick Ashton. In her classes at the church hall in Notting Hill Gate, later to become the Mercury Theatre, Rambert gradually molded Chappell into a fine artist, one of the first generation of dancers to form the nucleus of what became the Ballet Club and later Ballet Rambert.

Chappell's first ballet design was for a student charity performance of Ashton's *Leda and the Swan* (1928), in which he also danced. His first professional performance as a dancer was in the play *Jew Süss* (1929). After that engagement, he toured Europe with Ida Rubinstein's company, working with Léonide Massine and Bronislava Nijinska.

Returning to England in 1930, Chappell became involved with the Ballet Club as a dancer and designer, creating many roles over the years, among them a memorable Faun in Rambert's 1931 revival of Nijinsky's *L'Après-midi d'un Faune.* Meanwhile, he was dancing in the commercial theater, mainly in productions by Charles B. Cochran and in ballets given by the Camargo Society. For the Camargo Society, Chappell created roles in Ninette de Valois's *Job* and Ashton's *Façade* (both 1931), as well as designing de Valois's *Cephalus and Procris* (also 1931).

In 1934 Chappell joined the Vic-Wells Ballet, dancing leading roles in the first productions of the classics given by a British ballet company and creating many roles in new works. The most notable were in those by de Valois: the Stranger Player in *The Haunted Ballroom* (1934), the Rake's Friend in *The Rake's Progress* (1935), and the Second Red Knight in *Checkmate* (1937).

It is as one of the first designers of British ballet that Chappell will be most remembered, particularly because of his ability to design economically and to work on small stages such as the one at the Mercury Theatre. For Rambert he designed some fifteen ballets, the most notable being Ashton's *Capriol Suite* (1930), Antony Tudor's *Lysistrata* (1932), and de Valois's *Bar aux Folies-Bergère* (1934). For the Vic-Wells Ballet he designed Ashton's *Les Rendezvous* (1933) and *Les Patineurs* (1937), as well as early productions of *Giselle* and *Coppélia*. For René Blum's Ballets Russes de Monte Carlo, he designed Boris Romanov's production of *The Nutcracker* (1936), under the pseudonym A. Alexeett. His most famous decor is his evocation of a wintry public garden, probably in Vienna, for *Les Patineurs*, with its white trellis arches, Japanese lanterns, and bare, shadowy trees.

After World War II Chappell gave up dancing but had a highly successful career designing, directing, and arranging dances for an enormous number of musicals, revues, straight plays, operas, and ballets. He also wrote two books, *Studies in Ballet* (1948) and *Fonteyn: Impressions of a Ballerina* (1951), and edited several others. In 1980, after an interval of more than three decades, Chappell once again collaborated with Frederick Ashton, providing the designs for Ashton's *Rhapsody*, mounted for the Royal Ballet and premiered at the Royal Opera House, Covent Garden. In 1985, Chappell's design for Ashton's *La Chatte Métamorphosée en Femme*, also done for the Royal Ballet, marked the final collaboration of these two pioneers of British ballet.

BIBLIOGRAPHY
Anthony, Gordon. "William Chappell." In Anthony's *A Camera at the Ballet: Pioneer Dancers of the Royal Ballet.* Newton Abbot, 1975.
Chappell, William. "A Fragment from an Autobiography." In *Ballet Rambert: Fifty Years On*, rev. ed., edited by Clement Crisp et al. London, 1981.
Clarke, Mary. *Dancers of Mercury: The Story of Ballet Rambert.* London, 1962.
Sorley Walker, Katherine. "The Camargo Society." *Dance Chronicle* 18.1 (1995): 1–114.
PETER WILLIAMS

CHARACTER DANCING. The term *character dancing* is usually understood to signify some form of ethnic dance adapted for use in a ballet, although this definition may also include other Western theatrical forms, such as opera and musical comedy. Most commonly, it refers to folk and national dances, but some writers extend the term to any nonballetic dance genre presented as part of a ballet. Hence, social dances, such as the waltz or tango, and theatrical dance, such as jazz and tap, may sometimes be called character dances.

The idea of role-playing implied by the word *character* applies both to the dancers, who are usually ballet dancers performing in a style outside their basic training, and to the dances themselves. Role-playing may be enhanced by ethnic costumes, headdresses, and footgear, · the last often consisting of boots or heeled "character shoes." Character dances are usually not performed on pointe, but they are also not intended to be accurate reproductions of ethnic dances; instead, they have been tailored to serve particular purposes—to play specific roles within the context of a given ballet.

The very act of placing a dance on stage often creates a self-awareness foreign to the original dance, and the primary purposes of many dances—for example, propitiation of a deity, courtship, or simple pleasure—may be lost in the overriding concern with theatrical presentation. According to Lincoln Kirstein (1970), "National dances characteristic of various people and places cannot be transposed to theater without compromise of authenticity. Folk dancing is more fun to do than to watch; making it both legible and entertaining to non-participants depends on tactful translation, in which a pure flavor, if not the form, of characteristic simplicity is retained." Igor Moiseyev has pointed out that character dances are meant to serve the ballet, and not the other way around. He maintains, "One must not turn the national dance in the ballet into an ethnographic document. It is not slavish photographic reproduction of folk dance that can stimulate the classical ballet" (quoted in van Praagh and Brinson, 1963).

Character dancing may serve many purposes within the framework of a ballet. It provides local color and helps to set the scene. It may be contrasted with the *danse d'école* both formally and as an ingredient of characterization. For example, the Scottish dances in *La Sylphide* (1832) establish the earthly nature of the mortals in contrast to the otherworldly nature of the sylphides. Character dances may also contrast with each other to give variety to a *divertissement*, as do different ethnic dances (Spanish, Neapolitan, Polish, and Hungarian) in the ballroom scene of *Swan Lake* (1895).

The term *character dancing* is related to the terms *character dancer* and *character role*, although the latter two usually suggest individual personality traits rather than ethnic or national characteristics. For example, the character role of Petrouchka emphasizes his personal qualities rather than his Russian nationality. In the eighteenth and nineteenth centuries, a character role was often determined by the portrayed individual's rank or station in life, occupation or profession, and occasionally by age; hence, character roles might include a notary, peasant, washerwoman, or old man. In today's usage, character roles usually connote age, lack of good looks, and a strong personality (often evil). Some examples are Alain and Widow Simone in *La Fille Mal Gardée* (1789), Madge in *La Sylphide*, Doctor Coppélius in *Coppélia* (1870), Carabosse in *The Sleeping Beauty* (1890), Drosselmeyer in *The Nutcracker* (1892), von Rothbart in *Swan Lake*, and Kastchei in *The Firebird* (1910). *Character dancer* partakes of both meanings and may be used to denote a dancer who is especially skillful in ethnic dances or one who specializes in the type of role discussed above. Some famous character dancers include Jean Babilée, Léonide Massine, Alexander Grant, Lydia Sokolova, Adolph Bolm, Leon Woizikowski, and Valery Panov.

The derivation of these terms may be traced to the three genres that were used to classify dancers at the Paris Opera during the eighteenth and early nineteenth centuries: the *noble*, also called the serious and heroic; the *demi-caractère*, or semiserious character; and the *comique*. The utmost in academic perfection was displayed by the *danseur noble*, who was required to be tall and perfectly proportioned, with an air of majesty in his movements. His direct opposite was the *danseur comique* of short and stocky build, who performed grotesque and eccentric dances in addition to folk and national dances. The *demi-caractère* represented a midpoint between the two extremes: the dancers of this category had to be of medium height, but slender and elegant in form, and their dancing blended elements of the other two genres. Over the years, the three genres gradually overlapped more and more until such categorization was abandoned in the 1830s.

Character dancing borrows various elements from given dance forms in order to create the illusion that an authentic folk or social dance is being performed. Among these elements are steps and leg gestures, head and arm movements, carriage of the body, partnering and linking, group formations, floor patterns, and dynamic qualities such as rhythm, flow, and sense of weight. Representative costumes may be worn, and the ballet's score may incorporate musical characteristics of the dance type. Many character dances tend, however, to select the most salient characteristics of a dance type, sometimes to the point of stereotype, such as the gesture of the hand behind the head in "Slavic" dances and the undulating arms of "Hindu" dances. Although a country such as Spain or India may have many different dance forms, these differences are often glossed over or ignored in the creation of character dances.

Classes in character dancing are offered as a supplement to ballet training in many dance academies. Students usually wear heeled character shoes or boots for these classes, and the females often wear full skirts. Classes may begin with a warm-up at the *barre* and progress to center exercises. The study of character dancing is widely required by dance academies in Great Britain, Canada, and eastern Europe but far less so in the United States.

The systematic teaching of character dancing was pioneered in Russia by Aleksandr Shiriaev, a teacher at the Imperial Ballet School (later the Vaganova Choreographic School). Drawing upon his study of Russian and other folk dances, he developed an academic syllabus with the aid of the dancer Alfred Bekefi and, in the 1920s, instituted the first daily character dancing classes in Russia. He and his pupils Andrei Lopukhov and Aleksandr Bocharov published the manual *Osnovy kharakternogo tantsa* (Rudiments of Character Dancing) in 1939. England's Royal Academy of Dancing and the Imperial Society of Teachers of Dance have also developed methods of teaching character dancing to ballet students, as have dance instructors in Canada and Denmark. In the United States there is no single method, although character dancing has been taught by Edward Caton, Yurek Lazowski, Walter Camryn, and others. Camryn's system, published in 1958, includes exercises in dramatic expression, mime, mimicry, and grotesque and eccentric movement, as well as folk and national dances.

Although there has been an interest in ethnic diversity since the early days of ballet, the ethnic element was often confined to sets and costumes, while the dancing was couched in the vocabulary of the *danse d'école*. In surveying the history of character dancing, it is sometimes difficult to judge the degree to which ethnic dance actually shaped the choreography. Some ballets used little more than token gestures, often many times removed from the originals, such as the upward-pointing fingers of many "Chinese" dances. Some character dances, however, result from long study or consultation with an expert, such as the Spanish dances in Léonide Massine's 1919 ballet *Le Tricorne*.

In his *Letters on Dancing and Ballets* (1760), Jean-Georges Noverre expressed the opinion that ethnic dance was a raw material in need of refinement:

> If one were too scrupulous in depicting the characters, manners, and customs of certain nations, the pictures would often be poor and monotonous in composition. . . . Neither a Turkish nor a Chinese festival would appeal to our countrymen if we had not the art to embellish it, and I am persuaded that the style of dancing common to those people would never be captivating. This kind of exactitude in costume and imitation will only present a very insipid spectacle.

Noverre's analysis of the three genres of dancers almost ignores ethnic dance as a component of character dancing. He states that the *danseur noble* should "draw his themes from history and mythology," the *demi-caractère* dancer from pastorals, and the comic dancer from "boorish and rustic sources" (which might include folk dances).

The interest in character dancing was on the rise in the eighteenth century. Charles Le Picq's *Le Tuteur Trompé* (1783) included a *seguidillas* and a bolero that were later performed as *Les Folies d'Espagne*. Vincenzo Galeotti's *The Whims of Cupid and the Ballet Master* (1786) was basically a suite of character dances: Styrian, Quaker, Greek, Norwegian, French, Amager (Danish), and African. In keeping with the broader definition of character, a dance by an aged couple was also included. Jean Dauberval's *La Fille Mal Gardée* (1789) based some of its dances on those of southern France and the Basque provinces.

In the early nineteenth century, the French dancer and choreographer Jean Aumer created a *pas nègre* in *Les Deux Créoles* (1806), a bolero and a tarantella in *Les Pages du Duc de Vendôme* (1815), a Cossack dance in *La Fête Hongroise* (1821), and Spanish and Italian dances in Daniel Auber's opera *La Muette de Portici* (1828).

In his *Traité élémentaire, théorique et pratique de l'art de la danse* (1820) and *The Code of Terpsichore* (1828), Carlo Blasis (1828) speaks of ethnic dances chiefly as the province of comic dancers and advises them to "render themselves servile imitators of every kind of dancing peculiar to different countries, giving their attitudes and movements the true national stamp of the dances they are performing." He lists the most frequently performed character dances as the bolero, the tarantella, the forlana, and Provençal, Russian, Scottish, German, Tyrolean, and Cossack dances; in the category of the "lower comic style" are clog, Chinese, English, and caricature dancing.

The Romantic period was a high point for character dancing, which represented a distinct alternative to the "white ballets" then in vogue. A rage for Spanish dancing began in London and Paris in the 1830s, sparked by the visits of Spanish dancers and the triumph of Fanny Elssler in the *cachucha* from the ballet *Le Diable Boiteux* (1836). Elssler's magnetism made her the period's major popularizer of character dancing; she also popularized the *cracovienne* (derived from the Polish *krakowiak*), the tarantella, and the mazurka.

Romantic choreographers also turned to more exotic climes in their quest for local color. The *pas de l'abeille* in Jean Coralli's *La Péri* (1843) was a refined version of the *nahleh*, an Egyptian striptease dance. August Bournonville's *Far from Denmark, or A Costume Ball on Board* (1860) included dances for Eskimos, Chinese, *bayadères*, and American Indians—and any faults in authenticity could be overlooked because the dances were supposedly performed by costumed guests at a ball.

Although Arthur Saint-Léon is sometimes credited with having created the first national ballet (Russian) in *The Little Humpbacked Horse* (1864), he actually translated folk dance movements of various ethnic groups in Russia into the academic ballet vocabulary, as he also did in his *Coppélia* (1870). Marius Petipa used a similar process to create the many character dances in his ballets: *Don Quixote* (1869), *La Bayadère* (1877), *Raymonda* (1898), and his two collaborations with Lev Ivanov, *The Nutcracker* (1892) and *Swan Lake* (1895). In these ballets, arm and upper body movements derived from ethnic dances are often superimposed upon academic leg movements.

Although in the early twentieth century Michel Fokine popularized the use of folk and national themes in ballet, it was Léonide Massine who most successfully assimilated ethnic dance styles into ballet, both as a dancer and a choreographer. Massine's success lay in his ability to recognize each country's characteristic pulse and flow of melody and to reflect these in the coordinated movements of the whole body. Many of his ballets contain character dances, notably *Midnight Sun* (1915), *Le Tricorne* (1919), and *Capriccio Espagnol* (this last created in collaboration with the Spanish dancer La Argentinita in 1939).

Character dancing is most often associated with European folk dances and least often with Asian dances, but American and African dance forms have appeared with increasing frequency in ballets. Agnes de Mille used square dancing in *Rodeo* (1942) and *Texas Fourth* (1973), while Jerome Robbins used jazz dancing in *Fancy Free* (1944) and *N.Y. Export, Opus Jazz* (1958). African and African-American dance forms enriched Louis Johnson's *Forces of Rhythm*, first performed by the Dance Theatre of Harlem in 1971.

Choreographers continue to use character dancing both to extend the technical vocabulary of ballet and to give it greater immediacy and appeal for audiences of diverse ethnic backgrounds. Although ethnic dances are still adapted for stage presentation, there is more respect for their intrinsic value as expressions of the cultures they represent.

[*See also* Bolero; Mazurka; *and* Tarantella.]

BIBLIOGRAPHY

Arkin, Lisa C., and Marian Smith. "National Dance in the Romantic Ballet." In *Rethinking the Sylph: New Perspectives on the Romantic Ballet*, edited by Lynn Garafola, pp. 11–67. Hanover, N.H., 1997.

Berkut, Mikhail. "Character Dance." *New Dance*, no. 29 (Summer 1984): 14–15.

Berkut, Mikhail. "An Introduction to Character Dance." *Dance Teacher Now* 11 (January–February 1989): 48–52.

Blasis, Carlo. *The Code of Terpsichore: A Practical and Historical Treatise on the Ballet, Dancing, and Pantomime*. London, 1828.

Camryn, Walter. *An Analytical Study of Character Movement for Dancers, Singers, Actors*. Chicago, 1958.

Jones, Alan. "Character Dance Returns with Panache." *New York Times* (19 June 1983).

Kelly, Brigitte. "Character Dancing." *The Dancing Times* 76 (March 1986): 513.

Kirstein, Lincoln. *Movement and Metaphor: Four Centuries of Ballet*. New York, 1970.

Lawson, Joan. *A History of Ballet and Its Makers*. New York, 1964.

Lopoukhov, Andrei, et al. *Character Dance*. Translated by Joan Lawson. London, 1986.

Noverre, Jean-Georges. *Lettres sur la danse et sur les ballets*. Stuttgart and Lyon, 1760. Translated by Cyril W. Beaumont as *Letters on Dancing and Ballets*. London, 1930.

Pagels, Jürgen. *Character Dance*. Bloomington, 1984.

van Praagh, Peggy, and Peter Brinson. *The Choreographic Art*. London, 1963.

SUSAN AU

CHARISSE, CYD (Tula Ellice Finklea; born 8 March 1923 in Amarillo, Texas), dancer and actress. Born with a homespun name (but nicknamed "Sid"), this eventual personification of dancing sophistication began ballet at the age of six with Constance Ferguson in Amarillo, Texas. While vacationing in Hollywood in 1935, her parents enrolled her in the Fanchon and Marco School, where French-born Nico Charisse taught ballet. Although only twelve, she remained in California, to continue training with Charisse, Adolph Bolm, and Bronislava Nijinska. Observing class one day in 1937, Colonel Wassily de Basil asked her to join his Ballets Russes. Calling herself Natacha Tulaelis or Felia Siderova, she toured with the company until her father's illness and eventual death caused her return to Texas. Ballets Russes co-worker David Lichine convinced her to rejoin the troupe for their 1939 European tour (as Maria Istomina). While in France, she and Nico Charisse were married. Returning to Hollywood, she danced at the Hollywood Bowl for Nijinska, and Lichine partnered her in a ballet film sequence he was choreographing, *Something to Shout About* (1943).

As Lily Norwood (her grandmother's name), she danced in the films *Mission to Moscow* and *Thousands Cheer* (both 1943). Broadway choreographer Robert Alton used her on pointe in Metro-Goldwyn-Mayer's *Ziegfeld Follies*, where she pirouetted around Fred Astaire in the film's opening and finale. Producer Arthur Freed took notice and signed her to a seven-year contract and adapted the spelling of her nickname to Cyd for her final screen name. After a speaking role in *The Harvey Girls* (1946) and a dramatic part in *Three Wise Fools*, she was partnered by Gower Champion in *Till the Clouds Roll By* (1946). She had a major role in the backstage ballet melodrama *The Unfinished Dance* (1947) and danced in *Words and Music* (1948).

Once she had a name, MGM sought an onscreen identity. They cast her as "ethnic exotics," dancing with Ricardo Montalban in *Fiesta* (1947) and *On an Island with You* and *The Kissing Bandit* in 1948. She and Charisse divorced, and she married singer Tony Martin. After the

CHARISSE. Fred Astaire dips the long-legged Charisse in *The Band Wagon* (MGM, 1953). (Photograph from the Dance Collection, New York Public Library for the Performing Arts.)

dramatic films *Tension* and *East Side, West Side* (both 1949), she continued in ethnic roles in *Mark of the Renegade* (1951), *The Wild North* (1952), and *Sombrero* (1953).

When Gene Kelly decided *Singin' in the Rain* (1952) needed a climactic "Broadway ballet," he first intended to use his assistant, Carol Haney, as the lurid gangster moll. Freed suggested Charisse and movie musical history was made. Appearing next opposite Fred Astaire in *The Band Wagon* (1953), their "Dancing in the Dark" duet (choreographed by Astaire) and her sensational dancing in the "Girl Hunt Ballet" (created by Michael Kidd) secured film stardom. She danced again with Kelly in *Brigadoon* (1954) and *It's Always Fair Weather* (1955), performed a sensual "One Alone" pas de deux with James Mitchell (choreographed by Eugene Loring) in *Deep in My Heart* (1954), co-starred with Dan Dailey in *Meet Me in Las Vegas* (1956), and was reunited with Astaire in *Silk Stockings* (1957). After several dramatic roles, she returned to dance in Roland Petit's *Black Tights* (1962).

In 1964, Charisse and husband Martin began performing cabaret engagements internationally, and she continued onstage in *Once More with Feeling* (stock); *Ilya Darling* (national tour); *No, No, Nanette* (Australia); and *Charlie Girl* (1986 London revival). She debuted on Broadway as the Russian ballerina in *Grand Hotel* in 1992 and that same year was honored with a Gypsy Lifetime Achievement Award from the Professional Dancer's Society.

Although a classically trained ballerina, Charisse found film immortality by adding sensuality to her lyrical femininity and reigned as dance goddess of the golden age of the movie musical. She was at her best when partnered: supported, lifted, and suspended by filmdom's best male dancers, creating stunning poses and images with her exquisitely proportioned, long-legged body. *Village Voice* critic Dale Thomajohn (1992) called her "the best-looking human being ever to appear on a movie screen." Astaire dubbed her, simply, "beautiful dynamite."

BIBLIOGRAPHY
Martin, Tony, and Cyd Charisse. *The Two of Us.* New York, 1976.
Shipman, David. *The Great Movie Stars: The International Years.* New York, 1972.
Thomajohn, Dale. *From Cyd Charisse to Psycho: A Book of Movie Bests.* New York, 1992.
Thomas, Tony. *That's Dancing.* New York, 1984.

LARRY BILLMAN

CHARLEROI/DANSES. Based in Charleroi, Belgium, the classical company Charleroi/Danses was founded in 1966, but it traces its origins to the 1950s, when dance groups were maintained by two theaters, the Charleroi and the Théâtre Royal in Mons. *Divertissements* were performed in various productions and occasional ballet evenings were organized featuring the best dancers. These activities led to the formation in 1959 of the Ballet de Hanaut, which was attached to the Palais des Beaux-Arts. This evolved into the Ballet Royal de Wallonie, formed in 1966. The leading dancers were Boris Tonin, who was also choreographer, Marie-Louise Pruvot, Monette Densy, Jo Savino, Jacques Sausin, and Jean de Cock.

Hanna Voos was appointed artistic director. She had studied classical ballet at the Teatro alla Scala in Milan and modern dance with Kurt Jooss at Dartington Hall in England. She had also received a teaching certificate from Sadler's Wells before returning to Belgium, where she taught at the conservatory in Charleroi. When she retired in 1976, her position was taken over by Juan Giuliano from Argentina; he was succeeded in 1980 by Jorge Lefebre from Cuba. With a varied background including ballet with Alicia Alonso and jazz with teachers in New York, Lefebre had also danced with Maurice Béjart's Ballet du XXᵉ Siècle.

The aim of the company is to promote the art of dance in the French-speaking part of Belgium. Integral to this is the revival of masterworks; consequently *Giselle*, *The Nutcracker*, and *Swan Lake* are in the repertory.

Since 1990 a new policy has been enacted whereby different choreographers are invited to mount works in various styles. Out of this came Michèle Noiret's *Chasse-Croise*, Micha van Hoecke's *Symphonie en Trois Mouvements*, and José Besprosvany's *Cap de Bonne Espérance*. In 1991 the name of the company was changed to Charleroi/Danses–Centre Chorégraphique de la Communauté Française. Frédéric Flammand was appointed artistic director in September 1991.

[*See also* Belgium, *article on* Theatrical Dance.]

BIBLIOGRAPHY

Como, William. "The New Theatricality." *Dance Magazine* (January 1986): 58–60.

Diénis, Jean-Claude. "Étoile du Ballet de l'Opéra de Wallonie: Eric Frédéric." *Danser* (April 1992): 42–43.

Dubrulle, Paulette. *Ballet de Wallonie.* Brussels, 1976.

Egan, Carol. "From Ballet Royal to Charleroi/Danses." *Ballet Review* 21 (Fall 1993): 85–90.

Jorge Lefebre au Ballet Royal de Wallonie. Mons, 1986.

Moffett, Luisa. "Charleroi." *Ballett International* 12 (September 1989): 28–30.

Philp, Richard. "The Belgian Miracle: Charleroi." *Dance Magazine* (January 1985): 54–55.

LUC VERVAEKE

CHARLESTON. *See* Social Dance, *article on* Twentieth-Century Social Dance to 1960; United States of America, *article on* African-American Social Dance Traditions.

CHARLIP, REMY (born 10 January 1929 in Brooklyn, New York), American dancer, choreographer, costume and set designer, writer, illustrator, actor, director, and teacher. Remy Charlip studied art at Straubenmuller Textile High School in New York and fine arts at Cooper Union, where he received his bachelor of arts degree in 1949 and an award in 1984 for professional achievement in the arts.

Charlip began dancing, directing, producing, and teaching in 1949. From 1950 to 1961 he danced with Merce Cunningham and Dance Company, simultaneously designing many of the company's costumes, posters, and flyers. He also danced with Charles Weidman, Jean Erdman, Katherine Litz, and Donald McKayle. From 1950 to 1962 Charlip worked as a director and performer with the original Living Theater company. He was a co-founder in 1958 of New York's longest-running children's theater, the Paper Bag Players, for which he wrote, directed, and produced numerous works through 1962. From 1964 to 1970 he also worked extensively with the Judson Poets' Theater as a choreographer, designer, performer, and director of musicals and of such plays as Ruth Krauss's *A Beautiful Day* (1965) and *The Sayings of Mao Tse Tung* (1968). As director of the National Theater of the Deaf he wrote and directed two plays, *Biography* (1970) and *Secrets* (1971). In 1980 he wrote thirteen dance plays for the Metro Theater Circus of Saint Louis, Missouri, collectively titled *Do You Love Me Still? . . . Or Do You Love Me Moving?*

As a choreographer Charlip has created well over two hundred dances, for theatrical works, for his own company (the Remy Charlip Dance Company, or latterly the International All-Star Dance Company; also known as Remy Charlip Dances for his solo programs), and for

soloists and repertory companies around the world. The diverse sources of his work include abstraction, improvisation, music visualization, eurythmy, biography and autobiography, the American Sign Language of deaf people (ASL), Native American poetry, *jin shin jyutsu*, healing, meditation, and bodywork. Gentleness and a wry, whimsical sense of humor inform most of his work.

Among his most notable pieces are *Hommage à Loie Fuller* (1969), created for the Osaka World's Fair; *The Book Is Dead* (1971), for the Caen Bibliothèque; *Quick Change Artists* (1973) for the Scottish Theatre Ballet; *Tiempo Azul* (1976), for Taller de Danza Contemporanea of Caracas, Venezuela; *Art of the Dance* (1977), in which Charlip created a painting with his foot that was auctioned off to the audience at the end of the dance; and *Danza por Correo* (1978) for José Ledezma of Caracas. Charlip has a particular gift for making charming occasional pieces, often incorporating text or song; among the best of these is *Every Little Movement, A Homage to Delsarte* (1980), made for his longtime friends and collaborators from the Judson Poets' Theatre, David Vaughan and composer-pianist Al Carmines. Among the many solos he has made in collaboration with celebrated dancers, one of the finest is *Growing Up in Public* (1984), for former Limón dancer Lucas Hoving. Many of Charlip's own solos have been autobiographical and included text, such as *Glow Worm* (1976) and *Before Me Peaceful* (1984). Since 1982 Charlip has choreographed many pieces for companies based in California, including *Pillows and Comforter,* with an original score by Lou Harrison for gamelan orchestra, created for Tandy Beal and Dancers (1985). Among Charlip's several site-inspired works are *Amaterasu* (1988), choreographed while he was the first artist in residence at the Los Angeles Museum of Contemporary Art (MOCA). Charlip has also made many pieces during teaching residencies in universities throughout the United States, most recently *Young Omelet* (1991), created with students at Hofstra University as an interpretation of *Hamlet* for a festival of Shakespeare plays. His works have been performed by the Joffrey Ballet; London Contemporary Dance Theatre; Welsh Dance Theatre; the Dance Company of New South Wales, Australia; Rotterdam Dans; and Rep West of Santa Barbara, California, among others. In 1997 he became an advisor to the artists and teachers in the San Francisco Arts Education Project for the production of his musical play *Harlequin,* with a cast of 650 schoolchildren.

In 1972 Charlip began a series titled *Air Mail Dances* or *Mail Order Dances,* in which he sent drawings of dancers, with twenty to forty figures on each page, to various dancers and companies who then created the necessary transitions to compose dances based on the images. These dances, some of which can be arranged for up to 250 performers, have been performed in the United States, Europe, South America, and Australia. Representative pieces from this series include *Garden Lilacs* (1979), *Dance in a Bed with a Pillow* (1979; filmed for WGBH Television, Boston, as part of a program of Charlip's dances), and *Six Mail Order Dances for Forty People in Six Open Spaces in Maine* (for the Bates College Dance Company, 1979).

The illustrator and/or writer of twenty-seven picture books, many considered classics, Charlip is also a unique figure in American children's literature. Like his dances, his books are full of puns, jokes, word games, fantasies, magical metamorphoses, and sweet-natured humor. One book, *Thirteen* (with Jerry Joyner), tells thirteen stories simultaneously; others, such as *Arm in Arm* (1967) dispense with narrative entirely. Among the best-loved of his other books are *Fortunately* (1964), *The First Remy Charlip Reader* (1986), *Handtalk: An ABC of Fingerspelling and Sign Language* (with Mary Beth and George Ancona, 1974); *Hooray for Me* (with Lillian Moore and Vera B. Williams), and Margaret Wise Brown's *The Dead Bird* (1958). In 1997 his books were honored with a special exhibition at the Library of Congress in Washington, D.C.

Charlip was head of the children's literature department at Sarah Lawrence College in New York for five years, where he taught a "Workshop in Making Things Up." He has been a Regent's Lecturer at the University of California at Santa Barbara; a visiting professor at Hofstra University; and taught at Mills College, the Walker Art Center, the Harvard Summer Dance Program, and the Colorado Dance Festival. He has received two OBIE awards, three Isadora Duncan awards, two Ingram Merrill awards, a United States/Japan Commission Arts Fellowship, and the first three-year choreographer's fellowship from the National Endowment for the Arts, among many other grants. His books have won awards in the United States, Japan, Italy, France, and Russia. His paintings and drawings have been exhibited in France, Russia, Japan, and in several museums and galleries in the United States. The Remy Charlip Library in Greenville, Delaware, houses a collection of archival material relating to his books, as well as a hundred-foot-long mural painted by him. His writings on dance have appeared in the *Village Voice, Contact Quarterly*, the *Movement Research Performance Journal*, and *Ballet Review*.

BIBLIOGRAPHY
Gow, Gordon. "The Versatile Talents of Remy Charlip." *The Dancing Times* (April 1974): 399–400.
Vaughan, David. "Making Things Up: About Remy Charlip." *On the Next Wave* 2 (October 1984): 30–32.

CHRISTOPHER CAINES

CHARRAT, JANINE (born 24 July 1924 in Grenoble), French dancer and choreographer. Charrat is credited with more than fifty ballets. She grew up in Paris and began her dance apprenticeship with a teacher of Eastern dance, Jeanne Ronsay, who recognized the precocious gifts of her young pupil. At the age of eight Charrat composed and created dances, and at thirteen gave full-length recitals in which her understanding of composition and her musical sense were immediately evident. At twelve she played a supporting role in the film *La Mort du Cygne* with Mia Slavenska and Yvette Chauviré. She then began her classical training with Lubov Egorova.

Between 1941 and 1944 Charrat joined young Roland Petit in recitals that helped develop her choreographic talent. Her first major ballet, *Jeu de Cartes* (Card Game; 1945, to music by Igor Stravinsky), for the newly established Ballets des Champs-Élysées, was a personal triumph, since she was only twenty-one years old. A small woman with a delicate, foxlike face and a slight, flexible body, Charrat was an expressive dancer, both forceful and lyrical. Her classical training never spoiled her melodic fluidity of movement and line. Fascinated by dramatic subjects, she herself was usually the heroine of her ballets. Charrat considered herself a faithful disciple of Serge Lifar, but she departed from his style in giving her own choreography more expressivity and lyricism.

In 1946 Charrat presented the ballet *Cressida*, in which she danced with Yvette Chauviré, for the Nouveau Ballet de Monte Carlo. In 1947 she danced in Paris, at the Opéra-Comique, in *Concerto*, with music by Prokofiev. Later that year she directed, for Roland Petit's Ballets de Paris, *La Femme et Son Ombre* (The Woman and Her Shadow) and Jean Genet's *Adame Miroir*. In 1951 she formed her Ballets Janine Charrat, which in 1955 became the state-sponsored Ballets de France. Her most important creations for her own company include *Le Massacre des Amazones, Héraklès, Les Liens* (The Bonds), and in particular *Les Algues* (Seaweed), created with the *régisseur* Bertrand Castelli to music by Guy Bernard (premiered 20 April 1953, Paris). Outside her own company, Charrat worked at the Teatro alla Scala in Milan, the Teatro Colón in Buenos Aires, the Paris Opera, and the Théâtre Royal de la Monnaie in Brussels, where she danced in *The Seven Deadly Sins*, choreographed by Maurice Béjart. Her major work remains *Abraxas* (1949), with music by Werner Egk; it was first performed in Berlin with Charrat in the principal role. [*See* Abraxas.]

In 1961 Charrat suffered severe burns when her tutu caught fire in a television studio. The next year, however, she was able to resume activity as dance director at Le Grand Théâtre de Genève, where she directed and danced *Tu Auras Nom Tristan* (Your Name Will Be Tristan). She participated in a newly formed company at the Dance Festival in Paris (1964) with *Alerte . . . Puit 21 (Warning . . . Shaft 21)* and won an award for *Paris*, with music by Henri Sauguet; her partners were Milorad Miskovitch and Karl Musil. At the Vienna State Opera she created roles in *The Firebird* and in *L'Enfant et les Sortilèges* (1964). In

1973 she performed at the Paris Opera in *Offrandes*. Charrat's robust nature kept her dancing despite the problems caused by her severe burns. Her last appearances on the stage were during a tour in 1967–1968 with Milorad Miskovitch's company in Central and South America, where she danced one of her great roles in *Concerto*, to music by Edvard Grieg, and performed *The Dying Swan* with great sensitivity.

In 1980 Charrat became dance consultant for the Centre Pompidou, where she regularly introduced contemporary dance companies; she retired from this position in 1989. In 1982 she had created, for the Grand Théâtre of Bordeaux, a modern work, *Hecuba*, which was restaged at the Nice Opera. In 1987, for the Pompidou Centre, she had staged a new ballet, *Palais des Glaces*, based on a book by Pierre Rhallys. In September 1988 she had organized a short season in the Casino de Paris, reviving her old successes *Adame Miroir* and *Concerto*, as well as *Palais des Glaces*.

Both as a dancer and as a choreographer, Janine Charrat holds a special place in ballet. First and foremost, she has always been a creator, and with rare exceptions she did not dance ballets by other choreographers. Her only appearance in the classical repertory was in *Giselle*, as a guest artist with the Grand Ballet du Marquis de Cuevas.

In 1996, Janine Charrat was decorated by France's Ministère de la Culture with the Ordre National du Mérite.

BIBLIOGRAPHY

Baril, Jacques. "Poétes-visionnaires et chorégraphes." *Saisons de la danse*, no. 26 (Summer 1970): 18–19.

Humbert, Michel. *Janine Charrat, Antigone de la danse*. Paris, 1970.

Lidova, Irène. *Dix-sept visages de la danse française*. Paris, 1953.

Lidova, Irène. "Janine Charrat." *Saisons de la danse*, no. 26 (Summer 1970): 10–15.

Stranciu-Reiss, Françoise. "Entretien avec Janine Charrat." *Recherche en danse*, no. 2 (1983): 86–96.

IRÈNE LIDOVA
Translated from French

CHASE, LUCIA (born 24 March 1907 in Waterbury, Connecticut, died 9 January 1986 in New York City), American dancer and codirector of American Ballet Theatre. The driving force behind American Ballet Theatre for thirty-five years, Chase originally sought a career as an actress. After receiving her academic education at Saint Margaret's School in Waterbury, Connecticut, Chase studied acting at the Theatre Guild School in New York City. Her artistic focus shifted when she undertook ballet training from Mikhail Mordkin. As a ballerina with the Mordkin Ballet Company (1938–1939), she danced leading roles in *La Fille Mal Gardée*, *Giselle*, and Mordkin's *Goldfish*, among other ballets.

Chase's eminent role in American ballet began in 1939, when Richard Pleasant launched Ballet Theatre. The company drew, in part, from the Mordkin Ballet for dancers and productions, and Chase was among the founding members who provided financial backing when Ballet Theatre presented its first season in 1940. Chase continued to dance, performing with American Ballet Theatre (the company amended its name in 1957) until the 1970s. Although she was never a true *prima ballerina*, Chase was a talented actress and mime in dramatic roles. The critic Walter Terry called her "a superb dramatic dancer and a brilliant comedienne."

Through the years Chase created a number of roles in works by major twentieth-century choreographers. For Antony Tudor she performed Minerva in *The Judgment of Paris* (1938), the Eldest Sister in *Pillar of Fire* (1942), and the Nurse in *Romeo and Juliet* (1943), as well as a leading role in *Dark Elegies* (1940). She created the role of the Greedy One in Agnes de Mille's *Three Virgins and a Devil* (1941) and the Innocent in *Tally-Ho* (1944). She was the first to dance Pallas Athena in *Helen of Troy* (1942) and Khivria in *Fair at Sorochinsk* (1943), both by David Lichine, and she danced Queen Clementine in Michel Fokine's *Bluebeard* (1941) and the Little Girl in Eugene Loring's *Great American Goof* (1940). She also performed leading roles in de Mille's *Fall River Legend*, Anton Dolin's *Pas de Quatre*, and Fokine's *Les Sylphides*, *Petrouchka*, and *Le Carnaval*.

In 1945 Chase was named co-director (with Oliver Smith) of Ballet Theatre. She was responsible for selecting dancers, setting the repertory, arranging the programs, and making casting decisions. During her tenure she saw the company through various financial crises, and it is generally acknowledged that she contributed generously from her private fortune to its maintenance and survival. In her writings and public statements, however, Chase has minimized her role, preferring instead to recall Richard Pleasant and his vision of Ballet Theatre as a showcase for the best in classic and contemporary ballet, a company international in scope and national in spirit.

When American Ballet Theatre marked its thirty-fifth anniversary in 1975, Chase was awarded the Handel Medallion by the City of New York. In June 1980 she was presented the Presidential Medal of Freedom by Jimmy Carter. She resigned her directorship that same year, and Mikhail Baryshnikov assumed the leadership of American Ballet Theatre.

[*See also* American Ballet Theatre.]

BIBLIOGRAPHY

Ballet Review 18 (Spring 1990): 54–66. Special section entitled "Lucia Chase Remembered."

Gruen, John. *People Who Dance: Twenty-Two Dancers Tell Their Own Stories*. Princeton, N.J., 1988.

Hunt, Marilyn. "Lucia Chase, 1897–1986." *Dance Magazine* (March 1986): 50.

Kisselgoff, Anna. "Lucia Chase Helped Create the Ballet World We Know." *New York Times* (19 January 1986).

Louis, Murray. "Lucia Chase, 1907–1986." In *Murray Louis on Dance.* Pennington, N.J., 1992.

Payne, Charles, et al. *American Ballet Theatre.* New York, 1977.

Rosen, Lillie F. "Lucia Chase and the American Ballet Theatre." *Attitude* 4.1 (1986): 16.

THOMAS CONNORS

CHAUVIRÉ, YVETTE (born 22 April 1917 in Paris), French ballet dancer, teacher, and coach. Yvette Chauviré is one of the most illustrious ballerinas of the second half of the twentieth century and one of the few French ballerinas who have achieved international renown. Trained at the Paris Opera Ballet School, where she studied with Carlotta Zambelli, Madame Rousanne, Albert Aveline, and others, she began to appear onstage in 1930, as a member of the *second quadrille,* the lowest rank in the company hierarchy. As a result of her training, she acquired a personality and style once considered typically French, characterized by an acidulous charm, personal mannerisms, and coquetry. Small and dark, with a short torso and square shoulders but with long, slender legs, a wonderful neck, a small head, and a pretty face, she was accepted into the Paris Opera Ballet as a principal dancer in 1936.

Chauviré quickly attracted notice and by 1937 had been named a *première danseuse.* That same year she gained international fame as one of the stars of the film *La Mort du Cygne* (released in Anglophone countries as *Ballerina*), although she was clearly surpassed by her co-star, Mia Slavenska. Soon thereafter, however, she began a process of training that would transform her from a talented ballerina into a dancer of incomparable artistry, thanks to her director at the Opera, Serge Lifar, and to two remarkable Russian teachers, Boris Kniaseff and Victor Gsovsky.

Although already a principal dancer, Chauviré submitted herself to an apprenticeship to her new teachers and willingly endured the iron discipline and hard work they demanded. Gradually, a completely new dancer began to emerge, a dancer who seemed suddenly to have grasped the mystery of classical dance. Kniaseff found in Chauviré a sensitive and enthusiastic student, and under his tutelage her body stretched, her arms lengthened and acquired a languourous fluidity. Her style of dancing became one of rigorous refinement, clarity, and perfect equilibrium. Not blessed with exceptional elevation, she suggested a flower rather than a bird, for she seemed to blossom in space. The lines of her legs and arms had an absolute purity. In rapid measures, in running and *batterie,* she showed a crystalline precision, and in adagio passages she exhibited an exceptional musical sensitivity, being vibrant, flexible, and expressive from head to toe.

Chauviré became one of Lifar's favorite ballerinas at the Opera. She had danced her first solo in 1936 in his ballet *Le Roi Nu,* a one-act ballet based on the fairy tale "The Emperor's New Clothes," and in 1937 she had created roles in his *David Triomphant* and *Alexandre le Grand.* In 1941, she stunned Parisian audiences when she danced *Istar,* an eighteen-minute solo that Lifar had made expressly for her. Her long-lined flexibility was admirably suited to Lifar's neoclassical choreography, and her triumphant interpretation of Istar, the Mesopotamian goddess of love, won her promotion to *première danseuse étoile.* Subsequently, she created roles in Lifar's *Le Chevalier et la Demoiselle* (1941), *Joan de Zarissa* (1942), and *Suite en Blanc* (1943) as well as dancing the ballerina roles in such classics as *Sylvia, Coppélia,* and *Swan Lake,* act 2. In 1942 she starred in a new production of Louis Mérante's *Les Deux Pigeons,* staged by Albert Aveline with the assistance of Carlotta Zambelli, and in 1943 she danced for the first time the title role of *Giselle,* with which she would be identified throughout her career.

In 1946, when Lifar left the Paris Opera because of political allegations, Chauviré followed him to Monte Carlo, where he established a short-lived company, Nouveau Ballet de Monte Carlo, and continued to fashion works

CHAUVIRÉ. In the film *La Mort du Cygne* (1937), Chauviré became widely known as a rising star of the Paris Opera. (Photograph by Maurice Seymour; used by permission.)

CHAUVIRÉ. The Shadow in Serge Lifar's ballet *Les Mirages* (1947) was one of the roles for which Chauviré was most famous. (Photograph from the Dance Collection, New York Public Library for the Performing Arts.)

around her. She was the flirtatious young wife in *Dramma per Musica* (1946); Queen Thamar, the inspiration and lover of the title character, in *Chota Roustaveli* (1946); and Leuchothéa, goddess of the sea, in *Nautéos* (1947). Returning to the Opera in 1947, she created the role for which she is, perhaps, most famous: the Shadow in Lifar's neo-Romantic work *Les Mirages*, set to music by Henri Sauguet. Bringing to it the perfect beauty of her classical technique and investing it with a tender, Romantic femininity, she made this role indelibly her own. The other single role with which Chauviré was most frequently identified is Giselle, the doomed heroine of the quintessential ballet of the Romantic era. She was acclaimed for her interpretation not only in France but in England, Russia, Italy, Germany, South Africa, and the United States.

From 1948 onward, Chauviré's career was that of an international artist, although she returned regularly to dance on France's national stage at the Paris Opera. She displayed her virtuosity in Lifar's *L'Écuyère* (The Equestrienne), created in 1948 as a showpiece for her tours, and in Victor Gsovsky's *Grand Pas Classique*, also known as

Grand Pas d'Auber, created for the Ballets des Champs-Élysées in 1949. At the Paris Opera she created leading roles in John Cranko's *La Belle Hélène* (1955) and Harald Lander's *Concerto aux Étoiles* (1956). In Monte Carlo, she created roles in Jean Babilée's *Balance à Trois* (1955) and Lifar's *Divertissement à la Cour* (1956), and at the Berlin Opera she appeared as Juliet in a 1957 revival of Tatjana Gsovsky's *Romeo and Juliet*. In 1960 she returned to Berlin to create the role of Marguerite in Gsovsky's expanded version of *Die Kameliendame* (The Lady of the Camellias). At the Festival du Marais in Paris in 1965, Chauviré and Milorad Miskovitch danced the title roles in Dimitrije Parlić's *Romeo and Juliet* with the Zagreb Ballet.

In a career that spanned more than thirty-six years, Chauviré also danced with La Scala Ballet in Milan, Ballet Russe de Monte Carlo in New York, London Festival Ballet, the Rome Opera Ballet, the Stuttgart Ballet, the Royal Ballet (London), and Le Grand Ballet du Marquis de Cuevas, and she toured extensively in western Europe, the Soviet Union, the United States, and Central and South America. In her gala performances—which frequently featured Lifar's *Adagio d'Albinoni* and Gsovsky's *Grand Pas Classique*—her customary partners were Youly Algaroff, Milorad Miskovitch, Cyril Atanassof, and Vladimir Skouratoff. She danced *The Sleeping Beauty* and *Giselle* with Rudolf Nureyev during tours of Germany and Italy in 1961, and Erik Bruhn partnered her in *Giselle* at the Paris Opera in 1964. She retired from the stage on 20 November 1972, after dancing *Giselle* with Atanassof, a performance that won for her a prolonged and deeply affectionate ovation.

Chauviré then, once again, devoted her energies to teaching. From 1963 to 1968, she had been director of the Paris Opera Ballet School and had exerted considerable influence on the rising generation of female dancers. Some of them, such as Noëlla Pontois, had become stars of the company while Chauviré was still dancing. Others would follow in later years. In retirement, Chauviré coached such luminaries of the Opera as Dominique Khalfouni, Florence Clerc, and Isabelle Guérin in various roles in the repertory, particularly Giselle, and occasionally conducted master classes at schools abroad, in Japan, Italy, and the United States. In a brief stint as an actress, she played the legendary Greek queen Leda at the Théâtre de la Madeleine in 1976/77.

In 1981 and 1982 Chauviré returned once more to the Opera as a teacher in the ballet school and thereafter made occasional stage appearances in mime roles. In 1984 she played the Countess Sybille de Doris in Nureyev's production of *Raymonda*, and in 1985 she was Lady Capulet in his production of *Romeo and Juliet*. In 1988 she appeared in a film dedicated to her art, *Yvette Chauviré: Une Étoile pour l'Exemple*, produced by Dominique Delouche, in which she is seen teaching seven ballerinas of the Opera fragments of her famous roles.

As the brightest star of the Paris Opera, Chauviré was widely admired in France and was the source of such pride that she was called "La Chauviré Nationale." She received many honors and awards in recognition of her achievements as a dancer. She is a Commandeur de l'Ordre National du Mérite and a Commandeur de l'Ordre des Arts et des Lettres. She was named a Chevalier de la Légion d'Honneur in 1964, an Officier in 1974, and a Commandeur in 1988.

BIBLIOGRAPHY

Anderson, Jack. *The One and Only: The Ballet Russe de Monte Carlo.* New York, 1981.

Baignères, Claude. *Yvette Chauviré* (in French). Paris, 1956.

Beaumont, Cyril W. "Four Giselles." *Ballet* (March 1951).

Chauviré, Yvette. *Je suis ballerine.* Paris, 1960.

Fargue, François. "Chauviré par Chauviré." *Saisons de la danse,* no. 250 (October 1993): 41–42.

Guest, Ivor. "Fair Exchange: The Stars of the Paris Opera." *Dance and Dancers* (September 1954): 9–11.

Guillot de Rode, François. *Yvette Chauviré* (in French). Paris, 1949.

Lidova, Irène. "Yvette Chauviré." In *Dancers and Critics,* edited by Cyril Swinson. London, 1950.

Lidova, Irène. "Yvette Chauviré." In *Saisons de la danse* (February 1968).

Moore, Lillian. "A New Choreographer." *The Dancing Times* (June 1950).

Nemenschousky, Léon. *A Day with Yvette Chauviré.* London, 1960.

Percival, John. "The French Revolution." *Dance and Dancers* (January 1984): 14–15.

IRÈNE LIDOVA
Translated from French

CHECKMATE.

CHECKMATE. Choreography: Ninette de Valois. Music: Arthur Bliss. Libretto: Arthur Bliss: Scenery and costumes: E. McKnight Kauffer. First performance: 15 June 1937, Théâtre des Champs-Élysées, Paris, Vic-Wells Ballet. Principals: June Brae (The Black Queen), Harold Turner (The First Red Knight), Pamela May (The Red Queen), Robert Helpmann (The Red King).

Checkmate is an allegorical ballet depicting a game of chess between Love and Death, who are seen in the prologue making their opening moves. The main action shows the game itself, in which the Black Queen seduces the Red Knight. Torn between desire and duty, he hesitates to deliver the coup de grâce when he has her in his power, whereupon she contemptuously stabs him to death. Alone and defenseless, the old Red King summons up the last remnants of his strength in defiance of the Black forces, then falls lifeless. It is checkmate: Love has been defeated by Death.

The ballet stands or falls by the strength of its interpreters. In the original cast—Brae as the glamorous, implacable Black Queen, Turner as the noble but weak Red Knight, Helpmann as the doddering Red King, and May as his gentle consort—all gave enormous conviction to their roles. (Margot Fonteyn was a Black Pawn.) In later casts Beryl Grey gave a powerful performance as the Black Queen, a role also danced by Violetta Elvin, Julia Farron, Svetlana Beriosova, Monica Mason, Natalia Makarova, and Maina Gielgud. Rudolf Nureyev has danced the Red Knight.

Structurally the ballet has several weaknesses. The allegory does not hold: the odds are too heavily weighted against the Red side; not only are the Red King and Queen weaklings, they cannot win because there is no Black King. Bliss's score is effective but sometimes emptily bombastic; some of the numbers, notably the Red Knight's mazurka, are too long. A stroke of genius was the choice of Kauffer, an American poster artist, to design the decor and costumes (especially the drop curtain), though his revised and enlarged version of the backdrop for the revival at the Royal Opera House in 1947 was inferior to the original.

Checkmate was one of the ballets lost when the Vic-Wells Ballet (soon to become the Sadler's Wells Ballet) was caught in the Nazi invasion of the Netherlands in the spring of 1940, and it was not restored to the repertory until the company's 1947 revival. Since then the ballet has been danced by both sections of the Royal Ballet. It was also revived by the Vienna State Opera Ballet in 1964. *Checkmate* was among the earliest ballets telecast by the British Broadcasting Corporation (BBC), in 1938 and again in 1939, with the original cast; the BBC telecast it again in 1963. A five-part series that aired in January 1984 on Britain's Channel 4 showed the choreographer rehearsing various sections of the ballet for a revival by Sadler's Wells Royal Ballet.

BIBLIOGRAPHY

Barnes, Clive. "Ballet Perspectives No. 29: *Checkmate.*" *Dance and Dancers* (February 1963): 31–33.

DAVID VAUGHAN

CHEERLEADING.

CHEERLEADING. *See* Dance as Sport.

CHEIRONOMIA.

CHEIRONOMIA. The word *cheironomia* is a compound of the classical Greek words for "hand" *(cheir)* and "name" *(onoma).* Recent scholarship has challenged the long-held belief that the ancient Greek dramatic chorus communicated the lyrics through a codified system of pantomimic hand gestures called *cheironomia.*

In Greece of the fifth century BCE, the term denoted an athletic or military skill learned in the gymnasium. Medical sources define it as a sort of shadowboxing. In Xenophon's record of a conversation between Socrates and his friend Charmides, Charmides explained that he practiced the exercises of *cheironomia* ("shadowboxing") because he did not know how to dance. Because exercises and drills learned by the Greeks in the gymnasium were often executed to music, the movements may have acquired a dancelike quality though the activities remained distinct from formal dancing. There is no indication, however, that fifth-century writers associated *cheironomia* with the practice of choral dancing.

Five centuries later, at the height of Roman arts, the term *cheironomia* acquired an association with the practice of contemporary *pantomimi*, who told stories through the use of hand gestures. [*See* Pantomime.] Many writers sought to compare their dance or link it to the choral dance of fifth-century BCE Greece because they admired the earlier culture.

One anecdote in Greek history (Herodotus 6) was particularly vulnerable to misinterpretation by the Romans. Hippocleides, a military officer, outshone the other suitors in an athletic competition to win the daughter of the Greek tyrant Cleisthenes. Just before he announced his choice of son-in-law, Cleisthenes provided a sumptuous feast for the suitors. Hippocleides indulged in so much wine that he danced on a table. Finally he stood on his head and "performed *cheironomia* with his legs." This particular figure lost Hippocleides the respect of Cleisthenes and with it his bride. Romans (for example Pollux in his *Onomasticon*) who retold this story ignored the military and athletic context of the incident and extolled it as an early example of theatrical or pantomimic dance.

Although the ancient commentators attributed a pantomimic dimension to *cheironomia* in their own time, they displayed confusion even within individual works as to the exact meaning of the practice. Lucian and Plotinus noted the similarity of dance (that is, pantomime) to *cheironomia*. Athenaeus equated *cheironomia* with the pyrrhic, an armed dance, which may have been his acknowledgment that *cheironomia* originated in a military or gymnastic context. [*See* Pyrrhic.] The discrepancies may be explained by the facts that the various Roman accounts span at least several centuries and that they were written in different locales across the empire. There is no assurance that the practices of *cheironomia* seen by each writer were identical.

Both Greek and Roman literary excerpts imply that *cheironomia* was a solitary practice. The shadowboxing would have been practiced in the absence of a sparring partner, and the Roman pantomime was always a solo performance.

[*See also* Greece, *article on* Dance in Ancient Greece.]

BIBLIOGRAPHY
Athenaeus. *Deipnosophists* 14.629–631.
Herodotus 6.126–130.
Lucian. *On the Dance* 78.
Plato. *Laws* 830c.
Pollux, Julius. *Onomasticon* 2.153.
Smigel, Libby. "The Case against Cheironomia in the Fifth-Century B.C. Greek Theatre." In *Proceedings of the Fifth Annual Conference, Dance History Scholars, Harvard University, 13–15 February 1982*, compiled by Christena L. Schlundt. Riverside, Calif., 1982.
Xenophon. *Symposium* 2.

LIBBY SMIGEL

CHEN WEIYA (born 11 July 1956 in Nanjing), Chinese dancer and choreographer. Chen began dancing leading roles in the restagings of the Chinese ballets *The White-Haired Girl* and *The Red Detachment of Women*, and the dance dramas *The Song of the Yimeng Mountain* and *The Dagger Society*, in productions by the Huaibei Municipal Dance Company in Anhui Province of southern China. He became better known as a choreographer, mainly through *Miners and Sunlight*, a short piece that won him a first-class prize in an eastern China dance competition in 1984. In 1989 he graduated from the choreography department of the Beijing Dance Academy, where he became an associate professor.

At the Beijing Dance Academy Chen has been a talented and productive choreographer. His notable works include *Hua Mu-lan Coming Home from the Frontline, Mu Gui-ying Taking Command in the Battle, Single-plank Bridge, Mong Dong, The Goddess Luoshen, Flying Apsaras, The Boat Trackers' Tunes, Back to the Heavens, Widowed Heroines from the Yang's Family, Youth in the Warring Fire, Sail Never Falls, Older Brother and Younger Sister under One Master, Nuo Zha Stirring the Sea, Skylight, The Fire Maker, Back and Forth*, and *Entries and Exits*. These dances, chiefly in the styles of Chinese folk and classical dance, all brought him regional or national prizes and recognition. His choreography (some in collaboration) for *Nuances of the Tang Dynasty, Series I and II*, included *Dancing to the Pi-pa Tunes, Beside a River on a Moonlit Spring Night, In the Deep of Night*, and *Hatred by the Wu River*, which combined classical nuances with contemporary concepts and aroused great interest among audiences in mainland China and Hong Kong. In 1990 he was invited to co-choreograph a full-length dance drama, *The Emperor Qin*, for the Hong Kong Dance Company. Chen created the innovative *Oratorio* (1992), his first ballet, for the French Youth Ballet, and *Greenfield* (1993), his version of Stravinsky's 1913 score for *The Rite of Spring*. Another full-length dance drama, *Fantasy of the Western Pilgrimage*, danced by both the Hong Kong Dance Company and the Beijing Dance Academy in 1992, showed the lightheartedness of Chen's imagination.

[*See also* China, *article on* Contemporary Theatrical Dance.]

BIBLIOGRAPHY
Chen Weiya. "Talking about My Classical Styled Creations from My Own Choreography: Hua Mu-lan Coming Home from the Frontline" (in Chinese). *Dance Art* (Beijing), no. 1 (1994).

OU JIAN-PING

CHHAU. Until relatively recently, *chhau* dance was not known outside Northeast India. In 1938 the European tour of a company of *chhau* dancers introduced both Indian and foreign audiences to three unique styles of dance—Seraikella *chhau* of the state of Bihar, Mayurbhanj *chhau* of Orissa, and Purulia *chhau* of Bengal. All three share some common features, but each has its own unique characteristics.

A general feature is the basic dance exercises, which are derived from regional martial arts traditions. They are classed as shield and sword exercises (*parikhanda; pari* means "shield," and *khanda* means "sword"). In general the exercises are focused on the lower torso, with special stances and poses coupled with various walks, kicks, and turns executed in progressively faster tempos forming the bulk of the exercise patterns.

Seraikella *Chhau*. This strikes the outside observer as the most lyrical of the *chhau* styles, perhaps owing to its royal patronage and the participation of local *rājas* as dancers in the court company. It appealed to the great Bengali poet Rabindranath Tagore, who championed Seraikella *chhau* outside the region.

The dancers wear beautifully conceived and executed masks painted in pastel yellow, blue, green, pink, and bone white. The design and execution of these masks have no parallel anywhere in India. Finely wrought headdresses of tinsel and jewels crown most of the masks.

Like the other *chhau* styles, Seraikella *chhau* emphasizes earthbound movements. The repertory consists of epic themes and purely lyrical numbers. Usually the dances are of short duration and involve only a few performers at a time. Owing to the snug fit of the masks, the dancers find it difficult to sustain long passages of movement. Typically the dances concern birds, animals, and purely interpretive and symbolic themes based on Indian myths and legends. Choreography is still part of the Seraikella *chhau* tradition, and new works are added to the repertory by leading teachers.

Because the mask must be made to live in performance, emphasis is placed on expression by the whole body in space, and a specific vocabulary of movements has evolved. There are various *cali*s, or directions, that movement may take—front, back, diagonal, curved, crescent, or rough. Three tempos, slow, medium, and fast, are used for the *topka*s, or styles of gait or locomotion; some *topka*s take their name and movement pattern from specific birds and animals. Out of these actions emerge the *ufli*s—the footwork and movements of the legs and torso that translate the elements of daily life into dance. These patterns are drawn from the daily routines of housewives and farmers, such as mixing and spreading cow dung and preparing a mud floor or collecting and winnowing grain. All these units combine into the *bhangi*s, basic sequences of movement that make up a dance on a particular theme.

Public performances usually take place in April during the Caitra Parva, a festival in honor of the sun. This is the hot season, so performances occur at night, on a specially demarcated plot of ground in front of the royal palace.

Mayurbhanj *Chhau*. This style takes its name from a region in the southeastern corner of Orissa. There is little written history of it, but as with Seraikella *chhau*, a regional tradition of martial arts has informed the basic dance movements and style. It similarly presents a range of simple themes such as hunting and fishing as well as dance dramas taken from Hindu myths and legends; newly choreographed pieces are also introduced by prominent teachers. Three classes of dance pieces are found in Mayurbhanj *chhau*—solo, duo, and group. Large-scale choreographed pieces in which many dancers participate make this unique among the *chhau* styles; in addition, the dancers of Mayurbhanj *chhau* do not wear masks.

The special occasions for the performance of Mayurbhanj *chhau* are the Dussehra and Caitra Parva festivals, in which competitions take place between two groups of dancers at a time. The groups are called the *uttara sahi* and the *dakṣina sahi*. The place of competition is a wide outdoor dance space, bounded on two sides by narrow platforms with steps leading up to them. Elevated seats for the teachers of the competing companies are located upstage of the open space. The spectators sit or stand in front of the open area between the two platforms and witness the entrance of the dancers to the accompaniment of deep, resonant drums and shrill wind instruments.

Each dance has four stages of development. It begins with *rangabaja*, a musical invocation performed in dance behind a curtain. Second, walking (*cali*) begins as the characters appear onstage in their characteristic stances (*dhāraṇa*s). This is followed by the *vidūṣaka praṇālikā*, in which there is dialogue, mime, and movement of two characters known as *kaji-paji*. Third, the *nāc* introduces the theme of the dance but does not move the dramatic action forward. The fourth phase is the finale (*nāṭkī*), which consists of intricate choreography in fast tempo.

Like Seraikella *chhau*, the dance movements are divided into *topka*s, *ufli*s, and *bhangi*s. Many of the movements correspond to the routines of daily life among the rural people of this region.

Mayurbhanj *chhau* is preserved by teachers (*ustād*s) who have passed down the tradition from generation to generation. Today, schools organized along modern institutional lines help to sustain the tradition.

Purulia *Chhau*. This style of masked dance is found in the Purulia district of West Bengal. There is little historical detail about its tradition or development. Today there are said to be three schools of performance: the Bandyoyan, generally regarded as the most conservative of the schools; the Bagmundi, which has been the focus of much

CHHAU. A dancer from West Bengal, India, in a typical stance of the Purulia *chhau*, an athletic dance drama related to martial arts. This genre is performed in village squares by men, traditionally of the lower castes, for the Dussehra and Caitra Parva festivals. (Photograph from the archives of The Asia Society, New York.)

recent anthropological research; and the Jhalda, which has been considerably influenced by urban cinema.

Purulia Chhau is performed during the Dussehra and Caitra Parva festivals by male dancers who are also agriculturalists, laborers, or rickshaw pullers. Many of these individuals belong to the lowest social strata of the region. Their teachers, or *ustāds*, generally come from the *mura* caste; musicians are from the *ḍom* caste, landless individuals who earn their living by playing music and weaving baskets.

In shape, construction, color, and design, the masks worn in Purulia *chhau* are unique in India and contrast markedly with those of Seraikella *chhau*. The headdresses of the characters are usually incorporated into the mask, forming a single unit. The colors of the faces and the designs and shapes of eyes, mouths, and noses, along with the shape of the headdress or hair, identify the type of character depicted. The repertory of Purulia *chhau* is drawn from India's epic literature, the *Rāmāyaṇa*, the *Mahābhārata*, and the Purāṇas.

Physically, the *chhau* dances of Purulia are different from those of the other *chhau* styles. There is a decided martial quality to the physical movement. Dancers often stand in wide knee bends, walk on their knees, pirouette on their knees, and leap high into the air and land on their knees or in wide knee bends. To demonstrate the prowess and temperament of the characters they portray, they sometimes quiver the upper torso, making the tinsel on the headdress shimmer in the light of the stage lamps.

Jerky, halting movements are also unique to Purulia *chhau*.

Performances commonly take place on a smooth open area in a village in which a space about twenty by twenty feet is reserved for the dancing. The musicians usually sit along one side; those who play the small drum move within the dancing area and seem to draw the characters into the action with their wild patterns of drumming. A number of groups may perform one after another, or they may perform at the same time, leading to considerable confusion in music and pace of execution. The competitive spirit is very much a part of Purulia *chhau*, as it is in Mayurbhanj *chhau*.

Performances usually begin around nine or ten at night with the entrance of the musicians, who demonstrate their considerable skill. This is followed by the actor who portrays Gaṇeśa, the elephant-headed god of good fortune. Typically, each character in the drama enters the dancing area slowly and establishes his personality with a particular stance. Once the characters are assembled in the dancing area, the pace increases and the dramatic action is completed. Songs are used in Purulia *chhau* to tell the story, but owing to the volume of the drums they are frequently inaudible. Themes of violence are prevalent, and it is not uncommon that hand-to-hand combat or encounters with weapons result in the wounding or death of one of the characters.

[*See also* Mask and Makeup, *article on* Asian Traditions.]

BIBLIOGRAPHY

Bhattacharyya, Asutosh. *Chhau Dance of Purulia.* Calcutta, 1972.

Khokar, Mohan. "The Seraikella Chhau Dance." *Quarterly Journal of the National Centre for the Performing Arts* 2 (June 1973): 25–32.

Kothari, Sunil. *Chhau Dances of India.* Bombay, 1968.

Mahapatra, Sitakant, and Jivan Pani, eds. *Chhau Dances of Mayurbhanj.* Bombay, 1993.

Massey, Reginald, and Jamila Massey. *The Dances of India: A General Survey and Dancer's Guide.* London, 1989.

Pani, Jivan. "Chhau: A Comparative Study of Sareikela and Mayurbhanj Forms." *Sangeet Natak,* no. 13 (July–September 1969): 35–45.

Ragini Devi. *Dance Dialects of India.* 2d rev. ed. Delhi, 1990.

Richmond, Farley. *The Chhau Dance of Purulia.* Asia Society, Monographs on Music, Dance, and Theater in Asia, vol. 1. New York, 1974.

Vatsyayan, Kapila. *Traditional Indian Theatre: Multiple Streams.* New Delhi, 1980.

FARLEY RICHMOND

CHILDS, LUCINDA (born 26 June 1940 in New York City), dancer and choreographer. Childs graduated from Sarah Lawrence College, studied with Merce Cunningham and Robert Dunn, and danced with James Waring. She was active in the Judson Dance Theater and in 1966 choreographed a work in collaboration with Bell Telephone Engineers for *Nine Evenings: Theater and Engineering.* In 1973, she formed the Lucinda Childs Dance Company.

Since her earliest dance, *Pastime* (1963), Childs has been concerned with contrasting points of view. In that dance, she moved in and out of a stretch-jersey bag (satirizing both Alwin Nikolais and Martha Graham's famous solo *Lamentation*) and presented movements in profile and from a back view. Her *Street Dance* (1964), in which she guided the audience in noticing a block of city landscape—by moving around on the street while her voice on tape told them what to look at—radically redefined dance by proposing that it is the spectator's act of framing movement, rather than the quality of the movement itself, that makes a dance a dance.

Several of Childs's dances of the 1960s used objects and monologues as springboards for movement. In *Carnation* (1964), Childs made sandwiches of foam-rubber curlers placed between sponges and put the curlers on the prongs of a colander placed on her head. Curlers, sponges, and colander all went into a plastic bag, then spilled out when Childs did a handstand. *Geranium* (1965) presented different aspects of a football game.

For five years (1968–1973) Childs presented no work in public performances. She taught, worked in the studio, practiced ballet, and worked on problems of cognition and perception. She founded the Lucinda Childs Dance Company in 1973, for which she has since created more than twenty-five works.

Child's interest in varying angles of vision took on a new form with *Untitled Trio* (1968; revised 1973). Here three dancers trace grid patterns on the floor, constantly regrouping in relation to one another and to space. In *Calico Mingling* (1973), four dancers trace similar but not identical paths consisting only of circles, semicircles, and straight lines. The solos *Particular Reel* (1973) and *Mix Detail* (1976), are two complex series of arm patterns that repeat both forward and retrograde. All these dances use pure movement to focus modes of attention, recognition, and points of view. Childs creates minute variations on the basic phrases by inserting new material, changing direction, or reversing or inverting the phrase. The detached, cool, concentrated presentation and the rhythmic stepping that generates and defines classical, flat, geometric forms has elements in common with the work of certain contemporary visual artists.

In 1976 Childs appeared in a leading role in the Robert Wilson–Philip Glass opera *Einstein on the Beach,* a work that led to future collaborations with both artists. Childs won a Village Voice Obie Award in 1977 for her performance. Childs appeared in the revival of *Einstein* in 1984 (and again in 1992), for which she also choreographed new versions of the opera's *Field Dances* for members of her company, who also filled many of the opera's nonsinging roles.

Beginning in the mid-1970s, Childs's choreographic style became more elaborate and dancerly, incorporating small leaps and turns into the vocabulary, increasing in rhythmic complexity, and maintaining a balletic verticality of the dancers' bodies. In *Dance* (1979), Childs's first evening-length work and the first to use music, the play of contrasts and comparisons was underscored by the alternation of solo and group sections and by Sol LeWitt's film (projected on a downstage scrim), which supplied contrasting sizes and points of view of the dancers. The music, by Glass, gave *Dance* a buoyant, celestial tone. *Dance,* whose creation was supported by a Guggenheim Fellowship (1979), has been revived several times. In 1983, Childs worked with architect Frank Gehry and composer John Adams on *Available Light,* in which the dancing took place on two different levels in space and the asymmetry of the set correlated to new asymmetries in Childs's choreography and shifting moods in the dramatic music.

Childs' major works in the 1980s and 1990s include collaborations with contemporary composers, including *Cascade* (1984; to music by Steve Reich), *Field Dances* (1984; to music by Philip Glass), and *Four Elements* (1990; to music by Gavin Bryars). *Portraits in Reflection* (1986), a collaboration with the photographer Robert Mapplethorpe, was set to music by four composers: Michael Galasso, Michael Nyman, Allen Shawn, and Elizabeth Swados. In it, dancers often mirrored one another's movements. In dances such

CHILDS. Members of the Lucinda Childs Dance Company, against a backdrop designed by Robert Rauschenberg, in Childs's evening-length work *Relative Calm*, at the Brooklyn Academy of Music, 1981. (Photograph © 1981 by Johan Elbers; used by permission.)

as *Mayday* (1989; with music by Christian Wolff) and *From the White Edge of Phrygia* (1995; to music by Stephen Montague), Childs's rigorously patterned choreography took on deeper expressiveness.

Childs frequently works in Europe, where she has choreographed for the Rambert Dance Company, the Lyon Opera Ballet, the Berlin Opera Ballet, the Bavarian State Ballet, the Paris Opera Ballet, and Charleroi/Danses. In the United States Childs has choreographed for the Pacific Northwest Ballet and the Ohio Ballet.

In the 1990s, Childs continued to experiment with music outside the minimalist idiom that defined her earlier group works, including scores by Iannis Xenakis, Henryk Górecki, Andrzej Kurylewicz, Zygmunt Krauze, and François-Bernard Mâche. She also began to choreograph extensively for opera in Europe, beginning with a "Dance of the Seven Veils" for Luc Bondy's production of Richard Strauss's *Salome* in Salzburg in 1992. Childs also performed in Bondy's production of *Reigen*, to music by Mozart, at the Théâtre Royal de la Monnaie in Brussels,

where she returned for her debut as an opera director, with Mozart's *Zaide* in 1995. She collaborated with director Peter Stein on De Nederlandse Opera's production of Arnold Schoenberg's *Moses und Aron* in the same year. In 1996, she rejoined Bondy to choreograph his production of Giuseppe Verdi's *Don Carlos*. In the same year she also staged a new "Dance of the Seven Veils" for Klaus Lehnhof's *Salome* at New York's Metropolitan Opera. In 1996 Childs was also inducted as an Officier de l'Ordre des Arts et des Lettres of France.

BIBLIOGRAPHY

Banes, Sally. *Terpsichore in Sneakers: Post-Modern Dance.* 2d ed. Middletown, Conn., 1987. Includes a bibliography.

Childs, Lucinda. "Notes: '64–'74." *Drama Review* 19 (March 1975): 33–36.

Chin, Daryl. "Talking with Lucinda Childs." *Dance Scope* 13 (Winter–Spring 1979): 70–81.

Kaplan, Peggy Jarrell. *Portraits of Choreographers.* New York, 1988.

Kreemer, Connie, ed. *Further Steps: Fifteen Choreographers on Modern Dance.* New York, 1987.

Sontag, Susan. "For *Available Light*: A Brief Lexicon." *Art in America* (December 1983).

FILMS. *Calico Mingling* (director, Babette Mangolte, 1975). *Making Dances* (Blackwood Productions, 1979). *Four Elements* (BBC-TV, London, 1991).

SALLY BANES

CHILE. [*This entry comprises three articles on dance traditions in Chile. The first article focuses on folk and traditional dance; the second explores the history of theatrical dance; the third provides a brief history of scholarship and writing.*]

Folk and Traditional Dance

Very little is known about pre-Hispanic dance in Chile, since descriptions by chroniclers and travelers of the mid-seventeenth and eighteenth centuries were brief. Most did not mention the arts. Eugenio Pereira Sales, a diligent researcher of Chilean musical history, has summarized the most important with respect to dance: The indigenous dances, orgiastic in nature, were performed in circles around a pole, with couples dancing, marching, bending, and stretching, as if to jump but without lifting their feet off the ground. The principal dances of the eighteenth century were, among others, the *nuin* danced by pairs of dancers holding hands in a circle; the *cunquen*, also for pairs; and the *hueyel*, "this son of Venus and Baccus invented in honor of the devil." According to the early twentieth-century researcher Ricardo E. Latcham,

> The initiated formed groups that could be called theatrical groups, with masked and costumed actors who often represented animals and performed songs and tableaux that dramatized their traditional legends.

From today's indigenous dance performances we may draw some inferences about choreographic expressions that persist from the ancient past. Of the magico-religious dance ceremonies where the Mapuche language is still used, the main dance is the *guillatun*. In it, the participants advance and fall back rhythmically, shaking tree branches, while the shaman (*machi*) accompanied by four youths (*choiques*) imitating ostriches expel evil spirits. Another important dance ceremony is the *machitun*, in which *choiques* accompany the shaman in healing rituals. Annual festivals strongly tied to work include the marking of the herds of sheep, llamas, alpacas, and vicuñas. Here, the participants sing in Aymara or Spanish to pre-Hispanic musical instruments, such as the *quena*, the *pinquillo*, and the *tarca*, accompanied by the *bombos* and other drums. For potato planting, the men dig holes and the women plant. The *mayordomo*, elected by the community, uses harvested potatoes to venerate the town's patron saint.

For patron saints' feast days, Aymara and *mestizo* communities celebrate them as a major social event. They are attended by all, including those who have migrated to the city or who are usually away from town because of herding activities. For example, the Festival of the Cross in Putre is held in May; there, the *cuculi* ("dove") is danced tirelessly. Holding hands, the dancers do a three-step to move in a circle to two-beat accompaniment. On the same occasion, for recreation, the *chaya-chaya* is danced to a *huayno* rhythm by many couples facing one another, and the *zonzo ternero* ("foolish calf") is danced as a zoomorphic game. The *sayare* is danced in a satirical penitential way so that the dancers' failings of the past year are sung out to them in Aymara; this is followed by a whipping in front of a shrouded cross. Some of these patron saints' feasts feature pilgrimages. The flutes used and the long *flautones* made of reeds or hollowed-out wood suggest the antiquity of the accompanying dances. The festival of San Pedro de Atacama is still celebrated with the *catimbanos* (or *catimbaos*), a dance with two lines of masked men, regarded by Pereira Sales as one of the oldest dances in Chile.

Early Christian Dances. From the early sixteenth century, the Roman Catholic missionaries who arrived in South America with the Spanish conquerors used music and dance to convert the Indians. Indigenous music and dance were, however, incorporated with Spanish rhythms. The Indian confraternities soon appeared in Christian processions, as did black brotherhoods after the introduction of African slaves to Chile. The Indian dances continue today in the *chinos* and *catimbanos*, dances of the religious fraternities. African dances, such as the *morenos*, are characterized by the dancers' use of rattles to accompany the three-beat steps done to two-beat marching music.

The dances described as the most important during that time of conversion have largely disappeared, as for example, the dance of the Tarascan—a monstrous dragon paraded in procession in some towns, which alluded to the apocalyptic Whore of Babylon. Still surviving are the dances of the Giants and Big Heads in processions in Santiago and Serena, the dance of the *parlampanes*, sponsored by the confraternity of tailors, and the above-mentioned *catimbanos*.

The *contradanza*, a European social dance popular at the time of the Conquest, must have been basic to the dances learned by most of the confraternities. They included elements probably taught by the missionaries, such as lively marching, crossover steps, turns, and circles.

Performances of allegorical religious plays, such as "El Cautivo" at La Tirana in the interior of the Province of Iquique or "Moros y Cristianos" and Christians at Quenal on the Island of Chiloe, ceased during the first half of the twentieth century. Dances in which good overcomes evil may still be seen in San Pedro de Atacama. These dramatizations involve old people wearing ostrich feathers and riders using horselike frames, a good example of Christian theater's presentation of Aymara-Spanish syncretism. As for expressions of Christian dance in the southern part of Chile, only vestiges remain of a Jesuit military-style festival. In the procession at this festival, rhythmic movements with flags and pennants vaguely recall Renaissance Europe.

Recreational Dance. The recreational aspect of dance in Chile may be expressed in what are called the "dances of this land," products of a mixture of folk music and dance, strongly influenced by those of Peru. The best known are the fandango and bolero, both of which have disappeared from Chile. The fandango was probably a forerunner of the samba and related dances; this dance style, which was spread from Spain to Europe and America in the mid-1700s, can still be recognized in them. Of the following dances, only the names remain: *cachupina, chocolate, guachambi, juana, jurga, llanto, oletas, soldado, solita, sorito,* and *verde y zapatero.*

With Chilean independence from Spain at the beginning of the nineteenth century, new dances became popular. The South American revolutionary leader José de San Martín and his army brought "El Cielito," "El Pericon," "La Sajuriana," and "El Cuando," a sort of minuet that ended with an allegro. The dances ranged from serious to flirtatious. There are two known versions of the music and dance for "El Cuando," although it lost popularity by the end of the nineteenth century. At times "La Pericona" (as it became known) was confused with the "Seguidilla de Cuatro." "La Sajuriana" has been said to have come from Argentina, yet its relation to dances derived from the *zambacueca* seems evident. By the mid-twentieth century, versions could still be found easily, and it is still performed in San Juan de la Costa.

Chilean folk dances of the twentieth century are under study by dance researchers for the time span when they were current, their geographic distribution, and their function. The information obtained from observations in the field, from information reported by participants in rituals, and from academic investigators will soon be published.

BIBLIOGRAPHY

Danzas de Chile. Santiago, 1964.
García Arribas, José Javier. *Los bailes religiosos del norte de Chile.* Santiago, 1989.
Garrido, Pablo. *Biografía de la Cueca.* 2d ed., rev. Santiago, 1976.
Loyola, Margot. *Bailes de tierra en Chile.* 2d ed. Valparaiso, 1980.
Pereira Salas, Eugenio. *Los orígenes del arte musical en Chile.* Santiago, 1941.
Poole, Deborah A. "Accommodation and Resistance in Andean Ritual Dance." *Drama Review* 34.2 (1990): 98–126.
Urrutia Blondel, Jorge. *Danzas rituales en las festividades de San Pedro de Atacama.* Santiago, 1968.
Van Kessel, Juan. *Danzas y estructuras sociales de los Andes.* Cuzco, 1982.
Van Kessel, Juan. *Lucero brillante: Mística popular y movimiento social.* Iquique, 1987.

ARCHIVE. Private collection of field research conducted and maintained by Raquel Barros Aldunate.

RAQUEL BARROS ALDUNATE
Translated from Spanish

Theatrical Dance

During the nineteenth century, travel to and through Chile was difficult, often requiring a sense of adventure. The prospering nitrate and copper mines in the deserts of northern Chile brought settlers who soon became the audience for itinerant performers. Additionally, between 1850 and 1862, four French dance groups went to Chile's two largest cities, Valparaiso and Santiago. One of these groups performed shortened versions of the ballet *Giselle.* As a result of these performances, such a frenzy was raised within the intellectual community that a journal appeared, called *La sílfide,* which extolled the virtues and beauty of the Romantic ballet. Chileans also saw the mid-century performances of *La Fille Mal Gardée, Catarina, ou La Fille du Bandit,* and *La Bayadère.* The Catholic church, however, a strong influence in the country's cultural life, soon mounted a moral attack on the performers, specifically complaining about the revealing costumes—the transparent tutus and tights.

During the latter years of the nineteenth century, various performers toured such full-length ballets as *Giselle* and *La Sylphide,* with varying success. Dance performances in these years also included the interludes between dramatic works and various *divertissements.* Several European dancers stayed in Chile, attempting to start what turned out to be short-lived dance academies.

Not until Anna Pavlova's visits in 1917 and 1918 was Chilean interest in dance, which had become somewhat dorment during the last decades of the nineteenth century, revived. Pavlova's visit was received with interest and admiration. The press noted that she was like a "breeze renovating the monotony of the enforced isolation imposed by the Andes mountain range." Other touring performers soon followed Pavlova but not until Jan Kaweski arrived in 1919 and founded a ballet school were local performances presented. At about the same time, the English ballerina Doreen Young also arrived in Chile, and she too opened a ballet school. By the early 1920s, however, Chile's social elite considered classical ballet a beautiful but dying feminine ornament, impractical in the harsh realities of Chilean life.

Influences from the currents of European expressionism soon began to contribute to the social and creative aspects of life in Chile and throughout hispanic America. As Chilean painters traveled to France and Germany, they discovered that expressionism was being communicated through dance, especially in the work of Mary Wigman and Kurt Jooss. Based on these new ideas, two dance academies were opened between 1933 and 1942 by Elsa Martin and Andréa Háas. Their objective was to create a unique body language, so they taught dance based on the methods of Émile Jaques-Dalcroze as well as gymnastic dance, pantomime, and choreography. Soon their stu-

CHILE: Theatrical Dance. A scene from *Alotria* (1954), choreographed by Ernst Uthoff for the Ballet Nacional Chileno. (Photograph courtesy of Luz Marmentini.)

dents were presenting successful performances in Santiago's Teatro Municipal. These schools and performances became an important part of university cultural life, a movement that during the early 1940s saw the creation of the Instituto de Extensión Musical, whose mission was to plan and promote professional music and dance performances. As a result of its work, the Chilean public enjoyed touring performances of such international companies as the Ballets Russes de Colonel W. de Basil, the Colón Theater Ballet from Buenos Aires, and Lincoln Kirstein's American Ballet. In fact, the premieres of two George Balanchine ballets for the American Ballet, *Fantasia* and *Brasileira*, took place in Chile.

During the winter season of 1940, Germany's Les Ballets Jooss, directed by Ernst Uthoff, toured South America. The modernist works of Kurt Jooss were held in high esteem by the Chilean public; Jooss was considered an innovator who revealed through dance the rhythmic emotional and expressive qualities of the music. Jooss was also appreciated for his multidimensional use of dance space. In the popular Jooss repertory was his classic, *The Green Table*. The political difficulties created by World War II almost ended the company's South American tour. When news of its impending demise reached influential Chileans, authorities from the university hired Ernst Uthoff, his wife Lola Botka, and the solo dancer Rudolph Pescht to form a dance school,

with a goal of creating a Jooss-style performing company.

Elsa Martin and Andréa Háas passed their students on to Uthoff and created a base for a university company. This venture would later become the Ballet Nacional Chileno, which was enormously successful, receiving substantial public and government support. Uthoff instilled in his dancers the importance of the artist as total interpreter. He not only provided most of the company's choreography but designed scenery and conceived the lighting plans. The contributions of Uthoff, Botka, and Pescht to the Chilean dance community were enormous; they trained outstanding dancer-artists who displayed a clear sense of discipline and technique, who were capable of a wide range of dramatic and musical interpretations. Out of this nurturing atmosphere, a number of Chilean dancers rose to prominence and went on to become successful choreographers with careers of their own, including Virginia Roncal, Patricio Bunster, Malucha Solari, and Maria Elena Aranguiz.

Chile's symphony orchestra and its chorus took advantage of the public's support for the ballet, to parallel its growth. All three groups cultivated audiences not only in the capital city of Santiago but throughout the interior regions. Additionally, the groups toured Germany, France, and England. While in Santiago, the ballet continued to perform seasons at the Teatro Municipal and virtually every premiere was considered a success. During his years in Chile, Uthoff maintained a program of exchange with European companies, and many Chilean students re-

CHILE: Theatrical Dance. Members of the Ballet Nacional Chileno in Patricio Bunster's *Calaucán* (1959). (Photograph courtesy of Luz Marmentini.)

ceived scholarships to study in other countries. The vision of Uthoff and his team was to create an atmosphere that provided basic academic technique without relying on pointe work or excessive virtuosity. Instead, the emphasis was on naturalism, emotional commitment, and theatrical expressiveness.

Uthoff created many successful dance works for the Ballet Nacional Chileno, such as expressionist versions of *Coppélia, Die Josephslegende,* and *Petrouchka.* His greatest triumph, however, was his version of Carl Orff's 1937 oratorio *Carmina Burana;* first performed on 12 August 1953, Uthoff's production utilized the musical resources of the University of Chile, including the chorus, soloists, and a new generation of dancers.

Russian Ballet in Chile. Although the Chilean dance public highly regarded the expressionist work of Ernst Uthoff, there was also a growing interest in classical ballet—enough, in fact, to support in theory, if not financially, a second professional dance company in Santiago. In the late 1940s, Russian refugees Nina Gisvova and her husband Vadim Sulima arrived in Santiago. A graduate of the Leningrad Choreographic Institute, not only was Sulima an outstanding dancer, he was an excellent teacher with a strong flair for painting and scenography. Together the couple created a ballet school based on the teaching system of Agrippina Vaganova and a company that hoped to establish a repertory in the Russian tradition. Established by the city of Santiago and invited to ap-

pear in the Teatro Municipal, by 1956 Sulima's company (later known as the Ballet de Santiago) was performing such standard Russian repertory as *The Fountain of Bakhchisarai.* One of Sulima's major contributions resulted from his interest in Chilean folklore, and this inspiration was evident in his choreographies *Las Tres Pascualas* and *Noche de San Juan.* The Ballet de Santiago toured outside Chile and was part of the first centenary celebrated by the Teatro Municipal. This era of ballet ended when the Sulimas emigrated to the United States.

Octavio Cintolessi was invited from Europe to continue the work of the Sulimas. Cintolessi's organizing skills and his solid traditional, classical training were mixed with influences from young European avant-garde choreographers, such as Maurice Béjart. By 1960, the company and school were reorganized under Cintolessi, and the repertory was expanded to include the works of Serge Lifar and Elsa-Marianne von Rosen. Among the guest artists appearing with the company in Cintolessi's early years was the British ballerina Margot Fonteyn.

While the Ballet de Santiago performed in the Teatro Municipal, Uthoff's Ballet Nacional Chileno wandered in search of an appropriate performing space. With Uthoff's retirement, the Nacional Ballet reached a low point. While some interesting choreography was presented, such as Patricio Bunster's *Calaucán,* the company's downfall continued. Subsequent directors were unable to produce a successful season. The various changes of directors and personnel interrupted its evolution as an avant-garde dance company.

The city of Santiago continued to support and assist the Ballet de Santiago and, with Iván Nagy (1982–1989) as director, the level of the ballet was elevated. During Nagy's tenure, the Ballet de Santiago saw the development of an outstanding ballerina, Sara Nieto. She is well known for her eloquent expression, technique, and control, as demonstrated in Hilda Riveros's *Carmen,* in her *Anna Karenina,* and as Odette-Odile in *Swan Lake.*

During Nagy's appointment, the majority of the company's soloists were foreigners, the presence of Chilean-trained dancers greatly reduced. Guest artists included soloists from American Ballet Theatre, including Julio Bocca. The ballet school thrived, however, and the company did well financially. By 1985 its seasons were sold out. Outstanding productions of this period included Ben Stevenson's *Cinderella,* with designs by Beni Montraesor; Harald Lander's *Etudes;* and John Cranko's *Taming of the Shrew.* The Ballet de Santiago seemed on the verge of becoming an international company when it made its North American debut on 21 January 1986 in New York's City Center. After Nagy's departure in 1989, however, a series of directors attempted to maintain the company's achievements. Imre Dózsa became artistic director in 1989, to be followed in 1991 by Luz Lorca, a former dancer and the assistant director since 1982.

In 1993, Marcia Haydée, head of the Stuttgart Ballet, also became artistic director of the Ballet de Santiago. Instituting a policy of exchange between her two companies, Haydée arranged for Chilean dancers to go to Stuttgart; Marcela Coloechea performed Cranko's *Romeo and Juliet* and Luis Ortigoza danced in Béjart's *Gaîté Parisienne*. In Santiago, *prima ballerina* Nieto performed Haydée's *The Firebird*, which was choreographed for the Chilean company in 1992; Stuttgart's Richard Cragun took part in a new version of Riveros's *Carmen*.

In 1995, Iván Nagy returned as artistic director of the Ballet de Santiago. The future looks bright for Santiago, for a new generation of Chilean dancers and choreographers.

Modern Dance. By the beginning of the 1960s, the dance companies and solid professional schools of Chile, which were supported and subsidized by the Teatro Municipal and the University of Chile, no longer offered a creative outlet for Chilean artists oriented toward a personal movement language. As a result of a change in regulations within the university, a chamber dance company called Balca was established in 1969. Directed by Gaby Concha, a graduate of the University of Chile and a recipient of a Fulbright grant to study in the United States with Martha Graham and Merce Cunningham, Balca was utilized by Concha for her choreographies. These were noted for their base of Latin American, especially Chilean, music and poetry. Her works were considered reflections of Chile's powerful nature, wisdom, and attitudes. Concha's subjects ranged from fairy tales and other literary works to the rich fertility of the soil, issues of ecology, and homages to Walt Whitman and Martha Graham. By teaching Graham and Cunningham technique classes at the university, as well as workshops opened to the general public, Concha spread ideas about modern dance.

This new dance scene was popularized by artists performing in the streets. Concha and her Balca company took performances out of the theaters to perform in town squares, schools, and throughout the suburbs. Other artists soon joined in this type of expression. Joan Turner's Las Condes Ballet was a company of professional and amateur dancers originally organized in a project by Alfonso Unanue. Patricio Bunster's Ballet Populaire, which presented works emphasizing the future of society, utilized professional dancers from the Ballet Nacional Chileno.

Postmodern influences were introduced in large measure by Gabriela Figuera, a dancer and choreographer from Uruguay. Known for her personality, strength, and vitality, her presence is still felt in students who worked with her, such as Gregoria Fassler. Well known in both Chile and Brazil, Fassler's work is popular for the use of dance space and works that are performed in series.

Other Kinds of Dance. In the late 1970s, visual artist Vicky Larrain began to experiment with combining move-

ment and images. The former classical dancer Magaly Rivano organized the Experimental Workshop of Dance and Theater and encouraged actors and dancers to experiment with this type of drama, utilizing language and dynamic dancing.

Karen Conolly, a dancer who emigrated from Australia, was dedicated to show dancing. She formed her own school and trained professionals for performances and television shows that were popular during the late 1970s.

Among other explorations that added to the growing dance community in Chile was the formation of the Taller de Danza Antigua, directed by Sara Vial. She reconstructs European court dance from the fifteenth through the eighteenth century, stressing accuracy and scholarship.

During the early 1980s, Hernan Baldrich, the well-known creater of beautiful and subtle choreographies, organized productions that used actors, artists, and scenic and costume designers. One of the most respected of Chilean costume designers, Marcos Correa, came out of this period. Apart from Baldrich, the creative forces at

CHILE: Theatrical Dance. A scene from the Ballet de Santiago's production of Ronald Hynd's *Rosalinda*, a ballet version of Johann Strauss the younger's operetta *Die Fledermaus*. (Photograph © 1986 by Jack Vartoogian; used by permission.)

CHILE: Theatrical Dance. Two dancers in Nelson Avilés's *Refugiados a Ras de Suelo* (1990). (Photograph courtesy of Luz Marmentini.)

this time were relatively weak. Most of the modern dance performers were adult college students inspired by local stimululi. They were strongly independent and displayed little influence from outside styles or schools of dance. However, training at the university became precarious, due in part to the military government.

One important exception was Bárbara Uribe, a former student of the Laban Center in London. She was in many ways considered the leader of future generations of dancers. Until her untimely death in 1991, Uribe's aptitude for teaching, stimulating, and supporting young dancers and choreographers was well known. She persisted in a climate unsupportive of independent dance, yet her students could count on solid training and a creative vision of dance.

In December 1984 Luz Marmentini organized the first Encuentro Coreográfico, a workshop for modern dance choreographers. Held annually, the workshop offers a performance venue and provides a forum for exchange of ideas. Works are critiqued by professionals and compositional methods are analyzed.

Several important choreographers emerged from workshops held in the late 1980s. Nelson Avilés, director of the company Andanzas, is one of the most productive of the experimental choreographers. Nuri Gutes has become well-known throughout South America for her refined style and expressive use of poetry and ritual. Working primarily as a soloist, Luis Eduardo Araneda creates poignant, sometimes humorous dances about pain and love. A new generation of choreographers has come forth during the 1990s, including Paulina Mellado, Elizabeth Rodriguez, Raquel Ramirez, Marcelo Rodriguez, and Luz Condeza.

As well as the Encuentro Coreográfico, the creative work of Chilean choreographers has also been influenced by the performances and workshops directed by such well-known artists as Pina Bausch, Susanne Linke, and Dominique Petit. Since Chile's return to democracy, exchange programs for both teachers and students have played a growing role in the development of performing and choreographic talent.

Modern dance trends that lean closer to performance art include the work of Andrés Perez and his company Gran Circo Teatro and Mauricio Celedon's group Teatro del Silencio. Internationally known theater specialist Eugenio Barba has made many trips to Chile to give lectures and to organize seminars and performances. By providing a stimulus for other ways to look at movement, Barba has been popular among young Chilean choreographers interested in the total theater of performance art.

It is extremely important to note that, unlike ballet, modern dance (known in Chile as "independent dance") has not been supported by state or municipal monies. It has existed and been nurtured with aid and support of Chilean-French, Chilean–North American, and Chilean-German cultural organizations and by the hard work and dedication of many dancers and choreographers.

BIBLIOGRAPHY

Bunster, Patricio. "El Dpto. de Danza de la Universidad de Chile." *Cuba en el ballet* 5 (May 1974): 22–25.

Caban Brenner, Alfonso. *Pequeño biografía de un gran teatro: El Teatro Municipal, ayer y hoy.* Santiago, 1967.

Cánepa Guzmán, Mario. *El Teatro Municipal en sus 125 años de sufrimientos y esplendor.* Santiago, 1985.

Ehrmann, Hans. "Jooss, Conquistadores, and the Wheel of Fortune." *Dance Magazine* (November 1964): 52–54.

Ehrmann, Hans. "News from Chile." *Dance Magazine* (March 1976): 105–106.

Ehrmann, Hans. "Ballet de Santiago at Teatro Municipal." *Dance Magazine* (January 1990): 79–80.

Flatow, Sheryl. "Northward Bound." *Ballet News* 7 (January 1986): 16–21.

Habel-Moreno, Shana. "The North American Influence on the Contemporary Dance in Chile." In *Proceedings of the Fifteenth Annual Conference, Society of Dance History Scholars, University of California, Riverside, 14–15 February 1992,* compiled by Christena L. Schlundt. Riverside, Calif., 1992.

Hardy, Camille. "Ballet de Santiago's Ivan Nagy." *Dance Magazine* (January 1986): 44–48.

Hardy, Camille. "Hungarian Directs Chilean Ballet." *Dance Magazine* (July 1989): 14–16.

Muñoz, H., Juan Antonio. "Lola Botka: Gran bailarina y maestra de la danza chilena." *Monsalvat* (September 1988): 29–30.

Rado, Claudia. "Recent Developments of Modern Dance in Chile with Reference to Its Roots in the 1940s." Master's thesis, American University, 1986.

Robilant, Claire de. "*Giselle* a través de la historia del ballet chileno." *Cuba en el ballet* 4 (May 1973): 28–29.

Robilant, Claire de. "Santiago." *Dance News* (May 1975): 8–9.

Sloat, Susanna. "Muevete!" *Attitude* 10 (Summer 1994): 14–15.

LUZ MARMENTINI

Dance Research and Publication

Exciting dance activity stimulates a certain amount of writing and research. Thus, the 1945 to 1965 period generated what little there is in the way of scholarly articles, while the period from 1965 to the mid-1990s has added little beyond reviews and standard journalistic pieces.

In the past, academic journal *Revista musical chilena* has published occasional pieces on dance, including a special ballet issue (no. 80, April–June 1962). The Sunday supplements of newspapers and magazines such as *Ballet*, a Peruvian-Chilean publication from the mid-1950s, which survived for twenty-one issues, are sources of data for ballet in Latin America. There is, however, a dearth of sources on ballet, compared to the amount of material available for the theater for the same period.

Folk dance in Chile, as elsewhere in Latin America, is entirely different from theatrical dance. Various regional dances have been researched over the years, and there have been publications from "how-to" manuals to academic treatises, such as Pablo Garrido's *La cueca*, and field studies, such as Jorge Urrutia Blondel's *Danzas rituales en las festividades de San Pedro de Atacama* (1968). Undergraduate group seminars, held since 1980 for students at the University of Chile dance school who wish to teach—although oriented to a large extent toward teaching—are a source for research into local dance history or the analysis of the background of locally created ballets.

A Municipal Dance Archive was created in 1965 by Claire de Robilant, who ran it until 1974. It was reopened in 1977 and managed by Hilda Soto, a former dancer. The archive comprises more than six hundred books, about four thousand photographs, some fifty pairs of signed ballet slippers (belonging to, e.g., Margot Fonteyn and Natalia Makarova), autographs of foreign dancers who, since 1979, have performed at the Teatro Municipal, plus newspaper clippings, mostly about the Ballet de Santiago. The archive receives only two dance periodicals regularly, *Les saisons de la danse* and *Dance Magazine*. The Municipal Dance Archive lacks a regular acquisitions budget and might be improved by a more systematic approach to the organization of its materials. In Chile, the scarcity of published materials on theatrical dance also causes the frequent lack of local reference materials necessary for productive and analytical scholarship.

The lack of a register of the visits of foreign companies has proven to be a significant omission because, given the cultural isolation of many Latin American countries, those tours have helped develop the ballet culture of both performers and audiences. However, Victoria García Victorica's *El Original Ballet Russe en América Latina*, published in Buenos Aires in 1948, does includes a detailed itinerary of Colonel Wassily de Basil's company tours. It provides a geographic view of the development of ballet in Latin America by noting the places where many dancers settled (e.g., Tatiana Lesksova in Rio de Janeiro at the Teatro Municipal and Nina Verchinina in Mendoza, Argentina). Pablo de Madalengoitia's *Panorama de danza*, published in 1954, offers details about the tours, dates, and programs of foreign companies and dancers who performed in Lima, Peru, between 1940 and 1953.

World War II proved to be a decisive moment for the Southern Hemisphere, since it brought many European dancers and ballet masters to settle in Latin American cities, a phenomenon whose artistic effects are worth studying. There have been, as well, the various attempts in Chile and other countries to use the ballet and modern dance idiom to express local subject matter with, in some cases, music by local composers. As so little is available, it is all too easy to suggest rewarding subjects for dance research in Chile.

HANS EHRMANN

CHINA. [*To survey the dance traditions of China, this entry comprises six articles:*

An Overview
Folk and Minority Dance
Dance in Opera
Classical Dance
Contemporary Theatrical Dance
Dance Research and Publication

The first article presents a historical overview of traditional dance and the introduction of Western forms of social and theatrical dance styles; the following four articles explore various genres of Chinese folk and theatrical dance; the concluding article provides a brief history of scholarship and writing. For related discussion in a broader context, see Asian Dance Traditions, *overview article. For discussion of more specific topics, see* Aesthetics, *article on* Asian Dance Aesthetics; Asian Martial Arts; Costume in Asian Traditions; *and* Mask and Makeup, *article on* Asian Traditions.]

An Overview

The immense time span of Chinese history permits only a subjective view of so transient an art as dancing. Dance in

China evolved from the socioreligious rituals of early agrarian communities, blossomed as secular entertainment under court patronage while also serving the needs of Confucian high ritual, and finally emerged as a great animating force of the theater. In theater lies China's most obvious contribution to the dance.

History. The texts of the Confucian canon, compilations dating from the Zhou (Chou) dynasty (c.1030–221 BCE), provide information on early dance and music in China. Three of these—the *Book of Changes (Yijing* or *I ching), Book of Rites (Li ji* or *Li chi),* and *Book of Songs (Shijing* or *Shih ching)*—are particularly relevant. The first began as a divination aid but became a treatise embodying a major concept of Chinese thought in its concern with intuitive insight, pertinent to all aesthetic theory in China. The *Book of Rites* explains ritualistic practices and has a section on the philosophy of music, a subject much speculated on by Confucian scholars. The *Book of Songs* is China's oldest poetic anthology. It is divided into four sections: folk songs of the states; eulogies of the emperor; eulogies of the feudal princes; and sacrificial rites of Zhou. The evocative imagery of the *Book of Songs* conveys vivid impressions of dance in a formative stage of China's cultural history.

The folk songs preserved in this text were the prototypes for a regional repertory of song and dance transmitted through generations. Simple in their rhythmic structure, Chinese folk songs expressed the uncomplicated emotions of ordinary people by means of conversational or narrative stanzas, or a combination of both. Such forms led naturally to the spontaneous use of mime—pantomimic gesture—and so the potential for dance was created.

In his pioneering study of the songs and dances of ancient China, the French scholar Marcel Granet (1884–1940) advanced the theory that in early times the spring festivals were used to sponsor courtship assemblies. There young men and women from various communities were brought together as potential marriage partners. The practice was designed to strengthen the federal union of neighboring districts and to ensure the stability of local society. In the assemblies a line of men faced a line of women; each side moved according to a common emotion, as representatives of their community and of their sex. An alternating structure of song and mime improvisation developed, often in a spirit of raillery. In this way, according to Granet, the "rhythmic principles underlying the language of poetry and dance were first given issue."

China's early agrarian communities worshiped the unseen forces of nature as spirits who controlled the elements and presided over rivers, fields, and mountains. Professional sorcerers known as *wu* were employed as intermediaries who performed invocatory rites to ensure

CHINA: An Overview. Han dynasty bronze ornament depicting two men dancing on a snake while holding saucers. The significance of this representation is not known. (British Museum, London.)

good harvests, bring on the rains, or exorcise evil spirits. Historians mention the sorcerers as being of both sexes, but not much is recorded concerning their methods. That they utilized some elementary dance forms and, sometimes, masks seems evident from allusions in the *Book of Songs* and *Book of Rites.* In both texts there are references to an exorcism dance performed by sorcerers. In the seventh century CE this was adapted as a court entertainment, suggesting that the sorcerer was one progenitor of dance invention. Another passage in the *Book of Songs* describes how drunken guests at a festival became noisy and danced around "like demon mask dancers," presumably an allusion to the sorcerers. These practitioners were eventually banished from public office and designated as outcasts in Confucian society, a stigma they shared with professional entertainers.

Confucius (c.554–479 BCE) and his followers stressed the educative and moral functions of music and ritual, including dance, as the desired attainments of high-minded men. Dancing was held to be a necessary discipline in the education of the young. Dance was divided into two categories, *wen* and *wu*, rendered in English as "civil" and "military." These terms relate to the Confucian worldview that humanity is one with a universe governed by the cosmic forces of *yin* and *yang*, the polarities inherent in all things and all activities. Through the fusion of these contrasting forces, order and harmony are established in the universe and in human activity. The word *wen* implies literary attainment and therefore cultural refinement. *Wu* indicates skill with combat forms and weapons as taught in the old calisthenic disciplines called *wu shu*. This term embraces a great variety of forms, ranging from those designed purely for physical exercise to those intended to train men for hand-to-hand combat, with or without weapons.

The Confucian novice was expected to master and perform both aspects of the dance in alternation and, in doing so, to achieve a harmonious reconciliation of body and mind. Dance became an aid to perception of the transcendent reality of the cosmos.

Confucian ritual favored large-scale dance formations. An example was the *Great Dance of Zhou*. The performers, holding flutes and pheasant plumes, danced in a long file while moving over a lozenge-shaped performance area. The general ground pattern of the dance was worked out as follows. Commencing at the southern tip of the dance area, the performers followed a diagonal path to the western periphery, where they paused before turning to the beating of a drum and proceeding in a horizontal direction toward the eastern tip; the process was repeated in movements to the northern, western, and eastern boundaries. At the last point the dancers split into two files; one returned southward to the starting point, and the other returned to the eastern boundary before turning south to complete the circuit.

We have limited knowledge of the secular dances mentioned by historians as a spectacular feature of court entertainments. Numerous references are scattered throughout musical treatises, Chinese encyclopedias, and the verses of Tang-dynasty (618–906 CE) poets. This information, however, is largely descriptive or incidental, and little can be gleaned about fundamental technique and method. Dance knowledge was transmitted directly from teacher to pupil in performance, and knowledge died when that continuity was broken. Notational methods in antiquity were improvisational at best. In one interesting passage, we read of an imperial concubine in the eighth century CE memorizing a new musical setting while sitting behind a curtain to hear it played and dropping beads into a bowl to count the measures and beats (Picken, 1969).

The Han dynasty (202 BCE–220 CE) was a period of expansion under a centralized government. Confucianism was promoted as a state doctrine, but Daoist metaphysical theories were explored. [*See* Aesthetics, *article on* Asian Dance Aesthetics.] The great caravan route to the West (called the Silk Road) was opened during this period, and communication was established with the peoples of central Asia. New styles of entertainment became popular at the court, including the Hundred Entertainments. These were a miscellany of events brought from various Asian areas, including acrobatics, juggling, stilt-walking, wrestling, animal impersonation, musical turns, balancing acts, and equestrian displays—in fact, all the elements of the circus ring and the variety stage in modern times. This profusion of forms stirred a new inventiveness that was later to influence dance and theater perfor-

mance. Acrobatics in particular had a significant influence, eventually seen in the choreographic structure of dance dramas that portrayed the exploits of warriors, heroines, and bandits.

It was also during Han times that the arts of *wu shu* came to maturity and experts laid down their rules in treatises used to train military conscripts. In time, martial techniques such as fighting with spears and swords were transposed as exercises to be taken up by the layman, much as people today practice fencing. Women too practiced these skills until the eighth century CE.

A bureau of music was established at the Han court in 120 BCE with responsibility for all palace musical activities, supplying music for solemn ritual and ceremonial occasions as well as more lighthearted events such as palace banquets. As a result of the bureau's activities, a collection of folk songs was preserved in the imperial archives. These marked an evolutionary step in Chinese poetic composition and became esteemed for the quality of their imagery. The music of the songs was lost, but some of the pieces characterized by repetition suggest choral singing, perhaps accompanied with gestural accentuation. Several of the literary styles developed during the long Han period suggest that there may have been mime representation within the framework of poetic narrative, presaging the tonal movement of language that became a focus for dance in later centuries.

In one dance of the Han period, it is recorded that sixteen boys in pairs sang as they danced out scenes from the farmer's calendar—cutting grass, reclamation, sowing, ploughing, driving away birds, reaping, threshing, and winnowing. This symbolic celebration of the land suggests more elaborate development from earlier work dances.

Another composition, the *Divine Altar Dance*, according to the great encyclopedia featured three hundred young girls dancing around a specially erected sacrificial altar. There was still a strong affinity between dance and religious ritual.

The many bas-reliefs and stone rubbings that exist from the Han period provide visual testimony of the variety of choreographic styles in vogue. They included dancing with weapons, scarves, or the long sleeves of a dancer's robe, and the leaps and somersaults of the acrobat. All bear remarkable similarity to techniques witnessed in the traditional stage repertory of today.

Chinese historians stress the significance of certain pieces played at court during the sixth century CE as germinal to the pantomimic dance genre. They were a further step in the synthesis of dance, narrative, and song that had been developing since Han times and was to continue as a central element of many types of performance. A much-cited example was based on the legend of Prince

Lan Ling, who went into battle wearing a mask. The mask may actually have been a painted facial design; whatever the facts, the Lan Ling theme was held to be the origin of using a "substitute face" to portray character. Several versions of this narrative dance were subsequently devised.

Another piece given prominence by Chinese writers was *The Swinging Wife*, a farce in song and dance about a drunken wastrel who ill-treated his wife. The actor playing the wife sang a rueful lament, providing rhythmic accentuation as he swayed to and fro on the stage, with the audience joining in the final refrain. This is reminiscent of the old English music hall, with the same possibilities for studied improvisation. Such a piece lent itself readily to interpolations, and several humorous side topics were eventually introduced into the main theme, providing opportunity for extended bouts of comic dancing and accompanying song.

The Tang dynasty (618–906) is regarded by the Chinese as an outstanding period in their cultural history. Western Asia was opened to caravans in the north and by sea in the south, resulting in a burgeoning of cultural exchange and an influx of many new dance and musical styles. Ambassadors from all over Asia converged on the Chinese capital, Chang'an (Ch'ang An), bringing their dancers with them. Dancing went on in palaces, great houses, and public festivals. The absorption of foreign choreographic and musical ideas during previous eras now coalesced in a flowering of new creativity. The Tang emperor, Ming Huang (712–756), has been immortalized as the founder of a palace training school called the Academy of the Pear Garden. Here hundreds of young men and women were instructed in dance and music, with the emperor reputedly assisting at rehearsals. The name *liyuan* (pear garden) became a metaphorical designation for the professional theater world of China, reflecting the common identity assigned to acting and dancing.

The Tang poets lauded dance in their verses, invoking images such as "the dance of the rainbow skirt and feathered jacket," with constant allusions to the long silk sleeves that extended the dancers' hand gestures. Sleeve dancing is perpetuated in traditional acting forms, particularly those employed for women's roles. Buddhist cave frescoes and tomb figurines vividly depict sleeve-dancing styles and confirm the relationship of ancient dance with today's stage forms.

During the Zhou dynasty (1027–256 BCE), troupes of trained women dancers graced every princely household and performed at official banquets and private drinking parties. Almost a thousand years later, the Tang dynasty marked the apogee of such dancers. Apart from the palace women, in the licensed quarters of the capital hundreds of talented courtesans entertained. As paintings and figurines show, these women performed in low-necked robes

CHINA: An Overview. Tang dynasty sculpture of a court dancer in a long-sleeved garment, the mark of a skilled performer. (Museum of Fine Arts, Boston.)

with long pleated and flared skirts; the rippling lengths of their silk sleeves added to the swirling of the dance lauded by the poets. In the licensed quarters, literati reigned as an aesthetic elite in a world of sensual pleasures, now thought of as a golden age of dance in China.

The decline of the Tang dynasty was followed by a half century of internal strife and external attacks on the northern and western frontiers. The Song dynasty (960–1279 CE) saw the country unified again and ushered in the rise of a new, pleasure-loving merchant class. Popular entertainments of several kinds arose to meet public demand. Storytellers and the shadow-puppet theater became particularly active. A novelty of the period was the variety play, consisting of a prelude, central feature, and musical epilogue. The prelude was usually a farce and the central feature a lyric episode accompanied by dancing and singing. A second innovation was the Big Song, a poetic form conceived as a succession of musical scenes conforming to a key rhythm, in which group dancing alternated with song and recitative. The dance leader at times sang solo or in response to the musician's narrative. A third significant development was the Southern Drama, a colloquial form with sustained themes in song and dialogue, marking it as an advanced step toward fully developed lyric drama.

Court performances continued their tradition of elaborate entertainments during the Song dynasty, and the emperors were surrounded by palace women as in the past. Nevertheless, the heyday of the Tang court dancers was over. Their art had long since been passed on to Japan and Korea, where it flourished independently.

Despite the cultural profusion and ongoing developments of Song times, dance suffered a setback that was to stifle creative participation by the majority of Chinese women. During the half-century between the Tang and Song periods, the practice of binding womens' feet came into fashion. This became an established social custom of the upper classes that persisted until the twentieth century in spite of many campaigns against it; it was finally proscribed by the government of the republic in 1911/12. The origin of the practice is often attributed to a palace dancer who indulged the aesthetic whim of her royal master and created a vogue. Girls' feet were deformed by tight binding, which broke the bones and stunted their growth, resulting in the tiny "three-inch lotus" foot that for centuries was a sign of social status and a sexual fetish. Not every woman in China had bound feet; the Manchus (of the Qing dynasty), who ruled from 1644 to 1911, forbade their own women the practice, although they failed to deter the Chinese. Women who worked outdoors, the Hakka women of the south, and autonomous tribespeople kept their feet unbound. Nevertheless, until the early twentieth century the practice remained so widespread that walking or running any distance without support, much less dancing and doing calisthenics, were impossible for many Chinese women.

The Yuan dynasty (1271–1368) resulted from China's conquest by the Mongols from the north, who imposed their traditions on a nationwide scale. Nevertheless, Chinese values proved equal to this imposition. Paradoxically, this age of alien domination marked the emergence of a mature Chinese theater, with a formal four-act structure and a standardized role system that was perpetuated in all future Chinese drama. It embodied the rhythmic elements of the variety play and the narrative dance, both of which had been moving toward integration. Dance became subsumed as an expressive inner force modulating the controlled, patterned progression of an actor's movements and gestures, contained by the rhythms of song, music, and declamation.

In the changing social conditions that emerged from the Yuan era, the theater inevitably passed through phases of stylistic change. New literary forms, metrical schemes, and sound patterns conditioned by regional dialects were some principal agents of change. Nevertheless, the basic premise of performance remained the same—fixed character roles with formalized combinations of song, poetry, and recitative, and dance as the underlying dynamic component and binding force. As the Ming dynasty (1368–1644) established itself, it became notable for the attention given music rather than theater, although the popularity of theater was never in question. During this period many wealthy families supported their own theatrical troupes for the instruction and entertainment of their large extended households—a practice responsible for widening the body of knowledgeable amateurs. Ming times were noteworthy for the advances made in musical research and in dance notation. Zhu Zaiyu

CHINA: An Overview. Yeh Funjun (left), as Fan Chung-yu, and Mao Fu-kuei (right) as the Old Woodsman Yun-chaio, in the Beijing Opera *Asking the Woodsman*, a production of Yen Lanching's company. (Photograph © 1992 by Jack Vartoogian; used by permission.)

carried out definitive study in the complementary areas of musical structure and dance notation.

Confucian ritual dances were often performed by boys during the Ming era. The choreography was bound by fixed rules, operative in every aspect of performance. When the emperor arrived to open the ceremonies, the dancers were ranged on either side of a marble terrace, eighteen on the western side and eighteen on the eastern. Each group had a leader who carried a banner to guide their movements. They performed to bells and bell chimes, stones and stone chimes, flutes, and large drums. The sacrificial hymn to Confucius was composed of six stanzas, during the second, third, and fourth of which the dancers performed in three cycles, assuming thirty-two positions for each stanza. The positions were based on the written characters for the words of a poem, so the performers danced out the shape of the inherent tones and melody of the words.

During the Qing dynasty (1644–1911), a new style of popular theater arose in Beijing, called Beijing Opera, supplanting the older, more lyrical style, which fell into public disfavor owing to its quietist literary approach. The new style Beijing theater was melodramatic—even vulgar—in its forcible approach. A synthesis of regional forms in which song, dance, mime, music, recitative, and acrobatics merge, Beijing Opera reflects the eclecticism of past traditions. It has persisted until today despite the vicissitudes of the Cultural Revolution (1966–1976), when it was singled out for attack.

Elements of Dance Theater. The choreographic nature of acting on the Chinese stage is patent in the formalized treatment of movement and gesture, integrated with passages of song and music, in which words are treated as time-movement units. Hand gestures symbolizing emotional reactions create a continuous visible element within the tonal movement of the actors' singing and declamation. Graceful passages of pointing with the fingers of one or both hands move through spatial sequences attended by the following glances of the performer, whose foot movements timed to music carry forward the motifs of the dance. Mime also contributes physical actions, such as opening and shutting a door, that are treated as a rhythmic sequence in the play's action.

The costumes and properties used by Chinese actors and actresses are associated with extensive vocabularies of formalized gestures and dance steps that must be mastered by the performer, much as a Western ballet dancer must master positions and steps as the language with which a dramatic idea is transmitted by dance. Typical costume elements are the long white silk cuffs, the "water sleeves," a functional extension of the ordinary sleeves of an actor's robe, as much as two feet long, and the sweeping pheasant plumes of six to seven feet, worn in pairs and attached to certain headdresses. These are manipulated while being held between the first and middle fingers of each hand. Even the long false beards worn in many of the male roles are flicked aside, shaken, or caressed in patterned gestures expressing emotional nuances.

The combat scenes that are a spectacular feature of Beijing Opera are based on techniques derived from *wu shu*. There are dozens of styles demanding skill with long swords, scimitars, or spears, which originated in ancient calisthenic exercises. There are two broad categories of movement: one stresses relaxation and flexibility, providing the means to counter violence through resilience; the second style emphasizes speed and strength. Both utilize weapons play and have their own variations of crouching, twists, turns, and leaps. Dance and stage movement have been profoundly influenced by these disciplines, which are essential to basic stage training. Dancing with weapons has always been an admired art in China, and theater was quick to take advantage of it. Chinese audiences relish the climactic moments provided by a graceful solo dance with a long sword, or a lightning display of footwork while the actor wields a scimitar. The poet Du Fu (712–770) wrote a long poem in praise of Lady Kongsan, who was accomplished in swordplay. Her strokes in attack he described as like "a thunderclap" but in cessation "as still as waters of the river and sea shining calm and still on a summer day." This is a lyrical interpretation of the forces of *yin* and *yang* as they invest the rhythms of dance.

Modern Theatrical Dance. With China's last Qing emperor deposed, the Republican era (1911–1949) had a successful transition of the old theater—in spite of a new generation influenced by Western culture—wishing to dispense with traditional art forms. In 1913 a young Beijing actor, Mei Lanfang (1894–1961), was welcomed as a rejuvenating force on the old stage because of his creative interpretations of female roles, traditionally played only by men. In 1915 he attracted attention with the stage dance *Zhang O's Flight to the Moon,* based on an old legend and employing motifs that owed much to historical precedents. It was the first of a series of such pieces he devised. These gave a new and innovational dimension to dance on the traditional stage. They were the result of a professional partnership with Qi Rushan (Ch'i Ju-shan; 1876–1962), a scholar and theater historian, who acted as Mei's artistic adviser and close collaborator for some twenty years. Mei perfected an acting style based on a synthesis of dance, song, and combat forms, creating an expressive new area of performance. He was a pioneer in breaking down the prejudice against women on stage by taking them as pupils. By the 1930s there was the nucleus of a school of young actresses, accomplished in dance and staged combat, ready to carry on the graceful symbolism that was devised by men to portray the theatrical quintessence of feminine character.

Mei traveled widely, providing an international public with a revealing introduction to Chinese theatrical art. His reputation in Japan was enhanced by his performances there in 1919, 1924, and 1958. In 1930 he toured in America, but his greatest international success was in the Soviet Union in 1935. One of his last engagements in the Soviet Union was a conference with leading theatrical personalities including the cinematic pioneer Sergei Eisenstein, the actor and director Konstantin Stanislavsky, the dancer Viktorina Kriger, and others. At this meeting Eisenstein called for the preservation of the Chinese classical theater as a foundation for a new theater and a new cinema in China. [*See the entry on* Mei Lanfang.]

While new performance styles were emerging in China's traditional performing arts, women's social roles were beginning to change as well in the new Republic of China. Several Western missionary schools for girls in and around Shanghai began to offer physical training and folk dancing. In 1915, the Shanghai YWCA opened the first girls' normal school for physical training; it was absorbed in 1935 by Ginling College for Girls. In the early 1920s, the Liangjiang College was founded near Shanghai as a school for female physical training instructors; three hundred were graduated in fourteen years, and group dancing was taught, as were piano and sight-reading. In 1924, female folk-dancing teams took part, for the first time, in the Third All China Athletic Meet, held at Wuchang. Dalcroze eurhythmics were then in vogue and, in 1934, women of the Shanghai Dongnan Physical Training School were being instructed in Broadway chorus–style legwork—tempered by Chinese decorum.

Several ballet teachers were among the large White Russian émigré colony in Shanghai between the world wars, among them George Goncharov, the first teacher of Margot Fonteyn. Only the wealthier Chinese could then send their children to ballet school, but there was little chance of seeing first-class professional ballet. Nevertheless, interest had been awakened in an art that was to dominate the new Chinese dance movement from the 1940s onward.

Modern Social Dancing. Social dancing, as practiced in the West, was unknown to the Chinese. By the 1920s, however, ballroom dancing had caught on in westernized Shanghai among the Chinese smart set, though frowned on by their elders. The Chinese proved to be good dancers, according to their Western instructors—graceful, light-footed, and too conservative to indulge in flashy effects.

The taxi-dance hall, where male customers hired female partners employed by the establishment, followed on the heels of ballroom dancing. Taxi dancing spread to New York and Chicago from the West Coast in the early 1920s (and had its ancestry in the "49 dance halls" of the 1890s Alaska gold rush). By the 1930s taxi dancing had become

CHINA: An Overview. A gleeful Monkey King, played by Chu Luhao, in a scene entitled "Raiding the Dragon King's Palace" from the Beijing Opera *The Monkey King*. (Photograph © by Jack Vartoogian; used by permission.)

a prominent feature of Shanghai night life, and the dance hostess had begun to replace the old style "singsong girl" as a public entertainer. Chinese hostesses had a reputation for agility on the dance floor and restrained comportment in public. Taxi dancers and ballroom dancing were anathema to Confucian prudery, however, and a constant cause of controversy.

During the 1930s public dancing became a burning question in Chinese government circles. Cabarets and dance halls were decried as steppingstones to prostitution. Ballroom dancing was held to be a symbol of China's foreign shackles. In 1937 a decree was issued threatening Nanjing students with summary dismissal from their colleges and universities if they were found in dance halls. Ten years later the campaign was still being waged. A ban on dancing was enforced in all nationalist Guomindang-controlled cities, and dance hostesses were treated as prostitutes by the police. In October 1947, the director of the government information office held a press conference to explain that the ban on dancing was for the purpose of "thriftiness, increasing production, maintaining social security and quelling the rebellion of the communists." The Shanghai public affairs commissioner pointed out that the ban would put 200,000 dance hostesses out of work. The hostesses themselves were outraged and threatened to stage a protest in Nanjing before the tomb of Sun Zhongshan (Sun Yat-sen), founder of the republic. The impending political collapse of the republic effectively shelved the dispute until the Communist administration came to power, when the ban was enforced immediately.

Regional Dance Revival. In 1940, a young Trinidad-born dancer, Dai Ailian (Tai Ai-Lien), arrived in Hong Kong en route to the mainland to study the regional dancing of the peasants and the autonomous tribal communities. Apart from the traditional theater and the annual Confucian ritual held in temples, the folk dances of distant rural areas were the only ones known to China at that time. They were sadly neglected and familiar only to a few. Dai Ailian began dancing in childhood and in the 1930s went to England to study at the Jooss Ballet School. She also studied under Anton Dolin and Margaret Craske. In Hong Kong she made two professional appearances, in one of which she performed a new sketch called *East River*, based on Cantonese folk dances. She went on to the

mainland and began to study local folk dances, aided by a group of pupil-assistants. She traveled as widely as circumstances permitted (Japan had invaded in 1937), researching and adapting regional dances for performance. Her interpretations of Uighur dances from Xinjiang were particularly well received. She also taught at the National School of Opera and the Academy of Social Education. In 1945, she regrouped her dancers and the following year visited the United States and gave dance recitals in New York. On her return to China, she opened a new school in Shanghai with former students.

The seizure of power in 1949 by the Communists resulted in a reorganization of China's cultural activities following the First All China Conference of Artists and Writers in Beijing, to which Dai Ailian was an invited delegate. Administrative committees were convened for each activity, including an All China Dance Association. Plans were drawn up for new training facilities and future goals.

In the first flush of Mao Zedong's victories, youths took to the streets dancing the *yangge* (yang-ko), a simple song-and-dance style that developed among farmers planting their ricefields. Taken up by the Communists during the war, it spread rapidly and became their victory theme. Students and schoolchildren paraded in the streets in long files, winding in and out to the repetitious rhythms of waist drum, cymbals, and a simple chanted stanza. The dance was elementary: three quick steps forward, one step

CHINA: An Overview. Members of the Chinese Performing Arts Company in *Lotus Dance*, a modern adaptation of a traditional genre, at the Metropolitan Opera House, New York. (Photograph © 1978 by Jack Vartoogian; used by permission.)

backward, pause, and repeat. Hand-clapping and body-swaying accompanied the pacing.

Similar dances are found throughout China where song and music help direct work movements. The related field song *(tiange,* or *t'ien-ko)* is found in Hubei and Shaanxi provinces, where tilling and sowing are done to singing accompanied by drumbeats. It is in the Dingxian area, however, that the most developed form of this folk genre is seen.

In 1932 two scholars, Li Jinghan (Li Ching-han) and Zhang Shiwen (Chang Shih-wen), published an anthology of Dingxian rice-planting songs as the result of a government-sponsored field study, anticipating Communist exploration of the subject by several years. Their anthology included pieces in forty-eight categories, such as love; piety and chastity; husband–wife, daughter–mother-in-law relationships; comedy; and a miscellany that included pieces adapted from professional theater. All were the work of villagers with no professional expertise, drawing on familiar experience. The early *yangge* had twenty to thirty dancers headed by a troupe leader. Male and female characters faced each other in performance, and singing followed a question-and-response formula. Three steps forward and one swing back constituted the basic pacing, with some variants and gestural embellishment according to the role played. Group movements could be extended in fanciful dance patterns, with body-swaying to express sex appeal. There was usually a comic character to add the necessary touch of farce—sometimes a Buddhist priest, the favored butt of the Beijing stage. Drum, gong, flute, and cymbals provided additional musical emphasis, although percussion predominated.

With the Japanese war (1937–1945), *yangge* was monopolized by the Communists and adapted to their propaganda needs. Rifles replaced agricultural implements as props; soldiers, farmers, and laborers became the characters portrayed. The clown was replaced by a Japanese aggressor or Chinese collaborator. This form even spread to the nationalist forces, since it was directed at the common enemy. At a 1944 spring festival in Communist-held Yenan, thirty-seven *yangge* troupes staged a selection of dances and plays, including *The White-Haired Girl,* as a retrospective recital. Originally a ballad recitative based on a reputedly true incident, *The White-Haired Girl* became a collective work that went through many revisions. Staged continuously in the late 1940s and early 1950s, it became a symbol of revolution in progress. Less partisan critics found it excessively long and lacking in unity. The original version ran for six hours—a later Shanghai version for four and one-half. Twenty years later it attained its final form as a three-hour ballet, choreographed by the Shanghai School of Dance (founded in 1960).

In 1949, the numerous *yangge* dance troupes of the People's Republic of China were organized as the dance unit

CHINA: An Overview. The Chinese have a strong acrobatic tradition that they have adapted to modern theatrical presentations. The balancing act of these Shanghai acrobats incorporates many elements of dance: fluidity, grace, and precision of movement. (Photograph © 1980 by Jack Vartoogian; used by permission.)

of the Central Drama Academy in Beijing. They presented their first dance spectacle at Shanghai in October 1950. Entitled *Doves of Peace,* it was eclectic in expression and political by intent. Staged with 150 dancers, it drew on classical ballet techniques and Jooss-style mime mingled with *yangge* forms, Chinese folk music, and Western musical rhythms. Critics saw it as promising, given China's lack of ballet tradition and the short time available for production. The choreography was the joint work of seven members of the troupe, led by Dai Ailian, whose influence the critics discerned in the more artistically credible scenes.

Dai Ailian was destined to become the guiding force of a rapidly growing new dance movement. In 1953 she toured China and Inner Mongolia to study folk dances before taking up her post in 1955 as principal of the new Beijing Academy of Dance (founded in 1954). A seven-year dance training program was set up, including general education to high-school level for students of eleven years and older; they were selected from talented children in primary and secondary schools and, in the case of older students, from song-and-dance troupes or from the different regional and minority areas with well-developed folk dance traditions.

Students in the last two categories usually spent an intensive year at the school studying Chinese classical and folk dances, elements of ballet, and the traditional dances of other nations before returning to their own troupes. The largest independent folk ensemble was the Central Song and Dance Ensemble, founded in 1953, which grew into a 200-member company in a decade; its repertory concentrated on the songs and the dances of China and its several minority ethnic groups. Many of their new dance compositions were adapted from regional theater. Members were recruited from among the experienced dancers and singers of the various local genres. Promising youngsters were also recruited for five years of basic training before being admitted as full members.

The first glimpse of the new eclecticism was given to the outside world in 1956 when the Chinese Folk Artists Troupe visited Hong Kong. Included in the lengthy program were folk dances from Fujian, Xinjiang, and Korea. A newly choreographed *Lotus Dance* strongly influenced by Russian folk-style footwork was offset by a comical lion dance, a trick wrestling bout, and a stately sword dance on classical lines. A female chorus, more than a score of folk-song soloists, a flute recital, and a musical mime on trumpet were followed by several excerpts from traditional Beijing plays. Disciplined, spectacular, and a little synthetic, it provided a new demonstration of the perpetual Chinese passion for variety shows.

In February 1962 a new song and dance group, the Dong Fang Art Ensemble, made its Beijing debut. The performance opened with a Balinese *pendet*, a traditional invocation given as a prelude to a recital, followed by a Japanese folk dance, a Cambodian classical dance, an Ethiopian harvest dance, a group of Burmese folk songs, and other pieces. Chinese dancers first began to learn Burmese, Indian, and Indonesian dances in the early 1950s when troupes from Beijing began visiting the other Asian countries on cultural good will tours. By 1957, so much enthusiasm had been generated that an Asian dance class was set up in the Beijing Dance Academy. Four well-known dancers from Indonesia were invited to give instruction in their national dance styles. In 1960, a Burmese cultural troupe visited China and a leading dancer from the group was invited to work with Chinese students. The Chinese took every opportunity to add the traditional dances of their Asian neighbors to their own repertory. By 1962, the group numbered more than one hundred members, drawn from several nationalities besides Chinese, and it began to tour regularly. A training class for children was also attached to the new company.

Ballet in China. Of all the Western performing arts, the Chinese perhaps feel the greatest affinity with classical ballet. Its synthesis of elements accords well with their attitudes toward the structure of dramatic form; it is concerned with story and character translated into dance terms, with which the Chinese feel at ease. The extreme abstraction of some modern Western dancing (whether ballet or modern dance) goes against the grain in China and opposes an insistence on socialist realism.

China's first ballet company, the Experimental Ballet Troupe, was set up in the Beijing Dance Academy in December 1959, six years after the founding of the school, where ballet training was a regular feature of the curriculum. The company members were drawn from fifth-year graduates and some of the younger instructors. The Sino-Soviet alliance was strong in those years and political prestige was involved in the taking up of Russian ballet. Whatever the political strings, Chinese novices became immersed in a great dance tradition and had to strive for high standards; from 1957 Soviet dancers and choreographers went to Beijing to teach. The first Soviet ballet instructor was Dimitri Saplain of the Bolshoi Ballet, who worked with the Chinese students on *La Fille Mal Gardée*. In 1959 they staged their first full-length ballet, *Swan Lake*, after four months of intensive rehearsal under Petr Gusev of Leningrad. In 1959 Gusev also directed their second full-length production, *Le Corsaire*, to music by Adolphe Adam. In 1957 the Novosibirsk Ballet Theatre visited China, followed by a tour of the Bolshoi Ballet in 1959; Galina Ulanova danced in *Giselle* and Maya Plisetskaya in *Swan Lake*. Elena Ryabinkina and Vladimir Tikhonov, soloists of the Bolshoi, danced with the Beijing Dance Academy group in November 1961 under an arts exchange program.

In return, the Beijing troupe visited Moscow, where they performed a new dance production, *The Magic Lotus Lantern*, in the Bolshoi Theater. It was based on an old legend, a typical Chinese romantic fantasy, and traditionally costumed. The choreographic basis of the composition was, however, an experiment in combining the technical lessons learned from ballet with traditional Chinese forms. Ballet had influenced the shape of steps, postures, and movements in certain passages of the dance, although the inner rhythm of the piece remained essentially Chinese. It was another exploratory step in the synthesis of forms that has been so creative a force in the long history of Chinese dance.

In 1962 the Beijing Ballet made its first overseas tour at the invitation of the Burmese government—a contemporary echo of a past when dance and dancers were offered as political tribute to neighboring Asian states. In February 1964 the British ballerina Beryl Grey, formerly of the Royal Ballet (in 1957, the first Western ballerina to dance as guest artist with the Bolshoi), was invited to China to dance with and instruct the Beijing Ballet. The company then consisted of eighty-eight dancers, five teachers, three choreographers, and an orchestra of seventy-three musicians and two conductors. There were also six pianists, four stage designers, and thirty stage technicians, costumers, and shoemakers. Grey wrote that Chinese classes were similar to the Russian, complimenting the quickness and concentration of the students. Of a rehearsal of act 2 of *Swan Lake*, she wrote:

> I had not expected to see such good limbs and well arched feet. Their backs were unusually supple and their extensions high without any apparent forcing. The Oriental fluidity of their arm movements was particularly suited to *Swan Lake* as were their long slender necks. But I was perhaps most impressed by the dignity and poise, the quiet composure and concentration with which they tackled everything.

Of audiences, she said, "New to ballet they were wholly attentive to every performance and were obviously keen to absorb all they could of this alien art form."

With the coming of China's Cultural Revolution (1966–1976), all that had been accomplished in those first productive years of ballet training was to be politically denounced. The Cultural Revolution was based on the following event: in July 1964, Jiang Qing, Mao Zedong's wife, launched scathing attacks on the performing arts; ballet, she said, had done untold harm to the cause of socialism and must be revolutionized. The outcome of her criticism was the decade of sociopolitical confusion that followed the autumn productions of two "revolutionary" ballets, *The Red Detachment of Women* (1964) and *The White-Haired Girl* (1964). Both were prepared under the personal supervision of Jiang Qing, and both remained the only ballets in the diminished repertory until the Cultural Revolution was ended.

The Red Detachment of Women was lauded as the first ballet on a contemporary revolutionary theme when shown before Mao, who approved its political orientation. The one choreographic element that could have been described as revolutionary was a corps de ballet armed with rifles. Western critics discerned only a resemblance to the heroic naturalism of Russian performances in the 1920s, steeped in melodrama.

The White-Haired Girl was the creation of the Shanghai School of Dance. Their first production of it ran about 30 minutes, but it was eventually amplified to a three-hour ballet. The final version became the subject of party dissension. Liu Shaoji, the party secretary, opposed Jiang Qing's interpretations and wanted more subtlety in the acting and directing. Mao's wife prevailed.

Both these ballets were made into films that were eventually shown on Western screens and television. U.S. President Richard M. Nixon was entertained with a performance of *The Red Detachment of Women* when he made his first visit to China. The technical competence of the dancers was acknowledged by Western critics, although they felt that budding talents were misdirected. Both the music and the choreography of the two ballets were dependent on an outmoded Western romanticism, with derivative elements superimposed on the compositional structure. [*See* Red Detachment of Women, The; White-Haired Girl, The.]

Dance in the People's Republic of China suffered severe setbacks owing to the political disruption of its formative years and the resultant aesthetic confusion. Today these revolutionary ballets belong to the past as Chinese dancers begin to distance themselves from the years of suppression. Their poise, concentration, and technical

CHINA: An Overview. Yin Mei manipulates a long swath of fabric in her *Ribbon Dance*. (Photograph © 1986 by Jack Vartoogian; used by permission.)

virtuosity are not in question, but they require the time and maturity to acquire that emotional charge that differentiates dance art from calculated propaganda.

BIBLIOGRAPHY

"A Ballet for Peace." *Peoples China* (1 October 1950).

Chai Ch'u and Winberg Chai, eds. *Li Chi Book of Rites: An Encyclopedia of Ancient and Ceremonial Usages, Religious Creeds, and Social Institutions.* New Hyde Park, N.Y., 1967.

"Chiang Ching, the Political Pickpocket." *Chinese Literature*, no. 2 (1977): 109–117.

Ch'i Ju-shuan. *Ch'üan-chi.* Collected Works, vols. 3, 5. Taiwan, n.d.

Chu Tsai-yu. *Yueh-lu ch'üan shu.* Taipei, n.d.

"Chu Tsai-yu." In *Dictionary of Ming Biography.* New York, 1976.

Confucius. *The Analects.* Translated by Arthur Waley. London, 1938.

Confucius. *Confucian Analects: The Great Learning and the Doctrine of the Mean.* Translated and edited by James Legge. New York, 1971.

Delza, Sophia. "Perspectives on the Aesthetics of Change from the Classical Chinese Theatre to the Revolutionary Peking Opera." *Chinoperl Papers* (March 1978).

DeWoskin, Kenneth J. *A Song for One or Two: Music and Concept of Art in Early China.* Michigan Papers in Chinese Studies, no. 42. Ann Arbor, 1982.

"Doves of Peace: October 1950." *China Monthly Review* (January 1951).

"Dunhuang Art Treasures." *China Reconstructs* 36 (May 1987): 1–14.

Goodrich, L. Carrington. *A Short History of the Chinese People.* 3d ed. London, 1969.

Granet, Marcel. *Festivals and Songs of Ancient China.* London, 1932.

Granet, Marcel. *Chinese Civilisation.* London, 1957.

Gray, Basil. *Buddhist Cave Paintings at Tun-huang.* London, 1955.

Grey, Beryl. *Through the Bamboo Curtain.* London, 1965.

Gulik, Robert Hans van. *Sexual Life in Ancient China: A Preliminary Survey of Chinese Sex and Society from c. 1500 B.C. till 1644 A.D.* Leiden, 1961.

Hsu Tao-ching. *The Chinese Conception of the Theatre.* Seattle, 1985.

Jing Cheng and Yeh Feng. "Li dai wuzi tu." *Wudao*, nos. 1–2, 4–6 (1962).

Karlgren, Bernhard. *The Book of Odes.* Stockholm, 1950.

Levy, Howard S. *Chinese Footbinding: History of a Curious Erotic Custom.* New York, 1966.

Li Ching-han and Chang Shih-wen. *Tinghsien Yang-ko.* Shanghai, 1933.

Liu Wu-chi. *An Introduction to Chinese Literature.* Bloomington, 1960.

Lobet, Marcel, et al. "The Living Dance." *World Theatre* 6 (Autumn 1957): 166–223.

Mackerras, Colin. *The Chinese Theatre in Modern Times: From 1849 to the Present Day.* Amherst, Mass., 1975.

Mackerras, Colin, ed. *Chinese Theater from Its Origins to the Present Day.* Honolulu, 1983.

"Mei Lanfang in Moscow." *China Weekly Review* (18 May 1935).

Mei Wu-ji. "New Dance Drama: Flying to the Moon." *China Reconstructs* 29 (1980): 21–25.

Needham, Joseph. *Science and Civilisation in China*, vol. 1, *Introductory Orientations*; vol. 2, *History of Scientific Thought.* Cambridge, 1954.

Ouyang Yu-chien. "The Dance in China." *Peoples China* (14 July 1957).

Pian, Rulan Chao, et al. "China." In *The New Grove Dictionary of Music and Musicians.* London, 1980.

Picken, L. E. R. "T'ang Music and Musical Instruments." *T'oung Pao* 55.1–3 (1969).

Scott, A. C. "The Dance in Contemporary China." *World Theatre* 6 (Autumn 1957): 211–216.

Scott, A. C. "*Hung Ten Chi* [The Red Lantern], an Example of Contemporary Chinese Dramatic Experimentation." *Modern Drama* 9 (February 1967): 404–411.

Scott, A. C., trans. and ed. *Traditional Chinese Plays.* 3 vols. Madison, Wis., 1967–1975.

"Shanghai and the 'Gang of Four.'" *China Reconstructs* 26 (November 1977): 2–10.

Snow, Lois Wheeler. *China on Stage.* New York, 1972.

Strauss, Gloria B. "The Art of the Sleeve in Chinese Dance." *Dance Perspectives*, no. 63 (1975): 1–47.

Tang-Loaec, R., and Pierre Colombel. *Chine, fresques du désert de Gobi: La route de la soie au jardin des plantes.* Paris, 1983. Exhibition catalogue, Musée National d'Histoire Naturelle.

Tu Fu. "On Seeing the Pupil of Kung-sun Dance the Sword Dance." In *Selections from the Three Hundred Poems of the T'ang Dynasty.* Translated by Soames Jenyns. London, 1940.

Waley, Arthur. *The Book of Songs.* London, 1954.

Waley, Arthur. *The Nine Songs: A Study of Shamanism in Ancient China.* London, 1955.

Wang Kefen. *The History of Chinese Dance.* Beijing, 1985.

Wang Xi and Liu Qingxia. "Along the Silk Road Dance Drama." *China Reconstructs* 29 (March 1980): 24–29.

Wan Kung. "How Our Revolutionary Operas and Ballets Were Produced." *Chinese Literature*, no. 5–6 (1977): 66–72.

Watson, Burton. *Hsun Tzu.* New York, 1963.

A. C. SCOTT

Folk and Minority Dance

China is a multiethnic country. The largest ethnic group, the Han, accounts for more than 90 percent of its population of some 1.3 billion. In addition, about fifty-five minorities exist with different cultures and languages, belonging to five main linguistic families. This diversity is further enriched by China's many geographical and climatic environments, influencing local modes of production, which in turn have caused these cultures to evolve divergently. This helps to explain why an enormous variety of folk dance traditions can be found in China to this day.

Han Folk Dance. In the popular tradition of the Han ethnic group, the origins of dance are associated with the deeds of mythic culture heroes. Fu Xi gave humans the fish net and the Harpoon Dance; Shen Nong created agriculture and the Plough Dance, and the Yellow Emperor, a legendary ruler of the twenty-sixth century BCE, is celebrated in the Dance of the Cloud Gate. Also mentioned in early texts are agriculture-related dances intended to enlist the help of the gods, such as the Constellation Dance—an incantation for as much seed grain as stars in the sky—and the Great Ode of Emperor Yao's period (about the twenty-second century BCE), a hunting dance. In ancient times dance was not an independent art; it was intimately linked to the struggle for survival and the heroes that emerged from it. Other elements of ancient dance were the influence of totems and pre-Confucian religious practices.

Totemic worship is common worldwide, and fragments of it survive in folk songs and folk dances as well as in legends, poems, costumes, religious practices, and graphic arts. One of the main totems of the Han ethnic group was the dragon. It can be traced in its primitive form to the great ancestor Fu Xi and to his sister, Nü Wa, who were both semi-human figures with snake bodies. The gradual assimilation of other ethnic groups into the Han added new totemic elements to the original reptile shape—animal legs, horse mane, rat tail, deer hooves, dog claws, and fish scales—to make up the dragon as we know it today. Although the dragon eventually lost its cultic value, its totemic symbolism has persisted. The emperor (who was both the master and the symbol of China and its people) was referred to as the Son of the Dragon—and the Chinese people have long associated themselves with the dragon image.

An example of the totemic value of the dragon is found in the popular Dragon Dance, more than seven hundred variants of which are still performed in different parts of the country. This dance is regularly performed for the Spring Festival, the traditional Chinese New Year, and for the Lantern Festival, fifteen days later. It enjoys mass participation by people of all ages, dressed in festive colors and holding balls and representations of clouds, following the frolicking dragons.

The dragon totem also pervades many other types of Han folk dance. The *yangge*, a rice-planting dance, is very common in the northern half of China. It is performed to the accompaniment of drums and singing, with alternating fast and slow rhythms and a succession of steps forward and back. In the countryside it may be part of a complex ensemble which includes drama and singing.

Another type of folk dance, more common in the south of China, is the Lantern Dance or Flower Lantern Dance. It is found under different names and forms in Anhui, Hunan, Guangxi, Yunnan, Sichuan, and Guangzhou provinces. Despite great differences in style, movements, and meaning between the northern *yangge* and the southern Lantern Dance, they share many characteristics, including circular or arc movements of the arms and hands, and undulating body motion with accentuated lower-back movements accompanied by upward elongation. The northeastern Chinese *yangge*, for example, has been described as "waves in stability," because of the characteristic waving motions of the upright body. The Shandong Jiaozhou *yangge* requires a triple bending of the torso and strong hip movements, described as "back-breaking," which give the impression that the dancers are floating on the sea. The same undulation, in which the body describes a figure eight is found in the southern Lantern Dance. These dances are also characterized by the same graceful circular arm and hand movements. In both the north and south, the general impression given is one of

continuous reptilian movement, reminiscent of the writhings of a dragon. This totemic association is reinforced by the age-old names given to the movements: dragon's-tail thrust, two dragons blowing their whiskers, and golden dragon curling around a jade pillar. Women's dance movements have such names as phoenix triple bow, phoenix wing spread, and two phoenixes facing the sun—the phoenix is the feminine totemic figure and represents the empress.

Ethnic Minorities. Among the national minorities whose economic development has been somewhat slower than that of the Han, traditional ways have been better maintained. This applies strongly to folk dance. Totemic associations vary from one group to another, but bird totems are common. The Mongols recognize the hawk, Genghis Khan's favorite bird, and the wild goose, symbol of heroes roaming the steppes in search of home. For the Evenki of northeastern China, it is the swan. The Tibetans consider the peacock an auspicious bird, and the movements of its tail are associated with the way men tie their gowns around their waists. Tibetan dance movements have names such as "the peacock's wingspread" and "the drinking peacocks."

In Yunnan along the Hong river live the Yi people, who have adopted the chicken as their totem. It appears in a dance usually performed at night. Dozens of people, barefoot and wearing hats with strings of beads arranged in the shape of chicken combs, move to the sound of the moon guitar. The steps are executed from the knee down, at a fast tempo, reinforcing the bird image.

In northeastern China, ethnic Koreans traditionally worship the purity of the crane, which is also considered a

CHINA: Folk and Minority Dance. Dancers and musicians with spectators in Inner Mongolia, an autonomous region of northern China. (Photograph from the Dance Collection, New York Public Library for the Performing Arts.)

symbol of happiness and longevity. Korean elders usually dress in white, with a black hat, black vest, and black shoes, in imitation of the bird's color pattern. Korean folk dance shows the influence of this totem: the steps are aptly described as "crane steps"; shoulder movements imitate the beating of wings, and the general attitude of the dancers, graceful reserve and inwardness—though male dancers tend to show some exuberance—is inspired by the bird's aloof demeanor.

In the Xishuangbanna area of Yunnan, the Dai people consider the peacock a holy bird. In their dances they imitate its movements, gait, and flight, perhaps as a form of worship, attaching special importance to tail and wing movements. Animal imitation among the Dai people has reached a high degree of sophistication, seen in the Dance of the Hundred Animals, a participation dance performed annually until 1956. Wearing masks and cos-

CHINA: Folk and Minority Dance. Li Zhongmei in her theatricalized presentation of a southern Chinese Peacock Dance. Traditionally, the Dai people of southern China have considered the peacock a holy bird. (Photograph © 1995 by Jack Vartoogian; used by permission.)

tumes, the dancers tried to recreate the movements of the animals they were representing, around the central figure of an elephant. Animal dances on a smaller scale are still common today in the villages. The observation of nature, the worship of the noble beauty of the peacock, and the pervasive influence of Hinayana Buddhism are the three major factors that make Dai folk dance so graceful, with a rich range of expression conveyed by delicate hand, finger, and eye movements. This grace is enhanced by the fluidity of the body, which is bent in three curves at all times.

Shamanistic Dance. Around the eleventh century BCE, Chinese society began to be divided into slaves and slave-owners. At the same time, dance moved away from its primitive status to emerge as an independent art form aimed at pleasing both spirits and humans. In the course of this evolution appeared the shamans (*wu*) whose function was to serve as intermediaries between the human and spiritual worlds. They gradually became invested with the powers of curing, divination, and sorcery. Because dance and incantation were their main means of communication with the supernatural world, they also became the first professional dancers, collecting and refining earlier dance forms. Later their art evolved into sacred dance, but it also permeated popular dances, lending them a number of elements that have survived to this day.

For example, the Rain Sacrificial Dance used to be performed by female shamans, who could be sacrificed to the spirits if their invocations proved unsuccessful. Elements of it can still be seen today in the Dragon Dance, particularly in the tradition of holding cloud representations around the dragon as a way of asking for rain. It can also be seen in the Shandong *yangge* traditionally performed in the first half of the eighth lunar month: the dancers first make offerings at the temple and burn incense and sacrificial paper money for the gods and the souls of the dead. Then, accompanied by the beating of gongs and drums, they form into long lines to dance for rain.

Another shamanistic element is found in the surviving fragments of the *luo* sacrificial dance. Originally performed to drive away evil spirits, or at funerals to insure a peaceful afterlife for the souls of the dead, this dance used to involve twelve animal role dancers moving violently around a central bear figure. A relationship may exist with the totemic tradition still alive among the Evenki of northeastern China, who (like other Tungusic Siberian groups) consider bears sacred animals protected by hunting taboos and feature them in a number of their dances. [*See* Siberia.] It is difficult to ascertain whether the folk dances still performed under the name *luo* in the southern provinces of Anhui, Jiangxi, Guizhou, and Hunan are related to the original shamanist *luo*, but the bear and other animal spirits are still commonly seen in a number of folk dances across the country, including the Bear Dance, the

Eight-Animal Dance, the Spirit Dance, and the Human Bear Dance.

The shamanistic dance tradition is still alive among some ethnic groups, particularly the Jingpo, Mongols, and Uighurs. Among the Tibetan people, Shamanism has been incorporated into Lamaist Buddhism, and temples often have several lamas whose role it is to perform sacred dances as a part of Buddhist worship.

Shamanist dance is also found in the Peace Drum dances performed under different names by Han people in northern and northeastern China. The dancers wear special costumes with little bells tied around their waists. They dance to the rhythm of drums in a ceremony aimed at inducing the gods to drive away evil spirits. The dance follows a strict five-stage procedure: invitation to the gods, welcoming of the gods, arrival of the gods, flight of the evil spirits, and send-off of the gods.

Rich in all these influences, Chinese folk dance benefits from ethnic diversity. Since the establishment of the People's Republic of China in 1949, tremendous changes have affected Chinese society. With the weakening of religious practice, progress in mass communications, and the trend toward urbanization, certain traditions, including dance traditions, are being neglected and forgotten. At the same time, however, folk dance has become the object of serious attention and study on the part of the country's cultural authorities. This has led to extensive research and preservation. Concurrent with this preservation effort, traditional folk dance elements are being used as the basis for creating new works or incorporation into the choreography of composite pieces—thus bringing folk dance to the stage as a performing art form.

CHINA: Folk and Minority Dance. Young dancers in a choreographed benefit performance for the Beijing Dance Academy, a school that teaches traditional, folk, and minority dances. (Photograph © 1994 by Jack Vartoogian; used by permission.)

BIBLIOGRAPHY
Bredon, Juliet. *Chinese Near Year Festivals*. Rev. ed. Singapore, 1989.
Chamberlain, Franc. "Fragments of a Dixi Training." *Drama Review* 36 (Summer 1992): 118–125.
Chen Weiya et al., eds. *Flying Dragon and Dancing Phoenix: An Introduction to Selected Chinese Minority Folk Dances*. Beijing, 1987.
"A Chinese Smorgasbord." *Folk Dance Scene* 30 (October 1994): 10–17.
Delza, Sophia. "The Dance-Arts in the People's Republic of China: The Contemporary Scene." In *Dance in Africa, Asia, and the Pacific*, edited by Judy Van Zile. New York, 1976.
Fairbank, Holly. "Chinese Minority Dances: Processors and Preservationists" (parts 1–2). *Journal for the Anthropological Study of Movement* 3 (Autumn 1985): 168–189; 4 (Spring 1986): 36–55.
Feng, Lide, and Kevin Stuart. "Delighting the Gods in 1990." *Asian Theatre Journal* 11 (Spring 1994): 35–63.
"Festivals Chinese Style." *Folk Dance Scene* 30 (November 1994): 7–12.
Flowers of Songs and Dances of Nationalities. Beijing, 1985.
Huang-pu, Chong-ching. "Dixi: Chinese Farmers' Theatre." *Drama Review* 36 (Summer 1992): 106–117.
Li Huailin and Jin Shaoqin, eds. *Local Cultural Festivals in China*. Beijing, 1992.
Ou Jian-ping. "Yunnan Province Miniorities Song and Dance Ensemble." *Dance Magazine* (April 1990): 76–77.

Qi Xing, comp. *Folk Customs of Traditional Chinese Festivities*. Beijing, 1988.
Stepanchuk, Carol, and Charles Wong. *Mooncakes and Hungry Ghosts: Festivals of China*. San Francisco, 1991.
Thompson, John. "Hubei Song and Dance Ensemble." In *The Tenth Festival of Asian Arts*. Hong Kong, 1985.
Thrasher, Alan R. *La-li-luo Dance-Songs of the Chuxiong Yi, Yunnan Province, China*. Danbury, Conn., 1990.
Tsung Wen. "The Art of the Working People." *Chinese Literature*, no. 3 (1965): 71–82.
Wang Kefen. *The History of Chinese Dance*. Beijing, 1985.
Wu Hsiao-pang. *A General Survey of the Development of the Chinese National Dance*. Paris, 1982.

XU SUYIN

Dance in Opera

Dance is an integral part of the classical Chinese theater (called "Chinese opera" in the West), and the actor is equally a dancer. In the Zhou dynasty (1027–256 BCE), music, dance, and pantomime were combined to pay homage to the kings by presenting their lives and exploits in choreographed dance dramas. This composite art may be considered the source of Chinese classical theater.

CHINA: Dance in Opera. Li Pao-chun (left) in his company's production of the Beijing Opera *The Story of Lin Chung*. (Photograph © 1992 by Jack Vartoogian; used by permission.)

The historic classical theater, the short-lived "revised opera" of the Cultural Revolution (1966–1976), and the "contemporary opera" since that date share certain basic principles. They stress political, social, and historic content, and they adhere to the aesthetic precepts of the traditional style. This last prescribes a harmonious synthesis of drama, acting, speech, song, dance, and orchestral music, with conventionalized flowing transitions to weave an aesthetic whole.

Basic training for theater students has historically begun at age eight or nine. It focuses on the art and science of body movement. The student is expected to be rhythmically coordinated and proficient in stylized movement; to master acting's technical and expressive aspects; and to develop physical prowess and the empathetic skills that imbue individual roles with feeling.

Although the actor's rhythmic, stylized movements give the impression that the Chinese opera is a dance theater, its acting is distinguishable from other kinds of choreography in terms of form, body placement, and thematic development. Self-contained dance is here architecturally composed and dynamically and spatially organized, with somewhat abstract rhythmic gestures and patterned combinations. Chinese opera dance, however, combines such form and structures within the context of the play's plot and roles.

Chinese theatrical dance is quite varied, owing to the wide range of the dramatic stories, which may be political and historical or ethical and philosophical, and which include themes of family relationships and the problems of scholars, as well as fantasy and legend. There are dances of courage, defeat, triumph, despair, love, intrigue, sadness, satire, and madness; moreover, dances are specific to the age, sex, status, education, character, and occupation of the role.

Concepts and Content. Dance is a natural medium for expressing sorrow, joy, fear, anger, or love. Formalized patterns are varied with subtle nuances of feeling and dramatic emphasis to give individuality to each dance.

In the classical opera *Rainbow Pass*, a woman warrior indicates with obvious gestures and body movements that she is attracted to the general with whom she is in combat. The general's aloof manner and tensed positions show his scorn of her flirtatiousness. Emotional expressiveness is sustained throughout, giving flavor to the conventional combat-duet.

In the operatic version of *The White-Haired Girl*, the heroine does a dance of sorrow and despair on discovering that her father has been brutally attacked. In balletic fashion she dances on demi-pointe, but she uses her head, torso, hands, and fingers in the lyric classical way. Such choreographic mixtures are typical of both contemporary and revised opera.

In the contemporary opera *Monkey Dramas* the action-dance forms remain as they were in the classical version, except that certain motifs are shortened. Anger, grief, annoyance, humor, wit, and jollity are each cleverly incorporated into the dance scheme, which utilizes the Monkey's unique ability to leap, bound, fall, gyrate, and somersault, making the choreography exceptionally rich.

In addition to the emotions of the moment, the character's dominant trait becomes the subject of dance. Whether the character is heroic, regal, modest, uncouth, sly, arrogant, or evil can determine the manner in which the dance is executed. The swaggering hero enters tossing and twirling his gown, kicking and striding with overdone vigor, showing that he is tough enough for any task. A modest person gestures subtly and dances with gliding steps. Consciously directing his eye movements, the spy performs speedy acrobatics with torso low and knees bent. Exaggerated undulating body and arm movement reveals the young flirt; a heavy, slow tread, the elderly woman. The hero, young or old, projects power and dignity in smooth-flowing action.

Because classical opera uses no scenery, the actor-dancer sets the stage by incorporating the idea of physical environment into gesture and movement. Facing upstage, the actor raises a foot as if stepping over a threshold to indicate entering a room. In contemporary opera, where sets are used, such functional gestures are not considered a structural part of the acting-dancing theme.

Action expands the stage when, from atop three stacked tables, the dancer does a double somersault to indicate he is running down a mountain. Many actor-dancers turn the stage into a sea with spread-eagle leaps, diving falls, and spiral-twisting turns. Swaying and rocking with irregular rhythmic patterns, as if trying to keep her balance, a dancer conjures up the image of being on a pitching boat. A general on a symbolic horse uses slipping, sliding, and collapsing movements to portray efforts to advance on icy ground. A pair of fighters on a lighted stage imbue their slow, groping movements with such tense caution that they convey being in utter darkness. Swordplay and acrobatic action gain new vitality with such portrayals of atmosphere and place.

Closely knit with emotion, character, and place, the dance of situation appears most frequently—to enhance, intensify, and illustrate the plot. A hero's sword dance is not merely a decorative technical interlude, but a display of prowess and a proof of his ability to overcome an adversary. A general fleeing from his camp performs elaborately with lance and whip, all the while singing the story of his plight.

In the classical opera *A Buddhist Nun Craves Worldly Love*, a sixteen-year-old nun plays out her life story choreographically, integrating song and speech with mimetic and symbolic gestures. While moving from convent to garden to temple, she describes her feelings in words, song, and dance, plaintively, flirtatiously, satirically, and finally cheerfully as she reaches the outside world. This half-hour solo playlet is a typical example of the harmonious use of all the arts.

Body Technique. Always present in the dance structure is the manner of moving used to define the specific individual being portrayed. Roles fall into genres—human beings, animals and birds, and supernatural beings. Qualities inherent in each type—psychological, physiological, emotional, and intellectual—are focused on creatively.

Body technique comprises the way the torso is held, how the head turns and where the eyes are directed, what form the hands and fingers take, how the arms are positioned and walking steps shaped, and the way the legs and feet are oriented. The range of body dynamics, the plasticity of muscle movement, the agility of joint action, and rhythmic phrasing specify the type—reinforced by special makeup.

Ghosts are conceived as being stiff, devils as curvaceous; they dance grotesquely and humorously. Heavenly beings, superhumanly handsome, dance with proud dignity. The intrinsic quality of each animal or bird is fancifully and fully exploited—the powerful tiger, the brazen leopard, the sly fox, or the wily eagle.

Within a generalized category, a character's role is individually assessed. The sympathetic old farmer with stooped back and bent knees gestures dramatically but quietly. The upper-class villain struts with widely spaced steps and gesticulates with tensed hands, fingers spread. Physical and emotional characteristics are the basic vocabulary for dance structure.

The contemporary operatic hero is not as relaxed as is the classical hero, who acts more subtly and less dynami-

CHINA: Dance in Opera. Liu Tsu-chu (top), as Yang Pa-chieh, threatens Lee Kuo-hsing (bottom), as Chiao Kuang-po, in *Journey to the Fatherland*, a production of Yen Lan-ching's Beijing Opera Troupe. (Photograph © 1992 by Jack Vartoogian; used by permission.)

cally. Although the contemporary hero is very forceful and determined, he nevertheless moves with ease and fluidity.

Ballet technique has altered the style of the classic gestures, resulting in arabesques, turns, and leaps that are tense and sharp. Women's carriage and body style have been completely changed. Instead of the classical willowy torso, curved arms, and lightly held head, the entire body form is now tensed and severe. The straight spine and taut head are a result of ballet training. Although the "flowery-fingered" hand is still part of dance form, women use the clenched fist, imitative of the man's resolute gesture. Backbends and turns are classical, but leg lifts and kicks show contemporary freedom. These changes were instigated by the revised opera to emphasize the emancipation of women—who now are, in spirit and action, the equals of men.

Certain acrobatic techniques are retained. The military dancer-actress retains the classical curvilinear posture because the acrobatic complexities intrinsic to this role cannot be executed from the tensed postures of ballet.

Even the spectacular acrobatics of many roles express concrete thematic elements. Sometimes the acrobatics are a display of strength, and sometimes they are symbolic of an emotional state. For example, a sudden backward "cat-turn" somersault is done by a general to express his anguish on learning of the death of his family.

Arrangement and Architecture. The dimensions of dance composition are designed floor-space patterns; body forms; costumes and properties; and the use of voice in song, speech, and other sounds.

Dance action in Chinese opera moves in combinations of diagonals, zigzags, spirals, arcs, waves, and circles, all precisely composed. Some movement forms are always performed in the same delineated areas, such as the act of adjusting the cuffs or the motion of tightening symbolic armor.

Walking around in a large circle depicts traveling to a distant place. Whether a journey is easy or difficult, in rain or wind, through forests or open terrain, is expressed in dance by the way the body behaves kinesthetically and by the diversity of rhythmic patterns. In *Journey on Horseback*, the dancer thus moves rapidly through lanes that twist and turn, using gown and whip choreographically to indicate that the horse is being spurred on, restrained, or redirected.

The basic stance of the hero in both old and new operas is the same: the torso is agile and erect, in profile; the head is turned sideways, toward the audience; and the feet are at a forty-five-degree angle, with the left toe pointed outward. The clenched left hand is below the open right hand, with both arms curved. The entire figure with its asymmetrical balance projects assurance and alertness, ready to move easily into action. No actor's stance is ever

statically square-set, because the body must always contain the potential for movement.

Manipulation of costumes—gowns, sleeves, fringed belt, and feathers—and of properties such as swords, flags, lances, or horsewhips is structurally part of the choreographic design, used to express emotion, to emphasize the plot, to depict place, and to reveal character qualities. The costume is used as if it were an appendage of the body.

Finally, voice—as speech, song, and other vocal sound—is a fourth dimension of drama. It is a vital element integrated into the composition, as illustrated by *The Buddhist Nun*, discussed earlier. Whatever political or social differences exist between classical and contemporary opera, both conform to and uphold the ethical and aesthetic philosophy expressed by a Ming-dynasty writer of the sixteenth century: "The theater [opera] must appeal to the emotions and instruct while entertaining . . . and unless it elevates the cultural standards of the people, it is worth nothing."

[*See also* Kunqu, *as well as entries on opera actors and actresses Pei Yanling, Ye Shaolan, Yuan Xuefen, and Zhou Xinfang. For treatment of a classical Chinese theater actor, known also for his singing roles, see the entry on Mei Lan-fang. For discussion of acrobatic feats and stylized combat used in Chinese opera, see* Asian Martial Arts.]

BIBLIOGRAPHY

Delza, Sophia. "The Classic Chinese Theater" (1956). In *Dance in Africa, Asia, and the Pacific*, edited by Judy Van Zile. New York, 1976.

Delza, Sophia. "The Dance in the Chinese Theater." *Journal of Aesthetics and Art Criticism* 16 (June 1958): 437–452.

Delza, Sophia. "The Dance-Arts in the People's Republic of China: The Contemporary Scene." In *Dance in Africa, Asia, and the Pacific*, edited by Judy Van Zile. New York, 1976.

Delza, Sophia. "Perspectives on the Aesthetics of Change from the Classical Chinese Theatre to the Revolutionary Peking Opera." *Chinoperl Papers* (March 1978).

Scott, A.C. *The Classical Theatre of China*. London, 1957.

Young, Stark. "Mei Lan-fang." *Orient et Occident* 1.9 (1935): 35–38.

Zucker, A. E. *The Chinese Theater*. Boston, 1925.

SOPHIA DELZA

Classical Dance

Chinese classical dance has a long history, dating back to the Han dynasty (202 BCE–220 CE) and perhaps even more ancient times. Since the late Song dynasty of the thirteenth century, dance has been combined with Chinese classical musical drama (called "Chinese opera" in the West), an important element of which is the combination of singing, dancing, dialogue, and mime. The dance element derives mainly from daily activities and military skills, along with a strong acrobatic element.

Through the work of many dancer-actors, classical dance gradually developed into a disciplined and established form of art with its own style and character in both aesthetics and technique. This art was transmitted through generations of classical musical drama performers.

After the establishment of the People's Republic of China in 1949, classical dance was not only maintained in classical musical drama but also established as an independent art form. Teachers at the Beijing Dance Academy, considering the need to train dancer-performers, to respect both tradition and the demands of modern life, and to reorganize, revise, and supplement the old form, worked out rules and established a new training system. In 1954 this new system was established as part of the curriculum at the Beijing Dance Academy and became the basic course for the training of dancer-actors.

A number of large-scale productions based on this new system were created, including *Lantern of Lotus, The Beauty Fish, Princess Wencheng,* and *Qu Yuan.* Since the 1950s, the classical dance system has been developed and refined. During the 1980s, some dancers became interested in tracing the history of the oldest sources of classical dance. They researched sculptures, grottoes, and archaeological objects and created such productions as *Colorful Sculpture of Dunhuang, Silk Road Flower Rain, Chime Bell Music and Dance,* and *Imitation Tang Dynasty Music and Dance,* each with a unique style. A new branch of Chinese classical dance has been created through this research.

BIBLIOGRAPHY

Delza, Sophia. "The Dance-Arts in the People's Republic of China: The Contemporary Scene." In *Dance in Africa, Asia, and the Pacific,* edited by Judy Van Zile. New York, 1976.

"Dunhuang Art Treasures." *China Reconstructs* 36 (May 1987):1–14.

Mackerras, Colin. *The Chinese Theatre in Modern Times: From 1849 to the Present Day.* Amherst, Mass., 1975.

Mackerras, Colin, ed. *Chinese Theater from Its Origins to the Present Day.* Honolulu, 1983.

Scott, A. C. *The Classical Theatre of China.* London, 1957.

Wang Kefen. *The History of Chinese Dance.* Beijing, 1985.

Wang Kefen et al., eds. *A Dictionary of Chinese Dance* (in Chinese). Beijing, 1994.

Zung, Cecelia. *Secrets of the Chinese Drama* (1937). New York, 1964.

LU WENJIAN

Contemporary Theatrical Dance

Ballet and modern dance are entirely Western imports in China, introduced in the 1930s by, respectively, Russian emigrés and a Chinese intellectual, Wu Xioxbang, who studied violin, ballet, and German modern dance in Japan after graduating from college (Wu is known as the "Father of China's New Dance Art"). Nevertheless, ballet has become the preferred national dance genre and has nearly monopolized theatrical dance in mainland China since 1949. The newly established People's Republic of China found ballet systematic and easy to adopt in reconstructing its theatrical dance under the principle of socialist realism that was to be practiced in literature and the arts. This provided a highly unified entertainment for the people. Modern dance, by contrast, was considered a symbol of invasion by Western, especially American, imperialism; it was totally rejected, called "fierce floods and savage beasts," until 1980, when China's central government began to adopt an open-door policy.

Ballet. The relationship between Western ballet and Chinese culture seemed predestined. Margot Fonteyn, in 1933, started her long and successful ballet career in Shanghai, where a Russian named George Goncharov operated a ballet school in the 1920s and 1930s. Vera Volkova taught in China beginning in 1929, and Anna Pavlova danced there in 1922. Other Russians also gave ballet lessons in Shanghai, Tianjin (where Edwin Denby was born in 1903), and Harbin, major cities in China. Nevertheless, all this elite activity took place exclusively within the concessions (foreign enclaves of China's ports), and only foreign diplomats and members of the Chinese upper class could afford to see the performances or send their children to the classes. Thus ballet, the "crystallization of Western civilization," did not enter China on a large scale until 1954, when the first theater-dance training base of the People's Republic, the Beijing School, predecessor of the present Beijing Dance Academy, was founded. Several important Soviet ballet experts, including Petr A. Gusev, were officially invited under a cultural exchange agreement between the Chinese and Soviet governments to teach technique and choreography and to restage classics. They also directed their Chinese students in creating a full-length national ballet in pointe shoes, *The Sea Maid,* a new version of which, also on pointe, was performed for American audiences by the Central Ballet of China in 1986.

When the Sino-Soviet entente broke down and the Soviet experts left China early in the 1960s, Western ballet had fully permeated its Chinese disciples. They have remained the backbone of the Chinese dance world and in turn have nurtured younger generations of dancers and choreographers, infusing ballet into all styles of Chinese dance. The domination of ballet over Chinese national dance forms is reflected in the fact that both the Chinese National Dance Drama and Chinese Classical Dance training systems were based on the narrative structure, the movement sequence, and above all the aesthetic ideal of Western aristocratic ballet. Even the dancer-singers of tiny cultural troupes of ethnic minorities in remote regions could not start their daily schedule of activities until they came to the *barre,* despite the fact that in their own

CHINA: Contemporary Theatrical Dance. *(top left)* The ensemble of the Central Ballet of China in the full-length nationalist ballet *New Year's Sacrifice*. *(bottom left)* Four of the company's leading ballerinas in a production of Perrot's *Pas de Quatre*. *(directly above)* Dancers of the Chinese Performing Arts Group in *The Red Detachment of Women*, a Revolutionary ballet first performed in 1964. (Top and bottom left photographs © 1995, right photograph © 1978, by Jack Vartoogian; all used by permission.)

dances they never really move, jump, or turn as in ballet. The situation may be seen as a tragedy, or a tragic comedy.

As for audience response, a sharp critical remark popular during the 1950s and 1960s expresses the resistance of the common folk in that period: "Big legs are running all over the stage, and the workers, peasants, and soldiers could not bear to see." Nevertheless, since 1980, as China has become more open to the outside world, more and more Chinese people are eager to see Ballet, to raise their personal level of cultural awareness. The premiere of the fifth Chinese ballet company, the Guangzhou Ballet, in October 1994 clearly marked the increasing demand of the Chinese people for this elite art. The other four existing companies are the Central Ballet of China, the Shanghai Ballet, Liaoning Ballet, and Tianjin Ballet.

Modern Dance. The history of modern dance in China is as old as that of ballet, beginning with the Denishawn tours of 1925 and 1926, Irma Duncan and her Russian students in 1927, and Wu Xiaobang's creative use of the form to serve patriotic needs during the war against Japan (1937–1945). Ten factors—economy, politics, sci-

ence and technology, society, ideology, education, aesthetics, literature, music, and dance technique—militated against its establishment. Today, however, modern dance has become a new and inspiring phenomenon to many Chinese. There is a professional company located in Guangzhou (Canton), the Guangdong Modern Dance Company, which has been generously supported by the American Dance Festival and the Asian Cultural Council since 1987. The Beijing Dance Academy established a two-year modern dance major under its choreography department in fall 1993, and eight of its graduates have become the core members of Beijing Modern Dance Company in this capital of Chinese culture and politics.

Meanwhile more and more Chinese have been able to study modern dance in the United States. The first series of books on its history, theory, choreography, and appreciation were published by Ou Jian-ping after two U.S. study tours, in 1988 and 1993, and a German tour in 1988. The author and others have presented many workshops and courses all over China. A few experimental performances are emerging while foreign experts, including Chinese Americans, are joining the effort. Modern dance is on the way to success in China, although it still obviously has a long way to go. Modern dance is not only an imported dance form, it is also a highly efficient catalyst; it might never directly solve all of China's artistic problems, but it can certainly help stimulate China's creative capacities.

Compared with ballet, modern dance in China has not yet become well known to its widest audience, including some editors, journalists, and even dance professionals. Many cannot distinguish ballroom dance from modern dance.

[*See also entries on Chen Weiya, Wu Xiaobang, and Yang Meiqi.*]

BIBLIOGRAPHY
Koegler, Horst. *The Concise Oxford Dictionary of Ballet.* New York, 1972.

CHINA: Contemporary Theatrical Dance. Feng Ying as Kitri is surprised by a kiss from Xu Gang as Basilio in the Central Ballet of China's production of *Don Quixote.* (Photograph © 1995 by Jack Vartoogian; used by permission.)

Ou Jian-ping. "From 'Beasts' to 'Flowers': Modern Dance in China." In *East Meets West in Dance: Voices in the Cross-Cultural Dialogue,* edited by John Solomon and Ruth Solomon. Chur, Switzerland, 1995.

Ou Jian-ping. *The Modern Dance: Theory and Practice,* vol. 1.5, *Oh, My Great Motherland* (in Chinese). Beijing, 1994.

Wang Ke-fen et al., eds. *A Dictionary of Chinese Dance* (in Chinese). Beijing, 1994.

World Ballet and Dance 1–5 (1989–1994). Each volume contains an annual overview of the national dance situation in mainland China by Ou Jian-ping.   OU JIAN-PING

Dance Research and Publication

Many passing references to dance may be found in early Chinese histories. One such document is the *Zuozhuan* (Chronicle of Zuo), written during the fourth century BCE by Zuo Qiuming, an official historian of the Spring and Autumn period (722–481 BCE) of the Zhou dynasty (1027–256 BCE). The chapter titled "Jizha Enjoys the Music and Dance Performance," written by Jizha, describes several dances, including *da wu* ("great dance"), *Shao wu* ("Shao dance"), and *da Xia* ("great Xia").

Other early references to dance may be found in such classics as the *Shangshu* (Book of Records) and *Lunyu* (Confucius's Statements and Actions), which were written by students of Confucius during the sixth and fifth centuries BCE. These works contain criticism articulated by Confucius on *ba yi*, a folk dance in which sixty-four dancers perform in eight rows, with eight dancers in each row; the works also contain profuse praise of the court dance *ya* (graceful dance).

The philosopher Mo Di (482–420 BCE) analyzed dance in the chapter "Fei yue" (Denying Music), in his *Mozi* (Collection of Works by Mo). Mo denied dance, claiming that it was harmful to politics. The philosopher Xun Kuang (313–238 BCE) also treated the subject of dance. In the volume titled *Yue lun* (A Discussion on Music), he opposed Mo's idea and recognized music and dance as an inevitable part of human life.

Dance theory was treated in detail in the *Yueji* (Treatise on Music and Dance), a book written by Gongsun Nizi, a disciple of Confucius, during the Warring States period (403–222 BCE). This was the first time an author made a full study of the nature, distinctive characteristics, and social function of Chinese dance.

Late in the Han dynasty (202 BCE–220 CE), the poet Zhang Heng wrote *Xijing fu* (Ode to the Western Capital). Included in the work are elaborate descriptions of costumes and of masked dances about such animals as tigers, monkeys, and elephants. Fu Yi's *Wu fu* (Poetic Description of Dance), also of the late Han, is distinctive because rather than focusing on dance as an educational, moral, or political tool, as many earlier works had done, it comments on dance as an independent art form and stresses the value of folk dance, which previously had often been relegated to a substantially lower rank than that of court dance.

De shou gongwu pu (Court Dance Notation in the Palace De Shou), written between 1162 and 1187, is noteworthy because it contains a form of dance notation in which Chinese characters from the written language are used to record movements.

Following the Song dynasty (960–1279), dance as a separate theatrical art began to decline. Dance that did exist was found largely in the context of *xiju* (drama-music), a forerunner of what is popularly known today as Chinese traditional opera, represented by the Beijing Opera. Although general historical documents written earlier contained occasional comments on dance, and the writings of early poets included colorful, though inaccurate, descriptions of selected dances, scholarly publications that dealt specifically with dance did not appear until very recent times. Such works are often based on early historical documents written in ancient Chinese languages, making some of the early writings accessible to contemporary researchers.

Prior to the establishment of the People's Republic of China in 1949, only a few articles on dance were published. Among the most valuable are "Shuo wu" (On Dance), written in the mid-1940s by Wen Yiduo, and "Guoji shinduan pu" (Dancing Movements in Beijing Opera), written in the 1920s by Qi Rushan. The former contains descriptions of indigenous dances in Australia and Africa.

In 1949, the Zhonghua Quanguo Wudao Gongzuozhe Xiehui (All-China Association of Dance Professionals) was formed. The organization has changed its name three times and since 1979 has been known as the Zhongguo Wudaojia Xiehui (China National Dance Artists Association). Wu Xiaobang, who studied violin, ballet, and modern dance in Japan, was instrumental in its establishment and served as its chair until 1991.

After the formal organization of Chinese dance artists, Wu Xiaobang, with Ouyang Yuqian and Sheng Jie (Wu's wife), was responsible for guiding students in serious dance research. Wu directed the work of his students to the relationship between dance and religion, particularly shamanism, Confucianism, Daoism, and Buddhism. An important film on dances from a Confucian temple, which Wu made with the assistance of his students, resulted from this work. The film is preserved by the China National Dance Artists Association in Beijing.

Ouyang Yuqian directed the work of his students in historical research, based especially on ancient manuscripts and archaeological sources. These efforts resulted in the five-volume work *Zhongguo wudaoshi* (Chinese Dance History). Sheng Jie guided her students in collecting folk dances from China's vast countryside.

In 1974 the Ministry of Culture established the Wudao Yanjiusuo (Dance Research Institute) within the Zhongguo Yishu Yanjiuyuan (China National Arts Academy). The Dance Research Institute has three sections, which are devoted to Chinese dance history, dance theory, and foreign dance. It has published numerous books on Chinese dance history and dances of minority nationalities in China, as well as Chinese-language translations of English-language books on Western dance forms. The institute is also responsible for many entries in *Zhongguo dabaike quanshu yinyue wudao juan* (The Chinese Encyclopedia: Music and Dance Volume).

In 1981, the Dance Research Institute embarked on a major project to research systematically, document, and publish in more than thirty volumes information on dances from all of China's fifty-six ethnic groups. This project has strong government support and was designated a key social science project in China's Seventh Five-Year State Plan.

Other organizations established since the end of in 1949 are, first, the Beijing Wudao Xueyuan (Beijing Dance Academy), which specializes in the technique and pedagogy of Chinese folk dance and classical dance, Western ballet and modern dance, and choreography, and, second, the dance section of Zhongyang Minzu Xueyuan (Central Minority Nationalities Institute), which specializes in the teaching of minority national dance.

The China National Dance Artists Association has published *Wudao xuexi ziliao* (Dance Data) three or four times a year from 1954 to 1957, and *Wudao* (Dance) bimonthly since 1958. These periodicals ceased publication during China's Cultural Revolution (1966–1976); when *Wudao* began publishing again in 1978, it was as a monthly. Both periodicals include articles on folk and classical dance, choreography, and ballet, calendars of current dance events, reviews, and articles on dance abroad. Today, there are branches of the association throughout the country; they organize lectures and discussions on issues of concern and publish various periodicals.

From 1980 to 1990, the association published the quarterly *Wudao luncong* (Dance Tribune), and from 1980 to 1994, the Dance Research Institute of the Wen Hua Bu (Ministry of Culture) edited *Wudao yishu* (Dance Art). Both publications treat traditional Chinese dance, classical European ballet, and modern dance. Most periodicals contain photographs whose quality varies in terms of both content and reproduction.

The China National Dance Artists Association and the China National Arts Academy provided financial assistance for these dance publications. The government sponsors research projects and supports the study of various types of dance. It provides grants to all students who attend the Beijing Dance Academy and the dance schools in many other Chinese cities.

Dance reviews appear regularly in newspapers, particularly in *Renminribao* (People's Daily), *Guangmingribao* (Guangming Daily, Beijing), *Wenhuibao* (Shanghai), and *China Daily* (published in English in Beijing), as well as in such periodicals as *Zhongguo renmin huabao* (China People's Pictorial), *Wenyibao* (Literature and Art), *Zhongguo wenhuabao* (Chinese Culture Newspaper), and *Xijubao* (Theater).

Two publishers specialize in dance: Shanghai Wenyi Chubanshe (Shanghai Literature and Art Press) and Renmin Yinyue Chubanshe (People's Music Press).

In 1982, the Zhongguo Dabaike Quanshu Chubanshe (Chinese Encyclopedia Publishing House) began to compile the music and dance volume of its encyclopedia. Hundreds of scholars and choreographers were involved in this work. More than four hundred articles are devoted to traditional dance forms, both Chinese and other, ballet, modern dance, and dance history and theory. The music and dance volume was published in 1989.

The most prolific Chinese scholar pioneering in the field of dance theory is Wu Xiaobang, a choreographer,

educator, researcher, and the former chair of the China National Dance Artists Association. His *Xin wudao yishu gailun* (Introduction to the New Dance Art), originally published in 1950 with an enlarged edition in 1982, is the first Chinese book to deal seriously with dance theory. It is also concerned with contemporary dance movements in China—those that blend modern styles with traditional Chinese forms. Wu has also published *Wudao xinlun* (New Theory on Dance) and three anthologies of his dance theoretical writings. Other dance writers who actively contribute to contemporary dance periodicals in China include Ye Ning, Hu Guogang, Jia Zuoguang, Lu Yisheng, Long Yinpei, Xu Erchong, Ou Jian-ping, and Yu Ping.

Forerunners in the study of ancient Chinese dance history include Sun Jingchen, Peng Song, Wang Kefen, and Dong Xijiu, whose five-volume series *Zhongguo wudao shi* (Chinese Dance History) took thirty years to complete. Wang Kefen's book *Zhongguo gudai wudao shihua* (A Primer of Ancient Chinese Dance History) appeared in Chinese in 1981 and also in English (1985), French (1988), and Japanese (1988) versions.

Zhu Liren, whose interpretation was responsible for introducing Russian ballet into China in the 1950s, focused on translations of works on the history and aesthetics of classical ballet, including Noverre's *Lettres sur la danse et sur les ballet* and (together with Liu Mengdie) Isadora Duncan's *My Life*.

Ou Jian-ping, after studying modern dance and dance criticism in the United States and Germany in 1988 and 1993, published seventeen books, including translations of works by Selma Jeanne Cohen, James Michael Friedman, John Martin, and Walter Sorell, as well as the first volume of his own *The Modern Dance: Theory and Practice (Xiandai wude lilun yushijian)*, which collects his theoretical and historical papers and reviews published in both Chinese and English as well as synopses of his courses in modern dance, "How to Appreciate the Modern Dance" (*Xiandai wuxin shangfa*), "Dance Aesthetics" (*Wudao meixue*), and others.

Other notable book-length works by Ou's generation include Yu Ping's *Zhongguo gudian wu yu yashi wenhua* (Chinese Classical Dance and the Scholar's Culture), Yuan He's *Zhongguo wudao yixiang lun* (Theory of Chinese Dance Imagery), and Zhang Hua's *Zhongguo minjian wu yu nonggeng xinyang* (Chinese Folk Dance and Agricultural Belief).

The highest achievements in Chinese dance writing and publication thus far are *Zhongguo minzu minjian wudao Jicheng* (Collection of Chinese National Folk Dance), edited by Wu Xiaobang, and *Zhongguo wudao cidian* (A Dictionary of Chinese Dance), edited by Wang Kefen, Liu Enbo, and Xu Erchong. The former, in more than thirty volumes recording all the folk dances of China's thirty provinces and minority autonomous regions, was to be completed by 1997; the latter appeared in 1994 and features more than 4,500 entries on historical, folk, operatic, and contemporary dances of all fifty-six Chinese ethnic groups, as well as dance personalities, books and records, journals and magazines, institutions and administrative systems, terminology, dance images, notations, and other topics, with a chronology from 5,800 years ago to 1989. More than 200 scholars and experts from all over the country contributed, and there are 150 photographs and more than 500 other illustrations. This work is a necessity for all interested in Chinese dance.

OU JIAN-PING
with Zhu Liren

CHIRIAEFF, LUDMILLA (Liudmila Aleksandrovna Otsup; born 10 January 1924 in Riga, Latvia, died 22 September 1996 in Montreal), Russian-Canadian ballet dancer, choreographer, teacher, and company director. Through an accident of history Ludmilla Otsup was born in Latvia, where her Russian father and Polish mother temporarily resided. While she was still an infant, her parents moved to Berlin and established a household that would, in time, become a central meeting place for Russian expatriates. Her father, Aleksandr Otsup, writing under the *nom de plume* of Sergei Gorny, became well known in literary circles and eventually established friendships with many prominent Russian artists and writers, including the poet and novelist Ivan Bunin, the singer Fedor Chaliapin, and the dancer and choreographer Michel Fokine, all of whom were frequent visitors to the Otsup home. Under the tutelage of her father and the

CHIRIAEFF. Brydon Paige, Eva von Gencsy, and Eric Hyrst in Chiriaeff's *Kaléidoscope* (1954), choreographed for television. (Photograph courtesy of Ludmilla Chiriaeff.)

influence of his friends, young Ludmilla was imbued with the highest values of Russian culture from an early age.

Having been enrolled at age six in a eurhythmics class at the Dalcroze Center in Berlin, Ludmilla Otsup began her ballet training the following year, 1931, with Alexandra Nikolaeva, who had been a principal dancer with the Bolshoi Ballet in Moscow. She studied with Nikolaeva, and with Nikolaeva's daughter and son-in-law Xenia and Edouard Borovansky, until 1939, and she took private classes with Evgenia Eduardova from 1933 to 1935. In 1936, at age twelve, she was accepted as an apprentice in Colonel de Basil's Ballets Russes and danced in performances of *La Boutique Fantasque* and *The Firebird* during the company's Berlin season. Her association with this company, which returned to Berlin in 1938, enabled her to continue her acquaintance with Michel Fokine, who became a lasting influence. In 1939, when she was fifteen, she secured a position as a demi-soloist at the Theater Nollendorf. There, she danced in operas and operettas and, encouraged by Sabine Ress and Margot Rewendt, made her first attempts at choreography. For the 1940/41 season, she was engaged as a soloist by the Berlin Opera Ballet.

The conflict of World War II disrupted the young dancer's career and brought hard times. Having survived being buried in a demolished building during an air raid on Berlin, she was banished to Oranienburg labor camp because the Nazis suspected she was Jewish. She escaped from the camp during a bombing raid, spent some days in outdoor hiding places, and eventually was rescued by the Red Cross and soldiers of the Allied forces, who helped her make her way to the neutral territory of Switzerland.

After the war, Otsup remained for several years in Switzerland. From 1946 to 1948, she was principal dancer and choreographer at the Théâtre Municipal in Lausanne and, in 1948/49, at the Théâtre Kursaal in Geneva. In 1949, she founded Les Ballets du Théâtre des Arts in Geneva, serving as artistic director, *première danseuse*, and choreographer until 1951. During these years, she continued her training in classes with Jacqueline Farelli, Madame Rousanne, Lubov Egorova, and Harald Kreutzberg. She also married the artist Alexis Chiriaeff and acquired the surname by which she would later become widely known.

In January 1952, with the aid of the International Rescue Committee, Chiriaeff and her family immigrated to Canada and settled in Montreal. There she opened a school and began to teach. Soon drawn into Montreal's flourishing cultural community, she was invited to choreograph and perform for Société Radio-Canada, the nascent French-language public television service. The group of dancers she then formed, later called Les Ballets Chiriaeff, regularly appeared on *L'Heure du Concert*, an ongoing cultural series, and in numerous special pro-

CHIRIAEFF. Ludmilla Chiriaeff in the opening scene of her production of *Petrouchka* (1957), staged for Les Ballets Chiriaeff, with the assistance of Joy McPherson, after Fokine. (Photograph by Varkony; courtesy of Ludmilla Chiriaeff.)

grams. [*See* Television, *article on* Dance on Television in Canada.]

The popularity of the early television appearances of Chiriaeff's troupe led to increased demands for new choreography, and Chiriaeff was more than equal to the task. From 1952 to 1957, she participated in some three hundred television broadcasts and produced an astonishing stream of works, including a good number set to music by Russian composers. *Cendrillon* (1953), *Jeanne d'Arc* (1953), and *Jeu de Cartes* (1954) were set to music by Sergei Prokofiev; *Tableaux d'une Exposition* (Pictures at an Exhibition; 1954) and *Nuit sur le Mont Chauve* (Night on the Bare Mountain; 1955) were danced to the familiar music of Modest Mussorgsky; and other works were mounted to music by Aram Khachaturian, Aleksandr Glazunov, Sergei Rachmaninov, and Igor Stravinsky. Notably, however, in the mid-1950s Chiriaeff began to choreograph works to music by French-Canadian composers: *Kaléidoscope* (1954), set to a score by Pierre Mercure; *Horoscope* (1955), to music by Roger Matton; *Valse Caprice* (1956), to music by Alexis Contant; and *Ti-Jean* (1956), to music by Michel Perrault.

From a company of television dancers, Les Ballets Chiriaeff was transformed into a theatrical troupe with its first appearance on a Montreal stage at a gala charitable performance in 1955. The following year, the company, now numbering eighteen dancers, was invited to perform during the Montreal Festival season. Three works by Chiriaeff were presented, including *L'Oiseau Phoenix* (1956), set to a score by Clermont Pépin, a Québécois, and *Les Noces* (1956), set to the score by Stravinsky. The popular and critical success of these performances attracted the support of municipal officials who encouraged Chiriaeff to incorporate her company so that it would qualify for government subsidies.

Thus, in 1957 came into being Les Grands Ballets Canadiens, its name reflecting both Chiriaeff's aspirations for her troupe and her devotion to furthering the art of ballet in French Canada. Despite severe difficulties at the beginning, she persevered in developing her company, acquiring for it a mixed repertory of classical and contemporary ballets. The company revived many of her earlier ballets, and Chiriaeff created additional works, including her second version of *Cendrillon* (1962), set to music by Mozart, which was Canada's first original three-act ballet. Continuing her interest in the music of French-Canadian composers, she set *Suite Canadienne* (1957), *La Belle Rose* (1959), and *Canadiana* (1961) to music by Michel Perrault, the company's musical director and resident conductor, and *Payse* (1962) to music by Jean Vallerand. Other works of the early 1960s included *Quatrième Concert Royal* (1961), set to music of François Couperin; *Pierrot de la Lune* (1963), set to music of various Russian composers; and *Fête Hongroise* (1964), set to music of Johannes Brahms.

In the meantime, Chiriaeff had led Les Grands Ballets Canadiens into international prominence. The company made its first appearances before American audiences, at the Jacob's Pillow Dance Festival, in 1959 and thereafter

CHIRIAEFF. Members of Les Grands Ballets Canadiens in Chiriaeff's *Farces* (1958), also known as *Commedia dell'Arte*. This work was performed during the company's first visit to Jacob's Pillow in the summer of 1959. (Photograph by Varkony; from the archives of Les Grands Ballets Canadiens, courtesy of Ludmilla Chiriaeff.)

undertook a five-week tour of the United States in 1960 and an extensive tour of eastern and western Canada during the 1963/64 season. In 1965, Chiriaeff invited the distinguished teacher and ballet master Fernand Nault, a native Montrealer, to become assistant artistic director of the company. Together, Chiriaeff and Nault, who was named associate artistic director in 1967, confirmed the international stature of Les Grands Ballets Canadiens with the signal success of the 1966/67 season, culminating during Canada's Expo 67 World Festival, and with subsequent tours of the United States and western Europe. They continued as joint artistic directors of the company until 1974. [*See the entry on Nault.*] One of Chiriaeff's final contributions to the company repertory was a new production of Stravinsky's *Les Noces* (1973), a ballet that she had first mounted for Les Ballets Chiriaeff in 1956 and that had helped to win the support of civic authorities in Montreal.

After 1974, Chiriaeff assumed full-time leadership of the company's associated schools: the Académie des Grands Ballets Canadiens, founded in 1958, and the École Supérieure de Danse du Québec, founded in 1966. She subsequently pioneered an innovative program with the Quebec Ministry of Education, enabling high school and junior college students from across the province to continue academic education in Montreal while receiving ballet instruction from company teachers. In 1978, Chiriaeff made her final appearances on stage as one of the Gossips in Nault's production of *La Fille Mal Gardée* and in the role of Bathilde in Anton Dolin's production of *Giselle*, in which she was escorted by Dolin himself as the Duke of Courland.

Chiriaeff was fiercely loyal to Canada, her adopted homeland, and to the province of Quebec, where she found such strong support for her art. She was the recipient of many honors and awards, including the Trophée Frigon de Radio-Canada (1955), for her contributions to Canadian television; the Centennial Medal (1967), for services to the nation; and the Diplôme d'Honneur of the Canadian Conference of the Arts (1975). She was named a Grande Montréalaise in 1978 and was awarded the Prix Denise-Pelletier for the Performing Arts, bestowed by the government of Quebec, in 1980. She was made a Companion of the Order of Canada in 1984 and a Grand Officier de l'Ordre National du Québec in 1985. She was awarded honorary doctorates by McGill University (1982), the Université de Montréal (1983), and the Université du Québec (1988). In 1992, the minister of culture of Poland gave her the Nijinsky Medal, for inestimable contributions to the world of dance, and in 1993 she was the recipient of one of the highest honors given to artists by the Canadian government, the Governor General's Performing Arts Award.

[*See also* Grands Ballets Canadiens, Les. *For discussion in a broader context, see* Canada, *article on* Theatrical Dance.]

CHIRIAEFF. The ensemble of Les Grands Ballets Canadiens in a 1979 performance of Chiriaeff's *Les Noces*, created in 1956 and revived in 1973. (Photograph by André Le Coz; from the archives of Les Grands Ballets Canadiens, courtesy of Ludmilla Chiriaeff.)

BIBLIOGRAPHY

Anderson, Jack. "Ludmilla Chiriaeff." Obituary. *New York Times* (25 September 1996).

Crabb, Michael, and Andrew Oxenham. *Dance Today in Canada.* Toronto, 1977.

Crabb, Michael. "Les Grands Ballets Canadiens." *The Dancing Times* (July 1982): 744–745.

Greenaway, Kathryn. "Ludmilla Chiriaeff." *Montreal Gazette* (17 August 1991).

Guilmette, Pierre. *Bibliographie de la danse théâtrale au Canada.* Ottawa, 1970.

Lorrain, Roland. *Les Grands Ballets Canadiens: Cette femme qui nous fit danser.* Montreal, 1973.

Maynard, Olga. "Ballet in Canada Today: Ludmilla Chiriaeff and Les Grands Ballets Canadiens." *Dance Magazine* (April 1971): 56–64.

Officer, Jillian. *The Original Ballets Appearing in the Repertoire of Les Ballets Chiriaeff 1955–1958 and Les Grand Ballets Canadiens 1958–1980.* Waterloo, 1982.

Tembeck, Iro. *Dancing in Montreal: Seeds of a Choreographic History.* Studies in Dance History, vol. 5.2. Madison, Wis., 1994.

Wyman, Max. *Dance Canada: An Illustrated History.* Vancouver, 1989.

FILM AND VIDEOTAPE. *Pas de Deux* (1966), with choreography and commentary by Chiriaeff, is an award-winning film starring Margaret Mercier and Vincent Warren, principal dancers of Les Grands Ballets Canadiens; it was directed by Norman McLaren and produced by the National Film Board of Canada. Videotapes of numerous special television programs and documentaries are in the archives of the Canadian Broadcasting Company and Radio-Québec; especially notable are *Profile* (CBC-TV, 1975), *The Achievers: Ludmilla Chiriaeff* (CBC-TV, 1989), and *La Vie N'Arrête Jamais* (Radio-Québec, 1991), three documentaries on Chiriaeff's life and work.

CLAUDE CONYERS

CHLADEK, ROSALIA (born 21 May 1905 in Brno, Moravia [now Czech Republic], died 3 July 1995 in Vienna), Austrian dancer, choreographer, and teacher. Chladek developed the Chladek technique, which is based on the natural possibilities of movement of the human body and is taught above all in the Rosalia Chladek International Company, founded in 1972 and represented in many European countries. The technique is applied in dance and in the pedagogical and therapeutic domain.

An encounter with a student of Émile Jaques-Dalcroze was a decisive factor in Chladek's career. From 1921 to 1924 she studied at the Hellerau School in Germany under Ernst Ferand, Christine Baer-Frissell, Valeria Kratina, and Jarmila Kröschlova. In addition to rhythm and music training according to the ideas of Jaques-Dalcroze, the school offered "artistic" dancing, which was considered the opposite of "unartistic" classical ballet. During her studies Chladek adopted the Jaques-Dalcroze viewpoint that rhythmic gymnastics was a condition for the artistic rebirth of dance. In 1923, in connection with the Hellerau Festival, Chladek danced in Kratina's *Der Holzgeschnitzte Prinz* (The Wooden Prince), to music by Béla Bartók and, later the same year in Vienna, in Kratina's *Der Mensch und seine Sehnsucht* (Man and His Desire), to music by Darius

Milhaud. While still a student, she made her debut as a solo dancer in Dresden and traveled with the Hellerau Dance Group under Kratina's leadership.

After receiving her apprenticeship certificate in physical education, Chladek was engaged as a teacher in the school, where she taught until 1928 (in 1925 the school moved from Hellerau to Laxenburg, near Vienna). She left to become the director of the center for gymnastics and artistic dance at the Basel Conservatory and a guest choreographer at the Basel Municipal Theater, where she presented *The Soldier's Tale, Petrouchka, Pulcinella,* and *Don Juan.* In 1930 she returned to the Hellerau-Laxenburg School as artistic director of the dance group and director of gymnastic and dance training and set about devising her own system. Before the school closed in 1939, it attracted about 3,500 students from all over the world.

With the Hellerau-Laxenburg Dance Group Rosalia Chladek received second prize in 1932 at the first international competition for choreography in Paris for her *Les Contrastes* (consisting of George Frideric Handel's *Alcina Suite,* and *Magische Suite* to Sergei Prokofiev's *Visions Fugitives*). Other significant performances with the dance group included *Festliche Tanzsuite* (to Georges Bizet's *L'Arlésienne*) and *La Danza* set to music by Gluck. In addition to this activity, Chladek had a thirty-five-year career as a solo dancer. She created pure dance works such as *Rhythmen-Zyklus,* abstract choreographies *(Elemente-Zyklus, Sancta Trinitas),* dramatic works on the lives of extraordinary women *(Jeanne d'Arc, Die Kameliendame),* mythological figures *(Narcissus),* and religious themes *(Marienleben, Erzengel-Suite). Afro-Amerikanische Lyrik* is an example of lyrics set to dance. Chladek created seventy solo works, which she presented on tours in about fifteen countries. At the first international competition for solo dancing in Warsaw in 1933, Chladek was awarded second prize.

Chladek's creative activity included also choreography for the chorus in plays by Aeschylus, Sophocles, and Euripides, performed at classical festivals at the Teatro Greco in Syracuse and at other historic sites in Italy. Her most important operatic productions were Gluck's *Orpheus und Eurydike* (1940) at the Vienna State Opera and Handel's *Julius Caesar* (1959) at the Salzburg Municipal Theater. She also created choreography for plays, operettas, films, and television.

In 1940 Chladek became the director of modern dance training at the German master classes for dance in Berlin. From 1942 to 1952 she was the director of the dance training center for theater and instruction at the Vienna Conservatory, and from 1952 to 1970 she headed the dance department at the Vienna Institute for Music and the Dramatic Arts, which offered a training program that included all phases of theater dance. In addition, from 1963 to 1977 she was the director of the institute's training program in modern dance education and dance pedagogy according to her system.

After World War II Chladek devoted increasing attention to group choreography. Works created for students and for the Rosalia Chladek Dance Group include the dance drama *Kleine Passion* (1948), to music by Heinrich Ignaz Franz von Biber; *Die Vier Temperamente* (1949), to music by Paul Hindemith; *From Morning to Midnight* (1951), to music by George Gershwin, Aaron Copland, and Irving Berlin; *Afro-Amerikanische Lyrick* (1952); and *Curriculum Aeternum* (1968). After a period that Chladek devoted solely to teaching, a new interest in her works grew in the 1980s. Her stagings of some of her most important solo creations for the Vienna State Opera were not only successful but also proved influential on young choreographers.

The impact of Rosalia Chladek as dancer and choreographer resulted from her personality. A tall, majestic woman, governed by intellect, she uncompromisingly executed her artistic principles, which were rooted in her education and her analytical abilities. As a teacher Chladek has had a decisive influence.

[*See also* Austria, *article on* Theatrical Dance; *and* Chladek Technique.]

BIBLIOGRAPHY

Amort, Andrea. "Die Tür öffnen: Die Auswirkungen Rosalia Chladeks auf die zeitgenössische Tanzszene." *TanzAffiche*, no. 23 (May 1990): 6–7.

Amort, Andrea. "Die Klassikerin der Moderne: Rosalia Chladek zum 90. Geburtstag am 21. Mai." *TanzAffiche* 8 (1995): 24–25.

Alexander, Gerda, and Hans Groll, eds. *Tänzerin, Choreographin, Pädagogin Rosalia Chladek.* 4th ed. Vienna, 1995.

Artus, Hans-Gerd. "Living Traditions in Ausdruckstanz: An Interview with Rosalia Chladek." *Ballet International* 8 (June–July 1985): 16–20.

Artus, Hans-Gerd, and Maud Paulissen-Kaspar. "Gesetzmäßige Bewegung als Grundlage tänzerischer Erziehung: Zu den Prinzipien nach dem Chladek-System." In *Ausdruckstanz: Eine mitteleuropäische Bewegung der ersten Hälfte des 20. Jahrhunderts,* edited by Gunhild Oberzaucher-Schüller. Wilhelmshaven, 1992.

Buschbeck, Axel C. "Rosalia Chladek: Eine Monographie." Ph.D. diss., University of Vienna, 1973.

Chladek, Rosalia. "Gesetzmäßigkeit körperlicher Bewegung als Grundlage tänzerischer Erziehung." In *Eutonie.* Ulm, 1964.

Chladek, Rosalia. "Aus der Werkstätte der Choreographie." *Jahresbericht 1967/68 der Akademie für Musik und Darstellende Kunst in Wien* (1968).

Chladek, Rosalia. "Was ist Tanz? Apologie für den freien Tanz." *Tanz Aktuell* 6.3 (1991): 20–21.

Chladek, Rosalia. "Von Hellerau bei Dresden nach Laxenburg bei Wien." In *Ausdruckstanz: Eine mitteleuropäische Bewegung der ersten Hälfte des 20. Jahrhunderts,* edited by Gunhild Oberzaucher-Schüller. Wilhelmshaven, 1992.

Donath, Martina. "Die Tanzschule Hellerau-Laxenburg und Rosalia Chladek: Pädagogik und Wirkung des Ausdruckstanzes." Ph.D. diss., University of Vienna, 1987.

Forster, Marianne. "Reconstructing European Modern Dance: Bodenwieser, Chladek, Leeder, Kreutzberg, Hoyer." In *Dance Reconstructed,* edited by Barbara Palfy. New Brunswick, N.J., 1993.

Garske, Rolf. "Rosalia Chladek: Sich an den Menschen in seiner Totalität wenden." *Tanzen* 5.1 (1987): 6–7.

Klingenbeck, Fritz. *Die Tänzerin Rosalia Chladek.* Amsterdam, 1936.

Kneiss, Ursula, and Edith M. Wolf Perez. "Von der Bewegungslust zur Methode: Ein biographischer Abriß." *TanzAffiche*, no. 23 (May 1990): 8–11.

Koegler, Horst. "Aus Rhythmus geboren—zum Tanzen bestellt: Hellerau-Laxenburg und die Anfänge des modernen Tanzes." In *Ballett 1977: Chronik und Bilanz des Ballettjahres,* edited by Horst Koegler et al. Velber bei Hannover, 1977.

Oberzaucher, Alfred, and Gunhild Oberzaucher-Schüller. "Eine Frau ohne Alter." In *Ballett 1985: Chronik und Bilanz des Ballettjahres,* edited by Horst Koegler et al. Velber bei Hannover, 1985.

Oberzaucher-Schüller, Gunhild. "Die große Schöpferin und Interpretin des Freien Tanzes: Hommage à Rosalia Chladek." *Bühnenkunst* 4 (July 1990).

Palme, Johanna. "Rosalia Chladek". In *Pipers Enzyklopädie des Musiktheaters,* vol. 1, edited by Carl Dahlhaus. Munich, 1986.

Potgieter, Brenda. "n'Choreografiese benadering vanuit die Chladekbewegingsopvoeding." Mag. art. diss., University of Potchefstroom, 1984.

Schneider, Detlev. "Hellerau." *Tanz Aktuell* 7.4 (1992): 20–25. Interview with Chladek.

Seidl, Roswitha. "Wege der modernen tänzerischen Erziehung: Lehrweise Chladek und Orff Schulwerk: Ein Vergleich." Mag. phil. diss., University of Vienna, 1974.

Selzer, Eva. "Das Ziel ist der Weg: Intentionen und Ziele der Chladek-Pädagogik" (parts 1–2). *Ballett International* 5 (March–April 1982).

Servos, Norbert. "Rosalia Chladek—Aristokratin des Tanzes." *Tanz Aktuell* 6.3 (1991): 18–19.

Welzien, Leonore. "Vom Rhythmus zur Bewegung—von der Bewegung zum Tanz: Interview mit Rosalia Chladek." *Tanzdrama Magazin* 11 (1990): 18–23.

ALFRED OBERZAUCHER
Translated from German

CHLADEK TECHNIQUE.

As a child Rosalia Chladek acquired knowledge of the causal connections of movement, the course of economic and harmonic movement, and the interrelationship of body and mind. She believed that the average human is alienated from his or her body. Based on a consideration of human anatomy and the physical laws that affect it, she developed the Chladek technique of movement.

Chladek classified the varieties of movement systematically, according to cause and effect, and reduced them to a few elementary principles. The central principle of her technique is the differentiation of movement according to a tension scale. According to Chladek, human beings operate in a force field, and a complete tension scale that ranges between the poles of total activity and total passivity can be derived from the varying adjustment between the force of gravity and one's natural energy. The neutral center of this scale is normal stasis, which is characterized by the equally strong effects of these two forces. For Chladek, movement is the result of one's point of attack, one's orientation, and the amount and duration of one's bodily energy and behavior, which can be classified according to degree of tension. Behavior is the decisive moment for the dynamic temporal–spatial course of movement, and Chladek distinguishes between the central and peripheral application of energy in normal, active, unstable, and passive body behavior. For example, central application as displacement of the center of gravity is the most direct and hence the most efficient application for changing the body's position in space. To increase or decrease tension throughout the body, an application of force in the center of the body is required. In turn, the central application realized in a wide variety of directions in unstable body behavior (that is, behavior that can be influenced) includes complete mobility of the spinal column as well as sensitivity of the entire body.

Chladek's teaching method reflected the nature of the technique she developed from her observation and analysis of natural possibilities of movement. She called students' attention to themselves, thereby eliminating the demand that they learn through imitation something that was outside themselves. She assigned tasks that students tried to solve independently. Instead of using music simply as background, she worked with a vocal accompaniment: that is, the music of movement, which in itself was only visible, not audible and was expressed dynamically and rhythmically through the medium of the human voice and thereby became acoustically perceptible.

Chladek preferred to work on the floor initially, since this offered the best possibilities for self-control and thus self-correction. The initially unconscious experience of movement was followed by attentive self-observation; repetition was followed by analysis of the experiencing subject. This reinforced knowledge of the causes and effects of movement—interacting with point of attack, orientation, extent, and duration of the force along with body behavior—became the key to mastering a variety of movements. The transition to independent organization was completed easily, since it was rooted in playful confrontation with the material. Similarly, preparation for the interpretation of music through vocal accompaniment began as early as the first hour of technique: the music of movement, which could be physically experienced and which was rooted in the direct correspondence of body tension and tonal pitch, brought students very early into a close relationship with music and sensitized them to musicality in dance.

BIBLIOGRAPHY

Alexander, Gerda, and Hans Groll, eds. *Tänzerin, Choreographin, Pädagogin Rosalia Chladek.* 3d ed. Vienna, 1980.
Artus, Hans Gerd. "Living Traditions in Ausdruckstanz: An Interview with Rosalia Chladek." *Ballett International* 8 (June–July 1985): 16–20.
Artus, Hans Gerd. "Rosalia Chladek stellt ihre Lehrweise vor: Ein Bericht." *Tanzforschung Jahrbuch* 5 (1994): 99–108.
Forster, Marianne. "Reconstructing European Modern Dance: Bodenwieser, Chladek. Leeder, Kreutzberg, Hoyer." In *Dance Reconstructed,* edited by Barbara Palfy. New Brunswick, N.J., 1993.
Schneider, Detlev. "Hellerau." *Tanz Aktuel* 7.4 (1992): 20–25. Interview with Chladek.
Selzer, Eva, "Das Ziel Ist der Weg: Intentionen und Ziele der Chladekpädagogik" (parts 1–2). *Ballett International* 5 (March–April 1982).

EVA SELZER

CH'OI SEUNG-HEE (born 1911 in Seoul; fate unknown), Korean dancer, choreographer, teacher, and writer. Originally she trained as a traditional dancer, but Ch'oi Seung-hee was inspired to become a modern dancer in 1922 when Ishii Baku, a pioneer of modern dance in Japan who had studied with Isadora Duncan, visited Seoul and performed the so-called *Neue Tanz* ("new dance") that he had learned in Europe. Ch'oi followed Ishii to Tokyo, became his student, and performed with him on his second visit to Seoul in 1927. She returned home from Japan in 1929 and opened a private dance institute in Seoul. There in 1930 she gave the first performance of her compositions, including such works as *They Seek after the Sun, The People Long for Liberation, Song of the World,* and *The Sorrow of India.* A tour of the provinces followed; however, her innovative style was not well received by Korean audiences and she returned to Japan in 1933.

In 1934, after performing such traditional numbers as *Buddhist Monk Dance* and *Sword Dance,* Ch'oi became known as Sai Shoki (Japanese for Ch'oi Seung-hee), the Queen of Korean Dance, and scored a great success with the Japanese public. Her fame increased when she became a model and starred in a film, *Peninsula (Korea) Dancing Girl.* In 1937 she embarked on a two-year tour of the United States, Latin America, and Europe under the aegis of impresario Sol Hurok, giving more than one hundred performances that won the acclaim of critics everywhere. She was later appointed a member of the judging committee at the Second International Dance Concours in Belgium. Returning to Japan, she took the role of a Korean dancer in a *kabuki* play, for which a traditional instrumental ensemble was brought from Korea to accompany her. In 1942, in line with Japanese colonial policy, Ch'oi was compelled to entertain Japanese troops and gave twenty-four solo performances in sixteen days.

With the end of World War II and the liberation of Korea from Japan in 1945, Ch'oi returned to Korea, but she was highly criticized by the public for her pro-Japanese activities. In 1947, she followed her husband, a pro-Communist proletarian writer, into North Korea. There she became a leader in the dance world and established an institute for the purpose of creating dance dramas with socialist themes. In 1948, she choreographed *Song of Liberation* and other works for a performance welcoming the return of Korean patriot Kim Ku from the People's Republic of China (PRC). In 1950 she made a performance tour in the Soviet Union and the PRC, where she undertook research on Chinese dances and presented such creations as *Mother of Korea*. In 1955, she was officially designated a People's Actress and performed her dance drama *Under the Clear Blue Sky*. She was elected a representative of the People's Congress in 1957.

After her husband was purged in 1958, her institute's name was changed from the Ch'oi Seung-hee Dance Research Institute to the National Dance Research Institute; as well as being excluded from the dance world, she fell from grace with the regime. In 1964 she wrote *A Dance Primer for Korean Children;* in 1966, she was cited in a literary gazette for her excellence in Korean folk dance movement and technique. She was purged in 1967 and has not been heard of since that time outside North Korea.

Ch'oi Seung-hee is most noted as an innovator in the modernization of Korean traditional dance, who gained fame and fortune both in Japan and on the international dance scene and who was the creator of epic dance dramas with a socialist aesthetic. She was also the teacher of many of today's leading dancers in Korea.

[*See also* Korea, *article on* Modern Dance.]

BIBLIOGRAPHY

Cho Dong-wha. "Dance." In *Korea: Its Land, People, and Culture of All Ages.* 2d ed. Seoul, 1963.

Ch'oi Seung-hee. *My Autobiography.* Seoul, 1937.

Chung Byong-ho. *Korean Folk Dance.* Seoul, 1992.

Kang Yi-hyang. *Dance of Spirit, Dance of Love.* Seoul, 1989.

Pak Yong-ku. "Young Dancers Seek to Create Fresh Stage Idioms." In *Korean Art Guide.* 2d rev. ed. Seoul, 1986.

Takashima Yusaburō. *Sai Shoki: Korean Dancer.* Tokyo, 1981.

ALAN C. HEYMAN

CHOPINIANA. *See* Sylphides, Les, *article on* Russian Origins.

CHORAL DANCING. The Greek word *choros*—the source of English *chorus*—designated simply a group dancing in unison. By contrast to *orchēsis*, the word for dancing in general, *choros* denoted the kind of dancing associated with public religious festivals, in which admission to a given type of chorus depended on such aspects of social identity as citizenship, age, or sex. Greek choral dancing thus had much in common with that of other tribal cultures. Its principal distinction lay in the way it united dance with poetry and made the latter dominant. The choral ode, in which dancers sang words whose meters formed the basis of a choreographic pattern, became the central form of artistic expression as well as of civic ritual from the seventh through the fifth centuries BCE, at the peak of Classical Greek civilization. When this *choreia*—unity of words, music, and dance—began to be disrupted by those who wished to give dominance to the music, conservative Greeks considered the center of their civilization shaken.

Choreography. Both the religious importance of choral dancing and its choreographic structure can best be understood by beginning with poetic accounts of the dancing of the gods themselves. Commonly, a chorus of subordinate deities surrounded a single god who was *exarchōn*, or leader of the dance, and who dictated rhythms by the words he sang, the instrument he played, and the steps he executed, as described in the Homeric Hymns. Early depictions of mortal choruses around an *exarchōn* are sometimes interpreted as epiphanies of the god; it is significant that the verb *choreuō* ("to dance in a chorus") often takes as its direct object the name of a god, for example, "to dance Apollo." Choruses of mortals with mortal leaders thus honored the gods and partook of their blessedness by imitating them.

Differences between divine and mortal *choreia*, however, are implicit in choral poets' descriptions of their multiple tasks. When Apollo meets the Muses he is capable, as a god, of improvising words, music, and choreography and somehow communicating these things instantaneously to them. He is moreover capable of executing vigorous dance steps while singing and playing the lyre, a coordination that seems just beyond mortal limits. When a choral poet was commissioned to compose an ode for a city, by contrast, he had to perform a series of tasks in sequence. First, he composed the words to an elaborate meter meant to govern both the music and the dance. He then came as an honored guest to train the chorus of locals, drilling them in the singing of the words as well as working out the choreography. At the performance, the poet himself normally played the role of *exarchōn;* it was specifically in his function as lyre player that he was thought to be leading. Typically an ode started with a solo prelude on the lyre by the poet, which led to the moment when the feet and voices of the chorus were prepared to begin the ode proper.

Apart from the fact that the poet was somehow present as lyrist in the midst of the dancers, what little we know about the choreography of a typical ode comes almost entirely from metrical analysis. Cryptic catalogs of the names of standard dance figures are given by ancient writers, such as Pollux and Athenaeus, but they were writing centuries after the choral ode had passed its prime and may have been influenced by the solo dances of Hellenistic and Roman pantomimes. Artistic representations on vases, reliefs, statues, and coins show at best a range of stylized groupings and postures, adapted by the artists to the spaces at their disposal within the strictures of certain conventions of depiction. T. B. L. Webster has classified

positions of legs and hands common to many different types of chorus as depicted by artists contemporary with the great age of choral poetry. His effort, however, to distinguish dance tempi ("walking," "dancing," "excited dancing") and then to assign them to specific meters is only conjectural. Even less persuasive is the effort of scholar Germaine Prudhommeau to find classical ballet positions in ancient representations and to assign metrical values to them.

The one metrical feature that points to a clearly definable choreographic convention is the division of most odes into triads, recurrent large metrical units subdivided into three stanzas called the strophe, antistrophe, and epode. The metrical scheme of the strophe (A) is repeated exactly by the antistrophe (A), while that of the epode is a variant (B), so that the stanzaic pattern of a three-triad ode was A-A-B A-A-B A-A-B. Metricians and scholiasts of later antiquity report that in triadic choreography the chorus circled in one direction while reciting the strophe and in the opposite direction while reciting the antistrophe, then stood still while reciting the epode. The triadic odes of Pindar, the only poet with a body of work large enough for statistical analysis, have been shown to reserve important themes for the epode, a pattern that tends to substantiate these later accounts of the epode's distinct choreographic realization. The words uttered by the chorus during its periods of epodic arrest must have struck the audience with special force; often Pindar's narrative climaxes in epodes that describe or imply the coming to a halt of the characters in the myth as well as of the chorus itself. These are moments of hieratic solemnity, and the cessation of action may have claimed some special sign of a god's favor or invoked special divine attention.

Genres. The classification of choral odes into genres by later Alexandrian editors, starting in the third century BCE, must be viewed critically, since it was made for the purpose of published editions, whereas the odes themselves had been performance events commissioned for occasions that were often complex. The language of many an ode shows that both patron and poet considered its occasion to be unique (and not simply cyclically repeatable), and that conventions of diction (and therefore possibly of choreography) appropriate to more than one genre were needed to reflect each occasion's special combination of elements. The following summary of the Alexandrian genres must therefore be qualified by careful study of the language of each particular ode. Such study should also keep in mind the genres of dance not accompanied by specially commissioned poetry or by language of any kind, such as the pyrrhic dance (a weapon dance in military dress) or the *anapalē* (a dance imitating wrestling holds), since these would offer conventions on which a choral poet might draw. In addition to the pure choral genres, the odes found in Athenian drama often have diction invoking traditional genres, as appropriate to the dramatic occasion in which the chorus finds itself.

The pure choral genres may be defined as follows:

1. Hymn *(hymnos; plural, hymnoi):* ode praising a god by narrating incidents connected with his birth and deeds.
2. Paean *(paian; plural, paianides):* hymn dedicated to Apollo and performed seasonally at Delphi, Delos, and other cult sites, or else on special occasions to avert disaster or celebrate escape from it.
3. Dithyramb *(dithyrambos; plural, dithyramboi):* hymn dedicated to Dionysus.
4. Processional *(prosodion; plural, prosodia):* hymn sung during a procession to the god's temple and altar.
5. Maiden-song *(partheneion; plural, partheneia):* ode performed by the virgin girls of a given town, arranged in a processional order with detailed attention to kinship and rank.
6. Hyporcheme *(hyporchēma; plural, hyporchēmata):* a confusing genre, defined differently by different sources.
7. Encomium *(enkōmion; plural, enkōmia):* ode in honor of a living individual, in whose presence it was performed.
8. Threnos *(thrēnos; plural, thrēnoi):* funeral ode.
9. Epinician *(hymnos epinikios; plural, hymnoi epinikioi):* a special kind of encomium commemorating one or more victories of an athlete, performed by his fellow citizens on his return home from the contest. Many other events in the fortunes of the athlete, his clan, and his city were also brought in, and the bulk of the ode usually had to do with deeds of ancient heroes. More epinicians survive than specimens of all the other pure choral genres combined.

Athenian Drama. There are three genres of Athenian drama: tragedy, comedy, and satyr plays.

Tragedy. The song sung by the chorus as it marched into the circular dancing space was called the *parodos*, and its exit song the *exodos*. Songs sung between blocks of dramatic action, while the chorus was in place in the *orchēstra*, were called *stasima* (singular, *stasimon*). In addition, many plays have one or more *kommoi* (singular, *kommos*), lyric dialogues between the chorus and one of the actors, in which the actor sang (and perhaps moved) in the same meters as the dancers. We are told that the choruses of tragedy were "rectangular," as opposed to the "circular" or "cyclic" choruses of the Athenian dithyramb, which like tragedy was performed during the spring festival dedicated to Dionysus. In a standard entrance or exit march (a convention not always adhered to, judging by the language and dramatic situations of many plays), the fifteen-member chorus was arranged in three ranks and five files, with the flute player preceding and the *koryphaios*, or "chorus leader," placed third in the rank closest to the audience. This arrangement explains why tragic choruses were said to be rectangular, but it tells us nothing about the choreography of the *stasima* and *kommoi*.

Comedy. Comic choruses were made up of twenty-four members and were divided into two semichoruses; they entered in ranks of six and files of four. Like tragedy, comedy had a *parodos*, an *exodos*, and odes between scenes; in addition, there was a central section called the *parabasis*, in which the poet himself addressed the audience through the medium of the chorus and the *koryphaios*. Moreover, comic texts suggest greater liveliness and variety in modes of entrance and exit than those of tragedy, motivated sometimes by the nonhuman roles the dancers were assuming (for example, frogs, wasps, birds, or clouds), and sometimes by the appropriateness of making the chorus fall into a *kōmos*, the traditional drunken triumphal procession out of which comedy evolved. In addition to its own choreographic conventions, the choral dancing of comedy borrowed richly from tragedy during scenes when tragic poets were being parodied, as in several plays of Aristophanes.

Satyr plays. A tragic trilogy was always followed by a satyr play, an obscene mythological burlesque with a chorus of twelve goat-men, or satyrs, led by a fat old drunkard named Silenus. A dance associated with the satyr play was the *sikinnis*.

Choreographers. Alcman (late seventh century BCE) is the earliest choral poet whose work has survived, in puzzling fragments often referring to details of performance difficult to reconstruct. He wrote maiden-songs for Sparta, which were sometimes led by one of the virgins and sometimes by himself as lyrist. Stesichorus (first half of the sixth century) is credited with having introduced triadic composition; the few fragments of his that we possess, stirring in both meter and diction, belong to immense choral epics that would have taken hours to perform. Corinna (late sixth century), in one of her fragments, fashioned new versions of the tales of her fathers and led the girls of Tanagra (in ancient Boeotia) in dances that presented these versions to the public.

Corinna was one of the teachers of Pindar (first half of the fifth century), the greatest of the Greek choral poets, from whom we possess complete odes or fragments in all the traditional genres. His career as a choreographer began young; there is an anecdote that another of his teachers, Apollodorus, entrusted the adolescent Pindar with the training of a chorus in his absence, and the youth acquitted himself so splendidly that he became immediately famous. His thirty-seven epinicians in triadic composition show astonishing variety in their management of epodic arrest. It is clear that he worked within highly developed conventions for a sophisticated audience, and that he insisted on solving formal problems afresh in each work.

The early tragedians had many talents, as Athenaeus recorded in *Deipnosophists:* "Thespis, Pratinas, Kratinus, Phrynichus . . . were called dancers because they not only realized their dramas through the dancing of the chorus but also, apart from their own poems, trained people who wished to learn to dance." Aeschylus (c.525–456) "devised many dance figures himself and assigned them to the dancers in his choruses . . . using no dance teachers but making up the dance figures himself for the choruses." Sophocles (c.496–406) was precocious in music and dance; after the Greek victory at Salamis he was the boy chosen to dance the paean around the trophy while accompanying himself with the lyre, naked and anointed with oil. When he produced his *Nausicaa,* he assumed the title role himself (all parts in tragedy were played by male actors); in this production he danced some kind of ball game with great virtuosity. In Sophocles the unity of poet, dancer, and musician reaches its perfection among dramatists, as in Pindar among pure choral poets; Sophocles is also said to have written a theoretical prose work, *On the Chorus.* Thereafter we read that Euripides (c.485–406) merely composed the words of his odes and had others choreograph them; Agathon (*fl.* 416–401) began the practice of writing *embolima,* choral interludes that could be transferred from play to play. From the fourth century on, we have neither the names of great choral poets nor surviving fragments.

[*For related discussion, see* Dithyramb; Hyporchēma; *and* Sikinnis. *See also* Greece, *article on* Dance in Ancient Greece.]

BIBLIOGRAPHY

Calame, Claude. *Les choeurs de jeunes filles en Grèce archaïque.* 2 vols. Rome, 1977.
Lawler, Lillian B. *The Dance in Ancient Greece.* Middletown, Conn., 1964.
Lonsdale, Steven. *Dance and Ritual Play in Greek Religion.* Baltimore, 1993.
Miller, James L. *Measures of Wisdom: The Cosmic Dance in Classical and Christian Antiquity.* Toronto, 1986.
Mullen, William. *Choreia: Pindar and Dance.* Princeton, 1982.
Pickard-Cambridge, A. W. *Dithyramb, Tragedy and Comedy.* Revised by T. B. L. Webster. 2d ed. Oxford, 1962.
Pickard-Cambridge, A. W. *The Dramatic Festivals of Athens.* Oxford, 1968.
Webster, T. B. L. *The Greek Chorus.* London, 1970.
Winkler, John J. "The Ephebes' Song: Tragöidia and Polis" in *Nothing to Do with Dionysos?: Athenian Drama in Its Social Context.* Princeton, 1990.

WILLIAM MULLEN

CHO T'AEK-WON (born 22 May 1907 in Hamhung, died 8 June 1976 in Seoul), Korean dancer, choreographer, and teacher. Cho T'aek-won's inspiration to become a modern dancer occurred in 1922 when Ishii Baku, a pioneer of modern dance in Japan who had studied with Isadora Duncan, visited Seoul and performed the so-called *Neue Tanz* ("new dance") that he had learned in Europe. Cho then left for Tokyo and became a student of Ishii, with whom he later performed. When Ishii became blind in 1932, Cho returned to Seoul, where he became a professor of dance at what is presently Choongang University and also opened a private dance institute.

In 1934 Cho made his Korean debut with a self-choreographed work entitled *Impressions of a Buddhist Monk,* along with twelve other compositions. A second performance of his works a year later included such compositions as *Poem* and *Curfew.* In 1936 he returned to Tokyo for a performance with some of Ishii's former students. In 1937 he made his first contact with the Western art world on a trip to Paris, later followed by a performance tour of Japan and Korea. In 1941 he presented two new compositions, *The Crane* and *Fragrance of Spring,* in Tokyo and Nagoya; in the following year he premiered an epic work entitled *Reminiscences of Old Puyo* in Seoul and Taegu. In line with the Japanese colonial policy of the time, Cho was compelled to form a dance group to entertain Japanese troops, performing for them in China, Mongolia, Manchuria, and Korea until World War II ended in 1945. After publicly criticizing himself for his pro-Japanese activities, he then assumed the chairmanship of the Korean Dance Arts Association.

In 1947 Cho debuted on the American stage in Los Angeles, Chicago, and New York. He then remained in the United States until 1960 because of his outspoken criticism of the Korean dictatorship that held power at the time. During his U.S. sojourn, he introduced Korean traditional and modern dance to the American public. In 1949 in New York he premiered his *Old in Age, but Still Young in Spirit.* He journeyed to Paris in 1953 to perform for the United Nations Educational, Scientific, and Cultural Organization (UNESCO), thereafter giving four hundred performances throughout France and the rest of Europe for a two-year period. During this time he became acquainted with such great dancers as Ruth St. Denis, to whom he taught Korean dance.

In 1960 Cho returned home and became director of the Korean Dance Association and the Korean Folk Arts Company. In 1966 he received the Seoul City Cultural Award; in 1972 he was appointed a board member of Korea's National Academy of Arts. Cho T'aek-won is most noted for being the first Korean male dancer of the modern school and for his distinguished contribution to the development of modern dance in Korea through his combination of modern Western dance techniques with the unique spiritual motifs of Korean traditional dance.

[*See also* Korea, *article on* Modern Dance.]

BIBLIOGRAPHY

Cho Dong-wha. "Dance." In *Korea: Its Land, People, and Culture of All Ages*. 2d ed. Seoul, 1963.

Chung Byong-ho. *Korean Folk Dance*. Seoul, 1992.

Korea Britannica, vol. 19, p. 541. Seoul, 1993.

Pak Yong-ku. "Young Dancers Seek to Create Fresh Stage Idioms." In *Korean Art Guide*. 2d rev. ed. Seoul, 1986.

ALAN C. HEYMAN

CHRISTENSEN BROTHERS, family of dancers and teachers who trained dancers and built ballet companies that contributed greatly to the establishment of a ballet tradition in the western United States. Members included **Willam Christensen** (William Farr Christensen; born 27 August 1902 in Brigham City, Utah), **Harold Christensen** (Harold Farr Christensen; born 25 December 1904 in Brigham City, died 20 February 1989 in San Anselmo, California), and **Lew Christensen** (Lewellyn Farr Christensen; born 6 May 1909 in Brigham City, died 9 October 1984 in San Bruno, California). As a family, the Christensens are probably the closest American equivalent to the European tradition of extended dance families. The brothers' cultural heritage can be traced to their grandfather, Lars Christian Christensen, who emigrated from Denmark to Utah in 1854. Lars taught folk and social dances in the community of Brigham City and, with his sons, formed a traveling orchestra to accompany dance events across northern Utah. Lars's sons Christian, Frederic, Moses, and Lars Peter became professional teachers of social dancing, opening ballrooms in Brigham City and Salt Lake City, Utah; Portland, Oregon; and Seattle, Washington. Active in the American National Association, Masters of Dancing. Moses served as its president for 1916/17. He introduced his family to ballet technique through the Italian teacher Stefano Mascagno. Trained in music by their father and in ballet by their uncles and Mascagno, the brothers Willam, Harold, and Lew acquired a firm commitment to the classical tradition during an era when many young American dancers were attracted by the modern dance of the Denishawn company. Willam later studied ballet with Laurent Novikoff and Michel Fokine.

A natural and charismatic leader, Willam spurred the brothers to performing careers, initially in vaudeville. During the late 1920s and early 1930s, Willam, Lew, and partners toured first as Russian character dancers, and then in a stunt-filled ballet act highlighting Lew's technical prowess, height, and commanding stage presence. Willam married his partner and former student Mignon Lee; when she contracted multiple sclerosis, the couple moved to Portland to teach in the dancing school established by Moses Christensen. Harold and another of Willam's students, Ruby Asquith, filled the vacant roles in the act until 1934, when Lew, Harold, and their partners joined the cast of an elaborate Broadway musical, *The Great Waltz*. At the same time, the foursome began studies with George Balanchine and Pierre Vladimiroff at the recently established School of American Ballet.

Harold and Lew joined Balanchine's American Ballet ensemble when it became the resident company of the Metropolitan Opera (1935–1937). Lew, who received special tutelage from Balanchine, earned critical acclaim in the title roles in *Orpheus and Eurydice* and *Apollon Musagète*. As the first American Apollo, Lew's unmannered athleticism and musicality set a standard for future interpretations of that role.

Lew was also the ballet master of Ballet Caravan, a small touring company sponsored by Lincoln Kirstein between opera seasons to nurture young American choreographers and generate repertory based on American themes. In this context, Lew choreographed *Pocahontas* (1936) and *Filling Station* (1938), the latter featuring himself as Mac the attendant and Harold as the confused Motorist. Choreographed to a commissioned score by Virgil Thomson, *Filling Station*'s choreography reflected Lew's vaudevillian roots, incorporating acrobatics, deadpan humor, allusions to social dance, and tap dancing into its episodic structure. Lew also created the role of Pat Garrett in Eugene Loring's *Billy the Kid* (1938). Through the seasons at the Metropolitan and the Caravan's tours, Lew earned a reputation as the preeminent American *danseur noble* of the early twentieth century. Harold also performed with Ballet Caravan, serving as stage manager rather than choreographing. In this era, Lew married Gisella Caccialanza, another Balanchine performer and a former protégée of Enrico Cecchetti.

While Lew and Harold performed with Balanchine and Ballet Caravan, Willam established a student company in Portland, which included Janet Reed (later a principal dancer with Ballet Theatre and the New York City Ballet). In 1937 he was hired as a leading dancer with the San Francisco Opera Ballet, and the following January he became director of that company, which included many of his Portland students. The highlights of his tenure in San Francisco were his evening-length ballets in an era otherwise typified by mixed programs of shorter works. He was the first American choreographer to set the complete *Coppélia* (1939), a four-act *Swan Lake* (starring Lew as Siegfried, 1940), and a full-length version of *The Nutcracker* (1944). In creating these works he drew on the knowledge of his conductors and the memories of White Russian émigrés in San Francisco. Balanchine and Alexandra Danilova advised Willam on *The Nutcracker*, which predated Balanchine's by ten years and established the tradition of presenting this ballet at Christmastime.

Willam's shorter works, such as *In Vienna* (1938) and *Winter Carnival* (1942), were in the tradition of Léonide Massine's *demi-caractère* depictions of high society; his Prohibition farce *Nothin' Doin' Bar* (1950) echoed the goals of Ballet Caravan in synthesizing classical and popular forms rooted in American themes. Although he experimented with abstract composition as early as 1938 in *Bach Suite*, he is best known for the narrative ballets that demonstrated his talent for characterization through movement. Several of the dancers he trained in San Francisco left to make their reputations in New York or abroad, including Peter Nelson, Scott Douglas, Norman Thompson, Onna White, Carolyn George, and Jocelyn Vollmar.

Willam also choreographed San Francisco Opera productions until 1955. When the Opera decided to discontinue its ballet troupe during World War II, Willam assumed responsibility for the company and, with Harold's help, bought out its school. Although company histories date the San Francisco Ballet's existence to 1933, the independent company, free of opera domination, did not exist until Willam assumed leadership in 1943. Harold became director of the San Francisco Ballet School, a post he held until his retirement in 1975. He maintained high standards of training and sought out talented students, with the result that the school supplied a steady stream of dancers for the company. His fiscal conservatism also benefited Willam and Lew, because income from the school paid the brothers' salaries and subsidized the company before the era of federal funding and corporate grants. Harold married his former vaudeville partner Ruby Asquith, who was a leading ballerina in San Francisco Ballet productions during the 1940s.

Lew and Gisella were principal dancers during American Ballet Caravan's 1941 South American tour. Lew subsequently joined Loring's Dance Players and choreographed *Jinx*, a haunting drama of superstition in a traveling circus. Drafted into the army in 1942 at the height of his performing career, Lew spent the remainder of the war in the European theater, first in the infantry and then as military governor of a German town. After leaving the service in 1946, he joined the latest Balanchine-Kirstein venture, Ballet Society, functioning once again as ballet master. Lew partnered Elise Reiman in the premiere of Balanchine's *The Four Temperaments*, but he never fully regained his prewar technique. Thus, although Kirstein viewed Lew as Balanchine's eventual successor, the youngest Christensen brother was drawn back into the family fold, joining his brothers Willam and Harold in San Francisco in 1948. He assisted Willam in directing the San Francisco Ballet from 1949 to 1951 and assumed leadership of the company in 1951, when Willam left to establish a ballet program at the University of Utah.

When Lew took over the reins of the San Francisco Bal-

CHRISTENSEN BROTHERS. Willam and Lew Christensen in a vaudeville dance act in the late 1920s or early 1930s. (Photograph from the San Francisco Performing Arts Library and Museum; used by permission.)

let, he and Kirstein instituted an exchange program by which the company and the New York City Ballet would share some repertory and leading dancers. Because the company's performing schedule was extremely limited, Lew was able to travel to New York regularly to serve as ballet master for the New York City Ballet through 1954. His involvement in both companies, and the teaching methods he brought to San Francisco, rendered him an important early disseminator of Balanchine's repertory and style in the American West. A gifted teacher as well as performer, Lew taught advanced classes at the San Francisco Ballet School and regularly lost dancers (such as Conrad Ludlow, Suki Schorer, Cynthia Gregory, and Terry Orr) to New York companies.

As a choreographer, Lew was not content to be seen as an imitator of his former master; he worked in a variety of styles to create balanced programming for the San Francisco company. The more than seventy ballets and operatic *divertissements* he created between 1951 and his death in 1984 display this diversity: the ebullient *Con Amore* (1953), a tongue-in-cheek takeoff on Romantic ballet lithographs; *Masque of Beauty and the Shepherd* (1954), a retelling of the story of Helen of Troy; *The Nutcracker* (1954); romances such as *The Dryad* (1954), *The Lady of Shalott* (1957), and *Beauty and the Beast* (1958); *Emperor Norton*, an essay in Americana inspired by the San Francisco UNESCO conference; abstract works such as *Sinfonia* (1959), *Divertissement d'Auber* (1959), *Stravinsky Pas de Deux* (1976), and *Vivaldi Concerto Grosso* (1981); *Original Sin* (1961, a jazzy retelling of the Adam and Eve story); *Jest of Cards* (1962), to an avant-garde score by Ernest Krenek; a pop art ballet entitled *Life* (1965); and *Il Distratto* (1967), a witty dissection of classical technique. Lew's choreography often featured virtuosic roles for men, from that of Mac in *Filling Station* to the dazzling Hoop Dance in *Scarlatti Portfolio* (1979), which won the 1979 bronze medal for choreography at the International Ballet Competition in Jackson, Mississippi.

Under Lew's direction, the San Francisco Ballet gained recognition through performances at Jacob's Pillow (1956) and three international tours sponsored by the U.S. State Department (to Asia, the Middle East, and South America, 1957–1959). Lew's and Harold's commitment and personal sacrifices to maintain the school and company attracted a Ford Foundation grant in 1963, which gave the company its first financial stability.

The conservatory-style program Willam founded at the University of Utah constituted an intentional departure from the tradition of modern dance training in colleges of physical education. Located institutionally in the theater department, Willam choreographed theater and opera productions in addition to works for his student company. Always able to attract male students, in Utah Willam oversaw the early training of Finis Jhung, Kent Stowell, Bart Cook, Jay Jolley, and Michael Smuin; the last co-directed the San Francisco Ballet with Lew from 1973 to 1984. Willam's student company went professional with the receipt of a Ford Foundation grant in 1963 and was rechristened Ballet West in 1968, in recognition of its extensive touring in the intermountain region of the West.

The Christensen brothers' geographical isolation from ballet activity on the East Coast was a major factor in their ability to establish and maintain their choreographic individuality. Their work contributed significantly to the decentralization of ballet in America in three ways: their companies acquired stability through Ford Foundation grants; their students carried on the Christensens' work in western cities and universities (such as Stowell with the Pacific Northwest Ballet); and their repertory was widely disseminated—by Lew's death in 1984 *Con Amore* had been staged by nine companies and *Filling Station* by six. Recognition of the brothers' contribution to dance in America came late in their careers: in 1973 they received a *Dance Magazine* Award (with Rudolf Nureyev), and in 1984 they shared the Capezio Dance Award.

[*See also* San Francisco Ballet.]

BIBLIOGRAPHY

Croce, Arlene. "Americana." *The New Yorker* (3 November 1980).

Dorris, George. "Willam Christensen Reminisces." In *Proceedings of the Twelfth Annual Conference, Society of Dance History Scholars, Arizona State University, 17–19 February 1989*, compiled by Christena L. Schlundt. Riverside, Calif., 1989.

Hastings, Baird. "Tribute to a Trio." *Ballet Review* 22 (Summer 1994): 8–9.

Kirstein, Lincoln. *Thirty Years: The New York City Ballet*. New York, 1978.

Kirstein, Lincoln. *Ballet: Bias and Belief—Three Pamphlets Collected and Other Dance Writings*. New York, 1983.

Kirstein, Lincoln. "American Apollo." *Ballet News* 6 (January 1985): 11–13.

Mason, Francis. "Lew Christensen." *Ballet Review* 12 (Winter 1985): 4–6.

Maynard, Olga. "The Christensens: An American Dance Dynasty." *Dance Magazine* (June 1973): 44–58.

Newman, Barbara. "Lew Christensen." In Newman's *Striking a Balance*. Rev. ed. New York, 1992.

Ross, Janice. "Lew Christensen: An American Original." *Dance Magazine* (December 1981): 66–69.

Siegel, Marcia B. "Filling Station." In Siegel's *Shapes of Change: Images of the American Dance*. New York, 1979.

Sowell, Debra Hickenlooper. "The Christensen Brothers: A Career Biography." Ph.D.diss., New York University, 1990.

Steinberg, Cobbett. *San Francisco Ballet: The First Fifty Years*. San Francisco, 1983.

ARCHIVES.   The primary source of information for all three brothers is the Christensen-Caccialanza Collection, San Francisco Performing Arts Library and Museum. The Utah Ballet Archives, housed at the University of Utah Marriott Library, Salt Lake City, also contains valuable documentation of Willam Christensen's career.

DEBRA HICKENLOOPER SOWELL

CHRISTIANITY AND DANCE. [*To survey the relationship between dance and the Christian church, this entry comprises three articles:*

Early Christian Views

Medieval Views

Modern Views

The first article focuses on Christian views in the Hellenistic and Roman periods; the second discusses the development of dance as part of the Christian liturgy; the third considers the growing opposition to dance that paralleled the rise of Protestantism. For related discussion, see Aesthetics, *article on* Western Dance Aesthetics; Bible, Dance in the; *and* Liturgical Dance.]

Early Christian Views

Religious dance has been widely practiced throughout the world and evidence for ceremonial dance is documented in history and prehistory. Its role in early Christianity is unclear, however; some scholars have argued that the early Christian church was always hostile to it, whereas others have argued that in the earliest days there was a custom of dancing and swaying while chanting the hymns of the faith. The records of the patristic period (written by the founders) provide little support for this; instead they abound with vigorous condemnations of dancing.

At the shrines of martyrs, however, some dancing was performed as we learn from a few unambiguous references. For example, a fourth-century homily commemorating Saint Polyeuctus includes the following: "If you wish it so, celebrate in his honor our customary dances" (Aubé, 1882). In Carthage on Saint Cyprian's Day in the year 360, there was dancing in the memorial church at the Area Macrobii, according to Saint Augustine (354–430). A declaration of Saint Augustine may also be cited as representative: "It is not by dancing but by praying . . . that the martyrs gained their victory." Within a few years of this, the Christians of Antioch were dancing in their churches at news of the death of their persecutor, the Roman general and emperor, Julian (331–363), called Julian the Apostate. John Chrysostom (c.350–407) related that women were attacked by Basil of Caesarea (c.330–379) when dancing on the martyrs' shrines on the outskirts of town; he opposed "gesticulating with hands and hopping with the feet" around the communion table. That dancing continued, however, is evidenced by the prohibitions of the next six hundred years.

Christianity began with Jesus of Nazareth during the Roman Empire's governance of Europe, the Near East, and North Africa. Jesus, his first followers, and the earliest Christian communities were Jewish Near Easterners; his followers interpreted the significance of his life and times within their own frame of reference. Ceremonial dancing had been, since prehistoric times, part of ancient Near Eastern religious life—and it was part of Roman ceremonies as well. To distinguish early Christians from other Near Easterners and from Romans—in an environment of great secrecy since Rome wanted no new religious group to disrupt local governance—certain policies of restraint were adopted. By the end of the first century CE, Paul had inspired his followers to transform a Jewish sect into a gentile movement, to challenge the Roman Empire, and to conquer it in Jesus' name. Opposition between empire and church during the second and third centuries sometimes took the form of persecution and martyrdom, which were replaced in the fourth century by the creation of a Christian Roman Empire when Emperor Constantine (306–337) first made the new faith legal; he soon made it his own and then established it as the official religion of the empire. If second and third century Christian writers tried to distinguish their faith from those of Greece and Rome, by the fourth and fifth centuries they undertook to interpret Christian theology as a perennial philosophy in which the aspirations of all religions had now been fulfilled.

More important than simply chronicling dancing in church, then, or attacks on it, is the understanding of any opposition to it. Christianity centers on the Incarnation—the enfleshment of God—and declares its faith in the resurrection; the sacraments thus affirm the body's spirituality. Dancing would seem to be in keeping with such beliefs, especially since nothing in the New Testament compels rejection of dancing whereas much in the Hebrew scriptures (Old Testament) encourages it. Why, then, was dance denigrated in the early centuries?

By the time Christianity was beginning to make headway, dance had become so degraded in comparison with its former sacred character that educated people shunned it. Plutarch (c.46–127) typified this when he remarked that "nothing enjoys the benefit of bad taste so much as dancing . . . she has lost her honor among men who have intelligence."

This cultural repudiation was shared by Christians, who as part of this same Greco-Roman culture wanted to avoid dancing, because it was still a part of contemporary pagan ceremonies: it accompanied bird and animal sacrifices and it often mimed the legends of the gods. Dance was a part of fertility rites, was usually bawdy, even pornographic, and was especially so at gatherings where alcoholic beverages (wine, mead) were featured. Through the sacrament of the Lord's Supper, Christianity sought to distance itself from this practice; such behavior was in marked contrast to the lifestyle being defined by its developing asceticism. The quest for God began to be interpreted in Platonic (idealistic) categories; the journey of the soul was regarded as a never-ending war against the flesh, because body and soul were conceived of as being in opposition. This quite unbiblical denigration of the physical aspect of human nature supported the view that dance had no place in Christian devotions.

In the early years of Christian expansion and conversion, several other new faiths were competing for new members. If other religious groups and heretical movements of the time allowed dancing, mainstream Christianity affirmed its own distinctiveness by refusing to imitate them. Other fast-expanding heretical groups then included the Gnostic sects as well as the Messalians and the Meletians. To condemn these groups meant rejection not only of their beliefs but also of their practices, including dancing.

Christianity did not remain in the founding era. As the centuries passed and differing philosophical and political challenges emerged, the various branches of Christianity responded in their own creative ways. In its historical context, the early condemnation is understandable, but it cannot be regarded as authoritative for all time.

BIBLIOGRAPHY
Arbeau, Thoinot. *Orchesography* (1589). Translated by Mary Stewart Evans. New York, 1948.
Aubé, Benjamin. *Polyeucte dans l'histoire*. Paris, 1882.
Backman, Eugène Louis. *Religious Dances in the Christian Church and in Popular Medicine*. Translated by E. Classen. London, 1952.

Bertaud, E. "Danse." In *Dictionnaire de spiritualité*. Paris, 1937–.
Davies, J. G. *Liturgical Dance: An Historical, Theological, and Practical Handbook*. London, 1984.
Sachs, Curt. *World History of the Dance*. Translated by Bessie Schönberg. New York, 1937.

J. G. DAVIES

Medieval Views

In the Middle Ages, preachers and theologians gave some attention to the issue of dance, but always within the larger context of church efforts at conversion, at unifying the liturgy, and at consolidating Roman Catholic authority. In a period of crusades, heresies, and demands for church reform, dance was of interest to churchmen only in terms of its orthodoxy or heterodoxy, of its utility or threat to the advancement of a unified religious force.

Sacred Dancing. Records of church-authorized dancing are so sparse and cryptic that they reveal almost nothing about choreography or even the context of the performance. Furthermore, references to dance contained in hymns or prayers may well have been intended purely symbolically: the soul might dance in spiritual rejoicing, but it is rarely clear that this dancing was to be performed physically.

Christian liturgy has an inherent theatricality that the early church was generally hesitant to exploit. Yet, by the twelfth century, plays illustrating religious themes were being performed in the churches of Italy, Germany, France, England, and Spain (Bevington, 1975). As the plays evolved, they were often supplemented with processionals and dancing, with the dance roles usually assigned to such characters as shepherds or devils.

In the thirteenth century, sacred dances formed a part of the Easter liturgy in some parts of France. The *bergerette*, performed in Besançon and elsewhere, may have been a dance depicting Jesus as Christ the shepherd, while the *pelota* of Auxerres has been described as a complex dance performed by the clergy and involving the passing of a ball along the stations of a labyrinth (Backman, 1952). In the fifteenth century, the church at Hildesheim, Germany, also included sacred dancing at Easter. The Pentecostal season was celebrated with dancing in Auxerre, Limoges, Liège, Salzburg, and Würzburg. Records from the twelfth through the fifteenth centuries indicate that the Christmas season gave rise to sacred dancing, especially for the Feast of the Little Bishop and for Epiphany. These holidays were celebrated with processions, plays, and dancing in France (Auxerre, Paris, Le Puy, Sens), Germany (Nuremburg), and Spain (Seville, Toledo).

In religious processions such as Corpus Christi (instituted in 1264), the pageantry, music, plays, and dancing were designed to both impress and inspire the population with the strength of Christian belief and rejoicing. Among the contributions of such groups as guilds, parishes, and civil authorities were those dances that best demonstrated that group's sense of rejoicing. In many parts of Spain, for example, the municipal government commissioned professional dancers to perform in the cathedral, as well as outside, along the procession route. Seville's cathedral council presented its elite choristers, *los seises*, in a special dance, a version of which is still performed.

Certain localities celebrated particular feasts with dance. The "jumping dance" of Echternach, Luxembourg, was performed in the Whitsun procession to celebrate the town's patron, Saint Willibrord. Dating from at least the eleventh century, this processional dance was credited with working cures in those who participated. Similar processions were held on Ascension Day in Prüm, Germany, in the fourteenth century, and also in Tournai, Belgium, to celebrate the raising of the cross. During the Easter season in Cologne, the *Gottestracht* procession was led by a harlequin-clad dancer.

Sacred dancing took root in local liturgies and in celebrations for patron saints, which provided the necessary freedom from standard Roman Catholic practices. Spain, for example, isolated from Rome by the Muslim invasion of the early eighth century, nurtured its own liturgy and permitted the development of sacred dancing. In England there was some church-approved dancing in the early Middle Ages; France had a tradition of liturgical dance, at least from the tenth through the fourteenth centuries.

Popular Religious Dancing. Several factors conspired to ensure that, with or without church approval, there was barely a religious event from which dancing was absent. Daily labor was prohibited on Sundays and feast days, and the enforced leisure made such holidays the perfect opportunity for the public to entertain itself with songs, games, and dances. The church was the gathering place for the community, and dance was a frequent obvious choice for communal entertainment. Furthermore, because the Christian calendar had essentially been superimposed on pre-Christian celebrations, such ancient rituals as fertility dances and winter festivals continued to find their appropriate time for performance. Liturgical developments in the medieval period increasingly reduced public participation in the mass, so that other outlets for popular devotion were needed.

In Spain, France, the Low Countries, Germany, England, and Scandinavia, preachers and moralists bemoaned the unauthorized public entertainments held on holy days. As early as the sixth century, the bishop of Arles had condemned dances on feast days, but beginning in the twelfth century, concern over these abuses increased. Even in the later Middle Ages, the ancient tradition of celebrating saints' feasts with night-long revels was reported in Seville, Utrecht, and York. Lent was also celebrated with "rejoicings, vanities, and dances," according to preacher Johann Geiler of Augsburg (Coulton, 1910, vol. 4, p. 359). In the fifteenth and sixteenth centuries, feasts enlivened with unauthorized dancing were Easter, Whitsun, the Feast of Mary Magdalene, Assumption Day, Christmas, Shrove Tuesday, and Ash Wednesday. The Christmas season was particularly profaned by popular revelry, including mumming and dancing, provoking one Wycliffite reformer to condemn it as "a feast of words with dancing and ditties," lacking in any spiritual content (Pimlott, 1978, p. 17).

The lower clergy, often as illiterate and superstitious as their peasant parishioners, were known to violate the sanctuary with ribald satires, gambling, lewd songs, and dancing. Their most irreverent behavior was reserved for the Feast of Fools, when they would make mockeries of bishops, cardinals, and even the mass. These burlesques proved resistant to the repeated condemnations of prelates, kings, and popes, from the sixth through the fifteenth centuries. Some village priests were accused of leading their congregants in games and dancing, even in church. Convents and monasteries in late medieval Germany were the scenes of shameful dances of men and women together, according to preachers' sermons of the time (Schultz, 1892, vol. 2, p. 335). On the other hand, high prelates were as worldly as secular princes and took equal delight in banquets, theater, and dancing.

Preachers rightly suspected pagan roots for many popular forms of celebration. Ancient fertility rites reappeared in Christian guise at Easter, winter solstice feasts were transformed into Christmas celebrations, and demon-expelling rituals were submerged in the sword dance performed at Corpus Christi. Medicinal and fertility rites were the ancient sources of the Saint John's celebrations in England and Germany, where garland-clad townsfolk danced around bonfires lit in the square. Reports exist from Scotland and Germany of priests mixing idolatrous dances and incantations into their church services (Coulton, 1930, vol. 2, p. 128; vol. 4, p. 210).

Medicinal rites may have played some role in the dance manias that swept through Europe in the later Middle Ages. Exorcisms performed by Christian priests sometimes succeeded in curing those possessed, who were treated with compassion, rather than as heretics. The flagellants, in contrast, were condemned as a heretical sect in the fourteenth century. While these ascetics never described their performances as dancing, they are of interest from a movement perspective because of the rhythmic nature of the scourging and formularized movements accompanied by hymns. The gloomy world-view and extreme religious climate of the fourteenth and fifteenth centuries also contributed to the popularity of the image of the Dance of Death, frequently illustrated in painting and poetry. Such a dance may have actually been performed in the later fourteenth cen-

tury, in Montserrat, Spain, and in the Norman church of Candebec.

Theological Attitudes. The position of the medieval church regarding dance was ambivalent. Dance was condemned for its associations with paganism, with ceremonies of magic, and with wild behavior that distracted parishioners from solemn devotion at Christian feasts. Yet, the ancient Near Eastern concept of dance as a reflection of the harmonious movement of the cosmos had also influenced Christian theology. Legitimate spiritual rejoicing had been demonstrated in the Hebrew Bible by the dance of King David and in the early church at celebrations of Christian victories at Antioch (363 CE) and Constantinople (380 CE). Early theologians, such as John Chrysostom, Saint Ambrose, Pseudo-Dionysius, and Basil of Caesarea attempted to mediate these two positions on dance: the orderly, devotional dance of the faithful was a valid demonstration of orthodox Christian joy; yet, when dancing became wild and immodest, the devil was at work, distracting the Christian from his or her spiritual devotions. As summarized by John Chrysostom, "God gave us feet not to use in a shameful way, but to join one day in the choirs of angels" (*Homilia* 48).

In the Middle Ages, theological positions on dance were built on the foundations laid by the church fathers. From the eighth through the fifteenth centuries, preachers from every corner of western Europe condemned dance as "the sport of Venus," invented and led by the devil (Coulton, 1930, vol. 1, p. 90). Franciscan and Dominican orders forbade their followers to attend wedding celebrations and dances, and church councils prohibited priests from dancing at mass, in church, or in cemeteries. Stories were circulated of God's wrath visited in thunderbolts, floods, paralysis, consuming fires, and other calamities upon those who refused to cease their dancing. Nevertheless, masquerading, burlesques, and dancing continued to plague church celebrations, despite preachers' threats of excommunication and hellfire. Church councils were forced to take up this persistent issue in a period when such crucial matters as doctrinal heresies and threats to papal authority were demanding the attention of churchmen. Among those councils that issued prohibitions of dancing on holy days or in churches were the Council of Laodice in 343, Toledo in 589, Rome in 826, and Avignon in 1209 and the Synod of Lyon in 1566.

In counterbalance, Gregory the Great (died 604) had recognized dance as a legitimate expression of a jubilation too powerful for words. Eighth- and ninth-century psalters had illustrated such dancing in David's performance before the ark. Ascetics and mystics from the twelfth century onward, among them Saint Victor, Mechthilde of Magdeburg, and Sister Berthe of Utrecht, reported that their souls were moved to dance in spiritual intoxication.

Christian concepts of heavenly music and dance, although rooted in pre-Christian philosophies, were elaborated by the scholastics. Their concepts of a heavenly hierarchy influenced Dante Aligheri's *Commedia* (1472), in which dance and music are depicted as the activities of the angels in the highest spheres of paradise (Meyer-Baer, 1970).

In the visual arts, both the positive and the negative perspectives on dance were represented. In illustrations of Hell, the damned were depicted in grotesque versions of popular dances and steps—limbs flailing and bodies contorted—as demons delighted in their torment. A witches' sabbath illustrated in the decree of the tribunal of Arras, France, in 1460 shows witches and demons dancing around a tree and women performing a circle dance to the accompaniment of lutes and viols (Lacroix, 1877). These instruments, usually associated with aristocratic dance, demonstrate that courtly as well as popular dances were reprehended by some moralists. Yet, as jongleurs gained admission at court, so did dancing and music gain a more positive image in Christian art. Heavenly musicians began to appear in eleventh-century illustrations and, by the fifteenth century, depictions of heaven were rich in dancing angels. Andrea da Firenze, Fra Angelico, Luca della Robbia, and Sandro Botticelli were among those whose works illustrated these themes. Fifteenth-century art brought religious dancing back down to earth: in a miniature in Charles d'Angoulême's Book of Hours, shepherds are depicted in a lively dance celebrating Christ's birth.

Nevertheless, dance remained acceptable only as a symbol of spiritual emotion: the soul might dance in Christian rejoicing, but the corporeal dance too quickly disintegrated from heavenly harmonies to scandalous diversions. Although dance was not associated with any organized heresy, it was never admitted into the official Roman Catholic rite, and sacred dancing was protected only in exceptional cases of local liturgies. Yet, the church's maintenance of learning in the Middle Ages permitted the transmission of classical culture to later generations of artists, and those sources inspired the golden age of theater and dance in the Renaissance. No effort of the church was ever successful in entirely suppressing dance in the popular, the courtly, or even the clerical community. It is the church's own records that provide documentation for the popularity of dance in the Middle Ages.

BIBLIOGRAPHY

Backman, Eugène Louis. *Religious Dances in the Christian Church and in Popular Medicine.* Translated by E. Classen. London, 1952.

Bevington, David, comp. *Medieval Drama.* Boston, 1975.

Brooks, Lynn M. *The Dances of the Processions of Seville in Spain's Golden Age.* Kassel, 1988.

Coulton, G. G., ed. *Life in the Middle Ages.* 4 vols. in 1. New York, 1930.

Davies, J. G. *Liturgical Dance: An Historical, Theological, and Practical Handbook.* London, 1984.

Donovan, Richard B. *The Liturgical Drama in Medieval Spain.* Toronto: Pontifical Institute of Medieval Studies, 1958.

Hecker, J. F. C. *The Dancing Mania of the Middle Ages.* Translated by B. G. Babington. 1837; reprint, New York, 1970.

Jungmann, Josef A. *The Mass of the Roman Rite: Its Origins and Development.* 2 vols. Translated by Francis A. Brunner. New York, 1951–1955.

Lacroix, Paul. *Moeurs, usages, et costumes au moyen âge et à l'époque de la Renaissance.* Paris, 1871.

Lacroix, Paul. *La vie militaire et religieuse au moyen âge et à l'époque de la Renaissance.* 4th ed. Paris, 1877.

Lázaro Carreter, Fernando. *Theatro medieval: Textos íntegros.* Salamanca: 1958.

Manor, Giora. "The Bible as Dance." *Dance Magazine* (December 1978): 55–86.

Meredith, Peter, and John E. Tailby. *The Staging of Religious Drama in Europe in the Later Middle Ages: Texts and Documents in English Translation.* Kalamazoo, Michigan, 1983.

Meyer-Baer, Kathi. *Music of the Spheres and the Dance of Death.* Princeton, 1970.

Miller, James. *Measures of Wisdome: The Cosmic Dance in Classical and Christian Antiquity.* Toronto, 1986.

Pimlott, J. A. R. *The Englishman's Christmas: A Social History.* Hassocks, England, 1978.

Schultz, Alwin. *Deutsches Leben in XIV. und XV. Jahrhundert.* 2 vols. Vienna, 1892.

LYNN MATLUCK BROOKS

Modern Views

From the sixteenth century through the early twentieth century the general attitude of the Christian church and its clergy toward dance had been neutral or negative.

In the sixteenth century the leaders of the Reformation, having broken with the Church of Rome on the doctrine of justification by grace through faith alone, stressed the Bible and individual conscience as their primary authorities, thereby dismissing the importance of pope and church council. Although knowledgeable about the dancing mentioned in the Bible, reformers did not use it to approve contemporary dancing. Instead they asserted that the ancient Israelites had danced for religious purposes and with the sexes separated; such dancing was therefore different from that of the sixteenth century. Furthermore, they pointed to the idolatrous dancing around the golden calf described in *Exodus*, and invariably declared it was because of the infamous Salome's dancing that John the Baptist was beheaded (*Exodus* 32.19; *Matthew* 14.6–11; and *Mark* 6.21–28). Thus, behavior associated with dancing became a major issue.

One of Christianity's fundamental tenets is that humans, sinful by nature, cannot achieve the obedience God requires except through faith in Jesus and the guidance of the holy spirit. In preaching repentance, or turning from sin, Protestant clergy have exhorted people to reform their behavior. With the splintering of the Western Christian church, which began in the sixteenth century, the existence of several denominations permitted various scriptural interpretations of what constituted correct conduct. "Mixt" dancing invited degrees of censure; while not proscribed in the Bible, many saw it as the open door to temptation and sinful behavior. Theater, gambling, and other pastimes, as well as women's dress, also could invite lustful behavior, wasting of time, and squandering of money. Thus they became targets for reform along with dancing. Not all Christians agreed that such pastimes tempted to sin, however.

The values of the upper classes in Europe, who fostered dancing as a courtly and ballroom art, differed somewhat from those of Protestant reformers. The ideal of the gentleman required that he be a Christian and that he seek virtue and shun vice. Life was to be ordered around service to God and country; the mind was to rule over the passions; and the care of the body was important. The gentleman was to present an aesthetically pleasing appearance on the dance floor, as was his lady. Their dancing was to be skilled and graceful but not virtuosic. It was to display ordered form and to be pursued in moderation. The English Catholic Sir Thomas Elyot (1531) even asserted that learning to dance enabled one also to acquire prudence, the mother of all virtue, but his Spanish contemporary, Juan Luis Vives, likened schools of dancing to baudy houses. Their differing perceptions point to the conflict in the valuing of dance that continued among Protestants and Roman Catholics well into the twentieth century.

Although church officials had periodically spoken out against dancing since the patristic era, opposition to dancing intensified with the growth of Protestantism in the sixteenth century. Criticisms issued from English, Dutch, French, German, and Swiss preachers and theologians affiliated with the Anglican, Puritan, Calvinist, Huguenot, and Lutheran churches. Their opinions circulated as whole treatises, chapters in books, and explications to the seventh commandment. Their intent was to exhort readers to lead a life of Christian virtue and holiness by avoiding the temptations of mixed dancing and other allegedly immoral pastimes and amusements. (A comprehensive listing of Catholic and Protestant antidance writers appears in William Prynne's *Histrio-Mastix*, 1633.)

In general, critics from the sixteenth to the twentieth century condemned the abuses accidental to contemporary dancing rather than censuring all dance *per se*. Allegations of sin or vice focused on: sins of the body—drunkenness, lust, fornication, adultery—viewed as attendant upon dancing; disorderly movement, considered unbecoming to the Christian ideal of sobriety and gravity; fatigue and ill health, claimed to result from immoderate dancing; immoral musical accompaniment; profaning the Sabbath; and wasting both time and money. Arguments opposing dance developed from a Christian moral

ground, rather than from an aesthetic base. Support from the Bible relied heavily on the seventh commandment and passages such as Paul's injunction to prepare for the final judgment (*Romans* 14.10–12), at which time, warned dance opponents, it will be necessary to account for every idle word and deed.

Verifiable opposition to dance in the English North American colonies dates from early New England laws and from Increase Mather's 1685 treatise, *An Arrow against Profane and Promiscuous Dancing Drawn out of the Quiver of the Scriptures*. Protestant influence from the previous century appears in Mather's citations of Prynne, Pietro Vermigli, John Calvin, Lambert Daneau, and William Perkins. New England Puritans neither universally opposed dancing nor objected to dance *per se*, but in general, their early laws opposed dancing associated with civil disorder, Indians, and witchcraft.

By 1714, New England Puritan influence had waned sufficiently that the Anglican Church in Boston could bring Edward Enstone from England, as organist, with permission to supplement his salary by giving dancing lessons. A common figure in eighteenth-century America, the itinerant dance and music master tended to find more business in places where Puritans and Quakers were not the majority. Revival preaching by George Whitefield and publications from the Reverend Oliver Hart in Charleston (1778) and Sir Richard Hill in England (1761) indicate that opposition to dancing had subsided but not vanished.

The nineteenth century, characterized by revival and reform, produced strong opposition to dance in the United States and England. Like their sixteenth-century counterparts, nineteenth-century evangelicals dismissed the argument that biblical examples of dancing should be interpreted as approval for contemporary dancing. Baptists, Methodists, Presbyterians, Congregationalists, and Disciples of Christ produced the most treatises on the subject. Scandinavian and German Lutheran immigrants to America, however, brought antidance attitudes. Opposition, by mid-century, focused on the evils of the round dances, such as the waltz and the polka. Purists argued that even square dances, such as the quadrille, should be avoided because they inevitably led to round dancing.

Additionally, it was also thought that late hours, low necklines, undue excitement, and nervous exhaustion particularly threatened women's health. The extravagance of dress for balls fostered a vanity that was contrary to the Christian ideal of humility. Yet the greatest concentration of concern focused on the freedom permitted by the embrace in round dances, which, opponents argued, threatened female virtue.

Although many objections thus derived from gender roles, the arguments based on spiritual growth applied to both men and women. Worldly pleasures like dancing, critics declared, countered the development of a truly spiritual nature, stealing time and energy from pious practices, such as attendance at prayer meetings and Sunday worship, as well as regular Bible reading.

In the early twentieth century, American clergy and evangelists of conservative and fundamentalist persuasions continued to oppose dancing. The tango and subsequent "modern" dances were attacked as they became popular. Once again the opposition concentrated on the immoral behavior between the sexes that dancing was thought to evoke. Some claimed the new jazz inflamed evil. Others attacked the "modern woman" who smoked, drank, and wore trousers. The diffusion of black dances and dancers fueled fears of still other dance opponents. The public's association of dancing with liquor and sex targeted the dance hall for censure until it became controlled by city and state legislation. By World War II, however, dancing had become so popular and churches faced so many more issues than that of appropriate amusements that the outcry against dancing had markedly decreased.

Little evidence is available concerning the impact of Christian missionaries on the dancing of the native cultures they encountered. Given the historic absence of dance in churches and the traditional assumptions and training of missionaries, it is unlikely that, until recently, the typical worker would have found indigenous dancing compatible with Christian faith and doctrine.

Dance within the Church. Dancing throughout the modern era has been primarily a secular activity. From the Reformation to the present, dance has been practiced in church worship and festivals only on disparate occasions. Yet both active and passive approval of dance can be found in Roman Catholic countries during the modern era.

Support for ballet and courtly dancing came from at least three sources. First, the Jesuit colleges in Italy, France, and Germany from the sixteenth through the eighteenth centuries included theater as a central part of their curricula. Despite Jansenist opposition, ballet flourished in these liberal arts colleges, which trained the sons of gentlemen. Second, among the extant sixteenth-century dance manuals is one by Jehan Tabourot, the canon at Langres. Written in French in 1588 under the pseudonym Thoinot Arbeau, his manual was translated into English as *Orchesography* (1589); it describes contemporary dances, music, and cultural context. Third, ballet as a courtly art and then a stage art developed and flourished in France, beginning in the seventeenth century, under Catholic monarchs. [*See* Ballet de Collège.]

Other evidence points to examples of spontaneous movement outbursts. According to Backman (1952), scattered "dance epidemics" broke out on the European continent into the nineteenth century. A continuation of the medieval phenomenon, such dancing usually was done by afflicted persons seeking to be healed by the curative power of particular saints. The dancing occurred in front of graves, statues, and relics of the saint. These epidemics, though labeled dance by early chroniclers, actually resulted from periodic and widespread ergot (a fungus on grains) poisoning, according to Backman.

Nineteenth-century American revivals also elicited a behavior described by contemporaries as dancing. For example, Barton W. Stone gives accounts of a camp meeting in Cane Ridge, Kentucky, in 1809, indicating that people overcome by the spirit displayed bodily movements called the "dancing exercise," "falling exercise," and "jerks." How frequently such behavior occurred is not known.

Despite the prohibitions of southern Protestant denominations American slaves retained their sacred dancing, which was characterized by singing, shouting, and possession by the holy spirit. The fiddle and the drum were banned, so the slaves used their bodies to produce a rhythmic accompaniment to their dancing, which W. E. B. Du Bois labeled "frenzy."

A spontaneous, frenzied movement also characterized the dance of the early Shakers; gradually they formalized their movements into set steps and patterns. Dancing symbolized shaking off lust and pride and gave the restrained Shakers a form of physical expression within their strict daily regimen. In marked contrast to traditional churches, Shaker meeting houses were simple and spacious, with a floor sufficiently large to accommodate group dancing. [*See* Shaker Dance.]

Religious dances dating back to the Middle Ages are still performed on certain holy days in various parts of Europe. Backman's account of these traditions states that they mostly flourished in Spain. *El baile de los seizes* began at least by the fifteenth century in the Seville Cathedral; it involved six young choristers who danced annually before the high altar at Corpus Christi, Annunciation Day, and the end of Carnival. Some groups presently perform reconstructions of this dance in American churches during Holy Week. In Luxembourg, the centuries-old Whitsuntide pilgrimage to Echternach also continues. Honoring Saint Willibrod, whose relics reputedly carry healing power, the processional dance occurs in both church sanctuary and yard. Christmas carols and ring dances around the Christmas tree are still performed in Scandinavian countries, and every year Austrian youth gather out-of-doors before sunrise for traditional Easter dancing.

For centuries, processionals have been part of Christian worship and festivals. Worship services opening with processionals and ending with recessionals to and from the chancel area occur regularly in the more liturgical denominations. Weddings, funerals, and special celebrations also occasion processionals in many churches today. Another broad interpretation of the word *dancing* suggests that the ritual of the Mass may itself be viewed as a dance.

Though dancing is not part of its regular worship, the Mormon church is unique for its positive attitude toward dance. Some opposition existed within its ranks, during the nineteenth century, but Mormon officials chose to control rather than ban dancing. Each district traditionally had a dance director; festivals and contests helped teach youth how to dance. Today Brigham Young University in Salt Lake City, founded by Mormons, supports a large dance curriculum and sends performing groups on national and international tours.

By the mid-twentieth century, many American denominations began to experience a renewal of interest in sacred dance. Pioneered by Ruth St. Denis and others in the modern dance movement, liturgical dance is becoming increasingly known and accepted. The pervasiveness of dance today, the changes in moral and social values, as well as in gender roles, and the varieties of contemporary church music and architecture have all combined to produce a climate favorable to dance as a form of religious expression. Yet within that framework, new questions have arisen, for example, should dancing that is intentional and choreographed be permitted in churches or should there be only spontaneous dancing inspired by the holy spirit? This and similar questions point to more basic issues about the place of fine art in the church and about the authority and interpretation of the Bible.

[*See also* Aesthetics, *article on* Western Dance Aesthetics; *and* Liturgical Dance.]

BIBLIOGRAPHY

Adams, Doug, and Diane Apostolos-Cappadona, eds. *Dance as Religious Studies.* New York, 1990.

Andrews, Edward D. *The People Called Shakers.* New York, 1953.

Arbeau, Thoinot. *Orchesography* (1589). Translated by Mary Stewart Evans. New York, 1948. Reprinted with corrections, introduction, and notes by Julia Sutton. New York, 1967.

Backman, Eugène Louis. *Religious Dances in the Christian Church and in Popular Medicine.* Translated by E. Classen. London, 1952.

Boiseul, Jean. *Traité contre les danse.* La Rochelle, 1606.

Clive, H. P. "The Calvinists and the Question of Dancing in the Sixteenth Century." *Bibliothèque d'Humanisme et Renaissance* 23.2 (1961): 296–323.

Daneau, Lambert. *Traité des danses: Auquel est amplement resolue la question, à savoir s'il est permis aux Chrestiens de danser.* Geneva, 1579.

Daniels, Marilyn. *The Dance in Christianity.* New York, 1981.

Elyot, Thomas. *The Book Named The Governor* (1531). Edited by S. E. Lehmberg. New York, 1962.

Emery, Lynne Fauley. *Black Dance from 1619 to Today.* 2d rev. ed. Princeton, 1988.

Hart, Oliver. *Dancing Exploded.* Philadelphia, 1778. Reprinted in *The Patriot Preachers of the American Revolution*, edited by Frank Moore. New York, 1860.

Hill, Sir Richard. *An Address to Persons of Fashion*, 3d. ed. rev. and enl. London, 1761.

Malinowski, Bronislaw. "Native Education and Culture Contact." *International Review of Missions* 25 (1936): 480–515.

Marks, Joseph E., III. *The Mathers on Dancing.* Brooklyn, 1975.

Nordhoff, Charles. *The Communistic Societies of the United States from Personal Visit and Observation.* London, 1875. New York, 1971.

Orfila, Ansley. "Dancing in the Church." *The Evangelist* (October 1987): 53–54.

Perkins, William. *A Discourse of Conscience.* Cambridge, 1608.

Prynne, William. *Histori-Mastix.* London, 1633.

Rock, Judith. "The Jesuits Go for Baroque." In *Proceedings of the Seventh Annual Conference, Society of Dance History Scholars, Goucher College, Towson, Maryland, 17–19 February 1984*, compiled by Christena L. Schlundt. Riverside, Calif., 1984.

Rock, Judith, and Norman Mealy. *Performer as Priest and Prophet.* San Francisco, 1988.

Scholes, Percy. *The Puritans and Music in England and New England.* London, 1934.

Stone, Barton W. *The Biography of Elder Barton Warren Stone.* Cincinnati, 1847. New York, 1972.

Taylor, Margaret Fisk. *A Time to Dance.* Aurora, Ill., 1976.

Vermigli, Pietro. *A Briefe Treatise, Concerning the Use and Abuse of Dauncing.* London, c.1580.

Vives, Juan Luis. *A Very Frutefull and Pleasant Boke Called the Instructiõ of a Christen Womã.* Translated by Richard Hyrde. London, c.1529.

Wagner, Ann. *Adversaries of Dance: From the Puritans to the Present.* Champaign, Ill., 1997.

Walsh, John J. "Ballet on the Jesuit State in Italy, Germany, and France." Ph.D. diss., Yale University, 1954.

Weiser, Francis X. *Handbook of Christian Feasts and Customs.* New York, 1958.

Wesson, Karl. "Dance in the Church of Jesus Christ of Latter-Day Saints, 1830–1940." Master's thesis, Brigham Young University, 1975.

ANN WAGNER

CHRISTOUT, MARIE-FRANÇOISE (born 13 February 1928 in Neuilly-sur-Seine, France), dance critic and historian. Christout holds the degree of Doctor of Letters and a Diploma from the Institute of Art and Archaeology of the Sorbonne, Paris. In 1960 she became a specialist curator in the theater department of the Bibliothèque Nationale there.

Although best known for her extensive research in the area of the formal French ballet of the seventeenth and eighteenth centuries, Christout is also a perceptive writer on contemporary dance and has maintained a special interest in popular forms. Her early concern with the theater of marvels combined these facets, as she noted that each epoch creates its own mode of fantasy theater, which—although the particular configuration changes with time—always reflects an evasion of contemporary constraints, a revolt against the ordinary. For her, the genre represents a special and fascinating aesthetic category.

A meticulous scholar, Christout combines rigorous historical narrative and argument with vivid description, as in her portrayal of a scene at the Louvre during the reign of Louis XIII in her 1964 article "The Court Ballet in France, 1615–1641." In that scene, students, soldiers, and pickpockets manage to slip secretly into the hall where the new ballet is to be performed.

For Christout, the seventeenth-century *ballet de cour* was characterized by its protean quality, its multiplicity of elements—spoken verse, music, dance, decor, costumes, and machinery—amplified by numerous changes of scene and style as engineered by numerous composers. Yet each work achieved a kind of harmony, attaining a kind of logic (albeit an unrealistic logic) of its own. Product of a collective imagination, the ballet transported the viewer to another world. Christout observed that changes occurred as the seventeenth century drew to a close; dancers became professionals, and the attraction of elaborate floor patterns was replaced by the allure of virtuoso steps. The fantasy of Proteus, she noted somewhat sadly, had given way to the order of Apollo.

Christout found a similar protean quality in the work of a later choreographer, Maurice Béjart, whose ballets also combined multiple elements of movement and spectacle. In Béjart she also found a deeper meaning, however, a sense of fundamental values and a search for truth underlying the profusion of images.

Christout has served as a contributing editor to numerous professional journals, including *Dance Chronicle* and *Dance Magazine* in America; *Dance and Dancers, Dance Research,* and *Theatre Research* in England; and *Les saisons de la danse* in France.

Christout has published catalogs for a number of exhibitions and has contributed to many encyclopedias; she supervised the entries on dance in France for the *Enciclopedia dello spettacolo.* A member of several learned societies, she has frequently presented papers at international conferences.

BIBLIOGRAPHY

Christout, Marie-Françoise. "How to Succeed in Ballet: The Court Ballet in France, 1615–1641." *Dance Perspectives,* no. 20 (1964).

Christout, Marie-Françoise. *Le merveilleux et le théâtre du silence.* Paris, 1965.

Christout, Marie-Françoise. *Histoire du ballet.* 2d ed. Paris, 1966.

Christout, Marie-Françoise. *Le ballet de cour de Louis XIV, 1643–1672.* Paris, 1967.

Christout, Marie-Françoise. *Iconographie du ballet de cour à paraître Genêve.* Geneva, 1986.

Christout, Marie-Françoise. *Le ballet de cour au XVIIe siècle.* Geneva, 1987.

Christout, Marie-Françoise. *Maurice Béjart.* Paris, 1987.

Christout, Marie-Françoise. "L'influence vénitienne exercée par les artistes italiens sur les premiers spectacles à machines montés à la cour de France durant la régence (1645–1650)." *Venezia e il melodramma nel Seicento.* Florence, 1994.

Christout, Marie-Françoise. "Ballet: Incarnation of Allegory." *Dance Chronicle* 18, no. 3 (1995).

SELMA JEANNE COHEN

CHUMA. The choreographer in her work *Human Voice*, at Saint Mark's Church in The Bowery, New York. (Photograph © 1988 by Beatriz Schiller; used by permission.)

CHUMA, YOSHIKO (born 25 December 1950 in Osaka), Japanese dancer, choreographer, and performance artist. One of the forerunners of New York City's downtown dance movement of the 1980s, Chuma was born in postwar Osaka. From age eight to thirteen she was one of ten children selected to participate in an education experiment. The group, led by a young, enthusiastic teacher, took part in all aspects of creating dramatic works—directing, acting, scripting, and performing—with the aim of encouraging self-esteem, creative problem-solving and individual thinking. Chuma learned to be bold, to improvise, and to persevere.

In the 1960s Chuma participated in the peace movement in Japan and was active in avant-garde theatrical demonstrations. These two early experiences formed the foundation for Chuma's daring approach to performance and choreography. When she moved to New York in 1977, she was armed only with her curious mind and a bold sense of experimentation. She soon became instrumental in the development of postmodern "downtown" dance theater. By the mid-1980s, she was receiving grants and had a full-time dance company, and her community-based performances had made an international impact.

In 1980, at the invitation of the Venice Biennale, Chuma collaborated on a performance work with filmmaker Jacob Burckhardt and composer-musician Alvin Curran, titled *The School of Hard Knocks.* Later she adopted the title as her company's name. Since 1982, The School of Hard Knocks has grown into a collective of performing artists including dancers, musicians, visual artists, media artists, theater technicians, and designers. In the course of the company's history, more than one thousand people have performed under Chuma's direction in works ranging from theatrical dance concerts and street performances to large-scale performance art spectacles.

Known widely as a community activist, Chuma became aware of the declining funding in the arts in the 1990s and began to curate an intimate monthly series called *Brand New Dance* for the fifty-seat alternative space Dixon Place in New York City. The series offered mature choreographers a forum to develop new work in a low-budget, noncompetitive atmosphere.

Chuma's work has been characterized as "rapscallion vaudeville," by critic Marcia Siegel because of its seemingly wild, "unleashed" appearance. What appears as chaos, however, is actually a well-conceived structure in which Chuma associates numbers and letters with choreographed gestures. The choreography, created in collaboration with all the individual players, is mathematically structured by Chuma, using her delightful sense of timing, rhythm, and surprise.

Major company works created by Chuma include *Three Stories* (1995), *Crash Orchestra* (1995), *A Night at the Millionaire's Club* (1984, 1994), *Jo Ha Kyu* (1992, 1993, 1994), *DUO* (1992), *Suspicious Counterpoint* (1990), *The Man Who Never Wasn't* (1989–1990), *Da Costakada da da, A Letter to Van Gogh* (1989), *Pennsylvania Kaffeeklatsch* (1988), *You-You O Solo Mio* (1988), *The Big Picture* (1987), *Five Car Pile-Up* (1983), and *Pikkadon* (1982).

Chuma has been commissioned by other dance companies to create performance spectacles and proscenium works. Spectacles often integrate noted artists with nonprofessionals drawn from the local communities. *Here Here There There,* created with Danny Yung and Zuni Icosahedron, was a mile-long parade of forty performers around Hong Kong harbor for the 1994 Hong Kong International Arts Festival. For the opening for the 1992 Annual Greenwich Village Halloween Parade in New York City, Chuma mixed sixty students and professionals; in *Five Car Pile-Up,* a work she toured throughout Europe and the United States, she used one hundred community members and a core of ten dancers.

Among her many proscenium works, two in active company repertories are *Crash into Zero,* choreographed for the Dutch Reflex Dance Company, which premiered in Groningen in 1993; and *8, Letters from Eight* a work made for Belgium's Charleroi/Danses Company in 1993. With the idea of continuing long-time artistic relationships, Chuma often brings her company collaborators to these commission sites: costume designer Gabriel Berry, lighting designer Pat Dignan, and composers Jacob Burckhardt, Mark Bennett, and Robert Een have collaborated closely on most of her 1990s works.

Chuma has received many awards and honors, including The New York Dance and Performance Award ("Bessie"), and fellowships from the Guggenheim Foundation (1985), several from the National Endowment for the Arts, and two from the New York Foundation for Artists (1985 and 1995). In 1995–1996 Chuma was honored with a fellowship from the Japan Foundation to return to Japan as a professional artist for the first time after eighteen years abroad.

BIBLIOGRAPHY
Aloff, Mindy. "Yoshiko Chuma." *Dance Magazine* (June 1985): 74–75.
Fleming, Donald. "Yoshiko Chuma and the School of Hard Knocks." *Drama Review* 29 (Summer 1985): 53–64.
Svane, Christina. "The Pro Series." *Contact Quarterly* 18 (Summer–Fall 1993): 15–20.
Tobias, Anne. "Different Drummers." *Dance View* 12 (Summer 1995): 26–29.
Zimmer, Elizabeth. "Out of Left Field." *Dance Magazine* (October 1988): 64–65.

BONNIE SUE STEIN

CICERI, PIERRE (Pierre-Luc-Charles Ciceri; born 17 or 18 August 1782 in Saint-Cloud, Paris, died 22 August 1868 in Saint-Chéron, France), French scenery designer. Much of Pierre Ciceri's success as a stage designer lay in his ability to move with his times. He began his career in the transitional period when romanticism was just starting to establish itself, first at the boulevard theaters, then at the more conservative Paris Opera. He was both able to satisfy the needs of the new movement and to make his own contribution to it. He kept abreast of new technological developments and devised ways to apply them in the theater. His influence extended beyond his lifetime, for his workshop trained the next generation of French stage designers.

He originally planned a musical career, but injuries received in a carriage accident forced him to turn to painting. During his early years he worked as a scene painter, specializing in landscapes at the Paris Opera, and was also employed by the Comédie Française and the Théâtre de la Porte-Saint-Martin, one of the most progressive and influential boulevard theaters. In 1816 he was promoted to chief designer at the Paris Opera, a position that he shared with Louis-Jacques-Mandé Daguerre, inventor of the diorama and the daguerreotype, from 1820 to 1822. He and Daguerre introduced gas lighting to the Paris Opera's stage in their designs for Nicolò Isouard's opera *Aladin, ou La Lampe Merveilleuse* (1822).

Although the Opera's scenic department was reorganized in 1822 so that the designers became independent contractors, Ciceri and his workshop continued to receive many important commissions. Henri Duponchel, leader of the committee set up in 1827 to supervise the department, encouraged his innovations. At Duponchel's instigation, Ciceri went to Milan to study theatrical machinery in order to devise the eruption of Vesuvius in *La Muette de Portici* (1828). He mounted a painted canvas on rollers for the moving panorama of *La Belle au Bois Dormant* (1829). In 1829 Duponchel introduced the practice of lowering the curtain between acts, thus allowing Ciceri to create more complex sets, which became increasingly naturalistic, for example, in 1841 real reeds were used to border the lake in the second act of *Giselle*.

The precedent-setting ghostly cloister scene of Giacomo Meyerbeer's opera *Robert le Diable* (1831), conceived by Duponchel but carried out by Ciceri, achieved its effects partly through evocative painting and partly through the use of recent inventions such as gas lighting and the *trappe anglaise*, which sprang shut to conceal the actors' means of entry. Ciceri's forest scene for the ballet *La Sylphide* (1832) exploited a similar atmosphere of shadowy mystery as well as equally ingenious machinery, used for the flights of the sylphides.

Ciceri also designed a wide range of historical and geographical settings for the numerous ballets of local color. Between 1815 and his retirement in 1848 he worked on many of the most important ballets of the time, among them *Clari* (1820), *Alfred le Grand* (1822), *Aline* (1823), *Zémire et Azor* (1824), *La Somnambule* (1827), *La Belle au Bois Dormant* (1829), *Manon Lescaut* (1830), *La Sylphide* (1832), *Nathalie* (1832), *La Tempête* (1834), *La Fille du Danube* (1836), *Giselle* (1841), *La Jolie Fille de Gand* (1842), and *Le Diable à Quatre* (1845).

[*See also* Scenic Design.]

BIBLIOGRAPHY

Allevy, Marie-Antoinette. *La mise en scène en France dans la première moitié du dix-neuvième siècle.* Paris, 1938.

Daniels, Barry V. "Cicéri and Daguerre: Set Designers for the Paris Opera, 1820–1822." *Theatre Survey* 22 (May 1981): 69–90.

Guest, Ivor. "Stage Designers: VI. Pierre Ciceri." *Ballet and Opera* (July 1949).

Guest, Ivor. *The Romantic Ballet in Paris.* 2d rev. ed. London, 1980.

Join-Diéterle, Catherine. *Les décors de scène de l'Opéra de Paris à l'époque romantique.* Paris, 1988.

Wild, Nicole. *Décors et costumes du XIXe siècle*, vol. 1, *Opéra de Paris.* Paris, 1987.

ARCHIVE. Walter Toscanini Collection of Research Materials in Dance, New York Public Library for the Performing Arts.

SUSAN AU

CIEPLINSKI, JAN (Jan Ciepliński; born 10 May 1900 in Warsaw, died 17 April 1972 in New York), Polish dancer, choreographer, teacher, and writer. Cieplinski was one of the generation of Polish dancers who came of age during World War I and contributed to the later development of dance both in Poland and abroad. A graduate of the ballet school affiliated with Warsaw's Wielki Theater, Cieplinski performed there from 1917 until 1921. He then joined Anna Pavlova's company for a season before directing his own company from 1922 to 1925. For the next two years he performed with Serge Diaghilev's Ballets Russes; he then worked as a choreographer and ballet director in Stockholm (1927–1931) and Budapest (1931–1934).

Cieplinski continued his wandering: in the mid-1930s he worked in Buenos Aires, Budapest, and Warsaw. In 1938/39 he choreographed for the Polish Ballet. During World War II he worked first in Warsaw, where his choreography for the official music theater was condemned by the underground government, and then in Budapest. From 1948 to 1959 he lived in London and worked with the Anglo-Polish Ballet, Legat Ballet, Mercury Theatre, and many Polish amateur groups. From 1959 until his death in 1972 he lived in New York, where he choreographed only occasionally, working mostly as a teacher, lecturer, and writer. His *Outline of Polish Ballet History* was published in 1956.

Brought up with very traditional schooling and company work, Cieplinski rebelled against the classical style of ballet. His choreographic creations were therefore his own, even in versions of such well-known ballets as *Coppélia*. In pursuit of novelty, he used a rich but difficult to contain imagination. In his works, extremely interesting pieces alternated with strange or even plain motifs. He knew and appreciated Polish national culture and folk dances, creating some very interesting stage versions. He introduced to ballet a Silesian folk dance, *trojak*, with enormous success.

He choreographed only to the best music of the past and present. Thus he introduced to the Polish ballet repertory Beethoven's *The Creatures of Prometheus* (*Prometeusz*, 1922), as well as some newly composed pieces by Karol Szymanowski. He particularly favored Polish composers from the past but was lauded for his version of Szymanowski's *The Highlanders*, created for the Polish Ballet in 1938.

BIBLIOGRAPHY

Dąbrowski, Stanisław, and Zbigniew Raszewski, eds. *Słownik biograficzny teatru polskiego.* 2 vols. Warsaw, 1973–1994.

Dienes, Gedeon P. "History of the State Opera Ballet, Budapest: Part 6." *Hungarian Dance News*, no. 1–2 (1981): 5–6.

Körtvélyes, Géza, and György Lőrinc. *The Budapest Ballet: The Ballet Ensemble of the Hungarian State Opera House.* Vol. 1. Translated by Gedeon P. Dienes and Éva Rácz. Budapest, 1971.

Mamontowicz-Łojek, Bożena. *Terpsychora i lekkie muzy.* Kraków, 1972.

JANINA PUDEŁEK

CINDERELLA. Charles Perrault's classic popularization of the ancient fairy tale has been treated choreographically by many ballet masters since 1815, when the first known version was performed in Saint Petersburg. François Decombe, known as Monsieur Albert, created his *Cendrillon* in 1822 and restaged it at the Paris Opera in the following year. Charles-Louis Didelot's version was premiered in Paris on 9 June 1824. As *Aschenbrödel, Cinderella* received its Viennese debut on 4 October 1908 at the Hofoperntheater. It was the only ballet composed by Johann Strauss the younger. The choreography was by Josef Hassreiter after Emil Graeb, and the scenery was by Heinrich Lefler. The title role was danced by Marie Kohler; her consort, by Karl Godlewski. Frederick Ashton's version, premiered by the Sadler's Wells Ballet at the Royal Opera House of Covent Garden on 23 December 1948, was the first full-evening English ballet to be composed in the wake of nineteenth-century models.

There has been considerable variation in imaginative scope and details. The Viennese incarnation portrayed Cinderella as a young apprentice named Grete and the Prince as Gustav, a department store magnate. The production's nearly floor-length costumes ruled out technical virtuosity; the story's origins as a fairy tale also were routed. In contrast, Paul Meija's fanciful version, colored by an infusion of creatures from nature (for example, ladybugs and mushrooms) danced by children, was premiered by the Chicago City Ballet at the Auditorium Theater on 25 November 1981 and provided Suzanne Farrell with one of her few full-length narrative vehicles.

The story of Cinderella has spoken throughout the ages to the need for personal and social fulfillment. A virtuous young woman, mistreated by her family, is presented with the opportunity by her Fairy Godmother to attend the Prince's ball, providing that she depart by midnight. During the course of the evening the Prince falls in love with her, but she disappears before he can learn her name. He then travels the globe in search of his mysterious love, carrying one of her glass slippers, which she accidentally left behind. Eventually Cinderella and the Prince are reunited and her family is forgiven.

Cinderella entered the repertory of the Royal Danish Ballet on 25 September 1910. Emilie Walbom choreographed the work to a score by Otto Malling. (No scenery or costumes were credited. It is likely that the scenic elements were borrowed from other productions.) Ellen Price and Hans Beck assumed the principal roles, while the famous Danish composer Carl Nielsen conducted.

Andrée Howard choreographed and designed a version of the ballet to the music of Carl Maria von Weber (*Rondo Brillant*, parts of *Konzerstück*, and various overtures) for the Ballet Rambert. It was presented at the Mercury Theatre in London on 6 January 1935, with Pearl Argyle in the title role; Frederick Ashton performed the role of the Prince. Ballet Rambert also appeared in the pantomime *The Glass Slipper*, a three-act, eleven-scene version of the Cinderella tale by Herbert and Eleanor Farjeon. Howard

CINDERELLA. Svetlana Beriosova as Cinderella in act 1 of Ashton's ballet. Beriosova first performed this role in 1958. (Photograph from the Dance Collection, New York Public Library for the Performing Arts.)

choreographed this production as well, with music by Clifton Parker and designs by Hugh Stevenson. It was presented at the Saint James Theatre, London, during Christmas 1944. The cast included Sally Gilmour, Joyce Grame, Walter Gore, and Lulu Dukes.

As *Zolushka, Cinderella* was premiered at the Bolshoi Theater in Moscow on 21 November 1945. The choreography was by Rostislav Zakharov, the music by Sergei Prokofiev. Olga Lepeshinskaya portrayed the heroine, and Mikhail Gabovich was the lovestruck Prince. The decor was by Petr Williams. Prokofiev had started work on the ballet in the winter of 1940, when it was intended for the Kirov Ballet in Leningrad. His plans were interrupted, however, by the outbreak of World War II, and he did not complete the ballet until the spring of 1944. Prokofiev's version follows in the classical tradition, containing pas de deux, adagios, a gavotte, a mazurka, and waltzes. Each main character dances an individual variation. The composer drew on simple yet vivid means to suggest Cinderella's inner life. Prokofiev was pleased with the Bolshoi production, though he objected to changes made in the orchestration and disliked the extravagant decor. The Kirov production, which premiered on 8 April 1946, was more in line with his original conception. It marked the choreographic debut of Konstantin Sergeyev, who also danced the Prince to Natalia Dudinskaya's Cinderella. The decor was by Boris Erdman. The ballet's music won Prokofiev the State Prize of the USSR.

Among the most remarkable versions was that of Ashton, who cast Moira Shearer (followed by Margot Fonteyn) and Michael Somes as the leads with Ashton and Robert Helpmann as the Ugly Stepsisters. In *The Dancing Times*, Mary Clarke praised Fonteyn's characterization, noting that "she was not afraid to look a drab and frightened waif . . . [which] lent her transformation an added radiance." This production, seen in New York City during the Sadler's Wells Ballet's first visit to the United States in 1949, greatly influenced American versions of the ballet.

Ben Stevenson's *Cinderella*, first performed by the National Ballet of Washington at the Lisner Auditorium in Washington, D.C., on 24 April 1970, was one of the most distinguished descendants of Ashton's version. Choreography was by Stevenson, scenery was by Edward Haynes, costumes were by Norman McDowell, and the principal performers were Gaye Fulton and Desmond Kelly. Like Ashton, Stevenson had the stepsisters played *en travesti*, providing a brilliant role for Frederic Franklin in the original production. Omitting the stepmother, Stevenson employed two main leitmotifs: traveling lifts to emphasize the fantastic, fairy-tale element and quick, unexpected changes in direction.

Cinderella has been staged by many choreographers in Russian cities. Additional versions have been performed in Czechoslovakia, Poland, Yugoslavia, Germany, Japan, and elsewhere. Most productions have delighted in maintaining an air of childlike naiveté, but in 1987 Rudolf Nureyev broke with that tradition and staged a version for the Paris Opera that took place in a Hollywood studio, with the heroine the stepdaughter of a deranged stage mother.

BIBLIOGRAPHY

Goodwin, Noël. "Cinderelliana." *Dance and Dancers* (November 1979): 18–19.
Maynard, Olga. "The Ballet of Cinderella." In Maynard's *The Ballet Companion*. Philadelphia, 1957.
Milnes, Rodney. "Prokofiev's Ballet Scores." *Dance Gazette* (October 1984): 18–20.
Reynolds, Nancy, and Susan Reimer-Torn. *Dance Classics*. Pennington, N.J., 1991.
Slonimsky, Yuri. *Sovetskii balet*. Moscow, 1950.
Williams, Peter. "A Northern Cinderella: Cinders for All Seasons." *Dance and Dancers* (January 1980).

MOLLY McQUADE
Based on materials submitted by Reba Ann Adler,
Natalia Levkoyeva, and Ruth Sander

CINEMA. *See* Film Musicals.

CIRCUS. The mime Marcel Marceau once observed that "the circus and choreography, expressions of the same art, turn up their noses at one another today, after having been in the eighteenth century one and the same spectacle" (preface to Winter, 1962). This is a deliberate exaggeration, but dance did start to loom large in the circus when buildings meant to showcase equestrian shows also began to house miscellaneous entertainments, including dance. The commixture of popular balletic figures with fairground attractions became commonplace: all circus folk learned to dance at the age of four or five, and clans such as the Chiarinis with their "Mimo-Choréographique" troupe and the Zanfrettas worked with equal facility in ballets and circuses. On the eve of the French Revolution, Jean-Baptiste Nicolet's company of acrobats and equilibrists bore the distinction Les Grands Danseurs du Roi.

In 1788 Astley's Amphitheatre in London hosted a pas de trois, the "New Comic Dance called the 'Ethiopian Festival' . . . representing the whimsical actions and attitudes made use of by the Negroes," one of the earliest analogues to blackface minstrelsy. Five years later a "Fricasee Dance" executed by clowns was seen at London's Royal Circus. In 1792, when Alexandre Placide imported his English circus pantomimes to the John Street Theatre in New York City, he danced a *menuet de la cour* and a gavotte with his wife, a skilled hornpipe artist. Later, at Pepin's Circus in 1819, the city witnessed a ballet of ten dancers on stilts in the costumes of La Lande. The introduction of a precision dancing corps came in 1811, when the ballet master Renauzy drilled an army of Cupid soldiers at the Cirque Olympique, Paris, to celebrate the birth of the king of Rome.

Rope dancing, as the name implies, meant tripping the light fantastic on a rope elevated above the heads of the crowd: the performer might sketch a few elementary *pas* or dance a hornpipe on his head. The genre was tremendously popular in the late eighteenth century: the Comte d'Artois took rope dancing lessons from the great Forioso. The most renowned of these artistes was Madame Saqui (Marguerite Lalanne, 1777–1866), who, with her rival La Malaga, had learned to execute *ronds de jambe* and *pas croisés* on the high rope. Saqui's most famous feat was to dance on a cable stretched between the towers of Notre Dame cathedral in Paris. Another of her competitors, Mademoiselle Rose, a brilliant *danseuse*, was celebrated for a sword dance that won her the nickname "la belle Tourneuse": she could pirouette for more than twenty minutes with the points of ten blades set against her nostrils and bosom. She was the first rope dancer to wear gauze sylphide's wings, a practice later adopted by equestriennes. Balletic rope dancing was brought to the United States by Marietta Zanfretta, and a whole dynasty of such performers was founded in Germany by Jean Weitzmann; by the 1870s, however, dancing had been eclipsed by acrobatic stunts and feats of strength and agility performed on the rope. In the early twentieth century the dashing Con Colleano revived the art by dancing, in torero costume, tangos, *jotas*, and *fandangos* atop a cable seven millimeters in diameter. His number has been described by a circus historian as

> an obsolete and charming art, as simple and graceful as a Tanagra vase of chaste outline which has come down tens of centuries to reach us in its integral purity. (Thétard, 1947)

Bird Millman (Jennadean Engelmann, 1895–1940), who was known as "the Genée of the Air," perfected a dance on pointe that moved Florenz Ziegfeld to erect a tightrope for her in one of his revues.

Philip Astley (1742–1814) gained prominence as an equine choreographer: horses trained to dance were exhibited at his London amphitheater as early as 1782, and the circus he established in the Faubourg du Temple, Paris, featured a "Minuet d'Exaudet" of quadrupeds, directed by Antoine Franconi. In 1808 Astley's horses went through a cotillon and a country dance, and quadrilles were soon added, but by 1830 the dancing horse had been superseded by the dancer on horseback.

Minette Franconi (1805–1835), billed as "La Fille de l'Air," danced on top of a horse, reportedly with much grace, thus swelling the receipts of Cirque Olympique. Hornpipes on horseback were performed in Salem, Massachusetts, in 1808. It is significant that the greatest equestrian of the age, Andrew Ducrow (1793–1842), studied as a child with James Harvey D'Egville, ballet master of the King's Theatre Opera House, and that he was cited for his dancing talent by the time he was eight. Both Ducrow's *poses plastiques* on horseback, such as *Le Bouquet de l'Amour, ou Les Jeux de Zéphyre et de Cupidon* (c.1820), and his pyrrhic dance reflected analogous passages in the *ballets d'action* staged by his master. Ducrow's best partner, Louisa Woolford (1814–1900), known as "The Sylph of the Circle" and "The Taglioni of Horse-

CIRCUS. A *contredanse* performed on four slack ropes as depicted in *Observations sur les modes et les usages de Paris*, 1827. (Metropolitan Museum of Art, New York; Harris Brisbane Dick Fund, 1938. [no. 38.38.5]; used by permission.)

women," had begun with stilt dances before transferring her Terpsichorean graces to a horse's back. In Paris, at the Cirque Olympique, Madame F. Dumos danced a *pas de shawls* under Ducrow's tutelage in 1839.

What the French called an *écuyère à panneau* came to be known in England as a ballerina, an equestrienne in tutu dancing bareback or, occasionally, on a large flat saddle, made fashionable by James Morton in 1849. The standard routine was to leap through paper hoops (called *ballons*), vault over taut ribbons (a stunt invented by Laurent and Henri Franconi for Laurent's wife), and blow kisses to the crowd. While horse and rider caught their breath, the clown would chatter with the ringmaster; at the crack of the whip, the ballerina, ankles joined, would remount her steed in a bound as it galloped apace, venture a few more *entrechats*, and ride out of the ring. The most celebrated of these ballerinas were Louise and Adelheid Tourniaire, Minna Hinné, the lyrical Virginie Kenebel ("*prima ballerina di gracia*"), Ellen Kremzov, and Coralie Ducos. A popular pas de deux, obviously borrowed from the Romantic ballet, was *L'Ecossais et la Sylphide*, performed on two horses.

The balletic ride was effaced by the acrobatic ride, which was used to begin the first half of the show; its performer became known as an *écuyère à voltige* or Lady Principal Act. Often carried out by teams, such as Mitty and Tillio, Rachel and Zoiga, or the Kitchen Pirates, these turns merely suggested a few dance steps before showing off the performers' acrobatic prowess. The Mona-Tymga troupe consisted of three bareback carriers who tossed a supple female tumbler back and forth between them like a ball. Helen Gontard introduced the serpentine dance on horseback, but the decline of the ballerinas was illustrated by clown parodies, such as those of Footit and Achille Zavatta. By the twentieth century, according to Thétard (1947), "mighty few" riders fooled "with dancing masters."

European circuses of the late nineteenth century, expanding in size, tried to appeal to mass audiences by introducing the properties of pantomime and extravaganza: crowd scenes, sumptuous costumes, complicated technical effects, and exotics, such as Adráá in her Greco-Roman sacrificial dance. The great Russian circuses all boasted their own ballet troupes and ballet masters: Foma Nijinsky at Krutikov's, Yuri Oposnansky and D. Martini at Nikitin's, V. Reizinger at Ciniselli's, and P. Prozerpi at Truzzi's. Their creations ranged from simple gladiatorial combats or Spanish dances to full-scale ballets, such as Reizinger's *David's Victory over Goliath* (1905–1906), employing one hundred children, or the "Carnival on Ice." The Soviets continued these traditions, often imbuing them with satirical or theatrical themes that bore little relation to the circus format, the exceptions being William Truzzi's works of the 1920s and 1930s, among them *Texas Cowboy, Thousand and One Nights,* and *The Black Pirate.* Lavish ballets-pantomimes also were mounted in Paris in the 1930s to excite a flagging public: the Cirque d'Hiver staged *Les Fratellini Détectives* and *Les Fratellini en Afrique* (1933–1934) with a mélange of dancers and swimmers, and the Cirque Napoléon followed suit by mingling ballerinas and stags in *Blanche-Neige* (1935). As late as 1963 an equestrian ballet, *The Fountain of Bakhchisarai,* was put on in Moscow.

Dance dwindled in importance in the American circus with its competing three rings and emphasis on immediate sensation. Massed chorines continue to be used for the grand entries and the finales, however, and choreographers are still employed by the larger concerns. George Balanchine devised an elephant ballet to Igor Stravinsky's *Circus Polka* for Ringling Brothers, Barnum & Bailey in 1942. The brother and sister team of Richard and Edith Barstow, who became Ringling's official dancing masters in 1948, made the discovery that elephants could simulate *glissades* and giraffes *bourrées*, and the siblings built on that find. The diminution of dance's importance is seen most clearly, however, in the aerial ballets.

These combinations of acrobatics and ballet confected by Professor Risley (Richard Carlisle, c.1814–1874) and his adopted sons had been widely influential in Europe in the mid-nineteenth century. Théophile Gautier had cited them in 1844 as an inspiration to dancers for a new type of fantastic ballet that could use the springboard and acrobatic tricks. By the late twentieth century the aerial ballet had become a fill-in that used any available staff member: in a number such as "The Spanish Web," scantily clad girls (or boys in wigs and tutus) clamber up canvas-covered ropes to a point twenty-three feet above ground where they pose, do simple acrobatics, revolve or hang by their teeth, all in unison. When they wave silk scarves in "kaleidoscopic gyrations," the Spiders are dubbed "Butterflies." These acts are popular with the management because they require minimal training and rehearsal and yet make a vivid impression on naive audiences. The pirouettes, pas de deux, and other balletic standbys once native to the ring are more likely to be found at the Aquacades and the Ice Follies.

BIBLIOGRAPHY

Adrian. *Le cirque commence à cheval.* 2d ed. Paris, 1979.
Cornell, Joseph. "Clowns, Elephants, and Ballerinas." *Dance Index* (June 1946): 136–156.
Goleizovsky, Kasyan. "Tsirk v moei zhizni." *Sovetskaiia estrada i tsirk* 1 (1964).
Lijsen, H. J. *Mounted Quadrilles, Carousels, and Other Equestrian Manoeuvres.* London, 1957.
Saxon, A. H. *The Life and Art of Andrew Ducrow.* Hamden, Conn., 1978.
Shneer, A. I., and R. E. Slavskii, eds. *Tsirk: Malenkaia entsiklopediia.* 2d ed. Moscow, 1979.
Stahl, Norma G. "The Circus Dances." *Dance Magazine* (April 1954): 29–31.

Strohl, D. "La danse à cheval: L'ecuyère de panneau." *La danse* (June 1922): 3–4.

Thétard, Henry. *La merveilleuse histoire de cirque.* Paris, 1947.

Winter, Marian Hannah. "Theatre of Marvels." *Dance Index* (January–February 1948): 3–39.

Winter, Marian Hannah. *Le théâtre du merveilleux.* Paris, 1962.

LAURENCE SENELICK

CLERICO, FRANCESCO (born c.1755, died after 1838), Italian ballet dancer, choreographer, and composer. Clerico was a prolific choreographer and a frequent composer of music for his ballets. Early in his career he was influenced by the theories of Jean-Georges Noverre, having appeared in Noverre's ballet *Giasone e Medea*, produced by Charles Lepicq, in 1773 in Milan. His first known choreographic work, in which he also danced, was *Diana e Endimione*, mounted in 1776 at the Teatro Sant'Agostino in Genoa. From the beginning, Clerico's work fully adhered to the principles of neoclassicism, and he remained substantially faithful to them until the end of his career.

Clerico composed his most widely reproduced ballets from 1776 to 1800: *Zemira e Azor* (Teatro San Samuele, Venice, 1783); *Il Ritorno di Agamenone* (Teatro San Benedetto, Venice, 1789); *Ercole e Dejanira* (Teatro Nuovo, Padua, 1789); *La Conquista del Vello d'Oro* (Teatro alla Scala, Milan, 1792); *Il Fantasma in Sogno, o Il Finto Oracolo* (Teatro La Pergola, Florence, 1796); and *Cleopatra* (La Scala, 1801, but previously presented in 1800 at the Vienna Hofoper under the title *Cleopatra's Tod*). Clerico excelled in tragic ballets in which, according to Carlo Ritorni (1838), he used "mute action as the only vehicle of communication." Ritorni also believed that Clerico knew better than his contemporaries how to "infuse the spirit of sublime, silent poetry into the great design of heroic action." Of Clerico's style and poetry, Ritorni wrote,

His programs were composed with poetic reason and expanded with tragic import beyond the limits of any previously composed, but the principal means with which he emulated the effects of classic tragedy were in essence himself and some of his relatives, the great mime actors, and the ability to compose such scenes, which they were able to perform with true poetic expression and action, not hitherto achieved.

(Ritorni, 1838)

In many productions Clerico was assisted by his sister Rosa (later the wife of choreographer Lorenzo Panzier) and by his brother Gaetano, both of whom possessed great interpretive gifts. Clerico was not skilled, however, in handling a corps de ballet. Regarding ensemble movement, Ritorni observed less development in the works of Clerico than in those of his contemporary Salvatore Viganò, where "everybody has to assume different figures, with the most elaborate but disguised picturesque group work" (Ritorni, 1838).

Clerico produced his ballets in many Italian cities, including Turin, Parma, Trieste, Naples, and Rome. He also worked from 1798 to 1800 in Vienna, where he staged several of his earlier productions. In spite of his fame and the success also of his comic ballets, such as *Il Convalescente Innamorato* (San Samuele, Venice, 1784) and *Il Tamburo Notturno* (La Pergola, Florence, 1793), in the later part of his career the unavoidable competition with the new generation of choreographers and the change in taste by the audience moved him to search for new solutions, not always with successful results.

A study by Giovanna Trentin (1987) of the libretti of Clerico's ballets produced in Venice before 1802 reveals that in most of them the effective rendering of the characters is made possible by simple recurrent structures consisting of a limited number of significant episodes. For the ballets produced in Venice after 1822, on the other hand, Trentin points out a less favorable reception, due to an overgrowth in the number of characters and in the complexity of the action paralleled by the drying up of the poetic vein.

Notwithstanding this, the collation of the chronologies of the major Italian theatres reveals a steady presence of Clerico's productions up to 1830 (Celi, 1995). Among his later ballets were *La Morte di Ettore* (La Scala, 1821), *Adelaide di Guesclino* (La Fenice, 1822), *Matilde e Malekadel* (La Scala, 1824), all with music by Agostino Belloli, and *Il Bardo della Scandinavia* (La Scala, 1830).

BIBLIOGRAPHY

Celi, Claudia. "Il balletto in Italia." In *Musica in scena: Storia dello spettacolo musciale*, edited by Alberto Basso, vol. 5, pp. 89–138. Turin, 1995.

Hansell, Kathleen Kuzmick. *Il ballo teatrale e l'opera italiana.* In *Storia dell'opera italiana*, vol. 5, pp. 175–306. Turin, 1987.

Ritorni, Carlo. *Commentarii della vita e delle opere coreodrammatiche di Salvatore Viganò e della coreografia e de' corepei.* Milan, 1838.

Tozzi, Lorenzo. "Clerico, Francesco." In *Dizionario biografico degli italiani.* Rome, 1960–.

Trentin, Giovanna. "Francesco Clerico, il poeta del ballo pantomimo." *La danza italiana* 5–6 (Autumn 1987): 121–149.

Winter, Marian Hannah. *The Pre-Romantic Ballet.* London, 1974.

ARCHIVE. Walter Toscanini Collection of Research Material in Dance, New York Public Library for the Performing Arts.

CLAUDIA CELI
Translated from Italian

CLEVELAND–SAN JOSE BALLET. In 1976, two dancers from American Ballet Theatre returned to their midwestern roots and founded the Cleveland Ballet. They were Ian Horvath, a Cleveland native, and Dennis Nahat, who grew up in Detroit. Although the company had its first official season in 1976, the school had been established in 1972 with Charles Nicoll as director. A nonprofessional company of better-than-average quality called

Ballet Guild of Cleveland had previously existed under the direction of Alex Martin. His board of directors aligned itself with the new organization.

The Cleveland Ballet identified itself as "classically based, contemporary in style, eclectic in nature." Unlike most young companies, it had immediate access to substantial support. Provided with an initial grant in 1974 by the Cleveland Foundation, the second largest community-based funding entity in the United States, the company was fully launched with Horvath as artistic director, Nahat as resident choreographer, and Nicoll as ballet master. It had twenty-four dancers and a budget of $124,000.

From the outset, the Cleveland Ballet enjoyed solid community support. The city had a well-established tradition of arts involvement. Its art museum, orchestra, and playhouse were nationally respected. A ballet company was virtually inevitable. Horvath and Nahat were in the right place at the right time. In addition, both were charismatic performers, and in the early days they danced with the company. Thus they became readily identifiable by the funding community. Only ten years later, the budget had reached $4.5 million. But a major change took place. Horvath left the company to become a freelance choreographer. Nahat became artistic director.

From the beginning, the major portion of the Cleveland Ballet repertory was created by Nahat, whose choreographic career had been launched at American Ballet Theatre. His musical taste was on the whole traditional, with composers such as Brahms, Mozart, Shostakovich, Stravinsky, and Tchaikovsky figuring among his choices. For his most ambitious production, the evening-long *Celebrations and Ode*, Nahat selected Beethoven's Seventh Symphony and the final movement of his Ninth Symphony. The ballet elicited highly conflicting critical reactions because some felt that the structural density of Beethoven's music rendered it unsuitable for choreographic interpretation. Nevertheless, it was a challenge to both dancers and audience.

Aware of the conservative element among its subscribers, the Cleveland Ballet quickly developed a solid repertory of full-length dramatic ballets staged by Nahat. Among them were *The Nutcracker, Romeo and Juliet, Giselle, Coppélia*, and *A Midsummer Night's Dream*. After George Balanchine's death in 1983, many regional companies began ambitiously to acquire his works, but they remain minimal in the Cleveland Ballet repertory. The company also has a limited listing of ballets by guest choreographers.

In 1986 the Cleveland Ballet established a second home in San Jose, California. On the West Coast the company is usually referred to as the Cleveland–San Jose Ballet or the San Jose–Cleveland Ballet.

By 1992, the company's budget had climbed to $5.1 million, but it contained a $2.47 million debt. Collapse loomed. Only a courageous grass-roots effort on the part of dancers and board succeeded in pointing the company in the right direction. The following year, Nahat and Robert Barnett, artistic director of the Atlanta Ballet, presented a highly successful *Swan Lake* using both companies, with Nahat's choreography. It was performed in Cleveland, Atlanta, and San Jose.

BIBLIOGRAPHY

Fay, Kenneth. "Cleveland Ballet, the Last Step toward Professional Status." *Dance Magazine* (January 1976): 106.

Hardy, Camille. "Crisis at Midlife: Ian Horvath Hangs Up the Shoes." *Dance Magazine* (August 1985): 48–51.

Hardy, Camille. "On a Roll with Cleveland and San Jose." *Dance Magazine* (October 1986): 56–59.

Salisbury, Wilma. "An Ensemble Grows Up." *Dance Magazine* (May 1978): 75–77.

Salisbury, Wilma. "Cleveland Ballet Is Saved." *Dance Magazine* (May 1992): 22.

Sexton, Jean Deitz. *San Jose/Cleveland Ballet: A Legacy for the Future.* San Francisco, 1993.

Zuck, Barbara A. "Cause for Celebration." *Dance Magazine* (December 1992): 44–50.

DORIS HERING

CLOGGING. [*This entry comprises two articles. The first article provides a historical overview; the second explores clog dancing in Appalachia. For related discussion, see* Step Dancing.]

Historical Overview

The history of clog dancing is sketchy at best, but can be inferred to some extent from folklore and the few written sources available. Determining the heritage of folk dance steps in such styles as clogging is difficult; it is easy to be misled by similarities between dance forms that are not in fact directly related historically. With such forms as clog dance that are widely dispersed, it is important to research the settlement patterns of the communities in which the form is practiced and, in cases where different cultural groups live in the same area, their social habits. It is also important to discover the origin of any traveling performers who passed through a given area, since their dances were often copied.

Percussive dancing in wooden clogs on a hard surface (usually flagstones) has been known in various lowland and coastal parts of England for centuries, and the term *clog dance* is attested from at least the nineteenth century. A clog formerly danced in England that mimed the actions of a clock gave rise to a false etymology deriving *clog dance* from "clock dance." A more plausible derivation attributes the invention of the term to eighteenth- and nineteenth-century English mill workers, who developed a form of challenge dance in which they pounded out elaborate rhythms on floors and cobblestone streets with their wooden-soled shoes. When this exciting percussive noise was added to the complex footwork already existing in such step dances as the jig, hornpipe, and reel, and in Morris dances, a new dance form, sometimes called the "noisy shoe," was created.

Whatever the source of the name, English clog dance is without question directly descended from the step dances of England. It is possible that the English step-dance style began and evolved separate from the Irish tradition; in the last two centuries, however, it is likely that the two styles have influenced each other reciprocally. (The more intricate Irish music and dance rhythms, of Celtic origin, are also believed to have been influenced by Moorish dance and music, suggesting a relationship to the percussive flamenco footwork of Spanish Gypsies.) English clogging may in turn have influenced the development of step dancing in Quebec (which is based mainly on Irish step dance) and in Cape Breton (thought to be based largely on a native Scottish tradition now vanished in Scotland). A simple, direct relationship between English clog dance and Appalachian clogging should not, however, be taken for granted.

Appalachian clogging, which apparently originated in North Carolina, first as a solo dance that had several other names, then as part of a big circle dance (forerunner of the square dance), has never been done with wooden shoes. A comment by the future Queen Elizabeth II during a visit to the United States in 1939, reported in newspapers, that a square dance team doing some fancy stepping looked like British clog dancers, is sometimes said to be the source for the name. (According to another etymology, the term derives from "clod dance," named for the clods of dirt kicked up by people dancing outdoors.) Solo dancing (outside the context of the big circle dance) is known in various places as buck dance, flatfooting, hoedown, jigging, sure-footing, and/or stepping. These names vary in meaning from place to place, and dancers do not always agree on their use, but some general observations can be made. Jigging in Arkansas is the same as stepping and sure-footing in Tennessee and Alabama, and is similar to the Kentucky back step. It consists of a fast stepping on the balls of the feet while crossing the feet and without traveling much, in a manner similar to Irish soft-shoe jigs. Flatfooting is the same as, or very similar to, buck dance in many areas; however, in the West Virginia mountains a style of flatfooting is done with twisting foot movements like the African-American Jump for Joy dance of the Georgia Sea Islands. The hoedown can be found in Missouri as a jumping-and-stamping dance similar to the Mexican Norteño Polka and may have the same European polka heritage.

The body movement in North Carolina big-circle Appalachian clogging is different from the style prevailing in the solo dances done in the same area, and appears to be similar to the old version of African-American buck dance. The term *buck dance* came to the United States from the West Indies, where "buck" was a nickname for the freebooting sailors called the *boucaniers* in French, buccaneers in English, and *bockorau* or *buckorau* in West Indian pidgin. (The word derives from a Tupi Indian word denoting a frame for drying and smoking meat; the original buccaneers were sailors who smoked meat and fish after the manner of the Indians.)

The old-style African-American buck dance consisted essentially of a stamp and slip of the weight-bearing foot backward, often with an incidental toe bounce, with the body leaning forward. The Appalachian-mountain buck dance, as done by European-Americans, generally begins with a stamp, followed by a forward heel brush and a toe slap with the free foot. The dancer's posture is straighter than the Appalachian clogger's, but more relaxed than the English and Irish step dancer's. The English clog begins with a step on the downbeat of the music; the toe of the free foot is then brushed forward and backward. The Irish hard-shoe jig has a similar beginning step, but is much more elaborate in rhythm. Appalachian cloggers (except modern-style cloggers) tend to lean forward, snapping the toe, rather than brushing the foot, forcing it to bounce before stepping heavily on the downbeat. Appalachian cloggers also use large swinging movements of the legs. It is possible that big-circle clogging may have been influenced more by the older African-American buck dance, and the mountain buck dance influenced more by Irish step dance. Certainly few African-Americans have traditionally lived in the Appalachian mountains, while many have lived in the eastern Carolinas and in Georgia. However, some African-American dance styles such as the Buzzard Lope and Jump for Joy are done by European Americans in the context of buck dance or flatfooting. The term *Buzzard Lope*, originally applied to a dance that mimed a buzzard swooping for a meal, has come to include any solo buck dance done with flailing arms (this may also be the origin of the buck-and-wing dance). There is a Georgia Sea island song called "Buzzard Lope," but it is not very danceable and its connection to the dance of the same name is unclear. Several other influences for the North Carolina big-circle clog style may be conjectured: the Cherokees who live in that area dance with similar body movement, and the Scots and Germans who settled in the region dance with large swinging movements of the legs.

The recently invented styles called *precision* or *modern clogging* are somewhat similar in movement style to English and Irish step dancing. Choreographed line clog dancing became popular in the 1970s. In this form, dancers stand in rows and lines to do a series of choreographed steps, standing straight with little or no specified body movement, then turn and repeat the steps in another direction. Most of these routines are choreographed to specific music.

The name *clog dance* is also often imposed on Dutch *klumpfen* and Belgian and Spanish *sabot* dances (both performed in wooden shoes), in which the figures of the dance, and not fancy footwork, are the most important feature. Dancers of these two styles do not refer to them by terms equivalent to "clog dance." *Clog dance* is also the name of a dance style taught in schools in the United States in the 1920s and 1930s, though it was not always done with wooden shoes.

American clogging also has a kind of sibling relationship with tap, the other great form of percussive dance developed in the United States. On the U.S. stage of the nineteenth and early twentieth centuries an English-style Lancashire Clog was performed with wooden shoes. With the extensive borrowing of steps from Irish and African-American dance, and the addition of wooden and eventually metal taps to leather-soled shoes, tap dance was born.

[*See also* Great Britain, *article on* English Traditional Dance.]

BIBLIOGRAPHY

Ajello, E. *The Solo Irish Jig.* London, 1932.

Bonner, Frank. *Clogging and the Southern Appalachian Square Dance.* Acworth, Ga., 1983.

Bridenbaugh, C. *Myths and Realities: Societies of the Colonial South.* New York, 1973.

Duke, Jerry. *Clog Dance in the Appalachians.* San Francisco, 1984.

Evans, B. and M. *American Indian Dance Steps.* New York, 1931.

Fairchild, A. *Appalachian Clogging: A Handbook on What It Is and How To Do It.* Privately published, 1982.

Frost, H. *Clog Dance.* New York, 1931.

Jones, Bessie, and Bess Lomax Hawes. *Step It Down: Games, Plays, Songs and Stories from the Afro-American Heritage.* New York, 1972.

Raffe, W. G. *Dictionary of the Dance.* London, 1964.

Stearns, Marshall, and Jean Stearns. *Jazz Dance: The Story of American Vernacular Dance.* New York, 1968.

JERRY C. DUKE

Clogging in Appalachian Dance Traditions

Clogging is an energetic American folk dance that involves beating out rhythms on the floor by tapping, stamping, shuffling, and sliding the feet to lively reels or "hoedowns" played on the fiddle (violin) or banjo. Contemporary clogging is most often performed in leather-soled shoes, with two-piece metal "jingle" or "jiggle" taps. Clogging is descended from a number of styles of solo step dancing called variously clog dance, buck dance, flatfoot, jigging, and hoedown. The names for these styles and the styles themselves vary from region to region, and even from dancer to dancer.

Although fancy footwork often played a part in the social dances of eighteenth-century America, the history of solo step dances is largely undocumented. Even the relationship of American clogging to its ancestor, the English clog dance, is unclear. Clogs (wooden-soled shoes with leather uppers) were worn in Europe but were not commonly worn in England until the nineteenth century, and only in the last half of that century did the so-called Lancashire Clog, a stage dance, come to America. It mingled with older solo dance forms from the English, Scottish, Irish, and African traditions to give birth to such American dances as hoofing and tap, as well as clogging.

Although clogging's solo-dance roots are poorly documented, its beginnings as a team exhibition dance can be traced to Pack Square, Asheville, North Carolina, on 6 June 1928. On that evening Bascom Lamar Lunsford, a local lawyer, editor, and folk musician, produced a square dance contest as part of Asheville's Rhododendron Festival and invited groups of dancers and musicians from the surrounding mountain communities. Here, exhibition clogging was first demonstrated. The event drew an enthusiastic audience of five thousand and has continued as the annual Mountain Dance and Folk Festival.

The history of Lunsford's festival provides many clues to the development of clogging and its relationship to Appalachian square dance. In the early years of the festival, square dance teams performed the traditional mountain figures almost exactly as they had at social dances in their own communities. Some teams used more of a shuffle or scuff in their steps than others, but the only clog dancers mentioned in press reports were solo dancers who entertained the audience during the intervals between square dance team performances. Because winners of the square dance competition were decided largely on the basis of audience reaction, teams gradually danced faster and arranged or embellished the traditional figures for visual effect. Some of them came to rely on the heavily accented clog style of stepping to excite the spectators. In the early 1950s matching costumes began to appear, over the objections of critics who complained that the result looked more like a ballet than a square dance.

At the 1958 festival, a major change took place. The *Asheville Citizen* reported that "a new trophy, equal in value to the Pless Cup [first prize in the square dance competition] will be given to the team judged best in the 'clogging' style of dancing." Henceforth the square dance competition was in effect divided into two categories: clog and smooth. Lunsford himself sponsored the new prize, giving the clog division added prestige.

Two further developments took place in the 1950s: throughout the Southeast, television stations began to broadcast segments of *The Grand Ole Opry*, which featured some excellent clogging teams, and "precision" clogging first appeared. Until this time individual dancers on a team were free to use steps of their choice as long as everyone kept the basic rhythm. In precision clogging, all dancers were required to perform exactly the same step at the same time. Many clogging contests began to include both precision and freestyle divisions.

Although team clogging became a well-defined activity during the 1950s, it was mostly confined to the Appalachian region. It began to spread to the rest of the nation in the mid-1970s through two different channels. The first was a folk-music revival that focused on rural music styles. Many young people in towns and cities across the country became proficient folk dance musicians and developed an attendant interest in traditional square dancing and clogging to live music. Folk festivals in both the United States and Canada featured clogging groups that not only performed but also offered instruction in basic technique. The 1970s also witnessed the formation of clogging clubs modeled after and loosely associated with the modern western square dance movement. Like their square dance counterparts, most members of these clubs danced exclusively to phonograph records of contemporary popular music and sought to standardize the terminology and performance of steps through various regional and national associations.

By the mid-1980s, performing clogging teams were found throughout America as well as in Europe and Japan. New step combinations of increasing complexity were being created, sometimes using techniques from English, Irish, and Canadian step dances. Books, records, videotapes, and periodicals about clogging began to be sold. In November 1984, the first national clogging convention was held in Mobile, Alabama. After little more than a half century, a regional folk dance had become a significant international recreational activity.

BIBLIOGRAPHY

Bernstein, Ira. *Appalachian Clogging and Flatfooting Steps.* Malverne, N.Y., 1992.
Bonner, Frank X. *Clogging and the Southern Appalachian Square Dance.* Acworth, Ga., 1983.
Duke, Jerry. *Clog Dance in the Appalachians.* San Francisco, 1984.
Jones, Loyal. *Minstrel of the Appalachians: The Story of Bascom Lamar Lunsford.* Boone, N.C., 1984.
Popwell, Sheila. *Clogging.* Huron, Ohio, 1975.
Popwell, Sheila. *Teaching Clogging.* Huron, Ohio, 1980.
Whisnant, David E. "Finding the Way between the Old and the New: The Mountain Dance and Folk Festival and Bascom Lamar Lunsford's Work as a Citizen." *Appalachian Journal* (Autumn–Winter 1979–1980).

ROBERT G. DALSEMER

CLUSTINE, IVAN (Ivan Nikolaevich Khliustin; born 10 [22] August 1862 in Moscow, died 21 November 1941 in Nice), Russian dancer, ballet master, and choreographer. Clustine had an important pioneering career in both Russia and the West: as one of the early native ballet masters in Russia he inspired nationalist pride; as choreographer at the Paris Opera and for Anna Pavlova he transmitted the ideals of the Moscow school of ballet beyond Russia's borders. His career was unique in that he reversed the practice of foreign ballet masters being brought into Russia when he went to Paris after retiring from the Imperial Theaters, some years before Serge Diaghilev's company and the events of the Russian Revolution made this a common occurrence.

Clustine trained in Moscow with Gustav Legat in the Theater School, from which he graduated in 1882. While still a student he made his Bolshoi debut in 1878 in a pas de deux with Maria Stanislavska; he was appointed premier danseur in 1886. His repertory at the Bolshoi Theater closely paralleled that of Pavel Gerdt at the Maryinsky: he danced Colin in *La Fille Mal Gardée,* Phoebus in *Esmeralda,* and Albrecht in *Giselle.* He was particularly praised as a partner, but his own dancing, which stressed refinement and elegance in the *danseur noble* tradition, was not highly valued in Moscow, where the *demi-caractère* style had taken hold.

Following a serious injury in 1892 Clustine began to set new dances and to revive old ballets, including *Le Corsaire, The Naïad and the Fisherman,* and *Katarina,* and to revise some of the dances in *La Halte de Cavalerie* and *The Magic Flute.* He also choreographed many parts of the ballets credited solely to the Moscow ballet master José Mendes. By 1898, on the basis of his choreography of the *Polovtsian Dances* for the premiere of Aleksandr Borodin's opera *Prince Igor* and of his own three-act ballet *Stars,* Clustine was appointed ballet master of the Bolshoi Theater, replacing Mendes. That year he attempted to reconstruct the original version of *Coppélia,* eliminating interpolated numbers and restoring the dances of Arthur Saint-Léon. In 1900 he staged his own version of *The Fairy Doll* and revived *Cinderella* with many of the original dances. His principal original works at the Bolshoi were *Stars* (1898), *Magic Dreams* (1898), and *The Magic Shoes* (1899).

Coinciding with his 1898 appointment as ballet master, Clustine began to teach at the Moscow Theater School, where he remained until 1902. Upon his 1903 retirement from the Bolshoi after twenty years of service, he opened a ballet school in Paris. With the success of Diaghilev's Russian ballet there, Clustine was offered the position of ballet master and teacher at the Paris Opera, where he served from 1909 to 1914. At the Opera he choreographed *Russalka* (1911), *Les Bacchantes* (1912), *Suite de Danses* (1913), and *Philotis* and *Hansli le Bossu* (both 1914).

In 1913 Pavlova invited Clustine to become ballet master of her company, a post he held intermittently until her death in 1931. For Pavlova he choreographed a series of selections from the longer works of Marius Petipa and the Legat brothers as well as original divertissements, theatricalized social dances during the ragtime rage, and an abridged version of *The Sleeping Beauty,* produced at the New York Hippodrome in 1916. Clustine also taught with Pavlova at the Free Ballet School at the Hippodrome. Among the many dances he staged for her were *Ajanta Frescoes, Assyrian Dance, Dance of the Hours, Dionysus, Egyptian Ballet, The Fauns, Gavotte, La Péri, Raymonda, The Romance of a Mummy, Russian Dance, Scène Dansante, Une Soirée de Chopin,* and *Valse Triste.* Following Pavlova's death, Clustine left the stage to teach and occasionally mount ballets.

BIBLIOGRAPHY

Como, William, and Richard Philp. "Pavlova." *Dance Magazine* (January 1976): 43–74.

Krasovskaya, Vera. *Russkii baletnyi teatr vtoroi poloviny deviatnad-tsatogo veka.* Leningrad, 1963.

Lazzarini, John, and Roberta Lazzarini. *Pavlova: Repertoire of a Legend.* New York, 1980.

Money, Keith. *Pavlova: Her Art and Life.* New York, 1982.

SUZANNE CARBONNEAU

CLYTEMNESTRA. Choreography: Martha Graham. Music: Halim el-Dabh. Scenery: Isamu Noguchi. Costumes: Martha Graham and Helen McGehee. Lighting: Jean Rosenthal. First performance: 1 April 1958, Adelphi Theater, New York City, Martha Graham Dance Company. Principals: Martha Graham (Clytemnestra), Bertram Ross (Agamemnon and Orestes), Paul Taylor (Aegisthus), Helen McGehee (Electra), Yuriko (Iphigenia), Ethel Winter (Helen of Troy), David Wood (The Messenger of Death), Matt Turney (Cassandra), Gene McDonald (Hades, Paris, The Ghost of Agamemnon, The Watchman).

Graham's only full-evening dance, *Clytemnestra* is considered by many to be the crowning achievement of her works based on Greek drama and myth. Clytemnestra is, in the words of the libretto of el-Dabh's score for orchestra and two singers, "dishonored among the dead," and she searches back through her life for vindication. Summoning up the past, she witnesses the rape of Helen, the Trojan War, and the sacrifice of her daughter Iphigenia. She reenacts her lustful liaison with Aegisthus and, in a brilliant dramatic passage, her murder of Agamemnon: a huge red velvet cloak becomes by turns ceremonial carpet, snare, shielding curtain, and finally a river of blood. The sumptuous work, part ceremony, part dream, part drama, shows its most sustained dancing in a choral passage for six Furies. El-Dabh's score, written for orchestra and male and female solo vocalists, evokes a dire and tempestuous atmosphere. In her *Notebooks,* Graham likened Clytemnestra's torment to "the private hell of a woman who has killed her love because her love killed her creative instinct—her child." The designer Halston created new costumes for the *Dance in America* videotape of the work; these have been used in performances since the late 1970s.

BIBLIOGRAPHY

Gardner, Howard. "Martha Graham: Discovering the Dance of America." *Ballet Review* 22 (Spring 1994): 67–93.

Graham, Martha. *The Notebooks of Martha Graham.* New York, 1973.

VIDEOTAPE. *Clytemnestra, Dance in America* (WNET-TV, New York, 1979).

DEBORAH JOWITT

COCTEAU, JEAN (born 5 July 1889 in Maisons-Lafitte, France, died 11 October 1963 in Milly-la Forêt, France), French writer and artist. Cocteau's world held many personal myths that he repeated and varied again and again in his books, plays, films, and ballets. Fascinated by the ballet because he found it, as well as film, to be the most appropriate art form from which to bring forth "le spectacle intérieur," Cocteau used ballet to reach toward the unreal, which he believed was integral to everyday existence. This world and "the other" were merged in Cocteau's art, and his own life, itself a kind of myth, became closely associated with the universal myths.

In his early years Cocteau, concerned primarily with the aesthetics of dance language, strove to make ballet a new modern art. He rebelled against classical ballet, which he felt had grown stiff and had lost the capacity to move one emotionally; his goal was to open up new possibilities with a movement pattern inspired by everyday life. When Léonide Massine choreographed Cocteau's *Parade* (1917), Cocteau gave concrete suggestions regarding how the dancers should move: these included the skipping and typewriting American Girl, the Acrobats' pas de deux with movements inspired by the trapeze and the tightrope walk, and the Conjurer's imitation of an act of illusion.

The farce *Le Boeuf sur le Toit, ou The Nothing Doing Bar* (1920) as well as *Les Mariés de la Tour Eiffel* (1921) were experimental works. In the first, Cocteau renewed the dance language by working with acrobats as well as by giving the dancers big cardboard heads and transferring the action to a kind of surrealistic world. In *Les Mariés,* created for Les Ballets Suédois with music by the group of French composers known as Les Six, Cocteau reacted against naturalism and realized a new theatrical approach that became important for French playwrights from Jean Anouilh to those of the avant-garde theater. Dance and talk were mixed in a Dadaist way. The ballet, a caricature of a bourgeois family on a Sunday afternoon, is at the same time a surrealistic vision: strange things happen on the platform of the Eiffel Tower when the unborn child rebels against its parents and when the general is eaten and later thrown up by the lion. Cocteau never lost interest in the movements themselves, but he later became more occupied by the thoughts, ideas, and myths that his ballets were to express. For him, ballet was a way of reaching toward the unconscious, toward the dream.

Diaghilev's Ballets Russes in Paris first elicited Cocteau's interest in the ballet. Through interviews and articles he publicized the troupe in the newspapers; he created posters of Tamara Karsavina and Vaslav Nijinsky; and he wrote libretti for *Le Dieu Bleu* (1912) and *Parade*. Cocteau suggested ideas for both the choreography of *Parade* and its music, composed by Erik Satie. Cocteau wanted typewriters, sirens, even spoken text to be included in the score, but he did not get it exactly the way he wanted it and was never quite satisfied with the ballet.

Nor was Cocteau satisfied with his position as librettist. He always wanted to play a more prominent part in the creative process and to blur the line between librettist and choreographer. In *Les Mariés*, Cocteau directed the choreography through the young Swedish dancer and choreographer Jean Börlin. Cocteau wanted to take an active part also in the choreography and the *mise-en-scène* for *Le Train Bleu* (1924), but he ran into problems with Bronislava Nijinska. Again Cocteau's goal was to renew the vocabulary of ballet, in this case by using movements from the world of sport. That same year he staged a much-discussed and admired production of *Romeo and Juliet*, his own adaptation, in which ballet and drama merged. In this, Cocteau was inspired by the Russians Aleksandr Tairov and Vsevolod Meyerhold.

From the mid-1920s to the mid-1940s, Cocteau participated little in the ballet world, but he made a strong comeback after World War II as the inspiration and the man with the ideas behind Roland Petit's emerging group of young French dancers. In Petit's cruel, morbid, and sadomasochistic *Le Jeune Homme et la Mort* (1946), Cocteau's inspiration lay behind every step and every feeling. This was the closest he ever came to becoming a choreographer—and again in opposition to classicism he worked with slow motion and with acrobatic elements in a violent movement language. In *Le Jeune Homme*, the most fully realized of Cocteau's ballets, Love and Death are represented by the same woman—Love as the young girl in a yellow dress, Death as the elegant lady in an elaborate evening gown. Death as a female figure often inhabited Cocteau's universe, both when he described his early memoirs of his mother dressing for the theater and when he portrayed death in his film *Orphée* (1950).

In 1950 Cocteau created text, costumes, and sets for a *Phèdre* ballet at the Paris Opera, but he and Serge Lifar, the choreographer, did not see eye to eye, Cocteau holding the view that Lifar was unable to get into his world. Whereas for Lifar dance was a continuous stream of movement, Cocteau wanted to achieve *tableaux vivants* and sculptural effects. In 1952 Cocteau did in fact stage and narrate his own *Oedipus Rex* as a series of *tableaux vivants* set to music by Igor Stravinsky.

More successful than Cocteau's collaboration with Lifar was his ballet *La Dame á la Licorne*, created in Munich in 1953. In Heinz Rosen, Cocteau found a young choreographer who was more willing to serve as his "medium." Cocteau's last two libretti, *La Poète et sa Muse* to the music of Gian-Carlo Menotti (1959) and *Le Fils de l'Air, ou L'Enfant Changé en Jeune Homme*, written in 1962 but not realized in his lifetime, were, like all his other works, closely linked to his personal existence. *La Poète et sa Muse* concerned his art; *Le Fils de l'Air*, his eternal fight against the bourgeois milieu in which he grew up, an ongoing artistic struggle to the end of his life.

BIBLIOGRAPHY

Aschengreen, Erik. *Jean Cocteau and the Dance*. Translated by Patricia McAndrew and Per Avsum. Copenhagen, 1986.

Cocteau, Jean, et al. *Théâtre Serge de Diaghilew: Les Fâcheux*. Paris, 1924.

Cocteau, Jean. *Le Coq et l'Arlequin: Notes autour de la musique 1918*. Paris, 1979.

Debold, Conrad. "*Parade* and *Le Spectacle Intérieur*: The Role of Jean Cocteau in an Avant-Garde Ballet." Ph.D. diss., Emory University, 1982.

Garafola, Lynn. *Diaghilev's Ballets Russes*. New York, 1989.

Ries, Frank W. D. *The Dance Theatre of Jean Cocteau*. Ann Arbor, Mich., 1986.

Sprigge, Elizabeth, and Jean-Jacques Kihm. *Jean Cocteau: The Man and the Mirror*. New York, 1968.

Steegmuller, Francis. *Cocteau: A Biography*. Boston, 1970.

ERIK ASCHENGREEN

COE, KELVIN (born 8 September 1946 in Melbourne, died 9 July 1992 in Melbourne), Australian dancer and teacher. Kelvin Coe was the first male dancer to rise through the ranks of the Australian Ballet to the position of principal artist. He joined the company as an apprentice in its inaugural season in 1962 and was promoted to soloist in 1965 and principal in 1969. Throughout his career Coe partnered every principal female dancer to emerge from the Australian Ballet in the 1960s and 1970s as well as some of the world's leading ballerinas, including Margot Fonteyn and Carla Fracci.

In an interview recorded shortly before his death in 1992 from an AIDS-related illness, Coe said he felt he was never a strong dancer in terms of physical stamina. He was, however, a favorite with audiences who admired him for his masculinity and elegance. He had an acclaimed partnership with Marilyn Rowe, which blossomed after they won silver medals in the Moscow International Ballet Competition in 1973. While he danced all the leading roles in the Australian Ballet's repertory, he was especially admired for his performances in the ballets of Frederick Ashton, especially *La Fille Mal Gardée* and *The Dream*.

Coe's first dance training was in tap, and his early ambition was to follow in the footsteps of Fred Astaire. But he took up ballet at age twelve and shortly afterwards joined classes that were being given for dancers who found themselves unemployed between the folding of the

Borovansky Ballet and the formation of the Australian Ballet. When Coe joined the Australian Ballet for its opening season, he was overcome by the performances and the working ethic of Erik Bruhn, also dancing with the company in the inaugural season. He continued to admire Bruhn, and later Nureyev, both of whom fueled his ambition to be a classical dancer.

Coe spent almost his entire career in Australia with the Australian Ballet, and his popularity and star status were largely confined to his home country. In 1981 when the Australian Ballet was divided by an acrimonious strike over pay and conditions and what was claimed were falling artistic standards, Coe became the elected representative of the dancers. He did not find this role, which constantly required him to face a confrontational and demanding press, an easy one. He left the Australian Ballet shortly after the strike was resolved. He did, however, work in England briefly with the London Festival Ballet in the 1970s and, after he left the Australian Ballet, with the Sydney Dance Company and the Australian Opera.

He was encouraged by Anne Woolliams, who directed the Australian Ballet in 1976 and 1977, to consider teaching. In 1985 was invited by Dame Margaret Scott to join the faculty of the Australian Ballet School, and he taught there until 1991 when his illness became too debilitating for him to continue. He danced infrequently after 1988, including an appearance with the Australian Ballet in a gala performance at Covent Garden, performing the lead-

ing role in Graeme Murphy's *Beyond Twelve,* the only work ever created on him. His last performances were as an Ugly Sister, Clothilde, in the Australian Ballet School's production of Ray Powell's *Cinderella* in December 1991.

BIBLIOGRAPHY
Christofis, Lee. "True Blue Artist." *Dance Australia* 84 (June–July 1996): 22–26.
Pask, Edward H. *Ballet in Australia: The Second Act, 1940–1980.* Melbourne, 1982.

INTERVIEW. Kelvin Coe by Michelle Potter (May 1992), National Library of Australia (TRC 2807).

MICHELLE POTTER

COLE, JACK (John Richter Cole; born 27 April 1911 in New Brunswick, New Jersey, died 17 February 1974 in Los Angeles), dancer and choreographer. The work of Jack Cole spanned four decades. Shortly after beginning study at Columbia University, Cole dropped out to join the Denishawn ensemble, then in its last days, making his first professional appearance with the company at Lewisohn Stadium in August 1930. (His early training had also included Cecchetti ballet technique.) The following August, he danced Elihu in Ted Shawn's version of Vaughan Williams's *Job: A Masque for Dancing,* adopting the name of J. Ewing Cole. He decided not to join Shawn's new male ensemble; instead, he went on to work with

COLE. A dance number staged by Hermes Pan from the film *Moon over Miami* (Twentieth Century–Fox, 1941), with Jack Cole and Florence Lessing in front. In publicity rosters for this film, Cole and his company were billed along with the Condos Brothers as "Specialties." (Photograph from the Dance Collection, New York Public Library for the Performing Arts.)

Doris Humphrey and Charles Weidman, appearing with them on Broadway in *School for Husbands* in 1933. When they dismissed him, he decided to make a career of dancing in supper clubs, such as the Rainbow Room, Casa Mañana, Chez Paree, and Ciro's. His partner in his early successes was Alice Dudley; later he was joined by the duo of Anna Austin and Florence Lessing.

Disdaining the imitation Orientalia of Ruth St. Denis, Cole mastered *bharata nāṭyam* techniques, the oldest form of dance in India, but he and his partners performed them first to a swing beat and later to jazz. He also added dance steps, linked to jazz, from Africa, the Caribbean, and Harlem; these innovations earned him the title "Father of Jazz Dance," which he disclaimed, preferring the phrase "Theater Dance." Noted for his perfection of isolations and placement, his frenetic choreographies were distinguished by abrupt changes in direction, including long, punishing knee slides.

Cole danced and choreographed in casinos and clubs for over three decades. On Broadway, he danced in a number of shows and contributed notable choreographies to musicals such as *Magdalena* (1948), *Kismet* (1953), and *Jamaica* (1957). He both directed and choreographed *Donnybrook!* and *Kean* in 1961. While he was involved with nearly thirty musicals, not all of them reached Broadway.

Called to Hollywood in the mid-1940s, Cole was able to establish a unique dance workshop at Columbia Pictures, providing a core of Cole-trained dancers for film musicals such as *Eadie Was a Lady* (1945) and *Down to Earth* (1947). In the 1950s, he worked for Twentieth Century–Fox and choreographed *On the Riviera* (1951). He worked with stars such as Ann Miller, Betty Grable, Rita Hayworth, Jane Russell, Mitzi Gaynor, and Marilyn Monroe, and he devised movement that would make nondancers appear competent. He coached Monroe on her walk, her manner, and her interpretation of songs. His dancers included talents such as Gwen Verdon, Marc Platt, Carol Haney, Rod Alexander, and Matt Mattox. He also choreographed for major television shows but was proudest of his work for New York City Opera's production of *Bomarzo* (1968).

[*For further discussion, see* Jazz Dance.]

BIBLIOGRAPHY

de Mille, Agnes. *America Dances.* New York, 1980.
Hirschhorn, Clive. *The Hollywood Musical.* New York, 1981.
King, Eleanor. *Transformations: The Humphrey–Weidman Era.* Brooklyn, 1978.
Loney, Glenn. "The Legacy of Jack Cole: Rebel with a Cause" (parts 1–12). *Dance Magazine* (January 1983–).
Loney, Glenn. *Unsung Genius: The Passion of Dancer-Choreographer Jack Cole.* New York, 1984.
Terry, Walter. *I Was There: Selected Dance Reviews and Articles, 1936–1976.* Edited by Andrew Mark Wentink. New York, 1978.

GLENN LONEY

COLES, HONI (Charles Coles; born 2 April 1911 in Philadelphia, died 12 November 1995 in New York), American tap dancer. Coles started to dance as a teenager, performing on street corners in Philadelphia, and then he began to enter amateur talent shows. In 1931 he joined George and Danny Miller in an act called the Miller Brothers (later the Lucky Seven Trio), doing fast tap routines on giant dice, pedestals, and boards suspended in the air. After an unsuccessful attempt to break into show business in New York City, Coles returned to Philadelphia, where he locked himself in a room and practiced eight hours a day for a year. When he returned to New York in 1933, Coles had the fastest feet in show business. Ironically, it was his celebrated slow soft-shoe, co-choreographed with his partner, Charles ("Cholly") Atkins, some years later, and performed to a slow tempo rendition of "Taking a Chance on Love," that made Coles and Atkins one of the great class acts.

Coles's self-taught and complicated rhythm tap was ahead of its time. In 1934 he played at the opening of the Apollo Theater in Harlem. "Nobody knew what I was doing," he later said. "All the white cats would come up to the Apollo and tell the agents about the black cat uptown, but the agents felt I had no routine."

Between 1934 and 1940 he worked with such bands as those of Duke Ellington, Count Basie, and Cab Calloway. He also made film shorts of the type known as "Snader Telescriptions" (short films made for television), but he was never given the opportunity to appear in feature films. Joining together as a team after World War II, Coles and Atkins toured with several big bands from 1946 to

COLES. Tapper Coles grooves with Brenda Bufalino, his protégée and a leading exponent of jazz tap. (Photograph courtesy of the American Tap Dance Orchestra.)

1949. In 1949 they went into the Broadway musical *Gentlemen Prefer Blondes* and later toured with *Kiss Me, Kate*. By the late 1950s, tap had gone out of fashion, and from 1960 to 1976 Coles worked as production manager of the Apollo Theater.

Coles was in the forefront of the tap revival of the late 1960s, and beginning with his return to Broadway in *Bubblin' Brown Sugar* in 1976, he became the most-renowned tap dancer in the 1970s and 1980s. In 1983 he was featured in the musical *My One and Only*, for which he won a Tony award. Honorary chairman of the Copasetics, the black fraternity of tap dancers who have performed throughout America and Europe, Coles was generous throughout his career, passing his rhythms onto students throughout the world. With Atkins he danced in a brilliant, thirty-minute television show, on which he collaborated with tap historian Marshall Stearns. The show originally aired on the CBS television program *Camera Three* in 1965. Coles often appeared with his protégée Brenda Bufalino and with the Jazz Tap Ensemble, whose mentor he was. He was featured in the original television film of *The Tap Dance Kid*, on which the successful Broadway musical was based, and he was the subject of a profile on the *McNeil-Lehrer News Hour* in 1984. Coles's widow, Marion Coles, a former chorus dancer from the Apollo, was also active in preserving and performing tap dancing.

[*See* also Tap Dance.]

BIBLIOGRAPHY

Frank, Rusty E. *Tap! The Greatest Tap Dance Stars and Their Stories, 1900–1955.* Rev. ed. New York, 1994.

Mihopoulos, Effie. "Honi Coles Interviewed." *Salome* 44–46 (1986).

Stearns, Marshall, and Jean Stearns. *Jazz Dance.* Rev. ed. New York, 1994.

FILM AND VIDEOTAPE. Jolyon Wimhurst, *Masters of Tap* (1983). "Tap," *Dance in America* (WNET-TV, New York, 1989). Stephan Chodorov, *Honi Coles: The Class Act of Tap* (1993). Louise Tiranoff, *Milt and Honi* (1994).

JANE GOLDBERG

COLLIER, LESLEY (born 13 March 1947 in Orpington, Kent), English dancer. A scholarship student at the Royal Ballet School, Collier joined the company in 1965, having danced the leading role in Frederick Ashton's *The Two Pigeons* at her graduation performance. Her first solo roles, in 1968, were in the Bluebird pas de deux in *The Sleeping Beauty* and the peasant pas de deux in *Giselle*. Her performances of classical variations showed her to be a dancer who exemplified the lyricism, delicacy, and precision of the British style and led to promotion to soloist in 1970 and to principal in 1972.

Collier continued to be an ideal interpreter of the romantic but plucky heroines of Ashton's *Two Pigeons, Cinderella*, and *La Fille Mal Gardée*; more surprising, perhaps, were her passionately dramatic portrayals of Kenneth MacMillan's Juliet, Anastasia, Manon, and Mary Vetsera in *Mayerling*. She danced the ballerina roles in the first performances of Ninette de Valois's 1977 revision of *The Sleeping Beauty*, Norman Morrice's *Swan Lake* in 1979, and Peter Wright's *The Nutcracker* in 1984 and *Giselle* in 1985. In 1980, Ashton cast her opposite Mikhail Baryshnikov (with whom she had earlier danced *Romeo and Juliet* and *La Fille Mal Gardée*) in his *Rhapsody*, creating for her a role that exploited her rare musicality, crystalline phrasing, and quicksilver technique. She frequently appeared abroad as guest artist, often partnered by Rudolf Nureyev. She retired from the stage in July 1995, performing Giselle for one last time, but went on to teach at the Royal Ballet School.

BIBLIOGRAPHY

Nugent, Ann. "Images, Changes, and Joy . . ." *Dance Now* 3 (Summer 1994): 2–11.

Rigby, Cormac. "Fleet of Foot, Melting Hearts." *Dance and Dancers* (November 1986): 24–27.

DAVID VAUGHAN

COLLINS, JANET (born 2 March 1917 in New Orleans), dancer, choreographer, and teacher. "If dancing has ever peopled your nocturnal dreams, then you can achieve a fairly good idea how Janet Collins looks on stage," wrote Doris Hering in 1949 about New York's latest discovery. Newly transplanted east, Collins was raised in Los Angeles, where she studied with Adolph Bolm, Carmelita Maracci, and Mia Slavenska, among others. A talented artist, her family hoped that she would pursue painting as a career rather than dance which, at the time, offered limited opportunities to blacks. Collins did major in art at Los Angeles City College, later transferring to the Los Angeles Art Center School when she received a scholarship. But she continued to dance, performing in musical theater productions of *Run Little Chillun* and *The Mikado in Swing*, the 1946 film *The Thrill of Brazil*, and with the companies of Lester Horton and Katherine Dunham.

A 1945 Julius Rosenwald Fellowship helped Collins develop a diverse choreographic repertory. Often reflecting her African-American and French heritage, some works were created to spirituals, others based on life in New Orleans. Her first concert, on 3 November 1947 at the Las Palmas Theater, left critics hailing her as a unique performer. "Seldom indeed is anyone able to convey meaning and mood as does Miss Collins," said the *Los Angeles Daily News*, for not only is her pantomime telling, her grace matchless, but she has the rare talent, even in her almost stylized numbers, of reaching out to her audience and making them share emotions that her characters are portraying." The New York critics were equally stunned upon her appearance at the Ninety-second Street YM-YWHA's audition winners' concert on 20 February 1949. "It took no more (and probably less) than eight measures of movement in the opening dance to establish her claim to dance distinction," wrote Walter Terry in the *Herald Tribune*, adding that "she could, and probably would stop a Broadway show in its tracks as easily as she could and will cause a concert-going audience to shout for encores." After another shared concert at the Ninety-second Street Y in March and one of her own in April, Collins was named in the May 1949 *Dance Magazine* "The Most Outstanding Debutante of the Season."

Terry's predictions came true. Hanya Holm, choreographer of Cole Porter's *Out of This World*, cast Collins in the minor role of Night. After the show's Broadway premiere on 21 December 1950, the *Savannah Evening Press* declared: "It is the completely captivating Janet Collins that gives the show a wallop. Only she is truly out of this world." *Mademoiselle* agreed, naming Collins "Young Woman of the Year" and presenting to her its Merit Award. The Committee for the Negro in the Arts lauded her "for outstanding contributions as an artist to the cultural life of the United States and to the struggles of the Negro people and their artists for full equality and freedom." Finally, the Donaldson Award for the best dancer on Broadway was bestowed upon Collins in 1951.

That same year Zachary Solov, the new ballet master of the Metropolitan Opera, saw her in *Out of This World*. "She walked across the stage," he recalled, "pulling a chiffon curtain, and it was electric. The body just spoke." He immediately went to Rudolph Bing, the Met's general manager, and told him that he wanted to hire Collins for the upcoming production of *Aida*, and that she was black. "Is she good?" Bing asked. "She's wonderful!" exclaimed Solov. "Hire her," Bing decreed. Inspired by her movement, Solov was able to prepare the choreography in only a few rehearsals. He featured her as an Ethiopian slave in the second-act Triumphal Scene where, partnered by two Watutsi warriors (actually white men in body tights and blackface), she danced for the Pharoah's entertainment.

After the premiere on 13 November, P. W. Manchester (in *Dance News*) praised "the supple ferocity of the lithe and feline Janet Collins," observing that "the ballet rightly becomes the peak of the scene instead of, as usually happens, the somewhat embarrassing anticlimax." Collins remained Solov's muse for three other new productions: she appeared in *Carmen* (1952) as a gypsy; in *La Gioconda* (1952), notably the only Met opera in which she performed on pointe, as the Queen of the Night in "The Dance of the Hours"; and in *Samson et Dalila* (1953) as leader of a bacchanale. Although all her opera appearances attracted excitement, it was *Aida* that firmly established Collins as a dancing sensation. And while the Met had previously engaged blacks for specialty roles, Collins, as its first full-time black company member, was considered the pioneer who broke the color barrier.

She left the Met in 1954, exhausted. Throughout her contract, Collins had toured cross-country not only with the company but also, when it was on vacation, as a solo performer under Columbia Artists Management, presenting her own choreography. She continued, however, in the offstage role of a teacher, one with which she had been familiar since 1949, when she began teaching at the School of American Ballet. Her greatest challenge as an educator came in 1957, at Saint Joseph's School for the Deaf in the Bronx, where dance was part of the curriculum as a means of rehabilitation. Collins devised her own teaching method and wrote an article on the experience.

Eventually teaching became entwined with her increasing commitment to Catholicism. She joined the faculty of Marymount Manhattan College in 1958 and in 1959 accepted a concurrent position at Manhattanville College of the Sacred Heart at Purchase. Over the years, she restricted her own performances to academic and charity events but continued to choreograph for her students on liturgical themes. Marymount was the site of the premiere in 1965 of *Genesis*, a piece that Collins had been working on since 1954, when she first commissioned its music from Heitor Villa-Lobos. Depicting the evolution of primordial man and his eventual awareness of the power of God, *Genesis* was Collins' quintessential dance, the culmination of her deep-rooted religious feelings.

She entered the opera world but one more time, choreographing *Nabucco* for the San Francisco Opera in 1970. By then, Collins had relocated to California, and continued to teach and choreograph at Scripps College and the Mafundi Institute, among other places. Her last work to premiere in New York City was *Canticle of the Elements*, which she set on the Alvin Ailey Dance Company in 1974. She then seemingly vanished into thin air. Only on 28 January 1995, when Collins emerged in Philadelphia as the keynote speaker at the Eighth International Conference of Blacks in Dance, was the world told that for the last twenty-one years she had devoted herself exclusively to religious painting.

Loren Hightower, Collins's partner at the Met, perhaps best described the rare quality of her dancing that amazed critics and colleagues alike: "You could show Janet a movement and immediately it became something that nobody else could do. But she did not alter it," he explained. "It was as if Janet looked inward, and a strange power that she had seemed to come from there . . . it was magic, hypnotic. It was totally intuitive, and when anything is that unadornedly genuine, it's absolutely compelling."

BIBLIOGRAPHY
Stahl, Norma G. "The First Lady of the Metropolitan Opera Ballet." *Dance Magazine* (February 1954): 27–29.

INTERVIEWS. Loren Hightower and Zachary Solov, by Yaël Lewin (New York, 1995).

ARCHIVES. Dance Collection, New York Public Library for the Performing Arts. Metropolitan Opera Archives, New York.

YAËL LEWIN

COMBAT DANCES. *Many cultures have dances that take the form of mock or stylized combats or competitions, usually between male dancers. Dances may also be based on military forms, or may utilize sticks, swords, daggers, knives, or rifles. For traditions in western Europe and the Americas, see* Armed Dances; Barriera, Torneo, and Battaglia; Capoeira; European Traditional Dance; Matachins; Morris Dance; Moresca; Pyrrhic; *and* Sword Dance. *For discussion of combat dances in the Middle East and neighboring regions, see* Algeria; Arabian Peninsula; Egypt, *article on* Traditional Dance; Lebanon; Middle East, *overview article;* Morocco; Turkey, *and* Yemen. *Related discussions can also be found in the following entries:* Central and East Africa; Micronesia; *and* Southern Africa. *See also* Asian Martial Arts.

COMMEDIA DELL'ARTE is the name given to a form of theater that flourished first in Italy then elsewhere in Europe between 1550 and 1750. It is usually considered to have been distinctive in the history of postmedieval European theater in that it mingled masked and unmasked performers who would improvise plays rather than interpret the scripted words of a playwright. From the beginning, dance and dancelike movement, including pantomime and acrobatics, were essential features of *commedia dell'arte.*

The origins of *commedia dell'arte* have been much disputed: Michele Scherillo, Lorenzo Stoppato, and Allardyce Nicoll have argued for its descent from Latin theater, particularly from early mime shows and farce; while Paolo Toschi and Ireneo Sanesi have emphasized the importance to the evolution of the form of vestigial elements of ritual, ceremonial, and carnival entertainments, notably in the antics of clowns, buffoons, and jesters. Others (Benedetto Croce, Vito Pandolfi, Roberto Tessari, and Ferdinando Taviani) have in different ways stressed the importance to its birth of the emergence in the sixteenth century of professional acting companies. Here, at least, we are on slightly surer ground. Although it is not known when the first Italian professional troupe was formed, a convenient point of origin is provided by actors' contracts and articles of association, the earliest of which date from the 1540s and bear witness to the players' awareness that it was advantageous to their status and livelihood to organize in groups and to regularize the nature and terms of their professional commitments. The company idea prospered, and by the last decades of the century the players traveled far beyond Italy, to Spain, the German states, the Low Countries and England, as well as France.

In France, the popularity of players *all'improvviso* is well-attested. In the late sixteenth and early seventeenth centuries many of the most celebrated of the early troupes, like the Gelosi and the Confidenti, played there. In 1661 a permanent company of Italian players was formed in Paris and remained until 1697 when, for a supposed slight to Louis XIV's mistress, they were banished. French scripted comedy was much influenced by the *commedia all'improvviso* and Molière in particular drew on the strategies and materials of the Italian players with whom he worked at various times in the provinces and in Paris. But, despite the banishment of the Italians from Paris, and although the companies traveled even further abroad in the late seventeenth and eighteenth centuries (as far north as Sweden and as far east as Russia) and semipermanent companies were formed in foreign cities such as Warsaw, the French cultural domination of Europe at this time ensured that French influences on the development of the *commedia dell'arte* remained paramount. In 1716 a company of Italian players returned to Paris under troupe manager Luigi Riccoboni and sought to revive a kind of improvised playing, but the old style of performance was now much modified by Riccoboni's own literary interests, by French culture, taste, and expectations, and by an iconographic tradition that had begun to refine, idealize, and prettify the form. Increasingly, in the late seventeenth century and in the eighteenth century, the *commedia dell'arte* in Italy itself fell into decline. As materials became exhausted through repetition, some lead players turned to vulgarities or crowd-pleasing extravagances in order to hold audiences. Additionally, the gradual embourgeoisement of theater, and a concomitant taste for the naturalistic, undermined the performance aesthetic of the comedians *dell'arte.* By midcentury the Venetian dramatist Carlo Goldoni had begun his reform of Italian comedy that contributed substantially to the gradual demise of improvised playing.

Use of masks and improvisation has generally been seen as the defining characteristic of the *commedia dell'arte* and the feature that links it with popular modes of theatre—thus distinguishing it from the academic theater of the *dilettanti* who performed scripted plays before socially and intellectually sophisticated audiences in the courts, academies, and religious houses of the Italian *ducati* and *principati.* But the relationship of the *commedia dell'arte* to the academic theatre and to the entertainers of the streets and piazzas is complex. The players *dell'arte* took over, and turned to their own purposes, much of the materials of the academic drama: plots, character types, and some staging techniques. Indeed, during their heyday in Italy they performed not only "improvised" but scripted drama, and some leading actors and actresses were celebrated for their playing in such work. The troupes were, on the whole, economically better placed than the many itinerant jugglers, ropedancers, musicians, and mountebanks who also made up the world of Renaissance professional entertainment. But much depended on the quality and status of the individual company: the position of troupes in the lowest reaches of the profession was precarious, and the gap between them and the street entertainers very narrow. The more stable companies were not of the streets, but played in the theaters of patrons or in hired rooms and halls before paying spectators: they organized their theater as business. Some could even exercise a measure of independence when faced with patrician demand or bureaucratic opposition. Church enmity could be formidable, as is witnessed in the criticisms of Giovanni Domenico Ottonelli or in Niccolò Barbieri's attempt to defend the profession in *La supplica* (1634). So too could be the hostility of local administrators. Throughout the history of the *commedia dell'arte* improvised, rather than scripted drama, presented a problem to officials seeking to control the moral, religious, and political content of plays. The more economically secure the company, the easier was the task of resisting such pressures. What distinguished the *commedia dell'arte* performers from the academic *dilettanti* is that the *dell'arte* players at all levels were professional, and sought to make a living by acting: theirs was not only the *commedia all'improvviso* or *italiana*, it was also the *commedia mercenaria*.

They have become best known, of course, as the *commedia dell'arte*, a term that has been variously interpreted to mean the drama of the profession or the drama of skill, and perhaps carries an implication that theirs was a drama collectively composed. The companies were generally small (twelve to fifteen members), close-knit, and bound by family ties. Their improvised playing was based on *scenari, soggetti,* or *canovacci* (action outlines), which the actors elaborated into full dramas only in performance. To do so they drew on a wealth of stock or assembled material—soliloquies, dialogues, comic set pieces *(lazzi),* and extended passages of comic business, transmitted orally or gathered in *zibaldoni* (notebooks). It can be seen in most *commedia dell'arte* comic *scenari* that the parts are symmetrically organized; the key figures are two masked *vecchi* ("old men": Pantalone, Graziano), two masked *zanni* ("servants": Pedrolino, Burattino, Arlecchino), and two pairs of *innamorati* ("lovers": Flavio, Orazio, Flaminia, Isabella). To these eight must be added a number of less firmly fixed parts, the functions of which vary from scenario to scenario. They include the witty, or scolding, or flirtatious *servetta* (Franceschina), and the boasting military dandy, often a Spaniard or Calabrese, the Capitano (Spavento, Matamoros, Giangurgolo). Cos-

COMMEDIA DELL'ARTE. Jacques Callot's intalgio etching *Balli di Sfessania* (c.1615) portrays imaginative, comic, and grotesque characters of Italian street entertainments during the Florentine Carnival. (Metropolitan Museum of Art, New York; Harris Brisbane Dick Fund, 1928 [no. 28.98.44]; photograph used by permission.)

tume and regional dialect particularized the different comic types, as did certain recurring accoutrements, such as Pantalone's dagger, the Capitano's sword, or Arlecchino's wooden sword or baton.

The extent to which dance was used in the *commedia dell'arte,* and the nature of the dancing involved, are thinly documented. But it is inescapable that dance was an important feature of court and popular entertainment, and the *commedia dell'arte's* links with both were close. Tradition sanctioned the use of dance in comedy, and production of the earliest Italian scripted plays included dance sequences. There were opportunities for dance in the popular plays of Andrea Calmo and Angelo Beolco, and it was a feature of performances by carnival clowns like Zan Pollo. Indeed, a condition of employment for *commedia dell'arte* players was that they should possess skill with musical instruments and be able to sing and dance. To most of the actors and actresses, popular and regional dances would have been familiar enough, while descriptive handbooks and manuals of instruction in more formal and sophisticated dances were, where necessary, available to help refine skills. These included Fabritio Caroso's *Il ballarino* (1581) or Cesare Negri's *Le gratie d'amore* (1602 and 1604). Many factors would have shaped the kind of dancing undertaken; for example, the particular skills of individual players, the requirements of the *scenari,* the nature of the performance place, the social complexion, and entertainment expectations of the audience. Flexibility according to the needs of the market place was a *sine qua non* of the profession and doubtless applied to dance as much as to other aspects of *dell'arte* performance. Again, the distinctions between dancing, leaping, and acrobatic movement, often called for in the *scenari*, are not easy to make. Much *commedia dell'arte* dancing was perforce comic and it could be satirical, sometimes expressly ridiculing or parodying the ceremonial dances of the social elite and the extravagances of professional dancers.

Illustrative material certainly suggests that dance was important. Perhaps most familiar are the twenty-four prints in Jacques Callot's *Balli di sfessania*, etched c.1620 and based on drawings made some years before in Italy. These are not reliable visual records of actors in performance; rather, Callot's artistic imagination seems to have been fired by the grotesquerie and the birdlike quality of the figures he depicts. By no means are all of them *dell'arte* figures and none is clearly shown to be dancing on a stage, save for those in the very striking frontispiece in which three characters sing, dance, and play musical instruments on what may be a carnival or fairground setting. Another plate shows performers more formally

COMMEDIA DELL'ARTE. An eighteenth-century engraving entitled *Le Théâtre Italien*, after a painting by Nicholas Lancret. The central figure is Pierrot; he is flanked by Pulcinella and Arlecchina (at left) and Trivellino and Colombina (at right). (Metropolitan Museum of Art, New York; Harris Brisbane Dick Fund, 1953 [no. 53.600.4205]; photograph used by permission.)

dancing in a circle and may reflect recollections of a stage dance pattern; yet another foregrounds dancing figures, and shows, in the background, a performance on a trestle stage. Callot's world is an imagined one of buffoons, entertainers, and types, and insofar as it depicts *commedia dell'arte* characters, they have descended from the play into the piazza to carry the spirit of *dell'arte* performance with them into the wider world of public carnival. Their dance postures are variously witty, ebullient, and grotesque. [*See the entry on Callot.*]

It is the amusing and bizarre that also tend to be emphasized in Gregorio Lambranzi's 1716 figures published in his *Deliciae theatrales*, with plates by Johann Georg Paschner. Lambranzi, a Venetian *maestro del ballo*, claimed to have performed these dances in Italian, German, and French theaters. In his introduction he stresses the importance of confining the dances of comic and ridiculous figures to eccentric styles and (significantly alert to late Baroque notions of stage decorum) considers it inappropriate to allow characters like the *zanni* to dance a "minuet, courante, sarabande or *entrée.*" Notable among Lambranzi's plates are those depicting Dottore and his wife dancing peasant steps, and Scaramuccia performing a *pas de Scaramouche* (a long, exaggerated step in which the hams nearly touch the ground) together with cabrioles and pirouettes. However, Lambranzi's emphasis is on popular and character dancing, and we cannot conclude from his illustrations that *commedia dell'arte* players eschewed more socially refined dances. Much of the illustrative material we possess depicts the visually striking masked figures; aesthetic decorum would have assigned more socially gracious dances to the *innamorati.*

Both Callot and Lambranzi, in their different ways, serve to remind us of how essentially balletic was the *commedia all'improvviso.* Vigorous, physical, and rapidly paced, it depended greatly for stage effect on fluid, if often informally, choreographed movement. Certainly many *commedia dell'arte* performers were noted for the quality of their dancing, or for allied balletic or acrobatic movement, including the actresses Isabella Andreini, Vittoria Piissimi, and Antonia Veronese, and the actors Pier Maria Cecchini, Pietro Gandini, Tommaso Antonio Visentini, and Giuseppe Domenico and Pietro Francesco Biancolelli. The *pas de Scaramouche*, depicted by Lambranzi, took its name from the *dell'arte* comedian Tiberio Fiorilli whose physical agility was legendary, according to the seventeenth-century writer Angelo Costantini. But such illustrative material may be deceptive in its suggestion that dance was a very prominent feature of *commedia dell'arte* performance. On the other hand, the naive watercolor depictions of stage scenes in the Corsiniana collection of *scenari* occasionally depict a character in a pose possibly suggestive of dance.

The first, and indeed only, early printed collection of *scenari* is Flaminio Scala's *Il teatro delle favole rappresentative* (1611). Several of the *scenari* expressly call for dance. In act 2 of *Le Burle d'Isabella*, Pantalone and Pedrolino flirt with Isabella and Flaminia. and the women, before leaving, invite the men to come at night and serenade them. Convinced they have made amorous conquests, the *vecchio* and *zanni* dance for joy, their absurd antics watched by Franceschina and Burattino, the mocking servants. Here the dancing is manifestly ridiculous and may have been more in the nature of random, excited cavorting and leaping than a choreographed dance. Perhaps more carefully organized was the set piece called for in act 2 of *Il Vecchio Geloso*, where in front of Pantalone's house, and to the accompaniment of three vagabond musicians, *vecchi*, *zanni*, and *innamorati* "dance, first with one partner, then with another." This dancing, even if formally composed, would certainly have been in the popular vein, as doubtless too was that required in act 3 of *Il Capitano*, where wedding guests must dance out at the end of one scene and dance in at the start of another. However, it is noticeable in the Scala *scenari* that the dancing is not extensive; nor is it merely decorative and extraneous to the plot. In *Il Capitano*, for example, the bustle and excitement of the dance provide opportunity for the villain, Capitano, to kidnap the heroine, Flaminia. Much more decorative is the dance that closes act 1 of Scala's *L'Arbore Incantato*, but this is a special case. The pastoral conventions governing this scenario license a dance of wood spirits; nevertheless, the dance is largely an embellishment. There is little indication in most *scenari* that a closing dance was a characteristic of *commedia dell'arte* performance. However, the endings of most *scenari* do observe the comic convention of bringing the action to a close with happy pairings in marriage, and a final dance may have been so recurrent a feature as to require no scripted stipulation in the *scenari* themselves.

Although dance clearly occurred, and occasionally played a significant part in early *dell'arte* comic performance, opportunities for the introduction of much formal dance were probably limited to *intermezzi*. *Intermezzi* were farcical comedies with complicated plot lines and rapid movement of scenes, which could easily lose cohesiveness if the thrust of the comic action were slowed or halted by the interpolation of lengthy dance sequences within the acts. For the most part such dancing is likely to have been brief and occasional, either an extension of comic business or closely integrated to it, and serving directly to further, the comic action.

In later *commedia dell'arte* performance the case may have been different. Elements of the *commedia dell'arte* gradually permeated court musical drama and ballet, whether in *intermezzi* or *entrées comiques*. The colorful, stylized masked figures in particular lent themselves to balletic treatment in sophisticated masques and burlesques, providing sharp theatrical contrast to the high formality of Baroque opera and dance. From the 1660s Molière and Jean-Baptiste Lully evolved forms drawing heavily on the stock materials of the *commedia all'improvviso*, and eventually these exercised reciprocal influence on *dell'arte* performances. In some eighteenth century Italian and French *scenari* dance was exploited for considerable scenic effect; for example, Luigi Riccoboni's scenario *Il Giocatore*, composed about 1715, places much of act 2 in a ballroom, and the setting provides the opportunity for a sequence of formal dances, including a *minuette*. It also gives cues for comedy in the inability of Capitano to dance *à la mode*. Dance is very much in evidence in late seventeenth- and eighteenth-century illustrations of the *commedia dell'arte*. It is found in engravings, in paintings by Jean-Antoine Watteau, Claude Gillot, and Giambattista Tiepolo, as well as in the ceramic figurines of the time. But this iconographic material cannot be taken as providing reliable evidence of the style and characteristics of the earlier *commedia dell'arte*—a qualification that probably applies equally to the Lambranzi illustrations mentioned above. Indeed, nearly all the surviving visual records of the *commedia dell'arte*, from the sixteenth century to the eighteenth century, need to be taken with caution. In most, the artistic imagination will have selected, modified, and distorted, and one must not suppose them to possess any quasi-photographic authenticity. To date, the iconography of the *commedia dell'arte* has received little detailed and systematic study, and it presents considerable interpretive problems.

The second half of the eighteenth century saw the gradual decline and dispersal of the *commedia dell'arte*, although its presence was felt in contemporary and later forms such as the harlequinade, the pantomime, and the Pierrot show. Sometimes that presence was particular, as in E. T. A. Hoffmann's *Harlekins Reise* (1809). In the mid- and late nineteenth century there was a reconstructuralist revival of interest in the *commedia dell'arte*. If the form itself was irrecoverable, the "idea" (what it was assumed to have been and what were thought its essential characteristics) came to exert a considerable influence on twentieth-century drama, opera, and dance. Major directors, from Copeau and Reinhardt to Barrault and Strehler, have drawn inspiration from the example of, or staged plays in the supposed manner of, the *dell'arte* players. In Russia the idea of the *commedia dell'arte* was particularly fertile. Directors like Vaktanghov, Tairov, and Eisenstein were inspired by the form. So too was Meyerhold, who included study of *commedia dell'arte* performance techniques in his actor training programs. Michel Fokine drew on the *commedia dell'arte* for *Petrouchka* in 1911. Plays scripted in the manner of the *commedia dell'arte* have provided the libretti for opera, as has Carlo Gozzi's mid-eighteenth century *fiaba, The Love of Three Oranges,* on which Sergei Prokofiev's opera of the same name is based; the plot materials and stock types of the *scenari* have given scope for composers, designers, and choreographers either to stage new work, or imaginatively to rework early *commedia dell'arte*-based plays and musical dramas—for example Léonide Massine's *Pulcinella* in 1920 (with Stravinsky's arrangements of music by Pergolesi and designs by Picasso). Elements of the *commedia dell'arte,* particularly the decorative qualities found in the masked figures, however modified by a romantic view and accommodated to modern theatrical needs, continue to permeate dance and musical theater, and can, when used with discretion, imbue productions with something of the color, wit, and brio that were among the hallmarks of the companies *all'improvviso* in their prime.

COMMEDIA DELL'ARTE. Michel Fokine used *commedia dell'arte* characters in two ballets, *Le Carnaval* (1910) and *The Adventures of Harlequin* (1922). In this 1916 studio portrait, Lydia Lopokova as Columbine and Vaslav Nijinsky as Harlequin strike a pose from *Le Carnaval.* (Photograph by Jean de Strelecki; from the Dance Collection, New York Public Library for the Performing Arts.)

BIBLIOGRAPHY

Andreini, Francesco. *Le bravure del Capitano Spavento.* Venice, 1607.

Apollonio, Mario. *Storia della commedia dell'arte.* Rome, 1930.

Aronco, Gianfranco d'. *Storia della danza popolare e d'arte, con particolare riferimento all'Italia.* Florence, 1962.

Attinger, Gustave. *L'esprit de la commedia dell'arte dans le théâtre français.* Paris, 1950.

Barbieri, Niccolò. *La supplica.* Venice, 1634.

Bartoli, Francesco. *Notizie istoriche de' comici italiani.* 2 vols. Padua, 1782.

Bragaglia, Anton Giulio. *Pulcinella.* Venice, 1581.

Bragaglia, Anton Giulio. *La danza popolare in Italia.* Rome, 1945.

Carrieri, Raffaele. *La danza in Italia, 1500–1900.* Milan, 1946.

Caroso, Fabritio. *Il ballarino* (1581). New York, 1967.

Cecchini, P. M. *Frutti delle moderne comedie.* Padua, 1625.

Comici dell'arte: Corrispondenze 2 vols. Edited by S. Ferrone. Florence, 1993.

Costantini, Angelo. *La vie de Scaramouche.* Paris, 1695.

Courville, Xavier de. *Un apôtre de l'art du théâtre au XVIIIe siècle, Luigi Riccoboni, dit Lélio.* 2 vols. Paris, 1943–1945.

Croce, Benedetto. "Intorno alla commedia dell'arte." In Croce's *Poesia popolare e poesia d'arte.* Bari, 1930.

Duchartre, Pierre-Louis. *The Italian Comedy.* Translated by Randolph T. Weaver. London, 1929.

Ferrone, Siro. *Attori mercanti corsari. La commedia dell'arte in Europa, tra cinque e seicento.* Turin, 1993.

Fitzpatrick, Tim. *The Relationship of Oral and Literate Performance Processes in the Commedia dell'Arte.* Lampeter, 1995.

Gherardi, Evaristo. *Le théâtre italien de Gherardi.* 6 vols. Paris, 1700–1738.

Gozzi, Carlo. *The Memoirs of Carlo Gozzi.* 2 vols. Translated by John Addington Symonds. London, 1890.

Lambranzi, Gregorio. *Neue und curieuse theatralische Tantz-Schul. Deliciae theatrales.* Nuremburg, 1716. Translated by Friderica Derra de Moroda as *New and Curious School of Theatrical Dancing.* London, 1928.

Lea, K. M. *Italian Popular Comedy.* 2 vols. Oxford, 1934.

Marotti, Ferruccio. *Il teatro delle favole rappresentative.* 2 vols. Milan, 1976.

Mic, Constant [Miklashevskii, Konstantin]. *La commedia dell'arte.* Paris, 1927.

Molinari, Cesare. *La commedia dell'arte.* Milan, 1985.

Negri, Cesare. *Le gratie d'amore.* Milan, 1602.

Nicolini, Fausto. *Vita di Arlecchino.* Milan, 1958.

Nicoll, Allardyce. *Masks, Mimes, and Miracles: Studies in the Popular Theatre.* London, 1931.

Nicoll, Allardyce. *The World of Harlequin.* Cambridge, 1963.

Oreglia, Giacomo. *The Commedia dell'Arte.* Translated by Lovett F. Edwards. New York, 1968.

Ottonelli, Giovanni Domenico. *Della christiana moderatione del theatro.* Florence, 1652.

Pandolfi, Vito. *La commedia dell'arte: Storia e testi.* 6 vols. Florence, 1957–1961.

Pandolfi, Vito. *Il teatro del rinascimento e la commedia dell'arte.* Rome, 1969.

Papetti, Viola. *Arlecchino a Londra: La pantomima inglese, 1700–1728.* Naples, 1977.

Perrucci, Andrea. *Dell'arte rappresentativa premeditata ed all'improvviso.* Naples, 1699.

Petraccone, Enzo. *La commedia dell'arte: Storia, tecnica, scenari.* Naples, 1927.

Rasi, Luigi. *I comici italiani.* 2 vols. Florence, 1897–1905.

Riccoboni, Luigi. *Histoire du théâtre italien.* Paris, 1728.

Riccoboni, Luigi. *Discorso della commedia all'improvviso e scenari inediti.* Edited by Irene Mamczarz. Milan, 1973.

Richards, Kenneth, and Laura Richards. *The Commedia dell'Arte: A Documentary History.* Oxford, 1990.

Sand, Maurice. *The History of the Harlequinade* (1860). 2 vols. Philadelphia, 1915.

Sanesi, Ireneo. *La commedia.* 2 vols. 2d ed. Milan, 1954.

Scala, Flaminio. *Scenarios of the Commedia dell'Arte: Flaminio Scala's Il Teatro delle Favole Rappresentative* (1611). Translated by Henry F. Salerno. New York, 1967.

Scherillo, Michele. *La commedia dell'arte in Italia.* Turin, 1884.

Smith, Winifred. *The Commedia dell'Arte.* New York, 1912.

Stoppato, Lorenzo. *La commedia popolare in Italia.* Padua, 1887.

Studies in the Commedia dell'Arte. David J. George and Christopher J. Gossip, eds. Cardift, 1993.

Tani, Gino. *Storia della danza dalle origini ai nostri giorni.* 3 vols. Florence, 1983.

Taviani, Ferdinando. *La commedia dell'arte e la società barocca: La fascinazione del teatro.* Rome, 1969.

Taviani, Ferdinando, and Mirella Schino. *Il segreto della commedia dell'arte.* 2d ed. Florence, 1986.

Tessari, Roberto. *La commedia dell'arte nel seicento: Industria e arte giocosa della civiltà barocca.* Florence, 1969.

Tessari, Roberto. *Commedia dell'arte: La maschera e l'ombra.* Milan, 1981.

Toschi, Paolo. *Le origini del teatro italiano.* Turin, 1955.

KENNETH RICHARDS

COMPETITIONS. *See* Ballet Competitions; Ballroom Dance Competition; *and* Ice Dancing. *For related discussion, see* Dance as Sport.

CONCERTO BAROCCO. Ballet in three movements. Choreography: George Balanchine. Music: Johann Sebastian Bach; Double Violin Concerto in D Minor, BWV 1043. Scenery and costumes: Eugene Berman. First performance: 27 June 1941, Teatro Municipal, Rio de Janiero, American Ballet Caravan. (Preview: 29 May 1941, Little Theater of Hunter College, New York.) Principals: Marie-Jeanne, William Dollar, Mary Jane Shea.

Concerto Barocco was George Balanchine's homage to Bach's polyphonic craftsmanship. Created for American Ballet Caravan's South American tour in 1941, it is a work of shimmering restraint, exactitude, refinement, and continuous motion for all involved. The eight women in the corps are onstage throughout, while the principal ballerina is absent for only a few moments. With Bach's score as its only subject matter, the ballet stands as an austere architectural monument to absolute dance and polyphonic texture.

The work's three movements are marked *vivace, largo ma non tanto,* and *allegro.* The lively opening movement establishes the ballet's rhythmic drive and its complex, though impeccable and precise, spatial patternings. An expansive adagio is the centerpiece, with sustained phrasing and ravishing lifts adding emotional color to the for-

CONCERTO BAROCCO. Members of the original cast of Balanchine's 1941 ballet, including the principals (in front) Marie-Jeanne, William Dollar, and Mary Jane Shea. (Photograph from the Dance Collection, New York Public Library for the Performing Arts. Choreography by George Balanchine © New York City Ballet.)

mal invention. The playful finale, featuring Charleston-like steps and pelvic thrusts, brings the work to a jocular conclusion. Throughout the work, each female soloist dances to one of the two violin lines, while the corps dances to the orchestral foundation. Yet the ballet's own polyphonic structure and the interrelationships of movements among large and small groups transcend any sense of simple correspondence to the musical score.

Concerto Barocco was begun as an exercise in stagecraft with students at the School of American Ballet, who of course wore standard practice clothes—black leotards and pink tights for the girls—at rehearsals. When the ballet was mounted for the Ballet Russe de Monte Carlo in 1945, Balanchine once again dressed his dancers in practice clothes, an innovative step in costuming that has now become accepted practice for many modern choreographers. A few years later, on 11 October 1948, *Concerto Barocco* was presented on the first program of the New York City Ballet, along with *Orpheus* and *Symphony in C,* and thereafter became a staple in the company's repertory. After 1963, the black attire of the dancers was replaced by white leotards and skirts for the female dancers and a white shirt and black tights for the lone male. Thus simply clad, the dancers perform Balanchine's elegant inventions to Bach's engaging score before a luminous blue cyclorama at the back of the stage.

Of all Balanchine's ballets, *Concerto Barocco* is perhaps the most widely performed. With the sanction of the Balanchine Trust, it has entered the repertories of many companies in the United States and in many other countries around the globe. In the mid-1990s it was estimated to be one of the two most frequently performed works by regional ballet companies in North America—outstripped in popularity only by various ballets based on the legend of Dracula.

BIBLIOGRAPHY

Balanchine, George, with Francis Mason. *Balanchine's Complete Stories of the Great Ballets*. Rev. and enl. ed. Garden City, N.Y., 1977.

Choreography by George Balanchine: A Catalogue of Works. New York, 1984.

Denby, Edwin. Review. *New York Herald Tribune* (16 September 1945).

Kaplan, Larry. "Corps Choreography by Balanchine." *Ballet Review* 15 (Winter 1988): 64–75.

Kirstein, Lincoln. *Thirty Years: The New York City Ballet*. New York, 1978.

Kirstein, Lincoln. *Ballet, Bias, and Belief: Three Pamphlets Collected and Other Dance Writings*. New York, 1983.

Reynolds, Nancy. *Repertory in Review: Forty Years of the New York City Ballet*. New York, 1977.

Reynolds, Nancy. "Balanchine: An Introduction to the Ballets." *Dance Notation Journal* 6 (Winter–Spring 1988–1989): 15–74.

Selleck, Nancy. "*Barocco* Turns Fifty." *Ballet Review* 19 (Spring 1991): 88–96.

Willis, Thomas. Review. *Chicago Tribune* (16 August 1967).

NOTATED SCORE. *Concerto Barocco*, Benesh notation by Jürg Lanzrein (1973).

VIDEOTAPE. *Concerto Barocco*, with Jerilyn Dana and Les Grands Ballets Canadiens, *L'Heure du Concert* (SRC, Montreal, 1969). Second movement of *Concerto Barocco*, performed by the Pennsylvania Ballet, *Dance in America* (WNET-TV, New York, 1976).

REBA ANN ADLER

CONCHEROS. In Mexico, the *concheros* dance is known by various names "Azteca," "Chichimeca," "The Dance of the Conquest," "The Dance of Great Tenochtitlan," and "Cuerudos." It is performed in Mexico's Federal District and in the states of Queretaro, Guanajuato, Hidalgo, Tlaxcala, Puebla, San Luis Potosí, Jalisco, Morelos, and Mexico.

The dance of the *concheros* dates from the time of the Spanish conquest of Mexico, when the Cañada region (a part of what is now Queretaro), some one hundred miles (170 kilometers) northwest of Mexico City, was inhabited by the Chichimecas Pames, Mesoamerican hunters and food gatherers. Their culture was influenced chiefly by that of the Otomí to the south, who maintained trade relations with them.

According to legend, the Chichimeca trader Conin fled his native town, Nopala (which was ruled by the chieftains of Xilotepec), accompanied by his seven brothers, relatives, and friends, when he learned of the approach of the Spanish conquerors. Subsequently Conin was baptized, taking the Christian name Hernando de Tapia. He then undertook the conquest of Queretaro with Nicholás de San Luis Montañez and Xilotepec chieftains, commanding an army of Spanish soldiers, Tlaxcalan soldiers, and Christianized Otomí. His campaign culminated in the battle of El Cerro del Sangremal on 25 July 1531. The Spanish victory was allegedly due to the appearance in the heavens of a blazing cross and Saint James the Apostle (Santiago), at the sight of which the Chichimeca laid down their arms and surrendered. The Spanish forces then erected a cross, around which the defeated Chichimeca gathered and began to dance, crying out, "He is God." Most *conchero* groups regard this event as the origin of the dance, which then spread to other areas.

The dance is now performed in a religious context that includes the veneration of the cross, Saint James the Apostle, and the dead. It takes place at religious festivals, including those held in Queretaro in honor of the cross; in San Miguel de Allende, in honor of the archangel Michael; in Tlatelolco in honor of Saint James the Apostle; and in Villa de Guadalupe in honor of the Virgin of Guadalupe.

Each dance is organized in a society called a *conformidad* or a *mesa;* it assigns various tasks in a military-type hierarchy with a captain, sergeants, and soldiers. Several *mesas* are in turn combined under the command of a captain-general.

The night before the festival a vigil is kept and offerings of fruits, *cucharilla* flowers, tortillas, bread, and other items are prepared. During the day a pilgrimage is made to the temple. Upon arrival the offering is presented and a petition is made to the holy image for permission to dance. The dance is performed in the courtyard by men and women, and in some cases by children. The circle is the dominant element in its choreography, a pre-Christian influence. The dance begins with a salutation in cross formation and a turning to the four cardinal points and to the directions of major sanctuaries at which dancing is performed—the Basilica of Guadalupe, Chalma, Los Remedios, and Amecameca.

The musical accompaniment uses both pre-Christian and European instruments, including the *teponaztli* (a type of drum made from a hollowed tree trunk), the *huehuetl* (a percussion instrument), a rattle, a conch shell, and armadillo-shell mandolins (*conchas,* for which the dance is named).

Costumes vary from one dance to another. The male dancers wear a crest made of feathers, a cape with various decorations, and a loincloth. The women wear a straight dress open on the sides and decorated with small ornaments; they wear bird bones and small bells on their ankles. Dancers sometimes dress as Aztec warriors carrying shields.

[*For related discussion, see* Mexico, *article on* Traditional Dance.]

BIBLIOGRAPHY

Kurath, Gertrude Prokosch. *Los concheros*. Ann Arbor, 1946.

Moedano, Gabriel. "Los hermanos de la Santa Cuenta: Un culto de crisis de origen chichimeca." In *Los procesos de cambio en Mesoamérica y áreas circunvecinas*. Mexico City, 1977.

Rostas, Susanna. "The Concheros of Mexico: A Search for Ethnic Identity." *Dance Research* 9 (Autumn 1991): 3–17.
Stone, Martha. *At the Sign of Midnight: The Concheros Dance Cult of Mexico.* Tucson, Ariz., 1975.

César Delgado Martínez

CONGO. *See* Central and East Africa.

CONGO DANCES, a variegated complex of dramatic dances (Sp., *los congos*) widely dispersed throughout the Americas under various names and varying in details of performance and costume. Originally, the word *Congo* was employed as a designation for slaves brought from the Congo–Angola region of Africa; however, in most contemporary situations, *Congo* simply signifies dance traditions of African descent, especially in New Orleans, the Caribbean, and in South America.

Although the folklore in the Roman Catholic colonial regions of the Americas (Spanish, Portuguese, French) incorporates many traditions long practiced in the religions of both Africa and Europe, Congo dances were created in the Americas, from Louisiana to Brazil, as a response to emerging social, political, and religious situations. Their origins rest partly in the practice of electing monarchs within slave communities as a form of local governance. These leaders were often called *governors* in the Protestant colonies of North America.

Historically a tradition of some religious importance, Congo was sometimes characterized by brotherhoods (*cofradías*) that collected alms for the mutual benefit of members, organized processions for patron saints, elected officials for their organizations, and met regularly to celebrate religious festivals.

There are wide divergences in the stylistic elements of the dance drama called "El Juego de los Congos" (The Congo Play), its musical features, choreography, and costume. Nevertheless, the existence of kings and queens, their courts, ministers, ambassadors, secretaries, the Devil, animal characters, and other supernatural beings seem universal. The characters mentioned above need not all appear in any one local tradition, for Congo performances (*Congadas*) include a measure of improvisation. It is common for *Congadas* to be celebrated during the Carnival season.

Congo also has developed strong secular elements within its area of influence. The events represented in Congo dance drama may include almost any event of significance to local groups, as well as elements relevant to their lives. The oral history of slave rebellions, pirates, relationships among Native Americans and *cimarrones* (Maroons, or escaped slaves), life within their fugitive communities (*palenques*), and the biblical stories of conflicts between good and evil (as represented by the archangel Michael and the Devil) form the material presented in dramatic dance tableaux accompanied by singing, drumming, and sometimes the playing of maracas.

In Panama, the religious focus is no longer a major factor; however, remnants of the strong religious component may be seen in the connection between one of the names for Panama's Congo queen, Maria Mercé and the Virgin of Mercy (La Merced), as well as the king, Saint John of God (Juan de Dioso).

One of the distinctive features of Congo dances in each country is the relationship between men and women. Roberto Benjamin (1977) reported that in Paraíba, Brazil, Congo is quite similar to a dramatic dance called "Los Diablos de los Espejos" (Mirror Devils) or "Gran Diablos" (Grand or Great Devils) in Panama. Both these forms emphasize male dancers. Not only do Panamanian Congos have a devil tradition separate from these forms but the role of queen is of great importance and women characters play important parts in the dramatic action and dance. This version emphasizes couple dancing rather than line dancing as in some Brazilian variants. Some undiscovered connections still exist between the many devil-dance traditions in the Americas and various aspects of Congo traditions.

Individual studies of Congo dance drama were made for localities in Central America, the Caribbean, and South America. To find additional documentation, however, one must search the general folkloric literature of specific countries as well as publications that describe African-American dramatic dance genres.

[*See also* Brazil, *article on* Ritual and Popular Dance; *and* Caribbean.]

BIBLIOGRAPHY
Arosemena Moreno, Julio. *Danzas folklóricas de la villa de Los Santos.* Panama, 1994.
Ayesteran, Lauro. *El folklore musical Uruguayo.* Montevideo, 1972.
Bastide, Roger. *Las Américas Negras.* Translated from French by Patricio Azcárate. Madrid, 1969.
Benjamin, Roberto. *Congos da Paraíba.* Rio de Janeiro, 1977.
Brandão, Théo. *Quilombo.* Rio de Janeiro, 1978.
Cable, George Washington. *The Dance in Place Congo and Creole Slave Songs* (1886). New Orleans, 1974. Also contains "The Congo Dance" (1884).
Cheville, Lila, and Richard A. Cheville. *Festivals and Dances of Panama.* Panama, 1977.
Drolet, Patricia L. "The Congo Ritual of Northeastern Panama: An Afro-American Expressive Structure of Cultural Adaptation." Ph.D. diss., University of Illinois, 1980.
Joly, Luz Graziela. *The Ritual "Play of the Congos" of North-Central Panama.* Austin, 1981.
Nuñez, Benjamin. *Dictionary of Afro-Latin American Civilization.* Westport, Conn., 1980.
Ortiz Fernández, Fernando. *Los bailes y el teatro de Los Negros en el folklore de Cuba.* 2d ed. Havana, 1981.
Smith, Ronald R. "The Society of Los Congos of Panama: An Ethnomusicological Study of the Music and Dance-Theater of an Afro-Panamanian Group." Ph.D. diss., Indiana University, 1976.

Szwed, John F., and Roger D. Abrahams. *Afro-American Folk Culture: An Annotated Bibliography of Materials from North, Central, and South America and the West Indies.* 2 vols. Philadelphia, 1978.

Zárate, Manuel F., and Dora P. de Zárate. *Tambor y socavón.* Panama, 1962.

RONALD R. SMITH

CONSERVATORIET. *See* Konservatoriet.

CONTACT IMPROVISATION. *See* Improvisation.

COOK ISLANDS. *See* Polynesia.

COPES, JUAN CARLO. *See* Nieves and Copes. *See also* Tango.

COPLAND, AARON (born 14 November 1900 in Brooklyn, New York, died 2 December 1990 in North Tarrytown, New York), composer. Copland's trio of ballet scores for Eugene Loring, Agnes de Mille, and Martha Graham established him as the leading American composer for the dance. *Billy the Kid, Rodeo,* and *Appalachian Spring* were not instances of writing bars of music to dancers' counts, but genuine collaborations between musician and choreographer.

Born to emigrant parents from the Polish and Lithuanian parts of Russia, Copland studied piano with Leopold Wolfsohn, Victor Wittgenstein, and Clarence Adler, and wishing to be a composer also, studied harmony and counterpoint with Rubin Goldmark. These private lessons instilled rigorous discipline, but Goldmark's conservative approach moved Copland to seek out newer music, such as that of Claude Debussy. In addition to attending concerts, Copland also went enthusiastically to performances by Isadora Duncan and the Diaghilev company.

The year 1921 was a watershed for Copland as he set out for France to study at the American Conservatory in Fontainbleu under Nadia Boulanger. Thus Copland set the style for other Americans—including Virgil Thomson and Walter Piston—who followed him to France to work with her. He and the others assimilated French influences, but with an ear to creating a genuinely American music. (Of the genuinely American Charles Ives, Copland was then only peripherally aware.)

Copland studied with Boulanger for three years, shaping a jazz-tinged style that transformed traditional counterpoint into something uniquely his. Among his student pieces was a projected ballet score, for dance was everywhere in Paris and as Arthur Berger noted, it was a must among Boulanger's students to write for dance. The vampire plot of *Grohg* (prepared with his friend Harold Clurman) was based on the German film *Nosferatu.* Although without either commission or choreographer, Copland worked on it intermittently for two years in Paris, continuing work after returning to New York in 1924. In 1929 he reworked it into a concert piece, *Dance Symphony.* (Tomm Ruud's ballet *Polyandrion,* set to *Dance Symphony* with a scenario based on *Grohg,* was performed by American Ballet Theatre on 6 July 1973 but was not a success.)

In New York, Copland set to work with a missionary zeal for the cause of the new American music. From 1928 to 1933, with Roger Sessions, he presented an influential series of concerts that introduced works by many young and later important composers. After teaching privately, he became a lecturer at the New School for Social Research from 1927 to 1937, in 1933 presenting the music of new composers dubbed simply "The Young Composers Group," including Paul Bowles, Henry Brant, Vivian Fine, and Bernard Herrmann.

Copland's own early music was a great deal more dissonant, even avant-garde, than his popular scores of later date. Chief among the early works, perhaps, is *Piano Variations* (1930), a thorny set of technically demanding variants on an original theme, but to the composer's surprise, Martha Graham used it for *Dithyrambic* (1931). Nor was Copland then concerned with the practicalities of writing music for use. *Music for the Theatre* (1925) and *Dance Symphony* were not functional theater pieces, but commentaries on these genres, although the former was used by Antony Tudor for *Time Table* (1941) for American Ballet. The jazz elements felt in *Music for the Theatre* and *Piano Concerto* (1926) suggest Copland's openness to the rhythms of popular music; whereas contemporary French composers reveled in such influences as exotic flavoring, Copland approached them in a natural manner. A trip to Mexico in 1932 introduced Copland to Latin rhythms, which he used for his portrait of a Mexico City dance hall, *El Salón México* (1933–1936), to the delight of Mexican musicians. A trip to Cuba resulted in the very different *Danzón Cubano* (1944), showing his subtle understanding of dance rhythms.

Copland's first full score in collaboration with a choreographer was *Hear Ye! Hear Ye!* (1934), composed for Ruth Page about a nightclub murder trial in which everyone told a different story. The score was praised for "a modernist sting in harmony and pungent rhythms, and its incursions into the realm of jazz" (Copland and Perlis, 1984). Although Copland made a suite from the ballet in

1939, he eventually withdrew the score but salvaged one number as the second of his *Four Piano Blues*.

Berger (1953) notes that the great Copland scores came in the wake of "a drastic revision of attitude in the middle thirties." Part of a wider populism, this revision took the form of greater accessibility, a deliberate attempt to reach a wider audience than he had with his earlier music. Berger quotes Copland as saying, "I felt that it was worth the effort to see if I couldn't say what I had to say in the simplest possible terms."

According to Virgil Thomson (1966), Copland had been offered a commission by Ballet Caravan prior to *Billy the Kid* but had declined; "it was not till he had heard the scores we three [Thomson, Paul Bowles, and Robert McBride] had done and watched the new troupe in action that he undertook the medium again." Copland's tunefulness and "American" sound in *Billy the Kid* (1938) come from his extensive use of folk material. Cowboy songs are quoted and varied throughout the score. He stretched and refracted a folk melody to give it a feeling of space and of almost distorted repose. The pas de deux between Billy and his sweetheart, for example, is largely a lyrical extrapolation of a much rougher original, "Come Wrangle Yer Bronco." The score's bright, western flavor made it a permanent success. [*See* Billy the Kid.]

For Agnes de Mille's *Rodeo* (1942) he once again utilized and refracted folk tunes and vernacular modes like ragtime to give a western flavor to the score, but *Rodeo* is warmer than *Billy*. Although it too evokes the wide spaces of the Southwest, there is nothing like the striking opening and close of *Billy*, in which the music suggests the difficult yet inevitable drive westward. But his unusual handling of chords and intervals had by then become a virtual Copland trademark. In *Rodeo*, premiered by the Ballet Russe de Monte Carlo at New York's Metropolitan Opera House, the music has an affable quality that never condescends to the ranch people or to the heroine's plight. In evoking the music of western dances and the loneliness of the prairie, he handles the material differently than in *Billy* or in his music for the film *Of Mice and Men* (1940). [*See* Rodeo.]

Appalachian Spring began as a scenario without a title by Martha Graham. Copland proceeded with what he later described as a sort of portrait of the choreographer's personality; "Ballet for Martha" was his working title even after Graham chose her striking title from a Hart Crane poem.

Copland made slight suggestions for changes in Graham's scenario, which she readily accepted, and he set down to work in June 1943, completing the score exactly one year later. Although the popular suite he made from the score is for full symphonic orchestra, the size of the pit in the Library of Congress auditorium where the ballet was to be premiered forced the composer to mold his music for only thirteen musicians with instruments limited to flute, clarinet, bassoon, piano, and strings. The entire sound of the work is different from his other ballet scores, taking advantage of the smaller forces to create delicate as well as powerful effects, while the sonorities are consistently open. The rhythmic drive of the Evangelist's sermon contrasts strikingly with the gentler music for the Pioneer Woman, the controlled excitement of the Young Bride, and the twittering of the Evangelist's Followers. As in *Billy* and *Rodeo*, a world is evoked by seemingly the simplest of means, and while each score is recognizably Copland's, they are also different in many important ways. Copland's use of folk tunes is at its subtlest in *Appalachian Spring*. While in *Billy* he had depended for effect on a number of borrowed melodies, and even in *Rodeo* some music (such as the hoedown) was little more than an orchestral transcription of his source, most of *Appalachian Spring* consists of "composed folk melodies" shaped by the composer to resemble genuine folk tunes. The exception is the Shaker hymn "Simple Gifts," which he subjects to a group of plainly hewn variations. [*See* Appalachian Spring.]

As *Appalachian Spring* capped Graham's American period, so it completed the American period of Copland's work. From 1945 onward, he turned to more abstract and contrapuntal music, slowly moving toward serialism, in which he was totally immersed by the time of *Inscape* (1962). But choreographers (perhaps inspired by the success of the Loring, de Mille, and Graham scores) increasingly used Copland's music for dance. Doris Humphrey took the 1941 Piano Sonata for her *Day on Earth* (1947) and Jerome Robbins borrowed the Clarinet Concerto for his lighthearted *Pied Piper* (1948). But the only score written specifically for dance after *Appalachian Spring* was *Dance Panels*. Originally written in 1959 for Robbins's Ballets: U.S.A., it was intended as the score for the work that eventually became *Moves* (1963), which is danced without any accompaniment. Revised in 1962, the score was first performed by the Munich Opera Ballet with choreography by Heinz Rosen, but the ballet was not a success. When John Taras used the score for the New York City Ballet for *Shadow'd Ground* (1965), Allan Hughes noted in the *New York Times* that "the music sounds as though it could have been created much earlier, for it is akin to the style Copland used as far back as 1940 for *Our Town* or a few years later for *Appalachian Spring*."

Copland wrote nothing after the early 1970s, but one of his last compositions, *Three Latin American Sketches* (1973), once again shows his abiding involvement with dance rhythms. Copland's gifts as a composer for dance include his sense of theater, his willingness to work in union with the choreographer, and his ability to write music that is danceable without being overtly pulsive. In 1982, before a performance of *Appalachian Spring* conducted by the composer, Copland was asked by the *New*

York Times dance critic Jack Anderson why he had not composed more dance scores. "No one asked me." This was not literally true—de Mille, for one, reports asking him for a score in the 1950s, but he said that he did not want to repeat himself. It is this insistence on making each work its own tonal and rhythmic world, rather than repeating successful formulas, that made him such a striking composer for dance.

BIBLIOGRAPHY

Berger, Arthur. *Aaron Copland.* New York, 1953.
Copland, Aaron, and Vivian Perlis. *Copland, 1900 through 1942.* New York, 1984.
Copland, Aaron, and Vivian Perlis. *Copland since 1943.* New York, 1989.
Goodwin, Noël. "Copland Musical Americana." *Dance and Dancers* (November 1990): 21–23.
Martin, John. *Ruth Page: An Intimate Biography.* New York, 1977.
McDonagh, Don. *Martha Graham.* New York, 1973.
Tempo (Winter 1970–1971). Special issue on Copland.
Thomson, Virgil. *Virgil Thomson.* New York, 1966.

KENNETH LaFAVE and GEORGE DORRIS

COPPÉLIA. Full title: *Coppélia, ou La Fille aux Yeux d'Émail.* Ballet in three acts. Choreography: Arthur Saint-Léon. Music: Léo Delibes. Libretto: Charles Nuitter and Arthur Saint-Léon, adapted from a story by E.T.A. Hoffmann, "Der Sandmann" (1815). Scenery: Charles Cambon, Édouard Despléchin, and Antoine Levastre. Costumes: Alfred Albert. First performance: 25 May 1870, Théâtre Impérial de l'Opéra, Paris. Principals: Giuseppina Bozzacchi (Swanilda), Eugénie Fiocre (Franz), François-Édouard Dauty (Doctor Coppélius).

The creation of *Coppélia,* or *The Girl with Enamel Eyes,* took almost three years. Impressed by the 1866 success of the ballet *La Source,* Émile Perrin, then director at the Paris Opera, asked Charles Nuitter to collaborate again with Saint-Léon and Delibes on a new ballet. Nuitter suggested using a doll story by E.T.A. Hoffmann as a basis for the libretto, to which his collaborators quickly agreed. However, as Saint-Léon was then dividing his time between France and Russia, the ballet did not begin to take its final form until the summer of 1869. In the meantime, the music and the dances were created simultaneously, as if molded to each other. Saint-Léon, a musician and folklore enthusiast, sent Delibes information about what he wanted, along with popular songs he collected during his travels. The result was a successful blend of classical variations with such folkloric dances as the mazurka, the czardas, the bolero, and the jig.

Synopsis. *Coppélia* takes place in a village in Galicia, an Austro-Hungarian province, and despite its title, the heroine is a spunky village lass named Swanilda. Swanilda is in love with Franz and is inclined to be jealous of Coppélia, the quiet, enigmatic girl who attracts his attention as she sits reading in an upper window of the house of the mysterious Doctor Coppélius, a toymaker. In a tender pas de deux, Swanilda tests her sweetheart's devotion with an ear of wheat, which when shaken will rustle if he loves her truly but will remain silent if he is false. The results are disappointing: the wheat is silent. Swanilda suspects that Franz loves Coppélia. Both Swanilda and Franz try to forget their troubles by dancing with their friends. During a boisterous encounter with Franz and a few of his companions, Doctor Coppélius drops the key to his house, which Swanilda and her friends use to enter and satisfy their curiosity about Coppélia.

Once inside Coppélius's workshop, they discover that Coppélia is one of a number of fantastic automatons, merely a doll. As they play with the dolls, Coppélius returns and drives them away in a fury, except for Swanilda, who hides in the curtained alcove where Coppélia is kept. Franz climbs through a window on his own quest to make acquaintance with Coppélia. Doctor Coppélius nabs him and tricks him into taking a drug that causes him to fall asleep. At last Coppélius has the opportunity to carry out his greatest experiment: he will transfer Franz's life force to Coppélia and truly animate his beloved creation.

Doctor Coppélius is overjoyed when Coppélia indeed appears to come to life. He delights in her doll-like waltzing and in her spirited performance of a Spanish dance and a Scottish jig, not realizing that she is actually Swanilda in disguise. But "Coppélia" is wilfull and disobedient, and as she proceeds to wreak havoc in his workshop, Doctor Coppélius becomes increasingly alarmed. Swanilda manages to rouse Franz from his stupor, he realizes his mistake, and the two flee the premises. Coppélius discovers the limp form of Coppélia, minus her dress and wig, slumped behind the curtain. His despair is not assuaged by the payment offered to him during the village festival and wedding celebration for Swanilda and Franz that ends the ballet.

History. The role of Swanilda was to have been created by Adèle Grantzow, a protégée of Saint-Léon. Work with her on the first scenes began in 1868, but she fell ill in 1869, and the authors had to look for another dancer. They found her in the class of Madame Dominique, a famous teacher of the day: the prodigiously talented Giuseppina Bozzacchi was just fifteen when she began to work with Saint-Léon in May 1869. The ballet was practically finished by the end of the summer, but Saint-Léon had to leave for Russia then, and rehearsals did not resume until January 1870.

The leading figures of Parisian society attended the ballet's premiere on 25 May 1870. The audience loved the music, and Bozzacchi scored a triumph in all her variations. Trained in Paris since the age of ten, she danced in a style that was essentially French, although noticeably influenced by the somewhat more gymnastic Italian

COPPÉLIA. A Ballet Russe de Monte Carlo production of *Coppélia*, staged by Nicholas Sergeyev after Marius Petipa, with Alexandra Danilova (center) as Swanilda. The company first mounted this classic in 1938, and it remained a staple in the repertory through the 1950s. (Photograph from the Dance Collection, New York Public Library for the Performing Arts.)

school. Thus, she displayed both technical mastery and a winning charm. Only six months after the premiere, on the morning of her seventeenth birthday, she died of smallpox during the German siege of the city in the Franco-Prussian War. When the theater reopened, Léontine Beaugrand danced Swanilda in 1871 and was followed later by Julia Subra, Emma Sandrini, and, in 1908, Carlotta Zambelli. In 1937, Zambelli handed the role over to Solange Schwarz, whose *demi-caractère* style was perfectly suited to it.

The first Franz was a woman performing *en travesti*, Eugénie Fiocre, who was a specialist in such roles. In 1870, male dancers were held in low esteem at the Paris Opera, but if a male had been wanted, no doubt Saint-

Léon would have taken pains to engage one from outside the Opera if necessary. The members of the Jockey Club, who profoundly influenced artistic matters at the Opera, were not interested in having male dancers share the stage with their female favorites. Thus, for almost a hundred years, the role of Franz was performed *en travesti*. Notable interpreters were Marie Sanlaville, Pepa Inverzinni, Olga Soutzo, and Paulette Dynalix.

In 1961, the ballet disappeared briefly from the repertory of the Paris Opera. In 1966, it returned in a more modern form, with the peasants transformed into students, the previously eliminated third act restored, a sound track that seemed more chemical than magical, and Franz played by a male. This version, choreographed by Michel Descombey and danced by Claude Bessy and Cyril Atanassoff, was quickly abandoned. With the help of old models and records in the Paris Opera archives, Pierre Lacotte staged a new version in 1973 that was faithful to the style of Saint-Léon, with Ghislaine Thesmar and Michaël Denard in the principal roles.

Outside France, *Coppélia* has proved popular in many countries. Joseph Hansen staged his version at the Théâtre de la Monnaie in Brussels in 1871 and presented it at the Bolshoi Theater in Moscow in 1882. Aleksandr Gorsky mounted his version in Moscow in 1902. In Saint Petersburg the ballet has been produced numerous times by various choreographers: Marius Petipa in 1884, Enrico Cecchetti in 1894, Fedor Lopukov in 1934, Nina Anisimova in 1949, and Oleg Vinogradov in 1973. Many other productions, literally too numerous to mention, have been mounted in Poland, Sweden, Denmark, Germany, Switzerland, England, South Africa, Australia, and the United States.

There are several reasons for the universal popularity of *Coppélia*. Chief among them is the score by Léo Delibes, which is widely considered to be the first great score written for ballet. Delibes traveled to Hungary with Jules Massenet to transcribe folk music, and his score for *Coppélia* thus has an authentic ethnic quality missing from other "nationalistic" pieces of the era. It was the first ballet score to contain a czardas, and the first-act mazurka has become, independently, a well-known concert piece. Delibes had been a student of Adolphe Adam, the composer of *Giselle*, and Tchaikovsky was inspired to write for ballet by Delibes's achievement. The book for *Coppélia* also has great appeal, dealing as it does with fallible human beings and their emotions and exhibiting the Romantic era's preoccupation with the notion of man creating life, as exemplified by Mary Shelley's *Frankenstein* (1818).

But the book can be adapted and emended to suit the cultural biases and interests of various producers while maintaining its inner logic. For example, the Royal Danish Ballet's production, first presented in Copenhagen on 27 December 1896, was generally faithful to Saint-Léon's original structure but was considerably more virile in effect, as male dancers had been held in high esteem in Denmark for many years. In this version, which was staged by Hans Beck after Max Glasemann's Swedish production, only Swanilda dances on pointe. Although extremely successful with both dancers and audience, Beck's version was criticized because he made extensive cuts in the score. Harald Lander restaged the ballet in 1934, restoring most of the cuts, clarifying the mime scenes, and adding a brilliant male solo for Børge Ralov at the end of the first act. Hans Brenaa staged the work again in Copenhagen in 1951.

In 1975, for the Ballet National de Marseille, Roland Petit created a substantially revised version of *Coppélia* in which Doctor Coppélius, played by himself, was the starring role. The Canadian ballerina Karen Kain danced Swanilda, alternating in the role with the Cuban dancer Loipa Araujo, and Rudy Bryans was Franz. Petit placed the story in a garrison town around 1880, and Coppélius

was transformed from an elderly toymaker into a young *premier danseur*, the better to seduce the woman he loves. In Petit's interpretation of the role, laughter blends with drama when he dreams he is dancing with Coppélia.

Yet another departure from the traditional book was made by Heinz Spoerli in his mounting of *Coppélia* for the Basel Ballet in 1984. Drawing many details of his production from Hoffmann's original story, Spoerli set his version in a German university town, transformed the villagers into students, and named his heroine Antonia. The graduation ball in act 3 is disrupted when, during a wild chase, the students smash the doll Coppélia to pieces. Franz and the brokenhearted Doctor Coppélius lovingly gather the fragments as Antonia, her hopes dashed, flees the scene in tears. In this production, Chris Jensen gave a memorable performance as Franz.

Throughout the twentieth century, however, most productions of *Coppélia*, wherever they have been mounted, have remained faithful to Saint-Léon's original structure, and, it seems, most of them derive from Marius Petipa's reconstruction for the Imperial Ballet in Saint Petersburg in 1884. This important production, as revised ten years later by Lev Ivanov and Enrico Cecchetti, has provided the basis for numerous productions around the globe, notably in England and the United States.

In London, the Danish ballerina Adeline Genée triumphed as Swanilda in a new production of *Coppélia* staged by her uncle Alexander Genée at the Empire Theatre on 14 May 1906. He had earlier staged a version for her at the Munich Hoftheater in 1896. Swanilda was to prove one of Genée's most frequently performed roles, a perennial favorite with London audiences. In 1933 the Vic-Wells Ballet presented the version of Nicholas Sergeyev, based on the Petipa-Cecchetti production, with Lydia Lopokova as Swanilda. This version was also staged by Ballets Russes de Monte Carlo in both London and New York in 1938. Later productions in London were mounted by the Sadler's Wells Ballet (1940), with Mary Honer and Robert Helpmann; by London Festival Ballet (1956), with Belinda Wright and John Gilpin; and by Ballet Rambert (1957), with Violette Verdy and Norman Dixon.

The first American production of *Coppélia* was staged by Mamert Bibeyran for the American Opera in New York on 11 March 1887, with Marie Giuri and Felicita Carozzi in the leading roles, but the first Russian-derived production was presented by the Metropolitan Opera Ballet for the debut performance of Anna Pavlova on 28 February 1910. Later productions in the United States were mounted by Willam Christensen for the San Francisco Ballet (1939) and by Simon Semenov for Ballet Theatre (1942); Semenov's one-act version starred Irina Baronova and Anton Dolin as Swanilda and Franz. American Ballet Theatre presented a new, three-act production by Enrique

Martinez in 1968, with Carla Fracci and Erik Bruhn in the principal roles on opening night.

The New York City Ballet's production, staged by George Balanchine and Alexandra Danilova, was first presented in Saratoga Springs, New York, on 17 July 1974, with Patricia McBride as Swanilda and Helgi Tomasson as Franz. Not unexpectedly, this version, too, derived from the Imperial Ballet production, with an expanded pure dance divertissement in the third act. It is noteworthy that Balanchine, often charged with being interested only in the ballerina in his work, added music from the Delibes ballets *Sylvia* and *La Source* to give the male role more importance. Tomasson was hailed for his interpretation of Franz, and McBride was highly praised for her dazzling realization of Swanilda.

Despite the fact that *Coppélia* is a comedy, many of ballet's greatest classicists have danced the leading roles. The choreography for Swanilda is very demanding, and the role requires her to be onstage almost constantly, a grueling assignment in the three-act version. Alexandra Danilova, as *prima ballerina* of the Ballets Russes de Monte Carlo, is indelibly associated with the role of Swanilda. Edwin Denby once called her "the most wonderful *Coppélia* heroine in the world" (Denby, 1968, p. 87). But other great ballerinas, from the time of Carlotta Brianza in 1896, have also excelled in the part, among them Margot Fonteyn, Svetlana Beriosova, Natalia Makarova, Margot Lander, Toni Lander, Solveig Østergaard, Cynthia Gregory, Carla Fracci, Liliana Cosi, and Gelsey Kirkland. Notable Franzes have included Frederic Franklin, Igor Youskevitch, Flemming Flindt, Niels Kehlet, Ugo dell'Ara, Iván Nagy, Mikhail Baryshnikov, Peter Martins, and Damian Woetzel. The mime role of Doctor Coppélius has been performed memorably by Simon Semenoff, Norman Morrice, Roland Petit, and Niels Bjørn Larsen, among others.

BIBLIOGRAPHY

Anonymous. Program note, New York City Ballet, 17 February 1987.
Balanchine, George, with Francis Mason. *Balanchine's Complete Stories of the Great Ballets*. Rev. and enl. ed. Garden City, N.Y., 1977.
"Coppélia." *L'Avant-Scène / Ballet-Danse*, no. 4. Paris, 1981.
Croce, Arlene. "I Have Made You and You Are Beautiful." *New Yorker* (Date unknown, 1974).
Croce, Arlene. "The Other Royal Ballet" (1966). In Croce's *Afterimages*, pp. 316–319. New York, 1977.
Denby, Edwin. "Coppelia Tells the Facts of Life" (1944). In Denby's *Looking at the Dance*, pp. 84–87. New York, 1968.
Goldner, Nancy, and Lincoln Kirstein. *Coppélia: New York City Ballet*. New York, 1974. With photographs by Richard Benson.
Guest, Ivor. *Two Coppélias*. London, 1970.
Guest, Ivor. *The Ballet of the Second Empire*. London, 1974.
Kirstein, Lincoln. "Decadence: The Dancing Doll." In Kirstein's *Movement and Metaphor*, pp. 170–173. New York, 1970.
Krokover, Rosalyn. *The New Borzoi Book of Ballets*. New York, 1956.
Poesio, Giannandrea. "A Controversial Ballet: Reflections on *Coppélia*." *The Dancing Times* (June 1993): 889–893.
Saint-Léon, Arthur. *Letters from a Ballet Master: The Correspondence of Arthur Saint-Léon*. Edited by Ivor Guest. New York, 1981.
Terry, Walter. *Ballet Guide*. New York, 1976.
Tobias, Tobi. "Travels with *Coppélia*." *Dance Magazine* (February 1987): 52–53.

CLAUDE CONYERS
Based on materials submitted by
Monique Babsky and Zelda Pulliam

CORALLI, JEAN (Giovanni Coralli Peracini; born 15 January 1779 in Paris, died 1 May 1854 in Paris), French dancer and choreographer. Coralli's name is inextricably linked with the Romantic ballet thanks to his collaboration with Jules Perrot on the ballet *Giselle* (1841), which became the epitome of the period's offerings. In his early years he and his wife formed the celebrated dancing couple of Giovanni and Teresa Coralli; they were often pictured together in contemporary prints. From 1831 to 1850 he occupied the position of *premier maître de ballet* at the Paris Opera, where he created a number of important ballets, among them *Giselle*, *Le Diable Boiteux*, *La Tarentule*, and *La Péri*.

CORALLI. Adèle Dumilâtre and Jean Coralli in act 2 of his ballet *La Gypsy* (1820), which premiered at the Académie Royale de Musique, Paris, with Fanny Elssler in the title role. This lithograph, by J. Rigo after Achille Devéria, is from *Album de l'Opéra*, Paris, c.1845. (Courtesy of Madison U. Sowell and Debra H. Sowell, Brigham Young University, Provo, Utah.)

Coralli was of Bolognese descent, the son of a comedian at the Théâtre Italien in Paris. As a child he studied at the ballet school of the Paris Opera but went to Vienna to make his debut as a dancer and choreographer. He danced briefly at the Paris Opera in 1802, then joined Sébastien Gallet's company at the King's Theatre in London. In 1805 he returned to Vienna to assume the position of ballet master at the Hoftheater (Court Theater). His Viennese ballets tended to follow the standard repertory of choreographers of the period, according to Marian Hannah Winter (1974). For example, *Helena und Paris* (29 June 1807) was an Anacreontic ballet based on an episode from the *Iliad*, while *Die Inkas, oder Die Eroberung von Peru* (31 March 1807) was a sentimentalized version of a historical event that took place in an exotic setting. Coralli and his wife often danced leading roles in these ballets, as did Filippo Taglioni, father of the famous ballerina Marie.

Beginning in 1809 the Corallis appeared as principal dancers at the Teatro alla Scala in Milan, where they danced in ballets by Urbano Garzia, Giuseppe Derossi, Gaetano Gioja, and Salvatore Viganò. During the 1810s and early 1820s they also danced at the Teatro La Fenice in Venice and the Teatro São Carlos in Lisbon.

In 1815 Coralli became one of the choreographers at La Scala. The titles of his ballets suggest that he worked predominantly in the mythological mode popular at the time; examples are *Imene Deificato* (9 August 1815), *Le Nozze di Zefiro e Flora* (autumn 1816), and *La Statua di Venere* (spring 1825), the last created for the ballerina Therese Heberle. He also choreographed ballets in Lisbon and Marseille.

His ballet *Belisa, ossia La Nuova Claudina*, presented at La Scala on 4 April 1825, was an early treatment of a theme that appears to have become an *idée fixe* for him: that of a young girl who is seduced by a nobleman and then abandoned. This theme recurs in *Lisbell, ou La Nouvelle Claudine* (1825), *Léocadie* (1828, revived at the Paris Opera as *L'Orgie* in 1831), and the celebrated *Giselle*.

From 1825 to 1829 Coralli served as ballet master of the Théâtre de la Porte-Saint-Martin in Paris, where he created ten full-length ballets and *divertissements* for fourteen plays. His company included Jules Perrot and Joseph Mazilier, both of whom were to become well-known choreographers. Many of Coralli's works for the Porte-Saint-Martin were created to display the comic gifts of the dancer Charles-François Mazurier. Among them were *Monsieur de Pourceaugnac* (28 January 1826), based on the play by Molière, with musical interludes by Lully; *Gulliver* (9 May 1826), a fairy pantomime adaptation of Jonathan Swift's satire; *La Visite à Bedlam* (19 September 1826), in which Mazurier played an Italian dancing master and at one point performed all the roles in a ballet within a ballet; and *La Neige* (6 October 1827), which fea-

tured a highly realistic ice-skating ballet with the dancers on hidden wheels.

The Porte-Saint-Martin was known at the time for its championship of the Romantic drama and its innovative ballets, many of which anticipated the Paris Opera's own Romantic productions. In the play *Faust* (1828), a fairy melodrama version of Goethe's verse drama, Coralli created a *pas de sylphides* that foreshadowed the supernatural "white scenes" of Romantic ballets such as *La Sylphide* (1832) and his own *Giselle*.

In 1831 Coralli was engaged as *premier maître de ballet* of the Paris Opera, replacing Jean-Louis Aumer. As his first work there, Coralli revived *Léocadie*, which he had previously presented at the Porte-Saint-Martin in 1828. With a new scenario by Eugène Scribe and a new score by Michele Carafa, it reemerged on 18 July 1831 as *L'Orgie*. The action of the ballet was transferred from Portugal to Spain as a pretext for introducing Spanish-style character dances, always popular with the audience. The story, which depicted a girl who is seduced and bears an illegitimate child, introduced "a certain realism . . . new to the Opéra stage" (Guest, 1980) but failed to retain an enduring place in the repertory. The principal roles were danced by Amélie Legallois and Mazilier, the latter another veteran of the Porte-Saint-Martin.

The Romantic ballet came of age in 1832 when Marie Taglioni created the title role of *La Sylphide*, choreographed for her by her father, Filippo. This ballet created a vogue for the supernatural, upon which Coralli's next work, the ballet for the opera *La Tentation* (20 June 1832), also capitalized. The germ of Edmond Cavé's scenario came from an ambulatory ballet composed in 1462 by King René of Anjou. The story concerns the struggle of an angel and a demon for the soul of a hermit (Mazilier). The demon creates the beautiful Miranda (Pauline Duvernay) to tempt the hermit. One of his trials takes place in a harem, a setting motivated by the Romantic period's love for exotic locales. Coralli's *Roméca*, a chain dance choreographed for this scene, was one of the bright spots in a work that owed more of its success to Duvernay's performance than to the strength of its choreography.

La Tentation was the first of Coralli's many works for opera. He also choreographed *divertissements* for Luigi Cherubini's *Ali-Baba* (1833; with ballet music by Fromental Halévy), Mozart's *Don Giovanni* (1834), Louis-Abraham Niedermeyer's *Stradella* (1837) and *Marie Stuart* (1844), Daniel Auber's *Le Lac des Fées* (1839), Gaetano Donizetti's *Les Martyrs* (1840), Michael Balfe's *L'Étoile de Séville* (1845), and others.

During the early 1830s the young Viennese ballerina Fanny Elssler began her rise to fame. When Dr. Louis Véron engaged her to dance at the Paris Opera, it was decided that she should make her debut in Coralli's *La Tempête, ou L'Île des Génies*, which was already in preparation.

The ballet was first presented on 15 September 1834. It was freely adapted by Adolphe Nourrit, who had written the scenario of *La Sylphide*, from Shakespeare's play *The Tempest*. Duvernay and Mazilier danced the lovers Léa and Fernando, while Elssler danced the fairy Alcine, who attempts to lure away Fernando by appearing in Léa's place. Coralli's choreography successfully exploited the brilliance and precision of Elssler's dancing—particularly her pointe work, which was still a relatively new technique. The bacchanal of gnomes in the tempest scene was highly praised for its originality. Also contributing to the ballet's success were the score by Jean Schneitzhoeffer, the composer of *La Sylphide*, and a new, highly realistic scenic effect that simulated the movement of water.

If *La Tempête* served to introduce Elssler to Paris, Coralli's next ballet, *Le Diable Boiteux* (1 June 1836), made her the toast of the city. The ballet's scenario, adapted from Alain-René Lesage's eponymous novel, was a Faustian tale in which a young student, Cléophas (Mazilier), frees a demon who promises to serve him. As part of his service the demon conjures up three women, Paquita (Pauline Leroux), Dorotea (Legallois), and Florinda (Elssler). [*See* Diable Boiteux, Le.]

Ironically, the most famous dance in *Le Diable Boiteux*, Florinda's *cachucha*, may not have been choreographed by Coralli. Elssler's friend and sometime manager, Henry Wickoff, later claimed that the dancer herself had arranged the dance; it is also possible that she learned it from a Spanish dancer who performed in Paris. "La Cachucha" was undoubtedly the high point of the ballet; Elssler performed it until the end of her career, and it inspired numerous prints, parodies, and a fashion for character dances in general.

La Chatte Metamorphosée en Femme (16 October 1837) was also designed as a vehicle for Elssler, but it met with considerably less success. Elssler played a Chinese princess who wins the love of a student by pretending to be his beloved cat, transformed by magic into a woman. Coralli's choreography was considered inferior to his usual quality, and the ballet was compared unfavorably to Louis Henry's Chinese ballet *Chao-Kang* (1834).

Coralli was more successful with *La Tarentule* (24 June 1839), in which Elssler played an Italian girl who saves her beloved by pretending to be bitten by a tarantula. The traditional remedy for such a bite, the dance known as the tarantella, offered an excellent pretext for a character dance of the type that had made Elssler famous.

The pinnacle of Coralli's choreographic career was in 1841, when the ballet *Giselle, ou Les Wilis* was first presented at the Paris Opera on 28 June. The scenario, written by Gautier in collaboration with Jules-Henri Vernoy de Saint-Georges, was inspired by a legend told in Heinrich Heine's *De l'Allemagne*. Giselle, a peasant girl, is courted by the nobleman Albrecht, who is disguised as a peasant. She discovers that he is already betrothed to a woman of his own class, goes mad, and dies. Act 2 is set in the ghostly domain of the wilis, spirits who entice men to dance to their deaths. Although Giselle has become a wili, her love for Albrecht endures beyond death and she saves him from the fate decreed by the Queen of the Wilis. [*See* Giselle.]

Coralli had previously treated the theme of seduction and betrayal in several ballets, including *Belisa* (1825) and *L'Orgie* (1831). The scenario that Gautier and Saint-Georges provided for *Giselle* differed in two important respects: the courtship does not proceed to the point of a secret marriage and a child, and the plot does not end with the reunion of the lovers. Giselle was less earthy than her earlier counterparts, and the tragic ending was possibly more satisfying to the Romantic sensibility than the glibly happy endings of Coralli's previous ballets.

The scenario reached Coralli through Perrot and Adolphe Adam, the ballet's composer. Although Perrot was not at this time an official member of the Paris Opera, he was present to look after the interests of his protégée Carlotta Grisi, and he recognized the role of Giselle as an ideal vehicle for her. He choreographed her dances in the ballet, although for contractual reasons he was not credited either on the playbill or the scenario. Coralli was responsible for the rest of the choreography, including the first-act ensembles and the peasant pas de deux (danced by Nathalie Fitzjames and Auguste Mabille to interpolated music by Friedrich Burgmüller) and the act 2 dances of the wilis. The cast also included Lucien Petipa as Albrecht and Adèle Dumilâtre as the Queen of the Wilis.

Giselle brought together in a single ballet many of the elements that had made the Romantic ballet successful. Act 1 offered local color, tinged by the medievalism of the troubadour style. The heroine's physical delicacy and emotional intensity, culminating in madness, marked her difference from the common herd—a distinction valued by the Romantics. Act 2 exploited the love of the supernatural and presented man's pursuit of the unattainable as a purifying experience. The ballet won immediate success and was widely imitated throughout Europe. Of all the Paris Opera's productions of the Romantic period, it alone has survived. Although the choreography has undergone inevitable changes during the years, most present-day productions are attributed to Coralli and Perrot.

Gautier and the composer Burgmüller were again Coralli's collaborators in his next ballet, *La Péri* (17 July 1843). Gautier's scenario told the story of a péri, an oriental fairy, danced by his beloved Grisi. Achmet (Petipa) sees her in an opium dream and falls in love with her. She comes to earth in the body of Leila, a runaway slave, who wins Achmet's love through her resemblance to the Péri. Leila's owner tries to reclaim her and imprisons Achmet for refusing to surrender her. His love and loyalty are rewarded in an apotheosis, when the walls of his prison vanish and he is seen entering paradise with the Péri. [*See* Péri. La.*]

In *La Péri*, Coralli created two striking dances for Grisi. The *pas du songe* of Achmet's opium dream required her to fling herself from a six-foot-high (two-meter) platform, representing the Péri's celestial court, into Petipa's waiting arms. This leap was much applauded for its daring and proved to be a drawing point for the ballet.

The *pas de l'abeille* in act 2 was also highly praised. As the slave girl Leila, Grisi pretended to have been stung by a bee, the pretext for a decorous striptease. This dance, however, was soon replaced by a Spanish dance. Coralli's choreography also included the use of pupils from the ballet school, a practice new to the Paris Opera.

Coralli's penultimate ballet, *Eucharis* (7 August 1844), was a failure. Based on an unfashionable mythological scenario by the Opera's director, Léon Pillet, it presented a love triangle involving the goddess Calypso (Leroux), Telemachus (Petipa), and Calypso's handmaiden Eucharis (Dumilâtre). Several of Coralli's dances in this ballet won praise from the critics, although Édouard Deldevez, the ballet's composer, complained of his lack of musicality.

Ozaï (26 April 1847) was Coralli's last ballet, although he continued as titular principal ballet master until 1850. The scenario, inspired by the travel book of the French explorer Louis-Antoine de Bougainville, presented Adeline Plunkett in her first created role as Ozaï, a native of the South Seas. She falls in love with a shipwrecked sailor and accompanies him to France, but relinquishes him upon learning of his love for Bougainville's daughter. The ballet was performed only ten times.

Coralli's duties as ballet master were taken over by Mazilier, Perrot, and Mabille, and Coralli died four years after his retirement, on 1 May 1854. His survivors included his son, Eugène, a dancer, mime, and *régisseur*.

[*See also entries on Elssler, Grisi, Mazilier, and Perrot.*]

BIBLIOGRAPHY

Beaumont, Cyril W. *Complete Book of Ballets*. London, 1937.
Binney, Edwin, 3rd. *Les ballets de Théophile Gautier*. Paris, 1965.
Christout, Marie-Françoise, and Gino Tani. "Coralli, Jean." In *Enciclopedia dello spettacolo*. Rome, 1954-.
Guest, Ivor. *The Romantic Ballet in Paris*. 2d rev. ed. London, 1980.
Guest, Ivor. *Jules Perrot: Master of the Romantic Ballet*. London, 1984.
Winter, Marian Hannah. *Le théâtre du merveilleux*. Paris, 1962.
Winter, Marian Hannah. *The Pre-Romantic Ballet*. London, 1974.

ARCHIVE.   Walter Toscanini Collection of Research Materials in Dance, New York Public Library for the Performing Arts.

SUSAN AU

CORNAZANO, ANTONIO (also Cornazzano; born c.1430 in Piacenza, Italy, died December 1484 in Ferrara), Italian dancing master, theorist, humanist, and statesman. Cornazano came from one of Piacenza's leading noble families. A figure of major literary importance, he was educated in classical and contemporary European languages and well versed in the theory and practice of the military arts, of politics, and of the art of dancing. He spent most of his first twenty years in Piacenza, except for a five-year period of study at the Studio di Siena (c.1443–1448; see Poggiali, 1789, vol. 1, pp. 72–73).

Cornazano's dance instructor in Piacenza was the great Domenico da Piacenza, whom he called "mio solo maestro e compatriota" (my only master and compatriot) and whose dance theory and aesthetics are restated in Cornazano's own manual *Libro dell'arte del danzare* (The Book on the Art of Dancing; 1st ed., 1455; 2d extant ed., 1465; for a full list of primary sources, see bibliography). Cornazano's manual also provides a selection of Domenico's finest choreographies.

Early in 1454 Cornazano joined the household staff of Duke Francesco Sforza as "Consigliore, Segretario, e Ciamberlane" (counselor, secretary, and chamberlain; see Poggiali, 1789, vol. 1, p. 80) and as educator of the duke's children. His friendship with the young princess Ippolita, whom he instructed in the art of dancing and to whom the original *Libro* was dedicated, lasted a lifetime (see the affectionate reference to her in Cornazano's *Vita di Maria Vergine* [Life of the Virgin Mary]; quoted in Poggiali, 1789, vol. 1, p. 80).

In 1465 Cornazano was one of the Lombardic nobles who accompanied the princess to her wedding with Alfonso, duke of Calabria. After Francesco Sforza's death in 1466, Cornazano went to Venice and spent the next eleven years as military adviser to General Bartolommeo Coleone. During this period he became actively involved in the blossoming book-printing trade in that city (Castellani, 1888, p. 22). Two years of political and diplomatic activities in and for his hometown of Piacenza followed.

In autumn 1479 Ercole d'Este called Cornazano to Ferrara, where he was warmly welcomed and "con molto onor . . . intertenuto" (entertained with much honor; Poggiali, 1789, vol. 1, p. 82). Soon after his arrival he married Taddea de Varro, a member of one of the oldest and noblest Ferrarese families. He died at Christmas 1484 and is buried in the Chiesa de' Servi.

Cornazano's *Libro* is the second dance instruction book of the Renaissance, preceded only by Domenico's treatise, to which it is closely related in theoretical content as well as in repertory. The theoretical material is arranged in almost exactly the same manner as that found in the manuscript of Domenico's treatise held by the Bibliothèque Nationale in Paris, beginning with the six *particelle principali* (primary requisites) necessary for all good dancing, followed by definitions and descriptions of the basic step-units *(tempi)* for the four dance meters, the individual steps and their tempo relationships, and the ladder that graphically illustrates the dance speeds from the slowest *(bassadanza)* to the fastest *(piva)*, and concluding with the rules for interchanging the *tempi* in the four meters.

The dances themselves (*Libro*, folios 12'–34), eight *balli* with their mensurally notated music *(in canto, in canto da sonare)* and three *bassedanze*, are also taken from the work of the older master. About the *balli* Cornazano says that they were "recently made by the king of the art," that is, Domenico. Domenico's manual was compiled in 1440 (Inglehearn and Forsyth, 1981) or 1450 (Gallo, 1979; Heartz, 1966); the *ballo* choreographies in Cornazano must therefore belong to the original version of the *Libro*, dated 1455. The date of the second extant version of the *Libro* has been much discussed (for a summary of opinions prior to 1915, see Mazzi, 1915, pp. 2–3). In the treatise as we know it, the dedicatory sonnet to Ippolita, duchess of Calabria, is preceded by a poem in *terza rima* honoring Sforza Secondo, Ippolita's natural brother. In that poem Cornazano mentions that the princess has just "gone across Italy to take a husband." Because her marriage to Alfonso took place in June 1465, the extant version of the *Libro* must have been written in the second half of that year (Mazzi, 1915) or shortly thereafter.

Unique to Cornazano are the three model "tenori da bassedanze et saltarelli gli megliori et piu usitati degli aetri" ("tenors for *bassedanze* and *saltarelli*, the best and most used of all"; folios 32ff.), written in even-note values (semibreves) reminiscent of the French Burgundian *bassedanze* tenors (facsimiles in Mazzi, 1915; transcriptions in Crane, 1968; Jackman, 1964; Kinkeldey, 1959; Inglehearn and Forsyth, 1981; Smith, 1995). Their presence in the *Libro* gives us an idea of at least one of the procedures used in providing musical accompaniment for Italian *bassedanze* of the fifteenth century, all of which are notated choreographically only: if the length of the tenor corresponded to that of the step sequence, any melody could be used to accompany for any *bassadanza*.

Particularly noteworthy is Cornazano's definition of *balletto* as a dramatic dance form: "che po contenire in se tutti gli . . . mouimenti corporei . . . ordinate ciascun con qualche fondamento di proposito" ("which can contain all bodily motions, each with its own characteristic design"; *Libro*, folios 7'–8). Here, for the first time in the history of the art of dancing, the term *ballet* is used in a modern sense, thus clearly placing the beginnings of a major art form in the elegant surroundings of the *ballo nobile* of the fifteenth century.

PRIMARY SOURCES

Fraudiphilia. N.p., c.1449–1455. Comedy in Latin.

La Sforzeide. N.p., c.1450. Poem in terza rima dedicated to Francesco Sforza.

De proverbiorum origine (c.1455). Milan, 1503.

Libro dell'arte del danzare. N.p., 1455–1465. Manuscript located in Biblioteca Apostolica Vaticana, Capponiano 203. Edited by Curzio Mazzi, "Il 'Libro dell'arte del danzare' di Antonio Cornazano," *La Bibliofilia* 17 (1915): 1–30. English translation by Madeleine Inglehearn and Peggy Forsyth, *The Book on the Art of Dancing* (London, 1981). Text and English translation by A. William Smith in *Fifteenth-Century Dance and Music* (Stuyvesant, N.Y., 1995).

Vita di Maria Vergine (c.1460). Venice, 1471.

Vita Christi (Vita di Gesù Cristo). [Venice], 1462.

De excellentium virorum principibus. N.p., c.1465. Edited by F. Gabotta. Pinerola, 1889.

Commentatorium de vita et gestis invictissimi bellorum principis Bartholomaei Colei. N.p., c.1476.

De re militari (c.1476). Venice, 1493.

Sonetti, e canzone del preclarissimo poeta messere Antonio Cornazano Piacentino. Venice, 1502.

De modo regendi. Venice, 1517.

Proverbi di mess. Antonio Cornazano. Venice, 1518.

La vita del Signor Pietro Avogadro Bresciano. Venice, 1540.

La reprensione del Cornazzano contra Maganello. N.p., n.d.

SECONDARY SOURCES

Bertoni, Giulio. "La morte di Antonio Cornazano." *Giornale storia della letteratura italiana* 74 (1919): 176–178.

Brainard, Ingrid. "Die Choreographie der Hoftänze in Burgund, Frankreich und Italien im 15. Jahrhundert." Ph.D. diss., University of Göttingen, 1956.

Brainard, Ingrid. "Bassedanse, Bassadanza, and Ballo in the Fifteenth Century." In *Dance History Research: Perspectives from Related Arts and Disciplines*, edited by Joann W. Kealiinohomoku. New York, 1970.

Brainard, Ingrid. "La Fia Guilmin in canto/Filia Guilielmino in canto (Domenico/A. Cornazano)." Appendix I in Isabel Pope-Masakata Kanasawa, *The Musical Manuscript Montecassino 871*. Oxford, 1978.

Brainard, Ingrid. "The Role of the Dancing Master in Fifteenth-Century Courtly Society." *Fifteenth-Century Studies* 2 (1979): 21–44.

Brainard, Ingrid. "Cornazano, Antonio." In *The New Grove Dictionary of Music and Musicians*. London, 1980.

Brainard, Ingrid. *The Art of Courtly Dancing in the Early Renaissance.* West Newton, Mass., 1981.

Brown, Howard M. "The Book on the Art of Dancing." *Early Music* 11 (1983).

Castellani, Carlo. *I privilegi di stampa e la proprietà letteraria in Venezia.* Venice, 1888.

Cestaro, Benvenuto. "Cornazano, Antonio." In *Enciclopedia italiana.* Rome, 1929–.

Crane, Frederick. *Materials for the Study of the Fifteenth-Century Basse Danse.* Brooklyn, 1968.

Dolmetsch, Mabel. *Dances of Spain and Italy from 1400 to 1600.* London, 1954.

Franko, Mark. *The Dancing Body in Renaissance Choreography, c.1416–1589.* Birmingham, Ala., 1986.

Frati, Lodovico. "Un volgarizzamento ignoto del Cornazano." *Bollettino Storico Piacentino* 10 (1915): 241ff.

Gallo, F. Alberto. "Il 'ballare lombardo,' circa 1435–1475." *Studi musicali* 8 (1979): 61–84.

Gombosi, Otto. "About Dance and Dance Music in the Late Middle Ages." *Musical Quarterly* 27 (July 1941): 289–305.

Guasti, Cesare, ed. *Lettere di una gentildonna fiorentina/Alessandra Macinghi Negli Strozzi.* Florence, 1877.

Guglielmo Ebreo da Pesaro. *On the Practice or Art of Dancing* (1463). Translated and edited by Barbara Sparti. Oxford, 1993.

Heartz, Daniel. "A Fifteenth-century Ballo: *Rôti bouilli joyeux.*" In *Aspects of Medieval and Renaissance Music. A Birthday Offering to Gustave Reese*, edited by Jan LaRue, pp. 359–375. New York, 1966.

Jackman, James L. *Fifteenth-Century Basse Dances.* Wellesley, Mass., 1964.

Kinkeldey, Otto. "Dance Tunes of the Fifteenth Century." In *Instrumental Music: A Conference at Isham Memorial Library, May 4, 1957*, edited by David G. Hughes. Cambridge, Mass., 1959.

Lockwood, Lewis. *Music in Renaissance Ferrara, 1400–1505.* Cambridge, Mass., 1984.

Lo Monaco, Mauro, and Sergio Vinciguerra. "Il passo doppio in Guglielmo e Domenico: Problemi di mensurazione." In *Guglielmo Ebreo da Pesaro e la danza nelle corti italiane del XV secolo*, edited by Maurizio Padovan. Pisa, 1990.

Luzio, Alessandro. *I precettori d'Isabella d'Este.* Milan, 1887.

Marrocco, W. Thomas. "The Derivation of Another Bassadanza." *Acta Musicologica* 51.1 (1979): 137–139.

Marrocco, W. Thomas. *Inventory of Fifteenth-Century Bassedanze, Balli, and Balletti in Italian Dance Manuals.* New York, 1981.

McGee, Timothy J. "Dancing Masters and the Medici Court in the Fifteenth Century." *Studi Musicali* 17.2 (1988): 201–224.

Meylan, Raymond. *L'énigme de la musique des basses danses du quinzième siècle.* Bern, 1968.

Michel, Artur. "The Earliest Dance-Manuals." *Medievalia et Humanistica* 3 (1945): 117–131.

Padovan, Maurizio. "Guglielmo Ebreo e i maestri del XV secolo." In *Mesura et arte del danzare: Guglielmo Ebreo da Pesaro e la danza nelle corti italiane del XV secolo*, edited by Patrizia Castelli et al. Pesaro, 1987.

Poggiali, Cristoforo. *Memorie per la storia letteraria di Piacenza.* 2 vols. Piacenza, 1789.

Pontremoli, Alessandro, and Patrizia La Rocca. *Il ballare lombardo: Teoria e prassi coreutica nella festa di corte del XV secolo.* Milan, 1987.

Renier, Rodolfo. "Osservaziono sulla cronologia di un'opera del Cornazano." *Giornale storia della letteratura italiana* 17 (1891).

Silvestri, Michele A. *Gli antenati e la famiglia di messer Antonio Cornazano.* Turin, 1914.

Silvestri, Michele A. "Appunti di cronologia cornazaniana." In *Miscellanea di storia, letteratura e arte piacentina.* Piacenza, 1915.

Smith, A. William, trans. and ed. *Fifteenth-Century Dance and Music: The Complete Transcribed Italian Treatises and Collections in the Tradition of Domenico da Piacenza.* 2 vols. Stuyvesant, N.Y., 1995.

Southern, Eileen. "Some Keyboard Basse Dances of the Fifteenth Century." *Acta Musicologica* 25.2–3 (1963): 114–124.

Southern, Eileen. "A Prima Ballerina of the Fifteenth Century." In *Music and Context: Essays for John M. Ward*, edited by Anne Dhu Shapiro. Cambridge, Mass., 1985.

Sparti, Barbara. "The Fifteenth-Century *Balli* Tunes: A New Look." *Early Music* 14.3 (1986): 346–357.

Sparti, Barbara. "Style and Performance in the Social Dances of the Italian Renaissance: Ornamentation, Improvisation, Variation, and Virtuosity." In *Proceedings of the Ninth Annual Conference, Society of Dance History Scholars, City College, City University of New York, 14–17 February 1986*, compiled by Christena L. Schlundt. Riverside, Calif., 1986.

Tani, Gino. "Cornazano, Antonio." In *Enciclopedia dello spettacolo.* 9 vols. Rome, 1954–1968.

Wilson, D. R. "'Damnes' as Described by Domenico, Cornazano, and Guglielmo." *Historical Dance* 2.6 (1988–1991): 3–8.

Wilson, D. R. *The Steps Used in Court Dance in Fifteenth-century Italy.* Cambridge, 1992.

Wilson, D. R. "'Finita: Et larifaccino unaltra volta dachapo.'" *Historical Dance* 3.2 (1993): 21–26.

Zannoni, Giovanni. "Il 'Libro dell'arte del danzare' di A. Cornazano (1465)." In *Rendiconti della Reale Accademia dei Lincei*, ser. 4, vol. 6. Rome, 1890.

INGRID BRAINARD

CORSAIRE, LE. Ballet in three acts, five scenes. Choreography: Joseph Mazilier. Music: Adolphe Adam. Libretto: Jules Henri Vernoy de Saint-Georges and Joseph Mazilier, after *The Corsair*, by Lord Byron. Scenery: Édouard Despléchin, Charles Cambon, Joseph Thierry, and A. Martin. Costumes: A. Albert. First performance: 23 January 1856, Théatre Impérial de l'Opéra, Paris. Principals: Carolina Rosati (Medora), Domenico Segarelli (Conrad).

Although it originated in France, *Le Corsaire*, like *Giselle*, found its second birthplace in Russia. First staged at the Bolshoi Theater in Saint Petersburg by Jules Perrot on 12 January 1858, the ballet had a long life and many recensions in the repertory of Russian ballet. *Le Corsaire* enjoyed particular popularity after the Revolution of 1917. Although it never left the repertory, the 1960s and early 1970s saw a period of renewed interest in the work. It was then that the pas de deux of a slave and the heroine, Medora, became a popular concert number, a staple in the

LE CORSAIRE. A lithograph by Alexandre Lacauchie depicting Carolina Rosati as Medora in the original production of Joseph Mazilier's 1856 ballet. (Photograph from the Dance Collection, New York Public Library for the Performing Arts.)

repertory of leading dancers and frequently performed at ballet competitions.

A product of the late period of Romantic ballet, *Le Corsaire* differed in important ways from the usual Romantic ballets. Works such as *La Sylphide* and *Ondine*, with their fantastic subjects drawn from fairy tales and legends, centered around the contest between supernatural and earthly forces and followed the aesthetic tradition of the *ballet blanc*. In the 1850s choreographers began to take a greater interest in drama in ballet, with quite realistic, if exalted, characters, usually devoid of the fantastic element. This late period of ballet romanticism was characterized by subjects drawn from adventure literature. Thus, Perrot ignored the philosophical message of Byron's poem and focused instead on its dramatic action, the adventures of a gallant rover. The oriental motif of the poem also appealed to the creators of *Le Corsaire*, who idealized its exotic, mystic, and languidly sensuous imagery.

Perrot's version of the ballet was a typical Romantic-realistic drama. The role of Conrad, the noble pirate, was played by Marius Petipa, while Perrot himself appeared as his adversary, Pasha Seyd, who holds captive Conrad's beloved, Medora, the young Greek girl he abducted from her guardian, the slave-dealer Isaac Lanquedem. Perrot created a theatrical pageant celebrating the Romantic idea of a chivalrous lover rescuing his fair lady. Conrad plucks Medora from captivity and, although his ship is wrecked as they try to escape, the lovers miraculously overcome the raging elements and safely gain the shore. Despite its neat, straightforward dramaturgy, Perrot's version suffered from an unconvincing dance treatment for the character of Conrad as well as from the absence of significant dramatic conflicts. Nor was Adam's score conspicuous for its integrity. Starting with Perrot's *Corsaire*, excerpts from other composers' music were incorporated into the ballet's score; for example, a *pas d'esclaves* (slaves' dance), choreographed by Petipa, was set to music by Prince Petr Oldenburg. Later, excerpts from Léo Delibes, Riccardo Drigo, and Cesare Pugni were added. Aleksandr Gorsky's revised version of the ballet used music from Chopin, Tchaikovsky, Grieg, and other composers.

A new version of the ballet was staged by Petipa at Saint Petersburg's Bolshoi Theater on 24 January 1863. It drew on Perrot's production as well as on the Mazilier original. Petipa repeatedly returned to *Le Corsaire*, producing his last revival of the ballet at the Maryinsky Theater on 13 January 1899. This version was in strict academic style, in which the plot-motivated succession of events receded to the background, leaving center stage to the dancing. In his 1868 version Petipa incorporated a new scene, "Le Jardin Animé," to music by Delibes. The scene represented a festal dream and went down in the annals of Russian ballet as one of Petipa's best creations, a ballet

LE CORSAIRE. Tatiana Terekhova of the Kirov Ballet performs a *grand jeté* in "Le Jardin Animé," a famous scene in act 3. (Photograph © 1989 by Jack Vartoogian; used by permission.)

within a ballet, which somewhat anticipated the genre of one-act ballets. Petipa was not actually the inventor of the scene; it first appeared in the original Mazilier production in 1867 as the *pas de fleurs* (flowers' dance). As was often the case with Petipa, while he borrowed something from the work of his fellow choreographers he nevertheless made it completely his own. Successive Soviet productions emphasized the dramatic aspect of the ballet's storyline and cut "Le Jardin Animé," as it tended to retard the action. However, later revivals, including Konstantin Sergeyev's 1973 version for the Kirov Ballet in Leningrad, attempted to return to Petipa's original production. The best of Petipa's choreography in *Le Corsaire* lives on. Over the years the role of Medora was taken by leading dancers, including Anna Sobeshchanskaya, Anna Pavlova, Tamara Karsavina, Olga Preobrajenska, and Ekaterina Geltser.

In 1912 Aleksandr Gorsky partly reworked Petipa's production for the Bolshoi Ballet in Moscow, trying to add unity to the ballet. In the old version oriental pirates and merchants mingled with ballerinas in tutus. Gorsky and the artist Konstantin Korovin, who designed the decor and costumes, reduced everything to a common denominator. Medora wore a Greek chiton, and the classical "Jardin Animé" had an Oriental flavor. A unity of styles was not

LE CORSAIRE. Inna Dorofeeva and Vadim Pisarev of the Düsseldorf-Duisberg Ballet in the *grand pas de deux*, set to music by Drigo. This pas de deux, a famous showpiece in the West, is an adaptation of Petipa's original pas de trois, which can be seen in most full-length Russian productions. (Photograph by Gundel Kilian; used by permission.)

attained because the Petipa classicism opposed the new choreography. Nevertheless, the ballet was greatly admired thanks to its romantic exoticism, passionate dances, and love duets danced by Ekaterina Geltser and Vasily Tikhomirov, all crowned by the storm scene and the sinking of the ship, realized by the machinist Karl Walz.

BIBLIOGRAPHY

Beaumont, Cyril W. *Complete Book of Ballets*. Rev. ed. London, 1951.

Guest, Ivor. *The Ballet of the Second Empire*. London, 1974.

Guest, Ivor. *Jules Perrot: Master of the Romantic Ballet*. London, 1984.

Krasovskaya, Vera. *Russkii baletnyi teatr nachala dvadtsatogo veka*, vol. 1, *Khoreografy*. Leningrad, 1971.

Reynolds, Nancy, and Susan Reimer-Torn. *Dance Classics*. Pennington, N.J., 1991.

Vaughan, David. "Annals of *Le Corsaire*." *Ballet Review* 15 (Fall 1987): 45–48.

Vazem, Ekaterina. "Memoirs of a Ballerina of the St. Petersburg Bolshoi Theatre." Translated by Nina Dimitrievich. *Dance Research* 3 (Summer 1985): 3–22; 4 (Spring 1986): 3–28; 5 (Spring 1987): 21–41; 6 (Autumn 1988): 30–47.

ALEXANDER P. DEMIDOV
Translated from Russian

CORTESI, ANTONIO (born December 1796 in Pavia, died April 1879 in Florence), Italian ballet dancer, choreographer, and composer. Cortesi was the son of the dancer Margherita Reggini and the choreographer Giuseppe Cortesi, who had danced in the roles of the *primo grottesco* beside Salvatore Viganò in the ballets of Viganò's father, Onorato, between 1790 and 1800. Details of Antonio's early years are obscure, but it seems that he began his dancing career when he was quite young. The *Indice de' spettacoli teatrali* (1794–1795, p. 22), mentions him as a dancer with the Teatro di Como in 1794. If authenticated, this information would lead to establishing a birth date for him earlier than that now accepted.

In the records of Giuseppe Cortesi's ballets, Antonio's name appears next to that of his sister, Giuseppa. In 1808, he danced the principal role in *Armida Abbandonata da Rinaldo* in Ravenna at the Teatro Comunale at his sister's side. From that time onward, he enjoyed a successful career in numerous Italian theaters. In 1812 he danced at the Teatro San Moisè in Venice and in 1813 in Padua. At the 1814 Carnival in Padua he performed in his father's ballet *Catterina di Coluga* at the Teatro degli Obizzi. In 1815 and 1816 he aroused the enthusiasm of audiences at the Teatro Comunale of Trieste in the ballets of Giovanni Galzerani and Giovanni Monticini. In 1817 and 1818 he returned to the Teatro Nuovo in Padua. He was at the Teatro della Comune in Reggio Emilia and the Teatro Comunale in Ravenna in 1820 and at Teatro La Pergola in Florence in 1821. According to Francesco Regli (1860), Cortesi injured himself in 1822 in Lisbon and was forced to stop dancing.

In 1822 or 1823, Cortesi accepted the post of choreographer at the Teatro São Carlos in Lisbon and presented his first ballet works there, including a *Septimino* for Luigi Astolfi and his version of Gaetano Gioja's *Gabriella di Vergy*. (Gioja had formerly favored Cortesi's dancing career by retaining him for his productions.) Toward the end of 1825, Cortesi was invited to be the principal teacher at the Teatro Regio in Turin. There, he created numerous ballets and presented in 1827 his masterpiece, *Inès di Castro*. Notwithstanding his commitment to the Turin theater, Cortesi presented his works at various other ballet centers. In 1827 he staged *Zaira* and *Alceste* at the Teatro alla Scala in Milan, and in 1831 he revived there *Inès di Castro* with new scenery created by Alessandro Sanquirico. The outstadnding dancer Antonia Pallerini, Viganò's favorite interpreter of his dance dramas, performed it.

The savage plot of *Inès*, conceived in an age that was still poised between neoclassicism and romanticism, while being visibly affected by Romantic motifs, nevertheless cannot be defined as Romantic if it is compared with French ballet of the time. The words of a critical observer indicate that Cortesi's taste must have been strongly influenced by the contemporary dramatic theater:

The mediocrity of talents has already led the surviving ballet composers to take a very different road, or to tread the old and more vulgar path, thanks to which choreography is treated like a written drama, and lengthy poetic concepts are translated into gesticulations . . . and sometimes they obtain popular applause, as for example when Inès di Castro raves for the children ravished by the wardens, or when she writhes in the agony of death after taking poison. These are scenes in which the situation or the performer has the greatest merit.

(Ritorni, 1838)

Notwithstanding such criticism, Cortesi continued to win success with his ballets, including *Imelda e Bonifacio*, presented at La Scala in 1831 after having had its premiere the year before at La Pergola in Florence.

Among the many choreographies that are attributed to Cortesi, including at least some sixty ballets and perhaps as many as a hundred (see Schmidl, 1926), mostly with music he wrote or adapted, some reveal that he showed greater sensitivity to the Romantic dimension than his contemporaries did. This is the case with his personal versions of *La Sylphide*, first given in Genoa in 1837, and *Giselle*, for which he retained Fanny Cerrito. These two ballets, presented at La Scala in 1841 and 1843, respectively, differed markedly from the originals. Giovanni Bajetti's music was used for *Giselle* instead of Adolphe Adam's, and the action was resolved in a happy ending. In the 1845 revival of Cortesi's *Giselle* at La Scala, the Austrian ballerina Fanny Elssler danced the principal role. In the same year Cortesi also adapted *La Fille du Danube* with Marie Taglioni at the Teatro San Benedetto in Venice. In ballets such as *L'Ultimo Giorno di Missolungi*, performed in Venice at Teatro La Fenice in 1832, and *Masaniello*, performed at La Fenice in 1836, to music by Giacomo Ferrari and Daniel Auber, Cortesi treated contemporary events (e.g., the Greek war of independence) and patriotic subjects.

Cortesi's indefatigable activity was not limited to Italy; he expanded it to foreign capitals, including London, Lisbon, and Vienna. He enjoyed the support of his wife, Giuseppa Angiolini, by whom he had two children, Francesco and Adelaide. Giuseppa died in 1852. She had been Cortesi's close collaborator, both as a performer and a teacher of his ballets, and her death led to a pause in the choreographer's productions. He eventually recovered from his grief, however, and in 1859 presented two new creations: *Fior di Maria* and *La Liberazione di Lisbona*, both composed for La Pergola in Florence.

On the whole, Cortesi was appreciated for his clear, expressive style, enriched with situations that were sometimes powerful and sometimes touching. "Cortesi's ballets," wrote Gino Monaldi, "while more simple in their images and in their technical development than those of his contemporary [Giovanni] Casati, were enlivened by a characteristic geniality of mimic action and extremely lively dances that almost always won the favor of the audiences" (Monaldi, 1910).

BIBLIOGRAPHY
Ascarelli, Astrid. "Cortesi, Antonio." In *Dizionario biografico degli italiani*. Rome, 1960–.
Cambiasi, Pompeo. *La Scala, 1778–1906*. Milan, 1906.
Celi, Claudia. "L'arivamento de la gran maravija der ballo ossia il ballo a Roma dal 1845 al 1854." *La danza italiana* 8–9 (Winter 1990): 73–107.
Monaldi, Gino. *Le regine della danza nel secolo XIX*. Turin, 1910.
Regli, Francesco. *Dizionario biografico dei più celebri poeti ed artisti melodrammatici, tragici et comici, maestri, concertisi, coreografi, mimi, ballerini, scenografi, giornalisti, impresarii, ecc. ecc. che fiorirono in Italia dal 1800 al 1860*. Turin, 1860. Facsimile reprint, Bologna, 1990.
Ritorni, Carlo. *Commentarii della vita e delle opere coreodrammatiche di Salvatore Viganò e della coreografia e de' corepei*. Milan, 1838.
Schmidl, Carlo. *Dizionario universale dei musicisti*. Milan, 1926.
Schüller, Gunhild. "Antonio Cortesi: Ines di Castro." In *Pipers Enzyklopädie des Musiktheaters, Oper, Operette, Musical, Ballett*, edited by Carl Dahlhaus. Munich and Zurich, 1986–.
Sowell, Debra Hickenlooper. "Virtue (Almost) Triumphant' Revisited." *Dance Chronicle* 18.2 (1995): 293–301.

ARCHIVE.   Walter Toscanini Collection of Research Materials in Dance, New York Public Library for the Performing Arts.

CLAUDIA CELI
Translated from Italian

COSTUME IN AFRICAN TRADITIONS. The visual, kinetic, and aural attributes of costume dramatically affect the expressive qualities of dance in sub-Saharan Africa. At once a personal and social statement, African costume ranges from total lack of adornment, or nudity, to dramatic transformations of the human form. Such transformations are inextricably related to movement, either facilitating or restricting it.

History. Early African costumes can be seen in paintings, engravings, stone carvings, and sculpture. Travelers' accounts also provide descriptions and illustrations. The beginnings of dance costume are difficult to establish, however, because visual arts and verbal descriptions can only hint at the nature of such ephemeral and irretrievable events as dance.

Despite these limitations, the rock paintings and engravings in the central Sahara's Tassili Plateau, provisionally dated to about 6000 BCE, document both costume and gesture. Silhouetted figures with round heads, horned and plumed headdresses, and objects in their hands are shown in active dance poses with knees flexed and backs rounded. By about 4000 BCE, the images were more elaborate, detailed, and polychromatic, showing necklaces, bracelets, anklets (probably cut from ostrich shell and schist), belts, ornaments for head, arm, and shoulder, and body paintings or decorative scarification. The figures depicted are engaged in dynamic movements—legs apart,

COSTUME IN AFRICAN TRADITIONS.
Masked figures of *dye (gye)*, a
secret-society rite of the Guru people, in
Dabruza, Côte d'Ivoire, 1975.
(Photographs by Eberhard Fischer and Hans
Himmelheber; used by permission.)

torso inclined, and arms upraised. One painting from this era portrays a group of eight people: the males are adorned in leggings, loincloths, and elaborate head-dresses that may mask both head and face; the females wear waistbands, arm and shoulder ornaments, leggings, and coiffures that crown their uncovered faces. If we have interpreted these paintings correctly, this is the earliest pictorial evidence that masking in Africa has for millennia been restricted to males—a tradition that persists today with rare exceptions. In this work, the postures and gestures of the figures, almost all of whom hold sticks, suggest a dance context, as do many of the images from the period of the first cattle herders (4000–1000 BCE), particularly the second millennium BCE. The elaborations of the human form depicted in these ancient works—necklaces, bracelets, anklets, and various other ornaments on shoulders, elbows, waists, and knees—cluster at the body's points of articulation, suggesting that costume in Africa has long been viewed as integral to gesture, in dance.

Diversity in African Costume. Limited or portable body adornment tends to be found among nomadic peoples, such as hunters and gatherers like the San of the Kalahari region or the Mbuti of the Ituri forest; among pastoralists, such as the Nuer, Samburu, and Masai; and among small-scale agriculturalists, such as those of the interior of Guinea, northern Ghana, Burkina Faso, and the plateau region of central Nigeria, Cameroon, and Sudan. In Sudan, for example, from childhood until the onset of pregnancy, the dress of Nuba girls consists of a coating of oil and strands of waist beads, bells, and necklaces; these enhance and dramatically define the musculature of their bodies and the textured surface of their tattooed torsos during energetic dances.

Significantly more clothed—in loose-fitting body-length robes, baggy trousers, wraparound skirts, loose blouses, and headwraps, turbans, or veils—are the peoples of North and Sudanic Africa, who have been influenced strongly by the dress of the Islamic world. Portuguese travelers in 1455 first recorded this mode of dress. Such attire flutters, ripples, and flows as the body moves, lending an added dimension to their dance. West African male dancers of northern Ghana—those of the Dagomba and Mamprussi—wear a pleated smock that swirls outward and then twists around the body during their dances' characteristic turns. One of the marks of a good dancer is the skill with which this smock is handled.

Among the Yoruba of Nigeria, men wear long gowns, probably influenced by northern Nigerian and Islamic kaftans with sleeves that often extend far beyond arm's length when fully stretched. During dances, these are folded over the shoulders as part of an arm and upper torso movement that draws attention to the lavish wealth of cloth. This gesture, elaborated and repeated, is a distinctive element in the choreography. Young boys, who do not wear the gowns when dancing, pantomime this cloth-arranging movement in imitation of their elders.

At the extreme of sumptuous costuming are ensembles that completely surround or envelop the wearer, almost totally concealing his or her identity. These great elaborations seem to occur most often in sub-Saharan Africa's settled, centralized, and stratified societies. Emphasis is put on displaying the acquisition of material wealth in the context of high rank or prestige, especially that of royalty or other social leaders. Examples of this type of dress include the costumes of the kings and chiefs of the Asante in Ghana, the Bakuba of Congo (formerly Zaïre), and the Yoruba and peoples of Nigeria.

Traditional costume as worn in the Benin Kingdom capital (now Benin City, Nigeria) highlights sumptuous royal regalia and its effect on movement and dance. Ornate coral crowns, elaborately beaded garments, and jewelry of coral enclose the torso of the king, while a large, full skirt gives him great bulk below the waist. Such costuming creates an impressive girth and presence while imposing limits on movement. These restrictions empha-

size the wearer's station, for it is believed that by divine right the king personifies the grandeur, stability, strength, and endurance of his nation-state. His ritual acts therefore convey the pomp and circumstance of the event through correspondingly slow, dignified, stately movement.

Costume, Dance, and Occasion. In African societies, costume marks the rites of passage in people's lives—their changing roles and identities from childhood to adulthood, from courtship to marriage and parenthood, from initiation to the assumption of authority, and from physical existence to the afterlife. Such transitions are almost always occasions for display and performance in which costume's effect on dance is evident.

In the Ubangi region of the Central African Republic, the Gbaya, Banda, and Ngbaka girls undergo initiation into womanhood in a rite known as *gaza* or *ganza* (that which gives force). Secluded in the bush, initiates begin to learn dances and songs. After circumcision (genital excision), the girls ritually bathe in pools and receive rigorous dance instruction. When they have perfected their dances and songs, they emerge from the bush for a celebration of their newly achieved adult status. Their rigorous dancing attests to their attainment of *ganza*, which has given them strength. Their attire for this debut consists of elaborate and close-fitting beaded headpieces covered with animal fur and leaves, numerous strands of beads or shells hung about the neck and crossed between their breasts, beads at the waist strung over loincloths or short grass skirts, and several rows of leg rattles made from plant materials.

This costume accentuates the choreography of the dances.

Boys in the liminal stage between childhood and manhood undergo similar trials and celebrations. In southeastern Angola, for example, young boys wear dance skirts of reddish wood that highlight the principal movement of their *kuhunga* dance, a sideways twisting of the pelvis. The anthropologist Gerhard Kubik reported that the dancers believe that "a good dancer . . . should make the dance skirt swing out continuously in perpetual motion so that it seems to stand still like a 'little cloud'" (1977, p. 267).

Courtship rites are also celebrated in performance, and personal adornment plays a crucial role. In Kenya, Herbert M. Cole writes, among the young unmarried Samburu men known as *moran*,

> long pigtails, the longer the better, figure in flirtatious dance gestures when a *moran* more or less casually but deliberately throws his pigtails, with wooden pendants, over his head to strike the bare head of a girl dancing opposite him. No doubt the aesthetic dimension of hair in motion, in the characteristic leaping dances and head-thrusting dance gestures of the Samburu, is important. (Cole, 1979, p. 72)

An example of the celebration of the rights and responsibilities of acquired or inherited status exist in Rwanda, where the Tutsi aristocracy is supported by royal drummers and warriors known as the Ntoré. Their courtly choreography of high leaps and stamps performed in a narrow, vertical plane is visually accentuated by long, tightly wrapped skirts, by white headdresses made of long strands of animal fur that fly up and down when the dancers are in motion, and by spears, staffs, bows, and arrows held in their hands.

Funerals, which mark the end of life and the passage to the other world, often contain reversals or inversions in costume and dance. Thus, coiffures are completely undone or heads shaved, and the dancers wear dirt and ashes or unkempt clothing, or they go completely naked. These visible, tangible signs of mourning accompany the gestures and postures in dances of sorrow.

Percussive Qualities of Costume and Dance. Percussion, a dominant trait in African music and dance, is also evident in costuming. Both dress and accessories are frequently designed with auditory attributes meant to enhance and contribute to the dance rhythms. For example, Kamberi male dancers in Nigeria wear heavy iron leg rattles and perform a stamping action; the weight and sound of the leg rattles partly determine the dancers' movements. Similarly, large copper disk anklets force titled Igbo women to walk, and presumably to dance, in a peculiarly restricted fashion.

African dancers make extensive use of bells, rattles, and idiophones of every description on different parts of the

COSTUME IN AFRICAN TRADITIONS. A masked performer in a Senufo Panther Dance. The Senufo are a people living mainly in the northern savannas of Côte d'Ivoire. (Photograph by Phyllis Galembo; used by permission.)

body. For example, Samburu girls wear neck beads that make an audible "whoosh" as they flop up and down; even more dramatic are the large iron anklets that clank rhythmically as they walk or dance. In some societies, such auditory accompaniments to dance are not only aesthetically pleasing but also have sacred functions. Among the Yoruba in Nigeria, the sounds of certain leg rattles and bells are said to dispel negative forces, thus protecting as well as complementing the performer (Drewal and Drewal, 1983).

Costume, Dance, and Change. The dynamics of cultural change in Africa continuously shape modes of dance and dress. In the nineteenth century, the Beni (dance societies, from the English word *band*) of Mombasa, on the eastern African coast, adapted their tradition of competitive communal dancing to parody European military drill procedures. One resulting dance was the *mganda*. According to T. O. Ranger (1975, p. vii), the dance is performed with "unflagging vigour and disciplined precision to the steady booming of a large military drum and to the drone of kazoos made out of gourds." The lead dancer wore "appropriately dignified clothes, with a cap of rank, with shoulder badges, with a row of fountain pens in his breast pocket. He paraded up and down the ranks of his men" (Ranger, 1975, p. 15). Members of the Sadla (Settler) Beni wore bush hats and khaki clothes and acted with an exaggerated "rough vigour" as they imitated and mocked the attitudes of European settlers (Ranger, 1975, p. 46).

Similarly, in South Africa, Zulus on the docks in Durban developed the *isicathulo*, or Boot Dance, using large rubber Wellington boots. They found that the boots made good percussive instruments and performed in them by stamping, clapping their feet together, and slapping the boots with their hands.

The long history of costume in Africa demonstrates sensitivity to movement in general and dance in particular. For all kinds of dance occasions, Africa preferences for accumulation, improvisation, and the use of both visual and auditory attributes of various media have resulted in richly inventive costuming and performance traditions.

[*For related discussion, see* Mask and Makeup, *article on* African Traditions.]

BIBLIOGRAPHY

Aronson, Lisa. "Patronage and Akwete Weaving." *African Arts* 13 (May 1980).

Beier, Ulli. *Yoruba Beaded Crowns.* London, 1982.

Ben-Amos, Paula. *The Art of Benin.* New York, 1980.

Biebuyck, Daniel P. "Nyanga Circumcision Masks and Costumes." *African Arts* 6 (Winter 1973).

Biobaku, Saburi O., ed. *The Living Culture of Nigeria.* Lagos, 1976.

Blacking, John, ed. *The Anthropology of the Body.* London, 1977.

Blum, Odette. "Dance in Ghana." *Dance Perspectives,* no. 56 (Winter 1973).

Borgatti, Jean. *Cloth as Metaphor: Nigerian Textiles from the Museum of Cultural History.* Los Angeles, 1983.

Boser-Sarivaxévanis, Renée. *Les tissus de l'Afrique occidentale.* Bâle, 1972.

Brain, Robert. *The Decorated Body.* New York, 1979.

Cole, Herbert M., et al. *African Arts of Transformation.* Santa Barbara, Calif., 1970.

Cole, Herbert M. "Vital Arts in Northern Kenya." *African Arts* 7 (Winter 1974).

Cole, Herbert M., and Doran H. Ross. *The Arts of Ghana.* Los Angeles, 1977.

Cole, Herbert M. "Living Art among the Samburu." In *The Fabrics of Culture,* edited by Justine M. Cordwell and Ronald A. Schwarz. The Hague, 1979.

Cordwell, Justine M., and Ronald A. Schwarz, eds. *The Fabrics of Culture: The Anthropology of Clothing and Adornment.* The Hague, 1979.

Cornet, Joseph. "The Itul Celebration of the Kuba." *African Arts* 13 (May 1980).

Court, Elsbeth, and Michael Mwangi. "Maridadi Fabrics." *African Arts* 10 (Fall 1976).

Donovan, Nancy. "Tsion Andom of Ethiopia." *African Arts* 7 (Fall 1973).

Drewal, Henry John. "Pageantry and Power in Yoruba Costuming." In *The Fabrics of Culture,* edited by Justine M. Cordwell and Ronald A. Schwarz. The Hague, 1979.

Drewal, Henry John, and Margaret Thompson Drewal. *Gelede: Art and Female Power among the Yoruba.* Bloomington, 1983.

Drewal, Margaret Thompson. "Symbols of Possession: A Study of Movement and Regalia in an Anago-Yoruba Ceremony." *Dance Research Journal* 7 (Spring-Summer 1975).

Drewal, Margaret Thompson. *Yoruba Ritual: Performers, Play, Agency,* Bloomington, 1992.

Eicher, Joanne B. *African Dress: A Select and Annotated Bibliography of Subsaharan Countries.* East Lansing, Mich., 1969.

Eicher, Joanne B. *Nigerian Handcrafted Textiles.* Ile-Ife, Nigeria, 1976.

Fagg, William B., ed. *The Living Arts of Nigeria.* London, 1971.

Faris, James C. *Nuba Personal Art.* London, 1972.

Forge, Anthony, ed. *Primitive Art and Society.* London, 1973.

Gardi, René. *African Crafts and Craftsmen.* Translated by Sigrid MacRae. New York, 1969.

Glaze, Anita J. *Art and Death in a Senufo Village.* Bloomington, 1981.

Heathcote, David. "Hausa Embroidered Dress." *African Arts* 5 (Winter 1972).

Heathcote, David. *The Arts of the Hausa.* Chicago, 1977.

Huet, Michel. *The Dance, Art, and Ritual of Africa.* New York, 1978.

Idiens, Dale, and K. G. Ponting, eds. *Textiles of Africa.* Bath, 1980.

Jefferson, Louise E. *The Decorative Arts of Africa.* New York, 1973.

Kubik, Gerhard. "Patterns of Body Movement in the Music of Boys' Initiation in South-East Angola." In *The Anthropology of the Body,* edited by John Blacking. London, 1977.

Lamb, Venice. *West African Weaving.* London, 1975.

Lamb, Venice, and Judy Holmes. *Nigerian Weaving.* Roxford, 1980.

Lambrecht, Dora, and Frank Lambrecht. "Leather and Beads in N'gamiland." *African Arts* 10 (Winter 1977).

Lhote, Henri. *The Search for the Tassili Frescoes.* Translated by Alan H. Brodrick. New York, 1959.

Menzel, Brigitte. *Textilien aus Westafrika.* 3 vols. Berlin, 1972–1973.

Mickelsen, Nancy R. "Tuareg Jewelry." *African Arts* 9 (Winter 1976).

Paulme, Denise, and Jacques Brosse. *Parures africaines.* Paris, 1956.

Paulme, Denise. "Adornment and Nudity in Tropical Africa." In *Primitive Art and Society,* edited by Anthony Forge. London, 1973.

Picton, John, and John Mack. *African Textiles.* London, 1979.

Plumer, Cheryl. *African Textiles: An Outline of Handcrafted Sub-Saharan Fabrics.* East Lansing, Mich., 1971.

Polakoff, Claire. "The Art of Tie and Dye in Africa." *African Arts* 4 (Spring 1971).

Ranger, T. O. *Dance and Society in Eastern Africa, 1890–1970.* London, 1975.

Sieber, Roy. *African Textiles and Decorative Arts.* New York, 1972.

Thompson, Robert Farris. "The Sign of the Divine King." *African Arts* 3 (Spring 1970).

Tracey, Hugh T. *African Dances of the Witwatersrand Gold Mines.* Johannesburg, 1952.

Trowell, Margaret. *African Design.* 3d ed. New York, 1960.

Vrydagh, P. Andre. "Makisi of Zambia." *African Arts* 10 (July 1977).

Warren, Dennis. "Bono Royal Regalia." *African Arts* 8 (Winter 1975).

Zahan, Dominique. "Colours and Body Painting in Black Africa: The Problem of the 'Half-Man.'" *Diogenes* (Spring 1975).

FILM.   Frank Speed and R. E. Bradbury, *Benin Kingship Rituals* (1962).

VIDEOTAPE.   Henry John Drewal, *Yoruba Performance* (1991).

HENRY JOHN DREWAL

COSTUME IN ASIAN TRADITIONS. The importance of costume in the Asian dance drama should not be underestimated; in fact, at times the costume becomes the character itself. Through shape, color, and texture the costume may represent a complex convention; it may also convey a strong emotion or transmit a definite symbolic message to the audience.

Japan. Sometimes costumes signify the splendor of an ancient era, such as the adaptations of Japan's Heian period (794–1185) costume that have been used in *bugaku,* the masked ceremonial dance of the Japanese court.

COSTUME IN ASIAN TRADITIONS. Performer of *bugaku*, the ceremonial court dance of Japan, wearing a *koto-yō-shōzoku* type of costume; the fringed apron-shaped overgarment is called a *ryōtō*. (Photograph from the archives of The Asia Society, New York.)

Bugaku. These costumes are combinations of Chinese concepts mixed with Japanese design. Before Buddhism came to Japan from China and Korea in the sixth century, most clothing was white—the color symbolic of purity in Japan's Shintō religion. When Buddhism reached Japan, silks called *aya* (a solid-colored patterned weave) and *nishiki* (with its brilliant multicolored patterns) were in use. The Japanese also had a color system that denoted rank, similar to one used by the Chinese imperial court. These colors, ranging from purple to dark green, were worn by the nobles during the dedication ceremonies of the Great Buddha at Nara in 752 (later the court colors underwent many revisions). The people who had no rank were required to wear yellow, and servants wore black. Red was then associated with Chinese families in Japan and green usually with Korean families, so in *bugaku*, the *samai* costumes of the left dance (associated with the Tang-dynasty music of China) became red and the *umai* costumes of the right dance (associated with the Pokai music of Korea), a dark green. The basic color white was reserved for *utami*, through its Shintō affiliations.

There are three categories of costume in *bugaku*. The most popular is the layered costume (*kasane-shōzoku*), worn for civil dances as well as other dance roles. The second type is *ban-e-no-shōzoku*, worn for the same type of dances as the first, but in this case the costumes are closer in authenticity to Heian prototypes. The third category has special costumes (*koto-yō-shōzoku*), used in children's dances, running dances, and military roles. These can include wings, armor, and unusual fabrications.

Clothing in the *bugaku* performance is layered similar to Heian court regulations. Although the weight of the costume during Heian times could exceed twenty pounds (8 kilograms), this is lightened for *bugaku*. In the first costume type, *kasane-shōzoku*, the outer robe is usually sheer red or green silk gauze, depending on the two groups of required dancers. The front of the outer robe (*hō-ue-no-kinu*) has two sections and is knee length. The back has a train, which during the Heian period signified rank according to its length. The robe has a rolled collar, and the sides of this garment are not sewn. Its large square sleeves contain an inner sleeve that makes the sleeves longer than the dancer's hands—this convention reverts back to the aristocratic customs of Chinese and Japanese imperial courts.

The inner garment called *shitagasane* is worn under the *hō-ue-no-kinu*; it is constructed of white *aya*, with red trim and a purple silk lining. The *hanpi*, a stiff sleeveless coat, is worn over the *shitagasane* but under the *hō-ue-no-kinu*. The bodice of the *hanpi* is of navy or black bamboo-and-phoenix patterned silk, and a short red silk skirt, pleated at the sides, is sewn to the bodice. The *hanpi* is lined with silk in floral colors, then tied with a navy blue sash (*wasureo*). One end of the sash is embroidered with the same patterns found in the *hanpi* fabric.

Under the *shitagasane*, there are a basic white kimono (*hakui*) and full checkered-patterned silk trousers with a red lining (*sashinuki*). The *sashinuki* are pleated in the front and back and open at the sides. The cucumber-and-hail pattern (*mon*) is embroidered in five colors on each leg; this motif, the principal one seen on *bugaku* costume, was originally the official seal of *gagaku* (Japanese court music). Multiple variations of the motif have been embroidered on the outer garment of *hō-ue-no-kinu*. Lined sashes are attached to the top of the pants to hold the garment in place, and cords are sewn into the bottom of the trousers to tighten the pants around the ankle.

Fukake (leg guards) are worn over the trousers. The leg guards are made in two identical parts and are tied around the ankle. Their construction consists of gold-cloth-covered paper lined in red silk and trimmed with a loosely woven fabric.

Perhaps the most important part of the *kasane-shōzoku* attire is the helmet (*kabuto*), which comes in several shapes; the most common is the head of the phoenix. Paper forms the basic construction of the helmet; *samai* covers it in gold cloth and *umai* uses silver cloth. The helmet is lined with red silk and has cords that tie under the chin. Metal disks, in the *kiri*-tree-branch design, are placed on each side of the crown. Another accessory is the belt worn over the *hō-ue-no-kinu*, which can be made of gold, silver, or stone decoration; this is necessary to keep everything in place.

The second category of *bugaku* dress, *ban-e-no-shōzoku*, has an outer garment called the *ban-e-no-hō*, which is very similar to the *hō-ue-no-kinu* in size, shape, and fabric. Here the embroidery consists of the lion-in-a-circle, depicted in five colors. Under this outer garment is a *shita-gasane* and *hakui*, which are similar to those in the first category; the exception is the lining of the *shitagasane*—white instead of purple.

The outer trousers (*omote-hakama*) are white without any textured design and have a red silk lining and no drawstrings at the ankle. Underneath are *o-guchi*, similar in shape to the outer pants. The *o-guchi* are constructed of fine fabric and are also lined in red.

The hat worn with this outfit is the *kammuri*, which was popular in the Heian court. A large black pin is inserted through the *koji*—a vertical projection at the back of the hat—and holds the knotted hair in place. A black cord wrapped around and crossed in front of the *koji* is then tied under the chin. The *kammuri* is made of paper, covered with silk, then lacquered black. Various cords, fringe, and flower decorations can be attached to the *kammuri* according to the dance role.

The third category, *koto-yō-shōzuku*, is the special type of costume used for the military, for running, and for children's performances. The garment called *hashiri-mai-no-hō* corresponds to the *hō-ue-no-kinu* in its shape, but its sleeves are narrower, with drawstrings at the wrists to free the hands when necessary. This is another detail inspired by the Heian court practices, when it was necessary to free the hands quickly for fighting in the palace. This red or green outer garment is decorated with the cucumber *mon*.

Ryōtō, an apronlike circular garment, lined with silk and trimmed with fringe, is worn over the *hashiri-mai-no-hō*; this garment has a round or jewel-neck opening, for ease of slipping over the head, and is the same length as the *hashiri-mai-no-hō* in the front, when it is worn, but the train of the *hashiri-mai-no-hō* sticks out in the back. Various designs are embroidered on the *ryōtō*, according to the dance. Sometimes, its shape is square instead of round; then fabric trim is used to decorate the edge rather than fringe.

Sashinuki, the full silk trousers, are also a part of this costume category, and *ate-obi*, a metal belt lined with silk, is worn at the back and sides of the waist, tied with cords at the front. *Ate-obi* can have a peony or other design and

is gold colored, with red cording for the *samai* and silver with green cords for the *umai*.

The masks used in *bugaku* are always painted, and they are usually classified according to their construction. There are paper as well as wooden masks called *zōmen*. The usual type is the one-piece mask, which sometimes has some attached hair. The second type has movable parts, such as eyes, ears, or a nose. Before the *bugaku* dancer dons a mask, a thin cotton towel is wrapped around the head.

Bugaku dancers wear special shoes called *skikai*, with natural-colored silk tops and diamond-patterned openwork at the sides. The shoes are tied with strings at the ankles with two types of knots, square and bow shaped. The shoe sole has two layers of rice straw, and its lining is of ox leather. White *tabi* (socks with a separation for the big toe) are worn with the shoes. [*See* Bugaku.]

Nō drama. Dance in *nō* drama is very structured, and some scholars say that all *nō* movements are choreography. The costumes have great aesthetic appeal and probably became more lavish under the patronage of the Tokugawa shogunate (1603–1868). It was earlier, during the Muromachi period (1392–1573), that *nō* developed tremendous refinement, and this was also seen in the cos-

COSTUME IN ASIAN TRADITIONS. Dancer and musicans from the Kita Nō Theater Company performing the *nō* drama *Momiji-Gari*. (Photograph © 1989 by Jack Vartoogian; used by permission.)

tumes. One theory is that new costumes were not made for *nō* but were received instead from the shogun's household. A custom then also existed of rewarding an employee by the employer removing a garment and presenting it as a gift. During the Heian period, bolts of cloth and sometimes garments were used as rewards for distinguished service. The garment was draped around the recipient, who would then leave. If a dancer was involved, an encore performance would be held with the garment in the dancer's hands, as is documented by scrolls and other sources. Inferior costumes were thought to be a bad reflection on the dignity of the company, creating tremendous concentration on developing superior costumes.

Nō costumes have a basic straight-line cut; they come to life only onstage when the performer fills out the costume. At first the performer will wear a plain white cotton undershirt with white cotton tights and white *tabi*. A knee-length padded silk robe *(dogi)* is then put on over a small pillow, which is used to give the abdomen a rounded shape. Over these undergarments is worn the *kitsuke* (under robe). On top of the *kitsuke*, depending on the role, is worn the *hakama*, a long, stiff divided skirt (similar to modern culottes). The outer robe *(uwagi)* is either left to hang loose or tied with a hip band *(koshi-obi)*. Accessories such as wigs and fans are used. The mask, the symbol of the character's mind and heart, is essential to *nō*, setting the emotional tone.

Nō performers are dressed by their fellow colleagues today; the professional dresser is of the past. The highly competent dresser-actors are known as *gakuya no meijin* (dressing-room maestros).

For *nō* female roles (played by men), the *karaori* is an outer robe of heavy, stiff silk brocade, with small sleeves in a colorful pattern. The heavy-weave costume called *atsuita*, principally used for male roles, is another outer robe. Both of these weaves are too heavy for any complicated structures, so the designs are straight and simple and hide the body's lines. This angular effect makes them suitable for representing ghostly visions. The female inner robes *surihaku* and *nuihaku*, the first a white satin weave with gold and the second a silver-foil appliqué or a gold-thread embroidery, both have small sleeves and are supposed to represent women's skin. Gold foil on a red fabric indicates a young woman; silver foil without any red indicates a middle-aged or older woman.

The *karaori*, which literally means "Chinese weave," can be combined with the inner garments, *surihaku* and *nuihaku*, in four ways. The first, most popular method, is to wear the outer garment over the inner garment, tied at the waist. Here, the outer robe *shōzoku* is left open in a wide manner. In the second method, the right sleeve of the *karaori* is slipped off and draped down the performer's back—an indication of active movement or madness. The third version is to tie the inner garment at the waist, al-

lowing the bodice to fall; the outer robe is then pulled up at the hips, over the under robe. At times, the actor will wear only the under robe without the outer, in which case the term *mogidō* (half-dressed) will be used. In the fourth method, the outer robe is picked up and tucked in over *ōkuchi*, the stiff *hakama* (pants)—indicating a lady of the court wearing *hakama* with soft pleats in the front and large leg openings. *Hakama* come in various colors, but they are usually white and decorated with an allover *mon* pattern. *Ōkuchi* are used for male as well as female roles. When older females are represented, kimono edges are tightly held—overlapped and close to the body.

When a female role calls for dancing, loose lightweight outer robes, like the *chōken* and the *mai-ginu*, are worn. The *chōken* is broad sleeved and unlined, with colors varying from white to pale greens and blues; at times it has gold embroidery. The sides are not seamed, and two red braids with bows across the chest hang, each from a side of the garment's front. Although this is primarily a woman's costume, it is also used for the role of effeminate young noblemen, instead of the *happi*. The *mai-ginu* costume is similar to the *chōken* but has sewn sides and no ties.

The *atsuita* is the under robe worn by *nō* male characters. Usually of geometric-patterned brocade, a thick fabric, this costume is sometimes used as an outer garment. The *noshime* is another male under robe, small sleeved in a plain, horizontal-striped or checkered fabric. The plain version is usually reserved for old men and Buddhist priests, while the stripes are used for low-ranking samurai (warriors). Sometimes the striped *noshime* is worn by low-class elderly women.

The short coat called *happi* (the *nō* word for *hō*) is found in lined and unlined versions. Its sleeves are very wide and shaped at right angles. Lined versions are often used by generals or demon gods; the unlined for young noblemen's battle costumes. Armor costume is called *sobatsugi*—a lined *happi* with sleeves removed.

The *kariginu* costume, with very full sleeves and wide openings, is known as *hirosode*. Cords set into the wide openings tighten the sleeves. Lined versions are used for males of high rank and gods; an unlined *kariginu* is worn in Shintō priest roles.

The elaborateness of *nō* costume was spurred by the rivalry between the samurai (aristocratic-warrior) class and the imperial court. The samurai did not wish to accept *gagaku* as their ceremonial music, so they had *nō* performed in contemporary (fourteenth- to nineteenth-century) samurai dress; in this manner they expressed their antagonism toward the court. *Nō* drama represented the samurai view of court conduct.

The mask is essential to *nō*; its beginnings have been traced back to rice planting and exorcism rites, where the mask was worn by the monk or the farmer. About sixty basic types of masks exist with their own names. Several have variations, so counting these, there are almost two hundred types. Rules define which masks are to be worn in certain performances, but these rules are not as strictly followed as they were during the Tokugawa period. Many *nō* schools have their own masks, which are hundreds of years old, the earliest being Okina gods and demons. It was not until Zeami perfected *nō* that the masks of young women and men expressing *yūgen* (the quiet beauty of the inner self) were developed.

Some of the older wooden *nō* masks are made from paulownia (*Paulownia tomentosa*) or camphor *(Cinnamomum camphora)* trees, but the *hinoki* cypress *(Cupressus sp.)* is more suitable and commonly used, since this wood has very few knots and a straight grain. The mask is carefully carved with a lack of symmetry in the features, a stage convention which allows for more expression as the head is moved. A white pigment called *gofun*, composed of ground seashells and animal glue, is painted in three or four layers and then sandpapered, both steps repeated several times until a very smooth surface is achieved. Shading *(furubi)* was applied with a brown liquid made from soot boiled in rice wine. The earliest masks do not have *furubi* shading, and today's mask makers use other antiquing techniques.

Most facial features are painted, using India ink for the hair, eyes, and teeth. Heian-period aristocrats had blackened their teeth for aesthetic reasons, and this became a *nō* convention. If a mask is to have a supernatural quality, gold dust mixed with glue and water is painted on the teeth and eyes. Brass is often used for the eyeballs of warriors and demons and was also used on the teeth of antique *nō* masks. The back of the mask is painted Indian red and waxed, chemically burned, or lacquered—this last being the most common method in use. The tradition of making *nō* masks was handed down from father to son; the masks are often considered family treasures. To some, the public exposure or handling of a mask is an irreverent act. [*See* Nō.]

Kyōgen. Costume for *kyōgen* basically depicts the dress of the common people. Performed between *nō* plays, *kyōgen* provides comic relief and often portrays simple folk in realistic everyday scenes. Most of the plots, dialogue, and costuming date from the Muromachi period. Masks are sometimes used but the uncovered face is more common. The *noshime* and *hakama* are used in *kyōgen* costume, but the most distinctive garment is the *kataginu*, a sleeveless, wide bodice made of hemp fiber. The *kataginu* usually has bold patterns, like gourds and arrows, and these designs were probably hand-drawn or stencil-dyed. From these patterns we have a good concept of what the commoner wore in the Muromachi period. The *kataginu* is worn over the *noshime* robe.

Another interesting feature in *kyōgen* costume is the use of simple stripes for undergarment patterns. These striped cloths are coarse and practical, with a distinctive color scheme.

Kyōgen Tojin-Zumo uses a special kind of curved sleeve and body shaping in its costume. Set in China, the scene of a Japanese character wrestling many men, including the king, to win his right to return to Japan is the occasion to view exotic costume variations. (Many of the fabrics used for *nō* were originally imported from China.) [*See* Kyōgen.]

Kabuki. The dance theater called *kabuki* is believed to have originated about 1600 from the dance performance of Okuni, a female attendant at the Izumo Shrine, and her troupe. Some of the elements of *nō* drama were added to it. *Kabuki* reached its peak during the Tokugawa shogunate, when only men were allowed onstage. Many of the *kabuki* costumes followed the social trends of the day, but others were highly imaginative and often beautiful; thus, in *kabuki* it is possible to have strange costumes that are nonexistent in life. (*Kabuki* means "offbeat" or "outrageous" in Japanese.)

During the early years of *kabuki* it was not possible to copy the dress of the samurai or the nobility, since feudal laws prohibited this. The display of sumptuous fabrics was also prohibited, and the task of making the costume indicative of an important person through color, design, and pattern became a challenge. The public craved glamour, and the *kabuki* actor supplied it by selecting special colors and patterns for onstage effects. The public then copied the actor's kimono and his way of tying his sash *(obi)*. Accessories and *mon* were also followed by the public during the eighteenth century, based on *kabuki* fashions.

The earliest *kabuki* costumes have not survived, since they were made for the moment and kept by the actor in theater warehouses. They did not have the protection of *nō* costumes, which were carefully guarded by the nobility and military. *Kabuki* costume today is based on information supplied by *ukiyo-e* woodblock prints and from generations of theater people involved with *kabuki*. *Kabuki* costume is not only complicated but very heavy, sometimes weighing over fifty pounds (20 kilograms). There is a lot of layering in the costume, which must be carefully arranged when the actor is seated, shifts his position, or performs a *mie*—the contained, tense pose.

No masks are used in *kabuki*, but there is exaggerated, colorful facial makeup *(kumadori)*, with areas of skin showing through. This stylized makeup was originally based on the actor's changing facial expressions and later followed the shadows made by the muscles. (The Chinese had also used this stylized type of makeup, but it was solely a design that disregarded facial structure and expression.) The Japanese actor learns to apply his own

COSTUME IN ASIAN TRADITIONS. Bandō Tamasaburō V, perhaps the finest *onnagata* (female impersonator) of the *kabuki* theater, delicately holds a fan in a solo performance of *Kanegamisaki*, the Osaka version of the famous Tokyo *nō* play *Dōjōji*, at the Japan Society, New York. (Photograph © 1984 by Linda Vartoogian; used by permission.)

makeup at an early age, but he often has to simplify conventional forms when changing roles quickly within the same scene. The face is divided into the section around the jaw and the area of the small bone of the nose. Emotion is expressed through color, and fierce anger and forcefulness are seen by a deep red on a white base. Ghosts often have a blue tinge on the face or blue veins sketched in a branch shape, a black outlined red mouth, and red-and-black eyes. A brown face signifies selfishness and dejection, while a light green face is indicative of tranquility. The samurai have white faces with black eyebrows and red touches at the mouth. The female roles (*onnagata*, portrayed by men) always have white faces.

The wig *(katsura)* is essential to the *kabuki* actor's role, and each costume has its own type. The *katsura* is shaped over a copper base by the *katsura-ya*, who measures the actor's head size to fit the base properly. The *toko-yama* maintains and dresses the wig during the performance. Some *toko-yama*s work only with the *onnagata* roles; others only with male wigs. In 1803, a method for sewing the hair—one strand at a time onto a piece of silk—became popular, and this technique produced great naturalism. Most wigs are made with human hair but some types require horsehair, yak-tail hair imported from China or Tibet, bear fur, sheep's wool, silk thread, and other materials.

Kabuki costume has several categories, including *otoko*, clothing for actors in male roles, and *onnagata*, costumes for actors in female roles. The kimono, which developed from the undergarment called *kosode* (small sleeves), is of major importance, as is the *obi*—the sash symbolic of beauty. *Hakama* (the pleated trousers) are worn for male and female roles. In both roles the actors are padded at the midriff to eliminate body curves, since the straight, flat figure is the epitome of beauty. The *onnagata* often wears two basic kimonos plus the woman's ceremonial outer robe, with a rolled and padded hemline called an *uchikake*. Since there are many *otoko* roles in *kabuki*, men's garments can range from one outer garment for commoners to a combination of several undergarments *(jubans)*. Also worn is the *haori*, a short outercoat with *mon* that has ties in front.

Costume changes in *kabuki* are a true art—known as *hada wo nugu*, the partial change; *hikinuki*, pulling out; and *hayagawari*, the quick change. In *hada wo nugu*, the upper section of the kimono is removed to reveal another underneath; sometimes the outer is totally removed. *Hinkinuki* is primarily used in dance pieces, since the outer kimono is basted together with loose stitches, and the stage dresser pulls the thread, allowing the kimono pieces to fall and reveal a new costume. This is done without any pause in the dance movement and requires timing and skill. When the costumes are discarded on the stage, they must be quickly removed. *Hayagawari*—the quick change—is performed offstage; here, the actor leaves and immediately reappears as an entirely different character wearing a new costume and makeup.

One of the essential accessories for *kabuki* is the fan. It can be used to symbolize the wind, a sword, a tobacco pipe, waves, or food. It is an indispensable item to the *kabuki* actor because of its versatility. [See Kabuki Theater.]

Festivals and folk dance. Japanese festivals are often the occasion for many types of folk dances. The annual rice planting festival, Otaue, is held in late June in Chiyoda. Women dancers, wearing wide-brimmed straw hats and cotton kimonos (the *yugata*) with large indigo patterns on a white background, plant the rice. The darkness of the fermented indigo depends on the number of times the fabric was placed in the dye bath. The *yugata* is used for the bath and during the summer, and the dancers wear this garment over a dark blue bodysuit that covers the arms and legs. *Obis* and narrow ties hold the *yugatas* in place. Male drummers, who are similarly dressed but with a narrower *obi*, beat their drums to invoke the gods' blessings.

The Izumo Kagura Dance performed in the Sanin area during autumn uses masks for the snake-dragon, the princess, and the noble warrior. The snake-dragon wears a blue-and-white costume with a very long tail, its scales outlined in black.

The Heron Dance *(sagi mai)*, also performed in the Sanin district, is held on 20 and 27 July at Yasaka Shrine in Tsuwano. (This dance, dating back to the seventeenth century, was once held in Kyoto.) White fabric strips cover the dancers' bodies from the shoulders to the ankles. The arms when spread form heron's wings. The heron's long neck head is a mask and headpiece. Under this costume is a red leotard with a white top and white shoes. A heron chick dance for children, inspired by the four-hundred-year-old adult dance, has become popular. A baby chick's head made from paper sits amid four large silk flowers. This is tied around a child dancer's head, leaving the child's face exposed.

The folk dances in Okinawa (the largest island of the Ryukyus, northeast of Taiwan, under Japanese sovereignty) often express feelings of love. A female dancer wears a blue scarf covered with a poppy and other flowers around her head. Her colorful kimono, in a floral abstract design of blue, green, gold, and red, is tied in front with a red-and-blue sash. Red undergarments, red shoes, and a lotus flower held in her hand complete her traditional Okinawan folk dance costume.

Butō. This is a modern form of Japanese dance, for which the dancers shave their heads, concentrate all their emotions, and are trained to move every muscle and joint in their bodies. With bared torsos, white painted faces, or weird masks of molten shape over their faces, they make a striking sight. Skirts of various lengths are tied to the side and represent the basic costume. Sometimes one long earring resembling rope suspends from an ear. *Butō* is esoteric and mysterious, with minimal costuming. [See Butō.]

China. Chinese opera costume may be traced to folk dances, ballet, and ancient Chinese lyrics. Costumes were designed to coordinate with dancers' movements, and very little thought was given to realism. Chinese opera is believed to have started during the Song dynasty (960–1279).

Chinese opera. Originally a type of song-and-dance act with a connecting story, Chinese opera gave more importance to dance actions than to the actor's role. In the Ming dynasty (1368–1644), the opera plots became more complex and the costumes underwent change; actors started to dress in period fashions, forgetting that the opera costumes were supposed to be for dancing. A costume mixture ensued where almost 70 percent of the stage costume was conventional and 30 percent contemporary fashion. This did not last long, for most opera companies soon used a standard set of costumes, a practice that lasted until the Qing dynasty (1644–1912). Any changes that occurred made little impact on costuming convention.

One major type of costume is the ceremonial robe with dragon designs known as *mang*. It is worn by high officials and honored courtiers and has wave patterns on its lower border. Military leaders wear *kao* (a padded armor), covered with ornaments. *Pi* are long sleeveless vests worn by both sexes. A girl's black vest is worn by an elderly maidservant, an ugly chambermaid, or a common woman, but a maid in the Imperial Palace would wear the same garment richly embroidered.

A dancer wearing a formal noblewoman's costume would have a multicolored skirt and a silk bodice with full sleeves embroidered with the phoenix, the lotus, and the Buddhist endless knot. Long white inner sleeves are attached to the embroidered sleeves; longer than the arms, these are part of the Confucian tradition, with its strong emphasis on moral conduct. This tradition promoted covering the entire body from sunlight, thus the extra-long sleeves that must be tossed back to view the sensitive and beautiful hand movements of the dancer.

China once had sumptuary laws governing the use of color for officials and their wives, but in Chinese opera these are not strictly followed. As a general rule, red signifies loyalty and righteousness; brown is reserved for the aged; white is associated with the educated; the vulgar often wear black and the virtuous green; yellow is reserved for the Chinese emperor and empress. When these conventions are not adhered to, it is usually because the story or setting demands adjustment.

Mandarin or rank badges designated the military and civil ranks in imperial China. Specific birds were used for each civil rank and different animals for the military ranks. Opera costume does not follow this custom, often filling the rank badges or Mandarin squares with flowers and symbols of longevity like the *wan* character (swastika pattern).

In the Chinese opera, masks are worn only for animals, such as the tiger, wolf, and pig; otherwise, actors and actresses use painted faces. Admirable characters use simple colors, while enemy generals, rebels, and bandits have complicated patterns. Red indicates courage, blue cruelty, and black impulsiveness. Mustaches and beards can also indicate character: a beard divided into three parts represents a man of integrity; a short mustache is found on a crude, rough man; a mustache that curls up belongs to a sly and tricky fellow.

High-soled boots are worn by all male actors except clowns, whose boots are lower. Some shoes have Chinese characters written on them, like *fu*, meaning "happiness and good fortune"; these are often worn by poor scholars or the elderly.

The cloud collar is an important accessory worn over robes. It can be small or large enough to fall over the shoulders; sometimes it has pearls or fringes but is commonly embroidered in silk or metal threads on a satin background.

COSTUME IN ASIAN TRADITIONS. Qi Shufang, wearing an ornate costume embroidered with gold and silver threads, in the Beijing Opera *The Green-Stone Mountain*. (Photograph © 1989 by Linda Vartoogian; used by permission.)

Beneath the costumes are the undergarments. One is a cotton jacket—the "fat coat" *(pang'ao)*—padded thickly or, sometimes, thinly to change the actor's silhouette. Protective white cotton collars are also worn underneath the robes to keep them clean.

Folk heritage. In China, many national songs and dances are performed by song-and-dance companies. The fifty-five minority nationalities in China produce their own dances and wear their own costumes—each of which is highly identified with each region. The Uighur people in the Picking Grapes Dance from Xinjiang Province of western China wear the *dorba*, a pillbox-type hat often made in black velvet covered with floral patterns of silver sequins and trimmed with black feathers. A red long-sleeved dress with a circular skirt is worn over tight tapered silk trousers with embroidery at the ankles. A black velvet vest decorated with gold sequins is worn over the dress.

The Tajik people from the same area express their deep feelings for their grasslands in the Shepherdess, a solo dance. Here the traditional Muslim veil can be seen attached at the back of the dancer's hat, flowing to her hips. A red long-sleeved coat is worn over a circular dress and tapered narrow pants.

The Dai people dance the White Peacock Dance, where a white long-sleeved silk chiffon dress with a full skirt has multiple painted peacock eyes trimmed with sequins. Sometimes the sequins and dress are blue-green; then the dance is simply called the Peacock Dance. The peacock is revered by the Dai people, since it represents prosperity, luck, and the wish for a peaceful existence.

Mongolia's Bowl Dance has a dancer balancing three bowls on top of a red-sequined turban. A green velvet sleeveless coat is worn over a white long-sleeved dress with borders trimmed in gold appliqué. Red boots complete this dance costume.

People's Republic of China. After the establishment of the People's Republic in 1949, many dances were choreographed to be political in content. In 1945 *The White-Haired Girl* was a folk opera; in the early 1960s it was performed as a ballet in Japan. The ballets *The Red Detachment of Women* (1964) and *The White-Haired Girl* (1965) were choreographed by the Chinese and performed in China, and Chinese military uniform adaptations were worn, including the peaked cap with the red star. The female costume was the blue jacket with short sleeves and four patch pockets and two red fabric tabs on the edges of its mandarin collar; blue Bermuda shorts with matching leg warmers were worn over flesh-colored tights. Blue satin ballet slippers, a brown leather belt worn over the jacket, and a red armband on the left arm completed the women's costumes. The male military dancers wore costumes similar to the womens' but in lighter blue, with knickers instead of Bermuda shorts. The female peasant dancers wore Chinese cotton jackets with right side closings and wide ankle-length trousers. Straw coolie hats, some decorated with sickle and star motifs, were tied under their chins.

Chinese dance companies often perform the traditional dances of Sri Lanka, Indonesia, India, Malaysia, Thailand, Cambodia, Nepal, Myanmar (formerly Burma), Pakistan, Bangladesh, and the Philippines. The costumes used are those of the individual countries, and the performances are held in China as well as on tour in other Asian countries.

Tibet. The Tibetans are one of China's minority nationalities, and many of their sacred (Buddhist) dances are still performed within Tibet as well as by refugees in parts of India, like Kangra Valley. *Cham,* the sacred dance of Tibet, is performed yearly in honor of Padmasambhava's birth. In the seventh century, Padmasambhava, an Indian yogi-saint, brought Buddhism to the Tibetan plateau and danced the original *cham;* there are many variations of *cham* today, danced in monasteries.

Cham masks are made from papier-mâché and have facial designs in black, red, and white paint. There usually is a gilt crown worn with the mask, and this type is indicative of a fierce guardian king. The monks can wear a brownish brocade robe and a diamond-shaped collar of blue-and-gold brocade. The robe is cut loosely, with wide pointed sleeves and deep side pleats. Historically, Chinese brocade had often been given to the Tibetans as tribute.

In *cham,* the Black Hat Dance performer can wear a robe of black-and-yellow Chinese satin trimmed with yellow-and-red brocade. Satin appliquéd eyes decorate the sleeves and the back of the skirt. A black satin apron with the wild face of Yama, the lord of death, is part of the costume. Skulls and fierce faces alternating with diamond sceptors *(dorjes)* border the apron. These patterns are composed of appliquéd silks and gilded leather. A collar with two types of angry guardians is also worn. Brocade and rope are the materials used for *cham* boots. The black hat is made of *papier-mâché* and has a finial comprising a skull, a *dorje,* and jewels. A ritual dagger *(phurbu)* and a small skull are held in the hands of all the unmasked dancers performing the Black Hat Dance. Rich Chinese robes, cloud collars, aprons made from silk or bone, and black hats lined in red silk complete the costumes of the sixteen to twenty performers who join the lead dancer. [*See* Black Hat Dance.]

A skeleton costume is used in the Lamaist Devil Dance (Lamaism is the form of Buddhism practiced in Tibet). The skeleton represents the Master of the Cemetery, and this dance is well known in Tibetan tantric traditions. The skeleton dancers wear coats, trousers, gloves, and shoes made from red flannel with a skeleton pattern appliquéd in white satin damask over the flannel. Velvet panels imitating tiger skin form the skirt. The paws are padded in white and pinkish red satin, and bones form the devil's claws. Sometimes, the costume details are made in black or in blue satin with gold-and-silver brocade. A bull mask

COSTUME IN ASIAN TRADITIONS. A dancer from Mongolia performing the traditional Bowl Dance. (Photograph from the archives of The Asia Society, New York.)

made of *papier-mâché* is worn with this costume. Streamers of satin brocade with gilded paper hang from the mask's finial, the gloves, the shoes, and at the five panels on the front, back, and sides of the costume. These mitered streamers are decorated with red, green, and white silk tassels and small brass bells. A velvet sash with two overlapping flounces keeps the outfit in place.

Korea. The dances of the Korean court are stately and dignified. These graceful dances are performed at special celebrations and royal ceremonies. The women's costumes were in pastel or brightly colored silks, with long skirts and full sleeves. In ancient times, many Chinese traits influenced the court dancers' headpieces. During the Paekche Kingdom of the Three Kingdom's Period (57 BCE–668 CE) the dancers wore a headdress. The dancers' costumes consisted of purple jackets with big sleeves, full skirts, and leather shoes. Later, the court dancers of the Silla period (57 BCE–935 CE) also wore a headdress, and the costume of this period was also purple with big sleeves, but a red leather gilded belt and black leather boots accessorized this outfit.

The historical Korean court dancers were impeccably coiffed, and their dress and dance movements were highly controlled. Today, the "Ball Throwing Dance" *(po'gurak)* is still performed; it was at one time performed in the court.

The dancers wear silk brocade tunics and small beaded crowns decorated with tassels. In a solo court dance, the "Nightingale Dance" (ch'unaenajŏn), the dancer wears layered skirts.

An elegant stately dance is the "Flower Crown Dance" (hwagwanmu). The dancers—with their crowns, yellow dresses, and red sashes—hold very long horizontally striped sleeves in their hands. The stripes are red, green, yellow, blue, white, and turquoise, and they create streaks of color as the dancers move. Striped sleeves have long been associated with court dress as well as the Korean bridal gown (hwalot).

The "Drum Dance" (mugo) is mentioned in the Korean writings of the Koryo dynasty (918–1392). It was performed in the ancient court and was combined with court music in the thirteenth century of the late Koryo period. The "Victory Drum Dance" (sŭngjonmu) came into existence during the sixteenth century when a Korean naval commander decided to boost his men's morale through musical entertainment. This dance is performed in Ch'ungmu, a southeastern coastal city, at a local shrine dedicated to the naval commander, during the spring and fall.

The dancers wear a small jeweled crown with a pendant in the middle of their foreheads, and they hold either a drumstick or a flower in their hands. Their long-sleeved silk tunics are constructed with two panels in the front and two in the back. Silk sashes are tied high under their breasts, forming an empire waist. They also hold the long flowing striped sleeve extensions in their hands. The

sleeve extensions have elastic at their wrists to hold them in place.

The sword dance was developed by women entertainers attached to Korea's royal court and to provincial magistrates' offices. In the southern town of Chinju, a sword dance is still performed where the eight dancers carry two swords apiece. They wear brightly colored military uniforms such as those worn in the Yi dynasty (1392–1910). Their brimmed black hats have huge red tassels attached to a metal finial on top of the crown. Sometimes, the tassels are attached to a button that gyrates when the dancers move. Red and yellow beads form chin straps to keep their hats on securely. The dancers wear white blouses trimmed with royal blue at their necklines and cuffs, royal blue skirts, and red sashes worn high above their waistlines. White padded socks (bosun) and white shoes complete their costumes. Sword dancing is recorded as far back as the Silla period, thus making it one of the court's oldest forms of entertainment. According to ancient records, such as *The Chronicles of the Three Kingdoms*, the sword dance was originally performed with masks, but the masks are no longer used.

There are many masked dances in Korea. The *pongsan*, a masked dance drama, pokes fun at the *yangban* ("upper class") and at corrupt monks. The masks are white with the eyes outlined in black. The mouths are painted red and the eyebrow furrows are lined in black. A red-masked dancer is also present, wearing a long-sleeved green satin jacket with yellow trim. This jacket can also be made in blue, trimmed with red or red-violet, with turquoise bind-

COSTUME IN ASIAN TRADITIONS. A lion and tamer in the Korean Lion Dance of the masked dance genre *pongsan t'alch'um*. (Photograph from the archives of The Asia Society, New York.)

ings. Sashes are worn over the jacket, and multicolored streamers are used to tie the baggy trousers and the sleeves of this male dancer's costume.

Gourd masks are used by the twenty-two performers in the "Mask Play of Yangju," performed in the provincial town of Kyonggido, outside of Seoul. Many villages also have their own mask dances, but this one goes back to about 1840. Sometimes a lion is featured in a mask play, so a lion dance is often a part of these plays. It is believed that lion dances derive from the ancient mask dances of north-central Asia. Often two people are needed to form the lion; the costume can be made of wool, fabric, brocade, paper, yarns, and various combinations. Lion dances are also performed in many parts of Asia, such as China and Japan.

One of the most graceful Korean dances is the "Monk's Dance" *(sungmu)*, which probably had its origins in an old Buddhist temple ritual; this dance uses a blue transparent robe with extremely large sleeves and a white hood (the *hansam*). White long trousers, a red sash decorated with tassels at each end, and a red-silk baldric worn diagonally across the body make this an eye-catching ensemble.

When Korean villagers wish to give thanks for good crops and to pray for blessings, they play farmer's music *(nongak)*. Using gongs, drums, and reed instruments and wearing white outfits with black hats decorated with a red flower, the men dance and work up the enthusiasm necessary for transplanting or harvesting. Green, yellow, and red cotton sashes are criss-crossed over their chests and backs and tied at the waist. Their white cotton pants are fuller at their knees and taper at their ankles.

The Korean national costume, the *hanbok*, is worn for the "Girl's Circle Dance" *(kanggangsuwollae)*. This dance is popular along the south coast of Korea and is part of the Autumn Moon Festival. A legend tells of an impending war with Japan in the sixteenth century that was averted when a Korean officer sent hundreds of women to dance in circles around bonfires at the seashore. The *hanbok* consists of a full skirt or solid colored *chima* that ties above the breasts, and a very short complementing jacket *(jugori)*, that ties with a looped knot at the right side. The padded socks *(bosun)* and the shoes with upturned toes and rubber soles *(komuchin)* complete the national costume.

India. Four major traditional dances exist in India today: *kathakaḷi*, *bharata nāṭyam*, *kathak*, and Manipuri.

Kathakaḷi. From Kerala in the south of India, *kathakaḷi* is performed solely by males. This dance drama dates to the late 1600s and copies the art (carvings and paintings) of Karala's old temples. Young boys train from the age of eight and practice for thirteen hours a day. This flamboyant dance drama is related to the martial arts. Its makeup and costuming are intricate and time consuming. The

COSTUME IN ASIAN TRADITIONS. Korean dancer Lee Mae-bang, designated an Intangible National Treasure, wears a traditional elongated-sleeved *hansam*, in the "Monk's Dance" *(sungmu)*, derived from the Buddhist ritual "Butterfly Dance" *(nabi ch'um)* (Photograph © 1986 by Jack Vartoogian; used by permission.)

makeup used in *kathakaḷi* has its roots in the ancient demon folk masks, and its themes often come from Indian mythology. The performer, clad in a loincloth, is given a foot massage before his makeup is applied. The colors are stored in a jar, waiting for use, freshly ground every morning and mixed with oils by the makeup specialist. First, the actor's face is marked with a black pencil as he reposes on the ground. Rice paste is applied in a curved shape from his chin to his jawline. The thick rice paste hardens, and this rice-paste coating is reapplied until it is a half-inch thick. Patterns are then painted on the face in red, green, or black depending on the actor's role. The performer is not permitted to move his face or lips, since he can destroy the white rice-paste frame or the makeup. (Some say that a few great *kathakaḷi* dancers have learned to control their facial muscles so that they can laugh on one side of their faces and cry on the other.)

The *kathakaḷi* dancer learns to meditate and often goes to sleep during the four-hour makeup process. Before dressing, the performer usually prays and bows before his costume, including the *mudi-kritam* (divine headdress). The dance drama is usually held at night, in a temple or a courtyard. The bare-chested actor ties bells to his knees over his white cotton tapered trousers, which have been tied at the ankles with narrow red and green ties. Then two green padded sections of fabric are tied around the waist and secured at the back with an off-white strip of material. Approximately fifty-five yards of fabric are used to make the *kathakali* costume.

Two pleated, bluish white, stiff skirts are then tied above the front waistline over each other. Finally, a third skirt of lightweight, white broomstick-pleated cotton gauze is tied below the breasts and this results in a mushroom silhouette. This cotton gauze outerskirt has horizontal stripes in orange and black at the bottom edge. A red cotton sash holds the three skirts in place, in addition to holding two long rectangular pieces of red cotton cloth at the sides of the body. The red cotton cloths are heavily decorated with blue-and-gold foil trims and are edged in multicolored fringes. A short jeweled piece shaped like an elongated petal is placed in the center front. This is also decorated with multicolored fringes and a large red pom-pom in the center front. On top of this a jeweled girdle is worn. At one time all the jewelry was pure gold but today the performers use imitations. The actor wears two jackets. The first one is of white cotton, collarless with long sleeves. This is tied around the neck and in front. The second long-sleeved jacket is of red felt and ties at the back. Two sets of jeweled gold bracelets trimmed with green pom-poms are worn on the forearms. Gold shoulder pieces, gold necklaces, and a gold jeweled breastplate backed with leather add glitter to this lavish costume.

Long black wigs and jeweled domed headpieces are worn with three to four sets of scarves around the neck. Some of the scarves form lotus-shaped ends containing mirrors, so the actor can check his makeup. All the actors have crimson eyes because they put the seeds of the wildflower *cunda-poo* into each eye before a performance. This causes irritation and the red eyes become more expressive.

Female roles are played by young boys who wear synthetic breasts and cover their heads with the end of the sari (the long fabric wound skillfully to form a dress). The female role is called *minukku,* but this term can also apply to a yogi or Brahman. The *minukku* do not require extensive makeup preparation; their faces are often lightly painted with yellow and sprayed with mica. The soles of their feet and the palms of their hands are dyed pink.

Generally, green makeup signifies godliness, evil is expressed by the color black, and yellow indicates a passive nature. Thus, in the depiction of Pacca, a noble hero, there is a white and parrot-green face, red lips, and a flame decoration on his forehead. His headpiece is a jeweled, domed, triple crown with a halo attached at back.

The upturned mustache and white mushroom warts on the forehead and nose tip indicate the role of majestic Katti. Two walrus tusks emerge from the ends of his mouth, and blue and white stripes outline his eyebrows. His fingers are fitted with long silver nail guards, and his headdress can sometimes rise to two and a half feet (almost 1 meter).

Red Beard, the fiend, does have a full red beard, as well as mushroom warts on his nose and forehead. White Beard, a noble person, has a black upper face and a red lower face decorated with curved white lines. His nose is green, his lips black, and black outlines his eyes. Two red spots decorate his forehead. A gray beard, a large fur coat, and the bell-shaped headdress tell us that he is Hanuman, the monkey. [*See* Kathakaḷi].

Bharata nāṭyam. This is the old South Indian temple dance to Śiva (Shiva) by the *devadasi*s, female Hindu dancers who give their lives to the Divine. The sanctity of the temple ritual was violated when the *devadasi*s started to please the feudal landlords, so a law was passed prohibiting any girl from being dedicated to a temple. In the late 1890s there was a revival of interest in the ancient culture, and the dances—carved in high relief on temple stones—were renewed. The female dancers then wore rich silk blouses (*choli*) with brightly colored silk saris. A section of the sari was pleated in front and fastened high, so that a pleated fan shape occurred when the dancer's legs spread. Today, a pleated fan is worn over constructed trousers, achieving the same effect.

The palms and soles of the feet are dyed pink, and a red dot is placed in the center of the forehead. Collyrium (eye salve) and black pencil accent the eyes. Diamonds are placed in the nostrils and a jewel in the center of the nose. A gold chain decorates the hair, and a pendant hangs from the center of the forehead. The braided hair is decorated with jasmine flowers, tassels, pom-poms, or pearls. Rings, gold necklaces, and bracelets add luster to the costume.

Kathak. This sensuous dance is performed in North India. Its source was Hinduism, and it is sometimes referred to as the whirling dance of the north. It is intricate and performed by both sexes, but women dominate. The *kathak* female dancer often wears a long-sleeved brocaded jacket with a central front slit over a long wide skirt. Sometimes the jacket is long, reaching to the ankles, and this is used over tapered trousers. A long head veil or a transparent fringed scarf worn across the chest gives this outfit a Mughal influence. The hair is braided into one long, hanging braid. The eyes are outlined in mascara. Anklets of miniature brass bells are worn. Some dance masters, however, insist on the traditional *sari* for this dance. The male dancers usually wear white tapered trousers, a waistcoat, and a *topi* cap. [*See* Kathak.]

Manipuri. This is a traditional dance of Northeast India. The female Manipuri dancer appears elegant in a tunic, a skirt, and a peaked headdress—a costume close to its seventeenth-century prototype. Manipuri dancing takes place in the Assam hills during Holī, the full-moon "festival of colors" (March–April), and the dancer's costume follows the hues of the surrounding landscape, with stiff skirts sometimes decorated with mirror pieces. The forehead and cheeks have dots of sandalwood paste; mica powder covers the face; and the hair is rolled up and crowned with white flowers. Short veils are attached to a pointed ornament on the headdress. Short-sleeved vests, multiple necklaces, and diagonally draped, ornamented shoulder sashes are often worn as well.

Folk dances. In India, these dances often have the same themes as in other parts of Asia. The folk theater, *yakṣagāna*, combines song and dance and uses epics and religion to maintain the constant theme of good overcoming evil. *Yakṣagāna*, or "the song of supernatural beings," is performed in western India, in the southern state of Karnataka; it has several styles according to its location.

Male *yakṣagāna* performers apply their own makeup, mixing it in the palms of their hands. Yellow orpiment (arsenic trisulfide) and white zinc oxide mixed with coconut oil are applied to the face, neck, and arms. For female roles, red coloring is applied to this basic mixture and put on the cheeks and chin. Coconut oil is used to remove the makeup. According to old beliefs, the female look should be fair skinned, with black-lined elongated eyes and full red lips; false breasts and a sari are worn to complete the costume.

When the demoness Surapankhi is portrayed, her facial makeup consists of a rice paste and cockle lime putty called *chuti*. Dots are formed from the rice paste and placed over the red, green, and pink facial makeup. Her eyes are elongated to the temples with yellow and black coloring. Giant coconut breasts, a long-sleeved blouse, a full skirt, gold belts, necklaces, armbands, and shoulder ornaments are components of her costume. A tall crown with peacock feathers is placed over her long hair.

The most interesting costume used in this performance is a headdress known as *mundasu*. Fabric is wrapped around the head until it reaches a height of more than two feet (0.7 meter). The resulting shape is a flattened disc with a long point at the top. Since the performer's hair is long, it must be tied in a bun at the top of the head before it is covered with fabric to form the *mundasu*'s foundation. Stuffed cloth tubing is placed around the hairline, then tied at back to the bun with strings; the tubes are placed on top of each other until the proper height is reached. The tubes can be covered with red or black cloth before multicolored ribbons are tied in a criss-cross direction, forming rays. The *mundasu* is decorated with jeweled collars, pom-poms, silk, and gold disks; a large jeweled ornament is fixed on top.

The trainee performers play the roles of buffoons (*ko-*dangis). They wear black pajamas with red tops and put mango leaves in their hair. They watch and learn by imitating the seasoned performers. [*See* Yakṣagāna.]

Bhutan. In Thimphu, the capital of the kingdom of Bhutan, the dancers in the Deer Dance wear shorts with a leopard print and wrap another leopard-patterned cloth around their bodies. A second cloth with tiger stripes is then wrapped over the first. Four yellow scarves are attached by their corners to a waist belt, forming a skirt. A broader belt is then put over this to keep everything in place. The dancers are bare chested but wear a wide scalloped collar and a red cloth hat with ear flaps.

A deer mask with long antlers is placed over the head, so that the dancer can see out of the mouth opening. This dance is symbolic of Padmasambhava, who while riding on a deer stopped the demon of the wind. Bhutanese Buddhism has many tantric practices, such as spells and symbolic mysticism, and these are often seen in the dances.

The monks who live in Bhutan's temple-monastery centers continue the Buddhist dance traditions. They also

COSTUME IN ASIAN TRADITIONS. *Yakṣagāna* performer wearing the elaborate headress known as *mundasu* or *kēdage mundale*. (Photograph from the Dance Collection, New York Public Library for the Performing Arts.)

make the masks. (Lay dancers are supported by the royal government but are not permitted to perform all of the dances.) The Black Hat Dance is performed by the monks. They dress in long, full brocade robes with wide sleeves. Their orange pants are tucked into their boots. Their hats are broad-brimmed; beads, carved bone aprons depicting gods, and Buddhist symbols are often worn over their robes. During this dance they carry scarves in one hand and a three-sided dagger in the other.

There are many forms of the dance drama in the kingdom of Bhutan. Religious dances are performed by the monks, and secular dances by lay people. Public entertainment (tsechu) is held annually in Thimphu, during late September to early October, lasting for more than four days. Prior to the tsechu, the monks perform a religious rite (domchae) for a few days, using masks to dispel evil forces and encourage good ones. In the tsechu, lay people and monks dance masked and unmasked dances as well as folk dances. Manuals exist in which the masks, costumes, and choreography are outlined, but most people know the specifics by heart.

The masks are composed of papier-mâché or sometimes carved from pine wood, with design and dimensions following the old descriptions. Every mask is blessed before it is used, and openings are made through the eyes, nose, and mouth. All the dancers are male. Generally, the lay costumes are simple and colorful and no shoes are worn; the dancing monks require more elaborate costumes with knee-high embroidered boots. A monk's costume color usually matches the color of his mask, and each deity has its own color. The choreography, costumes, masks, and music are symbolic; it is believed that the details follow the pre-Buddhist rites of Bon, an early animistic religion.

Nepal. Jumla is a town in the Karnali section of western Nepal. During the farmer's slow season in September, there is a dance pageant honoring the Hindu god Kṛṣṇa (Krishna). The dancer portraying Kṛṣṇa wears a wrapped yellow silk skirt, a sleeveless red coat, and a silver metallic breastplate over a short-sleeved black top. His hat is fashioned after a silver crow and has ear flaps. His face is painted red and white. Ankle bells are above one bare foot. He wears a silver-trimmed apron made from the same black fabric as his shirt. Flower chains (leis) decorate his neck.

Kṛṣṇa's princely brother, Balarāma, is dressed in a similar fashion but he does not wear a lei. In this epic Hindu conflict, Kṛṣṇa slays the evil demon Lakhe, who wears a mask with hair from yak tails attached to it. His skirt is full, with other skirts bunched and tied around his waist. His shirt is short sleeved, and the skirts are held up around his waist with a leather belt.

Pakistan. On 4 August 1947, Pakistan was established, and it is a melting pot of Islamic Indo-Aryan people. Be-

fore it was formed, pre-Dravidian and Dravidian groups of the Indian subcontinent mixed with people from central Asia—Aryans, Persians, Arabs, Bactrians, Moguls, and Turks. Today, Iranians and Turks predominate. Folk songs are often in Urdu, the country's national language, or in the regional Punjabi, Pushtu, Baluchi, Brohi, and Sindi.

Since more than three quarters of Pakistan's people are engaged in farming and herding, music and dance are often concerned with the agricultural duties of sowing, reaping, and harvesting. The most popular folk dance during harvest is Luddi. The men wear tunics with side slits, baggy trousers, and sleeveless vests with trimming. Bells decorate their ankles and long cotton scarves are placed around their shoulders. Cloth is often wrapped around their heads like turbans, and multicolored necklaces adorn their necks. The women are also clothed in tunics with side slits over wide, loose trousers.

In the Kalat valley of Pakistan, peasants perform ritual dances at harvest, weddings, birth, and death. The women wear loose blouses outside of full skirts, braids, headdresses of cowrie shells and coral, and silver wrist bracelets.

Sind jhooman, a folk dance of the Sind Province of Pakistan, honors a national hero. The women wear garments with hand-blocked red resist dyes.

Myanmar. The dances of the Burmese are often gay and exuberant, with movements ranging from the acrobatic to short, angular motions. Sometimes the movements of a marionette are imitated. The Burmese puppet theater has a long history. At first it was a children's show, but after the capital of Siam (now Thailand) was captured in 1769, the Burmese took the stories of the Rāmāyaṇa and the Jātaka tales and incorporated them. The Burmese were influenced by the masks, costumes, and dance of the neighboring Thai court. Today it is possible to see a marionette dancing on stage with Burmese dancers imitating the marionette's movements. The dancers paint their bodies with whitish makeup to look like the wooden marionettes; they wear the same headdresses and costumes.

Burmese female dancers wear semitransparent, long-sleeved, white silk fitted jackets that open in front. The jacket has a small peplum at the waist. The dancers' wrapped narrow skirts (longyis) have an extension of white fabric sewn to a hem that reaches beyond the feet and forms a train to accent their movements. Under the fitted jacket is a short-sleeved blouse or a strapless top densely decorated with sequins. The hair is worn back from the face and rolled up at back. Pearls decorate the hair, ears, and neck of the dancers. Sequins and metallic embroidery decorate most Burmese costume (similar to that of Thailand).

During the annual Burmese nat festival at Mount Popa, an extinct volcano, the dancers become possessed by a

COSTUME IN ASIAN TRADITIONS. Performers from the Burmese State Theater enacting a dance version of the Hindu epic, the *Rāmāyaṇa*. The characters holding bows chase the golden deer, represented by the helmets of the kneeling dancers. (Photograph from the archives of The Asia Society, New York.)

spirit and appear trancelike. The Burmese believe that it is possible for male dancers to become possessed by female spirits and vice versa. The mother of Mount Popa is usually played by a male. The dancers wear spirit masks and long scarves. The masks are often revered and are kept in small shrine houses next to the theater entrance. The demon masks are kept separate.

Thailand. The oldest formalized dance drama in Thailand is *khōn*. Of classical Indian origin, it developed over many centuries. The roles in *khōn* are traditionally played by men, including those of women. *Khōn* uses wigs, makeup, masks, side singers, and an orchestra. Every performance is based on an episode from the Hindu *Rāmāyaṇa* (known as *Rāmākien* in Thailand). Full-length *khōn* performances are only presented at the government-subsidized National Theater. The costumes are densely sequined, and with more than one hundred performers wearing these elaborate brocade costumes, it is a spectacular sight. The performers wear knee-length trousers with draped skirts over them. Silver buckles, spangled jackets, sparkling shoulder wings, jeweled collars, and boldly designed rhinestone pendants are worn. Gold head crowns rise upward—like temple spires—to complete the outfits. Some performers use vividly colored masks with playful to fierce expressions. The white mask represents Hanuman, the monkey, who is a chief character in the Hindu stories. The Thais, being primarily Buddhist, tell the Hindu stories as folk tales rather than as religious epics. Within the dances there are sixty-eight finger gestures that are gracefully portrayed. [*See* Khōn.]

The Thai term *lakhōn* means "theater." There are many types of *lakhōn*, such as *lakhōn nai*, the dance that was held solely in the king's palace. *Lakhōn* resembles *khōn*, but here the women play the male roles, since no males except the king were permitted in the inner courts of the palace. Another type is *lakhōn nok*, the dance troupes found outside of the royal palace. *Lakhōn duk damban* are dance plays with scenery. Today, a blending of many types of *lakhōn* exists, since *Rāmāyaṇa* stories, Thai legends, and Hindu and Indonesian folk tales are often combined. [*See* Lakhōn.]

A typical Thai female dancer performing nonclassical dance can wear a diagonally draped cotton or silk top with one end hanging down her right shoulder (the *pasabai*). Her draped ankle-length print skirt forms pants; necklaces, bracelets, and a hair flower are the accessories. The Thai male dancer can wear the same type of draped skirt that forms pants. A short-sleeved collarless shirt is worn outside the trousers, and this is sashed at the waist with a plaid fabric in a half bow. Necklaces, makeup, and a flower in the left ear complete the male dancer's costume.

A modified folk dance called *ramwong* is popular today. Couples form a large circle and repeat simple dance steps. There is almost no contact between their bodies, as the dancers hold their arms high and make finger gestures.

Cambodia. Some of the folk dances have probably been in existence since prehistory. The animist spirit *(pi)* is often subdued by the performance of a spirit dance. Several early dances have Indian influences, since the Śiva (Shiva) cult has been in evidence here from the fourth century.

COSTUME IN ASIAN TRADITIONS. A female performer and monkey character (right) of *khōn,* a dance drama of Thailand with origins in the sixteenth century. Generally, the only *khōn* figures to appear in masks are monkeys and demons. (Photograph from the Dance Collection, New York Public Library for the Performing Arts.)Il-

The Javanese dance style was introduced during the founding of the Khmer dynasty in 802. Angkor (the Khmer capital) was later captured by the Thais, and this influence created new directions in dance.

Classical Khmer ballet has about two thousand gestures, but its costumes are close to those of Thailand's classical *khōn.* The same type of domed headdress with a pointed spire is used. Flowers are added to the gilded headdress. The dancers wear a wide, round, heavily jeweled collar, a basic sleeveless bodice, and a huge jeweled pendant around their necks. Their draped brocaded skirt is short enough to expose their bare feet. A densely sequined and jeweled scarf is worn diagonally across the left shoulder. Gold bracelets and anklets accessorize these elaborate costumes, which sometimes have the same winged constructions worn by Thailand's *khōn* performers.

The folk dances often use masks. In the Deer-Hunting Dance *(trott),* there are masks for the hunter, the deer, the demon, and the girls. For other folk dances, masks for elephants, monkeys, horses, and princes are used.

Most of the people wear the *krama,* a checkered cotton head cloth used not only in the dance but also as a vital part of a person's wardrobe since birth. The *krama* covers the body for modesty, protects the body from the sun, carries food, and is used for bathing.

Sri Lanka. The Kandy Perahera, a yearly procession, takes place during parts of July and August. This period, referred to as Esala, honors the Sacred Tooth—one of the most important relics in Buddhism. Lasting fifteen nights and ending on the evening of a full moon, this spectacular procession originating at the Temple of the Sacred Tooth, includes close to one hundred elephants, drummers, torch carriers, dancers, and chieftains. A beautifully decorated elephant, the Temple Tusker, carries a gold copy of the tooth relic. Two lines of male dancers with small hand drums perform the *uddekki* dance. They are barechested, but sometimes have beaded straps across their chests. White cotton turbans with the ends hanging down, silver earrings, and brass arm bracelets form the upper part of their costume. Their white cotton skirts have three rows of ruffles at the hips, edged in a solid color; these ankle-length skirts are tied at the waist and belted. [*See* Kandy Perahera.]

In ancient times, dance performances were not usually given for pleasure but were an essential part of sacred religious traditions. The ascetic properties of Buddhism have been incorporated in the dances of Sri Lanka since the third century BCE. The first written record of song and dance occurs in the two-thousand-year-old *Mahavamsa* chronicle. The preservation of the traditions was the responsibility of the priests—the *yakdessa*s, *kattaduja*s, and *kapurala*s. The three basic categories of dance in Sri Lanka today are the hill country's *udarata* dance from around the city of Kandy in the central mountains; *ruhunu* from the southern coastal interiors; and *sabaragamuwa* from the base of the western highlands.

The dances from Kandy are considered the purest type of Sinhala dancing. Usually performed by men, this art is handed down from father to son, creating families of dancers. The national dances of Sri Lanka have been performed since 600 BCE. The *ves* dance is named for an intricate silver headdress, which is worn by the *yakdessa* while he is performing this Kandyan dance. The *yakdessa* must be initiated in an elaborate Buddhist temple ceremony after he has completed many years of training. The *ves* dance is part of the ancient ritual of *kohomba kankariya,* where the deity living in the *kohomba* tree is exorcised. [*See* Kohomba Kankariya *and* Ves Dance.]

The *ruhunu* dances are devil dances performed in the southern section of Sri Lanka. These dances are concerned with exorcism, and the mask is very important. Gods such as Nagaraksha, king of the serpents, and Garuda, king of the birds, are represented by these wooden masks, some of which are very old and are great treasures. The Nagaraksa wooden mask has a huge cobra in between three smaller cobras on either side. The mask has bulbous eyes, a nose, teeth, and long fangs. With this mask, the male dancer wears a cotton, appliqued collarless, long-sleeved midriff with ruffles at the wrists. His double-tiered ruffled skirt reaches his knees, bells are tied to the sides of his legs, and matching cotton ruffles decorate his bare feet. A long striped scarf hangs around his neck, and silver bracelets are around his wrists.

The *sanni* dances in the South use eighteen masks to represent the individual demons. The dancer wears the mask to exorcise the particular disease that each demon signifies. In the central and southern parts of Sri Lanka it is believed that evil influences can possess a person. The *sabaragamuwa* dance uses a huge barrel drum, and the dancers' costumes have accessories that are related to this region. In the *goyam kapeema* harvest dance the female dancers invoke guardian deities to the sound of background drums. The costume consists of a gold crown, gold ear ornaments that encircle the ears, small earrings, a black cloth-and-metallic necklace, and a black short-sleeved midriff and skirt that are decorated with appliqué and rickrack in red, gold, orange, and blue.

Women dancers are now allowed to take part in the national dances of Sri Lanka, which in the past were an exclusive male prerogative. These women wear a short-sleeved silk midriff with a flowing semi-transparent skirt. Earrings, an ornamental belt, and a triple-domed hat are included in their costume.

The men of Sri Lanka wear *sarongs*, which are tubular rectangles draped around their bodies. The women wear the *hette*, a blouse with puffed sleeves, a scooped neckline, and a buttoned center-front closing. The *redda*, a long wrapped cloth, covers their hips and legs. The top of the *redda* is draped over the tied waist to form a peplum-like ruffle.

Malaysia. The Federation of Malaysia consists of eleven states on the Malay Peninsula and two states on the island of Borneo. Thai and Indonesian dance dramas have had a strong effect on the dance dramas of Malaysia. All three have borrowed from India's classical style of dance, but Malaysia does not adhere to any one style. Much Malaysian dancing expresses emotion and moods and contains a lot of action.

The *mak yong* of the state of Kelantan is very similar to the southern Thai *lakhōn jatri*. Malaysian repertory includes exorcism rites from Kelantan, but a sophisticated court style had emerged under the patronage of the Kelantan sultans. Under turn-of-the-century British influence, the sultans were no longer able to support the *mak yong* performers; government support is used today. The *joget gamelan* is a court-inspired dance from the nineteenth-century courts of the Malaysian states of Pahang and Trengganu.

Malaysian costume is very bright in color and highly decorated with sequins, embroidery, and gold braid. Many female dancers wear a red, crown-like sequined headdress, pink flowers at each ear, and a collarless orange blouse with elbow-length ruffled sleeves. Their narrow skirts, often with side closings, are heavily sequined. A pink satin sash with a large silver buckle is

COSTUME IN ASIAN TRADITIONS. A dancer and two drummers from Sri Lanka perform *tovil*, a Sinhala ritual of exorcism related to Buddhist rites. (Photograph from the archives of The Asia Society, New York.)

worn as well as bracelets and earrings. The dancer is barefoot.

Some of the wraparound skirts are in gold brocade and worn with orange velvet long-sleeved, knee-length tunics, open in front from the waist down. The barefoot dancer wears gold ornaments in her hair, which is pulled back in a chignon.

The male dancers wear orange collarless long-sleeved shirts, buttoned in front and trimmed with gold sequins. Their trousers are of the same fabric and reach to their ankles above bare feet. A short black-and-gold apron is wrapped around their hips and tucked in front. A black velvet pillbox hat completes the outfit.

Philippines. According to legend, the Philippine Archipelago was formed when a goddess threw emeralds into the sea. Geologists have demonstrated that these 7,107 islands in the shallow seas a few hundred miles from southeastern Asia were part of an exposed land bridge thousands of years ago. The Philippine aborigines are Negritos, who most probably came from Asia more than thirty thousand years ago and settled in the hills of Zambales and Tarlac (of Luzon province). The Indonesians of Mongoloid and Caucasian stock who came later, and the Malays who came in three migrations and brought Indian, Chinese, and Arabian influences, helped create a vast cultural diversity. Ferdinand Magellan's voyage of 1521 brought 350 years of Spanish rule after he discovered the Philippines. Thus Roman Catholicism joined Asian and other customs to influence Philippine dance.

On the northeastern coast of the island of Luzon, the Wedding Dance *(maskota)* is popular in the provinces of Cagayan and Isabela; this dance is named for the skirt known as *maskota*, which is very full and usually has a large floral print. Newly married couples and couples at social functions often perform this dance. The *maskota* is worn with a *camisa* ("blouse") and a stiff *pañuelo* ("shawl"). A handkerchief is suspended from the right side of the girl's waist. The male dancer wears the Filipino shirt known as *barong tagalog* with colored trousers. The *barong tagalog*, which today is worn for formal occasions, dates back to the time of colonial oppression; when the Spanish arrived in the sixteenth century, the natives retained their own costume, with its mixture of Chinese, Indonesian, and other influences. By the seventeenth century, Spanish and other foreign influences had become stronger; in the eighteenth, they became dominant.

The *barong tagalog* was worn by the town natives, but the colonizers forbade them to tuck the shirt into their pants. Today the *barong tagalog* made from *piña* (woven from the fibers of pineapple leaves) and *jusi* (made from banana fibers), both found in the Philippines, are remnants of the organdy and lightweight starched muslin used during the Spanish days. The shirt has side slits and is shaped like a Western suit coat, similar to those of Pierre Cardin in 1969.

A *barong tagalog* and white trousers are worn by the male dancer in the *pinggan-pinggan pino*, an old courtship dance of the island of Visayan that was performed from early times, when chinaware was rare. The female dancer wears a wrapped skirt, or *patadyong;* the *camisa;* a soft *pañuelo* on her left shoulder; and a handkerchief from her waist. The male dancer carries a china saucer in his pocket to give to the female as a love token.

Another Visayan dance is the *sangig,* performed by the older people of Malinao, Aklan, and Capiz. After harvest time, only one couple dances this ballroom dance. The woman wears the *patadyong*, a *camisa* or *kimona* (a loose blouse), and the *pañuelo* over one shoulder. The man wears the *barong tagalog* with red trousers.

During the first week of August, the War Dance *(sumbali)* is performed on the town plaza of Bayombong in Nueva Vizcaya. This is the dance of the aboriginal Aetas (Negritos) from the interior of Luzon; they also live in Negros, Panay, Mindoro, and Mindanao. The male dancers wear narrow loincloths and wigs of dry cornsilk. They blacken their bodies with soot or burned cork and carry spears, bows, and arrows.

Filipino Muslims have their own dances, with costumes often in green, gold, blue, red. A popular Muslim dance is the *singkil*, which uses multiple crossed bamboo poles to form a ring in which the dancer's bare feet weave in and out. Young women of aristocratic birth are taught this dance, which derives its name from the heavy metal anklet called *singkil,* worn by the dancers. The dancer portraying the princess manipulates fans; her attendant carries a sequined umbrella. The dancer wears a printed narrow wrapped skirt, a white cotton short-sleeved blouse with embroidery on the V-neckline, and a crown headdress.

A sensual Muslim dance from Mindanao is the *sua sua,* with its graceful motions. The woman's costume consists of a tight long-sleeved blouse, a wrapped skirt to her ankles, and a rectangular scarf draped on one shoulder. The man wears a headband, a long-sleeved jacket with a front opening and no closings, pants with embroidered bands on the edges, and a matching sash around the waist.

The *subli* or *subil* is a ceremonial dance of Batanes, originally from two Tagalog words, *subsub* ("to stoop") and *bali* ("to bend"); Tagalog is the Western Austronesian language of Manila and the surrounding region. This is a dance based on the adoration of the Holy Cross, one of the major Roman Catholic rites for Good Friday; its beginnings go back to Spanish times. The choreography in Leonor Orosa's *Filipinescas* shows the men crouching and the women standing straight. During Spanish times only the men were permitted before the altar to adore the cross. The woman dancer is covered with a male hat while the male dancer is barefooted and crouches at her side, his head barely touching her waist. The costume is minimal.

The *maglalatik* or *magbabaó* dance originated in Laguna, where coconut oil *(latik)* is extracted. Two groups of male dancers representing Moors and Christians fight over the oil with forceful movements. The Moors have red trousers and long-sleeved black shirts, and the Christians wear blue pants and white shirts. Two circular coconut shells are attached to the dancer's chests, shoulder blades, and waists. Triangular coconut shells cover each knee and are held in the dancers' hands. For boy performers the torso is bared, and the trousers rolled up.

During the dancing of *la jota moncadeña*, a regional version of the Spanish *jota*, male dancers wear the formal *barong tagalog* and females the *terno* dress. This dance comes from Moncado and Tarlac. The beautiful *terno* dress, often embroidered, beaded, and sequined, has high rounded sleeves that resemble a butterfly. This dress can still be seen today at weddings, balls, and at many other festive occasions in the Philippines.

Similar to the Muslim *singkil* is the *tinikling*, probably the best known of all Philippine dances. The dancer imitates the movements of the long-legged *tikling* bird trying to avoid the farmer's bamboo trap. The dance uses crossed bamboo poles and is performed barefoot with everyday workers' costumes.

Indonesia. This is an extremely diverse country, with 13,677 islands stretching across a vast archipelago. Major islands include Bali, Bangka, Borneo (part), Celebes, Ceram, Flores, Java, Lombok, Madura, Sumatra, Timor, and New Guinea (part). The principal religion is Islam, but Christian religions and spirit worship exist.

In ancient times, the court dances of central Java were highly developed. The ceremonial dance *bedaya* was only performed at the sultan's court. Nine girls were dressed in gold-brocaded clothes and moved with slow, graceful motions. At present, the *bedaya* is danced during Garebeg, a Muslim sacrificial festival.

In the Javanese *rejog*, an ancient dance drama, fierce masks are worn by the actors. They will sometimes dance until exhaustion, as in the village of Ponorogo, where the dancers enact the legend of a king who loses his fiancée to another man but wins her again using disguise and a hobbyhorse army to frighten his enemy.

The Dance of Great Birds takes place on Java. Girls in pink-brocaded blouses and skirts and jeweled gold headpieces ride birds (as the god Vishnu rode Garuda, the king of the birds, in Hindu mythology); gold bracelets and armbands are also part of the dancers' costumes in this performance, which relates an Islamic story.

The finest of dances to be found on the island of Bali is the *légong*, performed only by young girls who have not reached womanhood. The girls wear silk garments with gold overleaf and gold headdresses decorated with frangipani flowers. At one time the dancers also wore gold earplugs, but these are no longer in use; instead, earrings are used, and heavy powder covers the dancers' faces. A white dot, the *priasan*, is painted in the center of the eyebrows, with three dots at each temple. The eyebrows are shaved and redrawn with black paint. The two main dancers wear a wrapped skirt, a sleeveless bodice, and a long narrow apron *(lamak)*. Their torsos are bound from their breasts to their hips with yards of fabric, which helps to support the dancers' spines; a gold sash is wrapped on top of the yards of fabric. A jeweled mirrored collar covers their necks, and a silver gilded belt covers their waists. Sometimes scarves are worn at the hips. The *tjondong*, the *légong*'s assistant, wears a simpler costume and carries fans. When the *tjondong* dances the crow role, she wears gilded leather wings. [*See* Légong.]

Once a year the Balinese celebrate the Kuningan festival, and *sanghyang dedari* is performed. Two small girls dressed in *légong* costumes go into a deep trance amid incense smoke. While in a trance the girls are able to dance without having had any instructions. There is chanting

COSTUME IN ASIAN TRADITIONS. Balinese *légong* dancer wearing a traditional costume, including an ornate headdress decorated with frangipani flowers. (Photograph © 1989 by Jack Vartoogian; used by permission.)

throughout, but the girls cease dancing when the chanting stops. It is believed that the young virgin girls are closest to the heavenly spirits, and this will protect and bring good fortune to the people.

The word *baris* means "in line," denoting a type of military formation. The ceremonial war dance called *baris gede* is performed in old Balinese villages. From ten to a dozen older men cover their heads with flowers and put scarves, supposedly containing magic powers, around their necks. They carry long silver and black spears with peacock feathers at the end. Dancing in a double line, they pretend to battle each other. This dance is often performed at important cremation ceremonies, but a large group of dancers is rare today.

A special type of *baris* is the *baris tekok djago*, where dancers wear *polen*, black-and-white checkered cloths thought to possess magical powers. The major costume element in the *baris* is the high triangular headdress of white fabric called *udeng-udengan*. This is worn at the back of the head, and a diadem of wired, fresh gardenia flowers is in front.

In Bali's *topéng* drama, dancers and clowns wear headdresses, masks, brocaded garments, and beaded fringed collars. The clowns, whose training is lifelong, are highly respected artists who provide the narration accompanying the dance movements. The clowns sing in Kawi, the

COSTUME IN ASIAN TRADITIONS. Barong is a Balinese mythological figure animated by two male performers. He bears a slight resemblence to the lion character in ancient Chinese dances, and an influence is suspected. In the Balinese *Calonarang* drama, this type of Barong is depicted as a force of good who battles the evil witch Rangda. (Photograph by Robert Wihtol; used by permission.)

ancient language of Bali, and also in modern Indonesian and Balinese. In the *topéng*, the masked dance often performed during a temple anniversary celebration is called *odalan;* this occurs every 210 days—the length of the Balinese year.

Some masks used in *topéng* are more than a hundred years old and have mother-of-pearl teeth. The king and god masks cover the entire face. Clowns wear partial masks leaving their jaws and mouths uncovered so they can speak. This half mask is symbolic of the fact that the clowns represent or exist in two worlds—the world of the audience and the world of mythology—since many of the plays are based on real or legendary events in Bali's history. The wearer of the mask becomes involved with the spiritual magic inherent in the mask itself. Some masks, according to the Balinese, are so powerful that they can put the wearer into a trance from which there is no recovery. Others are often brought into the presence of the ill in order to cure them. The *topéng* performers are generally older men who, by changing masks, can become many different characters. Although the clowns do speak, most of the *topéng* is in mime.

The Balinese clowns often poke fun at foreigners in the past and present. They ridicule the old Dutch colonialists and the modern foreign visitors by giving the mask a long nose, carrying a camera, and portraying bad manners. This satire enables the Balinese to cope with unpleasant situations.

Barong is one of Bali's oldest dances, in which two actors, wearing a half-lion and half-dragon wooden mask, portray the title character. His costume is of shaggy hair and jeweled, golden scales decorated with peacock feathers and minute bells. Rangda, the horrible queen of the witches, also has a mask. She is barely a female and symbolizes the dark, evil side of Balinese cosmology. Barong is a male role that represents human goodness, although he can also appear to be an amusing creature.

Conclusion. In the study of costume, the complexities and the nuances of the garment, the mask, and the accessories are telling objects. Asian costume is often mysterious, bedazzling, frightening, and exciting. It can be literal, allegorical, mythical, or metaphorical. It is so varied and culturally diverse that it provides study possibilities for many specialists in several disciplines. Since dance has become a theatrical showcase for touring national companies, the rich and varied costumes are increasingly on display.

[*See also the entries on the countries mentioned herein.*]

BIBLIOGRAPHY
Achjadi, Judi. *Indonesian Women's Costumes.* Jakarta, 1981.
Alley, Rewi. *Peking Opera.* Peking, 1957.
Ambrose, Kay. *Classical Dances and Costumes of India.* London, 1950.
Anand, Mulk Raj. *The Indian Theatre.* London, 1950.
Arensberg, Susan. *Javanese Batiks.* Boston, n.d.

Arnott, Peter D. *The Theatres of Japan.* London, 1969.

Barker, David. *Designs of Bhutan.* Bangkok, 1985.

Benjamin, Bonnie. *Sashiko: Quilting of Japan from Tradition to Today.* 1983.

Beny, Roloff. *Island Ceylon.* New York, 1971.

Bhushan, Jamila B. *The Costumes and Textiles of India.* Bombay, 1958.

Bloefeld, John. *The Great Cities: Bangkok.* Amsterdam, 1979.

Brandon, James R. *Theatre in Southeast Asia.* Cambridge, Mass., 1967.

Catalogue of the Tibetan Collection and Other Lamaist Articles. Vol. 4. Newark, N.J., 1975.

Chang Ta-hsia and Hwang Ti-pei, eds. *Chinese Opera Costumes.* Taipei, 1961.

Chou, Hsun. *Five Thousand Years of Chinese Costumes.* San Francisco, 1987.

Costumes of the Minority Peoples of China. Kyoto, 1982.

Covarrubias, Miguel. *Island of Bali.* New York, 1937.

Dalby, Liza C. *Kimono: Fashioning Culture.* New Haven, 1993.

Dar, S. N. *Costumes of India and Pakistan.* Bombay, 1969.

Dickinson, Gary, and Linda Wrigglesworth. *Imperial Wardrobe.* Wappingers Falls, N.Y., 1990.

Dorje, Shakya, and Guna Vidyarthi. "Cham: Sacred Dances of Tibet." *Orientations* 6 (July 1975).

Dragon Robes of China. Tokyo, 1982.

Ernst, Earle. *The Kabuki Theatre.* New York, 1956.

Gargi, Balwant. *Theatre in India.* New York, 1962.

Garrett, Valery M. *Traditional Chinese Clothing in Hong Kong and South China, 1840–1980.* Hong Kong and New York, 1987.

Ghurye, Govind S. *Bhāratanatyā and Its Costume.* Bombay, 1958.

Ghurye, Govind S. *Indian Costume.* Bombay, 1966.

Gittinger, M., and H. Lefferts. *Textiles and the Tai Experience in Southeast Asia.* Washington, D.C., 1992.

Gluckman, Dale. *When Art Became Fashion: Kosode in Edo-Period Japan.* New York, 1992.

Greeley, Alexandra. "The Revival of Thai Dance Culture." In *The Seventh Annual Festival of Asian Arts.* Hong Kong, 1982.

Haga Hideo. *Japanese Festivals.* Osaka, 1968.

Hibi, Sadao. *Japanese Detail: Fashion.* San Francisco, 1989.

Hitchcock, Michael. *Indonesian Textiles.* New York, 1992.

Hoass Sobrun. "Noh Masks." *Arts of Asia* (July–August 1977).

Jaffrey, Madhur. "Yakshagana: Karnataka's Lively Folk Theater." *Asia* 1 (March–April 1979): 8–15.

Jenkins, Ron. "Holy Humor of Bali's Clowns." *Asia* 3 (July–August 1980): 29–35.

Kartiwa, Suwati. *Sonket Weaving in Indonesia.* Djambatan, 1986.

Kartiwa, Suwati. *Indonesian Ikats.* Djambatan, 1987.

Kennedy, Alan. *Japanese Costume: History and Tradition.* New York, 1990.

Kesuma Dance Troupe. "Malaysia: Dance Drama of the People." In *The Seventh Annual Festival of Asian Arts.* Hong Kong, 1982.

Kim Jin-goo. *Korean Costume: An Historical Analysis.* Madison, Wis., 1978.

Kincaid, Zoë. *Kabuki: The Popular Stage in Japan.* New York, 1925.

Kirihata, Ken. *Kabuki Costumes.* Kyoto, 1994.

Komparu Kunio. *The Noh Theater: Principles and Perspectives.* Translated by Jane Corddry and Stephen Comee. New York, 1983.

Korean Folk Costume. Pyongyank, 1985.

Korean Overseas Information Service, Ministry of Culture and Information. *Korea: Contrast and Harmony.* Seoul, 1980.

Liddele, Jill. *The Story of the Kimono.* New York, 1989.

MacIntyre, Michael. *Spirit of Asia.* London, 1980.

Marshall, Mary. "The Vanishing Plummage: The Tribal Dress of the Northern Philippines: An Appreciation." *Archipelago* (May 1975).

Masakatsu Gunji. *Buyo: The Classical Dance.* Translated by Don Kenny. New York, 1970.

McKie, Ronald. *Bali.* Sydney, 1969.

Mele, Pietro F. *Ceylon.* Rome, 1958.

Myers, Diana K., and Susan S. Bean, eds. *From the Land of the Thunder Dragon: Textile Arts of Bhutan.* London, 1994.

Niessen, S. A. *Batak Cloth and Clothing.* Oxford, 1993.

Nishikawa Kyōtarō. *Bugaku Masks.* Tokyo, 1978.

Noma Seiroku. *Japanese Costume and Textile Arts.* New York and Tokyo, 1974.

The Oriental Song and Dance Company. Beijing, 1982.

Pakistan Cultural Troupe. "Pakistan: The Place of Folk Music." In *The Seventh Annual Festival of Asian Arts.* Hong Kong, 1982.

Pang, Mae Anna. *Dragon Emperor: Treasures from the Forbidden City.* Melbourne, 1989.

Precious Place: Costumes and Textiles of Guizhou China. San Francisco, n.d. Exhibition catalog, San Francisco Craft and Folk Museum.

Quraeshi, Samina. *The Legacy of the Indus.* New York and Tokyo, 1974.

Reilly, Theresa M. *Richly Woven Traditions: The Miao of Southwest China and Beyond.* New York, 1987.

Reyes Aquino, Francisca. *Philippine Folk Dances.* Vol. 2. Manila, 1976.

Reyes Urtula, Lucrecia. *The First Philippine Folk Festival: A Retrospective.* Manila, 1981.

Reynolds, Valrae. "From a Lost World: Tibetan Costumes and Textiles." *Orientations* 12 (March 1981).

Robes of Elegance: Japanese Kimonos of the Sixteenth–Twentieth Centuries. 1988.

Sahay, S. *Indian Costume, Coiffure, and Ornament.* New Delhi, 1973.

Salisbury, Charlotte. *Mountaintop Kingdom: Sikkim.* N.p., c.1975.

Seneviratne, Maureen. "The Music and Dance of Sri Lanka." In *The Seventh Annual Festival of Asian Arts.* Hong Kong, 1982.

Shaver, Ruth M. *Kabuki Costume.* Rutland, Vt., 1966.

Shaw, Brian. "Bhutan: Land of the Dragon People." In *The Seventh Annual Festival of Asian Arts.* Hong Kong, 1982.

Sichel, Marion. *Japan/Marion Sichel.* New York, 1987.

Smith, Captain. *Asiatic Costumes: A Series of Designs from Life.* London, 1828.

Thailande: Tissus royaux, tissus villageois. Honolulu, 1989. Exhibition catalog, University of Hawaii Art Gallery.

Tilke, Max. *Orientalische Kostume in Schnitt und Farbe.* Berlin, 1923.

Tokogawa Yoshinobu. *The Tokugawa Collection: Nō Robes and Masks.* New York, 1977.

Wells, Pru. *Costumes and Embroideries of the Ethnic Minorities of Southwest China.* 1991.

Wolz, Carl. *Bugaku: Japanese Court Dance.* Providence, R.I., 1971.

THERESA M. REILLY

COSTUME IN WESTERN TRADITIONS.

[*To describe the relationship between movement and clothing in Western theatrical and social dance, this entry comprises three articles:*

An Overview

Modern Dance

Film and Popular Dance

The overview provides a survey from the ancient Greek theater through the development of Western ballet and modern dance. This is followed by a discussion of costumes from the Greek-inspired tunics and draperies of the early dancers to the popularity of sneakers and sweatsuits as accepted modern dance attire. The third article considers costume styles that focus audience attention on the performer in film and popular entertainments. See also Footwear; Film Musicals, *article on* Hollywood Film Musicals; Practice Clothes; *and* Tutu.]

An Overview

In warmer regions of the world, where humanity had its beginnings, protection from the elements was not a primary motive for clothing. More likely, an increased sense of power was gained from decorating the body. When prehistoric peoples draped themselves in skins and amulets while imitating the movements of animals and birds or the forces of nature, they were trying to enter into ceremonial rapport with them, to control them through sympathetic magic. Some of the first clothing then, for this kind of activity, would come to be the category called dance costume.

Ancient Mediterranean Civilizations. The inhabitants of the ancient Near East and Egypt, where the recorded history of Western costume begins, believed in a more significant world beyond the immediate reality—a realm of part-human, part-animal gods. They dressed themselves to resemble their deities in religious rituals. Assuming the characters of other people was the next step in the evolution of theater. By the seventh century BCE, practices emerged in ancient Greece that shaped the theater of today. In religious festivals, actors and choruses gesticulated and executed series of expressive gestures and descriptive poses that were choreographed. In tragedies, the chorus (always male) moved in unison, within broad limits, wearing masks like the actors but not the *cothurni* (shoes with raised soles) and long gowns. To move more freely, they were costumed in short garments resembling the chiton or himation commonly worn daily by both sexes. They also wore less padding than the actors, in keeping with their normal height and mobility. When the chorus had a fantastic character or was meant to suggest a supernatural atmosphere, the costumes were appropriately expressive—the vengeful Furies appeared in black, with disheveled hair simulating snakes.

In satyr plays—rough sensual comedies that eventually superseded tragedy—the chorus wore long bandages made of animal skin to which were attached phalli of red leather and tails, reminiscent of the cult of Dionysus. When representing allegorical figures and animals, their costumes were vividly expressive: clouds appeared in loose robes and long noses; birds in Aristophanes' comedy wore tight body stockings decorated with feathers, with wings fixed to their arms; wasps were symbolized by narrow waists and a stinger. Horsemen in one comedy sat on the shoulders of other men who wore horse's heads, and thick tails were attached to padded posteriors.

In addition to mimetic dance used in the theater, dances in ancient Greece related to athletics, military training, celebration, devotion, mourning, courting, and recreation. Dancing became the idiom of Western symbolic expression to a degree that has not been approached before or since. From ancient Greek art we derive a concept of the body as an instrument capable of expressing all sentiments and passions; sculptors created a standard of perfection for the nude human form in representations of the gods. Thus nudity was associated with their divine *ethos*—balance, harmonious proportion, reason. It was believed that men and boys should know how to wear their nakedness in athletics and military training with its pyrrhic dances. If the image of the nude dominates ancient Greek art, almost equally important is that of the dancer, whose movements are articulated by garments or some accessory of dress. In art as in dance, fabric extended the motion of the body—intensifying its lyricism and emotionalism—or it hung in vertical folds, indicating repose.

Greek dancers had experimented with the possibilities of changing character by rearranging their draperies, but it remained for the Romans with their preference for mime to develop and refine this concept. Roman mimes were skilled impersonators who could play all rolls in an entertainment by manipulating the outlines of their costumes. Their techniques involved dance in the sense that their movements were rhythmic and expressive. Masks were used, and since some performances were of an extremely sensual nature, much attention was given to costumes that increased the performer's sexual allure. Costly sheer to transparent fabrics from the East were used to cover the body but conceal nothing—an effect considered more seductive than nudity. The Romans, who had little use for dance as the Greeks understood it—as personal expression—were more apt to hire professional entertainers to perform in their homes. Male and female dancers, jugglers, and acrobats usually appeared naked or in briefs.

Middle Ages. After the fall of the Roman Empire, the essence of theater survived in the medieval ceremonies and pageantry of Western Christianity. Although the church condemned dancing, except within its precincts, celebrations of good events by singing and dancing could never be eradicated. As the clothes of courtiers ceased to be like those of peasants, cloth was used lavishly as a means of displaying wealth. The inconvenience of lengthy trains, sleeves, and capes prevented a lady from doing anything useful or workaday, and therefore was symbolic of status. The hennin, a towering conical headdress inspired by a Near Eastern fashion, was introduced to Europe by returning Crusaders; it further hindered movement. Since women were the focus of courtly dancing, to be partnered or gallantly assisted by men (or sometimes dancing in all-female groups), the dances that evolved were stately and processional, always moving forward or in a circular pattern, which avoided reversals of direction entailing awkward adjustments of clothing. Although it might seem that the long hose worn by men allowed considerable freedom of movement, they were fashioned of woven fabric or of leather; both had little give. They were released from fastenings at the waist for any strenuous action. The formal atmosphere of the ballroom precluded this, and hose remained an inhibiting factor in dancing until the end of the sixteenth century, when knitted versions became available.

Dances of courtship provided opportunities for fanciful experimentation with costuming. They often took the form of simple dance-pantomimes with themes suggesting the use of props such as flowers, scarves, or pillows to make the action more interesting. Young lovers might be dressed as glamorous rustics or in some exotic or foreign style. Even more fanciful costume elements could be used by the addition of mythological figures—Venus, Cupid, Muses, Nymphs, Nereids, or Wildmen.

Of all the popular dances, the moresca offered the greatest opportunity for bizarre costuming. It was a dueling dance between the Christians and the Moors (North African Muslims who tried to conquer Europe in the seventh to fifteenth centuries); it sometimes included fencing and pantomime with those taking part masked or with faces blackened. In Germany, the moresca costume was of white fabric with painted flowers, leaves, stars, and various bright patterns, or it was striped. Sometimes half the costume was one color and the other half another, horizontally or vertically divided; sometimes bells were added to hemlines, presaging the later jester or fool's costume.

By the end of the fourteenth century, dances with well-defined dramatic action were organized by troubadours for the entertainment of princes and their courts. These aristocratic arbiters of style and taste traveled from castle to castle with retinues of entertainers and serving men, devising themes and programs and arranging every aspect of them, including the giving of instructions to tailors and seamstresses for costuming.

Renaissance through Eighteenth Century. The Renaissance in Italy introduced the idea of humans as independent agents free of mysterious forces, with their own intelligence being their greatest asset in a life organized around the pursuit of pleasure. People not only rejoiced inwardly in a new-found dignity and free will but also celebrated a resurgence of the spirit in expressions of beauty. To perceive oneself as beautiful and original was reason enough to dress beautifully and with originality. Both men and women took renewed interest in their outward appearance with a new passion for color, elegance, and personal distinction. By the beginning of the fifteenth century, all those who could afford it knew what fashion was and followed it as best they could. To be stylishly dressed

was reason enough to display oneself, and dancing was one of the best ways of doing so. Dancing masters flourished in Italy's courts, and such artists as Pisanello (Antonio Pisano), Leonardo da Vinci, and later Jacapo da Pontormo delighted in devising fashions. They applied their genius freely in creating costume designs for maskings and lavish celebrations in the palaces of their benefactors.

At first, the costumes were elaborate adaptations of current styles (so-called disguise gowns), with little attempt at characterization. Gradually, however, with the renewed interest in themes from Greek and Roman mythology, allusions were made to classical styles of dress. This neoclassical influence first appeared as a kind of romantic asymmetry that was associated with antiquity when applied to current fashions. Eventually, dancers impersonating gods and heroes wore costumes designed to suggest, but not reproduce, those of antiquity. In a time when clothing usually kept the female figure well hidden, light draperies and delicate sandals created heightened sexual allure. Over time, the standard dance costume for women or young men performing *en travesti* became a somewhat shortened skirt of gauzy fabric falling from a high-waisted girdle that, combined with the bodice, outlined the breasts. Male costume began to simulate the military musculated cuirass of classical armor, with knee-length skirt below. The nakedness of the ancient world could only be simulated. Arms and legs had to be covered with flesh-colored materials unless the performers were very young, in which case arms and legs (but not feet) could be left bare.

Toward the end of the fifteenth century, changes in fashion, emanating from Spain, profoundly altered the history of dress for the next four hundred years. In broad terms, the transfiguration that occurred was a disregard for softness in favor of straight, stiff forms—rigidly structured garments that altered the wearer's natural silhouette and manner of moving. Dancing—as it developed in courtly ballrooms and was transferred to stages—was subjected to the limitations these new styles imposed.

Women, preoccupied with shrinking the measurement of their waistlines, wore rigid corsets (hinged iron cages, eventually replaced by steel or whalebone stays), reshaping the torso from abdomen to neckline and virtually eliminating the natural contour of the bust. Their construction held shoulders down, preventing the upper arms from rising much above shoulder level. Forward flexion at the waist was made impossible by a busk (a strip of metal, whalebone, or wood inserted in the front of the corset), but waistlines cut slightly higher at the sides and back to prevent the overall weight of garments and stays from pressing onto hip bones and the lower back permitted some torsion and sideways flexion. Layered skirts were supported by the farthingale, a stiff bell-shaped underskirt encasing hoops.

If somewhat less burdensome in terms of poundage than women's, men's clothing was nearly as restrictive. Doublets were heavily padded, stiffened with stays, and very snugly fitted. Ruffs of stiffened and wired laces worn by both men and women at the neckline restricted movement of the neck and kept heads held high. The padded bulk of sleeves for both sexes, the breadth of men's upper hose (trunks), and women's farthingales, kept arms well away from the body and limited their action for the most part to prescribed arcs in front of the torso. Compelled by court protocol to stand for long hours in these uncomfortable fashions, aristocrats learned to distribute their weight as evenly as possible around the central axis of their spine in a carefully balanced stance that, transmitted by dancing masters, became the basis for the *danse d'ecole* and ballet.

In the increasing luxury with which spectacles were conceived for the courts, costumes left no possibility untried. All classes were represented wearing rich costumes; as long as the correct social relationship was indicated in the action, it was felt that sumptuousness enhanced all situations. Even rustics wore rich fabrics with encrustations of embroidery and stones. Performances were often in daylight, so costumers could not rely on the illusion of richness produced by stage lighting. Consequently, gemstones, cloths of gold and silver, and embroideries were used in abundance. Courtiers bore the expense involved in return for the privilege of attendance at court; many fortunes were dissipated in producing the constant festivities.

By the end of the sixteenth century, dancers' costumes offered an unprecedented freedom of movement. Designs of this period, which include those of Inigo Jones, show soft skirts cut well above the ankles or even abbreviated to the knees (resembling the ballet skirt to come of the Romantic-era ballet). Contemporary accounts make clear that one of the main delights of court spectacles was the unfamiliar glimpse of female calves and knees; however, female roles were often played by boys or young men, masked and padded to appear more feminine (in which case female modesty was only indirectly abused by scanty costumes). [*See the entry on Inigo Jones.*]

Some of the most ingenious designs ever created for dancing were for the comic antimasques popular at the court of James I of England (ruled 1603–1625). The masque proper followed the pattern of elaborate *entrées*, featuring courtiers performing dances in dignified courtly style. Antimasque interludes featured the faster tempi, buffoonery, and acrobatics performed by professionals. Fools, Satyrs, Baboons, Wildmen, Beasts, and other characters offered a wide range of possibilities for the choreographer, who created an atmosphere in which the more expressive and fantastic aspects of costume could develop.

Throughout most of Europe, wherever there was courtly dancing, the neoclassical convention prevailed, making use of symbols that were easily recognizable to an audience. Neptune always had his trident, Diana her crescent moon and hunting bow, Juno her peacocks, and so forth. Allegorical figures were depicted with wit and originality: Water was festooned with bulrushes; Fire was enveloped by tongues of flame; Air was given a plumed hat and wings; and Music's breeches and doublet was constructed from all manner of musical instruments.

Fashions of the first third of the seventeenth century became lighter and less deforming than those of the previous period, but silhouettes remained exaggeratedly full. The introduction of heeled footwear for both men and women presented new problems for the dancing master. The principal designer for the ballets at the court of Louis XIII of France (ruled 1610–1643) was Daniel Rabel, one of the first specialists—a designer by profession rather than a painter moonlighting in the theater. Rabel had a rare gift for grotesque invention. His sketches show women (probably young men *en travesti*) with two faces, one young and one old; men walking on all fours with heads between their legs; doublets reaching to the ankles with the dancer's head at the height of his stomach; breeches reaching all the way to the neck; characters armed with swords, clubs, and axes, whose false arms and hands were struck off during a dance. Deformity, misfortune, crime—nothing escaped burlesque. Even fantastic representations existed for various professions, for example, an innkeeper's costume composed of a barrel, a funnel, and a pair of pots.

Court entertainments reached their apex in France under Louis XIV (ruled 1643–1715), who inherited his fa-

COSTUME IN WESTERN TRADITIONS: An Overview. *(top left)* A ▶ sculpture of a maenad in classical-style drapery. This is a Roman copy of a Greek original from the last quarter of the fifth century BCE, perhaps by Kallimachos. *(top center)* A drawing by Inigo Jones of Basilino's costume for *The Shepherd's Paradise* (1633). Jones was a designer of the English court masques. *(top right)* A print of Marie Taglioni in a gauzy dress with wings, a popular costume for the nineteenth-century *ballet blanc. (bottom right)* An actor wearing a skirt known as a *tonnelet* in this print entitled *Beaupré, Danseur à l'Opéra*, after Antoine Watteau. *(bottom left)* An engraving by Jean-Baptiste Martin of an eighteenth-century woman's opera costume, an ornamented version of a court dress that included sturdy corsets coming to a point and panniers (hoops) at the hips. (*Top left*: Metropolitan Museum of Art, New York; Fletcher Fund, 1935 [no.35.11.3]; photograph used by permission. *Top center*: Courtauld Institute of Art, London; photograph used by permission. *Top right*: photograph from the Dance Collection, New York Public Library for the Performing Arts. *Bottom right*: Metropolitan Museum of Art, New York; The Elisha Whittelsey Fund, 1957 [no. 57.559.48]; photograph used by permission. *Bottom left*: photograph from the Dance Collection, New York Public Library for the Performing Arts.)

ther's passion for the ballet and was himself an excellent dancer and noble figure on the stage. The fashions he inaugurated—preposterous breeches, coats, and capes, all decked with masses of lace and ribbons (the women not half so elaborate as the men) reflected the extremely formal manners required of all who were privileged to participate in the panorama of life at Versailles. Etiquette required performing ladies to appear in court dress, which became the traditional costume of tragedy and the ballet. Local color, character, and allegorical significance were suggested by adding ornaments. Both outer and inner skirts had trains, and the caught-up overdress, heavier and more upholstered, required the support of whalebone, metal, or basketwork panniers (hoops) at the hips. The corset was low waisted, coming to a point in the front as in the preceding century, but the breasts were now forced upward and displayed prominently. It was a physical ordeal to carry the weight of a dress suitable for an appearance at court, and ladies lay about in their private chambers in comfortable robes *(dishabille)* except for the few hours or even minutes of formal attendance.

Male dancers wore costumes following the lines of civil dress less closely, offering more opportunity for invention. An adaptation of the Roman warrior's uniform, the *habit francais à la romaine,* became the accepted costume for the male dancer in the noble style. The cuirass, borrowed from Roman military dress, reproduced the torso in metallic fabric or gilded leather embossed with allegorical motifs. Beneath it was a knee-length kilt, sometimes divided into panels (lappets). This costume was completed by a plumed helmet and laced leather boots or halfboots (buskins). Costume for male demi-caractère roles was often a body stocking of knitted fabric or soft leather decorated with symbolic ornaments.

The most important designers of Louis XIV's early reign were Stefano della Bella (who had gone to France from Italy about 1640) and Henry Gissey, who presented the splendid horse ballet *Carousel de Louis XIV* before the Louvre in 1662. In 1671, Jean Berain undertook the design of French court presentations. Under the influence of the bigoted Madame de Maintenon, court fashions became severe. As many engravings from the studio of Berain illustrate, his costumes were often closer to contemporary fashions than they were previously. Those for women may be distinguished as costume only by their added richness and symbolic trimmings. [*See the entry on Berain.*] About 1685, the silhouette of the male dancer expanded to a fuller style, to balance the enormous wigs that Louis XIV's baldness brought into vogue. By 1718, panniers had been introduced in both male and female costumes; the kilt of the male gradually became a short hooped skirt (called *tonnelet,* "little cask"), and it remained in use until the French Revolution (1789).

In 1661 Louis XIV created the Académie Royal de Danse in Paris. Soon afterward professionally trained dancers began to replace courtiers in ballet performances. They eventually succeeded in lightening the female costumes, most notably about 1726 when Marie Carmago shortened her skirts (to just above the ankles) to reveal her brilliant footwork. In 1734 Marie Sallé discarded panniers and wig and appeared in a revealing neoclassical gown of soft muslin. After a brief scandal, the logic of Sallé's innovation was accepted as precedent for the neoclassical style, but Jean-Georges Noverre's *Lettres sur la danse et les ballets,* published in 1760, makes it clear that designers continued to prefer hampering artifices. Since drawers were not then a standard part of women's underclothing, dancers executing the more vigorous steps of the *danse haute* of the first quarter of the eighteenth century in shortened skirts were in danger of embarrassment if they fell or happened to catch their dresses on a piece of scenery. In 1720 the first of several edicts was issued requiring all actresses and dancers to wear *caleçon de précaution* ("precautionary drawers").

Design for the theater under Louis XV (ruled 1715–1774) was distinguished by the elegance, playfulness, and refinement of form that characterized the age of rococo. Jean-Baptiste Martin's sketches for *Les Indes Galantes* (1735) were masterpieces of exotic invention: delightful rococo fantasy mingling Turks, Persians, Incas, and American "savages" with Olympian deities and a current vogue for chinoiserie. Martin published a well-known series of engravings after his designs. His use of gentle colors (water green, pale blue, ivory, pink) touched with gold and silver was based on prevailing taste for delicate, airy effects. Instead of heavy embroideries, trailing brocade, and Baroque formality, the gay ribbons, billowing tissue, and garlands of fragile silk flowers created the effect of a graceful hedonism.

Louis-René Boquet replaced Martin as designer to the French court in 1760. His designs, some of the most charming ever devised for dancing, provide a record of an almost absurdly frivolous court; there, modes changed from day to day and a courtier might find it necessary to change clothes several times a day to be suitably dressed. The panniers of these years extended to the sides, producing an elliptical shape echoed in the men's tonnelets. Towering hair styles, popularized by Louis XVI's queen Marie Antoinette (ruled 1774–1792), were modified for the stage, but heels became so high that walking was precarious, and women carried staffs for security. Consequently, the minuet and other popular court dances lost any remnants of their origins in light carefree folk dance and became stately exercises in stylistic precision. [*See the entry on Boquet.*]

Jean-Georges Noverre, ballet master of the Paris Opera from 1776 to 1780, wrote derisively of the ostentation and inappropriateness of stage costuming; of the tinsel that glittered everywhere on Peasants, Warriors, Fauns, Tritons, and Priests, all cut from the same pattern and all loaded with gewgaws, spangles, gauze, and net. He asked for light simple draperies to reveal the dancers' figures and for the elimination of tonnelets, which he said transported the male dancer's hips to his shoulders. Noverre suggested that three-fourth's the width of the panniers be eliminated to restore elegance and proportion to a dancer's lines. His strongest diatribe was against masks, which he said deprived dancers of their most important means of expression. Noverre's demands for costuming reform were in keeping with his hatred of all the artificial conventions of the *ballet d'action*. He would have preferred more unity, relevance to real life, and greater lyric expressiveness in dancing. Reactionary influences prevented him from achieving all his ideals, but masks did become obsolete in the early 1770s, and dress reforms that occurred at the time of the French Revolution freed dance of all the encumbrances he detested. [*See the entry on Noverre.*]

The elaborate court costume of Louis XVI's time became prohibited, as part of Revolutionary policy. In its stead, the women of Napoleon's family and the painters of his official program of art promoted neoclassical modes. These dresses were formed in the simplest possible manner, of muslin tubes gathered at the neckline and again with ribbon or cord just below the breasts—the high Empire waistline. Corsets were abandoned, and fashionable women even appeared barefoot with rings on their toes. Men's clothing expressed the prevailing ideology—Liberty, Equality, Fraternity—by becoming uniform and practical in what has been called the "great male renunciation" of color, decoration, and beauty.

Nineteenth Century. As a result of liberating ideas and modes, ballroom forms expanded rapidly, and society amused itself with an amazing variety of stylistic mutations. Professional dancers found themselves freed of everything but the filmiest of muslin gowns for women and equally comfortable styles for men. Stage dancing was altered to the point of being almost unrelated to what had been seen before the Revolution. Prints of the period depict startling acrobatic postures; seemingly impossible distortions of the human anatomy attest to the effects of the new freedom.

As styles in costume, like dance technique, became more international, distinctive designs identified the three main types of professional dancer. *Danseur sérieux* (a male dancer in the noble style) wore a theatrical version of the ancient Greek chiton, a belted, one-piece tunic ending in a narrow skirt effect just below the knees. It often left one shoulder bare. He wore sandals, a plumed hat or Roman helmet, or dressed his hair forward and held it in place with a fillet. The costume of the *danseuse* in the noble style was a filmy neoclassical gown, always high-

waisted, and ending between calf and ankle. Like the man's tunic, it could be decorated with characteristic motifs to lend interest and local color. Both wore silk *maillot* (knit tights) named for the costumer who manufactured hosiery for the Paris Opera. These were usually pink to simulate flesh tones in the yellow light of candles or oil-burning lamps, except in the Papal States and Spain, where pontifical decree required that they be blue, to avoid even the suggestion of nudity.

In *demi-caractère* roles, male dancers wore a long-sleeved doublet, trunks, long hose, and a beplumed hat—a forerunner of *le style troubadour*, an anachronistic mélange of historical dress used by actors and singers as well as dancers throughout the remainder of the eighteenth century (and not altogether extinct in provincial theaters even today). The female partner's costume resembled a contemporary ball gown—a high-waisted sheath—decorated with ribbons, ruffles, insets, or jeweled embroideries affecting some historic or ethnic provenance.

Costumes for character roles—usually comic dances based on rural themes—resembled peasant dress: for the male, an open-necked shirt, short coat or vest, and breeches held up by suspenders; for the female, a high-waisted version of a country girl's dress. Though the techniques that once defined these distinct types of dancers have become blurred, echoes of the costumes that identified them are still apparent in today's ballet.

The most popular ballets of the period between 1830 and 1860 were peopled with specters, sprites, enchanted nymphs, incarnations of butterflies, and other transmutations whose special appeal to the imagination was that they could levitate, ascend, float, or fly, and make themselves invisible. The prototype of this enchanted aerial creature was the ballerina Marie Taglioni in the title role of *La Sylphide*, which premiered in Paris in 1832. In this milestone ballet, the art of dancing *sur les pointes* and the Sylphide's filmy white dress emerged as two of the most salient characteristics of the Romantic ballet. The origin of the costume is somewhat mysterious because, although there are sketches for other characters by the ballet's designer Eugène Lami in the Paris Opera's archives, no sketch exists for the Sylphide. None may have been necessary, since Taglioni had worn a very similar gown in *Flore et Zéphire* two years before. Basically the gown was in keeping with the mode of the day, but this earliest prototype of the tutu (a word not invented until much later) was also subtly neo-Grecian. Two or three soft white (some say pink) muslin skirts were caught at the waist by a slender blue ribbon; the front of the bodice was gathered in vertical folds, similar to the look of the chiton; bell-shaped sleeves fell from the points of the shoulders. By 1845, when Alfred Chalon published his famous series of lithographs of Taglioni as the Sylphide, the skirt had become considerably longer, a billowing froth of layer upon layer of tulle or tarlatan. The sleeves were fitted, the bodice no longer neo-Grecian, and the original simple wings of gauze stretched on wire had become those of the earthbound peacock.

Soon after the resounding success of *La Sylphide,* clouds of white dancers—principals and corps de ballet alike—invaded opera houses. These regiments of spirit-beings in whitest white constituted *le ballet blanc,* a late but one of the most vivid expressions of that fanciful state of mind that gave the Romantic-era ballet its name.

The frothy skirt was the secret of the costume's success and its persistence as a tradition. It was not just a beautiful embellishment for its wearer—it actively assisted in the interpretation of an idea. The buoyancy of skirts

caused them to billow around and around the body, suspended at the apex of a leap for a fraction longer than the body itself, coming to rest at a decreasing rate after the foot touched the floor. The momentary impression was of suspension—an illusion that the dancer had come to rest with diminishing speed. The white gown fused with the whiteness of her makeup to create a shimmering, unearthly presence. It took on the coloration of any light happening to fall on it, and thus was an ideal foil for experimentation with the new limelight and gas fixtures. Pale figures enveloped in a floating mist of white gauze were made to merge and emerge from the distance, to float in a flat hazy middle distance, or to seem to materialize out of the ether in a doorway or window. White was not only the most effective choice for this costume from the point of view of illusion, it was the inevitable choice from the point of view of symbolism—the perfect metaphor for virginity and all its poetic associations.

With the addition of decorative touches to delineate local color, character, or ethnicity, the Sylphide's dress became the uniform of the ballerina. To suggest a Spanish

COSTUME IN WESTERN TRADITIONS. Royal Danish Ballet dancers in a group pose from August Bournonville's *Napoli* (1842). For historical works in the repertory, the costumers of the Royal Danish Ballet reproduce both the materials and the construction of original costumes. The company also pays strict attention to the historical accuracy of footwear and hairstyles. (Photograph from the Dance Collection, New York Public Library for the Performing Arts.)

girl, it might be trimmed with black lace over red; an Italian background could be indicated by incorporating familiar details from Roman or Neapolitan peasant costume (an apron, a ribboned headdress); fur would be enough to indicate Poland, or plaid, Scotland. Once the convention was established, it was not difficult for audiences to recognize clues.

The ballet skirt, which was worn in the classroom as well as onstage, had a significant effect on the evolution of the ballet's vocabulary as it expanded to include sustained pointe work. Steps and positions that were most effective in the prevailing costume were consequently most likely to be popularized, codified, and handed down.

During the era of the Romantic ballet, male dancers were relegated to the role of *porteur*, existing for the glorification of wraithlike ballerinas. After 1830 the neoclassical tunic of the *danseur noble* lost its authenticity in being made of velvets and satin and decorated with anachronistic devices. It was gradually replaced by *le style troubadour* or combined with other influences, notably the fanciful reform styles of the Empire period, to produce a hybrid one-piece coat, somewhat full skirted and falling to midcalf. As worn by the *danseur noble*, it implied that he was a hero figure of refined sentiments.

A variety of styles proliferated in costuming male dancers in character and *demi-caractère* roles. Among the most popular were those depicting officers in ornately braided tunics with boots and trousers molded to their legs; bandits in short breeches with colorful sashes; peasants in the rustic tunics and tights of the Middle Ages; nobility of the same period in richer tunics and plumed hats; and other characters wearing hats, vests, jackets, and capes of vague historical origin. There was the curious convention of dressing the corps de ballet and soloists in traditional ballet costumes while presenting supernumeraries in more or less accurate period styles.

By far the most eccentric development was the popularity of women dancing male roles. In keeping with the biblical taboo against cross-dressing, moralists until this time had perceived as indecent the separation of a woman's legs by any garment resembling male trousers. This prejudice gave a distinctly prurient connotation to adaptations of male costume for the *danseuse en travesti*. Such portrayals had tongue-in-cheek simulations of masculine mannerisms and manners, and the costumes were fitted to achieve the most voluptuous effect, with no attempt to disguise the robust curves of female anatomy. Travesty contributed to the decadence of the ballet of the last part of the nineteenth century, except in Russia, where the tradition of virile male dancing was maintained. [*See* Travesty.]

The metamorphosis of the Sylphide's dress into a tutu

was a gradual one, commencing in the late 1860s as Italian ballerinas trained in acrobatic techniques of pointe work and high leg extensions shortened their skirts to reveal the full effect of their virtuosity. By the 1890s, the skirt had become an arrangement of graduated ruffles, resembling the shape of a mushroom or powder puff, covering the hips and upper thighs. Ballet masters concentrated on geometric perfection away from the lyricism of the Romantic ballet, and the abbreviated skirt reflected this trend by becoming a rigid affair, carefully constructed to maintain its own shape and to alter that of the dancer. The bodice was heavily boned and sometimes worn over a corset. To keep the starched ruffles of the skirt neat, and to counteract any sagging caused by atmospheric moisture, a clock spring was stretched out and sewn into a channel in one of the skirt's top layers; those underneath were loosely tacked in place. [*See* Tutu.] Coiffures for the stage were ponderously *à la mode*, and soloists were permitted to vulgarize their already resplendent costumes by wearing personal jewelry.

Twentieth Century. The first to confront standardized costumes was the young Russian choreographer Michel Fokine. One of his major concerns was authenticity for costume in works set in the past. Under impresario Serge Diaghilev's direction, Fokine collaborated in Paris with painter-designers Léon Bakst and Alexandre Benois in dance spectacles that established the Ballets Russes in Paris and later worldwide as a major influence in the art of the twentieth century. Bakst's decor and costumes for *Cléopâtre* (1909), *Schéhérazade* (1910), and *Thamar* (1912) seethed with barbaric color and bold design that had been influenced by Art Nouveau and his Russian-Jewish background. He abandoned the traditional tutu and devised costumes that were total transformations—bizarre shapes executed in lustrous textures, displaying astonishing craftsmanship and invention in embroidery, painting, appliqué, and the use of feathers and stones. Their exaggerated forms were extensions of the exotic qualities of scenic environments, fantastic mobile elements in shifting atmospheric canvases. Bakst's Orientalism featured a degree of nudity that, though only simulated with insets of flesh-colored material or brown fleshings, seemed deliciously risqué to the Edwardian *beau monde*, who were soon clamoring for real-life fashions and furnishings inspired by his designs. [*See the entries on Bakst and Benois.*]

Diaghilev's Ballets Russes basically dismissed costume conventions that had been one hundred years in the making. Diaghilev soon introduced other Russian designers: Mstislav Dobujinsky, Natalia Goncharova, Konstantin Korovin, Serge Soudeikine, Nikolai Roerich, and Aleksandr Golovin, all of whom fed the excitement with costumes and settings of unprecedented originality. The misunderstood choreographic genius of Vaslav Nijinsky soared, decades ahead of its time, introducing both modern sports clothing in the enigmatic *Jeux* and Roerich's startling abstractions of peasant costume in *Le Sacre du Printemps*. With the onset of World War I in 1914 and the Russian Revolution in 1917, access to Russian talent diminished. After 1917, the blazing Orientalism of Léon Bakst and the refined historical evocations of Alexandre Benois gave way to the influence of cubism, surrealism, and constructivism. Experimentation in design was continued by Marie Laurencin, André Derain, Henri Matisse, George Braque, Juan Gris, André Bauchant, and Georges Rouault, as well as from the more radial avant-gardists Pablo Picasso, Max Ernst, Joan Miró, Naum Gabo, Antoine Pevsner, Pavel Tchelitchev, and Giorgio de' Chirico. Until Diaghilev's time, designs for the ballet had been in the hands of specialists, often hacks. The opportunities offered painters by the Ballets Russes encouraged some who otherwise might never have thought of expressing themselves in terms of theater to consider it a legitimate avenue. By 1929, the year of Diaghilev's death and the dispersion of his company, his choreographers, composers, dancers, and designers had begun to explore most of the concepts associated with modernism in dance and design.

In the decades that followed, Ballets Suédois, founded in 1920, and the companies that formed from Diaghilev's Ballets Russes—Blum and de Basil's Ballets Russes de Monte Carlo, George Balanchine's short-lived Les Ballets 1933, Massine's Ballet Russe de Monte Carlo—all imitated his formula of evenings of short colorful ballets. They catered to the public's taste for glamorous personalities displayed in choreographic novelties, and there were few significant changes in the shapes or function of ballet costumes. When Ballet Theatre was launched in New York in 1939, one of the goals of its founders was to integrate the talents of designers and choreographers more fully than before. This was achieved in the first decade of the company's existence by a roster of designers that included Eugene Berman, Motley, Marcel Vertes, Raoul Pêne du Bois, Jo Mielziner, Marc Chagall, and Oliver Smith (who became co-director of the company in 1945). In mounting revivals, original design concepts were respected or sensitively updated; in contemporary works, designers were encouraged to explore new ways of dressing ballet. Under Smith's guidance, designers sought new contexts for choreographic exploration. Sensitive costuming defined character, period, social milieu, mood, and underscored movement.

The American Ballet, founded in 1935, and its successors, which culminated in New York City Ballet in 1948, gave Balanchine the opportunity to establish his own standards of production for nearly half a century. While under the influence of Diaghilev, from 1925 to 1929, Balanchine's ballets had been mounted very stylishly. He continued in this vein while choreographing for both of the

COSTUME IN WESTERN TRADITIONS. An unrealized costume design c.1909, by Léon Bakst, for one of Kastchei's retinue in Diaghilev's production of *The Firebird*. (Photograph from the Dance Collection, New York Public Library for the Performing Arts.)

Monte Carlo companies. The American Ballet's funds for production were very limited, however, so Balanchine was forced (or perhaps used the excuse) to present ballets in practice clothing—in tights, leotards, and simple tunics. With the formation of Balanchine and Lincoln Kirstein's Ballet Society in 1946, designers were again very much in evidence, as they were to be in many New York City Ballet programs. For those ballets in which Balanchine explored his increasingly idiosyncratic classicism, he seemed to need no visual exposition. These were presented in the simplest of settings—plain drops and wings—with dancers in black-and-white practice clothing. Without traditional decor and costumes, Balanchine made no attempt to tell stories, but his abstract works were not devoid of emotion, humanness, and ideas. The absence of costume (or the simplicity of practice clothing as costume) encouraged audiences to disregard the superficial conventions of ballet and respond to its intrinsic poetry.

A number of Balanchine's works originally presented in costume have been successfully remounted in simpler style. They seem to gain in significance what they loose in atmosphere. New York City Ballet has, for the most part, presented beautifully costumed works, constructed and in some cases designed by Karinska until her death in 1983. [*See the entry on Karinska.*]

In 1946, Sadler's Wells Ballet (now the Royal Ballet) re-opened London's Royal Opera House after World War II with *The Sleeping Beauty*, designed by Oliver Messel. After years of wartime austerity, the beauty and opulence of this production were received as a reaffirmation of British high culture. Messel's superbly crafted dresses, gossamer tutus, and resplendent cavaliers—in clear hues touched or overlaid with gold and silver to produce an iridescent effect against the more neutral tonalities of grandiose Baroque architecture—were a major factor in the ballet's great success. [*See the entry on Messel.*] In subsequent seasons the Royal Ballet mounted other full-evening ballets: *Cinderella* (1948) designed by Jean-Denis Malclès; *Sylvia* (1952) designed by Robin and Christopher Ironside; and *Swan Lake* (1952) designed by Leslie Hurry. Their frankly decorative treatments achieved a nice balance between the demands of spectacle and the English tendency to-

COSTUME IN WESTERN TRADITIONS. David Blair as the Prince in a costume reflecting his *danseur noble* role, and Margot Fonteyn as Cinderella in a bouffant classical tutu. (Photograph by Houston Rogers; from the Dance Collection, New York Public Library for the Performing Arts.)

COSTUME IN WESTERN TRADITIONS. A costume design by Pavel Tchelitchev for George Balanchine's *Balustrade* (1941). (Photograph from the Dance Collection, New York Public Library for the Performing Arts.)

ward understated choreographic effects and introverted performance techniques. British taste, which values refinement as much as invention, affords the designer opportunity to manipulate subtle stylistic elements with the assurance that aesthetic references and historicity will be appreciated. In costume construction and, in particular, in the reinterpretation of period clothing for the stage, the Royal Ballet has had the advantage of superb craftsmanship—expert tailors and seamstresses—since English schools offer the best training in this field.

In preserving its nineteenth-century Bournonville traditions, the Royal Danish Ballet has given as much attention to costumes as to choreography, carefully reproducing the materials and construction of original costumes. Footwear, coiffeurs, and other details are historically accurate, and great care is taken to avoid the almost inevitable influence that contemporary fashion tends to have on the authentic look of the past.

French ballet, in contrast, tends to disregard authenticity in revivals of nineteenth-century works, preferring stylish reinterpretations of history. In modern works, the

Parisian predilection for novelty and wit has been satisfied by painters and *couturiers* such as Carzou, Alexandre Cassandre, Jean Cocteau, Leonor Fini, Christian Bérard, and Dior, whose stylishness usually competed for attention with the choreography and the dancers themselves. In 1949, Antoni Clavé's designs (decor and costumes) for Roland Petit's version of *Carmen* crystalized this format in both sketches and actualizations that were the epitome of Gallic chic and sophisticated playfulness.

Soviet ballet rejected both historicity and experimentation in design, preferring a somewhat updated treatment of nineteenth-century costume and a very conservative approach to modernism in contemporary ballets. The huge size of the Russian theaters necessitated a sacrifice of subtle stylistic detail in favor of boldness in both design and the execution of costumes. The use of a large scale was very much in keeping with the flamboyant techniques of gesture and the vivid personalities that Soviet dancers characteristically portrayed.

Classification of Ballet Costumes. Throughout the history of dance and what is worn, a formalism has established broad metaphor for costume design—conventions instantly verifiable in the collective imagination of an audience. These conventions distinguish the dancer from other types of performers and clarify the substance of a dance or ballet. They are a matter of familiarity and recognition, rather than discovery, on the part of the audience. In contemporary ballet, durable stereotypes that provide frame of reference for both designers and audiences are as follows:

- *Romantic tutu.* The nineteenth-century calf-length Sylphide costume and its variants, reinterpreted by Benois for Michel Fokine's *Les Sylphides* (1909); used in reconstruction of ballets from the Romantic era and in modern works that by nature of their plot, music, choreographic style, or mood, relate to that time. Examples are the many revivals of *Giselle* and Balanchine's *La Valse* and *Serenade,* both designed by Karinska.
- *Classical tutu.* The shortened ballet costume of the late nineteenth century, associated with the ballets of Marius Petipa; sometimes diminished or distorted almost beyond recognition in contemporary ballets. Its basic form—a mass of light material surrounding the female dancer's hips—persists as the most universal symbol of the ballet. Examples are Balanchine's *Symphony in C* (Karinska) and Ashton's *Birthday Offering* (André Levasseur).
- *Style troubadour.* In both Romantic and classical ballets, males often wear this abbreviated form of the Renaissance doublet and tights, a convention descended from the nineteenth-century actor and *danseur noble.*
- *Neoclassicism.* The use of soft draperies to enhance movement, one of the most enduring of theatrical traditions, is inherited from ancient Greece. Chiffon tunics and bias-cut dresses of the ballet (as well as the capes, shawls, scarves, trains, and jersey gowns of the modern dancer) reflect the classical concept of the dancer's body as an instrument of lyrical expression and the use of fabric in relation to it as a dramatic foil. Examples are Frederick Ashton's *Symphonic Variations* (Sophie Fedorovitch) and *Ondine* (Lila de Nobili); Antony Tudor's *The Leaves Are Fading* (Patricia Zipprodt); and Balanchine's 1936 *Orpheus and Eurydice* (Pavel Tchelitchev).
- *Ethnic clothing.* Peasant modes and ethnic clothing may be used in near-authentic form but are usually reinterpreted. Examples are Fokine's *Petrouchka* (Alexandre Benois) and Jerome Robbins's *Les Noces* (Patricia Zipprodt).
- *Historical clothing.* Authentic reconstructions of historical styles are rarely used, because of their weight and tendency to interfere with dance movement. Period styles are usually adapted to suggest, rather than replicate, history. Examples are Ashton's *A Month in the Country* (Julia Trevelyan Oman); Tudor's *Pillar of Fire* (Jo Mielziner) and *Romeo and Juliet* (Eugene Berman);

COSTUME IN WESTERN TRADITIONS. In many of George Balanchine's neoclassical works, the dancers wear plain leotard-and-tights costumes. Women sometimes wear short, softly draped skirts, as seen here on Maria Tallchief, Diana Adams, and Tanaquil Le Clercq, dressed as the Muses in *Apollo* in 1951. In the title role, André Eglevsky is seen in a pseudo-Greek tunic that was soon abandoned in favor of black tights and a simple white drapery across the chest. (Photograph © 1951 by George Platt Lynes; used by permission. Choreography by George Balanchine © The George Balanchine Trust.)

Agnes de Mille's *Rodeo* (Kermit Love); Balanchine's *The Seven Deadly Sins* (Rouben Ter-Arutunian); and Todd Bolender's *Souvenirs* (Rouben Ter-Arutunian).

- *Painterly designs.* The images, textures, colors, and other aspects of painting on canvas are often interpreted in costume design, either first hand by the artist as designer or by other designers. Examples are Balanchine's *The Prodigal Son* (Georges Rouault), *Orpheus* (Isamu Noguchi), and *Firebird* (Marc Chagall); Massine's *Aleko* (Marc Chagall); and Merce Cunningham's *Summerspace* (Robert Rauschenberg).

- *Contemporary clothing.* The schism between the metaphors of dance and the reality that familiar clothing brings to mind may be used intentionally for dramatic effect. When this is not the intention, designers tend to schematize contemporary clothing. Examples are Robbins's *Fancy Free* (Irene Sharaff); Twyla Tharp's *Sue's Leg* (Santo Loquasto); and Roland Petit's *Le Jeune Homme et la Mort* (Christian Bérard).

- *Practice clothing.* The dancer's work clothing used as costume tends to neutralize aesthetic distance, focusing attention on the dancer as an instrument of the choreography. Thus the intrinsic drama of choreographic patterns—linear relationships, musicality, and energy expended in movement—are revealed in full force. Examples are Robbins's *Interplay* and *Afternoon of a Faun* (Irene Sharaff); Michael Kidd's *On Stage!* (Alvin Colt); and Balanchine's *Concerto Barocco*, *Episodes*, and *Agon*.

- *Nudity.* Flesh-colored leotards and tights give the illusion of nudity; G-strings, briefs, and minimal bras imply it. The spectator is encouraged to imagine the dancer "as if" nude. Since the liberal 1960s, actual nudity has been within the range of possibility for designers working in dance, but for audiences accustomed to seeing bodies clothed, the effect is apt to be too distracting. Examples are Robbins's *Watermill* (Patricia Zipprodt) and *The Cage* (Ruth Sabotka); Alvin Ailey's *The River* (Frank Thompson); Glen Tetley's *Le Sacre du Printemps* (Nadine Baylis) and *Mutations* (Emy van Leersun and Gijs Bakker); and Flemming Flindt's *Triumph of Death* (Paul Arnt Thomsen).

- *Adaptations from popular theater and modern dance.* Dance costumes for Broadway musicals, films, television, and nightclubs—where theatricality is more important than stylistic unity, authenticity, and expressiveness—are designed to enhance the individuality and sexual allure of the performer, a decorative approach catering to current attitudes on personal attractiveness. When borrowed for the concert stage, the conventions of popular theater are usually stereotyped and broadened.

Modern dance has established its own costume conventions and become a source of inspiration for designers working in other dance formats. Some examples in ballet are Tudor's *Dark Elegies* (Nadia Benois) and *Undertow* (Raymond Breinin); and John Taras's *The Song of the Nightingale* (Rouben Ter-Arutunian).

[*See also* Scenic Design. *Many of the figures and works mentioned herein are the subjects of independent entries.*]

BIBLIOGRAPHY

Beaumont, Cyril W. *Ballet Design: Past and Present.* London, 1946.

Bech, Viben. "Bournonville: The Costume." In *Theatre Research Studies.* Vol. 2. Copenhagen, 1972.

Benois, Alexandre. *Reminiscences of the Russian Ballet.* Translated by Mary Britnieva. London, 1941.

Buckle, Richard. *Modern Ballet Design.* London, 1955.

Chaffee, George. "Three or Four Graces: A Centenary Salvo." *Dance Index* 3 (September–November 1944): 136–211.

Davenport, Millia. *The Book of Costume.* New York, 1948.

Engel, Lehman. *The American Musical Theater.* Rev. ed. New York, 1975.

Feuer, Jane. *The Hollywood Musical.* Bloomington, 1982.

Flugel, J. C. *The Psychology of Clothes.* London, 1930.

Garafola, Lynn. *Diaghilev's Ballets Russes.* New York, 1989.

Hirschhorn, Clive. *The Hollywood Musical.* New York, 1981.

Kirstein, Lincoln. *Dance.* New York, 1935. Republished as *The Book of the Dance* (Garden City, N.Y., 1942).

Kirstein, Lincoln. *Movement and Metaphor: Four Centuries of Ballet.* New York, 1970.

Komisarjevsky, Theodore, and Lee Simonson. *Settings and Costumes of the Modern Stage.* London, 1933.

Laver, James. *Costume in the Theatre.* New York, 1965.

Lieven, Peter. *The Birth of Ballets-Russes.* Translated by Leonide Zarine. London, 1936.

Martin, John. *America Dancing.* New York, 1936.

Martin, John. *Introduction to the Dance.* New York, 1939.

Martin, John. *The Dance.* New York, 1946.

Noverre, Jean-Georges. *Lettres sur la danse et sur les ballets.* Stuttgart and Lyon, 1760. Translated by Cyril W. Beaumont as *Letters on Dancing and Ballets* (London, 1930).

Payne, Charles, et al. *American Ballet Theatre.* New York, 1977.

Priddin, Deirdre. *The Art of the Dance in French Literature from Théophile Gautier to Paul Valéry.* London, 1952.

Reade, Brian. *Ballet Designs and Illustrations, 1581–1940.* London, 1967.

Reynolds, Nancy. *Repertory in Review: Forty Years of the New York City Ballet.* New York, 1977.

St. Denis, Ruth. *An Unfinished Life.* 2d ed. New York, 1939.

Smith, Cecil, and Glenn Litton. *Musical Comedy in America: From the Black Crook through Sweeney Todd.* 2d ed. New York, 1981.

Strong, Roy. *Splendour at Court: Renaissance Spectacle and Illusion.* Boston, 1973.

Waugh, Norah. *Corsets and Crinolines.* London, 1954.

Wigman, Mary. *The Language of Dance.* Translated by Walter Sorell. Middletown, Conn., 1966.

Winter, Marian Hannah. *The Pre-Romantic Ballet.* London, 1974.

MALCOLM MCCORMICK

Modern Dance

The conventions associated with costuming in modern dance have evolved out of the combined achievements of five pioneers: Isadora Duncan, Ruth St. Denis, Mary Wigman, Doris Humphrey, and Martha Graham. Though each used costume in a manner that was as idiomatic as her choreography, collectively their methods form a homogeneous lineage.

According to John Martin, we inherit from Duncan the basic concept that the dancer is essentially a nude figure upon which is placed the minimum of costume required to obtain a desired theatrical effect. In rediscovering the dance as a transcendent, lyric art, she acknowledged the whole of her body; defying convention by dancing barefoot and barelegged without the obligatory corset, in loosely draped neoclassical costumes. Though she was by no means the first to do so (neoclassical dress had been a well-established theatrical convention for five hundred years), Duncan's genius lay in inventing a valid and expressive context for the Victorian association between Greek draperies and artistic inspiration. Preferring soft textures that permitted her to move comfortably and echoed the fluid dynamics of her gestures, she used fabrics that ranged from the lightest gauze and Chinese silk to homespun and heavy velvet. In keeping with the directness of her expression, she avoided elaborate detail, richly woven brocades, cloth ornamented with embroidery, or jewelry. However, the black-and-white photography of her era fails to convey Duncan's love of vibrant color, red being her favorite. There are descriptions of her in pink, gray, raspberry, violet, blue, cream, white, and purple, frequently with fresh flowers woven loosely in her hair or attached to her costume.

The question of immodesty and exhibitionism often arises in connection with Duncan's costumes. She was an outspoken and emotional woman, and with her rise to worldwide celebrity, the press became avidly interested in the details of her rather unorthodox private life. Inevitably, audiences (particularly those in the United States) were unable to disassociate these reports from her art and focused their disapproval on her costumes. She denounced prurience and defended nudity as "truth, beauty, art," and in so doing helped bring about the dress reforms for women that occurred in the first quarter of the twentieth century. Her costumes were at all times true to her intuition for artistic harmony and beauty, demonstrating that costume should develop on the pattern of the body itself, never hiding the communicative instrument of the dancer under superfluous trappings.

In the 1890s an American actress who had had some success as a skirt dancer, Loie Fuller, caught the public's imagination with a style of performance that was antithetical to Duncan's in that her dances contained few expressive movements—their choreographic substance being patterns created by undulating fabric. The hundreds of yards of floating silk that Fuller manipulated obscured

COSTUME IN WESTERN TRADITIONS: Modern Dance. *(left)* Loie Fuller in her *Lily Dance*, 1895. Fuller created dramatic visual effects by spinning cloth into motion and using innovative lighting techniques. *(right)* Doris Humphrey in *New Dance*, wearing a costume designed by Pauline Lawrence. Humphrey generally performed in long, simple, inexpensive dresses designed to enhance the flow of her movement. Critics considered her austerity inelegant. (Left photograph from the Dance Collection, New York Public Library for the Performing Arts. Right photograph by Thomas Bouchard; used by permission.)

her rather stocky figure, and her dance numbers usually occurred on one spot, taking full advantage of cleverly placed lights. Nevertheless, La Loie enjoyed tremendous international popularity as a dancer. Her use of fabric as a means of creating startling theatrical effects was much imitated and came to be popularly associated with the lyric expressiveness of modern dance.

Though they were contemporaries, Ruth St. Denis and Duncan expressed divergent tastes in costume. Whereas Duncan thought of herself as an embodiment of Walt Whitman's America and disdained theatrical glamour, St. Denis turned to the exotic mysticism of the East for inspiration and utilized all the illusory effects that stage magic—lights, makeup, scenery, and costumes—could offer. St. Denis's *Radha* established a pattern in 1906 that she was to follow throughout her career. As Radha—her metaphor for the human soul, derived from Hinduism— St. Denis appeared in an elaborate temple setting wearing stage jewelry attached to a flesh-colored foundation. She wore a glittering crown, arm bracelets, and jewels on otherwise naked ankles and feet. As the dance progressed, she made use of a series of props and costume accessories: a strand of pearls, a garland of flowers, finger cymbals, a cup, and a nautch skirt. Each had its choreographic symbolism but, like other aspects of the work,

made no claim to authenticity. For those who were not receptive to the metaphysical overtones, St. Denis's personal beauty, her rippling arms and shoulders, the illusion of near nudity, the colors and textures of beautiful fabrics, and beguiling stage pictures were enough to make her famous in America and Europe. Throughout her long career, St. Denis's ability to integrate costume, particularly flowing draperies, with dance was one of her most valuable assets—one that often provided a basis for choreographic inspiration.

Ted Shawn shared St. Denis's love of flamboyant theatrical effects. They were both masters of illusion in costuming, adept at combining ordinary materials to give the impression of great richness under stage lighting. These tricks, as well as traditional techniques of costuming, were taught as part of theater-training programs in the Denishawn schools. Shawn introduced American dances about cowboys and laborers and costumed them innovatively in simple, untheatrical designs. He believed that dancers should have the same prerogative as athletes to wear whatever was most comfortable and convenient for their physical effort. On these grounds, he sometimes appeared nearly nude and dressed his all-male company, formed in 1933, in loincloths, bathing briefs, and early versions of the unitard or tank suit. Shawn's men intro-

COSTUME IN WESTERN TRADITIONS: Modern Dance. *(left)* Alwin Nikolais, a choreographer noted for his integration of design elements and dance, created innovative costumes that extended the form of the body, like this one from *Totem* (1960). *(right)* Modern dance choreographers since the 1960s have often performed in casual street clothes. Here, choreographer Wendy Perron and percussionist David van Tieghem wear T-shirts, men's suit jackets, cargo pants, and sneakers in her *Divertissement* (1986). (Left photograph © 1993 by Johan Elbers; right photograph © 1986 by Beatriz Schiller; both used by permission.)

duced and popularized the simple trousers and shirts of contemporary working men as costume for dance.

Starting in the 1920s, Mary Wigman appeared in tense, introspective works, costumed in starkly modern gowns or in eccentric designs that were her transposition of subjective experience into the components of costume: color, texture, and form. She developed these elements exactly as she did the kinetic aspects of her work, as natural extensions of an underlying mood, thought, or intuition through the process of synesthesia, the sensory phenomenon wherein modalities of perception, sight, hearing, and smell interact. She did not think of "costuming" her dances. Rather, what she wore was in her mind an inseparable and essential part of an expressive synthesis—the dance, the dancer, sound, light, space, and costume. In some instances her designs made use of very subtle effects: the light rustling of a skirt lining, for example, which was probably audible only to herself. On other occasions her costumes were vivid expressionistic metaphors using her materials at the highest intensity to convey a theatrical idea. Wigman's process, rather than her costuming, became her lasting contribution to design.

Doris Humphrey and Martha Graham both emerged from Denishawn training with a thorough knowledge of costume. Both applied it advantageously but very differently. Humphrey rejected St. Denis's flamboyant decorativeness. After developing a theory of movement based on the simple process of fall and recovery, she used simply designed floor-length gowns of soft fabric to dramatize the effects of inertia and vivify the relationship between the dancer and gravity. Her movement was a life metaphor—and she usually dealt with prototypes and archetypal patterns of behavior. Her use of simplified gowns for women and their corollary, trousers for men, reflected both the essential humanism of her themes and the broadly abstract level on which she developed them.

Martha Graham's work embraced all the traditional techniques of the theater, including innovative and sometimes spectacular use of costume. She borrowed from all the aforementioned artists but created a style of costuming that was unmistakably her own—as recognizable as her idiosyncratic movements. Both Graham and her female dancers usually wore long, simply styled gowns that fitted closely through the torso but flared into long, wide skirts, revealing the visceral origin of movement and accentuating the drama of extended leg action. Like Shawn, Graham often stripped men down to loincloths, and, in the manner of St. Denis, she used elements of costume as symbolic props or even scenic devices. Whether developing ideas with a costumer or a designer, Graham imposed her own unmistakable sense of style—at once personal, modern, elegant, and timeless.

The creative aspects of designing for dance remain somewhat mysterious and seem to depend to a large extent on intuition and the degree to which the designer can share the creative sensibility of the choreographer. The subjective nature of most modern dance makes this collaboration a very intimate one; for the designer, difficulties abound. The convention of dancing barefoot precludes certain choices for the designer, and the dancer's need for an unlimited range of movement—for floor work and acrobatic partnering—imposes another kind of limitation. Since the main purpose is to reveal the dancers' bodies as fully as possible, everything extraneous or not functionally expressive must be eliminated, and the designer is forced to rely on the most minimal devices.

The long-skirted gowns and pants, which were the uniforms of the 1930s to 1950s, have given way to leotards and tights for both sexes in revealing stretch fabrics. Postmodern choreographers exploring alternative performance spaces and innovative forms often utilize studio apparel and streetwear as noncostume, to minimize the element of aesthetic distance in works that explore the boundaries of presentationalism. In this vein, Merce Cunningham's 1950s' use of sweat suits and sneakers set an example that many have followed; but even this approach has been absorbed into the mainstream of theatrical convention by familiarity and the use of designs that represent nondesign.

In the reciprocal interchange that has occurred between modern dance and the ballet in recent decades, this utilitarian approach and the characteristic simplicity of costume design for modern dance have had a distinctly freeing effect on ballet costume. Whereas the tutu has not invaded the modern field (except in jest), ballet dancers often perform in costume styles that are clearly modern in origin.

[*See also* Practice Clothes *and the entries on the principal figures mentioned herein.*]

BIBLIOGRAPHY

Martin, John. *America Dancing*. New York, 1936.
Martin, John. *Introduction to the Dance*. New York, 1939.
Martin, John. *The Dance*. New York, 1946.
St. Denis, Ruth. *An Unfinished Life*. 2d ed. New York, 1939.
Wigman, Mary. *The Language of Dance*. Translated by Walter Sorell. Middletown, Conn., 1966.

MALCOLM McCORMICK

Film and Popular Dance

Costumes for ballet and modern dance usually relate to thematic development, having an expository function enhancing the expressiveness of the choreography. Dancing in popular theater—films, musical comedy, television, nightclubs—is purely presentational and calls for costuming that focuses attention on the performer, enhancing his or her personal attractiveness in terms of prevailing concepts of beauty. For the designer this disparity in ap-

COSTUME IN WESTERN TRADITIONS: Film and Popular Dance. A retouched photograph of the Moulin Rouge quadrille stars—Grille d'Egout, La Sauterelle, La Goulue, and Rayon d'Or—shows the black stockings and frilly petticoats that typified the can-can costume. (Photograph by Harlingue-Viollet; reprinted from Peter Leslie, *A Hard Act to Follow: A Music Hall Review*, New York, 1979, p. 89.)

proach is enough to set the two fields distinctly apart, creating specialists in each.

Beginning in the last quarter of the nineteenth century with the designs of C. Wilhelm at the Alhambra Theatre in London, the roster of designers who have specialized in dance in popular theater includes Barbier, Cecil Beaton, Joseph Urban, Miles White, Irene Sharaff, Oliver Smith, Jo Mielziner, and Erté (adopted name of Romain de Tirtoff, 1892–1990) to name only a few of the most notable. Their work has been of lasting significance within that context and has also influenced fashion design and costuming in the fields of ballet and modern dance. Most have worked effectively in all these fields, but the aesthetic premise of specialization underlies their work in musical theater.

By the late 1800s, the vogue for the Romantic *ballet blanc* had passed, and exhibitionistic productions like *The Black Crook* in the United States, Luigi Manzotti's *Excelsior* in Italy, and the ballets at the Alhambra and Empire theaters in London replaced them. These combinations of scenic extravaganza, dramatic spectacle, and revue featured dancers in elaborate costumes of the type then fashionable—heavily ornamented with lace, silk flowers, ribbons, and ruffles and usually made top-heavy by headdresses or hats balanced on bouffant coiffeurs. Ample figures were nearly severed at the waistline by tight lacing, a distinctly erotic feature of female fashion, which was the object of fetishism even more onstage than off. Apart from Russia, male dancers were not popular; in their stead, women *en travesti* (in male dress) lent an air of naughtiness to these productions. [*See* Travesty.] Even had they made an effort to do so, designers of this period could hardly have disguised the fashionable curvilinear female form to pass for that of a man. Instead they made the most of tights and doublets, peasant blouses and breeches, or military garb, which satisfied a predominantly male audience usually deprived of a glimpse of women's legs by floor-length gowns.

Before the 1920s, the taboo in the West against showing women's legs and underclothing also explains the popularity of the French can-can, which caused an outbreak of that special form of prudery that concerns itself with dancing. Originating in the late 1840s as a social dance, albeit a rowdy one, in which women lifted their skirts to do high kicks displaying their undergarments (or sometimes the absence of undergarments), it was soon brought to the stage by Jacques Offenbach, closely followed by Hervé (Florimond Ronger) and Charles Lecoq, danced by ballet girls *en travesti* or wearing ballet skirts with high-heeled boots laced to the calves. The famous amateurs of the Moulin Rouge cabaret in Paris—the so-called laundresses—who danced the can-can, also popularized another costume: the black stockings, garters and suspenders, frilly petticoats, and underdrawers that became the stereotype for Edwardian eroticism in the musical theater over several decades.

The typical chorus girl's costume of the 1890s was a knee-length dress heavily ornamented with passementerie, chenille balls, and sequins, with a bell-shaped skirt that flared exaggeratedly at the hemline over elaborately ruffled petticoats. For skirt dancing, a form loosely based on the ballet that was popular through the last quarter of the nineteenth century and into the twentieth, the prerequisite was a long, full, colorful skirt of some

COSTUME IN WESTERN TRADITIONS: Film and Popular Dance. Outfitted to personify easeful elegance, Ginger Rogers and Fred Astaire hold hands in the film *Carefree* (1938). (Photograph by Hohn Miehle for RKO Radio Pictures, Inc.)

light material that could be manipulated by the dancer to billow and cascade around her as she moved to the rhythm of a pleasant waltz or gavotte. These costumes were often high-waisted to increase the mass of manipulable fabric. After her initial success as a skirt dancer around 1900, Loie Fuller had only to exaggerate its length and fullness to arrive at her *Serpentine Dance,* with its diaphanous rainbows of silk and colored light, which astonished audiences in Europe.

The arrival in the United States of the Gilbert and Sullivan operetta *H.M.S. Pinafore* in the 1878/79 season led to a veritable eruption of comic opera. Until that time comic opera was imported from Paris but sung without translation, so that it appealed to a discriminating but limited audience. The field was wide open for comic opera in English, and for several decades stars like Anna Held, Lillian Russell, Della Fox, and Edna Wallace Hopper—in tights and wearing revealing costumes like the chorus dancers who backed them up—were the rage of Broadway. In 1907 Florenz Ziegfeld presented the first of his famous revues in New York, featuring large choruses of scantily clad models and dancers. The success of the *Ziegfeld Follies* induced his competitors to offer more of the same, and by the 1920s the ubiquitous Broadway chorine was bare-legged, corsetless, and even sometimes nearly topless.

Sophisticated revues featured concert dancers from the ballet or the developing field of modern dance. Their costumes were often reminiscent of Léon Bakst's designs for Diaghilev's Ballets Russes: jeweled loincloths and halters, chiffon draperies, elaborate headdresses, turbans, and harem pants, lending an air of high art and exoticism. The

ballerina of the musical stage was apt to perform her technically bogus routine wearing the plumed costume of a showgirl, a fashionable evening gown, or the scanty panties and halter of the typical chorine. When the tutu was adapted to musical comedy, it acquired modish decorative details and lost most of its nineteenth-century construction. Without its traditional fitted and boned bodice and wire in its top skirt, it resembled a currently fashionable frock. Hairstyling, a matter of strict conformity in a ballet company, was left to individual preference or taken care of by identical wigs dressed in the current fashion. Male dancers wore jeweled loincloths in acrobatic adagio numbers, top hat and tails for sophisticated tap routines, and all manner of freely adapted male attire, but tights were eschewed as having distinctly effeminate or highbrow connotations. Dancing chorines in rehearsal costume—briefs, shorts, and outfits designed along the lines of bathing costumes—or in the glittering seminudity of elaborate production numbers have become a fixture in both musicals and films.

Irene and Vernon Castle had popularized exhibition ballroom dancing before World War I, in which she appeared in modest but trend-setting fashions offset by his immaculate formal wear. Their elegant mode of presentation was imitated by other dance teams, including Fred and Adele Astaire, who graduated from vaudeville to appear in Broadway musicals. Fred began a career in films in partnership with Ginger Rogers, whose flowing gowns influenced a Hollywood fashion in evening wear; they were as much a part of the team's theatrical signature as Astaire's beautifully tailored top hat and tails.

In the 1940s innovative choreographers working in both Broadway musicals and films developed concepts

COSTUME IN WESTERN TRADITIONS: Film and Popular Dance. A publicity shot of Vera Zorina in a star-spangled costume for the film *Star Spangled Rhythm* (1942). (Photograph from the Dance Collection, New York Public Library for the Performing Arts.)

that introduced nearly every aspect of ethnic Americana—from the cowboys and Plains women of Agnes de Mille's *Oklahoma!* to the gangsters of the New York underworld in Michael Kidd's *Guys and Dolls*. Astaire, Gene Kelly, Jack Cole, and others developed a style of Hollywood film dancing that featured elaborate costumes and settings presented in an overlapping montage of spectacular visual effects connected by dancing and choreographic camera work. For the most part, dance was exploited as a vehicle for film extravaganzas, featuring glamorous personalities like Cyd Charisse, Vera-Ellen, Rita Hayworth, and Betty Grable; designers concentrated on enhancing a star's personal allure. As in most forms of popular theater, stylistic consistency and authenticity were sacrificed to effects that would appeal to the taste of the average viewer. The designer's approach was apt to be more decorative than expressive and the results sentimental or deliberately kitsch.

By the 1960s George Balanchine's plotless and characterless ballets had won a general acceptance, and an abstract approach to form and theatrical effect was the prevailing mode in modern dance as well. Reflecting this trend (and because of rising costs of production), choreographers working in the popular theater began to eliminate narrative or thematic content requiring characterization and local color in costuming. Relying on the old principle that clothing draws attention to that which it speciously conceals, designers created provocative outfits by exaggerating current fashions popular in sports and in disco dancing. Deprived of any creative challenge, they concentrated on making various parts of the dancer's anatomy more interesting to watch than the generally vapid choreography.

By the 1980s the film musical was a thing of the past and there was little outlet for popular dancing on television. Although on the commercial stage new musicals continued to flourish, the greatest successes concentrated on singing and highly elaborate production effects containing little or no dance. Andrew Lloyd Webber's nearly plotless spectacles epitomized this format: in *Cats* (1982) dancers and singers, assuming feline identities, competed with stunning production gimmickry; *Starlight Express* (1987) featured all performers, including dancers, on roller skates, costumed in wildly futuristic gear as trains traversing ramps, bridges, and catwalks; in *The Phantom of the Opera* (1988), lavishly costumed dancers were used primarily to enrich the operetta on a grand scale.

In conjunction with the dance boom since the 1970s, the clothing worn by dancers in rehearsal had an unprecedented influence on general fashion. Stretch fabrics initially used in dancers' leotards and tights and their wrapped and layered sweaters and leggings were imitated by manufacturers and sold to the general public for use in sport activities and as everyday wear. This influence on

COSTUME IN WESTERN TRADITIONS: Film and Popular Dance. Ricardo Montalban and Cyd Charisse in a Spanish-style number from the film *The Kissing Bandit* (1951). "Ethnic" costumes were a prominent feature of many contemporary Hollywood films. (Photograph from the Dance Collection, New York Public Library for the Performing Arts.)

fashion has resulted in the layered, unstructured, and form-revealing clothing popular (but not necessarily appropriate) for almost all occasions.

[*See also* Film Musicals, *article on* Hollywood Film Musicals; United States of America, *article on* Musical Theater; *and entries on the principal figures mentioned herein.*]

BIBLIOGRAPHY

Engel, Lehman. *The American Musical Theater.* Rev. ed. New York, 1975.

Feuer, Jane. *The Hollywood Musical.* Bloomington, 1982.

Hirschhorn, Clive. *The Hollywood Musical.* New York, 1981.

Smith, Cecil, and Glenn Litton. *Musical Comedy in America: From the Black Crook through Sweeney Todd.* 2d ed. New York, 1981.

MALCOLM McCORMICK

CÔTE D'IVOIRE. *See* Sub-Saharan Africa, *overview article. For discussion of masking traditions of the Baule people and stilt-dancing among the Dan people, see* Mask and Makup, *article on* African Traditions.

COTILLON. In 1706 the French dancing master Raoul-Auger Feuillet (compiler of a celebrated notation system for Baroque dance) published a ballroom dance for two couples entitled "Le Cotillon." He described it as a *danse ancienne* (dance of former days) so in fashion at court at that time that he felt obliged to include it in his annual publication on dance. He called it a kind of *branle* (group dance) for four that anyone could dance without being taught. He notated the steps as *"contretemps, demi-contretemps, rigaudon,* and a *sauté"* on both feet to mark the cadences. Later *chassé, balancé, glissade, allemande,* and other Baroque steps were used.

The addition of two more couples to form a square allowed more people to dance at the same time and gave those unfamiliar with the figure a chance to observe it before commencing. This four-couple formation was the typical form of the eighteenth-century *cotillon.*

Dances for two or four couples had long been known, among them *corales* and *branles.* Feuillet's *cotillon,* however, contains the *rondeau* (figure and chorus) format that distinguishes it from the progressive English country dance and nonprogressive French *contredanse.* In English progressive dances, the dancers move mainly down the set and return to place, having danced with each couple in turn, often as many as twenty couples. In the French *cotillon,* such progression does not occur and most sets use only four couples.

The *cotillon* is said to have taken its name (meaning "underpetticoat") from a popular song of the period: "Ma commère, quand je danse, comment va mon cotillon? Il va de ci, il va de ça, comme le queue de notre chat." (My gossipy companion, how does my petticoat look when I dance? It goes like this, it goes like that, like the tail of our cat.)

A typical cotillon begins (after the usual honors) with Le Grand Rond, a circular figure involving all eight dancers. Following this the figure proper begins; one couple dances with the couple standing opposite across the set. The remaining two couples then duplicate this maneuver. Next follows "the first change," or refrain, during which all four couples simultaneously turn their partners, first with the right hand and then with the left hand. The figure proper is then repeated by the leading couples and the side couples, as before. Then "the second change" begins—usually a turn with both hands performed by all couples simultaneously. The figure is then repeated, always alternated with a different change, until ten changes have been danced.

The following list of popular changes is given by Giovanni Gallini in his *Critical Observations on the Art of Dancing,* published in London around 1770:

Change 1—Each couple join their right hands and turn, then back with the left. Change 2—Each couple join both hands and turn to their right, then back to the left. Change 3—The ladies *Moulinet* to the right, then to the left. Change 4—The gentlemen *Moulinet* to the right, then to the left. Change 5—The ladies join hands and go round to the right, then to the left. Change 6—The gentlemen join hands and go round to the right, then to the left. Change 7—Each couple *Allemande* to the right, then to the left. Change 8—*La Grande Chaine* (grand right to left). Change 9—*La Course,* or *La Promenade,* to the right. Change 10—*Le Grand Rond.*

The music for the *cotillon* consisted of popular airs of the day, older traditional tunes, and new compositions by dancing masters, hacks hired by publishers, and sometimes even well-known composers. It was written in 2/4 or 6/8 time and usually had two eight-measure phrases, each

COTILLON. The French *cotillon,* a group dance for four couples popular during the eighteenth century, presented an elaborate series of figures. In this English print from 1771, the couples begin the *cotillon* with Le Grand Rond. (Courtesy of Elizabeth Aldrich.)

COTILLON. A popular parlor game, the cotillon (later known as the German) consisted of a variety of figures. Here, in a figure called The Fan, the lady intends to dance with the gentleman who does not receive the fan. The unfortunate gentleman with the fan must follow and fan the dancing couple while hopping on one leg. (Reprinted from Leborde, *Le Cotillon,* Paris, c.1860.)

repeated and usually followed by a third sixteen-measure section in the minor key.

According to Claude Marc Magny, whose dance manual was published about 1765, the steps for the *cotillon* suitable for going forward on a straight line or for going backward are a *contretemps* and an *assemblé;* the steps for going diametrically to either side are three *chassés,* the third of which (the quadrille step) is an *assemblé.* For oblique directions, *contretemps,* *demi-contretemps,* or *chassés* are suitable, but the choice is arbitrary since these are rarely required. For circular lines *demi-contretemps* are appropriate, especially for more than two measures; for only two measures the steps are a *contretemps* (turning) and an *assemblé. Rigaudons, balancés,* and *pirouettes* are inserted as required.

Once dancers had mastered the complex vocabulary of steps required by Baroque dance technique and the ten or so cotillon changes, which remained more or less stable throughout the eighteenth century, they had only to keep abreast of the latest figures introduced each season to perform the cotillon at court balls, assemblies, and other social gatherings. These lively group dances were a welcome contrast to more decorous display dances such as the *menuet.* The *menuet* step was occasionally included as part of the figure of a *cotillon;* the music changed to 6/4 time to accommodate it. When the *allemande* became fashionable, with its intricate interlacing of arms done while turning and its dainty *jeté-coupé* step, it too was incorporated into the *cotillon.*

Toward the end of the eighteenth century, the ten familiar changes were shortened to four and eventually discarded altogether, leaving only the figure, which was too brief to be a complete dance. When several popular *cotil-*

lon figures were linked together without the changes, the *cotillon* was transformed into the quadrille.

As late as 1840 the quadrille was still erroneously referred to as the *cotillon,* even though the older *cotillon*-form had passed out of fashion. At this time, however, a new and entirely different dance, the German cotillon, appeared and usurped the name. It held a featured position in nineteenth-century dance evenings.

This new cotillon (also spelled *cotillion*), often two or more hours long, was led by a master of ceremonies or a popular guest chosen by the hostess. This leader directed a series of musical dance games, which allowed any number of dancers to exchange partners through humorous chance encounters and to intermingle in a playful, informal manner not formerly possible in the formal ballroom. The German cotillon was often held after supper, following the more formal ball. The music was taken from favorite waltz, polka, galop, mazurka, quadrille, and march airs.

Remnants of both the German cotillon and the eighteenth-century *cotillon* may still be found today in square dancing, European folk dances, and children's games.

[*See also* Social Dance, *articles on* Court and Social Dance before 1800 *and* Nineteenth-Century Social Dance.]

BIBLIOGRAPHY

Feuillet, Raoul-Auger. *Dances pour l'année 1706.* Paris, 1705.

Gallini, Giovanni. *Critical Observations on the Art of Dancing, to Which Is Added a Collection of Cotillons or French Dances.* London, c.1770.

La Cuisse. *Le répertoire des bals.* 3 vols. Paris, 1762–.

Magny, Claude-Marc. *Principes de chorégraphie, suivis d'un traité de la cadence.* Paris, 1765.

Malpied. *Les caractères des contre-danses.* Paris, c.1780.

DESMOND F. STROBEL

COTILLON. Ballet in one act. Choreography: George Balanchine. Music: Emmanuel Chabrier. Libretto: Boris Kochno. Scenery and costumes: Christian Bérard. First performance: 12 April 1932, Opéra de Monte-Carlo, Ballets Russes de Monte-Carlo. (Preview: 17 January 1932, Opéra de Monte-Carlo, at a gala in honor of Prince Louis II of Monaco.) Principals: Tamara Toumanova (Daughter of the House), Nathalie Strakhova (Her Friend), David Lichine (The First Guest), Valentina Blinova (Mistress of Ceremonies), Léon Woizikowski (Master of Ceremonies), Lubov Rostora and Valentin Froman (The Hands of Fate pas de deux).

Cotillon remains an important link in the Balanchine repertory because it was the first work he created specifically for Tamara Toumanova and because it is an early example of his use of the ballroom as the backdrop for dramatic events. The performance of the thirteen-year-old

Toumanova, as a young girl attending her first ball, established her reputation as a leading dancer. Balanchine selected the score from among Chabrier's *Pièces Pittoresques* for piano and *Trois Valses Romantiques* for two pianos; the score was orchestrated by Chabrier, Felix Mottl, and Vittorio Rieti. Bérard's set was a vast marble Victorian ballroom with a few red-curtained boxes and gilt chairs. The program had titles for each episode and a short description of the action.

The traditional cotillion had comprised a series of structured social dances that were popular during the nineteenth century. Balanchine's version utilized some of these formal figures and rigid manners. In the early parts of the ballet, the guests engage in party games and superficial flirtations. The mood shifts, however, to suggestions of spiritual and sexual loneliness, culminating in the Hands of Fate pas de deux. In it, a woman lures a man away from the crowd to dance with her and ultimately reveals herself to be a vampire.

Throughout these scenes, the Daughter of the House searches in vain for a kindred spirit among the strangers. In the final episode, "Grand Rond and End of Cotillon," her frustration explodes in a set of furious *fouettés* whose power summons the scattered guests back to the stage. They link arms in a circle and revolve feverishly around her as the curtain descends.

Similar motifs are found in other Balanchine ballets, including *Le Bal* (1929); *La Sonnambula*, originally titled *Night Shadow* (1946); and especially *La Valse* (1951). These works have in common formal dance settings against which themes of erotic tension, alienation, and death are played out. *Cotillon* ceased being performed in 1940. In 1988 Millicent Hodson and Kenneth Archer reconstructed the work for the Joffrey Ballet; it was presented 26 October 1989.

BIBLIOGRAPHY

Archer, Kenneth, and Millicent Hodson. "The Quest for *Cotillon*." *Ballet Review* 16 (Summer 1988):31–46.
Beaumont, Cyril W. *Complete Book of Ballets*. London, 1937.
Cellarius, Henri. *The Drawing-Room Dances*. London, 1847.
Coton, A. V. *A Prejudice for Ballet*. London, 1938.
Deakin, Irving. *To the Ballet!* New York, 1935.
García-Márquez, Vicente. *The Ballets Russes: Colonel de Basil's Ballets Russes de Monte Carlo, 1932–1952*. New York, 1990.
Goodman, G. E. "Decor at the Alhambra: Les Ballets Russes de Monte Carlo." *The Dancing Times* (October 1933):45–47.
Kirstein, Lincoln. "Ballet as We Know It: Dancers Working with Painters, with New Music." *Vogue* (November 1933).
Kirstein, Lincoln. *Thirty Years: The New York City Ballet*. New York, 1978.
Leighton, Luca. "Emmanuel Chabrier: Cotillon." In *The Decca Book of Ballet*, edited by David Drew. London, 1958.
McDonagh, Don. "'Lost' Balanchine Rediscovered." *Ballet Review* 17 (Fall 1989):26–32.
Review. *New York Sun* (16 November 1940).
Sitter Out. "Les Ballets Russes." *The Dancing Times* (August 1935).
Stokes, Adrian. *Russian Ballets*. London, 1935.

FILM. Laird Goldsborough, *Cotillon* (1933), Dance Collection, New York Public Library for the Performing Arts.

DIANE J. ROSENTHAL

COUNTRY DANCE is a social dance of English origin in which a number of couples perform a set pattern of figures. This dance achieved great popularity in the seventeenth century. The *contredanse*, which is the corresponding French form, reached its greatest popularity in the eighteenth century. Current English country dance derives largely from a revival early in this century of the original English dances of the seventeenth century, while the modern contradance has evolved over the centuries from the two early forms.

The earliest use of the specific term *countrye dauncis* occurs in Thomas Richardes's play *Misogonous*, composed in the second half of the sixteenth century. References to specific country dances, such as "Sellengers Round" and "Shaking of the Sheets," also began to occur in the sixteenth century. Sir John Davies's poem *Orchestra* (1594) provides the first indication of the nature of these dances. Stanzas 62 through 64, which in the second edition of 1622 bear the marginal title "Rounds or Country Dances," describe the formation of a weaving or serpentine line of dancers ("winding Heyes") leading into a ring around a tree. This accords with the suggestion that the English country dance derived from ritual dances. A connection between ritual and country dances is similarly suggested by Thomas Middleton's reference in his *Father Hubbards Tales* (1604) to the "dancing of Sellengers Round in moonshine nights about Maypoles."

The first detailed description of the English country dance is in *The English Dancing Master* (1651) by John Playford. This work, under the modified title *The Dancing Master*, went through seventeen subsequent editions from 1652 to 1728, the editor John Playford being succeeded first by his nephew Henry Playford and later by John Young. In addition, second and third volumes appeared early in the eighteenth century. In the first edition, Playford provides instruction and music for 105 dances. Several of these are round dances, either for a specific number of dancers or "for as many as will." There are also dances for two couples facing each other and for four couples in a "square Dance for eight." The overwhelming majority, however, involve longways sets of three, four, or as many couples as wish, arranged in a column. Dances are added and omitted in each subsequent edition of *The Dancing Master*, with the "Longwayes for as many as will" form gradually becoming so dominant that it accounts for nearly all of the approximately nine hundred dances in the final three-volume edition of 1728.

The longways formation does not conform to Davies's description of country dances but is typical of proces-

COUNTRY DANCE. An engraving depicting a country dance lesson at a dancing school. Musicans play at each side, as does the naked figure of Cupid (center). This illustration was printed on the title page of the seventh edition of the first volume of *The Dancing Master* (1686), by John Playford. (Dance Collection, New York Public Library for the Performing Arts.)

sional court dances of the fifteenth and sixteenth centuries. Moreover, the various patterns or figures that develop in these longways country dances also have parallels in the court dances of previous centuries. These similarities prompted Melusine Wood in 1937 to suggest that the adoption of country dances by the court early in the seventeenth century resulted in a transformation from the earlier serpentine or round dance into the longways pattern that eventually predominated. That new country dances were being composed within the court setting is supported by references—in such documents as a letter from Rowland Whyte to Sir Robert Sidney—to Queen Elizabeth's coming "to see the ladies daunce the old and new Country dances." A likely example of a "new" country dance is the "Longways for Six" in Playford's first edition called "Confesse" (or "Confesse [,] his Tune" in the table of contents), for Confesse was the name of a late sixteenth-century dancing master and composer.

Many of Playford's early country dances follow a formula of three parts: The first part begins with all leading up and back, the second with partners "siding" (approaching each other until they are side by side, and returning to places), and the third with partners "arming" (turning with arms joined). In some cases, the figure that follows the initial leading up and back is repeated as a refrain in the second and third parts. This use of a set pattern of opening figures followed by a repeating chorus figure, as well as the longways formation of three or four pairs of dancers, is common in modern Morris dance practice. As the Morris dance, or more properly the *moresca*, is known to have existed as a ritual or pyrrhic dance since the Middle Ages, this similarity in pattern has been taken as further evidence for the ritual origins of the country dance. The evidence available on Morris dancing in the sixteenth and seventeenth centuries, however, suggests that the Morris dance acquired this form only later, adopting it from the country dance.

French Contredanse. By the end of the seventeenth century, the English country dance had been exported to France, where it was referred to as the *contredance* (later spelled *contredanse*). This term has been taken to indicate a French origin to this form of dance, the name supposedly deriving from the arrangement of the dancers on contrary sides. Early in the seventeenth century, however, François de Lauze refers in his *Apologie de la danse* (1623) to *"mesures & contredanses"* as the characteristic dances of the English. The French *contredanse* manuals that began to appear by the end of the century also ascribed an English origin to these dances.

The French manuals of the late seventeenth and early eighteenth centuries did, however, introduce major changes in the method of describing the figures and in the specification of steps. The earliest of these is a pair of unpublished manuscripts composed by André Lorin in the years following a visit to England in the mid-1680s. Lorin's first manuscript provides diagrams for thirteen dances, most of which can be identified as dances published in England in contemporary editions of Playford's *The Dancing Master.* Lorin's second manuscript provides nearly a hundred pages of illustrations of a single dance, "Les Cloches ou le Carillon, Contredance du Roy" (the English dance "Christchurch Bells"), depicting the dancers at every stage of the dance. While this level of detail is unique, the use of diagrams with lines showing the paths of the dancers became widespread for depicting all forms of dance in the eighteenth century. It was adopted by Raoul-Auger Feuillet in his *Recüeil de contredances* (1706), the first published French manual of these dances.

Other French collections of country dances of the early eighteenth century, such as Jacques Dezais's *Recüeil de nouvelles contredances* (1712) and Feuillet's annual collection of dances for 1708, also use this diagrammatic approach. John Essex's English collection of dances, *For the Further Improvement of Dancing* (1710), displays a strong French influence both in its use of diagrams and in its recourse to a translation of the introduction from Feuillet's 1706 collection. Nicholas Dukes's *A Concise & Easy Method of Learning the Figuring Part of Country Dances*

(1752) also provides diagrams to explain each figure. Nevertheless, while English manuals of court dance rely upon the French method of diagrams, the English country dance collections produced in the eighteenth century tend to favor Playford's verbal approach to describing dance figures.

The rise in France of the minuet and other court dances involving the elaborate steps characteristic of the Baroque period had an effect not only on the representation of the *contredanse* but also on its performance. Playford's brief comments on dance steps in the various editions of *The Dancing Master* indicate no more than a plain walk. Lorin commented on the variety of steps employed as a matter of individual whim by the English dancers (Guilcher, 1969). He disapproved of this practice, describing in detail an approved repertory of steps to be used for the proper performance of each dance figure. The delineation of specific Baroque steps also occurs in Feuillet's introduction to his *Recüeil* and in most French works on *contredanse*.

Square Form. All the dances in the French collections mentioned previously are of the longways form. In the annual collection of *Danses pour l'année 1716*, Dezais presented a dance entitled "Le Cotillon des Fêtes de Thalie." This dance is labeled a *"Contre-danse,"* but instead of following the longways formation offered by Lorin and Feuillet, it calls for four couples arranged in a square. Examples of this formation appear in the early editions of Playford's *The Dancing Master*, but few are retained in the later editions. By the second half of the eighteenth century, this square formation had largely displaced the longways set in France, as illustrated by manuals such as de la

COUNTRY DANCE. Although its popularity in the ballroom eventually waned in preference to the quadrille, the country dance remained a staple in the early nineteenth-century social dance repertory, as evidenced by this anonymous French print from the 1820s. (Dance Collection, New York Public Library for the Performing Arts.)

Cuisse's *Le répertoire des bals, ou Théorie-pratique des contredanses* (1762). A method was devised of expanding the duration of these French dances by repeating the square figure several times, with a series of figures (called changes) interposed between each repeat. This dance, which came to be known as the cotillon, was the direct ancestor of the ballroom quadrille and of the square dance of rural America.

The square form of the *contredanse*, or cotillon, gained some popularity in England through works such as G. A. Gallini's *Critical Observations on the Art of Dancing* (c.1770) with its appended "New Collection of Forty-four Cotillons," but the dominant form remained the longways set for an unlimited number of couples. Volumes containing verbal descriptions of hundreds of such dances continued to be published throughout the eighteenth century (by Walsh, Johnson, Thompson, Rutherford, and others). John Walsh's several volumes of Scottish or *Caledonian Country Dances* (c.1733, etc.) indicate that the longways form was popular in other parts of Britain as well. Walsh provided no indication that these dances involved distinctively Scottish steps. The frequent instruction to "foot it" does not correspond to any step in Playford's descriptions but does occur in some of the English country dances in Thomas Bray's 1699 collection. The *Ten New Fashionable Irish Dances* described by Alexander Wills (c.1800) are likewise of the longways form, differing from English dances only in the specification (without explanation) of "running steps," single and double "Irish footing," and "back steps."

In other parts of Europe, both the longways and square formations of country dances achieved considerable popularity in the eighteenth century. In Germany, works such as Carl Lange's *Choreographische Vorstellung der englischen und französischen Figuren in Contretänzen* (1762) feature both longways *englischen Contretänzen* and square *französischen Contretänzen* or *Cotillons*. The association of the longways form of country dance with England was so complete that these dances came to be known as "Anglaise," the term *contredanse* then applying to the square formation. In describing both forms, the German manuals in general adopt the French manner of diagrams rather than relying on verbal instructions. An extreme example is Joseph Lanz's *Portefeuille englischer Taenze* (1784), which consists of a set of cards, each bearing an illustration of a single country dance figure, from which a combination may be drawn to create a variety of individual dances (Taubert, 1983). Mozart and Beethoven are among the composers of contradances for public balls. Both the English longways and French square formations were popular in the Low Countries as well, with works such as P. N. Gautier's *Dix contredanse engloises et deux françoises* (c.1780) providing verbal descriptions of both forms. Italy also felt the influence of the country dance, and Gennaro Magri included in his *Trattato teorico-prat-tico di ballo* (1779) not only longways and square dances, but also far more elaborate configurations.

Wilson's Work. By the early years of the nineteenth century, the square form of *contredanse* had evolved in the ballrooms of France beyond the cotillon into the quadrille. At the same time, the longways country dance was receiving new treatment by the English dancing master Thomas Wilson. Several of Wilson's works are simply collections of dances described in much the same way as had been common in England since Playford's time. *An Analysis of Country Dancing* (1808) and *The Complete System of English Country Dancing* (c.1820), however, present a systematic analysis of country dances into their component figures. More than three hundred basic figures such as Turn Your Partner, Swing Corners, and Reel of Six are individually described with diagrams and verbal accounts, while an elaborate set of tables shows the way these figures can best be combined to produce a huge number of different dances. Wilson admitted receiving the basic idea of displaying figures independently from Dukes's 1752 manual but seemed unaware of the late eighteenth-century works (such as Lanz's set of cards) that more nearly anticipated his program.

Wilson provided detailed instructions on the manner of performing country dances, indicating at least two new features. The elaborate steps of the Baroque ballroom, if indeed they ever achieved widespread use in country dancing, give way to somewhat simpler steps. In *The Complete System*, Wilson instructed dancers to proceed through figures with step combinations such as "three Chasses, one Jetté Assemblé." This step combination was employed in the quadrille in this period, though Barclay Dun stated in *A Translation of Nine of the Most Fashionable Quadrilles* (1818) that the steps in a country dance "are of a more prompt and pointed kind than those generally used in the quadrille, and are performed upon a more contracted scale" (p. 19). Also new was the idea of the "minor set": the dividing of a longways set into smaller groups, usually of four couples, with the first couple of each group beginning simultaneously rather than having everyone wait for the first couple to reach them.

An apparently American innovation of the early nineteenth century was the practice of "calling" the figures rather than requiring the dancers to memorize them. The square form of *contredanse* or cotillon, replaced in European ballrooms by the quadrille, evolved into the square dance of the rural United States. The longways country dance, which also lost its European popularity during the first half of the nineteenth century, continued as an active tradition in New England. The fancy quadrille steps mentioned by Wilson were soon abandoned (indeed, they were also dropped from the quadrille), and the country dance (or contradance) of the mid–nineteenth century was exe-cuted with a simple walk. Elias Howe, one of the most prolific publishers of contradances, concurred with Wilson in advocating minor sets of four couples. Modern country and contradance takes this practice further still, usually with every second couple beginning the dance.

Modern English country dancing owes its revival largely to the work of Cecil Sharp early in the twentieth century. In an effort to show that England possessed as strong a folk dance tradition as the other nations of Europe, Sharp looked first at the dances still being practiced in rural England. He published a number of these dances in part 1 of *The Country Dance Book* (1909). In parts 2, 3, 4, and 6, Sharp turned his attention to history, publishing his own reconstructions of dances from the various editions of Playford's seventeenth- and early eighteenth-century manuals (part 5 presents some dances of rural America). Sharp's versions of the Playford dances have achieved great popularity and are danced with enjoyment throughout Britain and the United States.

Modern contradancing (distinct from English country dancing) has evolved from the nineteenth-century New England forms and includes many dances originally published in the manuals of Howe and others. Today's Scottish country dances derive ultimately from Walsh's eighteenth-century collections of Caledonian dances but exhibit several individual features (such as four-couple minor sets and the use of a "skip-change" step similar to Wilson's chasse step) of the nineteenth-century English country dance. English country dancing and contradancing are administered today by the English Folk Dance and Song Society in London and by the Country Dance and Song Society, the main branch of which is in Northampton, Massachusetts. Scottish country dancing is administered by the Royal Scottish Country Dance Society in Edinburgh and its branch offices.

[*See also the entries on Playford and Sharp. For related discussion, see* Anglaise; Cotillon; Figure Dances; Quadrille; *and* Social Dance, *article on* Court and Social Dance before 1800.]

BIBLIOGRAPHY

Bray, Thomas. *Country Dances*. London, 1699.

Chambers, E. K. *The Elizabethan Stage*. Vol. 4. Oxford, 1923.

Cunningham, James P. "The Country Dance: Early References." *Journal of the English Folk Dance and Song Society* 9 (1962): 148–154.

Damon, S. Foster. *The History of Square-Dancing*. Worcester, Mass., 1952.

Emmerson, George S. *A Social History of Scottish Dance*. London, 1972.

Feldtenstein, C. J. *Erweiterung der Kunst nach der Chorographie zu tanzen*. Braunschweig, 1772.

Flett, J. F., and T. M. Flett. *Traditional Dancing in Scotland*. London, 1964.

Guilcher, Jean-Michel. *La contredanse et les renouvellements de la danse française*. Paris, 1969.

Guilcher, Yves. "Dance as a Reflection of Society." *Choreography and Dance* 2.1 (1992): 77–107.

Helwig, Christine, and Marshall Barron. *Thomas Bray's Country Dances, 1699*. New Haven, 1988.

Hilton, Wendy. *Dance of Court and Theatre: The French Noble Style, 1690–1725*. Princeton, 1981.

Howe, Elias. *American Dancing Master, and Ballroom Promptor*. Boston, 1862.

Lorin, André. *Livre de contredance presenté au Roy*. N.p., n.d. Manuscript located in Paris, Bibliothèque Nationale, fr. 1697–1698.

Millar, John Fitzhugh. *Country Dances of Colonial America*. Williamsburg, Va., 1990.

Playford, John. *English Dancing Master, 1651*. Edited by Margaret Dean-Smith. London, 1957.

Roodman, Gary M. *Calculated Figures: A Set of Twelve English and American Country Dances*. Tunnel, N.Y., 1987.

Sharp, Cecil, and A. P. Oppé. *The Dance: An Historical Survey of Dancing in Europe*. London, 1924.

Taubert, Karl Heinz. *Die Anglaise . . . mit dem Portefeuille Englischer Tänze von Joseph Lanz, Berlin, 1784*. Zurich, 1983.

Wittman, Carl. "An Analysis of John Playford's 'English Dancing Master' (1651)." Master's thesis, Goddard College, 1981.

Wood, Melusine. "Some Notes on the English Country Dance before Playford." *Journal of the English Folk Dance and Song Society* 3 (1937): 93–99.

Wood, Melusine. "English Country Dance Prior to the Seventeenth Century." *Journal of the English Folk Dance and Song Society* 6 (1949): 8–12.

PATRI J. PUGLIESE

COUNTRY-WESTERN DANCE is an American social dance style originating in Texas, from which it has spread to many parts of the United States. It is also known as cowboy dance, Texas dance, and kickin'. Country-western dance consists mainly of two specific styles of foxtrot known as the Texas Two-Step (not related to the two-step popular at the turn of the century, which developed from the polka) and the Progressive, together with versions of the waltz, polka, schottische, varsovienne, and beginning in the 1980s, unpartnered line dances. The dancing is done by all ages at certain social occasions, but is found mostly in dance and beer halls.

Social dancing has been popular in Texas since the arrival of the first settlers from Europe and the eastern United States in the 1820s. Throughout the nineteenth century square, round, and contradances were fashionable. These dances were done by couples, but only as part of a larger group. They continue to be popular in special clubs and organizations, but are not considered part of the country-western dance scene. The waltz and the polka arrived in the mid-nineteenth century; these dances allowed couples to dance away from the group and allowed them a more intimate (some have said too intimate) hold on each other. The varsovienne was more acceptable: it allowed couples to dance alone, but side by side rather than cheek to cheek.

The country-western dances now current, mainly couples dances done in a modified ballroom position, became popular in Texas after World War II, with the emergence of the style of music called Texas Swing, which offered a perfect tempo and rhythm for dancing. The foxtrot, from which the Texas Two-Step derives, is thought to have been named after Harry Fox, a New York stage dancer of the early 1900s, even though his dance did not much resemble the dance codified after World War I as the foxtrot (the dance may have been named for him simply because he and the dance were both popular at the same time). The foxtrot may be a variation of certain African-American (and Caribbean) dances and children's games that have a stepping and hand-clapping rhythm (the Calypso rhythm) very similar to the slow-slow-quick-quick of the foxtrot (and the Texas Two-Step).

The Texas Two-Step is done in modified ballroom position, partners facing with the man holding the top of the woman's left shoulder or the nape of her neck with his right hand. The woman's right hand is placed on top of the man's left shoulder, drooped from his left elbow, or held by the thumb in his left belt loop. The man's left arm

COUNTRY-WESTERN DANCE. Outfitted in cowboy hats and boots, a couple performs a country-western partner dance. (Photograph by Patrick K. Snook; from Leisner, 1980, p. 55).

may hold the woman's left hand or simply hang free—often holding a bottle of beer or a cigarette. The dancers travel counterclockwise around the floor, the man moving forward, the woman backward, sometimes turning or executing figures with the arms. The steps involve a step-close-step-pause sequence, beginning with the man's left foot and the woman's right, followed by a simple step-pause on the other foot. This crosses over the duple measures of the music, but does not confuse the dancers. The Progressive is done in the same way, but the footwork is more involved. The dancers perform the step-close-step-pause sequence twice. The man steps first on his left foot, the woman on her right; they begin on the opposite feet for the second sequence, then complete the step unit with a simple step on each foot (for a total of eight steps). The counts are one-and-two, three-and-four, five, six, which again crosses over the phrasing of the music in a manner similar to the Texas Two-Step. The country-western waltz also travels around the floor, but with few turns. The man travels forward, beginning with the left foot, the woman backward, beginning with the right. The basic step sequence is step-close-step, step-close-step, with each step falling on one beat of the music, exactly in time with the three-count rhythm of waltz music.

Two older dances still popular in country-western dancing are the polka, which is danced like the Progressive (but omitting the last two steps in each phrase, and including many turns), and the schottische, a side-by-side dance done by couples holding each other with an arm behind the partner's waist. The steps are step-close-step-hop (twice), then four step-hops, traveling forward around the floor with occasional turns. The varsovienne, a smooth three-count dance that predates the foxtrot, is not common today. In this dance, the dancers stand side by side and begin together on the same foot. The man holds his partner's hands from behind at shoulder height and moves across behind her from side to side; they then move forward together side by side. The steps change from one step per beat of music to a low hop, or pause, at the beginning of each three-count measure. Among the obsolete forms of country-western dance is the Texas Tommy, a swing dance popular at saloons and brothels (prostitutes were formerly called "Tommys") earlier in this century. The exact steps are not known—possibly because there were no exact steps. The common assumption is that the dance looked like a swing dance with partners holding hands and executing figures with their arms.

One line dance has been popular among country-western dancers for many years, named for the song "Cotton-Eyed Joe," to which it is always danced. For this, any number of dancers stand side by side, with their arms behind their neighbors' waists. The dancers travel forward with eight sets of a step-close-step-pause sequence, followed by four sets of two forward kicks, then three steps in place. It is believed that this dance is the origin of the term *kickin'*, which can encompass all forms of country-western dancing. The Cotton-Eyed Joe is believed to be a variation of the heel-and-toe polka, traditionally danced by men when there were no women available as partners. In other country-western line dancing, dancers stand in columns and rows (without partners and without touching) and do a series of choreographed steps in a small area, then turn and repeat the steps facing a different direction. Many of the line dances are set to specific pieces of music. Today strongly identified with the country-western scene, this form of line dance is actually of recent invention, an evolution of the simple disco line dance called the Hustle, popular in the 1970s.

BIBLIOGRAPHY

Leisner, Tony. *The Official Guide to Country Dance Steps*. Secaucus, N.J., 1980.

Livingston, Peter. *The Complete Book of Country Swing and Western Dance*. Garden City, N.Y., 1981.

Rushing, Shirley and Patrick McMillan. *Kicker Dancin' Texas Style*. San Antonio, Texas, 1984.

JERRY C. DUKE

COURANTE. A triple-meter court and theater dance, the *courante* is of obscure origin. In Baroque music, there are two distinct types, although the names are not used with discrimination: the slow French *courante*, and the faster and differently structured Italian *corrente*. The earliest known musical examples date from the mid-sixteenth century. The earliest known dance is a lively duple-meter *courante*, with a springing step-pattern given in Thoinot Arbeau's *Orchesography* (1589). Arbeau says that an earlier version of the dance, popular in his youth, contained an element of mime, after which partners danced away helter-skelter.

The oft-repeated theory that the name derives from the Latin *currere*, "to run," may well be applied to these early examples, and to the *corrente* for which dance evidence is scant, but not to the seventeenth-century *courante* popular at Louis XIV's court, which was the slowest and most noble of the triple-meter *danses à deux* (couple dances).

The eight *courantes* extant in Beauchamps/Feuillet notation have two essential characteristics: a rhythmic liveliness in the interplay of triple and duple elements, and an inherent nobility.

Almost one hundred years separate the two dance treatises in which appreciable space is devoted to the *courante*: François de Lauze's *Apologie de la danse* (1623), published soon after the courante became fashionable, and Gottfried Taubert's *Der Rechtschaffener Tantzmeister* (1717), written long after it began to lose its place of favor to the minuet during the 1660s. In 1725, in *Le maître à danser*, Pierre Rameau wrote about the seventeen-century *courante*, the dance Louis XIV preferred above all others. Unfortunately, none of these accounts is comprehensive.

Courantes are dances for the connoisseur. To the uninitiated, they may appear simple and technically undemanding, but, in practice, they require unwavering concentration and considerable physical control. Above all, they demand the bearing and presence of an aristocrat. Perhaps the most famous *courante* is "La Bocanne," composed to an air by Jacques Cordier, a famous dancing master and violinist known as Bocane or Bocanne. An example of a popular ballroom dance beginning with two figures of *courante* is Guillaume-Louis Pecour's "La Bourgogne."

There are two types of *courante*: the *courantes simples*, in which dancers circle the dancing area performing only the basic steps of the dance, and the *courantes figurées*, with developed spatial figures and step-sequences.

The *pas coupé* and the *temps de courante* are the characteristic steps of the dance. They are the only Baroque steps in which the ball of the foot glides gently along the floor before weight is put on it, an action that expresses the sustained, flowing quality of the courante. The other actions used are *pliés* (bends of the knees), which always precede and rhythmically lead to the *élevés* (rises up from the bends). The *élevés* are the strongest rhythmic moments in the steps; they usually coincide with the strongest beats in the musical measures. An *élevé* used at the end of a measure becomes the smallest possible spring from one foot to the other.

Courante airs are distinguished by a 3/2, or occasionally a 6/4, time signature with the recurring rhythm of ♪ | ♩. ♪ ♩ ♩ ♩. ♪ | ♩. ♩ ♩. ♪ | and a duple pulse of ♩. ♩ ♪ ♪ | in the concluding measures of strains. The courante is usually in binary form, and in the notated dances the musical strains are most frequently composed of a number of measures divisible by three.

The courante is built upon three basic metric principles: the triple-dactyl foot, the iambic foot, and *proportio sesquialtera*. In stanza 69 of his poem *Orchestra, or A Poeme of Dauncing* (1596), Sir John Davies writes:

> What shall I name those current traverses
> That on a triple dactyl foot do run
> Close to the ground with sliding passages,
> Wherein the dancer greatest praise hath won.

The triple-dactyl foot was evolved to facilitate medieval polyphonic writing, which made use of six *modi*, later named after the metric feet of Greek verse. The only two duple feet used, the dactyl and the anapest, were made triple, the dactyl being extended from ♩ ♩ ♩ to ♩. ♩ ♩.

In *Harmonie universelle*, book 2 (1636), Marin Mersenne says that the air of a *courante* is measured by the iambic foot, ◡–(♩ ♩), and that its movement is called

sesquialtera, or triple. *Sesquialtera*—one whole plus its half—was a musical proportion in which three notes were introduced in the time of two of the same kind. Thus, a change from duple to triple time was facilitated, the length of the measure remaining constant. *Sesquialtera* was most often employed with minims and denoted by the time signature 3/2, meaning three in the time of two:

♩ ♩ | **3** ♩ ♩ ♩ | ♩ ♩ ♩ | etc.
　　　2 ♩ ♩

Sesquialtera does not necessarily imply an interplay of two against three, but in the *courante* this is used as a significant element.

The relationship of the above elements in a measure is:

triple-dactyl foot　　　♩. ♩ ♩

proportio sesquialtera　**3** ♩ ♩ ♩
　　　　　　　　　　2 ♩. ♩.

two iambs　　　♩ ♩ ♩ ♩ ♩

In the final measure of a strain of *courante*, the duple element of *proportio sesquialtera* and of the two iambs in a measure emerges unencumbered.

All the above elements are reflected in courante step-patterns. The *courante's* structure of one whole plus its half is found in Raoul-Auger Feuillet's explanation of the notation of the dance contained in his *Chorégraphie* (1700):

> It is to be observ'd, nevertheless, that in Courante Movements, two Steps are put to each Barr or Measure; the first of which [a whole unit] takes up two parts in three of a Measure, and the second [half unit] takes up the third part.

The *courante* is the only dance in which one whole and one half step-unit are performed in a measure. (In most dances, one step-unit is performed in a measure.) This is indicated by the line of liaison that joins step-symbols to show that together they form a step-unit. A measure of courante should be notated with the half step-unit detached from the whole unit:

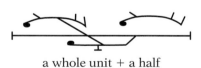

a whole unit + a half

The whole unit is composed of a *pas coupé* and the half is composed of a *demi-coupé*. (The *demi-coupé* is performed as a *demi-jeté*, a very small spring from foot to foot.) The whole step-unit might be a *temps de courante*. This step, the slowest and most sustained of the Baroque step-units, has only one weight change, but it nevertheless equals the time taken by the *pas coupé*.

In *courantes, élevés* and *sautés* have equal rhythmic strength. When executing the step-units, the simple steps (the weight changes) will occur on the three half-note beats, but the additional actions divide these beats to the quarter-note level. The rhythmic stresses in the basic courante step-patterns occur on the first and third half-note beats, just as they do in the fundamental music pattern: ♪ | ♩. ♪♪♩. ♪ |

The more complex rhythmic characteristic of the courante is a constant interplay of duple and triple elements. The basic one-and-a-half unit step-pattern of *coupé–demi-coupé (jeté)* provides a total of three single steps per measure, yet each unit is danced in duple time:

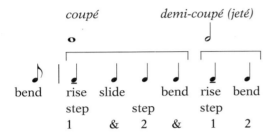

Occasionally the half unit will be placed first:

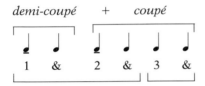

Frequently two whole step-units are used in a measure giving a double beat, while the execution of the units is in triple-meter:

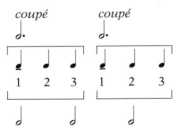

As has been shown, the rhythm of each of the above step-patterns has its musical equivalent. These do not, however, always occur simultaneously, the most common juxtaposition being:

Writing twenty-five years after Feuillet, Rameau (1725) describes the courante steps differently. According to him, the last single step in a measure (the half unit), and the *pas coupé* in the following measure (the whole unit), combine to make a *pas de courante*. The performance, the rhythmic values, and the notation of the steps are unaltered.

[*See also* Ballet Technique, History of, *article on* French Court Dance.]

BIBLIOGRAPHY
Arbeau, Thoinot. *Orchesography* (1589). Translated by Mary Stewart Evans. New York, 1948.
Collins, Michael B. "The Performance of Coloration, Sesquialtera, and Hemiola, 1450–1750." Ph.D. diss., Stanford University, 1963.
Davies, Sir John. *Orchestra Or a Poeme of Dauncing* (1596). London, 1945.
Feuillet, Raoul-Auger. *Chorégraphie, ou L'art de décrire la danse.* Paris, 1700. Translated by John Weaver as *Orchesography, or, The Art of Dancing.* London, 1706.
Hilton, Wendy. "A Dance for Kings: The Seventeenth-Century French Courante." *Early Music* (April 1977).
Lauze, François de. *Apologie de la danse, 1623: A Treatise of Instruction in Dancing and Deportment.* Translated by Joan Wildeblood. London, 1952.
Mersenne, Marin. *Harmonie universelle.* Book 2. Paris, 1636.
Morley, Thomas. *A Plaine and Easie Introduction to Practicall Musicke.* London, 1597.
Negri, Cesare. *Le gratie d'amore* (1602). Bologna, 1969.
Rameau, Pierre. *Le maître à danser.* Paris, 1725. Translated by Cyril W. Beaumont as *The Dancing Master.* London, 1931.
Sachs, Curt. *Rhythm and Tempo.* New York, 1953.
Taubert, Gottfried. *Rechtschaffener Tantzmeister, oder Gründliche Erklärung der frantzösischen Tantz-Kunst.* Leipzig, 1717.

WENDY HILTON

COURT DANCE. *For court dance traditions in western Europe, see* Ballet Technique, History of, *article on* French Court Dance; *and* Social Dance, *article on* Court and Social Dance before 1800. *For similar traditions in Japan, see* Bugaku; Gagaku; *and* Japan, *overview article. See also* Cambodia; China, *overview article*; Ghana; Indonesia, *article on* Javanese Dance Traditions; Korea, *overview article*; Malaysia; Okinawa; *and* Taiwan.

CRACOVIENNE, LA. *See the entry on the Elssler sisters.*

CRAGUN, RICHARD (Richard Allan Cragun; born 5 October 1944 in Sacramento, California), American ballet dancer, active in Germany. As a boy, Richard Cragun was inspired by watching the film musicals of Gene Kelly and Donald O'Connor. Determined to emulate these engaging performers, he took tap dance lessons with Jean Lucile and ballet classes with Barbara Briggs in his hometown of Sacramento. As a teenager, he began to realize the expressive possibilities of ballet, and he continued his dance training at the Banff School of Fine Arts in Canada, where he studied with Betty Farrally and Gweneth Lloyd, and at the Royal Ballet School in London, where his teachers were Errol Addison and Harold Turner. Thereafter he spent a year polishing his technique in private classes with Vera Volkova in Copenhagen.

Engaged as a corps de ballet member by John Cranko in Stuttgart in 1962, when he was barely eighteen years old, Cragun quickly progressed to soloist status. Soon after his appointment as principal dancer in 1965, he began his legendary partnership with ballerina Marcia Haydée. With the Stuttgart Ballet, where he remained throughout his performing career, Cragun danced in most of the company's major productions and enjoyed great popularity with German audiences. Thanks to the company's tours abroad and to frequent guest appearances with other ballet companies, he also achieved a formidable reputation as an international star. In addition to the Stuttgart Ballet and other leading companies in Germany, he danced with major companies in the United States, the United Kingdom, Belgium, Denmark, the Netherlands, Canada, Austria, Sweden, Japan, and Italy.

During his many years as principal dancer of the Stuttgart Ballet, Cragun created numerous roles made especially for him by John Cranko. Notable among them were leading parts in *L'Estro Armonico* (1963), *Opus 1* (1965), *Présence* (1968), *The Taming of the Shrew* (1969), *Brouillards* and *Poème de l'Extase* (both, 1970), *Carmen* (1971), *Initialen R.B.M.E.* (1972), and *Traces* (1973). During the 1960s and 1970s, he also created roles in Peter Wright's *The Mirror Walkers* (1963) and *Namouna* (1967), Kenneth MacMillan's *Das Lied von der Erde* (1965) and *My Brother, My Sisters* (1978), Glen Tetley's *Voluntaries* (1974) and *Daphnis and Chloe* (1975), John Neumeier's *The Lady of the Camellias* (1978), and William Forsythe's *Orpheus* (1979). During the 1980s and 1990s he appeared in the original casts of works by many of the leading choreographers of western Europe: Jiří Kylián's *Forgotten Land* (1981), Neumeier's *A Streetcar Named Desire* (1983), Maurice Béjart's *Operette* (1985), Heinz Spoerli's *Abschied* (1985), Norbert Vesak's *Death in Venice* (1986), Mats Ek's *Like Antigone* (1988), Renato Zanella's *Stati d'Animo* (1991) and *Man in the Shadows* (1992), David Bintley's *Edward II* (1995), and Roberto de Oliveira's *The Last Poem* (1996), among others.

A big, handsome man, with a powerful physique, and a dancer of dazzling virtuosity and distinct virility and sexiness, Cragun was not without a streak of humor, which showed brilliantly in his interpretation of Petrucchio in *The Taming of the Shrew* and in his portrayal of Junior in the Stuttgart revival of the Broadway musical *On Your Toes* (1990), where he finally had a chance to exhibit his tap dancing skills. He also excelled in such character roles as Carabosse in Haydée's idiosyncratic production of *The Sleeping Beauty* (1987). But it was in the wide repertory of roles in which he danced as partner to Haydée—from the classical purity of *Swan Lake* to the passionate romanticism of *Onegin*—that the range of his interpretive powers

was allowed full play. Their professional partnership endured more than thirty years, from 1965 until Cragun's retirement in 1996, making it one of the longest lasting in ballet history. [*See the entry on Haydée.*]

Cragun has been the recipient of numerous awards and honors, among them the German Order of Merit and a *Dance Magazine* award in 1985, a Golden Ballet Shoe award in 1987, and the John Cranko Medal in 1988. In his later Stuttgart years he became one of the company's ballet masters, and upon finishing his career as a dancer he was appointed artistic director of the German Opera Ballet in Berlin, starting a three-year contract with the 1996/97 season. A gifted cartoonist, Cragun has had several exhibitions of his caricatures.

BIBLIOGRAPHY

Cragun, Richard. "Zum Thema (11): Altern im Ballett." *Ballett 1985*: 44–45.

Cragun, Richard. "Sehnsucht nach Vollkommenheit." *Jahrbuch Ballet 1987*: 52–53.

Gruen, John. "Stuttgart Profiles: Marcia Haydée and Richard Cragun." *Dance Magazine* (August 1975): 66–71.

Hardy, Camille. "Richard Cragun: Prince in the Straw Hat." *Dance Magazine* (July 1985): 40–41.

Koegler, Horst. "Zum Beispiel Marcia Haydée und Richard Cragun: Über Partnerschaften im Ballett." *Jahrbuch Ballet 1987*: 45–47.

Percival, John, and Alexander Bland. *Men Dancing: Performers and Performances*. London, 1984.

Regitz, Hartmut. "Ballettmeister Richard Cragun." *Stuttgarter Ballett Annual 15/16* (1993): 29–36.

Taub, Eric. "Richard Cragun." *Ballet News* (May 1982).

Terry, Walter. *Great Male Dancers of the Ballet*. New York, 1978.

Terry, Walter, and Fritz Höver. *Richard Cragun*. Pfullingen, Germany, 1983.

HORST KOEGLER

CRAIG, GORDON (Edward Gordon Craig; born 16 January 1872 in Stevenage, England, died 29 July 1966 in Vence, France) actor, stage designer, producer, and theater theoretician. Craig was one of the foremost theater theoreticians of the twentieth century. Although he was not a choreographer, concern with dance and movement played a significant role in his practice and writings.

As the son of Ellen Terry, the principal British actress of her time, and Edward W. Godwin, architect and theater critic, Craig possessed special theatrical qualifications almost as a birthright. He gained practical experience in the theater through nine years as an actor with Henry Irving's theater company and as director-designer for the Purcell Operatic Society; he became knowledgeable in the other arts by virtue of friendships with the painters William Rothenstein and James Pryde, the musician Martin Fallas Shaw, the writer Max Beerbohm, and the American dancer Isadora Duncan. His growing intimacy with these other art forms contributed to his becoming a prophet of the New Movement in the theater.

In his productions for the Operatic Society, Craig swept away the tradition of historical-archaeologically accurate stage pictures. He replaced these visual trappings with simplicity in all elements—settings, costumes, lighting, staging, and choreography—placing primary emphasis on the emotion and mood of the work to create a unity of expression.

Craig's unflagging curiosity led him to study human movement, which motivated him to expect a director not only to plot floor positions, but also to write incidental music and to create choreography. He had already taken on these tasks in his operatic productions and did so again for the celebration of Ellen Terry's golden stage jubilee in 1906.

His early investigation of human movement was set aside for an opportunity to work in Germany. Within a few months of his arrival there, he met Isadora Duncan. Craig saw in Duncan's work a manifestation of his nebulous ideas about the theatrical potential of the human figure and came to yearn for a return to nature, as did Eleanora Duse and Konstantin Stanislavsky in their work. He came to feel, as Duncan clearly demonstrated in her art, that the embodiment of all theater lay in ancient Greece, where movement, dress, and even lighting stemmed from the natural. He felt further that Greek scene building was the ideal background for the play of light and shadow across the stage, along with the movement of the actors and the dancing of the chorus. All this led to Craig's revolt against the trappings and affectations of turn-of-the-century acting. Craig urged the actor of the future to create his art "Out of ACTION, SCENE, and VOICE. . . . And when I say *action*, I mean both gesture and dancing, the prose and poetry of action. When I say *scene*, I mean all which comes before the eye. . . . When I say *voice*, I mean the spoken word or the word which is sung" (Craig, 1912). Today this concept is called total theater.

His liaison with Duncan led Craig deeper into the pondering of human movement. After the huge success of the Russian ballet in western Europe, he denounced classical ballet as the antithesis of natural movement. He did this in a series of antiballet articles in the periodical he founded, *The Mask,* generally considered the best magazine ever published on theater. (After the premiere of *Apollon Musagète* in 1928, however, he had the foresight to hail George Balanchine's "creative talent.")

Traveling with Duncan as her manager, Craig drew many sketches of her dancing, some of which were handsomely printed and sold in now rare portfolios during the tours.

These experiences ultimately led Craig to think of the actor's environment as another source for movement. He had seen Duncan evoke an emotional response with her art and thought he could do the same with the setting. He conceived of a nonverbal performance in which the stage floor would be divided into cubes, mirrored by a set above, with each capable of moving singly or in groups; this required a vertical stage opening for its up-and-down motion, rather than the traditional horizontal stage opening. Unfortunately, the vision never became reality because of Craig's insufficient mechanical knowledge. The only record of this vision is a group of etchings, each comparable to a motion-picture frame, that lacks the essential uniting element—motion. Much of Craig's work survives as literature and graphics, neither of which is capable of demonstrating the New Movement in the theater that he espoused.

[*See also* Scenic Design.]

BIBLIOGRAPHY

Craig, Edward. *Gordon Craig: The Story of His Life.* New York, 1968.

Craig, Gordon. *On the Art of the Theatre.* Chicago, 1912.

Innes, Christopher. *Edward Gordon Craig.* Cambridge, 1983.

Rood, Arnold. "'After the Practise, the Theory': Gordon Craig and Movement." *Theatre Research* 11.2–3 (1971).

Rood, Arnold, ed. *Gordon Craig on Movement and Dance.* London, 1977.

Splatt, Cynthia. *Isadora Duncan and Gordon Craig: The Prose and Poetry of Action.* San Francisco, 1988.

ARNOLD ROOD

CRAMÉR, IVO (Martin Ivo Frederick Carl Cramér; born 5 March 1921 in Göteborg), Swedish dancer, choreographer, and ballet director. Before founding his first dance company in 1945, Cramér worked with Birgit Cullberg and Sigurd Leeder. He founded the Swedish Dance Theater with Birgit Cullberg in 1946, an enterprise that was choreographically interesting but financially disastrous. The company toured Sweden and central Europe.

Cramér won second prize in the International Choreographic Competition in Copenhagen, 1947, sponsored by Rolf de Maré, the founder of Les Archives Internationales de la Danse, with his ballet *Biblical Pictures*, with music by Christoph Willibald Gluck and George Frideric Handel. This ballet was broadcast by BBC Television under the title *The Message*.

Cramér was ballet director in the Verde Gaio Company of Lisbon in 1948 and 1949. He subsequently made a round of guest performances and produced operas, operettas, musicals, and cabaret revues in Oslo, Göteborg, and Malmö, and with the Royal Swedish Ballet. His ballet *The Prodigal Son,* first produced for the Royal Swedish Ballet in 1957, told a familiar folktale set in the Dalecarlia region of Sweden, to music by Hugo Alfvén. It was to become a national ballet; for some time it was given as a command performance for visiting dignitaries at the opera.

In 1967, under the auspices of the Swedish Riksteatern, Cramér founded his second company, with the intention of creating a repertory based on Scandinavian folklore

CRAMÉR. The Royal Swedish Ballet's production of Cramér's folk-nationalist ballet *Den Förlorade Sonen* (The Prodigal Son; 1957). In this work, probably his most famous, Cramér reenvisioned the biblical story as a folk tale set in the Dalecarlia region of Sweden. The quotation on the backdrop is from *Luke* 15.11–12, the opening verses of the parable. (Photograph from the Dance Collection, New York Public Library for the Performing Arts.)

and history. Cramér was nominated ballet director of the Royal Swedish Ballet in 1975 and remained until 1980, when he returned to his own company.

Throughout his life Cramér has had two strong sources of inspiration for his choreography, religion and Nordic folk art. He has not expressed his own religious credo but has used images from Christian history as symbols for universal human behavior. The best-known such work is *The Lord's Prayer* (1971). The elements of its choreography are based on the sign language of the deaf; in enlarging the hand gestures to include the whole body, Cramér created a prayer in dance of extraordinary purity and sincerity that has been performed in churches all over Scandinavia. Other ballets with religious themes are *Peasant Gospel* and its latest version, *Golgotha*.

Some ballets based on Nordic folk art and history are *A Bowl of Pea Soup* and *Good Evening Beautiful Mask*. They both visualize the moments before the death of a king—that of Erik XIV by poison and that of Gustaf III, who was shot at a masquerade at the opera in Stockholm. Cramér has encouraged young Swedish choreographers to create for his company and has chosen to work with contemporary Swedish composers such as Ralph Lundsten.

Cramér created some of his most important ballets for the Court Theater in Drottningholm, some in cooperation with Mary Skeaping and others on his own. These include *Pierrot in the Park* (1982), a homage to Lambranzi; *Harlequin, Magician of Love* (1984), staged in Paris with the Paris Opera Ballet, starring Rudolf Nureyev, at the Opéra Comique; *La Dansomanie* (1985), to music by Étienne Méhule, also with the Paris Opera Ballet and Nureyev; *Nemesis* (1985) a ballet about Don Juan, to music by Ilja Cmiral; *La Fille Mal Gardée* (Nantes, France, 1989), to anonymous music found in the library of the Royal Swedish Opera; *The Fishermen*, or *The Girl from the Archipelago*, to music by Méhul; and *Harlequin's Death*. Among his most appreciated works are ballets for children—*Peter and the Wolf, Cat's Journey,* and *Girl from the Woods*.

BIBLIOGRAPHY

Cramér, Ivo, et al. *Dansens villkor.* Stockholm, 1983.
Goodwin, Noël. "Masks and Bergamasks." *Dance and Dancers* (December 1983): 33–34.
Guest, Ivor. "Ivo Cramér's *La fille mal gardée* at Nantes." *Dancing Times* (April 1989).

Sjögren, Margareta. *Skandinavisk balett.* Stockholm, 1988.
Ståhle, Anna Greta. "Dans taler med: Ivo Cramér." *Dans* (October 1975): 26–32.
Ståhle, Anna Greta. "Cramérbaletten." *Dancing Times* (August 1983): 860–861.

LULLI SVEDIN

CRANKO, JOHN (born 15 August 1927 in Rustenberg, South Africa, died 25 June 1973, en route from Philadelphia to Stuttgart), dancer, choreographer, and company director, active in South Africa, England, and Germany. After his formative years with the Sadler's Wells Ballet and the Royal Ballet, John Cranko became artistic director of the Stuttgart Ballet, which he built into one of the foremost European companies.

Cranko started ballet lessons at the age of thirteen or fourteen with Nina Runich in Johannesburg, proceeding to Marjorie Sturman, one of the city's most accomplished ballet teachers. He saw his first ballet performances when the University of Cape Town Ballet appeared for its occasional seasons in Johannesburg. Cranko became acquainted with some of the dancers, making himself useful backstage and even stepping in occasionally to replace an injured dancer. In August 1944 he enrolled at the University of Cape Town Ballet School, where he continued to appear in the company's performances. It soon became apparent that Cranko would never become a classical dancer but that he was destined to become a choreographer. His first work was set to the concert suite from Igor Stravinsky's *The Soldier's Tale* (Cape Town Ballet Club, 24 November 1945), followed in quick succession by two short pieces set to music by Eduard Grieg and Claude Debussy and by *Tritsch-Tratsch* (1946), to Johann Strauss's popular polka (op. 214), his first fully successful ballet.

Late in 1945 Cranko went to London to continue his studies at the Sadler's Wells Ballet School. There was a dearth of male dancers in postwar Britain, and Cranko was immediately invited to join the recently established Sadler's Wells Theatre Ballet, occasionally dancing as a guest with Sadler's Wells Ballet at Covent Garden. He soon began to choreograph, first in the Christmas 1946 production of Engelbert Humperdinck's opera *Hansel and Gretel* at Sadler's Wells. Encouraged by Ninette de Valois and Peggy van Praagh, he continued to choreograph opera ballets and small works for the Royal Academy of Dancing Production Club and the St. James's Ballet. As in Cape Town, *Tritsch-Tratsch* became an instant hit when he mounted it for Sadler's Wells Theatre Ballet in September 1947.

For the 1947/48 season Cranko was transferred to Sadler's Wells Ballet at Covent Garden to broaden his experience as a dancer by working with such choreographers as Léonide Massine, Frederick Ashton, and Robert Helpmann. His first major ballet was *Sea Change* (1949),

set to music by Jean Sibelius, with designs by John Piper, who became a favorite collaborator. This was followed by an extended pas de deux, *Beauty and the Beast* (1949), to music of Maurice Ravel, which he later mounted for several other companies.

The failure of his next work, *The Witch*, commissioned by Lincoln Kirstein for the New York City Ballet while the company was in London in the summer of 1950, did not deter Cranko. At the beginning of the 1950/51 season, when he was only twenty-three years old, he stopped dancing altogether and accepted an appointment as resident choreographer of Sadler's Wells Theatre Ballet. His first popular success was *Pineapple Poll* (1951), a *ballet bouffe* in the manner of Massine, set to music by Arthur Sullivan, arranged by Charles Mackerras. It was followed by the mysterious, poetic *Harlequin in April* (1951), to a commissioned score by Richard Arnell.

The breadth of Cranko's tastes as well as his ability to work in different styles can be seen in a list of his next ballets: *Bonne-Bouche*, another broad comedy ballet, with music by Arthur Oldham (1952, Sadler's Wells Theatre

CRANKO. John Cranko as the Devil in his first ballet, *The Soldier's Tale* (1945), presented by the Cape Town Ballet Club. (Photograph by Anne Fischer; from the Dance Collection, New York Public Library for the Performing Arts.)

Ballet); *The Shadow* (1953, Sadler's Wells Ballet) and *The Lady and the Fool* (1954, Sadler's Wells Theatre Ballet), two Romantic ballets with music by Ernő Dohnányi and Giuseppe Verdi, respectively; *La Belle Hélène*, based on Jacques Offenbach's operetta (1955, Ballet de l'Opéra de Paris); *The Prince of the Pagodas*, his first full-length ballet, with a score by Benjamin Britten and designs by Piper (1957, Royal Ballet); his realistic and influential version of Sergei Prokofiev's *Romeo and Juliet* (1958, La Scala Ballet, Milan, subsequently revived for many other companies); a stark treatment of the Greek tragedy *Antigone* with music by Mikis Theodorakis (1959, Royal Ballet); and the farcical *Sweeney Todd*, with music by Malcolm Arnold (1959, Royal Ballet Touring Section). To these must be added the two cabaret-style revues *Cranks* (1955) and *New Cranks* (1960), as well as Cranko's direction of the first production of Benjamin Britten's opera *A Midsummer Night's Dream* at the 1960 Aldeburgh Festival.

Late in 1960 Cranko was invited to stage his *Prince of the Pagodas* in Stuttgart. He found there a company run by Nicholas Beriozoff very much on the lines of the Ballet Russe de Monte Carlo, but without that company's stars. The repertory consisted of Beriozoff's routine productions of the classics and one or two ballets by Michel Fokine, plus newer ballets, mostly by Cranko. The Stuttgart Ballet had its own school, albeit a minor operation, and its dancers were somewhat better trained than those of most other companies attached to the larger German opera houses.

Cranko was appointed ballet director of the Württemberg State Theaters in Stuttgart in January 1961. Gradually he assembled his own team of collaborators, starting with Peter Wright as ballet master and second choreographer and Anne Woolliams as ballet mistress and director of the completely reorganized school. Most of Beriozoff's leading dancers left; only Ray Barra remained. Younger recruits, notably Marcia Haydée, Birgit Keil, Richard Cragun, and Egon Madsen, were trained to fill the vacancies. Cranko's *Katalyse* (The Catalyst), set to music of Dmitri Shostakovich and premiered in November 1961, was his first Stuttgart creation to remain in the repertory for several years and to be mounted for other companies.

In 1962 the company began to develop an identity of its own, with the summer Ballet Festival, when Cranko's beautiful production of *Daphnis and Chloë* was given, with Erik Bruhn and Georgina Parkinson as guest artists, and with the revival in November of his *Romeo and Juliet*, with designs by the newly discovered Jürgen Rose, which

CRANKO. A scene from *Pineapple Poll* (1951). The original cast of this Sadler's Wells Theatre Ballet production included David Poole (center) as Jasper and Elaine Fifield in the title role. Osbert Lancaster designed the sets and costumes. (Photograph by Denis de Marney; from the Dance Collection, New York Public Library for the Performing Arts.)

CRANKO. Scene from a 1979 revival of *Initialen R.B.M.E.* The title of Cranko's ballet refers to the initials of the first names of the four principals of the original 1972 Stuttgart Ballet production: Richard Cragun, Birgit Keil, Marcia Haydée, and Egon Madsen. Here, Haydée's role is danced by Jean Allenby. (Photograph from the Dance Collection, New York Public Library for the Performing Arts.)

Second Piano Concerto in B-flat) and newly envisaged versions of such classics as *Swan Lake, The Nutcracker,* and *The Firebird.* (The title of *Initialen R.B.M.E.* refers to the initials of the given names of his quartet of principals: *R.* for Richard Cragun, *B.* for Birgil Keil, *M.* for Marcia Haydée, and *E.* for Egon Madsen.) What seemed closest to his heart, however, were his full-scale treatments of works from world theater and literature, such as *Romeo and Juliet* (1958, 1962), *Onegin* (1965, 1967), *The Taming of the Shrew* (1969), and *Carmen* (1971). At the time of his death, Cranko was working on an ambitious production of *Tristan,* set to music by Hans Werner Henze.

As a creator of steps, gestures, and patterns, Cranko proceeded rather eclectically; among his artistic forebears, he was closer to Massine than to Balanchine. If his choreography showed any personal style, it was in his unashamedly spectacular lifts—he clearly had learned a lesson from the Bolshoi. By the time of his death in June 1973, he had built the Stuttgart Ballet into one of the most important companies not only in Germany but in Europe as a whole, with a varied team of principal dancers, headed by Marcia Haydée, and a repertory that displayed their individual gifts. He also left the flourishing John

were to become a company signature. The company's first appearances abroad were at the Edinburgh Festival in 1963 and at the Festival of Two Worlds in Spoleto in 1965. However, the seal on its international status was set by its first New York season in 1969, chiefly through the advocacy of Clive Barnes, dance critic of the *New York Times.* The company visited the USSR in 1971 and London in 1974.

Cranko was equally gifted as artistic director, choreographer, ballet master, teacher, and educator of the public, for whom he analyzed new works at special matinées. He developed new choreographers from within the company, among them Ashley Killar, Gray Veredon, Jiří Kylián, and John Neumeier. He became a kind of paterfamilias to his dancers, whose group loyalty survived his death and was still to be found among the second generation. As a choreographer Cranko developed in Stuttgart a quite remarkable versatility, an absolute necessity at a theater that could only occasionally afford guest choreographers such as George Balanchine or Kenneth MacMillan (who created for the company two of his most durable works, *Las Hermanas* and *Das Lied von der Erde*).

Cranko was a master of many kinds of ballet, from abstract works such as *L'Estro Armonico* (1963, to music by Antonio Vivaldi) and *Concerto for Flute and Harp* (1966, to music by W. A. Mozart) to humorous pieces like *Jeu de Cartes* (1965, to the Stravinsky score) and *Salade* (1968, to music by Darius Milhaud), from poetic ballets such as *Opus 1* (1965, to music by Anton Webern) and *Brouillards* (1970, to music by Debussy) to a large-scale symphonic work such as *Initialen R.B.M.E.* (1972, set to Brahms's

CRANKO. Marcia Haydée and Richard Cragun, popular stars of the Stuttgart Ballet, in a 1979 performance of Cranko's 1958 *Romeo and Juliet.* (Photograph from the Dance Collection, New York Public Library for the Performing Arts.)

Cranko Ballet School, the first one in Germany to include a boarding school. In addition, he had been chief choreographer of the Munich State Opera Ballet from 1967 to 1971.

Cranko's ballets, particularly his full-length pieces, have been mounted for companies all over the world, ten years after his death they had become an integral part of the international repertory. That his company continued to thrive, with dancers who had never known him, and to produce its own new choreographers such as William Forsythe and Uwe Scholz, proves that the vitality with which Cranko endowed the Stuttgart Ballet is undiminished.

The John Cranko Gesellschaft was established in 1975 to preserve and further Cranko's legacy. It awards an annual prize, the John Cranko Medal, to a person who has rendered outstanding service in maintaining his works. Recipients include Anne Woolliams (1975), Marcia Haydée (1976), Jürgen Rose (1978), Georgette Tsinguirides (1980), Egon Madsen (1981), Alan Beale (1983), Birgit Keil (1985), Heinz Clauss (1987), Richard Cragun (1988), Fritz Höver (1989), Alexander Ursuliak (1991), and Reid Anderson (1995). The society has published the *Stuttgarter Ballett Annual* since 1978.

[*See also* Stuttgart Ballet *and the entries on Cragun, Haydée, Keil, and Madsen.*]

BIBLIOGRAPHY

Cranko, John. *Über den Tanz: Gespräche mit Walter Erich.* Frankfurt am Main, 1974.
Croce, Arlene. "John Cranko (1927–1973)." *Ballet Review* 4.5 (1973): 101.
Koegler, Horst. *Stuttgart Ballet.* London, 1978.
Percival, John. *Theatre in My Blood: A Biography of John Cranko.* London, 1983.
Royal Ballet, London. *A Tribute to John Cranko.* Souvenir program, Sadler's Wells Theatre, 3 October 1973.
Woodcock, Sarah C. *The Salder's Wells Royal Ballet.* London, 1991.

HORST KOEGLER

CRASKE, MARGARET (born 26 November 1892 in Norfolk, England, died 18 February 1990 in Myrtle Beach, South Carolina), dancer, choreographer, teacher, writer, and a leading exponent of the Cecchetti method. Craske was coauthor of two of the three authoritative textbooks that codified the Cecchetti technique: *The Theory and Practice of Allegro in Classical Ballet* and *The Theory and Practice of Advanced Allegro.* Her own teaching career spanned more than sixty years.

Craske studied with Enrico Cecchetti for five years after he opened his London school, from 1918 to 1923. Concurrently, she was one of the first English dancers to appear with Serge Diaghilev's Ballets Russes, of which she was a member for two seasons. By 1924 she had opened the Craske-Ryan School in London. During the 1920s, Craske

choreographed works for London shows and for the Carl Rosa Opera Company, where she was also ballet mistress. She performed in music halls with Ninette de Valois and in 1928 was sent to South Africa to further propagate the Cecchetti method of ballet pedagogy. She taught in London throughout the 1930s, attracting such notables as Antony Tudor, Anton Dolin, Frederick Ashton, Peggy van Praagh, Mary Skeaping, Keith Lester, and the young Margot Fonteyn. In the early 1930s, Craske was also a guest instructor at the Vic-Wells Ballet.

Following a seven-year absence from dance during a residence in India (1939–1946), where she had become a disciple of the guru Meher Baba, Craske returned to England. Throughout the rest of her life she believed in two masters: Baba, her spiritual master, and Cecchetti, her dance master.

In 1946, Craske accepted an invitation to the United States to become ballet mistress for Ballet Theatre. Shortly thereafter, she became a member of the faculty of Jacob's Pillow Dance Festival, where she taught for many summers. In 1950, when Ballet Theatre and the Metropolitan Opera Ballet formed a joint school, Craske became its assistant director; she remained on the faculty until the school was disbanded in 1968. She also served on the dance faculty of the Juilliard School of Music, New York, during the same period.

In 1968, following the closing of the Metropolitan Opera Ballet School, Robert Ossorio chose Craske to become director of his newly formed Manhattan School of Dance. When that school closed in 1983, she joined the faculty of the Ballet School NY, where she taught until her retirement in 1986.

Throughout her teaching career, Craske dedicated herself to expounding the principles of the Cecchetti method; yet, her classes were stamped with the mark of her own personality. Indeed, in the latter part of her career, she altered certain aspects of the traditional Cecchetti class. Although she continued to teach the prescribed Cecchetti *enchaînements*, she relaxed the custom of practicing a fixed set of them for each day of the week. Similarly, she discarded the rule of beginning all *enchaînements* on the left one week and on the right the next. To her children's classes she added a set of warm-up exercises on the floor—as a result of having observed European therapeutic exercises. Another unique feature of a Craske ballet class was the absence of or reduction in the number of mirrors. She urged her pupils to feel a correct movement rather than merely to see it.

Confronted by those who treated dance as an Olympic or commercial competition, Craske asserted other values. Her allegro training fostered *ballon* rather than athleticism, and she always insisted on "the pause in the air" at the top of a high jump. In her adagio work, proper placement was never to be sacrificed to achieve higher leg extensions or more extreme turnout. As to the arms, head, and upper body, Craske strove for simplicity and elegance in *port de bras* and for an unaffected lyricism of *épaulement*.

Possessed of an acute intellect (and delightful wit), Craske was able to teach ballet analytically, as well as of only by demonstration, imitation, and repetition. Nevertheless, she urged that all intellectualization of dance should finally be discarded in performance and that dancers and audience alike should experience dance as flow and feeling, not as a series of concepts.

Because Craske perpetuated the *pas* and *enchaînements* of Cecchetti (who, through Giovanni Lepri, Carlo Blasis, Pierre Gardel, and Jean Dauberval, formed part of an unbroken chain to eighteenth-century ballet), observing or participating in her classes was, in fact, an exercise in the historical continuation of choreography. Because of this, and because of her analytical teaching style, choreographers as well as dancers flocked to her classes.

The great dramatic ballerinas and *danseurs* Sallie Wilson, Melissa Hayden, Nora Kaye, Bruce Marks, and Hugh Laing were Craske's students, as was the distinguished modern dancer Carolyn Brown. The list of choreographers who attended her classes is especially impressive. In addition to Tudor and Ashton in England, American choreographers Paul Taylor, Agnes de Mille, Glen Tetly, Gerald Arpino, James Waring, Ron Sequoio, Pauline Koner, Viola Farber, and Janet Collins studied with and were influenced by her. In her nineties, Margaret Craske lived at the Meher Baba Center in South Carolina and continued to advise students who journeyed there for her counsel until her death.

BIBLIOGRAPHY

Craske, Margaret, and Cyril W. Beaumont. *The Theory and Practice of Allegro in Classical Ballet (Cecchetti Method).* London, 1930.
Craske, Margaret, and Friderica Derra de Moroda. *The Theory and Practice of Advanced Allegro in Classical Ballet (Cecchetti Method).* London, 1956.
Craske, Margaret. *The Dance of Love.* Myrtle Beach, S.C., 1980.
Craske, Margaret. *Still Dancing with Love.* Myrtle Beach, S.C., 1990.
Gale, Joseph. "Margaret Craske." In Gale's *Behind Barres: The Mystique of Masterly Teaching.* New York, 1980.
Greskovic, Robert. "Ballet, Barre, and Center, on the Bookshelf." *Ballet Review* 6.2 (1977–1978): 1–56.
VanderWerf, Klasina. "Uncompromising Champion: Teacher Margaret Craske." *Ballet News* 4 (January 1983): 28–31.

GLORIA B. STRAUSS

CRETE. [*To survey dance traditions of Crete, this entry comprises two articles. The first article focuses on dance in ancient Crete; the second on dance in modern Crete.*]

Dance in Ancient Crete

Homeric legend pictures Crete as a populous and prosperous island, encompassing nearly one hundred towns inhabited by peoples speaking many languages. The island's geographic location allowed for the absorption of cultural influences from the older civilizations of Egypt, Mesopotamia, Syria, and Asia Minor, which the Cretans adapted to their own purposes with remarkable ingenuity. In turn they transmitted these influences to Greece and the European mainland. Indeed, the island nurtured the development of the first major civilization in Europe more than two thousand years before the Christian era.

Among the important legacies Crete left to ancient Greece was the legend of Minos, the powerful ruler of Knossos who avenged the death of his son at the hands of King Aegeus by making war against the Athenians. Victorious, Minos demanded the sacrificial tribute of seven Athenian youths and seven Athenian maidens. The victims were let loose in a labyrinth designed by Daedalus and there devoured by the Minotaur, a monster half man and half bull. In the early seventeenth century, George Sandys was the first British traveler to enter the legendary labyrinth, which he correctly understood to be nothing more than a quarry at the foot of Mount Ida. His account describes a folk dance that could well have survived from antiquity:

> The Country people do dance with their Bows ready bent on their arms, their Quivers hanging on their backs, and their swords by their sides, imitating therein their Ancestors (a custom also among the Lacedemonians) and called by them *Pyrricha:* and, as of old, so used they to sing in their dancings, and reply to one another.

This combination of singing and dancing seems characteristic of performance forms in Crete and in ancient Greece as well. J. D. S. Pendlebury cites another example that shows the persistence of this tradition. Pendlebury first quotes the ancient *Song of Hybrias the Cretan*, which may well date from the sixth century BCE or even earlier. Presumably dancing accompanied the performance of the poem, declaimed by a Cretan aristocrat:

> My spear and my sword and that fine shield which guards my skin are my great wealth. For I plough with this, I reap with this, I tread the sweet wine from the vine with this, I am called master of the serfs with this. But those who dare not hold the spear and sword and that fine shield to guard their skin, all fall and kiss my knee calling me master and great lord.
>
> (Pendlebury, 1939)

Pendlebury also refers to a five-step dance called the *pentozalīs*, popular in Crete at the time of his investigations. The words accompanying the dance recall the ancient poem:

> He who is not a man of taste and skilled in arms has no right to tread the soil of Crete,
> He who is not a man of taste had much better die,
> Why should he clutter up the earth by merely living?

An intermediate stage in the survival of this singing and dancing tradition is the epic poem *Erotokritos*, composed in the Cretan dialect by Vincent Cornero around 1645. More than ten thousand lines long, the epic blends romance and heroism and has become a popular performance piece.

It seems that dancing and singing played an important role in the ritual and religious practices of ancient Crete. Indeed, the parallels among Cretan, Greek, and Near Eastern cults are too close to be coincidental. Although no one can prove that a single cult pattern was transmitted from the Near East to the Aegean, we cannot dismiss the possibility that such a pattern existed. Evidence suggests that the Minoan-Mycenaean variation on this pattern involved vegetation worship, a great goddess, a young male cult figure, animal daemons, and, significantly, ecstatic dancing. This ecstatic element focused attention on a male divinity who took mortal form—who was born, matured, and died—and who also appeared in the form of a bull.

The unanswerable scholarly question remains whether or not Minoan religion was monotheistic. Clearly, an anthropomorphic female divinity played a central role in Minoan religion. A rich variety of associations accompanied representations of this great goddess: animals, birds, and snakes; the baetylic pillar and sacred tree; the poppy and the lily; the sword and the double ax. She had male and female attendants and exercised dominion over mountain, earth, sky, and sea, over life and death. She was both household goddess and vegetation goddess, both mother and maid. A huntress and goddess of sports, she was armed and, significantly, presided over ritual dances.

The Curetes of Crete were initiated young men who guarded the infant male divinity and attended the great female divinity. According to Hesiod, they were lovers of sport and dancing. Demetrios of Skepsis considered it likely that the Curetes were also known as Corybantes and were chosen to perform the war dance associated with the rituals of the great goddess. The Corybantes were so-called because they walked with a butting of their heads, as if dancing. Homer called them *bētarmones* ("dancers"), which one commentator has translated as "those who go in harmony."

The labyrinth at Knossos and the emblem of the bull also were associated with rituals and dancing. Because the sun was conceived as a bull, it is not unlikely that the labyrinth was considered a solar symbol and that its arena or orchestra became the performance space for a mimetic dance in which a dancer masqueraded as a bull and represented the movement of the sun. This constellation of associations also underlay bull-leaping, a combination of acrobatics and dancing that is naturalistically represented in Cretan art. For example, a fresco panel from the Palace of Minos shows a bull-leaping scene in three phases. As the bull charges, an athlete grasps its horns and somersaults over its back, landing on his feet behind the bull. This sport probably had religious significance. During antiquity the bull—a symbol of virility, power, and fertility—became the focal point for rituals from India to the Mediterranean.

Homer makes a clear connection between the dancing tradition associated with the labyrinth and the design of Achilles' famous shield wrought by Hephaistos. According to Homer, Hephaistos depicted on the shield a dancing floor much like that which Daedalus once fashioned in Knossos for Ariadne, one of King Minos's daughters. Courting youths and maidens, holding one another's wrists, danced on this floor. The maidens wore dresses of fine linen and lovely garlands, the youths well-woven tunics with daggers attached to their silver belts. Now they ran "ever so lightly with cunning feet, as when a potter sits gripping his wheel with his hands and tries it out to see how it spins." Now again they ran in lines opposite to each other. A big crowd stood around enjoying the passionate dance, and two spinning tumblers set the rhythm of the performance.

An early commentator interpreted this passage as a sort of mythological allegory: after rescuing the Athenian youths and maidens and escaping from the labyrinth, Theseus wove a circling dance for the gods that resembled his own entrance to and exit from the labyrinth. Later commentators have noted that Homer's literary devices may imitate the movement of the dancers. The simile of the potter's wheel turning now this way, now that, imitates the labyrinthine progress of the lines of dancers, rushing forward and then doubling back, following the intricate course marked on the dance floor.

Plutarch associated a dance performed on Delos with this tradition of the labyrinth. According to his account, Theseus stopped at Delos on his way home from Crete. There he sacrificed to the gods, dedicated the image of Aphrodite that he had received from Ariadne, and performed with the young men a dance that apparently survived among the Delians in Plutarch's time. The mazelike pattern of the dance imitated the circuits and exits of the labyrinth. In Greek the dance was called *geranos*, which means "crane," in the sense both of the bird and of a mechanism for grinding grain or for lifting weights, especially in the theater. Many scholars have interpreted the dance as imitative of the movements of the bird, but Lillian Lawler has argued that *geranos* derives from the root *ger* ("to wander"). Her interpretation underscores the labyrinthine spatial pattern of the dance noted by Plutarch.

Lucian summarized the variety of Cretan dance themes. These included the stories of Europa, Pasiphaë, the two bulls, the Labyrinth, Ariadne, Phaedra, Androgeus, Daedalus, Icarus, Glaucus, the seer craft of Polyeidus, and the bronze sentinal Talos.

The civilization of ancient Crete developed before the advent of historical writing. Only fairly recently have scholars revealed its distinctive culture—and its contribution to the repertoire of world dancing—as tenacious survivals from the past.

[*For related discussion, see* Greece, *article on* Dance in Ancient Greece. *See also* Labyrinth Dances *and* Pyrrhic.]

BIBLIOGRAPHY

Davaras, Costis. *Guide to Cretan Antiquities*. Park Ridge, N.J., 1976.
Lawler, Lillian B. "The *Geranos* Dance." *Transactions and Proceedings of the American Philological Association* 77 (1946): 112–130.
Lawler, Lillian B. "The Dance in Ancient Crete." In *Studies Presented to David Moore Robinson on His Seventieth Birthday*, vol. 1, edited by George E. Mylonas. St. Louis, 1951.
Mandalaki-Spanou, Stella. "The Dance in Ancient Crete." Paper presented at the Fifth International Conference on Dance Research: Dance and Ancient Greece, Athens, 4–8 September 1991.
Pendlebury, J. D. S. *The Archaeology of Crete*. London, 1939.
Petrides, Ted. *Greek Dances*. Athens, 1975.
Sparti, Barbara. "Report on the Fifth International Conference on Dance Research: Dance and Ancient Greece." *Dance Research Journal* 24 (Spring 1992): 52–54.
Willetts, R. F. *Cretan Cults and Festivals*. New York, 1962.
Willetts, R. F. *The Civilization of Ancient Crete*. London, 1977.

R. F. WILLETTS

Dance in Modern Crete

Traditional dance thrives in modern Crete and among Cretan emigrant communities. Of about fifteen known dances, five make up today's active repertory—the *syrtós*, *sighanós*, *pentozalís*, *soústa*, and a dance known variously as *maleviziótikos*, *kastrinós*, or *pidihtós*. Currently, revivalists are reintroducing a number of the others.

Sentiments. Cretans believe that being and feeling Cretan is inextricably tied to the act of dancing. They talk passionately about their dances and travel far at the prospect of good dancing. Cretan emigrants are particularly sensitive to the significance of dance to their identity. There are many traditional performance troupes both in Crete and abroad. Sentiments about specific dances evolve and change, but the *syrtós*, regarded as the most delicate and beautiful of Cretan dances, is especially well loved; the *pentozalís*, especially in the 1970s, was held in something akin to awe; and the *maleviziótikos*, once declared the king of Cretan dances, became, in the 1980s, the favored dance among the younger generation.

Social and Cultural Context. As in the rest of Greece, dance is a feature of feast days, during Carnival, at civic festivals, at family celebrations such as weddings and baptisms, at balls, and in coffeehouses and places of entertainment. The relationship of dance to social and cul-

tural values can be sensed. For example, the *soústa* contains a tension between sensuality and conformity in the dancer's limited self-expression and the potential for loss of reputation (Coros, 1983). In the *syrtós*, cultural and personal imperatives give the dancer the responsibility to express cultural norms but also the potential to transcend them in a greater range of self-expression and authenticity (Coros, 1992).

Choreography and Protocol. The common Greek form prevails: a line of dancers is linked into a near-circle; the dancers hold each other's hands (in the *syrtós* and *maleviziótikos*) or shoulders (in the *sighanós* and *pentozalís*) and move counterclockwise around the dance space. In the *soústa*, male-female couples are scattered randomly about the dance area.

A protocol for dancing—grounded in concepts of social identity, gender, and interrelationships—determines when one dances, where one's position is in the dance line, and when one moves to the leader's position. Preferred practice is for one *paréa* (group with various relationships) to occupy the dance space for the duration of their dancing time; otherwise, as is the general practice, many *paréas* occupy the dance space together. Within a *paréa*, the leader of the line and the second person are the most active. The rest of the dancers perform basic patterns occasionally interspersed with variations; especially at the end of the dance line, they may even walk. Eventually, the leaders retire to another place in the line or to the end as others move up.

Movement Behavior. Supporting a variety of regional movement styles and dance-pattern variations is an underlying, invariable structure for all dances. The structure of the *syrtós* uses sixteen musical beats; the *pentozalís*, eight; the *soústa*, four; the *maleviziótikos*, twelve; and the *sighanós*, either six or eight. The basic posture is upright with the torso moving as a single unit. Departing from this posture are two distinguishing male "breakaway" torso positions—the vertical curve with shoulders rolled forward and head lowered, with arms outstretched and often elevated; the virtuosic figure, *talími*, a combination of leg and foot slaps, jumps, and corkscrewlike sideways leaps.

Desired and admired movement qualities recognizable as distinctly Cretan are clarity of articulation, with precise placement of the leg and foot in space and time, outstanding in the *tsákisma* (sharp and brisk rearward movement of the foot); poise and smoothness in a small yet perceptible up-and-down movement flow, achieved by the touted "dancing on toes" and slight bending of the knees; a general sense of subtle understatement accomplished by restraint and economy of movement, even in the man's *talími*; and a playing around with the rhythmic beat so as to not land a step on the mark. Important also is the common Greek expectation of larger and more energetic movement from men than from women. Despite these generalizations, each dance has its own prevailing movement quality, a description of which may be helped along by effort concepts of weight, tension, and time (appearing in parentheses), as in the *soústa*, a supple springiness (light, free, slow); *pentozalîs*, robust and forceful (strong, bound, quick); *maleviziótikos*, a vigorous spiritedness (light, bound, quick); *syrtós*, smoothly, gently and carefully stepped (neutral, free, slow); and *sighanós*, smoothly and forcefully stepped (strong, free, slow). Further, movement qualities of any dance may appear and provide accent in another dance, particularly in the leader's dancing.

Music is used to provide the external force for all dances, which continue through a consecutive repetition of basic patterns. The improvisatory character is the internal force that keeps them continuing. While members of the dance line execute basic patterns, each leader in turn improvises a sequence of basic patterns, stock variations, and innovative figures that build to a climax: a man to a *talími*, a woman to the currently popular turns. *Soústa* couples improvise using stock phrases and little innovation.

Change over Time. Even though the underlying structures do not change, the general feel and look of dance does. Each generation has its own preferences in dance and movement. Technical skill increases owing to formal teaching, and new variations develop. Troupe choreography tends to straighten out the near-circle, while set sequences of variations somewhat inhibit improvisation. The musical style becomes contemporary. Nevertheless, old and new appear at a dance event and sometimes even together in the dance space.

Music. Live music is a necessary component of an event; so musicians travel from event to event around the globe. The preferred musical ensemble comprises two *laouta* (lutes) and a *lyra* (pear-shaped fiddle) or, especially in the prefectures of Hania, eastern Irakleion, and Lassithi, a violin. Since the 1970s and 1980s, revivalists have included the obsolete *askomadoúra* (bagpipe), *sfirochábiolo* (flute), *mantolíno* (mandolin), and *tamboúrlo* (drum). The musical texture for dance thickens when musicians sing *mantinádes* (rhymed couplets) and contemporary and traditional *rizítika* songs; the latter are sometimes followed by a *syrtós* or *pentozalîs*. The music of the *syrtós* and *sighanós* appears to be the most open to innovation.

Dress. At dance events almost everyone wears contemporary Western fashion, although usually a few men wear traditional attire. Performance troupes, however, use traditional dress that dates from the nineteenth century. The most prevalent costumes are the woman's *sártza* from central Crete (white chemise and baggy ankle-length trousers, dark jacket with gold embroidery, red pleated backskirt, white apron with woven designs and tassels, woven red sash, and fringed red headscarf), and the man's *vráka* (dark baggy breeches, black or white shirt, vest, jacket and cape, woven red and blue sash, black net headscarf with fringe that lies on the forehead, and black or white boots). Silver-sheathed knives and chains embellish both *sártza* and *vráka*. Less often seen is the woman's town dress from western Crete (white chemise, dark jacket with gold embroidery, long brocade skirt that is usually crimson, and either a red soft fez with a long tassel or a silk kerchief on the head), and the man's *kilóta* (riding breeches, black shirt, black net headscarf with fringe, and black boots).

BIBLIOGRAPHY

Anoyanakis, Fivos. *Greek Popular Musical Instruments.* 2d ed. Athens, 1991.

Benaki, Antony E., ed. *Hellenic National Costumes.* 2 vols. Athens, 1948–1954.

Coros, Mary. "Sousta." *Reflections: Essays in Phenomenology* 4 (Summer-Fall 1983).

Coros, Mary. "A Crossing from Dance into Language." Ph.D. diss., University of Toronto, 1992.

Dell, Cecily. *A Primer for Movement Description Using Effort-Shape and Supplementary Concepts.* New York, Dance Notation Bureau, Inc., 1970.

Frangaki, Evangelia K. *Laiki texni tis kritis.* 2 vols. Athens, 1960.

Hatzidakis, Yiorgios I. *Kritiki mousiki: Istoria, mousika sistimata, tragoudia kai hori.* Athens, 1958.

Kaloyanides, Michael G. "The Music of Cretan Dances." Ph.D. diss., Wesleyan University, 1975.

Papantoniou, Ioanna. *Ellenikes phoresies.* 2 vols. Nauplia, Greece, 1973–1974.

MARY COROS

CROATIA. *See* Yugoslavia.

CROFTON, KATHLEEN (born 1902 in Fyzabad, India, died 30 November 1979 in Rochester, New York), dancer, teacher, director, and critic. A dedicated dancer and highly individual teacher, Crofton was trained entirely in the Russian style, by Nikolai Legat, Olga Preobrajenska, and Laurent Novikoff. She danced in Anna Pavlova's company from 1923 to 1928 and for Novikoff at the Chicago Lyric Opera Ballet from 1929 to 1931. She toured Europe with Bronislava Nijinska's company in 1932 and 1933, traveled across Australia with the Levitov-Dandré Russian Ballet in 1934, and performed as a soloist in the Markova-Dolin Ballet from 1935 to 1937. Her important work still lay ahead, however.

Having retired from dancing in 1938, Crofton returned to ballet as a teacher in 1950, encouraged by Alicia Markova and by an intensive study period with Preobrajenska. Remembered now and respected then for her perceptive comments in the classroom, she taught in her own London studio and as a frequent guest at the Royal Ballet School until 1966, when she accepted Markova's invitation to teach at the Metropolitan Opera Ballet in New York City. Crofton was also London dance critic for the *Christian Science Monitor* from 1958 to 1966.

In 1967 she moved to Buffalo, New York, where she established a small company, the Niagara Frontier Ballet, with an astonishing repertory that included Nijinska's revival of her own *Chopin Piano Concerto,* Markova's staging of *Le Carnaval,* David Lichine's *Graduation Ball,* and bits of the Pavlova repertory culled from Crofton's exceptional memory. After touring Europe unsuccessfully as the American Classical Ballet, the company suffered a fire in Buffalo and disbanded. Undaunted, Crofton continued to teach—with the San Francisco Ballet and the Maryland Ballet in Baltimore in 1974—before settling in Rochester. Determined to build another classical company, she held a fund-raising gala for the prospective Ballet Concordia in the fall of 1979 but died at her desk several weeks later.

BIBLIOGRAPHY
Obituary. *The Dancing Times* (January 1980): 251.

BARBARA NEWMAN

CUBA. [*To survey the dance traditions of Cuba, this entry comprises four articles:*

> Folk, Ritual, and Social Dance
> Ballet before 1959
> Ballet since 1959
> Modern Dance

The first article explores Iberian and African influences on folk and ritual dance and the assimilation of Cuban popular dance into urban Western culture; the three companion articles focus on the history of theatrical dance. For further general discussion, see Caribbean Region.]

Folk, Ritual, and Social Dance

The Republic of Cuba is the largest island in the West Indies, about 45,000 square miles (115,000 square kilometers), with some small adjacent islands. Cuba, in the Caribbean Sea, lies some ninety miles (145 kilometers) south of the Florida Keys. The island was discovered by the 1492 expedition of Christopher Columbus and colonized by Spain in 1511; it was first used as an exploration base and as a massing point for the treasure fleets that brought gold and ceremonial objects from the New World civilizations to the king. In the 1600s tobacco and sugar plantations were started. Slaves from Africa were then brought as laborers to replace the Native Americans who had lived there for thousands of years, fought the Spanish, fled, and died of epidemics in large numbers. Cuba's Ten Years' War for Independence (1868–1878) was unsuccessful, so it remained a Spanish colony, and slavery was abolished only in 1886. In 1895 a new war for independence culminated in the Spanish-American War of 1898 and the establishment of the Cuban republic that year. On 1 January 1959 Fidel Castro's Marxist government, based on agrarian reform, replaced a series of dictators. The population, some 12 million, are of Spanish *(criollos),* African, and mixed Spanish-African descent. They are mainly Roman Catholic, which is tolerated by the government.

CUBA: Folk, Ritual, and Social Dance. Dancers of the folkloric troupe Raices Profundas collectively represent the *orisha* Ochún at the Teatro Miramar, Havana. The goddess of the river, Ochún, is associated with female sensuality in the Afro-Cuban Santería religion. (Photograph © 1994 by David Garten; used by permission.)

CUBA: Folk, Ritual, and Social Dance. Four members of the company Los Pinos Nuevos represent four different *orishas*: (from left to right) Ochún, Oggun, Oyá, and Chango. The two male figures, Oggun, the *orisha* of work, and Chango, the *orisha* of thunder and lightening, are traditionally archrivals. (Photograph © 1994 by David Garten; used by permission.)

Since the mid-nineteenth century urban Western culture has assimilated Cuban popular dance, from the habanera performed in the salons of New York City in the 1860s to the conga, rumba, cha-cha, *son-montuno*, and dance-hall mambos of more recent vintage. Much of the island's culture, including some of its most popular dance forms, results from what historian Fernando Ortiz has termed "Cuban counterpoint," the interplay among Cuba's main crops—tobacco and sugar—and the Iberian and African cultural elements brought to Cuba by their respective cultivators. Perhaps the best musical example of such an interplay is the *son-montuno*. The *son* began as a couple dance in Cuba's Oriente Province, accompanied by a mix of Spanish-based folk guitars and Afro-Cuban percussion; moving west to Havana, it expanded musically and choreographically, with a marked increase in percussive elements, especially in the final *montuno* section. This dance became internationally popular in the 1930s, sometimes mistakenly called "rumba." The *son-montuno*'s synthesis of Spanish and African musical elements forms the basis of contemporary New York City salsa, whose dance elements have been derived from the mambo.

In Cuba, enclaves of Iberian or African culture developed around the separate zones of tobacco and sugar cultivation. Tobacco was grown on relatively small plots by farmers originating from Spain or from the Canary Islands, and Spanish couple dances, such as the *zapateo*, were preserved in these tobacco-growing zones.

The labor demands of the island's booming sugar economy in the early and mid-nineteenth century resulted in an accelerated slave trade with central and West Africa. Urban religious brotherhoods known as *cabildos* and concentrations of slaves of the same African ethnicity in sugar-growing areas, especially in Matanzas Province, helped to conserve a great body of religious and secular dance from four African traditions—the Yoruba and the Dahomean from West Africa, the Ejagham from southeastern Nigeria and Cameroon, and the Kongo-Angola from west-central Africa. The polytheistic Yoruba and Fon (Dahomean) religions produced an extensive repertory of dances for the deities (the *orisha* and *vodunsi*) honored and summoned in their rituals. Because the deities are invoked in dance, possession trance is a choreographed activity, and those who enter trance express in gesture and movement the personalities who come to "dance in their heads."

The most important dance element in the Ejagham-based men's secret society, known in Cuba as Abakuá, is expressed by masked figures called *íreme* (and in Spanish *diablitos*, "little devils"). These dancers represented ancestral figures in the Abakuá ceremonies and also danced in the processions forming part of the secret society's rites; they appeared as well in the street carnivals of Havana, the capital, and Santiago de Cuba.

Many Kongo-Angolans were brought to Cuba via the slave trade, and their music and dance have had a profound impact on Cuban popular culture. At the sugar mills (called *ingenios* or *centrales*), their nonritual celebrations (*conguerías*) often featured the dances called *makuta* and *yuka* (similar to some forms of modern rumba and including the pelvic movement known as the *vacunao*). The *yuka* is still danced in some parts of Cuba; although it now resembles the rumba, two distinctive steps may come from the older *yuka*—the *ronquido* and the *campanero*. The *ronquido* is a series of lateral steps; the *campanero* is a figure-eight pattern described by the dancer's feet on the ground. In both cases the dancer follows the master drum's patterns very closely. In the nineteenth century a Kongo ritual combat dance called *maní*, comparable to Brazilian *capoeira*, was also performed at the *conguerías*.

The drum-and-dance complex known as rumba is related to older Kongo forms and comprises the *yambú*, *guaguancó*, and *columbia*. All three are mimetic. The *yambú*, performed in slow tempo, is often thought of as an old people's dance. The dancers' gestures may mimic old age and the difficulty of daily tasks; they do not use the *vacunao*, the pelvic movement typical of the *guaguancó*, a more modern variety of rumba. In *guaguancó*, the dance element "breaks out" in the second section—a couple, dancing apart, simulates the man's pursuit of the woman, his partner, and the *vacunao* symbolizes his sexual conquest. Although the theme of sexual pursuit may be found in European couple dances including the *zapateo*, the *vacunao* is clearly a Kongo element, comparable to the *umbigada*, the pelvic thrust that characterizes early forms of samba, a Brazilian dance of Angolan origin (from Africa).

The *columbia* began in rural Matanzas Province and is a male solo dance that features many acrobatic movements. This may be the most complex form of rumba. In it the dancer imitates a ball-player, a bicyclist, a cane-cutter, a cripple, or other figures; he may also imitate the Abakuá *íreme* mentioned earlier. The *columbia* soloist and the master drummer challenge each other with improvisations.

Rumba also found its way into the Cuban Carnival. Here it was danced by groups known as *comparsas*, large organized Carnival associations that included paired male and female dancers who performed an outdoor or "street" rumba, as well as line dancers who executed choreographed routines. In Santiago de Cuba, *comparsas* were organized within neighborhoods. Santiago de Cuba's Carnival included many styles of dance—some popular, such as the rumba; some derived from Haitian elements in the local culture, such as the *cocoyé;* and still others derived from the Abakuá. The most popular dance was the conga, which attracted masses of "second-liners" as the conga musicians paraded through the city's streets. The conga was also found in Havana's Carnival as a street dance. Popularized in the United States and elsewhere in the late 1930s, a simplified form of this Havana street conga preserves some of the collective and processional features of the original.

Cuba's two most important social dances, the *son* and *danzón*, emerged from radically different social environ-

ments. The *danzón* is a descendant of the French *contredanse*, introduced into Havana in the late eighteenth century, then again into eastern Cuba at the end of that century by French planters fleeing the Haitian revolution. (Black Haitians also had a lasting impact on the culture of Santiago de Cuba, as witnessed in the Carnival *cocoyé*.) By the mid-nineteenth century the courtly French *contredanse* had become the Cuban *contradanza*, a collective line or figured dance led by a *bastonero* (dance master). It evolved into a somewhat simplified figured dance, called the *habanera* or *danza*, and then into the *danzón*. When this dance emerged from the habanera in 1879, it still bore traces of the habanera's figured choreography, but it soon evolved into a couple dance. The *danzón* is considered the national dance of Cuba.

Until the opening decades of the twentieth century the *danzón* remained an upper-class genre for private clubs and literary societies. By the late 1920s the *danzón* featured a syncopated final section, borrowed from the *son-montuno*. In the late 1930s an important innovation was introduced by musicians Israel Lopez (Cachao) and his brother Orestes, who were playing with a *charanga* orchestra of flute, strings, piano, and percussion led by Antonio Arcaño. They created what was then called the "new rhythm" *danzón*, which came to be the mambo. This new name was originally applied to the more swinging, riff-

CUBA: Folk, Ritual, and Social Dance. A dancer and drummer of the folkloric troupe Los Muñequitos de Matanzas in a rumba. In Spanish, *muñequito* (literally, "comic" or "comic book") connotes fun, happiness, and good times. (Photograph by Cynthia Carris; from the archives at Jacob's Pillow, Becket, Massachusetts.)

based final section of the *danzón-mambo*. The *danzón-mambo* caught on quickly among blacks and working-class Cubans, at one time rivaling in popularity the *son-montuno*. The cha-cha, one of the most popular of all Cuban dances, is an extension of the *danzón-mambo;* through a long series of steps it too may be traced back to the French *contredanse.*

The mambo was adapted to big-band versions by Pérez Prado in Mexico City and by Mario Bauzá and Machito in New York City. During the 1940s and 1950s a great popular urban dance tradition grew up around the big-band mambo. In New York City dance halls, such as the Palladium in midtown and the Chateau Gardens in lower Manhattan, mambo dancing reached heights of solo improvisation that rivaled the glory days of the Lindy Hop at the Savoy Ballroom in Harlem. New Yorkers of all backgrounds were united on the Palladium's dance floor, and mambos were danced at weddings, proms, *bar mitsvah*s,

and patio parties, as was the cha-cha in the craze of the late 1950s and early 1960s. Mambo lives on in salsa dancing, which probably reached its peak in New York City in the late 1970s and early 1980s.

[*See also* Congo Dances.]

BIBLIOGRAPHY
Bettelheim, Judith. "Carnaval and Festivals in Cuba." In *Caribbean Festival Arts,* edited by John Nunley and Judith Bettelheim. Seattle, 1988.
Daniel, Yvonne. *Rumba: Dance and Social Change in Contemporary Cuba.* Bloomington, 1995.
Galán, Natalio. *Cuba y sous sones.* Valencia, 1983.
Giro, Radamés. *El mambo.* Havana, 1993.
Guerra, Ramiro. *Teatralización del folklore.* Havana, 1989.
León, Argeliers. *Del canto y el tiempo.* Havana, 1984.
Millet, José, and Rafael Brea. *Grupos folklóricos de Santiago de Cuba.* Santiago de Cuba, 1989.
Moore, Robin. "The Commercial Rumba in Afrocuban Arts as International Popular Culture." *Latin American Music Review* 16 (Fall-Winter 1995): 165–198.
Ortiz, Fernando. *Cuban Counterpoint: Tobacco and Sugar,* translated by Harriet de Onis. New York, 1947.
Pajares Santiesteban, Fidel. *Ramiro Guerra y la danza en Cuba.* Quito, 1993.
Pérez Rodríguez, Nancy. *El Carnaval Santiaguero.* 2 vols. Santiago de Cuba, 1988.
Robbins, James. "Practical and Abstract Taxonomy in Cuban Music." *Ethnomusicology* 33 (Fall 1989): 379–389.

MORTON MARKS

CUBA: Ballet. Scene from Alicia and Fernando Alonso's 1948 staging of *Giselle*, after Coralli and Perrot, for the Ballet Nacional de Cuba. (Photograph from the Dance Collection, New York Public Library for the Performing Arts.)

Ballet before 1959

During the nineteenth century, occasional performances by European dancers sparked the interest of the *criollos* (Cubans of Spanish ancestry). Among the ballets seen in the capital, Havana, at that time were *La Fille Mal Gardée* (Teatro Principal, 14 February 1816); *La Sylphide* with Fanny Elssler (Teatros Tacón and Principal, 1841 and 1842); *Giselle*, presented twice in 1849 (Teatro Tacón, 14 February and Teatro del Circo, 17 November), featuring Madame Augusta (Caroline-Augusta Fuchs) in the second staging. In the early twentieth century Anna Pavlova danced with her company and her partner Alexandre Volinine at the Teatro Payret in 1915 and at the Teatro Nacional in 1917 and 1918.

From 1918 until 1931 there were only intermittent dance presentations. Classical ballet received its main impetus in August 1931, when the Sociedad Pro-Arte Musical (SPAM) founded the first dancing school of importance. Its first director (1931–1938) was the Russian Nikolai Yavorsky. The first of its students to graduate into a major company were Alberto Alonso and Delfina Pérez Gurri, who were engaged in 1935 by Colonel W. de Basil's Ballets Russes. Others followed, among them Fernando Alonso and Alicia Alonso (engaged by Ballet Caravan in 1939), Luis Trápaga (Original Ballet Russe, 1941), Aníbal

Navarro (Original Ballet Russe, 1945), and Dulce Anaya and Enrique Martínez (Ballet Theatre, 1947).

In 1938 Georges Milenoff succeeded Yavorsky as director of the school. Milenoff was followed in 1941 by Alberto Alonso, with the Canadian ballerina Alexandra Denisova (Patricia Denise) as co-director. Denisova left Cuba in 1944, and Alonso remained as director until 1959 (when Fidel Castro took over the government); SPAM ceased operation in 1967.

From 1942 to 1967 the school also had on its faculty Léon Fokine (nephew of Michel Fokine), Valrene Tweedie, Adelina Durán, and former students Luis Trápaga, Elena del Cueto, Finita Suárez, Cuca Martínez, and Hilda Canosa. Until 1958 advanced pupils performed annually alongside guest artists in the Teatro Auditorium. Among the principal dancers appearing at this time were Alicia and Fernando Alonso, John Kriza, Rosella Hightower, André Eglevsky, Marjorie Tallchief, Barbara Fallis, Igor Youskevitch, Alicia Markova, and Michael Maule, performing in works from Diaghilev's Ballets Russes repertory. In addition, several ballets were created by Alberto Alonso for Denisova—*Preludios* (to music by Franz Liszt), *Concerto* (music by J. S. Bach), *Forma* (music by José Ardévol). Among other works by Alonso were *Sombras* (music by Jean Sibelius), *Antes del Alba* (music by Hilario González-Iñiguez), *La Valse* (music by Maurice Ravel), *Orfeo* (music by Christoph Willibald von Gluck), *Nocturnos* (music by Claude Debussy), and *Petit Ballet* (music by Aleksandr Glazunov).

In September 1948 Ballet Alicia Alonso was formed, initially utilizing the facilities, costumes, sets, props, and musical scores of SPAM. The original company included members of the temporarily disbanded American Ballet Theatre and SPAM's school. In 1950 Ballet Alicia Alonso founded its own academy of ballet, directed by Fernando Alonso. The faculty was made up of local teachers and the school offered courses by guest teachers such as Aleksandra Fedorova and Phyllis Bedells. Ballet Alicia Alonso—renamed Ballet de Cuba in 1955—received artistic grants from the administrations of Cuba's presidents Carlos Prío and Fulgencio Batista. Its repertory included *Romeo and Juliet*, choreographed by Alberto Alonso; *Swan Lake*, staged by Mary Skeaping; *Coppélia, La Fille Mal Gardée; The Nutcracker,* and works by local choreographers such as Enrique Martínez, Ramiro Guerra, and Cuca Martínez. Ballet de Cuba also presented such guest dancers as Mia Slavenska, Nora Kaye, Royes Fernandez, Jean Babilée, and Nathalie Philippart. Ballet de Cuba stopped performing in 1956 because its government subsidies were cancelled.

Other dancers created ballet schools and ensembles in Cuba. Among them were Anna Leontieva and Nina Verchinina from the Original Ballet Russe (1941); Alberto Alonso and the choreographer Elena del Cueto, who started the group Ballet Nacional (1950); and Luis Trápaga, who established the Escuela de Danza Ballet Nacional in 1952.

Television helped to spread interest in all kinds of dance in Cuba. It presented, especially, classical ballets and theatricalized folkloric dance vignettes. These, although pleasant and tasteful, were commercialized to enhance their popular appeal. They were staged by Alberto Alonso, who combined authentic Antillean folklore with academic dance in an attempt to create an indigenous Cuban ballet. [*See also the entry on Alicia Alonso.*]

BIBLIOGRAPHY
García Cisneros, Florencio. "Augusta Maywood: Prima ballerina assoluta nunca bailó en Cuba." *Noticias de Arte* (January 1979).
González, Jorge Antonio. "El ballet en Cuba hasta 1948." *Cuba en el Ballet* (September 1973).
Guest, Ivor. *Fanny Elssler.* London, 1970.
Money, Keith. *Anna Pavlova: Her Life and Art.* New York, 1982.
Parera Villalón, Célida. *Historia concisa del ballet en Cuba.* New York, 1974.
Parera Villalón, Célida. *Pro-Arte Musical y su divulgación de cultura en Cuba, 1918–1967.* Montclair, N.J., 1990.

CÉLIDA PARERA VILLALÓN

Ballet since 1959

Dance in Cuba since 1959 (when Fidel Castro took over the government) has been placed under the auspices of Ballet Nacional de Cuba, formerly Ballet de Cuba. Inactive since 1956, Ballet de Cuba had been revived in early 1959 by Alicia and Fernando Alonso to appear at Havana's Teatro Blanquita on 2 and 3 February in a command performance in honor of the new revolutionary government, which had come to office on 1 January. Alicia Alonso and Igor Youskevitch were featured performers.

After the state agreed to subsidize the ballet company, the Alonsos proceeded to reshape Ballet de Cuba and held auditions in Havana presided over by a jury that included Igor Youskevitch, Alexandra Danilova, Anna Leontieva, and the dance critic Ann Barzel. The new ensemble left Havana in late 1959 for an extended South American tour. Its principal stars were Alicia Alonso and Youskevitch, whose famous partnership came to an end during this tour. Fernando Alonso shared the artistic direction of the company with Alicia until 1974 (when their divorce led him to leave his post).

Ballet Nacional de Cuba, with Alicia Alonso as sole director and artistic ambassador of the Cuban government, has undertaken extensive tours. In 1960 the company toured for eight months from Czechoslovakia to China, giving ninety-six performances. Rodolfo Rodriguez was Alonso's partner at that time and until 1967.

Upon the company's return to Cuba in 1961, the government abolished private schooling and created the official Escuela Nacional de Arte and the Escuela Provincial de

CUBA: Ballet. *(left)* Alicia Alonso with Bolshoi dancer Azari Plisetsky in act 2 of *Swan Lake*. The political ties between Cuba and the Soviet Union fostered dance partnerships like this one. *(right)* Alonso with a Cuban partner, Jorge Esquivel, in a revival of *Carmen Suite*. Alberto Alonso choreographed this ballet for his sister-in-law in 1967. (Top photograph by Michel Petit; from the Dance Collection, New York Public Library for the Performing Arts. Bottom photograph © 1976 by Linda Vartoogian; used by permission.)

Ballet. In the latter, Fernando Bujones started his training under Joaquín Banegas. The curriculum of the ballet school included, in addition to classical dance, character dance, historical dance, Cuban folklore, and dance history, supplemented by ideological courses. The Escuela de Danza Moderna and the Escuela de Camagüey—the latter in an eastern province of the island—are annexed to the Escuela Provincial.

The Ballet de Camagüey came into existence in 1969 under the artistic guidance of Jorge Riverón, a soloist of Ballet Nacional de Cuba. Its first principal dancers were Menia Martínez, trained in Russia and later a soloist with the Ballet Royal de Wallonie, and Miguel Campanería, who defected in Montreal in 1971 and later danced with American Ballet Theatre and the Pittsburgh Ballet. The Ballet de Camagüey at one time attempted works with progressive themes, but it returned to the traditional repertory favored by Fernando Alonso, who became its director in 1974. One of its principal dancers was Aida Villoch, trained in Escuela Provincial de Ballet in Havana.

Through the years some non-Cuban teachers have been invited to offer courses in the Escuela Provincial. Among the best known are the Bolshoi's Viktor Zaplin and Azari Plisetsky (who partnered Alicia Alonso for more than a decade), José Parés from Puerto Rico, and Olga Krilova and Nadia Rochepkina from the Soviet Union. The permanent faculty is made up of Cubans, including Joaquín Banegas, Laura Alonso, and Adolfo Roval.

In 1966 Ballet Nacional de Cuba won the grand prize at the Fourth Dance Festival of the city of Paris for their presentation of *Giselle*. Aurora Bosch, who danced the Queen of the wilis in the second act, was also awarded first prize by the critics.

In 1967 the Cuban choreographer Alberto Alonso was invited by Maya Plisetskaya to compose for the Bolshoi the ballet *Carmen*—based on a musical arrangement of the Bizet opera by Rodion Shchedrin—the first time a foreign choreographer created for the Bolshoi; the premiere was in Moscow on 28 April 1967, with Plisetskaya in the title role.

Carmen entered the Ballet Nacional de Cuba's repertory the same year and has been seen in various countries, including the United States. It has also been mounted for companies in Finland, Japan, Argentina, and Mexico. Other major works by Alberto Alonso for Ballet Nacional de Cuba are *Conjugación, Un Retablo para Romeo y Julieta* (music by Hector Berlioz), *Diógenes ante el Tonel,* and *El Güije* (music by Juan Blanco). In 1968 Alberto Alonso won first prize for choreography in the Varna Dance Competition with his work *Espacio y Movimiento,* set to a Stravinsky score.

The first visit of Maurice Béjart to Cuba, in 1968, interested several dancers in the freer idioms practiced by the Béjart group. Some members of the Ballet Nacional were stimulated to begin choreographing, including Jorge Riverón and Alberto Méndez. Riverón composed three works for the 1978 Havana Dance Festival: *Tarantos* (music by Leo Brouwer), *Canción* (music by Antonio Lauro), and *Enlaces* (music by Darius Milhaud).

Méndez has become a well-known choreographer in Cuba, having won the first prize for choreography in the 1973 International Ballet Competition in Moscow with his ballet *El Río y el Bosque,* to music by Félix Guerrero. Other works by Méndez are *Plásmasis* (music by Sergio Fernández Barroso), *Tarde en la Siesta* (music by Ernesto Lecuona), *Canción para la Extraña Flor* (music by Scriabin), and *Muñecos* (music by Remberto Egües). Other active choreographers working with Ballet Nacional include Iván Tenorio (*La Casa de Bernarda Alba* and *Leda y el Cisne*), and Jorge Lefebre *(Edipo Rey* and *Salomé),* who was a choreographer with the Ballet Royal de Wallonie.

Ballet Nacional de Cuba generally performs in the Teatro García Lorca (formerly Teatro Nacional); its main rehearsal hall is located in the colonial home that once housed the ballet school of Sociedad Pro-Arte Musical. Its repertory includes the new works already mentioned along with the traditional ballets that have been staples for Alicia Alonso throughout her long career. The company performs continuously and tours regularly. Its activities help intensify enthusiasm for classical ballet in Cuba.

Ballet Nacional de Cuba has also hosted dance festivals in Havana every two or three years. The first, held in March 1960, included an appearance by American Ballet Theatre with Erik Bruhn, Lupe Serrano, John Kriza, and Royes Fernandez. Subsequent festivals have featured many prominent non-Cuban dancers, such as André Eglevsky (who was Alicia Alonso's partner as a guest in *Coppélia* during the first dance festival).

The company has achieved recognition at dance festivals abroad as well, being most successful in Japan and Paris. Several Cuban dancers have achieved high honors at the International Ballet Competition: gold medalists Loipa Araujo (Varna, 1965), Aurora Bosch (Varna, 1966), and Amparo Brito (Moscow, 1973); silver medalists Josefina Méndez (Varna, 1965), Marta García (Varna, 1970), and Mirta Plá (Varna, 1964 and 1966); and bronze medalist Maria Elena Llorente (Varna, 1966).

CUBA: Ballet. *(top)* A tableau from Jules Perrot's Romantic ballet *Pas de Quatre,* with Alicia Alonso as Marie Taglioni, Maria Elena Llorente as Lucile Grahn, Mirta Plá as Fanny Cerrito, and Marta García as Carlotta Grisi. Seen here in a 1978 revival, Alonso first danced this role in her 1941 staging of the ballet. *(middle)* Laura Alonso, daughter of Alicia and Fernando, with Jorge Riverón in *Giselle,* Paris, 1966. *(bottom)* María Elena Llorente leaps over Lázaro Carreño in Alberto Méndez's *El Río y el Bosque.* (Top photograph © 1978, bottom photograph © 1977 by Linda Vartoogian; both used by permission. Middle photograph courtesy of Jorge Riverón.)

The principal female dancers of Ballet Nacional de Cuba are Loipa Araujo, Aurora Bosch, Marta García, María Elena Llorente, Josefina Méndez, Mirta Plá, and Rosario Suárez. The male soloists are Lázaro Carreño, Olando Salgado, and Jorge Esquivel, who partnered Alicia Alonso in the 1980s. Alonso danced with Rudolf Nureyev on 30 July 1990 in Palma de Mallorca, *The Poem of Love and the Sea*, choreographed by Alberto Méndez to music of Ernest Chausson (including a soprano part by Victoria de Los Angeles). Only one performance joined these two remarkable dancers.

BIBLIOGRAPHY

Alonso, Alicia. *Diálogos con la danza.* Edited by Pedro Simón. Buenos Aires, 1988.
Baker, Rob. "Ballet Nacional de Cuba." *Dance Magazine* (October 1978): 112, 116–119.
Cabrera, Miguel. "El Ballet de Camagüey." *Cuba en el ballet* 2 (September 1971): 25–29.
Cabrera, Miguel. "Jorge Esquivel, primer bailarin del Ballet Nacional de Cuba." *Cuba en el ballet* 4 (May 1973): 2–9.
Cabrera, Miguel. *Orbit: Cuba Ballet, 1948–1978.* Havana, 1978.
Cabrera, Miguel. *Festival Internacional de Ballet de la Habana: Tres décades de historia.* Havana, 1990.
Cashion, Susan V. "Educating the Dancer in Cuba." In *Dance: Current Selected Research,* edited by Lynnette Y. Overby and James H. Humphrey. New York, 1989.
Concepción, Alma. "U.S. Ballet and Modern Dance in the Caribbean: Cuba and Puerto Rico, 1940–1980." In *Proceedings of the Fifteenth Annual Conference, Society of Dance History Scholars, University of California, Riverside, 14–15 February 1992,* compiled by Christena L. Schlundt. Riverside, Calif., 1992.
Draegin, Lois. "A Cuban Portfolio." *Dance Magazine* (July 1979): 78–79.
Dudinskaya, Natalia. "Ballet Nacional de Cuba." *Cuba en el ballet* 1 (September 1970): 27–38.
Gamez, Tana de. *Alicia Alonso at Home and Abroad.* New York, 1971.
Garske, Rolf. "Chances for Ballet and Dance." *Ballett International* 6 (January 1983): 6–11.
Horosko, Marian. "Diary of a Trip to Havana." *Dance Magazine* (August 1971): 44–58.
Hunt, Marilyn. "The Cuban Connection." *Dance Magazine* (May 1991): 66–68.
King, Jane. "The Need for a New Look: Cuban Dance." *Ballett International* 16 (May 1993): 22–23.
Kirchner, Birgit. "Triumphs and Afflictions of the Revolution." *Ballett International* 13 (January 1990): 43–46.
Mahoney, John F. "Dance in Castro's Cuba." *Dance Teacher Now* 5 (September–October 1983): 13–16.
Maynard, Olga. "Alicia Alonso and Ballet Nacional de Cuba." *Dance Magazine* (June 1978): 50–58.
Patrick, K. C. "Building a Bridge from Cuba." *Dance Teacher Now* 12 (September 1990): 44–48.
Parera Villalón, Célida. *Historia concisa del ballet en Cuba.* New York, 1974.
Simón, Pedro. "La música cubana en la danza." *Cuba en el ballet* 2 (September 1971): 36–45.
Sociedad Pro-Arte Musical y su Diuulgacion de la Cultura de Cuba, *1918–1967.* New Jerey, 1990.
Terry, Walter. *Alicia and Her Ballet Nacional de Cuba.* Garden City, N.Y., 1981.
Zimmer, Elizabeth. "Havana." *Ballet Review* 19 (Fall 1991): 75–82.
Zürner, Inge. "The Ninth International Ballet Festival in Havana." *Ballett International* 8 (April 1985): 26–31.

ARCHIVE.   Jorge Riverón Collection, Havana and New York.

JORGE RIVERÓN

Modern Dance

In 1959, directly after the Cuban Revolution, the Department of Modern Dance was formed within the Teatro Nacional, under the direction of dancer/choreographer Ramiro Guerra. Pulling together a talented group of amateur and professional ballet, modern, folkloric, and nightclub dancers, Guerra created the National Dance Company of Havana, now called Danza Contemporánea de Cuba. Synthesizing African-Cuban, folkloric, ballet, and North American modern dance, Guerra pioneered a uniquely Cuban dance form: *La Tecnica Cubana* (the Cuban technique).

Guerra created choreography that reflected the deeply integrated African, Spanish, and Caribbean roots of Cuban culture within the modern dance genre. Non-Cuban teachers and choreographers also worked with the young company to provide artistic and technical insight. Lorna Burdsall and Elfreda Mahler, from the United States, were instrumental in the process: Burdsall staged dances by Doris Humphrey while Mahler helped develop the Escuela Nacional del Arte (National School of Art). Beginning with a single school in Havana, the system has expanded to fifteen elementary-level schools of art, nationwide, which continue to train dancers in the Cuban technique. Elena Noriega and Manuel Hiran, from Mexico, participated in designing the curriculum.

The development of Cuban artists has been a goal of the government under Fidel Castro, which continues to provide state support for dance education and performance. The government subsidies reflect the importance of dance in Cuban society, where social dances are a part of everyday life. Dance is at the core of the widely practiced religion called Santería, which incorporates the practice of African Yoruba with Roman Catholicism; each deity (*orisha*) is associated with particular dances. The mythology, music, and movement of the *orishas* were essential elements in the technique and repertory explored by Guerra and his collaborators—and in the choice of traditional drumming and song to accompany classes in the Cuban technique. Guerra's highly acclaimed *Suite Yoruba* from 1960 is representative of the marriage of Cuban ritual with the theatricality of modern dance.

The Cuban technique today has strong influences from Merce Cunningham and Martha Graham, used in concert with the fluid and percussive torso movements associated with African-Cuban dance. Most of Cuba's professional modern dancers have been trained in the National School of Art, undergoing a rigorous six-year course of study that includes the Cuban technique, ballet, folklore, improvisation, composition, music, repertory, dance history, Labanotation, and academics. Fluent in the complexities of Cuban folklore and folkloric dance, these modern dancers reflect their cultural heritage through the isolations of torso and hips, spinal undulations, flexed birdlike feet, mobile ribcages and shoulders, sudden changes of direction, rhythm, and syncopation. The versatility of their training is evident in their multiple pirouettes, luxurious balances, pitch turns, contractions, torsion, graceful leaps, and complex floor work.

Danza Contemporánea has produced many artists of renown. Eduardo Rivera, its principal and choreographer for many years, currently directs Teatro de la Danza del Caribe in Santiago, Cuba. Rivera's works *Okantomi* and *Súlkari,* examples of the strong African influence in Cuban art, are favorites in the repertory of Danza Contemporánea. Cuban National Ballet choreographer Alberto Méndez began his career as a modern dancer with the company. Marianela Boan, director and choreographer of Havana's independent group Danza Abierta, performed with Danza Contemporánea for more than a decade. Master teacher and principal dancer Manolo Vasquez continues to expand and refine the Cuban technique with Danza Contemporánea and abroad. Cofounder Lorna Burdsall now leads Asi Somos, an experimental group in Havana. Elfreda Mahler lives in Guantanamo, where she directs the contemporary folklore ensemble, Danza Libre.

In the late 1980s, a new generation of dancers and choreographers began branching off from Danza Contemporánea to form small independent companies. Following the demise of the Soviet Union in 1991 and the stringent economic restrictions of Castro's "Special Period" in the early 1990s, the rules governing private enterprise were loosened. Small self-financed dance schools and troupes emerged in Havana and the provinces.

In the 1990s, Cuban modern dance choreographers are pursuing individual philosophies and movement vocabularies. Unorthodox venues are being discovered to present new work, rehearse, improvise, and invite community involvement. Despite common roots in the Cuban technique, contemporary choreographers exhibit vast differences in movement styles, subject matter, and theatrical presentation.

One of the first unsubsidized, independent academies was created in 1993 by Narciso Medina, a Danza Contemporánea principal dancer and choreographer. Medina's signature piece, *Metamorphosis,* winner of the Prix de Lausanne in 1986, appears in the repertories of several Cuban and Mexican companies. The aesthetic of Dance

CUBA: Modern Dance. Narciso Medina and members of his troupe, Gestos Transitorios, in a perilous moment from his *Metamorphosis* (1996). (Photograph by David Garten; used by permission.)

Company Narciso Medina reflects an increased awareness of dance forms outside Cuba, culled from international tours, workshops, and cultural exchanges. Medina integrates the influence of *butō* (Japanese modern dance theater), dance theater, and performance art into his unmistakably Cuban style.

Other leaders in Cuban modern dance include Isabel Bustos and her Retazos company and Rosario Cardenas, director of Combinatoria. Among the roster of newly formed modern dance troupes are Fuera de Balance, directed by Lesme Grenot; Codanza, directed in Oguin by Marised Godoy; and Lilian Padron's Grupo Espiral of Matanzas.

Modern dance is flourishing in Cuba. In April 1996, the first national festival of Cuban contemporary dance was held at the Teatro Mella in Havana. Plans exist for the festival to continue on an annual basis as a showcase for the rapidly emerging voices of Cuban modern dance.

BIBLIOGRAPHY

Concepción, Alma. "U.S. Ballet and Modern Dance in the Caribbean: Cuba and Puerto Rico, 1940–1980." In *Proceedings of the Fifteenth Annual Conference, Society of Dance History Scholars, University of California, Riverside, 14–15 February 1992,* compiled by Christena L. Schlundt. Riverside, Calif., 1992.

Danza Nacional de Cuba: XX aniversario, 1959–1979. Havana, 1979.

Guerra, Ramiro. *Teatralización del folklore.* Havana, 1989.

Guerra, Ramiro, ed. *Se Danza.* Havana. Published quarterly, 1994–.

Haselberger, Gabriele. "Teatro de la Danza Cuba: 'You Will Eat the Fruit of My Heart.'" *Tanz Affiche* 8 (December 1995–January 1996): 101–111.

Kirchner, Birgit. "Triumphs and Afflictions of the Revolution." *Ballett International* 13 (January 1990): 43–46.

Manings, Muriel. "Modern Dance in Cuba." *Dance Magazine* (August 1971): 59–61.

Pajares Santiesteban, Fidel. *Ramiro Guerra y la danza en Cuba.* Quito, 1993.

Pérez León, Roberto. *Por los orígenes de la danza moderna en Cuba.* Havana, 1986.

Rausenberg, Esther. "In Cuba." *Dance International* 21 (Winter 1993–1994): 14–17.

Witzeling, Klaus. "Last Days and Visions." *Ballett International/Tanz Aktuell* (October 1994): 33–36.

SUKI JOHN
Based on materials submitted by Muriel Manings

CUCCHI, CLAUDINA (born March 1834 in Monza, died 8 March 1913 in Milan), Italian ballet dancer. In her memoirs, Claudina Cucchi wrote that at the age of six she was encouraged to take up dancing by the famous ballerina Sofia Fuoco. Reared in Monza, near Milan, Cucchi was soon enrolled at the ballet school of the Teatro alla Scala, where she received her entire training as a dancer, first with Carlo Blasis and his wife Annunciata Ramaccini, then with Auguste Hus. Reflecting on the different teaching styles of the two masters, Cucchi wrote:

> The school of the Blasis couple did not have the severity and rigor of the school of Mr. Hus, who succeeded them at La Scala. . . . Mr. Blasis demanded from his students to get an education, to read much, within the limits of the greatest attainable culture and gentility. He did not content himself with them performing correctly *pirouettes* and *entrechats*, but he wanted every movement to be given a characteristic imprint of grace and beauty, to form which must concur a serious education of the soul and of the intellect. . . . In Hus's method, on the other hand, the foundation of teaching was technical severity coupled with continuous training; but grace and the moral and intellectual part were much neglected.
>
> (Cucchi, 1904, pp. 5–6)

After gaining distinction as an *allieva emerita* (distinguished student), Cucchi performed an important role in *Un Fallo* by Giuseppe Rota at La Scala in 1853.

Subsequently, Cucchi went to Paris, where she made her debut at the Opera in the world premiere of Giuseppe Verdi's opera *Les Vêpres Siciliennes* on 13 June 1855. In the *divertissement* choreographed for this opera by Lucien Petipa, Cucchi interpreted the role of Spring, dancing with Victorine Legrain (Winter), Adèle Nathan (Summer), and Caterina Beretta (Autumn). A leading critic described her thus: "It was spring in person in the form of Miss Couqui [Cucchi], energetic, graceful, light-footed dancer with the physique for the role, and her first step placed her among our best ballerinas" (Castil-Blaze, 1855). Cucchi also experienced success at the Opera in January 1856, when she created the role of Gulnare in Joseph Mazilier's ballet *Le Corsaire*, sharing the stage with Carolina Rosati as Medora and Domenico Segarelli as Conrad. In 1857 Cucchi scored another hit when she danced *La Bonne Aventure*, the *pas d'action* that Verdi had composed for the Paris production of *Il Trovatore*.

In the following ten years, until 1868, Cucchi danced as *prima ballerina* at the Kärntnertor Theater in Vienna, appearing in ballets by Pasquale Borri, Giovanni Casati, Paul Taglioni, Giuseppe Rota, and Antonio Pallerini, among others. During vacations from the Viennese theater, Cucchi performed in various European capitals: in London, Berlin, Prague, Budapest, Warsaw, Hamburg, and Saint Petersburg, where she interpreted *Giselle, Catarina,* and *La Esmeralda* in productions mounted by Marius Petipa.

At the height of her success, Cucchi performed at the Teatro Comunale in Trieste in Rota's *Il Conte di Montecristo* in 1857 and 1858; at La Scala in Rota's *La Contessa di Egmont* in 1864; at the Teatro La Fenice in Venice in Borri's *Nefte, ossia Il Figliuol Prodigo* (reproduced by Giovanni Rando), in Raffaele Rossi's *La Capricciosa,* and in Arthur Saint-Léon's *Fiammetta* (reproduced by Rossi) in 1868 and 1869; and at the Teatro Carlo Felice in Genoa in Borri's *Uriella* in 1870. In 1872 she performed in Cairo. On her return to Italy she danced in Padua (1872), Naples (1873), and Rome (1874), where she ended her career.

In spite of her splendid career and her marriage to Baron Ferdinando Zemo, Cucchi ended her days impoverished, sheltered by the Trivulzio, a charitable institution in Milan. Her fame and popular success, to which contributed also the fame of the public character she created, were not always equaled by her appreciation by the critics. In Italy, after 1868, she aroused the hostility of patriotic circles, which accused her of Austrian sympathies. In Russia her performance was criticized as merely technical and lacking in expression and grace. On the whole, Cucchi was considered a graceful dancer with excellent technique, and a particularly good actress. Her greatest successes were in ballets such as *Catarina* and *La Esmeralda,* which fully complemented her temperament.

BIBLIOGRAPHY

Ascarelli, Astrid. "Cucchi, Claudina." In *Dizionario biografico degli italiani.* Rome, 1960–.

Castil-Blaze, François. *L'Académie Impériale de Musique.* Vol. 2. Paris, 1855.

Cucchi, Claudina. *Venti anni di palcoscenico.* Rome, 1904.

Guest, Ivor. *The Ballet of the Second Empire.* London, 1974.

Jürgensen, Knud Arne. *The Verdi Ballets.* Parma, 1995.

Regli, Francesco. *Dizionario biografico dei più celebri poeti ed artisti melodrammatici, tragici e comici, maestri, concertisti, coreografi, mimi, ballerini, scenografi, giornalisti, impresarii, ecc. ecc. che fiorirono in Italia dal 1800 al 1860.* Turin, 1860. Facsimile reprint, Bologna, 1990.

Souritz, Elizabeth. *Carlo Blasis in Russia, 1861–1864.* Studies in Dance History, vol. 4.2. Pennington, N.J., 1993.

Vazem, Ekaterina. "Memoirs of a Ballerina of the St. Petersburg Bolshoi Theatre" (part 2). Translated by Nina Dimitrievitch. *Dance Research* 4.1 (Spring 1986): 3–28.

CLAUDIA CELI
Translated from Italian

CULLBERG, BIRGIT (born 3 August 1908 in Nyköping), Swedish dancer, choreographer, and ballet director. Cullberg did not begin to train in dance until after she was more than twenty years old. Growing up in a wealthy home in a small town, she showed early artistic talent; she acted in plays, practiced the violin, wrote poetry, painted, and danced in a free and personal manner, inspired by dancers she had seen. She even appeared publicly in Nyköping and made a name for herself as "the bank director's dancing daughter."

In 1929, Cullberg left home to attend the university in Stockholm, studying literature there from 1931 to 1935. During this period she began her real dance studies—classical with Russian-born Vera Alexandrova and modern with Jeanna Falk, a student of Émile Jaques-Dalcroze and Mary Wigman. When Kurt Jooss's ballet company appeared in Stockholm, a generation of young dancers, tired of classical ballet, was swept away by the company's deep involvement in contemporary life. When Jooss established a school in England, Cullberg in 1935 chose to be among the many Swedish female dancers who studied there, spending four years at the Jooss-Leeder school.

Jooss was Cullberg's true mentor, and whatever she created revealed his basic attitude toward dance: a movement without content is meaningless; it must have an inner motivation and must be more than simply decorative. The sociopolitical side of Jooss's ballets influenced Cullberg deeply, as did the Jooss-Leeder movement technique. Its very personal shape was the foundation of Cullberg's vocabulary, although she has added other movement languages as she felt its limitations. After World War II, she resumed her classical studies; encounters in the 1960s with American modern dance, notably that of Martha Graham, further influenced her dance idiom.

Returning home to Sweden in 1939, Cullberg had formed her own little dance group with some comrades from England. It performed in revues and also gave recitals. In 1942, she gave her first public solo recital in Stockholm. She also taught and choreographed for the theater. In 1944, she gathered a new group; from 1946 to 1977, she took part in the Swedish Dance Theater—which was set up by her pupil, choreographer Ivo Cramér—and toured successfully all over Europe. In 1942 she married the actor Anders Ek and bore a son, Niklas, in 1943 and the twins, Malin and Mats, in 1945.

Cullberg was an extraordinary dancer with a famous sense of humor and characterization. Her solos and group works from the 1940s were often comical, satirical, and during the war years strongly political. In 1944 she also performed a one-act version of a new *Romeo and Juliet*, to music by Sergei Prokofiev.

After the war Cullberg's career entered a new phase. In Paris during the summer of 1949, Roland Petit's version of *Carmen* was a revelation. Cullberg understood for the first time that classical technique could be used to depict human psychology and relations. In the spring of 1950, she used this new understanding to create a dance drama based on August Strindberg's play *Miss Julie*. She used her renewed classical studies in the portrayal of the heroine and effectively contrasted classicism with a free dance vocabulary. She was quick to fuse the two apparently disparate styles and became one of the forerunners of the modern European ballet style.

Miss Julie's strong psychological acting and openly erotic atmosphere were not previously encountered in Swedish dance and caused a sensation, as the ballet did when it made its international tour. *Miss Julie* attracted new audiences to ballet and opened a new phase in Swedish dance life. Cullberg and ballerina Elsa-Marianne von Rosen were engaged by the Royal Swedish Ballet, and Cullberg served as choreographer there from 1951 to 1956. She then received a commission from the Royal Danish Ballet, resulting in *Moon Reindeer* (1957). Her collaboration with this company was long and fruitful, and she played an important part in its modernization. *Moon Reindeer* was an international triumph, leading to her successful U.S. debut with two 1958 productions, American Ballet Theatre's *Miss Julie* and New York City Ballet's *Medea*. She then embarked with a case of ballets to guest with companies in Europe, North America, South America, Iran, and Japan.

CULLBERG. Danish dancer Lizzie Rode in Cullberg's *Medea* (1950), a dark, psychological ballet. (Photograph from the Dance Collection, New York Public Library for the Performing Arts.)

CULLBERG. *Rapport* (1976) was set to music by Allan Pettersson. The dancers pictured here are Pasi Nieminen, Charlotte Stålhammar, and Mats Wegman. (Photograph by Enar Merkel Rydberg; used by permission.)

Although in 1960 Cullberg was engaged as theater producer to Stockholm's newly opened City Theater, she somehow seemed almost lost to Sweden. To secure her work there and give her a platform on which she could create new ballets, the Swedish government in 1967 founded the Cullberg Ballet; in 1968, it was put under the roof of a touring organization, the Swedish National Theater Center. The company tours extensively in Scandinavia and abroad. In 1969, the Cullberg Ballet was awarded the gold medal as the best company at the Paris Autumn Festival. In Italy it became something of a permanent guest company.

The company has also commissioned works from other Swedish choreographers, such as Ulf Gadd and von Rosen. From the international scene it has drawn works by Merce Cunningham, Alvin Ailey, Kurt Jooss, Flemming Flindt, Maurice Béjart, Lar Lubovitch, Jiří Kylián, and Christopher Bruce. Mats Ek, Cullberg's son, has been the company's principal choreographer since 1976; he shared artistic direction with his mother from 1982 to 1994, when he became the artistic director.

In 1961, Cullberg made her debut as a television choreographer with *The Evil Queen*, which was awarded the Prix Italia. Since then she has become one of the world's foremost producers of television ballet. Her method of composition is unique. She believes that it is the dancers who are to move in the image, not the cameras; therefore, she has the performers move within a frame as if seen within a painting. With the duet *Red Wine in Green Glasses* in 1970 she made a refined artistic use of the chromakey technique and was once again awarded a Prix Italia.

Cullberg has been active as a lecturer and writer. She was dance critic in the daily *Dagens Nyheter* in the late 1940s, continued to write on various subjects in the 1950s, and published the book *The Ballet and Us* in 1952 (it was published in a somewhat different form—as "Ballet: Flight and Reality"—in *Dance Perspectives* in 1967).

Ever since her debut as a choreographer, Cullberg has used her early studies of literature as inspiration. By focusing on a story from a drama, a myth, or a biblical tale, she can disguise the fact that much of her work derives from her personal situations. Her artistry shows, in that she can always turn the personal into the universal. Like her mentor Kurt Jooss and her son Mats Ek, she is very engaged in sociopolitical issues, and all her productions can be seen as social commentary. She has revolted against oppression and has been carried along by her passion for freedom and equality. Her greatest strengths, however, are her ability to portray human relations and her keen psychological perceptions.

[*See also* Sweden, *article on* Theatrical Dance since 1900.]

BIBLIOGRAPHY

Cullberg, Birgit, and Lilian Karina. *Balettskolan*. Västerås, 1960.
Cullberg, Birgit. *Baletten och vi*. 2d ed. Stockholm, 1965.
Cullberg, Birgit. "Television Ballet." In *The Dance Has Many Faces*, edited by Walter Sorell. 2d ed. New York, 1966.
Cullberg, Birgit. "Ballet: Flight and Reality." *Dance Perspectives*, no. 29 (1967).
Freeston, Brian. "Birgit Cullberg i helfigur." *Dans*, no. 14 (March 1977). Includes an English translation.
Lidova, Irène. "Birgit Cullberg." *Saisons de la danse* (May 1972). Includes a complete list of works.
Näslund, Erik. *Birgit Cullberg*. Stockholm, 1978.
Näslund, Erik. "The Cullberg Ballet Is Sweden's Cradle for Dance." *New York Times* (7 November 1982).
Näslund, Erik. "The Joy of Living." *Ballett International* 6 (July-August 1983): 18–27.
Näslund, Erik, et al. *Speglingar Birgit Cullberg 75 år*. Stockholm, 1983.
Näslund, Erik. "Alles ist Leben: Für Birgit Cullberg ist das alter kein Thema." In *Ballett 1985: Chronik und Bilanz des Balletjahres*, edited by Horst Koegler et al. Zurich, 1985.
Näslund, Erik. *Birgit Cullbergs "Fröken Julie," en Svensk balettklassiker*. Stockholm, 1995.
Ståhle, Anna Greta. "Birgit Cullberg's 'Fröken Julie.'" In *Perspektiv på "Fröken Julie,"* edited by Ulla-Britta Lagerroth and Göran Lindström. Stockholm, 1972.
Törnqvist, Egil, and Barry Jacobs. *Strindberg's "Miss Julie": A Play and Its Transpositions*. Norwich, 1988.

ERIK NÄSLUND

CUNNINGHAM, MERCE (Mercier Cunningham; born 16 April 1919 in Centralia, Washington), American modern dancer and choreographer. As a boy, Cunningham studied tap and ballroom dancing with a local teacher, Mrs. Maude M. Barrett. He later wrote in "The Impermanent Art" (1955) that her "devotion to dancing as an instantaneous and agreeable act of life" and her belief that "dance is most deeply concerned with each single instant as it comes along" made a deep impression on him. Cunningham spent an unproductive year at George Washington University, in Washington, D.C., before deciding that he wanted some formal, professional theater training; in the fall of 1937 he enrolled in the Cornish School (now the Cornish College of the Arts) in Seattle. His schedule there included classes with Bonnie Bird, a former member of Martha Graham's company, in Graham technique. Bird's classes rekindled his enthusiasm for dancing, and he soon changed his major from acting to dance.

At the beginning of Cunningham's second year at Cornish, Bird engaged John Cage, a young composer from California, as dance accompanist. In Bird's absence, Cage occasionally took over her dance composition classes, and he introduced her students to some unorthodox ideas about dance structure. Cage was beginning to devise ways in which dance and music could be composed at the same time, and he even encouraged the dance students to compose their own music. Cunningham's first student choreographies date from this time (1938/39).

In the summer of 1938 Bird had obtained a scholarship for Cunningham at a summer school at Mills College in Oakland, California, where she was to teach. Cunningham studied there also with Lester Horton, who asked him to dance opposite Bella Lewitzsky in *Conquest*, a piece he had choreographed for his workshop students. In 1939 the Bennington School of the Dance (usually held in Vermont) was held at Mills, and again Bird arranged scholarships for Cunningham and some of her other students. At the end of the session Cunningham performed not only in a dance of his own composition but also in the men's section from Doris Humphrey's *New Dance Trilogy*, choreographed by Charles Weidman. When Martha Graham saw Cunningham dance, she told him that if he came to New York she would use him in her company. He decided to accept her informal invitation and did not return to Cornish for what would have been his third and final year.

Cunningham danced in Graham's company from 1939 to 1945, creating roles in *Every Soul Is a Circus, El Penitente, Letter to the World, Punch and the Judy, Deaths and Entrances*, and *Appalachian Spring*. He also began to take classes at the School of American Ballet, an unusual step for a modern dancer at that time but one suggested by Graham.

Cunningham's most notable quality as a dancer was his extraordinary elevation, which Graham exploited in her choreography for him, especially in *Letter to the World*. Soon, however, he started to work on his own, gradually evolving a personal technique that incorporated elements of both Graham technique and ballet—the speed and elevation of ballet, the use of weight and the flexibility of the

spine of Graham—as well as his own movement discoveries.

In the summer of 1942, as in former years, the Graham company was in residence at Bennington College in Vermont. On 1 August Cunningham and two members of the Graham company, Jean Erdman and Nina Fonaroff, gave a joint concert of their own works at the College Theater. Each gave solos, and Erdman and Cunningham performed three dances that they had choreographed jointly. One of these, *Credo in Us*, a satire on contemporary American mores, had music by John Cage, who had recently arrived in New York. The program was repeated at the Humphrey-Weidman Studio Theater in New York on 20 and 21 October 1942, with the addition of a new solo by Cunningham, *Totem Ancestor*, also with music by Cage. These concerts initiated a collaboration between choreographer and composer that lasted for five decades—it was as important as the partnership of Petipa and Tchaikovsky or of Stravinsky and Balanchine.

On 5 April 1944 Cunningham and Cage presented their first joint concert of solo dances and music, again at the Studio Theater. Cunningham performed six solos, including *Root of an Unfocus*, all with music by Cage. Cunningham's dances still had psychological content, but he and

CUNNINGHAM. In his early twenties, Cunningham is pictured in a Graham-style leap. (Photograph © 1942 by Barbara Morgan; used by permission.)

CUNNINGHAM. The choreographer serves as support for (left to right) Marianne Preger-Simon, Carolyn Brown, and JoAnne Melsher in *Septet* (1953). (Photograph courtesy of the Cunningham Dance Foundation.)

Cage were already developing an unorthodox relationship between music and dance. Instead of choreographing movement to existing music, as was done in the ballet, or composing music to follow the counts of a dance made in silence, as was often done in modern dance, Cunningham and Cage worked within a common rhythmic structure; dance and music came together at certain specified points but they otherwise pursued independent existences.

In the summer of 1944 Cunningham created *Four Walls*, an ambitious dance play with his own text, choreography, and direction, music by Cage, and design by Arch Lauterer. The piece was rehearsed and performed at the Perry-Mansfield Workshop in Steamboat Springs, Colorado, where Cunningham was teaching for the summer. Although choreographically the work was still strongly influenced by Graham's expressionist style and turbid psychological content, by this time Cunningham was becoming acquainted with the work of contemporary painters and with the idea that the process of painting could be the subject of a work of art. He was also becoming more and more dissatisfied with Graham's aesthetic and with what he perceived to be her stereotyped notion of the kind of character he could portray in dance. During the 1944/45 season he informed her that he wanted to leave her company; his final role, in October 1944, was as the Revivalist in *Appalachian Spring*.

Cunningham continued to give concerts of his own work with Cage; their New York concerts were annual events, and they also began to tour in the United States. To introduce greater musical variety into these concerts, Cage invited other composers to write scores for dances.

Cunningham's first dance to the music of French composer Erik Satie, *Idyllic Song*, set to Cage's arrangement of the first part of *Socrate*, was performed at their first out-of-town concert, in Richmond, Virginia, on 20 November 1944. Their 1946 New York concert, at Hunter College on 12 May, included three solos: one to music by American composer Alan Hovhaness, one to a jazz drum improvisation by Baby Dodds, and one to music by Cage. There was also *The Princess Zondilda and Her Entourage*, danced by Cunningham, Katherine Litz, and Virginia Bosler, with a score by the Russian neoclassical composer Aleksei Haieff and a text written by Cunningham.

In 1947 Cunningham and Cage received a commission from Lincoln Kirstein to create a work for Ballet Society, then planning a program of pieces by young choreographers (Balanchine, its own choreographer, was away in Paris that spring). Cunningham originally wanted his contribution, *The Seasons*, to be designed by the northwestern American painter Morris Graves, but because Graves was unable to accept the commission, the ballet was designed by Isamu Noguchi, who had worked with Graham and who was to design Balanchine and Stravinsky's *Orpheus* for Ballet Society the following year. This change in designer entailed a change in the nature of the imagery to be presented onstage, but the cyclical structure envisaged by Cage and Cunningham remained. Cunningham himself danced in *The Seasons* with members of the Ballet Society company, including Tanaquil Le Clercq and Gisella Caccialanza. First performed at the Ziegfeld Theater in New York on 18 May 1947, *The Seasons* was the most successful of the non-Balanchine pieces in Ballet Society's brief history. It was revived the following year and again in January 1949, during the first season of Ballet Society's successor, the New York City Ballet.

In the early spring of 1948 Cunningham and Cage made their first cross-country tour of the United States. Before heading west they paid their first visit to Black Mountain College, the progressive liberal arts school in North Carolina, which led to an invitation to spend the summer. At Cage's suggestion, Josef Albers, head of the art faculty, also invited the artists Willem and Elaine de Kooning to join the summer faculty, which already included the engineer–social philosopher Buckminster Fuller, sculptor Richard Lippold and his wife, dancer Louise Lippold, and poet M. C. Richards. Cunningham and Cage taught classes, and Cage also presented the complete works of Erik Satie in a series of concerts. The climax of the summer was a production of Satie's play *Le Piège de Méduse* (translated by Richards as *The Ruse of Medusa*), with a cast that included Cunningham as a mechanical monkey, Fuller, and Elaine de Kooning. The de Koonings designed the sets, and stage and film director Arthur Penn directed.

Both Cage and Cunningham had attended D. T. Suzuki's lectures on Zen Buddhism at Columbia University, and during the late 1940s Cage became involved in the study of Eastern music and philosophy. Their collaborations were often described as, or accused of being, Dadaist in nature—Dadaism was anathema to the dance establishment at that time—and both men were certainly influenced by the ideas, not to mention the life and work, of Marcel Duchamp, whom Cage had met in the summer of 1942. Cunningham's dances did have a Dadaist quality in their inconsequentiality, use of nondance movement, and general iconoclasm; thus they were perhaps more closely linked to certain avant-garde ballets than they were to any previous works of American modern dance. Ballets presented in the early twentieth century by Diaghilev's Ballets Russes and by Rolf de Maré's Les Ballets Suédois, such as *Parade* and *Relâche*—both of which had music by Satie— are prime examples of that link.

Not only was Cunningham's approach to the content of dance and its relationship to music unorthodox, he was also moving toward a radically different use of space. In classical ballet the action traditionally radiates from a central point, usually occupied by the ballerina; in modern dance spatial patterns are more likely to be asymmetrical, though—as designated by Doris Humphrey in her book *The Art of Making Dances*—certain stage areas are "stronger" or "weaker" than others. In Cunningham's choreography, each dancer is his or her own "center," and the action may take place at any point in the space or in two or more places simultaneously; this technique perhaps derived from his study of Buddhism and his awareness of the concept of decentralization implicit in the principle that every creature is the Buddha. However, it was also clearly analogous to the New York school of painters' "field" approach to composition, exemplified by Jackson Pollock's "drip" canvases. These abstract expressionist painters were concerned with self-expression— their subject was, in critic Calvin Tomkins's phrase, "the heroically suffering artist." Yet self-expression was precisely what Cunningham and Cage wanted to eliminate from their respective crafts of choreography and composition.

In the early 1950s Cage began to use chance operations in his musical composition, drawing up charts for elements such as tempo, duration, and dynamics and choosing among them by tossing coins. Cunningham saw that similar methods could be applied to choreography, and he experimented with them initially in a large work entitled *Sixteen Dances for Soloist and Company of Three* (1951)— the music by Cage also composed by chance. Cunningham used chance procedures chiefly to determine the order of the dances, but in one quartet he used chance in the actual dance arrangement. Drawing up a gamut of movements for each dancer, he determined their sequence, duration, and direction by tossing coins. Thereafter, Cunningham habitually employed such methods in his choreography, in the belief that they would free him from the limitations of intuition and habit and open up possibilities that his own imagination might not present. In some cases he adapted processes used by Cage. For example, the notes in Cage's *Music for Piano* were determined by imperfections in the paper on which the piece was written. Cunningham's *Solo Suite in Space and Time* (1953) and *Suite for Five* (1956–1958, an expansion of the solo work) were both danced to *Music for Piano*, using such imperfections to determine the placement in space of the dancers.

There was, however, one significant difference between Cage's use of chance and Cunningham's. Cage did not wish to control the final result of his compositions; he left the performers free to make their own choices. Cunningham, in contrast, used chance processes primarily as an aid to composition, but once the choreography had been set, the dancers had, if any, strictly limited freedom in its performance.

The year 1952 was crucial in the development of the Cage-Cunningham aesthetic. Cunningham had been invited by conductor Leonard Berstein to choreograph two works for a festival of contemporary music to be held at Brandeis University in Waltham, Massachusetts; these

CUNNINGHAM. Viola Farber curves over Carolyn Brown in *Summerspace* (1958). Robert Rauschenberg designed the pointillist costumes and set. (Photograph by Richard Rutledge; courtesy of the Cunningham Dance Foundation.)

were a new version of Igor Stravinsky's *Les Noces* and some excerpts from Pierre Schaeffer and Pierre Henry's *Symphonie pour un Homme Seul* (1950), the first piece of *musique concrète* (taped music using pre-existing naturally produced sound) to be heard in the United States. Cunningham choreographed *Les Noces* in a fairly orthodox way, following the music, but the *Symphonie* was done by chance. It was clearly impossible for the dancers to count the beats of the *Symphonie* in the usual manner, so Cunningham decided simply to make a dance of the same duration; the sound and the movement proceeded independently. (The music was played twice, with two different choreographic versions, one a solo for Cunningham, the other a group dance.) This simultaneity of independent music and movement—itself a logical development of the way that he and Cage had been working for the last ten years—became a fundamental principle in Cunningham's work.

The dancers in the Brandeis performance included some experienced professionals, some who had been working with Cunningham in New York, and several Brandeis students with limited training. The problem was to find a way of putting them all onstage together, with very little rehearsal time. It occurred to Cunningham that he could give the dancers not only steps that he had invented but also ballroom dances and even everyday, nondance movements and gestures that would not require

great technical ability. He made three charts, each comprising movements from one of the categories of dancers, from which the movements were to be selected by chance processes. The dance was later renamed *Collage*.

Later that summer Cage and Cunningham were again in residence at Black Mountain, where Cage devised the famous untitled theater piece, a seminal work in the history of contemporary art. The performance lasted forty-five minutes and was completely unstructured except for rough time brackets, drawn up by chance methods, within which the participants were free to perform their various activities. Cage read a lecture; Cunningham danced; David Tudor played the piano; Robert Rauschenberg projected slides of his paintings on the walls and ceiling and played old phonograph records; Nicholas Cernovitch showed his films; and M. C. Richards and Charles Olson read their poetry. In devising this event Cage was influenced not only by his study of Zen but also by his reading of Antonin Artaud, the French surrealist actor and poet, author of *The Theater and its Double* (1938).

These performances at Brandeis and Black Mountain decisively established Cage and Cunningham as leaders of the avant-garde in the United States, with a wide and deep influence in painting and theater as well as in dance and music.

The following summer Cunningham was again in residence at Black Mountain, and this time he arranged to

CUNNINGHAM. Scene from *Nocturnes*, a work Cunningham created in 1956 that remained in the company's repertory until 1964. Here, William Davis and Steve Paxton support Carolyn Brown; Shareen Blair holds an arabesque in the background. The costume design is by Robert Rauschenberg. (Photograph by Richard Rutledge; courtesy of the Cunningham Dance Foundation.)

CUNNINGHAM. Chris Komar, Karole Armitage, Louise Burns, Rob Remley, and Cunningham in *Sounddance* (1975). An ear-shattering score by David Tudor accompanies this intricate, tumultuous work. (Photograph © 1975 by Johan Elbers; used by permission.)

bring a group of dancers who had been studying with him during the previous year or two. Cunningham had been teaching for the last few years, chiefly in order to train dancers who could perform his choreography—students from other modern dance classes could rarely move as lightly and swiftly as he wanted.

Cunningham technique, as it evolved over the years, is characterized by somewhat balletic leg action, with a progression from *pliés* to "foot stretches" (the equivalent of *battements tendus*), through "brushes" *(battements tendus jetés or dégagés)*, to "leg lifts" *(grands battements)*. These movements are combined with exercises designed to improve the flexibility of the back and torso. The technique emphasizes quick changes in rhythm, direction, and balance. Apart from the more or less standard progression of warm-up exercises, Cunningham resisted codification of his technique and did not impose rigid teaching methods on the instructors in his studio. He believed that good teachers do not get in the way of their students.

At the end of the summer of 1953 Cunningham and his dancers, among them Carolyn Brown, Viola Farber, Remy Charlip, and Paul Taylor, gave two performances of dances they had been rehearsing, including *Dime a Dance, Septet,* and *Untitled Solo.* These performances marked the inception of what would become the Merce Cunningham Dance Company. The first New York season of The Merce Cunningham Dance Company ran from 29 December 1953 to 3 January 1954 at the Theater de Lys on Christopher Street in Greenwitch Village. No reviews appeared in the New York daily press.

Very few of Cunningham's dances were ever made to ex-isting music. He used music by Erik Satie for three early solos, *Idyllic Song* (1944), *The Monkey Dances* (1948), and *Two Step* (1949), and three later group works, *Rag-Time Parade* (1950), *Septet* (1953), and *Nocturnes* (1956). He set *Dime a Dance* (1953) to nineteenth-century salon pieces for piano, selected by David Tudor. *Banjo* (1953) and *Picnic Polka* (1957) were to piano pieces by Louis Moreau Gottschalk. *Labyrinthian Dances* (1957) was to pieces by the little-known early twentieth-century Viennese composer Josef Matthias Hauer.

Otherwise Cunningham continued to work with Cage and with composers associated with him, such as Earle Brown, Morton Feldman, Christian Wolff, and Toshi Ichiyanagi. Much of the experimentation that Cage, David Tudor, and these composers were conducting was in the field of electronic music; at first they worked with magnetic tape but later with means of creating "live" electronic music, using equipment largely developed by Tudor. Increasingly electronic music became the accompaniment for Cunningham's dances. Tudor began to compose important scores for Cunningham, and scores were also supplied by Gordon Mumma, David Behrman, Pauline Oliveros, Maryanne Amacher, Takehisa Kosugi, Jon Gibson, Yasunao Tone, and Emanuel Dimas de Melo Pimenta, among others.

In the early years of its existence the dance company worked sporadically. Performances in the New York area—at the Brooklyn Academy of Music and occasionally in Manhattan—were few and far between. Cunningham kept the company together by giving them classes, followed by rehearsals. On tour, the company drove in a

Volkswagen microbus that accommodated the six dancers, two musicians (Cage and Tudor), a stage manager, and all the costumes and props. Cunningham paid all the food and lodging expenses and a small honorarium for each performance, and he collected the fees from the sponsors himself; touring usually resulted in a personal loss for him, unless he could make extra money by teaching master classes. Many of the performances were in colleges and universities, where the company gradually built up a small but devoted following for a kind of dancing that was quite unfamiliar and that often aroused antagonism at first.

For four consecutive summers, from 1958 to 1961, the company was in residence at the American Dance Festival, then held at Connecticut College in New London. The festival afforded Cunningham the luxury of several weeks of rehearsal, during which his dancers were housed and fed. The American Dance Festival commissioned several important works from the company, beginning with *Antic Meet* and *Summerspace* (both 1958), *Rune* (1959), and *Crises* (1960). In 1979 the festival, by then at Duke University in Durham, North Carolina, commissioned *Roadrunners* from Cunningham, who also received commissions from the festival for *Doubles* in 1984, the year of its fiftieth anniversary, and for *CRWDSPCR* in 1993.

In 1954 Cunningham asked Robert Rauschenberg, whom he and Cage had met in the winter of 1952 at the time of the painter's first New York exhibition, to design a set for *Minutiae*. (The costumes were by Remy Charlip, who had designed costumes for several dances in the early years.) For the next ten years Rauschenberg was, in effect, the company's resident designer, and often he toured as technical director and lighting designer as well.

During the 1950s avant-garde dance activity outside the Cunningham company was limited to a few choreographers, most of whom worked in isolation. The work of such soloists as Sybil Shearer, Katherine Litz, and Merle Marsicano was uniquely personal and belonged to no school. Jean Erdman, Nina Fonaroff, Erick Hawkins, and Shirley Broughton had broken away from Martha Graham to choreograph independently at about the same time that Cunningham had left her company. James Waring's highly theatrical pieces influenced not only younger dancers who worked with him but also the composers and painters with whom he collaborated. Alwin Nikolais, who had worked with Hanya Holm, began making his multimedia abstract dance works with his own company. Paul Taylor's early concerts, before he worked with Graham, were boldly experimental—he too collaborated with Rauschenberg, who contributed ideas as well as designs.

In the 1960s avant-garde activity suddenly proliferated. Much of it originated from the Judson Dance Theater, which had grown out of a dance composition course conducted at Cunningham's studio by the musician Robert Ellis Dunn, whose wife, Judith Dunn, was a member of the Cunningham company. Dunn's classes were based on ideas derived from experimental composition classes given by Cage at the New School for Social Research in New York during the late 1950s. Although the choreographers associated with the Judson Dance Theater and with the postmodern movement that stemmed from it rejected certain aspects of Cunningham's work—its technical finish, its theatricality, the fact that Cunningham himself re-

CUNNINGHAM. Alan Good, Helen Barrow, and Robert Swinston in a revival of *RainForest* (1968). The floating Mylar pillows that form the set were designed by Andy Warhol. (Photograph © 1988 by Jed Downhill; used by permission.)

CUNNINGHAM. The choreographer stalks away from his bouyant dancers (Patricia Lent, Helen Barrow, Victoria Finlayson, and Karen Radford) in *Fabrications* (1987). (Photograph © 1987 by Jed Downhill; used by permission.)

mained firmly in control—they were undoubtedly deeply influenced by it.

Cunningham, in turn, was aware of the Judson experiments. In the summer of 1963, while in residence with his company at the University of California, Los Angeles (UCLA), he made two works that introduced a greater degree of indeterminacy than he had previously allowed, *Field Dances* and *Story*. In both pieces the dancers learned a number of phrases. A running order for the phrases used in *Story* was posted in the wings at each performance, and the dancers were free to choose where in the space they would perform a given step, how many times, how fast, and so on. In *Field Dances*, Cunningham came as close as he ever came to allowing the dancers to improvise—they decided for themselves which phrases to perform. In both pieces the interaction with the other dancers also influenced their choices. Rauschenberg constructed his set for *Story* from whatever materials he found at the theater before the performance. The women wore yellow tights and leotards and the men black tights and blue leotards, adding "found" garments dumped out of a duffel bag in the wings.

The year 1964 marked a turning point in the company's history. Cunningham and Cage had done some traveling abroad in previous years but never with a full company; in 1949 they had spent the summer in Paris, giving performances with Tanaquil Le Clercq and Betty Nichols, Ballet Society dancers who happened to be on vacation there; in 1958 and 1960 they had appeared with Carolyn Brown and David Tudor at a number of European music festivals. In June 1964 the whole company embarked on a world tour that would last six months and take in thirty cities in fourteen countries across Europe (including eastern Europe) and Asia. In London the company opened at Sadler's Wells Theatre for a week at the end of July and then moved to the Phoenix Theatre for an additional three weeks, the longest continuous engagement ever played by the company, or any other modern dance company, at that time.

The company was also invited to perform in Vienna and Stockholm—but in museums, not in theaters. Because conventional performances of repertory pieces were not feasible, Cunningham devised a different kind of presentation for these spaces, which he called *Museum Event No. 1* (Museum of the Twentieth Century, Vienna, 24 June 1964), *No. 2*, and *No. 3* (Moderna Museet, Stockholm, 8 and 14 September 1964). These consisted of excerpts from dances, and even complete works, put together in a

CUNNINGHAM. Kimberly Bartosik, Patricia Lent, Emma Diamond, and Carol Teitelbaum leap together in Cunningham's *Five Stone Wind* (1988). (Photograph by Michael O'Neill; used by permission.)

new sequence, sometimes performed simultaneously or overlapping with one another. The events did not use the original musical accompaniment to each piece; instead, Cage's *Atlas Eclipticalis* (events 1 and 2) and *Variations IV* (event 3) were performed continuously by a mixture of company and local musicians. The performances lasted about eighty or ninety minutes, without intermission. In a sense, they were an extension of the idea behind the 1952 untitled theater piece at Black Mountain.

Cunningham was so pleased with the result that he continued to present such performances, simply called "Events," whenever his company had an opportunity to perform in a nontheatrical space, such as a basketball court, a gymnasium, a stadium, or even the open air; in 1972 an Event took place in the Piazza San Marco in Venice. Events were also given at Cunningham's studio in Westbeth, New York, and occasionally in theaters. Later Events often included material from works in progress or material specially made for them as well as sections from pieces no longer in the repertory. When presented on tour or as part of a regular engagement, Events were accompanied by the company musicians; however, some special series of Events, at Cunningham's studio, for example, used scores specially composed by guest musicians.

During the 1964 tour, in London and Paris especially, Cunningham's work was taken seriously and reviewed at length and in depth. When word got back to the United States, audiences and critics there also began to regard Cunningham's work as more than marginally important.

The world tour was financed in part by private subsidy and in part by grants from foundations, including the JDR 3rd Fund and the Foundation for Contemporary Performance Arts. Because of this funding, a more formal orga-

nization of the company's business side was required, and shortly before the tour began the Cunningham Dance Foundation was formed. It was the first nonprofit corporation to administer the affairs of a dance company, but since then almost every dance company that has achieved any kind of permanency has formalized itself in the same way.

Artistically some important internal changes had been made in the company by the end of the 1964 tour. Rauschenberg had become an internationally celebrated artist—he received the Venice Biennale Gold Medal that summer—and no longer found it possible to tour with the company. In addition, several dancers left the company; Viola Farber, one of the original company members, was among them.

In subsequent years the company toured more extensively in the United States, through programs initiated by the New York State Council on the Arts and the National Endowment for the Arts that helped to finance residencies in colleges and museums. These residencies in turn fostered the development of a large and knowledgeable audience for modern dance. The company also toured abroad more frequently, returning to Europe—especially to France—regularly as well as visiting Asia, South America, and Australia.

With Rauschenberg's departure, the company lacked a resident designer. The costumes for *Variations V* and *How to Pass, Kick, Fall and Run* (both 1965) were street or practice clothes. The set and costumes for *Place* (1966) were designed by Beverly Emmons, then the company's lighting designer. In 1967 Jasper Johns was appointed artistic adviser, responsible for choosing artists to design scenery and costumes as well as designing some himself. Many highly distinguished, if cumbersome, decors resulted. For *Scramble* (1967), Frank Stella designed strips of canvas, of different lengths and colors, mounted on mobile stands that the dancers moved about during the piece. Andy Warhol's decor for *RainForest* (1968) was in the form of a number of floating silver Mylar pillows, inflated with air and helium. Johns himself adapted Marcel Duchamp's *Large Glass* for *Walkaround Time* (also 1968), silk-screening the images onto a number of plastic inflatables. Robert Morris's set for *Canfield* (1969) featured a vertical beam that moved back and forth across the front of the stage; Bruce Nauman's set for *Tread* was a row of industrial fans that also stood between the dancers and the audience; and Neil Jenney built several tubular sculptures for *Objects* (1970). In some way all of these sets modified the stage space instead of simply decorating it with traditional painted flats or cloths. Johns designed the costumes for *Second Hand* (1970) and *Landrover* (1972), leotards and tights dyed in a variety of colors, which in *Second Hand* formed a spectrum that became apparent only when the dancers lined up across the stage for their final bow.

In 1973 the Paris Autumn Festival and the Paris International Dance Festival jointly commissioned a major work from Cunningham, Cage, and Johns for the Paris Opera Ballet. Cunningham had created large works before—*Aeon* (originally done with an augmented company), *Canfield, Landrover*—but *Un Jour ou Deux* was epic in length, size of cast, and use of space. It ran for ninety minutes without an intermission and required twenty-six dancers—Cunningham's largest cast ever—and Johns opened up the vast stage of the Paris Opera to its full depth. This was Cunningham's first choreography for a company other than his own since *The Seasons* in 1947.

Cunningham worked with the Paris Opera dancers for several weeks, teaching classes as well as rehearsing the piece. Although some of the dancers responded eagerly to the challenge of a new idiom—notably Wilfride Piollet and Jean Guizerix, two of the company's stars—others remained inflexible. Perhaps Cunningham's increased interest in the technical aspects of his choreography originated in reaction to this experience. Another factor was the loss of Carolyn Brown, his dance partner for almost twenty years, who had decided to leave the company at the end of the 1972 European tour. After *Un Jour ou Deux*, Cunningham began to work much more on ensemble, even unison, choreography of great technical complexity, as shown in *Torse* (1976), and even in *Sounddance* (1974/75) and *Rebus* (1975), despite the dramatic nature of these two dances. The term *dramatic* is not used here to denote specific narrative content; rather it refers to the effect of the dances' sheer dramatic intensity—and to the effect of the contrast between the virtuosity of the younger dancers and Cunningham's charismatic presence that often gave

those pieces in which he did appear an inescapable sense of drama. For Cunningham's power did not diminish, though he inevitably became less agile with the passing of time. Sometimes, as in *Roadrunners* (1979) and *Gallopade* (1981), the effect was comic; for example, a section of *Roadrunners* had him scurrying about the stage to avoid a woman who kept dancing in his direction while he frantically tried to put on pants, socks, and shoes. In contrast, *Quartet* (1981) seemed to be a meditation on tragic matters, perhaps even on death itself.

Jasper Johns was assisted on *Un Jour ou Deux* by Mark Lancaster, a young British painter, who thereafter became resident designer to the Cunningham company. In 1980 Lancaster was appointed artistic adviser, Johns having given up that position. In 1977 Rauschenberg had once again collaborated with Cunningham and Cage on a new work, *Travelogue;* his designs had their own title, *Tantric Geography.* Later that year Cunningham and Cage were able to realize the plan they had discussed thirty years before, at the time of *The Seasons*, to collaborate with Morris Graves: together they produced *Inlets*, which (appropriately) was rehearsed during a residency at the Cornish Institute in Seattle and presented at the University of Washington. A new version, *Inlets 2*, was made in 1983, with designs by Lancaster; this was presented by both the Cunningham company and the Groupe de Recherche Chorégraphique de l'Opéra de Paris (GRCOP).

Travelogue was first performed on the opening night of the Merce Cunningham Dance Company's first independent season in a Broadway theater, the Minskoff. From 1968 to 1973 the company had been resident at the Brooklyn Academy of Music and early in 1969 had participated

CUNNINGHAM. Four of the original cast members, Larissa McGoldrick, Victoria Finlayson, Alan Good, and Robert Swinston, in *Neighbors* (1991). This work was accompanied in performance by a score by Takehisa Kosugi; the backdrop was designed by Mark Lancaster. (Photograph © 1991 by Jed Downhill; used by permission.)

in a dance repertory series at the Billy Rose Theater in Manhattan. In the fall of 1978 the company gave a two-week season at New York's City Center where a spring season became an annual occurrence from 1979 to 1994 (with the exception of 1988, when the season was at the Joyce Theater). There were also new Events series at Cunningham's studio in Westbeth and at other New York venues—in fact, from 1974 to 1976 these were the only New York appearances the company made.

During the 1964 world tour several dances from the Cunningham repertory had been televised in Sweden, Finland, and Belgium. Cunningham made original pieces for television in Montreal (1961) and San Francisco (1968). In 1974 he collaborated with the television director Merrill Brockway on "A Video Event," broadcast in two parts on the Columbia Broadcasting System (CBS) program *Camera Three*. Cunningham concluded that if dance was likely to be seen on television more frequently in the future, and if he wanted to control how his dances would appear, he would be wise to learn about the medium. Charles Atlas, an independent filmmaker, was working with the company as technical director and had made a film of *Walkaround Time*. He and Cunningham acquired some video equipment and began to experiment. Their first video collaboration, *Westbeth*, taped at Cunningham's studio in 1974, was basically an exercise in the various properties of the medium.

In the next few years Cunningham and Atlas collaborated on several video and film dances, using more sophisticated equipment as time went on. *Blue Studio: Five Segments* (1975) was a short videotape, featuring Cunningham alone, that used chroma key and other optical devices. In 1976 they adapted *Squaregame*, which had been choreographed earlier that year, and called it *Squaregame Video*. Also in 1976 there was another collaboration with Merrill Brockway, "Event for Television," produced for the Public Broadcasting Service (PBS) *Dance in America* series. Like Cunningham's live Events, this program consisted of excerpts from dances in the repertory together with one segment, *Video Triangle*, created specially for the program.

Fractions I and II (videotape, 1977), *Locale* (film, 1979), *Channels/Inserts* (film, 1981), and *Coast Zone* (film, 1983) were all choreographed for the camera and, in a reversal of the usual procedure, were subsequently adapted for the stage. Each piece explored different aspects of choreography for the camera. Atlas also made films of *Torse* (1977) and *Exchange* (1978, unedited).

In 1984 Atlas was succeeded by Elliot Caplan as resident filmmaker with the Merce Cunningham Dance Company; his first collaboration with Cunningham was a videotape called *Deli Commedia* (1985). In 1986 they made *Points in Space*, co-produced by the Cunningham Dance Foundation and the British Broadcasting Corporation (BBC). This piece was adapted for the stage and taken into the company's repertory. Cunningham and Caplan also produced two technical videotapes, *Cunningham Dance Technique: Elementary Level* (1985) and *Intermediate Level* (1987), as well as a video version of the 1973 dance *Changing Steps* (1989).

Several of Cunningham's works have gone into the repertories of ballet and dance companies in the United States and abroad. In 1966 *Summerspace* was revived by the New York City Ballet, with the choreography slightly revised (the women were on pointe); it was later presented by the Cullberg Ballet, Sweden, in 1966, the Boston Ballet, in 1974, and the French company Théâtre du Silence, in 1976. The Boston Ballet also presented *Winterbranch* in 1974. Other revivals have included *Duets*, revived by American Ballet Theatre in 1982, and *Fielding Sixes*, by London's Ballet Rambert in 1983. In 1986 Cunningham restaged *Un Jour ou Deux* for the Paris Opera Ballet in a revised, shortened form; the Paris Opera Ballet also revived *Points in Space* in 1990. *Septet*, revived for Cunningham's own company in 1987 for the first time in more than twenty years, was staged by Chris Komar for the Rambert Dance Company (as it was now called) later that year; in 1990, the Rambert company acquired Cunningham's *Doubles*. *Septet* was also revived by Pacific Northwest Ballet in 1989 and by Mikhail Baryshnikov's White Oak Dance Project (which had acquired Cunningham's *Signals* in 1994) in 1996.

In 1985 Cunningham choreographed *Arcade* for Pennsylvania Ballet; soon after, the work entered the repertory of his own company. *Touchbase*, choreographed simulta-

CUNNINGHAM. In this scene from *Beach Birds* (1991), Michael Cole (center) perches on one leg for a prolonged, concentrated moment, as others dancers continue moving behind him. (Photograph by Michael O'Neill; used by permission.)

CUNNINGHAM. A portrait of the choreographer with members of his company in *Enter* (1992). Cunningham generated the movement for this work using the computer animation program Life-Forms. (Photograph © 1993 by Lois Greenfield; used by permission.)

neously for his own company and for dancers from the Rambert company in 1992, was first presented by Rambert in London later in the year and by Merce Cunningham Dance Company in March 1993. *Breakers*, commissioned by the Kennedy Center's Ballet Commissioning Project for the Boston Ballet in 1993, entered the repertory of Merce Cunningham Dance Company in March 1994.

Into the fifth decade of his career Cunningham continued to choreograph with unabated creativity, although he performed in fewer pieces himself. The 1983/84 season unveiled another product of the continuing collaboration between Cunningham and Cage; *Roaratorio: An Irish Circus on Finnegans Wake* was Cunningham's full-company choreography for a work Cage had made for radio in 1979. The text was Cage's adaptation of words from the 1939 stream-of-consciousness novel by James Joyce, and the music was a complex collage of sound and music that Cage and his assistant John Fullemann had recorded in Ireland. *Roaratorio* was given for the first time at the Festival de Lille, France, in October 1983. *Roaratorio* has also been performed at France's Avignon Festival, in July 1985, at the Brooklyn Academy of Music Next Wave Festival, in October 1986, and at the BBC Promenade Concerts, London, in July 1987.

In 1984 Cunningham choreographed three dances: *Pictures*, generally regarded as a masterpiece, *Doubles*, and *Phrases*. The latter was the first piece designed by William

Anastasi and Dove Bradshaw, who had succeeded Mark Lancaster in the post of artistic adviser. *Native Green* and *Arcade* were both created in 1985; *Grange Eve* and *Points in Space*, in 1986; *Fabrications, Shards,* and *Carousal*, in 1987; *Eleven* and *Five Stone Wind* (designed by Lancaster, with music by John Cage, David Tudor, and Takehisa Kosugi), in 1988; *Cargo X, Field and Figures, Inventions,* and *August Pace*, in 1989; *Polarity*, in 1990. Mark Lancaster frequently returned to design works by Cunningham, such as *Neighbors* (1991), *Touchbase* (1992), and *CRWDSPCR* (1993).

In 1990 Cunningham began to work with the computer program LifeForms (A Tool for Creating Human Movement). Starting with *Trackers* in 1991 every dance was choreographed in part with the use of this program, including the limpid and meditative *Beach Birds*, first presented at a James Joyce/John Cage Festival in Zurich in the summer of 1991. A film version, *Beach Birds For Camera*, was made by Elliot Caplan in December of the same year. Later works made with LifeForms showed an increasing complexity of movements and rhythms, beginning with *Loosestrife* (1991) and *Change of Address* (1992).

John Cage died in August 1992. At that time Cunningham was creating a major new dance, *Enter;* he continued to work on the piece, which was first presented at the Paris Opera Garnier in November 1992. *Doubletoss* and *CRWDSPCR* followed in 1993; the creation of the latter was recorded in another new film by Elliot Caplan, also called *CRWDSPCR* (released in 1996). Cage and Cunningham had originally planned to collaborate on a large work for the Joyce/Cage Festival in Zurich, to be called *Ocean*,

performed in the round, with the audience surrounding the stage and an orchestra of 112 surrounding the audience. At that time the project had to be abandoned for lack of a suitable venue. In 1994 it became possible to realize it, thanks to a joint commission from festivals in Brussels and Amsterdam, where *Ocean* was first performed in May and June of that year. The orchestral score was composed by Andrew Culver, according to Cage's original concept, with an electronic component by David Tudor. The design was by Marsha Skinner, who had previously designed *Beach Birds, Change of Address,* and *Enter.* Further performances of *Ocean* took place at the Teatro La Fenice in Venice in July 1995, at the University of California at Berkeley in April 1996, and at New York's Lincoln Center Festival '96 in August 1996.

Cunningham's posthumous collaboration with Cage continued with *Windows* (1995), with decor from one of Cage's paintings, and *Rondo* (1996), with music from one of his last compositions. Also in 1995, Cunningham choreographed *Ground Level Overlay*, with music by Stuart Dempster and decor by Leonardo Drew. *Installations* (1996) was performed in a video installation devised by Elliot Caplan, with music by the German composer Trimpin. Costumes for all these dances were designed by Suzanne Gallo, the company's long-time costume supervisor.

David Tudor died in the summer of 1996; he had already been succeeded as Musical Director (a title he assumed after the death of Cage) by Takehisa Kosugi, who continued the policy of musical innovation originated by Cage in the company's earliest years.

CUNNINGHAM. Jean Freebury and Frédéric Gafner glide past with open arms as Thomas Caley and Jeannie Steele (right) curve forward in *CRWDSPCR* (1993). Cunningham developed this work using the computer program LifeForms; the title can be read as "crowd spacer" or "crowds pacer." (Photograph by Jed Downhill; used by permission.)

Recognition of the importance of Cunningham's work has been reflected in numerous honors and awards, including two Guggenheim fellowships for choreography (1954 and 1959), the *Dance Magazine* Award (1960), and the Gold Medal for Choreographic Invention at the Fourth International Festival of Dance, Paris (1966). In 1972 he received an honorary doctorate of letters from the University of Illinois. Cunningham won a New York State Award (1975), the Capezio Dance Award (1977), and the Samuel H. Scripps / American Dance Festival Award (1982). Also in 1982 the French minister of culture named him Commander of the Order of Arts and Letters. In 1983 he received the Mayor of New York's Award of Honor for Arts and Culture, and in 1984 he became an honorary member of the American Academy and Institute of Arts and Letters. In 1985 he was awarded a MacArthur Foundation Fellowship, was a recipient of the Kennedy Center Honors, and won the Laurence Olivier Award for the best new dance production in London *(Pictures)*. In 1986 Cunningham and Cage received a Bessie (New York Dance and Performance Award) for sustained achievement. In 1987 Cunningham was the fifth recipient of Southern Methodist University's Algur H. Meadows Award for Excellence in the Arts. In January 1988 Cunningham was awarded the Dance/USA National Honor. At the end of his company's residency in Arles in July 1989 he was made Chevalier of the Légion d'Honneur by President François Mitterand of France. In September 1990 Cunningham was awarded the National Medal of Arts by U.S. President George Bush, and in October he became the recipient of the Digital Dance Premier Award in London.

In 1990 the Cunningham Dance Foundation produced a film *Cage/Cunningham*, directed by Elliot Caplan, on the collaboration of Merce Cunningham and John Cage. In 1993 the Wexner Prize was awarded to Cunningham and (posthumously) Cage by the Wexner Center for the Arts, Ohio State University. In the same year Cunningham received a Medal of Honor from the Universidad Complutense of Madrid, Spain; a second Bessie; and a Dance and Performance Award for the Best Performance by a Visiting Artist in London. In 1995 he received an Honorary Degree of Doctor of Fine Arts from Wesleyan University, Middletown, Connecticut; the Golden Lion of the Venice Biennale; and in Stockholm the Carina Ari Award (Grand Prix Video Danse to Merce Cunningham and Elliot Caplan). In 1996 he received the first Nellie Cornish Arts Achievement Award from his alma mater, the Cornish College of the Arts in Seattle, Washington.

[*See also* Canfield; Ocean; Suite for Five; Summerspace; Walkaround Time; Winterbranch; *and the entry on Cage.*]

BIBLIOGRAPHY

Cunningham, Merce. *Changes: Notes on Choreography.* Edited by Frances Starr. New York, 1968.

CUNNINGHAM. The choreographer in an Event, a program consisting of sections of different works spliced together, at the Joyce Theater, New York, February 1996. (Photograph © 1996 by Jed Downhill; used by permission.)

Cunningham, Merce, in conversation with Jacqueline Lesschaeve. *The Dancer and the Dance.* Rev. ed. New York, 1991.
Dance Perspectives, no. 34 (Summer 1968). Issue entitled "Time to Walk in Space," edited by Selma Jeanne Cohen.
Klosty, James, ed. *Merce Cunningham.* New ed. New York, 1986.
Kostelantz, Richard, ed. *Merce Cunningham: Dancing in Space and Time.* New York, 1992.
Tomkins, Calvin. *The Bride and the Bachelors: Five Masters of the Avant-Garde.* New York, 1965.
Vaughan, David. *Merce Cunningham: 50 Years.* New York, 1997.

FILMS.   The following films and/or videos are available from the Cunningham Dance Foundation, New York. *Story* (1964). *Variations V* (1966). *Walkaround Time* (1973). *Westbeth* (1974). *Blue Studio* (1975). *Squaregame Video* (1976). *Fractions I* (1977). *Grant for Television* (1977). *Torse* 1978. *Locale* (1979). *Channels/Inserts* (1981). *Coast Zone* (1983). *Deli Commedia* (1985). *Points in Space* (1986). *Changing Steps* (1989). *Cage/Cunningham* (1991). *Beach Birds for Camera* (1993). *CRWDSPCR* (1996). Two instructional films are also available. *Cunningham Dance Technique: Elementary Level* (1985) and *Cunningham Dance Technique: Intermediate Level* (1987).

ARCHIVE.   Cunningham Dance Foundation, New York.

DAVID VAUGHAN

CURRY, JOHN (born 3 September 1949 in Birmingham, died 15 April 1994 in England), English ice skater and choreographer. Curry began his ice-skating career at

CURRY. The innovative male skater John Curry with Cathy Foulkes in Norman Maen's *L'Après-midi d'un Faune*. (Photograph © 1978 by Jack Vartoogian; used by permission.)

the age of seven and by the age of fifteen had won many regional competitions; in 1967 he became the Junior British Champion in figure skating. At the time of his first victory in the British Men's Skating Championship (1970), he was acknowledged to be one of the most creative and arresting ice skaters to have come out of England. That very creativity made his career somewhat embattled, however. From an early age Curry had been interested in classical ballet, and he had thought briefly of training as a dancer. Though he chose to remain a figure skater, his interest in and natural instinct for balletic line and rhythm began to permeate his performances in competitions, particularly in the short program and free style sections, in which the competitor is expected to display a number of technical moves within an orchestrated presentation (in the short program, these are predetermined; in the long, they are chosen by the individual competitor).

Following World War II, men's figure skating developed along increasingly robust lines, with an emphasis on virtuosity rather than grace, as exemplified by such skaters as Dick Button (the first man to perform a triple axel, which entails three-and-a-half revolutions in the air, in competition). Thus, Curry's style, which emphasized fluid line and musicality over isolated, discrete displays of technical skill, was considered incorrect by some judges, decidedly unmasculine by others. Nevertheless, Curry

persisted and eventually prevailed. Despite uneven performances in a number of major international competitions, by 1975 he had won his fifth consecutive British men's title and, under renowned trainer Carlo Fassi, had honed his technique to a competitive edge. In 1976 he became European champion and followed this victory with an Olympic gold medal and the world championship. He skated his winning freestyle routine to Léon Minkus's rendition of music from the ballet *Don Quixote;* it featured liquid turns; buoyant, musically supported jumps; and a triumphant, spread-eagle circuit of the arena.

For Curry, this was the start, not the end, of a career. For some time he had cherished the idea of carrying figure skating out of the competitive arena and into the theater. The Olympic victory gave him the prominence to implement a style that had become a vision. Curry conceived of skating as a theater art capable of complexity of thought and design and of generating and sustaining a body of lasting work, such as exists for drama and dance. To this end, he assembled a small company, John Curry's Theatre of Skating, and in late 1976 began to give a series of performances, first in England and then in the United States. These programs, like a mixed bill in ballet, featured a series of varied solos, pas de deux, and ensemble pieces designed to create, and then display, a new style of skating—one influenced by the values and the lexicon of classical ballet. In 1978 the name of the company was changed to Ice Dancing. Curry's style required on the one hand a different approach to training and on the other a different type of material from that employed in traditional figure skating. Curry's training utilized a ballet *barre*, and his skaters were encouraged to display flowing lines and flexible backs, working out of *pliés* through relaxed, turned-out hips. This soft line compensated for one of skating's obvious differences from dance: the fact that the skating boot prevents any flexion of the foot and can truncate the body line. It was what the booted foot could do that contributed significantly to the hybrid style Curry was in search of, however.

In his desire to substitute skating choreography for skating routine, he went to the most likely source—dance choreographers. Among his earliest collaborators were Norman Maen, Jean-Pierre Bonnefous, Peter Martins, Kenneth MacMillan, Donald Saddler, and Twyla Tharp. The works they created for Curry and his company ranged from amiable period pieces for the corps, such as Saddler's *Palais de Glace*, in which skating was treated as a literal environment, to balletic skating pieces such as Bonnefous's *Ice Moves* and Maen's *L'Après-midi d'un Faune* to solos such as Tharp's *After All*, a piece about skating and particularly about Curry as a skater (at once a confident technician and a contemplative dreamer).

All the choreographers who have worked with Curry have been fascinated by ice skating's unique attributes:

speed, the possibility of executing virtually limitless turns, and the ability to make the transition from forward to backward motion invisibly, as well as the intriguing problems of balance. Those who began to work with Curry in the mid-1980s—among them Laura Dean, Eliot Feld, and Lar Lubovitch—have made technical challenges the center of remote, urgent, and emblematic pieces. Curry's work, which at first was somewhat genteel and directly generated by ballet, began to move toward increasing abstraction in the group pieces; at the same time, his solos and duets moved toward character skating in vignettes of varying tones reminiscent of *demi-caractères* in ballet but making full use of skating technique and imagery. Curry realized that for a new style of skating to be established and maintained, not a single company but a succeeding generation of skaters was needed. He founded a school that included in its methodology a ballet *barre* and the inculcation of a visceral approach to skating reminiscent of the Vaganova system, which dictates the Kirov manner. Financial exigencies made Curry's company internally fluid and transient, although a number of skaters, including Cathy Foulkes, remained with him for more than a decade, with a different corps and featured artists, such as Patricia Dodd, Jo Jo Starbuck, and David Santee. The two poles of its existence were New York and London, though it performed extensively throughout the United States and Britain.

Like dance pioneers before him, Curry attempted to create his own more balletic, articulate, and emotional style of skating as the basis for a new skating language, one that, under the performance heading, *Ice Dancing*, negotiates between ice and dance. His premature death from AIDS in 1994 left the field without its brightest light; companies such as the Ice Theater of New York, inspired by his example and modeled on his group, are his heirs.

BIBLIOGRAPHY

Money, Keith. *John Curry.* New York, 1978.
Montague, Sarah. "Art of Ice." *Ballet Review* 13 (Spring 1985): 64–73.

VIDEOTAPE: *John Curry: Dance on Ice* (1978), Dance Collection, New York Public Library for the Performing Arts.

SARAH MONTAGUE

CURZ, DANIEL (also spelled Curtz, Kurtz; born 23 December 1753 in Venice, died after 1818), dancer and ballet director. Curz worked with Gaspero Angiolini in Venice in 1773, and his later career in Poland shows how thoroughly he adopted his teacher's aesthetic of the *ballet d'action*. From 1774 to 1776 he performed as a soloist in Vienna, then went to Warsaw, where he remained for the rest of his career. With François Gabriel Le Doux, he co-directed His Majesty's Dancers from 1785 to 1794; this company originated as an aristocrat's avocation and be-

came Poland's first national ballet company. Thus Curz played an important role in establishing ballet in his adopted country.

Curz staged works by Angiolini, Jean-Georges Noverre, and Charles Le Picq in addition to choreographing about eighty original ballets. His notable works included *La Forête Enchantée* (1785), *La Partie de Chasse d'Henri IV* (1786), *La Pupille Espagnole* (1787), *Les Cracoviens et Cosaques* (1788), *Cléopâtre* (1789), and *L'Enrôlement* (1794).

After His Majesty's Dancers disbanded, Curz served as ballet master in Lemberg (1795–1798). He later taught at noble estates and secondary schools in eastern Poland.

[*See* Poland, *article on* Theatrical Dance.]

BIBLIOGRAPHY

Chynowski, Paweł, and Janina Pudełek. *Almanach baletu warszawskiego, 1785–1985/Le ballet de Varsovie, 1785–1985.* Warsaw, 1987.
Pudełek, Janina. *Two Hundred Years of Polish Ballet, 1785–1985.* Warsaw, 1985.

PAWEŁ CHYNOWSKI

CYGNE, LE. *See* Dying Swan, The.

CZARDAS (Hung., *csárdás;* Ger., *Tschardasch*) is a generic name for Hungarian couple dances, performed to newer-style folk music, that have been popular since the eighteenth century. Today a variety of czardases exist as solo, couple, and group forms, some combined with archaic and ritual dances—hence the numerous regional terms (*lippentős, mártogatós, dobogós, szapora, csendes, ugrós, rezgő*). The name *csárdás* derives from Persian, transplanted to Hungarian soil during the Ottoman occupation; in the mid-sixteenth century, *csárda* was used as a term for a military resting place, then later for a guesthouse or a roadside inn. Dances performed in these taverns were varied in style and kinetic elements; however, during the early nineteenth century they became homogenized through the conscious efforts of Hungary's anti-Habsburg elite, who were trying to fashion a genuine national culture for their emerging independent nation-state.

Ethnohistorical documents of the 1840s speak of peasant dances executed with a characteristic hold: the man places his hands on his partner's waist, and the woman places her hands on her partner's shoulders. Other noted elements are single and double sidesteps, various turns, and the fancy footwork often referred to as *cifrázás* or *figurázás*. Descriptions also mention the czardas's three distinct tempi (*három a tánc*), gradually increasing from slow to medium to fast, an attribute transplanted from earlier dance practices. Although the actual kinetic attributes of the czardas are in many ways analogous to move-

CZARDAS. A painting of Hungarian musicians and dancers outside a *csárda* ("roadside inn") in the mid-nineteenth century. (Photograph courtesy of the Dance Research Department, Ethnomusicological Institute, Hungarian Academy of Sciences, Budapest.)

ments of pre-1840s dances, many of the characteristics depicted in the nineteenth century are still discernible.

Both musical and rhythmic qualities of czardas dancing are based on the the so-called punctuated or *verbunkos*-style (men's "recruiting" dance) pattern in 2/4, 4/4, and 3/4 time, with musical fourths rather than eighths playing a determining role (Martin, 1979). The accompanying instrumental beat is always the slower *dűvő* (stressing every quarter) and the faster *esztam* (stressing every other eighth). Aside from the few movements mentioned, there are no prescribed spatial or movement patterns in the czardas: couples execute steps according to their own knowledge and desire. Perhaps this prompted one early eyewitness to observe that this "dance is characteristic of a people who feel free and independent" (Szentpál, 1954; p. 42).

Although dances of Hungarian character were known elsewhere in the late fifteenth and early sixteenth centuries *(ballo ungaro, ungaresca,* and *ungarischer Tantz),* it was only from the middle of the nineteenth century that the czardas gained worldwide acclaim (Kürti, 1983). Its elevation to the national and international stage was facil-

itated by a growing number of patriotic balls and traveling theater ensembles (Pesovár, 1980). From Paris to Venice, from Berlin to Prague, plays and folk ballets dazzled audiences: their simple plots recalled the Austro-Hungarian monarchy's rural cultures, embellished with color and stereotyped ethnic characters (Szentpál, 1954).

During this cultural awakening, illustrious dance masters (Szöllősy, Farkas, Lakatos, and Veszter) and popular composers (Rózsavölgyi, Lavotta, and Bihari) emerged. Their creations *(palotás, toborzó, körmagyar,* and other ballroom dances) were instrumental in welding international dances of the time—the cotillon, quadrille, minuet, waltz, polonaise, polka, *Zwei-Drei Schritt,* gavotte, and galop—with the czardas (Szentpál, 1954). These new dances made their way back into the countryside, creating an amalgam of dance culture in which local elements fused with steps recognizable today in classical ballet, ballroom, and European folk dances.

[*See also* Hungary, *article on* Traditional and Popular Dance.]

BIBLIOGRAPHY

Kürti, László. "The Ungaresca and Heyduck Music and Dance Tradition of Renaissance Europe." *Sixteenth-Century Journal* 14 (Spring 1983): 63–104.

Martin, György. "Die Kennzeichen und Entwicklung des neuen ungarischen Tanzstiles." *Acta Ethnographica Academiae Scientiarum Hungaricae* 28 (1979): 155–175.

Pesovár, Ernő. "A csárdás kialakulása" and "A lengyel tánczene és társastáncok hatása a csárdásra." In *Magyar néptánchagyományok*, edited by Lajos Lelkes. Budapest, 1983.

Szentpál, Olga. *A csárdás: A magyar nemzeti társastánc a 19. század első felében.* Budapest, 1953.

ARCHIVES. The Folk Dance Research Department of the Ethnomusicological Institute, Hungarian Academy of Sciences, Budapest, houses the largest collection of written, visual, and Labanotation material concerning Hungarian folk dances. In addition, there are archival films and photos in the Ethnological Collection of the Hungarian Ethnographic Museum, Budapest, an institution that also possesses important written materials on peasant dance, games, and customs. Regional and local museums throughout Hungary offer smaller databases, while private collections, mostly of recent vintage, are also numerous.

LÁSZLÓ KÜRTI

CZECH REPUBLIC AND SLOVAK REPUBLIC.

[To survey the dance traditions of the Czech Republic and the Slovak Republic, this entry comprises three articles:

    Folk and Traditional Dance
    Theatrical Dance
    Dance Research and Publication

For further discussion of theatrical dance, see the entries on individual companies, choreographers, and dancers.]

Folk and Traditional Dance

The rich traditions of folk music and dance in the Czech Republic and the Slovak Republic are rooted in the long coexistence of two closely related nations, the Czechs and the Slovaks. Differences in the forms of folk art in different regions stem from the influence of these two separate but intertwined traditions. The tradition of folk music and dance in the Czech lands (Bohemia and Moravia) is an integral part of Central European culture, while in earlier times the southern and eastern regions of Moravia and Slovakia, especially the area along the Carpathian Mountains, identified more with the Slovak cultures to the east. From these complex currents, many interrelated and transitional types of dances emerged.

Since the seventeenth century the aristocratic and folk cultures influenced each other not only in the larger cities but also in the areas around the numerous châteaux of Bohemia and Moravia and in the rich mining towns of Slovakia. This exchange is documented by the names of folk dances that appear in the scores of many types of musical compositions, including various lute and clavichord scores. The principles of the Baroque dance suite, together with features retained from the older Renaissance dance forms, encouraged the stabilization of many types of folk dances. Among the most important of these is a two-part suite, common as early as the sixteenth century, consisting of a slow 2/4 dance followed by a fast 3/4 version of the exact same melody (called the *tripel* or *pro-*

porce in Czech). Known as the *Vortanz* and *Nachtanz* in German, this two-part dance resembles the pairing of pavane and galliard in the Renaissance, or the minuet and gavotte in the Baroque era.

In Bohemia and Moravia, the so-called teachers' music played an important role. The influence of teachers, who had a prominent role in church and château music, was enhanced by their extensive participation in the bands that played for various dancing events. Dancing teachers, too, gave lessons not only in Prague but also in the inns on the outskirts of town, which were frequented by young artisans. Toward the end of the eighteenth century and in the first half of the nineteenth, many ballroom dances then in vogue found their way into the repertory of village dances. Their influence manifested itself in multiform folk adaptations of these fashionable dances and in an enrichment of the choreographic motifs and figures in the older folk dances.

Of the European types of contredanses, the ecossaise or schottische was the closest to the Czech type of duplemeter dance similarly called *šotyš*, a word used also for the "pushing" or "changing" step that characterizes the dance. Dances based on this step were often performed as line dances; when turning steps were added, they changed into couple dances. This innovation is behind the origin of the Czech polka, as a couple dance based on a turning-and-weight-changing step continuously repeated in a circle. Together with the long-prevailing minuet, the triple-meter folk dances of Czech provenance developed in parallel with the general conquest of the parquet floor by the enormously popular waltzes, which were often danced at a feverish tempo. The exchange between ballroom and folk forms led to the invention of several new triple-meter dances, including the *hulán* and the *rejdovák*, a line dance based on waltz steps. Most of the surviving local variations of waltzes and older types of triple-meter dances for couples show the folk influence.

The Carpathian region, reaching deep into Slovakia and eastern Moravia to the area called Wallachia, is home to the dances connected with the shepherds' culture. They are represented by men's jumping dances called the *odzemek* ("off the ground"), the *skok*, and the *hajduch*, danced by both soloists and groups.

Forms and Styles of Czech and Slovak Folk Dances. The oldest forms of dances in the Czech and Slovak lands are the *chorovod* (leaders' dances), which are performed to unaccompanied songs, and whose basic formations and motifs have survived in such Bohemian and Moravian children's games as *zlatá brána* ("golden gate"), *hélička*, and *žalman* (a line or circle dance). The original chain form has been preserved in wedding and later in Carnival dances in the *kotek* ("cat"), still danced at parties, and in the Moravian ceremonial women's dance called the *konopice* (hemp dance), which was connected with magi-

CZECH REPUBLIC AND SLOVAK REPUBLIC: Folk and Traditional Dance. A wall painting dating from the 1780s at the castle of Velké Meziříčí in the Czech-Moravian highlands. In this characteristic scene, villagers perform couple dances for the entertainment of the noble von Lichenštejn family. Performances by peasants for nobility were customary in central Europe at this time and were considered displays of loyalty. (Photograph courtesy of Hanna Laudová.)

cal practices. In Bohemia, housewives used to jump *na len* ("on flax").

Slovak dances of the *chorovod* type may be of an archaic character and are always accompanied by ceremonial songs, mostly about spring. They are danced in semicircles, circles, and in a chain formation in which girls move from one end of their village to the other. Such dances include also *kola* ("rounds"), often very fast, danced either by girls only or by girls and boys together. Similar rounds have also survived in amusing dances for young people in Moravia and Bohemia. The basic steps of the closely formed ring of dancers, who join hands behind each others' backs, are running, galloping, and skipping steps, either in 3/4 or 2/4 rhythm. The dancing is interrupted by short tunes during which the dancers keep still. In Bohemia, the accompaniment is provided by bagpipes, in western Moravia by a rustic form of the medieval fiddle.

Another typical choreographic form in Slovakia is the *šorový* (line dance, from the Hungarian *sor*, "line") with short steps and stamps executed with a wide range of dynamics. Group dances also include those in imitation of military recruits, called Bašistovská and Marhaňská (after places in eastern Slovakia). These imitate military drills in a witty, yet rather demanding, dance form. They are based on decorative variations of movements in the *verbunk* ("recruiting dance") and characterized by typical cries and a proud posture. They are danced mostly with a long-handled ax or, in northern Slovakia, with sticks decorated with metal rings that emphasize the rhythms of the dance. The character of the steps, high and low jumps, shifts of pose, and squats, and the order of the dance figures vary from region to region and village to village. They are sometimes the basis of mimic improvisations on animal motifs, such as the *medvědka* ("bear"), *žabský* ("frog"), and *zaječí* ("hare"). The same magical purpose has been ascribed to the high jumps of the men during dances at Carnival, which in south Moravia developed into a rather demanding jumping contest called *hošije*.

An older and rather remarkable category of dances includes variations on ancient guild "dances of honor," which are rare in Europe today. They are chain dances performed with weapons, and their variations are danced with both real and wooden sabers, sticks, hoops, and other props, according to the customs of the respective professions. They have survived as part of Carnival rounds, in southern Bohemia as *švertance* ("sword dances," from the German *Schwertänze*, "heavy dances"), in Moravia as dances *pod šable* ("under sabers"), and in Slovakia as dances belonging to various trades—for example, the *debnársky* (coopers' dance) and the *kordovnický* (rope-makers' dance). Similar in spirit are the *turecký* (Turkish dances), which recall battles with the Turks.

The largest category of Bohemian, Moravian, and Slovak dances consists of the couple dances, which represent many different regions, periods, and styles. The oldest group includes couple dances called *točivé* (turning dances), whose main feature is the gradual or rapid spinning of the couple, who hold one another tightly. The dance begins with men singing in front of the band while the couple begin the swinging step in place. Then the male partner improvises shorter *odzemok* ("jumping") steps around the woman, who turns in place; sometimes both perform solo variations simultaneously in a fast tempo while traveling in a circle. Next the couple whirls on the spot; the individual variations are then repeated. A 2/4 rhythm is used in the south Moravian dances, which include the *sedlácká* (farmers' dance) and the *danaj* as well as *starosvětská* ("old-fashioned"), *skočná* ("hopping"), and the Wallachian *gúlaná* ("rolling") and *točená* ("turning") dances. In Slovakia similar forms are the *do krutu* ("in the round"), *skakaná* ("jumping"), and *šuchon* ("pushing-step") dances. Czech and Moravian couple dances often end with waltz and polka codas.

Triple-meter couple dances are adapted from the polonaise type, such as the Silesian *starodávny* ("old-fashioned") and the central Moravian *coufavá* ("sauntering") dances. In Bohemia, the fast whirling style has survived in a reel-like dance performed by couples and accompanied by bagpipes, the rhythmical polyphonic play of which is supported by a characteristic declamation of the lyrics. The triple-meter dances also include loose variations of such forms as the minuet, deutsch, and ländler used as wedding dances; local variations called *zdlouha* ("slow"), *houpavá* ("swinging"), and *loudavá* ("sauntering"); and extravagant dances, such as the *hulán* and *rejdovák*. The last is the model for the *redowa*, a social dance based on a typical swinging two-step that changes from one foot to the other, or on a special form of the waltz step. The *redowa* became well known in Europe as a ballroom dance in the nineteenth century.

CZECH REPUBLIC AND SLOVAK REPUBLIC: Folk and Traditional Dance. A drawing dating from the 1820s depicting Fidlovačka, the Prague festival of the bootmakers. In this scene, the honored instruments of the trade are raised on a pole amidst dancing couples. Note the variety of partnering holds the dancers use as they spin. (Photograph courtesy of Hanna Laudová.)

Another group includes the duple-time two-step dances characterized by a sudden step or jump from one foot to the other with a simultaneous turn of 180 degrees or more by both partners, a movement known as *obkročák* (circular step). This difficult step is considered a specialty of Bohemian dance. Another important type of step is *skočná*. The dance called the *vrták* ("the fool"), like the waltz, was forbidden in the eighteenth century; it includes an intricate combination of different steps and jumps. Some older dances in 2/4 time contained an elementary polka step enriched with various turns, stamps, and slip-steps, as in the *dupák* (stamping dance). Influenced by the écossaise, these dances multiplied and developed new spatial patterns. From the first quarter of the nineteenth century onward, various types of mazurkas became popular in addition to the dances of the *šotyš* (schottische) type.

A special group of Czech dances are those with alternating rhythms, called *matenik* ("muddles"), which testify to the extraordinary rhythmical sense and skill of Czech folk dancers. Their structure consists of triple- and duple-meter sections in a steady tempo; about 130 variations are known. The basic steps are drawn from the *obkročák*, the polka, and the waltz. Their names and song texts are rich in concrete images drawn from rural culture: *slepička* ("hen"), *kozel* ("buck"), *Jidás* (Judas), and so on. A singular case of polyrhythm in a Czech dance is the combination of duple- and triple-meter steps performed in 3/4 rhythm in the *furiant* ("the swaggerer"), in which the dancers execute three *obkročák* steps in duple time during the first two bars of every verse of the song.

CZECH REPUBLIC AND SLOVAK REPUBLIC: Folk and Traditional Dance. Performers of the *verbunk* ("recruiting dance") in a village near Břeclav in southern Moravia, c.1950. The man in the center performs a characteristic "wallowing" step in which one knee skims the ground. (Photograph by Ludvík Baran; courtesy of Hanna Laudová.)

In the first half of the nineteenth century, a period of national revival, many dances with more complex musical accompaniment were invented as ballroom dancing grew in popularity in towns and villages alike. Two-part dances with one section in duple and the other in triple meter reemerged, such as the pair of *rejdovák* and *rejdovačka*—old dances that had been danced separately in the folk repertory—which however reversed the old sequence of meters and tempos, since the slow 3/4 *rejdovák* in this case preceded the fast 2/4 *rejdovačka*. The sturdy old rule according to which the musicians changed rhythm while continuing to play a metrically altered version of the same melody was also broken, and there now appeared many dances that used a polka with a new melody as a kind of coda for their first section.

The choreographic figures of couple dances became more varied; many followed the model of the *kadryla* (quadrille) and were based on several popular dance songs, for example the *čtyřpárová* (for four couples), and the Slovak *rosička* ("morning dew"). The most popular national quadrille was the *beseda*, a suite of slightly stylized Czech folk dances. For this dance the original music and lyrics and the steps and their variations were integrated into the sections of the *quadrille française* (including its La Visite, La Chaine, and Le Moulin). The link that united the various sections, fulfilling the ritornello function in a rondo, was the *furiant*. The dances were enriched with amusing motifs of the *Pusseltanz* type (a kissing dance, from a German word meaning "to putter about"): *líbání* ("kissing"), *šáteček* ("kerchief"), or the playful *honivá* ("chase") and *koníček* ("horse"). Artisans' dances, using imitations of working movements, also became widespread.

The climax of revivalist national tendencies was the introduction of the Czech polka into the repertory both at home and abroad. The origin of the polka form as a folk dance is uncertain. It was first documented as a new ballroom dance around 1830 in compositions written by conductors; it bears traces of folk melodies but corresponds to the new compositional requirements of ballroom dances. One element was the standard repeated changing step (the Czech polka step, derived from the *šotyš*, as described above) that had appeared in various combinations in Czech folk dances. The model for the steps and the character of the dance was probably the écossaise, and the name *polka* was likely adopted out of sympathy for the Polish emigrants who found refuge in eastern Bohemia after the unsuccessful uprising against Russian rule in 1830. The polka was also danced in this region to short tunes like those used for the the *krakowiaks*, with which it shared the same basic steps. Because the polka was often danced to older songs well known from older local dances, it had a folk appearance that was further emphasized in the new polka compositions of village conductors. As an expression of the genius of Czech dance culture, the

CZECH REPUBLIC AND SLOVAK REPUBLIC: Folk and Traditional Dance. Men performing a Moravian chain and sword dance called *pod šable*, which literally means "under sabers," 1964. This dance is generally performed during Carnival as a procession from house to house. (Photograph courtesy of Hanna Laudová; from the Institute of Ethnography, Czech Academy of Sciences, Prague.)

polka found an important place in the works of leading Czech composers such as Dvořák and Smetana.

Many folklore ensembles draw from the rich native folk dance tradition in both the Czech Republic and Slovak Republic. Folk dances are now adapted for stage performance, often in connection with demonstrations of traditional and contemporary customs. They are based on information from material provided by village groups from rural areas, where folk culture is kept alive.

Contemporary folk dance groups have evolved enormously in the Czech Republic in recent years. Today there are about thirty-five regional folklore festivals in Bohemia and Moravia, in addition to the important international folklore festival in Strážnice (in southern Moravia) and the international festival of bagpipe music and dance in Strakonice (southern Bohemia). In the Slovak Republic there are international festivals in Východná and Košice as well as about thirty regional events.

[*For related discussion, see* European Traditional Dance.]

BIBLIOGRAPHY

Bartoš, František. *Národní písně moravské, v nově nasbírané.* Brno, 1889.

Corrsin, S. D. "Sword Dancing in Bohemia in the Late Nineteenth Century." *Country Dance and Song* 24 (1994): 1–13.

Erben, Karel Jaromír. *Prostonárodní české písně a říkadla.* 2 vols. Prague, 1862–1864.

Holas, Čeněk. *České národní písně a tance.* 6 vols. Prague, 1906–1910.

Hošková, Jana. "On Dance Research and Publicity in Czechoslovakia." In *Beyond Performance: Dance Scholarship Today,* edited by Susan Au and Frank-Manuel Peter. Berlin, 1989.

Janáček, Leoš, and Lucie Bakešová. *Moravské národní tance.* Brno, 1891.

Jelínková, Zdenka. *Valašské lidové tance.* Prague, 1954.

Jelínková, Zdenka. *Točivé tance.* Gottwaldov, 1959.

Jelínková, Zdenka. "Oberlausitzer 'Reja.'" *Lětopis Instituta za Serbski Ludozpyt, Rjad C,* no. 4 (1959–1960): 58–79.

Jelínková, Zdenka. "Choreologic Types of 'Choro-Leading' Dances." *Věstník,* no. 1–2 (1967): 1–45.

Jelínková, Zdenka. *Peasant-Dance of Southern Moravia* (in Czech). Hodonín, 1983.

John, Alois. "Egerländer Tänze." *Österreichische Zeitschrift für Volkskunde* 14 (1908): 96–108.

Kresánek, Jozef. "Historické korene hajdúckeho tanca." *Hudebnovedné Študie* 3 (1959): 136–162.

Kröschlová, Eva. *Dobové tance 16. až 19. století.* Prague, 1981.

Laudová, Hannah. "Die figuralen Formen der älteren Paartänze auf dem Gebiet der ČSSR." *Veröffentlichungen des Instituts für Volkskunde der Universität Wien* 12 (1968): 289–303.

Laudová, Hannah. "Lidové slavnosti-jejich formy a funkce v jednotlivých obodobích národního obrození." In *Etnografie národního obrození,* vol. 1, 3, and 4, by Hannah Laudová et al. Prague, 1975, 1978, 1978.

Laudová, Hannah. *Trodice mečových tanců v lidové kultuře v Čechách a na Moravě.* Prague, 1996.

Markl, Jaroslav. *Nejstarší sbírky českých lidových písní.* Prague, 1987.

Mátlová, Ludmila. *Lidové tance a taneční hry z Hané.* V Prostejove, 1979–.

Nejedlý, Zdeněk. *Bedřich Smetana.* Vol. 4. Prague, 1951.

Pavlicová, Martina. "Research Results." *Viltis* 55 (September–October 1955): 15–17.

Pecka, Jindrich. "Tradition and Present of Czech Folk Music." *Viltis* 50 (May 1991): 4–5.

Podešvová, Hana. *Polka a lidové tance na Opavsku.* Opava, 1956.

Rittersberg, Jan. *České národní písně.* Prague, 1825.

Soukupová, Zora. *Folkdances of Southern Bohemia* (in Czech). 2 vols. České Budějovice, 1979.

Tanec/Dance. Prague, 1991.

Taneční listy 2. Prague, 1968.

Torp, Lisbet. *Chain and Round Dance Patterns: A Method for Structural Analysis and Its Application to European Material.* 3 vols. Copenhagen, 1990.

Vetterl, Karel. "K historii hanáckého tance 'coufavá.'" *Český Lid* 46 (1959): 277–286.

Vetterl, Karel. *Collection of Songs, Music, and Dances of Moravia and Silesia from the Year 1819* (in Czech). Strážnice, 1994.

Vycpálek, Josef. *České tance.* Prague, 1921.

Vycpálek, Vratislav. "The History of Polka" (in Czech). *Československá Etnografie* 4 (1961): 358–373.

Zálešák, Cyril. *Ľudové tance na Slovensku.* Bratislava, 1964.

Zich, Otakar. "Tance s proměnlivým taktem." *Národopisný Věstník Českoslovanský* 11 (1916): 6–53, 141–174, 268–311, 388–427.

Zírbt, Čeněk. *Jak se kdy v Čechách tancovalo* (1895). 2d ed. Prague, 1960.

ARCHIVES. Ethnographic Society, Czech Academy of Sciences, Prague. Institute for Anthropology and Ethnography, Masaryk University, Brno. Institute for Ethnography, Slovak Academy of Sciences. Institute for Folk Culture, Strážnice, South Moravia. Institute of Ethnography and Folklore, Czech Academy of Sciences, Prague. National Center of Folk Culture, Bratislava. The institute in Strážnice has available a series providing complete audiovisual documentation of the folk dances of Bohemia and Moravia, created by Hannah Laudová and Zdenka Jelínková 1993–1997, in English, French, German, and Czech.

HANNAH LAUDOVÁ

Theatrical Dance

It is possible to talk about Czech ballet in the strictest sense only after 1918, when the independent Czechoslovak Republic was born after the fall of the Austro-Hungarian empire. The first reports of theatrical dance in the historic Czech lands date from the fifteenth century, when ballet played a part in the lavish ceremonial observances of coronations, royal weddings, and other grand occasions. In 1479 Vladislav II, king of Bohemia, met with Matyàs of Hungary in Olomouc, and the two weeks of celebrations associated with their meeting were accompanied by theatrical scenes, music productions, and dances as well as the customary knightly games and tournaments.

Dancing with masks was cultivated in the second half of the sixteenth century at noble palaces as well as at royal courts. Extant from the early seventeenth century are records of ballets performed by noblemen at the Prague court. This development was interrupted by events following the Battle of White Mountain (1620) and other battles of the Thirty Years' War, during which the Protestant intellectual core of the nation emigrated, the country was ravaged, and the Czech population decreased almost by half. After the royal court moved to Vienna, Prague gradually became more provincial.

Italian opera, in which ballet was prominently featured, made its way to Bohemia in the seventeenth century. The first such performance was held in Prague in 1627, during the coronation of Ferdinand III of Bohemia. By the second half of the seventeenth century ballet was practiced at most noblemen's seats. The dancers were either hired professionals from Vienna or local groups made up of subjects of the estate. Also by this time, troupes of traveling comedians from Italy, England, and Germany regularly visited the country. In their comedies, stemming from the *commedia dell'arte*, pantomime and ballet played important roles.

From 1724 on, Italian opera was cultivated on Prague's first permanent stage, the Špork Theater. After 1737 opera also appeared at the Kotce Theater, where impresarios and their troupes performed pantomimes and ballets as well. Among the ballet masters was a Bohemian, Vojtěch Moravec-Alberti. A pupil of Jean-Georges Noverre, Moravec-Alberti presented excerpts from his master's *Les Petits Riens* and *Vénus et Adonis*, in Prague in 1776. For a short time beginning in 1777, a pure ballet theater also worked in Prague, performances by Moravec-Alberti alternating with those by Anton Roessler (for example, of Noverre's ballet *Les Horaces et les Curiaces*). Ballets were also performed in Brno and Bratislava. Most Bohemian ballet composers, however, could find work only outside the country. Leopold Koželuh (1747–1818) and Pavel Vranický (1756–1808) had ballets performed in Vienna;

Vojtěch Jírovec (1763–1850) composed ballets for companies in Paris, London, and elsewhere. After 1783 the center of opera in Prague was the Nostic Theater (later the Stavovské Divadló, Theater of Estates), now a branch of the National Theater.

In pantomime-ballets, which from 1768 on were also produced at the Patriotic Theater, preference was given to comic genres over tragic and heroic themes, the comic impulse having profited from the popularity of the burlesque. The result was a colorful mixture of images, scenic effects, music, and dance numbers held together by a simple plot with a main comic character in the spirit of Hanswurst or Harlequin. This emphasis lasted until the mid-nineteenth century. The repertory was influenced also by the suburban Vienna theaters; the level of choreography and interpretation was provincial.

The influence of Romanticism first became evident in 1841, when Françoise Crombé staged in Prague Filippo Taglioni's *La Sylphide* with Julia Springer in the title role. It is not known whether Springer danced on pointe, but Lucile Grahn, who performed in Prague in 1850 and 1851 (as the Sylphide and Giselle, among other roles), certainly did, thrilling her audiences. Guest stars from western Europe, such as Pepita da Oliva in 1853, and from Russia, such as Ekaterina Friedberk from Saint Petersburg in 1863, brought news of ballet developments abroad. The position of local ballet was still inferior, however. Without text or dialogue, this art form could not be used in the massive process of national awakening, in which drama and opera played a major role.

The effort to demonstrate national independence, cultural maturity, and the constantly growing social and economic power of the Czech bourgeoisie culminated in 1883 with the building of the National Theater in Prague, funded by donations from throughout the country. [*See* Prague National Theater Ballet.] Augustin Berger, who became ballet master in 1884, founded a ballet school at the theater, put the company on a firm professional base, and produced serious, high-quality works of the worldwide repertory as well as new local works of lasting importance. The theater's predecessor, the temporary Royal Theater of the Bohemian Lands, had opened in 1862, when a small ballet ensemble was formed to serve in opera or drama. It is only with the building of the National Theater, however, that the continuous heritage of Czech ballet can be traced.

The Gradual Development of an Independent Ballet. In the beginning, the technique of the Czech dancers was based on the Italian school. Indeed, until 1904, when Anna Korecká became the first Czech to be awarded the title of *prima ballerina*, the *prima ballerinas* had been Italian, even though some Czech dancers were of equal technical skill. Pantomime roles often were filled by actors and opera singers, while ballet was used as *divertissement;*

travesty was common. The ballet was a servant to the opera, and although the opera itself enjoyed international renown, the social and artistic prestige of the ballet was very low. Even visits by such celebrities as Tamara Karsavina, Anna Pavlova, Ruth St. Denis, and Diaghilev's Ballets Russes did not enhance the status of ballet before World War I.

A marked change, however, was brought about by the establishment of Czechoslovakia as an independent republic in 1918. The repertory was modernized with the addition of works such as *Petrouchka* in 1925 and *Salade* in 1926, both adapted from the Diaghilev repertory. At the same time, the Czech style, influenced by Jelizaveta Nikolská, was moving in the direction of the Russian school. Nikolská danced at the Národní Divadló (National Theater), first as a guest but later as *prima ballerina* and then

as chief of the ballet. She also had her own ballet school. Gradually the artistic level of the Czech ballet rose.

Meanwhile, wide use was made of stage dance in operetta and revue theaters, with troupes of girls, and sometimes boys, doing acrobatics and tap dancing. The most important of the strong national choreographers to emerge at this time was Josef Jenčík, whose revue troupe Jenčík's Girls was featured in the late 1920s at the Cabaret Lucerna and at the Liberated Theater of Jiří Voskovec and Jan Werich. Jenčík, widely known as "Joe," also choreographed large dance events for workers' sports and gymnastics festivals. Saša Machov and Ivo Váňa Psota were among the younger choreographers who began to work in this period.

In the 1920s and 1930s interest in a wide range of modern styles grew, influenced mostly by Émile Jaques-Dalcroze but also by Rudolf Laban and Isadora Duncan. The most prominent representatives of this movement produced numerous concerts, alone or together with their pupils, and some of them, including works by Milča Mayerová, Mira Holzbachová, and Jarmila Kröschlová,

CZECH REPUBLIC AND SLOVAK REPUBLIC: Theatrical Dance. A scene from the Prague Chamber Ballet's 1972 revival of Josef Jenčík's *Špalíček* (1933), a folkloric "singing" ballet composed by Bohuslav Martinů (Photograph by Josef Svoboda; courtesy of Vladimír Vašut.)

were incorporated into the theatrical avant-garde. The merit of these reformers lay in their unconventional repertory, often accompanied by "absolute" (that is, non-programmatic) music, both old and contemporary; their handicap lay in their lack of professional instruction and technique.

The promising rise of ballet was interrupted by the Nazi occupation of Czechoslovakia in 1939. Some choreographers, including Machov and Psota, managed to escape abroad; others, such as Nina Jirsíková, were imprisoned; still others, including Jenčík, were not allowed to work. Many Czech dancers were forced to take engagements in Germany and other countries of the Third Reich.

With the liberation of Czechoslovakia in 1945, a completely new developmental phase began, bringing with it a surprising flourishing of ballet. The boom of theater in general led to the birth of new ballet companies, and Machov and Psota, after their return from exile, became the leaders of the new developments in Prague and Brno, respectively. The high standard of their productions helped ballet develop independently of opera. A key influence on this development was the example set by the Soviet guest ensembles; the performance of the Moiseyev Dance Company, for example, led to the establishment of national professional folk companies. A great contribution was also made by the Soviet dance masters and choreographers working in Czech theaters. The social standing of dance professionals improved, and they began to receive official recognition in the form of artistic distinctions.

In the 1950s the ballet aesthetic changed in favor of the Soviet-type, full-length dance drama, with a complex plot, a real-life hero, and a clear ideological intent. The dominance of narrative pantomime and the lack of attention paid to the beauty of choreographic shape in these ballet dramas provoked a reaction at the end of the decade. Called the "new wave" of Czechoslovak choreography, the emerging approach accented the subtleties specific to ballet. Movement itself became the carrier of the dramatic message, first by stepping out of the narrowly defined, canonized territory of the classical *pas*, thereby searching for and creating new movement solutions and revitalizing concepts such as suggestion and metaphor. This new approach, whose main representatives were Luboš Ogoun and Pavel Šmok, projected itself also onto the repertory by increasing the number of shorter ballets, often inspired by "absolute" music not necessarily intended for dance.

This "new wave" eventually led to the establishment of Studio Ballet Prague (Balet Praha), the first completely independent professional ballet company in Czechoslovakia. Founded as Studio Ballet Prague in 1964 by the choreographers Luboš Ogoun and Pavel Šmok and by the critic Vladimír Vašut, its goals were to provide a creative laboratory dedicated to experimental dance to seek new avenues for the development of a national dance art. This type of experimentation and development was not possible within the traditional "stone theaters" because of prevailing public tastes, working conditions, and the necessity of cooperating with a theater's opera company or other performers.

With fewer than twenty dancers, Ballet Prague spent most of its time touring, primarily abroad. The company visited many European countries, Canada, and South America. In its eight full-evening programs it presented a total of twenty-two works that ranged widely in genre, music, and style. Most of the scores were not originally intended for the stage; seventeen of these ballets were presented for the first time. Ogoun, artistic director between 1964 and 1968, and Šmok, who succeeded him from 1968 to 1970, were both nonconformist choreographers with individual compositional styles. Since the early 1960s they have been considered the most original representatives of the progressive spirit in Czech ballet. Their choreography enriched the classical vocabulary with motifs from sports, acrobatics, and jazz, folk, and social dance, which soon gave the company an original dramatic and interpretive profile.

The most successful works in the repertory were Ogoun's *Hiroshima*, with music by Viliam Bukový, the first eastern European ballet performed to *musique concrète;* Šmok's comic *Nedbaliana*, with music by Oskar Nedbal; and Ogoun's *The Miraculous Mandarin*, to music by Béla Bartók. The artistic peak of the repertory was Šmok's staging of Leoš Janáček's String Quartet no. 2, *Intimate Letters*. Before it was dissolved in 1970 as an outcome of extremely unfavorable political and artistic conditions following the Soviet occupation in 1969, the company often collaborated on television productions in Prague, Vienna, and Munich; it filmed a total of ten ballets for television. In 1969, the core of the company, including Šmok, relocated to Basel, Switzerland, and continued to perform until 1973. At that time, the company had a group of distinguished dance artists including the lyrical Marta Synácová, the dramatic Marcela Martiniková, the robust Rudolf Brom, the expressive Petr Koželuh, the elegant Vladimír Klos (who later became a soloist with the Stuttgart Ballet), the technically mature Petr Vondruška (who later became a soloist in Dusseldorf), and others. During its seven years of existence, the Ballet Prague strongly influenced the development of Czechoslovak theatrical dance, especially in the area of choreographic innovation. Many productions mounted by Ballet Prague have been revived by other Czech and foreign dance companies. [*See the entries on Ogoun and Šmok.*]

By the 1970s Martha Graham's modern dance had come to Prague via the amateur Charles University Dance Company led by Jan Hartmann and Ivana Kubicová, both of whom had studied at the London Contemporary Dance School. This progressive trend became more and more

CZECH REPUBLIC AND SLOVAK REPUBLIC: Theatrical Dance. Mìchaela Vitková and Bohumil Reisner as the young lovers in the Prague Chamber Ballet's 1971 production of *Romeo and Juliet*, set by Miroslav Kůra to the score by Sergei Prokofiev. (Photograph by Josef Svoboda; courtesy of Vladímr Vašut.)

pronounced, and in the second half of the 1980s a few small, modern-oriented, semiprofessional groups were founded. On the professional level, these new choreographic trends became most evident in the work of the Prague Chamber Ballet.

The Prague Chamber Ballet is an independent chamber company of eight to twelve dancers and is in permanent residence in Prague. The company was formed in 1975 by choreographer Pavel Šmok. The company began its work during the politically difficult years of the so-called normalization process following the Soviet occupation. The Prague Chamber Ballet was formed under the auspices of Prague City Theater and performed full-evening programs in the Rokoko theater, gaining considerable popularity with audiences. With this small company, Šmok participated in an international festival in Nancy, France, in 1977 and in the Interballet festival in Budapest in 1978. In 1980 the company became independent of the Prague City Theater and has since performed as the Prague Chamber Ballet. During its early years, the company represented the artistic underground; consequently, it was the only active company in the socialist system of theater administration not to receive state support. Because of the company's high artistic level and with the assistance of international intervention, the Czech Ministry of Culture was finally pressured into providing the company with minimal financial support. However, by touring the Czech Republic and abroad, the company's more than one hundred performances each year pay the bulk of its administrative costs. The repertory consists of short ballets, usually performed as world premieres. The core of the repertory is the choreography to the music of Czech composes, primarily choreographed by the artistic director, Pavel Šmok, including *Trio in G Minor* (1991), to music by

Bedřich Smetana, and *Diary of One Who Disappeared* (1992), to music by Antonín Dvořák. Other guest choreographers have included Jiří Kylián, who mounted *Evening Songs* (1988) and *Stoolgame* (1996), both to music by Dvořák. Choreographer Gerhard Bohner's last work, *Angst und Geometrie* (1990; to music by Walter Zimmermann), was created for the Prague Chamber Ballet. Young Czech choreographers who have contributed works to the company include Kateřina Franková, Jan Klár, Vladimír Kloubek, Petr Tyc, and Petr Zuska, who is emerging as a special talent. Zuska's choreographies include *Small Gallows* (1994), *Seul* (1995) to songs by Jacques Brel, and *In the Mist* (1996) to music by Janáček. Several outstanding performers, including Kateřina Franková, developed their potential at the Prague Chamber Ballet and later became soloists with the Prague National Theater and other theaters abroad. Current outstanding dancers include Markéta Plzáková and Petr Kolář; both received the prize for the best dance performer in the Czech Republic in 1995. The company as a whole, and its artistic director Pavel Šmok in particular, have received several awards for excellence. The Prague Chamber Ballet's style can be classified as neoclassical with a distinctive Czech resonance.

By the 1990s, twelve dance companies were affiliated with theaters, nine in the Czech state and three in Slovakia. In addition to the major groups in Prague, Bratislava, and Brno, theater dance companies were based in Ostrava, Košice, Ústí nad Labem, Liberec, Pilsen, České Budějovice, Olomouc, Opava, and Banská Bystrica. Several operetta and musical theaters had their own dance ensembles as well. Among the folk dance companies that frequently toured Europe and overseas were the Czechoslovak State Ensemble of Song and Dance and the Army Artistic Ensemble, both in Prague, the Slovak Folk

Art Collective and "Lúčnica" in Bratislava, and the Ukraine Folk Ensemble in Prešov.

The emphasis that Czechs place on large, dramatic ballets bespeaks a cultural orientation toward understandable plots and full-length productions rather than more sophisticated, multiwork evenings. Another typical aspect of Czech ballet is the focus on child audiences, toward whom the overall premiere production often is directed. Young ballet spectators are educated, but the genre is thus necessarily infantilized. Perhaps because of this emphasis adult audiences still tend to undervalue ballet.

Overall, neither the creative nor the interpretational profiles of the individual Czech companies have been highly developed or original, except perhaps in the choreography of Pavel Šmok for the Prague Chamber Ballet. Although no specifically Czechoslovak choreographic style or interpretational school has emerged, Czech dancers show a pronounced ability for dramatic projection and lively expression.

At the beginning of the 1990s and after the fall of the totalitarian regime, many changes took place in the management of ballet companies. Now, many young, talented choreographers are active in a variety of theaters, for example, Libor Vaculík at the Prague National Theater Ballet, Petr Zuska at the Prague Chamber Ballet, Igor Vejsada in Ostrava, Ondrefj Šoth in Ústí nad Labem, Robert Balogh in Pilsen, and Petr Šimek in Liberec.

The economic recession of the late 1990s has led to the reduction of state subsidies. As a result, some companies have had to cut their number of dancers, and other companies have ceased to exist, as, for example, Prague's Bohemnia Balet and the television ballet. The absence of

good dancers continues to plague the theaters as the best conservatory graduates leave for well-paid contracts in the West and, consequently, their places are often taken by dancers from the former Soviet Union.

There is an active sphere of nonclassical dance in the form of independent companies that concentrate on modern dance. Often these companies are short-lived; however, Tanec Praha, an international dance festival held annually, supports modern dance activities.

Dance Education. Before 1945, dance in Czechoslovakia was taught in various private studios and ballet preparatory schools affiliated with theaters. Since 1945, the educational system has been state run and is strictly divided by discipline. The dance department program of the music conservatories originally lasted four years but gradually was extended. By the end of the 1980s, dance education programs in schools of dance in Prague, Brno, and Bratislava, lasted eight years, and the programs in Ostrava and Košice lasted five years, both culminating with high school graduation exams. The education of choreographers, teachers, and theoreticians was carried on by the departments of the academies of musical arts in Prague and Bratislava.

The Prague Dance Conservatory has graduated the most distinguished students, among them Hana Vláčilová, Michaela Černá, Jana Kurová, Lubomír Kafka, Libor Vaculík, Daria Klimentorá, Otto and Jiří Bubeníček, and Barbora and Vendula Kohoutek, all of whom have taken the honors at international ballet competitions. Jiří Kylián, director of the Netherlands Dance Theater, also graduated from the Prague school. The number of graduates, however, has remained insufficient to meet the needs of anything but the largest central theaters.

The social and economic changes after the fall of the communist regime were accompanied by changes in the sphere of dance education. Apart from state-subsidized schools, such as Prague's Duncan Center Conservatory and Jaroslav Ježek's conservatory, dozens of private ballet schools were founded. However, after the fall of the Iron Curtin, many of the best graduates left the country to work in theaters throughout Europe.

[*See also* Brno Ballet; Slovak National Theater Ballet; *and the entries on Augustin Berger, Emerich Gabzdyl, Miroslav Kůra, Saša Machov, Jiří Němeček, and Ivo Vána Psota.*]

CZECH REPUBLIC AND SLOVAK REPUBLIC: Theatrical Dance. Members of the Prague Chamber Ballet in Pavel Šmok's *Trio in G Minor,* set to music by Bedřich Smetana. (Photograph by Ivan Drábek; courtesy of Vladimír Vašut.)

BIBLIOGRAPHY

Apple, Jacki. "Voyage to Prague." *High Performance* (Spring 1991): 26–29.

Brodská, Božena. *Dějiny českého baletu do roku 1918.* Prague, 1983.

Černý, František, ed. *Dějiny českého divadla.* 2 vols. Prague, 1968–1969.

Dufková, Eugenie, and Bořivoj Srba, eds. *Postavy brněnského jeviště.* 2 vols. Prague, 1989.

Hošková, Jana. "On Dance Research and Publicity in Czechoslovakia." In *Beyond Performance: Dance Scholarship Today*, edited by Susan Au and Frank-Manuel Peter. Berlin, 1989.

Jaczová, Eva. *Balet Slovenského národného divadla*. Bratislava, 1971.

Jenčík, Josef. *Taneční letopisy*. Prague, 1946.

Jenčík, Josef. *Skoky do prázdna*. Prague, 1947.

Kamilov, S., ed. *Taneční umění v Československu*. Prague, 1932.

Kersley, Leo. "Prague Chamber Ballet." *Dance and Dancers* (November 1991): 22–23.

Kreuzmannová, Yvona. "Hopes and Prospects." *Ballett International* 16 (April 1993): 35–36.

Kröschlová, Jarmila. *Výrazový tanec*. Prague, 1964.

Nosál, Štefan. *Choreografia ludového tanca*. Bratislava, 1984.

Paseková, Dana. "Report ČSSR." *Ballet International*, no. 10 (1984): 34–37.

Percival, John. "Prague Chamber Ballet," *New York Times* (24 September 1991).

Procházka, Vladimír, ed. *Národní divadlo a jeho předchůdci*. Prague, 1988.

Regitz, Hartmut. "Pavel Mikulástík." *Ballet-Journal/Das Tanzarchiv* 38 (February 1990): 68–69.

Rey, Jan. *Psychologie tance*. Prague, 1928.

Rey, Jan. *Tanec jako divadlo*. Prague, 1938.

Rey, Jan. *Učebnice akademického tance*. 2 vols. Prague, 1946–1948.

Rey, Jan. *Jak se dívat na tanec*. Prague, 1947.

Scheier, Helmut. "Twenty Years of the Prague Chamber Ballet." *Ballet International/Tanz Aktuel* (November 1995): 56–57.

Schmidová, Lidka. *Československý balet*. Prague, 1962.

Siblík, Emanuel. *Tanec mimo nás a v nás*. Prague, 1937.

Studio Balet Praha. Mexico City, 1968. In Spanish and English.

Tanec/Dance. Prague, 1991.

Vašut, Vladimír, ed. *Le ballet en Tchécoslovaquie*. Prague, 1962.

Vašut, Vladimír. "Prága balett." *Tánctudományi tanulmánvok* (1975): 95–112.

Vašut, Vladimír. *Baletní libreta*. Prague, 1983–.

Vašut, Vladimír. *Dramaturgie baletu v ČSSR*. Prague, 1983.

Vašut, Vladimír. *Saša Machov*. Prague, 1986.

Vašut, Vladimír, and Emerich Gabzdyl. *V hlavní roli Emerich Gabzdyl*. Ostrava, 1988.

Windreich, Leland. "Ballerina-Entrepreneuse: Jana Kurova and the New Czech Ballet Theatre." *Danceview* 10 (Spring 1993): 2–5.

Windreich, Leland. "Budapest and Prague." *Ballet Review* 21 (Summer 1993): 10–12.

Zíbrt, Čeněk. *Jak se kdy v Čechach tancovalo*. Prague, 1895.

VLADIMÍR VAŠUT
Translated from Czech

Dance Research and Publication

Institutions in the former Czechoslovakia (now the Czech Republic and the Slovak Republic) dedicated to dance theory and history include the Theater Institute—founded in 1957 as a department of the Theater and Literary Agency and independent since 1959—and the Academy of Arts in Prague and the Arts School in Bratislava, where university-level courses began in 1949. The periodical *Taneční listy* (Dance Journal), concerned with theory and criticism in all branches of dance, has been published from 1947 to 1952 and from 1963 to the present.

These institutions, all established after World War II in a period of intense dance development, have been staffed by scholars specializing in dance theory and history. Their work on the history of Czech and Slovak dance and on theoretical problems in dance production illuminated the historical contributions of Czech and Slovak artists to both the national dance culture and that of the world, particularly to ballet, which has been important here for more than two centuries.

Research on folk dance has been a special focus of interest, especially since World War II. Dance folklorists have concentrated on defining principles for the comprehensive analysis of folk dances as the basis for further research, particularly the classification of individual dances. The problem of conserving and developing folk dance has been most important. Theoretical concerns about the stage presentation of folk dance and its choreography have been studied at several institutions, such as the Ethnographic and Folklore Institute of the Czechoslovak Academy of Sciences in Prague and Brno, the Folk Art Institute in Strážnice, the Ethnographic Institute and Arts Institute of the Slovak Academy of Sciences in Bratislava, the Adult Education Institute of Bratislava, and the Institute for Cultural Education in Prague. The works of ethnochoreologists and musicologists are both published and applied in collaboration with dance groups.

A major goal of dance research has been to document and evaluate the history of ballet in the country. The subject of expressive (modern) dance, which was performed by a number of Czech women dancers both before and after World War II, is still awaiting thorough analysis and contact with archives abroad.

Archival material on dance is scattered through many collections in museums, libraries, former homes of the nobility, theaters, institutes, and private collections. Efforts are under way to establish a central archive that will function not only as a site for preservation but also as a coordinating agency for scholarship, international cooperation, and the dissemination of information.

JANA HOŠKOVÁ

D

DAFORA, ASADATA (John Warner Dafora Horton; born 1890 in Freetown, Sierra Leone, died 4 March 1965 in New York City), West African singer, dancer, composer, choreographer, and writer. Born into the Temne tribe of West Africa, son of a Freetown city treasurer and great-grandson of a Nova Scotian slave, Dafora became during the 1930s a leading exponent of authentic African dance in the United States. After completing his education in England he studied voice for two years at Teatro alla Scala in Milan before abandoning a possible singing career in 1912 to join other Africans who were touring Europe in performances of African dance.

In 1929 Dafora went to the United States, where he organized Shogola Oloba (Dancers and Singers), a company of Africans supplemented with some black Americans, especially women, which the original troupe had lacked. The company produced a series of dance dramas based on West African legends and folk tales. The most successful of these was the dance opera *Kykunkor* (The Witch Woman) in 1934. Based on a Temne legend of a bewitched courtship and marriage between a Temne maiden and a young man from the nearby Mende tribe, and performed and sung in three African languages without translation, *Kykunkor* played to enthusiastic reviews and overflow crowds in four different locations in New York City, where it ran for sixty-five performances.

Other works by Dafora include the dance dramas *Zunga* and *Zungure* and coauthorship, with Orson Welles, of the radio play *Trangama-Fanga*, in which he acted with Welles. During the Great Depression members of the dance troupe became the basis of the Federal Theatre African Dance Troupe, and Dafora choreographed, supervised, and performed in the Vodun witches' scene of Shakespeare's *Macbeth* set in Haiti in the famous Federal Theatre production by John Houseman and Orson Welles.

Dafora promoted the musical and dramatic arts of Africa at a time when they were either unknown or dismissed as savage mumbo jumbo. His attempts to present authentic African forms outside of their tribal settings anticipated such later African traveling troupes as the Yoruba folk opera performers of Nigeria. Although he never repeated the success of *Kykunkor*, he continued to win the attention and praise of American musicians as different as Leopold Stokowski and George Gershwin,

and he performed at the White House at the request of Eleanor Roosevelt. He was also responsible for developing among black American musicians and dancers pride in and appreciation of their African heritage, inspiring artists such as Pearl Primus to study further the incorporation of African elements into their art.

BIBLIOGRAPHY

"Dafora, Asadata." In *The Dance Encyclopedia*, edited by Anatole Chujoy and P. W. Manchester. Rev. and enl. ed. New York, 1967.
Obituary. *New York Times* (7 March 1965).

KENNETH K. MARTIN

DAFORA. Seen here in a 1944 performance, Dafora was one of the first choreographers to present African dances on the American concert stage. (Photograph © 1980 by Barbara Morgan; used by permission of the Barbara Morgan Archives, Hastings-on-Hudson, New York.)

DALCROZE, ÉMILE. *See* Jaques-Dalcroze, Émile.

DALE, MARGARET (Margaret Bolam; born 30 December 1922 in Newcastle upon Tyne, England), British dancer, and producer and director for television. Dale studied ballet with Nellie Potts in Newcastle and appeared in pantomime before joining the Sadler's Wells Ballet School in 1937. She made her company debut, as the Child in Ninette de Valois's *Le Roi Nu*, while still a student. A soloist with the Sadler's Wells Ballet from 1942, Dale was often called a "ballerina in miniature"; her diminutive stature and dainty, precise style perfectly suited roles like Swanilda, the Sugarplum Fairy, the Polka in *Façade*, and the Bride in *A Wedding Bouquet*. She danced both the Fairy of the Golden Vine (the "finger variation") and the White Cat in the company's first Royal Opera House performance of *The Sleeping Beauty* in 1946 and also created several small roles.

After Dale had choreographed five ballets for children's television and one, *The Great Detective* (1953), for Sadler's Wells Theatre Ballet in 1954, she enrolled in a six-month training course at the British Broadcasting Corporation (BBC) and retired from dancing. Her second and more important career, for which her performing experience had provided unique preparation, was as a producer and director of more than one hundred ballet productions on BBC television. Between 1954 and 1968, she concentrated on ballets staged specifically for the medium—either shortened versions of the classics or original works. These included the Bolshoi Ballet's *Swan Lake*, the Kirov Ballet's *The Stone Flower*, Ballet Rambert's *La Sylphide*, and Royal Ballet productions of *Giselle*, *Coppélia*, *The Nutcracker*, *The Sleeping Beauty*, *La Fille Mal Gardée*, *Petrouchka*, *The Firebird*, and *Checkmate*.

From 1967 to 1976, Dale made documentary films for television, focusing in turn on Tamara Karsavina, John Cranko, Anna Pavlova, Marie Rambert, Gene Kelly, the International Ballet Competition in Varna, Bulgaria, and Japan's *kabuki* theater. She left the BBC in 1976 to become associate professor and chairman of the Department of Dance at York University in Ontario, Canada, positions she held for one year. In 1969 she won the Society of Film and Television Arts Award.

BIBLIOGRAPHY

Clarke, Mary. *The Sadler's Wells Ballet.* New York, 1955.
Dale, Margaret. "Ballet and BBC-TV." *The Dancing Times* (March 1963): 332–334.
Penman, Robert, comp. *A Catalogue of Ballet and Contemporary Dance in the BBC Television, Film, and Videotape Library, 1937–1984.* London, 1987.

INTERVIEW. Margaret Dale, by David Vaughan (1978), Dance Collection, New York Public Library for the Performing Arts.

BARBARA NEWMAN

D'AMBOISE, JACQUES (Joseph Jacques Ahearn; born 28 July 1934 in Dedham, Massachusetts), American dancer, choreographer, director, and teacher. D'Amboise was trained at the School of American Ballet; he began studying there in October 1942, the same year he had completed his very first classes with Madame Seda, an Armenian ballerina who also taught Leon Danielian. At age twelve d'Amboise performed with Ballet Society, and in 1949, at fifteen, he joined its successor, New York City Ballet, the company in which he pursued his career. His first principal role was Tristram in Frederick Ashton's *Picnic at Tintagel* (1952), and in 1953 he had great success as Mac in the revival of Lew Christensen's *Filling Station*.

D'Amboise created leading roles in many Balanchine ballets, including *Western Symphony* (1954), *Stars and Stripes* (1958), *Episodes* (1959), *The Figure in the Carpet* (1960), *Raymonda Variations* (1961), *Movements for Piano and Orchestra* (1963), *Meditation* (1963), *Brahms-Schoenberg Quartet* (1966), *Jewels* (1967), *Who Cares?* (1970), *Union Jack* (1976), and *Robert Schumann's "Davidsbündlertänze"* (1980). He was also especially well known for his performance of the title role in Balanchine's *Apollo*, which he first assumed in 1957.

An engaging performer with an outgoing personality and a strapping physique, d'Amboise also appeared in the films *Seven Brides for Seven Brothers* (1954), *Carousel* (1956), and *The Best Things in Life Are Free* (1956) and often performed on television. He was New York City Ballet's first male virtuoso to come from the ballet's own school. As a dancer he maintained the purity of the classical style yet infused it with an athletic quality. His energetic and expansive dancing greatly influenced the image of the male ballet dancer in America.

D'Amboise began choreographing in 1960 with the Uruguay section of New York City Ballet's *Panamerica*. Among the ballets he choreographed are eighteen other New York City Ballet productions, including *Irish Fantasy* (1964), set to music by Camille Saint-Saëns, *Tchaikovsky Suite No. 2* (1969), and *Celebration* (1983), to music by Felix Mendelssohn. A major aspect of his choreographing was identifying and working with young dancers who had star potential. He brought both Suzanne Farrell and Kyra Nichols to Balanchine's attention.

In 1976 d'Amboise founded the National Dance Institute, an organization designed to expose public school children—especially boys—to dance; the institute also has programs for hearing-impaired and visually impaired children. For the institute he writes, choreographs, and directs the annual Event of the Year, productions that have involved up to one thousand children. D'Amboise has also written, choreographed, and directed the films *Event of the Year* (1981) and *Fifth Position* (1983). *He Makes Me Feel Like Dancin'* (1984), a documentary about his work with the National Dance Institute, won an Oscar from the Academy of Motion Picture Arts and Sciences. In 1990 he received the Capezio Award and was awarded a MacArthur Foundation Fellowship. In 1995 he was the recipient of a Kennedy Center Honor.

In 1956 d'Amboise married former New York City Ballet soloist Carolyn George, who later became a photographer. They had four children, two of whom became professional dancers: Christopher d'Amboise, who was also a New York City Ballet principal dancer, later became artistic director of the Pennsylvania Ballet; Charlotte d'Amboise has starred in many Broadway productions.

BIBLIOGRAPHY
Barboza, Steven. "The Man Who Is Called the Pied Piper of Dance." *Smithsonian* (March 1990): 84–95.
Barboza, Steven. *I Feel Like Dancing: A Year with Jacques d'Amboise and the National Dance Institute.* New York, 1992.
d'Amboise, Jacques, with Hope Cook and Carolyn George. *Teaching the Magic of Dance.* New York, 1983.
Farrell, Suzanne, with Toni Bentley. *Holding On to the Air.* New York, 1990.
Gelb, Barbara. "Jacques d'Amboise: The Pied Piper of Dance." *New York Times Magazine* (12 April 1981).
Goodman, Saul. "Spotlight on Melissa Heyden and Jacques d'Amboise." *Ballet Today* (May–June) 1970.
Mason, Francis. *I Remember Balanchine: Recollections of the Ballet Master by Those Who Knew Him.* New York, 1991.
Rosen, Lillie. *Jacques d'Amboise.* Brooklyn, 1975.

WILLIAM JAMES LAWSON

DANCE AND MOVEMENT THERAPY. The first dance therapists practiced primarily with patients confined to the back wards of mental hospitals. As a result of the natural integration of dance with self-expression, however, dance educators found themselves practicing dance therapy in their private studios. A few of these private practitioners began functioning as primary therapists, utilizing dance therapy with both normal and neurotic individuals. During the 1980s there was a resurgence of interest in body movement and dance, accompanied by a growing recognition of the profound benefits of motor activity on mind and body. Simultaneously, the need for individualized styles of self-expression and communication received greater recognition. Thus, having built upon the foundations laid by the pioneers and having been shaped by a rich heritage of modern dance and psychoanalytic thought, dance therapists achieved professional status within the mainstream of the mental health field.

Dance therapy serves not only creative, social, emotional, and physical goals but also interpsychic and intrapsychic aims. It is being used in medical and mental hospitals, in clinics, rehabilitation centers, and schools, and in private practice. Dance therapists function as primary therapists, as ancillary therapists, and as family and couples counselors. They serve a wide spectrum of patients of all ages, from individuals with severe emotional and physical problems and handicaps to healthier individuals seeking in-depth self-exploration through expressive movement.

Most often referred to as dance therapy or dance/movement therapy, the discipline has also adopted many branch names, such as movement psychotherapy, psychoanalytic movement therapy, Jungian dance movement therapy, psychomotor therapy, and so on. The American Dance Therapy Association (ADTA) has adopted the policy of referring to the discipline as dance/movement therapy. The alternation in the field between the designations *dance* and *movement* stems largely from concern over preconceived ideas of what *dance* means to people. Some people feel inadequate, silly, or embarrassed when the word is used. Others fear they will have to perform dance steps or display an aptitude for body movement, as opposed to simply expressing their thoughts and feelings. In fact, the psychomotor expression witnessed in sessions does not at times resemble dance in any formal—or even informal—sense. For example, an arm reaching out, a fist gesturing in rage, the symbolic rocking of a child, or even the tilt of a head may all be elements of the expressive and exploratory process. While some still joke about the "angry mambo," the "inspirational cha-cha," and "dancing one's troubles away," these stereotypes are quickly fading. Today the field, broad in its applications and diverse in its methodology and theoretical foundations, extends into every area of mental health. The American Dance Therapy Association defines dance therapy as the "psychotherapeutic use of movement as a process which furthers the emotional and physical integration of the individual."

History. Dance therapy is rooted in the idea that the body and the mind are inseparable. Its basic premise is that body movement reflects inner emotional states and that changes in movement behavior can lead to changes in psyche, thus promoting health and growth. Helping individuals—those who are generally healthy as well as those who are emotionally or mentally disturbed, physically or mentally disabled—to regain a sense of wholeness by experiencing the fundamental unity of body, mind, and spirit is the ultimate goal of dance therapy.

The use of body movement, particularly dance, as a cathartic and therapeutic tool is perhaps as old as dance itself. In many primitive societies, dance was as essential as eating and sleeping. It provided individuals with a means to express themselves, to communicate feelings to others, and to commune with nature. Dance rituals frequently accompanied major life changes, thus serving to promote personal integration as well as the fundamental integration of the individual with society.

In contrast, the complexity and stress of modern living have led many people to feel alienated, out of touch with themselves, with others, and with nature. Much of Western thought at the turn of the century subscribed to the credo of dualism, or the distinct separation of body and mind. Formal dance developed as a performing art, emphasizing technique, with little attention to how it affected the dancer. Medicine and psychotherapy developed as forms of treatment, with the former focusing on the body and the latter focusing on the mind. Psychotherapeutic treatment approaches were almost entirely verbal and nonactive.

During the first half of the twentieth century, a trend began within many fields to break away from the limitations of these traditions. The modern dance movement sought to replace the rigid and impersonal forms of the art with more natural, expressive movements that emphasized spontaneity and creativity. In the area of psychotherapy, there was a growing interest in the nonverbal and expressive aspect of personality. Out of this changing intellectual climate, dance therapy emerged in the 1940s and 1950s. All of the major dance therapy pioneers began their careers as accomplished dancers. It was their experiences as performers and teachers that led them to realize the potential benefits of using dance and movement as a form of psychotherapy.

According to Levy's (1988) research, one woman from the modern dance world can be pointed to as the seminal influence on contemporary dance therapy—Mary Wigman. Wigman was concerned with pure movement expression, sometimes referred to as natural movement or the "inner dance." Wigman was a colleague and student of the movement philosopher Rudolf Laban, and like many of the pioneering dance therapists, she studied eurythmics (i.e., the representation of musical rhythms in movement) with Swiss musician Émile Jaques-Dalcroze and was also a student of François Delsarte. She incorporated these progressive teachings, all of which had in common natural, expressive movement, and from this created a unique teaching style. Its major requirement was that the student, once given the elements of dance upon which to build, find his or her own movements. That is, Wigman's movement medium was expressive-improvisational. Her technique provided a strong foundation for exploring human emotion, both personal and universal.

In the 1920s, one of Wigman's counterparts in improvisational and expressive movement in America was Bird Larson. Larson's major contributions to modern dance and dance therapy are not well known, owing to her early death in the 1930s. However, dance therapy pioneers in New York, such as Blanche Evan and Franziska Boas, were profoundly influenced by her. The expressive opportunities that Larson and Wigman afforded their students in the 1920s can be viewed as some of the earliest forms of dance therapy in the twentieth century.

The overall intellectual climate of this early period revolved around the acceptance of the unconscious as a potent source for deepening self-realization and reflection.

The revolutionary work of Sigmund Freud in psychology, first introduced in the late nineteenth century, had a great impact on modern dance and dance therapy. Freud's work prompted an examination of the motivation behind human action and self-expression through verbalization, in contrast to the nineteenth-century attitude that private thoughts and feelings were to be concealed. The innovative belief in the open expression of feeling gave dance both fresh subject matter and structure. The environment was ripe for the translation of self-expression through dance into psychotherapy through dance.

As the dance therapy pioneers continued to explore the power of movement as a form of psychotherapy, they began to seek further understanding of the nature of personality and the effects that movement had on personality. This led them to investigate the works of Freud, Alfred Adler, Carl Jung, Harry Stack Sullivan, and others, which gave verbal expression to their own intuitive-experiential knowledge.

Pioneers. Foundations of the theory and practice of dance therapy were laid, in large part, by six major pioneers in the United States: Marian Chace, Blanche Evan, and Liljan Espenak on the East Coast and Mary Whitehouse, Trudi Schoop, and Alma Hawkins on the West Coast.

Marian Chace. Considered by many to have been the grande dame of dance therapy, Chace (1896–1970) began her work in the early 1940s with severely disturbed psychiatric patients at Saint Elizabeth's Hospital in Washington, D.C. Chace, influenced by Harry Stack Sullivan, had a profound respect for the rights and needs of hospitalized patients. Believing that every patient had a desire to communicate, however buried that desire might be, Chace always sought and engaged those parts of the patient's personality still available and wanting to "be heard and be well." Chace achieved this by closely observing and responding to the small, idiosyncratic movements and gestures that constituted her patients' emotional expressions. Such direct movement expression, she believed, could break through verbal defenses. It is harder to disguise the physical expression of, or defense against, emotions than to hide their verbal counterparts. It was Chace's profound ability to use dance or movement and music for self-expression and communication and her capacity to perceive, encounter, reflect, and interact with the movement expressions of her patients that enabled her to draw them out of their psychotic isolation. She engaged them in a dance or movement dialogue that since has become known as the therapeutic movement relationship.

This concept of therapists involving themselves in a movement relationship or interaction with patients as a way of reflecting a deep emotional acceptance and communication was Chace's revolutionary contribution to dance therapy. The theoretical assumption in the process of "mirroring" or "reflecting" is simple—and perhaps this is why it is so effective. By taking the patient's nonverbal and symbolic communications seriously, and by helping to broaden and clarify them, Chace demonstrated her desire and ability to meet the patient "where he/she is" emotionally. In essence, Chace said to her patients, in movement, "I understand you, I hear you, and it's okay." In this sense she helped to validate the patients' immediate experience of themself.

In addition, through the use of what Levy (1988) calls the Group Rhythmic Movement Relationship, Chace facilitated and supported the expression of thoughts and feelings in an organized and controlled manner. Even severely withdrawn patients can be mobilized by the contagious aspect of rhythm, with safe and simple rhythmic sequences providing a medium for the externalization of otherwise chaotic and confusing emotions.

Rhythm not only organized the expression of thoughts and feelings into meaningful dance action, it also helped to modify extreme behaviors, such as hyperactivity or hypoactivity, or a tendency toward the use of bizarre gestures and mannerisms. During the process of rhythmically exaggerating gestures and other nonverbal communications, Chace would elicit and suggest symbolism and content. This would enhance the patients' awareness of language and its symbolic meaning and gradually enable them to modify extreme behavior and verbalize underlying conflicts.

In essence, the group rhythmic movement relationship provided a structure in which thoughts and feelings could be shaped, organized, and released within the secure confines of rhythmic action and group structure and support. Patients previously considered nonverbal began to speak in Chace groups. She reached the "unreachable."

Blanche Evan. Like all of the pioneers, Evan (c.1909–1982) began her career in dance as a dancer, choreographer, and performer. She later moved into dance instruction, becoming a pioneer in teaching creative dance to children, and then, in the 1950s and 1960s, she gradually moved into the use of dance as a primary form of psychotherapy for the "normal neurotic."

In describing the relationship between dance therapy and creative dance, Evan once said that "creative dance broke the crust, but dance therapy unraveled the knots of one's being" (personal communication, 1980). Evan felt that some forms of modern dance and ballet geared themselves to the separation of mind and body, thus severing the dynamic quality she called "the life of Dance." The challenge of integration became the major thrust of her work.

In accordance with Adlerian psychology, of which Evan was a student, Evan believed that repressed aggression and anger are the major maladies of the neurotic. Because the neurotic's anger is repressed, so is his or her assertive-

ness and commitment to growing up. This is reflected clearly in the body musculature. "With action repressed, the energy is diverted to different kinds of tension: rigidity at one extreme, apathy at the other" (Evan, 1945–1978). If the body is trained for years in nonexpression, the need to express may eventually become lost. In severe cases, the resiliency of the muscles can be totally destroyed. "Body and spirit split and begin to atrophy; ego power shrinks to low self-esteem with an ineptness for both anger and love" (Evan, 1945–1978).

Evan's goal was to reeducate individuals to the natural unification and identification with organic bodily responses and needs that, she believed, preexisted the repressive influences of family and society. For Evan, dance is a language very similar to that of words, but, unlike words, dance represents a more direct communication and language of the self. She thus worked with the whole person, that is, she emphasized the person in his or her world. She did not believe, as the traditional psychoanalysts did, that insight and the awareness of unconscious material alone constituted the goals of treatment. If an individual, after completion of psychotherapy, was not better equipped to cope with his or her life, both intrapersonally and interpersonally, Evan believed that the treatment was not successful (personal communication with B. Melson, Evan's protégée, 1987).

Evan's methodology is composed of four major modes of intervention: the warm-up, her system of "functional technique" (corrective movement work), improvisation/enactment, and verbalization of thoughts and feelings. This sequence was popular among many of the pioneers and is still in use. The warm-up, a process of releasing superficial or excess tension, helps the individual to achieve a state that mediates between relaxation and tension and thus paves the way for receptivity to bodily feelings, emotions, and possible expressive actions.

Functional technique includes postural work, coordination, placement of body parts, and rhythmicity. Evan stressed the strengthening and alignment of the spine as the foundation of all action. Evan's concern with the spine centered on her belief that the functioning of the spine determines the overall ability to use the body as an "Instrument of Dance" (1964) and therefore as an instrument of self-expression.

Finally, Evan also emphasized in-depth improvisation, a form of psychomotor free-association in which the unconscious is made conscious. She worked with patients to structure dance improvisations and dramatic dance enactments that focused on significant themes and problems in the individual's life, past and present.

In contrast to Chace, Evan quietly observed with empathy and compassion when individuals moved. She never moved with patients. This differentiation is characteristic of those dance therapists who worked with hospital patients rather than privately with higher-functioning patients.

Liljan Espenak. Born in Bergen, Norway, Espenak (*fl.* late 1920s–1988) studied movement and dance in Germany with Mary Wigman. Fleeing Hitler's Germany, Espenak went to England and then to the United States. In the 1950s she studied psychotherapy at the Alfred Adler Institute and integrated the knowledge she obtained there with her already well-developed understanding of the expressive nature of dance. In 1961 Espenak became director of the Division of Creative Therapies, Institute for Mental Retardation, New York Medical College. Subsequently she became assistant professor and coordinator of a postgraduate course in psychomotor and dance therapy at New York Medical College's Mental Retardation Institute (personal communication, 1980).

Espenak believed that the aggression drive in humans is natural and that if it is repressed, the life-giving source in the personality is repressed also (personal communication, 1986). She also felt that children have to overcome inevitable feelings of inferiority. These beliefs supported her use of dance as a vehicle through which individuals can safely express their aggressive side. Working directly on the body to develop physical strength, grounding, and an expressive movement vocabulary can help to counteract feelings of inferiority and dependency.

Espenak incorporated Adler's emphasis on developing social feeling and cooperation. He believed that if the individual's abilities in this area were either unused because of personal isolation or repressed owing to personal rejection, a sense of self in the broader community would be unattainable. In order to combat this she brought her isolated patients out of individual dance therapy and into group dance therapy as soon as they were able.

Finally, Espenak is known for her development of specific psychomotor tests for use in patient diagnosis and assessment. In 1981 she published *Dance Therapy: Theory and Applications*, which has also appeared in a German edition. She also taught in the United States, Germany, and Austria.

Mary Whitehouse. A profound influence on many major contemporary dance therapy leaders, Whitehouse (1911–1979), in her private studio in California, worked one-on-one and in groups as well as with her dance students. In working with her students, Whitehouse placed emphasis on uncovering unconscious material, whereas with hospitalized patients, owing to their more fragile ego structure, she stressed structured forms of expressive movement. The two most profound influences on Whitehouse were Wigman and Jungian psychoanalysis.

Whitehouse's basic goal was to release unconscious emotions, which she believed became "buried in the body, in tissues, muscles, and joints" (Wallock, 1977). In other words she strove to make the unconscious conscious. To that end she utilized the psychoanalytic practice of releasing repressed material through the process of loosening and relaxing the ego's defenses against spontaneous expression. In addition, she supported Jung's concept of the personal unconscious being united with an unconscious that extends beyond the individual self to a universal or "collective" unconscious. Finally, she pointed to the importance of the conscious self, or ego, as the observer who watches and participates but does not censor or control the individual's expressions.

If individuals are able to release themselves from external controls and allow movement improvisation, Wigman style, to simply happen as eruptions from the depths of their being, then they are engaged in what Whitehouse referred to as "authentic movement" or "movement in-depth" and are participating in the Jungian method of "active imagination." The role that Whitehouse took while her students improvised was that of empathic observer. Sitting nearby as individuals moved, at times she offered suggestions or themes to help start the action; at other times she just gave individuals the time and space necessary for movement to evolve spontaneously. If she saw movements that seemed contrived as a result of an individual's anxiety or fear of letting go, she would reflect this back to the mover and help him or her to start over and be patient.

Trudi Schoop. Swiss-born Trudi Schoop was trained as a dancer and mime before coming to the United States and pursuing her career as a dance therapist in California. Building characters through mime profoundly influenced her dance therapy techniques. In order to build characters onstage, she said, "I had to find out how they felt, how they would move, and how they would behave" (Wallock, 1977).

Schoop's approach to mime was one of externalizing or "objectifying" her personal conflicts on the stage. "If other people could laugh, then the conflicts were not so terrible" (Wallock, 1977). The combined use of mime and humor for the expression of conflict became the cornerstone of her dance therapy practice, and it constituted her major contribution to the field.

Schoop believed that who we are is reflected and manifested in our bodies. What happens in the mind has a concomitant reaction in the body and the reverse: what happens in the body has a concomitant reaction in the mind. For this reason, posture and body alignment are reflective of one's mental state. It is the harmonious interaction between psyche and soma that promotes conflict-free functioning.

Schoop found this harmony painfully lacking in her hospitalized psychiatric patients. In their posture she saw all of the stresses and tensions indicative of internal conflicts and stemming from opposing and repressed drives. Schoop believed that all individuals are pulled by opposites and that all individuals encompass the entire spectrum of human emotion but that, owing to societal taboos, one side of the individual must go "under cover." This repression exerts pressure on the individual and in so doing undermines his or her integrity and performance. One of Schoop's major therapeutic goals was to bring the patient's repressed side to consciousness.

Schoop stressed the importance of teaching proper body use in order to build the individual's capacity for self-expression and exploration. She believed that through movement one's self-esteem could be improved via more efficient physical functioning. After building the body image by expanding the movement repertory, developing increased body awareness, and experimenting with postural attitudes, she gradually moved to thematic movement explorations, which she often initiated herself. When it was evident that the patients' tolerance of dynamic movement expression had increased and that they had developed a sufficient movement vocabulary, Schoop, like many of the other dance therapy pioneers, moved on to spontaneous movement expression in the form of improvisation. In contrast, however, she would stay in this mode only long enough to bring out new personalized material. As this material surfaced, she helped patients to organize their new experiences through movement "performances," that is, the planned reproduction and repetition of movement themes (Schoop, 1974). The process of formulating dance or movement sequences served the function of slowing down the expressive process and in this way allowed more time for the exploration of inner conflicts. Schoop believed that patients could gain some control, insight, and mastery over their problems by choreographing conflicts. [*See the entry on Schoop.*]

Alma Hawkins. As chairperson of the Dance Department at the University of California, Los Angeles (UCLA), from 1953 to 1974. Hawkins introduced dance therapy there in 1963 and her work evolved into a comprehensive dance therapy program. Hawkins had been deeply influenced by the work of Harold Rugg, professor at Columbia University Teachers College in New York City. Rugg was interested in the nature of creativity as it relates to all of the arts. He believed that movement plays a fundamental role in the arts and that it is an integral part of the thought process (Hawkins, personal communication, 1985).

While teaching at UCLA, Hawkins sought to increase her understanding of the nature of the creative process and the fully functioning person through the writings of and personal study with specialists such as Edmund Jacobson (relaxation), Robert Ornstein (modes of consciousness), and Eugene Gendlin (inner sensing). In psychology, she was influenced by the humanistic psychologists.

Marcia B. Leventhal, a protégée of Hawkins, remembered her early training in the 1960s.

We always returned to the basic premise of Dr. Hawkins: that there is an inherent talent and creativity residing within each individual, waiting only to be [tapped and] guided. . . . She has dedicated her life to the art of dance with the belief that there is no swifter, truer way for an individual to reach his/her fullest growth potential.   (Leventhal, 1984)

Hawkins also believed that relaxation is a highly significant factor affecting one's movement potential. A high degree of residual tension not only increases anxiety but also blocks perception. This results in a narrow, rigid pattern of response, which keeps one from his or her own creative influences and from establishing a complete body image. Authenticity in movement, according to Hawkins, implies that the externalized movement pattern is congruent with inner sensing (personal communication, 1985). Through relaxation, one opens the threshold to inner sensing (i.e., attentiveness to the inner self) and makes possible a new connection with early, often unconscious experiences. The movement that develops from this state can be filled with meaning and insight.

Hawkins believed that as long as the creative process is based on "inner sensing, feeling and imagery, healing will occur" (Leventhal, 1984). "Man seeks creative and aesthetic experiences because they enrich him . . . help him become an integrated individual and help him feel in harmony with his world" (Hawkins, 1972).

Midwestern influences. Margaret H'Doubler, a landmark dance educator at the University of Wisconsin from 1918 to 1953, influenced many early dance therapists and therapy pioneers, especially Rhoda Winter Russell. H'Doubler, not actually a dancer herself but rather a movement educator, saw the value of dance and fought for its inclusion as an academic discipline in universities across the country.

By the early 1950s interest in dance therapy was growing at the University of Wisconsin. H'Doubler's student, Rhoda Winter Russell, and her colleagues Maja Schade and Shirley Genther actively pursued the study of movement for therapeutic ends and went on to become leaders in the field. Russell developed her own dance therapy methodology, Schade specialized in movement relaxation techniques, and Genther experimented with the integration of psychodramatic techniques and dance/movement and referred to this as movement-drama.

Although the University of Wisconsin was an important center for early dance therapy leaders in the 1950s, it was not the only source from which dance therapy took root in the Midwest. Other important leaders and contributors were experimenting independently during these formative years, including Alice Bovard-Taylor with psychiatric patients and Billie Logan with retarded children, both in Minnesota, and Norma Canner with psychiatric and cerebral palsy patients in Ohio.

Literary contributions. Elizabeth Rosen wrote the first book on dance therapy, *Dance in Psychotherapy* (1957), originally prepared as a dissertation for her education doctorate at Columbia University Teachers College. Rosen's book stands out as the first comprehensive study of dance therapy within the hospital milieu.

Franziska Boas's 1941 article "Creative Dance" was the first comprehensive study of dance therapy techniques with children (Costonis, 1978). Boas was part of a research team at New York City's Bellevue Hospital in the early 1950s that included the work of two psychiatrists, Lauretta Bender and Paul Schilder. Boas integrated into her work three concepts being explored at that time: the building of body image through movement; the use of projective techniques in psychotherapy; and free association through movement.

Laban Movement Analysis (LMA). The theories of Rudolf Laban, which originated in the early 1900s, became integrated into the therapeutic use of dance and movement among English dance therapists in the 1950s. Warren Lamb was a protégé of Laban who expanded on Laban's original concepts. It was not until the mid-1960s that the theories of Laban and Lamb became popular among dance therapists in the United States. At that time, when dance therapy was still a fledgling profession, Laban's teaching provided a method of movement analysis and a system of notation that placed dance therapists on their own professional ground by giving them a language for describing patients' movements and by eliminating the need to rely on less accurate jargon borrowed from other disciplines.

Laban viewed body movement in a complicated and multifaceted way. He saw its potential use as an expressive medium of both conscious and unconscious thoughts, feelings, and conflicts and also viewed it as a vehicle through which societies pass on traditions, coping behaviors, and religious rituals. Laban continually impressed on his readers the variety of ways in which we express ourselves and our particular styles of coping through what he termed our movement configurations. He also stressed the individual's capacity, as compared with that of animals, to change his or her style of communication and adaptation through both conscious and unconscious mechanisms.

The primary leader responsible for the timely introduction of Laban and Lamb's concepts in the United States was Irmgard Bartenieff, a pioneering leader in movement who integrated her expertise as a physical therapist with her expertise in Laban Movement Analysis (LMA) and her knowledge of dance. Bartenieff's work stressed perceiving movement as a complex interrelated whole. "Change in any aspect [of movement] changes the whole configuration" (Bartenieff and Lewis, 1980). Bartenieff believed that each individual's movement style was an amalgam of his or her congenital activity type, psychological influences, and cultural milieu. Respecting each individual's unique adaptation to and physical expression of these influences, she worked creatively to help her patients make better use of what was already present in their movement repertories.

In clinical work with patients Bartenieff always looked at the total movement configuration with a major focus on the *potential* movement expression. The idea that potential movement was inherent in one's physical actions and movement preferences was derived from Laban's concept of "a diminished Effort." If an "effort" (movement quality) was diminished, it remained present but in small quantity. Hence, certain effort and shape factors that for one reason or another were not fully activated would continue to exist but only in a beginning or partially utilized form. Bartenieff did not attempt to explain, in formal psychological terms, why a specific movement factor might appear only in its diminished state, or why a certain quality of movement would not fully materialize. The view was simply accepted and incorporated into the total configuration.

Bartenieff cautioned the therapist against pointing out to a patient what movement qualities were lacking or asking the patient to work consciously at producing a particular movement. Rather, she believed that the therapist should study the total movement configuration available to the patient and then nonverbally engage him or her in movement activities that, in accordance with the individual's specific movement preferences, would eventually draw out the diminished movement factor.

In the mid-1960s, around the time Bartenieff began working at Bronx State Hospital, she and her disciple Martha Davis wrote an article entitled "Effort/Shape Analysis of Movement. The Unity of Expression and Function?" This article presented the following three assumptions regarding the use of Laban Movement Analysis: it is a replicable technique for describing, measuring, and classifying human movement; it describes patterns of movement that are consistent for an individual and distinguish him or her from others; and it delineates a behavioral dimension related to neurophysiological and psychological processes (Costonis, 1978).

In accordance with these beliefs, Bartenieff used Laban Movement Analysis as an observational, diagnostic, and assessment tool in her dance therapy work at Bronx State Hospital. Her work became formally integrated into the discipline of dance therapy in the late 1960s when the dance therapy department at Bronx State Hospital was expanded and training programs for dance therapists and other hospital staff were instituted. These developments owed largely to the pioneering efforts of Elissa White and Claire Schmais, in collaboration with Bartenieff and Davis.

Both White and Schmais had previously taken courses in Laban Movement Analysis with Bartenieff and in dance therapy with Marian Chace. Their joining the staff at Bronx State Hospital resulted in a historical and timely coming together of two previously distinct movement disciplines: Chacian dance therapy and Laban Movement Analysis.

Marion North, also a protégée of Laban and one of the leading dance therapists in England, made several important contributions to the practice of dance therapy. Her work typified the clinical use by English dance therapists of Laban's work as a tool to diagnose, assess, and plan treatment programs for patients. Reliance on Laban's movement framework as a guide for dance therapists is an integral part of dance therapy in England. This is in contrast to dance therapy in the United States, where other theoretical frameworks, such as psychoanalytic, ego-psychological, humanistic, and Gestalt therapy, are often utilized in addition to Laban's concepts. North correlated personality assessment through movement analysis with psychological and behavioral assessments, and played a significant role in emphasizing the clinical attributes of Laban Movement Analysis.

Judith Kestenberg, a psychiatrist and psychoanalyst, also borrowed concepts from Laban and Lamb and organized them into a theory of development. Some dance therapists trained in her theoretical model find it a helpful framework for the practice of dance therapy. A leading dance therapist and one of the major proponents of the Kestenberg model is Penny Lewis (previously Bernstein), who has trained many dance therapy students in the Kestenberg Movement Profile. [*See also* Laban Principals of Movement Analysis.]

Trends. The melding of influences among younger generations of dance therapists is inevitable. Levy's survey shows that most dance therapy leaders at the end of the twentieth century had studied the work of at least two of the pioneering leaders, and many of these later leaders had taught throughout the United States and abroad. Levy believes that work with patients is conducted on a continuum from most to least directive and that, over time, patients let the therapist know what they need and when. Because the therapeutic interaction takes place on a continuum, and because it is an oversimplification to say that all hospitalized patients need one way of working, whereas all nonhospitalized patients need a distinctly different way, it is important to take an eclectic approach to dance therapy. In addition to integrating various trends in dance therapy, some dance therapists also integrate aspects of action-oriented psychotherapies, such as psychodrama and other creative arts therapies.

Of particular interest is the integration of drama and art with dance therapy; there is at times a fine line between dance and art and dance and drama. The incorpo-

ration of dramatic movement into dance therapy practice is a natural phenomenon and can be traced back to each of the early dance therapy pioneers. In recent years Fran Levy (1979, 1988) has formalized this merger into a creative, action-oriented approach to group and individual psychotherapy, which she calls psychodramatic movement therapy. This approach blends East and West Coast dance therapy trends but also includes drama and dance, alone and in combination, along with drawing, visualization, and creative writing.

According to Levy, the incorporation of other artistic modalities into a patient's treatment evolves naturally when the therapist is both attuned to a patient's needs and in touch with the unique expressive qualities of other idioms. Each insight has its own way of deepening and clarifying the dance movement experience.

[*This overview of dance therapy was abstracted from Fran Levy's* Dance/Movement Therapy: A Healing Art *(1988) by permission of the publisher, the American Alliance for Health, Physical Education, Recreation and Dance, Reston, Virginia.*]

BIBLIOGRAPHY

Bartenieff, Irmgard, with Dori Lewis. *Body Movement: Coping with the Environment.* New York, 1980.

Bender, Lauretta. *Child Psychiatric Techniques.* Springfield, Ill., 1952.

Bernstein, Penny L., ed. *Eight Theoretical Approaches in Dance-Movement Therapy.* Dubuque, 1979.

Bernstein, Penny L., ed. *Theoretical Approaches in Dance-Movement Therapy.* Dubuque, 1984.

Chaiklin, Harris, ed. *Marian Chace: Her Papers.* Kensington, Md., 1975.

Costonis, Maureen Needham, ed. *Therapy in Motion.* Urbana, Ill., 1978.

Espenak, Liljan. *Dance Therapy: Theory and Application.* Springfield, Ill., 1981.

Hawkins, Alma. "Dance Therapy Today: Points of View and Ways of Working." In *Creativity and the Art Therapist's Identity: The Proceedings of the Seventh Annual Conference of the American Dance Therapy Association,* edited by Roberta Hastings Shoemaker and Susan E. Gonick-Barris. Pittsburgh, 1977.

Hawkins, Alma. *Moving from Within: A New Method for Dance Making.* Pennington, N.J., 1991.

Kestenberg, Judith S., and J. Mark Sossin. *The Role of Movement Patterns in Development.* Vol. 2. New York, 1979.

Laban, Rudolf. *The Mastery of Movement.* Edited by Lisa Ullmann. London, 1960.

Lefco, Helene. *Dance Therapy: Narrative Case Histories and Therapy Sessions with Six Patients.* Chicago, 1974.

Leventhal, Marcia B., ed. *Movement and Growth: Dance Therapy for the Special Child.* New York, 1980.

Leventhal, Marcia B. "An Interview with Alma Hawkins." *American Journal of Dance Therapy* 7 (1984): 5–14.

Levy, Fran. "Psychodramatic Movement Therapy: A Sorting Out Process." *American Journal of Dance Therapy* 3.1 (1979): 32–42.

Levy, Fran. *Dance-Movement Therapy: A Healing Art.* Reston, Va., 1988.

Mason, K. C., ed. *Focus on Dance VII: Dance Therapy.* Reston, Va., 1974.

North, Marion. *Personality Assessment through Movement.* Boston, 1972.

Rosen, Elizabeth. *Dance in Psychotherapy.* New York, 1957.

Sandel, Susan L., and David Read Johnson. *Waiting at the Gate: Creativity and Hope in the Nursing Home.* New York, 1987.

Schilder, Paul. *The Image and Appearance of the Human Body.* New York, 1950.

Schoop, Trudi, and Peggy Mitchell. *Won't You Join the Dance? A Dancer's Essay into the Treatment of Psychosis.* New York, 1974.

Siegel, Elaine V. *Dance-Movement Therapy: Mirror of Our Selves.* New York, 1984.

Wallock, Susan F. "Dance-Movement Therapy: A Survey of Philosophy and Practice." Ph.D. diss., United States International University, 1977.

Whitehouse, Mary. "C. G. Jung and Dance-Therapy: Two Major Principles." In *Eight Theoretical Approaches in Dance-Movement Therapy,* edited by Penny L. Bernstein. Dubuque, 1979.

ARCHIVE. B. Evan, *The Child's World: Its Relation to Dance Pedagogy* (New York, 1964), and B. Evan, ed., *Packet of Pieces by and about Blanche Evan,* a collection of published and unpublished articles, 1945–1978, both available from Barbara Melson, ADTR, Brooklyn, New York.

FRAN LEVY

DANCE AS SPORT. [*This article focuses exclusively on the United States, where various sports incorporating dance have become popular as healthy recreational exercises and as competitive events.*]

American popular concern with physical fitness expanded in the 1970s and 1980s. Exercise facilities proliferated and public attention to physical activity, including televised coverage of sporting events and competitions, increased and intensified; corporations and government agencies issued new policies encouraging regular physical activity to cut down on work and school days lost because of illness. Responding to a perceived crisis in American health—in particular to high cholesterol rates and emergence of heart disease as the leading cause of death in the United States—the popular emphasis on physical fitness created an atmosphere in which original types of exercise and competition developed. A new orientation toward dance and its relationship to athletics facilitated the emergence of contemporary forms that blur the traditional distinction between dance and sport. In addition to enduring functions of dance as performance and social activity, forms such as aerobic dancing and competitive cheerleading now began to utilize dance movement in new contexts of competition and the pursuit of physical fitness.

Aerobic Dancing. Aerobic dancing was invented and copyrighted by Jacki Sorenson, who taught her first class in 1969. A former professional dancer and the wife of an Air Force officer, Sorenson began teaching classes to other military wives as a form of recreation and physical exercise. Influenced by Air Force physician Kenneth Cooper, whose pioneering book *Aerobics* first articulated the value of regular, continuous exercise requiring increased oxygen output for overall cardiopulmonary fitness, Sorenson

designed classes that set simple movements to energetic music, which made the exercises more engaging and encouraged nondancers to join in. By setting repetitive calisthenics such as jumping jacks and marching in place to music and naming it "aerobic dancing," Sorenson discovered a way to counteract the boredom that many people associate with regular exercise. Sorenson's classes were an immediate success, which she transformed into a profitable business, inspiring many others—particularly women—to pursue aerobic dancing as a means of recreation, physical fitness, and business opportunity.

By the mid-1970s aerobic dancing was a national trend whose popularity shows no sign of waning. As innovations in household technology and large-scale entry into the corporate workforce transformed the nature of middle-class women's work in the 1970s and 1980s, aerobics was deliberately designed and marketed to appeal to women with the leisure time and funds to afford classes. Additionally, the rise of aerobic dancing complemented the changing popular rationale for strictures surrounding the proper shape for women's bodies. Preoccupations with health as an absence of fat—either in food or on the body—began to be used to justify prescriptions of thinness for both men and women. Aerobic exercise was seen as a new, paradoxically healthy form of addiction, which could replace the amphetamines that doctors had prescribed for women throughout the 1950s and 1960s to help them maintain a trim figure. Books, audiotapes, and videotapes such as *Jane Fonda's Workout* proliferated in the early 1980s, giving people the opportunity to follow an aerobics instructor in the privacy of their own homes while eliminating the cost of individual class fees or gym membership. The chance to participate in structured exercise without having to endure the scrutiny of instructors or participants alleviated the self-consciousness many people experienced in an aerobics classroom. Ballet, jazz, social dances, and calisthenics provided the vocabulary of movements initially included in aerobics class routines, but as aerobics has spread and expanded across the United States—and internationally—distinctive forms emphasizing country line dancing, hip-hop, martial arts, and other forms have emerged. [*See* Aerobic Dance.]

Cheerleading. Structured cheering for sports teams is generally acknowledged to have begun formally at Ivy League universities at the turn of the century with groups of men who led the audience in cheers and fight songs. Cheerleading squads developed gradually as a (primarily) female auxiliary to male sports teams, providing entertainment and encouraging team and school spirit. While the squads were originally contingent upon and peripheral to the male sports teams for which they galvanized support, cheerleading has developed over time into a competitive sport in its own right. Cheerleading squads are now so popular that the schools and universities that have traditionally sponsored them cannot accommodate the demand for training. In consequence, cheerleading gyms have sprung up all over the country, which sponsor and train independent "all-star" squads not connected to any other institution. National cheerleading organizations began organizing nationwide collegiate competitions in 1978. Competitions are now conducted on the local, regional, and national levels and are divided into categories according to the squad's age and institutional affiliation.

Contemporary cheerleading competitions are now regularly televised like any other spectator sport on cable networks (including USA and the all-sports channel ESPN). Hosted by "expert" commentators, such programs are watched by enormous audiences. Cheerleading squads create elaborate combinations of military drill, acrobatics, and dance movement, combining floor patterns and grouping structures as well as specific movements derived from these other forms. Both all-female and coed squads of up to thirty people perform routines divided into sections accompanied alternately by vocal cheering or rapid techno and hip-hop music. Routines combine unison dancing (usually hip-hop derived); acrobatics; intricate group architectures requiring strength, balance, and cooperative weight-sharing; individual and unison group tumbling passes like those in gymnastics floor exercises; and aerial maneuvers in which one competitor is thrown into the air by other competitors from a "basket toss" and performs twists, turns, and positions that would only otherwise be possible with the use of an apparatus such as a trampoline or diving board. In fact, small trampolines had become staples of competitive cheerleading until they were banned in the mid-1980s because of concern about the severe injuries that had resulted from their use.

The importance of difficulty and balance contribute an element of danger to competitive cheerleading. While the pursuit of height and complexity in cheerleading stunts continued unchecked until the mid-1980s, incidents of severe injury including paralysis and death created an atmosphere of alarm in the competitive cheerleading community and in the public at large. Representatives from cheerleading organizations argue that cheerleaders actually sustain far fewer injuries than do people who play basketball or other team sports, but it is the severity of the injuries suffered by even skilled cheerleaders that has caused nationwide concern. Since the mid-1980s competitive cheerleading has been strictly regulated to prohibit the performance of excessively risky stunts and to ensure the presence of trained spotters during both training and competition. However, the policing of competition does not prevent cheerleaders from executing such dangerous moves in other contexts. Similar concerns about severe, recurring injuries resulting from excessive or uninformed participation in aerobic dance exercise has led to the de-

DANCE AS SPORT. To encourage team spirit at the 1997 Rose Bowl, the Arizona State University Dance Line performs a high-energy routine to the accompaniment of the marching band. (Photograph © 1997 by Tim Trumble; used by permission.)

velopment of low-impact and no-impact aerobics, step aerobics (executed with individual low platforms to increase muscular effort by simulating climbing); slide aerobics (in which slippery floor pads and cloth covers on the shoes facilitate side-to-side gliding movements); and various forms of resistance training using rubber bands or tubing and small weights, choreographed like aerobics classes. Knee and ankle injuries, shin splints, and lower back strain were regularly suffered by participants in the early days of high impact aerobics classes, which emphasized jumping and rarely included appropriate or sufficient warm-ups.

Like other institutionally organized dance competitions, such as ballroom, modern clogging, Highland, or Irish dance, competitive cheerleading performances are evaluated according to a set of predetermined criteria. Emphasis is placed on high-energy, cheerful performance, synchronization, precision and clarity of movement, and degree of difficulty. While cheerleading has always been an audience-oriented activity, aerobics was originally designed as a nonperformance form. Nonetheless, the popularity of aerobics and the high level commonly attained by aerobics instructors and regular participants has led inevitably to its organization as a competitive form as well. Aerobics competitors are additionally judged according to their overall degree of physical fitness, muscle definition, flexibility, and the creativity of their choreography. Both aerobics and cheerleading emphasize precision and regimentation over spontaneous individual expression, facilitating their assimilation to competitive evaluation.

Racial Issues. The enormous prevalence of hip-hop music and movement in cheerleading and aerobics choreography raises complex questions involving the dynamics of race and bodily movement in American society. Black high schools and colleges have a long history of excellence in cheerleading, step shows, and marching bands, which are sometimes televised on the cable television network BET (Black Entertainment Television). While African-American choreographic innovations have clearly influenced the predominantly white cheerleading squads who frequent competitions, black and white cheerleading are institutionalized and televised nationally as separate entities. This situation reflects some of the nuances of choreographic exchange between black and white communities in the United States, and the prevalent crossover and appropriation of black music and dance styles in American popular entertainment forms. The popularity of MTV (Music Television, originally an all-music channel), hip-hop's ascendence as one of the dominant forms of jazz dance technique, and the emphasis on hip-hop dance among professional basketball cheerleaders—in particular Paula Abdul's innovations with the Laker Girls (the Los Angeles professional basketball team's cheerleaders) before she went on to pop stardom—both represent this phenomenon and reinforce it. The adaptation of hip-hop, an African-American improvisational dance form, to the regimented protocol of aerobics and cheerleading is another example of the crossover, appropriation, and transformation that have characterized the dissemination of African-American dance forms throughout American history.

Gender Issues. From the start, both aerobic dancing and competitive cheerleading were designed as outlets for female activity, although men currently participate widely in both forms. The 1990s has seen growing participation of coed cheerleading squads and enthusiasm from male athletes formerly involved in such male sports as football for both aerobics and competitive cheering. However, the traditional "femaleness" of cheerleading and its auxiliary role in football and other team sports have had a strong impact on the controversy surrounding its potential status as a sport. Jane Gottesman (1994) wonders whether designating cheerleading as a girl's sport is a way of shirking the responsibility to establish equal "athletic opportunities" for girls and boys on the high-school level as mandated by the U.S. Department of Education's Title IX. Recognizing cheerleading's second-class position within the athletic community, she further argues that to call cheerleading a "sport" is to institutionalize girls' sports as contingent upon male sports. Her concern is legitimate, given that the function of providing support for the school, the community, or the team is fundamental to the structure of cheerleading performances. While the image of a cute girl in the short skirt jumping up and down with pompoms certainly reflects one element of cheerleading, contemporary cheerleaders achieve athletic excellence and enjoy competitive opportunities that do, in fact, give cheerleading an independent life and status.

BIBLIOGRAPHY
"Aerobics: What Teachers Need to Know." *Dance Magazine* (January 1984): 107.
Casten, Carole, and Peg Jordan. *Aerobics Today.* Saint Paul, Minn., 1990.
"Gimme an 'S'—for Safety." *New York Times Magazine* (15 January 1995): 14.
Gottesman, Jane. "Is Cheerleading a Sneaky Way around Title IX?" *New York Times* (23 October 1994).
Loken, Newt. *Cheerleading.* New York, 1961.
Neil, Randy, and Elaine Hart. *The All New Official Cheerleader's Handbook.* New York, 1986.
Perkins, Janet. "Aerobics: The Dance Form to Promote Good Health." *Dance Teacher Now* (September–October, 1982): 28–37.
Polley, Maxine J. *Dance Aerobics.* Mountain View, Calif., 1981.
Thomas, Robert McG., Jr. "New Heights, and Dangers, for Cheerleaders." *New York Times* (15 November 1986).
Thompson, Terri L. "Greg Carelli: National Aerobics Champion." *Dance Teacher Now* (March 1990): 34–38.

KATHERINE FRIEDMAN

DANCE MARATHONS. Often thought of as entertainments paradigmatic of the Great Depression of the 1930s, dance marathons actually began as early as 1923. In the spring of that year, a thirty-two-year-old woman named Alma Cummings danced nonstop for twenty-seven hours, capping her endurance feat to the blaring of "The Star Spangled Banner." Trampling cigarette butts and inhaling the odor of stale coffee, Cummings breathlessly danced a victory waltz with her sixth and final partner. Her feat, reported nationally, engendered both brief fame and challenges to break her record. In these early marathons, both victory and loss were understood as public-spirited endeavors. Celebrating the winner did not necessitate debasing the loser; it was the spectacle of the effort that mattered. The greatest number of hours danced nonstop in the spring of 1923 was 217, reached on 10 June.

In the months and years that followed, dance marathons were held at local dance halls across the United States. Publicized by the local press, they became bigger and bigger attractions to ever-increasing audiences. Dance marathons persisted as local contests with local contestants until the late 1920s, when professional promoters began experimenting with large-scale urban shows that combined professional and amateur entertainment. The most famous of these promoters in the 1920s was Milton Crandall, who would later be shot to death by a drive-by gunman outside a marathon in Chicago. Crandall's slick and professional 1928 Madison Square Garden marathon, called "The Dance Derby of the Century," set the tone for what was to follow.

From the beginning, marathons combined grit, endurance, patriotic blather, and popular dances. At their heyday in the 1930s, these endurance events, characterized by grueling competition and lasting weeks and sometimes months, included comedy sketches, songs, audience giveaways, and elimination contests. Participants were seasoned professionals who toured from marathon to marathon as well as wide-eyed newcomers hoping to win fortune, fame, and maybe a Hollywood contract.

Professionally promoted marathons were primarily a between-the-wars American phenomenon, although some were staged in the 1930s by American promoter Hal J. Ross in Paris and Frankfurt. They began as part of the insouciant fads of the 1920s for who could do the most, be the quickest, perform the longest, and, sometimes, act the silliest. Flagpole sitting, transatlantic flights, tree sitting, all kinds of tests of human record setting marked post–World War I society. Beginning as authentic contests, marathons increasingly became staged events. Once professional promoters such as Ross and Crandall got involved, moneymaking replaced record setting as the driving force behind the marathon craze. "Staged" is a crucial concept because although dance marathons were presented as contests, they were, in fact, carefully planned theatrical events knitting together endurance dancing with acts from vaudeville, band music, and audience participation.

Whereas in the 1920s marathons were part of the mood of liberated living in the name of patriotism, in the 1930s they represented the arduous struggle (actual as well as sham) for survival while also offering cheap, around-the-clock entertainment to audiences who had very little money but lots of time. What linked the dance marathons of the 1920s to those of the 1930s was the overarching framework of a dance contest that kept contestants moving, on average, forty-five minutes out of every hour, twenty-four hours a day; the remaining fifteen minutes were used as rest periods, during which contestants left the dance floor to collapse onto their cots in either the "boys" or "girls" rest quarters. Rest periods enabled contestants to dance for weeks at a time. Dragging around the dance floor for such an extended period of time was not enough to hold an audience, however, so promoters punctuated the unrelenting endurance contest with nightly diversions provided by emcees, singers, and other entertainers.

Dance marathons truly came into their own, and earned their infamous reputation, during the Great Depression. What had been a fun and voluntary activity in the 1920s became a kind of forced labor in the 1930s. The seemingly innocent postwar entertainment turned into a spectacle of survival in a world where individual humans seemed not to count for much. The prosperity of the 1920s was as fleeting as it had been spectacular; the Depression quickly exposed a widespread culture of poverty. Marathons toyed with the perdurable American Dream of luck and wealth even as they demonstrated that most people would drop out long before they could cash in. The emcee fast talked the crowd. Everything could be had—fame, food, and fortune—by winning a contest, and to win, all the contestant had to do was keep moving until everyone else had dropped. How was anyone to know that most marathons were fixed?

The spectacle was not simply a display of the dispossessed and the self-deceived struggling against each other—and the odds—to earn prize money; it was also a

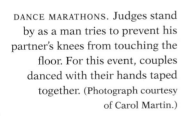

DANCE MARATHONS. Judges stand by as a man tries to prevent his partner's knees from touching the floor. For this event, couples danced with their hands taped together. (Photograph courtesy of Carol Martin.)

type of American theater featuring vanishing entertainments drawn from vaudeville, exhibition dancing, burlesque, and popular dance. Many contestants, a veritable professional troupe of marathoners, traveled all over the country and entered contest after contest. Others, once their dancing days were over, migrated to Hollywood, where they took small roles or worked as extras in films. A very few—June Havoc, Red Skelton—found real fame or success in theater or the movies.

Depression dance marathons relied on audiences that were out of work and on contestants who were willing to work for very little. Admission generally was twenty-five to forty cents, and prize money was most often $1,000 or $1,500 to the one winning couple. For the promoters,

marathons could be big business, as spectators often returned to follow the progress of their favorite couples. Contestants became adroit at exploiting the emotion of the moment, whether it entailed falling out of the contest or falling in love with one's partner. Promoters were quick to serialize dramatic occurrences by elaborating on them in daily episodes. As a marathon wore on, contestants either dropped out or, more likely, were eliminated by floor judges when they stopped moving or collapsed, the latter defined as touching one's knee to the ground. Slow ticket sales prompted promoters to add cleverly devised elimination features: "grinds," "zombie treadmills," "hurdles," "dynamite sprints," and "duck waddles" were special, demanding, and demeaning races conducted within the larger marathon and contrived to eliminate contestants. The last couple to finish was eliminated along with anyone who fell during the race. These well-planned exhibitions of pain and struggle enhanced ticket sales.

DANCE MARATHONS. Dance endurance competitions often featured other entertainments to break the monotony for spectators. Here, a boxing ring forms the centerpiece of the arena. (Photograph from the Mansell Collection, London.)

DANCE MARATHONS. Exhausted contestants slump against their partners in a 1930s dance marathon. (Photograph by Lawrence Matthews; from the Dance Collection, New York Public Library for the Performing Arts.)

The accomplishments of Cummings and others who broke records with their dancing might seem relatively unimportant when compared to more heroic achievements, yet the meanings produced by the bodies of dance marathon contestants were multiple and complex. The spectacular endurance of the dancers was often coupled with a flippant attitude, but what was hyped as a great triumph ultimately turned out to be an inconsequential victory. Winning was not as fascinating as the ritualized display of a highly regulated set of procedures that governed every activity: dancing, sleeping, eating, using the toilet, and bathing. In this array of pure physicality the body became the primary subject and dancing became an opportunity not for art but for the primacy of unmasked physical exigency. The Charleston, fox trot, ballroom, and other popular dances became the media through which contestants displayed their stamina. Everything "fun" was performed in the context of basic living: eating, sleeping, bathing, using the toilet, and sex.

Dance marathons and what the body was permitted to do at them became a battleground for civic authorities and reformers who wanted to wage a war against unscrupulous entertainments. Were dance marathons dangerous? Crooked? Immoral? A few deaths were associated with the early contests, especially those without rest periods, but the real danger, as perceived by the reformers, was the threat to public morals posed by corrupt promoters. Many unethical promoters did in fact leave contestants stranded when they abandoned shows that were not drawing enough spectators to pay the bills, thus also aggravating local authorities who had to face enraged businessmen who had not been paid for the food, medicine, laundry, and advertising they had provided on credit. From the point of view of morality, reformers were troubled by the rejection of Victorian womanhood implicit in the spectacle of female bodies on display. Some were afraid that such a public display of physicality in an unregulated entertainment might provoke sexual exploitation. There is, in fact, every indication that this was a real possibility. The larger issue, however, was autonomy. That women were able to make independent decisions about their social, sexual, political, and economic welfare in public alarmed some. An early press report questioned whether "girls" were so successful as dance marathon contestants because of their loyalty to their partners or because of competition with their partners. Others were enthusiastic, viewing women's superior staying power as a new point of departure for women and what they could achieve.

For all that ailed dance marathons regulation seemed to be the answer. Standardized rules would make the shows a legitimate athletic entertainment. A professional organization could, by regulating its membership, eliminate inexperienced and unprincipled promoters who were ruining the reputation of marathons. Such were the organizing principles of the National Endurance Amusement Association (NEAA), which sought not only to regulate dance marathons but also to fight growing legislative efforts to ban them. But despite the determination of some promoters, the NEAA never got off the ground. Even attorney Richard Kaplan's address in the pages of *Billboard* warning promoters about the legal issues facing them failed to summon the enthusiasm necessary to legitimate these spectacles.

What Kaplan and others did not seem to realize was that resistance to authority was part of what made the genre so appealing. Dance marathons were about tenacity and the desire to beat the odds. Realization of that dream had to be remote in order for the victory to seem so sweet. Regulation would destroy the wild card nature of the entertainment. Regulation also meant that the sensibilities of athletic jurors and legal officials would prevail. In the end, though, it was the theatricality of struggle within the framework of entertainment that gave marathons their meaning. It was not simply that scam and illegality were intriguing aspects of some shows; dance marathons constituted a kind of sociological discussion of the principal realities of poverty and struggle and patriotism. When in the late 1930s these "conversations" no longer dominated social discourse, dance marathons faded from the American scene, disappearing altogether after World War II.

BIBLIOGRAPHY

Calabria, Frank. "The Dance Marathon Craze." *Journal of Popular Culture* 10 (Summer 1976): 54–69.

Eells, George. "Some 20,000 Were in 'Marathon Dance' Biz at Zenith of Craze." *Variety* (7 January 1970): 154.

Gilmartin, Eddie. "Why a Successful Walkathon—Marathon?" *Billboard* (30 June 1934).

Gingrich, Arnold. "Poor Man's Night Club." *Esquire* (Autumn 1933).

Kaplan, Richard. "An Appeal to Reason." *Billboard* (29 June 1935).

Kaye, Joseph. "Dance of Fools." *Dance Magazine* (February 1931): 12–13.

Martin, Carol. *Dance Marathons: Performing American Culture of the 1920s and 1930s.* Jackson, Miss., 1994.

Mix, Ruth. "Are Dance Marathons Dangerous?" *Journal of Social Hygiene* (March 1934).

Ross, Hal J. "Is the Endurance Show Durable?" *Billboard* (14 April 1934).

Scott, Jimmy. "We Danced All Night—And All Day!" *Ballroom Dance Magazine* (July 1961): 8–9, 20–24.

CAROL MARTIN

DANCE MEDICINE. In its multitude of forms, dance is universal and generally vigorous; therefore, movements that are unfamiliar to the human body, repeated and practiced for hours, day after day, may result in acute and chronic injuries. For the treatment of these injuries, dancers have traditionally sought assistance from trainers, lay therapists, and physicians.

The practitioner of dance medicine as a physician works alone or in a partnership at a specialized medical clinic to provide and/or supervise the medical services that are needed by dancers of all ages involved in every type and category of dance activity. The physician works with dancers, instructors, choreographers, trainers, and therapists to avoid practices and schedules that may predispose to injuries and shorten the dancer's career. The teaching and practice of good and correct technique depends on the trained and experienced knowledge of anatomy and physiology. This knowledge informs recommendations on when to stop dancing for necessary treatment, what rehabilitative procedures can be effective, and when a full schedule of dancing may be resumed.

Medical treatment of injuries may be empiric based on the physician's knowledge of anatomy and function. Prevention, however, depends on the establishment of a scientific study of frequency of injury and characteristics of activities. One pioneer in these investigations was Bernardino Ramazzini, author of a treatise in 1700, *Diseases of the Workers*. Ramazzini and later writers laid a foundation for what became known as industrial medicine. Illnesses and injuries characteristic to athletes were described and reported in the nineteenth century. It was not, however, until the establishment of a committee during the second Winter Olympic Games at Saint Moritz in February 1928 that a plan was formulated for the First International Congress of Sports Medicine. Held in Amsterdam in August 1928, the congress was the first event that used the term *sport medicine*.

The first mention in the medical literature of injuries identified as characteristic to dancers appeared in Francisco Ronchese's 1948 publication, *Occupational Marks and Other Physical Signs*, in which he noted

One would expect to find some peculiarities in the toe dancer's toes, from the pressure of the whole body on half an inch of body surface, and perhaps, some slight changes in bones or joints appreciable on an x-ray film. However, nothing can be detected. . . . A moderately helpful sign of the dancing profession may be the peculiar divaricability of the legs as a result of performing the split and the hypertrophy of the muscles of the calves.

The first report in the medical literature of injuries identified specifically as occurring in dancers was published in 1935. Louis P. Pressman's study of neurovascular function discussed motor reaction and movement time in the lower extremities of ballet dancers. This was followed by additional publications, including Lulu E. Sweigard's study of psychomotor function in 1949, August Rutt's study of dancers' feet in 1952, Edward. G. Leiber and G. D. Roklin's examination of ballet dancers' skeletal characteristics in 1967, and William Hamilton's work on tendonitis in classical ballet dancers' ankle joints published in *Foot and Ankle*. Two symposia were also held in 1982 at the Sorbonne in Paris. However, none of the aforementioned publications or symposia used the term *dance medicine*.

The apparent first use of the term *dance medicine* occurred at the First International Symposium on Orthopaedic and Medical Aspects of Dance presented in September 1979 in Los Angeles and New York, where the topic "Dance Medicine—A New Challenge to the American Physician" was discussed. The symposium's organizer and director, Ernest L. Washington, M.D., also used the term in the 1982 issue of *Dance Medicine-Health Newsletter*. A former dancer, Washington did graduate work in dance at the University of California, Los Angeles (UCLA), and, as a resident in the Department of Orthopedic Surgery of the Cleveland Clinic Foundation became coordinator of Dance Orthopedics in the section of Sports Medicine. In 1971–1972 he organized a symposium entitled "Orthopedic Aspects of Dance and the Dancer's Environment," and the speakers included physicians on the faculty of the Department of Orthopedic Surgery and physicians for three dance companies.

The idea and concept for a comprehensive program addressing the medical health and environmental aspects of dance was originated and, to a large extent, implemented by Washington. While completing his training as a fellow (resident) at the Cleveland Clinic, he served as physician to the Dance Company of the Fairmont School of the Performing Arts in Cleveland. During the early 1970s he began to give lecture demonstrations at festivals including the American Dance Festival and Pacific Regional Ballet Festival and at the departments of dance at the University of California, Santa Cruz; New York University; and Saint Louis University.

As coordinator of Dance Orthopedics in the Sports Medicine section of the Cleveland Clinic, Washington developed a plan in 1972 for a comprehensive dance health program, the first of its kind. Although it was never fully implemented, it provided a pattern and model for subsequent cooperation and symposia leading to the establishment of a professional association.

A survey asking for information about dance injuries was mailed to every professional dance company, major university dance department, and dance school in the United States and several foreign countries. The survey was also sent to orthopedic surgeons who were identified as having experience in observing and treating dance injuries. During the course of four years, 1,662 dance-related injuries were reported and the results were published by Washington in 1978. Although other phases of the development of a comprehensive dance health program were never fully realized, Washington received a Fulbright grant to observe physicians working with the Bolshoi Ballet.

Washington also took part in the first general symposium on dance medicine organized by the editors of the newsletter *Kinesiology for Dance* scheduled around the program of the Seventh Annual Dance in Canada Conference in 1979. Reports and summaries of these discussions were later published in *Kinesiology for Dance*. Under his direction as medical director of the International Center for Dance Orthopedics and Dance Therapy, and with cooperation of UCLA and the Department of Orthopedic Surgery of Centinela Hospital Medical Center, the First Annual Symposium on the orthopedic and general medical aspects of dance was presented in Inglewood, California, in September 1979. The program was repeated several days later in New York City. Subsequent symposia were held in various cities, including London and Paris.

The stimulus provided by these symposia resulted in the presentation of similar events around the world during the years following the 1979 symposium. All were multidisciplinary, and sponsorships included universities, medical and educational associations, hospitals, and ballet companies. During this time, special clinics and services for dancers were established in many places, including the Dance Injuries Clinic at the University of Cincinnati Medical School; the Israeli Dance Medicine Center at Bat-Dor School of Ballet, Tel Aviv; the Center for Dance Medicine, New York City; and the Kathryn and Gilbert Miller Health Care Institute for Performing Artists at Saint Luke's–Roosevelt Hospital Center in New York City.

International attempts to bring together people working with dancers and their injuries began in Spain in 1985. This meeting resulted in the inauguration of the Spanish Association for Dance Medicine. On the occasion of the International Days of Dance Medicine held in Barcelona in 1990, people involved with dance medicine activities in England and Belgium joined with representatives from the United States and Spain to form the International Association for Dance Medicine and Science. The association has held annual meetings since 1990.

The term *dance medicine* identifies a concept of a type of specialization of established and generally accepted medical practice that is recognized in the United States of America in thirty-six categories. Licensure, however, which is controlled by the individual states, is general. Admission to each of these categories is made by satisfying specific qualifications in training beyond the medical degree and requires oral and written examinations approved by a Board of Medical Specialties. Neither sports medicine nor dance medicine have obtained such formal recognition for several reasons, the most important of which is that physicians who identify themselves as interested in these aspects do not, for the most part, devote their entire practice to them. Additionally, most are already recognized in one of the thirty-six categories that do provide certification.

Although the term *dance medicine* is often used broadly to describe many forms of counseling and therapy, *Webster's New World Dictionary*, third college edition, defines medicine as "the science and art of diagnosing, treating, curing, and preventing disease, relieving pain, and improving and preserving health" (1996). Instruction, counseling, treatment, and rehabilitation of dancers by people other than physicians and with a variety of backgrounds and qualifications is valuable, but the use of the term *dance medicine* should be limited to what a physician is expected to know and to do. Collaboration with a physician has encouraged the development and recognition of professionalism among those who provide services to dancers that may loosely be described as medical, even when they are primarily instructional or technical.

Dance Medicine Literature. The emergence of any medical specialty is demonstrated in book-length publications that eventually become parts of the body of knowledge that define and identify a specific field. This, in turn, develops an audience of readers and serves as a focus around which further and more definitive publications, which eventually serve as texts, are encouraged.

For dance medicine, the first of these books written in English is *Dancing through Danger: A Guide to the Prevention of Injury for the Amateur and Professional Dancer* (1970), by the English surgeon Donald F. Featherstone in collaboration with Rena Allen, a dance teacher. The book is divided into four parts: "The Human Body," "Prevention of Injury," "Vital Areas of the Body", and "Treatment of Injuries." The book's appendixes discuss physical activity during menstruation, fighting nervousness and tension, and preventing and fighting the common cold. It also includes a chapter, "Back to Work," by Lillian Moore, which was originally published in the August 1964 issue of *The Dancing Times.*

The second publication in this body of knowledge is Joan Lawson's *The Teaching of Classical Ballet: Common Faults in Young Dancers* (1973), which was followed by Beryl Dunn's *Dance! Therapy for Dancers* (1974) and I. A. Badnin's *Okhrana truda i zdorov' ia artistov baleta* (Orthopedic Problems in Classical Ballet Dancers; 1970). *Dance Injuries: Their Prevention and Care,* originally published in 1975 by D. D. Arnheim, was the second book after Featherstone's published on the subject of dance medicine in the United States. Important in this literature is Lawson's *Teaching Young Dancers: Muscular Coordination in Classical Ballet* (1975). These publications attracted the dance community, especially in the United Kingdom and the United States.

L. M. Vincent's *The Dancer's Book of Health* (1978) was unique in that it was directed to the dancer and not to the professional caregiver. Vincent, a physician and former dancer with the Kansas City Ballet Company, divided his book into four parts. He explains how the musculoskeletal system of the dancer works and how it may incur injuries, as well as how to prevent injuries. This is followed by a discussion of particular injuries and their management and concludes with recommendations on nutrition and rehabilitation following injury. While this book primarily attracted an audience of dancers, his next book attracted the attention of the general public in addition to dancers and physicians. *Competing with the Sylph: Dancers and the Pursuit of the Ideal Body Form* (1979) identified the theatrical and aesthetic image of the female ballet dancer as an unrealistic ideal and pointed out the dangers involved. This book marked a significant step in the promotion of better health, especially in young dancers.

Elvind Thomasen's 1982 publication *Diseases and Injuries of Ballet Dancers* summarizes twenty-five years of experience in working with and treating dancers as company physician to the Royal Danish Ballet. It is a comprehensive work that includes a history of classical ballet, discussion of dance movements and terminology, descriptions of injuries to the different parts of a dancer's body and their treatment, and a review of the literature on dance injuries up to 1982. Although Thomasen never uses the term *dance medicine,* he can truly be called the father of this specialty because of the extent of his experience and the development of surgical techniques that made his work widely known and respected throughout the dance world.

The Dancer as Athlete, edited by Caroline G. Shell (1988), records the presentations of thirty-five participants who addressed the Olympic Scientific Congress in Eugene, Oregon, in 1984. The Congress presented issues of (1) musculoskeletal considerations—the classical dancer versus the athlete; (2) nutritional, physical, and physiological considerations in the dancer and the athlete—similarities and differences; (3) dance for fitness; (4) the use of body therapies and motor reeducation in dance and athletics; and (5) emerging research in dance science.

A similar conference was held in 1985 that resulted in *The Medical Aspects of Dance,* the proceedings of a conference held at the University of Western Ontario. It includes twelve presentations by eleven authors and a panel discussion on the medical aspects of dance and recommendations for action, as well as an extensive bibliography of scientific references.

Dance Medicine: A Comprehensive Guide (1987), edited by Allan J. Ryan and Robert E. Stephens, is considered the standard text and reference for dance medicine. Written primarily for the physician and other professionals who supervise, train, and treat dancers, its twenty chapters contain contributions by twenty-six authors on the epidemiology of dance injuries, the training of the young dancer, the physiological demands of dance, particular injuries in various forms of dance, the surfaces on which dance is performed, dancers' footwear, and psychological issues in the dancer's career.

Dance Technique and Injury Prevention (1988) was written by Justin Howse, orthopaedic surgeon to the Royal Ballet Schools, the Royal Academy of Dancing, and the Remedial Dance Clinic in London, and Shirley Hancock, principal therapist to the clinic. Its purpose was to fill the needs of dancers, teachers, or those treating dance injuries. Here it is possible to find, in one place, the essentials of anatomy and physiology of the dancer, the biomechanics of dance movements, the role that mechanical faults in technique play in producing injuries, the identification and correct treatment of injuries, steps in the prevention of injuries, and rehabilitation following them, with appropriate exercises.

Science of Dance Training (1988) was edited by Priscilla M. Clarkson and Margaret Skrinar, dancers, educators, and researchers. The sixteen chapters are divided into four parts: Perspectives in Dance Medicine and Science; Scientific Aspects of Dance Training; Medical Aspects of Dance Training; and Behavioral and Pedagogical Aspects of Dance Training. The writings, by seventeen authors in addition to the editors, had their origin in a symposium held at the 1993 national meeting of the American Alliance for Health, Physical Education, Recreation, and Dance.

The Dancer's Complete Guide to Healthcare and a Long Career (1988) by Ryan and Stephens was aimed particularly at the young beginning dancer. It can be readily understood by those without technical backgrounds and contains glossaries of dance and medical terms.

[*See also* Kinesiology. *For related discussion, see* Body Therapies.]

BIBLIOGRAPHY

Ambre, Tolen, and B. E. Nilsson. "Degenerative Changes in the First Metatarsophalangeal Joint of Ballet Dancers." *Acta Orthopaedica Scandinavica* 49 (1978): 317–319.

Arnheim, D. D. *Dance Injuries: Their Prevention and Care.* 3d ed. Princeton, 1991.

Badnin, I. A. *Okhrana truda i zdorov' ia artistov baleta.* Moscow, 1987.

Brodelius, Ake. "Osteoarthritis of the Talar Joints in Footballers and Ballet Dancers." *Acta Orthopaedica Scandinavica* 30 (1961): 309–314.

Burrows, H. Jackson. "Fatigue Infraction of the Middle of the Tibia in Ballet Dancers." *Journal of Bone and Joint Surgery* 3813 (1956): 83–84.

Chapchal, George. "Schaden beim Ballett. I. Praxis." *Schweizeriche Rundschau für Medizin* 55 (1966): 191–194.

Clarkson, Priscilla M., and Margaret Skrinar, eds. *Science of Dance Training.* Champaign, Ill., 1988.

Dance Medicine-Health Newsletter 1 (Winter 1982).

Desoille, Henri, et al. "Étude statistique de la frequence de l'Hallux Valgus et des différentes formes de pied chez les danseuses classiques." *Arch. des Mal. Frof.* 21 (1960): 343–349.

Dunn, Beryl. *Dance! Therapy for Dancers.* London, 1974.

Featherstone, Donald F., and Rena Allen. *Dancing through Danger: A Guide to the Prevention of Injury for the Amateur and Professional Dancer.* South Brunswick, N.J., 1970.

Foot and Ankle Problems in Classic Dance III 2 (September–October 1982).

Grieg, Valerie. *Inside Ballet Technique.* Pennington, N.J., 1994.

Hamilton, William. "Tendinitis about the Ankle Joint in Classical Ballet Dancers." *American Journal of Sports Medicine* 5 (1977): 84–88.

Howse, Justin. "Orthopaedists Aid Ballet." *Clinical Orthopaedics and Related Research* 89 (1972): 52–63.

Howse, Justin, and Shirley Hancock. *Dance Technique and Injury Prevention.* Rev. ed. London, 1992.

LaCava, Giuseppe. "The International Federation of Sports Medicine." *Journal of the American Medical Association* 162 (November 1956): 1109–1111.

Lawson, Joan. *The Teaching of Classical Ballet: Common Faults in Young Dancers.* London, 1973.

Lawson, Joan. *Teaching Young Dancers: Muscular Coordination in Classical Ballet.* New York, 1975.

Leiber, Edward G., and G. D. Roklin. "Some Characteristics of Skeleton in Ballet Artists" (in Russian). *Archiv Anatomii, Gistologii, Embroyologii* 63 (1967): 42–47.

Mashkara, Kaio T. "Dynamics and Symptoms of Working Hypertrophy of the Osseous System in Certain Physical Working Ballet Dancers" (in Slavic). *Rado Medicinskogo Fakuitet Zagreb* 50 (1960): 131.

Miller, William, et al. "A New Consideration of Athletic Injuries: The Classical Ballet Dancer." *Clinical Orthopaedics and Related Research* 111 (1975): 181.

Nikolaev, Isador A., and S. Najdenov. "Osteo-arthropathies professionelles et danse classique." *Arch. des Mal. Prof.* 31 (1970): 39–42.

Nikoloc, Vlasic, and B. Zimmerman. "Functional Changes on Tarsal Bones of Ballet Dancers" (in Slavic). *Rado Medicinskogo Fakuitet Zagreb* 58 (1968): 131–146.

Peterson, Donna, et al., eds. *The Medical Aspects of Dance.* London, Ontario, 1986.

Pressman, Louis P. "Neurovascular Function in Limitation of Muscular Reaction in Ballet Dancers." *Kinesiology of Medicine* 13 (1935): 43.

Ramazzini, Bernardino. *Diseases of the Workers* (1713). Translated and edited by W. C. Wright. Chicago, 1940.

Ronchese, Francisco. *Occupational Marks and Other Physical Signs.* New York, 1948.

Rutt, August. "Studie über die Fusse von Tanzern und Tanzerinnen." *Zeitschrift für Orthopädie* 82 (1952): 370–375.

Ryan, Allan J., and Robert E. Stephens, eds. *Dance Medicine: A Comprehensive Guide.* Chicago, 1987.

Ryan, Allan J., and Robert E. Stephens. *The Dancer's Complete Guide to Healthcare and a Long Career.* Chicago, 1988.

Shell, Caroline G., ed. *The Dancer as Athlete.* Olympic Scientific Congress Proceedings, vol. 8. Champaign, Ill., 1986.

Sweigard, Lulu E. "Psychomotor Function as Correlated with Body Mechanics and Posture." *Annals of the New York Academy of Science* 2 (1949): 243–248.

Thomasen, Elvind. *Diseases and Injuries of Ballet Dancers.* Aarhus, 1982.

Vincent, L. M. *The Dancer's Book of Health.* Kansas City, 1978.

Vincent, L. M. *Competing with the Sylph: The Quest for the Perfect Dance Body.* 2d ed. Princeton, 1989.

Volkob, Volda. "Occupational Accidents in Ballet Performers and Their Prevention." *Orthop. Traumatol. Protezim.* 31 (1957): 57.

Washington, Ernest L. "Musculoskeletal Injuries in Theatrical Dancers: Site, Frequency, and Severity." *American Journal of Sports Medicine* 6.2 (1978): 75–98.

Allan J. Ryan, M.D.

DANCE OF DEATH

DANCE OF DEATH (Ger., *Totentanz;* Fr., *danse macabre;* It., *trionfo della morte;* Sp., *danza de la muerte*). All cultures through the ages have searched for ways to deal with the inevitability of dying. The arts in Europe created an imagery of death that brought it closer to human comprehension. The Dance of Death is part of this imagery, poignant and emotionally disturbing because, says Tilde Sankovitch (1979), it juxtaposes "the illusion of the dance, an activity connoting celebration, festival, companionship, and the reality of death with its inexorable joylessness and isolation."

Although representations of encounters between the living and the dead can be traced back to at least the thirteenth century, genuine dances of death do not appear until the fourteenth century. Two factors contributed decisively to their creation: the bubonic plague, which swept through and annihilated much of Europe, and the new eschatology formulated in a papal bull of 1336, according to which eternal bliss or damnation begin at the moment of death and not, as had been previously believed, after a long period of waiting for the Last Judgment.

Artists and poets from France and the southern German territories initiated the great wave of Dances of Death that began to appear in the second half of the fourteenth century and flourished in the fifteenth and sixteenth centuries. Although they gradually declined in the Baroque era, the Dance of Death continued to inspire artistic works in the nineteenth and twentieth centuries. Even though the oldest extant record of a Dance of Death, a fifteenth-century copy of a lost, illuminated fourteenth-

DANCE OF DEATH. A fifteenth-century German woodcut depicting a Dance of Death. One decaying figure leads a skeleton couple, as another plays a pipe. This print was published in Hartmann Schedel's *Weltchronik*, Nuremberg, 1493. (Reprinted from Sachs, 1933.)

century codex, is a textual source only, most such records combine rhyming stanzas and pictorial illuminations.

The texts of the dances developed from older monologue forms into dialogue forms (Death in altercation with the doomed mortal, not unlike the *débat* in mystery plays) and from texts in Latin into mixed Latin and vernacular texts and, finally, into texts in the vernacular alone. In most cases the actual Dance of Death is surrounded by an opening and closing penitential sermon in verse warning humankind of the brevity of life.

In the iconography of Dances of Death three major forms predominate. One is the long line of dancers holding hands, in which skeletons alternate with mortals, the latter depicted in descending order of their stations in life: princes of church and state, officials, lesser clerics, artisans and other craftspeople, beggars, children, the old, the infirm, and minstrels. The antecedents of this line are the processions of the damned in representations of the Last Judgment of the twelfth and thirteenth centuries. The second predominant form is the procession of couples, each mortal led by a figure of Death, also in strict hierarchy. The third form has cycles of separate, often intensely dramatic, scenes of Death dancing or interacting with a living partner. All three forms have counterparts in dances of the real world: linear Dances of Death are reminiscent of the medieval *carole*, the linear *bassedanze* of the fifteenth century and the *branles* of the sixteenth century; processions evoke the processional *bassesdanses* of the fifteenth century and the *pavanes* of the sixteenth century;

scenes for solo couples are reflections of the *balli* and *balletti* of the Renaissance, both early and late.

Some scholars disagree, but many believe that most pictures of a Dance of Death do in fact show dancing. The pictures show a wealth of leg and arm gestures, body and foot positions, and speed and vigor of motion, especially in the depictions of the skeletons that are the principal figures in the dances of death. Furthermore, the textual glosses to the illuminations reveal that the writers had substantial familiarity with contemporary dance practices since they make use of an extensive movement vocabulary and refer to specific dance types. Besides conventional formulas for dancing and an extensive general movement vocabulary (to tread, glide, jump, drag, crawl, lead, follow), the glosses make reference to specific dances, ranging from the *baixa dança* in a Spanish source from about 1400 to the *Bettler, Schwarzer Knabe, moresca, Hupff-auff, Hopperdantz,* and even the minuet mentioned in a variety of German sources dating from the late fifteenth through the early eighteenth century. At times, Death assumes the role of the dancing master and instructs the various social classes in his manner of choreography.

All this, however, does not mean that Dances of Death were ever performed. With only a few exceptions, they are artistic, symbolic representations of moral and ethical (less often theological) concepts. In keeping with their symbolic qualities, most Dances of Death—whether they are frescoes or carvings on church and cemetery walls, stained glass windows, engravings or painted book illuminations—move from left to right, that is, in the "negative" direction, toward the charnel house in front of which a band of skeletons provides the musical accompaniment for the approaching dancers.

In addition, individual Deaths play for the dance of their doomed partners on a wide variety of wind and stringed instruments, among which the pipe—*fistula diaboli*—predominates. Indicative of the irony of death is the occasional "perversion" of musical instruments: the gravediggers' spades are played as shawms or trumpets, skulls as drums with bones for drumsticks, wine bottles as lutes, and so on. The occasional depiction of Death, the trumpeter of doom or guardian of hell, as a black man merges the heritage of ancient vegetation rites with classical and medieval concepts of the identity of Death and the Devil, which lived on in the *moresca* and the *matachin,* in *Totentanz* tunes of the sixteenth century, and in specific references in Dances of Death.

BIBLIOGRAPHY

Beerli, C.-A. "Quelques aspects des jeux, fêtes et danses à Berne pendant la première moitié du XVIe siècle." In *Les fêtes de la Renaissance,* vol. 1, edited by Jean Jacquot. Paris, 1956.

Böhme, Franz M. *Geschichte des Tanzes in Deutschland.* 2 vols. Leipzig, 1886.

Boyd, Malcolm. "Dance of Death." In *The New Grove Dictionary of Music and Musicians*. London, 1980.

Brainard, Ingrid. "An Exotic Court Dance and Dance Spectacle of the Renaissance: *La Moresca*." In *Report of the Twelfth Congress, International Musicological Society [Berkeley 1977]*, edited by Daniel Heartz and Bonnie C. Wade. Kassel, 1981.

Brainard, Ingrid. "Tanz und Musik des Todes." *Speculum* 54 (1983).

Brown, Howard M. *Instrumental Music Printed Before 1600: A Bibliography*. Cambridge, Mass., 1965.

Clark, James M. *The Dance of Death in the Middle Ages and the Renaissance*. Glasgow, 1950.

Cosacchi, Stephan. "Musikinstrumente im mittelalterlichen Totentanz." *Die Musikforschung* 8 (1955).

Cosacchi, Stephan. *Makabertanz: Der Totentanz in Kunst, Poesie und Brauchtum des Mittelalters*. Meisenheim am Glan, 1965.

DuBruck, Edelgard E. *The Theme of Death in French Poetry of the Middle Ages and the Renaissance*. The Hague, 1964.

Freitag, Hartmut, ed. *Der Totentanz der Marienkirche in Lübeck und der Nikolaikirche in Reval (Talinn)*. Cologne, 1993.

Hammerstein, Reinhold. *Tanz und Musik des Todes: Die mittelalterlichen Totentänze und ihr Nachleben*. Bern, 1980.

Harrison, Ann Tukey. "La grant danse macabre des femmes." *Fifteenth-Century Studies* 3 (1980).

Harrison, Ann Tukey, ed. *The Danse Macabre of Women: Ms. fr. 995 of the Bibliothèque Nationale*. Kent, Ohio, 1994.

Kastner, Georges. *Les danses des morts*. Paris, 1852.

Kirstein, Lincoln. *Dance: A Short History of Classic Theatrical Dancing*. New York, 1935.

Manasse, Ernst M. "The Dance Motive of the Latin Dance of Death." *Medievalia et Humanistica* 4 (1946): 83–103.

McDonald, William C. "On the Charnel House as a Poetic Motif: Villon and German Poetry on Death." *Fifteenth-Century Studies* 19 (1992): 101–145.

Meyer-Baer, Kathi. *Music of the Spheres and the Dance of Death*. Princeton, 1970.

Rosenfeld, Hellmut. *Der mittelalterliche Totentanz: Entstehung, Entwicklung, Bedeutung*. 2d ed. Cologne, 1954.

Rowlandson, Thomas. *Drawings for "The English Dance of Death."* San Marino, Calif., 1966.

Sankovitch, Tilde. "Death and the Mole: Two Fifteenth-Century Dances of Death." *Fifteenth-Century Studies* 2 (1979).

Wickham, Glynne. *The Medieval Theatre*. 3d ed. Cambridge, 1987.

INGRID BRAINARD

DANCES AT A GATHERING. Choreography: Jerome Robbins. Music: Frédéric Chopin. Costumes: Joe Eula. Lighting: Thomas Skelton. First performance: 8 May 1969, New York State Theater, New York City Ballet. Principals: Allegra Kent, Sara Leland, Kay Mazzo, Patricia McBride, Violette Verdy, Anthony Blum, John Clifford, Robert Maiorano, John Prinz, Edward Villella.

Dances at a Gathering is sometimes likened to Mikhail Fokine's *Les Sylphides* because of its use of Chopin's piano pieces and its lack of plot. Jerome Robbins's ballet, however, is more timeless than Fokine's evocation of the Romantic era. *Dances at a Gathering* is performed on a bare stage against a cyclorama, a blank slate of a dancing ground that the viewer's imagination can transform into an open field or a ballroom at will. Although Robbins has said that the men's flowing sleeves were influenced by the counterculture fashions of the late 1960s, when the ballet was created, this is not obvious. Indeed, the men's loose shirts and boots and the women's simple dresses and hair ribbons, coupled with the refined behavior of both sexes, conjure up some gracious bygone period rather than the modern age.

Though several of the dances portray emotional interactions that could be the seeds of dramatic situations, Robbins foils any attempt to impose a unifying narrative upon the ballet by having the dancers change partners from dance to dance and by refusing to assign them distinctive qualities other than their own personalities. The dancers also seem to be performing for their own pleasure rather than for an audience; this is established from the ballet's beginning, when a man steps onstage and starts to dance as quietly and ruminatively as if he were alone in a rehearsal studio. In a letter written to *Ballet Review* in 1972, Robbins made clear his intentions: "The dancers are themselves dancing with each other to that music in that space."

In formal terms, the choreography of *Dances at a Gathering* abandons the hierarchical conventions of classical ballet—the symmetrical placement of the corps around a centrally positioned and spotlighted ballerina and danseur. In the cast of ten (five women and five men), everyone is at once a principal dancer and a member of the ensemble. The focus of attention shifts from one dance to another, and no single dancer or couple dominates the action either choreographically or dramatically.

In downplaying though not entirely eschewing the presentational aspects of the production, Robbins in 1969 seemed to have assimilated and adapted some of the precepts of Yvonne Rainer's avant-garde manifesto of 1965:

> NO to spectacle no to virtuosity . . . no to the glamour and transcendency of the star image . . . no to seduction of spectator by the wiles of the performer.

Robbins's earlier ballet *The Concert* (1956) is perhaps the true precursor of *Dances at a Gathering*. It too is a suite of dances to piano pieces by Chopin, here given a slyly humorous twist that is by no means absent in *Dances*. Its cast, like that of *Dances*, is unassuming in demeanor, depicting the fantasies of concertgoers with an engaging lack of pretension. Both ballets use Chopin's music as a basis for keen-eyed observations about human emotions and relationships. Unlike Fokine's dreamlike vision in *Les Sylphides* of a poet and sylphs in a woodland glade, both *The Concert* and *Dances* place before us people much like ourselves.

The intimate scale and atmosphere of *Dances at a Gathering*, coupled with its simple costumes and deceptively effortless, unself-conscious dancing, have inspired many imitators and at least one parody, Peter Anastos's *Yes, Virginia, Another Piano Ballet* (1977).

BIBLIOGRAPHY

Balanchine, George, with Francis Mason. *Balanchine's Complete Stories of the Great Ballets*. Rev. and enl. ed. Garden City, N.Y., 1977.

Denby, Edwin. "Jerome Robbins Discusses *Dances at a Gathering*." *Dance Magazine* (July 1969): 47–55.

Reiter, Susan. "Twenty Years of *Dances*." *New Dance Review* 2 (July–August 1989): 10–14.

Reynolds, Nancy. *Repertory in Review: Forty Years of the New York City Ballet*. New York, 1977.

Reynolds, Nancy, and Susan Reimer-Torn. *Dance Classics*. Pennington, N.J., 1991.

SUSAN AU

DANCE THEATRE OF HARLEM was founded in 1969 by Arthur Mitchell. While still a principal dancer with the New York City Ballet, Mitchell had envisioned a ballet school in New York's Harlem district to serve the community. It was the assassination of Martin Luther King, Jr., in 1968 that spurred him to realize his ambition. With the help of grants from the Ford Foundation and from private donors, a school was established with an initial enrollment of thirty students that grew to four hundred within the year. Mitchell's larger aim was to create an all-black ballet company. Dance educator Karel Shook shared artistic direction of the school and company with Mitchell. Regularly scheduled open houses encouraged students and permitted invited audiences to monitor their progress. By 1971 the school had trained enough talent to warrant an official debut: on 8 January, the Dance Theatre

DANCE THEATRE OF HARLEM. Arthur Mitchell, a principal dancer of the New York City Ballet before founding Dance Theatre of Harlem, created the male role in the pas de deux in George Balanchine's *Agon* (1957). Here, Mel Tomlinson dances this role with Lydia Abarca in Dance Theatre of Harlem's 1979 production. (Photograph © 1979 by Jack Vartoogian; used by permission. Choreography by George Balanchine © The George Balanchine Trust.)

of Harlem appeared at the Guggenheim Museum in New York, performing three works choreographed by Mitchell. George Balanchine allowed two of his best-known ballets, *Agon* and *Concerto Barocco*, to enter the repertory, waiving royalties. Subsequently, *Allegro Brilliante*, *The Four Temperaments*, *Serenade*, *Bugaku*, and *Square Dance* were added. Jerome Robbins permitted the company to perform his *Afternoon of a Faun*. Louis Johnson's *Forces of Rhythm* and Lester Horton's 1928 modern dance work, *The Beloved*, also were included in the 1971 repertory.

From the first, the company toured internationally, appearing in 1971 in Italy, at the Spoleto Festival of Two Worlds, and visiting the Netherlands and Switzerland. Another European tour in 1972 took it to several countries, but it was not until 1974 that the company had its first New York City season, performed in the ANTA Theatre. Subsequently, the company appeared at the Uris Theatre and for several successive years at City Center. Touring has taken the company all over the United States and to Japan, Australia, and Europe. In 1981, Dance Theatre of Harlem made history as the first black ballet company to appear at the Royal Opera House, Covent Garden.

From an original nucleus of neoclassic ballets, the repertory expanded to encompass classical, modern, and ethnically oriented works. A number of ballets associated with Diaghilev's Ballets Russes and other Ballet Russe companies have also been revived. *Schéhérazade* made a popular debut in 1981; *Les Biches*, staged by Nijinska's daughter, Irina, after her mother's original choreography, was a more controversial revival in 1983. The first nineteenth-century ballet, *Swan Lake, Act II*, was staged by Frederic Franklin for the 1980 season. In that year, Alexandra Danilova also supervised the staging of a suite of dances from *Paquita*. In 1982 John Taras's reworking of Stravinsky's *The Firebird* proved a success and, as part of the *Kennedy Center Tonight* television series, won a Peabody Award. Other notable revivals include David Lichine's *Graduation Ball* (1983), Ruth Page and Bentley Stone's *Frankie and Johnny* (1981), and Valerie Bettis's *A Streetcar Named Desire* (1982); Agnes de Mille's *Fall River Legend*, revived in 1983, proved a great personal success for the company's leading ballerina, Virginia Johnson. Ballets closely identified with the company include Geoffrey Holder's *Dougla* and *Belé* and Robert North's *Troy Game*, a ballet that shows off the strength and virtuosity of male dancers.

Several distinguished Dance Theatre of Harlem alumni have gone on to other ballet companies and to Broadway: Mel Tomlinson joined New York City Ballet; Paul Russell, the San Francisco Ballet; Ronald Perry, American Ballet Theatre; and Lydia Abarca and Hinton Battle have been featured in Broadway musicals.

The school continues to hold open houses and has expanded its original allied arts training program, which en-

DANCE THEATRE OF HARLEM. Virginia Johnson and Eddie J. Shellman with the female corps de ballet in *Giselle*, staged in a Creole setting for the company in 1984 by Frederic Franklin, after Jean Coralli and Jules Perrot. (Photograph © 1984 by Jack Vartoogian; used by permission.)

compasses stagecraft, technical and administrative skills, fashion and stage design, and choral and instrumental music. In recent years Dance Theatre of Harlem has moderated its all-black policy and is now considered interracial. The company's policy of bold, if sometimes redesigned versions of well-known ballets is one of its distinguishing features. Its strength lies in its dancers' sound and thorough classical ballet training and in the Balanchinian and ethnically oriented ballets that remain the core of its repertory.

In 1985 Dance Theatre of Harlem marked its fifteenth anniversary with its debut at New York's Metropolitan Opera House. During 1987 its Creole version of *Giselle* was a featured telecast on NBC. In May 1988, as part of a renewed United States–Soviet cultural exchange, the company made an acclaimed debut at the Palace of Congresses, Moscow, with Soviet leader Mikhail Gorbachev's wife Raisa present. The program consisted of *The Firebird*, *Voluntaries*, *Othello*, and *Dougla*. During the five-week So-

viet tour, the company also visited Leningrad (now Saint Petersburg) and Tbilisi, capital of Georgia.

As the scope of the company has grown, it has engaged in educational as well as performance activities. Its outreach program "Dancing Through Barriers[TR]" is designed to make children worldwide aware of dance, through lecture demonstrations, master classes, and open rehearsals. Started when the company visited South Africa in 1992, the program has grown and developed into an important part of Dance Theatre of Harlem, whether on tour or at home.

[*See also the entry on Mitchell.*]

BIBLIOGRAPHY

Dunning, Jennifer. "A Dance Troupe Rebounds." *New York Times* (25 January 1983).

Emery, Lynne Fauley. *Black Dance from 1619 to Today*. 2d rev. ed. Princeton, 1988.

Finkel, Anita. "Dream Dancer." *Ballet News* 4 (January 1983): 10–13.

Ghent, Henri. "Dance Theatre of Harlem: A Study of Triumph over Adversity." *The Crisis* (June 1980): 199–205.

Gruen, John. "Toe Shoes in Harlem." *Geo* (July 1983).

Hodgson, Moira. *Quintet: Five American Dance Companies*. New York, 1976.

Levin, Anne. "The Pied Piper of Ballet." *New York Alive* (September–October 1983).

Maynard, Olga. "Arthur Mitchell and the Dance Theater of Harlem." *Dance Magazine* (March 1970): 52–64.
Mitchell, Arthur, et al. "NYCB and DTH: Anniversary Reflections." *Ballet Review* 22 (Fall 1994): 14–28.

HILARY B. OSTLERE

DANCING MASTER (Fr., *maître à danser;* It., *maestro da ballo* or *di danza;* Sp., *maestro del dançar;* Ger., *Tanzmeister*). Charles Compan's *Dictionnaire de danse* (1787), although it comes late in the history of the profession, pinpoints some of the essential traits of the dancing master. The person who teaches dance must be proficient in the art himself; he must be a competent choreographer and dance writer. But dancing masters did much more. At court they were in charge of the physical education, and also part of the intellectual and artistic education, of their students. They taught fencing, riding, vaulting, and other athletic skills; they were teachers and composers of music as well as competent instrumentalists; they served as masters of ceremonies and conceived the grand spectacles as well as the daily repertory of the court. They were learned in poetry, mathematics, geometry, aesthetics, philosophy, rhetoric, painting, and sculpture. Dancing masters also taught the polished manners and social graces that were an important part of the training of a prince. The evolution of the dancing masters' profession went hand in hand with the evolution of attitudes toward dance itself. In Europe during the Middle Ages, dance was considered mainly a companionable pastime that united the inhabitants of castles and palaces and of cities and villages at the end of the day or after a battle, tournament, hunt, or harvest. Court dances and the dances of urban and country people seem to have been simple enough to be learned on the spot. As a consequence, dancing masters are seldom mentioned in the sources. The only medieval instructor known by name is the Rabbi Haçen ben Salomo, who in 1313 taught a dance to the congregation of Saint Bartholomew's church in Tauste, in the Spanish province of Zaragoza.

Even in the highly refined aesthetic atmosphere of the court of Burgundy in the fifteenth century, the identity of the persons in charge of dance remains obscure. It is not known who compiled the beautiful black-and-gold-and-silver Brussels *bassedanse* manuscript nor who developed the subtle technique needed for the proper execution of its repertory. One of the few teachers mentioned in Burgundy during the late Middle Ages is Thomas Reed, a harpist who, from 1473 through 1475, taught a wealthy merchant of Calais forty dances, seven songs and a *Hornepype* [hornpipe] on the harp and the lute and instructed him in "ffotting off bass daunssys." For this he received an honorarium.

The example of Thomas Reed demonstrates one of the principal difficulties of identifying dancing masters: in many instances the teaching of dance was adjunct to the teaching of music and, therefore, salary lists often record only payment for teaching music without mentioning whether dance was also taught.

Italy in the fifteenth century presents a very different situation. Here, with the dawning of the Renaissance, the prevailing attitude toward dance had fundamentally changed. Dance was now considered an art and as such was governed by rules and a fully developed aesthetic; it possessed a refined technique and a large repertory of choreographies designed to express every mood and emotion. The representatives of the new art were the court dancing masters, erudite and of high repute, for whose services the most cultured houses—Este, Gonzaga, Sforza, Medici, Bentivoglio, Aragon—were in constant competition. The earliest and most important of these dancing masters was Domenico da Piacenza, author of the first dance instruction book ever written (c.1445). Domenico trained two of the most notable dancing masters active between c.1455 and 1500, the courtier Antonio Cornazano and Guglielmo Ebreo (William the Jew, also known as Giovanni Ambrosio). Both were authors of important dance manuals. Also of note were Lorenzo Lavagnolo, dancing master of Bona di Savoia in 1480, and Giovanni Martino, dancing master at the Aragonese court in Naples during the 1470s. While Domenico and Cornazano appear to have been court dancing masters exclusively, Guglielmo (as Giovanni Ambrosio), mentions in his manual that his commitments included arranging dances for many festivities for commoners, which, however, he does not enumerate. The remark is evidence that, with the increasing wealth of the urban upper classes, interest in skillful dancing spread from the courts to city ballrooms and assembly halls, whose patrons now sought the services of the dancing masters. To dance well and according to the latest fashion was rapidly becoming a status symbol. [*See the entries on Cornazano, Domenico da Piacenza, and Guglielmo Ebreo.*]

The anonymous *L'art et instruction de bien dancer,* printed in Paris c.1488, is the first dance manual made for urban use; it was soon followed by others in Germany, England, and Italy. Examples include *Die Wellschen Tenntz,* compiled in Bologna for the daughters of the Nuremberg *Ratsherr* Willibald Pirckheimer in spring 1517 (Brainard, 1984); Antonius de Arena's *Leges dansandi* (c.1519 and later editions), originally written for his fellow students at the University of Avignon; Robert Coplande's small manual (London, 1521); the Moderne treatise (c.1540); and the Italian "Il papa" manuscript (New York Public Library Dance Collection, c.1535–1540). *Orchésographie* (1588), by Thoinot Arbeau, is another book for persons not of the nobility who wished to develop refined manners and solid dancing skills. Although Fabritio Caroso (*Il ballarino,* 1581, and *Della nobiltà di dame,* 1600) and Cesare Negri

(*Le gratie d'amore,* 1602) dedicate their treatises as a whole to members of the highest social echelons, many of their individual choreographies are addressed to the lesser nobility and gentry, and their lists of subscribers and patrons include wealthy commoners along with high-ranking personages.

The number of dancing masters apparently increased significantly in the late 1500s. Negri, for example, mentions forty-one men—among them Caroso, his own teacher, Pompeo Diobono, Virgilio Bracesco, and Giulio Cesare Lampugnano—who after completion of their training were called into royal service or opened schools in Italian cities and abroad (*Le gratie d'amore,* 1602, pp. 2–6), teaching dance as well as music and the military arts. Contemporary to Caroso and Negri were Lutio Compasso, Prospero Luti di Sulmona, and Livio Lupi da Caravaggio, all three writers of technical reference books. [*See the entries on Arbeau, Caroso, Diobono, and Negri.*]

While affluent citizens could afford to engage the services of a dancing master in their own houses, others needed to seek him out. As a consequence, dancing schools flourished everywhere. In England, as early as 1533, ordinances were passed to suppress those already in existence and to prevent new ones from being formed. By 1574 dancing schools were allowed under regulations that, if disobeyed, subjected the offender to a fine or imprisonment. In 1572 the city of London granted a monopoly to dancing masters Richard Frythe, Robert Warren, and William Warren, who were well known at court and enjoyed a reputation for honesty and an excellent knowledge of dancing. The Inns of Court in London paid considerable sums to dancing masters Rowland Osborne and Robert Holeman to instruct their members in everything pertaining to dance. The citizens of Lisbon had a choice between regular dancing schools and others that specialized in the teaching of *mouriscas* at the height of their popularity. Spanish dancing masters were among Negri's students, and forty years later Juan de Esquivel Navarro in his *Discvrsos sobre el arte del dançado* (Seville, 1642) named many outstanding teachers who ran their own schools in Madrid and Seville.

Court dancing masters were as important throughout Europe as ever. They taught social dancing to the princes and their families, arranged *ballets de cour* and masques, composed the dances and sometimes also the music for banquets, theatrical interludes, intermezzos, operas, and so on. They were rewarded not only with money and goods but also with prestigious positions and titles independent of the dance. Baldassare Belgiojoso (Beaujoyeulx) was not only court choreographer but *valet de chambre* to Catherine de Médicis in the late sixteenth century. Leone de' Sommi, distinguished choreographer and theorist, had connections with the court of Urbino from the mid-1560s (Fenlon, 1980, p. 42). Isacchino Massarano was ballet master to the Gonzaga family in 1592. Jacques Cordier, alias Bocan ("Mr. Bochan"), born 1580, supervised the masque dances at the court of James I in 1610–1611; was dancing master to the queens of Spain, Poland, and Denmark; and served as royal violinist and dancing master of Henrietta Maria in Paris (c.1619–1640); during this same period his relative Jean Cordier was dancing master to the queen's daughters. Jean-Baptiste Lully (1632–1687) came to the court of Louis XIV as dancer and violinist; he soon became the king's favorite, was appointed supervisor of the royal music in 1661 and, as a dancer, shared the spotlight in several ballets with the king. [*See the entries on Beaujoyeulx and Lully.*]

In England during the reign of Elizabeth I, a French family of dancing masters, the Cardels, were established at court. In the early seventeenth century John Ogilby taught dancing in London; among his students were the great court dancing master Isaac (after 1631) and John Lacey. Members of the court's musical establishment also fulfilled dance obligations. Adam Vallet, one of James I's musicians for the lute, and John Tetart in April 1616 received "the sum of 80 £ . . . for their attendance on his Majesty . . . in the exercise of their several arts of fencing and dancing" (F. Devon, ed., *Issues of the Exchequer,* London, 1836, p. 21). Thomas Warren, violinist in the King's Musick, was known for his skill "in these artes of dancing and vaulting" (Ward, p. 21). Specifically hired as choreographers for the English court masques were Thomas Cardell, Thomas Giles, Jerome (Jeremy) Herne, "Mr. Confesse," and "Mr. Bochan." Thomas Caverley, who was Kellom Tomlinson's teacher, André Lorin, and William Jones dominated the scene in the second half of the century. Josiah Priest choreographed Henry Purcell's *Dido and Aeneas.* Francis Pendleton was dancing master to Mr. and Mrs. Samuel Pepys (Martin, 1977, pp. 66ff.). [*See the entries on Caverley, Priest, and Tomlinson.*]

Germany became a dance region of importance after the end of the sixteenth century. The many smaller and larger courtly establishments at Berlin, Stuttgart, Darmstadt, Celle, Braunschweig-Wolfenbüttel, Munich, Halle, Dresden, Leipzig, Vienna, Graz, and Innsbruck engaged the best talent available, first mainly from France and Italy, later from Germany, all well paid and, as was the custom everywhere, rewarded "in specie," that is, with grain, wine, beer, gifts of clothing, houses, and grounds in addition to their salaries. Through the seventeenth century the same names reappear in different locations as the best of the dancing masters, and they and their families often moved from one court to another. Paschal Beuce was dancing master in Celle from around 1653 to 1665, then went to Hanover only to return to Celle in the late 1660s. François d'Olivet (Dolivet) came to Dresden from the court of Kassel in 1651 and was "lent" to the courts of Braunschweig and Cologne for special occasions. Michael

DANCING MASTER. The frontispiece from Gottfried Taubert's *Rechtschaffener Tantzmeister* (1717) shows the dancing master in his various roles, as choreographer, teacher, musician, and theoretician. (Courtesy of Madison U. Sowell and Debra H. Sowell, Brigham Young University, Provo, Utah.)

du Bruil (various spellings) was musician and court dancing master in Celle from 1654; his contract, definitive after September 1660, obligated him to teach dancing at the ducal *Ritterschule* in the city of Lüneburg in addition to his duties as *Hof-Tantz-Meister* and choreographer in Celle. One of the first German dancing masters mentioned is Steffan Hauer, "Dantz-meister und Violist" to the princess of Heidelberg in the early seventeenth century. Hieronimus Pernickel von Hornburg (died 1662) was *Fürstlicher Tantzmeister* at the court of Halle; his successor was Ludwig Kanneberg, likewise a German. Julius Weilandt served the dukes of Braunschweig–Wolfenbüttel (c.1660) side by side with Ulrich Roboam de la Marche. The large dance establishment at Berlin under Frederick III (1688–1713) at times consisted of eight dancing and ballet masters of different nationalities (Desnoyers, de la Montagne, Doitu, Gericke, Butqven, Vetter, Brumeck, Flöricke) and a sizable ensemble of professional dancers in addition to the courtiers who regularly participated in the entertainments.

As the number of dancing masters on the international circuit increased, a need was felt to exert greater control over the representatives of the profession and to set standards for the quality of the product offered. This goal was served by the founding of academies. Charles IX of France created the Académie de Musique et de Poésie in 1570. In charge were the poet Antoine de Baïf and the composer Joachim Thibault de Courville, whose ideas contributed to the creation of the Balet Comique de la Royne (1581). The important Académie Royale de Danse grew out of the Confrairie des Maîtres de Danses & Joueurs d'Instrumens, whose statutes were formulated in 1658, confirmed by Louis XIV of France in 1659, and by the parliament of Paris in 1660. Its director was nominated by royal letters of accreditation; its thirteen masters were elected. Students committed themselves for four or occasionally five years, after which they took rigorous examinations and received a diploma that entitled them to enter into public or private employment. The dance school of the Académie Royale de Musique (the Paris Opera) came into being under the aegis of Jean-Baptiste Lully, its director from 1672 until his death in 1687. [*See* Académie de Musique et de Poésie *and* Académie Royale de Danse.]

Other countries, following the French model, also opened academies for the conservation, perfection, and renovation of the art of dance, including ballroom dance. One of the most famous is the Imperiale Regia Accademia di Ballo, which opened in 1812 at the Teatro alla Scala in Milan. The Royal Academy of Dancing in London has been in existence since 1920.

The first professional organization of dancing masters in the United States was The American Society of Professors of Dancing, constituted in 1879. It was followed by The American Association of Masters of Dancing, United States and Canada, founded in Boston in 1883, and the Western Association of Normal School Masters of Dancing, founded in 1894 in Saint Louis. The American Lyceum Movement under the early leadership of Josiah Holbrook also promoted the practice and teaching of dancing.

The period that saw the founding of the first academies also saw the separation of social dance and stage dance. The teaching of both, however, remained in the same hands. Dancing masters of international repute were active throughout Europe. Pierre Beauchamps, Raoul-Auger Feuillet, Louis Pecour, Michel Gaudrau, Jacques Bonnet, and Pierre Rameau worked in France in the first half of the eighteenth century; Johann Pasch, Louis Bonin, Gregorio Lambranzi, Gottfried Taubert, and Franz Hilverding dominated the German and Austrian region during the same period; John Weaver, John Essex, Edmund Pemberton, Kellom Tomlinson, Sir Isaac, Siris, and

Anthony L'Abbé created dances for English stages and salons. Many of these masters were theorists of their art as well; their books on technique, style, manners, and dance history are our main sources of information regarding all aspects of the art of dancing in the first half of the eighteenth century. Many of their choreographies are preserved in the notation developed by Beauchamps and Feuillet late in the seventeenth century. [*See* Feuillet Notation.]

This system remained in use into the early nineteenth century, by which time the separation between the professions of the dancing master and the ballet master had become increasingly pronounced. Each major city in Europe and some in the United States had, in addition to the theater ballet masters, teachers of ballroom dancing who instructed their clients privately and in classes, taught repertory as well as the etiquette of dancing, arranged and supervised balls and assemblies, and published books about their art. The full titles of these publications reflect the Victorian emphasis on self-improvement and proper social conduct, for example, the section called "Etiquette, Deportment, and the Toilet" in Charles Durang's *Terpsichore, or Ball Room Guide* (1847).

To supplement the dancing masters' personal lessons in the fashionable waltz, polka, mazurka, reel, écossaise, and especially the cotillon and quadrille, and to facilitate self-study, innumerable how-to books were written in the course of the nineteenth century. Thomas Wilson, dancing master in the city of London and at the King's Opera House, published several volumes from 1810 on; the sixth part of Carlo Blasis's *Code of Terpsichore* (London, 1828) is devoted to "private dancing." Henri Cellarius of Paris saw his famous *100 tours de cotillons* translated into English (London, 1847; New York, 1858) and German (Erfurt, 1898); also in Paris appeared Jules Perrot's and Adrien Robert's *La polka enseignée sans maître* (1845) and Philippe Gawlikowski's *Guide complet de la danse* (1859). Among the earliest German publications were Johann Heinrich Kattfuss's *Choreographie: Taschenbuch für Freunde und Freundinnen des Tanzes* (part 1, 1800; part 2, 1802, both in Leipzig) and the anonymous *Neuer Tanz- und Ball-Kalender für das Jahr 1801* (Berlin), followed in quick succession by Ernst Chr. Mädel's *Die Tanzkunst für die elegante Welt* (Erfurt, 1805), Andreas Schönwald's *Grundregeln der Tanzkunst* (Freiburg, 1812), and many others.

In America, too, there was considerable activity. Puritan leader Increase Mather's "Arrow against Profane and Promiscuous Dancing" (1685), aimed at dancing masters such as Henry Sherlott and Francis Stepney (Boston, seventeenth century) ultimately missed its mark. Peter Pelham continued his dancing school in Boston (founded 1732) for more than a decade despite the complaints of

the pious against this "Licentious and Expensive diversion" (Cole, 1942, p. 16); Harvard, Yale, Williams, and other colleges in the Northeast and in the South employed dancing masters for the benefit of their students. The Bourniques had their famous and elegant dance studio in Chicago (1867–1938), complete with reception area, dining room and ballroom; the de Garmo and Dodworth families maintained similar establishments in New York City; Louis Papanti taught in Boston. Many a "Call Book" and "Ball-Room Prompter" went to press in the nineteenth century: Boston's publishing firms printed teaching manuals by Elias Howe and C. H. Cleveland; Charles Durang's books appeared in Philadelphia; those by Edward Ferrero, Thomas Hillgrove, L. de Garmo Brookes, William B. de Garmo, and Allen Dodworth were published in New York. Henry Meyen, writing in Kentucky around 1850, was the first American dance teacher to illustrate dance steps by using woodcuts of footprints, a graphic device still favored by Arthur Murray and colleagues, who followed in the twentieth century.

[*For related discussion, see also* Social Dance, *articles on* Court and Social Dance before 1800 *and* Nineteenth-Century Social Dance; *and* Technical Manuals, *article on* Publications, 1440–1725. *See also the entries on the principal figures mentioned herein.*]

BIBLIOGRAPHY

Aldrich, Elizabeth. *From the Ballroom to Hell: Grace and Folly in Nineteenth-Century Dance.* Evanston, Ill., 1991.

Aschengreen, Erik. "August Bournonville: A Ballet-Poet among Poets." *CORD Dance Research Annual* 9 (1978): 3–21.

Astier, Régine. "Pierre Beauchamps and the Ballets de Collège." *Dance Chronicle* 6.2 (1983): 138–163.

Baron, John H. "Les Fées des forests de S. Germain ballet de cour, 1625." *Dance Perspectives*, no. 62 (1975): 3–15.

Beaumont, Cyril W. *Michel Fokine and His Ballets.* London, 1935.

Brainard, Ingrid. "The Role of the Dancing Master in Fifteenth-Century Courtly Society." *Fifteenth-Century Studies* 2 (1979): 21–44.

Brainard, Ingrid. "The Art of Courtly Dancing in Transition: Nürnberg, Germ.Nat.Mus.Hs.8842, a Hitherto Unknown German Dance Source." In *Crossroads of Medieval Civilization: The City of Regensburg and Its Intellectual Milieu*, edited by Edelgard E. DuBruck and Karl Heinz Göller. Detroit, 1984.

Brooks, Lynn Matluck. *The Dances of the Processions of Seville in Spain's Golden Age.* Kassel, 1988.

Brown, Bruce Alan. *Gluck and the French Theatre in Vienna.* Oxford, 1991.

Campardon, Émile. *L'Académie Royale de Musique au XVIIIe siècle.* 2 vols. Paris, 1884.

Caroso, Fabritio. *Nobiltà di dame* (1600). Translated by Julia Sutton. Oxford, 1986.

Christout, Marie-Françoise. *Le ballet de cour de Louis XIV, 1643–1672.* Paris, 1967.

Cole, Arthur C. *The Puritan and Fair Terpsichore* (1942). Brooklyn, 1966.

Cornazano, Antonio. *The Book on the Art of Dancing* (c.1455–1465). Translated by Madeleine Inglehearn and Peggy Forsyth. London, 1981. See also A. William Smith, below.

Cunningham, James P. *Dancing in the Inns of Court.* London, 1965.

Daye, Anne. "The Professional Life of the Italian Dancing Master, c.1550–1625." *The Dancing Times* (February 1991): 458–459.

Fenlon, Iain. *Music and Patronage in Sixteenth-Century Mantua.* Cambridge, 1980.

Feves, Angene. "Caroso's Patronesses." In *Proceedings of the Ninth Annual Conference, Society of Dance History Scholars, City College of the City University of New York, 14–17 February 1986,* compiled by Christena L. Schlundt. Riverside, Calif., 1986.

Friedhaber, Zvi, and Giora Manor. "The Jewish Dancing Master in the Renaissance in Italy, in the Jewish and Gentile Communities and at the Ducal Courts." In *Guglielmo Ebreo da Pesaro e la danza nelle corti italiane del XV secolo,* edited by Maurizio Padovan. Pisa, 1990.

Gallo, F. Alberto. "Il 'ballare lombardo,' circa 1435–1475." *Studi musicali* 8 (1979): 61–84.

Gallo, F. Alberto. "L'autobiografia artistica di Giovanni Ambrosio (Guglielmo Ebreo) da Pesaro." *Studi musicali* 12 (1983): 189–202.

Goff, Moira. "Edmund Pemberton: Dancing-Master and Publisher." *Dance Research* 11 (Spring 1993): 52–81.

Goff, Moira. "Dancing-Masters in Early Eighteenth-Century London." *Historical Dance* 3.3 (1994): 17–23.

Grattan, Thomas Colley. *Civilized America.* 2 vols. 2d ed. London, 1859.

Guest, Ivor. *The Romantic Ballet in England.* London, 1972.

Guglielmo Ebreo da Pesaro. *On the Practice or Art of Dancing* (1463). Translated and edited by Barbara Sparti. Oxford, 1993.

Guilcher, Jean-Michel. *La contredanse et les renouvellements de la danse française.* Paris, 1969.

Harris-Warrick, Rebecca, and Carol G. Marsh. *Musical Theatre at the Court of Louis XIV: Le Mariage de la Grosse Cathos.* Cambridge, 1994.

Heartz, Daniel. "Hoftanz and Basse Dance: Towards a Reconstruction of Fifteenth-Century Dance Music." *Journal of the American Musicological Society* 19 (1966): 13–36.

Hilton, Wendy. *Dance of Court and Theatre: The French Noble Style, 1690–1725.* Princeton, 1981.

Kendall, Yvonne. "*Le gratie d'amore* (1602) by Cesare Negri: Translation and Commentary." Ph.D. diss., Stanford University, 1985.

Kunzle, Régine [Astier]. "Pierre Beauchamps: The Illustrious Unknown Choreographer." *Dance Scope* 8 (Spring–Summer 1974): 32–42; 9 (Fall–Winter 1974–1975): 30–45.

L'Abbé, Anthony. *A New Collection of Dances* (1725). Edited by Carol G. Marsh. London, 1991.

La Gorce, Jérôme de. "Guillaume-Louis Pecour: A Biographical Essay." *Dance Research* 8 (Autumn 1990): 3–26.

Little, Meredith Ellis, and Carol G. Marsh. *La Danse Noble: An Inventory of Dances and Sources.* Williamstown, Mass., 1992.

Lowe, Joseph. *A New Most Excellent Dancing Master: The Journal of Joseph Lowe's Visits to Balmoral and Windsor, 1852–1860, to Teach Dance to the Family of Queen Victoria.* Edited by Allan Thomas. Stuyvesant, N.Y., 1992.

Lynham, Deryck. *The Chevalier Noverre: Father of Modern Ballet.* London, 1950.

Magri, Gennaro. *Theoretical and Practical Treatise on Dancing* (1779). Translated by Mary Skeaping. London, 1988.

Malpied. *Traité sur l'art de la danse.* Paris, n.d. (c.1785).

Marsh, Carol G. "French Court Dance in England, 1706–1740: A Study of the Sources." Ph.D. diss., City University of New York, 1985.

Martin, Jennifer K. L. "The English Dancing Master, 1660–1728: His Role at Court, in Society, and on the Public Stage." Ph.D. diss., University of Michigan, 1977.

McGee, Timothy J. "Dancing Masters and the Medici Court in the Fifteenth Century." *Studi musicali* 17.2 (1988): 201–224.

McGowan, Margaret M. *L'art du ballet de cour en France, 1581–1643.* Paris, 1963.

Mirabella, Bella. "Dance in Shakespeare's England." Unpublished ms., 1981.

Noack, Elisabeth. *Musikgeschichte Darmstadts vom Mittelalter bis zur Goethezeit.* Mainz, 1967.

Noverre, Jean-Georges. *Lettres sur la danse et sur les ballets.* Stuttgart, 1760.

Petipa, Marius. *The Diaries of Marius Petipa.* Translated and edited by Lynn Garafola. Studies in Dance History, vol. 3.1. Pennington, N.J., 1992.

Picker, Martin. *The Chanson Albums of Marguerite of Austria.* Berkeley, 1965.

Pontremoli, Alessandro, and Patrizia La Rocca. *Il ballare lombardo: Teoria e prassi coreutica nella festa di corte del XV secolo.* Milan, 1987.

Ralph, Richard. *The Life and Works of John Weaver.* London, 1985.

Roberts, Jane B., and David Vaughan, comps. *Looking at Ballet: Ashton and Balanchine, 1926–1936.* Studies in Dance History, vol. 3.2. Pennington, N.J., 1993.

Sabol, Andrew J. *Four Hundred Songs and Dances from the Stuart Masque.* Exp. ed. Providence, R.I., 1982.

Sachs, Curt. *World History of the Dance.* Translated by Bessie Schönberg. New York, 1937.

Sasportes, José. "Feasts and Folias: The Dance in Portugal." *Dance Perspectives,* no. 42 (1970).

Scholes, Percy. *The Puritans and Music in England and New England.* London, 1934.

Schwartz, Judith L., and Christena L. Schlundt. *French Court Dance and Dance Music: A Guide to Primary Source Writings, 1643–1789.* Stuyvesant, N.Y., 1987.

Smith, A. William. "Dance in Early Sixteenth-Century Venice: The *Mumaria* and Some of Its Choreographers." In *Proceedings of the Twelfth Annual Conference, Society of Dance History Scholars, Arizona State University, 17–19 February 1989,* compiled by Christena L. Schlundt. Riverside, Calif., 1989.

Smith, A. William, trans. and ed. *Fifteenth-Century Dance and Music: The Complete Transcribed Italian Treatises and Collections in the Tradition of Domenico da Piacenza.* 2 vols. Stuyvesant, N.Y., 1995.

Souritz, Elizabeth. *Carlo Blasis in Russia, 1861–1864.* Studies in Dance History, vol. 4.2. Pennington, N.J., 1993.

Suárez-Pajares, Javier, and Xoán M. Carreira. *The Origins of the Bolero School.* Studies in Dance History, vol. 4.1. Pennington, N.J., 1993.

Swift, Mary Grace. *A Loftier Flight: The Life and Accomplishments of Charles Louis Didelot.* Middletown, Conn., 1974.

Taubert, Karl Heinz. *Höfische Tänze: Ihre Geschichte und Choreographie.* Mainz, 1968.

Taubert, Karl Heinz. *Die Anglaise . . . mit dem Portefeuille Englischer Tänze von Joseph Lanz.* Zurich, 1983.

Terry, Walter. *Ted Shawn: Father of American Dance.* New York, 1976.

Théleur, E. A. *Letters on Dancing* (1831). Edited by Sandra Noll Hammond. Studies in Dance History, vol. 2.1. Pennington, N.J., 1990.

Thorp, Jennifer. "P. Siris: An Early Eighteenth-Century Dancing-Master." *Dance Research* 10 (Autumn 1992): 71–92.

Tomlinson, Kellom. *A Work Book by Kellom Tomlinson: Commonplace Book of an Eighteenth-Century English Dancing Master* (c.1708–1722). Edited by Jennifer Shennan. Stuyvesant, N.Y., 1992.

Vaughan, David. *Frederick Ashton and His Ballets.* London, 1977.

Veronese, Alessandra. "Una societas ebraico-cristiana in *docendo tripudiare ac cantare* nella Firenze del quattrocento." In *Guglielmo Ebreo da Pesaro e la danza nelle corti italiane del XV secolo,* edited by Maurizio Padovan. Pisa, 1990.

Ward, John M. "A Dowland Miscellany." *Journal of the Lute Society of America*, vol. 10 (1977).

Winter, Marian Hannah. *The Pre-Romantic Ballet.* London, 1974.

Witherell, Anne L. *Louis Pécour's 1700 Recueil des dances.* Ann Arbor, Mich., 1983.

Wynne, Shirley S. "The Charms of Complaisance: The Dance in England in the Early Eighteenth Century." Ph.D. diss., Ohio State University, 1967.

Yates, Frances A. *The French Academies of the Sixteenth Century.* London, 1947.

INGRID BRAINARD

DANIELIAN, LEON (born 31 October 1920 in New York, died 8 March 1997 in Canaan, Connecticut), American ballet dancer and educator. Danielian, the son of Armenian parents, studied with Madame Seda, Mikhail Mordkin, Michel Fokine, and Anton Dolin. He made his debut with the Mordkin Ballet in 1937, became a charter member of Ballet Theatre in 1939, and appeared with the Original Ballet Russe in 1941. Danielian is identified in the United States with Ballet Russe de Monte Carlo (1943–1961), where he became *premier danseur* (and later appeared as guest artist), with an unusually large repertory. Walter Terry quotes him as saying, "I was a *demi-caractère* dancer with a classical technique."

Danielian had a buoyant, virtuosic technique with clean, incisive *batterie* and a noble carriage in classics such as *Swan Lake* (in which his *entrechats huit* were famous), coupled with a highly theatrical manner and a flair for comedy in *demi-caractère* roles such as Harlequin in *Le Carnaval* and the Peruvian in *Gaîté Parisienne*. He made many guest appearances, including seasons with Ballets des Champs-Élysées, as partner of Yvette Chauviré, and with the San Francisco Ballet. He toured the globe, becoming one of the first internationally known American male dancers.

Danielian choreographed several works for Ballet Russe and received one of the first *Dance Magazine* Awards in 1949. He retired from performing in his late thirties, suffering from arthritis, and chose a teaching career. He was director of American Ballet Theatre School from 1968 to 1980 and of the Dance Program at the University of Texas, Austin, from 1982 to 1991.

BIBLIOGRAPHY

Anderson, Jack. *The One and Only: The Ballet Russe de Monte Carlo.* New York, 1981.

Gale, Joseph. "Leon Danielian." In Gale's *Behind Barres: The Mystique of Masterly Teaching.* New York, 1980.

Gruen, John. *The Private World of Ballet.* New York, 1975.

Stoop, Norma McLain. "Leon Danielian and the American Ballet Theatre School." *Dance Magazine* (January 1975): 59–62.

Terry, Walter. *Great Male Dancers of the Ballet.* Garden City, N.Y., 1978.

FILMS. Victor Jessen, *Gaîté Parisienne* (c.1940). Carol Lynn, *Nutcracker: Excerpts* (Jacob's Pillow, 1948). Carol Lynn, *La Boutique Fantasque: Can-Can* (Jacob's Pillow, 1950). William Richert, *First Position* (1972), with footage of Danielian teaching. With the exception of *La Boutique Fantasque*, all are held in the Dance Collection, New York Public Library for the Performing Arts.

MARILYN HUNT

DANILOVA, ALEXANDRA (Aleksandra Dionisievna Danilova; born 20 November 1903 in Peterhof, Russia, died 13 July 1997 in New York City), dancer and teacher. In about 1912, Alexandra Danilova entered the ballet section of the Imperial Theater School, Saint Petersburg, where her teachers included Varvara Rykhliakova, Vera Zhukova, Klavdia Kulichevskaya, Olga Preobajenska, Julia Sedova, Viktor Semenov, and Elisaveta Gerdt. (After graduation, Danilova studied with Agrippina Vaganova and Anna Johansson in Russia, Lubov Egorova and, briefly, Vera Trefilova in Paris, and Nikolai Legat in London.) As a student, she appeared in various ballets at the Maryinsky Theater (later, State Academic Theater for Opera and Ballet), including *The Talisman, Le Pavillon d'Armide,* and *La Fille Mal Gardée.*

On graduation in 1920, Danilova entered the corps de ballet of the State Academic Theater for Opera and Ballet, and by the end of her first season she had danced her first

DANILOVA. One of Danilova's most famous roles was the Glove Seller in Léonide Massine's *Gaîté Parisienne.* (Photograph by Constantine; from the Dance Collection, New York Public Library for the Performing Arts.)

DANILOVA. The stars of the Ballet Russe de Monte Carlo, Frederic Franklin and Danilova, seen here c.1950 in *Coppélia*, one of the company's most popular works. (Photograph from the Dance Collection, New York Public Library for the Performing Arts.)

solo role, Prayer in *Coppélia*. She was soon promoted to *coryphée* and given further featured roles, including the Diamond Fairy in *The Sleeping Beauty*, Ta-Hor in *Une Nuit d'Égypte*, and the title role in Fedor Lopukhov's *The Firebird*. From 1922 to 1924, she also participated in the avant-garde dance movement in Petrograd, taking leading roles in George Balanchine's experimental works for the Young Ballet and in Lopukhov's *The Magnificence of the Universe* (also called *Dance Symphony*, 1923).

In 1924 Danilova, as part of a small troupe called Principal Dancers of the Russian State Ballet (including also Balanchine, Tamara Gevergeyeva [later, Geva], and Nikolai Efimov), left Russia for a tour of Germany. Recalled by the Soviet authorities, the dancers declined to return. They proceeded to London and then to Paris, where they auditioned for Serge Diaghilev. Danilova joined Diaghilev's Ballets Russes in late 1924 and remained with the troupe until 1929, creating major roles in Léonide Massine's *Le Pas d'Acier* and in several Balanchine works—*The Triumph of Neptune* (Fairy Queen), *The Gods Go a-Begging* (Serving Maid), *Le Bal* (Lady)—and alternating with Alice Nikitina as Terpsichore in Balanchine's *Apollon Musagète*. Her Diaghilev repertory also included *The Firebird* (Firebird), *La Boutique Fantasque* (Can-Can Dancer), *Petrouchka* (Ballerina), *Aurora's Wedding* (Aurora), and *Les Biches* (Chanson Dansée). Danilova's liaison with Balanchine lasted from 1927 to 1931.

After the dissolution of the Diaghilev troupe, Danilova danced with the Monte Carlo Opera Ballet (1929–1931) and in the operetta *Waltzes from Vienna* (1931–1932, choreographed by Albertina Rasch) in London. She married Giuseppe Massera, an Italian engineer, in 1932 (1933?). She was widowed in 1936. In 1933 she joined Colonel Wassily de Basil's Ballets Russes de Monte-Carlo, where she remained (with one brief interruption, to dance in *The Great Waltz*, the New York production of *Waltzes from Vienna*) until 1938, creating roles in ballets by Massine (Allegro Giocoso in *Choreartium*) and David Lichine (e.g., Titania in *Nocturne*) and starring with great success in *The Firebird*, *Swan Lake*, and *Le Beau Danube* (Street Dancer), among other works.

In 1938 Danilova left the foundering de Basil troupe to become the *prima ballerina* of Léonide Massine and Serge Denham's new, rival company, soon also to be known as the Ballet Russe de Monte Carlo. Here she formed a famous partnership with Frederic Franklin and starred in new ballets by Massine, Balanchine, Bronislava Nijinska, and Ruth Page. Of these, her most fruitful connection was again with Balanchine, who created leading roles for her in his new *Danses Concertantes* and *Night Shadow* (Sleepwalker), collaborated with her on a staging of Petipa's *Raymonda*, in which she starred, and cast her prominently in revivals of his *Le Baiser de la Fée* (Bride), *Jeu de Cartes* (Queen of Spades), and *Mozartiana* (Adagio and Variations). Other famous Danilova roles with the Denham company were Myrtha in *Giselle*, Sugar Plum Fairy in a one-act version of *The Nutcracker*, Swanilda in *Coppélia*, and the Glove Seller in Massine's *Gaîté Parisienne*. In 1941 she married Casimir Kokitch, a soloist with the company. (The marriage was annulled in the late 1940s.) In December 1951 Danilova gave her last performance as a regular member of Ballet Russe de Monte Carlo.

Danilova's late career included guest appearances with various companies (Sadler's Wells Ballet, 1949; London's Festival Ballet, 1951, 1955; Slavenska-Franklin Ballet, 1952–1953). She also formed her own small company, usually billed as Alexandra Danilova and Her Ensemble (in a program called "Great Moments of Ballet"), which from 1954 to 1956 toured the United States, Canada, South America, the Far East, and South Africa. In 1957, at the Metropolitan Opera House, she gave her last New York ballet performance, as guest artist with Ballet Russe de Monte Carlo. Later in 1957, on tour in Tokyo, she gave her final ballet performance, in *Raymonda*.

Danilova then appeared in the Broadway musical *Oh, Captain* (1958) and began a fruitful second career staging ballets, including several opera ballets (Metropolitan Opera, 1959–1961), *Coppélia* (La Scala, Milan, with Frederic Franklin, 1961; Fort Worth Ballet, 1966; New York City Ballet, with Balanchine, 1974), *The Nutcracker* (Washington Ballet, 1961), *Paquita* (Ballet Russe de Monte Carlo, 1949; Cincinnati Ballet, 1979; Dance Theatre of Harlem, 1980), and *Chopiniana* (New York City Ballet, 1972). In 1964 she joined the faculty of the School of American Ballet (SAB), for whose "workshops," or annual recitals (first organized by her), she has staged numerous ballets, including Fokine's *Le Pavillon d'Armide* and his Polovtsian Dances, as well as sections from *The Sleeping Beauty, Swan Lake, Raymonda,* and *Paquita*. She taught at SAB, giving special attention to *épaulement* and to "ballerina" style until her retirement in 1989. Danilova received the Capezio Award in 1958, the *Dance Magazine* Award in 1984, and a Kennedy Center Honor and New York City's Handel Medallion in 1989.

In the 1930s and 1940s Danilova was one of the most celebrated ballerinas in the Western world. Her primary gifts as a dancer were an extraordinarily full and subtle rhythmic response, a seemingly spontaneous joyfulness ("pleasure like a little girl's" [Denby]), a commanding glamour and stage presence, and a pair of long and peerlessly shaped legs ("legs like luminous wax" [Kirstein]). Chiefly a dramatic dancer, she was fortunate enough to come to maturity in an age of character ballet. Though she excelled in several tragic roles—Odette, the Bride in *Le Baiser de la Fée*, the Sleepwalker in *Night Shadow*—she was adored by audiences above all in those ballets that drew on her wit and gaiety: *Coppélia* and her great Massine triad, *La Boutique Fantasque, Le Beau Danube,* and *Gaîté Parisienne*. Danilova had in her much of the late-nineteenth-century grand ballerina. In the mid-twentieth century, when a new image of the ballerina was being formed, her dancing, teaching, and stagings were crucial in ensuring that the best of the older tradition was incorporated into the new.

BIBLIOGRAPHY

Anderson, Jack. *The One and Only: The Ballet Russe de Monte Carlo.* New York, 1981.
"A Conversation with Alexandra Danilova." *Ballet Review* 4.4 (1973): 32–51; 4.5 (1973): 50–60.
Danilova, Alexandra. *Choura: The Memoirs of Alexandra Danilova.* New York, 1986.
Denby, Edwin. *Looking at the Dance* (1949). New York, 1968.
García-Márquez, Vicente. *The Ballets Russes: Colonel de Basil's Ballets Russes de Monte Carlo, 1932–1952.* New York, 1990.
Philp, Richard. "Danilova on Balanchine." *Dance Magazine* (July 1983): 62–63.
Sorley Walker, Kathrine. *De Basil's Ballets Russes.* New York, 1983.
Twysden, A. E. *Alexandra Danilova.* London, 1945.

FILM. *Spanish Fiesta* (1941), *Reflections of a Dancer: Alexandra Danilova, Prima Ballerina Assoluta* (dir. Anne Belle, 1981), and many archival films are housed in the Dance Collection, New York Public Library for the Performing Arts. The Barzel Collection, Newberry Library, Chicago, contains films of Danilova in performance with the Ballet Russe de Monte Carlo.

VIDEOTAPE. "Gaîté Parisienne" (Video Artists International, 1988).

JOAN ACOCELLA

DANOVSCHI, OLEG (born 9 February 1917 in Vosnesensk, Ukraine, died 21 October 1996), Romanian dancer and choreographer. Danovschi began his studies with his mother Malvina before training with Boris Kniaseff, Anton Romanowski, and Floria Capsali. He made his first appearances very early in Constantz, in the company of Ivan Dubrovin; in 1932 he danced at the Alhambra Theater in Bucharest and soon became the head ballet master of several musical theaters there. In 1938 he made his debut at the Bucharest Opera in Capsali's ballet *Wedding in the Carpathians*, to music by Paul Constantinescu; he served there as a leading dancer, ballet master, libretto writer, choreographer, and ballet company director until 1970. Between 1949 and 1953 he was dean and professor at the Faculty of Choreography of the Arts Institute in Bucharest. Since 1979 he has been the artistic director of Fantasio, a classical and contemporary ballet ensemble which he created as the first Romanian independent ballet company, based in Constantza; since 1993 the company has borne his name.

Danovschi has staged acclaimed versions of classics such as *Swan Lake, The Nutcracker, Coppélia,* and *Giselle*. His original works are set to scores by contemporary composers such as Béla Bartók, Paul Hindemith, Alban Berg, Edgar Varèse, and George Gershwin, or Romanian composers such as George Enescu *(Romanian Rhapsodies, Vox Maris)*, Mihail Jora *(Coming Back from the Depths, The Market Place)*, Laurenţiu Profeta *(Prince and Pauper)*, Cornel Trăilescu *(Miss Nastasia)*, and Mircea Chiriac *(Iancu Jianu)*. They are characterized by epic and dramatic force, a taste for the picturesque, and an impressive lyricism; Danovschi is considered to be one of the creators of Romanian national ballet.

Danovschi has staged ballets in Bulgaria, Yugoslavia, Italy, Austria, France, and Germany. He has toured with his company in many countries and has served on the juries of dance competitions in Varna, Moscow, Vercelli, Osaka, and Tokyo. Danovschi has been named Honored Artist and has been awarded the Cultural Merit, Hungary's Bartók Prize, and the USSR's Lenin Badge.

In 1991, Danovschi was elected president of the newly created National Committee of Dance, a branch of the

Conseil International de la Danse. Danovschi founded the first National Ballet Festival in Constantza and was named First Honorary Citizen of Constantza.

[*See also* Romania, *article on* Theatrical Dance.]

BIBLIOGRAPHY

Constantinescu, Marian. *Dirijorul de lebede: Intilniri cu Oleg Danovski.* Bucharest, 1989.

Finkel, Anita. "The Ballet Fantasio of Romania." *Ballet News* 3 (April 1982): 38–39.

Goldner, Nancy. "Ballet Fantasio." *Dance News* (March 1982): 9.

Negry, Gabriel. *Memoria dansului.* Bucharest, 1986.

Urseanu, Tilde, et al. *Istoria baletului.* Bucharest, 1967.

TEA PREDA

DANSE DU VENTRE (also called *belly dance* or *danse orientale*) most probably derived its name from one or both of two sources: (1) a corruption of the Arabic *raqs al-baladi*, meaning "dance from the countryside," and (2) a reference to the highly developed movement articulations of the torso and abdomen, which are the most characteristic movement practices of this widespread dance genre. Arabs outside Egypt often call it *raqs al-sharq* ("Oriental dance") or *raqs al-misri* ("Egyptian dance"), underscoring the widespread notion that this dance tradition originated in ancient Egypt. No historical documentation exists for the origins of this dance genre, which today is performed in many homes by both men and women and in cabarets and clubs by women throughout the Arab world (and in areas to which Arabs have migrated). Similar dance genres, such as the *cifte telli*, also exist in Turkey and Greece but not in Iran as is sometimes thought. Today belly dancing is performed outside the Middle East by professional dancers in nightclubs in Greece, western Europe, Canada and the United States as well as by many devoted amateurs. Numerous conventions for amateurs meet throughout the United States; they feature dance workshops by professional performers and by instructors.

Professional belly dance as seen in the urban cabaret—the form most generally known and popular in the West—is characterized by three elements: movement practices, music, and costume. The practices that mark this dance genre center on the sinuous and elaborate movements of the chest to abdominal musculature. To acquire professional levels of skill often takes years of arduous practice, articulating and isolating specific body areas, especially the shoulders, chest, abdomen, hips, and pelvis. The footwork and use of the hands are less elaborate, secondary to the focus on intricate torso movements. The dance space is often limited, so the dance may be performed in a restricted area or by executing movements while kneeling. Cabaret dancers often perform while moving among the patrons so money may be attached to their costumes as they dance. Like many of the primarily solo dance gen-

res throughout the Muslim East, belly dance is largely an improvised form. Today, however, some professional performers create their own or hire a choreographer to create intricate dances to pieces of music composed for a specific routine. Regional folk movement practices may also be incorporated into performances, giving regional flavor to some of the dances. Props such as canes, candelabra, snakes, tea trays, vases, swords, and other items may be balanced on dancers' heads or manipulated by their hands and bodies; some roll paper money or coins on their abdomens. In the United States, some dancers will pull a man from the audience onto the floor to "teach" him how to dance, in what is called the "Sultan Act."

The music that accompanies belly dance is generally Egyptian (although other Arabic, Turkish, or Greek music

DANSE DU VENTRE. The dancer known as "Artemis" in a typical cabaret-style costume with a spangled brassiere and low-slung skirt. In the United States, *la danse du ventre*, or belly dancing, is performed at restaurants, clubs, and private events, primarily by women who are not of Middle Eastern origin but who adopt Oriental-sounding names. (Photograph by Serpentine Communications Company; courtesy of Elizabeth Artemis Mourat.)

DANSE DU VENTRE. A postcard, of the type popular in the early 1900s, showing a posed grouping of *ghawāzī* dancers and musicans from Egypt. The *ghawāzī* are itinerant street performers believed to be descended from Indian Gypsies. Here, the central dancer plays the finger cymbals, one man plays a reed flute called *nāy*, and the other a *dumbeq*. The seated woman (at right) plays a *riq*, the others are either singers or are dancers waiting to perform. (Photograph courtesy of Elizabeth Artemis Mourat.)

may be employed), and the musical set is divided into parts, often two rhythmic sections separated by a *taqsim* (improvised instrumental selection). The most popular costume worn in a professional performance is called the "cabaret" costume; it derives from a concoction created through the combined influences of Russian artist and set designer Léon Bakst and the Hollywood and Broadway Orientalist fantasy productions (e.g., *Kismet*). It generally consists of a highly decorated brassiere or halter top and a full skirt, with panels open at the sides, worn low on the hips, and attached to a lavishly decorated belt or girdle band. Some dancers, especially in the West, utilize a large veil for the dance. Since this form of dance is often monitored by the government officials responsible for public mores, officially enforced modesty may alter aspects of the costume related to how much of the body may be revealed. (In Egypt during Gamel Abdel Nasser's regime in the 1950s, the abdomen had to be covered; Egyptians then used a stylized, tight form of the traditional village *[baladi]* costume—which remains popular for professional performances.)

Rural professional dancers use many of the movements described above, but they perform in regional costume to local music. They are not as sophisticated in using the myriad choreographic devices their urban counterparts use in a typical performance. Their costumes however still mark them as professional performers, since they differ from everyday clothing. These dancers are distanced from the local Muslim women because they do not cover themselves or wear the veil, and they dance before men in public. Such performers are typified by the *ghawāzī* of Egypt.

History. The origins of this dance genre are unknown, although authors with Orientalist fervor have speculated on ancient, even prehistoric, origins. The speculation reflects, in part, the abundance of pictorial evidence for solo dancing that exists from Pharaonic Egypt, pre-Islamic Iran, and ancient Mesopotamia. Ancient dance movements cannot, however, be reconstructed from still pictures. The Orientalist accounts of exotic ancient religious rites, goddess worship, and birthing rituals that circulate in the West have not been substantiated by scholars. The dance, as presented in current cabaret manifestations, reflects relatively modern sources, particularly those used for music and costume.

Dancers (both male and female) often functioned as prostitutes in more recent history, and this contributes to a general avoidance of this subject by Middle Eastern writers. These performers were occasionally highly paid and some had famous encounters with well-known people, such as Koutchouk Khanum, who enamored the nineteenth-century French novelist Gustave Flaubert; he described both her dancing and their amorous moments. More often, belly dancers were street performers who were hired for middle- and lower-class weddings and other festive occasions. Whole families might be involved in the business of dancing and prostitution, among whom the most famous were the Ouled Naïl of Algeria, whose young women earned their dowries in this manner. [See Ouled Naïl, Dances of the.]

Today's belly dancer uses both rural and urban movement practices as well as influences that come from the Egyptian movie industry. Many Egyptian films feature cabaret dance sequences. Fans have created sex icons and

DANSE DU VENTRE. A postcard, c.1910, showing an Algerian dancer doing a backbend and two female musicians, one playing a tambourine *(riq)* and the other a drum *(dumbeq)*. The performers' coin-decorated headdresses are typical of the Ouled Naïl, a confederation of tribes in Algeria. Although their dances are associated with prostitution, they have been a major influence on Egyptian and Oriental-style dancing. (Photograph courtesy of Elizabeth Artemis Mourat.)

movie star idols of dancers such as Nadia and Samia Gamal and Tahia Carioca. Filmgoers' expectations of naughty sex displays have influenced cabaret scenes in movie productions for both the East and the West. Belly dance was introduced in the West with demonstrations in the Egyptian pavilions at several *fin de siècle* expositions and world's fairs in large European and American cities. The performer then known as Little Egypt not only inspired the popular imagination about the "sinful East" but also spawned a number of "Little Egypt" burlesque acts.

If a few women in the Arab world attain fame and fortune through belly dancing in night clubs, five-star hotels, films, and high-society social events, by far the majority of such performers eke out a difficult, gritty existence. Their social status is very low due to both the historic associations with prostitution and the revealing of the body before strangers. Belly dancers are thus sometimes targets of Islamic zealotry and reform.

Traditional Belly Dancing. Although known in the West through its urban cabaret performances, this dance is most often performed within domestic settings by both males and females in family-oriented events—these are generally, but by no means always, sexually segregated. In every family one or two people are considered to be outstanding and are encouraged to dance. Children are often pushed into the performance area by doting relatives. The person who performs within the context of the family circle draws no moral criticism. The amateur often exceeds the professional in technical proficiency.

[*See also* Algeria *and* Egypt, *article on* Traditional Forms.]

BIBLIOGRAPHY

Arabesque: A Magazine of International Dance. New York, 1975–.
Berger, Morroe. "The Belly Dance." *Horizons* 8.2 (1966): 41–49.
Buonaventura, Wendy. *Serpent of the Nile: Women and Dance in the Arab World.* London, 1989.
Choudhury, M. L. Roy. *Music in Islam.* Journal of the Asiatic Society, Letters, vol. 2. London, 1957.
Danielson, Virginia. "Artists and Entrepreneurs: Female Singers in Cairo during the 1920s." In *Women in Middle Eastern History,* edited by Nikki R. Keddie and Beth Baron. New Haven, 1991.
Deaver, Sherri. "Concealment vs. Display: The Modern Saudi Woman." *Dance Research Journal* 10 (Spring–Summer 1978): 14–18.
Faruqi, Lois Lamya' al-. "Dance as an Expression of Islamic Culture." *Dance Research Journal* 10.2 (1978): 6–13.
Fraser, Kathleen. "Aesthetic Explorations: The Egyptian Oriental Dance among Egyptian Canadians." *UCLA Journal of Dance Ethnology* 17 (1993): 58–66.
Lane, Edward W. *Manners and Customs of the Modern Egyptians* (1836). New York, 1966.
Roberts, David. *Roberts' Journal.* London, 1849.
Saleh, Magda. "A Documentation of the Ethnic Dance Traditions of the Arab Republic of Egypt." Ph.D. diss., New York University, 1979.
Shiloah, Amnon. *Music in the World of Islam.* London, 1995. See chapter 11.
Van Nieuwkerk, Karin. *"A Trade Like Any Other": Female Singers and Dancers in Egypt.* Austin, 1995.
Wood, Leona, and Anthony V. Shay. "Danse du Ventre: A Fresh Appraisal." *Dance Research Journal* 8 (Spring–Summer 1976): 18–30.

VIDEOTAPE. Rhoda Grauer, "Dancing," eight-part series (WNET-TV, New York, 1993), especially part 3, "Morocco."

ANTHONY V. SHAY

DANTZIG, RUDI VAN (born 4 August 1933 in Amsterdam), Dutch dancer, choreographer, ballet director, and writer. Van Dantzig studied with Sonia Gaskell, who engaged him in 1954 as a dancer in her company Ballet Recital and who commissioned his first ballet, *Nachteiland* (Night Island), set to music by Claude Debussy, in 1955. Having continued his dance training with Martha Graham in New York, van Dantzig was among the dancers who founded the Netherlands Dance Theater in 1959, but in 1960 he returned to Gaskell's company, by then named the Netherlands Ballet. The company merged into the Dutch National Ballet in 1961, and van Dantzig subsequently became a member of the artistic council (1965), co-director (1968), and sole artistic director (1971). Most of his ballets were created for the Dutch National Ballet, but he also worked as guest choreographer for many companies outside the Netherlands.

Van Dantzig's ballets, based on both classical and modern techniques, are expressionistic and full of symbolism, usually displaying psychological conflicts within the individual. Most notable is their quality of excitement. The passionate choreographic patterns often show dynamic twists of rows or groups of dancers who first come together and then move apart with an explosive outburst of energy.

In the treatment of his basic theme, the acceptance of life's imperfections, van Dantzig's choreographic development has shown different emphases. In his earlier pieces the moral contrast between good and evil is stressed, often in an attempt to recover a lost ideal of purity and innocence, specifically in relation to homoerotic desires.

This dynamic is exemplified in his popular ballet *Monument voor een Gestorven Jongen* (Monument for a Dead Boy; 1965), set to music by Jan Boerman. A later dominant theme is the acceptance of death as the inevitable outcome of all life's struggles, as in *Epitaaf* (1969), to music by György Ligeti, and *Vier Letzte Lieder* (Four Last Songs; 1977), to music by Richard Strauss, which many consider to be his best work. Another important theme concerns the problems of modern society, which van Dantzig saw as threatened by both physical and mental pollution. *Geverfde Vogels* (Painted Birds; 1971), set to music by Niccolò Castiglioni, was the first socially engaged Dutch ballet after the war, and *Life* (1979), a spectacular co-production with Toer van Schayk, set to music by various composers, dealt with the oppression of revolutionary ideals of freedom. In van Dantzig's psychodramatic and elegiac ballets, relations between people always play an important role and are often colored by aggression, frustration, or fear.

Other works created by van Dantzig for the Dutch National ballet include *Jungle* (1961), to music by Henk Badings; two versions of *Romeo and Juliet* (1967 and 1976), set to the score by Sergei Prokofiev; *Ogenblikken* (Moments; 1968) and *Antwoord Gevend* (Answering; 1980), both set to music by Anton Webern; *Ramifications* (1973), to music by Ligeti; and *Blown in a Gentle Wind* (1975), to music by Richard Strauss. Also created in 1975 was *Collective Symphony*, choreographed jointly with Hans van

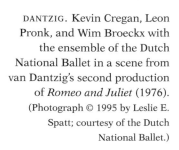

DANTZIG. Kevin Cregan, Leon Pronk, and Wim Broeckx with the ensemble of the Dutch National Ballet in a scene from van Dantzig's second production of *Romeo and Juliet* (1976). (Photograph © 1995 by Leslie E. Spatt; courtesy of the Dutch National Ballet.)

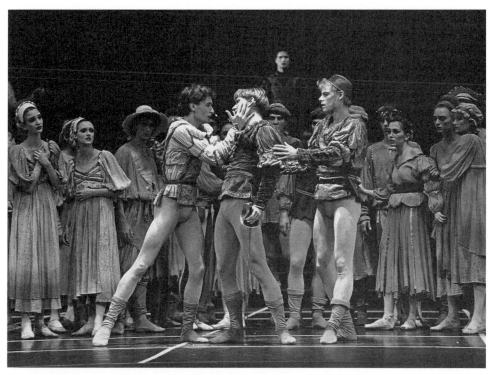

Manen and Toer van Schayk to music by Igor Stravinsky. Among van Dantzig's later works are *Onder Mijne Voeten* (Under My Feet; 1981), set to music by Peter Schat; *Buigen of Barsten* (Bend or Break; 1987), to music by Chiel Meijering; and *Aartsengelen Slachten de Hemel Rood* (Archangels Butcher the Heavens Red; 1990), to music by Giya Kancheli.

In the 1970s, van Dantzig began to exercise his talents as a writer. His early publications include *Ballet and Modern Dance* (1975), *Nureyev: A Biography* (1975), and *The Cry of the Firebird* (1977). In 1986, he was awarded the Geert Jan Lubberhuizen Prize for his autobiographical novel *Voor een verloren Soldaat* (For a Lost Soldier), later made into a popular film (Sigma-AVRO, 1994), directed by Roeland Kerbosch. In 1991, van Dantzig left the Dutch National Ballet in order to pursue a writing career. That same year he was named an Officer of the Orde van Oranje-Nassau, capping the numerous honors and awards he had previously received.

[*See also* Dutch National Ballet. *For discussion in a broader context, see* Netherlands, *article on* Theatrical Dance since 1945.]

BIBLIOGRAPHY
Dantzig, Rudi van. "A Question of Values." In *Visions: Ballet and Its Future*, edited by Michael Crabb. Toronto, 1978.

Dantzig, Rudi van. *For a Lost Soldier*. Translated from the Dutch by Arnold J. Pomerans. London, 1991. Reprint, Swaffham, Norfolk, 1996.

Loney, Glenn. "Evolution of an Ensemble: Rudi van Dantzig on the National Ballet of Holland." *Dance Magazine* (March 1974): 34–39.

Percival, John. "The Voice of the People." *Dance and Dancers* (June 1987): 32–34.

Schaik, Eva van. "Rudi van Dantzig." *Ballett International* 12 (November 1989): 10–17.

Utrecht, Luuk. *Het Nationale Ballet 25 jaar: De Geschiedenis van Het Nationale Ballet van 1961 tot 1986*. Amsterdam, 1987.

Utrecht, Luuk. *Rudi van Dantzig: A Controversial Idealist in Ballet*. Zutphen, 1992.

LUUK UTRECHT

DARK ELEGIES. Choreography: Antony Tudor. Music: Gustav Mahler. Scenery and costumes: Nadia Benois. First performance: 19 February 1937, Duchess Theatre, London, Ballet Rambert. Principals: Peggy van Praagh, Maude Lloyd, Agnes de Mille, Antony Tudor, Walter Gore, Hugh Laing.

Tudor had suggested to Marie Rambert a year or two earlier that he make a ballet to Mahler's song cycle on poems by Friedrich Rückert, *Kindertotenlieder*, but she had rejected the idea because she believed that Tudor—then only in his midtwenties—needed more experience of life before tackling the subject of death. By the time he was able to persuade her that he was ready to do the ballet, Tudor had eliminated all extraneous elements from a pure expression of grief, including any indication of its cause.

Like Vaslav Nijinsky's *Le Sacre du Printemps* and Bronislava Nijinska's *Les Noces*, Tudor's *Dark Elegies* depicts a

DARK ELEGIES. From left to right, Antony Tudor, Maude Lloyd, Peggy van Praagh, Agnes de Mille, and Walter Gore in Tudor's *Dark Elegies* (1937), a ballet exploring themes of bereavement. (Photograph by Houston Rogers; used by permission of the Board of Trustees of the Theatre Museum, London.)

community confronted with a momentous event, in this case, as indicated by the title of Mahler's song cycle, the deaths of its children. Individuals emerge from the group to perform a series of solos and one duet, only to be reabsorbed into the ensemble. The singer sits on the stage, clothed like the dancers in anonymous peasant dress, but the movement never pantomimes the words of the songs. In fact, at times the movement parts company with the music, forming a parallel structure with it, and that movement is not drawn from conventional ballet vocabulary. Even though the women go on pointe, *Dark Elegies* is essentially a modern dance work. The movement and patterns are often derived from folk dance or from everyday life; the dancers turn their feet into parallel, and the movement is always weighted into the ground.

Dark Elegies was among the ballets that Tudor took with him when he formed his own company, the London Ballet, in 1938. The following year he also took it to the United States, where he joined the newly formed Ballet Theatre (now American Ballet Theatre); it went into the repertory of that company in January 1940. The ballet has remained in the repertories of both Ballet Rambert (now Rambert Dance Company) and American Ballet Theatre and has also been revived by the National Ballet of Canada in 1955, the Royal Swedish Ballet in 1961, the Royal Ballet in 1980, and the Paris Opera Ballet in 1985.

BIBLIOGRAPHY

Anderson, Jack. "The View from the House Opposite: Some Aspects of Tudor." *Ballet Review* 4.6 (1974): 14–23.

Chazin-Bennahum, Judith. "Shedding Light on *Dark Elegies*." In *Proceedings of the Eleventh Annual Conference, Society of Dance History Scholars, North Carolina School of the Arts, 12–14 February 1988*, compiled by Christena L. Schlundt. Riverside, Calif., 1988.

Coton, A. V. *A Prejudice for Ballet*. London, 1938.

Dance Research Journal 24 (Fall 1992): 17–30. Special section entitled "What Constitutes a Dance? Investigating the Constitutive Properties of Antony Tudor's *Dark Elegies*."

Huxley, Michael. "A History of Dance: An Analysis of *Dark Elegies* from Written Criticism." In *Dance Analysis*, edited by Janet Adshead. London, 1988.

DAVID VAUGHAN

DARK MEADOW. Choreography: Martha Graham. Music: Carlos Chavez. Scenery: Isamu Noguchi. Costumes: Edythe Gilfond. Lighting: Jean Rosenthal. First performance: 23 January 1946, Plymouth Theater, New York City, Martha Graham Dance Company. Principals: Martha Graham (One Who Seeks), Erick Hawkins (He Who Summons), May O'Donnell (She of the Ground).

The four sections of Graham's *Dark Meadow* are "Remembrance of Ancestral Footsteps," "Terror of Loss," "Ceaselessness of Love," and "Recurring Ecstacy of the Flowering Branch." In it, an individual's passionate quest is structured as a cryptic rite and given mythic dimension.

Noguchi's four set pieces stud the stage—stones or phallic herms in a desert landscape. A chorus of five women and three men threads through the work. The women begin with a primal stamping dance; later, three couples in unison perform duets that are erotic, yet formal and angular. She of the Ground often brings in symbolic props or turns the set pieces to signal change. In "Terror of Loss," the heroine dances alone, walking upon and winding herself in a long piece of dark fabric. In "Ceaselessness of Love," the masterful male figure pursues her and they dance together.

This potently enigmatic work, influenced by the writings of Carl Jung, links one of Graham's most consistent themes—the artist-seeker entering a dark place, undergoing an ordeal, and being reborn, illumined—with the Persephone myth, which relates the tides of a woman's passions to the changing of the seasons. Perhaps because the work was considered difficult for audiences to understand, it was not performed on tours immediately following its creation. It was revived, however, most recently in 1994.

BIBLIOGRAPHY

Jowitt, Deborah. *Time and the Dancing Image*. New York, 1988.

Shelton, Suzanne. "The Jungian Roots of Martha Graham's Dance Imagery." In *Proceedings of the Sixth Annual Conference, Society of Dance History Scholars, the Ohio State University, 11–13 February 1983*, compiled by Christena L. Schlundt. Milwaukee, 1983.

Siegel, Marcia B. *The Shapes of Change: Images of American Dance*. New York, 1979.

DEBORAH JOWITT

DARRELL, PETER (Peter Skinner; born 19 September 1929 in Richmond, Surrey, died 1 December 1987 in Glasgow), British dancer, choreographer, and company director. Having been trained at the Sadler's Wells Ballet School, Peter Darrell was accepted into the Sadler's Wells Ballet in 1944, when he was only fifteen years old. He danced with the company during the last two, dangerous years of World War II, and in 1946, after the war in Europe was over, he became a founding member of the Sadler's Wells Opera Ballet (later called the Sadler's Wells Theatre Ballet). He left the company in 1947 to dance abroad—in Paris with Léonide Massine, in Sweden at the Malmö Opera—and to dance in musicals, in cabaret, and on television in England. In 1952, while with London's Festival Ballet, he choreographed his first major work, a revised version of David Lichine's *Harlequinade*. He also choreographed several pieces for Ballet Workshop (1951–1955), at the Mercury Theatre, and for a pioneering television dance series, *Cool for Cats* (1959).

While appearing in a musical, Julian Slade's *The Duenna*, Darrell met Elizabeth West, who later invited him to create a work for her Bristol School of Ballet—

Celeste and Celesthina (1956), set to music by Carlos de Seixas. Darrell and West founded Western Theatre Ballet in 1957, but Darrell became sole director of this Bristol-based company when West died in a climbing accident five years later. From the outset, Western Theatre Ballet's policy was to combine dance with acting and drama to form a dance theater that also reflected current trends and attitudes; in this respect it was unique in British ballet at that time.

A strong dramatic sense was the dominant feature in most of Darrell's creative work. It brought great impact to Western Theatre Ballet's repertory, which ranged from pieces set to music by Béla Bartók—*The Prisoners* (1957), *A Wedding Present* (1962), and *Home* (1965)—to *Jeux* (1963), set to the score by Claude Debussy, and *Mods and Rockers* (1963), set to music of the Beatles. *Mods and Rockers* brought the company its greatest success in the pop era of the 1960s. Darrell's first two-act work, *Sun into Darkness* (1966), set to a commissioned score by Malcolm Williamson, was based on David Rudkin's story of the effects of ancient pagan rituals on life in a Cornish village.

In 1969, Western Theatre Ballet moved to Glasgow and became Scottish Theatre Ballet, the first major ballet company to be based in Scotland. In the same year, Darrell produced his second full-length work, *Beauty and the Beast,* set to a commissioned score by Thea Musgrave. In the following years, he would produce numerous works for the company, which soon became known as the Scottish Ballet. Notable among his shorter works are *The Scarlet Pastorale* (1975), created for guest artist Margot Fonteyn and set to music by Frank Martin; *Five Rückert Songs* (1978), to music by Gustav Mahler; *Such Sweet Thunder* (1979), to music by Duke Ellington; and *Midnight Masquerade* (1982), to music by Richard Rogers.

Darrell's major contributions to the repertory of the Scottish Ballet were, however, a half dozen full-length, original works: *Tales of Hoffmann* (1972), *Mary, Queen of Scots* (1976), *Cinderella* (1978), *Chéri* (1980), *Gardens of the Night* (1983), and *Carmen* (1985). Of these, *Mary, Queen of Scots,* set to music by John McCabe, and *Chéri,* a passionate dance treatment of Colette's novels, set to music by David Earl, attracted particular praise, and the rollicking *Tales of Hoffmann* proved to be a perennial audience favorite. Darrell also mounted productions of three of the great classical ballets for the company: *Giselle* (1971), *The Nutcracker* (1972–1973), and *Swan Lake* (1977).

In addition to his works for the Scottish Ballet, Darrell staged works for several other British companies—including *Othello* (1971) and *Tristan and Iseult* (1979) for the New London Ballet and *La Péri* (1973) for London Festival Ballet—and for companies in Australia, Canada, Czechoslovakia, Denmark, Germany, Holland, Ireland, Japan, Sweden, Switzerland, the United States, and Yugoslavia.

Despite the large number of works he made for the Scottish Ballet, he did not neglect to diversify the company's repertory with works by other leading choreographers, including Rudi van Dantzig, Flemming Flindt, and Walter Gore.

As a choreographer, Peter Darrell brought a sharp dramatic focus to all his creations; as a director he was unstinting in his encouragement of new and experimental work by established choreographers and promising young creators. For his services to British ballet, he was named a Commander of the British Empire in the Queen's Honours List of 1984.

[*See also* Scottish Ballet.]

BIBLIOGRAPHY

Darrell, Peter. "Settling Over the Border." *Dance and Dancers* (June 1979): 22–24.

Goodwin, Noël. "Nutcracking over the Border." *Dance and Dancers* (May 1974): 30–35.

Massie, Annette. "Elizabeth West and Western Theatre Ballet." *Dance Research* 6 (Spring 1988): 45–58.

Percival, John, and Noël Goodwin. "Tales of Hoffmann." *Dance and Dancers* (June 1972): 31–35.

Percival, John, and Noël Goodwin. "Towards the Source of *Swan Lake.*" *Dance and Dancers* (June 1977): 22–27.

Percival, John, and Noël Goodwin. "A Scottish Cinderella." *Dance and Dancers* (December 1979): 18–22.

Sandler, Ken. "Peter Darrell." *Ballet News* 2 (May 1981): 8.

West, Geoffrey. "The Darrell Legacy at Scottish Ballet." *Dance Now* (Winter 1994): 29–37.

Williams, Peter, and John Percival. "Mary, Queen of Scots." *Dance and Dancers* (May 1976): 14–18.

PETER WILLIAMS

DARSONVAL, LYCETTE (Alice Perron; born 12 February 1912 in Coutances, in Normandy), French ballet dancer, teacher, and choreographer. In 1920 the Perron family moved from Coutances to the Montmartre section of Paris, where two of the children, Alice (called Lycette) and Serge, would later become well-known ballet dancers, Lycette Darsonval and Serge Perrault.

Enrolled as Alice Leplat at the Paris Opera Ballet School in 1924, when she was twelve, Lycette was taken into the company at age fourteen, while she was still a student. Blessed with both beauty and strength, she became the favorite pupil of Carlotta Zambelli. She was graduated from the ballet school in 1930 and assigned the rank of *petit sujet.* Disappointed in her ranking, she left the company, married, and traveled abroad. When she returned to Paris, she resumed her ballet training with Lubov Egorova, Olga Preobrajenska, and Madame Rousanne (Rousanne Sarkissian).

In 1933, having changed her name to Lycette Darsonval, she won first prize at the International Classical Ballet Competition in Warsaw, where Serge Lifar noticed her and invited her to be his partner on an American tour. After touring the United States with Lifar, she danced for two years as guest artist with a Russian company, Ballets d'Esprilova, on tours of central Europe and North Africa. Encouraged by Lifar, she rejoined the Paris Opera Ballet in 1936 and, in a special competition that he arranged, soon won the exclusive right to perform the role of Giselle, which she held for many years. She was immediately promoted to *première danseuse* and was made a *danseuse étoile* in 1940. She continued to dance with the company until 1959, appearing as a guest after 1955.

Darsonval also danced at the Opéra-Comique from 1946 to 1951, and in 1953 she formed her own small troupe, Ballets Lycette Darsonval, with which she made occasional tours of Europe and the United States. From 1957 to 1959 she was the director of the Paris Opera Ballet School, and from 1963 to 1965 she served as ballet mistress of the Nice Opera Ballet and taught classes at the Nice Conservatoire. She later founded her own school in Nice but returned to Paris in 1975 to teach the *classe de perfectionnement* at the Paris Opera Ballet School and to give private classes in her own studio.

Fair-haired, tall for her time, and possessing a strong technique, Darsonval was the opposite of petite, brunette Yvette Chauviré, to whom she passed the role of Giselle in a historic performance at the Paris Opera in 1949 in which Darsonval danced the first act and Chauviré the second. Darsonval was at her best in dramatic ballets, and Lifar gave her some of her best roles in *Oriane et le Prince d'Amour* (1938), *Sylvia* (1941), *Joan de Zarissa* (1942), *Suite en Blanc* (1943), *Phèdre* (1950), *Cinema* (1953), and *Variations* (1953). In *Phèdre* she first danced the role of Oneone before taking over the title role created by Tamara Toumanova. Darsonval was also a favorite of Albert Aveline, for whom she created roles in *Elvire* (1937), *Les Deux Pigeons* (1942), *La Grande Jatte* (1950), and *La Tragédie de Salomé* (1954).

Darsonval's command of *taqueterie* (speed and lightness on pointe), for which she was famous, was especially notable in the first movement of George Balanchine's *Le Palais de Cristal*, which she created at the Paris Opera in 1947. She also exhibited a dazzling technique in the Black Swan pas de deux at the Opéra-Comique in 1951 and in the title role of *The Sleeping Beauty* in a broadcast on British television in 1952. She gave her farewell performance in *Giselle* at the Paris Opera in 1959, still dancing with flawless technique and great artistry.

Darsonval presented her first choreography at the Paris Opera in 1939, when she danced in *La Nuit Venitienne*, set to music by Maurice Thiriet. She was partnered by Max Bozzoni and Serge Peretti. For her own troupe she mounted a program called *Trois Siècles de Danse a l'Opéra* (1953), based on lecture-demonstrations she had first given at the Sorbonne in 1941. She also created *Rondo Capriccioso* (1952), to music by Camille Saint-Saëns, and

Combats (1957), to music by Rafaello de Banfield. But her greatest success was her restaging of *Sylvia*, basing her choreography on the previous productions of Serge Lifar and Léo Staats, after the original by Louis Mérante. [*See* Sylvia.] It was presented by the Paris Opera Ballet in 1979 and by the Central Ballet of China in Beijing in 1980 and was also broadcast on French television.

Darsonval was the recipient of many honors and awards. She was elected to the Légion d'Honneur in 1959 and was elevated to the rank of officer in 1980. She was named Commandeur de l'Ordre National du Mérite and in 1980 was the recipient of the Medaille de Vermeil de la Ville de Paris.

BIBLIOGRAPHY

Cadieu, Martine. *Lycette Darsonval* (in French). Paris, 1951.
Darsonval, Lycette. *Ma vie sur les pointes*. Paris, 1988.
Fabre, Dominique. *Lycette Darsonval* (in French). Paris, 1956.
Guest, Ivor. "Fair Exchange: The Stars of the Paris Opera." *Dance and Dancers* (September 1954): 9–11.
Hersin, André-Phillipe. "Reprise de Sylvia." *Saisons de la danse*, no. 119 (December 1979): 6–8.
Lifar, Serge. *Ma vie, de Kiev à Kiev*. Paris, 1965. Translated into English as *Ma Vie, from Kiev to Kiev* by James Holman Mason (New York, 1970).
Prudhommeau, Germaine. "Giselle première." *Danser* (October 1991): 35–40.
Vaillat, Leandre. *Le Ballet de l'Opéra de Paris*. 3 vols. Paris, 1943, 1947, 1951.

MONIQUE BABSKY
Translated from French

DAUBERVAL, JEAN (Jean Bercher; born 19 August 1742 in Montpellier, died 14 February 1806 in Tours), French dancer, choreographer, and ballet master. Jean Bercher, subsequently known as Jean Dauberval, was born during the reign of Louis XV, the son of an actor. Within the theatrical world of his early life the pretty graces of the rococo style supplied the setting for his development into an accomplished dancer and brilliant choreographer. It was a time of wars—the War of the Austrian Succession (French participation 1741–1748) and the Seven Years War (1756–1763)—but these conflicts were far removed from the young performer's experiences. He identified with the world represented in paintings by François Boucher and Jean-Honoré Fragonard, and in music by François Couperin and Jean-Philippe Rameau, a world of polite and elegant playfulness where Baroque grandeur had been discarded for expression on a more human scale. It was also the world within which great writers were turning their craft to the task of social criticism; Voltaire published *Candide* in 1759, and Jean-Jacques Rousseau published *Du contrat social* in 1762. Indeed, even dance people shared this reforming spirit; Jean-Georges Noverre presented his *Lettres sur la danse* in 1760.

Dauberval trained as a dancer at the Paris Opera under Jean-Barthélemy Lany, whose varied career included a time as ballet master in Berlin (1743–1746) and in London at the Haymarket Theatre (1775). Dauberval began his career with the Paris Opera in the summer of 1761 and spent the next twenty-one years there, progressing rapidly through the ranks from corps de ballet to *premier danseur demi-caractère* (1763), to *danseur seul* (1764), and finally to *premier danseur noble* (1770). During seasonal absences from Paris he was, in keeping with the status of a Paris Opera dancer, employed as a premier danseur in Stuttgart in 1762 and 1763 and at Covent Garden in 1763 and 1764.

One of Dauberval's Paris Opera partners was Marie Allard, famous both as a dancer and as the mother of the virtuoso dancer Auguste Vestris. A contemporary gouache by Carmontelle shows Allard and Dauberval in the opera *Sylvie* by Pierre-Montan Berton and J.-C. Trial (1766) performing a dialogued scene that, according to Noverre, "expressed all the sentiments which love might inspire." The image presented is one of pretty and graceful sentiment, not of grand passions, a scene of nature humanized, a pastoral playground for grown-ups.

Dauberval and Allard were more than stage lovers though, for upon seeing the dancing of Vestris, son of Gaëtan Vestris and Allard, Dauberval remarked, "What talent! He is the son of Vestris and not mine! Alas! I missed him but by a quarter of an hour" (Guest, 1960).

Dauberval's dancing, as well as his good humor, graceful manners, and skill as a hunter, gained him access to the highest levels of society. Madame du Barry, mistress of Louis XV, was his patroness, and when in 1774 he threatened to avoid his creditors by fleeing to Russia, she organized a subscription, raising the considerable sum of ninety thousand francs, including a donation from the king. Indeed, with a sumptuous residence on rue Saint-Lazare containing a salon that could be transformed into a theater, Dauberval's personal expenditures must have been princely. His extravagance did not prohibit generosity, however. When London's Pantheon Theatre burned in 1792, he offered to forgo the £150 he was offered for lost work if performances could be resumed as soon as possible for the sake of the regular dancers, for whom the loss of work would have been a considerable hardship.

Dauberval's major achievements were not as a gentleman, or as a protector of less well-off performers, or even as a dancer, but as a choreographer. His visits to Stuttgart in 1762 and 1763 brought him into contact with Noverre, who was the ballet master there and whose approach to ballet as a dramatic art was adopted by Dauberval. Already from 1763 to 1764 he was arranging dances during his time at Covent Garden, the fashionable themes of which were pastoral or redolent with local color—*The Turkish Coffee House, A Tyrolese Wedding, Le Matelot Provençal, The Encampment, Le Marriage du Village, La Femme Maîtresse, Le Tambourin,* and *La Masquerade.*

In 1772, at the age of thirty-two, Dauberval became assistant ballet master at the Paris Opera jointly with Maximilien Gardel, who was the first dancer to appear on the Paris Opera stage without a mask. Dauberval must have anticipated a brilliant future, for his progress toward the post of ballet master had thus far been smooth. However, in 1776, when Gaëtan Vestris retired as ballet master, both Dauberval and Gardel were sidestepped in favor of Noverre, who possessed the right connections through his former pupil, Marie Antoinette. The two young hopefuls did not let any prior associations they may have had with Noverre inhibit their scheming against him. Noverre survived under pressure for several years before retiring in 1781. Dauberval and Gardel at last shared the post of ballet master, but the partnership was an uneasy one; in 1783 Dauberval resigned.

Dauberval's departure from the Paris Opera was not a setback for the ballet master; a reputation based on long and distinguished service at this theater guaranteed him high salaries and artistic freedom almost anywhere in Europe. The 1784 season was spent at the King's Theatre in London. It was here that Dauberval introduced audiences to one of his most enduring ballets, *Le Déserteur, ou La Clémence Royale,* for the benefit of Mademoiselle Théodore (Marie-Madeleine Crespé), whom he had married in 1783. First presented in Bordeaux in 1772, the ballet tells a highly dramatic story in which the lover is saved from a firing squad at the last possible instant.

Mademoiselle Théodore was known as the *philosophe* of the stage; she is said to have written to Rousseau to ask how she should order her life in a fitting manner in the theater. Acting upon his notion of the noble savage, she wrote a pamphlet to raise money for the unfortunate "savages" shipped as slaves through French ports. Of a determined character, she opposed the Opera management in 1782 and was imprisoned. She fought a duel with the opera singer Mademoiselle Beaumesnil (the guns failed to fire). Yet as progressive as some of her ideas and actions may have been, she enjoyed aristocratic society, and as the Revolution was shaking France, she had a medallion struck of herself in the attitude of an empress. Noverre called her "the image of Terpsichore. She had ease, facility, and brilliance. Her *ballon* made her so light that, without jumping, with the elasticity of her foot alone, she convinced everyone that she did not touch the earth."

The year 1785 found the Daubervals in Bordeaux. There Dauberval commenced the most productive phase of his career, and continued his dogged harassment of anyone who opposed either his artistic freedom or his economic prosperity. The Grand Théâtre in Bordeaux was second only to the Paris Opera in the quality of its productions. The management allowed Dauberval a freedom of artistic creation he would never have enjoyed in the capital, though it was grudging in its willingness to pay the large sums he demanded for the production of his ballets and for his wife and himself. Nevertheless, audiences were strongly behind the Daubervals, and the theater, for the most part, had to agree to their demands. It was at this provincial theater that Dauberval created two of his most popular masterpieces, *La Fille Mal Gardée* and *Le Page Inconstant* (based on Pierre-Augustin Caron de Beaumarchais's *Marriage de Figaro*); with *Le Déserteur* they became the most consistently popular French ballets for almost fifty years, far outliving works produced at the Paris Opera. It was also in Bordeaux that many of the important ballet masters of the next generation learned their craft, including Jean-Louis Aumer, James Harvey D'Egville, Charles-Louis Didelot, and Eugène Hus.

Despite Dauberval's artistic successes, intrigue and his own extravagance created an uneasy atmosphere. In 1787 the Bordeaux theater proposed to release Mademoiselle Théodore from her contract to save on salaries, a move successfully countered by audience support for her. More serious was Dauberval's refusal to accept a Bordeaux native of second-rate talent, the chevalier Peicam, into the company. As an intriguer, Peicam was almost a match for the great ballet master, managing to make life so uncomfortable for him that he and Théodore left Bordeaux early in 1789. Yet Dauberval was not a man to take defeat lightly. He returned on 3 May with a *lettre de cachet* from Louis XVI exiling Peicam from the environs of the city. The triumphant Dauberval pressed his claims for a new contract and a guarantee of a company of at least ninety dancers, including eight premier performers. Such was the atmosphere within which *La Fille Mal Gardée* premiered on 1 July 1789 under the title *Le Ballet de la Paille, ou Il N'est Qu'un Pas du Mal au Bien* (Ballet of Straw, or It Is Only One Step from Bad to Good). [*See* Fille Mal Gardée, La.]

The Daubervals' departure from Bordeaux in March 1790 must have brought a huge sigh of relief to those responsible for the city's ballet, even if they did regret the couple's absence on artistic grounds. Bordeaux never regained the choreographic preeminence it had enjoyed, though a school established by Hus trained dancers of merit well into the nineteenth century; both Monsieur Albert, the great nineteenth-century *danseur noble*, and Monsieur Paul, known as "The Aerial," were trained in Bordeaux.

When the Daubervals returned to London in 1791, they became involved in the rivalry between the theater managers, Robert Bray O'Reilly and William Taylor, both of whom claimed the sole right of presenting operas and ballets. Dauberval formed an impressive company for O'Reilly at the Pantheon Theatre—Didelot, Salvatore Viganò, D'Egville, Louis Boisgirard, Aumer, Mademoiselle

DAUBERVAL. This etching (c.1780) by Pierre Lelu, depicts a merry pas de trois. From left to right are Marie-Madeleine Guimard, Dauberval, and Marie Allard. Dauberval and Allard were noted stage partners and were presumed to be lovers. (Bibliothèque National, Paris.)

Théodore, Maria Medina (Viganò), and the Simonet sisters. The ballets Dauberval presented during these two seasons were similar to those popular throughout the theatrical world: the pastoral—*La Fille Mal Gardée* and *La Fête Villageois;* the Anacreontic—*Le Triomphe de la Folie* and *La Fontaine d'Amour;* the sentimental—*L'Amant Déguisé;* and the neoclassical—*Telemachus in the Island of Calypso* (in which Madame Hilligsberg donned male attire).

After Dauberval returned briefly to Bordeaux in 1796, his artistic productivity appears to have ceased. He was fifty-four when his thirty-six-year-old wife died in Audenge on 9 September 1796. The great ballet master died in Tours in 1806.

Dauberval wrote no books and established no lasting school or company. His importance lies in his ballets, and since the art of ballet is ephemeral, nothing concrete has survived by which we can evaluate his achievements. Therefore it is all too easy to underestimate his importance, especially in light of the more readily evident legacies of men such as Noverre and Carlo Blasis, who left books, or those of Didelot and August Bournonville, who left ballet companies. Yet Dauberval was possibly the greatest choreographer of his age, if importance is measured by the impact of ballets upon contemporary artists, critics, and audiences. His ballets became the bread and butter of many a traveling choreographer who could be guaranteed success by reviving *La Fille Mal Gardée, Le Page Inconstant, Le Déserteur,* and others. In this way his ballets outlasted all rivals, and though often in radically altered form, *La Fille Mal Gardée* has continued to be produced, which is a tribute to the sturdiness of its construction.

The idea that ballet should be dramatic and that all elements should contribute to the dramatic purpose (the *ballet d'action*), an idea most clearly stated by Noverre, was fairly common during the late 1700s. Yet its realization presented most ballet masters, including Noverre, with overwhelming problems, because dancing, which is a major part of ballet, was in their eyes essentially nonexpressive and hence incapable of contributing to dramatic development. Thus most works in the *ballet d'action* idiom relied on mime to convey the story line, and in some instances dance was almost eliminated. Dauberval's achievement was to make dance an essential part of the action, to make it expressive of both character and situation. A Parisian critic wrote that "his ballets are motivated, and one does not dance simply for the sake of dancing. Thus in the ballet of *Le Page Inconstant*, each dance has its special interest which characterizes it." Another French critic, writing for *Le journal de Paris* (15 July 1805), commented that Dauberval "knew how to put dances into the action. By suppressing the dance in his productions there would no longer be any action, nothing would remain. . . . Dauberval, by his happy creations, by his brilliant executions, had associated his art with dramatic art." So successful was Dauberval at integrating action and dance that to remove a dance sequence from one of his ballets was to render a section meaningless. Whereas people remembered Noverre for his theories, they remembered Dauberval for his ballets.

Noverre, who jealously guarded his self-appointed position as creator of the *ballet d'action*, did not write of Dauberval's success in this genre. Nevertheless, he paid him considerable tribute in the 1807 edition of his *Lettres*. "Dauberval was thus the first who zealously battled preconceived ideas to overcome old prejudices, to triumph over the Opera's outworn rules, to abolish masks, adopt a more natural costume, and present himself as Nature's engrossing interpreter." Didelot's homage was that of a grateful pupil to his master. "May I, oh! Master, inspired by thee, retain still in my Sappho a spark of thy genius! My thankful heart would enjoy it but as thy gift!" And in his preface to *Jenny* (Théâtre de la Porte-Saint-Martin, 1806), Aumer proudly calls himself "student of Dauberval, whose loss the arts weep."

Dauberval left few recorded statements about his art. One rare example, recorded by Carlo Blasis in his *Elementary Treatise* (1820), is, like his ballets, succinct and unpretentious.

I conceive that a multiplicity of decorations and of mechanical effects can dazzle a multitude; but I dare to disdain this means when it does not hold essentially to the subject; I deal with pantomime and the dance; I wish to leave all the honor of success to these two arts; it is not sufficient for me to please the eyes, I wish to interest the heart.

[*See also entries on the principal figures mentioned herein.*]

BIBLIOGRAPHY

Blasis, Carlo. *An Elementary Treatise upon the Theory and Practice of the Art of Dancing* (1820). Translated by Mary Stewart Evans. New York, 1944.

Chazin-Bennahum, Judith. "Wine, Women, and Song: Anacreon's Triple Threat to French Eighteenth-Century Ballet." *Dance Research* 5 (Spring 1987): 55–64.

Chazin-Bennahum, Judith. *Dance in the Shadow of the Guillotine.* Carbondale, Ill., 1988.

Costonis, Maureen Needham. "Dauberval's *Le Siège de Cythère*, 1791: A Commentary in Translation." *Dance Chronicle* 14.2–3 (1991): 175–202.

Guest, Ivor. *La fille mal gardée.* London, 1960.

Guest, Ivor. *The Romantic Ballet in England.* London, 1972.

Guest, Ivor. "*La fille mal gardée:* New Light on the Original Production." *Dance Chronicle* 1.1 (1977): 3–7.

Guest, Ivor. *The Romantic Ballet in Paris.* 2d rev. ed. London, 1980.

Milhous, Judith. "Dancers' Contracts at the Pantheon Opera House, 1790–1792." *Dance Research* 9 (Autumn 1991): 51–75.

Noverre, Jean-Georges. *Lettres sur les arts imitateurs en général et sur la danse en particulier.* 2 vols. Paris, 1807. Edited by Fernand Divoire as *Lettres sur la danse et les arts imitateurs* (Paris, 1952).

Price, Curtis A., et al. *Italian Opera in Late Eighteenth-Century London*, vol. 1, *The King's Theatre, Haymarket, 1778–1791.* London, 1995.

Swift, Mary Grace. *A Loftier Flight: The Life and Accomplishments of Charles Louis Didelot.* Middletown, Conn., 1974.

JOHN V. CHAPMAN

DAVIES, SIOBHAN (Susan Davies; born 18 September 1950 in London), dancer and choreographer. Davies studied at the Hammersmith College of Art and Building from 1966 to 1967; in 1967, she became one of the first students at the London School of Contemporary Dance. She appeared with the London Contemporary Dance Theatre from its first season in 1969 and danced with Ballet for All in 1971. Davies began choreographing for company workshops in 1970, was appointed associate choreographer in 1974, and became resident choreographer in 1983. Between 1972 and 1987 Davies created seventeen works for the company.

In 1980, Davies was one of the first choreographers to receive a dance award from the Greater London Arts Association; thereafter, she spent part of each year as artistic director of an independent company—Siobhan Davies and Dancers in 1981 and Second Stride in subsequent years. Second Stride, whose co-director was Ian Spink, derived its name from Strider, the first independent British group, founded by Second Stride's third choreographer, Richard Alston. Second Stride was recognized immediately as a major force in British dance, both at home and by several American critics during the group's 1982

U.S. tour. In addition to her success as a choreographer, Davies has also danced in her own groups and in several Richard Alston works outside as well as within the London Contemporary Dance Theatre repertory. She performed with Alston in New York during a study leave in 1976.

In 1986 Davies was awarded the first Fulbright Fellowship in choreography, enabling her to take a study trip to America. On returning home, she launched the Siobhan Davies Company (1988) and became associate choreographer of the Rambert Dance Company (1989), a position she held until 1993. During her time at Rambert she created works such as *Embarque* (1988), *Sounding* (1989), *Signature* (1990), and *Winnsboro Cotton Mill Blues* (1992), for which she won the 1993 Olivier Award for outstanding achievement in dance. In 1990 she received her first commission from a ballet company, the English National Ballet, formerly the London Festival Ballet.

The titles of Davies's works often suggest the nature of their content: *Relay,* her first work for the London Contemporary Dance Theatre, is based on sports movement; *Pilot* is based on images of travelers with suitcases; and *Sphinx* is framed by the choreographer's own enigmatic solos. During the 1970s, however, Davies's work tended toward abstraction: its literal content was combined with and even subsumed under abstract concerns, and its movement vocabulary, structure, and spatial patterning became increasingly intricate. Concentrating on developing a dance language, she commissioned music to support her dance statements.

For works in the 1980s, Davies turned most often to existing sources and used a more clearly defined dramatic content—human character and relationships. *Something to Tell* (1980) suggests the loneliness and sorrow of a woman who, with her partner, conducts "several conversations as in a play" with various younger characters who may represent aspects of her past. *Minor Characters* (1983), with a text by Barbara McLauren, explores the interplay between words and movement that reveals personality. *Silent Partners* (1984), the subject of a London Weekend Television documentary in 1985, expresses the progress of a relationship through a series of encounters leading up to a final meeting.

In the 1970s, Davies's style was characteristically gentle and understated; she introduced a more intimate, cushioned quality of movement, unseen in other London Contemporary Dance Theatre work. Even so, she could contrast this intimacy with broad ecstatic statements that emphasize the risk of fall and the recovery of weight. *Rushes* (Second Stride, 1982) revealed a harsh new angularity in her work; since she produced this piece, Davies has enriched her works with a sharpness of attack and greater speed. Beginning in the late 1970s, design became increasingly important in Davies's work. In the 1980s and

1990s, her regular collaborators have been photographer David Buckland, lighting designer-television director Peter Mumford, and costume designer Anthony McDonald.

The Siobhan Davies Dance Company was formed in 1988, founded in order to create work on a more intimate scale. The company has performed all over Europe and in South America and Russia. Davies has most often commissioned music scores, notably five from Kevin Volans, including *White Man Sleeps* (1988) and *Wild Translations* (1995)—both drawing upon Volans's South African background, which in turn obliquely influences the choreography—and two from Gerald Barry: *White Bird Featherless* (1992) and *Trespass* (1996). Her dances show a remarkably sensitive response to the score, with themes that are abstracted yet deeply evocative of place and/or situation; they have often been described as neither narrative nor abstract but somewhere in between. In *Wanting to Tell Stories* (1993), for example, Davies seems to hint at episodes in peoples' lives, wanting "to tell the essence of a story without being literal or abstruse."

The company has won four Digital Dance Awards, and *The Art of Touch* (1995), set to Domenico Scarlatti's harp-

DAVIES. Poised here in one of the solos framing her work *Sphynx* (1977), Siobhan Davies is noted for the soft, understated quality of her movement. (Photograph by Anthony Crickmay; used by permission of the Board of Trustees of the Theatre Museum, London.)

sichord sonatas, and the young Italian composer Matteo Fargion's *Sette Canzoni* won a second Olivier award, as well as an *Evening Standard* Award for Best Dance Production. The company won the 1996 Prudential Award for Dance. Davies was awarded the M.B.E. (Member of the British Empire) in honor of her choreographic achievement in 1995 and has held the position of Senior Research Fellow at Roehampton Institute, London, also since 1995.

BIBLIOGRAPHY

Davies, Siobhan. "The Artist's View." *Dance Theatre Journal* 7 (Autumn 1989): 8–9.

Gow, Gordon. "Extremes of Energy: Siobhan Davies." *The Dancing Times* (December 1976): 142–143.

Heaton, Roger. "Music for Dance." *Dance Theatre Journal* 11 (Spring 1995): 12–15.

Jordan, Stephanie. *Striding Out*. London, 1992.

Jordan, Stephanie, and Helen Thomas. "Dance and Gender." *Dance Research* 12 (Autumn 1994): 3–14.

Kane, Angela. "Siobhan Davies." *The Dancing Times* (March 1990): 1–8.

Mackrell, Judith. *Out of Line: The Story of British New Dance*. London, 1992.

Preston, Sophia. "Beyond Words." *Dance Now* 1 (Winter 1992–1993): 11–15.

STEPHANIE JORDAN and BONNIE ROWELL

DAY, MARY (born 1919 in Washington, D.C.), dancer, teacher, founder of the Washington School of Ballet, and artistic director of the Washington Ballet. Day studied dance with Lisa Gardiner (a former dancer with the Anna Pavlova Company), the School of American Ballet, and Ella Daganova. In 1944 Day and Gardiner established the Washington School of Ballet. Presenting students dancing to the accompaniment of the National Symphony Orchestra, Day and Gardiner's ballets for children were popular in Washington. Among their successes were *Cinderella*, *Hansel and Gretel*, and *Adventures of Oz*. In 1956 the company took the title of the Washington Ballet. In 1960 the company was invited to dance at the Jacob's Pillow Festival. Day choreographed a number of ballets for the company, including *Hi Spri*, *Schubertiana*, and *Ondine*, and she welcomed guest choreographers, including Louis Johnson, who created *Wing Suite*.

In 1961, sponsored by the U.S. State Department and as a guest of the former Soviet Union, Day visited the schools of the Kirov and Bolshoi ballets to study their teaching methods. After she returned she established the Washington School of Ballet, now entirely under her supervision. The company, now completely professional, performs in Washington and tours nationally and internationally. In the 1980s the company gained artistic recognition through the ballets of its late resident choreographer, Choo San Goh. Kevin McKenzie was appointed artistic director in 1991. When McKenzie left to become artistic di-

rector of American Ballet Theatre in 1992, Mary Day was thereafter listed as artistic director of the Washington Ballet.

As a teacher, Day's understanding of the physical aspects of dance, her appreciation of the possibilities and aims of ballet, and her intrinsic taste have combined to imbue her students not only with meticulous technique but also with the deceptive simplicity that is good style. Among her students who have achieved eminence are Kevin McKenzie, Marianna Tcherkassky, Patricia Miller, Peter Fonseca, Suzanne Longley, and Virginia Johnson. Her students have collected medals at the International Ballet Competitions in Moscow and Varna: McKenzie won the silver and Longley the bronze in 1974, Amanda Mc-Kerrow won the gold in 1981, and Bonnie Moore won the bronze in 1983.

[*See also* Washington Ballet.]

BIBLIOGRAPHY

Gamarekian, Barbara. "The Washington Ballet Abroad." *New York Times* (26 September 1982).

Hering, Doris. "Washington Ballet's Mary Day." *Dance Magazine* (March 1992): 58–59.

ANN BARZEL

DAY ON EARTH. Choreography: Doris Humphrey. Music: Aaron Copland. Costumes: Pauline Lawrence. First performance: 10 May 1947, Beaver Country Day School, Brookline, Massachusetts. Principals: José Limón, Letitia Ide, Miriam Pandor, Melisa Nicolaides.

The four archetypal figures in *Day on Earth*, a plotless dance about work, love, loss, and continuity, represent a man, his first love, his wife, and their child. Using movement and stage space thematically and guided by the music, Doris Humphrey derived her dance material partly from the gestures of work, domesticity, and play and partly from the instrinsically dramatic motifs of human interaction: solitude, companionship, desire, flight, sorrow, nurturing, and constancy.

The man who is the central figure has a pattern of gestures that look like those of planting, cultivating, and harvesting without literally imitating them. As the other characters enter his life, the man's work motif is interrupted and sometimes varies with slight or large distortions, but he always returns to work for consolation.

The girl of his youth is temperamentally his opposite. They dance in counterpoint briefly, and she leaves him. A more mature woman comes, with whom he can move in complete harmony. Their child—played by a real child, whose choreography derives from simple games—eventually slips away, and the movement of the man and woman becomes violent and broken. Even after his wife leaves him, however, the man still plants and harvests. The dance ends as it began, with a formal procession, and then a final, beautiful image of continuity as the adults lie down, drawing over them a silk cloth, and the child seats herself above them with calm expectancy.

BIBLIOGRAPHY

Humphrey, Doris. *Doris Humphrey, an Artist First: An Autobiography.* Edited by Selma Jeanne Cohen. Middletown, Conn. 1977.

Siegel, Marcia B. *The Shapes of Change: Images of American Dance.* New York, 1979.

Siegel, Marcia B. *Days on Earth: The Dance of Doris Humphrey.* New Haven, 1987.

MARCIA B. SIEGEL

DAYTON BALLET. The second-oldest regional company in the United States, the Dayton Ballet was founded in 1937 by Dayton, Ohio, natives Josephine and Hermene Schwarz. The sisters came from a close-knit, middle-class family that encouraged their talents. Although Josephine, born 8 April 1908, was six years younger than Hermene, she provided the initiating creative energy. Hermene designed costumes and decor. Both taught at the Schwarz School of the Dance (later renamed the Dayton Ballet School), which they opened in 1927.

A performing career was Josephine's initial goal. She extended her ballet studies beyond Dayton, taking classes in Chicago with Russian choreographer Adolph Bolm and touring briefly with his Ballet Intime. In 1926 she also danced in Ruth Page's Ravinia Park Ballet. A performance of German dancers Harald Kreutzberg and Yvonne Georgi attracted her to modern dance. In 1928 the sisters studied in Germany, principally with Mary Wigman.

Josephine then selected the New York school of Doris Humphrey and Charles Weidman. She soon taught for Humphrey and performed at the Roxy Theater and in the 1935 production of *Life Begins at 8:40*. A 1937 knee injury threatened her career. That same year in Dayton, she and her sister formed the Experimental Group for Young Dancers. It was retitled Dayton Theater Dance Group in 1941 and subsequently became the Dayton Civic Ballet in 1958 and the Dayton Ballet in 1978.

The school and company placed equal emphasis on modern dance and ballet, and the choreographers they produced, notably Bess Saylor Imber and Stuart Sebastian, had impressive stylistic range. Until the 1960s, Josephine's choreography dominated the repertory. Although tasteful, it was somewhat pedagogical in outlook. Among her more effective works were *Lincoln Portrait* (1949), *I Watched Myself Grow Up* (1953), *Archaic Fragments* (1954), and *Dance Overture* (1964).

The 1960s were a time of accelerated progress for the Dayton Ballet. In 1959 it became a charter member of the Northeast Regional Ballet Association, and Josephine initiated the organization's pioneering Craft of Choreography Conferences. Four years later, David McLain became

DAYTON BALLET. Christopher Grider, Rachel Carmazzi, and Jennifer Ingle in the company's premiere of *Romeo and Juliet*, choreographed by Septime Webre to the Prokofiev score. (Photograph by Andy Snow; used by permission.)

the Dayton Ballet School's first male teacher. He introduced into the company several male dancers, notably Jon Rodriguez, who also became a prolific choreographer. By 1972 the company had performed in New York as one of three major companies (along with the Atlanta Ballet and the Sacramento Ballet) of the National Association for Regional Ballet.

Stuart Sebastian became artistic director in 1981 and held the position until his death in 1990. Sebastian produced many original ballets, among them *Ballet à la Carte* (1980), *"and they were not ashamed"* (1981), and *Oh, My, Murder?* (1982). James Clouser was artistic director for two seasons, and in 1992 the Dayton Ballet board selected Dermot Burke to succeed him. In tune with the 1990s, Burke combined business acumen and artistic sensibility. His first gesture was to raise funds for and mount a new version of *The Nutcracker*.

Over the years, the company has produced outstanding artists, such as Rebecca Wright (American Ballet Theatre), Donna Wood (Alvin Ailey American Dance Theater), Jeraldyne Blunden (artistic director, Dayton Contemporary Dance Company), Joseph and Daniel Duell (New York City Ballet), Jeff Gribler (Pennsylvania Ballet), and Stuart Sebastian (National Ballet).

BIBLIOGRAPHY

Hering, Doris. "Dayton Civic Ballet: A Merging of Currents." *Dance Magazine* (May 1959): 56–57.

Hering, Doris. "Why Ohio?" *Dance Magazine* (September 1971): 48–62.

Morris, Terry. "Remarkable, by Jo." *Dayton Daily News* (18 April 1993).

Our Fiftieth Year. Dayton Ballet souvenir program, 1987.

ARCHIVE.   Josephine Schwarz Papers, Wright State University, Department of Archives and Special Collections (MS–218).

DORIS HERING

DAYTON CONTEMPORARY DANCE COMPANY.

Taste and well-rounded training have characterized the Dayton Contemporary Dance Company since its founding by Jeraldyne Blunden in 1968. The taste is innate with Blunden; the training began in 1947 when, as an eight-year-old child, she was taken by her mother to a Dayton, Ohio, recreation center where African-American children studied dance. The visiting teacher was Josephine Schwarz, co-founder, with her sister Hermene, of the Dayton Ballet. Blunden later transferred to the Schwarzes' own school, where she received equal exposure to ballet and modern dance. Blunden's own company has since taken this dual approach.

Because performing opportunities for African-American dancers were limited, Blunden decided early on to teach and to establish her own company. Two summers spent studying modern dance at the American Dance Festival in New London, Connecticut, confirmed her desire that it be a modern dance company. In 1960, she opened her own school and through it began developing the Dayton Contemporary Dance Company, also known as DCDC.

At first most of the repertory was by Blunden, but her dancers, notably Kim Carter and later Dwight Rhoden, were encouraged to contribute original works. Two gifted resident choreographers have emerged: Kevin Ward and Debbie Blunden-Diggs (Blunden's daughter). Both are also associate directors, and each has created more than a dozen works for the company. Ward is a versatile composer as well. Other key members of the DCDC artistic structure are Dawn M. Wood, rehearsal coach and tour coordinator; Sheri Williams, fitness trainer; and Calvin Norris Young, men's rehearsal coach, all of whom also perform with the sixteen-member company.

A salient trait of DCDC, in addition to its quality training, is the humanity of its performing style. The works it acquires from outside choreographers usually are chosen to reinforce this image. Among them have been Doug Varone's *Home* and *Kiss My Eyes Goodnight*, Lynne Taylor-Corbett's *Diary*, and Lester Horton's *With Timbrel and Dance Praise His Name*, staged by James Truitte.

Since 1988, the company has had access to important African-American repertory works through the American Dance Festival's Black Tradition in Modern Dance. The project has enabled the Dayton Contemporary Dance Company to acquire Talley Beatty's *Mourner's Bench* and *The Stack-Up*, Donald McKayle's *Rainbow 'Round My Shoulder* and *District Storyville*, Dianne McIntyre's *Take-Off from a Forced Landing;* and Eleo Pomare's *Las Desenamoradas, Blues for the Jungle,* and *Missa Luba.* Under American Dance Festival auspices, DCDC also has toured extensively.

In 1994, the Jacob's Pillow Dance Festival awarded a grant to be shared by the Dayton Contemporary Dance Company and Philadanco (Philadelphia Dance Company), also an African-American ensemble. It was for *BAMM*, a fourteen-dancer work incorporating seven dancers from each company. Created by Donald Byrd, *BAMM* was performed in 1994 to celebrate DCDC's twenty-fifth anniversary and in 1995 to hail that of Philadanco.

BIBLIOGRAPHY

Dayton Contemporary Dance Company. Souvenir program. Dayton, 1994.

Hering, Doris. "The Future of Dance Is in Dayton." *Dance Magazine* (December 1993): 66–69.

DORIS HERING

DEAN, CHRISTOPHER. *See* Torvill and Dean.

DEAN, LAURA

(born 3 December 1945 in Staten Island, New York), American dancer, choreographer, and composer. Dean graduated from New York City's High School of the Performing Arts, where she studied with Lucas Hoving. She also attended the School of American Ballet, studied piano and music theory at the Third Street Music School, and studied dance with Martha Graham, Merce Cunningham, Paul Sanasardo, and Mia Slavenska.

Beginning in 1965, Dean danced for a year with the Paul Taylor Dance Company; she also performed with the Paul Sanasardo Company and with Kenneth King. She began to choreograph in 1966. For her first company, Laura Dean and Dance Company, she created *Stamping Dance* (1971); *Square Dance, Circle Dance, Jumping Dance* (all 1972); *Changing Pattern Steady Pulse* (1973); and *Spinning Dance* and *Response Dance* (both 1974). *Square Dance, Walking Dance* (1973), and *Drumming* (1975) were all performed to the music of American composer Steve Reich, whose use of repetition and of rhythmic structures inspired by African music has continued to influence Dean.

In 1975 the Dean Dance and Music Foundation was formed to support the creation of music and dance works by Laura Dean. Her own company of eleven dancers and four musicians was renamed Laura Dean Dancers and

Musicians. Dean both choreographed and composed the music for *Song* (1976), in which the dancers were required to sing as they danced; *Dance* (1976); *Spiral* (1977); *Music* (1979); *Tympani* (1980); *Sky Light* (1982); *Solo in Red* (1982), later incorporated into *Enochian* (1983); and *Inner Circle* (1983). In 1984 she choreographed *Tehillim*, to music by Reich, for the Bat-Dor Dance Company of Israel.

Dean's first commissioned work for a ballet company was *Night* (to her own music), created for the Joffrey Ballet in 1980. This was followed by three more works for that company: *Fire* (1982) with music by Dean and designs by the architect Michael Graves (revived by the Frankfurt Ballet in 1989); *Force Field* (music by Reich, 1988); and *Structure/Light Field* (music by Glenn Branca, 1992). She has also made three works for the Ohio Ballet: *Patterns of Change* (music by Philip Glass, 1985); *Gravity* (music by Dean, 1987); and *Quantum* (music by Mark Isham, 1990). In 1988 Dean was invited to contribute a work to New York City Ballet's American Music Festival; the result was *Space*, to music by Reich. Also in 1988 she created *Dream Collector* (music by Terry Riley) for the Concert Dance Company of Boston. *Arrow of Time* (music by Totem, 1989) was commissioned by the Berkshire Ballet, and *Delta* (music by Gary Brooker, 1990) by the Royal Danish Ballet. In 1993 she choreographed "Sometimes it Snows in April" as a section of *Billboards* for the Joffrey Ballet, a full-evening work to rock music by Prince. Dean has also made several works for ice skaters, including *Burn*, for the John Curry Skaters in 1983; *Ocean*, for the Next Ice Age Company in 1989; and *Sedona Sunrise*, for the Ice Theater of New York in 1991.

In 1988 Laura Dean Dancers and Musicians took part in the New Contemporary Masters series at the New York's City Center, featuring the New York premiere of *Equator*, first performed in Amsterdam earlier that year. In 1989 the company presented *Memory* (music by Egberto Gismonti) at the University of California, Los Angeles. In spring 1990 the Joyce Theater in New York produced a retrospective of her work in a fifteenth-anniversary season, and in July the company presented a new work by Dean, *Infinity*, at the American Dance Festival in Durham, North Carolina. *Sacred Dances* was presented at a residency at Dartmouth College in Hanover, New Hampshire, in March 1991.

From the beginning, Dean has worked with a deliberately minimalist movement vocabulary; her energetic, abstract dances, usually ensemble works, are characterized by repetitive phrases, geometric patterns, unison and canon phrases, semaphoric arms, and spinning. "With spinning, I just got involved in the energy of it, and in a curious way, the dances have always been about that ever since," Dean has said. Her driving, motoric, highly percussive music features ostinatos and an underlying steady pulse; her early work focused on piano music, but later she included autoharps, synthesizers, strings, and percussion. Many of her mature scores are for synthesizers and drum kit.

Laura Dean Dancers and Musicians were featured on the Public Broadcasting System's (PBS) *Dance in America* program, "Beyond the Mainstream." *Tympani* was the subject of another PBS program produced by KTCA-TV, Minneapolis. Dean has received two Guggenheim fellowships as well as grants from the National Endowment for the Arts, the New York State Council on the Arts, and the Creative Artists Public Service Program. She has published articles in *Dance Scope*, *Drama Review*, and *Contemporary Dance*. In 1982 she received a *Dance Magazine* Award, and in 1986 the Brandeis Creative Arts Award, as well as a Bessie (New York Dance and Performance Award).

Following her New York season at the Joyce Theater in 1994, Dean disbanded her company and relocated to North

DEAN. Spinning is a characteristic element in Dean's choreography. Here, she whirls (center) with her dancers in *Drumming* (1975), performed to music by Steve Reich at the Brooklyn Academy of Music, New York. (Photograph © 1975 by Johan Elbers; used by permission.)

Carolina. She continues to accept commisions from other repertory companies, and taught in 1995 and 1996 at the American Dance Festival (ADF). Dean was among several choreographers hosted in an extended residency with performances and community outreach by the ADF in 1997 with a grant from the Lila Wallace–Reader's Digest Fund.

BIBLIOGRAPHY

Dean, Laura. "Notes on Choreography." *Dance Scope* 9 (Fall–Winter 1974–1975): 8–13.

Dean, Laura. "Seven Dances by Laura Dean and Company." *Drama Review* 19 (March 1975): 18–25.

Livet, Anne, ed. *Contemporary Dance.* New York, 1978.

McDonagh, Don, ed. *The Complete Guide to Modern Dance.* New York, 1976.

AMANDA SMITH

DEATHS AND ENTRANCES. Choreography: Martha Graham. Music: Hunter Johnson. Scenery: Arch Lauterer. Costumes: Edythe Gilfond. Lighting: Jean Rosenthal. First performance: 26 December 1943, Forty-sixth Street Theater, New York City, Martha Graham Dance Company. (Preview: 18 July 1943, Bennington College Theater, Bennington, Vermont). Principals: Martha Graham, Jane Dudley, Sophie Maslow (The Three Sisters), Ethel Butler, Nina Fonaroff, Pearl Lang (The Three Remembered Children), Erick Hawkins (The Dark Beloved), Merce Cunningham (The Poetic Beloved), John Butler, Robert Horan (The Cavaliers).

Inspired by the lives and works of the Brontë sisters, Graham presented the heroine of *Deaths and Entrances* as one of three women cooped up together in a gloomy house. There is no "story" in the traditional sense. Visited by dreams, memories, and terrors, the central figure descends into madness, but in the end achieves illumination and self-mastery. The rancorous dancing for the three close but dissimilar sisters reveals aberrant emotions and perilous states of mind, heightened by repression and the suffocating atmosphere. The dancing of three "children" identifies them at times as the sisters when young. They also bring onto the stage various props—a shell, a vase, a bowl, and a blue goblet—that summon up vivid recollections. As in dreams, real time is suspended, and imagined time permits odd juxtapositions of characters and events. The two men that figure prominently in the heroine's visions are sometimes joined by two others, billed as "Cavaliers," who dance with the sisters. Although *Deaths and Entrances* is not an easy dance for audiences, critics were immediately impressed by the originality of its movement and by Graham's remarkable performance. The first of several notable revivals was mounted in 1970, with Mary Hinkson taking over Graham's role.

BIBLIOGRAPHY

Jowitt, Deborah. *Time and the Dancing Image.* New York, 1988.

Sears, David. "Graham Masterworks in Revival." *Ballet Review* 10.2 (1982): 25–34.

Siegel, Marcia B. *The Shapes of Change: Images of American Dance.* New York, 1979.

DEBORAH JOWITT

DEBUSSY, CLAUDE (Achille-Claude Debussy; born 22 August 1862 in Saint-Germain-en-Laye, France, died 25 March 1918 in Paris), French composer. Debussy graduated from the Paris Conservatory (which he had entered at the age of eleven), winning the Prix de Rome in 1884. While a student, he took summer employment in 1880 as domestic musician to Nadezhda von Meck, the wealthy Russian widow who was then financially supporting Petr Ilich Tchaikovsky, and accompanied her to Switzerland, Italy, and Moscow.

Debussy warmed to Russian music, Tchaikovsky's in particular, and the German music of Richard Wagner, especially the opera *Parsifal*, which he saw at Bayreuth in 1888. The first Debussy compositions date from 1876, and by the early years of the twentieth century he had achieved his major orchestral works, *Nocturnes* (1897–1899), *La Mer* (1903–1905), and some of *Images* (1905–1912), and his only completed opera, *Pelléas et Mélisande* (1893–1902). With his piano music and songs, these identified his so-called impressionist style of composition, in which he ignored conventional methods of musical development in favor of line, color, immediate sensations, and the expression of "waking dreams."

In the 1890s, Debussy had discussions on ballet projects with the writers Paul Valéry and Pierre Louÿs regarding *Amphion* and *Daphnis et Chloé*, respectively, but neither was composed. Nor was *Masques et Bergamasques*, for which he wrote a scenario in 1910 at the invitation of Serge Diaghilev. He composed incidental music for Gabriele d'Annunzio's play *Le Martyre de Saint-Sébastien* (1911), declaimed and danced by Ida Rubinstein with choreography by Michel Fokine and designs by Léon Bakst. The next year he agreed to Diaghilev's request that the *Prélude à L'Après-midi d'un Faune*, composed as early as 1893, be used for Vaslav Nijinsky's first choreography, premiered by the Ballets Russes in Paris in 1912.

Khamma (1912) was composed for the Canadian dancer Maud Allan, but she never performed it and the work remained unknown in the theater until 1947, when it was staged in Paris at the Opéra-Comique, with choreography by Jean-Jacques Etchévery. Its subject was an Egyptian temple dancer who engages in heroic self-sacrifice. Debussy completed a piano score but orchestrated only the first few bars, handing over the rest to Charles Koechlin to finish.

Diaghilev planned a ballet on Debussy's *Fêtes*, but it did not materialize; his only direct commission to the composer resulted in *Jeux*, a "poème dansée" with choreography by Nijinsky, which premiered in 1913. His instrumentation is diaphanous, with luminous colors and often audacious polytonal writing. Dreamlike transitions are propelled by varied rhythms and the use of rubato, ending with an effect of enigmatic fantasy as darkness steals over the music and finally snuffs it out. The ballet had little success, and the music (Debussy's last orchestral score) was virtually forgotten for many years. Later it was found to contain some of his most subtle invention, moving from one idea to another without any references back but with germinal motives linked in a seamless musical flow.

Loie Fuller choreographed and danced in *Nuages* and *Sirènes* in Paris in 1913, the same year Debussy began *La Boîte à Joujoux* (The Toy Box), a children's ballet in four tableaux devised by André Hellé, an illustrator of children's books. Only some of the orchestration was sketched by Debussy before the outbreak of war in 1914, and the work was completed after his death by André Caplet. A ballet of sorts was staged by Hellé in Paris in 1918, and a choreographically more definitive production was mounted by Jean Börlin for Les Ballets Suédois in Paris in 1921.

Despite declining health caused by the onset of cancer, Debussy began another score for dance in 1914 as a commission from the Alhambra Theatre in London. It had the strange title of *No-ja-li*, alternatively called *Le Palais du Silence*, but the music did not progress beyond some preliminary sketches before being abandoned.

It can be accepted that Debussy never understood the art of dance and that he composed for it primarily for financial reasons, but his music has continued to interest choreographers. An updated version of *L'Après-midi d'un Faune* was done by Jerome Robbins as *Afternoon of a Faun* (1953) and by Jiří Kylián as *Silent Cries* (1986). *Jeux* has been choreographed by Jean Börlin (1920), Peter Darrell (1963), John Taras (1966), Roland Petit (1982), and William Tuckett (as *Gare*, 1990). Petit and Oscar Araiz have choreographed ballets to *La Mer* (both 1982), and John Cranko's *Brouillards* (1970) took its title from one of the nine Debussy piano preludes that made up the music. The String Quartet has been adopted for dance by Todd Bolender (1955) and Ron Sequoio (1967); *Epigraphes Antiques* by Rudi van Dantzig (1956) and Jerome Robbins (1984); *Chansons de Bilitis* by Geoffrey Cauley (1970); *La Damoiselle Élue* by Erich Walter (1966); and *La Cathédrale Engloutie* by Kylián (1975). *Khamma* was newly choreographed by Uwe Scholz (1986), and *Le Martyre de Saint-Sébastien* was choreographed entirely as a ballet by Maurice Béjart (1986). Numerous solos have been danced to "Clair de Lune."

BIBLIOGRAPHY

Austin, William W., ed. *Debussy: Prelude to the Afternoon of a Faun.* New York, 1971.
Garafola, Lynn. *Diaghilev's Ballets Russes.* New York, 1989.
Lesure, François. Claude Debussy: Lettres 1884–1918. Paris, 1980. Translated by Robert Nichols as *Debussy: Letters.* London, 1987.
Lockspeiser, Edward. *Debussy: His Life and Mind.* 2 vols. London, 1962–1965.
Neagu, Philippe, et al. *Afternoon of a Faun: Mallarmé, Debussy, Nijinsky.* New York, 1989.
Orledge, Robert. *Debussy and the Theatre.* Cambridge, 1982.
Pasler, Jann C. "Debussy, Stravinsky, and the Ballets Russes." Ph.d. diss., University of Chicago, 1981.

NOËL GOODWIN

DECOMBE, FRANÇOIS. *See* Albert, Monsieur.

DEGAS, EDGAR (Hilaire-Germain-Edgar Degas; born 19 July 1834 in Paris, died 27 September 1917 in Paris), French painter, engraver, and sculptor. Degas devoted a major part of his extremely long, prolific career to recording the Paris ballet world in all its aspects and in all artistic mediums. Beginning with oil paintings of specific Paris Opera productions (e.g., *La Source*, 1866–1868, Brooklyn Museum) and ending well into the twentieth century with bold sketches of anonymous dancers, the artist produced almost eight hundred known works on this subject alone. More than that, he photographed dancers, wrote sonnets about them (and to them), and confessed that they had sewn his heart "into a bag of pink satin, pink satin slightly faded, like their dancing shoes." As the nineteenth-century journalist Jules Claretie wryly observed, Degas was "le peintre des danseuses."

Degas did not record Paris ballet in its greatest period but rather at a time of stagnation, following the birth of Romantic ballet at the Paris Opera during the 1830s and 1840s. The sylphs and wilis of the great era had enchanted their predominantly male audience with newly acquired pointe technique and ethereal subject matter. By Degas's adulthood, the Marie Taglionis and Fanny Elsslers were gone, and their successors too often capitalized solely on male admiration, raising to new heights of notoriety the dancer's age-old reputation as "la crème du demi-monde." Male roles were increasingly danced by females *en travesti*, and serious male performers deserted Paris for more welcoming stages elsewhere, principally Russia. As the dancer's reputation waned professionally and personally, ballet itself suffered a loss of prestige as a serious art form, a loss also felt by its admirers. When asked to comment on Degas, Émile Zola snorted contemptuously that he could not take seriously a man who shut himself away to paint ballet dancers.

Degas's own personal background and artistic training, however, were impeccable. He was the son of a banker with a private income and as an artist trained briefly at the École des Beaux-Arts and on his own in Italy. It was his sensibility as a member of the *haute bourgeoisie* that he brought to his theatrical subject matter. Before turning to racetracks and cafés concerts, Degas systematically explored the traditional artistic challenges of history paintings and portraits. Whether his subject was ancient Greece or modern Paris, he drew and studied it, then drew and studied it again. "No work," he said, "is less spontaneous than mine."

Although early in his career Degas exhibited in the government-sponsored Salon, he was by nature a loner and an experimenter. It was natural for him, therefore, to join with other independent artists to exhibit outside the official Salon in 1874 at what came to be called the First Impressionist Exhibition. Degas's inclusion with these artists still troubles art critics, since he practiced few of impressionism's preoccupations—working in outdoor light, studying landscape as a primary subject matter, or applying scientific color theories. Although his fascination with scenes of modern life and with experimental compositional devices alone might justify aligning him with the impressionists, his decision to exhibit in seven of the eight impressionist shows, and never to disassociate himself from the group, validates his inclusion.

By age twenty, Degas had established a lifelong pattern as a season subscriber at the Paris Opera. He mixed freely with the famous personalities of that world, counting, for example, the Halévy family of composers and dramatists as close friends. He volunteered to illustrate Ludovic Halévy's satirical novel of the ballet *La Famille Cardinal*, producing a a number of monotypes which the author re-

DEGAS. Perhaps best known for his portrayals of dancers offstage, Degas often captured his subjects from unexpected angles. In *The Dancing Class* (oil on wood), the central figure is seen both from three-quarter view and, in her reflection in the mirror, from behind. (Metropolitan Museum of Art, New York; Bequest of Mrs. H. O. Havemeyer, 1929, H. O. Havemeyer Collection [29.100.184]; photograph used by permission.)

fused. In Degas's own correspondence he refers familiarly to Louis Mérante, ballet master at the Opera from 1869 to 1887, and to a number of *danseuses*, including Mesdemoiselles Sangalli, Malot, Sallé, and Sacré. He was, as he wrote to the co-director of the Opera, "one of the household": Opera dancer Suzanne Mante (herself portrayed by Degas in *La Famille Mante*, 1879–1880) recalled Degas as an old man wearing tinted glasses, stopping "les petits rats" (little girls studying ballet) and offering bonbons if they would pose for him.

Not surprisingly, Degas's understanding of ballet technique was superb. All his ballet works, even the roughest sketches, demonstrate his understanding of turnout and its effect on the body. He often noted the names of ballet positions and steps on his drawings, sometimes even indicating that an arm should be more rounded or a leg held at a different angle. The brothers Goncourt recorded with amusement that Degas had insisted on showing them a proper arabesque when they visited his studio.

His works establish his interest in all facets of a dancer's life, from her rigorous training to the more glamorous aspects of performing. Degas's eye for the telling gesture or characteristic movement caught the dancer as she rubbed sore muscles or slumped on a studio bench under the watchful eye of an ambitious mother. His respect for dancers as young working women gave them a place alongside his other series, which portrayed shop girls, laundresses, and prostitutes. Rarely did he show the dancer in what was then her most popular incarnation—the gauzy seductress of top-hatted dandies. He had scant interest in male dancers, although he did portray the famous instructors then at the Opera: Louis Mérante, Jules Perrot, and Ernest Pluque, themselves dance luminaries.

Degas became increasingly obsessed with his failing eyesight and as various cures proved useless, he turned more and more to sculpture. His *Fourteen-Year-Old Dancer*, a bronze shown at the Impressionist Exhibition of 1881 in a real tutu, ballet slippers, and satin hair ribbon, was the only one of his clay models to be cast in his lifetime. The majority of his work in clay was known only after his death in 1917; then, the contents of his studio were inventoried and some of the many little crumbling figures were saved through casting and circulated. What Degas's eye's had taught him about dance was transmitted by his undiminished hands into exquisite studies of dancers in arabesque and other readily identifiable dance positions, as well as tiny representations of strain, challenge, and beauty.

While Degas remained secluded and virtually forgotten in his late years, his reputation skyrocketed after his death. The revitalization of ballet as an art form in the twentieth century turned the contemptuous phrase "painter of dancers" into a compliment.

BIBLIOGRAPHY

Browse, Lillian. *Degas Dancers*. London, 1949.
Lemoisne, Paul-André. *Degas et son oeuvre* (1947–1949). 5 vols. New York, 1984.
Shackelford, George T. M. *Degas: The Dancers*. Washington, D.C., 1984.
Valéry, Paul. *Degas, danse, dessin*. Paris, 1936.

ARCHIVES.   Burrell Collection, Glasgow Art Gallery, Scotland. Norton Simon Museum, Pasadena, California.

JANET ANDERSON

D'EGVILLE, JAMES HARVEY (born c.1773 in England), ballet master. D'Egville was the most influential English ballet master since John Weaver. His father, Peter D'Egville had moved to England from France in 1770 and was himself ballet master at Drury Lane, at Covent Garden, and briefly at the major London opera house, the King's Theatre. Peter intended a ballet career for his son from an early age—James Harvey's first appearance at the King's was as a child in 1783.

After his initial training in England, the young dancer was sent to France, where he studied and performed until 1791, most notably under the great ballet master Jean Dauberval in Bordeaux. D'Egville returned with Dauberval for the 1791 and 1792 seasons to London, where he danced with Charles-Louis Didelot and Salvatore Viganò, who were also members of the company.

After Dauberval's departure in 1792, D'Egville worked under the new ballet master, Jean-Georges Noverre, during 1793 and 1794. It was during the first Noverre season that the young performer began to attract notice. When D'Egville danced Agamemnon in Noverre's *Iphigénia in Aulide* in 1793, the *Observer* commented that he "is entitled to share the laurels of the first Performer on the English Stage. . . . No English *Actor* can compete with him." Indeed, within Noverre's dramatic *ballet d'action*, D'Egville would have full scope for the development of his pantomime acting skills.

D'Egville was very strong, an attribute he exploited for experimentation with lifts. The *Morning Chronicle*, writing of his role in Noverre's *Les Ruses de l'Amour* (1794), described how he threw "one of the nymphs lightly over his shoulder, which he does with infinite neatness." In 1804 the same paper observed that "the giant power of D'Egville is well displayed in his raising and holding Deshayes on his thighs in a posture which is very striking." Muscular power stimulated one negative response, however; in 1793, D'Egville, still in his early twenties, was warned by one critic to take care not to become too fat.

D'Egville's first ballet at the King's Theatre, *Le Jaloux Puni*, was composed in five days and was presented near the end of the season on 1 June 1793. In it a nobleman is discovered by his wife in the act of wooing his farmer's wife. He is punished when his own wife is wooed by the farmer's wife in male disguise. The *Times* was impressed: "The departure of *Noverre* for Brussels was not felt; for *D'Egville*, who is by the bye one of the best actors on the stage, and also a very fine dancer, produced a Ballet of his own composition . . . which might rival the grand Ballet of IPHIGINIA." D'Egville's next work, *Le Bon Prince* (1794), was equally successful; its story, wrote the *Morning Chronicle*, "engages our interest and touches the soul." An eighteenth-century critic could not offer higher praise.

In 1799, D'Egville was appointed ballet master at the King's Theatre, a post he held with three interruptions (1803, 1806, 1807) until 1809. His first seasons were successes, with works such as the neoclassical *Hyppomène et Atalante* (1800), the exotic *Le Mariage Méxicain* (1800), the pastoral *Barbara and Allen* (1801), the comic *Le Jugement de Midas* (1802), and a revival of Dauberval's morally uplifting *Télémaque* (1799), a classical story well known at the time for its warnings against the dangers of love. The *Morning Chronicle* wrote that D'Egville's *Télémaque* was a "richer entertainment in point of Dancing than we ever saw." *Le Mariage Méxicain* "in point of merit, has claims far beyond the dull routine of what is technically termed a *Divertissement*," wrote an enthusiastic critic in the *Morning Post* (26 February 1800). *Le Jugement de Midas*, wrote another in the *Morning Post* (24 February 1802), boasted "a diversity of character seldom found in these little interludes, and considerable share of comic effect." *Barbara and Allen*, wrote the *Monthly Mirror*, "is very simple, but it shows how a trifle may prosper in the hands of a master."

D'Egville showed himself to be a good, if not brilliant, ballet master, who could create attractive dances and tell an effective story. In keeping with Dauberval's methods, he often chose simple plots that were particularly suitable for balletic representation. He allowed the best dancers (as opposed to pantomimes) to display their skills and had a special talent for inspiring designers. His ballets appealed to the mind through their dramatic action and to the eye through their dances and decor.

Subsequent seasons produced more favorites. In January 1804 the very popular *Achille et Déidamie* (in which Achilles is dressed in female attire and hidden among the daughters of Lycomedes) was produced. "Since the days of Naverre [sic]," wrote the *Morning Herald*, "we have never witnessed a Ballet which seemed so likely for the season to arrest the attention of the World of Fashion." It was in this ballet that D'Egville lifted André Deshayes to his thighs, a feat of strength he followed offstage when breaking down a jammed dressing-room door with his shoulder.

In 1805, D'Egville created the popular yet ill-fated *Ossian* (based on bogus poems supposed to have been written by a Gaelic warrior and bard). When its sixth performance was shortened because of a bishop's ordinance decreeing that all theatrical performances must end before midnight Saturday, a riot ensued. The *Morning Chronicle* wrote:

> The tumult now increased to an outrageous attack on the chandeliers, benches, musical instruments, and everything else within reach, and the theatre was threatened with utter demolition . . . several persons were observed to be active in the riot, whose rank in life ought to have prevented them from setting such an example to heedless boys.

Among the items destroyed was the ballet's music, without which *Ossian* could not be shown. There were, however, other ballets that season to compensate; *La Belle Laitière*, with its graceful shawl dance by Mademoiselle Parisot, and *La Fille Sauvage* were outstanding successes.

The 1808 and 1809 seasons were less successful. The best ballets were probably the revivals of *La Belle Laitière* and *La Fille Sauvage. Constance and Almazor*, a love story set in India, enjoyed moderate success in 1808. Others were not so popular—for example, *Les Amours de Glauque et Circe* (1809), *Don Quixote* (1809), and *Le Mariage Secret* (1808), which were criticized for their improbable stories, slowness, and excessive length.

D'Egville's involvement in ballet went beyond that of ballet master and performer, for he was also an important teacher. He ran a school (independent of the King's Theatre) whose best students—Miss Cranfield (debut 1802), Miss Twamley (debut 1808), the Misses Gayton (debut 1808), and Miss Smith (debut 1809)—though never as good as the better French dancers, could perform principal roles with credit. D'Egville's younger pupils also appeared regularly at the King's from about 1804. The critical reaction to these half-trained children was mixed, some commentators finding them beautiful, others disgusting.

D'Egville's demise at the King's Theatre came, not as the result of a fall from public favor, but through overambition. He was involved in a wide range of pursuits within ballet and in one dangerous pursuit outside it, that of theater management. William Taylor trusted D'Egville to manage the King's at a time when Taylor was fighting with co-owner Edmund Waters over control of the theater. The short-tempered D'Egville was not the man to handle such a difficult situation; he was arrested in 1808, for assaulting Waters, and dismissed in 1809. It appeared to be a light fate compared with that of Taylor, who was sent to the Fleet Street debtor's prison in 1813, and of Waters, who fled his creditors to France in 1820.

During his seasons at the King's, and those in between, D'Egville had produced ballets at other London theaters— for example, *The Brazen Mask* at Covent Garden in 1802 and *Love in a Tub* at Drury Lane in 1808. *The Brazen Mask* demonstrated the melodramatic demands of such theater—in his pursuit of a young peasant girl, an evil baron burns her house, drives her mother mad, scatters her brothers and sisters, and nearly kills her father. After 1809 D'Egville continued his activity for this type of theater, as well as his teaching. He also spent some time in Paris, possibly trying to show a ballet at the Paris Opera. Returning to the King's for the 1826 and 1827 seasons, he produced the very successful *La Naissance de Vénus* (1826).

D'Egville worked at a time when conditions were most advantageous for the development of an English school of ballet. The Napoleonic wars both necessitated the use of local dancers and intensified national pride so that English dancers were encouraged. With the end of the wars in 1815, the demand for English performers lessened. The ten or fifteen years available to D'Egville had not been enough for the creation of an English school of ballet. His involvement in his many activities probably diminished his effectiveness as well. It was not long before people had forgotten that it was possible to have a good English ballet master and properly trained English dancers.

BIBLIOGRAPHY

Chapman, John V. "A Grand Mythological Ballet." *The Dancing Times* (December 1977): 144–145.

Chapman, John V. "The Pre-Romantic Ballet World of London." *The Dancing Times* (October 1977): 24–25.

Fenner, Theodore. "Ballet in Early Nineteenth-Century London as Seen by Leigh Hunt and Henry Robertson." *Dance Chronicle* 1.2 (1978): 75–95.

Guest, Ivor. *The Romantic Ballet in England.* London, 1972.

JOHN V. CHAPMAN

DE HESSE, JEAN-BAPTISTE (also spelled Deshayes; born September 1705 in The Hague, died 22 May 1779 in Paris), French dancer. Trained by his parents during theatrical tours in the Netherlands, Flanders, and France, de Hesse started his acting career in the provinces before making his debut in November 1734 at Fontainebleau, during performances of the Théâtre Italien at the French court. He performed in Paris on 2 December 1734, demonstrating his ability as a comic actor in such roles as a valet, a Swiss mercenary, and a drunk. At the same time he displayed a mastery of dance, and particularly of choreography.

The constant interplay of dramatic technique and rhythmic pantomime close to the dance customary in the *commedia dell'arte* developed alongside the French public taste for classical dance. We do not know who de Hesse's teachers were, but he certainly mastered their rules, steps, vocabulary, and sense of sequences. He undoubtedly began by staging his own *entrées* before trying to compose for other dancers. From the start his dual training as an actor and a dancer endowed him with an individual style and competence evidenced in his work, which appeared at the end of the more or less hybrid spectacles put on at the Théâtre de la Foire. Following a principle Molière had already understood in his comic ballets, de Hesse applied himself to staging the numerous *divertissements* that formed part of the dramatic action; he often supplemented comedies with pantomime ballets that quickly became successful. He combined his sense of expression with a choreographic imagination that soon gained him a place on the periphery of the Opera, granted a freedom not shared by his famous contemporaries.

On 25 October 1738, de Hesse staged *Les Amants Trompés.* On 30 July 1742, he married Catherine-Antoinette Visentini, who made her debut as a little harlequin in Thomas-Simon Gueullette's *Arlequin-Pluton* before taking the courtesan roles in the Comédie Italienne, alternating with the famous Benedetta Balletti. Perhaps it was this relationship that inspired de Hesse to stage *La Parenté d'Arlequin* on 26 October 1746. Generally he preferred popular subjects, such as *Les Chasseurs et les Petits Vendangeurs*, to the mythological subjects he occasionally used; one example was *Ariane Abandonnée par Thésée et Secourue par Bacchus* of 1747, with music by Adolphe Blaise.

De Hesse enjoyed such tremendous success in Paris that he came to the attention of the court, particularly of Madame de Pompadour; she herself danced, along with the dukes of Chartres, Villeroy, Courtenvaux, Luxembourg, and Coigny, at the Théâtre des Petits-Appartements in Versailles, in the ballets de Hesse staged for *Erigone*, to music by Jean-Joseph Mondonville. An arrangement was made with Louis XV under which de Hesse regularly staged the ballets danced in this theater by Madame de Pompadour, Monsieur de Courtenvaux, and other dancers, along with four sons and four daughters of Paris dance masters, ranging in age from ten to fifteen. According to the duc de Luynes, the dances were always judged to be "extremely pretty" and "of an agreeable invention." The young professional performers included Lépy and Mesdemoiselles Puvigné and Camille, who were to have brilliant careers at the Opera.

The most popular pantomime-ballets included *Le Pédant*, with music by Blaise, and *L'Opérateur Chinois* (1748), with music by Louis-Gabriel Guillemain, which illustrated the contemporary rage for the Chinese-style scenes painted by François Boucher. The exotic costume of the Opérateur (Courtenvaux) was painted to look like Peking fabric decorated with the image of a monkey. De Hesse himself entered the theater with Camille in a sedan chair before dancing a pas de deux that was applauded by Louis XV. *Les Quatre Âges en Récréation* (1749) had seven *entrées*. De Luynes admired the choreographer's "surprising genius" in numerous spectacles inspired by rustic scenes, including *Les Bûcherons et le Médecin de Village* (1750), with music by Des Rochers, and *Les Sabotiers*. At

DE HESSE. A scene from *La Guinguette*, a ballet staged by de Hesse on 8 August 1750 at the Théâtre Italien, Paris. This engraving, c.1753, is by F. Bason after a painting by Gabriel de Saint Auben. (Widener Collection, National Gallery of Arts, Washington.)

the same time de Hesse was presenting fashionable rustic pieces at the Comédie Italienne, including *La Guinguette* (1750), *Les Vendangeurs, Le Mai, Les Meuniers,* and *Les Noces Bergamasques.* He staged *Vénus et Adonis* (1752) at Madame de Pompadour's Château de Bellevue, with music by Mondonville, and an impromptu to a text by Charles-Simon Favart. Favart and de Hesse were at this time the unchallenged masters of the Comédiens Italiens troupe. De Hesse composed such short works for it as *Belphégor* (1753), *Arlequin Génie* (1754), *Arlequin dans la Ville de Ceylon* (in collaboration with his student Antoine-Bonaventure Pitrot), *Les Femmes Corsaires, Le Ballet Turc et Chinois* (1755), and *Les Noces Chinoises* (1756). The titles and the libretti clearly evoke the variety of his invention, which heralded the pre-Romantic *ballet d'action* developed particularly by Jean Dauberval.

De Hesse apparently stopped creating new works around 1768, when he was awarded a pension of two thousand livres by the king. Though esteemed both in the city and at court, he was soon forgotten. He never published a theoretical treatise, and so he was eclipsed by the genius of Jean-Georges Noverre, who like de Hesse was inspired by comic genres close to the *commedia dell'arte.* De Hesse seldom ventured outside the *demi-caractère* style; by both inclination and necessity he ignored the noble or heroic genre, which was reserved for the Paris Opera. However, his accomplishments for a time gained him the reputation of "the most excellent ballet composer in Europe."

[*See also* Ballet de Cour.]

BIBLIOGRAPHY

Campardon, Émile. *La troupe italienne.* Paris, 1877.
Christout, Marie-Françoise. "De Hesse, Jean-Baptiste." In *Enciclopedia dello spettacolo.* Rome, 1954–.
Jullien, Adolphe. *La comédie à la cour.* Paris, 1883.
Luynes, Charles Philippe d'Albert, duc de. *Mémoires* (1735–1758). 17 vols. Edited by Eudoxe Soulié. Paris, 1860–1865.
Parfaict, François, and Claude Parfaict. *Mémoires pour servir à l'histoire des spectacles de la foire.* 2 vols. Paris, 1743.
Winter, Marian Hannah. *The Pre-Romantic Ballet.* London, 1974.

MARIE-FRANÇOIS CHRISTOUT

DE LAVALLADE, CARMEN (born 6 March 1931 in Los Angeles), American dancer, choreographer, and actress. Known primarily for her work with Lester Horton, Alvin Ailey, and her husband, Geoffrey Holder, de Lavallade has also been a successful interpreter of the works of John Butler and Glen Tetley.

De Lavallade grew up in Los Angeles, where she studied ballet with Carmelita Maracci and modern dance with Horton. She made her debut in 1950 in Horton's *Face of Violence,* dancing the role of Salome. When the Lester Horton Dance Theatre first performed in New York City in the spring of 1953, critic Walter Terry singled out de Lavallade for critical attention: "The body instrument is strong yet fluid, excellently disciplined, technically and wonderfully responsive to musical and dramatic nuance" (*New York Herald Tribune,* 5 April). These attributes continue to distinguish her beautiful performances.

From 1952 to 1955 de Lavallade appeared in four films produced by Twentieth Century–Fox, most notably *Carmen Jones,* choreographed by Herbert Ross. Ross then brought her to New York to be in the musical *House of Flowers,* and there she met Holder, whom she married in 1956. The couple often worked together. In particular Holder choreographed two solos that became de Lavallade trademarks: *Three Songs for One* (1963), set to songs from the Auvergne region of France, and *Come Sunday* (1968), set to folk songs sung by Odetta.

From 1956 to 1958 de Lavallade appeared in Metropolitan Opera productions of *Aïda* and *Samson and Delilah.* Meanwhile, she began to do television work with John Butler, and in 1959 she was a soloist in his production of *Carmina Burana* for the New York City Opera. In 1960 she created the lead role in Butler's *Portrait of Billie* at the Jacob's Pillow Dance Festival.

De Lavallade has been a guest artist with many companies. In 1962 she went with Ailey on a tour of the Far East sponsored by the U.S. State Department; she danced with Donald McKayle from 1963 to 1964 and was guest artist of American Ballet Theater in 1965, appearing in Agnes de Mille's *The Four Marys* and *The Frail Quarry.* In 1966 she performed with Tetley and also formed her short-lived Carmen de Lavallade Company.

In the 1970s de Lavallade turned to a combined career of acting and dancing. As a professor at Yale University, she was also a leading member of the Yale Repertory Theatre Company. A freelance artist who teaches acting and dance, de Lavallade has continued to choreograph and give guest appearances with the Alvin Ailey American Dance Theater, the Joyce Trisler Dance Company, and with other groups, such as the Harlem Boys Choir. In 1979 she choreographed *Sensemaya,* with music by Silvestre Revueltas, for the Dance Theatre of Harlem. She is noted especially for *The Creation* (1972), her interpretation of the poem by James Weldon Johnson, to music from Gustav Holst's *The Planets;* the solo was choreographed for her by Holder. In the early 1990s de Lavallade choreographed the Metropolitan Opera's productions of *Lucia di Lammermoor* (1992) and *Die Meistersinger von Nürnburg* (1993).

BIBLIOGRAPHY

Emery, Lynne Fauley. *Black Dance from 1619 to Today.* 2d rev. ed. Princeton, 1988.

Hering, Doris. "Carmen De Lavallade Makes Magic." *Dance Magazine* (February 1994): 32–33.

Terry, Walter. *I Was There: Selected Dance Reviews and Articles, 1936–1976.* Edited by Andrew Mark Wentink. New York, 1978.

ARCHIVE. Dance Collection, New York Public Library for the Performing Arts.

KITTY CUNNINGHAM

DE LAVALLADE. With Alvin Ailey as her partner, de Lavallade appeared in the Broadway show *House of Flowers* in 1955. Herbert Ross choreographed the dances to music by Harold Arlen. (Photograph from a private collection.)

DELIBES, LÉO (Clément-Philibert-Léo Delibes; born 21 February 1836 in Saint Germain du Val, France, died 16 January 1891 in Paris), French composer. Delibes entered the Paris Conservatory in 1847, where he studied composition under Adolphe Adam, the composer of the ballet *Giselle;* his work was, however, considered academically undistinguished. Consequently, Delibes began his career as a church organist, theater accompanist, and piano teacher. He continued as an organist until 1871, but his interest and ambitions were focused on the theater, and in 1856 he composed the first of his operettas, the one-act *Deux Sous de Charbon* (Twopence Worth of Coal).

Similar works followed at roughly yearly intervals for the next fourteen years, testifying to his popular success in this form. Russian sources indicate that he also contributed to Léon Minkus's score for *Fiammetta* (Little Flame; 1863), but André Coquis (1957) and other French sources make no mention of this. Delibes worked at the Théâtre-Lyrique and then at the Paris Opera, where he was appointed second chorus master in 1864. In that year his choral cantata *Alger,* celebrating the return of Emperor Napoleon III from the new French colony of Algeria, met with official favor, so he was asked to assist Minkus, then ballet composer to the Imperial Theaters at Saint Petersburg, on music for a ballet on an oriental theme, which reflected fashionable interest at that time.

La Source (The Spring) premiered at the Paris Opera in 1866, with a scenario by Charles Nuitter and choreography by Arthur Saint-Léon. Delibes and Minkus divided the music between them: Minkus composed act 1 and the second scene of act 3; Delibes composed act 2 and the first scene of act 3. Delibes's share was considered musically superior, but the whole ballet was a popular success. Saint-Léon choreographed a wholly new version for Saint Petersburg in 1869 called *Le Lys* (The Lily), and he revived it for the Vienna Court Ballet in 1878 as *Naïla*, the name of one of the ballet's principal characters.

Meanwhile, Delibes was asked to enhance the ballet *Le Corsaire* for a Paris revival in 1867; its original production had been mounted in 1856 with choreography by Joseph Mazilier and music by Adolphe Adam. Delibes composed an extra *divertissement* in the form of a *pas des fleurs* (flower dance), and in 1921 this was added to his share of the music for *La Source* to make the score for *Soir de Fête* (Gala Night). Choreographed by Léo Staats for the Paris Opera Ballet, *Soir de Fête* has been performed more than two hundred fifty times.

When the Paris Opera management made plans for *Coppélia*, Delibes, because of his earlier success, was given the sole commission for the music, again working alongside Nuitter and Saint-Léon. Delibes was very much the junior partner in this trio, but it was principally the music that kept *Coppélia* in the international repertory for more than a century after its 1870 premiere. Little is known about how the collaborators worked, but it is likely that they agreed on a structure based on Nuitter's story line, including several national dances that would reflect the latest trend for nationalism in music.

In musical idiom, Delibes began almost where Adam had left off, and he possessed the rare talents for illustrating incident, expressing emotional mood, and stimulating a sense of movement, all with equal facility. He could be called the first impressionist composer, for he shared similar principles with his contemporaries in pictorial art: he made color and rhythm the most important elements in his compositions. Delibes also extended Adam's tentative use of themes to identify mood and personality in relation to stage events.

Each leading character in *Coppélia* is portrayed in music and not just accompanied by it: Swanilda in her entry waltz, bright and graceful; Dr. Coppélius in stiff, dry counterpoint, the canonic device ingeniously applied also to Coppélia, the doll he has created; Franz in two themes, each sharing the same melodic shape of the first four notes, but the second having a more sentimental feeling than the sprightly first theme. Franz's role having been played originally by a woman *en travesti* (and so performed in Paris for more than ninety years) explains why the music for him lacks masculine vigor and resilience and why there is no specific pas de deux composed for the two principals.

National dances in *Coppélia* include the mazurka, czardas, bolero, and jig, with a waltz rhythm prominent at least once in each dance scene. The Thème Slav no. 6, to which Delibes added his own five variations, was noted down from a tune Saint-Léon believed to be a folk song. When it was identified as being a duet by the Polish composer Stanisław Moniuszko, a note was added to Delibes's score acknowledging its provenance from *Echos de Pologne* (1865), an album of Moniuszko's songs and duets with French lyrics, in which the duet in question is described as a Polish dance, the *krakowiak*.

The full *Coppélia* score comprises a prelude and twenty numbers, some subdivided, including a final *divertissement* in eight parts. This allegorical "Fête de la Cloche" establishes a celebration for the dedication of a new village bell, which will ring for dawn, for prayer, for work, for weddings, and for war and peace; the betrothal of Swanilda and Franz will, it is hoped, herald the bell's first wedding chime. Marius Petipa's Russian version (1884) and Enrico Cecchetti's (1894), which rearranged some of this music to furnish a conventional pas de deux, retained solos only for Dawn and Prayer and discarded the rest. Some of this music was restored many years later in performances of the ballet outside France; in Paris, however, it continued to be heard.

Only eighteen performances of *Coppélia* were given before its success was interrupted by the Franco-Prussian War, which closed the Paris Opera for a year. *Coppélia* was later restored to the stage, but it was not until 1876 that Delibes composed his next ballet, *Sylvia, ou La Nymphe de Diane*. The scenario by Jules Barbier and Baron de Reinach was based on *Aminta*, a classic pastoral drama by Torquato Tasso; choreography was by Louis Mérante. In this ballet, Sylvia herself is left unidentified in music, although her shepherd lover, Aminta, has two themes—a cool flute solo and a romantic cello tune—and even Eros is lyrically depicted.

Otherwise, the *Sylvia* music is richer and more imaginative than *Coppélia*, and it may be considered the finest score for ballet before Petr Ilich Tchaikovsky (whose *Swan Lake* premiered a year later, and who himself declared *Sylvia* the better music). The addition of expressive character to dance music was still relatively new, and Delibes was generous in providing it, as much in the tumultuous, almost Valkyrie-like entry of Diana's huntresses as in the well-known *intermezzo* and the later *pizzicati*, which were marked to be played *moderato maestoso*, not with the mannered hesitancy now often inflicted.

No full score of either *Coppélia* or *Sylvia* was published at the time. The piano reduction of *Sylvia* included stage directions and indications of instrumentation, such as the first balletic use of an alto saxophone for the Barcarolle, no. 15b. Later versions gave rise to other arrangements, such as Frederick Ashton's 1952 production at Covent Garden, with some orchestration by Robert Irving and Richard Temple Savage. Four numbers from *La Source* were interpolated into act 3; two of these were retained, along with twelve of the original numbers, when Ashton staged a one-act version for the Royal Ballet in 1967.

Most other productions of *Sylvia*, and the many versions of *Coppélia* by different choreographers, have kept to the musical structure as Delibes composed it, making it the foundation for the balletic narrative. Diaghilev's associate Alexandre Benois described enthusiastically the "higher inspiration penetrated with the essence of poetry" in Marius Petipa's first Saint Petersburg production of *Coppélia* in 1884, declaring that "this metamorphosis was *entirely due* to the music." Fifty years later, Fedor Lopukhov substantially rearranged the music for his Leningrad version, and his changes were thought to be out of character with the ballet.

After *Sylvia*, Delibes's only composition for dance was a suite of six dances for a Comédie-Française production in 1882: Victor Hugo's *Le Roi S'Amuse*, on which Giuseppe Verdi had based his opera *Rigoletto*. The dances, in a pastiche of seventeenth-century style, are seldom performed but show a keen ear for the nuances of period character. The remainder of Delibes's career brought three operas, of which *Lakmé* (1883) quickly achieved widespread success on both sides of the Atlantic. It was almost as successful as Georges Bizet's opera *Carmen* eight years before, and it helped to make audiences more aware of the imaginative quality at the heart of Delibes's music.

[*See also* Coppélia *and* Sylvia.]

BIBLIOGRAPHY

Balanchine, George, and Francis Mason. "Coppélia" and "Sylvia." In *Balanchine's Festival of Ballet*. London, 1978.

Coquis, André. *Léo Delibes: Sa vie et son oeuvre*. Paris, 1957.

Dunn, Thomas. "Delibes and *La Source*: Some Manuscripts and Documents." *Dance Chronicle* 4.1 (1981): 1–13.

Guest, Ivor. *Two Coppélias*. London, 1970.

Guest, Ivor. *The Ballet of the Second Empire*. London, 1974.

Saint-Léon, Arthur. *Letters from a Ballet Master: The Correspondence of Arthur Saint-Léon*. Edited by Ivor Guest. New York, 1981.

Studwell, William E. *Tchaikovsky, Delibes, Stravinsky: Four Essays on Three Masters*. Chicago, 1977.

Studwell, William E. *Adolphe Adam and Léo Delibes: A Guide to Research*. New York, 1987.

NOËL GOODWIN

DELL'ARA, UGO (born 13 April 1921 in Rome), Italian dancer, choreographer, and ballet master. Ugo dell'Ara received his dance training at the ballet school of the Teatro dell'Opera in Rome, where he spent most of his performing career. Tall, vigorous, and expressive, he was named *premier danseur* in 1938. In subsequent years he created roles in many works by Aurelio Milloss, the company's ballet master from 1939 to 1945: *La Bottega Fantastica (La Boutique Fantasque)*, *La Giara*, *Coppélia*, *Le Donne di Buon Umore (Les Femmes de Bonne Humeur)*, *Il Gallo d'Oro (Le Coq d'Or)*, *Petrouchka*, *The Creatures of Prometheus*, *La Rosa del Sogno*, and *Boléro*.

In 1945, dell'Ara left the Rome Opera Ballet to join Milloss's own ballet company, the Balletti Romani di Milloss, appearing in the entire repertory of his works, including *L'Isola Eterna*, *La Dama delle Camelie*, and *Danze di Galanta*. The next year, when Milloss closed his company and went to Milan to become artistic director of the ballet at the Teatro alla Scala, dell'Ara went with him. As Milloss's favorite dancer, he appeared often at La Scala in such works by Milloss as *La Follia di Orlando* and *Evocazioni* (both, 1947).

In 1947, dell'Ara was appointed ballet master at La Scala, and in 1950, after a successful tour of Europe in *Carosello Napoletano*, a musical he had also choreographed, he was named permanent choreographer. Thereafter he had an active career as artistic director and choreographer for ballet companies attached to numerous lyric theaters in Italy, including the Teatro dell'Opera in Rome, the Teatro Massimo in Palermo, and the Teatro San Carlo in Naples. He also frequently choreographed dances for television shows, and in 1955 he appeared in the film *Mario the Magician*, directed by Luchino Visconti. In 1965 he became director of the ballet company and school at the Teatro Massimo in Palermo.

Dell'Ara was an excellent dancer and a competent choreographer, but he may be best remembered for his reconstructions of two famous ballets in the late 1960s. For the Rome Opera Ballet in 1966, he recreated Filippo Taglioni's "Ballet of the Nuns" (1831) in Giacomo Meyerbeer's opera *Robert le Diable*—one of the earliest ballets in which Marie Taglioni rose *sur les pointes*, ushering in a century of Romantic ballet—and the following year he reconstructed Luigi Manzotti's spectacular ballet *Excelsior* (1881) for the Teatro Comunale in Florence. Dell'Ara's staging of the latter work was a detailed, impassioned, and truly impressive reconstruction based on Manzotti's notes and the memories of retired dancers. The ballet is rich in imagery and symbolism, showing the rise of civilization and the progress of technology as a struggle between the Spirit of Light and the Spirit of Darkness, a role that dell'Ara himself portrayed. When the Spirit of Darkness is finally defeated, the ballet ends in a Festival of Nations and an apotheosis of light and peace. This work was also later staged at La Scala, the Arena of Verona, the Teatro dell'Opera in Rome, and the Teatro San Carlo in Naples.

Among dell'Ara's own choreographies, two works are especially notable. *L'Urlo* (The Howl; 1967), set to music by Luciano Chailly and with decor by Misha Scandella, deserves to be remembered for its dramatic intensity and for its choreographic inspiration: the phenomenon of tarantism, a nervous disorder prevalent in southern Italy in the sixteenth and seventeenth centuries. The protagonist is a poor peasant woman who is bitten by a tarantula and who suffers a hysterical mania for dancing, a kind of magical, choreic possession. A work of a completely different nature was *Laudes Evangelii* (1975), set to music by

Valentino Bucchi, in which dell'Ara danced the role of Christ.

BIBLIOGRAPHY
Doglio, Vittoria, and Elisa Vaccarino. *L'Italia in ballo*. Rome, 1993.
Rossi, Luigi. *Il ballo alla Scala, 1778–1970*. Milan, 1972.
Testa, Alberto, et al. *Il balletto nel novecento*. Turin, 1983.

VITTORIA OTTOLENGHI
Translated from Italian

DELSARTE SYSTEM OF EXPRESSION. Although the name of François Delsarte is associated in the United States with a system of training in expression and physical culture, in his native France, Delsarte was known as a master teacher of singing, declamation, and aesthetics. The disparity in these views stems from the fact that Delsarte's theories were used in the United States as a basis for performance forms, training methods, and various reforms that never were a part of his own original interests or intentions.

Delsarte's Life and Career. François Delsarte (born 11 November 1811 in Solesmes, died 22 July 1871 in Paris) trained at the Conservatoire National de Musique et d'Art Dramatique in Paris from 1826 to 1829. In the mid-1830s, after a few years of unsuccessful work in musical theater, he acquired a post as choir director at a church and also began to offer classes in singing and to present annual concerts.

Reportedly, Delsarte began his research on expression and aesthetics around 1830. He was convinced his voice had been ruined by the Conservatory training; he objected to the current style of acting and singing as stilted and untrue; and he believed that training should not follow outworn formulas but be based on empirical data and scientific principles. He systematically observed the physical and vocal behavior of people in various situations and studied anatomy of the body and voice. Eventually he organized his data into a system based on the number three and its multiples, which he related to the Catholic trinity. In his opinion, trinities were the basis of every aspect and element, tangible or abstract, of life and the universe. Delsarte's second fundamental was his Law of Correspondence that posited a fixed relationship between the physical and the spiritual—in practical terms, between movement and meaning.

Reviews of Delsarte's concerts and discussions of his teaching and theories appeared frequently in French theater, music, and general publications between 1839 and 1866. At the peak of his popularity, from about 1853 to 1860, he was recognized not only as a distinguished artist and major authority on early music but also as a brilliant teacher. In addition to private lessons for individuals, he offered annually his *Cours d'esthétique appliqué*, a series of lectures on his theories as applied to the arts of oratory, painting, and music.

Delsarte's health began to decline after 1860, but he continued to teach and to develop his system. At his death he was lauded in obituary notices for the importance of his research in expression, the excellence of his teaching, and his leadership in promoting early music.

DELSARTE SYSTEM OF EXPRESSION. A prominent method of physical education in the late nineteenth and early twentieth centuries, Delsartism was based on gestures designed to facilitate the flow of breath, to balance relaxation and control, and to develop an easeful poise. *(left)* An instructional drawing showing an exercise for the hands and head. *(right)* In this illustration a man performs a defensive gesture. (Reprinted from Edward B. Warman, *Gestures and Attitudes: An Exposition of the Delsarte Philosophy of Expression*, Cambridge, 1892, pp. 75, 215.)

American Delsartism. The only American known to have studied with Delsarte was James Steele Mackaye (1842–1894), influential actor, dramatist, director, and inventor of theater innovations who worked with Delsarte from October 1869 to July 1870. Mackaye had already been working for almost a decade on his own approaches to expression including pantomime, gymnastics, and aesthetics. Delsarte recognized that the younger man's work could complement and enhance his own, so he invited the new pupil to teach with him. Thus began the series of developments that would lead to the American Delsarte system, something quite different from what was known in France.

After Mackaye returned to the United States in July 1870, he promoted the Delsarte system in courses and lectures. He taught a combination of theory from Delsarte and his own harmonic gymnastics, a method of training in techniques of emotional expression based on relaxation and naturalness in the body. Mackaye's material was designed for the training of actors and public speakers, but inherent in such an approach to expressive movement was the suggestion of a new way to think about dance as well as acting.

Genevieve Stebbins (1857–1914 or later), a pupil of Mackaye's for two years in the late 1870s, became the second important figure in the development of American Delsartism and was influential in developing the system in the direction of dance. Stebbins worked extensively as teacher, writer, and performer. Published in six editions from 1885 to 1902, her major treatise, *The Delsarte System of Expression*, delineated a training program that she claimed was derived from Delsartean aesthetic gymnastics, Swedish Ling gymnastics, and yoga breathing techniques.

To the combination of theoretical and practical material from Delsarte and Mackaye, Stebbins added energizing techniques (to complement Mackaye's relaxation techniques), breathing techniques, and the concept of human motion patterning itself on what she considered to be the basic motion in nature, the spiral curve. In the service of these concepts she collected and created a multitude of exercises, many of which are still relevant and continue to be used in acting and dance training.

Stebbins differentiated her work from the ballet tradition and identified it with the kinds of expressive movement that she felt existed in the sacred dances of Asia and ancient Greece. She thus directed attention to sources that later would inspire Ruth St. Denis and Isadora Duncan. Stebbins further developed and publicly performed two performance forms associated with American Delsartism: statue posing and pantomime. Ruth St. Denis saw one of her programs in 1892 and found it to be a crucial motivating experience. In Stebbins's ideals, her approaches to movement and expressive art, and her performances she introduced much of what would be credited by future generations as the invention of Isadora Duncan.

A third notable American Delsartean was Henrietta Russell (1849–1918), who had studied both in the United States and with Delsarte's son in Paris and who first taught under the name Henrietta Crane. Russell and her husband, Edmund, characterized as the "high priest and priestess of Delsarte," lectured on art; color; house decoration; dress; grace; gesture; and expression in oratory, acting, painting, and sculpture. Their range of interests was typical of late American Delsartism and reflected a connection between Delsarte enthusiasts and the arts-and-crafts movement in England. The Russells cultivated pupils among high society on both sides of the Atlantic and offered private lessons and classes to wealthy society ladies who wanted to learn "decomposing" (relaxation), spiral curves, falling gracefully, breathing, and other Delsartean techniques. Russell was active as a lecturer and teacher from the 1880s until her death in 1917. Ted Shawn first came in contact with the Delsarte system through one of her pupils, Mary Perry King, and later, in 1915, he met Henrietta herself, who by then was the widow of the poet Richard Hovey. Shawn studied with Hovey and brought her to Denishawn for lectures.

A corollary to the Delsarte movement in its later stages was clothing reform. Stebbins had recommended less-restrictive clothing, particularly for women, because the traditional corset hampered breathing. The Russells emphasized clothing reform for both sexes and for aesthetic as well as health reasons. The Delsartean ideals of full respiration and fluid movement necessitated clothing different from what was fashionable in the late nineteenth century. The public was hesitant to give up all its constraints, however, so instead of no corsets, Delsartean corsets were promoted.

American Delsartism was not an esoteric cult. Known and taught throughout the United States, it reached many in the middle and upper classes. The leaders—Mackaye, Stebbins, Crane-Russell-Hovey, and others—taught, lectured, and often wrote extensively. Their students and followers, in turn, spread the movement in ever-widening circles through their own teaching and writing. The system was taught in schools for speech and the dramatic arts and in private classes across the country. It was one of the three most prominent systems—along with German and Swedish gymnastics—to be discussed and used in physical education. The large number of published books and articles on the system spread its influence even further. Unfortunately, it also turned into a fad with commercialized products and uninformed promoters detracting from its real worth.

At its best, however, the American Delsarte system introduced new principles of movement based on relaxation, controlled and limited tension, easy balance, and natural flow of breath. It opened up possibilities for new kinds of design in movement and new, or rediscovered, thematic concerns. And in order to train students in the principles and techniques, the Delsarteans compiled and created a body of exercises that could be used both for general physical education and as a basis for further innovations in the art of movement.

Outside of professional speech and theater training, American Delsartism was mainly attractive to women. Nearly all of the teachers, students, and authors were women, and Delsartism did much to liberate middle- and upper-class ladies from Victorian strictures. The Delsarteans equated art with religion, the physical with the spiritual; and they identified their expressive arts with the glories of ancient Greece and the mystical East. Thus as well as offering a respectable, practical, and relatively easy form of physical training, they provided a rationale for women to engage in physical activity and expression. Delsartean statue posing and pantomime—the ultimate in refinement and gentility—became the opening wedge for the entrance of respectable women into the field of theatrical dance. Delsartism paved the way for two middle-class women, Ruth St. Denis and Isadora Duncan, not only to become professional dancers but also to initiate and lead a far-reaching renaissance of the art of dance.

BIBLIOGRAPHY

Burns, Judy. "The Culture of Nobility/The Nobility of Self-Cultivation." In *Moving Words: Re-writing Dance*, edited by Gay Morris. London and New York, 1996.

Harang, Myra White. "The Public Career of François Delsarte." Master's thesis, Louisiana State University, 1945.

Porte, Alain. *François Delsarte: une anthologie*. Paris, 1992.

Ruyter, Nancy Lee Chalfa. "American Delsartism: Precursor of an American Dance Art." *Educational Theatre Journal* 25 (December 1973).

Ruyter, Nancy Lee Chalfa. "The Intellectual World of Genevieve Stebbins." *Dance Chronicle* 11.3 (1988): 381–397.

Ruyter, Nancy Lee Chalfa. "Antique Longings: Genevieve Stebbins and American Delsartean Performance." In *Corporealities: Dancing, Knowledge, Culture and Power*, edited by Susan Foster. London, 1996.

Ruyter, Nancy Lee Chalfa. "The Delsarte Heritage." *Dance Research* (London) XIV/1 (Summer 1996): 62–74.

Shaver, Claude L. "Steele Mackaye and the Delsartean Tradition." In *History of Speech Education in America*, edited by Karl R. Wallace. New York, 1954.

Shawn, Ted. *Every Little Movement: A Book about Delsarte*. Pittsfield, Mass., 1954. 2nd ed. 1963. Reprint, New York, 1974.

Shelton, Suzanne. "The Influence of Genevieve Stebbins on the Early Career of Ruth St. Denis." In *Essays in Dance Research from the Fifth CORD Conference, Philadelphia, November 11–14, 1976*. Edited by Dianne L. Woodruff. Dance Research Annual IX. New York, 1978.

Stebbins, Genevieve. *Delsarte System of Expression*. 6th ed. New York, 1902. Reprint, New York, 1977.

Zorn, John W., ed. *The Essential Delsarte*. Metuchen, N.J., 1968.

NANCY LEE CHALFA RUYTER

DE MILLE, AGNES (Agnes George de Mille; born 18 September 1905 in New York, died 7 October 1993 in New York), American dancer, choreographer, director, and

writer. De Mille looms as a true Renaissance woman in the twentieth-century theater. The granddaughter of Henry George, she inherited on her mother's side a strong social conscience; from her father, William Churchill de Mille, playwright, director, and brother of filmmaker Cecil B. De Mille, she derived a profound identification with the theater.

Her early years, spent in New York City and at her family home at Merriewold in Sullivan County, are recounted in her memoir *Where the Wings Grow* (1978). In 1914, William de Mille summoned his family to Los Angeles, where he had cast his lot with his brother Cecil in the nascent film industry. There the impressionable child was taken to a matinee performance by Anna Pavlova and was fired with the inspiration to study ballet. Although her father remained opposed to her wish for a career in dancing, she was allowed two lessons a week at the studios of Theodore Koslov. Frustrated by her family's indifference, de Mille gave up dancing to attend the University of California, Los Angeles, where she learned "three important things—to use a library, to memorize quickly and visually, to drop asleep at any time given a horizontal surface and fifteen minutes" (*Dance to the Piper*, 1952). Graduating with a degree in English, *cum laude*, she settled in New York after her parents' divorce and resumed her dancing. Denied the long lines and compact torso of the ideal ballerina, she developed, as compensation, a capacity for endurance.

> Because I was built like a mustang, stocky, mettlesome and sturdy, I became a good jumper, growing special compensating muscles up the front of my shins for the lack of a helpful heel.
>
> (de Mille, 1952)

In 1928 de Mille made her professional debut on Broadway as Columbine in the Mozart opera *La Finta Giardiniera* and her solo dance debut in a recital shared by Jacques Cartier at the Republic Theatre. The following year brought her first assignment as a choreographer when, in Hoboken, New Jersey, she staged the dances for the Christopher Morley revival of *The Black Crook*.

After engagements as a soloist with the Roxy Theatre and her tour as a guest artist with the Adolph Bolm Company, de Mille embarked on a concert tour of Europe, appearing in Paris, Brussels, and Copenhagen with her partner Warren Leonard. Settling in London, in 1933 she devised dances for Cochran's *Nymph Errant* and studied at the Ballet Club with Marie Rambert and Antony Tudor. A sojourn in America offered two choreographic assignments: the dances for the Thalberg film of *Romeo and Juliet* (1936) and for the Broadway musical *Hooray for What* (1937). Returning to London, she resumed her concert work, with Hugh Laing as her partner and Antony Tudor serving as stage manager. Tudor created for her a moving solo in the Ballet Rambert production of *Dark Elegies* (1937) and the role of Venus in *The Judgment of*

Paris (1938), which de Mille had commissioned as a curtain raiser for a Gogol play.

Her association with Ballet Theatre began in 1939 when Richard Pleasant commissioned *Black Ritual* (or *Obeah*) for the company's charter season. Set to Darius Milhaud's score for *La Création du Monde* and requiring a pick-up group of sixteen black female dancers, the ballet drew negative press and was dropped after a few performances. In 1941 de Mille returned to set *Three Virgins and a Devil* on the company, dancing the role of the Priggish One in the premiere, a part she would return to many times as guest artist. An inventive work of high comedy, *Three Virgins* was judged by Martha Graham as "a classic of its kind . . . a little masterpiece," and it has survived in many revivals.

De Mille's breakthrough came in 1942 when she mounted *Rodeo* for Sergei Denham's Ballet Russe de Monte Carlo. [*See* Rodeo.] The story of her negotiations with the Russian management, of her collaboration with Aaron Copland and Oliver Smith, of her tour with the company to the West Coast to set and rehearse the ballet, and of the brilliant premiere that rewarded her with twenty-two curtain calls is told with great vitality in *Dance to the Piper*.

Rodeo offered de Mille entrée into the musical theater—an invitation to stage the dances for *Oklahoma!*, a new Rodgers and Hammerstein musical based on the 1931 play by Lynn Rigg, *Green Grow the Lilacs*. The premiere for *Oklahoma!* was on 31 March 1943. In June of that year de Mille married Walter Foy Prude. Over the next four decades, she divided her time among her various interests: creating new ballets and reviving her earlier pieces; designing dances for and directing Broadway shows; organizing and managing her own repertory companies; and writing.

The dances for *Oklahoma!* were unique in two respects: they were the first to be fully integrated with the dramatic action of a play, and they required the abilities of dancers with training in both ballet and modern dance. Hundreds of tap dancers were thus rendered obsolete, and the training patterns for the traditional Broadway hoofer were dramatically changed. The de Mille ballets for musicals opened up a broad new medium for many artists from the ballet and provided strong links between the two theatrical forms.

Most of de Mille's early musicals have become American classics: *One Touch of Venus* (1943), *Bloomer Girl* (1944), *Carousel* (1945), *Brigadoon* (1947), and *Allegro* (1947), which she also directed. Her directing assignments grew, and from Benjamin Britten's opera *The Rape of Lucretia* (1948) to *Come Summer* (1969), de Mille frequently took on broader, more demanding assignments in the theater. Her success never distracted her, however, from a deep commitment to Ballet Theatre, to which she returned frequently, to stage new works.

DE MILLE. Scene from de Mille's *Three Virgins and a Devil* (1941), with Annabelle Lyon as the Lustful One (left), Lucia Chase as the Greedy One (center), bedecked in outrageous finery, and de Mille as the Priggish One (right) who points the way to the church. Eugene Loring was the original Devil. (Photograph from the Dance Collection, New York Public Library for the Performing Arts.)

One does not expect money in the ballet world. Here, it is supposed, one makes the lasting statement. Our big ballet companies are our treasury and nursery. This is supposedly the matrix form.   (de Mille, 1968)

She created *Tally-Ho, or The Frail Quarry* (1944) for Ballet Theatre during its transcontinental tour, and it has been significantly revised over the years. In its 1965 revival, de Mille reset the work under its alternative title, achieving the structure and effect she desired. Set to a score by Paul Nordoff, based on melodies from Gluck operas, the ballet is a gay and bawdy romp in the style of the French Rococo painter Jean-Antoine Watteau.

In 1948 de Mille produced *Fall River Legend*, her first excursion into the genre of tragedy. Designed for the dramatic ballerina Nora Kaye, it was first performed by Alicia Alonso. It is based on the Lizzie Borden ax-murder case, which the choreographer researched with the assistance of a Massachusetts lawyer and senator, Joseph Welsh. The genesis, realization, and reception of the ballet are all described in de Mille's book *Lizzie Borden: A Dance of Death* (1968). In 1969, de Mille staged *Fall River Legend* for the Royal Winnipeg Ballet, and in 1983 it entered the repertory of the Dance Theatre of Harlem.

The Harvest According, her enlargement of the Civil War ballet in *Bloomer Girl*, was mounted for American Ballet Theatre in 1952. Set to concert music arranged for de Mille's needs by Virgil Thomson, this ballet was considered by many to be her finest creation. Its failure to enchant European audiences, however, during the company's tour that year, and Lucia Chase's indifference to preserving its choreography on film, consigned the ballet to history. De Mille's next original ballets for Ballet Theatre—her preferred company—were *The Four Marys* and *Wind in the Mountains* (1965), but neither survived because each relied on performers with special skills from other media. *A Rose for Miss Emily* (1970) and *Texas Fourth* (1976) were new productions for American Ballet Theatre of works originally performed by students at the North Carolina School of the Arts. In 1988 she created *The Informer* for American Ballet Theatre, using dance materials drawn from her musical *Juno and the Paycock*.

DE MILLE. Alicia Alonso (The Accused) and Ruth Ann Koesun (The Accused as a Child) kneel before Lucia Chase (The Stepmother) in de Mille's *Fall River Legend* (1948). This dramatic ballet is based on the story of Lizzie Borden, a Massachusetts woman who, in 1892, was accused of murdering her father and stepmother with an ax. (Photograph by Baron; used by permission of Camera Press, Ltd., London.)

De Mille devised *The Bitter Weird*, a reworking of her Scottish dances in *Brigadoon*, for the Royal Winnipeg Ballet in 1964 and staged for them a documentary piece called *The Rehearsal*. That company and the Harkness Ballet received productions of *The Golden Age* in 1967. In 1975 she staged *Summer* (later called *Death and the Maiden*) for the Boston Ballet; this work was set to songs and instrumental pieces by Franz Schubert. De Mille revised it for the Joffrey Ballet in 1978 under the title *A Bridegroom Called Death*, and two more recent resettings have been performed by companies in Richmond, Virginia, and Nancy, France, with yet another title, *Inconsequentials*. A final version of the Schubert-based ballet was staged by American Ballet Theatre in 1992 under the title *The Other*.

Always concerned with the preservation of her national dance heritage, de Mille formed two companies to foster American concepts. The Agnes de Mille Dance Theatre toured the United States in 1953 and 1954, sponsored by Sol Hurok. James Mitchell and Gemze de Lappe were the principal dancers in a repertory consisting of excerpts from de Mille's own Broadway works, items from her earlier concert programs, and some new material by contemporary choreographers. Grants from the Rockefeller Foundation and the National Endowment for the Arts enabled her to establish the Agnes de Mille Heritage Dance Theatre in 1973 at Winston-Salem, North Carolina. Thus, students in the theater arts program at the North Carolina School of the Arts became the nucleus of a company that toured sporadically over the next two years. It ceased performing in 1975, when de Mille suffered a stroke.

De Mille wrote frequently and fluently on a number of subjects for popular magazines, and publishers commissioned entertaining histories and treatises on various aspects of the dance. *To a Young Dancer* (1962) remains one of the finest handbooks for the aspiring performer ever written. Her most significant contribution to dance history is in the series of seven autobiographical works that tell the story of her own career and of an era that offered her a particularly stimulating theatrical life. *Dance to the Piper* (1952), *And Promenade Home* (1958), and *Lizzie Borden: A Dance of Death* (1968) recount her career chronologically.

The monograph *Russian Journals* (1970) accounts for de Mille's two visits to the USSR—the first as a journalist covering American Ballet Theatre's second Russian tour and the second as an adjudicator at an International Ballet Congress in Moscow. In *Speak to Me, Dance with Me* (1973), de Mille reevaluates in detail her London years in the 1930s, referring to letters and journals kept at that time. *Where the Wings Grow* (1978) concerns her earliest childhood memories, and *Reprieve* (1981) documents her hospitalization for stroke and her rehabilitation.

De Mille was also a frequent contributor to television. A pioneer in the making of documentaries, de Mille devised and narrated two presentations on ballet style and choreography for the National Broadcasting Corporation's *Omnibus* programs in 1956. Her *Fall River Legend* has been televised twice with de Mille as narrator: as part of an *Omnibus* documentary on the Borden case in 1957; and in a Canadian-German television collaboration (CBC-ZDF) with Sallie Wilson and the Royal Winnipeg Ballet in 1982. In 1987 de Mille participated in a documentary on her career called *The Indomitable Agnes*, directed for public television's *Great Performance* series by Merrill Brockway.

Active in labor organizations to promote the welfare of performing artists, and a frequent lobbyist for arts causes, Agnes de Mille is one of the most decorated persons in the history of dance. She received numerous awards, including the New York City Handel Medallion, a Kennedy Center Honor, three New York Critics Awards, two Antoinette Perry Awards, the Woman of the Year (Press Woman's Association and A.N.T.A.), and honorary degrees from fourteen American universities for her contributions to American life and the arts.

[*For related discussion, see* United States of America, *article on* Musical Theater.]

BIBLIOGRAPHY

Barker, Barbara M. "Agnes de Mille's Heroines of the Forties." In *Proceedings of the Twelfth Annual Conference, Society of Dance History Scholars, Arizona State University, 17–19 February 1989*, compiled by Christena L. Schlundt. Riverside, Calif., 1989.

Barker, Barbara M. "In Memoriam: Agnes de Mille, September 18, 1905–October 7, 1993." *Dance Research Journal* 26 (Spring 1994): 62.

Barnes, Clive. *Inside American Ballet Theatre*. New York, 1977.

Barnes, Clive. "Remembering Agnes: The De Mille Legacy." *Dance Magazine* (January 1994): 66–71.

de Mille, Agnes. *Dance to the Piper*. Boston, 1952.

de Mille, Agnes. *And Promenade Home*. Boston, 1958.

de Mille, Agnes. *Lizzie Bordon: A Dance of Death*. Boston, 1968.

de Mille, Agnes. "Russian Journals." *Dance Perspectives*, no. 44 (1970).

de Mille, Agnes. *Speak to Me, Dance with Me*. Boston, 1973.

de Mille, Agnes. *Where the Wings Grow*. Garden City, N.Y., 1978.

de Mille, Agnes. *Reprieve*. Boston, 1981.

de Mille, Agnes. *Portrait Gallery*. Boston, 1990.

Easton, Carol. *No Intermissions: The Life of Agnes de Mille*. Boston, 1996.

Edwards, Anne. *The DeMilles: An American Family*. London, 1988.

Gale, Joseph. "The Spirit of '76: The Agnes de Mille Heritage Dance Theatre." *Dance Magazine* (June 1974): 40–42.

Gere, David. "A Conversation with Agnes de Mille." *Ballet Review* 22 (Spring 1994): 52–60.

Gherman, Beverly. *Agnes de Mille: Dancing Off the Earth*. New York, 1990.

Lyle, Cynthia. *Dancers on Dancing*. New York, 1977.

Maynard, Olga. *The American Ballet*. Philadelphia, 1959.

Payne, Charles, et al. *American Ballet Theatre*. New York, 1977.

Rodgers, Richard. *Musical Stages*. New York, 1975.

Shearer, Sybil. "Agnes de Mille." *Ballet Review* 22 (Winter 1994): 10–12.

Speaker-Yuan. Margaret. *Agnes de Mille*. New York, 1990.

Windreich, Leland. "Agnes." *Dance International* 21.4 (Winter 1993–1994): 10–13.

LELAND WINDREICH

DENBY, EDWIN (born 4 February 1903 in Tianjin, China, died 12 July 1983 in Searsmont, Maine), American poet and critic. Denby published his first piece of dance criticism in 1936 in the New York journal *Modern Music*. The subject was Bronislava Nijinska's *Les Noces*, a ballet he prized.

> There is a realness in the relation of dance and music like a dual force, separate but inseparable. The movements, odd as they are and oddly as they come, often in counter accent, are always in what theoreticians call "motor logic"; that is, they are in a sequence you get the hang of to your own surprise, and that has a quality of directness when performed. (Denby, 1936)

In these sentences, the characteristic notes of Denby's criticism are sounded: the easy erudition; the fondness for paradox ("separate but inseparable"); the concentration on specific qualities of movement and on the meanings that arise from them, rather than on an intention either specified or implied; the offhand diction ("a sequence you get the hang of"); and the friendly, confidential tone that steadies the reader through passages of close textual analysis and assures us that these things can be understood—that, in fact, in some hitherto untouched part of our being we already understand and value them in much the same way that Denby does.

Denby was an aristocrat who wrote in a democratic spirit. The reviews that he published over the next three decades established him as the most evocative and discerning dance critic the English language has ever had and very likely the easiest to read. His word portraits of the great dancers of his day—Alexandra Danilova, Alicia Markova, Tamara Toumanova, André Eglevsky, Igor Youskevitch, Galina Ulanova, and Merce Cunningham—are models of communication. He was the first writer to give a clear account of the dynamic process of choreography—to capture in precise imagery the means by which dancing "in the abstract" exerts its power over the imagination. While Denby's voice was unusually close to the reader's ear, his eye acted like a corrective lens; vision and voice were magically allied. His influence on writers of the next generation has been widely noted.

He was born the son of an American diplomat and was educated at Hotchkiss, Harvard, and the University of Vienna. In Vienna, where he first became interested in dance, he attended the Hellerau-Laxenburg school, founded on Dalcrozian ideas. After graduating, he joined the dancing chorus of the State Theater in Darmstadt, famous for its productions of contemporary opera. In 1929, when the corps was disbanded, director Clare Eckstein formed a group to do comic modern dancing in Berlin cabarets; Denby became her partner. This enterprise, too, broke up, and eventually Denby migrated to New York, where he made his life among the action painters and art-conscious poets who were later to become known as the New York School (Willem de Kooning, Jackson Pollock,

Arshile Gorky, John Ashbery, and Frank O'Hara). He developed an attentive eye for street life, which informed both his critical articles and his poetry.

Denby's major assignment as a dance critic came in 1942–1945, when he took over the dance column of the *New York Herald-Tribune*, substituting for Walter Terry, who had joined the army. Denby reviewed the premieres of Jerome Robbins's *Fancy Free* and *Interplay*, Antony Tudor's *Romeo and Juliet*, *Dim Lustre*, and *Undertow*, and became an advocate of George Balanchine; his pieces on *Apollo*, *Balustrade*, *Ballet Imperial*, *Concerto Barocco*, *Danses Concertantes*, and other Balanchine ballets stand among the finest criticism written in the twentieth century. Nevertheless, he was primarily a poet. In addition to his two collections of dance criticism, *Looking at the Dance* (1949) and *Dancers, Buildings, and People in the Streets* (1965), he published three volumes of poetry, a novel, and six libretti—three originals and three adaptations.

BIBLIOGRAPHY

Ashton, Dore. *The New York School: A Cultural Reckoning.* New York, 1973.

Denby, Edwin. *Looking at the Dance.* New York, 1949.

Denby, Edwin. *Dancers, Buildings, and People in the Streets.* New York, 1965.

Denby, Edwin. *Collected Poems.* New York, 1975.

Denby, Edwin. *Dance Writings.* Edited by Robert Cornfield and William MacKay. New York, 1986.

ARLENE CROCE

DENISHAWN. A performing dance company and a dance school that existed in the United States from 1914 to 1931, Denishawn was an outgrowth of the marriage and performing partnership of the two American dancers Ruth St. Denis and Ted Shawn. Already famous as a solo dancer in the United States and Europe, St. Denis combined with Shawn in 1914 to form a dance company that always included at least one of them. It made some twenty-five tours of the United States, both in vaudeville and as concerts, until it was dissolved after their New York Lewisohn Stadium concert in the summer of 1931. The Denishawn school, begun in Los Angeles in 1915, was carried to New York by Shawn in 1921, flourished there with the development of a varied curriculum with national branches, and gradually phased out during the depression.

The performing entity, billed as "Ruth St. Denis, Ted Shawn and the Denishawn Dancers," was developed between 1914 and 1920. It began as a shakedown tour across the United States during the winter of 1914–1915, the two artists having married the previous August. A stop for the summer in Los Angeles in 1915, when the first Denishawn school was informally set up and dancers were recruited for performing, was followed by another tour back to New York. Floundering as a concert perform-

ing company without financial base, Denishawn in late May 1916 shortened concert numbers to "acts" and joined Keith's vaudeville circuit, a relationship that included a 1916–1917 tour. In those three seasons, the gradually recognizable Denishawn entity made some two hundred full-length theater performances, plus forty-six vaudeville stands (or weeks, with two, three, even four performances per day) in the United States and Canada. In addition, St. Denis, while her husband was in the army, made two more tours, one on the Orpheum and the other on the Pantages circuit, in 1918 and 1919. Growing out of St. Denis's solo career (international in extent), fed by Shawn's aesthetic (still naïve and local), and attracting developing artists—Louis Horst, Doris Humphrey, Martha Graham, Charles Weidman were all a part of Denishawn by 1920—Denishawn was St. Denis's show in the 1910s. Although other dancers were performing on the American stage at this time, including Anna Pavlova and Isadora Duncan, neither approached St. Denis's record in sheer coverage of the United States.

The dances presented included her old East Indian series (*The Spirit of Incense*, the *Cobras*, *Nautch*, *The Yogi* and *Radha*), solos taken from her full-evening works (*O-Mika* and *Egypta*), and her new works (*The Peacock*, *The Spirit of the Sea*, *Dance of Theodora* and *Dance of the Royal Ballet of Siam*). Shawn contributed nature studies, Christian religion rituals, pieces for students, and exhibition ballroom numbers. His mature works began to appear, such as *Japanese Spear Dance*, *Serenata Morisca*, and *Valse Directoire*. Collaborative works began with *The Garden of Kama* and the *Pageant of India, Greece and Egypt*, but up to 1920, Denishawn was largely carried by the St. Denis aesthetic: beautiful, exotic, romantic, with a clear message of spiritual value based on the assumption that dance could communicate a serious, uplifting message by means of movement.

Denishawn repertory during these formative years always remained in process. No dance ever really premiered; no one set form existed to be identified categorically. Long spectacles were taken apart and "arias" toured as short dances, or short studies were expanded into full spectacles. A series of dances were made into suites in one program or allowed to stand alone in another. In the 1910s, during which Denishawn performed mostly in vaudeville, the "act" generally lasted from twenty to twenty-five minutes and consisted of a dance mostly for St. Denis, whose personal presence carried it.

It was during the 1920s that Denishawn, composed of a performing company of dancers and a dance school of followers, spread from Los Angeles to New York and the Far East as well as England and operated as the entity historically remembered as Denishawn. As a company, it no longer performed in vaudeville but was presented by the national impresario Daniel Mayer in three concert tours of the United States. As vaudeville in the 1910s had carried Denishawn dancing to masses of people in large cities, the concert circuit in the early 1920s presented it to audiences in many small towns as well as metropolitan areas of the United States. The international impresario Asway Strok then carried it to the major cities of the Far East for fifteen months in 1925–1926, after which Arthur Judson presented new Denishawn dances made abroad in a cross-country tour from Los Angeles to New York from December 1926 to April 1927. The four concerts at Carnegic Hall that month marked Denishawn at the height of its powers as a performing unit. The subsequent Follies tour, 1927–1928, undertaken for the express purpose of earning enough money to build a permanent headquarters for the Denishawn school in New York City, began the disintegration of Denishawn. After the stock market crash of October 1929, the two artists could put together only short performing series, including a duet tour with a symphonic quartet in 1929–1930, or Shawn took some Denishawn Dancers and toured locally. In 1930

he went on his first solo tour to Germany, St. Denis picked up odd performances on the West Coast, and Denishawn touring was over.

Denishawn dance can best be described as romantic, combining the ethereal and the sentimental with local-color folk dance of myriad cultures. The dark side of life, the tragic, was omitted but not missed in Denishawn theater of the 1920s, for it was a dance accessible to new audiences, and it spread the appreciation of dance as an art form in a large way.

During the interval between 1919 and the first Mayer tour of 1922, St. Denis experimented with a kind of dance she called music visualizations. Costumed in simple tunics, her feet bare and her hair softly rolled, she danced choreography that mirrored selected music in melodic line, density, rhythm, and dynamics. No story was depicted, no national culture was suggested, no message was conveyed—other than the abstract musical concept visualized by moving dancers. The several dances that St. Denis made of this type were presented in a financially disastrous but critically successful tour in 1920 by her Ruth St. Denis Concert Dancers. These dances, augmented by Shawn (*Revolutionary Etude*, for example), became an important section of the first season of the Mayer tours. The group *Sonata Pathetique*, St. Denis's *Waltz* and *Liebestraum*, and the St. Denis and Humphrey *Soaring* for

DENISHAWN. Both Ruth St. Denis and Ted Shawn, a former divinity student, wished to embue their dances with spiritual significance. Often they placed themselves directly in the role of deity. *(left)* St. Denis as Guan Yin, the Chinese *bodhisattva* of mercy, in *White Jade*. *(right)* Ted Shawn as the Hindu deity Śiva Nāṭarāja (Shiva, Lord of the Dance), creator and destroyer of the universe. (Photographs from the archives at Jacob's Pillow, Becket, Massachussetts.)

five dancers gave a strong aesthetic base to Denishawn dance.

The first Mayer tour, in 1922–1923, carried these music visualizations, St. Denis' East Indian series, her Japanese *The Flower Arrangement,* and groups of dancers doing colorful nautches or St. Denis repeating her favorite solos, *The Peacock, The Spirit of the Sea, The Dance of Theodora, Greek Veil Plastique,* and *The Spirit of the Rose.*

Shawn's contribution to the first Mayer tour grew out of his earlier work in vaudeville, acts choreographed for Denishawn performers that were produced immediately following his stint in the army. Moved whole into the program of the Mayer tour was *Xochitl,* Shawn's first Native-American dance, choreographed for the fiery Martha Graham. She and Weidman, with Pauline Lawrence at the piano, had toured with *Xochitl* in vaudeville during 1921. Shawn also made *Spanish Suite,* extended St. Denis's *Siamese Suite,* and produced *divertissements* for company dancers—*Pierrot Forlorn* for Weidman, a trio to Carrie Jacobs Bond's *Betty's Music Box,* and two waltzes—as well as performed his strong solos (*Gnossienne* was especially striking) and his duet *Valse Directoire.* This combination was the romantic dance with the Denishawn aesthetic: austere music visualizations, ethereal St. Denis solos, vigorous Shawn solos, an exotic ethnic production number, and coy company pieces.

During the second Mayer tour, which ran from the beginning of October 1923 to 3 May 1924 with only five nights off, Denishawn came of age with souvenir programs, commissioned scores, major production numbers, and a large company of supporting dancers and production staff. Graham had moved to the Greenwich Village Follies, but Humphrey, on leave since the disastrous Ruth St. Denis Concert Dancers tour, returned to dance. Louis Horst still remained as musical director, having written music for some of the dances as well (this season's *Cuadro Flamenco* and *Flamenco Dances*). A Denishawn program had three parts: music visualizations, *divertissements,* and "Orientalia," St. Denis's and Shawn's presentations of their own versions of Oriental dances, presented by country: China, *Kuan Yin;* Crete, *Gnossienne;* India, *The Three Apsarases;* Siam (Thailand), *Siamese Ballet;* Japan, *Lantern Dance, Arranging the Flowers,* and *Servant and Parasol;* Java, *The Princess and the Demon;* and Egypt, *Egyptian Ballet. The Spirit of the Sea,* St. Denis's solo expanded into a drama, and *Xochitl,* danced by Graham's sister Geordie, remained in the program plus three new dance dramas, which filled the stage with drama and the souvenir program with color. St. Denis's *Ishtar* was based on Babylonian legend, Shawn's *Cuadro Flamenco* was Spanish, and *Feather of the Dawn* used original Hopi Indian costumes. Eclecticism and contrast—on the same program was Humphrey's music-less *Sonata Tragica*—were Denishawn trademarks during this second tour.

The souvenir program celebrated another aspect of Denishawn—its touted Americanism. Shawn called himself "American man dancer," St. Denis was advertised as the one who had led the dance away from the outworn traditions of the classic ballet (read "European"). Their dances were being inspired by themes indigenous to the American continent (Toltec, Hopi), their commissioned scores came from American composers, and their dancers, as their cameo photos showed, were strictly Anglo-Saxon. Like the decade in which they worked, they were positively American: "With this organization of dancers, American born and American trained, accompanied by music composed by American musicians, and with a repertoire of ballets the costumes and scenery for which have been designed by American artists, Miss St. Denis and Mr. Shawn expect in a few more years to tour the world, offering to the world America's contribution to the dance" (from the concluding lines of the souvenir program preface, "America and the Dance"). This posture would later come back at Shawn and St. Denis as antiminority, but in 1923 they were joined by their dancers in appealing to the large chauvinistic element of the American public of the 1920s.

The third Mayer tour carried essentially the same type of dance as had been developed in the previous two tours. Ensemble work by the "Denishawn Dancers" now had become equal in effect to the St. Denis mystical persona and the Shawn macho image. New music visualizations, often with Humphrey as focal point, were emphasized for these dancers. His pantomimic powers discovered and developed by Shawn in *Danse Américaine, The Crapshooter,* and *Pierrot Forlorn,* Weidman was also emerging as an artist out of Denishawn. Humphrey too was featured in solos, St Denis's *Scherzo Waltz* (dance with a hoop), Shawn's *Plasquinade,* and her own *Valse Caprice (Scarf Dance).* The major dance dramas from the previous season were repeated, with a new one, *The Vision of the Aissoua,* collaboratively choreographed by Shawn and St. Denis, adding Arabian themes to the Denishawn eclecticism, which was further enhanced by themes from Bali in *Balinese Fantasy,* a duet by Shawn for him and St. Denis—always the stars of Denishawn—and Shawn's impressions of North American historical dances in the five-part *American Sketches.* The scaled-down souvenir program stated: "The Denishawn Dancers being, in all essentials, the only actual American ballet, it is natural that this season's new creations should include themes of purely American inspiration."

The last years of the Denishawn company were spent touring the Asian countries of Japan, China, Burma, India, Ceylon, Malaya, Java, and the Philippines, followed by a tour of the United States to display the new dances that had been choreographed abroad. St. Denis and Shawn's controversial return to vaudeville in the 1927–1928 Follies tour, which led to the breakup of the

DENISHAWN. Members of the Denishawn ensemble c.1926 in *Cuadro Flamenco*, Shawn's vaudeville-style dance about a bull-fighter who woos a Spanish dancer by offering her a bundle of shawls. Ernestine Day and Charles Weidman stand in the center; at left are Ann Douglas, George Skares, and Doris Humphrey. Ruth Austin sits in the right-hand corner, and Ted Shawn, in a matador hat, leans forward. (Photograph by J. Walter Collinge; from the archives at Jacob's Pillow, Becket, Massachussetts.)

company when Humphrey and Weidman went off on their own (Horst had left in 1925), was the last extensive appearance of the Denishawn performing entity.

Research on the exact extent of the Denishawn school that underlay the Denishawn company has not been done, but presented as headed by the highly respected artist Ruth St. Denis, happily married to her artist husband Ted Shawn, it attracted middle-class children whose parents allowed them to come to dance in a controlled and uplifting environment. Being Denishawn, it was eclectic in its curriculum, proudly claiming that its system was to have no one system. A reassuringly middle-class organization,

Denishawn was instrumental in raising dance to a respected art in middle America.

In the 1970s, former Denishawn dancer Jane Sherman began publishing material about the dances, dance technique and philosophy of St. Denis and Shawn (see bibliography). Subsequently Sherman has recreated Denishawn dances for the Martha Graham Dance Company and others, especially the Denishawn Repertory Dancers (Michelle Mathesius, founder) who have toured in the United States and France.

[*See also the entries on St. Denis, Shawn, and the other principal figures mentioned herein.*]

BIBLIOGRAPHY

Brady, Susan, ed. *After the Dance: Documents of Ruth St. Denis and Ted Shawn.* Performing Arts Resources, vol. 20. New York, 1997.

Schlundt, Christena L. *The Professional Appearances of Ruth St. Denis and Ted Shawn: A Chronology and Index of Dances (1906–1932.* New York, 1962.

Schlundt, Christena L. *Into the Mystic. Dance Perspectives* 46 (Summer 1971).

Shawn, Ted, with Gray Poole. *One Thousand and One Night Stands.* New York, 1960.

Shelton, Suzanne. *Divine Dancer: A Biography of Ruth St. Denis.* Garden City, N.Y., 1981.

Sherman, Jane. *Soaring: The Diary and Letters of a Denishawn Dancer in the Far East, 1925–1926.* Middletown, Conn., 1976.

Sherman, Jane. *The Drama of Denishawn Dance.* Middletown, Conn., 1979.

Sherman, Jane. *Denishawn: The Enduring Influence.* Boston, Mass., 1983.

FILM AND VIDEOTAPE. "Denishawn Repertory Dancers Library of Videotapes" (1996)

ARCHIVE. Denishawn Collection and Ted Shawn Collection, New York Public Library for the Performing Arts. Jane Sherman Collection, New York Public Library for the Performing Arts. New Jersey Center Dance Collective, Trenton, N.J.

CHRISTENA L. SCHLUNDT

DENMARK. [*To survey the dance traditions of Denmark, this entry comprises four articles:*

> Traditional and Social Dance
> Dance in the Faeroe Islands
> Theatrical Dance
> Dance Research and Publication

For further discussion of theatrical dance, see entries on individual companies, choreographers, and dancers.]

Traditional and Social Dance

Danish medieval ballads mention dancing in connection with court festivities. The dances of the time were probably chain dances, in which the participants moved in a long line, linked hand to hand, accompanying themselves with songs. A similar tradition of song dance endures in the Faeroe Islands. The earliest recorded Danish ballad texts date from after 1550, and no tunes were collected until after 1800.

Early Danish dances also included singing games, some of which have survived to the present as children's games and in rural areas. Some folk dances performed to display individual athletic prowess also seem to be rooted in ancient times, and some dances still function as rituals.

An early mention of couple dances is in guild rules from about 1580, which mention penalties for indecent dancing and excessive turning and for unjustified performance of an introductory dance. This suggests the existence of a couple dance of two parts, perhaps with leaping and turning in the second part; such dances are known from elsewhere in Europe at this period. Dances performed at the Danish court in the sixteenth and seventeenth centuries seem to have been the same ones known at other European courts of the period.

In 1705 a book published in Glückstadt, *I. H. P. Maître de Danse, oder Tanz-meister,* described and gave music for the *menuet d'Anjou, passepied,* and *bourgogne.* The *polsk-*

dans (Polish dance) is mentioned in several eighteenth-century literary works; it was associated with the common people, often in a comical sense. About 1750 a writer named Holberg noted that complex dances such as the *rigaudon* and *folie d'Espagne* had gone out of fashion, replaced by minuets, English dances, and Polish dances.

The *polskdans* was probably a typical European couple dance with an introduction in duple meter, succeeded by a turning or leaping dance in triple meter. The term *engelskdans* (English dance) may have referred to both English longways country dances and French *contredanses;* a large repertory of both kinds of these contradances has survived in Denmark.

Several books and manuscripts from the late eighteenth century contain descriptions of dances and their music. Most are English longways country dances, but there are a few French *contredanses.* One collection is *Nye engelske danse* (New English Dances), with dance descriptions in Danish and French by the court ballet master Pierre Laurent. Another collection offers dance descriptions and music by Claus Schall, a composer, violinist, and dancer. During this period many dance teachers were also ballet masters in the theater.

DENMARK: Traditional and Social Dance. An illustration of two dancers performing the minuet, from Pierre Laurent's 1816 treatise *Vejledning ved Undervisning i Menuetten* (Guide to Instruction in the Minuet). This treatise demonstrates that the minuet, a court dance originating in eighteenth-century France, continued to be popular in Denmark in the nineteenth century. (The Theater Museum, Copenhagen.)

Stylized folk dances began to appear in ballets in the nineteenth century. Many of these dances passed from the theater to the social dance sphere through the teaching of the dancing masters, and some survived in dancing schools until the early twentieth century. The minuet and English country dances appear to have faded shortly after 1800, although teachers lamented the passing of the elegant minuet and tried to preserve it. The Baroque minuet, especially its step rhythm, has survived in the folk repertory.

Around 1830 the various contradances were replaced by a new version, the *contredanse française,* or *quadrille,* which consisted of figures such as Le Pantalon, L'Été, La Poule, and La Pastourelle, often performed *en suite* to music adapted from the popular stage. This dance was similar to the quadrilles of other European countries. From 1860 it appears in dance manuals coupled with the Lancers; the latter was especially popular and is still danced in Denmark.

The waltz *(vals)* came to Denmark about 1780 but was first incorporated in figures of contra dances. It was performed as an independent couple dance after 1800, when music books begin to include typical waltz melodies identified as such. Jørgen Gad Lund's *Terpsichore* (1823) describes several waltz variations, including the *Hopsa vals, Wiener vals, Russisk vals,* and *Tyroler vals;* the last was said to be the most graceful. The waltz became very popular and is an element of many folk figure dances.

Just after 1840 the polka was popularized in Denmark, largely through its theatrical use by the choreographer August Bournonville in Copenhagen. The first social polka was the *Pariserpolka,* with several figures, later simplified; it has survived as a folk dance. Over time the various polkas merged into a common form, with local variants.

Until the beginning of the twentieth century the models for social dancing were French. Many teachers of social dance came from the ballet, and others were educated at the military academy. Dancing schools had an important role in social life until the early twentieth century, when ballroom dances imported from England and America changed the nature of social dance. In earlier days the pupils were mostly children, but after the turn of the century the schools acquired a new clientele of adults eager to learn the new dances as a means to social success. Several associations of dancing teachers were formed—Danseringen in 1917 and Terpsichore in 1923. In 1951 the various Danish social dance associations united in Danse-organisationernes Fællersråd, which became a single organization in 1980.

From about 1920 the dancing schools taught primarily the new ballroom dances such as the one-step, two-step, tango, and English waltz as well as others that enjoyed short-lived popularity. A few nineteenth-century dances were maintained, especially for children. Gradually ball-

DENMARK: Traditional and Social Dance. Early nineteenth-century social dancers in Copenhagen performing an *engelskdans* (English country dance). Watercolor c.1807 by Johannes Senn. (Department of Prints and Drawings, Statens Museum for Kunst, Copenhagen. Photograph by Hans Peterson; used by permission.)

room dance teaching became uniform and governed by the international standards of medal tests and competitions; television has also contributed to the homogeneity of today's social dance.

Most of the existing descriptions of Danish folk dances were collected between 1900 and 1930. Systematic collection began in 1901 with the founding of Foreningen til Folkedansens Fremme (Association for the Promotion of Folk Dances), which published a series of booklets on folk dance and its music. In the following decades a number of folk dance societies sprang up all over Denmark; in 1929 they united as Danske Folkedansere (Danish Folk Dancers).

The revival of interest in folk dance early in the twentieth century was partly a reaction against the invasion of English and American social dances. In addition, at this time folk dance was introduced as an activity in youth leagues and folk high schools. Danish Folk Dancers began organizing courses for folk dance teachers. Today folk dance societies continue to offer courses for folk dancers and folk fiddlers, as well as yearly festivals. This activity has brought a certain uniformity to the performance of Danish folk dances, and distinctions among local styles have diminished.

The Association for the Promotion of Folk Dance published about eight hundred descriptions of dances, with their music; many are variants of a few main types. Nearly all are social couple dances, but there are a few competitive exhibition dances for men. In addition to the dances performed to instrumental music, there are many singing games characterized by pantomime.

DENMARK: Traditional and Social Dance. Watchful chaperons observe young performers at a 1950s end-of-season ball in Copenhagen. (Photograph courtesy of Henning Urup.)

Many of the dances to instrumental accompaniment are figure dances for a number of couples, especially contradances for sets of two or four couples. Their structure is the same as that of old French *contredanses*. The introductory figure, which varies in each repetition of the dance, may be a Grand Round (circle by all or some dancers), swinging in couples, or a Moulinet (Turning Star; lit., "windmill"). A refrain follows, with different figures performed by all the dancers simultaneously or by alternating pairs of couples.

There are many dances in which the dancers face each other in two lines and progress as in English longways country dances. In other dances the couples form a circle; many have a chain figure resulting in an exchange of partners. There are also couple dances consisting of series of figures.

Danish folk dance tunes are dominated by major tonality in tones of the tonic triad; most melodies are constructed of two to four symmetrical eight-measure phrases. The most common instrument used is the violin, which often reinforces the tune by playing on open strings with simple stops. An ensemble often includes two or more violins, along with clarinet or flute; a bass instrument may be added.

Local folk dance traditions survive in some parts of Denmark. The island of Fanø off southwestern Jutland has two couple dances that include a turning figure; the dancers alternate between this and an introductory figure. The step in this turning figure is known elsewhere in Denmark as the *polonaise* and is used in Norwegian regional dances, the *springar* and *pols*. The step is performed clockwise in triple meter, but in Fanø it is usually performed to music in duple meter. In one of the two Fanø dances the introductory figure is a procession; in the other, it consists of turning counterclockwise in place. Living folk dance traditions elsewhere in Denmark are limited to simple figure dances and couple dances of the waltz and polka types.

In recent years several new dance and music societies have arisen and united as Folkemusikhusringen (Circle of Folk Music Houses). Their goal is to reconnect living local traditions of music, dance, song, and storytelling into the larger fabric of social life. Their teaching emphasizes young people learning from elders. Their repertory is less extensive than that of the older associations, but their performances use more varied music.

Social dance schools today in Denmark focus on modern ballroom dances of both the standard and Latin repertories. Beyond the schools, however, people dance at private parties and in nightclubs, where dancing follows no set rules.

[*For more general discussion, see* European Traditional Dance.]

BIBLIOGRAPHY

Allenby Jaffe, Nigel, and Margaret Allenby Jaffe. *Denmark.* Skipton, 1987.

Aschengreen, Erik. "Tradition og kamp for fornyelse." In *Dansk teater i 60'erne og 70'erne,* edited by Stig J. Jensen et al. Teatervidenskabelige Studier, 8. Copenhagen, 1982.

Aschengreen, Erik, and Henning Urup. "Dance Research in Denmark." *Dance Research Journal* 27.1 (Spring 1995): 73–75.

Christensen, Anders. "Menuettraditioner på Randersegnen." *Meddelelser fra Dansk Dansehistorisk Arkiv* 12 (1993): 5–14.

Christensen, Anders, et al. "Gammeldanseforeninger i Danmark." *Meddelelser fra Dansk Dansehistorisk Arkiv* 4 (1985): 45–60.

Engberg, Harald. *Pantomimeteatret.* Copenhagen, 1959.

Holm, Ralph, and Klaus Vedel. *Folkedansen i Danmark.* Copenhagen, 1946.

Ibsen, Bjarne, and Jytte Kristensen, eds. *Sportsdans—i takt og utakt.* Copenhagen, 1994.

Koudal, Jens Henrik. "Ethnomusicology and Folk Music Research in Denmark and the Faeroe Islands." *Yearbook for Traditional Music* 25 (1993): 100–125.

Nørlyng, Ole, and Anders Christensen. "The Polka in Denmark." *Meddelelser fra Dansk Dansehistorisk Arkiv* 1 (1981).

Nørlyng, Ole. "Ti år for dansen." *Meddelelser fra Dansk Dansehistorisk Arkiv* 10 (1991): 5–13.

Schiørring, Nils. *Musikkens historie i Danmark.* 3 vols. Copenhagen, 1977–1978.

Schomacker, Judy Ryslander. "Folkelige dansemiljøer i Køben-havn." *Meddelelser fra Dansk Dansehistorisk Arkiv* 10 (1991): 20–30.

Torp, Lisbet, and Anca Giurchescu. "Folk Dance Collections and Folk Dance Research in Denmark and the Faeroe Islands." *Yearbook for Traditional Music* 25 (1993): 126–135.

Urup, Henning. "Spillemandsmusik og folkedans i Danmark omkring 1979: Vilkårenes indflydelse." In *Nordisk musik och musikvetenskap under 1970–talet,* edited by Anders Carlsson and Jan Ling. Göteborg, 1980.

Urup, Henning. "Dancing Schools in Denmark: Historical Dance." *Meddelelser fra Dansk Dansehistorisk Arkiv* 1 (1981).

Urup, Henning. "Dance Research in Denmark." *Dance Studies* 7 (1983): 7–20.

Urup, Henning. "Danseskolevirksomhed i Danmark før og nu." *Nordisk Forening for Folkedansforskning, Brev* 10 (1987): 4–7.

Urup, Henning, et al, eds. *Gammaldans i Norden.* Trondheim, Norway, 1988.

Urup, Henning, ed. "Rapport om projektet Vals i Danmark." *Meddelelser fra Dansk Dansehistorisk Arkiv* 7 (1988): 14–49.

Urup, Henning. "Finkultur og folkekultur danser arm i arm." *Humariora* 2 (1989): 28–30.

Urup, Henning. "Bidrag til en systematisk bibliografi for dans i Danmark—1980–94." *Meddelelser fra Dansk Dansehistorisk Arkiv* 14 (1995): 17–26.

ARCHIVE. Danish Dance History Archive, Copenhagen.

HENNING URUP

Dance in the Faeroe Islands

The Faeroe Islands, now part of the commonwealth of Denmark, were originally settled from Norway (with some Celtic influence); they remained under Danish rule after Norway left the commonwealth in 1814. Although small in population, these islands occupy a special niche in dance history. Here, more than anywhere else, the practice of dancing while chanting epic ballads has remained a living tradition, providing a glimpse into the original function and importance of this type of dance. Faeroese dance has served as a model for the reconstruction of similar dances in neighboring countries, especially Norway. The ballad dance remains the predominant dance form in the Faeroes and is simply called "Faeroese dance." That such distinctive and ancient dance traditions, exisiting alongside layers of several centuries of later social dances, should be fully alive in the Faeroe Islands puts the locale in a special position for scholars of traditional dance.

As a center of North Sea fishing, the Faeroes have had cultural exchanges with neighboring countries, which have led to the importation of various social dances now viewed as folk dances. These are locally termed "English dances," designating all dances done to instrumental music, including couple dances not actually of English origin. In addition, the Faeroes have a third genre, dance games; many of these correspond to singing games found in other parts of Scandinavia, but a number are unique to the islands.

The Faeroese dance is a simple chain dance in which the participants hold hands tightly and form a close chain or ring. The dance begins with the leader and a few others who take the floor and begin dancing. Gradually more dancers find places in the chain, and when enough have joined, the chain is closed into a ring. If the ring becomes too big, the leader or another dancer can break it and form internal loops, eventually filling all the floor space. The step motif is simple but precise. The same general pattern is found in many European folk dances, raising questions about the diffusion or spontaneous generation of dance patterns.

All evidence indicates that the Faeroese dance is one of the the oldest extant dance types. The first written mention of the dance dates from 1616, when the Icelander Jón Olafsson landed in the Faeroes in the service of King Christian IV. The Faeroese dance is probably even older than that. It is clearly related to medieval dances found in records throughout Europe; for example, Arbeau's 1588 description of the *branle* is virtually identical to the Faeroese dance in form and step motif. [*See* Faeroe Step.]

Gatherings to perform the Faeroese dance remain common, and it is a part of larger weddings. Since World War II, a number of dance societies have been founded expressly to maintain the Faeroese dance. These, however, do not resemble the usual folk dance clubs in other countries, where dance training is the chief concern. In meaning and function the dance is too different from the later folk repertory to be performed on the same programs; it is still viable enough that it can be done without special training, however.

Many scholars have written on the Faeroese dance. The work of the Danish musicologist Hjalmar Thuren, *Folkesangen på Færoerne* (Copenhagen, 1908), remains the main source.

Dancing to instrumental music is not new in the Faeroes. In *Indberetninger fra en Reise i Færoe, 1781 og 1782*, J. C. Svabo already could write, "At important weddings and merriments, especially in Tórshavn, the Faroese dance is phasing somewhat into disuse, and in its place, Minuets, Polish dances, English and Scottish Reels and Contredances are being introduced." In some of the larger towns where many foreign, especially Norwegian, fishing boats called, music traditions were also adopted from abroad, but in the Faeroese villages instrumental music was practically unknown and has remained so in many places to the present day.

Dance games and singing games are not easily traced through history. From the oldest written sources, scholars have found descriptions and texts which suggest singing games, but evidence of links to current singing games is thin. Only in the sixteenth and seventeenth centuries did glimpses of individual types emerge. Nevertheless, there are reasonable grounds to believe that these dances are quite old and have probably always been performed together with the ballad dance.

[*For related discussion, see also* European Traditional Dance, *overview article. For discussion of Faeroese ballads, see* Folk Dance History.]

BIBLIOGRAPHY

Allenby Jaffe, Nigel, and Margaret Allenby Jaffe. *Denmark*. Skipton, 1987.
Holm, Rurik, and K. Vedel. *Folkedansen i Danmark*. Copenhagen, 1946.
Koudal, Jens Henrik. "Ethnomusicology and Folk Music Research in Denmark and the Faeroe Islands." *Yearbook for Traditional Dance* 24 (1993): 100–125.
Torp, Lisbet, and Anca Giurchescu. "Folk Dance Collections and Folk Dance Research in Denmark and the Faeroe Islands." *Yearbook for Traditional Music* 24 (1993): 126–135.
Urup, Henning, et al. *Gammaldans i Norden*. Trondheim, Norway, 1988.

WILLIAM C. REYNOLDS
with Egil Bakka

Theatrical Dance

The Royal Danish Ballet has always held the predominant position among dance companies in Denmark. Few independent dance enterprises have been able to survive for

long. Before the first Danish-language theater opened in 1722, when the seeds for the Royal Danish Ballet were sown, there had existed a tradition of Danish court ballets.

As early as King Frederick II, who ruled from 1559 to 1588, dance was a favorite pastime at court, where troupes of dancers and mummers, especially of English origin, entertained. The true *ballet de cour* was introduced to Denmark by Christian IV (ruled 1588–1648), who on the occasion of a royal wedding in 1634 presented a ballet by Alexandre Kuckelsom at court. Danish court ballet reached its peak during the reign of Frederick III (ruled 1648–1670), whose queen, Sophie Amalie, was a ballet enthusiast, herself performing in them. During the first years of Frederick III's reign, the Frenchman Daniel Pilloy came to Copenhagen as court dancing master. Pilloy was the first in a long line of foreign artists who have dominated Danish theatrical dance throughout its history. Frederick's successors, Christian V (ruled 1670–1699) and Frederick IV (ruled 1699–1730), were more interested in drama and opera but nonetheless also sponsored dancers at court. In 1663 Copenhagen got its first theater, which, in its short existence, received many visiting companies. The king had his own theater at the palace, and an Italian opera company had its own theater for a short while as well. Dancing was performed on all these stages.

The development of dance led to the founding of the first Danish-language theater, which opened in Grønnegade in 1722, closed a few years later, and, in 1748, reopened in Kongens Nytorv. From 1767 on, the Kongens Nytorv troupe frequently competed with dancers at the new Hof (or Court) Theater (now maintained as a theatrical museum). As early as the 1600s, troupes of German actors had staged pantomimes in Denmark with characters from the *commedia dell'arte*. Italian and French dancers performed harlequinades and pantomimes at the Grønnegade theater and later at the Royal Theater (the formal name of the Kongens Nytorv theater after 1772). At the beginning of the nineteenth century, members of the Italian Casorti family and the English Price family, the two families of artists who founded the only Danish dance tradition besides the Royal Danish Ballet, arrived in Denmark.

Pasquale Casorti and his troupe arrived in 1800; his son, Giuseppe Casorti (1749–1826), a renowned portrayer of Pierrot—his portrayal of the character displayed the same characteristics as those still seen in performances at the Pantomime Theater in Tivoli—remained in Copenhagen and joined forces with the Prices. James Price (1761–1826), founder of the Price dynasty in Denmark, belonged to a family of English artistic equestrians. He visited Denmark for the first time in 1795, when he performed at Dyrehavsbakken, an amusement park outside of Copenhagen.

In addition to the Prices, who obtained their own theater in Copenhagen, the Englishman Joseph L. Lewin and the Italian Philippo Pettoletti also performed in Copenhagen, where—frequently in competition with each other and with much family strife—they developed the repertory and style that would become the basis of the Pantomime Theater in Tivoli (founded in 1843), where Niels Henrik Volkersen (1830–1893) in particular gained prominence as Tivoli's great, popular Pierrot. At Tivoli's Pantomime Theater, the Italian *commedia dell'arte* acquired a special Danish presentation as well as a tradition influenced by August Bournonville's ballet art, with its strong Biedermeier flavor—its emphasis on harmony. The Bournonville influence may also be related to mime artists in the nineteenth century being replaced by ballet performers in the twentieth century.

Ballet dancers began appearing at the theater in Tivoli as early as the 1860s—for example, Léontine and Fanny Carey, daughters of Gustave Carey, Bournonville's pupil. Adeline Genée also danced at the Pantomime Theater, in 1893, and in the twentieth century the ballet became even stronger, often with close ties to the Royal Danish Ballet. Poul Huld, a ballet dancer at the Royal Theater, headed the Pantomime Theater from 1911 to 1956. His successor, Niels Bjørn Larsen, was ballet master at the Pantomime Theater from 1956 to 1980 while at the same time being engaged at the Royal Danish Ballet as a character dancer and, during part of that period, as ballet master. Succeeding Larsen was Erik Bidsted, who had a lengthy career as dancer and choreographer at the Pantomime Theater, which he headed from 1980 to 1983. Palle Jacobsen, principal dancer with the Royal Danish Ballet, was ballet master in Tivoli from 1983 to 1993; he was succeeded by another principal from the Royal Theater, Flemming Ryberg. The theater has a permanent staff of pantomime artists and a changing roster of ballet dancers. The dance careers of Egon Madsen and Helgi Thomasson were launched at the theater around 1960.

With the exception of the Pantomime Theater, it has been difficult for a ballet master to break through in Denmark except through the Royal Danish Ballet. Birger Bartholin made an attempt in 1940 with the New Danish Ballet, which had a brief but noteworthy existence, and Niels Bjørn Larsen, Frank Schaufuss, and Else Knipschildt also experimented with small groups. Since 1960, there have been some notable successes in group theater despite the continuing difficulty of finding work outside the Royal Theater. In 1960, for example, Elsa-Marianne von Rosen and Allan Fridericia created the Scandinavian Ballet, which was intended to be a traveling ballet theater. Von Rosen choreographed her own ballets, and the work that the company started with the staging of *La Sylphide* in 1960 and *Holiday in Albano* in 1961 was influential in forming the present attitude toward the Bournonville tradition. The company was dissolved in 1966.

Also during the 1960s the new dance appeared in Denmark, inspired not only by modern dance but by the group theater movement as well. Among those active in the new dance was choreographer and dancer Eske Holm, who left the Royal Theater and in the mid-1970s created a dance group that, like others, had to struggle economically. Prominent among the pioneers of new dance in Denmark were the women's group Living Movement, formed in 1971, and Billedstofteatret (roughly translated as the Image Theater), which beginning in 1977 tried to break down the ordinary separations between art forms in an attempt to give dance theater a new shape. All these groups have since disbanded.

It is typical of theatrical dance in Denmark that during the early 1980s the new dance initiative was taken predominantly by foreign dancers who had settled in Denmark. This is a traditional trend in that from its very be-

DENMARK: Theatrical Dance. August Bournonville's *La Sylphide* (1836) is still a favorite in the repertory of the Royal Danish Ballet. In the company's 1979/80 season, Arne Villumsen appeared as James with Lis Jeppesen as the Sylphide. (Photograph by John R. Johnsen; used by permission.)

DENMARK: Theatrical Dance. Anna Lærkesen, a former principal of the Royal Danish Ballet widely acclaimed for her interpretation of the title role in *La Sylphide*, has created several of her own ballets. Here, Silja Schandorff and Nikolaj Hübbe appear in Lærkesen's *Partita* (1990). (Photograph © 1990 by David Amzallag; used by permission.)

aspirants in the company. The technical training is exclusively classical; academic subjects and ballet history are also taught. In 1985 the state began to support the House of Dance in Copenhagen, a center for the training of professional dancers outside the main company. There are many private dance schools as well. In 1992 Dansescenen, a stage for modern dance was established; and state support for modern dance education began that year.

[*See also* Royal Danish Ballet.]

BIBLIOGRAPHY

Aschengreen, Erik. "Tradition og kamp for fornyelse." In *Dansk teater i 60'erne og 70'erne*, edited by Stig J. Jensen et al. Teatervidenskabelige Studier, 8. Copenhagen, 1982.

Aschengreen, Erik, et al., eds. *Dance in Denmark*. Copenhagen, 1991.

Engberg, Harald. *Pantomimeteatret*. Copenhagen, 1959.

Flindt, Vivi, and Knud Arne Jürgensen, eds. *Bournonville Ballet Technique: Fifty Enchainements*. London, 1992.

Hallar, Marianne, and Alette Scavenius, eds. *Bournonvilleana*. Translated by Gaye Kynoch. Copenhagen, 1992.

Jürgensen, Knud Arne, ed. *The Bournonville Ballets: A Photographic Record, 1844–1933*. London, 1987.

Jürgensen, Knud Arne, and Ann Hutchinson Guest, eds. *The Bournonville Heritage: A Choreographic Record, 1829–1875*. London, 1990.

ERIK ASCHENGREEN

Dance Research and Publication

In Denmark and the other Nordic countries the study of folk dance is done apart from the study of theatrical dance. The central organization is the Nordisk Forening for Folkedansforskning (Nordic Society for Research in Folk Dance), founded in 1977 at a meeting held in the Dance Museum in Stockholm. The society, which has a board composed of members from each of the Nordic countries (Denmark, Finland, Iceland, Norway, and Sweden) as well as from the Faeroe Islands, has published a newsletter every year since 1978. In 1983 it published *Folkedanslitteratur i Norden* (Literature about Folk Dance in Nordic Countries), a bibliography that uses a system similar to that in Kurt Petermann's *Tanzbibliographie*. The society also has an ongoing project on the creation of an inter-Nordic terminology to describe and analyze Nordic folk dances, and it has completed research on *gammeldansformer* ("old dance forms") such as the waltz, the mazurka, the schottische, the *rheinlænder* (a German polka), and other dance forms, some of which arrived in the Nordic countries in the nineteenth century.

Another folk dance group, the Study Group for Ethnochoreology, under the International Council for Traditional Music, has as members four well-known scholars who work and live in Denmark: Anca Giurchesco, William C. Reynolds, Henning Urup, and Lisbet Torp, who wrote her 1990 doctoral dissertation, "Chain and Round Dance Problems," about structures in dance. These scholars have, among other things, expertise in notation, which

ginning, theatrical dance in Denmark has relied on inspiration from abroad, though subsequently it began to be adapted to take on a more specifically Danish expression. The new dance dancers in Denmark were the Swede Nanna Nilson and the Americans Cher Geurtze, Ann Crosset, and Warren Spears as well as the Norwegian Randi Patterson, who, along with Spears, founded, in 1982, the New Danish Dance Theater, the most professional and effectual alternative to the Royal Danish Ballet.

Since the mid-1950s Danish television also has done a great deal to promote ballet in Denmark. It has collaborated closely with the Royal Danish Ballet with respect to both dancers and choreographers but has also imported emerging choreographers from abroad for inclusion in special productions on Danish television.

In the area of education and training, the school of the Royal Danish Ballet was founded in 1771 by the French dancer Pierre Laurent. Students are admitted by audition and attend school until age sixteen, when they become

will be of great importance for future dance studies in Denmark. Because Giurchesco and Reynolds are foreigners, they bring important research traditions to complement those of Denmark.

Theatrical Dance. Much of the research on Danish theatrical dance centers on the work of August Bournonville, the most famous Danish ballet master. When, in 1972, the Institute for Theatre Research of the University of Copenhagen published *Theatre Research Studies II*, a series of articles in English, scholarly interest in Bournonville and his work began in earnest.

However, although music scholar Nils Schiørring wrote about Bournonville and his composers in *Theatre Research Studies II*, proper research on ballet—its history, its stage movements, and the interactions of ballet masters, choreographers, and composers—did not start until 1979, when Ole Nørlyng received a scholarship to study and teach ballet music at the University of Copenhagen. Nørlyng wrote several articles about the music in Bournonville's ballets; he also wrote the music chapters in Erik Aschengreen's *Balletbogen* (The Ballet Guide; 1982), the second Danish ballet guide to be published. (The first, published in 1954, was written by Svend Kragh-Jacobsen, a self-taught dance critic who also wrote several important dance histories.) Most important, Nørlyng put his knowledge at the disposal of professional theater people such as Peter Schaufuss, Toni Lander, Bruce Marks, Flemming Ryberg, Kirsten Ralov, Flemming Flindt, and Elsa-Marianne von Rosen, who, when staging Bournonville, came to him for information about the music. This linking of scholarly studies and live theater is not common in Denmark. Scholars have also assisted both Elsa-Marianne von Rosen and Peter Schaufuss in their productions of *La Sylphide*, *Napoli*, and *A Folk Tale*, Bournonville's three great Romantic ballets.

Several other scholarly works on Bournonville have been published. Theater historian Torben Krogh researched, taught, and wrote about the court ballet in Denmark as well as the eighteenth-century ballets of Vincenzo Galeotti and other Italian and French ballet masters who worked in Denmark. Krogh also co-wrote, with Kragh-Jacobsen, *Den Kongelige Danske Ballet* (1952), which, though not a complete scholarly work, still forms the backbone of the study of the history of the Royal Danish Ballet. In the late 1970s Birthe Johansen, a student of Krogh's, was employed at the Institute for Theatre Research to work on a project about Bournonville and the social condition of dancers in the nineteenth century. Her results were never fully published, but some of them can be found in *Perspektiv på Bournonville* (Perspective on Bournonville, 1980). Erik Aschengreen has published a series of books and articles on the Romantic ballet and on Bournonville. A few of these articles, "The Beautiful Dancer" (in *Dance Perspectives* 58 [1974]) and

"Bournonville: Yesterday, Today, and Tomorrow" (in *Dance Chronicle* 3, no. 2 [1979]), have been published in English. (In 1986 Aschengreen published, in English, *Jean Cocteau and the Dance*, the first Danish doctoral dissertation about dance.)

Foreign scholars interested in Bournonville also have contributed to the expansion of Bournonville research, and some source material is now available outside Denmark, in English. Patricia McAndrew's English translation of Bournonville's biography, *Mit Teaterliv*, titled *My Theater Life*, was published in 1979. She also translated Bournonville's ballet libretti in a series of articles for *Dance Chronicle*.

In 1979 Kirsten Ralov published, in New York, the so-called Bournonville schools, a training system established by Bournonville's pupils in the 1890s. The steps were notated in Benesh, Labanotation, and French terminology; a series of recordings of the music that went with the classes was published as well. The Bournonville system was the only training system for the Royal Danish Ballet until 1930, and it continues to be used by the Royal Theater, though not as its only system. In 1967 the six classes were presented on Danish television in a series by Elvi Henriksen, Allan Fridericia, Hans Brenaa, and members of the Royal Danish Ballet.

The first publication to date that focuses in depth on the Bournonville style is Erik Bruhn and Lillian Moore's *Bournonville and Ballet Technique: Studies and Comments on August Bournonville's Études Chorégraphiques* (1961). Another source is the oral history project that Tobi Tobias of New York carried out over a period of six to seven years during the 1980s. Danish dancers of all generations were interviewed about the style, the training, and the tradition. Completed tapes are housed in the Royal Theater in Copenhagen and as part of the Harvard Theater Collection. In 1985 and 1986 five dancers and mimes from the Royal Danish Ballet and two Danish and two American scholar-critics came together over a two-week period at the Bournonville Summer Academy in Midland, Michigan, where dancers, scholars, and dance students met to exchange ideas. The Summer Academy continued in Copenhagen until 1992.

Reconstruction of Bournonville Ballets. The Bournonville centennial in 1979 marking the one hundredth anniversary of Bournonville's death was in many ways a turning point for dance scholarship in Denmark. International interest in Denmark's national dance heritage was tremendously gratifying, but the success presented a challenge for the Royal Danish Ballet. How should the tradition be preserved for the future? How could the performances be renewed without betraying the original style? Reconstruction was seen as one way of preserving dance traditions in Denmark, and dance scholars have since been involved in the reconstruction of old, forgotten Bournonville dances and entire ballets. Toward this end they have used Bournonville's own notations, which can be found in various archives, especially in the Royal Library in Copenhagen.

Knud Arne Jürgensen, librarian at the Royal Library, has reconstructed a number of Bournonville dances and has staged them in Denmark, France, and the former Soviet Union. He has also published several books with material from his work with the Bournonville soloists such as dancer Dinna Bjørn, who created a new repertory for the group of Bournonville soloists from the Royal Danish Ballet. They have performed at home and abroad since 1976. Flemming Ryberg, Toni Lander, and Bruce Marks reconstructed Bournonville's 1855 ballet *Abdallah* for Ballet West in Utah in 1985.

Jürgensen has published a few articles about his work in *Dance Chronicle*, but more scholarly discussion of the problems of reconstruction is needed between artists and scholars. More discussion of the relationship and the delicate balance between faithfulness to tradition and the demands of the living theater also is needed.

Contemporary Scholarship. Until the late twentieth century, the subject of dance—aesthetics, history, and so on—was not regularly taught at the Institute for Theatre Research, though periodic seminars on dance—on ballet in particular—were held over the years. Interest in dance as a scholarly field has grown, however, as indicated by the fact that students from various related fields, such as music and theater, have written master's theses on dance topics. As a result of this growing interest in dance, in 1989 the faculty for the humanities at the University of Copenhagen instituted an educational program on the history and aesthetics of dance. It was expanded in 1996. The program coordinates interdisciplinary study among the Institute for Theatre Research, the Institute for Nordic Philology, and the Institute for Music as well as with teachers and scholars from outside the university. The program, made up of four courses, may be built into a five-year master of arts program in the humanities focused on theater, music, literature, and other arts.

Given that as yet there is no center for dance scholarship in Denmark and little education in the field, it is understandable that some of the best Danish critics and scholars have worked on an individual basis. Most of these independent researchers are self-taught, as are most of the few university-based scholars in other fields who have devoted themselves to dance research. A good deal of research has been conducted on theatrical dance in Denmark, and a handful of scholars have published a series of works that can form the basis for further studies, but these efforts have been scattered and somewhat desultory. Detailed studies of individual dancers and ballets must be undertaken before the history of the ballet in Denmark can be fully understood. With an expanding university program, younger scholars and critics may well bring dance study to serious recognition.

ERIK ASCHENGREEN

DESCOMBEY, MICHEL (born 28 October 1930 in Bois-Colombes, near Paris), French dancer, ballet master, and choreographer. Michel Descombey began his dance studies at the Paris Opera Ballet School in 1942, when he was eleven years old. He joined the company in 1947, at age sixteen, as a member of the corps de ballet, rising through the soloist ranks to become *premier danseur de caractère* in 1959. His best roles were in Harald Lander's production of *Les Caprices de Cupidon* (1952)—a revival of Vincenzo Galeotti's 1786 classic, *The Whims of Cupid and the Ballet Master*—and in Serge Lifar's *Daphnis et Chloë* (1958). In 1960 he had great success as the Buffoon in Vladimir Burmeister's production of *Swan Lake* and in featured roles in Gene Kelly's *Pas des Dieux* and Harald Lander's *Qaartsiluni*.

Descombey began choreographing with *Les Frères Humains* (1953) for a charity performance. It was presented at the Opéra-Comique in 1958. This was followed by *Le Clouchard* (1959), *Scaramouche* and *Les Baladins* (both 1960), and *Cláirière* (1961). In 1962, for the newly founded Ballet National Jeunesses Musicales de France, Descombey created *Piccolo et Mandolines*, to music by Antonio Vivaldi, and for the Paris Opera Ballet he choreographed *Symphonie Concertante*, to music by the Swiss composer Frank Martin. As danced by Madeleine Lafon and Francine Souard, *Piccolo et Mandolines* was highly praised for its humor and lightness.

The success of these early works led the new director of the Paris Opera, Georges Auric, to name Descombey ballet master and principal choreographer in 1962. In subsequent years, Descombey mounted *But* (1963), to music by Jacques Casterede; *Sarracenia* (1964), to music by Béla Bartók; a new production of *Coppélia* (1966); a new production of *Bacchus et Ariane* (1967), to music by Albert Roussel; and *Zyklus* (1968), to music by Karlheinz Stockhausen. *Zyklus* had already been performed by his own group, Ballet-Studio de l'Opéra, which had been formed to tour various cultural centers in France.

Descombey left the Paris Opera in 1969, but he returned in 1970 to create *Spectacle Berio*, three ballets set to music by Luciano Berio: *Sequenza*, *Visage*, and *Laborintus*. For Ballet-Théâtre Contemporain, he choreographed *Déserts* (1968), to music by Edgard Varèse; a part of *Hymnen* (1970), a collaborative work to music by Stockhausen; and *ES, le 8ème Jour* (1973), also set to music by Stockhausen. For the Tokyo Ballet Company he set *Mandala* (1970), to music by Toshirō Mayuzumi, and for the Zurich Ballet, which he directed from 1971 to 1973, he set

The Miraculous Mandarin (1971), to the Bartók score, and *Messe en Jazz* (1972), to music by Lalo Schifrin.

In 1972, Descombey began working for Ballet Teatro del Espacio, formerly the Ballet Independiente de México, and in 1977 he was appointed its associate director and chief choreographer. Ballets created for that company include *Ano Cero* (1975), *Dialogo* (1978), *La Opera Descuartizada* (1980), and *Pavana para un Amor Muerto* (1985).

BIBLIOGRAPHY

Bourcier, Paul. "Danser aujourd'hui." In Bourcier's *Histoire de la danse en Occident*. Paris, 1978.

Delgado Martínez, César. "Michel Descombey." *Niestro danza*, no. 6 (March 1990).

Hersin, André-Philippe. "Michel Descombey." *Saisons de la danse*, no. 136 (1981).

Nussac, Sylvie de. "Michel Descombey." *Musica disques* (June 1959).

Ruégger, Emmanuèle. "La danse contemporain en Suisse alémanique." *Danser* (October 1991): 22–24.

MONIQUE BABSKY
Translated from French

DESHAYES, ANDRÉ (André Jean-Jacques Deshayes; born 24 January 1777 in Paris, died 9 December 1846 in Les Batignolles, Paris), French dancer and choreographer. Deshayes, a member of a French theatrical family, was a dancer during the late eighteenth and early nineteenth centuries. He retired early, "at the peak of his powers" (Guest, 1980), and thereafter devoted most of his time to teaching and choreography. Almost all of his choreography was produced in London rather than in Paris, the city of his birth. In his later years he collaborated with Jules Perrot on two of Perrot's earliest works for Her Majesty's Theatre, but he did not survive to see the end of the Romantic period.

Deshayes's father, Jacques-François, was the ballet master of the Comédie Française and the director of the ballet schools of the Comédie and the Paris Opera. André entered the Paris Opera ballet school in 1788 and danced children's roles in the 1790s. He joined the company in 1794 and was named a principal dancer in 1795. He danced in the ballets of Pierre and Maximilien Gardel, who were then in power at the Paris Opera. Among his roles in Pierre's ballets were Zephyr in *Le Jugement de Pâris* and L'Hymen in *Psyché*. He also danced in Maximilien's *Le Déserteur*.

In 1799 Deshayes obtained leave from the Opera to appear in Lisbon and Madrid, and again in 1800 to dance in London, a city to which he was to devote a considerable part of his career. He made his London debut on 11 January 1800 in James Harvey D'Egville's revival of Jean Dauberval's *Les Jeux d'Églé*, presented at the King's Theatre.

Deshayes again left the Paris Opera in 1802 with his wife, Elisabeth Duchemin, to dance at La Scala in Milan. After two years there they went to London, where they were engaged as principal dancers at the King's Theatre. Deshayes retained this position until 1811, his wife until 1810. A souvenir of his achievements at this time is a print after a drawing by François Huet-Villiers, depicting a pose from D'Egville's ballet *Achille et Déidamie* (1804). Deshayes, who danced the role of Achilles, is shown in female disguise, held aloft by D'Egville as Ulysses. The print has sometimes been mistaken for a male-female pas de deux.

In 1810 and 1811 Deshayes's performing career was enlivened by his rivalry with Armand Vestris, son of the famous Auguste. Armand, who reportedly lacked the elegance and taste of his illustrious father, danced the bolero in Deshayes's restaging of Louis-Antoine Duport's *Figaro* (1811), in which Deshayes himself took part.

Deshayes staged four ballets at the King's Theatre between 1806 and 1811: *Figaro*; *La Dansomanie* (1806) and *Psyché* (1810), both staged with choreography by Pierre Gardel; and *L'Enlèvement d'Adonis* (1807), which appears to have been Deshayes's own work. This last was danced to music by Frédéric Venua, who also composed the scores of Deshayes's versions of *Psyché* and *Figaro*.

In 1815 Deshayes danced in Vienna in the ballets of Jean-Louis Aumer; he also danced in Germany and Naples. He was recalled to London in 1821 by John Ebers, who had just become the manager of the King's Theatre and wanted to improve the ballet. Deshayes was named ballet master; his company included the Paris Opera stars Lise Noblet and Monsieur Albert. His first ballet of the season was *Le Prix, ou L'Offrande de Terpsichore* (10 March), in which Noblet danced Terpsichore and Albert the role of Tymante. Ebers recorded in his memoirs (1828) that this was "a piece without any great pretensions in point of design, but comprising many pleasing groupings and situations, calculated to display the merits of the dancers."

During his single season under Ebers's leadership, 1821, Deshayes also produced the following: *La Paysanne Supposée* (10 April), with a cast headed by Noblet, Albert, and François Montessu; *Alcide* (21 July), choreographed in collaboration with Albert, who also danced the title role, and presented in honor of the coronation of George IV; and *Le Seigneur Généreux* (26 July), to music by Fernando Sor.

In 1822 Deshayes published a pamphlet, *Idées générales sur l'Académie Royale de Musique, et plus specialement sur la danse*, in which he proposed a number of reforms to be effected at the Paris Opera. These included the production of more new works, preferably by living authors; the reinstatement of the three genres of dance (noble, *demi-caractère*, and character); and the creation of a workshop theater where *aspirants* (students) could gain practical stage experience before making an official debut. He appended the scenario of a projected ballet, *Terpsichore, ou Le Tri-*

omphe des Grâces, which he had submitted to the Paris Opera in 1819.

He realized his dream of mounting a ballet at the Paris Opera in 1824, but it was not *Terpsichore.* The first and only ballet that he was to produce there, *Zémire et Azor,* was based on André Grétry's eponymous opera (1771). The story was an elaborate version of the fairy tale "Beauty and the Beast." The cast was headed by Amélie Legallois as Zémire (Beauty) and Louis Montjoie as Azor (the Beast). The ballet's scenery included many special effects, a number of which misfired at the first performance on 20 October, thus provoking the derision of the audience. However, Legallois won praise in two dances, a *pas de schalls* and a pas de deux with Montjoie, in which the dancers assumed poses inspired by classical sculpture.

Deshayes was reengaged by the King's Theatre from 1829 to 1831. His outstanding works during this period were a restaging of Jean-Louis Aumer's *La Somnambule* (31 January 1829), *Masaniello* (24 March 1829), and *Kenilworth* (3 March 1831). *Masaniello,* a ballet version of the opera *La Muette de Portici,* was especially popular and inspired many imitations on the London stage. Its attractions included not only Pauline Leroux's moving interpretation of Fenella, the mute girl, but also the spectacular eruption of Mount Vesuvius at the end of the ballet.

Kenilworth, one of Deshayes's most successful works, was the first ballet to be seen by Queen Victoria, then an eleven-year-old princess. Unlike most nineteenth-century ballets, it was unusually faithful to its source, the novel by Sir Walter Scott. Caroline Brocard played the role of the heroine, the ill-fated Amy Robsart. Her husband, the Earl of Leicester, was played by Lefebvre, while Zoé Beaupré formed the third part of the triangle, Queen Elizabeth. The featured dancers were Antoine Paul and Pauline Montessu, both from the Paris Opera. The ballet depicted many processions and pageants, including an Elizabethan masque. Loving care had been given to the sets, designed by William Grieve, and the costumes, which were carefully researched.

Deshayes returned to the King's Theatre in 1833, when he mounted *Faust* to music by Adolphe Adam, with Leroux as Marguerite. Adam later used parts of this score for the ballet *Giselle* (1841). Deshayes also worked as ballet master of the King's Theatre from 1835 until 1838, during which time the theater's name was changed to Her Majesty's Theatre in honor of Queen Victoria's accession in 1837.

During this period Deshayes created *Le Rossignol* (12 April 1836) for the London debut of Carlotta Grisi. The ballet included a pas de deux for her and her mentor Jules Perrot. Grisi also danced in *Beniowsky* (5 May 1836), a ballet set in Russia and based on a play by the German dramatist August von Kotzebue. Among the cast were Madame Copère, who played the role of Catherine the Great, and Antoine Coulon. *Beniowsky* was so successful

that it was revived for Pauline Duvernay in 1837; her famous *cachucha* from *The Devil on Two Sticks* (the London restaging of Jean Coralli's *Le Diable Boiteux*) was inserted into act 2.

Coulon also played the role of the bandit chief Fra Diavolo in *Le Brigand de Terracina* (25 February 1837), which Deshayes created as a vehicle for Duvernay. The ballet was an adaptation of Daniel Auber's opera *Fra Diavolo* (1830). Duvernay, in the role of Zerlina, won special praise for her looking-glass dance; later, Fanny Elssler also triumphed in the role. The ending of the ballet was applauded for its realism: Fra Diavolo, beleaguered by soldiers, plunges from an overhanging rock into an abyss and then is carried onstage for a pathetic death scene.

Deshayes shared his final season at Her Majesty's Theatre with Perrot in 1842. They collaborated on the first London production of *Giselle* (12 March), staged some nine months after Coralli and Perrot had first presented it at the Paris Opera. Grisi, the original Giselle, was present to re-create the role, while Perrot danced her lover, called Albert in this production. Deshayes was also responsible for the scenario and general staging of *Alma, ou La Fille de Feu* (23 June), to which Perrot and Fanny Cerrito contributed the principal dances.

BIBLIOGRAPHY

Deshayes, André. *Idées générales sur l'Académie Royale de Musique, et plus specialement sur la danse.* Paris, 1822.

Ebers, John. *Seven Years of the King's Theatre* (1828). New York, 1969.

Fenner, Theodore. "Ballet in Early Nineteenth-Century London as Seen by Leigh Hunt and Henry Robertson." *Dance Chronicle* 1.2 (1978): 75–95.

Guest, Ivor. *The Romantic Ballet in England.* London, 1972.

Guest, Ivor. *The Romantic Ballet in Paris.* 2d rev. ed. London, 1980.

Guest, Ivor. *Jules Perrot: Master of the Romantic Ballet.* London, 1984.

Winter, Marian Hannah. *The Pre-Romantic Ballet.* London, 1974.

SUSAN AU

DESIGNING FOR DANCE. The nature of decor and costumes for dance imposes an element of visual permanence upon an ephemeral, fluid art form that exists only through movement. Refined sensibility and altruistic discretion are essential in order to assimilate the design into a harmonious entity of music, movement, and vision; this assimilation frequently remains an elusive prospect for those who create a ballet: the triumvirate of composer, choreographer, and designer.

The search for an idea, the formulation of the mental image, and the representation of it through a composition of form, color, and light is a delicate process for the designer. The process depends upon a combination of various factors: affinity with the choreographer and his or her style of movement, response to music, the perception of an underlying dramatic content, inspiration, imagination, and good luck.

The devotion to excellence, which distinguishes the profession of dance to a formidable degree, cannot help but impress any outsider exposed to it during a related collaboration. The blend of athleticism and spiritualism, a characteristic of many dancers, and their relentless drive for self-improvement, infuse a performance of dance with the notion of an athletic event, celebrated with divine grace and touched by an aura of a religious ritual—a lasting revelation to the uninitiated, exposed to it for the first time. The idealistic commitment of the dancers to their work with a rigorous discipline in their pursuit of technical perfection is unique in the performing arts, as is the fervor of their dedication to a profession when their bodies are inevitably subjected to physical deterioration with passing time. This exemplary attitude, which marks dancers for their entire life, ought to inspire and challenge the sensitive designer to a creation of similar quality.

Stage Design. The primary function of a stage design for dance is to organize the stage to provide a musically and dramatically conditioned atmosphere that will complement and emphasize the movement. Decisions about the appearance of the stage, how to shape, back, frame, cover, color, surround, and light it—as well as how to dress the human figure—are the responsibility of the designer, with the assisting interference of the choreographer.

Though there are unlimited options for the look of the stage, it will derive from four basic categories: (1) bare stage; (2) dressed stage without apparent decor; (3) sculptural decor in space; and (4) traditional decor of illusionistic, painted, flat scenery.

Practical, financial, and artistic considerations of contemporary taste can produce a stage that eschews noticeable scenery and costumes, relying primarily upon the effect of lighting and dancers in their essence. The first category, the bare stage, thought by some to be the desirable setting to experience dance in unalloyed purity, would seem to qualify as a prototype of this cult of an aestheticism of utility. But it is an intellectual conceit to detect a "message" in the functionalism of technical paraphernalia—glaring lights, bare walls, ladders, and cables—and to relate any of it to the notion of an antiseptic laboratory for movement, an environment uncontaminated by design. Haphazard technical display on the stage is indicative of a misconceived decor by a dilettante. To expect that this kind of decor will provide a focus for the movement is presumptuous. Indeed, even the most accomplished lighting fails to eradicate an impression of centrifugal flight of dancers drawn against their will onto the periphery of the incoherent stage. The perverse appeal of theatrical naturalism seldom stimulates a fusion of music, motion, and image.

The second category, the dressed stage without apparent decor, is the most practical, neutral, and universally appropriate stage for dance behind the traditional proscenium arch, as it offers great versatility and easy change of appearance with a simple, traditional setup. The organization of this stage consists of a series of narrow panels of fabric ("legs") stretched over a frame, if possible, to give a clean, unobtrusive surface. These panels are placed parallel to one another on opposite sides of the stage and are topped by spanning borders; together they proceed toward a large full drop in the back of the stage. This arrangement may not seem to be a decor, but scrutiny will reveal a strong visual statement, particularly when the fabric is black velour. Exerting a dense, precisely defining ambiance, the space appears oppressive, airless, and claustrophobic—a hypnotic void. The impression of limitless confinement exudes a sensuous elegance and underscores the visible presence of beacons of lights. The play of the geometric patterns of these shafts of light alludes to an eerie mobile architecture of illuminated air. They are the only visual competition for the human figure, delineating it with crystalline sharpness. It is a harsh, merciless presence, not without a certain matter-of-fact beauty. This "black stage," beloved by modern dance and considered abstract, is in fact realistic in that it does not pretend to anything; there is no illusion or allusion.

The practicality of this setting is apparent from the ease with which it can change radically from an obsessive black enclosure to a liberation of air and sky, even during an ongoing performance, with the simplest raising of the drop in the back. Such an effect can be completed by using a white scrim (a drop of transparent open-weave fabric), invisibly backed by a drop of translucent white plastic, bathed in blue light. This setup can provide any desired mood, subject to the color of the scrim and suitable lighting. The elementary arrangement of the "black stage," with a white scrim, a black scrim, and white plastic, together with reasonable lighting equipment, ought to be the first decorative investment for a decorless dance company.

It is evident that the stage without decor depends upon lighting for an assumption of visual appeal. In the realism of the bare stage and the neutrality of the dressed stage, light is the only source of visual diversity, and it exercises a decisive function of great importance. Benefiting from the openness of a stage devoid of the obstructive physical presence of decor, lighting delivers results effectively and economically. The intangibility of light might account for its close affinity with dance's related characteristic of transience. Their appealing union enhances, defines, and lends character to movement, justifiably attracting a contemporary sensibility fascinated with instability, fluidity, and speed.

The popular response to the impact of stage lighting and the considerable sophistication of lighting equipment have advanced the highly reputable profession of "electrician" to that of "lighting designer," a title that claims artistic creation for a highly important act of practical execution. The change of appellation is understandable when the function is performed in the visual desert of a stage without decor, where there is no need to submit to a previously existing concept. On a dressed stage, however, it is the designer of the decor who is ultimately responsible for the stage's total visual appearance.

Creating a stage appearance without the use of decorative additions presents an important and necessary function for design, but it is a very minor challenge compared to the tantalizing prospect of the creation of decor and costumes to transform the stage and dress the human body. The choice of visual style is generally left to the designer to suggest to the choreographer. It is largely based on an instinctive response to the influences mentioned earlier, which have to be combined with the practical, technical, and financial resources of the company mounting the production.

Sculptural decor in space, the third category of stage design, is favored by contemporary taste. It concerns the creation and assemblage of dimensional elements, and the appearance of the stage in relation to them. The presence, position, and proportion of these two-dimensional and three-dimensional elements—voluminous or linear, textured and opaque or diaphanous and luminous, responsive to light—exerts an immediate and powerful impact upon the audience. It is not unlike a magnetic field attracting powerlines of attention and reverting them instantly to the viewer. This continuous interplay between feature and audience, which is stimulated by the intersecting movement of the dancers, is an integral part of the concept of the sculptural design. The considerable influence sculptural design has upon the dance is a major asset when it is understood by the choreographer.

The decisive impact of sculptural design upon the effect of choreography is equaled by the influence of the "surrounding" stage upon both. Placed within the bare stage, the assemblage might seem intentionally absorbed by the environment; whereas on the stage dressed in black, it might function as magical catalyst. Set against the simulated "air" of a scrim, colored by ingenious lighting, the stage assumes a totally different character, related to the traditional decor of painted scenery. The combinations, variations, and possibilities of sculptural decor are unlimited as is its susceptibility to lighting, another reason for its popularity.

The fourth category of scenic treatment for the stage, the traditional decor of illusionistic, painted, flat scenery, continues a centuries-old convention. It consists usually of a framing portal in front and a series of side panels and borders leading to a full backdrop. It is still the most effective and practical way to dress the full stage and to con-

jure any desired image, either of awesome realism or of fantastic invention, strictly through paint alone. Unfortunately the method has come into disrepute. Occasionally scene painters balk at the difficulty in transferring a maquette (the design in small scale) onto the large dimensions of the stage. Scene painting is also unpopular with some lighting personnel who are reluctant to accept the professional challenge of discreet, sensitive illumination of colorful scenery painted on canvas.

The possibilities of invention for painted scenery are as infinite as they are for an easel painting, but here the decor is meant to feed upon rhythm, sound, and the human figure in motion, in order to produce collectively an impression of an integrated totality. The painted rendering of forms, their simulated volume, the agitation of their outline, and their position have to blend to the right degree with the intensity and vibrancy of color and the harmony of the palette. The density, the variety, and the insistence and direction of patterns are also very significant in formulating a visual partnership with music and motion, as are other factors such as lighting and costumes.

Costumes. The design of costumes for dance follows similar basic principles that apply to the human figure in motion. The clear and immediate perception of the diverse patterns of stage movement requires a precise definition of the dancer's body, which is the very least the costume ought to provide. The concept of the design must relate to the structure of the human anatomy and approach it logically, almost in terms of an architectural blueprint.

The dominant feature is the emphasis on the central, vertical axis of the body. This can be achieved by accentuating the torso through the classic V-line, which descends symmetrically from the front of the armpit to the center of the waist. The emphasis of the shoulders, without incurring visual bulk and consequently reducing proportional height, and the exposure of the neck, setting off the head, are elementary features of costume design. Equally important is the presentation of the horizontal axis; the waistline must remain unobstructed and clearly visible, or at least perceptible. The dancer's wrists should also be exposed to show off the hands (although long sleeves give a more elegant appearance). The expressive gestures of the hands complement the general movement and bring it to its final conclusion. Awareness of the legs (even when covered by fabric) and of the feet is self-evident in a costume for dance.

Three categories typify the design of dance costumes: (1) the costume for classical ballet; (2) the body suit; and (3) the costume based on character, situation, and folklore.

In the first category, the costume for classical ballet, the correct dress for women is the tutu, a skirt of several layers of shirred net (tulle) attached between the waist and the hip and complementary to the formfitting bodice, which accentuates the waist. The length and character of the tutu is determined by choreography and design.

The tutu is being replaced by a body-revealing dress—or a stretch-fabric leotard with a skirt—of a flowing fabric that is generally a solid-color (usually pink) pastel. The arching waves of the diaphanous material of the skirt obscure the motion of the legs, cling to the body, and submit to the movement without comment or character. In contrast, the tutu accents the motion instantly and even seems to anticipate it. The soft cloud of pliant "air" of the calf-long romantic tutu envelops the legs in a sinuous caress, revealing their motion distinctly, though they remain fully covered most of the time.

The short tutu, extended from the hips, shows the legs in their entire length. The flexible disk of the skirt vibrates with the movement, responds to it in a perky dialogue, and sets up the torso with seductive flair. The layers of net encircling the body quiver with high-strung restlessness. They offer an alluring contrast to the determined precision of the stiletto-like pointe work of the feet. This pulsating extension of the movement is an ingenious function of the short tutu, particularly when it underscores the technical display of virtuoso bravura. It is also a necessary feature to balance the elongation of the body terminating on the tip of toe shoes. The perfection of the tutu's design is matched in ingenuity only by certain ecclesiastical garments and the ceremonial dress of ethnic tribes. The variations and adaptations of the design of the tutu and incidental decorations are restricted only by lack of imagination. The design of men's costumes is usually more restricted. Traditionally, men are dressed in tights and a body-hugging top garment.

The body suit, the second category of dance costume design, is worn by both women and men. It has gained immense appeal through the perfection of stretch fabric, which envelops the body like a second skin. The body suit offers infinite possibilities for presenting variations on the natural silhouette of the body, combining with different materials, exposing parts of the human anatomy, or creating a facsimile of nudity. Its favorable response to chemically advanced fabric dyes that provide greater permanence is a welcome attribute; it is also easy to maintain and has minimal storage requirements. But the body suit's main attraction is that it provides a heightened awareness of the dancer's body, unadorned, if so intended, or syncopated by either fragments or masses of sympathetic material.

The third category of dance costumes—those based on character, situation, and folklore—is obvious in its implications and is a subject too substantial for consideration in this limited space, except to note that it is completely susceptible to the previously examined principles of de-

sign for dance as they pertain to accurate historical contexts, period dress and habits, and locale.

The effect of costume on the human figure is an accepted fact, but the knowledge and effort required for the transfer of the design onto the human body is seldom appreciated. The function of the designer demands an understanding of fabrics and their properties and cut for construction, plus a cunning eye for proportion. The final impression of the design is critically dependent upon a magnitude of details constantly scrutinized during execution and fittings. A major concern, for example, is the size of headdresses and wigs. Contrary to common belief, a small head will provide an impression of greater height than will the addition of measurable substance, which will shrink the figure proportionally to the eye.

The fascination with physical glamour and youth and the relaxation of Victorian prudery have resulted in the acceptance of the nude body onstage. For the dance, however, certain parts of the anatomy defy choreography, especially with the male physique. Suggestion is usually more titillating, and the viewer's mind, directed by a calculated design, will be stimulated toward images reality cannot provide. Diaphanous fabrics most effectively reveal body structure without exposing surface detail. The popular obsession with the essence of the body also seems to motivate the reluctance of choreographers to entrust their creation to costumes of some fantasy, which might ostensibly obscure the beauty of the movement.

The Designer's Challenge. Suggestion is a powerful facet of design. The appreciation of the large space of the stage, required by dance to be left empty, and the creation of a design that will allow the human figure maximum freedom of movement challenge the imagination of the designer. Transforming these apparent limitations into a source of inspiration and deliberate motivation is a unique condition of the design of decor and costumes for the dance. The recourse to suggestion and evocation is a natural consequence and a positive step toward design's alliance with music and movement.

[*See also* Costume, History of Western; Footwear; Lighting for Dance; *and* Scenic Design.]

BIBLIOGRAPHY

Dance, Theatre, Opera: Costume and Decor Designs, Sculpture, Photographs, and Books. New York, 1977. Exhibition catalogue.
Hartnoll, Phyllis, ed. *The Oxford Companion to the Theatre.* 4th ed. Oxford and New York, 1983. In which, see "Costume" and "Scenery."
Rowell, Kenneth. *Stage Design.* London, 1972.
Ter-Arutunian, Rouben. "Decor for Dance." In *Contemporary Stage Design, U.S.A.*, edited by Elizabeth B. Burdick et al. New York, 1975.
Ter-Arutunian, Rouben. "In Search of Design." *Dance Perspectives* 28 (Winter 1966).
Tipton, Jennifer. "Innovation in Lighting Design." *Theatre Design and Technology* 22 (October 1970).

ROUBEN TER-ARUTUNIAN

DESNOYER, PHILIP (also known as Denoyer, Denoyers; born c.1700, died 1788), French dancer and dancing master. Desnoyer had a brilliant theatrical career in London during the two decades between 1721 and about 1740. Afterward, until the late 1770s, he was court dancing master to the House of Hanover in Britain.

Desnoyer's father may have been the ballet master Desnoyers who went from Paris to the summer palace of Queen Sophia-Charlotte (wife of Frederick I of Prussia) at Lictzenburg (Charlottenburg) to arrange ballets for the opera *La Festa del Himeneo* in 1701. Desnoyer was trained in France, presumably by his father, and first appeared in England at Drury Lane on 11 January 1721. In the following season he continued to appear in light entr'acte pieces at the same theater. In 1722 he was appointed dancing teacher to Prince Frederick, son of the Prince of Wales, with whom he was always on intimate terms, at an annual fee of £500.

On his return to Drury Lane for the 1731/32 season he composed formal pieces, such as *Grand Ballet d'Amour*, appeared in speciality dances, and began his distinguished career as a dramatic dancer. After a brief trip to Poland, he appeared in John Weaver's final composition for the stage, *The Judgement of Paris* (1733), in which he interpreted the role of Paris.

Throughout the 1730s Desnoyer danced a variety of pieces, ranging from grand ballets and speciality dances to comic and dramatic roles. He lived near Saint James's Palace in order to be close to his royal patrons.

In the early 1730s, Desnoyer partnered the English dancer Hester Santlow (Hester Booth). During the late 1730s and early 1740s, Desnoyer had three renowned partners with whom he appeared to great public acclaim: Catherine Violanta Roland, Maria Chateauneuf, and Barbara Campanini ("La Barberina"). At Drury Lane he and Roland had a disagreement that occasioned her move to Covent Garden the following season. In January 1740, riots occurred when he and Chateauneuf failed to appear at Drury Lane as billed. In 1740 Desnoyer moved to Covent Garden for the final two seasons of his career and appeared with La Barberina (with whom the painter William Hogarth depicted him in *Charmers of the Age*).

Desnoyer's successful genteel practice sustained him well after his retirement from the stage. He taught not only the future George III of England and his daughters but also members of the nobility such as the earl of Chesterfield's son. He moved close to the royal palace at Kew and created pieces for the amusement of his patrons at court. He became a party to court intrigue and, in 1773, confidant to Princess Caroline.

BIBLIOGRAPHY

Highfill, Philip H., Jr., et al., eds. *A Biographical Dictionary of Actors, Actresses, Musicians, Dancers, Managers, and Other Stage Personnel in London, 1660–1800.* Carbondale, Ill., 1973–.

Moore, Lillian. "The Adventures of La Barberina." *Dance Magazine* (December 1958): 68–69, 116–117.

Winter, Marian Hannah. *The Pre-Romantic Ballet.* London, 1974.

RICHARD RALPH

DEUTSCHE OPER BERLIN. *See* Berlin Opera Ballet.

DEVADĀSĪ. The Sanskrit term *devadāsī* denotes a female temple dancer in India. It comes from the Sanskrit words *deva* ("god" or "deity") and *dāsī* ("female servant"). The *devadāsī*s were women from good families chosen for their beauty and talent and consecrated to the temple at an early age. The exact date of this custom's origin is not known, but it is assumed that it began when temples were erected to honor the gods of the Hindu pantheon. Most temples are dedicated to Śiva (Shiva) or Viṣṇu (Vishnu), and dance was an integral part of ceremonies in these temples through the ritual performances of the *devadāsī*s. Their duties consisted of dancing before the god during worship rituals and when the sacred image was taken out in processions. The temple dancers came to form a community of their own, and the name *devadāsī* underwent local variations.

The first recorded evidence of the custom of dedicating dancers to temples is found in Orissa, the northernmost state on the eastern coast of India. Dated from the ninth century CE, it is in the form of a temple inscription commemorating the consecration of a number of dancers to the temple of Brahmeśvar. The *devadāsī*s of Orissa were called *maharis*, an abbreviation of the words *mahati nari* ("great woman"). This name was given to the dancers by the most illustrious ruler of Orissa, Sri Chudagangadeva. Their style of dance, formerly known as *oudra nṛtya*, came to be known as *mahari nṛtya*. It is the origin and source of the style now known as Oḍissi.

Around the thirteenth century, the custom of temple dancing began in the southern states of Andhra, Karnataka, and Tamil Nadu, where the temple dancers were called by the original Sanskrit name of *devadāsī*. Their style was called *dāsiāṭṭam* or *sadir nautch*; it is now known as *bharata nāṭyam*.

In Assam, in the northeast, there is an almost extinct tradition of temple dancing in which the temple dancers are called *deodhani*s ("women of god").

[*See also* Bharata Nāṭyam *and* Oḍissi.]

BIBLIOGRAPHY

Jordan, Kay. "From Sacred Servant to Profane Prostitute: A Study of the Changing Legal Status of the Devadasis, 1857–1947." Ph.D. diss., University of Iowa, 1989.

Kersenboom, Saskia C. *Nityasumaṅgalī: The Devadasi Tradition in South India.* Delhi, 1987.

Kopf, David. "Dancing Virgin, Sexual Slave, Divine Courtesan, or Celestial Dancer: In Search of the Historic Devadāsī." In *Bhārata Nāṭyam in Cultural Perspective*, edited by George Kliger. Delhi, 1993.

Marglin, Frédérique Apffel. *Wives of the God-King: The Rituals of the Devadasis of Puri.* Delhi, 1985.

Massey, Reginald, and Jamila Massey. *The Dances of India: A General Survey and Dancer's Guide.* London, 1989.

Mayo, Katherine. *Slaves of the Gods.* New York, c.1929.

Prasad, A. K. *Devadasi System in Ancient India: A Study of Temple Dancing Girls of South India.* Delhi, 1990.

Ragini Devi. *Dance Dialects of India.* 2d rev. ed. Delhi, 1990.

Shankar, Jogan. *Devadasi Cult: A Sociological Analysis.* New Delhi, 1990.

Tarachand, K. C. *Devadasi Custom: Rural Social Structure and Flesh Markets.* New Delhi, 1991.

RITHA DEVI

DE VALOIS, NINETTE (Edris Stannus; born 6 June 1898 in Blessingham, County Wicklow, Ireland), British dancer, teacher, choreographer, and administrator. The future founder of the Royal Ballet and its school was born to a father who was a career officer in the British army (he was killed in World War I) and a talented mother avidly interested in music and the performing arts. Her childhood, described in her evocative autobiography *Come Dance with Me* (1957), was happy and secure, and she characterized herself as an extraordinarily stubborn and determined child. Her first memory of dance was of learning an Irish jig from a household servant; she performed it with gusto at parties. She also remembered being enthralled by a pantomime version of *The Sleeping Beauty*, which she had seen in Dublin.

At about age eight she was sent to live with her grandmother in England, where, like many other girls of her age and class, she began lessons in what was then called "fancy dancing." These lessons taught elementary social dancing and ballroom etiquette, using a system that de Valois described as "a quaint compromise of rudimentary steps, such as the *chassé* and *glissade*, combined with other steps fancy beyond belief." Young Edris did so well in these classes and enjoyed them so much that at about eleven, she went to London to live with her mother, continuing her lessons with the prominent teacher Mrs. Wordsworth and eventually becoming a pupil assistant. She also began to learn about professional dance in London, where she was inspired by the performances of Adeline Genée and Phyllis Bedells at the Empire Theatre, as well as the visiting companies of Pavlova and Diaghilev.

De Valois was anxious to make a career in dance. She was encouraged by her mother, though her father disapproved; in his milieu dance was considered a profession unsuitable for well-bred girls. Around 1910 de Valois succeeded in persuading her family and began a course of theatrical training at the Lila Field Academy. She soon decided to specialize in classical ballet; early in 1913 she was selected to perform with Lila Field's company of "Wonder Children," a small troupe who toured the London music halls and pier theaters in resort areas along England's southern coast. Her mother chose her stage name, Ninette de Valois.

Billed as the troupe's *prima ballerina*, de Valois performed an imitation of Anna Pavlova's *The Dying Swan*, having learned the Fokine choreography by watching Pavlova from the upper circle at the Palace Theatre and taking careful notes. A number of child performers imitated Pavlova's most famous dance, but, as P. J. S. Richardson, editor of *The Dancing Times*, suggested, de Valois stood out by virtue of her "sensitivity and integrity."

In a typical "Wonder Children" performance, de Valois's dance was sandwiched between two music-hall turns, a telling indication of the position of ballet in England at that time. Ballet was not considered a serious art form equal to music, opera, or theater; although visiting Russian performers were lionized, English dancers were not accorded equal status with other creative and performing artists. In 1915, two years after de Valois began performing, the Empire closed—the last London theater to produce regular performances of British ballet—and British ballet dancers were forced either to join Diaghilev or Pavlova (disguised under Russianized names) or to dance in music halls, revues, and pantomimes.

In December 1914, de Valois won a place in the annual Christmas pantomime at the Lyceum, a position she held until 1919. In the small world of London dance, the post was an important one. Billed as the production's *première danseuse*, she attracted acclaim as she led a corps of dancers in the "grand fairyland" ballet that traditionally ended the first half of the pantomime.

De Valois studied from 1914 to 1917 with the French-trained dancer Édouard Espinosa, an outspoken advocate of good training. With P. J. S. Richardson, Espinosa had spearheaded the drive for the reform and standardization of dance training in Britain, resulting in the founding of the Association of Operatic Dancing (later the Royal Academy of Dancing) in 1920. De Valois was from its inception an enthusiastic participant in this organization. She became one of Espinosa's star pupils.

De Valois's schedule during the years of World War I (1914–1918) was increasingly hectic. To support herself and pay for her lessons, she performed in music halls. Accompanied by a partner (often a female in male costume), she took her act of operatic dancing (as ballet was then called) around many London music halls, playing the standard two shows a night (at the Palladium, three shows). In addition, the young dancer began to take pupils herself. On weekends she did volunteer war work.

In 1918, at the war's end, de Valois became involved in opera ballet, performing first as a guest artist with a company headed by Sir Thomas Beecham and then, in 1919, as *première danseuse* for the summer season of opera at London's Covent Garden. The same year she also began to work in musical comedy, appearing with Fred Leslie in *Laughing Eyes* (1919) and *Oh Julie!* (1920). In 1921, with the dancer Serge Morosoff, she briefly toured music halls with her own company of twenty dancers in a program of short pieces, some of which she choreographed.

Music hall appearances led to increasing disillusionment and boredom for the young dancer. Nevertheless, she continued to train assiduously. She could only afford two or three hours of tuition a week but, with characteristic determination, she wrote notes on her lessons and executed a class every day by herself.

One of her few sources of inspiration at this time was Diaghilev's Ballets Russes, whose annual visits to London she eagerly anticipated. In 1921 she repeatedly attended Diaghilev's *The Sleeping Princess* at the Alhambra, a production that was to have a profound influence on her own conception of ballet.

By this time, de Valois had had an opportunity to see the Russian dancers at closer range. In 1919 Enrico Cecchetti had accepted her as one of his first pupils in London, and Cecchetti's close connection with the Diaghilev company allowed her to mingle with these dancers.

During a respite in the activities of the Ballets Russes that followed the financial failure of *The Sleeping Princess,* Léonide Massine and Lydia Lopokova organized a small dance troupe and invited de Valois to join them. The experience was a revelation to de Valois, who wrote later:

> The choreography was of an order undreamt of in any of my experiences, and the disciplined routine of classes and lengthy rehearsals in preparation for the opening filled me with a sudden feeling of dedication that was an entirely new experience.
> (de Valois, 1957, p.48)

In 1923 Cecchetti left London and "for a few inspiring months," de Valois attended the classes of Nikolai Legat. In the fall of 1923, however, she was invited to join Diaghilev's Ballets Russes. Diaghilev's impact on the young dancer was crucial. He cultivated her taste and expanded her horizons; she always considered him the single most important influence on her ideas about the development of a British national ballet company.

In the Ballets Russes, de Valois perceived the example of a serious repertory dance troupe that far surpassed any contemporary British company; she also acquired first-hand knowledge of dancers and choreographers who had received rigorous and systematic training from a single, stable institution devoted entirely to dance—the Imperial Ballet School in Saint Petersburg. As a member of the corps and later in some soloist roles, she became intimately acquainted with some of the most innovative and important choreography of several decades. She danced in works by Michel Fokine, Léonide Massine, Vaslav Nijinsky, Bronislava Nijinska, and George Balanchine, as well as in truncated, one-act versions of *Swan Lake* and *The Sleeping Princess.*

In the Ballets Russes, Bronislava Nijinska singled out de Valois from the corps and made the role of the Hostess in *Les Biches* on her; Nijinska also coached her in sections of *The Sleeping Beauty* and in the role of Papillon in Fokine's *Le Carnaval.* Another choreographer with whom de Valois worked, and whom she admired, was George Balanchine, who joined the company in 1924. De Valois danced in some of the ballets he choreographed for operas produced by Diaghilev. When the company was in Paris, she also refined her technique "to its final point" by working with Olga Preobrajenska.

When de Valois left the Ballets Russes in 1925, she had already formulated the goal of establishing a native British ballet company that would eventually take its place beside the great state ballets of Russia and Europe. She hoped to create an institution that could ultimately raise ballet in the eyes of her countrymen to what she believed to be its rightful status—equal to the other arts. The idea of creating an English ballet had been in the air through most of the previous decade; as early as 1916, Richardson and Espinosa had agitated for it, while Phyllis Bedells made a professional statement by refusing to russianize her name.

De Valois turned all this talk into action and the dreams into reality. She began in March 1926 by establishing a school in Kensington, the Academy of Choreographic Art, to train the personnel for such a company. In the summer of 1926 she approached Lillian Baylis, director of the Old Vic Theatre, with a carefully planned scheme for the formation and development of a repertory ballet company to be attached to the theater, which then alternated performances of opera and Shakespeare. Baylis was favorably impressed, but she could only offer de Valois part-time work coaching actors in movement, arranging dances for Shakespeare plays, and giving a series of small dance performances as "curtain raisers" for operas. It was nevertheless a beginning, and on 13 December 1928, de Valois's ballet *Les Petits Riens* (to the music of Wolfgang Amadeus Mozart, and danced by pupils from her school) was presented at the Old Vic as a prelude to the Christmas performance of the Englebert Humperdinck opera *Hansel and Gretel.*

To support herself, de Valois continued to dance in revues, most notably *Whitebirds of 1927,* in which she appeared and arranged the ballet *Traffic in Souls* with Anton Dolin. On occasion, she also returned to the Diaghilev company for guest appearances.

In 1926 de Valois also became the choreographic director of the Festival Theatre at Cambridge, where she worked until 1931. There she collaborated with its young director, her cousin Terence Gray, in staging avant-garde experimental productions. The multilevel stage of the Festival Theatre had no proscenium, and naturalistic scenery and props were eliminated. Instead, atmosphere was created by subtle and varied colored lighting effects, and emphasis was placed on choreographed, stylized movement. Their first production together was in 1926, the *Oresteia* trilogy of Aeschylus, which featured de Valois's innovatively choreographed movements for the chorus. In addition to choreographing movement for plays (notably *Oedipus Tyrannus* and *Prometheus*), de Valois also arranged dance programs for the Festival Theatre, employing the students and repertory from her Academy of Choreographic Art. These programs mostly consisted of short dance pieces choreographed by de Valois to music of such modern composers as Anton Arensky *(A Daughter of Eve)*, Maurice Ravel *(Beauty and the Beast),* and Francis Poulenc *(Mouvement Perpetuel).* Her major work from this period was *Rout* (1927), with music by Sir Arthur Bliss, which she characterized as the revolt of modern youth against the older generation. It incorporated some of de Valois's and Gray's experimental ideas, mixing dance, music, and the spoken word. In the opening section the dance was performed (in soft shoes) to the recitation of a poem by Ernst Toller, and then continued to the music.

Among the admirers of de Valois's work at the Festival Theatre was her Irish compatriot William Butler Yeats, for whose 1927 Festival Theatre production of *On Baile's Strand* she did the choreography. In 1927 Yeats persuaded her to return to Ireland to work with him at the Abbey Theatre in Dublin. Undaunted by this addition to her schedule, she commuted by the night ferry to Ireland, where she established a school for dancers attached to the Abbey Theatre (the first government-supported ballet school in the British Isles). She staged and performed in a number of Yeats's plays for dancers, including *At the Hawk's Well, The Only Jealousy of Emer,* and *The King of the Great Clock Tower.* Yeats rewrote the latter specifically for her. The poet was so impressed with de Valois' performance in *The King of the Great Clock Tower* that he dedicated it to her "asking pardon for covering her expressive face with a mask." De Valois also choreographed several short ballets on Irish themes for the Abbey Theatre dancers: *The Faun* (1928), billed as the first entirely Irish ballet, with music by Harold White and *Fedelma* (1931), a mime ballet based on the Irish legend "The King of the Land of Mist."

Between 1930 and 1933, de Valois was active in the Camargo Society, another theater group that was to have a profound impact on the development of British ballet. Founded in 1930 by P. J. S. Richardson and Arnold Haskell (in part to fill the gap left by the death of Diaghilev in 1929), this organization produced a series of perfor-

DE VALOIS. For the Vic-Wells Ballet, de Valois choreographed *Douanes* (1932), in which she created the role of the Tightrope Walker. (Photograph by Gordon Anthony; used by permission of the Picture Library, Victoria and Albert Museum, London.)

mances by British dancers and choreographers to show the London public that British artists could succeed in ballet, formerly viewed as the preserve of Russians. De Valois helped plan the organization. Along with Marie Rambert, she provided dancers to perform in its productions, and she also contributed several of her own ballets to its repertory: *Danse Sacrée et Danse Profane* (1930, music by Claude Debussy), *Cephalus and Procris* (1931, music by André-Ernest-Modeste Grétry), *La Création du Monde* (1931, music by Darius Milhaud), *The Origin of Design* (1932, music by George Frideric Handel), *The Jackdaw and the Pigeons* (1931, music by Hugh Bradford), *Fête Polonaise* (1931, music by Mikhail Glinka)—and one of her most important and enduring works, *Job—A Masque for Dancing* (1931, music by Ralph Vaughan Williams).

By the time the Camargo Society was dissolved in 1933, de Valois's small company had expanded and was established at the newly opened Sadler's Wells Theatre, performing fortnightly evenings of ballet.

In 1934 de Valois left the Abbey Theatre to spend all her time with her London company. The remainder of her career was devoted to the development of the company's repertory, dancers, choreographers, and school. She was determined to create a stable organization that, like the state ballets of France, Russia, and Denmark, would provide British dancers with a consistent living wage and a congenial atmosphere in which their talents might be developed and displayed. From the beginning she planned well into the future. She observed, "If the company does not survive the existence of many a director it will have failed utterly in the eyes of the first dancer to hold that post." To accomplish her goals de Valois needed to develop not only a company of performers but also a school, a nursery and laboratory in which future dancers and choreographers could be trained rigorously and a company style developed. School and company together formed a continuous cycle, with company members drawn from the school and older artists returning to teach the young.

De Valois had to perform a multitude of difficult roles. No detail was too small for her attention. She became an administrator of genius, managing on a minimal budget not only the day-to-day running of the company but also the school. She planned programs, rehearsed and cast ballets, and sorted out the finances. In addition, she developed a training syllabus that instilled in her dancers a strong technique and artistry of movement; she was a strict and inspiring teacher. The result was a distinctive company style that would eventually make it one of the great dance ensembles of the century and produce some of the era's greatest dancers—foremost among them Margot Fonteyn, whom de Valois singled out as a child.

Drawing on her experience with the Diaghilev company, de Valois believed that her school and company must produce not only new dancers but also new choreographers and native modern repertory of British ballets. She served as the company choreographer during its first years but, perhaps in acknowledgment of her limitations, in 1935 she engaged Frederick Ashton as resident company choreographer. Ashton had been discovered and encouraged by Marie Rambert, but it was de Valois who gave him the security of a regular wage, placed her confidence in him for the long term, and, most importantly, gave him a laboratory and dancers on which to work out his ideas.

At the same time, de Valois was coaching actors and actresses of the Old Vic in dance movement. She choreographed for and, with members of her company, performed in dance interludes in operas. She used her skills as a persuasive and charismatic public speaker and writer to promote the cause of British dance in a series of lectures and articles in *The Dancing Times* (1933–1935). In her book *Invitation to the Ballet* (1937), she lucidly and forcefully assessed the situation of ballet in Britain (and Europe), outlined her own concept of ballet as a theatrical art form, and argued for the development of a national British ballet. Understanding the importance of audience development, in 1946 she became the president and an

DE VALOIS. The Gambling Scene from *The Rake's Progress* (1935), with Robert Helpmann (left) as the Rake and members of the Vic-Wells Ballet. Set to music by Gavin Gordon, *The Rake's Progress* featured scenery and costumes designed by Rex Whistler after those shown in the famous series of engravings (1735) by William Hogarth. (Photograph from the Dance Collection, New York Public Library for the Performing Arts.)

enthusiastic supporter of the London Ballet Circle, formed to educate the growing audience.

De Valois was not only the director of the Vic-Wells Ballet and school but also a performer in it. By necessity she danced in a wide variety of roles, but she particularly excelled in *demi-caractère* roles that exploited her precise footwork, strong attack, and spirited, forceful personality, such as the eccentric Tightrope Walker in her comic ballet *Douanes* (1932) or a cheeky, intelligent Swanilda in *Coppélia*. Aspects of her offstage personality were immortalized by Frederick Ashton in the role of Webster, the no-nonsense housemaid who rules the members of *A Wedding Bouquet* (1937).

Most important of all, de Valois was a choreographer. Although she did not consider choreography her true vocation, she provided the company with twenty-two of its thirty-seven ballets during its first seven years. Her ballets were able to draw and hold audiences accustomed to the Diaghilev repertory. Even after the emergence of Ashton as company choreographer in 1935, one third of the repertory between 1935 and 1950 (when she produced her last ballet) was hers. She favored the one-act form, popularized in England by Diaghilev, tailored to the small size of her company and its predominance of female dancers.

Her works encompassed a variety of types and subjects. Some were essentially a succession of short dances within a generalized setting, but dance dramas are her most characteristic and personal works. Included in the former category are *Danse Sacrée et Danse Profane* (1930, music by Claude Debussy); *Hommage aux Belles Viennoises* (1929, music by Franz Schubert); *Suite de Danses* (1930, music by Johann Sebastian Bach); and *Fête Polonaise* (1931, music by Mikhail Glinka). Carefully and skillfully crafted, these ballets often exhibit de Valois's strong interest in regional folk dance.

Dance dramas—ballets with a specific theme or narrative—make up the bulk of de Valois's work. Their variety reflects de Valois's wide-ranging interest in all the arts, drawing inspiration from pictorial, literary, historical, and musical sources. De Valois's style contrasts strongly with that of Ashton. Although she may employ a strictly classical style, de Valois usually favors less academic movements, freeing the dancer's head, arms, and torso, using them expressively to reveal character and to create dramatic effect. She has said her choreography was influenced by Massine's ballets for Diaghilev. In her use of mass choral movement, dramatic tableaux, and emphasis on vivid gesture, Nijinska's influence can be discerned. Critics have also noted a stylistic relationship to central European modern choreographers such as Kurt Jooss.

Despite severe limitations of time and money, de Valois tried to work whenever possible with commissioned scores and set designs in the manner of Diaghilev, to whose concept of synthesis of the arts she has remained

DE VALOIS. Using the same music and libretto by Vittorio Rieti that George Balanchine had used in 1925, de Valois choreographed her version of *Barabau* for the Vic-Wells Ballet in 1936. She herself created the role of the Peasant Woman. (Photograph by Gordon Anthony; used by permission of the Picture Library, Victoria and Albert Museum, London.)

strongly committed. She made a special effort to use the music of British composers, both past and contemporary, along with British themes, and British visual artists. She was by no means limited, however, to exclusively British ballets.

The earliest of de Valois's British ballets is one that many consider her masterwork: *Job—A Masque For Dancing*, created in 1931 for the Camargo Society, to music by Ralph Vaughan Williams. Based on an idea suggested by her friend Geoffrey Keynes (who devised the scenario), the ballet drew inspiration and many of the dancers' gestures from William Blake's illustrations for the biblical book of *Job*. Danced off pointe, her *Job* displays her interest in creating powerful male characters; in the role of Satan, she gave Anton Dolin one of his most memorable roles. Also for the Camargo Society, de Valois modified a scenario Blaise Cendrars had written for Jean Börlin's Ballet Suédois to music by Darius Milhaud, presenting in *La Création du Monde* (1931) her vision of an African myth of the origin of the world, using distinctive choral movement to the jazz-influenced modernist score. In *The Origin of Design* (1932, music by George Frideric Handel), de Valois delved into English dance history, basing the ballet on a scenario originally published by Carlo Blasis in *The Code of Terpsichore* (1828), when he was a dancer and choreographer at the King's Theatre, London. The designs of the English artist Inigo Jones were coordinated with the ballet. *Douanes* (1932) concerned the efforts of a group of nineteenth-century tourists to slip through French customs. Nursery rhymes, fairy tales, and the music of Edward Elgar inspired *The Nursery Suite* (1932), with dancers cast as Little Bo Peep, Georgie Porgie, Snow White, the Three Bears, and Jack and Jill. In choreo-

DE VALOIS. *Checkmate,* one of de Valois's best-known works, was premiered by the Vic-Wells Ballet during a season in Paris in June 1937. The ballet is a game of love and death, with characters named after the playing pieces in the game of chess. The original designs for scenery and costumes, by Edward McKnight Kauffer, were reproduced for the 1947 revival by the Sadler's Wells Ballet, seen here. (Photograph from the Dance Collection, New York Public Library for the Performing Arts.)

graphing *The Birthday of Oberon* (1933) de Valois, with music director Constant Lambert, again rediscovered and revived past English composers and scenarios, in this case Henry Purcell's *The Fairy Queen* (based on Shakespeare's *A Midsummer Night's Dream*). In 1934 she also created one of her most popular ballets, *The Haunted Ballroom,* with music by Geoffrey Toye and a scenario similar to that of *Giselle,* in which the protagonist is danced to death by ghosts. *The Jar* (1934) was a comic ballet based on a story by Luigi Pirandello, with music by Alfredo Casella, originally choreographed by Jean Börlin for Les Ballets Suédois. In 1934 de Valois also created a ballet for Marie Rambert's company; its inspiration was Manet's painting *The Bar at the Folies-Bergère,* which was re-created on stage by William Chapell. Around it de Valois developed a series of dances (including a witty role for Markova as the can-can dancer La Goulue), to music by Emmanuel Chabrier, as suggested by Constant Lambert.

De Valois's interest in specifically British themes and visual arts continued in *The Rake's Progress* (1935), a masterful dance drama inspired by a series of engravings by

William Hogarth. Using decor by Rex Whistler, based on Hogarth, and music by Gavin Gordon, de Valois chronicled the adventures of an English country boy who falls prey to the temptations of London life, squanders his inheritance, and ends up in an insane asylum. Here she created one of her most subtle and powerful character portraits, first for Walter Gore, who created the role; later Robert Helpmann became one of its finest interpreters, and even later it was danced by David Wall.

In 1936 de Valois looked back to her years with Diaghilev and to the work of Balanchine. She rechoreographed *The Gods Go a-Begging* (to music of Handel, arranged by Sir Thomas Beecham) and *Barabau* (words and music by Vittorio Rieti), originally choreographed by Balanchine for the Ballets Russes. The critic Arnold Haskell felt that de Valois's *Barabau* compared well with Balanchine. De Valois's enduring interest in dance history next turned to Beethoven's ballet *The Creatures of Prometheus* (1801), originally choreographed by Salvatore Viganò. In 1936, working with Lambert, she modified the original myth and worked out an arrangement of the score to fit the new choreography.

Checkmate (1937), another specifically British work, is one of the few of de Valois's ballets (along with *Job* and *The Rake's Progress*) that remains in the repertory of the Royal Ballet. [*See* Checkmate; Job; *and* Rake's Progress, The.] The dancers portray chess pieces which represent the opposing forces of love and death, performing on a brilliantly colored chessboard designed by E. McKnight Kauffer, to music of Sir Arthur Bliss. The distinctly French *Le Roi Nu* (1938), a version of the Hans Christian Andersen fairy tale "The Emperor's New Clothes," had music by Jean Françaix (originally composed for Serge Lifar) and decor by Hedley Briggs in the style of eighteenth-century chinoiserie.

The Prospect before Us, or Pity the Poor Dancers (1940) was a return to English dance history, the eighteenth century, and English composers and artists. Based on an incident chronicled in Ebers's *History of the King's Theatre*, it concerns a rivalry between two London impresarios. The music by William Boyce (1710–1779) was arranged by music director Constant Lambert. In setting and spirit, both designer Roger Furse and de Valois looked for inspiration to the witty caricatures of Thomas Rowlandson (1756–1837). *The Prospect before Us*, no longer in the repertory, contained one of de Valois' most inspired comic solos for Robert Helpmann as Mr. O'Reilly, one of the rival managers.

With the coming of the 1940s de Valois, burdened with other responsibilities and secure in the knowledge that Ashton could fill the company's need for a choreographer, gradually ceased choreographing. During World War II she choreographed only two works: *Orpheus and Eurydice* (1941) used music from Christoph Willibald Gluck's opera and was enhanced by the simple, white-on-white designs of Sophie Fedorovitch; *Promenade* (1943) was a suite of dances to music of Franz Joseph Haydn. De Valois created no more works until 1950, when she produced her last major ballet for the company, *Don Quixote*, a dance drama in five scenes, based on the seventeenth-century Spanish novel by Miguel Cervantes, with music by Roberto Gerhard and costumes and scenery by Edward Burra.

Subsequently, she gave up choreographing regularly; some works for the Turkish State Ballet, however, must be mentioned. In *Cesembasi* (At the Fountainhead; 1964), set to music by Ferit Tüzün, she incorporated Turkish folk dance and themes. *Sinfonietta* (1966) to music of Nevit Kodalli, is set in a rehearsal room in which the dancers contrast classical and character dances.

Along with building a native modern ballet repertory, de Valois was determined to remount and preserve French and Russian ballets of the previous century that she considered to be classics: *Giselle, Coppélia, Swan Lake, The Nutcracker,* and *The Sleeping Beauty*. She felt they were the foundation on which ballet in the twentieth century rested and from which it evolved. With her clear vision of dance history, de Valois believed that her dancers needed to learn not only from modern choreography but also from these works.

To mount these ballets in the 1930s (especially the Tchaikovsky ballets), in the hope that their importance would be recognized and that they would appeal to more than a limited audience of connoisseurs, was to risk a great deal. Their status as landmarks in the history of dance was by no means commonly acknowledged when de Valois conceived her plan. The Ballets Russes had accustomed audiences to the one-act form, choreographic innovations, and the music of modern composers, but Diaghilev's 1921 staging of Tchaikovsky's and Petipa's three-act *The Sleeping Beauty*, failed to engage more than a small group of enthusiasts. De Valois (along with Ashton and Rambert) also recognized Petipa's choreographic merit and the musical importance of Tchaikovsky. Thus, she reconstructed the classics for both British and American audiences.

In 1932, aided by her friend Lydia Lopokova, de Valois contacted Nicholas Sergeyev, the former *régisseur* of the Russian Imperial Ballet, then living in poverty in Paris, who possessed the Stepanov notation for many ballets. She gave him a ten-year contract to produce *Giselle, Coppélia, The Nutcracker, Swan Lake,* and *The Sleeping Beauty*. These ballets were mounted with every attempt to preserve them as accurately as possible. In this de Valois played a crucial role. With the aid of Lambert, she cajoled the ballets from Sergeyev, whom she described as "unmusical to a degree bordering on eccentricity" and often more interested in special effects than in the fine points of

DE VALOIS. Scene 4, "Opening Night at the Pantheon," from *The Prospect before Us, or Pity the Poor Dancers* (1940) in a 1951 performance by the Sadler's Wells Theatre Ballet. Scenery and costumes were designed by Roger Furse. (Photograph from the Dance Collection, New York Public Library for the Performing Arts.)

choreography (de Valois, 1957, p. 112). De Valois had to arrange numerous important details—arranging entrances and exits, choreographing crowd movement to suit the small Sadler's Wells and later Covent Garden stages, and deciding on details of lighting.

The late 1930s and early 1940s, when the company had acquired the classics and also a substantial repertory of modern ballets, presented de Valois with perhaps her severest test. Military service decimated her company's contingent of male dancers (in short supply in the best of times); and the company became briefly homeless when Sadler's Wells Theatre was closed (it was given new facilities at the New Theatre in 1941). On a state-sponsored tour of Holland in 1940, the company was caught in the German invasion and lost many sets, scores, and costumes, narrowly escaping internment. Despite these set-

backs, the company not only flourished but served as an important national morale booster during the war years, touring the provinces and giving regular performances in London for civilian and military personnel, often during air raids.

The war's end found the company stronger than ever in spirit and accomplishment. In 1946 they were given a home at London's Royal Opera House, Covent Garden. De Valois now expanded her organization and founded a smaller company to perform at the Sadler's Wells Theatre and tour the provinces.

When de Valois brought *The Sleeping Beauty* to the United States in the historic tour of 1949, it was clear that she had realized her ambition of creating a British national ballet of international stature. With a corps of dancers headed by Margot Fonteyn and including Beryl Grey, Moira Shearer, and Robert Helpmann, the company in their New York debut demonstrated conclusively that it had become one of the great performing ensembles of the century. Its enduring repertory also proved that London had become a world ballet center, producing not only superb dancers but also, in Frederick Ashton, a choreographer of genius.

Two years after the first American tour, de Valois, who had already received the honor of Commander of the British Empire in 1947, was made a Dame of the British Empire (1951). On 31 October 1956, she saw her dream of a state-sponsored national ballet come true when Queen Elizabeth II became the official patron of the company and school, granting them a charter under the general title "The Royal Ballet" and making official their status as Britain's national ballet.

Throughout the 1950s de Valois continued in her role as company director. The Royal Ballet school and companies produced a new generation of major dancers and choreographers. De Valois continued to work for the company as administrator, teacher, and promoter. The lecture tours she gave throughout the United States and Canada in the wake of the company's successful series of North American tours provided much-needed funds and helped educate the public. In 1957 she published her autobiography, *Come Dance with Me*.

De Valois retired in 1963, leaving the company in the hands of Frederick Ashton. She continued, however, to play an active role in the development of the Royal Ballet school (of which she is a Life Governor) and remains deeply involved in company and school activities well into her nineties. Her specialty classes for seniors at the school were a great influence on the dancers, and she continued to take a particular interest in promising young dancers and choreographers. In 1971 and 1972, she succeeded in having folk dance included in the curriculum, reflecting her conviction that native folk dance was vitally important in the development and maintenance of a particularly British style of dance. She also continued to advise and coach dancers in the production of her own ballets. In 1977 she mounted a new production of *The Sleeping Beauty*, which many believe to be the finest version extant. Also in 1977 she published a collection of essays, *Step by Step*. In 1985, a volume of her poems, *The Cycle*, was published by the Sadler's Wells Trust.

"Madame," the term of affection and respect by which her dancers know her, was also long influential in the international world of dance. In 1947, de Valois was asked to found a national ballet and school in Turkey. She stuffed it with dancers trained in her own company and supervised its successful development, making regular visits. Dancers and choreographers developed under her aegis have become important throughout the dance world: John Cranko in Stuttgart; Kenneth MacMillan, in Britain, Stuttgart, Berlin, and the United States; and Peggy van Praagh and Robert Helpmann in Australia. Dancers trained at the Royal Ballet school are prominent members of companies in western Europe, the United States, Canada, Australia, New Zealand, and South Africa

as well as noted teachers in many cities in Europe and the United States.

De Valois has always guarded her personal life closely. In 1935 she married a physician, Dr. Arthur Connell. Thereafter, in addition to her work with the ballet, she fulfilled the duties of a physician's wife, answering patients' calls, making appointments, and cooking regularly for family and guests.

In addition to being named a Dame of the British Empire, de Valois was made Chevalier of the Légion d'Honneur (1950). She received honorary doctorates from the universities of London (1947), Reading (1951), Oxford (1955), Sheffield (1955), Dublin (1957), and Aberdeen (1958). In 1954 she received the Erasmus Prize. In 1981 she was made a Companion of Honour, one of Britain's highest awards. Despite these honors, de Valois adamantly rejects the attempts of others to treat her as a great lady. She responded to fulsome praise with the remark, "It takes more than one person to make a ballet."

[*See also* Royal Ballet *and the entries on the principal figures mentioned herein.*]

BIBLIOGRAPHY

Bland, Alexander. *The Royal Ballet: The First Fifty Years*. London, 1981. Includes a foreword by de Valois.

Clarke, Mary. *The Sadler's Wells Ballet: A History and Appreciation*. New York, 1955. Includes a list of de Valois's ballets.

de Valois, Ninette. "The Future of the Ballet." *The Dancing Times* (February 1926): 589–593.

de Valois, Ninette. "Modern Choreography" (parts 1–5). *The Dancing Times* (January–May 1933).

de Valois, Ninette. "The Vic-Wells Ballet." *The Dancing Times* (October 1935): 28–31.

de Valois, Ninette. *Invitation to the Ballet*. London, 1937.

de Valois, Ninette. "Frederick Ashton." *The Dancing Times* (September 1941): 657–658.

de Valois, Ninette. "The Sadler's Wells Ballet School." *The Dancing Times* (July 1944).

de Valois, Ninette. "The Sadler's Wells Ballet in Western Europe." *The Dancing Times* (May 1945): 341–342.

de Valois, Ninette. "Constant Lambert: An Appreciation of His Work." *The Dancing Times* (October 1951): 7–8.

de Valois, Ninette. "The Sadler's Wells Organisation." *The Dancing Times* (August 1952): 654–657.

de Valois, Ninette. "Miss Sophie Fedorovitch: An Appreciation." *The Dancing Times* (March 1953): 344.

de Valois, Ninette. *Come Dance with Me*. Cleveland, 1957.

de Valois, Ninette. "Splendors and Miseries of the Diaghilev Days." *The Dancing Times* (October 1957).

de Valois, Ninette. "Folk Dance and the Royal Ballet." *The Dancing Times* (May 1960): 400–401.

de Valois, Ninette. *Step by Step*. London, 1977.

Farjeon, Annabel. "Choreographers: Dancing for de Valois and Ashton." *Dance Chronicle* 17.2 (1994): 195–206.

Genné, Beth Eliot. "Preparing for British Ballet." *The Dancing Times* (May 1981): 528–529.

Genné, Beth Eliot. *The Making of a Choreographer: Ninette de Valois and "Bar aux Folies-Bergère."* Studies in Dance History, no. 12. Madison, Wis., 1996.

Jordan, Stephanie. "A Conversation with Ninette de Valois." *Ballet Review* 18 (Spring 1990): 74–80.

Sorley Walker, Kathrine. "The Festival and the Abbey: Ninette de Valois' Early Choreography, 1925–1934" (parts 1–2). *Dance Chronicle* 7.4 (1984–1985): 379–412; 8.1–2 (1985): 51–100.

Sorley Walker, Kathrine. *Ninette de Valois: Idealist without Illusions.* London, 1987.

Sorley Walker, Katherine. "The Camargo Society." *Dance Chronicle* 18.1 (1995): 1–114.

Woodcock, Sarah C. *The Sadler's Wells Royal Ballet.* London, 1991.

ARCHIVE. The Oral History Archives, Dance Collection, New York Public Library for the Performing Arts, holds taped interviews with de Valois and many of her associates.

BETH ELIOT GENNÉ

DEVI. *See* Ragini Devi; Ritha Devi.

DE VOS, AUDREY (Audrey Mullins; born 24 January 1900 in Weymouth, Dorset, England, died 7 May 1983 in Shaftesbury, Dorset), British dance teacher. A student of Serafina Astafieva and Laurent Novikoff, de Vos first started teaching dance in her hometown of Weymouth, taking over the school started by her half sister Kathleen de Vos. During the 1930s she moved to London and opened a studio on George Street. During World War II she drove an ambulance in London. At the end of the war she moved to the studio at 42 Linden Gardens, Notting Hill Gate, where she taught for many years.

De Vos believed strongly in developing the individual talents of a dancer, both in terms of physical assets and mental ability. She was interested not so much in fitting a dancer into her ideas as in adapting her ideas to the greatest advantage of a dancer and each dancer's particular problems. She disliked the term *method*, believing that there should be continual growth, change, and adaptation in the training, to help the dancer cope, as easily as possible, with the demands, stresses, and strains of the present day.

Although de Vos was adamant on the importance of technique, she insisted that it should never be obvious; she saw the body as an orchestra with differing variations and muscular tones, always to be used expressively. She was a pioneer in combining both modern and balletic movement in her training, achieving both fluidity and control, with both strength and precision. Uniquely for her time and place, she devised and taught a form of modern technique to supplement her classes in ballet.

De Vos's classes were based on a particular problem of the moment rather than on following a set routine, so her training benefited most those students who were prepared to use their brains as well as their bodies. She constantly questioned theories, which she considered inappropriate to contemporary conditions, and always sought new ways of achieving her aims. Possessing a thorough knowledge of anatomy, she was particularly helpful to those with physical problems—and through her training was frequently able to develop bodies that other teachers might have regarded as unsuitable for dancing. The basic principle of her teaching was to work from a central focal point, with careful attention to the strength of the spine and the equal distribution of weight through the hips and the body in movement, thus relieving strain and preventing the building of unnecessary muscles. She always encouraged students with "difficult" proportions to use them to advantage.

Although her unorthodox way of teaching was for a time regarded with suspicion by the dance "establishment," de Vos attracted a wide range of students not only from the British Isles but also from the British Commonwealth countries, from Europe, and from the United States; many professionals found their way to her studio.

In the early 1960s, de Vos was guest teacher at the Joffrey Ballet's summer workshop (at the home of Rebekah Harkness, at Watch Hill, Rhode Island) and with the Royal Winnipeg Ballet (Canada). Notable among those who studied with her were Beryl Grey, Nadia Nerina, Doreen Wells, Pamela Foster, Joyce Graeme, Paula Hinton, Maggie Black, Marilyn Burr, Valda Setterfield, Richard Glasstone, and Domy Reiter-Soffer.

BIBLIOGRAPHY

Coton, A. V., and Piers Pollitzer. "Two Tributes to Audrey de Vos: The Critic and the Student." *Dancing Times* (October 1965): 20–21.

Cowper, Anthony. "Teacher with a Difference." *Dance and Dancers* (October 1953): 19.

Mason, Edward C. "Schools and Teachers: Audrey De Vos." *Dance and Dancers* (July 1957): 20–21.

DAVID VAUGHAN

DHANANJAYAN, V. P. AND SHANTA, Indian dancers, husband and wife: V. P. Dhananjayan (born 30 April 1939 in Payyanur, Kerala); Shanta Dhananjayan (born 12 August 1943 in Malacca, Malaysia). The Dhananjayans were trained from an early age at the Kalakshetra dance school of Rukmini Devi. V. P. Dhananjayan studied *bharata nāṭyam* under the supervision of Rukmini Devi and other noted teachers. He took part in several dance dramas choreographed by Rukmini Devi, receiving critical acclaim for his enactment of Rāma in her *Rāmāyaṇa* series. He also studied Sanskrit (India's classical language), music, and *kathakaḷi* dance under Chandu Panicker, acquiring proficiency in all these areas. His work with his wife Shanta adhered to the ideals of Kalakshetra. Shanta Dhananjayan also studied *bharata nāṭyam* at Kalakshetra, marrying her husband there.

The Dhananjayans embarked on an independent career in 1970, when they established their school, Bharata Kalanjali, in Madras. Their dancing is dignified, subdued, and pleasant. Rukmini Devi emphasized dignity and virility in male dancers; his training in *kathakaḷi* also contributed to V. P. Dhananjayan's masculine stage presence. His performance of Nandanar's *Varugalamo*, depicting the plight of a pariah (outcaste or untouchable) begging the deity Śiva (Shiva) to give him a divine vision, is memorable.

The Dhananjayans have choreographed a number of dances and dance dramas in the traditional format and have been presenting duets, solos, and group works. Their enjoyable compositions and group choreography are precise, with arresting patterns. Not deviating from the standards of Kalakshetra but extending its parameters, they have personalized their individual approach through a cohesive body of work.

For his contributions to dance, V. P. Dhananjayan has received many honors and awards, including the Nritya Choodamani and the Central Sangeet Natak Akademi award. Shanta Dhananjayan has been honored with the Nritya Choodamani award. Their son Satyajit is also a fine *bharata nāṭyam* performer. Both remain active, traveling, teaching, and choreographing in India and abroad from their school, Bharata Kalanjali, and home in Madras.

BIBLIOGRAPHY
Dhananjayan, V. P. *A Dancer on Dance.* 2d ed. Madras, 1992.
Kothari, Sunil, ed. *Bharata Natyam: Indian Classical Dance Art.* Bombay, 1979.

SUNIL KOTHARI

DIABLE À QUATRE, LE. Also known as *The Devil to Pay, Il Diavolo a Quattro, Weiberkur,* and *The Willful Wife.* Ballet in three acts. Choreography: Joseph Mazilier. Music: Adolphe Adam. Libretto: Adolphe de Leuven and Joseph Mazilier. Scenery: Pierre Ciceri, Édouard Despléchin, Charles Séchan, and Jules Diéterle. Costumes: Paul Lormier. First performance: 11 August 1845, Théâtre de l'Académie Royale de Musique, Paris. Principals: Lucien Petipa (The Count), Maria [Jacob] (The Countess), Joseph Mazilier (Mazourki), Carlotta Grisi (Mazourka).

The scenario of *Le Diable à Quatre* reverted to the out-of-date practice of adapting ballet plots from light opera. Using as its original source the 1686 play *The Devil of a Wife,* it was a down-to-earth ballet with a common sensical moral, more like *La Fille Mal Gardée* (1789) than the otherworldly ballets of the Romantic period.

Magic, however, catalyzes the plot by causing two wives to exchange places for a day. The proud Countess is humbled by Mazourki's rough treatment, while he in turn learns to appreciate Mazourka's gentle qualities.

Grisi surprised the critics with the humor of her acting. To display her dancing skill, she introduced two solos choreographed for her by Jules Perrot in an earlier suc-

cess, *La Esmeralda* (1844). Mazilier choreographed the ensemble dances in the style of the children's dance troupe Les Danseuses Viennoises, famed for its discipline and precision.

This popular ballet was revived, with choreography after Mazilier, in London, Milan, New York, Berlin, and Saint Petersburg.

BIBLIOGRAPHY
Beaumont, Cyril W. *Complete Book of Ballets.* London, 1937.
Guest, Ivor. *The Ballet of the Second Empire.* London, 1974.
Guest, Ivor. *The Romantic Ballet in Paris.* 2d rev. ed. London, 1980.
Guest, Ivor. *Jules Perrot: Master of the Romantic Ballet.* London, 1984.

SUSAN AU

DIABLE BOITEUX, LE. Also known as *The Devil on Two Sticks.* Ballet in three acts. Choreography: Jean Coralli. Music: Casimir Gide. Libretto: Edmond Burat de Gurgy and Adolphe Nourrit, based on a novel by Alain-René Lesage. Scenery: Léon Feuchères, Charles Séchan, Jules Diéterle, Humanité Philastre, and Charles Cambon. First performance: 1 June 1836, Théâtre de l'Académie Royale de Musique, Paris. Principals: Joseph Mazilier (Cléophas), Jean-Baptiste Barrez (Asmodée), Fanny Elssler (Florinda), Amélie Legallois (Dorothea), Pauline Leroux (Paquita).

The role of Florinda in *Le Diable Boiteux* gave Fanny Elssler her single most famous solo, "La Cachucha" (which she may have choreographed herself or learned from a Spanish dancer). It became the rage of Paris and "finally established her as the rival of [Marie] Taglioni, and presented her image as the prototype of the sensual facet of the Romantic ballet" (Guest, 1980). She is portrayed performing this dance in numerous prints, statues, and other visual images of Romantic-era ballet.

In the ballet, the dancer Florinda is one of three women pursued by the student Cléophas with the help of Asmodée, a demon whom he has freed from a bottle. Florinda's *cachucha* takes place at a supper party in her house, which Cléophas watches from the rooftops. After various misadventures Cléophas chooses Paquita, the woman he had initially rejected.

Pauline Duvernay also won a great personal triumph as Florinda when the ballet was revived, as *The Devil on Two Sticks,* at the Drury Lane, London, on 1 December 1836.

In 1967 Ann Hutchinson Guest reconstructed "La Cachucha" from the notated score of Friedrich Albert Zorn. Philippa Heale performed it with Peter Brinson's Ballet for All company, and Guest later restaged it for a number of companies. It was filmed in 1981 with Margaret Barbieri.

BIBLIOGRAPHY
Beaumont, Cyril W. *Complete Book of Ballets.* London, 1937.
Gautier, Théophile, et al. *Les beautés de l'Opéra.* Paris, 1845.

Guest, Ann Hutchinson. *Fanny Elssler's Cachucha.* New York, 1981.

Guest, Ivor. *Fanny Elssler.* London, 1970.

Guest, Ivor. *The Romantic Ballet in Paris.* 2d rev. ed. London, 1980.

Meglin, Joellen A. "*Le Diable Boiteau:* French Society behind a Spanish Facade." *Dance Chronicle* 17.3 (1994): 263–302.

Moore, Lillian. "Pauline Duvernay" (parts 1–3). *The Dancing Times* (January–March 1934).

Moore, Lillian. "Elssler and the *Cachucha.*" *The Dancing Times* (August 1936): 495–497.

SUSAN AU

DIAGHILEV, SERGE (Sergei Pavlovich Diagilev; born 19 [31] March 1872 in Selishchev Barracks, Novgorod Province, Russia, died 19 August 1929 in Venice), Russian ballet impresario and producer. Founder and artistic director of the Ballets Russes (1909–1929), Serge Diaghilev had a profound and far-reaching influence on the history of twentieth-century ballet. Under his aegis, the first of the century's classics came into being—works such as *The Firebird, Les Sylphides, Petrouchka, L'Après-midi d'un Faune, Parade, Les Noces, Les Biches, Apollon Musagète,* and *The Prodigal Son,* which transformed ballet into a vital, modern art. He nurtured several outstanding choreographers, including Michel Fokine, Vaslav Nijinsky, Léonide Massine, Bronislav Nijinska, and George Balanchine, and through them influenced the direction of ballet choreography until the 1970s. He brokered remarkable marriages between dance and the other arts, partnerships involving composers such as Igor Stravinsky, Claude Debussy, Maurice Ravel, Sergei Prokofiev, and Francis Poulenc and painters such as Léon Bakst, Natalia Goncharova, Mikhail Larionov, Pablo Picasso, André Derain, Henri Matisse, and Pavel Tchelitchev. From the numerous dancers who passed through the Ballets Russes came the performers, teachers, choreographers, and company directors who continued its work in the metropoles and outposts of the West. A man of ferocious will and infinitely discerning taste, encylopedic knowledge and passionate curiosity, Diaghilev was both a Napoleon of the arts and a Renaissance man.

The son of an army officer, Diaghilev was born into a gentry family descended from merchants and boyars who had settled in the eighteenth century in the city of Perm. Diaghilev's mother, Evgenia Evreinova, died a few days after his birth; two years later, his father married Elena Panaeva, a highly cultured woman and a distant relation of Petr Ilich Tchaikovsky. Like her husband, she was a gifted singer, and in Perm, where the couple settled, they became leaders of local musical life, participating in concerts and evenings of domestic music-making that awoke in Diaghilev a lifelong love for music.

After completing his secondary studies at the Perm gymnasium in 1890, Diaghilev made his first trip abroad, traveling to Berlin, Paris, Venice, and other cities with his cousin Dmitri Filosofov. In Vienna, they heard Richard Wagner's opera *Lohengrin,* an event that prompted numerous pilgrimages to Bayreuth and an enthusiasm for the composer, whose idea of *Gesamtkunstwerk* (synthesis of the arts) was a formative influence on the early Ballets Russes. After returning to Russia, Diaghilev entered law school at Saint Petersburg University. He also enrolled at the conservatory with the aim of becoming a composer. Although he gave up this ambition when Nikolai Rimsky-Korsakov pronounced his music "absurd," the training was critical to his later success as an impresario.

By the mid-1890s, Diaghilev's interests came increasingly to center on the visual arts. In 1895, with money from his mother's estate, he acquired his first pictures; the following year, he published his first art criticism. In 1897, at the Stieglitz Museum in Saint Petersburg, he organized his first exhibition, featuring German and British watercolors; it was followed by nearly a dozen others by 1906. However, the greatest accomplishment of his early career was the journal he founded in 1898 and edited until its demise in 1904.

Mir iskusstva (The World of Art) was to Russia what *The Yellow Book* was to England and *La Revue blanche* to France—a breath of fresh air in a stagnant art world. The journal took a keen interest in all forms of art that manifested a spirit of individuality (a criterion that earned the hostility of Russia's utilitarian-minded critics, who attacked it as "decadent"), and it promoted artists whose work challenged the methods and aims of the dominant school of realist painting. Catholic in outlook, *Mir iskusstva* covered developments at home and abroad, alerting the Russian public to Western artists associated with symbolism and Art Nouveau and to the younger generation of Russian painters working in Saint Petersburg and Moscow. In addition to editing the journal, Diaghilev contributed a number of critical articles, the most important being four polemical essays appearing in the first two issues. Here, in what amounted to a personal manifesto, he insisted that the value of art lay in the revelation of individual temperament and in the empathy this created between artist and spectator. He held to this idea throughout his life.

Although Diaghilev was its driving force, *Mir iskusstva* was a collaborative effort. At his side were old friends, including several who later formed the artistic nucleus of the Ballets Russes. Chief among them were Alexandre Benois and Léon Bakst, painters who found their true calling as designers and who were intimately associated with Diaghilev's early theater enterprises. Their friendship with Diaghilev dated to the beginning of the 1890s, influenced his ripening artistic taste, and drew his interest to ballet. They worked closely with him on *Mir iskusstva* and followed him to the Imperial Theaters, where in 1899 he was appointed a special assistant to the director, Prince

Serge Wolkonsky. Here, in addition to editing the 1899–1900 *Yearbook of the Imperial Theaters* (which, like *Mir iskusstva*, Diaghilev made a triumph of graphic design), he received his first stage assignment: to supervise a production of the ballet *Sylvia* at the Maryinsky Theater. The project, which involved Bakst, Benois, and other *miriskusstniki*, never materialized; however, it was a forerunner of the collaborative method adopted by Diaghilev in the early years of the Ballets Russes and during later periods of intense creativity.

Diaghilev remained at his post only two years. His dismissal, a result of bureaucratic intrigue and his refusal to share production credit for *Sylvia* with the Maryinsky management, closed the civil service to him, although he remained on the imperial payroll (thanks to a nominal post at the Ministry of the Court) until 1917. By the early 1900s, his interest in *Mir iskusstva* began to ebb. Disagreements surfaced among the collaborators, while Diaghilev's relationship with Filosofov—his lover since 1890 and the journal's literary editor—foundered. Meanwhile, other projects were absorbing Diaghilev, including a prize-winning monograph on the painter Dmitri Levitsky published in 1902, and the huge Exhibition of Historical Russian Portraits that opened in February 1905. For this extraordinary show, he combed museums, libraries, imperial collections, and private homes all over Russia in search of portraits from the time of Peter the Great to that of Alexander II, rediscovering in the process scores of unknown artists.

A grand visual record of Russia's imperial history, the exhibition opened during the first throes of the 1905 Revolution. For Diaghilev, the two events were not unconnected. As he told the guests at a banquet arranged in his honor in Moscow, "We are witnesses of the greatest moment of summing-up in history, in the name of a new and unknown culture, which will be created by us, and which will also sweep us away." As political pressures mounted, Diaghilev called upon the new government to make far-reaching changes in the organization of artistic life. They never took place. With the dashing of his hopes for a place at home, Diaghilev now looked abroad. In 1906, he organized the first of his Russian enterprises for export, a huge exhibition of Russian art at the Salon d'Automne in Paris, ranging from fifteenth-century icons to paintings by contemporary artists, including many of his future designers. The following year, at the Paris Opera, he presented the Russian Historical Concerts, a series of five programs that introduced the composers, works, singers, and conductors featured in his pre-1914 opera and ballet enterprises. In 1908, again at the Paris Opera, he made his debut as a theater producer with *Boris Godunov*, seen for the first time outside Russia. With music by Modest Mussorgsky and designs by members of the *Mir iskusstva* circle, the opera was both a summing-up and a harbinger of the future.

In all likelihood, it was Benois, a passionate balletomane, who induced Diaghilev to include dance along with opera in the 1909 Saison Russe at the Théâtre du Châtelet. All the ballets were by Michel Fokine, with whom Benois had previously worked, and two of them— *Le Pavillon d'Armide*, a rococo fantasy that he had conceived as well as designed, and *Les Sylphides*, an evocation of the Romantic *ballet blanc* that Benois now redesigned—reflected his cult of the past. By contrast, the *Polovtsian Dances* from *Prince Igor* and *Cléopâtre* mined the Orientalist vein of *Boris Godunov* and the season's opera offerings. The operas were greeted appreciatively, but the impact of the ballets was overwhelming. This triumphant season launched Diaghilev's career as a ballet impresario.

From the start, Diaghilev was a "hands-on" producer. Even when operating within a collaborative framework, he looked after every aspect of production, engaging dancers, attending rehearsals, and supervising scenery, as well as raising money, dealing with impresarios, and seeing to publicity. Initially he shared artistic control with a committee of *miriskusstniki* colleagues. However, with the shift by 1911 from a repertory for export to one based on in-house creation, Diaghilev's attitude toward the enterprise changed: whereas before he had acted as its midwife, now he increasingly viewed it as the instrument of his imagination, a vehicle to express his own creative vision.

Among the artists most closely identified with this vision was Léon Bakst, who provided the scenery and costumes for fifteen ballets between 1909 and 1914. As the designer of *Cléopâtre* (1909), *Schéhérazade* (1910), *Thamar* (1912), and *Le Dieu Bleu* (1912), he created the magnificent settings that were virtually synonymous with Ballets Russes orientalism. His renderings of classical antiquity in *Narcisse* (1911), *Daphnis et Chloë* (1912), and *L'Après-midi d'un Faune* (1912), and the Biedermeier charm of his *Le Carnaval* (1910) and *Le Spectre de la Rose* (1911), revealed his virtuosity as a stylist and the masterful orchestration of color that distinguished all his works. The fusion of art, music, and dance that critics discerned in the best of Diaghilev's pre–World War I productions owed much to the syncretism of Bakst.

Another artist who proved an even greater catalyst to Diaghilev's imagination was the composer Igor Stravinsky. The first of the impresario's great "discoveries," Stravinsky contributed scores to more than a dozen productions, including five landmark ballets—*The Firebird* (1910), *Petrouchka* (1911), *Le Sacre du Printemps* (1913), *Les Noces* (1923), and *Apollon Musagète* (1928). With Stravinsky's *The Firebird* and Rimsky-Korsakov's *Schéhérazade* as the linchpins of the 1910 season, Diaghilev made music fully equal in importance to dance and design. *The Firebird*, moreover, was the first of a long series of commissions that established Diaghilev as a leading patron of modern music. Apart from the Stravinsky ballets, these commissions included such major works as Maurice Ravel's *Daphnis et Chloë* (1912), Claude Debussy's *Jeux* (1913), Richard Strauss's *Die Josephslegende* (1914), Erik Satie's *Parade* (1917), Manuel de Falla's *Le Tricorne* (1919), Francis Poulenc's *Les Biches* (1924), and Sergei Prokofiev's *The Prodigal Son* (1929), along with lesser works by Georges Auric, Darius Milhaud, Vittorio Rieti, Constant Lambert, and Henri Sauguet. The literature of twentieth-century ballet music owes an enormous debt to Diaghilev's musicianship.

The third figure who exerted a powerful influence on Diaghilev's prewar imagination was Vaslav Nijinsky, who became his lover in the aftermath of the 1909 season. Diaghilev's growing attachment to him prompted the creation of numerous ballets celebrating the dancer's virtuosity and exploring his still-unripened personality. Beginning in 1910, Nijinsky was the star on whom the Ballets Russes centered. He played the Golden Slave in *Schéhérazade,* Harlequin in *Le Carnaval,* and the title roles in *Le Spectre de la Rose, Narcisse, Petrouchka,* and *Le Dieu Bleu*—parts that recreated the Maryinsky *Wunderkind* as an erotic androgyne or a symbolist hero. The presence of Nijinsky, Adolph Bolm, and many other fine male dancers in the company sparked a renaissance of male dancing, bringing to an end the nineteenth-century tradition of the *danseuse en travesti* (women dancing male roles).

Nijinsky the choreographer was Diaghilev's second great discovery—proof, again, of his remarkable gift for developing raw talent. In *L'Après-midi d'un Faune* (1912), Nijinsky abandoned the aesthetics of Fokine's "new ballet," while treating sexuality with an explicitness that many found shocking. The following year, with *Le Sacre du Printemps,* he crossed the threshold of choreographic modernism with a vision of ancient Slavic rites and human barbarism that gave rise to one of the century's legendary artistic scandals. Both these ballets were at least partly the creations of Diaghilev. Not only did he play a key role in their genesis by suggesting their general style and choosing their various collaborators, but he also placed extraordinary resources at Nijinsky's command: underwriting trips to Émile Jaques-Dalcroze's art center at Hellerau, Germany, and to Princess Maria Tenisheva's art colony at Talashkino, Russia; hiring Marie Rambert as the choreographer's assistant for *Sacre;* spending hours in the studio; and paying for untold hours of experiment and rehearsal. His generosity as a mentor knew no bounds.

Although Diaghilev typically reserved generosity of this magnitude to lovers, his embrace of modernism owed far more to his own artistic restiveness than to his attachment to Nijinsky. Surfacing in the aftermath of *Petrouchka* (1911), the culminating work of the Fokine period, this restiveness signaled Diaghilev's mounting dissatisfaction with the legacy of *Mir iskusstva.* Although Bakst remained a member of his inner circle until 1917, neither Benois nor Fokine survived Diaghilev's change in course: Benois broke with him in 1911, and Fokine in 1912. For the dancers, many of whom had worked with Fokine since childhood, his departure from the company was deeply unsettling. Diaghilev, however, had no compunction in discarding artists who had ceased to serve his purposes.

The emergence of modernism coincided with another major change in the company's identity. Initially a summer touring ensemble made up of vacationing dancers from the Bolshoi and Maryinsky companies, in 1911 the Ballets Russes became a permanent enterprise headquartered in the West. Although Russian works, including the half-dozen operas produced by Diaghilev from 1912 to 1914, continued to dominate the repertory, his commissions to non-Russian composers such as Debussy, Ravel, and Strauss revealed his growing internationalism. Like modernism, internationalism became a pillar of Diaghilev's empire.

Nijinsky's marriage in 1913 and his subsequent dismissal from the company brought a temporary halt to the modernist revolution initiated by *Faune.* Nevertheless, in the following months, when Diaghilev paid his last visit to Russia, he engaged two of the artists who accompanied him on the next stage of his modernist adventure. One was Natalia Goncharova, a leading cubofuturist and neoprimitivist painter, who designed *Le Coq d'Or,* the outstanding success of the 1914 season. The other was Léonide Massine, a young Bolshoi dancer who became Diaghilev's lover. Handsome, gifted, and intellectually curious, Massine reawakened Diaghilev's passion for mentorship. Massine's education as a choreographer coincided with the opening months of World War I, which he spent with Diaghilev in Italy exploring the artistic treasures of Florence and Rome. From there they went to Switzerland, where Diaghilev set up the first of his wartime headquarters in 1915. Here, under the tutelage of Goncharova's partner, the avant-garde painter Mikhail Larionov, Massine created his first choreographic works— *Liturgie* (which was never performed) and *Le Soleil de Nuit* (1915).

At the same time, Diaghilev was reassembling a company for an American tour under the aegis of the Metropolitan Opera. With Europe at war, money scarce, and few of the company's stars willing or able to travel, the task was herculean. Dancers arrived in twos and threes from Russia, England, and other countries, often by circuitous routes. Many were newcomers to the company; some were barely out of school. As they labored to master his old works, Diaghilev, amazingly, was immersed in plans for new ones. He discovered the Italian futurists and toyed with several ideas for collaborating with the group, although only *Fireworks* (1917), with music by Stravinsky and sets and lighting by Giacomo Balla, came to fruition. Under the influence of Larionov and Goncharova, moreover, he recast the treatment of Russian folk material, stylizing it and dressing it in the brilliant colors of neoprimitivism.

The American tour that began in January 1916 interrupted these exciting experiments, although it restored the Ballets Russes to financial health. However, when Otto Kahn, the chairman of the Metropolitan's board of directors, invited the company to return the following autumn under the direction of Nijinsky (who had rejoined the Ballets Russes in America), Diaghilev was only too happy to remain with Massine and a skeleton company in Europe. Settling in Rome, they embarked on two productions that did much to shape the company's postwar image: *Les Femmes de Bonne Humeur* (1917), which initiated the genre of "period modernism," and *Parade* (1917), which inaugurated the company's alliance with the French avant-garde.

Inspired by Carlo Goldoni's classical play, *Les Femmes de Bonne Humeur* was the first of several ballets that juxtaposed a period theme with a modernist treatment of music, dance, and design. All were choreographed by Massine, who infused them with the rhythm, speed, and angularity of his early signature style, and, with one exception, they were designed by painters of the emerging School of Paris. Musically, too, these ballets represented an accommodation of both past and present. With scores cobbled together by Diaghilev from little-known music by Domenico Scarlatti, Giaocchino Rossini, Domenico Cimarosa, and Giambattista Pergolesi, they traveled across time, laying the foundation for the neoclassicism born with Stravinsky's *Pulcinella* (1920).

In contrast to these period ballets, which drew on Italian sources, *Parade* owed its genesis and theme to the French avant-garde. Conceived by Jean Cocteau and laced with borrowings from popular culture, it had music by Erik Satie and designs by Picasso that were indebted both to cubism and to his newer, "classical" style. Although Diaghilev failed to follow up on the *Parade*'s contemporary subject matter for some years, most of his commissions now went to artists associated with the prewar cubists and Fauves, including André Derain and Henri Matisse. It was to Picasso, however, that Diaghilev turned again and again. Between 1917 and 1924, the painter created sets, costumes, and curtains for no fewer than five productions, while also contributing numerous drawings to Ballets Russes programs.

Picasso's second ballet for Diaghilev was *Le Tricorne* (1919), and like so many other works that had their origin in the war years, this, too, was the creation of Diaghilev's traveling studio. The ballet grew out of his love for Spain, where the company first performed in 1916, and his dis-

covery of Manuel de Falla's music. In 1917, as the Ballets Russes toured South America, the composer, Diaghilev, Massine, and the Spanish dancer Félix Fernández traveled throughout Spain in search of authentic dance and musical material for the ballet. *Le Tricorne* did not come to the stage for another two years; when it did, however, it initiated a postwar vogue for Spanish dance and became the model for La Argentina's ground-breaking ballets of the middle and late 1920s.

The experiments of the war years took place against a background of increasing financial difficulty. In 1917, the Revolution cut off Diaghilev's income from Russia. By the spring of 1918, he was holed up in Madrid, penniless. Until then, Diaghilev had refused to allow his company to appear in music halls; now, swallowing his pride, he accepted with gratitude an offer from Oswald Stoll for the Ballets Russes to dance at the London Coliseum. "London has saved me," he later wrote a friend. Indeed, between 1918 and 1922, the British capital virtually became his home. It was here, rather than in Paris, that the Ballets Russes performed for months at a time, danced the premieres of *Le Tricorne* and *La Boutique Fantasque* (1919), tapped an intellectual public enamoured of Diaghilev's modernist repertory, and built a huge popular following. And it was at London's Alhambra Theatre, another venerable music hall, that Diaghilev in 1921 mounted *The Sleeping Princess*.

This landmark enterprise, which introduced Marius Petipa's *The Sleeping Beauty* to the international repertory, revealed yet again Diaghilev's extraordinary resourcefulness in coping with personal and professional upsets. In 1921, Massine left the company after falling in love with the dancer Vera Savina. His place was not easily filled. Thadée Slavinsky, to whom Diaghilev entrusted the choreography of *Chout* (1921) under the tutelage of Larionov, proved to be a disappointment. With new works temporarily out of the question, Diaghilev looked to the nineteenth-century repertory for a possible substitute. This was a risky solution, given the lukewarm reception of his prewar productions of *Giselle* (1910) and *Swan Lake* (1911). Rejecting the suggestion of *Coppélia*, he settled on *The Sleeping Beauty*, inducing Stoll to underwrite the production on a grand scale. To design the ballet, Diaghilev turned for a last time to Bakst, with whom he had previously broken; he called on the former Maryinsky *régisseur* Nicholas Sergeyev to set the choreography, and engaged three Maryinsky ballerinas—Vera Trefilova, Lubov Egorova, and Olga Spessivtseva—to dance the role of Aurora. Despite the care he lavished on the work, and despite its relatively long run of three months, the production lost a fortune and brought the Ballets Russes close to financial ruin.

Even as the dancers abandoned what they perceived to be a sinking ship, Diaghilev was engrossed in plans for the future. At his side was Bronislava Nijinska, who had re-joined the company after an absence of several years. Formed as a choreographer in the experimental ferment of post-Revolutionary Kiev, she had proved her mettle in revising sections of *The Sleeping Princess*. Diaghilev's faith in her was soon rewarded: with *Les Noces* (1923) and *Les Biches* (1924), Nijinska produced a synthesis of modernism and the *danse d'école* that marked the beginnings of ballet neoclassicism.

Ironically, this important development coincided with Diaghilev's rediscovery of contemporary subject matter and his adoption of the young French composers known as Les Six. This newest shift in artistic direction partly reflected a change in location: after the failure of *The Sleeping Princess*, Diaghilev had moved the center of his operations from London to Paris and Monte Carlo, where the Ballets Russes now performed for several months of the year. It also reflected the influence of Rolf de Maré's Ballets Suédois, a Paris-based troupe of mostly Swedish dancers that had eclipsed the Ballets Russes in the early 1920s as the leading purveyor of avant-garde ballet.

During his years in Russia, Diaghilev had dreamed of founding a museum or ruling an enterprise like the Imperial Theaters. In Monte Carlo, where he enjoyed the support of the ruling Grimaldis, he thought his old dreams might be realized. In 1924, he put his encyclopedic knowledge of music to work again with a series of French historical operas, including several by Charles Gounod, attesting to his continued interest in lyric theater. This was also revealed in his production of Stravinsky's operas *Mavra* (1922) and *Oedipus Rex* (1927) and in the many ballets of the 1920s that called for vocal accompaniment, such as *Le Tricorne, Les Noces, Les Biches,* and *Barabau* (1925). Moreover, under the terms of his annual agreements with the Société des Bains de Mer, which controlled the Théâtre de Monte-Carlo, he provided not only the dancers but also the choreographers for most of its opera productions.

Although esteemed by Diaghilev both in her own right and as Nijinsky's sister, Nijinska never became an intimate of his circle. Nor did the choreographer who replaced her when she left the Ballets Russes early in 1925. Fresh from Soviet Russia, George Balanchine was only twenty when he joined the company, although, he already had experience as a choreographer. This, and the fact that he was married, precluded the intimacy that was a necessary condition of Diaghilev's mentorship. Still, Diaghilev contributed enormously to the young man's development, refining his musical taste, introducing him to several future collaborators, and, most important, entrusting him with the choreography of ten ballets and the dances in nearly three dozen operas. Again, Diaghilev's faith was not misplaced: under his tutelage, Balanchine created two

outstanding works—*Apollon Musagète* (1928), which marked his embrace of neoclassicism, and *The Prodigal Son* (1929).

For all his faith in Balanchine, Diaghilev continued to mold not only individual ballets but also the repertory as a whole. If previously he had typically relied on a single in-house choreographer, he now routinely called on Massine and others to supplement Balanchine's services. He confided the libretti to his secretary and assistant Boris Kochno, and most of the principal roles to his lover Serge Lifar, whom he promoted to stardom with Balanchine's assistance. He awarded commissions to ever younger composers and painters such as Constant Lambert, Pedro Pruna, Henri Sauguet, Joan Miró, and Vittorio Rieti.

Despite the prevailing internationalism of the period, several works testified to Diaghilev's renewed interest in Russian artists and themes, both Soviet and émigré. In 1924, he came close to accepting an invitation to visit the Soviet Union. Although the visit fell through, plans were soon under way to produce an all-Soviet ballet, *Le Pas d'Acier* (1927), with music by Prokofiev, constructivist designs by Georgi Yakulov, and choreography by Kasyan Goleizovsky (who was eventually replaced by Massine). Other productions drew on young émigré talent. *Zéphire et Flore* (1925) had music by Vladimir Dukelsky (Vernon Duke); *Ode* (1928) teamed the painter Pavel Tchelitchev and the composer Nicolas Nabokov. Kochno, Balanchine, and Lifar, along with several of the company's lead dancers—Anatole Vilzak, Felia Doubrovska, Olga Spessivtseva, Alexandra Danilova, and Alice Nikitina—and many of its lesser ones were also émigrés.

Russia was also present in another activity that increasingly occupied Diaghilev as the 1920s drew to a close. Over the years, he had collected as he commissioned, amassing the designs, portraits, and other objects that were sometimes exhibited in tandem with company seasons and that formed the basis of his collections for Massine and Lifar. Toward the end of his life, however, Diaghilev turned his connoisseurship to books, building up a collection of rare Russian volumes that included one of only seven known copies of the first Russian grammar, from the press of Ivan Fedorov, and, from the same press, a Book of Hours, dated 1564. As Diaghilev's passion for book collecting grew, his interest in the company waned, and he turned over the supervision of certain works, such as *Ode*, to Kochno. Still, he never lost the thrill of discovery. He was fascinated by the innovative classicism of Balanchine's *Apollon Musagète* and seemingly rejuvenated by his relationship with Igor Markevitch, a young émigré composer who made his debut at Covent Garden under Diaghilev's auspices in 1929.

Despite his willingness to discard collaborators who had outlived their artistic usefulness, Diaghilev could be remarkably loyal. During the years of Nijinsky's illness, he never forgot him. He came up with jobs for his old friends Walter Nouvel and Pavel Koribut-Kubitovich when they arrived penniless from Russia in the 1920s. In Spain he found money for the doctor who kept Lydia Sokolova's baby daughter from dying. "Judge of my love," he told Tamara Karsavina in 1929, explaining that he had left his sickbed to see her dance in *Petrouchka*. He could drive a hard bargain, but he could also be immensely generous. To his three loves—Filosofov, Nijinsky, and Massine—and his two "sons"—Stravinsky and Prokofiev—he gave unstintingly of his time, money, and knowledge. Without Diaghilev, it is doubtful whether Nijinsky or Massine would ever have become choreographers, or whether Fokine, Nijinska, or even Balanchine would have achieved international renown. The list of dancers he launched to stardom—Nijinsky, Karsavina, Bolm, Massine, Lydia Lopokova, Olga Spessivtseva, Anton Dolin, Alexandra Danilova, Alicia Markova, and Lifar—speaks for itself.

By 1929, Diaghilev's health was failing. For some time, he had been suffering from diabetes, and although he made a pretense of controlling his diet (he had a Russian weakness for sweets), he apparently never considered the use of insulin. In late July 1929, he bid farewell to the company in London and set off with Markevitch for an opera tour of Germany. From there he went to Venice. By 19 August he was dead. With him were Lifar, Kochno, and Misia Sert, a friend and patron of more than twenty years.

With Diaghilev's death, the Ballets Russes collapsed. Although he had contracts signed for most of the coming year, no one materialized to take the company in hand. In the final analysis, the Ballets Russes was a one-man show, resting on Diaghilev's unique combination of connoisseurship, critical acumen, business sense, social charm, and sheer willpower. He had a remarkable ability to make the marketplace of art serve his ends, to elicit the support of wealthy patrons, and to win over cultural tastemakers. Under his aegis, ballet not only prospered, but its prestige rose dramatically.

No less dramatic were the changes he wrought in the art form itself. By 1929, one-act ballets were the norm, as were scores and designs of high artistic quality. Male dancing occupied a place of eminence. Choreography was accepted on a par with composition in music. Although fewer than a dozen Ballets Russes works remain in active repertory, the true measure of Diaghilev's accomplishment lies in the artistry and high esteem of ballet today and in the legacy of his many artistic descendants around the world. Without Diaghilev, the history of twentieth-century ballet would be far different.

[*See also* Ballets Russes de Serge Diaghilev; Music for Dance, *article on* Western Music since 1900; Scenic Design; *and the entries on Bakst, Benois, Kochno, Massine, Nijinsky, Stravinsky, and other major figures mentioned herein.*]

BIBLIOGRAPHY

Baer, Nancy Van Norman, ed. *The Art of Enchantment: Diaghilev's Ballets Russes.* Exhibition catalog, Fine Arts Museums of San Francisco, 3 December 1988–26 February 1989. San Francisco, 1988.

Beaumont, Cyril W. *Bookseller at the Ballet: Memoirs, 1891 to 1929, Incorporating "The Diaghilev Ballet in London."* London, 1975.

Benois, Alexandre. *Reminiscences of the Russian Ballet.* Translated by Mary Britnieva. London, 1941.

Bowlt, John E. *The Silver Age: Russian Art of the Early Twentieth Century and the "World of Art" Group.* Newtonville, Mass., 1979.

Buckle, Richard. *Diaghilev.* New York, 1979.

Charles-Roux, Edmonde. *Chanel.* Translated by Nancy Amphoux. New York, 1975.

de Valois, Ninette. *Invitation to the Ballet.* London, 1937.

Dolin, Anton. *Last Words: A Final Autobiography.* Edited by Kay Hunter. London, 1985.

Egorova, E. I. "Sem'ia Diagilevykh i kulturnaia zhizn' Permi XIX veka." In *Sergei Diagilev i khudozhestvennaia kul'tura XIX–XX vv,* edited by N. V. Beliaeva et al. Perm, Russia, 1989.

Fokine, Michel. *Memoirs of a Ballet Master.* Translated by Vitale Fokine. Edited by Anatole Chujoy. London, 1961.

Garafola, Lynn. *Diaghilev's Ballets Russes.* New York and Oxford, 1989.

García-Márquez, Vicente. *España y los Ballets Russes.* Exhibition catalog, Auditorio Manuel de Falla, Granada, 17 June–2 July 1989. Granada, 1989.

García-Márquez, Vicente. *Massine: A Biography.* New York, 1995.

Gold, Arthur, and Robert Fizdale. *Misia: The Life of Misia Sert.* New York, 1980.

Grigoriev, Serge. *The Diaghilev Ballet, 1909–1929.* Translated and edited by Vera Bowen. London, 1953.

Haskell, Arnold L., and Walter Nouvel. *Diaghileff: His Artistic and Private Life.* New York, 1935.

Karsavina, Tamara. *Theatre Street: The Reminiscences of Tamara Karsavina.* London, 1930.

Kennedy, Janet Elspeth. *The "Mir Iskusstva" Group and Russian Art, 1898–1912.* New York, 1977.

Kochno, Boris. *Diaghilev and the Ballets Russes.* Translated by Adrienne Foulke. New York, 1970.

Lifar, Serge. *Serge Diaghilev, His Life, His Work, His Legend: An Intimate Biography.* New York, 1940.

Macdonald, Nesta. *Diaghilev Observed by Critics in England and the United States, 1911–1929.* New York, 1975.

Massine, Léonide. *My Life in Ballet.* Edited by Phyllis Hartnoll and Robert Rubens. New York, 1968.

Nijinska, Bronislava. *Early Memoirs.* Translated and edited by Irina Nijinska and Jean Rawlinson. New York, 1981.

Parton, Anthony. *Mikhail Larionov and the Russian Avant-Garde.* London, 1993.

Pastori, Jean-Pierre. *Soleil de Nuit: La renaissance des Ballets Russes.* Lausanne, 1993.

Schouvaloff, Alexander. *Léon Bakst: The Theatre Art.* London, 1991.

Sokolova, Lydia. *Dancing for Diaghilev.* Edited by Richard Buckle. London, 1960.

Steegmuller, Francis. *Cocteau: A Biography.* Boston, 1970.

Zil'bershtein, I. S., and V. A. Samkov, eds. *Sergei Diagilev i russkoe iskusstvo.* 2 vols. Moscow, 1982.

ARCHIVES. Archives Nationales, Paris. Bibliothèque de l'Opéra, Paris. Dance Collection, New York Public Library for the Performing Arts. Harvard Theatre Collection. Music Division, Library of Congress, Washington, D.C. Metropolitan Opera Archives, New York. Société des Bains de Mer, Monte Carlo. Theatre Museum, London. Tobin Collection, San Antonio, Texas. Wadsworth Atheneum, Hartford, Connecticut.

LYNN GARAFOLA

DIDELOT, CHARLES-LOUIS (born 1767 in Stockholm, died 9 November 1837 in Kiev), French choreographer. Didelot ranks high among the artists who formed nineteenth-century Russian ballet. His compelling drive for excellence in dance raised his own technique and performance to a high level, but his greatest fame came from his innovative choreography and imaginative staging. August Bournonville declared, "Didelot was undoubtedly the greatest choreographer after Noverre." His success as a teacher was equally remarkable.

Didelot was the son of two French ballet dancers, Charles Didelot and Magdeleine Maréchal, who had come to Stockholm to perform at the Royal Opera House. His early dance education, other than what he learned from his parents, was entrusted in Sweden to the competent Louis Frossard, a former dancer and choreographer at the Comédie Italienne in Paris. In his stage debut, young Didelot played the role of Cupid so successfully that he repeated this role often.

In 1776 Didelot was sent to study in Paris, where he was tutored by Jean Dauberval until Dauberval left the Académie Royale de Musique in 1783. A solid friendship developed between the two men, and later Didelot often acknowledged in print his great debt and affection toward his teacher. In particular, he paid tribute to Dauberval's expertise in pantomime and character portrayal, for which Didelot's own ballets were also noted.

Didelot took various jobs in Paris, including one at the Théâtre de l'Ambigu-Comique, where children took the parts of puppets. Perhaps it was there that Didelot developed the idea for the flights on wires that his dancers took in later ballets. After Dauberval's departure, Didelot studied briefly in Paris with Jean-Barthélemy Lany, but feeling out of place in Lany's elite clientele, he transferred to Jacques-François Deshayes, a ballet master at the Comédie Française. By 1782 Didelot was on the list of dancers there. Among the female dancers in the same company was Marie Rose Paul (or Pole), who became Didelot's first wife; she was a competent, stately, graceful dancer who enhanced Didelot's later productions. By 1783 Didelot was listed on the rolls of the Académie Royale de Musique as a conservatory pupil who danced in the theater.

On a visit to France in 1784, King Gustav III of Sweden saw Didelot perform and insisted that he return to Stockholm. Didelot unwillingly complied. At the Royal Opera House on 11 May 1786 he appeared as one of the Happy Shades in the first act of the opera *Orpheus and Eurydice*. Didelot suffered by comparison with his fellow dancer Antoine Bournonville, because Didelot was small and sinewy and had a complexion scarred by smallpox. He was thus better suited to *demi-caractère* dance than to noble roles.

When the opera *Armide* by Christoph Willibald Gluck and Philippe Quinault was staged in Stockholm in January 1787, Didelot headed the Pleasures in act 2. The same year, the twenty-year-old Didelot was asked to stage the dances for the opera *Frigga*, with lyrics by Carl Gustaf Leopold and music by O. Åhlström. As he was to do throughout his career, Didelot indulged his taste for idyllic themes and settings.

Nonetheless, Didelot knew that he would have difficulty competing in Stockholm with Bournonville. He returned to Paris in 1787 to study under the redoubtable Gaëtan and Auguste Vestris. Rose Paul was also a pupil of the Vestris brothers at the time.

Although he loved Paris, Didelot was willing to be lured away by lucrative salary offers. In 1787 Jean-Georges Noverre invited him to collaborate at the King's Theatre in London. On 8 December 1787, Didelot appeared there in *Les Offrandes à l'Amour*, along with the popular Madame Hilligsberg and Auguste Vestris. He also danced that season in Noverre's *L'Amour et Psyché*, *Les Fêtes de Tempé*, and *Euthyme et Eucharis*. Although these performances were not acclaimed, Didelot was to benefit from the collaboration with Noverre. He later staged his own versions of *Psyché* and *Euthyme*.

Didelot was given a benefit performance of his own on 22 May 1788, for which he created two new ballets—*La Bonté du Seigneur* and a five-act *Richard Coeur-de-Lion*. Neither was retained in the theater's repertory. During the remainder of the season, he danced in Noverre's *Adèle de Ponthieu* and in Noverre's revival of Dauberval's *Déserteur*.

Didelot returned to Paris to dance in an autumn presentation of Jean-Jacques Rousseau's opera *Le Devin du Village*. Although the French press declared this production a brilliant success, it brought Didelot no offers for permanent employment, so once again he crossed the channel to appear at the King's Theatre.

On 10 January 1789 Didelot produced a new ballet, *L'Embarquement pour Cythère*, and a new *divertissement*. On 31 January, when he danced in Noverre's *Les Fêtes Provençales*, the audience displayed such disapproval that Didelot and his fellow performers resorted to kicking off their shoes to get laughs. In April the management engaged the forty-six-year-old dancer Marie-Madeleine Guimard, whom Didelot partnered in several productions.

Two factors probably drew Didelot south to Bordeaux later that year. One was the presence of Dauberval and his wife, Madame Théodore, who danced at the Grand Théâtre of Bordeaux with her husband. The second was the Grand

Théâtre itself, which had few rivals in Europe for beauty and grandeur. In Bordeaux Didelot appeared on 21 October 1789 in the ballet *Amphion, Élève des Muses*.

During the Revolution, French theaters were often disrupted by partisans of both sides, and Bordeaux was no exception. Dauberval and his wife, who had many aristocratic connections, left Bordeaux in April 1790. During the next season, Didelot worked with Salvatore Viganò, who joined the Bordeaux troupe with his wife, Maria Medina. The new ballet master, Eugène Hus, presented a version of Maximilien Gardel's *Premier Navigateur*. Didelot's performance was praised by the local press, and in the summer of 1790 Didelot was allowed to stage the ballets for the opera *Chimène*.

Meanwhile, Gustav III continued to insist that because Didelot had been educated at court expense and was engaged in royal service, Sweden had a right to enjoy his talent. Didelot did not, however, return to Sweden.

In winter of 1791 Didelot, his wife, and Auguste Vestris were all engaged again by London's Pantheon Theatre. The Didelots danced in *Amphion and Thalia* in February 1791, and in March Didelot partnered Madame Dauberval in her husband's version of *Télémaque*. During the remainder of the season, Didelot took part in other productions by Dauberval.

On Dauberval's advice, Didelot made his debut on 31 August 1791 at the Paris Opera in the last act of *Le Premier Navigateur*, one of Gardel's more popular productions. He subsequently danced in the operas *Diane et Endymion* and *Castor et Pollux*.

When Didelot appeared on 11 December 1791 in *Bacchus et Ariadne*, choreographed by Sébastien Gallet, he changed the history of ballet with his reform of its costume. In the eighteenth century, male dancers, whether portraying gods, savages, or noblemen, usually dressed in buckled shoes with heels, powdered wigs, and knee breeches. In *Bacchus et Ariadne*, however, Didelot appeared in flesh-colored tights with a tiger's skin thrown over his shoulder. He wore a crown of grape leaves and held the staff of Bacchus in his hand. In July 1792, for the opera *Corisande*, he wore a gauzy tunic; his partner, Geneviève Chevigny, also appeared in a costume modeled after the Greek chiton. Before long, others imitated his audacity, and costumes more suitable for dancing became generally accepted.

Both Didelot and Rose Paul appeared with distinction at the Opera in Pierre Gardel's production of *Le Jugement de Pâris* in March 1793; however, they soon joined the company of the Théâtre National. There they took part in the patriotic piece *La Constitution à Constantinople*, the opera *Selico, ou Les Nègres*, and the patriotic *divertissement La Fête Civique*. When the company's director, Marguerite Brunet Montansier, was arrested during the Reign of Terror, the members formed a Society of Artists; Dide-

lot, Gallet, and others drew up a charter establishing a primitive communal rule for the company, which continued to perform in Montansier's theater, renamed the Théâtre de l'Égalité. Didelot danced there in Gallet's ballet *La Journée de l'Amour*, among other productions. The theatre nevertheless closed in December 1794.

Didelot and Rose Paul next found employment in Lyon at the Théâtre des Terreaux, where they appeared in Coindé's version of *Le Siège de Cythère* in September 1795. Didelot also staged a one-act version of *La Métamorphose* with decor in the spirit of the ancient Greek poet Anacreon, whose poetry extolled idylls of wine and love in dreamy meadows and sylvan dales (hence the term *Anacreontic*). In this ballet Didelot revealed his artistic credo, encouraging the use of mime. He also wished to emphasize certain ethical and moral ideas: for example, the idea that a man ruled by his passions could expect misfortune, and that the true love of a woman was a precious treasure. He also continued his campaign for costumes that harmonized with the setting and action.

On 11 February 1796 the Didelots opened another season at the King's Theatre. Although their first performance was in a *divertissement* by Didelot, most of the season featured works by Giacomo Onorati. Caricatures by James Gillray of their performances show Rose clad in Greek costume and Roman sandals.

In April 1796 Didelot produced a dance in Scottish setting, *Little Peggy's Love*, which became a great favorite. In his *L'Amant Statue*, Didelot took the part of a statue that is supposed to move according to the direction of the sculptor, but that is at last completely animated by the charms of a nymph. On 2 June 1796 Didelot presented a more elaborate version of *La Métamorphose*, titled *L'Amour Vengé, ou La Métamorphose*, as well as an Indian-style *divertissement*, *The Caravan at Rest*. On 7 July 1796 he produced the first version of his masterpiece *Flore et Zéphire*, a ballet *divertissement* in one act and seven scenes, with music by Cesare Bossi and scenery and machines by Liparotti. Rose Paul danced the role of Flora, with Didelot as Zephyr.

Didelot also staged another new work, *L'Heureux Naufrage, ou Les Sorcières Écossaises*. Although he acknowledged his debt to Shakespeare's *Macbeth* for the Scottish witches, the ballet has little in common with the play. Its plot uses the device of a danced dream. In the last act Didelot divided the stage into two parts, with one side showing action within a house while the other side showed action in a garden. Both works were well received in London.

In the season opening in November 1796 Didelot danced in the same productions, along with several new works choreographed by Gallet. On 6 April 1796 Didelot choreographed the impressive four-act production *Sappho et Phaon*. He danced the part of Phaon, the ungrateful lover of the poet Sappho, and was injured in jumping from a rock, leaving him unable to perform at his peak for several months. However, on 15 June Didelot presented *Acis et Galathée*, with a new score by Bossi. During the 1797/98 season Didelot continued to perform in Gallet's productions.

In 1798 Didelot's dancing costumes came under attack. In the House of Lords, Bishop Barrington of Durham declared that England's enemy France was using the licentious costumes and indecent attitudes of French dancers to corrupt the morals of English youth. The King's Theatre reacted by postponing performances of *Bacchus et Ariadne*, in which the offensive costumes had been seen, and by insisting that white stockings replace the flesh-colored ones Didelot had worn.

The next year James Harvey D'Egville replaced Gallet as choreographer, and Didelot appeared in three of his ballets. In 1800 Didelot choreographed a two-act version of *Laura et Lenza*, followed the next year by *Alonzo the Brave and the Fair Imogine*, based on a poem by Matthew ("Monk") Lewis. Didelot's last choreographic production in England during this phase of his career was a three-act Chinese-style ballet, *Ken-si and Tao*, given in May 1801.

Lured by a contract promising twelve thousand rubles over a period of three years, Didelot and Rose Paul left England for Russia. Didelot was also pleased with the prospect of training his own troupe in Russia, thanks to imperial support of the theatrical school.

The arrival of the Didelot couple set a new course for ballet in Saint Petersburg. No immediate predecessor had matched the drive and dedication he brought to choreog-

raphy and the training of young dancers. His first one-act ballet, *Apollo and Daphne*, was given at the Hermitage Theater on 4 April 1802, followed by a production at Pavlovsk in 1803 of *Roland and Morgana*.

With the death of Rose Paul in 1803, Didelot suffered both personal and professional loss, because she was the partner who attracted crowds. In December 1803 he took the chief role in his ballet *Le Pâtre et l'Hamadryade*, partnering the French dancer, Marie Rose Colinette, who had come to Saint Petersburg in 1799. Didelot married this new Rose in either 1805 or 1806. In Russia, his second wife seems to have used her dancing talent chiefly in teaching ballroom dancing to the nobility, which established connections that helped Didelot's turbulent career.

Didelot's *Flore et Zéphire*, retitled *Zéphire et Flore*, delighted the Hermitage audience in 1804 and later became part of the repertory of the Bolshoi Kamenyi Theater. At one point, to the amazement of the audience, Flora flew about the stage while a circle of cupids danced around her.

In 1806 Didelot's main works included dances in two operas by Adrien Boieldieu, *Le Calife de Bagdad* and *Télémaque dans l'Île de Calypso*. In 1807, for the debut of his pupil Maria Ikonina, Didelot revived the five-act ballet *Médée et Jason*, originally staged by Charles Le Picq. He choreographed *Don Quixote* for Jean Dutacq in 1808.

These efforts culminated in Didelot's five-act *Psyché et l'Amour*, given on 8 January 1809 during a state visit of Frederick William III of Prussia. In this work Didelot used a number of his famous flights, including one in which Venus flew into the clouds on a chariot "propelled" by fifty live white doves. Demons also flew across the stage by

DIDELOT. Late eighteenth- and early nineteenth-century dance prints typically depict idealized drapery, revealing the lines, and in this case the undergarments, of the dancers. The costumes in Didelot's ballet were notorious for their licentiousness. This representation, of Didelot's *Alonzo the Brave and the Fair Imogine* (1801), captures the sensual spirit, if not the precise detail of costuming, with (from left to right) Marie Rose Paul in bloomers, Didelot in a tight outfit, and Mademoiselle Parisot exposing a breast. (Theatre Museum, London.)

means of wires and stage machinery, brandishing torches above the spectators.

Before the end of 1809 Didelot produced the ballets *Solange Rose* and *Zélis et Alcindor*. A three-act version of *Laura and Henry*, given in 1810 at the Bolshoi Kamenyi Theater, was his last important production in Russia until his return several years later.

In 1805, after another serious injury, Didelot focused his energy on teaching, earning a reputation as a very strict but successful teacher. He doubled the hours of dance study in the theatrical school and strove to develop his students' acting ability as well as their dance technique.

In 1810, because of disputes with the theatrical management over money, Didelot was planning to leave Russia. The final blow came when the Bolshoi Kamenyi Theater burned down with all the machinery and accoutrements for *Psyché*.

On 5 March 1811 Didelot left for London. Although he and his wife arrived safely, the ship on which they sailed, the *Saint George*, was wrecked. With it went Didelot's music, manuscripts, dance compositions, drawings, and all the other records of his career. This loss cost him a year of work in London.

Despite many difficulties, Didelot continued to stage new ballets. *Zélis, ou La Forêt aux Aventures* (14 January 1812) was followed less than a month later by *L'Épreuve, ou La Jambe de Bois*. His favored mythological themes found expression on 7 April in *Zéphyr Inconstant Puni et Fixé*.

On 4 June 1812 Didelot brought forth the five-act *La Reine de Golconde*, based on a drama by Chevalier Stanislas de Bouffleurs, which became very popular. On one occasion when the management replaced this ballet with *Zéphyr*, the audience hissed and clamored so much that the cast, which included the Didelot couple, Fortunata Angiolini, and Armand Vestris, had to abandon the performance.

Didelot's first new work for the winter season of 1813 was *Le Pâtre et l'Hamadryade*. The English press praised his ability to convey the mythological story perfectly without language. In April 1812 Didelot produced a new heroic-comic ballet, *La Chaumière Hongroise*, dealing with the Hungarian national hero, Count Rákóczi.

During these three years Didelot produced a number of *divertissements*. The English audience was especially charmed by Russian folk dances he and his wife had learned during their stay in Saint Petersburg. His last major ballet of 1813 *L'Indorf et Rosalie, ou L'Heureuse Ruse*. In 1814 he presented new *divertissements* and two new ballets, *Karl et Lisbeth* and *Le Bazzard d'Algier*.

Didelot's long-sought-after chance to work in Paris again came, ironically, when Russian forces occupied Paris after the Napoleonic invasion of Russia. The Grand

DIDELOT. *Flore et Zéphire* was first staged by Didelot in London in 1796. He expanded it, as *Zéphire et Flore*, for a new production at the Hermitage Theater in Saint Petersburg in 1804 and subsequently staged it elsewhere in Europe. This lithograph by Salucci shows Adelaide Mersy as Flora and Giovanni Rousset as Zephyr in a performance at the Teatro La Pergola in Florence in 1828. (Dance Collection, New York Public Library for the Performing Arts.)

Duke Constantine Pavlovich, brother of Emperor Alexander I, was said to have helped Didelot obtain permission to stage a major work at the Académie Royale de Musique. Didelot himself offered to shoulder much of the financial risk. The work was a two-act version of *Flore et Zéphire*, first presented in Paris on 12 December 1815 with Geneviève Gosselin as Flora and Monsieur Albert (François Decombe) as Zephyr. The music was by Frédéric-Marc Venua, with added airs by Hus-Desforges and Lefèvre. It was a resounding success; 164 presentations were given before its temporary withdrawal in 1826, and in 1831 it was revived for Marie Taglioni and Jules Perrot. This appears to have been one of the first ballets in which dancers appeared on pointe. An 1821 print of Fanny Bias (who danced a lesser role in the original Paris production) clearly shows her on pointe in the role of Flora.

After suffering a financial loss despite the success of the production, Didelot once again accepted a position in

Saint Petersburg. Here he became so productive that contemporaries began to call him "the Shakespeare and the Byron of ballet."

Didelot choreographed *divertissements* and dances for a number of operas during these years. He also collaborated in the production of *vaudevilles* and other forms of musical theater. His own major ballets included *Acis et Galathée* (1816); *Don Carlos and Rozalba* (1817), *Theseus and Ariadne* (1817), *A Hunting Adventure* (1818), *Raoul de Créquis* (1819), *Karl et Lisbeth* (1820), *Cora and Alonzo* (1820), *Alcestis* (1821), *Lily of Narbonne* (1823), *The Prisoner of the Caucasus* (1823), and *Phaedra* (1825), along with new productions of many earlier works. In addition, Didelot frequently reworked the dances for ballets done by other choreographers with whom he collaborated, such as Auguste Vestris and Charles Le Picq.

Didelot's predilection for grand spectacles led him to produce the ballet *Raoul de Créquis*, which played more than one hundred times. Most of the story, dealing with the adventures of a crusader, was told through mime, but the ballet also contained many danced scenes. Didelot was especially praised for the beautiful scenic pictures incorporated into the work. Didelot studied art and was gifted at drawing. Themes and scenes in his ballets were often inspired by prints or paintings by such artists as Karl Pavlovich Bruillov and David Teniers.

Didelot took advantage of the Russian liking for realistic spectacle. In his version of *Cora and Alonso*, a volcano erupted, emitting sparks and torents of flames and lava. The earth was rent by cracks that spewed forth flames and smoke, and flocks of birds thrashing in the air heightened the aura of terror.

Didelot is especially remembered in Russia for his relationship with the great poet Aleksandr Pushkin. *The Prisoner of the Caucasus*, based on Pushkin's poem of the same name, remained in the Saint Petersburg repertory for thirteen seasons.

One of Didelot's reasons for returning to Russia was the opportunity to train his own young dancers. In the ten years after his return, seventy dancers were graduated from the Imperial School, freeing the theater from its dependence on foreign talent. Some of Didelot's pupils were Adam Glushkovsky, Maria Ikonina, and Anastasia Novitskaya. Glushkovsky achieved fame as a choreographer in Moscow and left one of the best accounts of his master's creativity and methods of work.

Although known for his harsh treatment of his pupils, Didelot never forgot his own poverty-stricken youth. He frequently interceded with Russian authorities to lighten the workload and increase the wages of his young dancers. He made the Imperial Theater School his residual legatee, and in his memory a Charles Didelot Scholarship was established to aid talented and needy students; one of its famous recipients was Vaslav Nijinsky.

Didelot's career at the Imperial Theater was fraught with conflicts with his superiors. The causes were varied; some were financial. He objected to the practice of assigning highly trained young dancers to other positions in the theater, such as costumer. He also deeply resented the importation, at high salaries, of foreign dancers who deprived his own dancers of roles in his ballets.

In the turmoil of the Decembrist Revolt of 1825, Didelot's superior became Prince Sergei Sergeevich Gagarin, a man known for haughtiness with his subordinates. On 30 October 1829 Gagarin berated Didelot because his corps de ballet was too slow in changing costumes between acts. When Didelot ignored his ranting, Gagarin had him arrested; he was officially dismissed in January 1830 from the Imperial Theater. However, he was missed by audiences; at a benefit given for him on 4 October 1833, Didelot was given wreaths of flowers along with an emotional, resounding display of appreciation from both the audience and his fellow workers. In Saint Petersburg, there was no one capable of succeeding him.

Because of his large output of choreography and his teaching, Didelot's influence on the history of ballet, particularly in Russia, was immense. As the titles of his work show, his vision served to bridge the gap between classical mythological ballets and Romantic works.

[*See also the entries on the principal figures mentioned herein.*]

BIBLIOGRAPHY

Bakhrushin, Yuri. *Istoriia russkogo baleta*. 3d ed. Moscow, 1977.

Borisoglebskii, Mikhail. *Proshloe baletnogo otdeleniia Peterburgskogo teatral'nogo uchilishcha, nyne Leningradskogo gosudarstvennogo khoreograficheskogo uchilishcha: Materialy po istorii russkogo baleta*. 2 vols. Leningrad, 1938–1939.

Bournonville, August. *My Theatre Life* (1848–1878). Translated by Patricia McAndrew. Middletown, Conn., 1979.

Chazin-Bennahum, Judith. "Wine, Women, and Song: Anacreon's Triple Threat to French Eighteenth-Century Ballet." *Dance Research* 5 (Spring 1987): 55–64.

Glushkovsky, Adam. *Vospominaniia baletmeistera*. Leningrad, 1940.

Guest, Ivor. *The Romantic Ballet in England*. London, 1972.

Guest, Ivor. *Jules Perrot: Master of the Romantic Ballet*. London, 1984.

Krasovskaya, Vera. *Russkii baletnyi teatr: Ot vozniknoveniia do serediny XIX veka*. Leningrad, 1958.

Krasovskaya, Vera. "Ballet Changes, Shakespeare Endures." *Ballet Review* 19 (Summer 1991): 71–80.

Milhous, Judith. "Dancers' Contracts at the Pantheon Opera House, 1790–1792." *Dance Research* 9 (Autumn 1991): 51–75.

Mundt, N. P. "Karl Ludovik Didlo." *Repertuar Russkogo Teatra* 3 (1840).

Price, Curtis A., et al. *Italian Opera in Late Eighteenth-Century London*, vol. 1, *The King's Theatre, Haymarket, 1778–1791*. London, 1995.

Roslavleva, Natalia. *Era of the Russian Ballet* (1966). New York, 1979.

Slonimsky, Yuri. *Didlo*. Leningrad, 1958.

Swift, Mary Grace. *A Loftier Flight: The Life and Accomplishments of Charles Louis Didelot*. Middletown, Conn., 1974. Includes a complete list of Didelot's productions.

Wiley, Roland John, trans. and ed. *A Century of Russian Ballet: Documents and Accounts, 1810–1910*. Oxford, 1990. Includes the libretti for *Raoul de Créqui* and *The Captive of the Caucasus*, as well as Adam Glushkovsky's "Recollections of the Great Choreographer Ch. L. Didelot."

MARY GRACE SWIFT

DIENES, VALÉRIA (Valéria Geiger; born 25 May 1879 in Szekszárd, died 8 June 1978 in Budapest), Hungarian theoretician, teacher, and choreographer. Dienes graduated from Budapest University with a doctorate in philosophy and a master's degree in mathematics and aesthetics; she also studied at the Academy of Music as a pianist and composer. She married Paul Dienes, a fellow student. She studied with Henri Bergson at the Collège de France from 1908 to 1912 and published mathematical theses accepted by the French Academy of Sciences in 1909, as well as studies in philosophy, sociology, and aesthetics in Budapest. She lectured in the Galilei Circle of progressive intellectuals in the 1910s and translated works by Lester F. Ward, Franklin Henry Giddings, George Berkeley, Alfred Binet, John Locke, and later almost all of the works of Henri Bergson, mostly published by the Hungarian Academy of Sciences.

Dienes three times saw Isadora Duncan dance in Paris at the Théâtre du Châtelet and was enthralled. She also frequented Raymond Duncan's "Greek gymnastic" courses. Back in Budapest, she started Duncan-style courses in 1912, developing the Duncan method into a system called *orchestics*. She first published these ideas in 1915 and first used them in artistic expression in April 1917, in a performance at the Urania Theater, where Isadora had danced in April 1902. Subsequently, dozens of Dienes's choreographies were performed by pupils of her school of orchestics to classical and modern music and to poetry by Mihály Babits, Rabindranath Tagore, and others. Dienes herself danced in Vienna and Belgrade but never in Budapest.

After 1919 Dienes immigrated with her sons Gedeon and Zoltán to Vienna, where she taught orchestics in a Montessori School in 1920, divorced Paul in 1921, and joined Raymond Duncan's colony in Nice and Paris from 1921 to 1922. On her return to Budapest she reopened her school in 1924, having turned her philosophically and mathematically trained mind to analyzing the principles governing human movement. In the early 1920s she established three physical criteria—space, time and force—and a spiritual criterion, meaning, to yield the four disciplines of orchestics: plastics (or kinetics), rhythmics, dynamics, and symbolics. She divided plastics into relative and absolute kinetics—that is, parts of the body moving in relation to other parts and the body traveling in relation to its environment. In the 1970s she developed her symbolics into a communication theory called *evologic* (consisting of time synthesis, irreversibility, emergence, and samelessness).

From 1929, Dienes was vice-president of the Society for Movement Culture, which protected the interests of art-of-movement teachers. She maintained her school until 1944, its amateur attendance often reaching two hundred. She also trained professionals beginning in the early 1930s. Inspired by medieval mystery plays, she choreographed several biblical and historical dance plays and fairy tales to her own librettos and texts (mostly in verse) and to music composed or selected by Lajos Bárdos. These works included *Waiting for the Dawn* (1925), to ancient Greek music; *Eight Beatitudes* (1926); and *Ten Virgins* (1934). The major historical plays were *Mystery of Saint Emery,* or *Hungarian Fate,* about heathen Hungarians converting to Christianity (1930); the *Lady of the Roses* (1932), about the charitable Hungarian queen Elizabeth; and *The Road of the Child* (1935), on how children were reared and treated through the ages. There were four fairy tales: *The White Princess* (1930), a shepherd boy's story by Countess Margit Bethlen; *The Sleeping Beauty* (1933); *Cinderella* (1934); and *Snow White* (1935), which featured her own text and preclassical musical arrangement. All these works were performed and revived several times until 1944. Discussions of the system of orchestics have been published in various Hungarian scientific periodicals, mostly in *Tánctudományi tanulmányok*. Her collected works on orchestics were published in 1996. The Orchestics Foundation was created in 1991 for reviving the stage- and health-oriented application of the Duncan-Dienes method of movement.

BIBLIOGRAPHY
Dienes, Gedeon P., trans. "Memories of Dr. Valéria Dienes." In *Proceedings of the Tenth Annual Conference, Society of Dance History Scholars, University of California, Irvine, 13–15 February 1987,* compiled by Christena L. Schlundt. Riverside, Calif., 1987.
Dienes, Valéria. "A relativ kinetika alapvonalai." *Tánctudományi tanulmányok* (1965–1966): 47–75.
Dienes, Valéria. "A mozdulatritmika alapvonalai." *Tánctudományi tanulmányok* (1969–1970): 91–114.
Dienes, Valéria. "Fejezetek az orkesztika történetéből." *Táncművészeti értesítő* 1 (1971); 2 (1971); 3 (1972).
Dienes, Valéria. Interview. *Valóság* 8 (1975).
Dienes, Valéria. "A szimbolika főbb problémái." *Semiotic Studies* 55 (1981).
Dienes, Valéria. *Orkesztika: mozdulatrendszer* (Orchestics: A System of Movement). Edited and introduced by G. P. Dienes. Budapest, 1996 (contents list and short summary in English).
Töttös, Gábor. *Dienes Valéria.* Szekszárd, 1991.
"Valéria Dienes." *Hungarian Dance News,* no. 1 (1987): 32.

GEDEON P. DIENES

DIGO DANCE. A small Bantu-speaking group, the Digo are farmers who live on the coast of Kenya, south of Mombasa. They are descended from nine tribes, known as the Nyika or Kenda group, who migrated to this area from southern Somalia at the beginning of the seventeenth century.

Digo dances are characterized by a sedate grace that arises from distinctive combinations of music, movement, and costume. The dances were originally celebratory but now are educational as well. They are often performed competitively at festivals.

The rhythms and structure of most Digo dances are dictated by the music, a song performed by a lead female singer who is sometimes also the principal dancer. The dance begins with a relaxed shuffling step, for both upright and crouched positions, and for either stationary or traveling modes. It is combined with a quick, light shoulder-shaking movement enhanced by the dancers' costumes—small shoulder capes edged with beaded fringes, worn over dresses or wrappers decorated with jewelry.

The dance groups usually consist of between twelve and twenty performers and include approximately equal numbers of men and women. The men also wear costumes that enhance their movements—wrappers and tunics having large feathers attached to their backs that vibrate when they shake their elbows and forearms. They also wear rattles and bells attached to bands on their ankles or knees.

In one of the best-known Digo dances, the *sengenya*, the dancers enter a cleared space in two lines, one male and one female, performing the shuffling step and the shoulder-shaking movement. They then form a crescent—women in front and men behind—and execute variations of the basic step. Sometimes the men's line comes through to the front, while the women repeat the basic movement from a kneeling position. The two lines also follow a counterclockwise oval path while continuing the basic step.

The *mzumbano* dance departs from the customarily smooth, graceful Digo style, although it begins similarly. The dancers enter in two lines and form a crescent with the men behind the women. They perform the shoulder-shaking and shuffling steps. The men, however, perform a variation much more vigorous and athletic, dancing to loud sounds created by their costumes as they move. The principal element of the costume is the *kiriba*, a skin covered with metal cowrie shells, which is worn by the men down the outside of the right leg, tied at the waist, knee, and calf. During the dance, the *kiriba* is rubbed with a *mugao* (metal shield), to produce a loud washboard sound. Simultaneously, the men leap around one another in pairs, twisting and turning in the air, or lie on their sides on the ground. The women continue shuffling and shaking their shoulders throughout this movement sequence.

The Digo have a strong tradition of vocal music, which may owe to their close links with neighboring Tavata or Mijikenda Segeju peoples, both renowned for their singing and music. The dances are accompanied by songs and various musical instruments, such as vertical wooden drums, large horns with deep loud sounds, *kivote* (flutes with three or four holes down one side), *kayamba* (raft rattles), and whistles.

To what extent these dances are unique and traditional to the Digo is difficult to determine, because Digo customs have been influenced by close relations with the neighboring Vumba and Segeju, with whom they intermarry, and because many Digos have converted to Islam since the 1880s.

[*For related discussion, see* Giriama Dance. *See also* Central and East Africa *and* Sub-Saharan Africa.]

BIBLIOGRAPHY

McKay, William F. "A Precolonial History of the Southern Kenya Coast." Ph.D. diss., Boston University, 1975.

Prins, A. H. J. *The Coastal Tribes of the North-Eastern Bantu*. Ethnographic Survey of Africa: East Central Africa, part 3. London, 1952.

VALERIE A. BRIGINSHAW

DIJK, PETER VAN. *See* Dyk, Peter van.

DIOBONO, POMPEO (*fl.* sixteenth century), Italian dancer and teacher. The dates of Diobono's birth and death are unknown. He is regarded as the link between the Italian tradition of fifteenth-century court dance and the theatrical dance of the 1600s. In the first half of the sixteenth century Diobono founded and directed a famous dance school in Milan which was attended by such noted pupils as Balthazar de Beaujoyeulx and Cesare Negri. Negri is our only source of knowledge about Diobono, whom he discusses in his treatise *Le gratie d'amore*, written in 1602. Negri considered Diobono the most remarkable dance teacher of the time, writing, "With all due respect for the others, it can in truth be said that among the masters of our art he was the most outstanding."

Negri reported that in 1554 Marshal de Brissac, viceroy of France in Piedmont, invited Diobono to go to Paris. Diobono accepted the invitation, taking with him his "group of violins," including Beaujoyeulx. In Paris he devoted himself to the physical and social education of the son of Henri II, the future Charles IX. He remained in Paris for the rest of his life in the service of Charles IX and his successor Henri III.

BIBLIOGRAPHY

Carrieri, Raffaele. *La danza in Italia, 1500–1900*. 2d ed. Milan, 1955.

Kendall, Yvonne. "Rhythm, Meter, and *Tactus* in Sixteenth-Century Italian Court Dance: Reconstruction from a Theoretical Base." *Dance Research* 8 (Spring 1990): 3–27.

McGowan, Margaret M. *L'art du ballet de cour en France, 1581–1643*. Paris, 1963.

Negri, Cesare. *Le gratie d'amore* (1602). Translated by Yvonne Kendall. Ph.D. diss., Stanford University, 1985.

Sealy, Robert J. *The Palace Academy of Henry III*. Geneva, 1981.

Tani, Gino. *Storia della danza dalle origini ai nostri giorni*. 3 vols. Florence, 1983.

ELENA GRILLO

DITHYRAMB is a genre of ancient Greek choral ode associated with the god Dionysus. The dance form of the dithyramb was called *turbasia*, a word implying confusion, riot, and revelry, qualities appropriate to a dance honoring the god of wine. The few surviving fragments of poetry classified as dithyrambic by later ancient editors, however, seldom exhibit these qualities; they are usually narratives about mythological figures other than Dionysus. The problem of the dithyramb is best addressed by dividing our knowledge of it into three historical phases: (1) origin and early development; (2) performance in the civic festivals of Athens down to the mid-fifth century BCE; and (3) transformation by the new music of later fifth-century Athens.

Origin and Early Development. Archaeological evidence has established that Dionysus was worshiped by the Mycenaean Greeks (second millennium BCE), a cult probably imported from Minoan Crete and ultimately from Asia. *Dithyrambos* may be an extremely old word whose etymology is not recoverable. Ancient writers were fond of the etymology "came through two doors" (Euripides, *Bacchae* 523ff.; Plato, *Laws* 700b)—alluding to the story that Dionysus was born twice, first from Semele when Zeus split her open with lightning, then from Zeus's thigh, where he had hid the babe he snatched from its mother's womb—but this is probably only a later wordplay. The etymology preferred by modern scholars connects *dithyrambos* to *iambos* and *thriambos*, both containing the root *amb*, "step" or "movement," but each with a different numerical prefix (*iambos* implying one- or two-step, *thriambos* three-step, and *dithyrambos* four-step). Following this logic, the dithyramb is named after a dance step characterizing it. Unfortunately, the meters of the surviving poems classified as dithyrambs have no features that throw light on this etymology.

Archilochus (first half of the seventh century BCE) is the first poet to mention the genre: "I know how to lead the dithyramb, splendid song of lord Dionysus, when my wits are fused with thunderbolts of wine" (fragment 77d). Aristotle maintains that tragedy arose from the improvisations of the poets "who led the dithyramb" (*Poetics* 1449a9), so Archilochus may be referring to a traditional practice in which a soloist improvised new words in alternation with a chorus singing some well-known refrain. Arion (c.652–585 BCE) is said by Herodotus (1.23) to have been "the first man we know of to have composed the dithyramb and named and taught it," implying that he transformed it from a loose improvisation to a formal ode in which the poet-choreographer composed words on a particular mythological subject beforehand and then taught them to the chorus along with the choreography. That Arion formalized the choreography as well as the language is suggested by two other ancient statements: that he "was the first to lead the circular chorus" (Proclus 12) and the first to "station a

chorus" (the *Suda* lexicon). Because dithyrambs were often later referred to simply as "circular choruses" (in distinction to the rectangular formation of the files of dancers in the choruses of tragedy), Arion's achievement may have consisted in fusing the solo leader and the singing chorus into a single choreographic unit occupying a defined circular space before an audience, rather than merely moving through the streets in procession.

Athenian Festivals. With Lasos's introduction of the dithyramb into the festivals of Athens under Hipparchus (c.527–514 BCE), it becomes possible to identify features that remained constant down to the second century CE. The principal occasion on which dithyrambs were produced was the Greater Dionysia (also called the City Dionysia), the late spring festival at which tragedies were also staged. Each of the ten tribes into which the Athenian population was divided would compete by sending one chorus of fifty men and another of fifty boys to perform a dithyramb. (Dithyrambic performances by female choruses are unattested.) In the fifth century the poet himself was often the choreographer and chorus trainer *(chorodidaskalos)*; later these functions became specialized. The chorus of fifty was crowned with ivy and did not wear masks. All we know of the choreography is that it was somehow circular, with the flute player standing amid the dancers.

The two principal fragments of the dithyrambs of Pindar (518–442 BCE) come closer than any others to fulfilling our expectations. One (fragments 75 and 83, Snell edition) announces the festal arrival of poet and dancers crowned with spring flowers. Its meter contains an extraordinarily high percentage of short syllables, and its diction a number of sonorous compound epithets unusual even for Pindar. The other (fragment 70b) begins with an account of the turbulent effects of Dionysus's rites on the gods in Olympus. These fragments constitute the only real textual evidence we have corresponding to the qualities attributed by the ancients to dithyrambic dancing.

Later Dithyramb and the New Music. Around the middle of the fifth century, Melanippides introduced into the dithyramb *anabolai*, passages of singing (probably always solo) in nontriadic meter with elaborate instrumental modulations that distracted from the choral unity of words and dance. Cinesias, Philoxenus, and Timotheus soon amplified this dominance of music over language, with the approval of Euripides and the disapproval of more conservative Athenians (Aristophanes, *Birds* 331–339; Plato, *Laws* 700a-701a; Aristotle, *Problems* 19.15). The language in the fragments from these poets is inflated and affected, suggesting a libretto whose words are only a pretext for the expression of emotion by music. The scores and choreography of this new music are lost, however, and we cannot judge whether the conservative criticism was fully justified.

[*For related discussion, see* Choral Dancing; Hyporchēma; *and* Sikinnis. *See also* Greece, *article on* Dance in Ancient Greece.]

BIBLIOGRAPHY

Pickard-Cambridge, A. W. *Dithyramb, Tragedy, and Comedy.* Revised by T. B. L. Webster. 2d ed. Oxford, 1962.

Pickard-Cambridge, A. W. *The Dramatic Festivals of Athens.* Oxford, 1968.

Sutton, Dana Ferrin, ed. *Dithyrambographi graeci.* Hildesheim, 1989.

Weiden, M. J. H. van der. *The Dithyrambs of Pindar: Introduction, Text, and Commentary.* Amsterdam, 1991.

Zimmerman, Bernard. "Dithyrambos: Geschichte einer Gattung." *Hypomnemata,* no. 98 (1992).

WILLIAM MULLEN

DIVERTIMENTO NO. 15. Original title: *Caracole.* Ballet in five sections. Choreography: George Balanchine. Music: Wolfgang Amadeus Mozart; Divertimento no. 15 in B-flat Major, K. 287. Scenery: James Stewart Morcom. Costumes: Barbara Karinska. Lighting: Jean Rosenthal. First performance: 31 May 1956, Mozart Festival, American Shakespeare Theater, Stratford, Connecticut; danced by members of the New York City Ballet. Principals: Diana Adams, Melissa Hayden, Allegra Kent, Tanaquil Le Clercq, Patricia Wilde, Herbert Bliss, Nicholas Magallanes, Roy Tobias. First performed as *Divertimento No. 15:* 19 December 1956, City Center of Music and Drama, New York, New York City Ballet.

Divertimento No. 15 epitomizes the harmonious liaison between perfection and humanity in the classical style as forged by George Balanchine. It is a harmony achieved through tension between idealism and mortal limitations. Poignancy and beauty are created by the executants' aspirations to achieve the sublime through a combination of stately eighteenth-century decorum and subtle, yet startlingly contemporary, ballet vocabulary.

Invited to mount a ballet for the 1956 Mozart bicentennial festival in Stratford, Connecticut, Balanchine had planned to revive his ballet *Caracole* (1952). When neither he nor his dancers could recall the choreography, he simply mounted a new work to the same Mozart score (K. 287) that he had used earlier. At its premiere in Stratford in May 1956 it retained its former title but was retitled *Divertimento No. 15* when it was presented in New York the following December. The production featured scenery by James Stewart Morcom, which he had originally designed for Balanchine's *Symphonie Concertante* (1947); costumes by Karinska; and lighting by Jean Rosenthal. For a revival in April 1966, a new garden-like setting of airy trellises was designed by David Hays, and beautiful new costumes, in yellows, white, and pale blue, were made by Karinska. Since the mid-1970s the ballet has been performed without scenery, although the dancers remain prettily dressed.

The ballet, for five women and three men, is in five sections: Allegro, Theme and Variations, Minuet, Andante, and Finale. Ironically, its asymmetrical structure (with the pivotal Andante placed near the end) and gender distribution give the work a curious sense of balance and equilibrium. The steps are fiendishly difficult, yet they transcend meaningless bravura; they contain subtle wit, passion, and drama, which brilliantly underscore Mozart's melodic invention. The intimate Andante is a series of pas de deux involving all eight soloists, as each of the five ballerinas is partnered by one of the three male cavaliers. The couples dance only for each other, disappearing into their private emotional realm with each exit, then reemerging to express their devotion to each other and to their art through the classical language.

Set to Mozart's sparkling score, *Divertimento No. 15* is one of Balanchine's most attractive creations. Still in the repertory of the New York City Ballet, it has also been mounted by the Vienna State Opera Ballet, the Bavarian National Ballet of the Munich Opera, the Cologne State Opera Ballet, the Dutch National Ballet, the Ballet du Grand Théâtre de Genève, the Hamburg Ballet, the Frankfurt Ballet, the Pacific Northwest Ballet, the Chicago Lyric Opera Ballet, the Pennsylvania Ballet, the Royal Danish Ballet, the Paris Opera Ballet, the San Francisco Ballet, Les Grands Ballets Canadiens, the Birmingham Royal Ballet, and the Finnish National Ballet.

BIBLIOGRAPHY

Choreography by George Balanchine: A Catalogue of Works. New York, 1984.

Greskovic, Robert. "Divertimento No. 15." In *International Dictionary of Ballet,* edited by Martha Bremser, vol. 1, pp. 386–387. Detroit, 1993.

Hunt, Marilyn. "Balanchine's *Divertimento:* A New Life." *Ballet Review* 13 (Fall 1985): 7–22.

Reynolds, Nancy. *Repertory in Review: Forty Years of the New York City Ballet.* New York, 1977.

Vaughan, David. "Midsummer Dancing." *Dance Magazine* (October 1975).

VIDEOTAPE. *Divertimento No. 15,* performed by the New York City Ballet, *L'Heure du Concert* (SRC, Montreal, 1961). Andante from *Divertimento No. 15,* performed by New York City Ballet, *Dance in America* (WNET-TV, New York, 1977).

REBA ANN ADLER

DMITRIEV, VLADIMIR (Vladimir Vladimirovich Dmitriev; born July 1900 in Moscow, died 6 May 1948 in Moscow), Russian designer and librettist. Dmitriev studied under the well-known painter K. S. Petrov-Vodkin in Petrograd from 1916 to 1917 and at the Art Academy from 1918 to 1922. He also took advanced courses in stage production under Vsevolod Meyerhold in 1918. Dmitriev was Meyerhold's pupil and follower and later a leading master of psychologically based design. He was a designer at the Moscow Art Theater, and ballet also occupied a significant part of his varied career. While still a student he was associated with George Balanchine's Young Ballet, designing original costumes in various nontraditional textures and materials for ballets such as *Marche Funèbre* (1923). From 1926 to 1929 he collaborated with the choreographer Fedor Lopukhov, devising new principles of costume and mask scenography based on Italian *commedia dell'arte* in *Pulcinella* (1926) and the Russian-style buffoonery of *Renard* (1927). For Lopukhov's production of *The Nutcracker* in 1929, Dmitriev proposed a series of vividly colored moving panels to be carried onstage by the dancers, which provided spectacular changes of color in the scenery.

Later in his career Dmitriev also worked as a librettist. In 1932, with Nikolai Volkov, he provided the libretto for Vasily Vainonen's *The Flames of Paris*, which marked the advent of drama ballet *(drambalet)* in the Soviet Union. In his decor for that production, as well as those for *Swan Lake* in 1933 and *Lost Illusions* in 1936—for which he was also the librettist—he created historically authentic locales in keeping with the principles of socialist realism. His last work in ballet was Vainonen's *The Nutcracker* in 1939, for which he produced traditional designs. The best of Dmitriev's decors had lyrical depth as well as dramatic impact. Dmitriev was named a Merited Art Worker of the Russian Federation in 1944 and won the State Prize of the USSR in 1946, 1948, and 1949.

BIBLIOGRAPHY

Berezkin, Viktor. *V. V. Dmitriev* (in Russian). Leningrad, 1981.
Braun, Edward. *The Theatre of Meyerhold: Revolution on the Modern Stage.* New York, 1979.
Kostina, Elena M. *Dmitriev* (in Russian). Moscow, 1957.
Souritz, Elizabeth. *Soviet Choreographers in the 1920s.* Translated by Lynn Visson. Durham, N.C., 1990.

VIKTOR I. BEREZKIN
Translated from Russian

DOBUJINSKY, MSTISLAV (Mstislav Valerianovich Dobuzhinskii; born 2 August 1875 in Novgorod, Russia, died 20 November 1957 in New York), Russian-American scenery designer. From 1885 to 1887 Dobujinsky studied at the School of the Society for the Encouragement of the Arts in Saint Petersburg, but he took a degree in law from Saint Petersburg University, graduating in 1898. His art vocation, however, ultimately won out, and in the early years of the twentieth century he gravitated toward the *Mir iskusstva* (World of Art) group, contributing to its journal and exhibitions. Thereafter, Dobujinsky worked as a designer for many journals, including *Zhar-ptitsa* (Firebird).

In 1907 he helped found the Antique Theater in Saint Petersburg and two years later designed Konstantin Stanislavsky's production of Ivan Turgenev's *A Month in the Country* at the Moscow Art Theater. In 1924 Dobujinsky immigrated to Kaunas, Lithuania, and in 1939 he moved to the United States. In the 1930s and 1940s Dobujinsky designed many stage productions in both the United States and Europe, including *The Sleeping Beauty* (Kaunas, 1934), *Mam'zelle Angot* (Metropolitan Opera, New York, 1943), and *Coppélia* (Cambridge Arts Theatre, Cambridge, England, 1956).

In a letter to Nina Berberova of 1949, Dobujinsky wrote that he had "drowned up to my ears in the theater"; certainly he had by then secured an international reputation as a first-rate stage designer. Perhaps his most celebrated designs were for the Stanislavsky production of *A Month in the Country*, in which he expressed his love for Russian *style empire* and for chinoiserie. These interests also showed in his fanciful designs for Serge Diaghilev productions of *Papillons* and *Midas* (both Paris, 1914) and even for much later pieces such as *Coppélia* (1933, 1936, 1956, and other productions). Dobujinsky's intelligent, imaginative evocations of past eras won the respect of his many notable collaborators in the dance world, including, among others, Léonide Massine, Marie Rambert, George Balanchine, and Nicholas Zvereff.

BIBLIOGRAPHY

Chugunov, Gennady. *Mstislav Valerianovich Dobuzhinskii, 1875–1957* (in Russian). Leningrad, 1988.
Dobujinsky, Mstislav. *Zhivopis, grafika, teatr/Painting, Graphic Art, Stage Design.* Moscow, 1982. In Russian and English.
Gusarova, Alla. *Mstislav Dobuzhinskii* (in Russian). Moscow, 1982.
Mstislav V. Dobujinsky. Oxford, 1975. Exhibition catalog, Ashmolean Museum.
Mstislav V. Dobujinsky: Half a Century of Theatrical Art. New York, 1979. Exhibition catalog, Center for the Arts, New York Public Library for the Performing Arts.

ARCHIVES.   Ashmolean Museum, Oxford. M. Rostislav Doboujinsky, Paris. New York Public Library for the Performing Arts. Tretiakov Gallery, Moscow.

JOHN E. BOWLT

DOGON DANCE. The Dogon, speakers of a distinctive Niger-Congo language, live in and around the spectacular Bandiagara cliffs of West Africa in southeastern Mali. Numbering about 400,000, the Dogon farm arid savannas and rocky plateaus, where they grow millet and corn. Because of their relative isolation, the Dogon have preserved their ancient religion and customs better than other ethnic groups in Mali. Since the 1960s, however, change has become inevitable. Young Dogon men who travel to cities and towns in search of work, schools, and medical care return home with new ideas. Muslim mosques now stand in villages that once had only family and communal shrines.

The Dogon are among the best known of African peoples, not only because of the spectacular terrain in which they live, the complexity of their cosmological concepts, and their continued use of widely admired art forms (including dance) but also because so many of their social and cultural traditions have remained intact. Dance is still ritually linked to religious ceremonies associated with funerals and death-anniversary ceremonies *(dama)*. Nevertheless, these masked performances have been adapted for presentation before tourists and as part of the theatrical program of the Mali National Folk Troupe.

Among the Dogon, all circumcised males are eligible members of the Awa, the society of masks; women are generally excluded. The members of a village Awa society conduct the masked dances associated with funeral rites and *dama*. The religious purposes of these masked dances is to conduct the souls of the deceased to the family altars and to consecrate their passage to the ranks of the ancestors. Every sixty years, the Dogon hold a ceremony (most recently, in 1967–1971) known as the *sigui*, which commemorates the replacement of one generation by another. Men who have participated in two *sigui* ceremonies are called *mulono* and head the village Awa society. After the *mulono*, a hierarchy is ranked according to age and *sigui* participation. All masks are destroyed during the *sigui*, and new ones are made thereafter.

Approximately eighty varieties of masks are used in Dogon dances; the total number and spectrum possessed by a village Awa is variable. The masks represent people, birds, mammals, reptiles, and objects; they are made of fiber, cloth, or wood and are strikingly elaborate. Masked performances at funerals consist of ritual acts rather than dances; however, at *dama* ceremonies, masked dancers perform dozens of carefully choreographed movements intended to convey moral and social messages as well as to fulfill religious requirements and to entertain. The same mask may be danced in different dances and to numerous rhythms provided by an orchestra of drums. Onlookers and officials of the Awa chant songs in both Dogon and *sigui*, the secret language known only to those who have witnessed the ceremony of the same name. Some of the more widely used masks depict animals of the region, including the hyena, antelope, lion, and crocodile. Numerous masks portray various Dogon and non-Dogon personages such as blacksmiths, healers, leatherworkers, hunters, and members of other ethnic groups.

Dances are usually performed in the village square. As the drums play, the masked dancers—sometimes numbering in the hundreds—march in single file through the village to the dance arena, accompanied by a drum rhythm known as *odu boy*. They then perform the *odu tonnolo* dance. The *kanaga* ("bird") masks are usually the most nu-

merous and, after the initial joint performance, they dance alone. During this dance, the crosslike superstructures of the *kanaga* are swept down across the ground. Among the most impressive dances are those performed by stilt-walkers representing spirits, and by the *sirige*, a ten-foot mask that represents a house.

During *dama* dances, pantomime and theater are mingled. For example, the hunter mask chases the rabbits through the crowd, and the hyena steals; at other times, they all dance. There are dozens of separate rhythms and dances.

Dogon masked dances fulfill religious and spiritual needs, entertain, and reinforce social and moral values: Deviation from societal standards is ridiculed and virtue is praised. The dances survive as part of a culture that shows a remarkable capacity to endure.

[*See also* West Africa.]

BIBLIOGRAPHY

Desplagnes, Louis. *Le plateau central nigérien*. Paris, 1907.
Dieterlen, Germaine. "Les cérémonies soixantenaires du Sigui chez les Dogons." *Africa* (April 1971).
Ezra, Kate. *Art of the Dogon*. New York, 1988.
Griaule, Marcel. *Les masques dogons*. Paris, 1938.
Griaule, Marcel, and Germaine Dieterlen. *Le renard pâle*. Paris, 1965.
Imperato, Pascal James. "Contemporary Adapted Dances of the Dogon." *African Arts* 5 (Autumn 1971).
Imperato, Pascal James. *Dogon Cliff Dwellers*. New York, 1978.
Lane, Paul J. "Tourism and Social Change Among the Dogon." *African Arts* 21 (August 1988).
Michaut, Pierre. "Les danses des Dogons d'après un film de Griaule." *L'Opinion* 31 (1938).
Pern, Stephen. *Masked Dancers of West Africa: The Dogon*. Amsterdam, 1982.

PASCAL JAMES IMPERATO

DOLGUSHIN, NIKITA (Nikita Aleksandrovich Dolgushin; born 8 November 1938 in Leningrad), Russian dancer, choreographer, teacher, and administrator. Noted both for technical refinement and dramatic expressivity as a *danseur noble*, Dolgushin has performed leading roles in classical and modern Russian and Soviet repertories, as well as in works by August Bournonville and José Limón. He trained with Mikhail Mikhailov and Aleksandr Pushkin at the Vaganova Choreographic Institute. After graduating in 1959, he joined the Kirov Ballet, where he began dancing principal roles. He left in 1961 when it appeared that Konstantin Sergeyev would not encourage his career.

For the next six years, Dolgushin performed as principal dancer with the Novosibirsk Ballet, under the direction first of Petr Gusev and then Oleg Vinogradov. At the time, the company was ranked third in the Soviet Union and was noted for its experimentation.

Dolgushin's repertory there included works by Vasily Vainonen and Yuri Grigorovich. From 1967 to 1968 he performed in Moscow with Igor Moiseyev's classical ballet ensemble. In 1968 he returned to Leningrad to become a soloist with the Maly Theater Ballet. There he created leading roles in Vinogradov's *Yaroslavna*, Lebediev's jazz ballet *Crossroads*, and Nikolai Boyarchikov's *Tsar Boris*. Concurrently, he appeared as guest artist with the Kirov Ballet in *Giselle* and *Don Quixote* and danced the title role in Sergeyev's *Hamlet*.

Dolgushin graduated from the Leningrad Conservatory Rimsky-Korsakov in 1980, where he studied under Vinogradov. Appointed director of the conservatory's choreographic department in March 1983, he also continued to perform. His particular interest in Western choreography resulted in the conservatory instituting a workshop program in Western styles, including a staging of Limón's *The Moor's Pavane* in 1984, and an exchange program with the dance department at Towson State University, Maryland, in 1989 and 1990.

Dolgushin made his choreographic debut in 1964 in Novosibirsk by reworking sections of *The Ice Maiden*. His choreography has favored one-act works with minimal plots and a modern ballet vocabulary, although he created a two-act ballet, *King Lear* (1990). Many of his works have been set to music of Tchaikovsky, among them *Meditations* (his version of *Hamlet*) and *Concerto in White*, both performed in 1969. He also staged *Giselle* (1973) and *Paquita* (1975) for the Maly company, each notable for its attempt at historical accuracy. In 1986 he organized a celebration of the work of the seminal Soviet choreographer Fedor Lopukhov, which included a staging of the final movement of the 1923 *Dance Symphony*.

In 1989 Dolgushin made his first visit to and performing debut in the United States (at Towson State University) and Canada (with the Vancouver Goh Ballet). His prior appearances in the West had been limited; they included appearances with Soviet companies in Vienna (1977), Paris (1967), and London (1963) and two months as guest artist with the Australian Ballet in early 1963. His staging of *Giselle* was seen in Avignon, France, in 1976.

Vera Krasovskaya (1985) has described the traits that for her distinguish Dolgushin's work. The first is a willingness to subordinate form in order fully to express the soul. The second, inseparable from the first, is the mastery of academic purity and nobility of manner characteristic of a representative of the precious tradition of the Leningrad school. The third is his taste for the experimental: a readiness to endeavor, to search, and to enter into alliance with choreographers of various artistic temperaments, opinions, and tastes.

BIBLIOGRAPHY
Greskovic, Robert. "Dancing in the Dark: Discovering Nikita Dolgushin." *Dance Theatre Journal* 5 (Spring 1988): 10–13.
Krasovskaya, Vera. *Nikita Dolgushin* (in Russian). Leningrad, 1985.
Matheson Katy with Marilyn Hunt. "Training Russian Choreographers: Interviewing Nikita Dolgushin." *Dance Theatre Journal* 6 (Fall 1988): 15–18.
Matheson, Katy. "Nikita Dolgushin: Work, Love, and Spirituality." *Dance Magazine* (June 1990): 44–47.
McDonagh, Don. "To Russia with TSU." *Ballet Review* 18 (Summer 1990): 82–92.
McDonagh, Don. "From Russia to TSU." *Ballet Review* 18 (Fall 1990): 80–89.
Smakov, Gennady. *The Great Russian Dancers*. New York, 1984.

KATY MATHESON

DOLIN, ANTON (Sydney Francis Patrick Chippendall Healy-Kay; born 27 July 1904 in Slinfold, Sussex, died 25 November 1983 in Paris), British dancer, director, choreographer, and teacher. Patrick Healy-Kay began his dance training in 1914, when he was about ten years old, at a school run by Grace and Lily Cone in Brighton. He made his first appearance on stage in a school recital at the Brighton Hippodrome. In 1915 his family relocated to London, where he continued his studies at the Italia Conti Stage School and soon found work as a child actor. He made his London stage debut playing Peter in *Bluebell in Fairyland* in 1916.

Upon seeing Serafina Astafieva's *Swinburne Ballet* at the London Coliseum in 1917, young Patrick determined that he must be trained by her. He lost no time in joining her classes or in proving himself a diligent and talented student. Four years later, in Astafieva's Chelsea studio, he was seen by Serge Diaghilev, who was then searching for extra dancers for his new, spectacular production of *The Sleeping Princess* for the forthcoming London season of his Ballets Russes. Under the name of Patrickieff, Healy-Kay danced in the corps de ballet of that famous production at the Alhambra for its three-month run beginning 2 November 1921. The performance of Olga Spessivtseva as Princess Aurora made an indelible impression on him, remaining an artistic inspiration throughout his life.

In 1923, with his name changed to Anton Dolin, he appeared in a ballet evening devised by Astafieva at the Albert Hall, for which he choreographed and danced two solos—*Hymn to the Sun* and *Danse Russe*. News of his success, his technical prowess, and his virile good looks reached Diaghilev, and Dolin was asked to audition in Paris. Engaged as permanent soloist with Diaghilev's Ballets Russes, he made his debut as Daphnis in Michel Fokine's *Daphnis et Chloë* in Monte Carlo in January 1924.

Dolin's time with Diaghilev falls into two periods, 1924–1925 and 1928–1929. In his first year with the company he created roles in two works by Bronislava Nijinska. In *Les Fâcheux*, as L'Élégant, he was one of the first men to dance on full pointe, but his outstanding success was as Le Beau Gosse in *Le Train Bleu*, in which he performed dangerous and daring acrobatic feats. In the same year he also danced featured roles in Nijinska's *Les Biches* and *Les Tentations de la Bergère*. In 1925 he created the role of Zephyr in Léonide Massine's *Zéphire et Flore*. He also danced in works from an earlier period, such as the condensed version of *Swan Lake*, Fokine's *Le Spectre de la Rose* and *Le Carnaval*, and in the Bluebird pas de deux in *Aurora's Wedding*. After quarreling with Diaghilev, Dolin left the company again until its final year, when he returned to create roles in George Balanchine's *Le Bal* and *The Prodigal Son* (both 1929).

During the years between his two Diaghilev periods, Dolin danced in a number of London revues for which he also arranged dance scenes, such as "Alabamy Bound" for *The Punch Bowl* (1925) and several numbers for *The Charlot Show of 1926*. He also danced in variety bills at the London Coliseum: in 1926 with Phyllis Bedells, when he arranged several of the dances, and in 1927 with Tamara Karsavina in Fokine's *Le Spectre de la Rose*. With Vera

DOLIN. From 1940 to 1946, Dolin danced with Ballet Theatre, based in New York. In 1943 he and Vera Zorina appeared in the leading roles of Frederick Ashton's *The Wanderer*, originally created for the Sadler's Wells Ballet in 1941. (Photograph by Alfredo Valente; from the Dance Collection, New York Public Library for the Performing Arts.)

Nemchinova he formed the Nemchinova-Dolin Ballet, also in 1927, for which he created *The Nightingale and the Rose*. Later, when the company appeared at the Théâtre des Champs-Élysées in Paris, he mounted a ballet based on George Gershwin's *Rhapsody in Blue* (1928). The company disbanded in that year, and he returned to Diaghilev.

After Diaghilev's death in August 1929, Dolin gave dance recitals with Anna Ludmilla and later went to New York, where he opened in *The International Revue* on 25 February 1930. The show closed after three months, and Dolin returned to England. There he was among those responsible for the formation of the Camargo Society, for which he created the roles of Vertumnus in Frederick Ashton's *Pomona* (1930) and Satan in Ninette de Valois's *Job* (1931). Dolin, always an outstanding partner, was Albrecht to Olga Spessivtseva's memorable performance in the title role of the Camargo Society's 1932 revival of *Giselle*.

For four years Dolin was principal dancer of the Vic-Wells Ballet, where he began his association with Alicia Markova, one of the great partnerships in ballet history. [*See the entry on Markova.*] They left in 1935 to form the Markova-Dolin Ballet and for three years toured both the English provinces and abroad, the first classical company to do so. In addition to the classics, the repertory included Nijinska's *Les Biches* and *La Bien-Aimée*, billed in English as *The House Party* and *Beloved*, and Keith Lester's *David* (1935) and *Pas de Quatre* (1936), a reconstruction of the famous work by Jules Perrot done in 1845 for the four leading ballerinas of the Romantic era. When the company disbanded in 1938, Dolin joined the Original Ballet Russe, which toured Australia in 1939.

Apart from the summer season of 1948, when he and Markova danced with the Sadler's Wells Ballet at Covent Garden, Dolin spent most of the 1940s in America. He was a principal dancer with Ballet Theatre from its inception in 1939, and during his seven-year association with the company, partly as guest artist, he restaged the classics—*Swan Lake, Giselle, Princess Aurora*—mounted his own version of *Pas de Quatre* (1941), and choreographed three original works: *Quintet* (1940), *Capriccioso* (1940), and *Romantic Age* (1942). Among the principal roles he created with Ballet Theatre were the title roles in Fokine's *Bluebeard* (1941) and in Léonide Massine's *Aleko* and *Don Domingo* (both 1942). He appeared with Markova in a revue, *The Seven Lively Arts* (1944–1945), for which he choreographed *Scènes de Ballet*, specially composed by Igor Stravinsky.

In 1945, Dolin and Markova formed another group of their own, which toured throughout the United States. He also made further guest appearances with Colonel de Basil's Original Ballet Russe—creating the role of Armand in John Taras's *Camille* (1946), again opposite Markova—and with Sergei Denham's Ballet Russe de Monte Carlo.

DOLIN. MICHEL FOKINE's *Petrouchka* was staged in 1950 by Nicholas Beriozoff for the newly founded London Festival Ballet. Dolin appeared in the title role. (Photograph by Scott Brothers, Edinburgh; from the Dance Collection, New York Public Library for the Performing Arts.)

Returning to England with Markova in 1949, Dolin formed another group surrounding the two stars, which appeared in sports arenas. Later it toured Britain's larger theaters under the title "Stars of the Ballet with Markova and Dolin," from which emerged London's Festival Ballet, which Dolin founded with Julian Braunsweg. As the company's first artistic director and principal dancer, Dolin, together with Markova as ballerina, launched London's Festival Ballet as a major British classical company. He continued to dance principal roles in the major classics during the company's early years but gradually moved on to character parts not only in the classics but also in new ballets. He revived his version of *Pas de Quatre* and later choreographed *Variations for Four* (1957) to display four leading male dancers. Retiring from Festival Ballet in 1961, Dolin served as director of the Rome Opera Ballet from 1962 to 1964.

After 1964, Dolin pursued a freelance career, mounting productions of classics—notably *The Nutcracker, Giselle,* and *Swan Lake*—and coaching, teaching, and giving master classes. He mounted his *Pas de Quatre* with several companies, including the Kirov in Leningrad. Dolin had acted in several plays during the 1930s; during the 1970s he played Herod in Lindsay Kemp's *Salomé* in London and abroad, and his one-man show on Diaghilev was seen in London, Tokyo, Cannes, Stockholm, Rome, Hamburg, and Monte Carlo. In Herbert Ross's film *Nijinsky* (1979), Dolin impersonated Enrico Cecchetti. A prolific writer, his books include four volumes of autobiography (1931, 1938, 1960, 1985), *Pas de Deux: The Art of Partnering* (1949), *Alicia Markova: Her Life and Art* (1953), and *The Sleeping Ballerina: The Story of Olga Spessivtseva* (1966).

For his services to ballet, Anton Dolin was given the Queen Elizabeth II Coronation Award by the Royal Academy of Dancing in 1954. Other awards and honors followed, in recognition of his extraordinary career as the first great British male ballet dancer and as a tireless and highly effective promoter of his art. The ultimate accolade came in 1981 when he was named to the knighthood on the Queen's New Year's Honours List.

[*See also* American Ballet Theatre; Ballets Russes de Monte Carlo; Ballets Russes de Serge Diaghilev; English National Ballet; *and* Royal Ballet.]

BIBLIOGRAPHY

"Celebrating Anton Dolin." *Ballet Review* 13 (Spring 1985): 74–91.
Dolin, Anton. *Divertissement.* London, 1931.
Dolin, Anton. *Ballet Go Round.* London, 1938.
Dolin, Anton. *Autobiography.* London, 1960.
Dolin, Anton. *Last Words: A Final Autobiography.* Edited by Kay Hunter. London, 1985.
Garafola, Lynn. *Diaghilev's Ballets Russes.* New York, 1989.
Haskell, Arnold L. *Anton Dolin: The "First Chapter."* London, 1929.
Nerina, Nadia, ed. *A Pictorial Tribute to Sir Anton Dolin, the First British Ballet Star, 1904–1983.* London, 1984.
Sorley Walker, Katherine. "The Camargo Society." *Dance Chronicle* 18.1 (1995): 1–114.
Wheatcroft, Andrew, comp. *Dolin: Friends and Memories.* London, 1982.
Williams, Peter. *Alicia Markova and Anton Dolin: A Legend of British Ballet.* London, n.d.

PETER WILLIAMS

DOLLAR, WILLIAM (William Henry Dollar; born 20 April 1907 in East Saint Louis, Illinois, died 28 February 1986 in Flourtown, Pennsylvania), American dancer, ballet master, and choreographer. As one of the first American *danseurs nobles,* William Dollar performed with the Philadelphia Opera Ballet, the American Ballet, Ballet Caravan, Ballet Society, Ballet Theatre, and the New York City Ballet. From the mid-1930s to the mid-1940s he created a number of roles in works choreographed by George Balanchine, among them *Alma Mater* and *Errante* (both 1935), *Orpheus and Eurydice* (1936), *The Card Party* and *Le Baiser de la Fée* (both 1937), *Ballet Imperial* and *Concerto Barocco* (both 1941), and *The Four Temperaments*

DOLLAR. As Tancredi, Dollar appeared with Melissa Hayden as Clorinda in *The Duel*, staged in 1950 for the New York City Ballet. (Photograph by Walter Owen; from the Dance Collection, New York Public Library for the Performing Arts.)

(1946). Balanchine's influence was also evident in Dollar's classical choreography, beginning with *Concerto*, their collaborative effort for the American Ballet in 1936.

Having studied with Catherine Littlefield, Mikhail Mordkin, Alexandre Volinine, and Michel Fokine, Dollar was already formed as a dancer when he first took class with Balanchine at the School of American Ballet in 1934. An accomplished technician, he joined the American Ballet as a soloist in 1935 and was soon dancing principal parts. He appeared in six of the seven ballets, all by Balanchine, in the repertory of the company's first New York season. He had an excellent facility for leaps and an expressive, committed presence onstage that not only made him stand out in Balanchine's ballets but also made him ideally suited for roles in Fokine's works, especially Harlequin in *Le Carnaval*, which he performed with Ballet Theatre in 1940. Edwin Denby, a leading critic of the time, also admired Dollar's "musical delight in dancing" (Denby, 1949).

Dollar's musical sensitivity and athletic prowess stemmed from early training on the piano and in gymnastics. He fought long and hard with his parents for ballet lessons, which he obtained in his midteens. Through these classes, he came into contact with popular dance directors such as Robert Alton and Russell Markert, who hired him for a number of vaudeville engagements. Dollar later appeared at Radio City Music Hall in New York; in movies, as Vera Zorina's partner in *Goldwyn Follies of 1938;* and on Broadway, as dance director of *Great Lady*, also in 1938.

Dollar's musicianship and acrobatic ability enhanced his ballet work. In *The Four Temperaments*, for example, Balanchine used Dollar's pliant, arching back to striking effcct in the Melancholic variation, extending the expressive possibilities of the classical vocabulary. Dollar's first choreographic venture, *Promenade* (1936), for Ballet Caravan, expanded his classical craftsmanship while exploring the irregular rhythms of Maurice Ravel's *Valses Nobles et Sentimentales*. In 1944, he reworked *Concerto*, which he and Balanchine had set to Frédéric Chopin's Piano Concerto no. 2, retitled it *Constantia*, and staged it for the debut season of the marquis de Cuevas's Ballet International. A finely crafted work, *Constantia* later entered the repertories of the Original Ballet Russe, Le Grand Ballet de Monte Carlo, and Ballet Theatre.

Dollar's best-known work, *The Duel*, mounted in 1949 as *Le Combat* for Roland Petit's Ballets de Paris, was a theatrical tour de force with the emotional validity and impact of a Fokine ballet. Set to a score by Rafaello de Banfield and based on an episode in Torquato Tasso's epic poem *Jerusalem Delivered* (1581), the ballet tells a tale of chivalry and tragic love during the time of the Crusades, reenacting the legend of armed combat between Tancredi of Normandy, a Christian knight, and Clorinda, the Saracen girl he loves. As Clorinda wears male armor and as both combatants fight with the visors of their helmets lowered, the lovers do not recognize each other; Clorinda's identity is revealed only when she removes her helmet as she lies dying. To heighten the exotic drama of the piece, Dollar added three more knights to the cast when he staged the work, as *The Duel*, for the New York City Ballet in 1950. Melissa Hayden made a powerful impression in the role of Clorinda, as did Janine Charrat and Colette Marchand with the Ballets de Paris and Lupe Serrano with Ballet Theatre.

While still continuing to perform, Dollar served as choreographer, ballet master, and coach for a variety of organizations. After the dissolution of American Ballet Caravan in 1941, he staged dances for several productions of the New Opera Company in New York, and in 1943 he founded the American Concert Ballet with Todd Bolender and Mary Jane Shea. For this short-lived troupe, he choreographed *The Five Boons of Life*, later called *The Five Gifts*, set to music by the Hungarian composer Ernő Dohnányi. In 1946, Dollar became ballet master of Ballet Society, and in 1948 he served in the same post for the marquis de Cuevas's Grand Ballet de Monte Carlo. For the New York City Ballet he choreographed *Ondine* (1949), using music by Antonio Vivaldi, and for Ballet Theatre he made a version of *Jeux* (1950), set to the music of Claude Debussy. For some years thereafter, he directed the Ballet Theatre choreographic workshop, for which he created several works, among them *Mendelssohn Concerto* (1954) and *The Parliament of the Birds* (1958).

Forced by arthritis to stop dancing, Dollar went to Tehran in 1956 to establish a state ballet school, and there he founded and supervised the Iranian National Ballet. The last decades of his life were devoted to guest teaching, choreographing, and staging ballets for regional companies in the United States and for several major companies in Europe and South America.

[*See also* American Ballet; Ballet Caravan.]

BIBLIOGRAPHY

Asinof, Lynn. "Where It All Began." *Ballet News* 2 (November 1980): 14–17.

Denby, Edwin. *Looking at the Dance* (1949). New York, 1968.

Dollar, William. Interview. *American Dancer* 18 (November 1944): 4.

Hastings, Baird. "Tribute to a Trio." *Ballet Review* 22 (Summer 1994): 8–9.

Hunt, Marilyn. "Promenade." *Dance Magazine* (September 1980): 44–46.

Kirstein, Lincoln. *Blast at Ballet*. New York, 1938.

Kirstein, Lincoln. *Thirty Years: The New York City Ballet*. New York, 1978.

Maynard, Olga. *The American Ballet*. Philadelphia, 1959.

Reynolds, Nancy. *Repertory in Review: Forty Years of the New York City Ballet*. New York, 1977.

FILMS. *Ballet Caravan* (1938–1940). *The Five Gifts* (1953). *The Duel* (1955).

REBA ANN ADLER
Amended by Claude Conyers

DOMENICO DA PIACENZA

(also known as Domenico da Ferrara; sometimes called Domenichino or Domenegino; born c.1400 in Piacenza, Italy, died c.1476 in Ferrara), Italian dancing master, theorist, choreographer, and founder of the first Lombardic school of dancing. Referred to by his contemporaries as *re dell'arte* (king of the art) and *saltatorum princeps* (the foremost among dancers), Domenico seems to have spent the years of his youth and early maturity in his native Piacenza, but he was later also active in Milan, Modena, Forlì, Faenza, and Ferrara. The fame of his teaching in Piacenza spread quickly and attracted personalities such as Guglielmo Ebreo and Antonio Cornazano, who in turn became leading figures in early Renaissance court dance.

Apparently, Domenico established contact with his future patron, Leonello, the marquis of Este, at Leonello's marriage to Margherita Gonzaga, which took place in Ferrara in 1435 and which Domenico attended. In 1439 Domenico is listed for the first time in the registers of the *mandati* (personnel) of the Este court; his name appears again in 1441, 1445, 1447, and 1450. In April 1455 Domenico, now at the height of his career, was in Milan at the request of Francesco Sforza as choreographer for the wedding of Beatrice d'Este and Tristano Sforza. On this occasion the dancing master himself performed in a *danza* as partner of Duchess Bianca Maria, together with seven of the most distinguished ladies and gentlemen of the court, including the bride and groom (Poggiali, 1989, vol. 1, pp. 36ff.). In October 1455, also in Milan, Domenico, assisted by Guglielmo Ebreo, choreographed *moresche e molti balli* for the engagement festivities for Ippolita Sforza and Alfonso of Aragon. Whether he was at this time resident dancing master at the Sforza court, as Daniel Heartz (1966) assumes, cannot be established with certainty. A few years later, in May 1462, Domenico and Guglielmo again collaborated, this time for the wedding celebrations of Pino de Ordelaffi and Barbara Manfredi in Forlì. By this time, Domenico seems to have made his permanent home in Ferrara. In 1456 he was being paid the substantial monthly salary of twenty *lire marchesani* (Lockwood, 1984, p. 70, n. 20) and can be found listed under the *salariati* of the Este court until 31 December 1472. His name appears intermittently in the Ferrarese records through 1475.

In recognition of his professional accomplishments Domenico was made a Knight of the Order of the Golden Spur, hence the references to him as *dignissimo cauagliere* ("most worthy knight") and *cauagliere aurato* ("golden knight") in the manuals of Guglielmo and Cornazano. Domenico was married to Giovanna Trotta, whose family served the Este family as courtiers and ambassadors.

Domenico's teaching, his theoretical concepts, and some of his most important choreographies (eighteen *balli* and five *bassedanze*) are preserved in the only extant copy of his work *De arte saltandi and choreas ducendi*, which is held by the Bibliothèque Nationale in Paris (see bibliography for complete information). This manual, which was compiled about 1445 or 1450 and which, as indicated by its frontispiece, was the property of the duke of Milan at an early point in its history, sets the example for all later dance instruction books. The first half contains the theory of dancing, the second half the dances themselves—*balli* with their music in mensural notation (*in canto, in canto asonare*) and *bassedanze* without. All choreographies are described verbally; they range from simple ornamental dances for two or three participants to elaborate creations for twelve or more, the latter frequently based on a thematic floor pattern ("La Tesara," "La Gelosia," "Anello," etc.) and dramatically intensified by the use of pantomimic gestures. Domenico's remarkable repertory also includes the first two genuine ballets in the history of the art: "La Mercanzia" and "La Sobria" are miniature dance dramas in the modern sense, employing all the steps and movements of the dancer's repertory "ordinato con qualche fondamento di proposito" (ordered with some fundamental intent), as Domenico's disciple Cornazano wrote in his *Libro dell'arte del danzare*.

As impressive as his choreographic inventiveness is Domenico's theoretical mastery of his subject. Fundamental to his work are those passages in which, for the first time in Western history, the aesthetics of the art of dancing are discussed. The frequent references to and quotations from Aristotle are not merely the conventional appeal of a dancing master to a classical authority for his own greater glory; Domenico has clearly studied Aristotle's *Poetics* and *Nichomachean Ethics* and makes connections between Aristotle's and his own concepts effortlessly. Particularly important are the *particelle principali* (primary requisites)—chapters dealing with style in dancing, with space, with musical accompaniment, and with dance technique, which Domenico understands as a means of artistic creativity rather than as mere physical exercise. The steps and movements are systematically grouped into *movimenti naturali* (movements given by nature) and *movimenti accidentali* (incidental movements); each of the four basic meters—*bassadanza, saltarello, quadernaria, piva*—is given its own characteristic step-unit *(tempo)*, but all good dancers are encouraged to interchange the *tempi* according to the requirements of each individual choreography and their own good taste. Such improvisation and the immense variety of steps and step combinations in the dances themselves make evident the complexity, the high degree of difficulty, the versatility, and the expressiveness of the Domenico dance style.

[*See also* Ballo and Balletto; Bassedanse.]

PRIMARY SOURCES

De arte saltandi & choreas ducendi. N.p., c.1455. Manuscript located in Paris, Bibliothèque Nationale, f.ital.972. Published by Dante Bianchi, "Un trattato inedito di Domenico da Piacenza," *La Bibliofilia* 65 (1963): 109–149. English translation by D. R. Wilson, *Domenico of Piacenza (Paris, Bibliothèque Nationale, MS ital. 972)*, corr. ed. (Cambridge, 1995). Text and English translation by A. William Smith, *Fifteenth-Century Dance and Music* (Stuyvesant, N.Y., 1995).

Otto bassedanze di M. Guglielmo da Pesaro e di M. Domenico da Ferrara. Foligno, 1887. Published by D. M. Faloci-Pulignano from a manuscript located in Foligno, Seminario Vescovile, Biblioteca Jacobilli, D.I.42.

SECONDARY SOURCES

Baxandall, Michael. *Painting and Experience in Fifteenth-Century Italy.* 2d ed. Oxford, 1988.

Bianchi, Dante. "Tre maestri di danza alla corte di Francesco Sforza." *Archivio storico lombardo* 89 (1962): 290–299.

Brainard, Ingrid. "Die Choreographie der Hoftänze in Burgund, Frankreich und Italien im 15. Jahrhundert." Ph.D. diss., University of Göttingen, 1956.

Brainard, Ingrid. "Bassedanse, Bassadanza, and Ballo in the Fifteenth Century." In *Dance History Research: Perspectives from Related Arts and Disciplines*, edited by Joann W. Kealiinohomoku. New York, 1970.

Brainard, Ingrid. *Three Court Dances of the Early Renaissance.* New York, 1971. Reconstructs an obsolete version of "Verçeppe."

Brainard, Ingrid. "La Fia Guilmin in canto/Filia Guilielmino in canto (Domenico/A. Cornazano)." Appendix I in Isabel Pope-Masakata

Kanasawa, *The Musical Manuscript Montecassino 871.* Oxford, 1978.

Brainard, Ingrid. "The Role of the Dancing Master in Fifteenth-Century Courtly Society." *Fifteenth-Century Studies* 2 (1979): 21–44.

Brainard, Ingrid. *The Art of Courtly Dancing in the Early Renaissance.* West Newton, Mass., 1981. Reconstructs the "Mignotta Vecchia" *(bassadanza)*, "La Gelosia" *(ballo* for six), and "Verçeppe" *(ballo* for five, new version).

Brainard, Ingrid. "The Art of Courtly Dancing in Transition: Nürnberg, Germ.Nat.Mus.Hs.8842, a Hitherto Unknown German Dance Source." In *Crossroads of Medieval Civilization: The City of Regensburg and Its Intellectual Milieu*, edited by Edelgard E. DuBruck and Karl Heinz Göller. Detroit, 1984.

Brainard, Ingrid. "Pattern, Imagery, and Drama in the Choreographic Work of Domenico da Piacenza." In *Guglielmo Ebreo da Pesaro e la danza nelle corti italiane del XV secolo*, edited by Maurizio Padovan. Pisa, 1990.

Celi, Claudia. "Talhor tacere un tempo e starlo morto: Il moto in potenza e in atto." In *Guglielmo Ebreo da Pesaro e la danza nelle corti italiane del XV secolo*, edited by Maurizio Padovan. Pisa, 1990.

Cornazano, Antonio. *The Book on the Art of Dancing* (c.1455–1465). Translated by Madeleine Inglehearn and Peggy Forsyth. London, 1981. Concordances to Domenico's *De arte saltandi.*

Daniels, Véronique. "Tempo Relationships within the Italian *Balli* of the Fifteenth Century: A Closer Look at the Notation." In *The Marriage of Music and Dance: Papers from a Conference Held at the Guildhall School of Music and Drama, London, 9th–11th August 1991.* Cambridge, 1992.

Daniels, Véronique, and Eugen Dombois. "Die Temporelationen im Ballo des Quattrocento: Spekulative Dialoge um den labyrinthische Rätselkanon *De la arte di ballare et danzare* des Domenico da Piacenza." *Basler Jahrbuch für Historische Musikpraxis* 14 (1990): 181–247.

Dolmetsch, Mabel. *Dances of Spain and Italy from 1400 to 1600.* London, 1954.

Francalanci, Andrea. "Le ricostruzione delle danze del '400 italiano attraverso in metodo di studio comparato delle fonti." *La danza italiana* 3 (Autumn 1985): 55–76.

Gallo, F. Alberto. "Il 'ballare lombardo,' circa 1435–1475." *Studi musicali* 8 (1979): 61–84.

Gallo, F. Alberto. "La danza negli spettacoli conviviali del secondo quattrocento." In *Spettacoli conviviali dall'antichità classica alle corti italiane del'400: Atti del VII convegno di studio, Viterbo, 27–30 maggio 1982.* Viterbo, 1983.

Gatiss, Ian. "The Puzzle of the Squiggle." *Historical Dance* 2.6 (1988–1991): 10–11.

Gatiss, Ian. "Realizing the Music in the Fifteenth-Century Italian Dance Manuals." In *The Marriage of Music and Dance: Papers from a Conference Held at the Guildhall School of Music and Drama, London, 9th–11th August 1991.* Cambridge, 1992.

Gombosi, Otto. "About Dance and Dance Music in the Late Middle Ages." *Musical Quarterly* 27 (July 1941): 289–305.

Guglielmo Ebreo da Pesaro. *On the Practice or Art of Dancing* (1463). Translated and edited by Barbara Sparti. Oxford, 1993. Contains approximately twenty Domenico choreographies.

Heartz, Daniel. "A Fifteenth-Century Ballo: *Rôti bouilli joyeux.*" In *Aspects of Medieval and Renaissance Music: A Birthday Offering to Gustave Reese*, edited by Jan LaRue. New York, 1966.

Kinkeldey, Otto. "Dance Tunes of the Fifteenth Century." In *Instrumental Music: A Conference at Isham Memorial Library, May 4, 1957*, edited by David G. Hughes. Cambridge, Mass., 1959.

Kinkeldey, Otto. "A Jewish Dancing Master of the Renaissance: Guglielmo Ebreo." In *Studies in Jewish Bibliography and Related Subjects, in Memory of Abraham Solomon Friedus.* New York, 1929.

Lockwood, Lewis. *Music in Renaissance Ferrara, 1400–1505.* Cambridge, Mass., 1984.

Lo Monaco, Mauro, and Sergio Vinciguerra. "Il passo doppio in Guglielmo e Domenico: Problemi di mensurazione." In *Guglielmo Ebreo da Pesaro e la danza nelle corti italiane del XV secolo,* edited by Maurizio Padovan. Pisa, 1990.

Luzio, Alessandro. *I precettori d'Isabella d'Este.* Milan, 1887.

Marrocco, W. Thomas. *Inventory of Fifteenth-Century Bassedanze, Balli, and Balletti in Italian Dance Manuals.* New York, 1981.

Mazzatinti, Giuseppe. *Inventario dei manoscritti italiani delle biblioteche di Francia.* 3 vols. Rome, 1886–1888.

McGee, Timothy J. "Dancing Masters and the Medici Court in the Fifteenth Century." *Studi musicali* 17.2 (1988): 201–224.

Michel, Artur. "The Earliest Dance-Manuals." *Medievalia et humanistica* 3 (1945): 117–131.

Monahin, Nona. "Leaping Nuns? Social Satire in a Fifteenth-Century Court Dance." In *Proceedings of the Sixteenth Annual Conference, Society of Dance History Scholars,* compiled by Linda J. Tomko. Riverside, Calif., 1993.

Padovan, Maurizio. "Da Dante a Leonardo: La danza italiana attraverso le fonti storiche." *La danza italiana* 3 (Autumn 1985): 5–37.

Padovan, Maurizio. "La danza di corte del XV secolo nei documenti iconografici di area italiana." In *Guglielmo Ebreo da Pesaro e la danza nelle corti italiane del XV secolo,* edited by Maurizio Padovan. Pisa, 1990.

Poggiali, Cristoforo. *Memorie per la storia letteraria di Piacenza.* 2 vols. Piacenza, 1989.

Pontremoli, Alessandro, and Patrizia La Rocca. *Il ballare lombardo: Teoria e prassi coreutica nella festa di corte del XV secolo.* Milan, 1987.

Pontremoli, Alessandro. "Estetica dell'ondeggiare ed estetica dell'aeroso: Da Domenico a Guglielmo, evoluzione di uno stile coreutico." In *Guglielmo Ebreo da Pesaro e la danza nelle corti italiane del XV secolo,* edited by Maurizio Padovan. Pisa, 1990.

Reyna, Ferdinando. "Origines musicales du ballet." In *La musique et le ballet: Numéro spécial de la Revue Musicale.* Paris, 1953.

Sachs, Curt. *World History of the Dance.* Translated by Bessie Schönberg. New York, 1937.

Smith, A. William. "Studies in Fifteenth-Century Italian Dance: *Belriguardo in due,* a Critical Discussion." In *Proceedings of the Tenth Annual Conference, Society of Dance History Scholars,* compiled by Christena L. Schlundt. Riverside, Calif., 1987.

Smith, A. William. "Una fonte sconosciuta della danza italiana del quattrocento." In *Guglielmo Ebreo da Pesaro e la danza nelle corti italiane del XV secolo,* edited by Maurizio Padovan, Pisa, 1990.

Smith, A. William, trans. and ed. *Fifteenth-Century Dance and Music: The Complete Transcribed Italian Treatises and Collections in the Tradition of Domenico da Piacenza.* 2 vols. Stuyvesant, N.Y., 1995.

Sonner-Ivers, Susanne. "Die Tanzbücher des XV. Jahrhunderts." *Die Musik* 34 (May 1942): 258–260.

Southern, Eileen. "A Prima Ballerina of the Fifteenth Century." In *Music and Context: Essays for John M. Ward,* edited by Anne Dhu Shapiro. Cambridge, Mass., 1985.

Sparti, Barbara. "Music and Choreography in the Reconstruction of Fifteenth-Century Balli: Another Look at Domenico's *Verçepe.*" *Fifteenth-Century Studies* 10 (1984): 177–194.

Sparti, Barbara. "Stile, espressione e senso teatrale nella danza italiana del '400." *La danza italiana* 3 (Autumn 1985): 39–53.

Sparti, Barbara. "How Fast Do You Want the Quadernaria? Or *Verçepe* and *Gelosia* Revisited: The Tale of the Three *Contrapassi* in *Quadernaria.*" In *The Marriage of Music and Dance: Papers from a Conference Held at the Guildhall School of Music and Drama, London 9th–11th August 1991.* Cambridge, 1992.

Sparti, Barbara. "Antiquity as Inspiration in the Renaissance of Dance: The Classical Connection and Fifteenth-Century Italian Dance." *Dance Chronicle* 16.3 (1993): 373–390.

Sparti, Barbara. "Rôti Bouilli: Take Two 'El Gioioso Fiorito.'" *Studi musicali* 24.2 (1995): 231–261.

Tani, Gino. "Domenico da Piacenza." In *Enciclopedia dello spettacolo.* Rome, 1954–.

Thomas, Emma Lewis. "Music and Dance in Boccaccio's Time." *Dance Research Journal* 10.2 (1978): 19–42. Publishes the "Mignotta alla Fila," "Leonzello," and "Ingrata" (in Labanotation), with music arranged by W. Thomas Marrocco.

Wilson, D. R. "'Damnes' as Described by Domenico, Cornazano, and Guglielmo." *Historical Dance* 2.6 (1988–1991): 3–8.

Wilson, D. R. "'La giloxia/Gelosia' as Described by Domenico and Guglielmo." *Historical Dance* 3.1 (1992): 3–9.

Wilson, D. R. *The Steps Used in Court Dance in Fifteenth-Century Italy.* Cambridge, 1992.

Wood, Melusine. *Some Historical Dances, Twelfth to Nineteenth Century.* London, 1952.

INGRID BRAINARD

DOMINICAN REPUBLIC. The Dominican Republic is situated on the eastern side of the Caribbean island of Hispaniola, discovered during the first voyage of Christopher Columbus in 1492. Haiti is on the western side of Hispaniola, and both originally comprised a single colony, Santo Domingo, Spain's first colony in the New World. The Spanish colonial empire in the Caribbean and the Circum-Caribbean during the sixteenth and seventeenth centuries was based on sugar cane, worked by an African slave labor force. Africans replaced the local Taíno, an Arawak people, who had inhabited the island for some five thousand years but were decimated by about 1530 by Spanish warfare and disease. With Spain's discovery of the riches of the mainland (especially the Aztec Empire in 1519 and the Inca Empire in 1532), Santo Domingo was virtually abandoned. This allowed the French to get a foothold in the eastern third of the island in 1697 and establish Saint-Domingue, the jewel of France's empire.

In the late 1790s, following the French and American revolutions, the slaves of Saint-Domingue revolted, winning the Haitian Revolution over France in 1804 to establish Haiti as the second republic in the New World (the first being the United States). Presumably to liberate the entire island of colonial domination, Haiti occupied Santo Domingo in 1822, abolishing slavery. With Spanish help, Dominicans reclaimed Santo Domingo in 1844, establishing the Dominican Republic. Spain reannexed the country in 1861, but independence was restored in 1865. Today almost eight million people live in the some 19,000 square miles (49,000 square kilometers); in addition, a recently emigrated expatriate population of more than a half million are in the United States, mainly in New York City. In the Dominican Republic, a recent marked trend is urbanization, and since the mid-1980s tourism has replaced sugar as the main source of national revenue. The people are largely racially and culturally hybrids of European and African ancestry, some 80 percent mulatto.

Traditional Dance. Culturally, the Dominican Republic is both an African-American and a Latin American country. Dominican dance today therefore reflects Spanish and African influences, creatively modified to form new genres, which vary in style according to region, social class, and rural or urban location.

Early Spanish chronicles report the *areíto* (or *areyto*) as the main Taíno dance event of the islands of Hispaniola, Puerto Rico, and Cuba. The *areíto* was a lengthy ceremonial dance accompanied by a slit-gong *(mayohuacán)* performed as a petition for fertility or protection, to render homage, for celebration, for funerary memorial, or for recreation. It was led by a singer-dancer with response by a chorus of as many as three hundred dancers—men, or both sexes—who assumed line, circle, or arch formations in close proximity with hand or arm contact.

The earliest documentation of African slave dance in the Caribbean is Father Jean-Baptiste Labat's description in 1698 of the *calenda*, a dance widely popular throughout the colonial Caribbean (also spelled *calinda* or *kalenda*). A century later, M. L. Moreau de Saint-Méry (1750–1819) described the *calenda* as a nonembracing couple dance that alternates a balancing step with circular turns symbolizing ritual pursuit, first in one direction and then in the other.

This description of the *calenda* is very similar to the drum dance, *baile de palos*, traditionally the most widespread Dominican dance and still frequent today. The *baile de palos* is the Dominican sacred dance, "a dance of respect," associated in particular with African-Dominican religious brotherhoods and their death rites and patron saints' festivals. Today's drum dance and music demonstrate the syncretism of Spanish and African elements. The dancer maintains a rigid posture, reflecting European influence, which contrasts with the greater African influence in the drum accompaniment; this posture and the lack of physical contact between the sexes differentiates this sacred dance from Dominican secular dance, which incorporates more hip movement and physical contact.

Secular and Social Dance. Dominican secular dance is much more subject to stylistic fashion than is sacred dance. Rural recreational dance differs in genres and style from urban dance—but dances of both rural and urban sectors have dialectically influenced each other. There is no documentation of specific dances until the early nineteenth century. The origins of many genres have legendary explanations that deny African influences; in fact, most dances are cultural hybrids.

Several groups of Dominican popular recreational dance can be identified. The earliest were genres based on Spanish folk dance, such as the *zapateo* (Spanish *zapateado*) in the Spanish-influenced north (Cibao) and northeast regions, with its variants, the *sarambo* in the

DOMINICAN REPUBLIC. Like the better-known merengue from the northern region of the country, the eastern *baile de priprí*, seen here, is a couple dance in which partners embrace. The accompaniment includes a button accordion, a *balsié* drum, and a *güira* or *guayo* (a metal scraper or grater). The occasion for this festivity is Pentecost, the Day of the Descent of the Holy Spirit upon the Apostles. (Photograph © 1978 by M. E. Davis; used by permission.)

Cibao and the *guarapo* in El Seybo (east). Derivatives of the fashionable seventeenth-century English country dance (Fr., *contredanse*) were characterized by a caller, like a quadrille *(cuadrilla)*, but were danced in a circle. These included the nineteenth-century *tumba* of the north (displaced by the *merengue* c.1850), the *carabiné* of the southwest, and the pan-Caribbean *bambulá* (Haitian *bamboula*) retained in the Haitian-derived enclave in Samaná. Variants of fashionable nineteenth-century ballroom dances of central European origin include the *vals* ("waltz") and mazurka (the latter is perhaps the basis of the *mangulina*, still danced in the south), and the *schotis* ("schottische"), allegedly danced in the north by Spanish officers during the period of annexation (1861–1865) and imitated in the *chenche* or *chenche matriculado*. Urban ballroom dances from the Hispanophone Caribbean of the late nineteenth century include the Puerto Rican *danza* and the Cuban *danzón* (based on the *habanera* rhythm, perhaps of Hispaniolan origin), and the bolero, as well as a Dominican serenade genre in 6/8 time, the *criolla*. Since the mid-twentieth century, the Cuban *son* (from Santiago de Cuba) has been popular in lower-class Santo Domingo and adjacent rural areas, such as Villa Mella. Finally, there are African-influenced "creole" (New World) dance creations, especially the northern *merengue* and its regional variants, such as the *merengue redondo* (round) based on circular turns (which includes the *baile de pripri* of the east and the *yuca* of the north); the *chivo* of Samaná, which resembles the *paso doble;* and the *pambiche* (Palm Beach), supposedly an imitation of U.S. soldiers trying to dance the merengue during the occupation of 1916–1924. Most genres except the merengue are currently in disuse or decline.

Before 1875, all recreational dance genres were accompanied by melodic stringed instruments—the *tres, cuatro,* and the *tiple;* however, trade with Germany led to their substitution by the Hohner button accordion. The contemporary rural recreational dance ensembles consist of accordion, metal scraper *(güira),* and a regionally specific short drum—in the north, this drum is the *tambora;* in the east, the *balsié* (Fr., *valser*), the ubiquitous Caribbean *juba* drum; and in the south, a vertical drum also called *balsié.* In addition, any type of dance rhythm may be adapted in a rural context to the widespread African-derived earth-bow *(gayumba,* called *tambour maringouin* in Haiti), which is now in disuse in practically all Dominican regions except Samaná and Puerto Plata.

The most popular ballroom genre of the early nineteenth century was the above-mentioned *tumba,* a variant of the quadrille. It was replaced at mid-century by the *merengue,* a rural dance from the northern region of the Cibao, popularized by General Juan Bautista Alfonseca (1810–1875) despite rejection by the elite. Until the 1930s, high-society dances included only the *vals* ("waltz"), *danza, danzón, criolla,* mazurka, polka, one-step, and two-step. The *merengue* was used only occasionally to close a dance. Today, the rural *merengue* of the Cibao, nicknamed *perico ripiao* ("deboned parrot," allegedly the name of a brothel), has diffused throughout the country and virtually displaced regional *merengue* variants and other genres of recreational dance. It coexists—albeit in different contexts—with the urban, commercialized, dance-band version that has evolved from it and has become internationally known.

The structure of both the *perico ripiao* and the urban merengue is a couple dance in 4/4 time, consisting of three sections: the brief *paseo* ("stroll"), for selecting the female partner and positioning the couple; the merengue proper; and the *jaleo* ("fuss," or "good time"), characterized by virtuosic figures, especially on the part of the man. The merengue, like most African-based Latin secular dances, breaks the rigid torso with lateral hip movement, emphasizing the hips and deemphasizing foot, leg, and arm

movement. In the country version there is more vertical movement, marking time, and less lateral hip movement.

The foot pattern is similar to that of the *paso doble,* but the feet are slid rather than lifted and slightly retarded with regard to the beat ("off-beat phrasing" reflecting African influence). The woman steps with the right foot to the right, and slides the left foot to meet it; the man does the same in mirror image, stepping with the left. In the ballroom *merengue,,* the couples on the dance floor move collectively in a counterclockwise direction, with an audible swish of sliding feet on the second and fourth beats. The *jaleo,* marked musically by the end of the soloist's stanzas and the beginning of the chorus section, entails a more improvisational call-and-response structure, shorter phrases, and heightened emotional intensity. The man directs the figures, which emphasize rapid and precisely synchronized body turns under and around the arms, largely by the woman, followed by the man to restore the initial position.

For the dance-band *merengue,* the accordion has been replaced by band instruments, notably the alto saxophone, introduced in 1925. As additional band instruments were gradually introduced, the *merengue* grew to be the musical symbol of national identity under the patronage of Rafael Trujillo Molina (1891–1961), Dominican dictator from 1930 to 1961. Luis Alberti (1906–1976),

DOMINICAN REPUBLIC. *Gagá* is the Lenten, Vodun-related, semi-secret society of a *batey,* the seasonal Haitian community who cut sugarcane in the Dominican Republic. An increasingly Dominican genre, because of immigration, intermarriage, and procreation, many *gagá* songs that were traditionally sung in Haitian Creole are now sung in Spanish. Here, in the Barahona region, are dancing *mayores,* young men who perform an acrobatic dance to a drum and aerophone ensemble. In their own *batey* their enactment of rebirth before dawn on Good Friday is a tradition that precedes performances in various communities on Holy Saturday and Easter Sunday. (Photograph © 1982 by M. E. Davis; used by permission.)

great-grandson of General Alfonseca, led Trujillo's official dance band. His *merengue* "Compadre Pedro Juan" (1936) could be considered the Dominican folk national anthem. Another key *merengue* and song composer is Julio Alberto Hernández (born 1900).

In the period following the Revolution of 1965, the *merengue* was commercialized by Johnny Ventura (born c.1940) and others. The contemporary commercial merengue is characterized by a markedly accelerated tempo, the addition of other band and percussion instruments, the elimination of the *paseo*, reduction of the merengue sections, and emphasis on the *jaleo* sections, risqué lyrics, and a more tightly embraced and sensual dance position. At the same time, certain trained popular musicians, singers, and dancers, such as Rafael Solano (born c.1932) and Casandra Damiró (1919–1983), promoted traditional genres and styles in the commercial repertory but without field research.

Since the early 1980s, the recorded *bachata*—a whiny, guitar-accompanied male lament influenced by the *son*— has joined the folk merengue in popularity in the rural and rural-derived marginal urban sectors. It has been legitimized for the middle and the upper classes by the conservatory-trained popular-music composer Juan Luis Guerra, director of the group "4–40."

Theatrical Dance. A genre of dance associated with the affirmation of national identity, as elsewhere in Latin America and worldwide, is the *ballet folklórico*. The professional folklorist Edna Garrido Boggs (born 1913), who pioneered Dominican folk dance studies with field documentation in the late 1940s, trained an authentically based performance troupe at the state university, now Universidad Autónoma de Santo Domingo. Today's university troupe continues to emphasize authenticity based on field research. The self-taught researcher, dancer, and teacher René Carrasco (c.1912–1978) was concerned with preservation, and he established a folk dance school nicknamed La Cueva Colonial in the colonial sector of Santo Domingo, where he taught research-acquired folk dance adapted for the stage. In the late 1970s, Fradique Lizardo (born 1930) succeeded in establishing a state-sponsored National Folk Dance Ballet; this company is directed in the 1990s by a Carrasco disciple, the dancer Josefina Miniño. The ministry of tourism followed suit with a troupe that presents well-rehearsed and picturesque albeit inauthentic dances as symbols of national identity. In the meantime, small-scale "folk dance ballets" largely associated with young peoples' neighborhood cultural clubs have proliferated throughout the country since political liberalization in the late 1970s. These groups, whose members sometimes engage in field observation, reflect a sincere search for Dominican identity. The ensembles of the 1990s in both Santo Domingo and New York City (expatriate Dominicans) emphasize music and dance genres of African and Haitian influence, in an effort to redefine Dominican identity through revivalist performance of selected traditional genres.

[*See also* Caribbean Region.]

BIBLIOGRAPHY

Alberti, Luis. *De música y orquestas bailables dominicanas, 1910–1959.* Santo Domingo, 1975.

Austerlitz, Paul. "Dominican Merengue in Regional, National, and International Perspectives." Ph.D. diss., Wesleyan University, 1993.

Boggs, Edna Garrido de. "Panorama del folklore dominicano." *Folklore Américas,* no. 1–2 (June–December 1961).

Boggs, Edna Garrido de. *Folklore infantil de Santo Domingo.* (Madrid, 1955). Reprint, Santo Domingo, 1980.

Brito Ureña, Luis Manuel. *El merengue y la realidad existencial del hombre dominicano.* Santo Domingo, 1987.

Castillo, José del, and Manuel García Arévalo. *Antología del Merengue/Anthology of the Merengue.* Santo Domingo, 1992.

Coopersmith, J. M. *Music and Musicians of the Dominican Republic.* Washington, D.C., 1949.

Davis, Martha Ellen. "Afro-Dominican Religious Brotherhoods: Structure, Ritual, and Music." Ph.D. diss., University of Illinois, Urbana-Champaign, 1976.

Davis, Martha Ellen. "Aspectos de la influencia africanna en la música tradicional dominicana." *Boletín del Museo del Hombre Dominicano* 13 (1980): 255–292.

Davis, Martha Ellen. "Música." *Encyclopedia Dominicana,* 2nd ed., 5:75–88.

Hernández, Julio Alberto. *Música tradicional dominicana.* Santo Domingo, 1969.

Incháustegui, Arístides. *Por amor al arte: Notas sobre música, compositores e intérpretes dominicanos.* Santo Domingo, 1995.

Jorge, Bernarda. *La música dominicana: Siglos XIX–XX.* Santo Domingo, 1982.

Lizardo, Fradique. *Danzas y bailes folklóricos dominicanos.* Santo Domingo, 1975.

Moore, Lillian. "Moreau de Saint-Méry and 'Danse.'" *Dance Index* 5 (October 1946): 232–260.

Pacini Hernandez, Deborah. *Bachata: A Social History of a Dominican Popular Music.* Philadelphia, 1995.

Rodríguez Demorizi, Emilio. *Música y baile en Santo Domingo.* Santo Domingo, 1971.

RECORDINGS

Gillis, Verna. *Music from the Dominican Republic.* Vol. 1, "The Island of Quisqueya." Folkways FE 4281 (1976); Vol. 2, "The Island of Española." Folkways FE 4282 (1976); Vol. 3, "Cradle of the New World." Folkways FE 4283 (1976); Vol. 4, "Songs from the North." Folkways FE 4284 (1978).

Gillis, Verna, and Daniel Pérea Martínez. *Rara in Haiti/Gaga in the Dominican Republic.* Folkways FE 4531, 2 disks. Republished with notes by Verna Gillis and Gage Averill as *Caribbean Revels: Haitian Rara and Domincan Gaga.* Smithsonian/Folkways CD SF 40402 (1991).

Llerenas, Eduardo, and Enrique Ramírez de Arellano. *República Dominicana: Merengues, cantos de vela y criollas.* Música Tradicional MT10 (México, D.F., 1987).

Roberts, John Storm. *Caribbean Island Music: Songs and Dances of Haiti, the Dominican Republic and Jamaica.* Nonesuch H-72047.

Roberts, John Storm. *Singers of the Cibao.* Original Music OML 403CC (Tivoli, New York, n.d.).

ARCHIVES. Archive of Folk Song, collections of J. M. Coopersmith (1945) and Edna Garrido de Boggs (1947–1948), Library of Congress, Washington, D.C. Archivo Nacional de Música, Secretaría de Estado de Educación, Bellas Artes y Cultos, Santo Domingo. Ethnomusicology Laboratory, Collection of Martha Ellen Davis (1972–1973), School of Music, University of Illinois, Urbana-Champaign.

MARTHA ELLEN DAVIS

DON JUAN. Full title: *Don Juan, ou Le Festin de Pierre.* Ballet-pantomime in three acts. Choreography: Gaspero Angiolini. Music: Christoph Willibald Gluck. Libretto: Gaspero Angiolini. Scenery and machines: Giovanni Maria Quaglio. First performance: 17 October 1761, Burgtheater, Vienna. Principals: Gaspero Angiolini (Don Juan), Giovanni Dupré, Vincenzo Turchi, Onorato Viganò, Camilla Paganini, Marianna le Clerc, Bettina Buggiano.

Don Juan is one of the first tragic ballets in history and one of the earliest and most important examples of the *ballet d'action.* It came into being because a chain of fortuitous circumstances brought together, in Vienna, the creative talents of three extraordinary artists of the eighteenth-century musical theater: the composer Christoph Willibald Gluck, the writer and librettist Count Rainero de Calzabigi, and the dancer, ballet master, and choreographer Gaspero Angiolini. In close collaboration they produced some of the most significant theater spectacles of all time: the tragic ballets *Don Juan* (1761) and *Sémiramis* (1765), the dramatic ballet *Alessandro* (1766), and the operas *Orfeo ed Euridice* (1762), *Alceste* (1767), and *Paride ed Elena* (1770).

In his famous and at times acrimonious correspondence with his colleague and competitor Jean-Georges Noverre, Angiolini laid claim to the invention of the *tragédie en ballet,* which he achieved "without help and without model" as the final stage of his "flowery and interesting path" from national dances, historical *balli,* and fables to a comedy, a drama, and "finally to a complete tragedy in pantomime." That tragedy was *Don Juan.*

On the occasion of the premiere performance of the work at the Burgtheater, a scenario was published in French (Vienna, 1761). In its preface Angiolini, through Calzabigi's pen, outlined his theories concerning the danced pantomime "dans le goût des Anciens" (in the style of the ancients):

Pantomime is the art to express the customs, the passions, the actions of gods, heroes, human beings through movements and body postures, through gestures and signs done rhythmically and appropriate for the expression of that which one wishes to represent. These movements, these gestures must, so to speak, constitute a running discourse: it was a kind of declamation created for the eye, whose comprehension was facilitated . . . by means of the music whose sonorities varied in accordance with the intentions of the pantomimic actor who wished to represent love or hate, anger or despair. . . . We must make the action visible. . . . We are capable of evoking all the passions by our mute representation. . . . If the public

does not want to deprive itself of the greatest beauties of our art, then it must get accustomed to be moved and to cry at our ballets.

The story of Don Juan had previously been dramatized by Tirso de Molina (*El Burlador de Sevilla,* 1630) and Molière (*Dom Juan, ou Le Festin de Pierre,* 1665). Angiolini and Calzabigi explain that the public's favorable acceptance of the Spanish tale of Don Juan determined their choice of this subject for their *coup d'essai:*

The unities of time and place are not observed, but the invention is sublime, the catastrophe terrible, and in our opinion it is believable. These qualities are more than sufficient for treatment in a Ballet Pantomime.   (preface f.4)

Act 1 shows a public street. The house of the Commander is on one side, that of Don Juan on the other. The action begins with a serenade offered by Don Juan to his mistress, Donna Elvira, daughter of the Commander. Don Juan gains admission to the house; the father surprises him. A duel ensues. The Commander is mortally wounded. Servants enter and carry the body away.

Act 2 takes place in Don Juan's house. Friends and mistresses are assembled for a banquet, preceded by a ball. All dance and then sit down at table. At the height of the festivity, the Commander, now a statue, knocks harshly at the door. The servant Sganarello opens it; the statue strides into the hall. The frightened guests flee. Don Juan remains alone with the statue. He mockingly invites it to the repast. The statue declines and in turn asks Don Juan to a meal at the gravesite. Don Juan accepts and accompanies the Commander outside. The guests, still anxious, return. Don Juan reenters. He tries to calm his guests, but they leave. He remains alone with his lackey, gives orders, and departs.

Act 3 takes place in "a cemetery for persons of noble birth." Center stage is the recently erected mausoleum of the Commander, who stands in front of it. Don Juan approaches, assuming a self-assured mien. The Commander takes him by the arm, urging him to mend his ways. Don Juan remains obstinate and impertinent. The earth opens, flames burst forth, demons and furies emerge "from the volcano" and torment Don Juan. They put him in chains and all are devoured by the fire. An earthquake turns the site into a heap of rubble.

The "musique admirable" that Gluck composed for *Le Festin de Pierre* made an immediate impact on the listeners. The monumental final scene of the Furies, which Gluck used again, verbatim, in his opera *Orfeo ed Euridice* is one of his most impressive compositions. Count Zinzendorf, eyewitness to more than one performance, reported that the Furies danced with torches and flew through the air—probably with the help of a flight machine constructed by the architect and designer Giovanni Maria Quaglio. The serenade in act 1 contrasts vividly with the furor of the duel and the death of the Commander. In act 2 social dances alternate with intensely dramatic pieces depicting all the moods from the tenderness of the Don Juan–Maitresse pas de deux to general celebration to fear in the "Entrée des Trembleurs." "M. Gluck . . . has perfectly captured the terrible of the action," wrote Angiolini. "He has attempted to express the passions . . . and the horror that reigns in the catastrophe" (Vienna, preface).

Choreographers and dancers such as Charles Le Picq (London, 1785), Vincenzo Galeotti (Copenhagen, 1781), and Onorato Viganò (Venice, 1787) created their own abbreviated versions of *Don Juan* to selected numbers of Gluck's score. In the twentieth century the story of *Don Juan* has fascinated many. Heinrich Kröller (1924), Rudolf Laban (*3 Don Juan Reigen*, 1925), Michel Fokine (1936), Léonide Massine (1959), Erich Walter (1965), Richard Adama (1969), and André Jerschik (1970) used as much of Gluck's music as suited their purposes and adjusted the original libretto accordingly. John Neumeier (1972, 1974) added music by Tomás Luis de Victoria to that of Gluck. Tatjana Gsovsky (1938) and Frederick Ashton (1948) choreographed their *Don Juan* ballets to Richard Strauss's score. Václav Kašlík composed the music for Nina Jirsikova's *Don Juan* (1941). Lew Christensen's version (1973) uses music by Joachín Rodrigo.

BIBLIOGRAPHY.   For a modern edition of *Don Juan*, see C. W. Gluck, *Sämtliche Werke*, Abt. 2, *Tanzdramen*, [Book 1], edited by Gerhard Croll (Kassel, Basel, Paris, London, New York, 1966), which includes a list of libraries and sigla of all known sources for both music and libretto, as well as an orchestra score. The volume also contains Gluck-Angiolini's *Sémiramis* ballet, with full apparatus and score. Biographical entries on Angiolini, Calzabigi, Durazzo, Gluck, Hilverding, and Noverre, with bibliographies and lists of works, are to be found in *The New Grove Dictionary of Music and Musicians* (London, 1980), *Enciclopedia dello spettacolo* (Rome, 1954–), *Die Musik in Geschichte und Gegenwart* (Kassel, 1949–), and *Riemanns Musiklexikon*, 12th ed. (Mainz, 1959–).

Angiolini, Gaspero. *Lettere di Gasparo Angiolini à Monsieur Noverre sopra i balli pantomimi*. Milan, 1773.
Angiolini, Gaspero. *Riflessioni sopra l'uso dei programmi ne'balli pantomimi*. Milan, 1775.
Brainard, Ingrid. "Angiolini, Gasparo: Don Juan." In *Pipers Enzyklopädie des Musiktheaters*. Munich, 1986–.
Brainard, Ingrid. "The Speaking Body: Gaspero Angiolini's *Rhétorique Muette* and the Ballet d'Action in the Eighteenth Century." In *Critica Musica: Essays in Honor of Paul Brainard*. Amsterdam, 1996.
Brown, Bruce Alan. *Gluck and the French Theatre in Vienna*. Oxford, 1991.
Croll, Gerhard. "Gluck's Don Juan freigesprochen." *Österreichische Musikzeitung* 31 (1976).
Gruber, Gernot. "I balli pantomimici viennesi di Gluck e lo stile drammatico della sua musica." *Chigiana* 29–30 (1972–1973): 508–512.
Haas, Robert. "Die Wiener Ballett-Pantomime im 18. Jahrhundert und Glucks Don Juan." *Studien zur Musikwissenschaft* 10 (1923): 6–36.
Haas, Robert. "Der Wiener Bühnentanz von 1740 bis 1767." *Jahrbuch der Musikbibliothek Peters* 44 (1937): 77–93.
Kirstein, Lincoln. *Movement and Metaphor: Four Centuries of Ballet*. New York, 1970.
Lynham, Deryck. *The Chevalier Noverre: Father of Modern Ballet*. London, 1950.
Raab, Riki. "Das k. k. Hofballett unter Maria Theresia, 1740–1780." *Jahrbuch der Gesellschaft für Wiener Theaterforschung, 1950–1951* (1952).
Testa, Alberto. "Il binomia Gluck-Angiolini e la realizzazione del balletto 'Don Juan.'" *Chigiana* 29–30 (1972–1973): 535.
Tozzi, Lorenzo. *Il balletto pantomimo del settecento: Gaspare Angiolini*. L'Aquila, 1972.
Tozzi, Lorenzo. "La poetica angioliniana del balletto pantomimo nei programmi viennesi." *Chigiana* 29–30 (1972–1973): 487.
Viale Ferrero, Mercedes. "Appunti di scenografia settecentesca, in margine a rappresentazioni di opere in musica di Gluck e balli di Angiolini." *Chigiana* 29–30 (1972–1973): 513.
Winter, Marian Hannah. *The Pre-Romantic Ballet*. London, 1974.

INGRID BRAINARD

DON QUIXOTE. [*To document some of the major productions of ballets based on episodes in the famous novel by Miguel de Cervantes, this entry consists of five articles:*
Early Productions
Petipa Production
Gorsky Production
Balanchine Production
Other Productions
For discussion in historical context, see entries on the principal choreographers and companies named therein.]

Early Productions

The masterpiece of the Spanish novelist Miguel de Cervantes Saavedra (1547–1616) is unquestionably *El ingenioso hidalgo Don Quijote de la Mancha* (part 1, 1605; part 2, 1615), a burlesque of the chivalric romances popular in Europe at the turn of the seventeenth century. A lengthy work that gradually deepens in character from burlesque to philosophical criticism of the human condition, it is generally considered the first and one of the greatest of modern novels. Translated into English as early as 1612 as *Don Quixote de la Mancha* and into other European languages soon thereafter, it has inspired numerous ballets in various countries around the world.

Since the mid-eighteenth century the absurd adventures of Don Quixote, also dubbed the Knight of the Woeful Countenance, and his faithful squire, the rustic Sancho Panza, have been frequently reenacted on the stages of Europe's great theaters. The earliest recorded production, on 12 February 1743, was in France. Set to a score by Joseph Bodin de Boismortier and mounted by an unknown choreographer at the Paris Opera, it was entitled *Don Quichotte chez la Duchesse*. Marie Allard danced the role of the Duchess. In Austria, Jean-Georges Noverre produced a *Don Quichotte* in Vienna in 1768 with music by Josef Starzer, possibly modeled on an earlier Viennese production by Franz Hilverding. In Italy, Paolo Franchi served as choreographer, librettist, and principal male dancer (in the role of Basilio), for his version of *Don Chisciotte*, presented at the Teatro alla Scala, Milan, during the Christmas season of 1783. The score was by Angelo Tarchi; the scenery was executed by Pietro Gonzaga; and the costumes were made by Francesco Motto and Giovanni Mazza. Some years later, in 1792, Antoine Pitrot also mounted a version of the ballet at La Scala, using a score by Niccolò Zingarelli, scenery by Paolo Landrian, and costumes by Motto and Mazza.

In the nineteenth century, the popularity of ballets about Don Quixote increased. Charles-Louis Didelot produced a two-act ballet about the errant knight in Saint Petersburg in 1808, and James Harvey D'Egville mounted a version in London in 1809. Paul Taglioni presented his version in Berlin in 1839, and Salvatore Taglioni mounted a production at the Teatro Regio, Turin, during the 1843/44 season.

All these ballets differed considerably in narrative and choreographic structure, as each choreographer fashioned his own libretto from different episodes in Cervantes's sprawling novel. Most of them were drawn from chapters in part 1, which frequently include the character of Dulcinea del Toboso, the good-looking peasant girl who unknowingly serves as inspiration for Don Quixote's chilvaric quest. The comic chapters from part 2 about the beautiful Quiteria (Kitri), her beloved Basilio (Basil), and the rich suitor Camacho (Gamache), who is preferred by Kitri's parents, were first used with notable success by Louis Milon, who mounted a production entitled *Les Noces de Gamache* at the Paris Opera in 1801. The part of Basilio was danced by Auguste Vestris.

Thereafter, Milon's libretto was widely used and adapted by choreographers who made ballets about Don Quixote. August Bournonville, for one, used it for his three-act ballet *Don Quixote at Camacho's Wedding*, produced at the Royal Theater, Copenhagen, in February 1837 with music by Gioacchino Rossini, Étienne Mehul, Gaspare Spontini, Jean Schneitzhoeffer, and others, arranged by Otto Zinck. Bournonville himself danced Basilio; Lucile Grahn was Kitri. In Milan, Bernardo Vestris also based his version on Milon's ballet, mounting his production at La Scala for the 1844/45 season. In Saint Petersburg, Marius Petipa, who was familiar with the Milon work, also retold the story of Gamache's comic wedding in his renowned version of *Don Quixote* mounted at the Bolshoi Theater in 1869.

Indeed, most later versions of ballets entitled *Don Quixote* would focus on, or include, the story of the captivating and mischievous Kitri; her sweetheart, the handsome barber Basil; and the comical proceedings surrounding the arrangements for the wedding of Kitri and her rich suitor Gamache. The characters of Don Quixote and Sancho Panza generally remain peripheral figures, often serving as links between various episodes.

BIBLIOGRAPHY
Beaumont, Cyril W. "Don Quixote." In *Complete Book of Ballets*. Rev. ed. London, 1951.
Cervantes Saavedra, Miguel de. *Don Quixote de la Mancha*. Translated by Charles Jarvis; edited with an introduction by E. C. Riley. The World's Classics. Oxford and New York, 1992.
Hurwitz, Jonathan. *Don Quixote* program notes and chronology. Souvenir program, PACT Ballet, 1994 season. Pretoria, 1994.
Koegler, Horst. "Don Quixote." In *The Concise Oxford Dictionary of Ballet*. Oxford and New York, 1982.

CLAUDE CONYERS
Based on material submitted by Reba Ann Adler

Petipa Production

Don Quixote. Ballet in four acts, eight scenes, a prologue, and an epilogue. Choreography: Marius Petipa. Music: Léon Minkus. Libretto: Marius Petipa, after Miguel de Cervantes. Scenery and costumes: Pavel Isakov, Ivan Shanguine, and Fedor Shenyan. First performance: 14 [26] December 1869, Bolshoi Theater, Moscow. Principals: Anna Sobeshchanskaya (Kitri), Sergei Sokolov (Basil), Dmitri Kuznetsov (Gamache), Wilhelm Vanner (Don Quixote), Vasily Geltser (Sancho Panza), Polina Karpakova (Dulcinea), Léon Espinosa (Harlequin).

The ballet's libretto is based on an episode in part 2 of Cervantes's novel involving a pair a young lovers, Quiteria (Kitri) and Basilio (Basil). The story of their courtship is central to the ballet and is framed by a series of scenes involving the principal characters of the novel, Don Quixote and Sancho Panza. Plot lines involving both sets of characters intertwine: Don Quixote helps the pair of lovers overcome obstacles blocking their path to marriage, such as the opposition of Kitri's father, Lorenzo, and the preference of Kitri's parents for her wealthy suitor, Gamache.

The first Moscow production emphasized the comic dimension of the ballet and was dominated by character dances (many of which were pure *divertissements*) and pantomime scenes (the prologue, epilogue, and Don Quixote's adventures). Only one scene, "Don Quixote's Dream," received pure classical treatment. The original production of the ballet contained several scenes that were omitted from subsequent reworkings (e.g., a colorful scene involving wandering comedians, a comic dance scene of a lark hunt, and some others).

Only two years later, for a production in Saint Petersburg Petipa reworked the ballet on a larger scale and in even more spectacular form. In five acts, eleven scenes, a prologue, and an epilogue, with additional music supplied by Minkus, and with the original, brightly colored scenery

DON QUIXOTE: Petipa Production. Erik Bruhn as Basilio and Lupe Serrano as Kitri in Petipa's famous pas de deux from the final act of *Don Quixote*. (Photograph by Maurice Seymour; used by permission.)

and costume designs, the new version was premiered at the Maryinsky Theater on 9 [21] November 1871. The cast included Aleksandra Vergina as Kitri-Dulcinea, Lev Ivanov as Basil, Timofei Stukolkin as Don Quixote, Alexandre Pichaut as Sancho Panza, and Nikolai Golts as Gamache.

The Saint Petersburg production featured a number of innovations and an increased emphasis on classical dance. Kitri and Dulcinea came together in a single character, and two new figures, the Duke and the Duchess, who receive Don Quixote and hold a fête in his honor, were introduced. The joyous celebration in the final act provided the occasion for an elaborate *grand pas espagnol*, in which none other than the *premier danseur* Pavel Gerdt partnered the ballerina in the pas de deux. This highly stylized dance, which is among the classic pieces of Petipa's choreographic art, has since been performed countless times the world over as a virtuoso concert piece. [*See* Pas de Deux.]

BIBLIOGRAPHY

Garafola, Lynn, ed. and trans. *The Diaries of Marius Petipa*. Studies in Dance History 3.1. Pennington, N.J., 1992.

Krasovskaya, Vera. "*Don Quixote*: A Dramatic Ballet" (in Russian). In *Ruskii baletnyi teatr vtoroi poloviny deviatnadtsatogo veka*. Leningrad, 1963.

Krasovskaya, Vera. "*Don Quixote* in Moscow and *Don Quixote* in Petersburg" (in Russian). In *Russkii baletnyi teatr nachala dvadtatogo veka*, vol. 1, *Khoreografy*. Leningrad, 1971.

Petipa, Marius. *Russian Ballet Master: The Memoirs of Marius Petipa*. Translated by Helen Whittaker; edited by Lillian Moore. London, 1958.

Slonimsky, Yuri. *Don Quixote* (in Russian). Leningrad, 1934.

NOTATED SCORE. *Don Quixote*, Pas classique espagnol, Benesh Notation score, notated by Jürg Lanzrein (1973).

VICTOR V. VANSLOV
Translated from Russian

Gorsky Production

Don Quixote. Ballet in four acts. Choreography and libretto: Aleksandr Gorsky, after Marius Petipa. Music: Léon Minkus and others. Scenery and costumes: Konstantin Korovin, Aleksandr Golovin, and N. A. Klodt. First performance: 6 [19] December 1900, Bolshoi Theater, Moscow. Principals: Liubov Roslavleva (Kitri-Dulcinea), Vasily Tikhomirov (Basil), Aleksei Yermolayev (Don Quixote), N. P. Domashev (Sancho Panza), Mikhail Mordkin (Espada), Sofia Fedorova (Street Dancer and Mercedes). Revival: 20 January [2 February] 1902, Maryinsky Theater, Saint Petersburg. Principals: Matilda Kshessinska (Kitri-Dulcinea), Nikolai Legat (Basil), Pavel Gerdt (Gamache), Aleksei Bulgakov (Don Quixote), Enrico Cecchetti (Sancho Panza), Olga Preobrajenska (Street Dancer), Marie Petipa (Mercedes), Tamara Karsavina (Amor), Anna Pavlova (Juanita). Restaged and remounted at the Bolshoi Theater, Moscow, in 1906.

Despite Petipa's complaint that Gorsky's production was a mutilation of his own masterwork by one of his former students, Gorsky's *Don Quixote* was in fact a truly imaginative and radical revision of the ballet. A number of innovations were introduced in the musical score, in the staging, and in the choreographic structure of the work. The score, for example, was augmented by music for a Spanish dance by Anton Simon and a fandango by Eduard Nápravík. Don Quixote's Dream scene was completely redesigned and moved to follow the famous Tilting at Windmills scene, and the classical pas de deux in the final act had begun to crystallize into the form that we know today.

The principal innovation that Gorsky introduced, however, was in his realistic staging of crowd scenes and in the individual character that he invested in members of the corps de ballet. Influenced by successful productions at the Moscow Art Theater and the Mamontov Opera House, Gorsky sought to make the action more logical and true to the period atmosphere of the ballet. To this end, he individualized the dancing of the corps de ballet in the scenes of the Square in Barcelona and the Tavern in Seville, thus avoiding the canonical symmetry of the dances in Petipa's production and so achieving a greater degree of dramatic verity. As a result the dances seemed to stem from the emotional excitement of the street crowd, arising as a natural result of high spirits rather than being set pieces of choreography.

Throughout the ballet, the dance and pantomime sequences followed each other in a freely interacting succession. The principal dancers' solo passages occurred as dramatic climaxes of mass dances, as the main characters emerged from the crowd, executed a choreographic phrase or two, and melted back into the crowd again. Gorsky's imaginative staging of individualized activities for various groups of dancers helped create a romantic, yet authentic period atmosphere of life in seventeenth-century Spain, which matched the spirit of the music. Lacking the usual stereotyped images and conventional

designs, the ballet's scenery and costumes looked more true to life but were not so realistic that they diminished the ballet's overall festive atmosphere or detracted in any way from the charm of the story.

Subsequently, Gorsky's production of *Don Quixote* underwent further marginal changes and modifications, acquiring, in particular, several new *divertissements*. With or without these latter changes, his version provided the basis for many subsequent productions of *Don Quixote* in Leningrad, Moscow, and elsewhere in the Soviet Union. In Petrograd/Leningrad, the work was revived at the Kirov Theater in 1923 by Fedor Lopukhov and in 1946 by Petr Gusev, with some new dances introduced by Nina Anisimova. Some of the foremost ballerinas at the Kirov have shone as Kitri, among them Olga Spessivtseva, Natalia Dudinskaya, Tatiana Vecheslova, Feya Balabina, Irina Kolpakova, and Gabriella Komleva, to name but a few. Vakhtang Chabukiani and Konstantin Sergeyev are among the leading male dancers to have appeared as Basil.

In Moscow the 1906 Gorsky version of *Don Quixote* was a staple of the repertory at the Bolshoi Theater until 1935. Revived in 1940 by Rostislav Zakharov, who added some dances, and again in 1942 by Kasyan Goleizovsky, it has survived largely intact for more than five decades. It can

DON QUIXOTE: Gorsky Production. One of Gorsky's innovations in his reworking of *Don Quixote* was a naturalistic, asymmetrical staging of the crowd scenes. In this scene from act 1 of a 1950s Bolshoi Ballet production, Maya Plisetskaya soars as Kitri, while the casually arrayed corps de ballet cheers her on. (Photograph from the Dance Collection, New York Public Library for the Performing Arts.)

still be seen on the Bolshoi stage today. Some of the best interpreters of Kitri in Moscow have been Olga Lepeshinskaya, Sofia Golovkina, Maya Plisetskaya, Ekaterina Maximova, Natalia Bessmertnova, and Nadezhda Pavlova. The best performers of the role of Basil at the Bolshoi have been Aleksei Yermolayev, Vladimir Vasiliev, Mikhail Lavrovsky, and Viacheslav Gordeyev.

During the Soviet era, *Don Quixote* was not only a perennial favorite with audiences in Leningrad and Moscow but was mounted by practically every theater of any importance in all the republics of the USSR. As a testament to the balletic heritage of both Petipa and Gorsky, it continues to enjoy exceptional popularity throughout Russia and the former Soviet republics to the present day.

BIBLIOGRAPHY
Bakhrushin, Y. A. *Aleksandr Alekseevich Gorskii.* Moscow, 1946.
"Don Quixote" (in German). *Tanzblätter* (October 1977): 8–19.
Krasovskaya, Vera. "*Don Quixote:* A Dramatic Ballet" (in Russian). In *Ruskii baletnyi teatr vtoroi poloviny deviatnadtsatogo veka.* Leningrad, 1963.
Krasovskaya, Vera. "*Don Quixote* in Moscow and *Don Quixote* in Petersburg" (in Russian). In *Russkii baletnyi teatr nachala dvadtatogo veka,* vol. 1, *Khoreografy.* Leningrad, 1971.
Slonimsky, Yuri. *Don Quixote* (in Russian). Leningrad, 1934.
Troziner, F. F. "Novoe v balete." *Saint Petersburg Gazette* 19–20 (January 1902).
Wiley, Roland John, ed. and trans. *A Century of Russian Ballet: Documents and Eyewitness Accounts, 1810–1910.* Oxford, 1990.

VICTOR V. VANSLOV
Translated from Russian

Balanchine Production

Don Quixote. Ballet in three acts. Choreography: George Balanchine. Music: Nicolas Nabokov. Libretto: George Balanchine and Nicolas Nabokov, after Miguel de Cervantes. Scenery, costumes, and lighting: Esteban Francés, assisted by Peter Harvey. Costumes executed by Barbara Karinska; giant devised by Kermit Love and Peter Saklin; masks and armor by Lawrence Vlady. First performance: 28 May 1965, New York State Theater, New York City Ballet. (Preview: 27 May 1965, New York City Ballet gala benefit performance.) Principals: Richard Rapp (Don Quixote), Deni Lamont (Sancho Panza), Suzanne Farrell (Dulcinea).

The first evening-length American ballet created to a commissioned score, *Don Quixote* is a somber tale of artistic alienation from society. An ambitious collaboration among the choreographer, composer, and scenic designer, the work approaches its themes—romantic aspiration and spiritual regeneration in a world of materialism, cynicism, derision, and death—with remarkable theatrical assiduousness and imagination. Basing their libretto on those portions of Cervantes's novel that portray the Don's madness against the social background of sixteenth-century Spain, Balanchine and Nabokov fashioned a

grim, twisted view of humanity and made a ballet quite unlike the festive, harmonious Petipa-Gorsky-Minkus work that they had known in their youth in Russia. (Balanchine performed in this ballet in 1916, when he was twelve.)

Balanchine's *Don Quixote* was first seen at a gala benefit performance on 27 May 1965 at the New York State Theater, Lincoln Center. Balanchine himself appeared as the Don, with Suzanne Farrell (then only nineteen) in one of her first starring roles as Dulcinea. The official premiere took place the following evening, with Richard Rapp as the Don, Deni Lamont as Sancho Panza, and Nicholas Magallanes, Jillana, and Francisco Moncion in supporting roles. The *divertissements* in act 2 featured many of the principal dancers and soloists in the company, as did the *pas d'action* in act 3.

There is a great deal of choreographic inaction in Balanchine's *Don Quixote,* primarily because most of the ballet is presented from the viewpoint of its philosophical title character, a mimed role. Dulcinea appears throughout in several different guises—a servant girl, the Virgin Mary, a shepherdess, a Gypsy woman, a high-born lady—but she essentially remains an ideal vision of womankind throughout the Don's spiritual quest, a role not unlike that of various women in Balanchine's own life. (In discussing the ballet, he stated that "everything man does he does for his ideal woman.") Only during the Vision scene of act 3, with its extended dance sequences, does the focus change from the Don to Dulcinea.

The knight's "crusades" in act 1 culminate in act 2, the heart of the dance drama, which takes place at the royal Spanish court amid an ominous, funereal atmosphere. After a series of dances, the courtiers, clad in heavy, brocaded, black and gold costumes, put on masks and indulge in rude pranks to mock and humiliate the Don, who is consoled by Dulcinea during the soft, gentle pas de deux that ends the act. As act 3 opens Don Quixote is captured in a huge net and left lying on the stage during a *pas d'action* danced by Dulcinea, a cavalier (the Knight of the Silver Moon), and a group of soloists. Thereafter the scenery breaks apart and the Don emerges as the central figure in action scenes of tilting with windmills, a battle with a giant, and a stampede of pigs, all well-known episodes in Cervantes's novel. At last the exhausted Don crawls into a cage to be carried home, where, on his deathbed, he experiences a hallucinatory vision of a funeral march, a long procession of black-clad figures: penitents in chains, monks bearing crosses, and priests swinging censers of smoking incense. In an apotheosis, Dulcinea appears and offers a final comforting gesture by placing a cross upon the dying man's chest.

Reviews of the work were decidedly mixed; it seemed that there had been insufficient time for the production to go through a stylistic maturation process. For a number of years Balanchine never stopped tinkering with it, including having new music added and scenery altered. As long as it remained in the New York City Ballet repertory, however, it continued to provide a fascinating subject for study of Balanchine's ideas on mysticism and creativity as well as a powerful vehicle for Farrell's absorbing interpretive achievement.

BIBLIOGRAPHY

Balanchine, George, with Francis Mason. "Don Quixote." In *Balanchine's Complete Stories of the Great Ballets*. Rev. and enl. ed. Garden City, N.Y., 1977.
Barnes, Clive. Reviews. *New York Times* (15 May 1966, 27 January 1967, 14 February 1969).
Choreography by George Balanchine: A Catalogue of Works. New York, 1984. The entry for *Don Quixote* includes full details of the cast and a list of major choreographic revisions.
Cornfield, Robert. "*Don Quixote:* Rehearsal and Performance." *Ballet Review* 1.2 (1965): 36–42.
Croce, Arlene. *Going to the Dance*. New York, 1982.
Denby, Edwin. "About Don Quixote." *Dance Magazine* (July 1965).
Farrell, Suzanne, with Toni Bentley. *Holding On to the Air: An Autobiography*. New York, 1990.
Kirstein, Lincoln. *Thirty Years: The New York City Ballet*. New York, 1978.
Kolodin, Irving. "The Durable Don Quixote." Program note, New York City Ballet, 22 May 1965.
Manchester, P. W. "Don Quixote." *Dance News* (June 1965): 13.
Reynolds, Nancy. *Repertory in Review: Forty Years of the New York City Ballet*. New York, 1977.
Taper, Bernard. *Balanchine: A Biography*. New rev. ed. New York, 1984.

REBA ANN ADLER

Other Productions

During the 1920s a ballet entitled *Don Quixote*, which was danced to music by Minkus and which was similar to the Gorsky version of the work, was introduced to the Western world by Anna Pavlova, not only one of the most beloved ballerinas of all time but surely one of the most widely traveled. The version presented by her company was staged by Laurent Novikoff in two acts, three scenes, and a prologue, with scenery and costumes designed by Konstantin Korovin. Although the prologue and act 1 faithfully followed the Gorsky staging, act 2 was entirely original with Novikoff and included dances to several passages of music not in Minkus's score.

In Gorsky's 1902 production in Saint Petersburg, Pavlova had appeared as Juanita, the fan seller, and had danced the last-act fandango with Georgi Kyaksht to music especially composed by Eduard Nápravík. A few years later she had taken on the role of Kitri and had enjoyed glowing notices in the Petersburg press. After leaving Russia she earned further acclaim wherever she danced the role in Novikoff's production, which was first seen in England on 8 September 1924 at the Royal Opera House, Covent Garden, London; in the United States on 17 October 1924 at the Manhattan Opera House, New York; and in Australia on 20 May 1926 at the Sydney Opera House.

In Europe, as ballet companies began to flourish again in the years following World War II, productions of ballets

DON QUIXOTE: Other Productions. Gelsey Kirkland as Kitri and Mikhail Baryshnikov as Basilio in Baryshnikov's 1978 staging of *Don Quixote*. Subtitled *Kitri's Wedding*, this American Ballet Theatre production premiered at the Kennedy Center for the Performing Arts, Washington, D.C., and remained in the company's repertory until 1989. (Photograph © 1978 by Eric Feinblatt; from the Dance Collection, New York Public Library for the Performing Arts.)

based on Cervantes's novel about Don Quixote were mounted by various choreographers using scores by various composers. In France, the Hungarian choreographer Aurelio Milloss created *Le Portrait de Don Quichotte*, to music by the Italian composer Gofredo Petrassi, for the Ballets de Champs-Élysées, which first performed it in Paris on 21 November 1947. Jean Babilée was the Don, and Nathalie Philippart was Dulcinea. A few years later, on 5 May 1950, Parisian balletomanes saw another work about the Don when Serge Lifar presented *Le Chevalier Errant*, which he had choreographed to music by Jacques Ibert for the Paris Opera Ballet. Lycette Darsonval danced Dulcinea to Lifar's Don Quixote.

In England, Ninette de Valois made a one-act ballet in five scenes to a commissioned score by Roberto Gerhard for the 1949/50 season of the Sadler's Wells (now Royal) Ballet. With scenery and costumes by Edward Burra, this *Don Quixote* was first performed on 20 February 1950 at Covent Garden, London, with Robert Helpmann as Don

DON QUIXOTE: Other Productions. The Central Ballet of China's production of *Don Quixote*, with Feng Ying as Kitri and Xu Gang as Basilio. (Photograph © 1995 by Jack Vartoogian; used by permission.)

Quixote, Margot Fonteyn as Dulcinea, and Alexander Grant as Sancho Panza. It included scenes of the Don tilting at windmills, his meeting with Dulcinea at the inn, and his delusions, madness, and death.

The first Western production of the complete ballet as it was known in Russia—that is, the full-length Petipa-Gorsky version—was staged by the Polish choreographer Witold Borkowski for Ballet Rambert in 1962. With scenery and costumes designed by Voytek, this production was first presented by the Rambert company at the Sadler's Wells Theatre, London, on 26 July 1962. John Chesworth played the role of Don Quixote, Lucette Aldous danced Kitri, and Kenneth Bannerman was Basilio. Chesworth was greatly admired for his interpretation of the Don's nobility of spirit, and Aldous, a brilliant technician, was especially praised for her virtuosity in the last-act pas de deux.

Most later versions of *Don Quixote* mounted in the West have also been patterned after the Petipa-Gorsky version performed at the Kirov Theater in Leningrad; most have proved widely popular and several are still performed in the present day. The first was mounted at the Vienna State Opera Ballet by Rudolf Nureyev. Set to the familiar score by Léon Minkus, with scenic designs by Barry Kay, Nureyev's *Don Quixote* was first performed at the Vienna Staatsoper on 1 December 1966, with the choreographer in the role of Basilio, Ully Wuehrer as Kitri, Michael Birkmeyer as Don Quixote, and Konstantin Zajetz as Sancho Panza.

This ballet not only provided Nureyev with one of the few comic roles in his large repertory, but it also allowed him to present the tale of the young Spanish lovers choreographically from the standpoint of *commedia dell'arte*, with Kitri as Columbine and Basilio as Harlequin. In his staging and choreography, Nureyev attempted to shift the focus of the ballet from Don Quixote's view of the world to other people's reactions toward the Don. In the process, he revealed the fanaticism of everyone, not just the misdirected zeal of a foolish idealist.

In 1970 Nureyev restaged his work for the Australian Ballet, where it proved an ideal vehicle for the company's principal dancers. In 1972 the Australian production was, fortunately, captured on film, with Nureyev and Lucette Aldous in the roles of the lovers and Sir Robert Helpmann in a memorable dramatic performance as the hapless knight Don Quixote. Nureyev's version was subsequently staged for the Zurich Ballet, the Norwegian National Ballet, the Paris Opera Ballet, the Boston Ballet, PACT Ballet (Pretoria), the Central Ballet of China, the Matsuyama Ballet, La Scala Ballet (Milan), and the Royal Ballet of Flanders.

A few years after Nureyev's version was first performed in Austria, a second popular version of *Don Quixote* was choreographed in the United States by Mikhail Baryshnikov, who, like Nureyev, had defected from the Soviet Union to find artistic freedom in the West. His version, subtitled *Kitri's Wedding*, was created for American Ballet Theatre and was first performed at the Kennedy Center for the Performing Arts in Washington, D.C., on 28 March 1978. With a libretto closely based on Petipa's 1869 original and with the Minkus score transcribed and orchestrated by Patrick Flynn, the production was handsomely mounted: the scenery and costumes were designed by Santo Loquasto, and the lighting was done by Jennifer Tipton. Baryshnikov himself danced Basil, Gelsey Kirkland was dazzling as Kitri, and Alexander Minz appeared as Don Quixote.

This production remained in the repertory of American Ballet Theatre until Baryshnikov relinquished his role as director of the company in 1989. New versions were staged for the company by Vladimir Vasiliev in 1991 and by Kevin McKenzie and Susan Jones, with assistance from Irina Kolpakova, in 1995; in both versions the choreography was credited to Petipa and Gorsky. Over the years, the roles of Kitri and Basil have proved ideal vehicles for displaying the talents of American Ballet Theatre's star-studded roster of ballerinas and premier danseurs. Outstanding among the many who have captivated audiences as Kitri are Natalia Makarova, Sylvie Guillem, Cynthia Harvey, Amanda McKerrow, and Paloma Herrera. Notable virtuosos who have danced Basil include Patrick Bissell, Fernando Bujones, Julio Bocca, Jose Manuel Carreño, and Angel Corella.

The infectious spirit of American Ballet Theatre's *Don Quixote* reminds one more of a raucous musical comedy than of a classical ballet or of the biting satire in Nureyev's version. Both versions, however, skillfully mix together classicism, pungent wit, and exotic atmosphere. And both openly acknowledge their debt to Petipa's theatrical treatment of the Minkus score and to Gorsky's lively staging of the crowd scenes. Baryshnikov's version was mounted for Britain's Royal Ballet in 1993, providing starring roles for Viviana Durante as Kitri and Irek Mukhamedov as Basilio.

Other notable productions of *Don Quixote* include those of the German State Opera Ballet (East Berlin), with choreography by Tajana Gsovsky (1949) to music by Leo Spies, and the Hamberg Ballet, with choreography by John Neumeier (1979) to music by Richard Strauss. Among the numerous productions by choreographers using the Minkus score are those by George Gé (1958) for the Finnish National Ballet, Veronica Paeper (1979) for CAPAB Ballet (Cape Town), Nicholas Beriozoff (1982) for the National Ballet of Canada, Yuri Gigorovich (1982) for the Royal Danish Ballet, Heinz Spoerli (1989) for the Basel Ballet, and Hilda Riveros (1991) for Ballet de Santiago (Chile).

BIBLIOGRAPHY

Aria, Barbara. *Misha: The Mikhail Baryshnikov Story*. New York, 1989.

Dorris, George. "Don Quixote in the Twentieth Century: A Mirror for Choreographers." *Choreography and Choreographers*, vol. 3, part 4 (1994): 47–53.

Fraser, John. *Private View: Inside Baryshnikov's American Ballet Theatre*. New York, 1988.

Hurwitz, Jonathan. *Don Quixote* program notes and chronology. Souvenir program, PACT Ballet, 1994 season. Pretoria, 1994.

Kirkland, Gelsey, with Greg Lawrence. *Dancing on My Grave: An Autobiography*. New York, 1986.

Lazzarini, John and Roberta. *Pavlova: Repertoire of a Legend*. New York, 1980.

Rambert, Marie. *Quicksilver: The Autobiography of Marie Rambert*. London, 1972.

Stuart, Otis. *Perpetual Motion: The Public and Private Lives of Rudolf Nureyev*. New York, 1995.

FILM.   Australian Ballet, *Don Quixote* (1973); co-directed by Rudolf Nureyev and Robert Helpmann; co-produced by Rudolf Nureyev, Robert Helpmann, and John Hargreaves. Released through the Walter Reade Organization.

CLAUDE CONYERS
Based on material submitted by Reba Ann Adler

DOUBROVSKA, FELIA (Felitsata Leont'evna Dluzhenevskaia; born 13 February 1896 in Saint Petersburg, died 18 September 1981 in New York City), dancer and teacher. Following preliminary studies with Enrico Cecchetti, Doubrovska entered the Imperial Theater School of Saint Petersburg in 1906. Upon graduating in 1913 she made her solo debut at the Maryinsky Theater in *La Source*. Her exceptionally sinuous physique confined her thereafter to appearances in minor *divertissements*, however.

In 1920 Doubrovska fled the Soviet Union, accompanied by *premier danseur étoile* Pierre Vladimiroff, whom she later married. Through his influence she was accepted into the Ballets Russes de Serge Diaghilev. With the exception of a one-year absence (1926–1927), she remained with the troupe until 1929. During that period she was chiefly noted for her interpretation of modern works and exotic revivals. In 1923 she created the role of the Bride in Bronislava Nijinska's *Les Noces;* in 1928, Calliope in George Balanchine's *Apollo;* and in 1929, the Siren in the same choreographer's *The Prodigal Son*. In the last role her serpentine bearing earned her praise as "an unbelievably fantastic seductress . . . thin, strong, and enticing," while her performances in Michel Fokine's *Schéhérazade* and *Thamar* caused W. A. Propert (1931) to call her "a dancer for whose equal in beauty of form . . . we have to go back to Ida Rubinstein." She was also noted for her portrayals of such Léonide Massine works as *Zéphire et Flore* (1925) and *Ode* (1928).

After Diaghilev's death, Doubrovska appeared with Anna Pavlova's company (1930); at the Teatro Colón in Buenos Aires (1930), where she danced the first full-length *Giselle* presented in Argentina; and with the Ballets

DOUBROVSKA. Noted for her elegant line, Doubrovska was perfectly suited to the streamlined costume designed by Pavel Tchelitchev for Léonide Massine's *Ode* (1928). (Photograph from the Dance Collection, New York Public Library for the Performing Arts.)

Russes de Monte Carlo (1932). In 1938 she joined the Metropolitan Opera Ballet, where she remained until her retirement from the stage the following year. With her husband, Doubrovska became a faculty member at the School of American Ballet (1948–1981), where, until her death, she trained generations of pupils in the classical purity and elegant bearing for which she had been known throughout her career.

BIBLIOGRAPHY

Ackerman, Gerald, and Susan Cook Summer. "Doubrovska Remembers." *Ballet News* 2 (August 1980): 24–29.

Gale, Joseph. *Behind Barres.* New York, 1980.

García-Márquez, Vicente. *The Ballets Russes: Colonel de Basil's Ballets Russes de Monte Carlo, 1932–1952.* New York, 1990.

Gruen, John. *The Private World of Ballet.* New York, 1975.

Horosko, Marian. "In the Shadow of Russian Tradition: Felia Doubrovska." *Dance Magazine* (February 1971): 40–42.

Huckenpahler, Victoria. "Felia Doubrovska: Imperial Ballerina." *Dance Chronicle* 5.4 (1982–1983): 361–437.

The National Atheneum (6 July 1929).

Newman, Barbara. *Striking a Balance: Dancers Talk about Dancing.* Rev. ed. New York, 1992.

Propert, W. A. *The Russian Ballet, 1921–1929.* London, 1931.

Sorley Walker, Kathrine. *De Basil's Ballets Russes.* New York, 1983.

VICTORIA HUCKENPAHLER

DOUVILLIER, SUZANNE (Suzanne-Théodore Taillandet, also known as Mademoiselle Théodore and Madame Placide; born 1778 in Dole, France, died 30 August 1826 in New Orleans, Louisiana), French-born dancer and choreographer. One of the most beautiful and popular pantomime dancers in Paris, Douvillier, under the name Madame Placide, was the first professional ballerina and first woman choreographer to tour the United States. Over the course of her American career she undertook almost one hundred and fifty roles, more than one hundred of them in full-length ballets, pantomimes, or *opéra-ballets.*

Under the stage name of Mademoiselle Théodore she was listed in the *Almanach des spectacles* as a child dancer at the Théâtre Français in 1784 and 1785. She was accepted into the Académie Royale de Musique in 1786 and for two years danced daily in the *opéra-ballets.* The *Almanach* noted that she was accorded the unusual privilege of dancing simultaneously at the Paris Opera and at one of the popular theaters. When, at only ten years of age, she played Columbine at Jean-Baptiste Nicolet's theater, she was admired as much for her beauty as for her talented interpretation.

Alexandre Placide, the renowned acrobat and pantomimist, appeared on the bill with her at Nicolet's. In 1788 the young girl and the thirty-eight-year-old star left for Haiti, where she adopted the stage name of Madame Placide. The Placides toured the island from October 1788 until July 1791, shortly before the Haitian Revolution began. They then embarked for the United States, and Douvillier, the leading ballerina with Placide's "French Company from Paris," appeared at Annapolis on 29 October 1791 and at theaters in other East Coast cities over the next eight years. [*See the entry on Placide.*]

In the United States, Madame Placide often danced Columbine in harlequinades created by her husband. Her repertory was widely varied, including not only comical roles but also serious dramatic roles from Jean-François Arnould-Mussot's pantomime-ballets, such as her favorite opening-night vehicle, *The Bird Catcher.* Madame Placide's repertory included roles in more than a dozen Arnould-Mussot pantomime-ballets, among them *The American Heroine, Sophie of Brabant, La Fôret Noire,* and *La Belle Dorothée.* [*See the entry on Arnould-Mussot.*]

In 1794, when the Placide troupe merged with Jean-Baptiste Francisqui's company in Charleston, South Carolina, their repertory expanded considerably with the new ballet master. For the next two years Madame Placide danced in *demi-caractère* ballets derived from the Paris Opera, where both she and Francisqui had danced. Jean-Georges Noverre's *Les Caprices de Galathée* and Maximilien Gardel's *Mirza*, for example, proved to be so popular that they became mainstays of her repertory for many years.

The troupe dissolved because of personal problems. In 1796 the jealous Alexandre Placide challenged Louis Douvillier, his leading singer, to a duel after Placide discovered that his wife was enamored of Douvillier. Half the town turned out to watch the two expert swordsmen; the duel was terminated after charges of foul play. Suzanne and Louis were reported to have married in Charleston on 30 June 1796.

The Douvilliers worked their way northward to Philadelphia in a series of minor engagements. In the spring of 1797 Madame Douvillier danced with Philippe Lailson's circus, a lavish spectacle of French opera, ballets, and Arnould-Mussot pantomimes alternating with equestrian exercises. Francisqui was the ballet master for the New York fall and the Philadelphia spring seasons.

The Douvilliers finally settled in New Orleans. Suzanne's third child was born in 1802 but did not survive. Neither did her marriage; Louis Douvillier abandoned his wife for the leading opera singer at the theater.

Almost no records of the New Orleans theater before 1805 survive, but Douvillier probably was the "Madame. . ." whose name was ripped off a rare surviving playbill dated September 1799. The unknown ballerina was to have danced opposite Francisqui, as Douvillier certainly did on many later occasions at the theater on Saint Pierre Street. Douvillier also appears to have been involved as ballet mistress, and perhaps even as proprietor, of a new theater, Le Théâtre de la Gaité [*sic*], which opened in the summer of 1808. She choreographed several Anacreontic ballets for it, such as *Echo and Narcissus, or Love and Vengeance* and *Amour et des Nymphes, ou Diane Vaincue par Cupidon*. She soon resumed her career at the Saint Pierre Street theater, however, performing as *première danseuse*, training a corps de ballet (which included her daughter Lise), and choreographing many ballets. A two-act pantomime with dances was one of her most successful; *L'Indépendance Americain, ou L'Apothéose de Washington* often was mounted for Fourth of July productions.

Sometime after 1814 Madame Douvillier retired from the stage, having been struck by a disease that disfigured her nose and mouth. Humiliated, she hid her face in a mask and withdrew from public appearances until April 1818, when poverty forced her to return to the stage, even though she could no longer speak. Theater manager Noah Ludlow described her in her last performance as "tall and commanding in her bearing" with "fine hair and eyes,

splendid bust, and beautifully rounded figure." Intrigued by the mysterious masked dancer, Ludlow claimed that he had never seen "such truly *speaking* pantomime." With "exquisite grace and ease" she performed the role of the abandoned Donna Anna in Christoph Willibald Gluck's *Don Juan*. Ironically, it was Louis Douvillier who enacted Don Juan's descent into the fiery pit while she danced the role of Vengeance in the "Ballet of the Furies."

Except for a few appearances that season and next, Madame Douvillier returned to her hermitlike existence and died in penury eight years later. Despite her tragic personal life, her career was marked by extraordinary achievements as America's first woman ballet mistress and choreographer and as the first trained Paris Opera *danseuse* to tour the United States.

BIBLIOGRAPHY

Almanach des spectacles de Paris, ou Calendrier historique et chronologique des théâtres. Paris, 1784–1788.

Campardon, Émile. *Les spectacles de la foire, 1595–1791.* Paris, 1877.

Costonis, Maureen Needham. "French Ballet in Eighteenth-Century Saint Dominique." In *Proceedings of the Sixth Annual Conference, Society of Dance History Scholars, the Ohio State University, 11–13 February 1983*, compiled by Christena L. Schlundt. Milwaukee, 1983.

Costonis, Maureen Needham. "The French Connection: Ballet Comes to America." In *Musical Theatre in America*, edited by Glenn Loney. Westport, Conn., 1984.

Costonis, Maureen Needham. "Ballet Comes to America: French Contributions to the Establishment of Dance in New Orleans and Philadelphia, 1792–1842." Ph.D. diss., New York University, 1989.

Fouchard, Jean. *Artistes et répertoire des scènes de Saint-Domingue.* Port-au-Prince, 1955.

Ludlow, Noah M. *Dramatic Life as I Found It.* St. Louis, 1880.

Moore, Lillian. "New York's First Ballet Season, 1792." *Bulletin of the New York Public Library* (September 1960).

Moore, Lillian. "Suzanne Theodore Vaillande [*sic*] Douvillier." In *Notable American Women*. Cambridge, Mass., 1971.

MAUREEN NEEDHAM

DOWELL, ANTHONY (born 16 February 1943 in London), British dancer and director. Dowell was one of the great *premiers danseurs nobles* of the twentieth century and the natural heir at the Royal Ballet to the classical tradition established by Harold Turner and Michael Somes.

After training for five years with June Hampshire in London, Dowell entered the Royal Ballet School at the age of ten, joined the Covent Garden Opera Ballet in 1960, and transferred to the Royal Ballet in 1961. If not the first to recognize Dowell's potential, Erik Bruhn—an incomparable *danseur* himself—was the first to display it, by giving him a variation in his 1962 staging of *divertissements* from August Bournonville's *Napoli*.

Once noticed, Dowell's quicksilver technique and impeccable line could not be ignored. With those very attributes in mind, Frederick Ashton chose him to create Oberon in *The Dream* (1964); it was Dowell's first created

DOWELL. Acclaimed for his lightness, elegance, and impeccable technique, Dowell appeared as the Boy with Matted Hair in an American Ballet Theatre revival of Antony Tudor's 1967 *Shadow-play*. (Photograph © 1979 by Max Waldman; used by permission.)

forgettably in three important creations: the tempestuous Troyte in *Enigma Variations* (1968), the ardent Des Grieux in *Manon* (1974), and the unprincipled Beliaev in *A Month in the Country* (1976). Appearing as a guest artist with American Ballet Theatre during the 1978/79 season and frequently thereafter, he added Natalia Makarova's three-act *La Bayadère* and Mikhail Baryshnikov's *Don Quixote* to his classical repertory and both Makarova and Gelsey Kirkland to his list of illustrious partners.

Away from the ballet stage, Dowell designed costumes in London for *Thaïs*, *Pavane*, and *In the Night* and acted as narrator for *Oedipus Rex* at the Metropolitan Opera House in New York City and for the Joffrey and Royal Ballet productions of *A Wedding Bouquet*. He even portrayed Vaslav Nijinsky, for the duration of a stunning tango with Rudolf Nureyev, in the film *Valentino* (1977).

When Dowell was made a CBE (Commander of the Order of the British Empire) in 1973, he was the youngest dancer ever to be thus honored. In 1986, he succeeded Norman Morrice as director of the Royal Ballet, for which he staged a new production of *Swan Lake* in 1987 and of *The Sleeping Beauty* in 1994. He was knighted for his services to ballet in 1995.

[*See also* Royal Ballet.]

BIBLIOGRAPHY

Bland, Alexander. *The Royal Ballet: The First Fifty Years*. London, 1981.

Dromgoole, Nicholas, and Leslie Spatt. *Sibley & Dowell*. London, 1976.

Gruen, John. *The Private World of Ballet*. New York, 1975.

Mosse, Kate. *The House: Inside the Royal Opera House, Covent Garden*. London, 1995.

Newman, Barbara. *Antoinette Sibley: Reflections of a Ballerina*. London, 1986.

BARBARA NEWMAN

role and his first teaming with Antoinette Sibley, with whom he quickly formed a lasting and legendary partnership. The next year he created Benvolio in Kenneth MacMillan's *Romeo and Juliet* and then danced Romeo, his first three-act role; he also created one of the two male parts in Ashton's *Monotones II*, a study in pristine elegance. When he was promoted to principal in 1966, he was already the embodiment of the English classical style: cool, lyrical, aristocratic, and restrained. With his creation of the Boy with Matted Hair in Antony Tudor's *Shadowplay* (1967) and as his repertory expanded, he developed into a dramatic artist as well.

He was a peerless prince of noble manner and bearing in *Giselle*, *Swan Lake*, *The Sleeping Beauty*, *The Nutcracker*, *La Bayadère*, and *Cinderella*. He was also richly comic as Colas in *La Fille Mal Gardée*, the Joker in *Card Game*, and Lo Straniero in *Varii Capricci*, with which, in 1983, Ashton celebrated his continued partnership with Sibley. As the Messenger of Death in *Song of the Earth*, as Daphnis in *Daphnis and Chloe*, and in *Dances at a Gathering*, he achieved a remarkable synthesis of passion and musicality. At his most theatrical, he fused dance and drama un-

DRAPER, PAUL (born 1909 in Florence, Italy, died 20 September 1996 in Woodstock, New York), Italian-born vaudeville performer and tap dancer. Draper's father, Paul Draper, Sr., was a lieder singer; his mother, Muriel Draper, was a noted author and lecturer; his aunt Ruth Draper was a famous monologuist. A largely self-taught tap dancer, Draper began to study ballet at the age of twenty-two, first with Anatole Vilzak and later with Anatole Oboukhoff at the School of American Ballet. At the time, Draper thought he was too stiff and rigid to become a ballet dancer. "But," he has since said, "I was able to learn to do what I set out to do, which was to tap dance larger, faster." Many elements of ballet technique were incorporated into his tap routines.

After working a variety of odd jobs in the United States—such as tap dancing on a pedestal—Draper began his formal professional career at a vaudeville theater in London in 1932. He later returned to the United States to

perform at Radio City Music Hall and in nightclubs in New York City and throughout the country. In June 1941 he married Heidi Vossler, a ballerina with Balanchine's American Ballet.

Draper was the first to tap to the music of Bach and other classical composers. From 1940 to 1949 he toured with Larry Adler, the harmonica virtuoso, with whom he developed a sophisticated act that played long engagements at various New York nightclubs during the heyday of tap. In 1948 Draper appeared in the film version of William Saroyan's *The Time of Your Life* (in the role created on stage by Gene Kelly); previously Draper had made an unmemorable film appearance as Ruby Keeler's partner in *Colleen* (1936).

In the early 1950s Draper lived abroad, having been blacklisted in 1951 during the McCarthy era. After returning to the United States in 1954, he continued to give solo concerts and eventually settled in Pittsburgh, where in 1974 he taught a tap dance workshop at Carnegie-Mellon University. He and Adler were reunited briefly in the early 1970s for a special Carnegie Hall concert in which many leading tap teachers and Draper's former students paid him homage.

Although known primarily as a soloist, Draper was brought back to New York City in the late 1970s to revive some of his vintage routines for American Dance Machine as part of the group's ongoing program to preserve the dance of American musical theater. He created a ballet-tap *barre* that has since influenced many of the tap teachers who train dancers for Broadway.

[*See also* Tap Dance.]

BIBLIOGRAPHY
Denby, Edwin. "Popular Though Super-Special." In Denby's *Looking at the Dance*. New York, 1949.
Goldberg, Jane. "A Conversation with Paul Draper." *Ballet Review* 5.1 (1975–1976): 56–62.
Frank, Rusty E. *Tap! The Greatest Tap Dance Stars and Their Stories, 1900–1955*. Rev. ed. New York, 1994.

FILM.   Roger Englander, *Paul Draper on Tap* (1979).

JANE GOLDBERG

DREAM, THE. Ballet in one act. Choreography: Frederick Ashton. Music: Felix Mendelssohn, arranged by John Lanchbery. Scenery: Henry Bardon. Costumes: David Walker. First performance: 2 April 1964, Royal Opera House, Covent Garden, London, Royal Ballet. Principals: Antoinette Sibley (Titania), Anthony Dowell (Oberon), Keith Martin (Puck), Alexander Grant (Bottom). Supporting cast: Vergie Derman (Hermia), Carole Needham (Helena), Derek Rencher (Lysander), David Drew (Demetrius).

A one-act précis of *A Midsummer Night's Dream, The Dream* was made by Ashton for a Royal Ballet program of three ballets in celebration of the quatercentenary of Shakespeare's birth. Omitting the characters of Theseus, Hippolyta, and Aegeus and the play of Pyramus and Thisbe, the ballet focuses on the amorous adventures of the mortals and fairies who enter the wood outside Athens. Ashton was influenced by Tyrone Guthrie's 1937 Old Vic staging of the play, which had employed Mendelssohn's music, Victorian dress, and choreography by Ninette de Valois. For Ashton, John Lanchbery culled a score from Mendelssohn's incidental music for the play. Henry Bardon's set and David Walker's costumes recreated the Victorian idiom in picturesque detail. *The Dream* initiated the dancing partnership of Antoinette Sibley and Anthony Dowell, giving the latter his first created role.

At its premiere *The Dream* was not generally received as a major work, but it steadily accumulated popularity and critical esteem. The ballet exemplified the Royal Ballet's skill in characterization. Ashton's varied vocabulary of gestures—some informal, some knit into dance steps, and some academic mime—demanded, as did his dances, detailed and full-bodied utterance. Victorian touches included genteel manners for the silly human lovers and Taglioni-style poses for the fairies. He also played up the comic elements of the plot.

In the choreography for the fairies, Ashton's art reaches its most complex and subtle form. These dances, especially the "Lullaby" (for Titania, soloists, and corps), "Scherzo" (for Oberon, Puck, soloists, and corps), and "Nocturne" (Titania and Oberon), show Ashton's response to Mendelssohn's rhythms and melodic lines at its most refined. The dances for the corps de ballet require fine detail and lively intricacy in positions of the torso, *épaulement*, *port de bras*, and footwork. These virtues had already been developed by Ashton but were brought to new refinement in *The Dream's* two principal roles. In Oberon, Dowell revealed an elegantly stretched line and brilliance, featuring steps then alien to the male dancer's lexicon, such as *arabesque penchée* and *piqué* and *soutenu* turns *en manège*. Sibley's Titania, with feathery *port de bras* and filigree footwork, showed caprice, power, and sensuality.

After the reconciliations of mortal and immortal lovers, Titania and Oberon dance the Nocturne pas de deux alone, combining in harmony or answering each other in solo passages. Here are the *frissons* of amorous contact, rebellious impulses melting into rapturous responses, and a soft close in which the queen is rocked to sleep in the arms of her king. It is the climax of the ballet and crowns a series of works in which love is Ashton's central theme.

A new production of *The Dream* was done by the touring company of the Royal Ballet in 1966, with scenery and costumes by Peter Farmer. This production was also used by the Royal Ballet at Covent Garden between 1971 and 1973, and for revivals by the Australian Ballet in 1969 and by South Africa's PACT Ballet in 1971. David Walker designed revivals for the Joffrey Ballet (1973) and the Royal Swedish Ballet (1975).

In June 1986 the Royal Ballet presented a new production of *The Dream* with decor and costumes by David Walker along the lines of the Bardon-Walker original. Sibley and Dowell danced in the first performances of this staging, and it was in this production that they later gave their final performances of the roles so significant to their careers, Dowell in June 1986 and Sibley in November 1987.

BIBLIOGRAPHY

Dromgoole, Nicholas, and Leslie Spatt. *Sibley and Dowell*. London, 1976.

Macaulay, Alastair. "In July." *The Dancing Times* (September 1983): 935–938.

Macaulay, Alastair. "A Summer Night's Ashton." *The Dancing Times* (August 1986): 960–963.

Vaughan, David. *Frederick Ashton and His Ballets*. London, 1977.

ALASTAIR MACAULAY

DRIGO, RICCARDO (born 30 June 1846 in Padua, died 1 October 1930 in Padua), Italian conductor and composer, best known for his work in Russia. Drigo came from a worthy, though unmusical, family: his father was a successful lawyer, his mother of noble lineage. There was no particular inclination among them toward music until Drigo, as a boy, gave himself eagerly to it.

He was enrolled at the Venice Conservatory at the age of fourteen. Two years later he was playing in an amateur orchestra in Padua, also composing and orchestrating, in his word, "naive" romances and waltzes for this group. In 1864, he completed his studies and began his career as a rehearsal pianist for Garibaldi Teatro in Padua.

Thereafter, he worked in provincial opera houses in Padua, Vicenza, Rovigo, Udino, and Venice. His debut as a conductor occurred in Padua's opera house in 1869, when he substituted for the regular conductor, who was ill. He conducted Costantino Dall'Argine's *The Two Bears* with such success that he was named permanent second conductor.

For the next ten years he conducted virtually all the repertory operas on tour with the Padua company throughout Italy and in Germany, France, and Spain, where he led one of the first performances of Georges Bizet's *Carmen* in Seville's Teatro San Fernando.

Because Drigo still did not think of himself primarily as a conductor, and because Italy was considered the land of composers, during this period he wrote two operas and assorted other works. His four-act *Don Pedro di Portugallo* premiered in Padua in 1868. His three-act comic opera *La Moglie Rapita* (The Abducted Wife) premiered in 1883 at the Italian Opera in Saint Petersburg. He also wrote several concert pieces, a cantata, two sinfoniettas, a mass, and some vocal works for the synagogue, requested by the chief rabbi of Padua.

In 1878, the *régisseur* of the Imperial Theaters in Saint Petersburg offered Drigo a contract to conduct their first six-month season of the Italian Opera. At the age of thirty-two, he made his debut in Russia with Giuseppe Verdi's *Un Ballo in Maschera*, followed by *Aïda*, which Drigo conducted without a score. Afterward, the theater director prophesied: "This young man is going to stay here a long time." Drigo remained in Russia for forty-two years. His contract with the Italian Opera theater was renewed each year until the opera house was condemned in 1886.

During the summers, Drigo returned to Italy, where he conducted important seasons of opera. The renown achieved in Russia preceded him. He was also in great demand in Spain, where, at San Fernando in April 1880, he conducted twelve operas in seventeen days. For this feat he was made a Cavalier of the Order of Charles III, in a ceremony that winter at the Spanish embassy in Saint Petersburg. It was the first of thirteen decorations and honors conferred on him during his career, including the highest in Italian opera—the silver baton and laurel crown from the orchestra and company at Teatro alla Scala in Milan.

In 1886, Drigo received an offer from Ivan Vsevolozhsky, director of Russia's Imperial Theaters, to conduct ballet performances for the coming season. His initial contract for three months was soon extended to three years. These triennial agreements were renewed until 1904, when Drigo was named an artist emeritus of the Imperial Theaters, equivalent to appointment for life. On this occasion the orchestra presented him with a huge silver plate engraved with the names of each musician. The faculty of the Moscow Conservatory gave him a large engraved cup in recognition of his musical merits. His students and colleagues referred to him as "the Good Father."

If originally unfamiliar with the requirements of ballet, Drigo had the confidence to face this new task. His first assignment was Cesare Pugni's *La Fille du Pharaon*, which he conducted on 3 September 1886 after only two rehearsals. His success was immediate, and his future assured.

Also in 1886, Russian choreographer Marius Petipa asked Drigo to compose an adagio and *danse bohemienne* for Pugni's *Esmeralda*. This, Drigo's first composition for ballet, was so well received that it earned him praise from Tsar Alexander III. The addition of musical numbers and reworkings of previously written music were common practices, and Drigo was responsible for more than eighty such insertions in old ballets.

Drigo was conscientous as well. He wrote a czardas in one day, a suggestion at the last moment by Lev Ivanov for his ballet *The Enchanted Forest*. A reworking from Mozart's opera *The Magic Flute* called for new orchestration from Drigo, which he accomplished in one day and one night after rehearsals had already begun. In *Les Millions d'Arlequin*, he composed and orchestrated a polka, at Petipa's request, also in one day. This ballet, preserved as *Harlequinade* in the repertory of the New York City Ballet, was Drigo's finest score for the dance and contains a delicious serenade, originally with mandolin accompaniment, that has become a popular piece.

The outbreak of World War I interrupted Drigo's return to Russia after his 1914 summer in Italy; against the advice of friends he did return in 1916, braving the perils of German submarines while crossing the Baltic. Despite his connections with nobility, the people received him with ovations and affection; during the 1917 Russian Revolution he resumed his career in Saint Petersburg under the hardships of rationed food and cold winters with little heat.

Two fur coats and a box containing most of his decorations, awards, and other valuables were stolen during his last years in Russia. One of the decorations, the Order of Commander of Saint Vladimir, elevated him to the status of nobility and assured him a comfortable pension. After the Revolution he was told he could receive the pension and his royalties if he became a Russian citizen, but Drigo, now seventy-four, preferred to spend his final years in the country of his birth. He was repatriated in 1920 (in exchange for eleven Russian prisoners of war), taking with him only the unpublished score of his last ballet, *The Romance of the Rosebud*, performed once during his lifetime, at his final benefit on 11 May 1919.

In the remaining decade of his life Drigo wrote little else, other than a few waltzes for special occasions. Yet these, too, bore his graceful and aristocratic style.

BIBLIOGRAPHY

Gregory, John. *The Legat Saga*. 2d ed. London, 1993.
Guest, Ivor. *The Divine Virginia: A Biography of Virginia Zucchi*. New York, 1977.
Scherer, Barrymore. "Toast of the Czars." *Ballet News* 3 (January 1982): 26–28.
Travaglia, Silvio. *Riccardo Drigo: The Man and the Artist*. Padua, 1928.
Wiley, Roland John. "Memoirs of R. E. Drigo." *The Dancing Times* (October 1990): 61–63.
Wiley, Roland John. *Tchaikovsky's Ballets*. Oxford, 1985.

ARCHIVES. Dance Collection, New York Public Library for the Performing Arts.

JOSEPH GALE

DROTTNINGHOLM COURT THEATER. *See* Sweden, *article on* Court Theaters.

DRZEWIECKI, CONRAD (born 14 October 1926 in Poznań), Polish dancer, choreographer, ballet director, and teacher. Conrad Drzewiecki studied in Poland with Mikołaj Kopiński, Jerzy Kapliński, and Leon Wójcikowski (also known as Woizikowski). In Paris from 1958 to 1963, Drzewiecki studied at the Académie de Danse Moderne with Lubov Egorova, Serge Peretti, Victor Gsovsky, Jerome Andrews, and others. Having debuted in Kopiński's company in Kraków in 1946, he danced in the Poznań Opera in 1947 and as a soloist of the Polish Army Ensemble in 1948. He returned twice to the Poznań Opera (1950–1956, 1963–1970), and danced at the Teatro San Carlo in Naples (1956–1957) and with the Théâtre d'Art du Ballet and other Parisian companies (1958–1963). He was a talented character dancer, appreciated particularly in grotesque, Spanish, and acrobatic roles. In addition to the Polish repertory, he danced in works by Michel Fokine, David Lichine, George Balanchine, Edward Caton, William Dollar, Serge Lifar, George Skibine, Roland Petit, and Paul Goubé.

In 1963 Drzewiecki returned to Poland as ballet director and choreographer of the Poznań Opera and as a teacher at the Poznań State Ballet School. His important works include *Valse Nobles et Sentimentales* and *La Valse* (music by Maurice Ravel), *Rhapsody in Blue* (music by George Gershwin), *The Soldier's Tale* (music by Igor Stravinsky), *Esik in Ostenda* (music by Grażyna Bacewicz), all in 1964; *Le Tricorne* (pas de deux; music by Manuel de Falla) and *Invitation to the Dance* (music by Carl Maria von Weber), both in 1965; *Improvisations after Shakespeare* (music by Duke Ellington), *4:4 Variations* (music by Franciszek Woźniak), and *Solemn Music* (music by Handel), all 1966; *The Firebird* (music by Stravinsky), *Adagio for Strings and Organ* (music by Tomaso Albinoni), and *Tempus Jazz '67* (music by J. Milian), all 1967; *Mother Goose* and *Pavane pour une Infante Défunte* (music by Ravel), 1968; *Divertimento* and *The Miraculous Mandarin*, both 1970, and *Sonata for Two Pianos and Percussions*, 1972 (music by Béla Bartók); and *Adagietto* (music by Gustav Mahler) and *Les Biches* (music by Francis Poulenc), both 1973.

Drzewiecki brought to the Polish stage new and fashionable tendencies current in western Europe. He created ballets in neoclassical, jazz, and modern dance styles and was partial to the utilization of grotesque and character dance. In 1973 he established, in Poznań, the Polish Dance Theater, which he also directed, staging several new works. There are many television films of his ballets, one of which, *Games*, was awarded the Prix Italia in 1970.

Drzewiecki also worked for the Dutch National Ballet (*4:4 Variations*, 1967, and *The Sleeping Beauty*, 1968); Conjunto Nacional de Danza Moderna, in Havana (*4:4 Variations*, 1971); German State Opera Ballet, in East Berlin (*The Miraculous Mandarin*, 1974); German Opera Ballet, in West Berlin (*The Moor of Venice*, 1975, and *Epitaph for Don Juan*, 1980); La Scala Ballet, in Basilica San Stefano (*The Childhood of Jesus*, 1980); the National Theater in

Prague (*Five Nocturnes, Immemorial Songs,* and *The Third Symphony,* 1982).

Drzewiecki taught summer courses in Poland and other European countries and in 1972 at the Juilliard School of Music in New York. He was awarded the Primo Premio Assoluto of the International Competition in Vercella, Italy, in 1956, and was many times given honors by the Polish government.

BIBLIOGRAPHY

Chynowski, Paweł. "Conrad Drzewiecki and His Polish Dance Theatre." *Dance Magazine* (August 1975): 88.

Gourreau, Jean-Marie. "Conrad Drzewiecki et le Théâtre Polonais de la Danse." *Pour la danse* (July–September 1981): 37–39.

Neuer, Adam, ed. *Polish Opera and Ballet of the Twentieth Century: Operas, Ballets, Pantomimes, Miscellaneous Works.* Translated by Jerzy Zawadzki. Kraków, 1986.

PAWEŁ CHYNOWSKI

DUATO, NACHO (born 1957 in Valencia), Spanish dancer and choreographer. Duato is one of the most prestigious figures in Spain's dance world today. A relative latecomer to dance, he began his studies in London at the Rambert School and later continued his professional training at Maurice Béjart's Mudra Centre in Brussels and at the Alvin Ailey American Dance Center in New York.

DUATO. Catherine Allard and Duato intertwine in his *Tabulae,* staged for the Compañía Nacional de Danza and set to music by Alberto Iglesias. (Photograph by Jorge Represa; used by permission.)

Duato joined Sweden's Cullberg Ballet in 1980. It was, however, his long relationship with Jiří Kylián's Netherlands Dance Theater from 1981 to 1990 that made a lasting mark on him as both a performer and choreographer. An outstanding performer, in 1987 Duato received Holland's Golden Dance Prize. His career as a choreographer began with the creation of *Jardi Tancat* in 1983 for Netherlands Theater II, set to popular Mallorcan folksongs performed by singer María del Mar Bonet. The work displayed the fluid musicality that has come to characterize Duato's work at its best, as well as a particularly Mediterranean flavor that won the choreographer fans throughout the world and first prize at Cologne's International Choreography Competition in 1983.

During the following years Duato created more than a dozen works for Netherlands Dance Theater I and II, almost all of them in collaboration with painter and set designer Walter Nobbe. These works included *Danza y Rito* to music by Carlos Chávez, *Ucelli* to music by Ottorino Respighi, *Synaphai* to music by Iannis Xenakis and Vangelis, *Arenal* to music by María del Mar Bonet, *Chansons Madacasses* to music by Maurice Ravel, and *Raptus* to Wagner's "Wesendonk Lieder." In 1988 Duato joined Hans van Manen and Kylián as a resident choreographer for the company.

Duato's growing reputation as a choreographer resulted in numerous requests for his work by such international dance companies as Les Grands Ballets Canadiens, the Cullberg Ballet, Ballet Gulbenkian, Frankfurt Ballet, and Spain's Ballet Lírico Nacional.

In June 1990 the INAEM, an agency of Spain's Ministry of Culture, offered Nacho Duato the artistic directorship of the Ballet Lírico Nacional. The company, founded in 1979, had been directed successively by Victor Ullate, María de Avila, and Maya Plisetskaya, with a repertory based on neoclassical and classical ballet. Under Duato's leadership the ensemble has changed both its name (it is now known as the Compañía Nacional de Danza) and its focus, concentrating on contemporary dance and ballet, incorporating foreign dancers for the first time in its history, and reducing the number of active performers. Although these changes have been controversial among Spanish dancers and balletomanes, during the past five years the company has increased its national and international touring and won much critical acclaim.

Duato's charisma has made him a popular personality on- and offstage in Spain where he has often been seen on television, as well as making forays into the worlds of fashion and film. His high profile has been instrumental in winning new audiences for the Compañía Nacional de Danza, especially among young people.

After assuming direction of the company, Duato had created ten new works for it by the end of 1995: *Concierto Madrigal,* to music by Joaquín Rodrigo; *Opus Piat,* to music by Beethoven; *Empty*, set to a collage of music; *Coming Together*, to music by Frederic Rzewski; *Mediterrania*, set to a collage of music; *Cautiva*, to music by Alberto Iglesias; *Alone, for a Second*, to music by Erik Satie; *Tabulae* to music by Iglesias; *Ecos*, to music by Stephan Micus; and *Cero sobre Cero* (Zero over Zero) to music by Iglesias. His choreography now forms the basis of the Compañía Nacional de Danza. Recent works are also performed by Les Ballets de Monte Carlo, revived in 1995 under the auspices of Princess Caroline of Monaco.

BIBLIOGRAPHY

Crow, Susan. "Nacho Duato and Contemporary Ballet." *Dance Theatre Journal* 11 (Winter 1993–1994): 4–5, 49–51.

Duato, Nacho. "They're Coming: Compañía Nacional de Danza." *Dance and Dancers*, no. 516 (1994): 15–16.

Howe-Beck, Linda. "Power Play." *Dance International* 22 (Summer 1994): 4–8.

Hunt, Marilyn. "Compañía Nacional de Danza." *Dance Magazine* (October 1994): 76–77.

Kumin, Laura. "Spanish Ballet Gets a New Image." *Dance Magazine* (April 1993): 28.

Mannoni, Gérard. "'J'aime faire danser mon âme': Nacho Duato." *Saisons de la Danse*, no. 272 (September 1995): 8–9.

Mazo, Joseph H. "Nacho Duato." *Dance Magazine* (September 1994): 50–53.

"Nacho Duato." *Saisons de la Danse*, no. 273 (October 1995): 25–28.

Planells, Martine. "Entretien: Nacho Duato." *Danser* (September 1995): 26–29.

Scheier, Helmut. "A Language of One's Own." *Ballett International* 9 (May 1986): 28–29.

LAURA KUMIN

DUDINSKAYA, NATALIA (Natalia Mikhailovna Dudinskaia; born 8 [21] August 1912 in Kharkov, Ukraine), ballet dancer and teacher. Dudinskaya graduated in 1931 from the Leningrad Choreographic Institute, where she studied under Agrippina Vaganova, and immediately joined the company of the Kirov Opera and Ballet Theater. She soon was given principal roles and remained a *prima ballerina* of the company until 1963. She danced all the major classical roles, enchanting audiences with the magical beauty of her Odette and the somber majesty of her Odile in *Swan Lake*. Her clarity of form and her temperament, dramatic power, and virtuosity were displayed in the heroines of *The Sleeping Beauty, La Bayadère, Don Quixote*, and *Le Corsaire*. She was equally impressive in Soviet ballets. Dudinskaya danced with many partners and worked with many choreographers, but her partnerships with Vakhtang Chabukiani and Konstantin Sergeyev, who was her husband, were the most significant. Her collaboration with Chabukiani had its culmination in his ballet *Laurencia* (1939). Her soaring flights and the steely resilience and brilliant technique of her leaps and turns created the image of a revolutionary heroine. Her other roles in the early productions of Soviet choreographers included Mireille de Poitiers in Vasily Vainonen's

The Flames of Paris (1932) and Maria in *The Fountain of Bakhchisarai* and Coralli in *Lost Illusions*, both choreographed by Rostislav Zakharov, which she danced in 1938.

Through the 1940s and 1950s Dudinskaya created leading roles in every significant premiere at the Kirov. The summit of her art as a dancer of dramatic roles was as Sari in Sergeyev's *Path of Thunder* (1957), an image of tragic appeal, psychological depth, and spiritual complexity. A major landmark of the intervening years was Sergeyev's *Cinderella* (1946), in which musical harmony and the integrity of the plastique distinguished her duet with Sergeyev. Depicting characters varied in genre and style, Dudinskaya's dancing expressed the magic power of the Polish Girl's beauty in Boris Fenster's *Taras Bulba* (1955), the transparent fragility of the Snow Maiden in Fedor Lopukhov's *Spring Fairy Tale* (1947), the wistful

DUDINSKAYA. The virtuosic Soviet ballerina Dudinskaya in a pose from *Swan Lake*. (Photograph from the Dance Collection, New York Public Library for the Performing Arts.)

gentleness of Pushkin's Parasha in Zakharov's *The Bronze Horseman* (1949), the desperate longing for flight of the bird maiden Syuimbike in Leonid Yakobson's *Shurale*(1950), the wanton passion of Baroness Strahl in Fenster's *Masquerade* (1960), the intransigence of the Mountain Girl in Nina Anisimova's *Gayané* (1942), and the fearlessness of the Slav girl in Vainonen's *Militsa* (1947).

As a teacher, Dudinskaya imaginatively applied Vaganova's methods, preserving and developing that school of dance. From 1951 to 1970 she taught the Class of Perfection at the Kirov Ballet, at the same time coaching for the company until 1963, and after 1963 she taught at the Leningrad Choreographic Institute. She occasionally assisted Sergeyev in staging new productions. She also directed two films for television, *Dialogue with the Stage* (1988) and *The Birth of the Dance* (1991). Dudinskaya was named People's Artist of the USSR in 1957 and was awarded the State Prize of the USSR in 1941, 1947, 1949, and 1951.

BIBLIOGRAPHY

Dudinskaya, Natalia. "My Philosophy Is Dance." In John Gregory's *Leningrad's Ballet*. London, 1981.

Gregory, John. "Natalia Dudinskaya." *The Dancing Times* (October 1970): 20–21.

Joel, Lydia. "A Friendly Visit." *Dance Magazine* (November 1964): 18–21, 68–69.

Krasovskaya, Vera. *Nataliia Dudinskaia* (in Russian). Leningrad, 1982.

Kremshevskaia, G. D. *Nataliia Dudinskaia* (in Russian). Leningrad, 1964.

Martin, John. "Reports from Russia." *Dance Magazine* (September 1956): 14–21, 58–64.

Movshenson, A. G. *Nataliia Dudinskaia* (in Russian). Leningrad, 1951.

Slonimsky, Yuri. "Natalia Dudinskaya." In *The Soviet Ballet*, by Yuri Slonimsky et al. New York, 1947.

Smakov, Gennady. *The Great Russian Dancers*. New York, 1984.

VALENTINA V. PROKHOROVA
Translated from Russian

DUDLEY, JANE (born 3 April 1912 in New York City), American dancer, choreographer, and teacher. Dudley was the daughter of a dance teacher. She began studying free, rhythmic dance at the age of six with Ruth Doing. After Mary Wigman's visit to the United States in 1930 had given Hanya Holm's studio prominence, Dudley began to train with Holm. From 1937 to 1944 Dudley was a member of Martha Graham's company, dancing such roles as the Ancestress in *Letter to the World* (1940) and the Sister in *Deaths and Entrances* (1943). She was a soloist for Graham in 1954 and continued to perform occasionally with the company for Graham. Dudley's dancing was both dramatic and sculptured, full of body and dimension yet capable of rapid transitions. She taught as an assistant to Graham at the Neighborhood Playhouse and at the Graham Studio from 1938 to 1958.

Dudley had begun to study with Louis Horst and Anna Sokolow at the Neighborhood Playhouse in 1936: the first year in preclassic forms, the second in modern forms. A concert shared with Sophie Maslow and William Bales sponsored by the *Dance Observer* in 1942 resulted in the formation of the Dudley-Maslow-Bales Dance Trio, in which she was both performer and choreographer until 1954.

Dudley performed and taught at the New London Summer School in Connecticut from 1948 to 1953; taught at Teachers College, Columbia University, from 1956 to 1964; and was on the dance faculty at Bennington College in Vermont from 1966 to 1967.

As a young choreographer Dudley was interested in presenting social themes, beginning in 1934 with *In the Life of a Worker, Time Is Money, The Dream Ends,* and *Death of Tradition* (with Maslow and Sokolow). Her signature piece, *Harmonica Breakdown,* which was created in 1938 and debuted in New York on 11 May 1941 at the Heckscher Theatre for an "America Dances" concert, has been especially enduring. Revived in 1966 for Martha Whitman and in 1967 for Ethel Winter, *Harmonica Breakdown* had its London debut in 1977 at the Sadler's Wells Theatre in honor of the queen's silver jubilee and was performed in the 1981 London "Dance Umbrella" series. Inspired by harmonica player Sonny Terry and his washboard accompanist Brownie McGhee, who performed in the first annual "From Spirituals to Swing" concert at Carnegie Hall in 1938, *Harmonica Breakdown* expressed the despair and resignation of a Dust Bowl woman in the 1930s. A heavy shuffle, repeated throughout the dance, characterized for Dudley "the effort that just living might seem to mean to black people, that shuffle."

In 1970 Dudley began an association with the London Contemporary Dance School. She served in various capacities including vice principal and senior teacher; she was director of Contemporary Dance Studies until 1991. Retrospectives of her work spanning fifty years were performed at both New York's Marymount Theater and at Dance Umbrella in 1988, and at The Place in London in 1989. In 1990 Dudley presented "After the Ark: A Celebration of Jewish Culture in Dance, Music, Song, and the Spoken Word" at South Bank's Purcell Room in London, featuring works by Dudley, Sophie Maslow, Anna Sokolow, and André Obey. In 1991 Dudley received an honorary Doctor of Music degree from the University of Kent, England.

[*See also* New Dance Group.]

BIBLIOGRAPHY

Dudley, Jane. "The Early Life of an American Modern Dancer." *Dance Research* 10 (Spring 1992): 3–20.

Lloyd, Margaret. *The Borzoi Book of Modern Dance*. New York, 1949.

Sears, David. "Breaking Down *Harmonica Breakdown*." *Ballet Review* 11 (Winter 1984): 58–67.

Tobias, Anne. "Jane Dudley Retrospective." *Ballet Review* 16 (Winter 1989): 50.

SARAH ALBERTI CHAPMAN

DUMOULIN BROTHERS (also spelled DuMoulin, Desmoulin), French dancers at the Académie Royale de Musique during the first half of the eighteenth century. The careers of the four Dumoulin brothers—Henri, François, Pierre, and David—are documented in the Parfaict brothers' *Les dictionnaire des théâtres de Paris* (1756).

Henri Dumoulin, the eldest, was only half brother to the others; his mother, having remarried a Sieur Dumoulin, brought him up with the other children born of this second marriage. He entered the Académie Royale de Musique as early as 1695, and his brothers, following his example, also became dancers. He continued in this profession until 1730 and died shortly afterward. Henri Dumoulin composed the ballets for the Opéra-Comique in Paris from 1714 until 1719.

François Dumoulin, eldest half brother to Henri, was also a dancer at the Académie Royale de Musique, who made his debut there in 1700. He adopted the character of Arlequin, which he performed in so many *entrées* of the academy's ballets. He retired from the theater at the end of 1748.

Pierre Dumoulin, next eldest, was also a dancer at the Académie Royale de Musique; he made his debut there in May 1705 and retired in 1748, at the same time as François. Among other dances, Pierre Dumoulin performed mostly those of Pulcinella, Pierrot, and other *demi-caractère* dances.

David Dumoulin, the youngest brother, entered the Académie Royale de Musique in December 1705. He was extremely acclaimed and danced the main *entrées* and the noble and serious dances until his retirement at Easter 1751.

J. C. Nemeitz, who visited the Paris Opera in 1713 and 1714, listed the Dumoulin brothers among the important dancers and added that

> one of them, who has an eye defect, is incomparable for the grotesque genre . . . another is famous for his canaries, such as gigues, bourrées, and other dances of this type.
>
> (Nemeitz, 1727)

Choreographer Jean-Georges Noverre wrote of David Dumoulin:

> Nobody has yet succeeded to Mr. Dumoulin. He danced his pas de deux with a superiority difficult to emulate; always tender, always graceful, be he a butterfly or a zephyr, at times inconstant, at others faithful, but always expressing new feelings, he could portray all the aspects of sensuous and tender love.
>
> (Noverre, 1760)

[*See also* Académie de Musique et de Poésie.]

BIBLIOGRAPHY
Nemeitz, J. C. *Séjour de Paris.* Paris, 1727.
Noverre, Jean-Georges. *Lettres sur la danse et sur les ballets.* Stuttgart and Lyon, 1760. Translated by Cyril W. Beaumont as *Letters on Dancing and Ballets.* London, 1930.
Noverre, Jean-Georges. *Lettres sur la danse, sur les ballets et les arts.* 4 vols. Saint Petersburg, 1803–1804.
Parfaict, Claude, and François Parfaict. *Les dictionnaire des théâtres de Paris.* Paris, 1756.

RÉGINE ASTIER

DUNCAN, ISADORA (Dora Angela Duncan; born 27 May 1877 in San Francisco, died 14 September 1927 in Nice, France), American modern dance pioneer. The image of a bold young American dancer taking Europe by storm, dancing from sheer inspiration in a way never seen before, runs through Isadora Duncan's autobiographical writings and pervades the views of many writers who have since echoed her self-proclaimed legend. Historical hindsight reveals, however, that Duncan developed her dance from nineteenth-century performance conventions, evolving a concept of performance that later dominated the

DUNCAN. A portrait of Duncan in 1898, at age twenty-one, wearing a costume fashioned from her mother's lace curtains. Later, she would abandon her slippers and perform barefoot. (Photograph by the Schloss Atelier, New York; from the San Francisco Performing Arts Library & Museum.)

twentieth century. Duncan's dances mark the transition from the nineteenth-century pictorial concept of performance to the twentieth-century architectural concept. The former conceived of the performer and the stage as realizations of pictorial motifs drawn from the other arts, while the latter conceives of the performer as one element in an onstage matrix of rhythm, space, and light.

Duncan never realized how much her early work employed nineteenth-century performance conventions, for she consciously rebelled against the ballet and spectacular theater of her time. Yet in evolving her performance beyond the limits of nineteenth-century pictorialization, she drew on the ideas of American transcendentalists and Delsarteans and on European neo-Romantics. Curiously, Duncan never entirely escaped the tradition of pictorialization; rather, she transformed it into a new concept of

DUNCAN. Isadora Duncan poses in 1897 as a fairy dancer in Augustin Daly's production of *A Midsummer Night's Dream*. (Photograph from the San Francisco Performing Arts Library & Museum)

performance appropriate to the twentieth century. This transformation resulted largely from her desire to elevate the aesthetic status of dance.

Duncan first encountered the professional theater in 1896 when she joined Augustin Daly's company in New York. The company's commercialism and hierarchy of authority elevated the director and the star performer above all other members of the cast, offending the sense of theater Duncan had nurtured during a San Francisco childhood of family theatricals. She remained with the company for only two years, taking minor roles in productions such as *The Geisha, Meg Merrilees, A Midsummer Night's Dream*, and *As You Like It*. While in New York, Duncan probably took ballet lessons, which she would have found no less crass, authority-ridden, and mechanical than the Daly productions. Unlike her contemporaries Loie Fuller and Ruth St. Denis, who transformed techniques acquired in the commercial theater for use on the concert stage, Duncan took little from her experience with Daly's professional theater.

Instead Duncan drew extensively on Delsartism, a mode of performance derived from the movement theories of French acting and singing teacher François Delsarte, which had been popular in the United States from 1870 to 1890. [*See* Delsarte System of Expression.] American Delsarteans dressed in classical robes and posed as Greek statues; Duncan later adapted this Hellenism to her own uses. The Delsarteans' emphasis on the body as a play of curved lines appealed to Duncan more than the vertical geometrics of ballet alignment, so she incorporated the Delsartean line into her own work. Delsarte-inspired entertainments often involved pantomimic illustrations of poetic recitations, reflecting the nineteenth-century concept of performance as a pictorialization of motifs drawn from the visual and literary arts. Duncan's first performances in New York City after leaving Daly's company used this mode of dance in illustrating poetry.

Although Daly's productions were also grounded in the concept of pictorialization, Duncan preferred the intimate scale of Delsartean theatricals to the large scale of Daly's spectacles. Not surprisingly, she returned to the family context of her earliest theater experiences for her intimate studio performances and appearances at society gatherings in New York. Her mother often accompanied her on the piano, and either her sister Elizabeth or her brother Raymond would recite poetry as Isadora danced. Many of her dances were inspired by poems, such as the *Rubaiyat of Omar Khayyam*, which Duncan danced to a waltz by Strauss and a song by Mendelssohn; other dances such as *The Story of Narcissus* and *Ophelia* derived from literary themes; these two were danced to compositions by Ethelbert Nevin, a friend of Duncan's.

The Duncan family moved to London in 1899, and Isadora performed at society gatherings there. Wider recognition resulted from a series of three subscription performances organized for Duncan by Charles Halle at his New Gallery in 1900. Each performance began with a lecture by one of Halle's associates on the relationship of dance to the other arts. Presenting a variety of media—lectures, recitations, music, and dancing—on the same bill was a format common to nineteenth-century theater that Duncan partially preserved in later performances by alternating dances with musical interludes and stage speeches. The first New Gallery concert reflected Duncan's Delsartean roots, and she presented new dances on literary themes as well as several dances previously performed in New York. But the second and third concerts shifted away from Delsartean theatricals and, in fact, became the basis for two programs that Duncan later toured widely in the professional theater. On the second program, dances to Chopin predominated; on the third, Arnold Dolmetsch's early music group accompanied pictorializations of paintings, including *La Belle Simonetta* (after Botticelli), *Angel Playing a Viol* (after De Predis), and *Bacchus and Ariadne* (after Titian).

In London, Duncan's aesthetic evolved. Though she never went beyond the sixth grade, she educated herself through voracious reading, museum going, and conversations with artists and intellectual friends. One member of Halle's circle suggested she dance to Chopin's music, another that she study the art in the British Museum as a choreographic source; her programs show that she responded to both suggestions.

As Duncan's aesthetic evolved, it incorporated a vision of a *Gesamtkunstwerk* ("total art work"), derived from the composer Richard Wagner and the German philosopher Friedrich Nietzsche. Duncan envisioned dance as the re-creation of the spirit of the Greek chorus. Unlike later modern dancers, who would call for dance to become an independent art, Duncan called for dance to serve as the basis for a reintegration of the arts. Duncan made sporadic attempts to realize this vision; in 1903 she trained a chorus of Greek boys to present Aeschylus's *The Suppliants*, and in 1915 she staged *Oedipus Rex* and *Iphigenia in Aulis* at the Century Theater in New York City. Yet this vision of a new *Gesamtkunstwerk* went largely unrealized in Duncan's work, and a tension remained between her solo dancing and her vision of dance as a choral form.

More fully realized in Duncan's solos were American transcendentalist ideas about the relationship of art, spirit, and nature. In an essay entitled "The Dance of the Future," Duncan describes the dancer as a channel for the movement of nature that translates into "natural" movement; this is how dance would connect the soul with the cosmos. Further, she says that natural movement acknowledges rather than denies gravity, employs successive rather than nonsuccessive movements, and adapts to the form of the individual body rather than adapting the

DUNCAN. This portrait of Duncan taken in Munich shows the loose, Grecian-style drapery she favored as her costume. (Photograph by Hof-Atelier Elvira; from the Dance Collection, New York Public Library for the Performing Arts.)

body to its form. The implied genre that opposes natural movement is, of course, ballet. In Duncan's view, ballet separates the body from the mind; her dance makes the body into a channel for the mind and spirit, in accordance with the transcendentalist view that art reflects the spirit of nature and of the human soul. Duncan considered herself an heir to the transcendentalists, especially the American poet Walt Whitman.

Duncan synthesized her reading, museum study, and her own dance experience into a theory of the interrelationship of form and movement. She defined beauty in dance as the direct correspondence of movement and form, for the lines of form suggest movement and the lines of movement suggest repose. This view originated largely in Duncan's study of ancient Greek sculpture; she perceived the sculpture as embodiments of the qualities of arrested motion and animate stillness that she attempted to re-create in dance. In this way, her dances pictorialized such sculpture.

DUNCAN. Isadora's Russian pupils in her dance *The Volga Boatmen*, choreographed in 1924 as one of the *Songs of the Russian Revolution*. Irma Duncan is at the far left. This suite was presented as part of the evening *Songs of the Revolution* at the Kamerny Theater in Moscow during Duncan's last visit to Russia. (Photograph reprinted from *Dance Perspectives* 64, 16 [Winter 1975], p. 30.)

Duncan's linking of dance to sculpture served to elevate the aesthetic status of the body, the essential medium of dance. Duncan projected a new image of the body akin to the turn-of-the-century ideal put forward by advocates of dress reform and physical culture—a body unhampered by the corset, draped freely with lightweight material, and capable of spontaneous movement. To make this new image aesthetic rather than erotic, the body had to be treated as form, like a work of sculpture, rather than as provocation, like a naked woman. Reviewers often noted that Duncan's dance, daringly costumed for its time, projected a spontaneous sensuality rather than eroticism.

Following her New Gallery concerts in London, Duncan and her family moved to Paris. There, at the Universal Exhibition of 1900, she saw Loie Fuller and Yakko perform (the Japanese dancer was known in Europe as Sada Yacco). In evolving her dance beyond nineteenth-century concepts of performance, she had used models such as these: Duncan did not work in a vacuum. Fuller and Yakko's dancing confirmed Duncan's belief that dance could be expressive outside the tradition of ballet. In 1902 Fuller took Duncan along on a tour of German cities and sponsored some performances for her that led to her first professional contract, as a solo dancer under impresario Alexander Grosz. Grosz booked Duncan into a theater in Budapest, where she appeared on a curtained stage with only costuming and lighting to support her solo dancing. Perhaps Fuller's own work inspired this basic configuration of elements. [*See the entries on Fuller and on Yakko and Kawakami.*]

After Budapest, Duncan never altered this configuration in performance. The curtains, depending on the lighting, ranged from gray to blue to green to burgundy; her costumes ranged from simple Greek tunics in any shade of silk to voluminous robes and swirling scarves. Duncan moved away from the nineteenth-century pictorial stage by reducing performance to her solo figure onstage, focusing the spectator's attention on the free play of the abstract elements of movement, light, and space. Her meeting with Edward Gordon Craig two years later served to confirm her modernist performance concept. Craig, a theatrical designer and reformer, saw in Duncan the realization of his vision of a new theater; Duncan found in Craig a theoretical definition of the performance mode she had evolved. Their union was personal as well as professional, and in 1906 Duncan gave birth to their daughter.

Increasingly, Duncan turned away from the pictorialization of painting and verse, though she never entirely abandoned it. (For example, as late as 1915 the solo *Marseillaise* presented images pictorializing statues from the Arc de Triomphe in Paris.) Beginning in 1904, she tended to create dances based on the musical compositions of Gluck, Beethoven, Brahms, Chopin, Schubert, and Tchaikovsky—compositions written not for the theater but for the concert stage. Duncan often required a large orchestra to dance these works, but sometimes she needed only an onstage pianist. Many critics were shocked by this "defamation" of concert music, but it was clearly part of Duncan's strategy to elevate the aesthetic stature of dance. Like Duncan's linking of dance to sculpture, this strategy extended the nineteenth-century pictorial tradition, for music also became a subject for pictorialization.

To pictorialize music, Duncan had to fuse music and movement in a new way. Traditional ballet scores were written to commission; thus, in performance the music often seemed to follow the dance or the dance to follow the music. Eschewing this approach, Duncan began not with a scenario that dictated a certain type of musical composition but with a musical composition itself. She worked intuitively rather than analytically, listening to the music over and over, meditating on it, improvising, evolving a structure for performance. In the end she seemed not to dance to the music, but to dance the music. Reviewers commented that Duncan's movement so completely fused with the music that to separate the one from the other seemed impossible.

The technique Duncan developed to accomplish this fusion centered the body in the solar plexus (the area of the upper body between the waist and the sternum). The focus on the solar plexus allowed her body to move as a single unit and with a sense of inner animation and anticipation as she walked, ran, skipped, and leapt, performing those natural movements that formed her basic vocabulary. The inner animation was especially clear in sequences when Duncan gestured rather than traveled or when she paused, in the course of traveling, in a momentarily static pose.

All these stylistic elements are clearly seen in *Brahms Waltzes*, a dance set to some Brahms pieces; it recently has been re-created by Annabelle Gamson. At the end of a long musical introduction, Gamson takes her place onstage; when she begins to dance the first waltz, her arms open toward the audience, as if she were inviting them into her dance. The second waltz, slower and stronger, begins as Gamson, standing in place, raises her arms against the resistance of the air above them; she ends by bending to touch the floor with her hand, straightening to touch her breast and forehead, and raising her arm overhead. This sequence of gestures, indicating first the self and then the space beyond the self, recurs through the third waltz: Gamson skips and turns lightly as in the first. This lightness gives way, as before, to a strong quality in the fourth waltz.

The pattern of alternating light and strong movement continues in the fifth waltz as Gamson again dances lightly, but this time she claps her hands together twice overhead to accent her movement. She ends in this pose and simply walks offstage as the sixth waltz sounds for piano alone. The seventh waltz varies the earlier handclapping gesture, for now Gamson claps at the level of her solar plexus as well as overhead—sometimes with an upward motion, sometimes with a downward. The eighth waltz breaks the pattern in its fusion of strength and lightness: Gamson ends standing, her arms weighted down at her sides. In the last brief waltz, Gamson remains still as the music surges; she ends as she did the second waltz, touching the floor, her chest, and her forehead, and raising her arm overhead. This final gesture fuses the dimensions within which she has danced—the strength of the ground, the lightness of the air, the center of the self, and the release of the space beyond.

Duncan never set her dances permanently; rather she changed their structure over the years as she reworked her physical response to the expressive qualities of the music. Her evolving series of works on the Orpheus theme exemplifies this working method. The London New Gallery concerts included both a minuet from Christoph Willibald Gluck's opera *Orfeo ed Euridice* and a dance inspired by Sir William Richmond's painting *Orpheus Returning from the Shades*, accompanied by an excerpt from Monteverdi's *Orfeo*. Thereafter, Duncan focused exclusively on Gluck's music, as in the *Orpheus* included on the Dance Idylls program that she toured widely until around 1910; in this version of *Orpheus*, she emphasized the celestial aspects of the myth, presenting the Elysian Fields and the meeting of Orpheus and Eurydice before finishing with an orchestral minuet and a danced gavotte. Around 1910, Duncan replaced this version with another that moved from Orpheus's lament through the dances of the Furies to the representation of the triumph of love. In some performances, an offstage chorus participated and, in others, a group of Duncan's students appeared; for the most part, however, Duncan herself represented all the varying characters and emotions of the work.

DUNCAN. Although she never allowed herself to be filmed, Duncan was a willing subject for still photographers. In this portrait, the camera captures the ethereal yet weighted quality that moved spectators of her art. (Photograph by Arnold Genthe; from the Dance Collection, New York Public Library for the Performing Arts.)

Duncan's students appeared in some other works too, such as *Igphigenia* and *Beethoven's Seventh Symphony*, yet she never fully integrated her students into her performances as equals. Duncan never expected them to become professionals; rather she wanted them to internalize all the spiritual benefits of a dance education. This spiritual emphasis was part of Duncan's strategy for elevating the aesthetic stature of dance; she wanted to reintegrate dance into life and hence render it essential rather than peripheral to modern living. Toward this end, in 1905 she founded a boarding school for young girls, in Grünwald, outside Berlin. It was directed by her sister Elizabeth and was moved to Paris before World War I, with the support of Paris Singer, an American millionaire and the father of Duncan's son, born in 1910. As the war approached, only six of the original forty students remained, acting as teachers for newer students. These six toured the United States alone during the war, as the Duncan Dancers, but only Irma Duncan—the six adopted their teacher's surname—rejoined Isadora after the war to open a school in Moscow, with the support of the new Communist government. Isadora left Moscow after the government withdrew its support, but Irma kept the school going commercially until after Isadora's death.

Duncan's involvement with the new state created by the Russian Revolution showed her willingness to cooperate with any institution or system that supported her work. (After all, she was also supported for a time by an American capitalist.) Duncan's involvement with the USSR also indicates the political program implicit in her dance.

Duncan believed she had made a fundamental discovery about how movement connects to emotion—what John Martin has termed her discovery of basic dance: "She was not seeking to invent or devise anything, but only to discover the roots of that impulse toward movement as a response to every experience, which she felt in herself and which she was convinced was a universal endowment." Duncan believed that this discovery, inextricably linked to the spiritual transformation of the individual, could lead to a larger social transformation—a utopia governed by spiritual rather than material values, where men and women were equals and free individuals. In Duncan's view, the new Soviet state seemed to be theoretically closer to this utopia than Europe or the United States were at that time.

Duncan attempted to embody her political vision in several of her solos. In 1917 she choreographed Tchaikovsky's *Marche Slav* to express her sympathy with the Russian Revolution; in the dance, Duncan represented a peasant rising from slavery to freedom. Reviews describe how she entered with slow and heavy steps, her hands apparently bound behind her back. When the melody of "God Save the Tsar" (which Tchaikovsky had interwoven into his music) was first sounded, she fell to the ground as if she were shuddering under the impact of blows. Then she rose, defying the melody with clenched fists and an expression of fury. When the tsarist hymn finished, and Duncan's fury passed, she explored the peasant's first response to freedom. She brought her hands forward in a gesture not of triumph but of bewilderment, as if she had forgotten how to use them. The dance ended as Duncan leapt about the stage with, in Carl Van Vechten's words, "the expression of frightened, almost uncomprehending joy."

When Duncan had arrived in Russia to open her school, she choreographed a dance to the Communist anthem, the *Internationale*. In this dance Duncan strode energetically in time with the music, as if to summon followers. At a concert to celebrate the fourth anniversary of the revolution, presented at the Bolshoi Theater in November 1921, one hundred children joined Duncan onstage during the *Internationale*, recalling her choreography to the French national anthem, the *Marseillaise*, during the early years of World War I. In both she seemed to implicate a multitude in her solo dancing: enfolded in a red robe, she seemed to confront an advancing enemy, suffer a nearly crushing defeat, but rise triumphant in the end.

Solos such as the *Marseillaise, Marche Slav,* and *Internationale* suggest a shift in Duncan's style after 1914. Her dances became more static, more sculptural, and they depended more on expressive gesture than on animated motion. This shift was perhaps the result not only of Duncan's personal tragedy—the accidental drowning of her two children in 1913—but also of the world tragedy of World War I. Works such as *Ave Maria,* presented as both a solo and a group work, and Scriabin's *Etudes* exemplified her new style by fusing the image of a grieving mother with the image of the grief of all persons over senseless death. In *Ave Maria,* Duncan repeated a gesture—"reaching toward the earth and then lifted upward"—that her sister-in-law, Margherita Duncan, in *The Art of the Dance,* interpreted as the suffering yet hopeful quality of maternal love. In one of the *Etudes,* Duncan repeated a gesture of her arms swinging overhead that lifted her body upward, her hands then plunging to the ground to bring her to her knees. The constant repetition of one expressive gesture became a major structural device in Duncan's works after 1914. Some commentators saw the new style as a decline in her work; they attributed it to her loss of discipline and her overindulgence in food and drink since the death of her children. Others saw the new style as a heightening of Duncan's artistry, an achievement of maximum expression through minimal means. The debate continued even after her accidental death in 1927.

There is no critical disagreement, however, over the enormous impact of Duncan's career as a whole. Her influence was more indirect than direct, because her direct followers, the six Duncan Dancers, did not develop her work further but imitated her dancing style. As fervently as Duncan desired to transmit her dance to great masses of people, her style rendered her wishes nearly impossible; her intuitive working methods and singular performing persona made it difficult for students to develop her work, leaving them with few options other than imitation.

Duncan's indirect heirs include not only individual dancers stirred by having witnessed, perhaps, only a single performance but also dance movements that might have developed differently if major practitioners had not felt Duncan's influence. Duncan's 1905 visit galvanized the Russian ballet world, confirming the notions of young choreographers such as Michel Fokine and Alexandr Gorsky that dance reform was imperative. Soon after Duncan's visit, Fokine choreographed the dance later called *Les Sylphides* by Diaghilev; setting several of the Chopin waltzes Duncan had danced on her visit, Fokine rendered the ballet style of his day more expressive by incorporating the fluid use of the upper torso and the flowing arm gestures he so admired in Duncan's dancing. While *Les Sylphides* showed Duncan's stylistic influence, Gorsky's *Etudes* (1908) showed a structural influence: these short dances by different composers were unified by the common theme of autumn, much as Duncan's programs of dances were unified by an abstract theme or quality of feeling.

Germany was also ready to receive Duncan's influence in the first decade of the twentieth century. German artists were then seeking an expressive art of movement, and Duncan's appearances—appropriately antiballet and, hence, anti-French—served as one catalyst in the emergence of a German dance movement. German dance soloists soon began to crisscross the country, their dances mingling Duncan's style with others more gymnastic and exotic.

The United States, like Germany, lacked a strong native ballet tradition, so when an American modern dance movement developed in the late twenties, Duncan was hailed as its precursor. Although Duncan had performed more extensively in Europe than in the United States, and although students of the Denishawn company and schools were largely responsible for the development of American modern dance, Duncan was appropriate as its originator. This allegiance resulted partly from the desire of Doris Humphrey, Martha Graham, and their contemporaries to distance themselves from Denishawn because, essentially, they wanted to establish a national repertory rather than an eclectic, international one. Duncan seemed a prototypical American and, moreover, one who had anticipated Humphrey's and Graham's preoccupation with the extension of basic movement experiences into dance idioms.

Duncan has influenced the development of twentieth-century ballet as greatly as she has influenced modern dance. The modernist concept of performance that she in-

DUNCAN. Many dancers were influenced by Duncan's free-spirited style. Here, Gertrude Hoffman and her dancers are caught in a Duncan-inspired moment. (Private collection.)

troduced—dance reduced to the dancer, the music, and the stage space—carries through in the ballets of George Balanchine and Merce Cunningham, to name only two of the important twentieth-century choreographers who are indirect heirs to Duncan's conception of dance.

Finally, Duncan's conception of dance is her most significant contribution and influence. In large part, twentieth-century audiences, dancers, and scholars view dance in terms that Duncan first articulated: dance functions as a revitalizing fusion of mind and body; participation in dance makes this revitalization accessible to all, while watching dance lets the spectator experience this revitalization vicariously; and the fullest realization of the fusion of mind and body is an innate rather than acquired talent. Duncan's view—our view—mingles egalitarian and elitist impulses: dance as an aspect of education for all and dance as a calling for a chosen few. This seeming contradiction generated much of the excitement of Duncan's performances, for everyone could imagine doing the movements Duncan performed, but no one could perform them as she could.

The twentieth century is heir to this contradiction in Duncan's conception of dance, as it is heir to the reduction of dance to movement, music, and space. Extending the mode of pictorialization beyond its own limits, Duncan made the transition to dance modernism.

[*See also* Costume in Western Traditions, *article on* Modern Dance; *and* Photography.]

BIBLIOGRAPHY. The best secondary source on Duncan is Ann Daly's *Done into Dance: Isadora Duncan in America* (Bloomington, 1995).

Also valuable is Deborah Jowitt's chapter on Duncan entitled "The Search for Motion" in *Time and the Dancing Image* (New York, 1988). Other recent studies include Fredrika Blair's *Isadora: Portrait of the Artist as a Woman* (New York, 1986), Millicent Dillon's *After Egypt: Isadora Duncan and Mary Cassatt* (New York, 1990), Dorée Duncan's edited volume *Life into Art: Isadora Duncan and Her World* (New York, 1993), and Lillian Loewenthal's *The Search for Isadora: The Legend and Legacy of Isadora Duncan* (Princeton, 1993).

Although Duncan's autobiography, *My Life* (Garden City, N.Y., 1927), contains many factual inaccuracies, it reveals some of the ways Duncan shaped her public persona. *The Art of the Dance* (New York, 1928), a collection of Duncan's writings on dance edited by Sheldon Cheney, presents Duncan's interpretation of her dances to the public. Contemporary reviews are republished in Henry Taylor Parker's *Motion Arrested: Dance Reviews of H. T. Parker*, edited by Olive Holmes (Middletown, Conn., 1982); André Levinson's *Ballet Old and New* (1918), translated by Susan Cook Summer (New York, 1982); and *Nijinsky, Pavlova, Duncan: Three Lives in Dance*, edited by Paul Magriel (New York, 1947), with reviews by Carl Van Vechten. The Magriel volume also contains John Martin's essay, "Isadora Duncan and Basic Dance," an analysis of Duncan's technique stressing its relationship to American modern dance as it emerged around 1930. Edwin Denby offers an equally illuminating view in "On Isadora's Technique," in his *Looking at the Dance* (New York, 1949). Irma Duncan presents more of a how-to approach in *The Technique of Isadora Duncan* (New York, 1937).

Irma Duncan recounts her years as a Duncan student in *Duncan Dancer: An Autobiography* (Middletown, Conn., 1966). Kay Bardsley compiles the facts on "Isadora Duncan's First School" in *CORD Dance Research Annual* 10 (1977):219–249. Natalia Roslavleva documents the history of the Isadora Duncan school in Moscow in *Dance Perspectives*, no. 64 (Winter 1975), and Elizabeth Souritz assesses "Isadora Duncan's Influence on Dance in Russia" in *Dance Chronicle* 18.2 (1995): 281–291.

Although no film exists of Duncan dancing, the Dance Collection of the New York Public Library for the Performing Arts includes film and videotape reconstructions of Duncan's dances by her students and others. Norma Adler discusses "Reconstructing the Dances of Isadora Duncan in the United States" in *Drama Review* 28 (Fall 1984): 59–66.

Images of Duncan herself appear in the many drawings, prints, photographs, and sculpture executed by artists of her dancing. Not all of these are published, but among the published volumes are Arnold Genthe's *Isadora Duncan: Twenty-Four Studies* (New York, 1929), Valentine Lecomte's *The Dance of Isadora Duncan* (Paris, c. 1952), and Abraham Walkowitz's *Isadora Duncan in Her Dances* (Girard, Kansas, 1945).

SUSAN A. MANNING

DUNHAM, KATHERINE (born 22 June 1909 in Glen Ellyn, Illinois), American dancer and choreographer. Dunham, who is best known for choreography based on African-American, Caribbean, West African, and South American sources, began her dance career in Chicago with the Little Theatre Company of Harper Avenue. That experience was followed by study with Mark Turbyfill and Ruth Page of the Chicago Civic Opera. Dunham's other primary influence during this period was Ludmilla Speranzeva, a Kamerny-trained modern dancer from Russia, whose teaching put equal emphasis on both dance and acting technique. She worked as well with Vera Mirova, a specialist in "Oriental" dance.

Out of her work with Turbyfill and Page, Dunham conceived the idea for a *ballet nègre*, and she later founded the

Negro Dance Group in 1934; the group performed Dunham's *Negro Rhapsody* at the Chicago Beaux Arts Ball, and Dunham herself made a solo performance in Page's *La Guiablesse* at the Chicago Civic Opera in 1931. While enrolled in the anthropology department of the University of Chicago, Dunham continued her experiments in ballet and modern dance, using her research to develop a choreographic style suited to the African-American sensibility. Support from the Rosenwald Foundation (1935–1936) enabled her to undertake an eighteen-month-long study trip to investigate the dance cultures of Jamaica, Martinique, Trinidad, and Haiti. This research, which resulted in a master's thesis entitled "The Dances of Haiti," became the basis for the uniquely African-American style that she was then developing. Her decision to appear as the scandalous Georgia Brown in the 1940 Broadway hit *Cabin in the Sky*, with choreography by George Balanchine, drew Dunham away from a career in anthropology, although her interest in the field continued, and the humanistic approach she brought to dance was founded in anthropological method.

During the 1940s the Dunham Company performed on Broadway in revues produced by Sol Hurok. Between 1943 and 1965, when it disbanded, her company toured the United States and fifty-seven other countries. The center from which this activity emanated was the Dunham School of Dance and Theater, which she established in New York City in 1945. It occupied the premises of the former Isadora Duncan Studio in Caravan Hall, but later relocated to 220 West Forty-third Street. The school provided training in rhythm, voice, and acting as well as dance and dance ethnology. Through her school, Dunham influenced several generations of prominent performers, among them Peter Gennaro, Marlon Brando, José Ferrer, Arthur Mitchell, Walter Nicks, Chita Rivera, and Eartha Kitt. Important members of the Dunham Company included Vanoye Aikens, Ricardo Avalos, Talley Beatty, Larl Beecham, Wilbert Bradley, Janet Collins, Jean-Léon Destiné, Lucille Ellis, Syvilla Fort, Tommy Gomez, Lawaugn Ingram, Charles Moore, Lenwood Morris, Pearl Reynolds, Carmencita Romero, Archie Savage, Glory Van Scott, Lavinia Williams, and Ural Wilson.

Dunham choreographed her first film, *Carnival of Rhythm*, in 1939, followed by *Star Spangled Rhythm* and *Pardon My Sarong* (1942), *Stormy Weather* (1943), *Casbah* (1948), *Botta e Risposta* (1950), *Mambo* with Silvana Mangano (Italy, 1954), *Liebes Sender* (Germany, 1954), *Musica en la Noche* (Mexico, 1955), *Green Mansions* (1958), and John Huston's *The Bible* (Italy, 1964).

Dunham's most important dances were *L'Ag'Ya* (1938), a story of love and revenge set in Martinique; *Rites de Passage* (1943), a celebration of puberty, fertility, and death rituals; *Shango* (1945), a reenactment of Trinidadian cult practices; and *Southland* (1950), a dance "documentary" about lynchings of blacks in the American South. Of the many musicals for which she created choreography, the most important include *Tropics and Le Jazz Hot* (1940), *Tropical Revue* (1943), *Carib Song* (1945), *Bal Nègre* (1947) and *Caribbean Rhapsody* (1948). The last major Dunham Company show was *Bamboche* (1962), a revue featuring sacred and secular dances of Haiti; among the performers were several members of the Royal Troupe of Morocco. At the Metropolitan Opera in 1964, Dunham provided the choreography for a production of Giuseppe Verdi's *Aïda*. In 1972 she directed and choreographed a presentation in Atlanta of Scott Joplin's folk opera *Treemonisha*, with musical arrangements by T. J. Anderson. In the same year the Alvin Ailey American Dance Theater revived Dunham's *Choros.*

In 1966 Dunham was a State Department representative to the first World Festival of Negro Arts in Dakar, Senegal. On her return to the United States, she began her long association with Southern Illinois University as director of the Performing Arts Training Center in East Saint Louis, Illinois. With poet in residence Eugene Redmond, she wrote *Ode to Taylor Jones* (1968), a play based on the death in an automobile accident of a local resident and his wife. East Saint Louis is also home to the Katherine Dunham Museum, which houses Dunham's collection of African, Asian, and Caribbean art as well as costumes and memorabilia from her stage career. Much of that material has been moved to the Missouri Historical Society in Saint Louis.

Dunham's work continues to thrill audiences. Performances at Carnegie Hall (1979) and a television documentary, *The Divine Dunham,* produced in 1980 for the *Dance in America* series, have reconstructed the Dunham style using the knowledge of three generations of her dancers trained in Dunham technique. In 1987 the Alvin Ailey Dance Theater presented fourteen of Dunham's works in a program entitled *The Magic of Katherine Dunham.* This performance signaled the reentry of a portion of Dunham's repertory onto the contemporary stage.

Dunham technique is African-American art in motion. Through isolations, Dunham taught performers to imitate the polyrhythms of African drumming; for example, a dancer can make the body "play" a battery of movements by isolating the rhythm of head movements from the rhythms of the trunk and feet. In Dunham's style, the head and neck were trained in movements from the Pacific, while material for the torso, arms, and feet derived from Africa and the Caribbean. When practiced for an extended period, these movements, isolated and repeated, lead the dancer toward an experience of total rhythmic immersion, to what in traditional religions is termed *possession.* Dunham's dances were not reproductions of actual rites, but rather artistic transformations capable of communi-

DUNHAM. Katherine Dunham (center) with Roger Ohardieno and Tommy Gomez in the "Rara Tonga" number from her musical *Tropical Revue* (1943). (Photograph from the Dance Collection, New York Public Library for the Performing Arts.)

cating the atmosphere and the social and religious function of dances from many cultures. Long before national folkloric troupes from outside Europe and the United States began to tour, the Dunham Company had paved the way for performing African diaspora folklore in the theater.

Critical response was generally favorable among African-American and European critics of the 1930s and 1940s. American dance critics of the time appreciated Dunham's accomplishments in promoting the "Negro dance," but were hard put to recognize the value of her work as part of the mainstream of either American dance or theater. Many could not share Dunham's attachment to the concept of a *ballet nègre* which, like Diaghilev's Ballets Russes, combined ethnic motifs with ballet, modern dance, and theatrical techniques. By the late 1960s, when more critics were able to appreciate Dunham's work on its own terms, her professional company was performing only on special occasions. The *Dance Magazine* Award presented to Dunham in 1969 and the Kennedy Center Honors in 1983 acknowledged the importance of her contributions to the profession well after the fact.

[*See also* Jazz Dance.]

BIBLIOGRAPHY

Aschenbrenner, Joyce. *Katherine Dunham: Reflections on the Social and Political Contexts of Afro-American Dance.* CORD Dance Research Annual, 12. New York, 1981.

Beckford, Ruth. *Katherine Dunham: A Biography.* New York, 1979.

Biemiller, Ruth. *Dance: The Story of Katherine Dunham.* New York, 1969.

Buckle, Richard, ed. *Katherine Dunham: Her Dancers, Singers, and Musicians.* London, 1949.

Clark, VèVè A., and Margaret B. Wilkerson, eds. *Kaiso! Katherine Dunham.* Berkeley, 1978.

Clark, VèVè A. "Katherine Dunham's *Tropical Revue.*" *Caribe* 7.1–2 (1983): 15–20.

Clark, VèVè A. "Performing the Memory of Difference in Afro-Caribbean Dance: Katherine Dunham's Choreography, 1938–1987." In *History and Memory in African-American Culture,* edited by Geneviève and Robert O'Meally. New York, 1994.

de Mille, Agnes. *Portrait Gallery.* Boston, 1990.

Dixon Gottschild, Brenda. *Digging the Africanist Presence in American Performance: Dance and Other Contexts.* Westport, Conn., 1996.

Dunham, Katherine. "The Negro Dance." In *The Negro Caravan,* edited by Sterling Brown. New York, 1941.

Dunham, Katherine. *Journey to Accompong.* New York, 1946.

Dunham, Katherine. *The Dances of Haiti.* Acta Antropológica, vol. 2.4. Mexico City, 1947. Reprinted by the Center for Afro-American Studies. Los Angeles, 1983.

Dunham, Katherine. *A Touch of Innocence.* New York, 1959.

Dunham, Katherine. *Island Possessed.* New York, 1969.

Dunham, Katherine. *Kasamance.* New York, 1974.

Emery, Lynne Fauley. *Black Dance from 1619 to Today.* 2d rev. ed. Princeton, 1988.

Harnan, Terry. *African Rhythm, American Dance.* New York, 1974.

Haskins, James. *Katherine Dunham.* New York, 1982.

Hill, Constance Valis. "Katherine Dunham's *Southland:* Protest in the Face of Repression." *Dance Research Journal* 26 (Fall 1994): 1–10.

Hodson, Millicent. "How She Began Her Beguine: Dunham's Dance Literacy." In *Kaiso! Katherine Dunham,* edited by VèVè A. Clark and Margaret B. Wilkerson. Berkeley, 1978.

Perpener, John O. "African-American Dance and Sociological Positivism during the 1930s." *Studies in Dance History* 5 (Spring 1994): 23–30.

Redmond, Eugene. "Cultural Fusion and Spiritual Unity: Katherine Dunham's Approach to Developing Educational Community Theatre." In *Kaiso! Katherine Dunham,* edited by VèVè A. Clark and Margaret B. Wilkerson. Berkeley, 1978.

Rose, Albirda. *Dunham Technique.* Dubuque, Iowa, 1990.

ARCHIVES.   The Katherine Dunham Archives are located in the Katherine Dunham Museum, East St. Louis, and the Morris Library, Southern Illinois University, Carbondale. Articles, scrapbooks, and a guide to visual materials may be found in the Dance Collection, New York Public Library for the Performing Arts.

VèVè A. CLARK

DUNN, DOUGLAS (born 19 October 1942 in Palo Alto, California), dancer and choreographer. Dunn graduated from Princeton University and danced with the Princeton Regional Ballet Company, Yvonne Rainer (1968–1970), Merce Cunningham (1969–1973), and was a member of Grand Union (1970–1976). He has collaborated with other choreographers, including Sara Rudner, David Gordon, Pat Catterson, and Sheela Raj, with filmmakers Charles Atlas and Amy Greenfield, and with poets Anne Waldman and Reed Bye.

As a choreographer, Dunn has created symmetrical structures that rigorously treat specific themes and their negations. In *Nevada* (1973), performed in a program at the New School in which choreographers comment on their work, Dunn juxtaposed pure movement invention to pure word play, incorporating the critique section of the evening into the format of his short dance. His next work, *Time Out* (1973), was just the opposite: a static work using various props and costumes but no words to create a series of theatrical tableaux peppered with small movement episodes. In *101* (1974), Dunn lay motionless for four hours a day on top of a large maze he had constructed in his Soho loft through which visitors wandered. *Gestures in Red* (1975) was a solo that explored space with a catalog of an extremely broad range of movement possibilities.

Many of Dunn's works have been solo dances, but since *Lazy Madge* (1976–1979), a long, changing, ongoing work for a stable group of dancers who could exercise independent choices in performance, he has worked with groups. *Celeste* (1977) had a cast of forty, and *Foot Rules* (1979) was a duet. In 1980, Dunn was commissioned to create *Pulcinella* for the Paris Opera Ballet.

His style since the late 1970s has a classical look shot through with slight awkwardnesses and gestural imagery. Dunn has an uncanny ability to evoke social behavior without literalism; many of his works are also infused with his wry, ironic, and multilayered sense of humor. His dances since 1980 reveal a predilection for collaboration, a dedication to exploring a variety of presentational formats, and an interest in evening-length works.

In 1981 Dunn returned to the Paris Opera to set *Cycles* on the Groupe de Recherche Chorégraphique, with music by Steve Lacey. Lacey also provided the scores for *Futurities* (1984) and *Landing* (1992), the former a duet for Dunn and Elsa Wolliaston, the latter for Dunn's company, Douglas Dunn and Dancers. Lacy's score for *Futurities* was based on poems by Robert Creeley; Dunn has also worked directly with poets on occasion, as in his video-dance *Secret of the Waterfall* (1983), commissioned by WGBH, Boston, and directed by Charles Atlas. Atlas also shot Dunn's solo *The Myth of Modern Dance* (1990), again for WGBH, based on his highly successful comic solo *Haole* (1988). *Haole* exemplifies the emphasis on comedic character that has emerged in Dunn's later work, particularly in his solo material. Dunn's other major work for film in the 1990s is *Rubble Dance. Long Island City* (1991), shot outdoors by Rudy Burckhardt in various industrial locations in Queens (Dunn reworked the material for the stage the following year). Two of Dunn's most frequent collaborators are painter Mimi Gross (sets and costumes) and Carol Mullins (lighting), who worked with Dunn on *Sky*

Eye (1989), *Caracole* (1995), and *Spell for Opening the Mouth of N* (1996). *Spell* (the title comes from the ancient Egyptian Book of the Dead) is one of Dunn's largest-scale works, involving ten dancers and eight singer-actors who are instructed to repeat without delay the fragmented texts they receive over headphones in composer Joshua Fried's score. The result, an alternately comic and macabre cacaphony, combines with Dunn's choreography to suggest both ancient ritual and a futuristic tribalism.

Since *Second Mesa* (1983), a dance installation work made in collaboration with sculptor Jeffrey Schiff and composer John Driscoll for the Institute of Contemporary Art, Boston, Dunn has been interested periodically in performance beyond the proscenium stage. *Stucco Moon* (1992), with sets, costumes, and sound by sculptor David Ireland, has been performed in a gymnasium, a museum, alternative performance spaces, and a conventional theater. The piece employs Dunn's own dancers as well as pick-up dancers from each city in which it is commis-

sioned; the choreography comprises modules and sets of material rearranged for each venue. In common with several of Dunn's later works, this dance allows the dancers some spontaneous choices in performance, including when to perform certain sections of material; in *Stucco Moon* the dancers are also free to alter their costumes, including total or partial nudity. *Disappearances* (1994) offered a completely different approach to site-specific work. For this dance Dunn dispersed his dancers among the lunchtime crowds of New York's Wall Street district, to execute everyday gestures in subtle unison and contrapuntal structures. The dance hovered on the edge of being perceptible as performance, a witty and poignant political comment on the state of dance in the harsh cultural climate of the United States in the 1990s.

DOUGLAS DUNN. The fleet-footed Dunn in his solo *Echo* (1980), performed at The Kitchen, New York. (Photograph © 1980 by Johan Elbers; used by permission.)

BIBLIOGRAPHY

Banes, Sally. *Terpsichore in Sneakers: Post-Modern Dance.* 2d ed. Middletown, Ct., 1987. Includes a bibliography.
Dunn, Douglas, with Sylvère Lotringer. "Interview." *Semiotext(e)* 3 (1978).
Dunn, Douglas, with John Howell. "Dunn on Dancing." *Live* 4 (1980).
Kreemer, Connie, ed. *Further Steps: Fifteen Choreographers on Modern Dance.* New York, 1987.

FILM AND VIDEOTAPE. *Making Dances* (Blackwood Productions, 1979). "Secret of the Waterfall" (WGBH–TV, Boston, 1983).

SALLY BANES

DUNN, ROBERT ELLIS (born 28 December 1928 in Clinton, Oklahoma, died 5 July 1996 in New Carrollton, Maryland), American musician, teacher, choreographer, and founding member of the Judson Dance Theater. Dunn studied and performed tap dance and music as a child in Oklahoma. He received a bachelor's degree in music from the New England Conservatory in 1958, studied dance at the Boston Conservatory with Jan Veen from 1955 to 1958, and received a master's degree in library science from Rutgers University in New Jersey in 1966. Dunn studied music with John Cage at the New School for Social Research in New York City from 1958 to 1960 and with Irmgard Bartenieff at the Dance Notation Bureau from 1972 to 1974. He was influenced by Zen Buddhism and Daoism, by the philosophers Martin Heidegger and Ludwig Wittgenstein, and by such literary artists as James Joyce, Marcel Proust, and Charles Olson.

During the early years of his career, Dunn worked as a musician, teacher, composer, choreographer, and occasional performer, mainly in Boston and New York. He was invited by Merce Cunningham in 1958, and subsequently by Martha Graham, to play for rehearsals, classes, and performances at the American Dance Festival in New London, Connecticut, and later in New York City. Dunn also played for Helen Tamiris and José Limón and performed with composers Richard Maxfield and La Monte Young. He was repertory coach for Boston Opera directors Boris Goldovsky and Sarah Caldwell. These opportunities, in addition to contact with Cage, Robert Rauschenberg, and other seminal art world figures of the 1960s, placed Dunn in a position to absorb and participate as an artist and teacher in the evolution of American dance.

At the invitation of Cage and Cunningham, Dunn led a series of classes on choreography from 1960 to 1962, which became the basis for the Judson Dance Theater. Based in part on Cage's ideas, these classes drew upon Dunn's rich notions concerning music and movement. They incorporated the projects of choreographers Trisha Brown, Yvonne Rainer, Judith Dunn, David Gordon, and Steve Paxton. Dunn's catalytic approach was to establish a climate of experimentation in workshop sessions and to provide a methodology for examining in detail the creative process and choreographic choices suggested by dances generated by workshop participants. Dunn arranged the order and spacing of the programs and contributed music for the first seven concerts of the Judson Dance Theater. Later participants, who gathered for the final workshop in the spring of 1964 at the studio of Judith Dunn, included second-generation dance innovators Lucinda Childs, Meredith Monk, Kenneth King, and Phoebe Neville.

Of particular importance to Dunn's approach to teaching were the influences of the Bauhaus art movement, emphasizing experimentation, basic materials, and design. In his analysis of choreography, Dunn focused on the strongest and most original qualities of what is seen—looking at the work as if it were one of a species. He analyzed the actual divisions of the piece with respect to temporal, imagistic, and narrative structures and considered the first interventions, or least changes, that might be undertaken to bring the piece into focus. From 1965 to 1972 Dunn was assistant curator for the New York Public Library's Dance Research Collection at the Library for the Performing Arts at Lincoln Center. He assisted with producing the collection's Dance Index for Research. From 1970 to 1985 Dunn taught choreography at Columbia University Teachers College, Hunter College, the American Dance Festival at Connecticut College, the Laban Institute, the Dance Notation Bureau, and the Baltimore County campus of the University of Maryland. In 1985 he became professor of dance at the University of Maryland at College Park. His residencies at the University of California at Santa Cruz, Southern Methodist University, the University of Wisconsin at Milwaukee, and elsewhere extended the scope of his influence.

Between 1994 and his death in 1996 Dunn directed the preparation of *Dance Findings*, a videodance installation for the Haggerty Museum of Art, Marquette University, with the cooperation of the University of Wisconsin–Milwaukee dance and film departments. This work, which was premiered at the Haggerty Museum in January 1997, was intended as a meditation on dance and the human body, and it documents Dunn's ideas on choreography. Dunn was the 1985 recipient of the New York Dance and Performance Award (the Bessie Award) and the 1988 recipient of the American Dance Guild Award.

BIBLIOGRAPHY

Banes, Sally. *Democracy's Body: Judson Dance Theater, 1962–64*. Ann Arbor, Mich., 1983.

Belloc, Danielle Marilyn. "Robert Ellis Dunn's Approach to Teaching Improvisation and Choreography." M.A. thesis, York University, 1996.

Carter, Curtis L., et al. *Dance Findings: Robert Ellis Dunn Videodance Installation*. Milwaukee: Haggerty Museum of Art, Marquette University, 1997.

Dunn, Robert. "Can Choreography Be Taught?" *Ballet Review* 4 (1971): 2.

Dunn, Robert Ellis. "Tradition and Innovation in Dance." *Contact Quarterly* 13 (Fall 1988): 14–17.

Dunn, Robert Ellis. "Judson Days." *Contact Quarterly* 14 (Winter 1989): 9–13.

Dunn, Robert. "Analysis in Context." *AALMA News* (Special Conference Issue, 1986; rep., April 1989).

Dunn, Robert. "Writing Dance." *Contact Quarterly* 14.2 (1989): 39–40.

Dunn, Robert. "Dance and Analysis." In *Compendium of Laban Movement Analysis*. Edited by Martha Eddy, Laban Institute of Movement Studies. New York, 1990.

Dunn, Robert. "Analysis and Notation." In *Compendium of Laban Movement*. Edited by Martha Eddy, Laban Institute of Movement Studies. New York, 1992.

Fisher, Berenice. "Master Teacher Robert Ellis Dunn: Cultivating Creative Impulse." *Dance Magazine* (January 1984): 84–87.

McDonagh, Don. *The Rise and Fall and Rise of Modern Dance*. Rev. ed. Pennington, N.J., 1990.

Parsons, Annie B., and Sharon True. "Notes on Dance/Improvisation/Music: Workshop Taught by Robert Ellis Dunn." *Contact Quarterly* 10 (Winter 1985): 19–23.

Smith, Nancy Stark. "High Contrast: Interview with Robert Ellis Dunn." *Contact Quarterly* 12 (Fall 1987): 29–33.

INTERVIEW.   Robert Dunn, by Pamela Sommers (1991), Oral History Project, Dance Collection, New York Public Library for the Performing Arts.

CURTIS L. CARTER

DUPOND, PATRICK (born 14 March 1959 in Paris), French ballet dancer and company director. An athletic boy, Dupond began taking ballet classes at a neighborhood studio when he became bored by soccer and judo. At age eleven, he began studying with Max Bozzoni, eventually entering the school of the Paris Opera Ballet at an advanced level. He was accepted into the company in 1975, at age sixteen. In 1976, his gold medal at the prestigious Varna ballet competition won him international recognition. His ascent through the Opera ranks began with his promotion to *coryphée* in 1977; he was named a *premier danseur* in 1979 and an *étoile* in 1980.

Dupond developed into an energetic, flamboyant dancer acclaimed for his high jumps and great theatrical magnetism. His body type did not conform to classical conventions, and many of his stellar roles, such as Mercutio in *Romeo and Juliet* and the Jester in *Swan Lake,* were character parts or *demi-caractère* in style. The role that confirmed his status was that of Vaslav Nijinsky—the man who set the mold for Dupond's type of bravura dancing—in John Neumeier's 1979 ballet *Vaslav.* Mounted on the Hamburg Ballet, this work was taken into the repertory of the Paris Opera Ballet in 1980.

Quickly becoming an international guest star, Dupond danced with companies all over the world. As guest artist with the Hamburg Ballet, he not only created the title role in *Vaslav* but danced in other Neumeier works as well. Ballets by Roland Petit also played an important part in his rise: Dupond's first solo role was Georges in Petit's *Nana,* mounted at the Paris Opera in 1976, and he danced an anguished, haunted young man in the same choreographer's *Queen of Spades* (replacing an injured Mikhail Baryshnikov) when it was produced at the Rome Opera in 1979. Other engagements took him to various countries of Europe, to Japan, and to the United States.

In contrast to his dramatic roles, Dupond also proved adept in such mischievous, playful roles as Alain in Heinz Spoerli's *La Fille Mal Gardée,* which he created in 1981, Puck in John Neumeier's *A Midsummer Night's Dream,* and the principal dancer in Twyla Tharp's *Push Comes to Shove.* Furthermore, he eventually did conquer much of the classical repertory, dancing Solor in *La Bayadère,* Albrecht in *Giselle,* Romeo in Rudolf Nureyev's *Romeo and Juliet,* and Prince Désiré in Rosella Hightower's staging of *The Sleeping Beauty* for the Paris Opera Ballet in 1982.

Among the works that Dupond has enlivened are many by twentieth-century masters, including Michel Fokine's *Le Spectre de la Rose* and *Le Carnaval;* Léonide Massine's *Le Tricorne;* Serge Lifar's *Icare;* George Balanchine's *Apollo, The Prodigal Son, Rubies,* and *Le Bourgeois Gentilhomme;* and Maurice Béjart's *Boléro, L'Oiseau de Feu, Symphonie pour un Homme Seul,* and *Salomé.* Most of these performances took place at the Paris Opera. Dupond also danced in modern pieces by innovators such as Daniel Ezralow, Robert Wilson, and Ulysses Dove.

During Nureyev's tenure as the Opera's ballet director, he cast Dupond in leading roles in many of his own ballets, including Caliban in *The Tempest* (1984), Morris Townsend in *Washington Square* (1985), and the Prince in *Cinderella* (1986). Nevertheless, the two were natural rivals. During the years of Nureyev's directorship, the number of Dupond's annual performances fell from seventy to seventeen. Dupond responded by intensifying his guest appearances and forming a small group of his own in 1985, the year he assumed the status of guest artist at the Opera.

From 1988 to 1990, Dupond was director of Ballet-Théâtre Français de Nancy, bringing in a number of works by Ulysses Dove and other contemporary choreographers. In 1990, after Nureyev left the Opera, Dupond

DUPOND. With Ballet-Théâtre Français de Nancy, Dupond appeared in *Salomé,* choreographed by Maurice Béjart. (Photograph © 1990 by Johan Elbers; used by permission.)

was appointed his successor as artistic director, a position he held until 1995. During his tenure, the Paris Opera Ballet mounted works by Twyla Tharp, Jerome Robbins, and Martha Graham, among others. At Dupond's invitation, Millicent Hodson and Kenneth Archer staged a reconstruction of Nijinsky's *Till Eulenspiegel* for the company in 1994. After leaving the directorship, Dupond continued to appear at the Opera as a permanent guest artist.

BIBLIOGRAPHY
Flatow, Sheryl. "Enfant Terrible: Patrick Dupond of the Paris Opera Ballet." *Ballet News* (July 1983).
Pastori, Jean-Pierre. *Patrick Dupond, la Fureur de Danser.* Lausanne, 1982.
Stoop, Norma McLain. "Opera Étoile Patrick Dupond." *Dance Magazine* (July 1984).

FILM AND VIDEOTAPE.   *She Dances Alone,* television film, with Kyra Nijinsky, features Dupond in a performance of *Le Spectre de la Rose* (1980). *Petrushka,* Neumeier production, with Dupond in the title role (Delouche, 1981). *Dancing Machine,* a documentary (1990).

ANITA FINKEL

DUPORT FAMILY. French family of dancers. The most notable member was Louis-Antoine Duport, who gained fame as both a dancer and choreographer. His sister, Marie-Adélaïde Duport, danced in a number of roles in her brother's ballets.

Louis-Antoine Duport (born 1781 in Paris, died 19 October 1853 in Paris), dancer, choreographer, and director. Duport debuted in 1799 at the Théâtre de l'Ambigu-Comique with his sister Marie-Adélaïde in Louis-Jacques Milon's *Pygmalion*, which they also danced at the Paris Opera as guest artists.

In 1800 Duport was lead dancer at the Théâtre de la Gaîté, where Eugène Hus was the choreographer; at the Opera, he danced the role of Zephyr in *Psyché* in 1801 and performed in *Héro et Léandre* in 1803. He first came to public notice when he replaced Auguste Vestris in Pierre Gardel's *Le Retour de Zéphire*, initiating a famous rivalry. In Gardel's *Achille à Sycros* (1804) Vestris danced Ulysses and Duport was Aiace. Duport himself choreographed several ballet-pantomimes—*Acis et Galathée* (1805) and *Figaro*, also known as *Le Barbier de Séville*, and a *divertissement* called *L'Hymen de Zéphire, ou Le Volage Fixé* (1806).

In 1808 Duport left Paris with his mistress, the actress Mademoiselle George, and went to Saint Petersburg, stopping en route to dance *Figaro* in Vienna. Tolstoy mentioned Duport's success in *War and Peace*. He danced in Charles-Louis Didelot's *Zéphire et Flore* with Marie Danilova, *Amour et Psyché*, and *Almaviva et Rosine*, and collaborated with Didelot in *Les Amours de Vénus et Adonis, ou La Vengeance de Mars*. He choreographed *La Fête chez le Hobereau, Les Américains, ou L'Heureux Naufrage* (1809), *Mélora et Sulima, La Rose de Solange*, and *Le Troubadour* (all in 1810), and danced in Pierre Gardel's *Le Jugement de Pâris*. He also danced in Moscow before leaving Russia in 1812 for Vienna, where he directed and danced in numerous ballets at the Hof Theater; there he married the beautiful Therese Neumann, his favorite partner. In 1817 he went to Naples, and then to London and the King's Theatre. Here, after the success of his ballet *Zéphire* in 1819, he danced in such new works as *Adolphe et Mathilde, La Rose*, and *Les Ingénus*. He danced for the last time in Naples in 1820.

From 1821 to 1836, in partnership with the impresario Domenico Barbaja, Duport was director of the Kärntnertor Theater in Vienna, where Marie Taglioni and Fanny Elssler made their debuts as soloists in 1822. He was a candidate to become director of the Paris Opera in 1831, but Louis Véron was appointed instead. In 1836 he retired to Paris.

A small man with a lively and animated face, Duport amazed and charmed the public with his technique and his gifts of expression. "He amazes through his skill and his brilliance, his daring and his vivacity, his vigor and his flexibility; his performance is full of rapid and difficult movements, which he performs with infinite ease; he pirouettes endlessly and at such speed that the eye is dazzled," wrote Jean-Georges Noverre. Noverre did not admire Duport's choreography, but he did acknowledge the success of *Figaro* and Duport's skill in translating the spirit of Beaumarchais "by the variety and charms of dance." Noverre applauded Duport's animation in the leading role, danced with "every resource of his art and the gaiety of his animated pantomime." His extraordinary lightness fascinated writers. Stendhal compared him to a kitten and admired his passion, his effortless élan, and his soft landings. In *La danse, ou Les dieux de l'Opéra*, the poet Joseph de Berchoux compared the young Louis-Antoine Duport with the aging Vestris; he was winged and elusive, "like a faint shadow that causes a ray of light to vanish," presaging the Romantic ideal of flight that was to be immortalized by Jules Perrot and the great ballerinas of the nineteenth century.

Marie-Adélaïde Duport (also known as Madame Petit; fl. 1800), dancer. The sister of Louis-Antoine, she made her debut at the Paris Opera in September 1800. She danced various roles in her brother's ballets, including Rosina in *Figaro* and Flora in *L'Hymen de Zéphire*. Noverre described her as a small woman who "danced with infinite charm," but he believed that Louis-Antoine's choreography was beyond her powers. She appears to have lacked her brother's elevation, agility, and daring; Noverre felt she would have been at her best with "a type of dance that would be less turbulent, simpler, more gracious, more pleasant," that would do justice to her agreeable talent.

In 1808 Marie-Adélaïde married the dancer Baptiste Petit. She continued her career until 1820, under the name Madame Petit, in Russia, Austria, and Italy.

BIBLIOGRAPHY

Berchoux, Joseph de. *La danse, ou, Les dieux de l'Opéra*. Paris, 1806.

Brooks, Lynn Matluck. "A Decade of Brilliance: Dance Theatre in Late-Eighteenth-Century Philadelphia." *Dance Chronicle* 12.3 (1989): 333–365.

Chapman, John V. "Auguste Vestris and the Expansion of Technique." *Dance Research Journal* 19 (Summer 1987): 11–18.

Guest, Ivor. *The Romantic Ballet in Paris*. 2d rev. ed. London, 1980.

Harel, François A. *Dictionnaire théâtral*. 2d ed. Paris, 1825.

Kara-Murza, S.G. "Le danseur Duport en Russie." *Archives Internationales de la Danse* (January 1935): 3–6.

Lifar, Serge. *A History of Russian Ballet* (1950). Translated by Arnold L. Haskell. New York, 1954.

Moore, Lillian. "The Duport Mystery." *Dance Perspectives*, no. 7 (1960).

Moore, Lillian. "How Does the Researcher Get the Facts?" In *Conference on Research in Dance, 1st, Riverside, N.Y., 1967*. New York, 1968.

Noverre, Jean-Georges. *Lettres sur les arts imitateurs en général et sur la danse en particulier*. 2 vols. Paris, 1807. Edited by Fernand Divoire as *Lettres sur la danse et les arts imitateurs* (Paris, 1952).

Pastori, Jean-Pierre. *L'homme et la danse.* Fribourg, 1980.
Swift, Mary Grace. *A Loftier Flight: The Life and Accomplishments of Charles Louis Didelot.* Middletown, Conn., 1974.

JEANNINE DORVANE
Translated from French

DUPRÉ, LOUIS (born c.1690, died December 1774 in Paris), French dancer. According to the historian Émile Campardon, Louis Dupré was a member of the orchestra at the Théâtre de Rouen before beginning his climb to fame with the Paris Opera. In 1701 he danced in T. de Gatti's *Scylla,* Jean-Baptiste Lully's *Phaëton,* Jean-Féry Rebel's *Ulysse,* and probably André Campra's *Tancrède.* On 29 November 1714, he performed with Marie-Catherine André-Cardinal Guyot in Destouches's *Télémaque.*

From that time Dupré began to define his artistic personality. He appeared in *Amadis de Gaule* and *Acis et Galathée* (1718), Lully's *Thésée* (1720), Destouches's *Sémiramis* (1718), and Pascal Collasse's *Thétis et Pélée* (1723), in which he danced a pas de trois with Mademoiselle Delisle and David Dumoulin. He left the Paris Opera for several years and moved to London, where he may have been the "Mr. Dupré senior" who danced Mars in John Weaver's *Loves of Mars and Venus.* He presented a group of students at the Lincoln's Inn Fields, and also at theaters in Dresden and Warsaw.

Dupré subsequently returned to the Paris Opera as principal dancer, replacing Michel Blondy, who had been named ballet master in 1728. He created nearly forty roles in ballets by the leading musicians of the day—Lully, Campra, Jean-Joseph Mouret, Michel-Richard de Lalande, and Destouches—usually evoking heroes whose greatness was well served by his noble style. On 21 August 1731, Dupré danced a pas de deux with Marie Sallé in Campra's *Les Fêtes Vénitiennes.* This performance was followed on 5 June 1732 by a premiere with Sallé and Antoine Bandieri de Laval in Mouret's *Ballet des Sens,* and on 16 March 1733 by a pas de trois with Marie Camargo and Dumoulin in Lully's *Isis.* He also danced in Lalande and Destouches's *Les Éléments* (1734), Lully's *Persée* (1737), Campra's *Tancrède* (1738), Lully's *Amadis de Gaule* (1740), Rebel and François Francoeur's *Pyrame et Thisbé* (1740), and Lully's *Proserpine* (1741). In 1739 he replaced Blondy as ballet master.

As a teacher, Dupré passed on his fondness for exalted themes to his famous students Gaëtan Vestris and Jean-Georges Noverre. His choreography accorded great importance to the carriage of the arms. He created a number of ballets for the Collège Louis-le-Grand in Paris, including *Le Portrait du Grand Monarque* (1748), *Le Temple de la Fortune* (1750), *Le Génie* (1751), and *La Prospérité* (1755). He left the Paris Opera in 1751.

He surpassed his teacher, Louis Pecour, and became one of the most famous dancers of his time. He is sometimes called Dupré *l'aîné* ("the elder") to distinguish him from Jean-Denis Dupré, a dancer with the Paris Opera between 1730 and 1754, whom Noverre described as "another [Louis] Dupré, much smaller than he from every point of view." He was also known as *le grand* Dupré for both his talent and his height, and *le dieu de la danse* ("the god of dance"), a title subsequently usurped by his pupil Gaëtan Vestris. He was admired for his elegance and noble serenity, qualities heightened by the masks he wore and the immense curled wigs of his day.

Noverre provided a knowledgeable analysis of Dupré's technique. He noted that Dupré danced with his legs turned in and was slender, adroit, and skillful on pointe and in landing nimbly from leaps. Noverre also praised "the flexibility, softness, and gentleness that govern all his movements, the careful balance of his limbs," which combined to make "an admirable ensemble." He was at his best in slow and majestic dances such as *chaconnes* and *passacailles.* Noverre also lauded his deliberate tempo, which was emphasized by his graceful line and his skill.

He put beauty of movement before acrobatics, with a somewhat systematic regularity that Noverre considered somewhat excessive—"He did not vary his styles, he was always Dupré—but the "divine harmony" of his style enchanted his admirers. Giacomo Casanova saw him dance in *Les Fêtes Vénitiennes* in 1750, toward the end of his career: "I see a handsome figure advancing with measured steps. At the edge of the orchestra pit he slowly lifts his rounded arms, moves them gracefully, extends them fully, then draws them in, moves his feet, taking small steps followed by half-*battements* and then a pirouette, after which he withdraws into the wings." At the end of the second act "he moves toward the orchestra, and holds his torso (which is very finely shaped, I must admit) still for a second. Then I hear hundreds of low voices murmuring from the pit, 'Oh, look, look, he's extending, he's extending!'" In *La déclamation théâtrale* (1771), Claude Joseph Dorat praised in verse the sovereignty of an art in which the dancer rises above mortals. "When the great Dupré moved onto the stage with his proud walk, set off by his plume, it was like a god demanding an altar and mingling in the dances of mortals."

[*See also* Indes Galantes, Les.]

BIBLIOGRAPHY
Campardon, Émile. *L'Académie Royale de Musique au XVIIIe siècle.* 2 vols. Paris, 1884.
Casanova, Giacomo. *Mémoires.* 3 vols. Paris, 1960–1963.
Marsh, Carol G. "French Court Dance in England, 1706–1740: A Study of the Sources." Ph.D. diss., City University of New York, 1985.
Moore, Lillian. "The Great Dupré." *Dance Magazine* (June 1960): 40–42, 62–63.

Nettl, Paul. "Casanova and the Dance" (parts 1–2). *Dance Magazine* (August–September 1945).

Noverre, Jean-Georges. *Lettres sur les arts imitateurs en général et sur la danse en particulier.* 2 vols. Paris, 1807. Edited by Fernand Divoire as *Lettres sur la danse et les arts imitateurs* (Paris, 1952).

Winter, Marian Hannah. *The Pre-Romantic Ballet.* London, 1974.

JEANNINE DORVANE
Translated from French

DUPUY, DOMINIQUE AND FRANÇOISE (Dominique born 31 October 1930 in Paris; Françoise Michaud born 6 February 1925 in Lyon), husband and wife, French dancers and choreographers. Françoise, daughter of the art critic Marcel Michaud, in her formative years studied music, painting, theater, and dance. She received further training in classical dance with Nicholas Zvereff, and in modern dance with Jean Weidt, Jerome Andrews, and Merce Cunningham. She considers her own work to be within the Hellerau-Laxenburg tradition. In 1951 she married Dominique, who received classical training with Olga Preobrajenska and Nicholas Zvereff and studied modern dance with Jean Weidt (in whose company, Ballet des Arts, both he and Françoise danced), Helen McGehee, Jerome Andrews, and Merce Cunningham. He also studied jazz dance and mime.

Dominique and Françoise Dupuy's careers are closely linked. In 1951 they founded the first important professional modern dance company in France, Ballets Modernes de Paris, which did extensive tours with a varied repertory and lecture demonstrations. As choreographers, they collaborated with composers, writers, and painters to produce works of true originality with clean theatrical impact, helping to gain a serious reception for modern dance. A number of the best dancers in France were at one time or another members of the company, which disbanded in 1979 when Françoise and Dominique turned more to teaching. In 1962 the Dupuys founded the Festival des Baux-de-Provence, the dance department of the Museum of Modern Art, now defunct, and in 1969 Rencontres Internationales de Danse Contemporaine, which covered a multiplicity of activities—a professional training school in Paris, summer courses, seminars, and performances.

Together and separately, the Dupuys have choreographed for other companies and for the theater. Their major works for Ballets Modernes de Paris include, by Françoise, *Paso* (music by Maurice Ohana, 1955); by Dominique, *Visages de Femmes* (1974); and by both, *L'Âme et la Danse* (music by Coquelin, 1962), *The Miraculous Mandarin* (music by Béla Bartók, 1965), *Antigone* (music by Charpentier, 1968), and *Incantations* (music by André Jolivet, 1971). In 1981 they created independent hour-long solos that epitomized their respective qualities, Françoise

with *Ana Non* and Dominique with *Trajectoires* and *Ballum Circus.*

Several important choreographers have created dances for Françoise. Her refined technique and her immense powers as an actress have enabled her to be equally at ease in tragic, lyrical, and humorous parts. Her richness as an artist and her wide experience add to her capacities as a teacher much in demand.

As a dancer Dominique brought to their joint repertory a note of virtuosity, whimsicality, and humor. As a performer and teacher he has included among his concerns the study of the relationship between body and voice, and Japanese martial arts.

Today the multiple abilities of the Dupuys have been well employed by official organizations. In 1985 Françoise, at the request of Maurice Fleuret, became a member of the staff of the Direction de la Musique et de la Danse at the Ministry of Culture; she was promoted to *inspecteur principal* in 1987 and put in charge of issues concerning dance training. In 1990 she was made director of the dance department of the recently created Institut de Formation à l'Enseignement de la Danse et de la Musique (since 1996 known as the Centre National de la Danse). In 1989 Dominique was appointed *inspecteur principal* at the Délégation à la Danse of the Ministry of Culture; from 1991 to 1995 he was director of the dance department of the Institut de Pédagogie Musicale et Chorégraphique; and he remains an active freelance teacher and performer.

[*For related discussion, see* France, *article on* Modern Dance.]

BIBLIOGRAPHY

Baril, Jacques. *La danse moderne (d'Isadora Duncan à Twyla Tharp).* Paris, 1977.

Hersin, André-Philippe. "L'animation chorégraphique en milieu scolaire." *Saisons de la danse,* no. 210 (February 1990): 9–12.

Hersin, André-Philippe, and Olivier Marmin. "Françoise et Dominique racontent." *Saisons de la danse,* no. 231 (January 1992): 55–58.

Koegler, Horst. *The Concise Oxford Dictionary of Ballet.* New York, 1987.

Marsyas. Paris, 1989–. Edited by the Institut de Pédagogie Musicale et Chorégraphique.

Reyna, Ferdinando. "Françoise et Dominique." *La scala* (December 1962): 32–35.

Robinson, Jacqueline. *L'aventure de la danse moderne en France, 1920–1970.* Paris, 1990.

JACQUELINE ROBINSON

DURANG, JOHN (born 6 January 1768 in York, Pennsylvania, died 1822 in Philadelphia), American dancer. Durang was the first native-born American to become known as a dancer; during his career he was also a puppeteer, tightrope walker, circus clown, acrobat, designer, scene painter, choreographer, property man, equestrian performer, pyrotechnic display artist, and theater manager. He was the eldest of seven children born to Jacob Durang of Strasbourg, Alsace-Lorraine, and Mary Arten of Wissembourg, who both came to the United States in November 1767 and settled in York County, Pennsylvania. John Durang was not a highly skilled artist, but he exhibited a certain showmanship, which with the fact that he was an American made him a popular favorite. His career was inextricably woven into the fabric of early theater in America, affected by public and political attitudes about entertainment, by the influence of the colonial British, and by the Europeans who came after the American Revolution.

Durang had no formal dance training. Professional dance instructors were seldom available at that time, a result of negative public attitudes toward dance. Nonetheless, Durang was fascinated by the theater at a very early age. He recalled in his memoirs the first time he saw a hornpipe, which "charmed his mind" and drew him to learn the intriguing dance that later became his trademark. At fifteen he left his parents to accompany a performer from Pennsylvania to Boston. This initiation into a performer's life was followed by the beginning of a long association with Lewis Hallam, who in 1784 had been one of the first actors to return to the United States after the Revolutionary War. In 1785 Hallam engaged Durang for his small company, in which Durang danced between the acts, performing his hornpipe and "La Fricassée," a comedy number. The same season, John Durang made the acquaintance of a German dwarf named Hoffmaster, who composed a melody for him; the tune became famous as "Durang's Hornpipe" and has survived, along with a description of Durang's steps, in *The Ball-Room Bijou*, a pocket guide to social and theatrical dance published in Philadelphia in 1855 by Durang's son Charles.

Hallam's company, later named the Old American Company, alternated between the John Street Theatre in New York and the Southwark Theatre in Philadelphia, with brief excursions to Hartford, Lancaster, Harrisburg, and other cities. Around 1787, Durang married Mary McEwen, a dancer who had made her debut at the Southwark Theatre.

After the war and the repeal of anti-theater laws, European performers began to come to the United States. Durang's skills matured through his collaboration with such noted eighteenth-century choreographers as Alexandre Placide, Jean Baptiste Francisqui, James Byrne, and William Francis.

As a member of the Old American Company Durang worked with the Placides and Francisquy. From the Placides he acquired skills in acrobatics, tightrope walking, and classical ballet, and from Francisquy he learned the art of mime. During an association with Ricketts' Circus, he acquired further pantomime skills working with James Byrne, former ballet master at Sadler's Wells and

DURANG. A self-portrait of the American showman as depicted in his memoirs, in a *pas seul à Vestris* (solo in the style of Auguste Vestris). (Courtesy of the Historical Society of York County, Pennsylvania.)

Covent Garden in London. On 19 October 1796, Durang produced his first pantomime for Ricketts. He remained with the circus for several years, trying his hand at writing with *The Death of Miss McCrea*, scenery artistry in *The Battle of Trenton*, and production with *The Battle of the Kegs*, a pioneering attempt at introducing American themes.

In 1799 the circus was destroyed by fire, and Durang soon became a member of the stock company for the Chestnut Street Theatre, where he remained until the end of his career. Here he worked with William Francis, one of the foremost dance instructors of the time; Durang collaborated with him in teaching as well as staging ballets.

Durang was involved in many firsts in American theater and dance history. In 1794 he appeared in *Tammany*, one of the first operas written in America with an American subject. Shortly thereafter, he danced with Madame Gardie in *La Forêt Noire*, the first serious ballet given in America. He also toured actively throughout the summer. He and his wife and their numerous children traveled to towns around Philadelphia, presenting bits of plays, ballets, acrobatics, pantomimes, equestrian feats, and the ever-popular hornpipe. In addition to his dancing, Durang performed Shakespeare in German for the Pennsylvania German population in the Lancaster area. True to the spirit of the times, he was a showman in every sense, a jack-of-all-trades, appearing in makeshift performing environments such as barns and taverns, bringing his craft to eager audiences during the early years of American theater and dance. It was on one of these tours, in 1812, that his wife died. He survived her by ten years and died in Philadelphia in 1822.

BIBLIOGRAPHY

Downer, Alan S., ed. *The Memoir of John Durang, American Actor, 1785–1816*. Pittsburgh, 1966.

Moore, Lillian. "John Durang: The First American Dancer." *Dance Index* 1 (August 1942): 120–139.

ARCHIVE. Historical Society of York County, York, Pennsylvania.

BARBARA FERRERI MALINSKY

DURGALAL. Durgalal is one of the foremost dancers of the Jaipur school of *kathak*, a North Indian classical dance genre that features intricate footwork and rhythmic spinning. (Photograph by Avinash Pasricha; courtesy of Sunil Kothari.)

DURGALAL (born 9 September 1948 in Mahendragarh, Rajasthan; died 31 January 1990), Indian dancer and teacher. Durgalal was trained in the Jaipur *gharānā* style of *kathak* dance by his father, Pandit Omkarlal, a noted singer and musician in Rajasthan. He also studied under his elder brother Devilal, a gifted dancer, vocalist, and *pakhavaj* instrumentalist. The brothers performed together, displaying some of the best features of the Jaipur school.

Durgalal then joined Sri Ram Bharatiya Kala Kendra in New Delhi and studied further under the great master Sundarprasad, accumulating a large repertory. He specialized in Jaipur *gharānā kathak*, of which he was considered the finest exponent, noted for his graceful yet powerful style of movement. A handsome man, he exuded zest in executing difficult *nṛtta* techniques, such as *parans*, breathtaking *chakkars*, and pirouettes. Meticulous endings, flawless footwork, and brilliant technique were strong points in his performances. Trained as a musician and percussionist, he had an uncanny sense of *tāla* (time cycles) and *laya* (rhythm). He presented some group choreographic works at the Kalka Bindadin annual dance festivals in Delhi; however, it was his solos that dazzled audiences.

Durgalal passed on his vast repertory generously to his disciples. After leaving Sri Ram Bharatiya Kala Kendra, he taught at George Town in Guyana and at Dartington Hall in England. On his return to India, he founded his own school; later he joined Kathak Kendra, training young dancers in the Jaipur *gharānā*.

Durgalal was at the height of his career when he died of a heart attack during a performance at a Lucknow dance festival. He is survived by his wife Bala and by a daughter, Nupoor, and a son, who are also dancers. Among his students, Harish Rawat, Urmila Dogra, Rakhi Badal Dhir, and Jayant Kastuar promise to carry on his legacy. Durgalal's dancing was recorded in a film series made by Prakash Jha for the Festival of India; in addition, the Central Sangeet Natak Akademi archives include videotapes of selections from his repertory.

BIBLIOGRAPHY

Kothari, Sunil. *Kathak: Indian Classical Dance Art*. New Delhi, 1989.

Misra, Susheela. *Some Dancers of India*. New Delhi, 1992.

SUNIL KOTHARI

DUTCH NATIONAL BALLET. Also known as Het Nationale Ballet, the Dutch National Ballet was formed in 1961 from the fusion of Sonia Gaskell's Netherlands Ballet (established in 1954) with Mascha ter Weeme's Amsterdam Ballet (formed in 1959). As the largest Dutch dance company, the ballet is subsidized mainly by the national government and its home city of Amsterdam. In the 1980s

DUTCH NATIONAL BALLET. Members of the company in Rudi van Dantzig's *Vier Letzte Lieder* (Four Last Songs; 1977), set to the music of Richard Strauss. (Photograph by Jorge Fatauros; from the Dance Collection, New York Public Library for the Performing Arts.)

the company had more than 135 members, including 80 dancers.

Sonia Gaskell was the first artistic director, from 1961 to 1968. She was assisted initially by Mascha ter Weeme, who took special responsibility for the subdivision that danced in productions staged by the Netherlands Opera Foundation; ter Weeme left the company after one year. From 1965 until her retirement in 1968, Gaskell was assisted artistically by Rudi van Dantzig and Robert Kaesen. Van Dantzig took over artistic direction in 1968, assisted at first by Kaesen (until 1970) and then by Benjamin Harkarvy (1970–1971).

From 1971 to 1991, the Dutch National Ballet was led by van Dantzig, who continued Gaskell's artistic policy, at least in principle. In 1991, van Dantzig left the company and artistic leadership was taken by Wayne Eagling, a former principal dancer with the Royal Ballet. The Dutch National Ballet's self-imposed task has been twofold: continuing the presentation of valuable older ballets of international merit, and performing contemporary ballets created specifically for the company. The repertory rests on three pillars: historical ballets, especially nineteenth-century Romantic classics and Michel Fokine's ballets; the contemporary world repertory, including more than twenty George Balanchine works; and the works of contemporary Dutch choreographers.

With its concentration on contemporary ballet, the Dutch National Ballet has one of the oldest and largest collections of Balanchine productions in the world. Other contributions from abroad have included *Aureole* (Paul

Taylor), *The Dream* (Frederick Ashton), *The Witch Boy* (Jack Carter), *Symphony for Fun* (Michael Charnley), *Symphonie Concertante* (Michel Descombey), *The Snow Queen* (Ronald Hynd), *La Sylphide* (Harald Lander), *Aimez-vous Bach?* (Brian Macdonald), *Time Out of Mind* (Macdonald), *Caprichos* (Herbert Ross), *The Prisoner of the Caucasus* (George Skibine), *Arcade* (John Taras), and *Dark Elegies* (Antony Tudor).

In the 1960s the principal contemporary Dutch choreographers were van Dantzig and Kaesen; the 1970s saw the celebrated trio of van Dantzig, Hans van Manen (beginning in 1973), and Toer van Schayk (beginning in 1971), whose different approaches added to the repertory's rich variety. Thanks to them, the Dutch National Ballet has played an important role in the renewal of academic ballet by combining classical and modern dance techniques.

The Dutch National Ballet's interest in modern dance was apparent when it became one of the first companies to revive Kurt Jooss's *The Green Table* in 1965; it also attracted such American modern dancers as Pearl Lang (for example, in *Shirah*) and Lar Lubovitch (*Clear Lake, Dark Woods*). The company also experimented with the Polish mime artist Henryk Tomaszewski in his early efforts to synthesize pantomime and ballet. The most experimental work has been contributed by Dutch modern dancer Koert Stuyf.

Among the leading ballet masters have been Karel Shook, Roland Casenave, Harkarvy, and several Russian guests in the 1960s; and Ivan Kramar, Reuven Voremberg, and Christine Anthony in the 1970s. The first generation

DUTCH NATIONAL BALLET. *(left)* Caroline Sayo Iura and Robert Bell in Hans van Manen's *Trois Gnossiennes* (1992). *(right)* Boris de Leeuw, Coleen Davis, and Jahn Magnus Johansen in the company's 1994 production of Glen Tetley's *Voluntaries*. (Photographs by Deen van Meer; used by permission.)

of soloists included Peter Appel, Sonja van Beers, Maria Bovet, Sylvester Campbell, Marianna Hilarides, Philip Kaesen, Leonie Kramer, Astrid Liefting, Clazina Nepveu, Panchita de Péri, Ben de Rochemont, Ronald Snijders, Maria Sylvaine, Chris Torenbosch, Irène de Vos, Conrad van de Weetering (who became a well-known dance publicist), and Billy Wilson.

Prominent Dutch National Ballet dancers of the 1960s were Simon André, Jan Arntz, Benjamin Feliksdal, Robert Fisher, Jessica Folkerts, Olga de Haas, Maria Koppers, Toer van Schayk, Kathleen Smith, Yvonne Vendrig, René Vincent, and Reuven Voremberg. The 1970s brought new soloists such as Maria Aradi, Laurel Benedict, Han Ebbelaar, Clint Farha, Henny Jurriëns, Sonja Marchiolli, Zoltan Peter, Alexandra Radius, Monique Sand, Francis Sinceretti, and Jeanette Vondersaar. New principal dancers during the 1980s included Fred Berlips, Coleen Davis, Lindsay Fischer, Alan Land, Robert Machherndl, Zoltán Solymosi, and Joanne Zimmerman. During the 1990s, principal dancers included Caroline Sayo Iura, Larissa Lezhnina, Jane Lord, Anna Seidl, Alexander Gouliaev, Jahn Magnus Johansen, and Boris de Leeuw.

The repertory continues to include classics such as *Giselle* (1977) and *The Sleeping Beauty* (1981), both staged by Peter Wright; *Swan Lake* (1988), staged by Rudi van Dantzig; and a completely revised version of *The Nutcracker*, set by Toer van Schayk and retitled *The Nutcracker and the Mouse King* (1996). Prominent modern

dance and experimental choreographers such as Carolyn Carlson, Jan Fabre, Édouard Lock, and Maguy Marin have also created works.

Works premiered by the company have included Kaesen's *Kringloop* (Cycle; 1962) and *You Can't Always Get What You Want* (1970); Pearl Lang's *Persephone* (1963); Sonia Gaskell's *De Spiegel* (The Mirror; 1964); Victor Jilek's *Don Juan* (1965); Henryk Tomaszewski's *De Stier* (The Bull; 1965); versions of *Swan Lake* by Igor Belsky (1965) and Zoltan Previl (1973); Koert Stuyf's *Visibility . . . by Chance* (1967) and *Mutation* (1968); Conrad Drzewiecki's restaging of *The Sleeping Beauty* (1968); and Harkarvy's *Contrasten* (1971). Wayne Eagling's works include *Frankenstein, the Modern Prometheus* (1993), set to music by Vangelis; *Symphony in Waves* (1994), to music by A. J. Kernis; and *Duet* (1995), to music by Richard Wagner.

[*See* Netherlands, *article on* Theatrical Dance since 1945; Netherlands Ballet; *and the entries on Dantzig, Gaskell, and Weeme.*]

BIBLIOGRAPHY

Fatauros, Jorge. "Choreographic Portraits." *Ballett International* 11 (June–July 1988): 18–27.

Loney, Glenn. "Evolution of an Ensemble." *Dance Magazine* (March 1974): 34–39.

Merrett, Sue. "Dutch National Ballet at the Crossroads." *The Dancing Times* (June 1991): 852–854.

Schaik, Eva van. *Op gespannen voet: Geschiedenis van de Nederlandse theaterdans vanaf 1900.* Haarlem, 1981.

Utrecht, Luuk. *Het Nationale Ballet 25 jaar: De Geschiedenis van Het Nationale Ballet van 1961 tot 1986.* Amsterdam, 1987.

Utrecht, Luuk. *Rudi van Dantzig: A Controversial Idealist in Ballet.* Zutphen, 1992.

Weetering, Conrad van de, and Luuk Utrecht. *Sonia Gaskell.* Zutphen, 1976.

LUUK UTRECHT

DYING SWAN, THE. Ballet solo. Choreography: Michel Fokine. Music: Camille Saint-Saëns. Costume: Léon Bakst. First performance: 22 December [4 January] 1907, Maryinsky Theater, Saint Petersburg. Dancer: Anna Pavlova.

The Dying Swan, Anna Pavlova's most famous role, is perhaps the most famous ballerina solo ever created. For people who are only casually acquainted with ballet, this work has come to symbolize the art. The first documented performance, under the title *The Swan,* occurred at a charity concert by the opera choir at the Maryinsky Theater in 1907. The choreographer, Michel Fokine, drew his inspiration from "Le Cygne," a section of Saint-Saëns's *Carnaval des Animaux,* and choreographed the work in less than half an hour, working directly with Pavlova.

The subject of this dance, which soon came to be known as *The Dying Swan,* is the longing for immortality expressed by the futile struggles of a dying swan to achieve freedom in a last flight. The movement of a swan gliding on the water is suggested by a continuous stream of *bourrées,* while the arms overhead, tensed and constrained, beat spasmodically. At the end the dancer lowers herself onto one knee, hands folded above her bowed head, as death triumphs on the final tremolo.

Fokine saw this dance as an early application of his reformist principles, reflected in its poetic appeal to the emotions and in its equal use of the upper and lower body in movement and expressive capacity. The choreographer claimed that this work was a paradigm for his new ballet in its combination of technique and expressiveness (*Dance Magazine,* August 1931).

Designed to suit the thin, fragile frame and tragic temperament of Pavlova, the solo was certainly as much her creation as it was Fokine's. Her image as the swan, in a white tutu designed by Léon Bakst, permeated Western culture. *The Dying Swan* became her signature piece, remaining in her repertory until her death in 1931. The dance has defied identification with its other notable interpreters, such as Alicia Markova, Galina Ulanova, Maya Plisetskaya, Natalia Makarova, Galina Mezentseva, and Susan Jaffe; perhaps only Ulanova created a critically satisfying interpretation.

A film of Pavlova dancing the role was made in Hollywood in 1924. In 1925 Fokine published an account of *The Dying Swan,* explaining exactly how the dance should be performed.

[*See also the entry on Pavlova.*]

BIBLIOGRAPHY
Fokine, Michel. *The Dying Swan.* New York, c.1925.
Lazzarini, John, and Roberta Lazzarini. *Pavlova: Repertoire of a Legend.* New York, 1980.
Levinson, André. *Ballet Old and New.* Translated by Susan Cook Summer, New York, 1982.
Money, Keith. *Pavlova: Her Art and Life.* New York, 1982.
Reynolds, Nancy, and Susan Reimer-Torn. *Dance Classics.* Pennington, N.J., 1991.
Ries, Frank W.D. "Rediscovering Pavlova's Dances." *Ballet Review* 11 (Winter 1984): 71–85.

FILM.   *Theatrical and Social Dancing in Film, 1909–1936,* Dance Collection, New York Public Library for the Performing Arts.
                                                    SUZANNE CARBONNEAU

DYK, PETER VAN (also spelled van Dijk; born 21 August 1929 in Bremen), German dancer and choreographer. Van Dyk studied dance in Berlin with Tatjana Gsovsky, then in Paris with Boris Kniaseff and Serge Lifar, for whom he performed. He was a soloist with the East Berlin Opera from 1946 to 1950, and then with the Municipal Opera of West Berlin.

As a soloist and choreographer with the Wiesbaden Opera in 1951, he created his first version of *Pelléas et Mélisande* (music by Arnold Schoenberg) and *Third Symphony* (music by Hans Werner Henze). With the Janine Charrat Ballets from 1952 to 1954, he evoked a triumphant and revolutionary romanticism in *Les Algues.* As *premier danseur étoile* with the Paris Opera from 1955 to 1970, he served the repertory remarkably well, particularly in two significant works by Lifar, *Chemin de Lumière* and *Les Noces Fantastiques.* He danced in *Swan Lake* with Vladimir Burmeister's choreography, which had not previously been performed at the Opera, and aroused enthusiasm in George Balanchine's *The Four Temperaments.*

At the same time, van Dyk was establishing his career as a choreographer. *Unfinished Symphony* (1957), *Pièce Chorégraphique* (music by Carl Maria von Weber, 1959), and *La Peau de Chagrin* (music by Simon Semenoff, 1960) attracted attention. After his *Pelléas* (second version), *Turangalîla* (music by Olivier Messiaen), and *Romeo and Juliet* were presented at the Hamburg Opera, he was named dance director there in 1962. From then until 1970 he produced a steady flow of creations, including *Sinfonia* (music by Dmitri Shostakovich), *The Firebird* (music by Igor Stravinsky), *Abraxas* (music by Werner Egk), *Poème* (music by Schoenberg), *Cinderella* (music by Sergei Prokofiev), and *Pinocchio* (music by Bibalo). After 1970 he devoted himself entirely to choreography. With the Ballet Royal de Wallonie he presented *Suite Lyrique* (music by Alban Berg). He spent some time in Hanover in 1973, then moved on to the Ballet du Rhin in Strasbourg (1974–1978), where he staged *Idéal* and *Suite de Danses* (music by Béla Bartók), *Vingt-quatre Préludes* (music by Marius Constant), and *Les Métaboles* (music by Henri Dutilleux). He was dance director at the Grand Théâtre de Genève from 1978 to 1980, where he presented *À la*

Mémoire d'un Ange (music by Berg) and *Manon* (music by Mozart). Beginning in 1981 he managed the Bonn Ballet, where he presented a new version of *Romeo and Juliet* and an adaptation of *The Sleeping Beauty;* at the associated experimental theater he presented *Variations Diabelli* (music by Beethoven) and *Gelobt Sei* (music by Roeder), inspired by Saint Francis of Assisi. The Zagreb, Sofia, and Athens operas have staged his ballets.

Both van Dyk's dancing and his choreography reveal his exacting nature and sensitivity. Purity of style determines his totally controlled language, in which the grace of an *épaulement,* the beauty of a *port de bras,* precision of *batterie,* clarity of pirouettes, and the dissolve that links one movement with another, rival each other for attention. His harmonious rigor ennobled the academic technique of *Études,* and his dramatic presence stamped works in which the human being expresses his anxieties—faced with madness in *Les Algues,* a pitiful toy of destiny in *Petrouchka,* a haunting phantom in *Les Noces Fantastiques.* Van Dyk's lyricism magnified the evocation of *Les Sylphides* and the intangible dream of *Giselle,* transmuted into poetry. An exceptional musicality governs his dancing and inspires his ballets. *Unfinished Symphony,* created for Jacqueline Rayet and himself, is broad, flexible, and vigorous, with flawless visual music and inexpressible emotion born of pure movement. Next to his logical and subtle narrative ballets, van Dyk prefers works whose abstract form reflects lyrical inspiration: *Poème,* a mysterious evocation of love; *Turangalîla,* a festival of the intellect; and *Suite Lyrique,* an exaltation of living classicism. He initiates choreographic composition after attentive listening to the scores. The concentration and diversity of Bartók's rhythms require endless innovation in dance; Mozart's joy and elegance, melodic scope, and somber consciousness of death are translated as well. The sonorous universe of Dutilleux is reflected in mysterious blossomings, gratuitous and necessary acts, and transformations of gesture. Berg inspires a solid and cautious architecture, movements that dissolve as soon as they have begun, and an infinite danced line interrupted by desperate violence. Van Dyk's originality is not expressed in novelty; rather, it resides in subtle inflections that unite and metamorphose movements.

The complexity of his choreography is concealed behind the appearance of ease he demands of his dancers. His instruction is supplemented by the performance of masterpieces in the repertory and lightened by elements foreign to dance. Anxious to expand the language of his performers, he brought in guest choreographers, including Balanchine and Lifar, and some stars, including Maria Tallchief and Nina Vyroubova, without diminishing the importance of dancers who have been discovered through his work—for example, Claire Feranne and Martial Bockstaele.

Peter van Dyk has won several prizes to crown his career of intense devotion to dance. He won the Critics' Prize in Germany and France for *Unfinished Symphony;* the Nijinsky Prize in 1959; the Gold Star for the most lyrical couple (with Maria Tallchief) for *Poème* at the Festival de Paris (1965); and the Prize of the Université de la Danse in 1979 for *A la Mémoire d'un Ange.*

BIBLIOGRAPHY

Dorvane, Jeannine. "Van Dyk." *Les Saisons de la Danse* (January 1969).

Dyk, Peter van. "Das Ballet." In *Theater bei Tageslicht,* edited by Jacob Hegner. Cologne, 1966.

JEANNINE DORVANE
Translated from French

E

EAST AFRICA. *See* Central and East Africa.

EASTER ISLAND. *See* Rapanui. *See also* Chile, *article on* Traditional Dance *and* Polynesia.

ECK, IMRE (born 2 December 1930 in Budapest), Hungarian dancer and choreographer. A pupil of Ferenc Nádasi, Eck became a member of the Budapest Opera Ballet in 1947 and was a soloist from 1950 until 1960. His first choreography for the Budapest Ballet was *Csonger and Tünde* (1959), based on a philosophical poem by Mihált Vörösmarty and set to Leó Weiner's music.

In 1960 Eck founded Ballet Sopianae at Pécs in southern Hungary, employing graduates of the State Ballet Institute. Eck had no stylistic precursors in Hungary and had not seen any modern ballets abroad, so he had to rely on his own inventiveness in molding a choreographic idiom to suit his new messages. Never denying classical technique as a foundation, he made excursions into the static world of postures and intercepted movements; his works had a strong pictorial quality. He toyed with contrasting dance and music and used symbols and a vocabulary drawing on acrobatics, jazz, and pantomime.

In the first two years at Pécs, Eck produced fourteen ballets, nearly all to music by young Hungarian composers. His *Variations on an Encounter* (1961, music by Tihamér Vujicsics) began a series of works addressing juvenile problems of choosing, of happy meetings and sorrowful partings; it was followed by *Spider's Web* (1962, music by László Gulyás) a ballet in the vertical dimension, danced on a steel framework, about a man trapped by two female spiders. *Ballad of Horror* (1961, music by Sánder Szokolay), a triumph of cruelty, was the first of his antiwar ballets, conceived in a naturalistic idiom; András Szöllősy's *I Lived in Those Days* (1962) proclaimed the ethical purity of the victims of wartime torture in an abstract style, and the Czech composer Viliam Bukovy's *As Commanded* (1962) depicted the guilty remorse of the pilot who dropped the first atomic bomb. In Frigyes Hidas's *Concerto to the Rainbow* (1961), White, as an absence of all color, defeats Black in concerted action. Eck's first his-

torical ballet, *Peasant Revolt of 1514* (1961, music by György Ránki), was designed in black and white, with simple stylized movements and sticks as multipurpose props. His *Miners' Ballad* (1962, music by Rudolf Maros), depicts the human struggle with nature.

Eck's series of abstract or plotless works was launched by *Études No. 2* (1962, music by François Couperin) in groups moving on platforms of different levels, and by *Études in Blue* (1964, music by Henry Purcell), consisting of three duets moving from orthodox academicism to a free handling of forms. The year 1965 was marked by five "miniatures" (five- to ten-minute sketches), including Emil Petrovic's *Passacaglia*, about the struggle with loneliness, alienation, and self-discipline, and György Kurtág's *Improvization and Aria*, about the power of generosity and unselfishness. This was also Eck's Bartók year: he staged the *Miraculous Mandarin* with himself in the title role, creating a vast canvas of human willpower in an idiom close to pantomime; *Concerto* was a visual counterpart of the music, with many colorful props; and *The Wooden Prince* was a revised revival of the previous year's premiere on the Szeged open-air stage. Eck's first full-evening ballet, Christoph Willibald Gluck's *Don Juan* (1966), and the exotic folklore of *Descent to Hell* (music by Franz Schubert) were uncharacteristic of his work.

In 1968, Eck ceded the directorship of the company to Sándor Tóth and became its artistic director. After a two-year interval, again inspired by Hungarian composers, he approached folklore in Zoltán Kodály's *Summer Evening* (1970), a village scene stylized in white, and Leó Weiner's *Hungarian Dolls* (1971), in which figures from a market stall come alive. Eck next explored the impact of power on people, as in László Lajtha's *Bonds* (1971), in which an animal-trainer cruelly triumphs over a vixen's love of her mate. He staged different aspects of the man-and-woman relationship: for example, Kodály's *Sonata* (1972) shows the daily bickering of a couple who know each other too well and have lived together too long, all in a humorous vein. Franz Liszt's *Faust Symphony* (1973) closed this Hungarian period with a powerful overview of the ups and downs of life in a highly artistic tableau, precursor of comprehensive, large-scale one-act ballets.

Spring 1975 was an evening of dances to Soviet music. Another evening program, *Brooding over This and That*

(1976), included nine miniatures of striking diversity, this time in silence, with music only during the intervals.

In following years Eck returned to painterly compositions characterized by synthesis, complexity of forms, and theatrical syncretism, including a wide range of musical styles, recitals in prose, and a diversity of visual environments. The most important examples of this trend are his dances set to Giuseppe Verdi's *Requiem* (1976), Eck's messages about death and life in a summary of his choreographic vocabulary; dances to Ludwig van Beethoven's sixth and seventh symphonies (1978) are rich in scenes of poetic beauty and dramatic power; those to Carl Orff's *Carmina Burana*, a variegated, colorful medieval merrymaking (1978); to Emil Petrovic's *Salome* (1980), scenes from the Bible in a combination of dance and pantomime; to Rudolf Maros's *Euphony* (1982), a trilogy of the soft female and the firm male principles combined in an encounter in subdued colors. *Dirge for a Bull* (1982), to György Kósa's *Cantata*, is a cavalcade of theatrical devices as a eulogy of the victimized; a dance to Johann Sebastian Bach's *Passion According to Saint Matthew* (1983) is a nightmare-like sequence of frantic images. Gluck's three-act *Don Juan* (1986) was revived after twenty years without sensational accessories, but rather as a personal confession. *Terror* (1987) to Vivaldi and Coptic music, shows the ethically and psychologically distorted relationships between torturers and tortured. *Blue Ballet* (1987) is a cavalcade of parapsychological happenings.

Another trend, perhaps in continuation of the miniatures or of the duet to Kodály's *Sonata*, was the series of mini-ballets that resumed in 1979 with the four-part *Song of Songs*, to the recital of the corresponding text from the Bible. Such works are meant to be performed in a small setting, close to the audience and without any stage, or else in the open, in a park, or in ruins of old castles; they rarely feature more than four dancers. Some of these are Verdi's *Otello* (1980), *Csángó Ballad* (folk music, 1981), *Violin Duos* (1981, music by Bartók), *Lot's Daughters* (1982, music by Károly Goldmark), the *Diamond Bird* (1983, music by the East Ensemble), and Béla Szakcsi Lakatos's *Danaides* (1963). Further chamber-size works are *Entropy* (1984), inspired by Thomas Pynchon's short story, to music by the Pastoral Ensemble; and *Nymphet* (1989) to a musical montage, telling of the duality of womanhood and maidenhood.

Eck was the artistic director of the annual Pécs Summer Festival since it began in 1978. He choreographed *Orpheus and Eurydice* (music by Franz Joseph Haydn) in 1967 for the British Minerva Ballet, Bartók's *The Wooden Prince* for a Boston company in 1969, and Hans Werner Henze's *Ondine* in Belgrade in the same year. In Helsinki he choreographed Jean Sibelius's *Tempest* (1974) and *Kalevala* (1976) and Bartók's *The Miraculous Mandarin* (1982). He has more than a hundred choreographies to

his credit but withdrew in the early 1990s owing to illness. His awards include the Liszt Prize (1962), Merited Artist (1970), the Kossuth Prize (1978), and Eminent Artist (1987).

[*See also* Ballet Sopianae.]

BIBLIOGRAPHY

Dienes, Gedeon P. "A Pécsi Balett reperteárjának koreográfiai elemzése." *Tánctudományi tanulmányok* (1967–1968): 7–28.

Dienes, Gedeon P., and Lívia Fuchs, eds. *A Színpadi tánc történeté Magyarországon*. Budapest, 1989.

Franks, A. H. "Young Hungarians." *The Dancing Times* (May 1963): 462–464.

Kaposi, Edit, and Ernő Pesovár, eds. *The Art of Dance in Hungary*. Translated by Lili Halápy. Budapest, 1985.

Peters, Kurt. "Interbalett '79 in Budapest." *Das Tanzarchiv* 27 (April 1979): 183–194.

GEDEON P. DIENES

ÉCOSSAISE, French for "Scottish," was a *contredanse* of French or German origin for four or more couples, danced to music in 2/4 time and based on actual or simulated Scottish airs. It was popular in Europe during the first two decades of the nineteenth century but was little known in Scotland.

The nineteenth-century *écossaise* was not the same as the *écosse* of the sixteenth century or the schottische of the mid-nineteenth century. It was part of a vogue for Scottish Highland music and dance that spanned several centuries, during a period when Scotland was politically and culturally allied with France against England.

Thoinot Arbeau's *Orchesography* (1589) describes two *bransles d'Écosse* (Scottish *branles*) known in France around 1568. Though not obvious in the music Arbeau gives, the Scottish association appears to lie in the *pied (en l'air) croissé* (one foot raised and crossed over the other leg). Whether Scottish or not, the *bransles d'Écosse* passed out of fashion along with other *branles* in the mid-seventeenth century.

The nineteenth-century *écossaise* used versions of the Scottish *strathspey* and *kemshoole* steps along with the *pas de basque* and *enchaînements* of three *chassés, jeté,* and *assemblé*. The *strathspey* and *kemshoole*, when combined with the newly introduced principle of revolving by couples, contributed directly to the development of the schottische and the polka.

Scottish music grew in popularity in the early nineteenth-century Romantic period, in part because the rebellious spirit of the Highland appealed to the Romantic sensibility combined with a new internationalism. The *écossaise*, more as a concept than as an original dance, found ready acceptance when introduced into such an ambience.

No less a master than Ludwig van Beethoven was attracted to the Scottish spirit, composing twelve *écossaises* in 1807 (for two violins, and for bass, two flutes, and two horns) and another in 1810, as well as musical settings for the songs of Robert Burns. Franz Schubert wrote eight *écossaises* in 1817 for piano and another set in 1823 and 1824. Interest in the Scottish mystique was made evident in Sir Walter Scott's poems and novels; in the popular new quadrille "The Caledonians," based on medleys of Scottish airs; and in Gaetano Donizetti's operas *Maria Stuarda* and *Lucia di Lammermoor* (both 1835).

Typically, many *contredanse* figures, such as Le Moulinet, the Hay, the English Chain, and versions of the Triumph and the Graces (in which one man dances with two women), were paired together in eight-measure phrases to form an *écossaise*.

The *écossaise* passed from favor by the 1820s. Supplanted by the quadrille, waltz, and polka, there followed a general decline in *contredanses*—the *écossaise* in particular.

[*For general discussion of nineteenth-century social dance, see* Social Dance.]

BIBLIOGRAPHY
Arbeau, Thoinot. *Orchesography* (1589). Translated by Mary Stewart Evans. New York, 1948.
Compan, Charles. *Dictionnaire de danse*. Paris, 1787.
Emmerson, George S. *A Social History of Scottish Dance*. London, 1972.
Lauchery, Herrn. "Gesellschaftliche Taenze." In *Taschenbuch zum Gefelligen Vergnügen*, edited by W. G. Becker. Leipzig, 1821.
Peacock, Francis. *Sketches Relative to the History and Theory but More Especially to the Practice and Art of Dancing*. Aberdeen, 1805.
Richardson, Philip J. S. *The Social Dances of the Nineteenth Century in England*. London, 1960.

DESMOND F. STROBEL

ECUADOR. Before the Spanish conquest of 1531, the Ecuadorean chiefdoms had been subjects of the Inca Empire for only a few decades, and the Ecuadorean ceremonial center of Quito had become the Inca capital of their northern province; Quechua, the Inca language, was in general use there. The Spanish refounded Quito as a Roman Catholic city in 1534, and Spanish land grants included total control over the indigenous peoples living on the land as long as they were Christianized. Many were converted and worked the land as serfs, but many also fled, fought, or died of epidemics and maltreatment; some retreated to Amazonia, the rain forest on the eastern side of the Andes. Simón Bolívar's independence movement against Spain was successful for Ecuador in 1822, although until 1830 it was part of Gran Colombia—a federation of Colombia, Venezuela, and Ecuador. Independence did not change the social order. Today, the population of some ten million are about 15 percent of European ancestry, 40 percent Native American (of which about half speak only native languages, including Quechua), 40 percent *mestizos* (part European and part Native American), and 5 percent of African ancestry. The majority are Spanish-speaking Roman Catholics, although indigenous and syncretic rituals continue in the Andean farming villages and in Amazonia.

Dance among the indigenous peoples of Andean Ecuador prior to colonization by Spain was associated with festivals, many of which were influenced by the practices of the Inca Empire and its courts. These festivals have been to some extent syncretized with both Roman Catholic celebrations and European dances. A second indigenous dance tradition in Ecuador is that of Amazonia, from the southeastern rain forests, where many ritual dances have been recorded.

Spanish chroniclers of the sixteenth century recorded four principal ritual occasions in Inca tradition. The Festival of the Sun (Raymi) was celebrated in Quito with great solemnity. Celebrants climbed to a nearby summit to watch the sunrise, playing instrumental dance music as the first rays broke through. Rituals were also held to initiate members of the nobility into warrior status; their ears were pierced, they were adorned with flowers, and they were given a yellow tassel. A related event, the Festival of Purifications, required that men fast and perform cleansing rituals. Finally, the Festival of Thanksgiving was held after the corn sprouted to honor the coming harvest; in it, people wearing elaborate bracelets, breastplates, and crowns danced to instrumental music.

Mimetic magical dance played an important role in the life of the Amazonian Shuar and Achuar peoples, speakers of Jivaroan languages. The Snake Dance was performed to follow the curing of a snake-bitten person by a shaman. [*See* Shamanism.] Once the cure had been accomplished, village members celebrated with a ritual festival. Adorned with feather crowns and neck ornaments, and carrying rattles and other instruments, dancers congregated at the house of a leader to hear the shaman guarantee the health of the patient. They then performed a dance imitating the events from the snakebite to the curing.

The Shuar and Achuar, who were hereditary enemies, used to sacrifice captured chiefs and shrink their heads. The prepared head was then displayed on a lance in the middle of the village. A singer *(ujaja)* chanted an account of the victory; a master of ceremonies *(wea)* directed the ritual; and warriors danced around the head.

Two agricultural festivals were recorded for the Shuar. The first, called Uwi Ijiambratei ("harvesting of fruits"), celebrates the ripening of the *tucuma* fruit and the beginning of the Shuar annual cycle. Dancers in ordinary attire mime the planting, growth, flowering, and ripening of the *tucuma*. A feast follows. The second is related to *yuca*, a tuber that is the mainstay of the Shuar diet and the source of a fermented beverage. Much like the *tucuma* festival.

the dance relates the growth cycle of *yuca* and the production of the beverage. Each of these Shuar festivals lasts for two weeks.

In the Hispanized villages of highland Ecuador one may observe several types of syncretic dances embodying both Inca and Spanish influences. As in much of Latin America, these dances are to some extent narrative and are performed in a religious context. The Danza del Abago involves dancers representing two angels and two devils (*abagos*), with one musician. The performance begins with a procession, followed by the *poroto-mayto* (a dance miming the agricultural cycle); next is the *largo*, a ritual performance; and finally the *yumbo*, which is believed to be derived from sacrificial rites to the sun god. The Danza del Abago has many variations.

The Danza de los Abagos de Cumbas is more elaborate. It is led by captains (*chaquis*), who dress elegantly, and danced by twelve *yumbos* wearing white and carrying *tucuma* spears, as well as a *sara-ñusta* in traditional regional costume. Its dance segments are the *poroto-mayto*, or agricultural mime; the *suche*, an imitation of a crippled person; the *tzagna*, performed with the feet tied together; the *obelo*, in which the mouth is covered; the *pilis-aspi*, which imitates the galloping of a horse; the *asúa-ufiay*, in which a wooden cup filled with *yuca* beverage is held as the dancer performs with his hands behind his back and his legs apart; and the *urcu-cayay*, an invocation to the mountains.

The Fiesta de Pendones (Festival of Banners) is said to derive from an ancient practice of suspending slain enemies from poles as a warning. It is organized by a Roman Catholic religious brotherhood, under the direction of a *prioste* ("steward"), who appoints members to sponsor the festival and carry out all the necessary tasks. The *prioste* himself handles food and beverage preparation and builds an arch indicating that the festival is to be held; he acquires prestige through these acts. The dances are full of splendor and beauty.

Brotherhoods also sponsor the Corazas, a festival commemorating the sun god and his avatar, the last Inca ruler Atahualpa. The *prioste* appoints a staff to carry out the tasks. The central figure, the *coraza*, performs a dance called *churay* on the eve of the festival. The next day he is dressed in an elaborate costume based on that of Atahualpa. The group dances begin with the preparation of *chicha* (a fermented beverage) and end with an expression of thanks to the staff. The celebrations go on for two weeks.

The celebration of the Fiesta de San Juan (Feast of Saint John), which takes place in Christian communities, is reminiscent of the precolonial Raymi festival. People organize themselves in *cuadrillos* (dance groups). The festival begins on 23 June with a ritual bath. The next day the groups dance in the streets and squares, traditionally conducting mock battles for the dancing grounds; the battles are said to purify the earth. The dances, performed in colorful costumes, include the *culebrillando, ras para abajo, copleros,* and *aruchicos.* Subsidiary events are the *rama*, a payment of tribute, and the *gallo capitán*, the sacrifice of a rooster.

The Danzantes de Pujili is essentially a precolonial rite, recorded as early as 1570 by Antonio Clavijo. This festival occurs on the Feast of Corpus Christi. Today the dancers dress in doublets made of transparent white gauze over brightly colored fabric, with tinsel, spangles, embroidery, and other ornaments, including a brilliant kerchief around the neck and chasubles like those of Roman Catholic priests. Their dancing is lively and colorful.

Pre-Lenten Carnival is celebrated in the town of Pillaro with bullfights, bands, bonfires, hawking for birds, and masses; dancers from from all the surrounding communities perform their regional specialties. The celebration ends with ceremonial and social dances.

A number of Ecuadorian folk dances honor or imitate animals, including the cat, bear, turkey, bull, or snake. The *llaminga* imitates the flamingo, sacred to the indigenous people, employing masks and other costume elements. In the *shararán*, dancers carry small bells and they bear stuffed animals on their heads. The *curiquinga* imitates the caracara, a raptor.

Another social folk dance is the *palalaibilli*, in which dancers progress through the streets performing a circle dance to instrumental music. In the handkerchief dance, each female dancer in turn passes between two rows of male dancers who hold handkerchiefs. A typical European Maypole dance is performed in town squares. In Ecuador a number of local dances are also performed, some borrowed from other Latin American countries, and some adapted from modern ballroom dances.

BIBLIOGRAPHY

Borregan, Alfonso. *Crónicas de la conquista del Perú.* Consejo Superior de Investigaciones Científicas Facultad de Estudios Americans, Series 7a, no. 3. Seville, 1940.

Carvalho-Neto, Paulo de. *Diccionario del folklore ecuatoriano.* Quito, 1964.

Cieza de León, Pedro de. *La crónica del Perú.* Madrid, 1947.

Coba Andrade, Carlos Alberto. *Relevamiento del Proyecto de Etnomusicología y Folklore.* Caracas, 1975.

Coba Andrade, Carlos Alberto. *La Fiesta del Coraza.* Otavalo, 1976.

Coba Andrade, Carlos Alberto. *Fiestas y bailes en el Ecuador.* Otavalo, 1976.

Coba Andrade, Carlos Alberto. *Prospección e investigación de las fiestas de San Juan y San Pedro.* 2 vols. Otavalo, 1976.

Coba Andrade, Carlos Alberto. *Carnaval en mi pueblo.* Otavalo, 1977.

Coba Andrade, Carlos Alberto. *Navidad en mi pueblo.* Otavalo, 1977.

Coba Andrade, Carlos Alberto. *Fiesta de Pendeneros.* Otavalo, 1980.

Coba Andrade, Carlos Alberto. *Literatura popular afroecuatoriana.* Otavalo, 1980.

Coba Andrade, Carlos Alberto. *Instrumentos musicales populares registrados en el Ecuador.* 2 vols. Otavalo, 1981–1992.

Coba Andrade, Carlos Alberto. *Danzas y bailes en el Ecuador.* Quito, 1985.

Fernández de Oviedo y Valdés, Gonzalo. *Historia general y natural de las Indias.* 5 vols. Edited by Juan Pérez de Tudela Bueso. Madrid, 1959.

Ferrario, Julio. "Descripción detallada de Quito." In *El Ecuador visto por los extranjeros: Viajeros de los siglos XVIII y XIX,* edited by Humberto Toscano. Puebla, Mexico, 1960.

González Suárez, Federico. *Historia general de la República del Ecuador,* vol. 1, *Tiempos antiguos, o, El Ecuador antes de la conquista.* Quito, 1969.

Hassaurek, Friedrich. "Un diplomático yanqui en el Ecuador." In *El Ecuador visto por los extranjeros: Viajeros de los siglos XVIII y XIX,* edited by Humberto Toscano. Puebla, Mexico, 1960.

Jijón y Caamaño, Jacinto. *Antropología prehispánica del Ecuador.* Quito, 1952.

Kauffmann Doig, Federico. *Manual de arqueología peruana.* 5th ed. Lima, 1973.

Mariño, Susana, and Mayra Aguirre. *Danzahistoria: Notas sobre el ballet y la danza contemporanea en el Ecuador.* Quito, 1994.

Muratorio, Ricardo. *A Feast of Color: Corpus Christi Dance Costumes of Ecuador.* Washington, D.C., 1981.

Peñaherrera de Costales, Piedad y Alfredo Costales. *El quishihuar, o, El árbol de Dios.* 3 vols. Quito, 1966–1982.

Peters, Kurt. "Que viva el Ecuador!" *Das Tanzarchiv* 23 (November 1975): 361–368.

Stevenson, William Bennett. "Cómo era Quito cuando se declaró libre." In *El Ecuador visto por los extranjeros: Viajeros de los siglos XVIII y XIX,* edited by Humberto Toscano. Puebla, Mexico, 1960.

Vega, Garcilaso de la. *Comentarios reales de los Incas.* Madrid, 1963.

Viajero Universal en America, Un. "Quito según una geografía de 1833." In *El Ecuador visto por los extranjeros: Viajeros de los siglos XVIII y XIX,* edited by Humberto Toscano. Puebla, Mexico, 1960.

CARLOS ALBERTO COBA ANDRADE

EDEL, ALFREDO (born 1856 or 1859 in Colorno, Italy, died 18 December 1912 in Boulogne-sur-Seine, France), Italian painter, illustrator, and set and costume designer. In dance, Edel's most fruitful collaboration was with Luigi Manzotti at the Teatro alla Scala in Milan. Exceedingly prolific, Edel was also extensively involved in opera and with other ballet choreographers in Italy, in addition to working abroad at such venerable institutions as the Comédie Française and the Folies-Bergère in Paris and P. T. Barnum's circus in London. In America he worked with the Hungarian impresario Imre Kiralfy and others in the production of theatrical extravaganzas at such houses of entertainment as the Hippodrome in New York. Edel's gift was unquestionably for the spectacular, and he is best known for his costumes. He began his career designing record covers for Casa Ricordi, Giuseppi Verdi's publishers, and after his first efforts with Manzotti (*Pietro Micca* in 1875; *Sieba* in 1876), he was put in charge of overhauling the costume stock at La Scala; between 1880 and 1890 he designed some three hundred costumes for major productions there.

With composer Romualdo Marenco, Edel was involved in producing Manzotti's trilogy of blockbusters at La Scala, of which the most famous was *Excelsior* (1881). This lavish production, involving five hundred performers, depicted the triumph of industrialized civilization over the forces of darkness. Peace, Glory, Industry, and Commerce were some of the leading characters, and such emblems of technological progress as the Brooklyn Bridge and the Suez Canal figured in the action. The entire spectacle, including Edel's elaborate, often low-cut women's costumes, might be considered a bit on the vulgar side for an opera house; however, *Excelsior* was an immediate hit. Manzotti, Mareno, and Edel then produced the even more gigantic *Amor* (1886), which used six hundred performers and an elephant; its theme was the achievement of order from primal chaos through love. *Amor* was followed by *Sport* (1897), which featured various chic sportive activities from around the world. Edel also provided costumes for Manzotti's *Rosa d'Amore* in 1899, but by then the choreographer's reputation was in decline.

Edel supervised every detail of the execution of his costumes, personally selecting the fabrics. Although he had a thorough knowledge of historical styles, it is the fantasy factor in his costumes that is memorable.

BIBLIOGRAPHY
Beaumont, Cyril W. *Ballet Design: Past and Present.* London, 1946.
Rossi, Luigi. *Storia del balletto.* Rev. ed. Milan, 1967.

NANCY REYNOLDS

EDWARDS, LESLIE (born 7 August 1915 in Teddington, England), British dancer, teacher, and ballet master. Edwards made his stage debut with Marie Rambert's Ballet Club and danced with her company from 1932 to 1939, appearing in the original production of *Jardin aux Lilas*. He also joined the Vic-Wells Ballet in 1933, and he performed with that company (now the Royal Ballet) until 1993, spending only two of the intervening sixty years away from it, in military service (1941–1943). He made periodic forays into the classical repertory, first in *The Nutcracker* and *Les Patineurs* and later as Benno in *Swan Lake*, Hilarion in *Giselle*, and assorted cavaliers. Two important creations—the evil magician Archimago in Frederick Ashton's *The Quest* (1943) and the pathetic Beggar in Robert Helpmann's *Miracle in the Gorbals* (1944)—pinpointed his extraordinary talents as a character dancer. Adding success to success, as a pompous Catalabutte in *The Sleeping Beauty*, a pitiable Red King in *Checkmate*, and a poetic Doctor Coppélius, he gradually abandoned dancing altogether to become the Royal Ballet's foremost mime.

A list of the ballets in which he performed during the years—often in four or five roles—numbers more than seventy and spans the entire history of the company; the finely detailed servility of his Catalabutte graced five different productions of *The Sleeping Beauty* between 1946 and 1968. His created roles—in nearly fifty ballets—range from Thomas, the bluff comic burgher in *La Fille Mal Gardée*, to the aristocratic Duke in *Marguerite and Armand;* his adopted roles encompass stylistic extremes from the sinister Charlatan in *Petrouchka* to the dignified Bridegroom's Father in *Les Noces*.

Edwards has also served as a mime teacher at the Royal Ballet School, as a company *répétiteur* (rehearsal director) from 1959 to 1970, as director of the Royal Ballet Choreographic Group from its first performance in 1967 until 1987, and as ballet master to the Royal Opera from 1970 until 1990. He was made an Officer of the Order of the British Empire (OBE) in 1975.

BIBLIOGRAPHY

Anthony, Gordon. "Leslie Edwards." In Anthony's *A Camera at the Ballet: Pioneer Dancers of the Royal Ballet*. Newton Abbot, 1975.

Steinbrink, Mark. "Leslie Edwards." *Ballet News* 3 (September 1981): 7–8.

Swinson, Cyril. *Six Dancers of Sadler's Wells*. London, 1956.

BARBARA NEWMAN

EGK, WERNER (Werner Mayer; born 17 May 1901 in Auschsesheim, Bavaria, died 10 July 1983 in Inning, Germany), German composer. Werner Egk grew up in Augsburg, where he studied at the local conservatory; he continued his studies in Frankfurt, and then in Munich with Carl Orff. His first contact with the theater occurred in Frankfurt, where he started to write incidental music. He was *Kapellmeister* (choral director) at the Berlin State Opera from 1936 to 1940. There he acquired a special interest in ballet, which he pursued in Nazi-occupied Paris in collaboration with Serge Lifar. After World War II he was in charge of many musical institutions, including the West Berlin Hochschule für Musik (1950–1953) and the Deutscher Komponistenverband (beginning in 1950).

As a composer Egk wrote in an extended tonality. His is a music of dexterous textures, heavy rhythms, and lush orchestrations that derives from Richard Strauss and Igor Stravinsky, although he confessed a preference for the lighter touch of the French composers who followed Erik Satie and Les Six. During the two decades after 1945 he became a vociferous advocate for the renaissance of classical ballet in Germany, basing his arguments mainly on his Paris experiences with Lifar. His ballet *Abraxas*, based freely upon Heinrich Heine's libretto *Der Doctor Faust* (1847) and choreographed by Marcel Luipart, was the first German evening-length ballet after World War II. Banned after only four performances (Bavarian State Opera Ballet, 1948) because of the alleged obscenity of its black mass in hell, it immediately became a hit at its second production with choreography by Janine Charrat (Municipal Opera, Berlin, 1949). After this it dominated the ballet repertory of German theaters during the 1950s and 1960s, with individual productions continuing well into the 1980s. [*See* Abraxas.]

Other ballets by Egk include *Joan de Zarissa* (choreography by Lizzie Maudrik, Berlin State Opera, 1940; choreography by Serge Lifar, Paris Opera Ballet, 1942); *Ein Sommertag* (A Summer Day; choreography by Charrat, Municipal Opera, Berlin, 1950); *Die Chinesische Nachtigall* (choreography by Tatjana Gsovsky, Munich State Opera, 1953); *Danza* (choreography by Heinz Rosen, Munich State Opera, 1960); and *Casanova in London* (choreography by Charrat, Munich State Opera, 1969). Of his concert pieces, the one most often adapted to ballet has been *Französische Suite* (French Suite; choreography by Manfred Taubert, Braunschweig, 1964; and by John Cranko, Munich State Opera, 1969).

BIBLIOGRAPHY

Egk, Werner. *Musik–Wort–Bild*. Munich, 1960.

Egk, Werner. *Die Zeit wartet nicht*. Munich, 1981.

Krause, Ernst. *Werner Egk: Oper und Ballett*. Wilhelmshaven, 1971.

Werner Egk: Das Bühnenwerk. Munich, 1971. Exhibition catalog, Theatermuseum, Munich.

HORST KOEGLER

EGLEVSKY, ANDRÉ (Andrei Evgen'evich Eglevskii; born 21 December 1917 in Moscow, died 4 December 1977 in Elmira, New York), Russian-born American dancer and teacher. As a classical dancer André Eglevsky was a uniquely gifted artist, technically brilliant and dramatically arresting. His flowing movements often seemed nearer those of a panther than those of a French courtier.

Born in 1917 in Russia, he was taken to southern France in 1921 by his mother, refugees of the Russian Revolution. When he developed a lung ailment, doctors recommended that he study dancing, and his mother arranged for ballet lessons in Nice. When Eglevsky was eleven, an audition with Michel Fokine was arranged, and the famous choreographer recognized Eglevsky's prodigious talent. As a result, the family moved to Paris, where Eglevsky studied with Alexandre Volinine and Matilda Kshessinska.

In 1931 Léonide Massine saw Eglevsky in the class of another Russian expatriate ballet teacher, Lubov Egorova. He asked the young dancer to join the newly forming de Basil Ballets Russes de Monte Carlo, to perform alongside many artists of the former Diaghilev company and some very young ballerinas (known as the "baby ballerinas"). As Eglevsky's only stage experience had been in school performances organized by Volinine, he began in the corps de ballet, but soon Massine gave him solo roles. His first starring role in a Massine ballet was in *Union Pacific*

(1934). In 1933 Eglevsky had begun to be featured in ballets of Fokine, including *Petrouchka, Les Sylphides, Prince Igor, Schéhérazade, L'Epreuve d'Amour,* and *Don Juan.* His first appearance in a George Balanchine ballet, the 1935 revival of *Concurrence,* marked the beginning of a long association with that choreographer; over the years Eglevsky danced in nearly thirty Balanchine ballets.

By the late 1930s Eglevsky had established himself as one of the foremost *danseurs nobles* with his performances in the classics. He became a resident of the United States and then a citizen in 1937; in 1938 he married Leda Anchutina, who had been a ballerina in Balanchine's first American company, American Ballet. After being associated with various companies, including Ballets Epstein (1934) and the Leon Woizikowski Ballet (1935), Eglevsky spent most of the war years with Ballet Theatre (except for a few months in 1944 with Ballet International) and joined the marquis de Cuevas's Grand Ballet de Monte Carlo in 1947. In 1950 Eglevsky returned to the United States to cap his dancing years with Balanchine and the New York City Ballet. His many roles included the virtuosic *Pas de Trois,* the witty *À la Françaix,* and revivals of Balanchine's ballets to music by Stravinsky, *Apollo* and *Le Baiser de la Fée.*

In a period when many considered the ballerina supreme, Eglevsky personified male dancing at its best. A favorite partner of Alexandra Danilova and later of Rosella Hightower and Maria Tallchief, Eglevsky was endowed with the muscles of an athlete, yet he also had a complete technique; Fokine said that while Eglevsky did not resemble Nijinsky, he could perform any step Nijinsky could. Eglevsky's five feet, eleven inches and 190 pounds were under amazing control. His apparently effortless pirouettes, performed without obvious preparation, were legendary. He often wagered Balanchine a lunch that he could turn fifteen times on one preparation, and Eglevsky never went hungry as a result. Another demonstration of Eglevsky's secure technical control occurs in Alicia Alonso's account of their many performances of act 2 of *Giselle.* The sound of her partner's descending *jetés* behind her were her cue to rise from a kneeling position, but because Eglevsky's descent was without sound, often Alonso had to be prompted. By the time Eglevsky retired in 1959, he had performed more than a hundred roles in both classical and modern ballets; about thirty of these were choreographed especially for him.

Eglevsky and his wife Leda (also a soloist with Massine) in 1955 founded a school of classical ballet in Massapequa, Long Island, New York. They also forged a small, well-trained ballet company in which their daughter Marina danced her first leading roles. Eglevsky, an excellent teacher, was a member of the faculty of the School of American Ballet for ten years. He was also coauthor of a

EGLEVSKY. As Paris in David Lichine's *Helen of Troy* (1942), Eglevsky demonstrates one of the technical feats for which he was famous: a single *cabriole* in which he seemed to hang suspended in the air. (Photograph by Roger Wood; used by permission.)

book with John Gregory, *The Heritage of a Ballet Master, Nicolas Legat* (New York, 1977).

BIBLIOGRAPHY

Denby, Edwin. *Dance Writings.* Edited by Robert Cornfield and William MacKay. New York, 1986.

García-Márquez, Vicente. *The Ballets Russes: Colonel de Basil's Ballets Russes de Monte Carlo, 1932–1952.* New York, 1990.

Hastings, Baird. "André Eglevsky." *Ballet Review* 8.1 (1980): 1–76.

Horwitz, Dawn Lille, and Don McDonagh. "Conversations with André Eglevsky." *Ballet Review* 8.1 (1980): 33–74.

Sheridan, Hope, "André Eglevsky." *Chrysalis* 2.3–5 (1949): 1–32.

Sorley Walker, Kathrine. *De Basil's Ballets Russes.* New York, 1983.

ARCHIVE.   Dance Collection, New York Public Library for the Performing Arts.

BAIRD HASTINGS

EGOROVA, LUBOV (Liubov' Nikolaevna Egorova; born 27 July [8 August] 1880 in Saint Petersburg, died 18 August 1972 in Paris, Russian ballet dancer and teacher.

Lubov Egorova studied with Enrico Cecchetti at the Imperial Ballet School in Saint Petersburg, entering the corps de ballet of the Maryinsky Theater in 1898. Promoted to *première danseuse* in 1903, she quickly became a public favorite as Lise in *The Magic Flute*, Ilka in *The Enchanted Forest*, and Pierrette in *Les Millions d'Arlequin*. In 1907, she danced Myrtha in *Giselle*, a performance Bronislava Nijinska recalled as "truly magnificent." In subsequent years she took on the major ballerina roles in *Raymonda*, *The Sleeping Beauty*, *Swan Lake*, and Michel Fokine's *Francesca da Rimini*.

Emigrating from her homeland in 1918, Egorova danced Aurora in Serge Diaghilev's production of *The Sleeping Princess* during his winter season (1921/22) at London's Alhambra Theatre and appeared the following spring in *Aurora's Wedding* at the Paris Opera, earning André Levinson's praise of her "delicate and noble craft."

In 1923, Egorova opened a studio in Paris, where for forty-five years she taught such well-known dancers as George Skibine, Catherine Littlefield, Solange Schwarz, Rosella Hightower, Janine Charrat, Marjorie Tallchief, and Muriel Belmondo. With students from her school, she organized the short-lived Ballets de la Jeunesse (1938). "To be present at her classes," Pierre Michaut wrote, "is always a great pleasure; one admires the inexhaustible combinations of steps and figures which she invents unceasingly." In 1949, she staged *Aurora's Wedding* for the Royal Danish Ballet. She married Prince Nikita Troubetskoy in emigration.

BIBLIOGRAPHY

Krasovskaya, Vera. *Russkii baletnyi teatr nachala dvadtatogo veka*, vol. 2, *Tantsovshchiki*. Leningrad, 1972.

Michaut, Pierre. "Notes on Some Paris Schools." *The Dancing Times* (June 1945): 389–392.

Nijinska, Bronislava. *Early Memoirs*. Translated and edited by Irina Nijinska and Jean Rawlinson. New York, 1981.

Scheuer, L. Franc. "Les Ballets de la Jeunesse." *The Dancing Times* (February 1938): 160–162.

Tugal, Pierre. "A Witness of a Glorious Past: Lubov Egorova." *The Dancing Times* (June 1952): 527–528.

FILM. Vladimir Forgency, *Adolescence* (M.K. Productions, 1966), with Lubov Egorova and Sonia Petrova.

LYNN GARAFOLA

EGRI, SUSANNA (born 18 February 1926 in Budapest), Hungarian-Italian dancer, teacher, and choreographer. Susanna Egri studied dance with Ferenc Nádasi at the Budapest Opera and with Sári Berczik at his own school, and in 1946 she received her diploma from the Hungarian State Institute for Choreography and Teaching. That same year she appeared in her first performance as a dancer at the Franz Liszt Society. She moved to Italy with her family in 1947, settling in Turin and eventually becoming an Italian citizen.

Much of Egri's activity, first as a dancer and then as a choreographer, has been in Turin, whence she consistently worked to spread the knowledge of dance throughout Italy. In an era when official culture tolerated theatrical dance only in the form of classical ballet, Egri taught and practiced her own modern dance technique of central European origin. Harald Kreutzberg with his expressive and distinctive dance was probably the strongest influence on her work as an interpreter and creator. The success and prestige of her famous countryman, Aurelio Milloss, certainly stimulated her to refine her technique and broaden her cultural awareness.

While still very young, Egri conquered Turin with her performances with the Centro di Studio della Danza (Center for Dance Studies), founded in 1953. Italian Radio-Television, which at that time had its headquarters in Turin, chose Egri and her pupils and collaborators for its first musical and variety programs conceived for the new medium. Her first television ballet was *Foyer de la Danse* (1952), set to music by Gioacchino Rossini; it was an affectionate evocation of the world of the subscribers of the Paris Opera as immortalized by the painter Edgar Degas. Over the years there followed a large number of "dance television originals." Egri's television activity culminated in a series inspired by the literary works that are the basis for so many lyric operas: *Bohème* (from *Vita di Boheme*, on which Puccini based his opera), *Turandot*, and *Cavalleria Rusticana* (from the story by Giovanni Verga), for which she received the international Città di Napoli award of the Premio Italia in 1963.

In 1953, despite many theatrical responsibilities, Egri founded her own company, I Balletti di Susanna Egri. From Turin, where she performed and choreographed between 1961 and 1972, sometimes at the Teatro Regio, she toured almost all of Italy and participated in the summer seasons of the main festivals. At Spoleto in 1963 she staged the scenic cantata *Plus Loin que la Nuit et le Jour* (Farther than Night and Day), set to music by Henry Sauguet. Among her company's productions were *Negro Spirituals* (1960), to original music; *Jazz Play* (1960), to music by Charlie Mingus; and *Three Parables* (1965), to popular Israeli music. Of particular interest among her works as guest choreographer is the reconstruction of Salvatore Viganò's famous ballet, *Il Noce di Benevento* (The Walnut Tree of Benevento), presented at the Teatro Romano in Benevento in September 1983, with the dance company of the Teatro di Torino.

Some of the best Italian dancers of recent years have come from Egri's school: Luigi Bonino, of the Ballet National de Marseille; Gabriella Cohen, guest ballerina with several European companies; Gianfranco Paoluzi, first dancer of the Eliot Feld company; and Loredana Furno, guest ballerina of the Teatro Regio of Turin and later director of the dance company of the Teatro di Torino. Egri has served as president of the Italian National Committee of the International Dance Council.

BIBLIOGRAPHY
Bentivoglio, Leonetta. *La danza contemporanea.* Milan, 1985.
Doglio, Vittoria, and Elisa Vaccarino. *L'Italia in ballo.* Rome, 1993.

VITTORIA OTTOLENGHI
Translated from Italian

EGYPT. [*To survey dance in Egypt, this entry comprises three articles. The first article considers the role of dance in ancient Egyptian culture; the second focuses on traditional dances in modern Egypt; the third discusses the introduction and development of European theatrical dance.*]

Dance in Ancient Egypt

The ancient Egyptians were a dance-loving people. Pictorial representations and the written records from as early as 3000 BCE offer indubitable evidence of dance in the early Egyptian civilization that developed along the Nile River. Dance was a part of the Egyptian ethos and featured prominently in religious ritual and ceremony, on social occasions, and in Egyptian funerary practices regarding the afterlife.

The study of ancient Egyptian dance involves identifying dance scenes from monuments, temples, tombs, and some royal and civic architectural remains, and translating and interpreting inscriptions and texts. It has been the domain of Egyptologists, many of whose findings concerning dance have been incidental. Major studies dedicated to dance are rare, published predominantly in German and French, but meticulously researched. Scholars have examined extant materials to propose the identification, if not classification, of the dances and their choreographic variety. This task requires a thorough understanding of the formal aesthetic conventions underlying ancient Egyptian art and has been made all the more arduous when, in some cases, the unique archaeological evidence has been partially or almost totally defaced or destroyed. These scholars' hypotheses on the function and probable shape and dynamics of dances are most ingenious. New discoveries can be expected to further elucidate the subject.

The oldest and most common term for dance is *ib*, or *iba*. Others are *rwi*, for the striding dance; *hbi*, for a special funerary dance and an acrobatic dance; *ksks*, for the leaping dance; and *trf* (later, *tnf*), for the pair dance. Classification according to these ancient terms has not proven possible, however, because they are not used consistently in the iconography for the dances. The dancers portrayed by the artists of ancient Egypt include children in rites of initiation; men and women (not always dance professionals); deities (Bes, Ihi, Shou, Thoth, Horus, Isis); kings dancing for such deities, including Mut (mother goddess), Nekhbet (vulture goddess), Nut (sky goddess); priests honoring Hathor (mistress of dance); divine dwarfs rendering the "dance of the gods"; animals (ostriches, baboons, desert fowl) rejoicing in the sunrise, sunset, or New Year; the long-tailed monkey and the goat capering in children's tales; and foreigners, such as Nubians, Libyans, and some Egyptian imitators practicing an exotic art. There is evidence of professional dance and music instruction for young girls. Female dancers, either the daughters or servants of the house, were attached to the harem of kings and high dignitaries. In the religious arena, such dancers were attached to a god's temple—in

EGYPT: Dance in Ancient Egypt. A copy of a wall painting depicting priestesses and dancers dating from the reign of Senwosret I, from the Tomb of Inyotefiker and Senet (twelfth dynasty). (Metropolitan Museum of Art, New York [30.4.160]; photograph used by permission.)

effect joining the harem in the service and worship of the god.

The functions of ancient Egyptian dance were many: for magical purposes; rites of passage; to induce states of ecstasy or trance; mime; as homage, honor, or entertainment; and even for erotic purposes. Dances took place in enclosed areas, open spaces, and in processions. The Egyptians danced singly and in pairs, mainly in sex-discrete groups.

Occasions for dance in ancient Egypt, both sacred and secular, were many, and they multiplied and diversified through the centuries. Sacred dances were offered to the goddesses—above all to Hathor—as well as to Isis and Mut. The gods, were also honored in dance, particularly Amun, and less frequently, Min (god of fertility), Montu (god of war), Ptah (the creator) and Osiris. The Osirian Festival of the Erection of the Djed (holy pillar) was accompanied by dancing, as was the month-long Opet Festival, during which the sacred bark of Amun sailed the Nile from Karnak to Luxor and back. There were dances in homage to the king at the receipt of foreign tribute, at ceremonies when the monarch conferred honors upon subjects; at agrarian work-associated festivities, such as thanksgiving, at harvest time; at postcircumcision initiation rites; at war or combat dances and games; as entertainment for the king and others of quality or rank; at banquets; at funerary feasts and in processions; and during the transport of the statue(s) of the deceased to a temple or tomb.

Even in this most conservative of ancient civilizations, with its strongly traditionalist views, an evolution in dance took place. Ancient Egyptian dance traditions displayed a rich variety of form, shape, and dynamic. In general, dance in the Old Kingdom (2664–2155 BCE) tended to be formal, measured and restrained. During the Middle Kingdom (2052–1786 BCE) leaps and stamping were introduced, and in the New Kingdom (1554–1075 BCE) dance acquired elements of grace, fluidity, and lightness.

Accompaniment for dancing was provided by the rhythmic sound of hand clapping, finger snapping, and body slapping. Musicians played percussion instruments (clappers, tambourines, drums) and string and wind instruments (lute, lyre, harp, flute, oboe, clarinet). Vocalizations such as rhythmic ejaculatory cries, choruses, and songs also accompanied the dance.

Costumes ranged from nudity to long flowing or pleated robes—fine, transparent, white, or exquisitely colored. There were loincloths and skirts of various shapes, sometimes held up by crossbanding in the back and front; tunics of various lengths and widths, from close-fitting to full, with shoulder straps or sleeves, and some wraparound; and even, in one instance, what is perhaps a culotte. Girdles and belts were not uncommon, and there

EGYPT: Dance in Ancient Egypt. A dancing ivory dwarf or a Pygmy figure, which was part of a mechanical toy, from the Tomb of Hepy at Lisht (twelfth dynasty). Pygmies were often brought from sub-Saharan Africa to serve as temple dancers or acrobats in the service of Re, the sun god. (Metropolitan Museum of Art, New York; Rogers Fund, 1934 [34.1.130]; photograph used by permission.)

was a wide selection of jewelry, including bracelets, armlets, anklets, earrings, a variety of collars and necklaces, and diadems. The hair might be cropped or long and loose. Much use was made of wigs of different shapes and lengths—short, tripartite, or huge and enveloping. Some dancers appear strangely coiffed with a braid that ends in the shape of a ball, or tightly capped, or with the hair built up in a conical tuft.

Accessories enhanced movement, provided rhythm, and served functional and symbolic purposes: gazelle-headed sticks, staffs, boomerangs, and clappers. The sistrum and rattling menat collared necklace were associated with Hathor, as were her other symbols, the mirror and a clapper topped by a human hand. In some dances the performers appeared bedecked with wreaths, crowned with lotus blossoms, or garlanded with trailing convolvulus (morning-glory) creepers.

The first representational evidence of dance appears in the Predynastic period (c.4000–3200 BCE), during the

Naqada II culture. Paintings on pottery vessels depict female figures (perhaps goddesses or priestesses) dancing with upraised arms. Similar female figures appear in conjunction with men brandishing clappers, in a scene now thought to represent mourners in a funeral procession. There appears no doubt that dances of celebration, worship, and the hunt existed in that remote period.

Old Kingdom (Third–Eighth Dynasties, c.2687–2165 BCE). Dance scenes from the period of the Old Kingdom are numerous, although they vary little. Dances were often, but not exclusively, performed by women or very young girls who might be mistaken for boys. Dances from the fourth dynasty appear not to have had the complexity, diversity, or speed characterizing those that followed the sixth dynasty. The aforementioned *rwi* appears solely in textual records. A group unison dance with a moderately paced gait, perhaps performed in a circle, with arms raised and rounded above the head, first appears in pictorial form. The accompaniment is rendered by a group of females clapping and perhaps calling out. Some doubt exists as to whether there was orchestral accompaniment, because the musicians are often depicted at some distance from the dancers. A connection with Hathor is possible, in that the upraised arms evoke one of her forms, the sacred cow. The advanced, slightly raised leg seems to be the position most characteristic of this early dance. A soloist performs a leg gesture (which survives in modern Egyptian dance), bent leg raised, thigh horizontal; a backward leg swing is also portrayed. The dancer is distinctive in her nudity, and her hair is coiffed in a braid terminating in a ball shape. This hairstyle was not exclusive to dancers but was primarily worn by them, no doubt to enhance their movements.

Pair dances, by men or women, holding hands, though not necessarily funerary in character, were sometimes performed at funerals. The range of movement varied, from moderate to expansive, and included agile *grands battements*. The pairs did not necessarily form a symmetry—one of the two might act as a partner or pivot. Acrobatic dance, probably performed in honor of Hathor and prototypical of dances associated with Hathoric worship in the Middle and New Kingdoms, was presented at funerals to the accompaniment of rhythmic clapping. Females in loincloths, sporting the ball-weighted braid, are shown in a precarious posture: one leg upthrust in a high kick with the torso thrown into a deep backbend. Several conjectures about the form of this dance have been proposed, perhaps the most likely being the alternation of this position with the upright stance. Erotic intent has been suggested.

The function of the Mirror Dance, which was presumably Hathoric, is unresolved, although the accessories belong to the goddess (mirrors and clappers topped by a hu-

EGYPT: Dance in Ancient Egypt. Three sculptural reliefs depicting the first *sed (top and middle)* and third *sed (bottom)* of Amenhotep III, from the Tomb of Kheruef, at the necropolis at Thebes, eighteenth dynasty. A *sed* is a ritual of renewal and regeneration celebrated by a king after a reign of thirty years. In these representations, the men and the women perform in segregated ceremonies. (Photographs courtesy of Ibrabim Farrah, *Arabesque Magazine,* New York.)

man hand). One such scene consists of a female quartet and a female duo together. In the first group, the object may be to capture the "hand of Hathor" reflected in a partner's mirror at the moment the clappers clash. In the second, one participant appears to perform a pirouette. Other dances reminiscent of this Mirror Dance are performed without the emblems.

Among the stick dances, both the object held and the type of dance vary. In one, men advance in a leisurely gait, grasping a boomerang in each hand. In another, at a funeral feast, very young nude girls appear to run at an easy pace in two counterdirectional, concentric circles around one girl who pivots in the center, each girl brandishing one or two boomerangs. The occasional symmetrical raising of two adjacent boomerangs seems to shape the horns of the cow goddess. Again, others advance in wide steps, legs uplifted, some leaning backward. At the harvest, aligned men stride forward, striking two sticks at neck level. Elsewhere, young boys form a joyous circle around a (masked?) stationary central figure, perhaps a benevolent demon (Bes?), warding off evil. Other scenes show female dwarfs. In one instance, a dwarf grasps a (pseudo- ?) sistrum and, in another, a boomerang. The so-called boomerang dances have been viewed as hunting dances of purported Libyan origin and magical purpose.

Illustrations of dance during the First Intermediate Period (ninth–tenth dynasties, c.2165–2040 BCE) are rare. Later, scenes of sports predominate. In a scene from the First Intermediate period, a "dance mistress" directs a group dance, conducting with a (pseudo- ?) sistrum, while another uses a wand, as a female monkey burlesques the dancers. All of this may be a religious agrarian entertainment or even a war dance.

The divine "god dance" of the dwarfs was greatly appreciated, and the performers much prized. If dwarfs were not available, the antics of Egyptian chondrodystrophic cripples supplemented the demand. Grotesque dwarf-figure toys for children have been discovered. The dwarf gods Aha and Bes figure as musicians and singers in the earliest royal rituals. Bes and the dwarfs dance not only for joy, but to ward off evil. The dancing Bes may be seen on artifacts from diverse periods, right up to the Ptolemaic and Roman periods, which ended in about 395 CE.

Middle Kingdom (Eleventh–Thirteenth Dynasties, c.2134–1665 BCE). In religious dance, the acrobatic Hathoric dances feature new configurations, most notably a pose formed by lying on the abdomen and deeply arching the torso, until the feet, nearing the head, close the circle. In an exaggeration, the feet pass over the head, with the abdomen and thighs nearly vertical. Hathoric funerary-cult dances were performed by the priestesses and musicians of Hathor in front of the deceased. As they were not dancers, their ritual rendition probably consisted of a series of gestures and attitudes.

A dramatic and erotic Hathoric dance by a skirted quartet of young girls, paired in opposing couples—one side short haired, the other sporting the ball-weighted plait—also had mythico-religious connotations. It referred to the union of the sun god Ra with the "mistress of the sky" Hathor—here in the guise of a funerary goddess, as is often seen in the New Kingdom. The Hathoric dance is only indirectly connected to funeral rites, endowing the deceased with the blessings of the goddess; in a curious confusion of sacred and profane, the dance could entertain as well because Hathor was the goddess of joy and love as well as of dance. In agrarian scenes, the dance becomes a thanksgiving to her. Thus, the Hathoric dances may be quite diverse—hieratic, fervid, sacred, profane, or acrobatic.

Dances performed during the transportation, in state, of the statue of the deceased (although rare and little developed in the Old Kingdom) acquired great importance in the Middle Kingdom period, with the participation of men and women in great numbers. The action presumably occurred when the procession stopped at several "stations" en route to the tomb, rather than during the actual procession. Various scenes include acrobatic dances; women perform a classic group dance, while the men's activity incorporates the whirl or turn of the pirouette. An inscription notes females mimicking the effects of the wind. Their hairdo, a raised tuft, recalls that of the dancing Muu; it also resembles the high crown of Upper Egypt. The Muu hark back to a form of ancestor cult: they were the shades of the kings of the Predynastic Lower Egyptian kingdom of Buto. Seldom seen in the Old Kingdom, the practice of incorporating the Muu passed from royal funerals to common usage in the Middle Kingdom period and continued unchanged until the eighteenth dynasty. Two dancers mime the king destroying a foe. Another pair imitates trees bending before the wind, while the fifth, the "wind," waves her arms toward them. The inscription reads, "Song of the Four Winds."

Dances in this period include a group of female couples; some of their postures and gestures reveal a strongly sculptural sensibility. Others dances are freer and less restrained, performed by individuals or in asymmetrical duets. An intriguing scene shows a man doing a squatting "Russian dance" movement—perhaps a war dance? The striding dance of the Old Kingdom period seems to have acquired an aerial dimension. Rhythmic accompaniment dominated—clapping, finger snapping (an innovation), and stamping. Rattles and percussion instruments provided sound, along with vocalizing. Dancer-musicians, so ubiquitous later in the New Kingdom, first appeared toward the end of the Middle Kingdom.

New Kingdom (Eighteenth–Twentieth Dynasties, c.1600–1076 BCE). Although the old dance forms endured into the New Kingdom, most of the paintings of dance

EGYPT: Dance in Ancient Egypt. A detail of a wall painting depicting dancers and musicians at a banquet, from the Tomb chapel of Nebamun, Thebes, eighteenth dynasty. (British Museum, London; used by permission.)

scenes (numerous in the eighteenth dynasty) adorn splendid representations of banquets and differ considerably from those decorating the tombs of earlier periods. These charming scenes are radiant with clarity, harmony, grace, elegance, and refinement—especially evident in the figures' fluid, sinuous curves and relaxed flow. They portray dancer-musicians in long, filmy gowns, delicately affecting head, arm, torso, or leg gestures while playing the lute, flute, double oboe, lyre, or tambourine, as well as the lustrous dancers so popular at these sumptuous events. The dance space was necessarily limited and the dances seem to have been performed solo or duo, almost in place. Many dancers are girls, very young and nude (albeit otherwise ornamented), some of them black. Movement was concentrated mainly in the upper body. Occasionally, clappers were used, branches held, or garlands of convolvulus trailed. One notable scene is interpreted as a belly dance, exalting fertility—a claim confirmed by the text of the related hymn celebrating the beneficent action of the Nile River flooding. The unprecedented style of this dance gives credence to a theory that it derives from an Asian form, a practice that became fashionable.

Dance movements were, however, also inspired by chanted hymns and incorporated in plastic dramatic dances that, although they existed in former times, were then usually reserved for religious purposes. Dance in the New Kingdom period was far removed from the great group dances of the Old Kingdom. A variety of dances were performed at the Festival of the Erection of the sacred Djed (see above), although no precise idea of the ceremonies has come to light. They may have included a mimed combat between the partisans and adversaries of Osiris. The former were victorious, providing an occasion for great rejoicing with music, dance, and acclamations. Certainly, the rich symbolism embodied in the choreographic figures was carefully studied and competently staged.

The acrobatic dance continued to thrive in the New Kingdom period. Dancers performed cartwheels and a forward somersault (this, done without benefit of support from the hands, was a perilous feat). Egyptologists have, upon close inspection, detected and differentiated between two versions of the backbend, each requiring a different technique—one belonging to the Middle Kingdom, the other to the New Kingdom. Acrobatic dancing occurred at the stations of the procession of the sacred bark of Amun up the Nile (the Opet Festival). It was escorted by clapping men, priestesses shaking sistra and rattling menat collars, and strumming harpists.

In the realm of the sacred, the Hathoric dance persisted, as did the funerary dance performed during the portage of statues. A profane, animated dance also figured at funerals, with robed women and naked girls beating tambourines in agitated, unconstrained movement, including deep forward torso bends. In contrast to this is a graceful funeral dance by flower-garlanded girls undulating their torsos. Other dances were performed at funerary feasts, of which two examples survive: one by a charming lute player and the other by a lyre player with a tattoo of Bes, the patron god of dancers, on her thighs (a not uncommon custom). Dances at official festivities were a frequent occurrence during the Amarna period (fourteenth century BCE) under Pharaoh Akhenaten, whose monotheistic doctrine exalted joy, nature, and spontaneity. Dance was frequently portrayed, showing little variation, but it often reached new heights of exuberance.

Foreign ("exotic") dances were probably much appreciated in ancient Egypt, notably Libyan and Nubian dances, but the scant evidence is found mostly in temple reliefs.

The dances were generally performed at official celebrations, such as the arrival of tribute or the procession of the divine barks of Karnak. Lively, scantily clad black-skinned male figures dance and leap wildly, even ecstatically, with an unruly spontaneity, accompanied by distinctive African drums. Female Nubian dancers appear more subdued, which would be to Egyptian taste. Libyan-type dance appears to have been part of a hunt dance with boomerangs. The performers wore phallic sheaths, and had ostrich feathers in their hair.

After the New Kingdom, into the Late Period of the twenty-first to thirty-first dynasties (c.1075–332 BCE) and beyond into Greco-Roman times up to 395 CE, the glory of pharaonic civilization gradually waned. With its aesthetic genius enfeebled, art, without creative inspiration, became imitative: artists resorted to reproducing scenes from a distant past. Foreign influences—Persian, Greek, Roman—introduced alien elements that produced hybrid forms. Pictorial records of dance become sparse, but it is mentioned in texts, hymns, and songs from the temples at Esna, Edfu, Philae, and Dendera. The joyous, sensual dances of New Kingdom worldly banquets and feasts became ritualized in performance at sacred and public festivities.

BIBLIOGRAPHY

Brunner-Traut, Emma. *Der Tanz im alten Ägypten*. Gluckstadt, 1938.
Brunner-Traut, Emma. "Tanz." In *Lexikon der Ägyptologie*. Wiesbaden, 1985.
Lexová, Irena. *Ancient Egyptian Dances*. Translated by Karel Haltmar. Prague, 1935.
Parker, Robert A. "The Calendar and Chronology." In *The Legacy of Egypt*, edited by J. R. Harris, Oxford, 1971.
Vandier, Jacques. *Manuel d'archéologie égyptienne*, vol. 4, *Bas reliefs et peintures*. Paris, 1964. See pages 391–486.
Wild, Henri. "Les danses sacrées de l'Égypte ancienne." In *Les danses sacrées*, edited by Jean Cazeneuve. Paris, 1963.

MAGDA SALEH

Traditional Dance

Egypt displays both venerable dance traditions and great variety within distinct subcultures. During the three thousand years of the pharaonic kingdoms, Egypt was a stable civilization. Through the succeeding epochs, leading to the Coptic Christian period (beginning in the first century CE) and the era of Islam (beginning in the seventh century CE), Egypt absorbed multiple cultural influences. Earlier influences from the ancient Near East (the Levant, Mesopotamia, and Persia) were succeeded by those of the Greeks, Romans, Arabs, Mamluks, and Ottoman Turks. Since the arrival of Europeans, spearheaded by the Napoleonic invasion in 1798, Egypt has experienced rapid change and remains a nation in transition. Although Egypt's history and culture have long been objects of serious study, its traditional dance forms have been neglected. A variety of dance traditions—urban, rural, communal, ritual, martial, and theatrical—are found; scholarly research in all these areas is in its initial stages.

Dhikr and Ecstatic Dance. For many centuries, religious expression in Islam was carried out on an individual basis. At most, a teacher gathered around himself a circle of disciples, which might persist for a generation or two. It was only in the twelfth century that institutions appeared, preserving the identity of organization and worship under a fixed name. These were the religious fraternities of dervishes. The spiritualization of Islam resulted in the founding of about one hundred fraternities, in which worshipers sought to achieve the highest state of attainment, identification with the divine by the practice of *dhikr* ("reminding oneself"). The basis of *dhikr* is found in two Qur'ānic texts. It implies the act of reminding, the oral reiteration of memory, the tireless repetition of a litany. Certain Sufi brotherhoods sought the equivalent by procedures purely physical and often extravagant, by means of esctatic dance and various thaumaturgical practices, generally opposed by the 'ulamā' (Islamic council) and the Muslim mainstream on grounds of unorthodoxy. The spiritual and physical exercises of *dhikr* (and other ceremonial performances that induce trance) enable the ordinary Muslim to obtain and renew emotional reinforcement and release. Collective *dhikr* sessions or circles are generally classifiable as *dhikr* of the commonality. Those well along the spiritual path practice the solitary *dhikr* of the privileged.

The *meglis*, the complete session of *dhikr*, includes dance; it is prefaced by recitations of the Fātiḥah (the opening surah of the Qur'ān), blessings, and invocations. The participants in the ecstatic dance, which proceeds slowly and then increases to a more rapid tempo, are seated or stand shoulder-to-shoulder in a row or in several rows. They first chant "Lā ilāha illā Allāh" (There is no god but Allah), bowing their heads and bodies twice in unison to each repetition. At the climax, they sink the whole body, twist sideways, and turn their heads or bend back and forth, swinging violently with greater latitude as their intensity increases. Jumps are also included. The chant may be shortened to "Allāh hayy" (God lives), just "hayy," or a guttural explosion of breath. Excited calls for spiritual aid burst out. An excess of fervor may cause a participant to become possessed and fall to the ground in a fit of frenzy. These exertions at the close of the ceremony contrast strikingly with the gravity of the earlier parts. A spiritual ode (*qaṣīdah*) or poetry (*muwashshaḥ*) are performed during *dhikr* by *munshidīn* singers, accompanied by the *nāy* (flute), *mazhar* (large frame drum with jingles), *bazah* (pair of kettle drums, one larger than the other), and *sagat turah* (cymbals). If music and song are dispensed with, the beat is maintained by various means—using a tambourine, tapping a rosary on a *turah*, or clapping by the leader. The celebration of a *mawlid* (a religious ceremony presided over by the spiritual and/or blood descendant of the founder, whose feast is being honored) whether it is great or humble, combines the secular activities and entertainments of a festive popular fair with ceremonial and devotional practices. The most important of the *mawlid*s celebrated in Egypt is that of the Prophet, Mawlid al-Nabī, an event unsurpassed in magnitude and lavishness. The dervishes are at the heart of the *mawlid* celebration. Multitudes of the laity, pilgrims and local people, attend and accompany them in the culminating procession, through the gaily, often brilliantly decorated quarter of the shrine. Dervishes engage in thaumaturgical feats, such as ritual piercing with a skewerlike rattle; swallowing fire, live coals, glass, snakes, and scorpions; licking red-hot knives; sustaining direct exposure to flames; and walking on burning ashes.

A nineteenth-century account describes how, in a dramatic spectacle—the treading—the *shaykh* of the order, accompanied by his entourage, would ride in ceremonial procession over a human causeway of prostrate dervishes and devotees, inflicting no harm (the supposed miracle was effected through supernatural power). This treading was suppressed, then revived, with the *shaykh* walking over the dervishes (it is not known whether the practice endures).

Zār. The earliest recorded reference to *zār* (a healing ceremony) in Egypt dates from 1862, supporting speculation that it was introduced following Egypt's 1820 conquest of the Sudan, and the ensuing influx of Sudanese into the country. Other theories trace it to earlier times. The etymology of the word *zār* is uncertain, but the ceremony, a ritual of pacification and propitiation enacted in cases of possession, is found in Egypt and other countries of the Middle East and North Africa. The practice is particularly widespread in Ethiopia, with the city of Gondar as its center. Transcending religion and social class, *zār*'s basic underlying premise is belief in the existence of spirits and the idea of spirit possession, which is ingrained in the traditional lore of many cultures. *Zār* is the means by which an individual in a perceived vulnerable position tries to neutralize the power of the spirit that is threatening him by placating and pacifying it. [*See* Zār.]

The spirits—infernal beings referred to in popular parlance as *jinn*, *asiyad*, '*ifrīt*, or *shaiṭān*—permeate solid matter and the firmament, roam the earth, and have the power to cause unhappiness, disease, and evil among humans. Their favourite haunts are ruined houses, graveyards, rivers, wells, baths, ovens, latrines. All human beings, and women in particular, are potentially vulnerable to possession caused by some supposed lapse or transgression.

A variety of ailments (hysterical and anxiety reactions, depressive neuroses, psychosomatic complaints, and some psychotic conditions) may afflict the victim, who resorts to *zār* as a remedy. It is the role of the *kodīah* (a female, rarely a male), the instrument and intermediary of the *asiyad*, to diagnose the patient's ills. The *kodīah* (often of Sudanese or Ethiopian origin) undertakes all the functions endowed with a spiritual mystique, in a role that is generally hereditary. She expresses the wishes of the spirits, revealed in a dream vision, and translates them into demands for material wealth. During a period of preparation, the patient may attend the weekly public *zār* held by the kodia on specific days in her own home; he or she must then continue to attend the "presence" regularly.

As a prelude to the ceremony, the *kodīah* wraps bread, salt and incense into a handkerchief tied to the patient's right arm. This signifies a pact or contract between her and the spirits. Violent and unrestrained dance is the core of the *zār*'s complex ritual, which can last up to seven days. The ceremony culminates with great pomp and celebration in a *laylah al-kabīrah* ("great night"). Most *zār* now last a day or two, out of financial considerations. The ritual procedure includes erecting at sunset an altar laden with edibles, mainly dried foods and sweetmeats. These are later distributed, the *kodīah* retaining a share. Arrayed in bridal finery and bedecked in jewelry and amulets, the patient, called the "bride," is paraded around the altar in a procession. Another ritual for the "bride" involves the use of henna and a crossing over fire; purification with incense is required all attending. A fee is exacted, considered a debt of the bride to be repaid in a similar situation. Invocations and incantations are intoned and blessings invoked; recitation of the Qur'ānic Fātiḥah is interspersed throughout the proceedings. At prescribed times, a sacrifice is made of animals with peculiar markings or coloring (pigeon, fowl, goose, duck, turkey, rabbit, kid, sheep, ewe, camel), which is first led in a procession. The patient establishes physical contact by handling or riding the creatures; the animals are then slaughtered in accordance with Islamic rites. The patient is smeared with their blood and may drink it. Sacrificial meats are apportioned between the *kodīah* (who secretly buries the offal), butcher, bride and participants, for whom a meal of allotted portions is prepared.

Singing and drumming heighten the charged, festive atmosphere and ensure the success of the *zār*. Emotion reaches an exceptionally high pitch: restraints are removed, repressed impulses reign, and learned norms are stripped away. The convulsive dance movements include forward and backward bends or plunges, jerking and twisting the head and torso from side to side with arms held close to the body, or swinging back and forth, stamping, tripping in a tight circle, or running in place. The dance peaks in crisis and subsides in exhaustion. While the musicians chant the refrain, the singer (*munshidah*)—also performing a hereditary function—renders songs from the entire and varied *zār* repertory, communing with the spirits. Each song is associated with a particular spirit. The musical instruments variously used include diverse *tabl'* (double-headed drums), *tār* (large frame drum without jingles), *tanbūr*, *bendir* (large frame drum with snares), *suffarah*, *sagat tura*, and *mangūr/oksh* (belt rattle of goat hooves).

A *zār* often accomplishes the therapeutic aims of symptomatic relief and improved functioning; it displays the universal characteristics of therapy in a primitive approach. It demonstrates a power to cope that is greater than some of the methods based on more "rational" assumptions. [*See* Zār.].

Bedouin Dance. The Arab conquest of Egypt took place in 642 CE. Waves of migration brought tribes of Arab settlers to the Mediterranean shores west of Alexandria, to the land east of the Nile River delta, to Upper Egypt, and to the Sinai desert. In Arabic, the word *bedouin* means "desert dweller" and refers to nomadic inhabitants of the region's deserts.

EGYPT: Traditional Dance. An Ababda bedouin man brandishes a sword in a traditional-style combat dance. (Photograph courtesy of Magda Saleh.)

Dance songs (kaf al-ʿArab). The *kaf al-ʿArab* (*kaf*, Arabic for the palm of the hand and, by extension, for clapping) is a dance genre peculiar to Arabs and is reportedly widespread in numerous variations throughout the Arab world. One or more veiled female dancers face a row of male singers who clap their hands as accompaniment. The dancer (*al-hashīyah*, "the attendant") advances and retreats, favoring with proximity the section of the male chorus that claps the most enthusiastically. Her movements consist of pelvic oscillations and rotations, with the hips sometimes padded to emphasize the motion. Central to the action is the interplay between the dancer and her male corps—and the fiction maintained in this rapport of dalliance and flirtation. The dancer can pretend to be a camel seeking food and water, whom the men cajole; at other times, the dancer snatches articles that the owner must redeem by paying a ransom. Her accessories include a stick, a rifle, daggers, or a sword that she may wield, both flat and on its edge, in a form of courage dance.

The dance song has three distinct parts: the *shitāwah*, sung by the entire group, during which the dance proper takes place; the *ghanāwah*, sung by a poet in free rhythm unsuitable to the dance; and the *magrūdah*, sung by the soloist and chorus, during which the dance usually stops. The form has variants with different names in various regions: *kaf* in the Faiyum; *hajjālah* in Marsa Matruh; *samar* in the neighborhoods of Asyut and Damietta; and *dahīyah* in the Sharqīyah governorate and in Sinai. Also in Sinai for the *samir* (an evening's socializing and [self] entertainment), women poets improvise the *khojar*, *razʿah*, and *mashraqīyah*, among others. Occasions for performance include weddings, circumcisions, and the *samir*.

Combat dance. In the hills around the Red Sea live the nomadic Ababda bedouin, who, with their kin, are not considered true Arabs by other Arab tribes. They display their martial and dancing skills in freely improvised mock combats, with pairs of warriors, armed with straight swords and round shields made out of hippopotamus or giraffe hide. This form is both ancient and widespread, being found on the east coast of Africa from Egypt to Somalia and on the southern Arabian Peninsula. The combatants circle each other and, brandishing sword and shield, leap into the air from both feet. Other movements include leaping from a crouch, squatting and lunging, thrusting, parrying, and feinting. In one notable feat, the combatant whips his sword arm to make the long blade quiver visibly along its entire length. No attempt can be made to wound the adversary. The display is accompanied by choral singing, clapping, stamping, and the strumming of the *tanbūr* (*qithar*, the zither), together with raucous taunting from the adversaries.

The Ababda bedouin are a branch of the Hamitic Beja tribes, in whose courage dance youths move in a circle around an elder who lashes out at them with a rawhide whip. Flinching is considered cowardly, and a weakling is barred from marriage until he passes the test. Until the beginning of the twentieth century, sword-and-shield dances were featured in the bridal procession and at other festive gatherings and celebrations.

Numerous ancient statuettes of the ancient Egyptian god Bes, the divine patron-god of dancers survive; the jovial pygmy or dwarf, grasping sword and shield demonstrates the great antiquity of combat dances. His image, tattooed on the legs of dancers, particularly temple dancers, can be discerned on their mummified remains. Sword dancers on Coptic textiles of the early Christian period confirm an uninterrupted tradition that continues today. [*See* Bedouin Dance.]

Kaf/Kaffafa Dance. The resemblance of the *kaf/kaffafah* dance to the *kaf al-ʿArab* suggests that Arab settlers may have influenced older dance forms native to the Nile Valley. The overall pattern opposes a straight or curved line of men to a lesser number of veiled women (sometimes only a soloist) who parade, pivot, advance, and retreat before the men. Many variations exist in Upper Egypt, especially in movement elements, motifs, sequences, and dynamics—most of which are performed by men.

Movements include stamping, sequences of jumps (sometimes combined with nodding), leaps, skips, hops, swaying, swinging, inclination of the torso, lunging, and short steps forward and backward. A southern form of this dance is known as *al-hamamah* ("the pigeon"), perhaps because the motion of the womens' veils resembles the flapping of birds' wings. This social dance is performed for weddings and circumcisions, to welcome returning pilgrims, and on other festive occasions. Sequences accompanied by a singer and drumming on a *tār* and/or *tabl'* are punctuated at intervals by choral response and rhythmic clapping by the men and switch to an accelerated tempo.

Bormāyah. The original inhabitants of the oasis of Siwah, near the Libyan border, are related to Berber, Arab bedouin, and African groups. Siwah was an important caravan station and slave market in the Middle Ages. Singing, dancing, and drinking enliven the leisure hours of the *zaqqalīn* (club bearers), a class of men who serve as fieldworkers and night guards, whose merry gatherings are the gayest and most frequented in Siwah. Traditionally, the *zaqqalīn* lived in enforced celibacy between the ages of twenty and forty, which commonly encouraged homosexuality among them. To this and to their popularity as entertainers might be attributed a dance style shared by both sexes. The *bormāyah* (Ar., *baramah*, "to twist") is a simple, almost stationary dance with minimal ornamentation; it is danced by men, by women (who perform veiled in the seclusion of the harem), and sometimes by female impersonators. Its most notable feature is a shuffling, hip-swinging action. Accessories include a stick and a scarf wrapped or held around the pelvic area.

Another dance performed by the *zaqqalin*, in character akin to an African animal dance, was disseminated by the descendants of black slaves and adopted locally. An energetic group forms a circle, dancing with a rhythmic swinging of the hips, jerks of the body, hops, and forward jumps. The dance climaxes in erotic movements punctuated by excited shrieks and shouts as the circle of girdled dancers closes in.

Musical instruments found in Siwah include *tabl'*, a metal flute *(tishbibt)*, and the double-horned *magrunah*. Other occasions for dance include the *samir*, weddings, and seasonal and religious festivals.

Suez Henna Ceremony and Dance. Almost everywhere in the Muslim world, one of the festive days preceding the *laylat al-dokhlah* ("wedding night"), is set aside for the ritual dyeing of the bride's (and sometimes the groom's) hands and feet with a thick paste of henna, celebrated in Egypt as henna night. Henna is a red-brown pigment obtained from *Lawsonia inermis*, a shrub of the loosestrife family known from the Atlantic to the Ganges. Used by the Egyptians and the Hebrews in ancient times, the plant is favored for its medicinal as well as its cosmetic properties; it has acquired ritual use of a prophylactic against the evil eye because of its red color, which symbolizes life and health.

In the city of Suez, a large circular tray of henna paste, gaily decorated, is prepared in the bride's home. In the evening it is carried through the streets by the male relations and friends of the uniting families, guests, and neighbors, who parade with song and merriment until dawn. The tray is deposited before the homes of the bridegroom, the relatives, and the friends of the couple. The men dance in a circle, led in song by a solo singer to the accompaniment of a *darabukkah* (a goblet drum similar to the *dumbeq'*), each sequence culminating in the complex, syncopated *saqfah suweisi* ("Suez clapping"). Movements include mimes of sail hauling, rope drawing, swimming, and rowing, accompanied by jogging, squatting hops, side-stepping across the body, and kicking.

It remains conjecture whether foreign influences over the ages have also shaped the Suez henna ritual itself, or whether the ritual parade through the streets is of ancient Egyptian origin, for Suez, once known as Kulzum, is an ancient city. It was and remains situated at the tip of the Gulf of Suez, at the mouth of an ancient Egyptian canal that joined the Red Sea to the Nile—a vital maritime link between the Mediterranean, Arabia, and India until it was filled in the Middle Ages.

Bambūtīyah. A dance from the Suez Canal zone, the *bambūtīyah* is particularly identified with the cities of Port Said, Ismailia, and Suez. Its name is a corruption of the English "bumboat" and refers to the boat peddlers in the harbor who sell their wares to passengers and sailors on ships. An evening's socializing can involve one or more individual male performers, who may wield a cane, knife,

EGYPT: Traditional Dance. Dancers of an Egyptian folkloric troupe perform a theatricalized version of *bambūtīyah*, a dance genre with Charleston-like steps. (Photograph © Folklore Film, Stockholm; courtesy of Ibrahim Farrah, *Arabesque Magazine*, New York.)

or shawl. The dance consists of a lively Charleston-like leg action with occasional pelvic shimmies, while the upper body gracefully manipulates accessories or mimes various kinds of work, such as rowing, winding ropes, and bargaining.

The instrumental accompaniment of the songs (some acquired from as far away as the Gulf region) is rendered by a soloist with a chorus. It is usually led by the five-stringed zither or *simsimāyah*, peculiar to the area, supported by the complex rhythmic interplay of a *riq* (a tambourine played with a virtuosic technique) and a *darabukkah* and by hand-clapping. The origins of the dance are uncertain. It may be an instance of the recent adoption and adaptation of a foreign dance form to a local dance culture. The Charleston enjoyed a vogue in Egypt after its appearance in the 1920s. The dockworkers and bumboatmen may have picked it up from the passengers on the great liners sailing through the canal, or at the gay entertainment spots catering to them. (One candelabrum dancer includes a "Charlestoon" in her routine, and dancing horses have attempted it).

Alexandrian Dance. In a practice now apparently defunct, the bellicose *sohbah* ("companions," "friends") was performed by young men from Alexandria's popular quarter of Ras al-Tin, demonstrating their talents in various feats. An individual exhibition dance demanding skill, balance, and strength and incorporating martial features, it reflected the indomitable character of the Alexandrians. According to local lore, the dance originated with popular resistance to the French and British at the turn of the nineteenth century.

Weapon dances have been common since antiquity, when dances with swords, knives, and daggers were part of ritual sacrificial processions and ceremonies. Representations of these rites survive in tattoo designs, and a link has been suggested between the old forms and those surviving in Alexandria and some towns in Lower Egypt. Dances using drapery are represented in Alexandrian Tanagra-type figurines dating back to 200 BCE. A shawl/sash dance performed by youths was popular in the Fatimid era, the tenth to twelfth centuries CE.

Alexandrian acrobat-dancers were a popular feature of the secular entertainments allied to the devotional celebration of *mawlid*s and associated processions. The dancers ran in front of the procession, carrying long poles bearing a kind of *sistrum* (rattle). More recently, feats have included the dancer's holding an inverted bicycle in his teeth or balancing a chair on his chin while dancing and spinning. The dance includes wide side-to-side hopping, undulating sidestepping, cross-stepping, balancing and pivoting on one leg, crouching and bouncing, and dancing on a chair. Mimetic gestures include stabbing, slashing, throat cutting, and a stylization of the formidable Alexandrian technique of *rusīyah* (using the head as a weapon to deal a stunning blow). Some dancers stab at themselves all over with knives, a dangerous trick. The modern version of the dance uses shawls, scarves, chairs, or knives (sometimes mimed by upright thumbs and pointed fingers) as accessories. The Alexandrian style, including the distinctive gesture of raising the hands alternately to the forehead, has been incorporated in other dancers' routines. The musical instruments used to accompany the dance include the *darabūkah*, the *mazhar*, *riq*, and the accordion.

Horse Dancing. The Arabian horse and his master perpetuate a fabled relationship of prowess and mutual devotion. First domesticated in central Asia, the horse early learned to dance. In the many cultures where horses feature as a companion in labor, sport, and warfare, a close and often mystical tie develops between man and beast. The equestrian principles recorded by Xenophon (c.430–355 BCE) in his treatises *Hipparchikos* (The Riding Master) and *Perihippikes* (Art of Horsemanship) served a martial purpose—training the horse for battle action. They remain mostly valid today as the foundation of the *haute école* of classical equestrianism, brilliantly epitomized by the Lippizaner horses of the Spanish Riding School in Vienna.

In his own territory, the Arabian horse plays an important role in social celebration. It is trained in forms of dressage and dancing peculiar to Arab societies. The horse was introduced into Egypt in the early seventeenth century BCE by the Semitic, nomadic shepherd Hyksos (kings of Egypt of the fifteenth and sixteenth dynasties). A variety of archaeological finds provide evidence of the participation of the horse with dancing youths in ancient and enduring seasonal ritual. Horse-inspired games and dances include the *kurraj*, a fourteenth-century combat dance by two men on stick horses. *Karg/karj*, named after wooden dummy horses suspended on an overdress, was a parallel female dance mimicking equine action. In Egypt, the combat *tardah*, presumably of bedouin origin, involves a large number of participants in two groups. They take turns pursuing each other wielding the spines of palm fronds with which a challenger attempts to touch his opponent. The game was formerly more dangerous, when the fronds were hurled after the fleeing horseman. Another game extant is the *birgas* ("tournament"), a form of jousting or mounted stick play *(taḥṭīb)*.

Among breeders, at the level of serious training and competition, the requirements for appearance and the high art of dressage are stringent. Dance is a prime feature, and the horse, to the rhythm of *wahdah wa nus* ("one and a half") played on the *tabl'* and *mizmār* (oboe), performs a variety of exercises. Among these are the *murabba'* (square), a cadenced on-the-spot trot; the *ta'qīlah*, in which the animal propels itself in rhythm off its hind legs while flexing one foreleg to the chest; and the *igwaz*, a combination of the *murabba'* in front and the *ta'qīlah* at the rear that even attempts an equine "Charleston," with the *ta'qīlah* in front and sideways kicking in the rear. In the *tahāyah* ("salute"), the horse firmly extends the foreleg. It can kneel and lie down, and the rider may dance, standing on the horse's back. Owners provide their horses with colourful, ornate harness, some of whose designs originated in the Abbasid, Fatimid, and Mamluk periods. Horse dance and games enliven *mawlids*, weddings, circumcisions, harvest festivities, and other popular events.

Nubian Dance. Nubia, the ancient land linking Egypt with sub-Saharan Africa, has disappeared under the waters of Lake Nasser, which was formed behind the new Aswan High Dam. The dam has permanently divided the Nubians of Egypt from those of the Sudan. In 1963, the Nubian communities (with a population of some fifty thousand) were relocated en masse to settlements in Upper Egypt, moving from a narrow, thousand-mile-long ribbon of sparsely populated, isolated villages lying along the Nile, to planned, compact, contiguous settlements near Kom Ombo. This was a radical shift in their basic demographic pattern. The rich Nilotic Nubian culture of the three main Nubian groups, the southern Fedija, the northern Kenuz, and the Arabic-speaking Nubians of Wadi al-'Arab in between, has been forever changed. Nubian culture has not been obliterated, but the Nubians are no longer a Nilotic people. Their society has had to adjust to a radically different environment.

Major occasions of ceremonial life—weddings, funerals, Islamic feasts, and, particularly among the Kenuz, *mawlids*—have sometimes been simplified or altered by the new residential situation and by exposure to the customs of Upper Egypt. A vital dimension of Nubian social relations, reciprocal obligation, has been affected. In old Nubia, the people were confronted with problems of limited resources and migration (well over half the inhabitants of every Nubian village lived in cities hundreds of miles distant, as migrant workers). For these problems the Nubians devised non-violent solutions. Nubian polity achieved a delicate balance between economy, ecology, and kinship organization. Intricate ceremony and pageantry, embodying a syncretism of popular Islamic and pagan customs, mark the crucial events of birth, circumcision, marriage and death.

The marriage ceremony—economically, socially, and ceremonially the most significant occasion in the life of Nubian men and women—embodied the network of relationships within the society. The most vital of these, illustrated by a ceremony rich and elaborate in detail and execution, is the system of mutual obligations by which the entire community mobilizes to produce ceremonies and complete tasks. The fundamental principle of the exchange relationship is total reciprocity. Monetary gifts offered to the groom are recorded as a debt to be repaid when the occasion arises. After the signing of the contract, the event culminates with the prenuptial bestowal

EGYPT: Traditional Dance. A hobby-horse dance performed by members of an Egyptian troupe at a festival in Lagos, Nigeria, 1977. (Photograph © Folklore Film, Stockholm; courtesy of Ibrahim Farrah, *Arabesque Magazine*, New York.)

of his share of wealth and gifts on the groom, and of gold jewelry on the bride. The actual wedding is the highlight of long days of arrangements, parties, and wedding announcements—a joyous but exhausting pattern of festive activity. Merrymaking, with dancing, singing, and drumming, is continuous. *Dhikr* is an essential feature of the celebrations (see above). At the end, the groom is danced in a procession to the bride awaiting him in the *diwani* ("marriage room").

Practiced by the ancient Egyptians, male circumcision remains universal in the Middle East. Female excision is also widespread in Islamic communities from India to Morocco. Although the Nubian wedding is more complex, the circumcision ceremony greatly resembles it, with marriage symbolism everywhere—the boy, usually aged between three and five, is called the "groom." (The girls' circumcision ceremony is relatively abbreviated and private.) Weddings and circumcisions are sometimes held simultaneously, or a cooperative ceremony is held for several boys, to minimize costs. As with a wedding, a lengthy period of preparation precedes the event. Music and dance begin with the first day of the ceremony and intensify while the procedure is taking place. The child is also taken in a ceremonial dancing procession to a saint's tomb, where an ecstatic *dhikr* is performed and a feast served. For the entire duration of a wedding or circumcision, and the forty days of Mushahara (the period of supernatural danger that attends a life crisis) following the event, many ritual precautions are observed to protect the couple or the little groom, who are particularly vulnerable at this time to the evil eye.

Nubian dance movement, delicate and supple, is accompanied by vigorous drumming on the *tār*. A variety of complex clapping or syncopated clapping-and-stamping rhythmic patterns supplement the drumming. The singing with choral response is punctuated by the women's piercing ululations. Men and women dance in discrete groups, simultaneously, generally separated by the singer; the musicians drum standing to one side.

In procession to a shrine, a large crowd of singing and dancing people spreads out along the path, the men moving backward with locked arms, the singer between them and the women regulating the progress of the procession. A distance of up to six miles (9.6 kilometers) could thus be covered in several hours. The tempo of the dance varies. In one dance, aligned participants clasp hands and, shuffling a step at a time, advance and then retreat. In another, girls in bright dresses and women clad in a transparent black overdress subduing their vivid colors, move in a semicircle, half a pace forward and then backward, with the right foot and then the left, clasping hands, swaying from side to side, and advancing with a slight inclination of the torso. A solitary woman may move forward to dance more rapidly. The men stand opposite, drumming,

clapping, and singing. Young men in a group vie with one another in the impetuosity of their clapping and dancing, occasionally moving apart to compete in pairs, to dance an inspired solo, or to join in a duet, flashing nimble footwork.

Nineteenth-century illustrations of Nubian dances depict scenes purported to represent "seasonal dances," during which youths, with martial display, selected their mates. Other illustrations show combat dances accompanied on a *qithar* (zither), which resemble the sword-and-shield dance of the Ababda (see above). This performance appears to be restricted to the Wadi al-'Arab Nubians, who also render a version of the *kaf* (see above). Arab influence may be inferred. Attempts have been made to trace this widespread form of combat dance to ancient Nubian practice in uninterrupted tradition. Such suggestions, supported by the evidence of artifacts such as the enduring image of the dwarf-god Bes thus accoutred, or ninth- to thirteenth-century Coptic textiles whose design incorporates sword and shield dances, remain conjectural.

Ringah. Ample archaeological remains in Egypt support evidence of continuous contacts with sub-Saharan Africa and the presence of sub-Saharan Africans in Egypt throughout the centuries. Black-skinned dancers were considered exotic and delightful by the ancient Egyptians. At the time of Sudan's conquest by Egypt's ruler Muḥammad 'Alī Pasha in 1820, there was an influx of Sudanese into Egypt as a result of migration, the slave trade, and the induction of Sudanese soldiers. In the late nineteenth century, Sudanese fleeing internal strife under the Mahdi (an Islamic messianic leader), settled in Egypt. (A large community in the town of Qena in Upper Egypt claims to have established itself there at that time). In about the mid-nineteenth century, Sudanese and Nubian performers were featured in bridal processions. They interspersed their acrobatic feats, clowning, and tricks with mock combat dances. This practice decreased by the turn of the century. The display of weapons was then banned because of serious political disturbances. Dance as entertainment became a form of soliciting, in the popular quarters—a practice that eventually faded.

By the first third of the twentieth century, the Sudanese *ringah* had gained prominence as a popular feature of *mawlid* entertainment. It has been described as a weird institution, always associated with the consumption of *boozah*, a kind of beer. The *ringah* enjoyed a steadily increasing vogue and was even permanently established in some places in Cairo.

Ringah performance, by male and female dancers, graceful and rhythmic, consists essentially of a "treadmill" step: a thrusting of a buttock to the rear and flapping arm movements close to the body. Men and women circle, group, and pair off. They may clasp hands and dance facing each other or back to back or side to side. The males display their talent—dancing and leaping, brandishing one or more rattles *(sistra)* shaken high, until they are "accepted" by the female they are "courting." Their use of the rattle recalls the *ringu* and *kurīah*, instruments traditionally associated with the dance. The *ringah* itself takes its name from the *ringu*, a xylophone made of gourds tied to wooden blocks and struck by mallets (similar instruments can be found in areas of western Africa). Metallic notes are struck with a pair of iron rods on the *kurīah*, a section of railway line. Singing in a crooning style may complement the accompaniment. The performance of *ringa* appears to be on the wane, if not extinct. The influence of Sudanese dance survives, in a restricted sense, in the *zār sudani* (Sudanese *zār*, see above).

Tahṭīb. Complex and highly structured, the *tahṭīb* is the oldest surviving form of Egyptian martial art. Its dynamically powerful offensive and defensive techniques were formulated centuries ago. Each of a pair of opponents wields against the other a thick, five-to-six foot bamboo or wooden stave, held in single or double-fisted grasp. This formidable weapon is still carried by the Egyptian peasant, particularly in Upper Egypt and used in self-defense. A fight involving *tahṭīb* techniques transforms graceful stick playing into a vicious and dangerous melee. Stylized, these techniques involve movement closely related to dance.

A favorite feature of *mawlid* entertainments and other festive occasions, the dueling of the *tahṭīb* is accompanied by the *tabl' baladi* (big drum), *naqrazan* (small kettledrum suspended from the neck), and *mizmār* (oboe). While maintaining his defense by circular sweeps of the stick about the body, each combatant seeks to penetrate his opponent's guard. He slashes, parries, feints, and eludes his adversary. Long intervening moments are spent nearly motionless, as each waits tensely for the other to flinch. Sometimes a combatant breaks away to hop, stick upheld, bent leg raised at a right angle to the body—a position prevalent in ancient Egyptian dance. He taunts, defies, and issues challenges verbally or with guttural bursts of sound. When practiced as a pastime, strict rules and restrictions apply during the game. Any infringement entails ejection from competition.

A demonstration of *tahṭīb* may be preceded or followed by a stick dance *(raqs bil asah)* in place or in a procession. This allows the individual performer to demonstrate musicality, skill, and inventiveness in the manipulation of his stick—solo or in harmonious ensemble combinations. The tempo and rhythms vary, as the men pace slowly through dignified evolutions, step out to the lilting *wahdah wa nus*, or perform mincing steps to a lively staccato. The musicians can mingle with the dancers, stepping and swaying rhythmically. The *tabl'* drummer, who, during *tahṭīb* can intervene to separate overly aggressive combat-

EGYPT: Traditional Dance. Two combatants of *tahṭīb*, a stylized martial art closely related to dance. (Photograph courtesy of Ibrahim Farrah, *Arabesque Magazine*, New York.)

ants and to regulate the game, often contributes a specialty tour de force. In one such feat, he spins incessantly on one foot, drum on upraised leg, and never misses a beat. Elements of *tahṭīb* are found in the *raqs al-jihayni*, a dance of the *ghawāzī* (public dancing girls) repertory (see below).

Dancing Girls. There has been far more reference to the voluptuous art of the dancing girls of Egypt than to all other Egyptian dance forms combined. The Western term *belly dance* (Fr., *danse du ventre*) refers only to the most familiar aspect of a dance genre that is ancient, various, widespread, and performed by both men and women. The defining element of this dance is a variety of articulated pelvic movements. Variants of the form exist from Morocco to Iran and from Greece to Turkestan to North India. It is, however, regarded as preeminently Egyptian, despite other cultural influences that have shaped the current style over a period of more than two millennia. Numerous theories have evolved to explain the origins and functions of this seductive dance, many associated with fertility and maternity. Some antique pottery figurines, of a type produced to this day to celebrate occasions, such as *sebu'* (the seventh day after a birth), represent dancers of both sexes. These figurines retain traces of long-vanished dances and rites. Celebration of *sebu'* was associated with ritual involving dance, and the "haloes" on the figurines (wreaths, crowns, other headgear) were held to possess magical properties.

The ancient practice of the execution of special feats requiring exceptional muscular control, skill, strength, and balance also survive in Egyptian dance. In the nineteenth century, a performer danced carrying a fowl settled on the head, a full water vessel, a sword balanced on its blade, or a stick. Other acrobatic dances involved vessels balanced

EGYPT: Traditional Dance. An 1869 engraving depicting a quartet of *ghawāzī* (dancing girls) performing a dance with finger cymbals. Note their loosened hair and flowing skirts. (Photograph courtesy of Ibrahim Farrah, *Arabesque Magazine*, New York.)

variously on the shoulders, arms, or head. "Specialties" included using spasmodic muscular contractions to transfer water from a full vessel on one side of the abdomen to an empty one on the other; and picking up from the floor a full cup of coffee between the teeth, then bounding from a kneeling position to the feet in one swift motion. Such skills seem to have all but died out.

An antique form of a striptease may have survived into the nineteenth century as the lively and risqué *raqṣat al-nahlah* ("dance of the bee"). The dancer, pretending a state of extreme agitation, teasingly sheds garment after garment as if to rid herself of a bee caught in her clothing. The most celebrated extant dance of this type is the *raqṣ al-sham ʿeddan* ("candelabrum dance"), in which the performer balances a tall, heavy, and ornate candelabrum, complete with lighted candles, on her head, simultaneously dancing and performing such tricks as shimmying,

spinning, doing splits, lying prone, and rolling. Based on the evidence of the *sebuʿ* dolls, dancers of the past may themselves have served as candelabra, with metallic candle-holding frames placed over their skirts, to add an element of danger. The present-day dance may derive from this older form, but its origin and function (if any) remain unknown.

Within the tradition of the *danse du ventre* is the distinctive form practiced by the *ghawāzī*, a unique style distinguished by a rapid vibration of the hips. In the past, these mostly itinerant dancers were the chief attractions at great religious and other public festivals; they were also engaged privately to dance at weddings, births, circumcisions, and all-male parties. Their origin is unclear, but they seem to derive from the Gypsies of India. They entered Egypt in 1517, in the wake of the conquering Ottoman army of Sultan Selim. The Egyptian name *Ghawāzī* for the people may refer to the predilection of their dancers for adorning themselves with quantities of an early Ottoman gold coin, the *ghāzī*, whose plural is *ghawāzī*. Their costume, a bolero and skirt overhung with long, tinseled strips, is derived from nineteenth-century dancers' apparel, although a tiara has been substituted for a kerchief. Padding is worn just below the waistline, under the skirt. *Ghawāzī* dancers usually perform in pairs, trios, or quartets, both in an improvised style and in choreographed or semichoreographed form. Their repertory includes *raqṣ al-takht* (an opening dance), *raqṣ al-na 'asi* (dance with cymbals), *asherat al-tabl'* (drum dance), *raqṣ al-jihayni* (a combat dance with sticks and elements of *taḥṭīb*), and *nizzawi* (using staffs manipulated as batons). Some dancers also sing. [*See* Danse du Ventre.]

After Egypt's ruler Muḥammad ʿAlī Pasha banned all dancing girls from Cairo in 1834 (not the first such stricture against dancers), the number of male dancers, already famous before the ban, increased markedly. Performing in a style that was not altered to accommodate performance by young males, these dancers almost inevitably wore female attire and were generally regarded with the opprobrium attaching to a male performer who does not create a masculine presence. The popularity of such dancing youths is rooted in ancient times, and the practice survives.

It is known that dance schools existed in the nineteenth century; a report of the period situates a "coffeehouse academy" at Kafr Mustanat in the "lower provinces." There, a colony of Ghawazi trained children who were bought or stolen from *fellah* ("peasant") mothers. Today, professional dancers in the metropolis of Cairo are drawn from sources other than the families of hereditary dancers to perform the *raqṣ sharqī* ("Oriental dance"), *raqṣ baladī* ("native dance"), *raqṣ misrī* ("Egyptian dance"), and *raqṣ ʿarabī* ("Arabian dance"). The *ghazīyah*—or *aʿlima* ("singer") as she was often erreonously termed—should now be distinguished from the better-paid and trained *raqiṣa sharqī* ("Oriental dancer") performing in night clubs, at private celebrations, or in films. Retired dancers, some famous, teach the refinements of interpretation, if not technique, and pass on routines.

BIBLIOGRAPHY

Alexandru, T., and E. A. Wahba. *The Folk Music of Egypt.* Cairo, 1967.
Berger, Morroe. "A Curious and Wonderful Gymnastic: The Arab Danse du Ventre." *Dance Perspectives*, no. 10 (Spring 1961): 4–41.
Fakhry, Ahmed. *The Oases of Egypt*, vol. 1, *Siwa Oasis.* Cairo, 1973.
Fernea, Robert A. "Initial Adaptations to Resettlement: A New Life for Egyptian Nubians." *Current Anthropology* (1966): 349–354.
Fernea, Robert A. *Nubians in Egypt: Peaceful People.* Austin, Tex., 1973.
Kennedy, John G. "Nubian Zar Ceremonies as Psychotherapy." *Human Organization* (1967): 185–194.
Khādim, Saʿd al-. *Al-raqṣ al-shaʿbī fī Miṣr.* Cairo, 1972.
Lane, Edward W. *An Account of the Manners and Customs of the Modern Egyptians.* London, 1836.
McPherson, J. W. *The Moulids of Egypt.* Cairo, 1941.
Mīṣrī, Fāṭimah al-. *Al-zār: Dirāsah nafsīyah taḥlīlīyah anthrūpūlūgīyah.* Cairo, 1975.
Mulouk, Q. el-. "The Mystery of the Ghawazi." *Habibi* 3–5 (n.d.).
Murray, G. W. *Sons of Ishmael.* London, 1935.
Saleh, Magda. "The Rise of the Egyptian Ballet." *Dance News* (April 1979): 8.
Saleh, Magda. "'Raqs el Kheil': The Dancing Horses of Egypt." *Arabesque* 8 (July–August 1982): 8–9.
Saleh, Magda. "The Ghawazi of Egypt: A Preliminary Report." *Arabesque* 19 (July–August 1993): 8–12.
Saleh, Maher. "Al-furusīyah wa-raqṣ al-kheil." *Al-Funūnal-Shaʿbīyah* 2 (April 1965).
Wood, Leona, and Anthony V. Shay. "Danse du Ventre: A Fresh Appraisal." *Dance Research Journal* 8 (Spring–Summer 1976): 18–30.

MAGDA SALEH

EGYPT: Traditional Dance. A pair of modern *ghawāzī* dancing with finger cymbals, probably in the 1970s. Note that their appearance is strikingly similar to their nineteenth-century counterparts: they wear a shimmery overskirt low on the waist, with padding at the hips, and are adorned with jewelry. (Photograph courtesy of Ibrahim Farrah, *Arabesque Magazine*, New York.)

Contemporary Dance Companies

Egypt today may be considered a bicultural nation in that it has maintained a broad base of local tradition alongside

Western imports. Some hybridization has also resulted from the combining of the two.

Folk Dance Companies. Inspired by the potential of colorful folkloric theatrical dance, as first revealed in the 1950s by the USSR's touring Moiseyev Dance Company and other Soviet-influenced European companies, Mahmoud Reda in 1959 formed the Firqat Reda Lil Funun al-Shaʻbīyah, popularly known as the Firqat Reda (Reda Troupe). Reda undertook extensive field surveys and pioneered the use of traditional Egyptian folk forms to create theatrical dance spectacle.

Reda's work ranged beyond the mere glamorization of original forms, generating vignettes of both rural and urban life, as well as pieces based on folk tales, history, and myth. For these and his full-length dramatic productions, claiming creative license, Reda borrowed movements from non-Egyptian sources to enliven and enrich his choreography. His sister-in-law, Farida Fahmy, was the company's longtime leading dancer and co-artistic director. His brother, the film director Ali Reda, also managed the company and was a contributing choreographer. This independent endeavor was an instant success and soon accepted a Ministry of Culture subsidy. In 1961 it became a state-sponsored entity. The initial company of eight male and eight female dancers peaked in the late 1970s at one hundred fifty. In 1963, Egypt's Ministry of Culture created a second folkloric ensemble, the Firqa al-Qawmīyah Lil-Funun al-Shaʻbīyah, the National Folkloric Troupe.

Soviet specialists were sent to Egypt to engage in nationwide fieldwork; they meticulously researched and documented the local dance genres, the music, vocalization, and costumes. A center for folk arts, the Markaz al-Funun al-Shaʻbīyah was soon founded by Egypt to become an ongoing national repository for ethnography and ethnology. Its collection was initially headed by Tiberiu Alexandru, a Romanian-born ethnomusicologist. The center is now attached to the Higher Institute of Folklore at the Academy of the Arts in Cairo, a graduate-level institution that offers master's and doctoral degrees in folklore scholarship.

The artistic directors of the performing group of the Firqa al-Qawmīyah were initially Soviet specialists, and the first was Boris Ramazin. Since 1979, this troupe has been headed by Egyptians, and the first was the dancer and choreographer Mohammed Khalil. The repertory consists mainly of "numbers," a series of theatricalized versions of a variety of authentic folk genres. Both dance companies now belong to the Folk Art sector of the Ministry of Culture. They have toured extensively, performing and participating in international festivals. The Reda troupe has been included in popular films. These companies have served as the inspiration and model for a proliferation of regional troupes in the various governorates (provinces) of Egypt, under the auspices of the Mass Culture sector of the Ministry of Culture (presently the General Organization for Palaces of Culture), housed in the Palaces of Culture in the governorate capitals. Several companies have achieved national prominence, with the Aswan (Nubian) and Sharqīyah (Eastern Delta) companies enjoying international recognition.

In 1956, Zakariah al-Heggawi, a devoted amateur of the traditional arts, saw the threat to these folk dances posed by their heightened promotion, popularization, and media exposure. He soon collected from all over Egypt a diverse, but select, group of authentic traditional musicians, singers, dancers, and epic poetry reciters; he named this unique ensemble Firqat al-Fellahin (Peasants' Troupe). In 1970, it became the Firqat al-Alaʿat al-Shaʻbīyah (Folk Instruments' Troupe). From 1970 to 1975, it was headed by musicologist Soleiman Gamil; since 1975, it has been under the direction of theater director Abdel Rahman el-Shafei, who is also director of mass culture for greater Cairo and Middle Egypt. The troupe has traveled worldwide, first appearing in Paris in 1974 as Les Musiciens du Nil; in 1976 it performed to critical and popular acclaim at the bicentennial folk festival in Washington, D.C., which was organized by the Smithsonian Institution. Its success abroad is not reflected in Egypt, where native arts do not have any cultural cachet but are regarded as primitive and nonaesthetic. The theatricalized versions are, however, considered a substantial improvement in the drive toward refinement.

Western Dance. Egyptian audiences were no strangers to classical ballet when the state-sponsored ballet school (Madraset al-Ballet) was founded in 1958 by Egypt's first minister of culture, Sarwat Okasha. The Cairo Opera House, built in 1869 by Khedive Ismail for the inauguration of the Suez Canal, became Egypt's venue for European music, opera, ballet, drama, and other theatrical productions. *Giselle* was the first ballet staged there, in 1882. After the building burned in 1971, this cultural hub was replaced by the National Cultural Center, inaugurated in October 1988 as a gift of the government of Japan to the people of Egypt. Its founding director was Magda Saleh, the *prima ballerina* of the original Cairo Ballet and a former professor and dean of the Higher Institute of Ballet. This new venue, completed after a hiatus of seventeen years, revitalized Cairo's cultural milieu.

Egypt's classical ballet school rapidly crystallized into the established institution that became the Higher Institute of Ballet; today it is one of the seven institutes constituting the Academy of the Arts. Soon after its founding, Enayat Azmi, a graduate and faculty member of the Higher Institute of Physical Education for Women, became dean. In 1984, Magda Saleh assumed this post, the first graduate of the school to be appointed. Alexei Zhukov, a former soloist of the Bolshoi Theater in

EGYPT: Contemporary Dance Companies. Egypt's *prima ballerina*, Magda Saleh, in a National Ballet of Cairo production of *Don Quixote*. (Photograph courtesy of Magda Saleh.)

Moscow was its first instructor. For more than twenty years, the school was staffed by Russian experts, who taught the full Russian academic ballet curriculum. In 1979, following the Soviet invasion of Afghanistan, Egyptian faculty who had obtained their degrees mainly from Russia but also from Bulgaria, France, and the United States assumed the instruction. Some Russian experts have returned to Cairo, in the 1990s, to resume their teaching duties at the institute. The Higher Institute offers undergraduate degrees in pedagogy and choreography, and the master's and doctoral degrees in classical ballet.

The first generation of Egyptian ballerinas were Aleya Abdel Razeq, Wadoud Faizi, Diane Haqqaq, Magda Saleh, and Maya Selim. After preliminary training in Cairo, they completed their studies in 1965 at the Bolshoi Academic Choreographic School in Moscow. One other Egyptian, Heba Abdel Fattah, born and bred in Moscow, graduated at the same school more than twenty years later. The all-Egyptian Cairo Ballet, with the five Russian-trained dancers in its cast, made its debut in December 1966, with *The Fountain of Bakhchisarai*, directed by Leonid Lavrovsky. As a success, the principals were decorated by President Gamal Abdel Nasser. Constantin Shatilov was the company's first artistic director; Anatoly Kuznetsov was the second. In rapid succession, *Giselle*, *The Nutcracker*, *Don Juan*, *Paquita Variations*, *Francesca da Rimini*, *Don Quixote*, *The Great Waltz*, *Gayané*, *Hamlet*, *Shéhérazade*, and other important ballets were added to the repertory. In 1970, Serge Lifar became the first Western choreographer to work with the recently formed company, creating his version of *Daphnis and Chloe*. The need

for a national expression in ballet idiom soon stimulated works by Egyptian choreographers. Early examples include the one-act *Al-Ayyam al-Assiba* (Days of Trial), also titled *Al-Soumoud* (Fortitude), on the theme of the 1967 Arab-Israeli conflict; it was created by Abdel Monem Kamel in 1971, to music by the Uzbeki composer Mokhtar Ashrafi. The full-length *Eyoun Bahīyah* (Baheyya's Eyes) was a 1975 collaborative work by premier danceur Kamel and Esmat Ali, composed by Gamal Salama. It was a political paean to Egypt's president Anwar Al-Sadat and imbued with nationalist symbolism. Magda Ezz transposed folkloric material in *Al-Moulid* (The Saint's Day Celebration). Magda Saleh, from 1974 to 1985, explored Egyptian themes in the medium of modern dance in choreographic miniatures, such as *Tahtib* (Stick Dance), *Mourning Isis*, *Seth Triumphant*, *Zār* (in collaboration with Margalit Oved), and *Bride of the Nile*, a *pièce d'occasion* for a pair of Egyptian contestants at the 1985 International Ballet Competition in Moscow.

Since 1972, the Cairo Ballet toured abroad, in full strength or in smaller troupes, in the USSR, Bulgaria, Japan, Germany, France, Italy, Mexico, Cuba, and North Korea, among others. In 1971/72, Saleh and partner Kamel starred as guest artists in *Giselle* and *Don Quixote* with the Kirov and Bolshoi ballets, as well as in other Soviet venues. Several of Egypt's male dancers, including Reda Sheta, Ahmed Ashour, and Gamal Gouda, have successfully pursued careers in Europe.

Until the inauguration of the New Opera House, the Cairo Ballet was affiliated with the Academy of the Arts. After 1988, the Cairo Opera Ballet was founded at this new venue as the resident company, and it has been directed since its inception by Kamel. The company is no longer all Egyptian, the majority of its dancers are Russian and Ukrainian. Their repertory combines such classics as *Swan Lake, Giselle, The Nutcracker, Les Sylphides, Le Corsaire, La Bayadère, Don Quixote*, and *Romeo and Juliet* with contemporary productions, including *Boléro*, as choreographed by Maurice Béjart, and *Carmina Burana*, as choreographed by Abdel Monem Kamel.

The pupils of the Higher Institute of Ballet are regularly pressed into service, to perform in national celebration super productions and other official, semi-official, and private-sector events. They are also in demand for appearances in children's television programs, festive productions, and commercials. The school continues to participate in international festivals and ballet competitions. The Higher Institute opened a satellite unit in Alexandria that was initially headed by Wadoud Faizi, one of the original five Egyptian dancers trained in Moscow. The curriculum is truncated and the courses abbreviated there, so it has not become a viable equivalent of its parent school in Cairo.

Modern Dance. Recognition and gradual acceptance of modern dance is coming from Cairo audiences. Their primary exposure was to its many variations by visiting world-renowned American and European companies. In 1993, the Firqat al-Raqs al-Hadith (the Cairo Opera Dance Theater) modern dance troupe was established under artistic director Walid Awni at the New Opera House. Of Lebanese origin, Awni was for seventeen years the director of the Tanit Dance Theater in Belgium and an associate of Maurice Béjart for six years. This fledgling company, which premiered at the fourth International Festival for Experimental Theater in Cairo with *Suqqout Ikaros* (The Fall of Icarus), claims a groundbreaking position for Arab theater in Cairo.

To date, choreographies have focused on eminent artistic and cultural icons and symbols, such as Nobel Prize–winning author Naguib Mafouz, painter Taheyya Halim, and film director Shadi Abdel Salam. Performances in Egypt attract particular critical attention and debate. Appearing abroad, the group of four female and nine male dancer-actors has been well received at international festivals in Tunisia, Germany, and South Korea.

Private Studios. A number of private ballet studios existed in prerevolutionary (1952) Egypt. Noted in Cairo were the schools of Sonia Ivanova, Magda Sami, Nelly Mazloum, and Michael Al-Dabh, among others. In Alexandria, the Conservatoire de Musique d'Alexandrie operated a ballet division. Teachers from the British Royal Academy of Dance, including Joyce Mackie and Sonia Chamberlain, taught there, training the beginner Magda Saleh. Maya Selim studied with Ivanova; Aleya Abdel Razeq with Sami; Diane Haqqaq with Michael Al-Dabh

before enrolling in the state school. Another Ivanova graduate, Persephone Samaropoulo, a Greek-Egyptian, left Egypt for a career in Europe.

A new group of dance studios is now flourishing in Cairo. In 1972, an enterprising administrative staff member at the Higher Institute of Ballet, Nagwa Shalabi, promoted the creation of a ballet program at the Shams Sporting Club, where she remains in charge. Teachers there are faculty members from the Higher Institute of Ballet, with one specialist from Azerbaijian, Ferkhat Ali. The all-girl student body numbers 250, rivaling the number at the ballet school of the Higher Institute. One of the Shams graduates has joined the Cairo Opera Ballet. The Nadi al-Shams Ballet, functioning under the auspices of the Higher Council for Sport and Youth, participated in international festivals in Yugoslavia, Turkey, Poland, and Germany. Less developed ballet programs are run at the Gezira Sporting Club in Cairo and the Alexandria Sporting Club. Two of the Ivanova Studio graduates, Samia Allouba and Indji Al-Solh, run successful businesses. Allouba's Creative Dance and Fitness Center's main branch is in a spacious, handsomely appointed location. Courses include classical ballet, jazz, folk, and belly dancing as well as fitness, aerobics, callanetics, and creative movement. A secondary facility is also in Cairo. Al-Solh offers a professional rather than a recreational approach. She teaches modern and jazz dance, as well as movement for actors at the theater department of the American University in Cairo. The American University also offers folklore dance as an extracurricular activity course. Ballet Institute faculty member Esmat Ali has two dance studios; Fatma Marzouq, a former Cairo Ballet dancer has one. A number of schools in Cairo and Alexandria offer ballet instruction as an extracurricular activity.

The private sector's dramatic, musical, and children's shows, seasonal extravaganzas, weddings, hotel dinner shows, and tourist entertainment (mostly folklore inspired) offer lucrative salaries to dancers and choreographers. Since they are far beyond those offered by state-sponsored troupes, they drain talented dancers from careers in the classical arts. Political realignment, socioeconomic dislocation, an altered cultural climate, and bureaucratic stagnation have also depleted the state-sponsored schools and troupes. In addition to the many male dancers who have pursued careers abroad, mainly in Europe, Egyptian dancers have established studios or teach abroad. Among them are Leila Amin, Hassan Sheta, and Nadia Abbas in Australia; Mary Abdel Malek in Canada; Diane Haqqaq, the couple Wagih Youssef and Mervat Nabarawi, Salwa Henery, and Nader Hamed in the United States; and Ahmed Ezzat in Germany. In a professional switch, Safwat Gerges and his sister Mona, Tharwat Murad, the couple Yousri Selim and Elham al-Amir, and Ahmed Mahgoub thrive in the domain of ballroom dance in the United States. Mahgoub also teaches Egyptian folklore and Oriental dance. Mahmoud Reda travels extensively in the United States and Europe, teaching Egyptian dance at workshops and conventions. Magda Saleh is the president of Performing Arts International, Inc., a New York–based agency promoting cultural exchanges between the United States and the Middle East.

BIBLIOGRAPHY

Karkabi, Barbara Farrar. "Choreography in Cairo." *Aramco World Magazine* 28 (March-April 1977): 16–23.
Matthews, Nancy. "Egyptian Arabesque." *Dance Scope* 13 (Fall 1978): 36–43.
Saleh, Magda. "The Rise of the Egyptian Ballet." *Dance News*.
MAGDA SALEH

EIFMAN, BORIS (Boris Iakovlevich Eifman; born 22 July 1946 in Rubtsovsk, Russian Soviet Federated Socialist Republic), choreographer. In 1964 Eifman graduated from the ballet school in Kishinev, capital of the Moldovan republic, and from the choreography department of the Leningrad Conservatory, where he trained under Georgi Aleksidze. From 1970 to 1977 he was choreographer for the Leningrad ballet school, where he staged his first ballets for graduation performances. He choreographed *Gayané* to Aram Khachaturian's score at the Leningrad Maly (now Modest Mussorgsky) Theater in 1972 and restaged it in Lodz, Poland, in 1975. He choreographed *The Firebird* for the Kirov Theater in 1975.

In 1977 Eifman founded his own company, which changed names several times: Leningrad New Ballet in 1977, Leningrad Ballet Ensemble in 1978, Leningrad Theater of Contemporary Ballet from 1983 to 1986, Leningrad State Theater of Ballet from 1986 to 1991, and Saint Petersburg Theater of Contemporary Ballet after 1991. Eifman's aim was to create ballets for young people, who considered the standard classics obsolete. Consequently, he used music by contemporary composers (often non-Russians), especially rock music and the music of popular groups. He also looked for subjects that could inspire youngsters: *The Interrupted Song* (1977) was set to music that Latvian composer Imant Kalninjs wrote for the death of Chilean rock singer Victor Jara; *Boomerang* (1979) was set to music by John McLaughlin, based on Bertolt Brecht's *Threepenny Opera;* and *Bivocality* (1977) was set to music of the rock group Pink Floyd. His untraditional style used ballet technique combined with acrobatics, modern dance, and jazz and rock movements.

By the 1980s Eifman shifted his interest and began to specialize in ballets on themes of classical literature, often choosing literary works depicting strong emotions. His first big success was *The Idiot* (1980), based on Dostoyevsky's novel, to the music of Tchaikovsky's Sixth Symphony. He then choreographed *Second Lieutenant Romashov* (1985) based on Aleksandr Kuprin's novel *The Duel*, to music by Valery Gavrilin; *The Master and Margarita* (1987), based on Mikhail Bulgakov's novel, to music by Andrei Petrov; *The Murderers* (1990), based on the novel *Thérèse Raquin* by Balzac, to music by Bach, Mahler, and Alfred Schnitke; and *Tchaikovsky* (1993), using his music. Eifman has also produced comedies, sometimes in farcical style, using acrobatics and buffoonery: *A Day of Madness* (1982), based on Beaumarchais's play *The Marriage of Figaro*, set to music by Rossini; and *Twelfth Night* (1985), based on Shakespeare, to music by Donizetti.

Eifman is a leading Saint Petersburg choreographer who has had an important influence on Russian choreography. He has the title, bestowed in 1988, of Honored Art Worker of the Russian Federation.

BIBLIOGRAPHY

Ballet Théâtre de Leningrad: Boris Eifman. Pamphlet, Théâtre des Champs-Elysées Festival de Danse Sovietique, Paris, 1990.
Degen, Arsen. "St. Petersburg State Theater Ballet of Boris Eifman." *Dance Magazine* (November 1994): 93–94.
Demidov, Alexander P. "New Choreographers Emerging in the Soviet Union." *Dance News* (March 1979): 8–9.
Hertling, Nele. "Dance Observations between East and West." *Ballett International* 13 (December 1990): 10–13.
Koegler, Horst. "One from Russia." *Dance and Dancers* (February 1990): 14–15.
Parks, Gary. "Soviet Artist in New Works." *Dance Magazine* (July 1987): 12.
Sokolov-Kaminsky, Arkady. "O mastere-masterski." *Balet*, no. 1 (1994): 37–38.
Uralskaya, Valeria. "Boris Eifman Warns of Passion's Consequences." *Dance Magazine* (November 1991): 24–27.
Uralskaya, Valeria, and V. Maranzman. "Boris Eifman." *Balet*, no. 3 (1995).
Vanslov, Victor V. "Leningrad Contemporary Ballet Theatre." *Dance Magazine* (July 1989): 53–57.
Vedekhina, O. "Tanzuinshchy *Tchaikovsky*." *Balet*, no. 3 (1994): 38–39.
Whyte, Sally. "St. Petersburg Ballet Theatre." *Dance and Dancers* (August 1992): 31.
ELIZABETH SOURITZ

EIKO AND KOMA, *butō* company established in 1972 by the wife-and-husband team Otake Eiko (born 14 February 1952 in Tokyo) and Otake Takashi (born 27 September 1948 in Niigata City, Japan). Eiko and Takashi both studied law and politics at Chuo University School of Law but left school before graduating. Both were involved in the late-1960s student movement in Japan. They met at Hijikata Tatsumi's dance school in 1971 and from 1971 to 1972 also studied with Ōno Kazuo. In 1972, Takashi, who had taken his wife's family name when they married, adopted the performance-name Koma; Eiko and Koma began to perform experimental dance events on the campus of Waseda University in Tokyo.

EIKO AND KOMA. Husband and wife cling to each other in their dance work *Trilogy*. (Photograph by Kazunobi Yanagi; used by permission.)

Their first collaborative piece, *White Dance*, premiered in Munich, Germany, in October 1972. In Cologne they won an award at a choreography competition; while in Germany they also studied expressionist dance with Manja Chmiel (who had studied with Mary Wigman). *White Dance* was performed again at the Japan Society in New York City in May 1976. Its great success encouraged Eiko and Koma to immigrate to the United States.

Eiko and Koma's dance style is very much akin to that of *Hijikata butō*, concentrating on the physicality of the body and expressing the mystery of eroticism. Eiko and Koma's pieces are always duets, and they themselves create the music and décor for their works. Many of their earlier works were danced without musical accompaniment.

Recent works include *Thirst* (1985), *Rust* (1989), *Passage* (1990), *Land* (1991), and *Wind*, which premiered at the Walker Art Center in Minneapolis in March 1993.

BIBLIOGRAPHY
Fullard, David. "Choreographers/Dancers of the Month." *Attitude* 2.8–11 (1984): 41–42.
Hunt, Marilyn. "A Terrible Beauty Attenuated." *Dance Theatre Journal* 9 (Spring 1992): 28–29.
Johnson, Robert. "Eiko and Koma." *Dance Magazine* (November 1991): 13–14.
Josa-Jones, Paula. "Delicious Moving." *Contact Quarterly* 11 (Winter 1986): 11–15.
Jowitt, Deborah. "Crawling into a Womb of Rice." In Jowitt's *The Dance in Mind*. Boston, 1985.
Kaplan, Peggy Jarrell. *Portraits of Choreographers*. New York, 1988.
Windham, Leslie. "A Conversation with Eiko & Koma." *Ballet Review* 16 (Summer 1988): 47–59.

HASEGAWA ROKU
Translated from Japanese

EK, MATS (born 18 April 1945 in Malmö, Sweden), dancer, choreographer, and ballet director. Ek is the son of choreographer Birgit Cullberg and actor Anders Ek. He made his dance debut at the age of seventeen, but then studied theater. He made his debut as a theater director in 1966 with the Japanese *nō* drama *Kagekiyo*, followed by Georg Büchner's *Wozzeck* in 1967, both at the Mari-

onetteatern of Stockholm. In 1969 Ek was invited by Ingmar Bergman to join the Royal Dramatic Theater. He worked as Bergman's assistant, but also staged plays (by Racine, Shakespeare, Pinter) on his own. Returning to dance in 1973, Ek joined the Cullberg Ballet.

Ek's debut as a choreographer came in 1976 with *Kalfaktorn*, based on themes from *Wozzeck*, followed by *Saint George and the Dragon*. In 1977 came *Soweto* and in 1978 *The House of Bernarda* (later called *Bernarda*), based on Federico García Lorca's play *The House of Bernarda Alba*. In 1981/82 Ek danced with the Netherlands Dance Theater, for which he choreographed, to music of Béla Bartók, *Memories of Youth*. In 1982 he became co-director with his mother of the Cullberg Ballet. That same year he created *Cain and Abel* for the Royal Swedish Ballet and gave his own company a modern, very personal version of *Giselle*, to music by Adolphe Adam, with the second act set in an insane asylum where Myrtha is the head nurse. In 1987 he produced a similarly iconoclastic interpretation of *Swan Lake*. A work that has remained in the repertory is *Pa Norrbotten* (1985), based on the northern folklore and music of Sweden.

EK. The Swedish choreographer in one of his early works, the satirical *Saint George and the Dragon* (1976). (Photograph by Lesley Leslie-Spinks; courtesy of Anna Greta Stahle.)

Ek left the Cullberg Ballet in 1993 to become an independant choreographer. He staged a performance for the Theater Unga Klara (Young Klara), letting the dancers speak and the actors dance. He also acted as guest choreographer for several companies. In 1995 he created a new ballet for the Cullberg Ballet, *She Was Black*. Through the years Ek has also choreographed for television; in 1995 a pas de deux called *Rök* (Smoke), to music by Arvo Pärt, was created for Sylvie Guillem and Niklas Ek as a co-production for Sweden's Channel 1.

Ek's ballets are intense dramas that express protest against oppression, be it in the form of political power, racism, colonialism, or within the family. His choreography is forceful, often violent, but there is also room for humor and satire. His theatrical experience is revealed in his use of light, props, and decor. Many of Ek's ballets have decor and costumes by Marie-Louise Ekman, a sophisticated "naive" painter with an expressive style that matches Ek's.

BIBLIOGRAPHY
Engdahl, Horace. *Swedish Ballet and Dance: A Critic's View*. Translated by Paul Kessel and Erika Svedberg. Stockholm, 1992.
Garske, Rolf. "Searching for a New Complexity: Interview with Mats Ek." *Ballett International* 12 (March 1989): 17–21.
Haglund-Hamp, Lotta. *"Kain och Abel," en balett av Mats Ek*. Stockholm, 1983.
Schmidt, Jochen. "It's the Way That You Tell It!" *Ballett International* 11 (March 1988): 16–21.
Vaccarino, Elisa. "Mats Ek." In Vaccarino's *Altre scene, altre danze: Vent'anni di balletto contemporaneo*. Turin, 1991.

ANNA GRETA STÅHLE

ELIZABETHAN PROGRESSES.

The customary migrations of Queen Elizabeth I of England and her court throughout her realm took place in summer from 1564 until 1603, with some interruption during the troubled decade of 1580. Recreational and political in purpose, progresses provided an escape from London's heat and plague, as well as occasions for exchanging courtesies and cementing bonds between the monarch and her subjects. Her state visits both won Elizabeth popularity and fostered the development of the masque, giving full scope to the Elizabethan taste for ceremonies and fantasy. The queen's favorite pastime, dancing, was an integral part of her progresses.

The royal household moved from one location to the next, sojourning at manor houses, nobles' palaces, and the homes of provincial gentry. Nobles and local officials vied for the privilege of spending vast sums on banquets, sporting events, and theatrical entertainments to glorify and amuse Elizabeth. Poets, musicians, and scholars were commissioned to devise such festivities as the "Princely Pleasures at Kenilworth," recorded by two eyewitnesses, George Gascoigne and Robert Laneham, in 1575 (Nichols, 1823).

In this event the queen, welcomed by a sybil's speeches, a porter costumed as Hercules, and a poet in flowing robes, crossed an elaborately adorned bridge and entered the castle under a shower of fireworks. She was treated to a debate between Savage and Echo, garden encounters with deities and nymphs, a water pageant featuring the Lady of the Lake with a Triton riding a mermaid and Arion on a dolphin, a medieval Hock-tide play, hunting, tilting, bear-baiting, the songs of madrigalists and lutenists, and constant dancing. Villagers feted the queen with Morris dancing; she and her courtiers danced galliards. Proud of her grace, Elizabeth danced vigorously all her life.

James I continued the tradition of progresses, but more in pursuit of the chase than of mimetic entertainment. When in 1613 Queen Anne made her own progress to Bath to take the waters, Morris dancing accompanied pageants offered in her honor. With the ascendancy of the Stuarts, who preferred hunting, masking and dancing lost their dominance and began to pass out of vogue.

BIBLIOGRAPHY
Kelly, William. *Royal Progresses and Visits to Leicester*. Leicester, 1884.
Nichols, John. *The Progresses and Public Processions of Queen Elizabeth*. 3 vols. New ed. London, 1823.
Nichols, John. *The Progresses, Processions, and Magnificent Festivities of King James the First, His Royal Consort, Family, and Court*. 4 vols. London, 1828.
Sieveking, A. Forbes. "Dancing." In *Shakespeare's England*. Vol. 2. Oxford, 1916.

ROBIN WOODARD WEENING

ELIZARIEV, VALENTIN (Valentin Nikolaivich Elizar'ev; born 30 October 1948 in Baku, Belarussian Soviet Socialist Republic), choreographer. Elizariev graduated from the Leningrad Ballet School in 1967 and in 1973 from the choreography department of the Leningrad Conservatory of Music, where he was a pupil of Igor Belsky. He produced several dozen choreographic miniatures and one-act ballets, among them *Contrasts*, to music by Rodion Shchedrin; *The Road*, to music by S. Samoilov (which won a prize at the 1970 USSR Choreography Competition); *Classical Symphony*, music by Sergei Prokofiev; *Poem*, music by Andrei Petrov (for the State Theater of Classical Ballet); *Adagietto*, using music from Gustav Mahler's Fifth Symphony; *Chamber Suite*, music by Shchedrin, for the Belarussian Theater of Opera and Ballet; *The Ballets of Valentin Elizariev*, a production of his one-act ballets by the Warsaw Ballet; and the ballet portion of *Fantasy*, a television film based on Ivan Turgenev's novella *Torrents of Spring* and directed by A. Efros.

In 1973 Elizariev became the artistic director of the Belarussian Theater of Opera and Ballet, where he has staged *Carmen Suite* (1974), music by Bizet orchestrated by Shchedrin; *The Creation of the World* (1976), by Andrei Petrov; *Till Eulenspiegel* (1978), by Evgeny Glebov; *Spartacus* (1980), music by Aram Khachaturian; Tchaikovsky's *The Nutcracker* (1982); and *Carmina Burana* (1983), to the cantata by Carl Orff. His most recent work is *Rogneda* (1995).

Elizariev usually writes his own libretti for his productions. He strives for broad generalizations so that the portrayals of individuals bring out features common to all mankind, national characteristics conjure up thoughts about all nations, and reflections on past events focus attention on current happenings. He makes wide use of the grotesque. Elizariev bases the structure of his ballets on the omission of secondary convolutions of the plot, placing greater emphasis on the culminative actions. His *Creation of the World* is distinguished by a philosophical approach and a high sense of civic commitment. This somewhat humorous dance translation of the biblical story turns into a dramatic tale about the lives of people today. In *Spartacus* and *Till Eulenspiegel* he deals with social problems and strives to disclose patterns of history that still obtain. *The Nutcracker* and *Carmina Burana* reflect an affirmation of beauty and harmony. Among the characteristic features of Elizariev's productions are a poetic picture of the world, rich imagery, a wealth of color, and new choreographic devices.

The Belarussian Ballet has presented Elizariev's productions while on tour in Hungary, Bulgaria, Poland, Kuwait, Syria, Vietnam, Thailand, and Germany. In 1979 Valentin Elizariev was awarded the title of People's Artist.

[*See also* Belarus.]

BIBLIOGRAPHY

Churko, Yulia M. *Belorusskii baletnyi teatr.* Minsk, 1983.
Uralskaya, Valeria, and Musa Kleimenova. "A World of Kindness and Joy" (in Russian). *Sovietskii balet*, no. 2 (1983).

YULIA M. CHURKO
Translated from Russian

ELSSLER SISTERS. Anna, Theresia, and Franziska Elssler, Viennese dancers, were the daughters of Johann Florian Elssler, valet and music copyist to Franz Joseph Haydn. The eldest, **Anna Elssler** (1804–1863), is today hardly remembered, as her career was overshadowed by those of her more famous sisters: Theresia, known professionally as **Thérèse Elssler** (born 5 April 1808, died 19 November 1878 in Merano, Italy), and Franziska, known professionally as **Fanny Elssler** (born 23 June 1810, died 27 November 1884 in Vienna).

Fanny Elssler occupies the place of the second great ballerina of the Romantic era; no mean achievement, considering that the first place belongs to Marie Taglioni, who is credited with popularizing if not creating the genre known as the Romantic ballet. In a period known for dichotomies, Elssler represented the sensuous and even erotic aspects of dance, as opposed to the illusion of disembodied purity projected by Taglioni's dancing. Théophile Gautier went so far as to contrast them in religious terms—Elssler being the desirable and attainable "pagan" dancer, Taglioni the virginal "Christian" dancer.

Elssler's genius in balletic national dances, epitomized by her solo "La Cachucha" in the ballet *Le Diable Boiteux* (1836), lent warmth and color to a stage that otherwise might have been dominated by the chilly whiteness of the sprites and fairies created in emulation of Taglioni's role as the Sylphide. Elssler's technical strengths differed from Taglioni's; Charles Maurice contrasted her *danse taquetée*, which emphasized small steps executed with rapidity and precision, with the more airborne *ballonné* style of Taglioni. She was also generally acknowledged to be a stronger mime than Taglioni. "She spoke without words, roared with soundless laughter, cried with pain though her lips remained sealed," wrote the Danish actress Johanne Luise Heiberg of Elssler's performance in *Le Diable Boiteux*. Her acting ability brought new life to the many roles she undertook, among them Lise in *La Fille Mal Gardée*, the Sylphide, Giselle, and Esmeralda. Her special gifts enriched the Romantic repertory, giving it dimensions it might have lacked had Taglioni alone dominated the field.

Thérèse Elssler, Fanny's elder sister, was also a dancer of note, although she never achieved Fanny's renown. She was unusually tall for a dancer of her day (five feet, six inches) but contrived to turn this into an asset by appearing *en travesti* or by assuming roles that required grandeur and majesty; an admirer called her a "biblical princess." She won some degree of success as a choreographer, creating many vehicles for her sister and herself. Among these was *La Volière* (1838), the first ballet choreographed by a woman to be produced at the Paris Opera.

Thérèse and Fanny trained at the ballet school of the Theater an der Wien. In 1818 they joined Anna in the ballet company of the Kärntnertor Theater, where Jean-Louis Aumer was ballet master. Fanny gave her first recorded performance at the age of seven, as Hymen in Aumer's *Die Hochzeit der Thetis und des Peleus*. Thérèse and Fanny made their first appearance outside Austria in 1825 at the Teatro San Carlo in Naples. (An unexpected result of this journey was the birth of Fanny's son, Franz Robert, in 1827.)

In Berlin, where the sisters first danced in the autumn of 1830, Fanny made her first venture into comedy in *The Swiss Milkmaid*, staged by Antoine Titus after Filippo Taglioni. Her success gave proof of a comic gift that later served her well in ballets such as *La Fille Mal Gardée* and *La Tarentule*.

Fanny and Thérèse first danced in London in March 1833, at the King's Theatre. There they met Marie Taglioni, who had been engaged for the same season. Although Fanny and Taglioni danced together on several occasions, their future rivalry was then unsuspected. Fanny took a leave of absence that autumn to bear a daughter, Thérèse.

Upon her return to the King's Theatre in May 1834, Fanny danced for the first time with Jules Perrot, whose choreography was to provide her with some of her most challenging roles. They first appeared together in a ballet by Thérèse, *Armide*. In the autumn the sisters were engaged to dance at the prestigious Paris Opera. Fanny made her debut there on 15 September 1834, dancing the role of the fairy Alcine in Jean Coralli's *La Tempête*. She was well received. "Her perfection has no rough edges, her grace is always controlled by technique," wrote a reviewer in *Le moniteur*. Marie Taglioni acknowledged "a certain perfection of timing with which she makes the rapid movements which characterise her style of dancing," but added that "hers . . . is a style which deprives the body of grace."

Thérèse first appeared at the Opera on 1 October in a pas de deux she choreographed, wearing male attire and partnering Fanny. Reviews state that she was accustomed to giving her sister first place; as Jules Janin wrote, "Without thought for herself, Thérèse has generously given Fanny the most beautiful poses and the liveliest pieces of music, she shows off her sister as much as she can, and dances herself only to give her time to recover her breath." Her first female role at the Paris Opera was Rosalie, the sister of the heroine Mathilde (Fanny) in Louis Henry's *L'Île des Pirates* (1835).

In 1836, Fanny had her first great triumph, the role of Florinda in Coralli's *Le Diable Boiteux*. Although Thérèse contributed a highly praised pas de deux, it was Fanny's *cachucha*, which she arranged herself, that became the highlight of the ballet. She was to perform this dance to the end of her career. Gautier vividly described it in an extended review:

> Now she springs forward and the resonant clatter of her castanets breaks out; she seems to shake down clusters of rhythm with her hands. How she twists! How she bends! . . . Her swooning arms flutter about her drooping head, her body curves back, her white shoulders almost brush the floor.

"La Cachucha" became to Fanny what the role of the Sylphide was to Taglioni. These two images, the Spanish dancer in pink satin and black lace and the Sylphide in diaphanous white, have become the twin emblems of the Romantic ballet. Jean-Auguste Barre made a statuette of each figure. The two also appear in *Les Trois Grâces*, a lithograph after a drawing by Eugène Lejeune; Fanny, however, is the central figure in this print.

Fanny's dramatic ability was further tested by the three great roles she first assumed in 1837. With its mad scene, *Nina, ou La Folle par Amour* was a prototype of *Giselle*.

Her interpretation of *La Fille Mal Gardée* was likened by Gautier to a pastoral goddess in disguise. The mime role of Fenella in Daniel Auber's opera *La Muette di Portici* earned her the praise of Hector Berlioz.

In Coralli's *La Chatte Metamorphosée en Femme* (1837), Fanny created the role of a cat that assumes human form. This rather slight work was followed on 5 May 1838 by Thérèse's first full-length ballet at the Paris Opera, *La Volière*. Thérèse played the role of a woman who has brought up her younger sister Zoé (Fanny) in complete ignorance of men. When a young man (Joseph Mazilier) arrives at their island retreat of San Domingo, Zoé is told that he is a bird. This misapprehension is corrected by the end of the ballet, and both sisters are united to the men of their choice. Although the ballet's plot was criticized, Thérèse won praise for her choreography, which concentrated on the dancing of her sister and herself. Gautier, approving fully of the lack of male dancing, singled out

ELSSLER SISTERS. Fanny Elssler in "La Cachucha," her solo from Jean Coralli's ballet *Le Diable Boiteux* (1836). (Dance Collection, New York Public Library for the Performing Arts.)

for special mention "one passage . . . when the two sisters run, hand in hand, from the back of the stage, thrusting their legs forward in unison, which surpasses everything that can be imagined for its effect, correctness and precision."

In 1838 the sisters, who had previously lived together, separated because of a disagreement between their lovers. They continued, however, to dance together. When Fanny undertook the role of the Sylphide in September, Thérèse created a pas de deux for Fanny and herself, which replaced the act 2 pas de deux of the Sylphide and James. Fanny's interpretation stressed the dramatic qualities of the role, particularly in the tragic denouement. "Her miming, when she is caught by her lover in the folds of the enchanted scarf, expresses sorrow and forgiveness, the sense of fall and irreparable error with rare poetic feeling, and her last long look at her wings as they lie on the earth is a moment of great tragic beauty," wrote Gautier.

The next ballet created for Fanny, Mazilier's *La Gipsy*, unfortunately led to a direct clash with Taglioni because of its similarity in theme and title to *La Gitana*, a ballet created for Taglioni by her father, Filippo, in 1838. *La Gipsy*, first presented at the Paris Opera on 28 January 1839, tells the story of a well-born girl who is kidnapped as a child by Gypsies. The ballet included a pas de deux for Fanny and Thérèse, who played the heroine and the Queen of the Gypsies, respectively. The high point was Fanny's solo, "La Cracovienne," a form of the mazurka. This dance, like "La Cachucha," was later performed independently. Another national dance, the tarantella, inspired Coralli's *La Tarentule* (1839), a comic ballet revolving around the folk belief that the poisonous bite of the tarantula can be cured by dancing. The role of Lauretta, the heroine, gave Fanny an opportunity to shine as a comedienne.

When the sisters restaged *La Gipsy* in London in the summer of 1839, they found that Taglioni had preceded them with a staging of *La Gitana*. The ill feeling arising from this confrontation led the Parisian critics to mount a campaign against the Elsslers. This unpleasantness may have hastened Fanny's decision to embark on a tour of the United States. On 30 January 1840 she and Thérèse danced together for the last time, at the Paris Opera. Fanny left for New York in April; Thérèse, who was to follow her, never did so, remaining in Europe and dancing in various cities until 1850, when she became the morganatic wife of Prince Adalbert of Prussia and was granted the title of Freifrau von Barnim.

Fanny made her American debut at the Park Theatre in New York on 14 May 1840. She remained in the United States for slightly more than two years, presenting six seasons in New York and appearing in Philadelphia, Washington, D.C., Boston, and other American cities. She also made two trips to Cuba. Her repertory consisted of her European successes augmented by works learned en route, such as the Cuban *zapateo*. Her partner for most of the tour was James Sylvain, who restaged his ballet *L'Amour, ou La Rose Animée* for her.

For the most part, she was rapturously received. U.S. president Martin Van Buren invited her to the White House, Ralph Waldo Emerson described "the winning fun & spirit of all her little coquetries" in his journal, and Henry Wadsworth Longfellow made a *cachucha* dancer the heroine of his verse-drama *The Spanish Student*. The journey was marred, however, by contretemps with Henry Wickoff, her American business manager and lover, and accusations of immorality from the press. In addition, the Paris Opera demanded that she return to honor her contract.

Fanny returned to Europe in July 1842. After weathering a final break with Wickoff and a suit for breach of contract from the Paris Opera, she went to London to give her first performance of *Giselle* in a production staged by Perrot at Her Majesty's Theatre. Her interpretation of the title role, which she first danced on 30 March 1843, was dramatically stronger than that of its creator, Carlotta Grisi, and gave particular emphasis to the mad scene. She always danced the full ballet, while Grisi often presented only act 2.

Elssler first danced at the Teatro alla Scala, Milan, in January 1844, winning praise for her performance of Antonio Cortesi's three-act version of *Giselle*. "She gave life to a character which until now had only been slightly hinted at," the *Corriere delle dame* reported. In May 1844 she danced in Hungary for the first time.

The 1844 summer season took her back to London where, on 3 August, she first performed one of her most powerful dramatic roles, the title role of Perrot's *La Esmeralda*. Like Giselle, Esmeralda had been created by Grisi, whose acting style was more low-keyed. Grisi excelled in depicting the softness and innocence of the Gypsy girl, while Elssler was at her finest in the moments requiring strong emotions. The *Morning Herald* gave a detailed description of the moving scene in which Esmeralda is accused of murder:

> At first she is overcome with terror, but presently she swells with pride and innocence, and indignantly confronts her denouncers; until, becoming sensible of her weak and forlorn condition, her courage forsakes her, and she droops into dejection and submissiveness.

During the next few years, Fanny's travels took her to Belgium, Germany, Ireland, Italy, and Hungary, with frequent engagements in her native Austria. In January 1847 she returned to La Scala to dance in Perrot's restaging of *Catarina, ou La Fille du Bandit*, in a role originally created by Lucile Grahn. This tale of a dashing female bandit who ultimately sacrifices herself for the man she loves was eminently suited to Elssler's dramatic gifts.

Given her resounding success in Perrot's ballets, it is ironic that neither of the two grand ballets he created for her at La Scala achieved lasting fame. *Odetta, o La Demenza di Carlo VI, Re di Francia* (16 March 1847) was a story of fifteenth-century intrigues at the court of the French king Charles VI. The characters were derived from history, although their relationships were somewhat bowdlerized: Odette de Champdivers (Elssler) was actually the king's mistress. In the ballet she is reduced to a mere sympathizer, who tries to cure the king's madness to save her father from the scaffold. "She probes all the secrets of the heart, passing brilliantly from a mere request to imploring, from calm to indignation, from reason to frenzy, from frenzy to madness," reported *Il pirata*. Though acclaimed as a masterpiece, the ballet is little known today.

Perrot's second grand ballet for Elssler, *Faust,* was injured by external events arising from an upsurge of anti-Austrian feeling in the Italian states, which were then struggling to cast off Austrian rule. Elssler became the target of political caricatures, pamphlets, and demonstrations. The ballet's German theme, based on Goethe's play, was an added insult to the Italians. Elssler danced the role of the ill-fated Marguerite only once in Milan, at the premiere on 12 February 1848, though she was to dance it with greater success in Vienna.

Later in 1848, Elssler went to Russia, where she made her official debut at the Bolshoi Theater in Saint Petersburg on 13 October, dancing the role of Giselle. The initial reception to her was cool, but her compelling acting gradually won over Russian audiences. Perrot, who arrived in Saint Petersburg late in 1848, restaged *La Esmeralda, Catarina,* and *La Filleule des Fées* for her. Her new partner Marius Petipa created *Lida* (1849), his first choreography for the Russian stage, for her and Perrot. She first danced in Moscow in May 1850 and became extremely popular there. She literally stopped the show when, dancing Esmeralda at her farewell performance on 2 March 1851, she impulsively wrote the word *Moscow* on the wall instead of the name of Esmeralda's lover.

She returned to western Europe only to make her final appearances onstage, appropriately enough in the Kärntnertor Theater, where she had first performed as a child. At her last performance on 21 June 1851, she danced Marguerite in Perrot's *Faust.*

After her retirement, Fanny spent most of her time in Vienna, where she occasionally coached dancers in her former roles and forged new friendships with the actors and actresses who came to seek her professional advice. Both of her children, who married and had children of their own, died before her. Her sister Thérèse, who left the Prussian court and came to live with her after the deaths

ELSSLER SISTERS. The highlight of Joseph Mazilier's ballet *La Gipsy* (1839) was Fanny Elssler's performance of "La Cracovienne," a variant of the mazurka. This engraving shows Elssler as Sarah, a Scottish girl raised by Gypsies, performing the dance on a street corner in Edinburgh. Engraving by W. Zinke, from *Costüme-Bilder zur Theaterzeitung* (Vienna, 1942). (Courtesy of Madison U. Sowell and Debra H. Sowell, Brigham Young University, Provo, Utah.)

of her husband and their young son, also predeceased her. Fanny's final years were spent in the company of her grandchildren and her cousin and companion, Katti Prinster.

[*Many of the figures and works mentioned herein are the subjects of independent entries.*]

BIBLIOGRAPHY.   Ivor Guest's *Fanny Elssler* (London, 1970) is generally considered the definitive biography of the dancer, and includes an extensive bibliography. Supplementary material on her career may be found in several volumes by Guest, including *The Romantic Ballet in Paris,* 2d rev. ed. (London, 1980), and *The Romantic Ballet in England* (London, 1972). Information on Thérèse Elssler may also be found in these sources.

Other biographies of Elssler include Cyril W. Beaumont, *Fanny Elssler* (London, 1931); Auguste Ehrhard, *Une vie de danseuse: Fanny Elssler,* 2d ed. (Paris, 1909); Emil Pirchan, *Fanny Elssler: Eine Wienerin tant um die Welt* (Vienna, 1940); and Riki Raab, *Fanny Elssler: Eine Weltfaszination* (Vienna, 1962).

Allison Delarue, ed., *Fanny Elssler in America* (Brooklyn, 1976), and Mary Grace Swift, *Belles and Beaux on Their Toes: Dancing Stars in Young America* (Washington, D.C., 1980), provide information on Elssler's American tour. Other recommended readings include the following.

Arkin, Lisa C. "The Context of Exoticism in Fanny Elssler's *Cachucha.*" *Dance Chronicle* 17.3 (1994): 303–325.

Aschengreen, Erik. "The Beautiful Danger: Facets of the Romantic Ballet." Translated by McAndrew. *Dance Perspectives*, no. 58 (Summer 1974).

Costonis, Maureen Needham. "The Personification of Desire: Fanny Elssler and American Audiences." *Dance Chronicle* 13.1 (1990): 47–67.

Costonis, Maureen Needham. "Fanny Elssler in Havana." *Choreography and Dance* 3.4 (1994): 37–46.

Denk, Liselotte. *Fanny Elβler.* Berlin, 1984.

Heiberg, Johanne L. "Memories of Taglioni and Elssler." Translated by Patricia McAndrew. *Dance Chronicle* 4.1 (1981): 14–18.

Meglin, Joellen A. "Fanny Elssler's *Cachucha* and Women's Lives." In *Dance Reconstructed*, edited by Barbara Palfy. New Brunswick, N.J., 1993.

Sorell, Walter. "She Came for Only Two Weeks, But She Stayed for Two Years." *Austria Kultur* 5 (March–April 1995): 12–13.

Wiley, Roland John, trans. and ed. *A Century of Russian Ballet: Documents and Accounts, 1810–1910.* Oxford, 1990.

ARCHIVES.   Fanny Elssler's correspondence, prints, and papers are housed in the Lunacharsky State Theatrical Library, Saint Petersburg; the Bakhrushin Central State Theatrical Museum, Moscow; and the Tanzarchiv, Cologne.

SUSAN AU

ELVIN, VIOLETTA

ELVIN, VIOLETTA (Violetta Prokhorova; born 3 November 1925 in Moscow), dancer. Elvin entered the Bolshoi Ballet School at the age of eight and received her entire training there; her senior teachers included Elizaveta Gerdt, Agrippina Vaganova, and Viktor Semenov. She graduated into the Bolshoi Ballet in 1942, but because World War II closed the Bolshoi Theater, in 1943 she danced at the State Theater in Tashkent, in taking the ballerina roles in *Swan Lake* and *The Fountain of Bakhchisarai*. She rejoined the Bolshoi Ballet in Kuibyshev in 1944 and was promoted to soloist when the company returned to Moscow. She immigrated to England in 1945 with her first husband, the English writer Harold Elvin.

Elvin joined the Sadler's Wells Ballet as a guest artist early in 1946 and made a dazzling debut in the Bluebird pas de deux in *The Sleeping Beauty* on the second night of the company's first Covent Garden season. A permanent member of the company by the second season (and billed officially as Elvin beginning in 1947), she quickly revealed the warmth of her temperament with the vivacity and stylistic panache of her Miller's Wife in *Le Tricorne* and proved the strength of her classical technique with the lyric amplitude of her Aurora.

Guided by Vera Volkova, her teacher and friend, Elvin went on to the leading roles in *Cinderella*, *The Sleeping Beauty*, and *Ballet Imperial;* dramatic performances as the Betrayed Girl in *The Rake's Progress* and the Black Queen in *Checkmate;* and the creation of the languorous Fairy Summer in *Cinderella*, before her promotion to ballerina in 1950. The title roles in *Giselle*, *The Firebird*, and *Sylvia*

followed, as did additional creations—the seductive Lykanion in *Daphnis and Chloe*, the Queen of the Waters in *Homage to the Queen*—and guest appearances in Milan, Copenhagen, Stockholm, and South America. In 1956, at the peak of her career, she retired to marry for the third time and settle in Italy. She became director of the ballet company and school of the Teatro San Carlo in Naples in 1985, but held the position for only six months.

BIBLIOGRAPHY

Clarke, Mary. *The Sadler's Wells Ballet.* London, 1955.

Fisher, Hugh, ed. *Violetta Elvin.* Dancers of Today, no. 3. London, 1953.

Percival, John. "The Ballerina from Moscow." *Dance and Dancers* (November 1992): 8.

BARBARA NEWMAN

EMMELEIA. In ancient Greek music, *emmeleia* (plural, *emmeleiai*) signified perfect harmony. Probably because of the close association of music and dance in Greek culture, the quality of *emmeleia* was ascribed to dance as well. When Plato recorded the types of dancing he deemed appropriate for citizens in his utopic state, he defined two categories: the warlike *(pyrrhic)* and the peaceful *(emmeleia)*. [*See* Pyrrhic.] The music and dance in the latter group, according to Plato, were to be performed at solemn and religious occasions. Therefore, *emmeleia* could have included dance for dignified rituals as well as the dance of the tragic chorus.

Although Plato did not associate *emmeleia* with the tragic theater directly, parodies of tragedy in excerpts from fifth-century BCE comedies suggest that *emmeleia* was in fact a dance genre used for the tragic chorus. In Aristophanes' *Wasps*, Philocleon challenges three sons of the tragedian Carcinas to a dance competition and threatens to vanquish one of them with a "knuckle-*emmeleia*."

The early indications of the existence of a tragic dance genre called *emmeleia* portray the mood of the dance rather than depicting movements. Later Roman commentaries give some additional information, but these basically juxtapose the three categories of theatrical dance: the *emmeleia* of tragedy, the *kordax* of comedy, and the *sikinnis* of satyr play. [*See* Kordax *and* Sikinnis.] Athenaeus further contrasted *emmeleia* with *kordax* by setting up two groups of dance according to the Greeks: the serious or noble dance *(spoudaios)* and the vulgar *(phaulos)*. The *emmeleia* belonged to the first category, and the *kordax* to the second.

[*See also* Greece, *article on* Dance in Ancient Greece.]

BIBLIOGRAPHY

Aristophanes. *Wasps* 1484–1537.

Athenaeus. *Deipnosophists* 14.631.

Centanni, Monica. "Emmeleia come parte strutturale (meros) della tragedia." *Quaderni urbinati di cultural classica* 38 (1991): 97–104.

Lawler, Lillian B. *The Dance of the Ancient Greek Theatre.* Iowa City, 1964.

Plato. *Laws* 816.

Smigel, Elizabeth [Libby]. "Redefinitions of the Fifth-Century Greek Chorus Using a Methodology Applied to Aristophanes' *Thesmophoriazusae.*" Master's thesis, York University, 1982.

LIBBY SMIGEL

ENGLISH NATIONAL BALLET. For almost four decades, the company now known as English National Ballet was known by a historic succession of names: Festival Ballet (1950–1951), London's Festival Ballet (1951–1969), and London Festival Ballet (1969–1989). The company came into existence as a result of a successful concert tour of Britain in 1949 and 1950, led by Alicia Markova and Anton Dolin with a corps de ballet recruited form the Cone-Ripman (later Arts Educational) School.

In January 1949 Markova and Dolin danced at the Empress Hall, a large arena in London, supported by a few professional dancers and students; from 27 August to 1 September 1949, they appeared at the Harringay Arena with Ballet Rambert. The Polish-born impresario Julian

ENGLISH NATIONAL BALLET. Company members of the Festival Ballet during its first London season in 1950. In a work entitled *Chopiniana*, Anton Dolin stands at left, extending his arm and his gaze toward Alicia Markova, held aloft at center. (Photograph from the archives of the English National Ballet, Markova House, London.)

Braunsweg, recognizing the interest these appearances generated, proposed that Markova and Dolin should follow the London performances with a regional tour to towns where they had not appeared since the demise of the first Markova-Dolin Company in 1937. Throughout the fall of 1949 their Gala Performances of Ballet appeared in town halls, rather than theaters. Initially only *divertissements* were performed, but for the final dates act 2 of *Swan Lake* was added to the repertory.

Following the success of the first tour, a second, eleven-week theater tour was arranged for the spring of 1950, and some of the *divertissements* were combined to form short ballets. The group pieces, solo variations, and pas de deux to Frédéric Chopin's music developed into *Chopiniana* and *Les Sylphides;* the pas de deux *Italian Suite,* choreographed by Dolin, and *Tarantella,* choreographed by Grace Cone, were combined with some additional choreography to create *Capriccioso (Italiana).*

That year Braunsweg decided to formalize his concert group as a company. Markova and Dolin would continue as its stars, and Nathalie Krassovska, Anna Cheselka, and John Gilpin were recruited to share principal roles. The present company dates its foundation from 14 August 1950, when—still under the name Gala Performances of Ballet—it performed at the King's Theatre, Southsea. The repertory for this inaugural season included *Les Sylphides, Petrouchka, Fiesta,* and a *divertissement* from *The Nutcracker.* Of these works only *Petrouchka* had not al-

ready been performed by the concert group; the Braunsweg troupe was the first British company to mount a production of *Petrouchka*.

Alicia Markova suggested that because 1951 would be the year of the Festival of Britain, it would be appropriate to call the company Festival Ballet. It first appeared under this name at Bournemouth on 2 October 1950. When the company first went abroad to Monte Carlo in April 1951, the name was extended to London's Festival Ballet, and in 1969 it became London Festival Ballet. In June 1989, to acknowledge its national status, it became English National Ballet.

Festival Ballet opened its first London season at the Stoll Theatre on 24 October 1950. With a strong company, guests Yvette Chauviré, Léonide Massine, and Tatiana Riabouchinska, and a series of charity galas attended by members of the royal family, Festival Ballet attracted the publicity, support, and audiences it needed to survive.

ENGLISH NATIONAL BALLET. *(left)* Founding artists Anton Dolin and Alicia Markova in *Giselle,* act 1, 1951. The year 1951 was the year of the Festival of Britain, for which the company was originally named. *(right)* Belinda Wright and Anjelko Yurésha in a pose from *Romeo and Juliet.* Wright was a leading dancer with London's Festival Ballet from 1955 to 1957. (Left photograph by Roger Wood, right photograph by Mike Davis; both used by permission.)

Julian Braunsweg regarded the London Festival Ballet as a successor to the Ballets Russes of the 1930s and 1940s. This was evident in the selection of Nicholas Beriozoff as the company's first ballet master (Beriozoff had learned Michel Fokine's choreography during their years together at the Ballet Russe de Monte Carlo); in the company's revivals of ballets created for Serge Diaghilev; in the many guest appearances of former Ballets Russes stars; and in the link Braunsweg cultivated with Monte Carlo, where the opera house served as the company's second home from 1951 to 1956.

Anton Dolin was the artistic director of the company from 1950 to 1960. It was his policy to make fine ballet available to the public at popular prices. The repertory was deliberately chosen to feature guest artists, including Alexandra Danilova, Mia Slavenska, Tamara Toumanova, Violette Verdy, Margot Fonteyn, Beryl Grey, and—after she left the company in 1952—Alica Markova. The guests provided inspiration to the young company members, who also benefited from the experience of working in different styles and learned to appreciate the traditions of ballet. Two other guests were Nóra Kovach and István Rabovsky, who defected from Hungary in 1953 and briefly created a sensation with their Soviet-style virtuosity.

ENGLISH NATIONAL BALLET. Members of London's Festival Ballet in the final pose of a 1957 performance of *The Nutcracker*. Over the years, *The Nutcracker* has been presented in seven different productions and has been given in almost two thousand performances. More than any other, it is the English National Ballet's signature work. (Photograph by Mike Davis; used by permission.)

The company's pattern of performances was established early in the 1950s and continued relatively unchanged throughout the first fifteen years of its existence. Summer seasons of eight or nine weeks were the main engagement in London; from 1952 these were usually given at the Royal Festival Hall. There were also Christmas seasons, often at the Royal Festival Hall and usually of four weeks, featuring seasonal works such as *Harlequinade* and *The Nutcracker*. These regular London seasons gave the company much-needed security.

During the 1950s London's Festival Ballet performed more than forty weeks of the year, spending considerably more time on tour in Britain and abroad than in London. Regarded as an important cultural ambassador, the company visited Europe, the Middle East, and North America. However, it was not until its 1957 visit to the Théâtre des Nations in Paris that it received support from the British Council for overseas touring.

London's Festival Ballet visited Canada for four weeks in 1953, to mark the coronation of Queen Elizabeth II.

The company returned during the 1954/55 season, for an eighteen-week tour of the United States and Canada, a mixture of one-night performances in small cities and seasons in major cities.

The company's most important overseas season came in 1956, when it was invited to participate in the celebrations marking the marriage of Prince Rainier of Monaco to Grace Kelly. In Monaco it performed Harald Lander's *Études* with Toni Lander, Flemming Flindt, and John Gilpin in the principal roles, during a gala televised internationally through the Eurovision network. This created a demand for further overseas touring and revived the company's fortunes after the failure of the full-evening ballet *Esmeralda* and the financial losses of the American tour.

Festival Ballet was the first ballet company to perform in Israel, where its initial visit in 1956 was so well received that the company returned again in 1958 and 1962. In 1960 the company made its first visit to Latin America on an eleven-week tour.

From 1950 to 1960, when Anton Dolin was artistic director, the company's repertory included Dolin's own stagings of the classics and featured choreographers David Lichine, Michael Charnley, and Harald Lander. Dolin's *Giselle* was particularly memorable for the galaxy of stars, both established and recently discovered, who appeared in the title role; among them were Markova, Krassovska,

Sally Gilmour, Paula Hinton, Yvette Chauviré, and Carla Fracci.

Lichine choreographed *Harlequinade* for the second part of Festival Ballet's 1950/51 Stoll season, when Riabouchinska was appearing as guest artist and the company was also appearing in matinees of the children's show *Where the Rainbow Ends*. Lichine also created *Impressions* to Bizet's Symphony in C. He returned to London's Festival Ballet in 1957, when he mounted *Graduation Ball* and *The Nutcracker*. His version of *The Nutcracker* replaced the Beriozoff and Dolin version with which the company had opened its first London season; it was designed by Alexandre Benois, who also guided the production according to his recollection of the 1892 Saint Petersburg production. In 1959 Lichine created his short-lived *Vision of Chopin* for the company.

Michael Charnley attracted Dolin's attention with the ballets he choreographed for Ballet Workshop at the Mercury Theatre. His first creation for London's Festival Ballet was the popular *Symphony for Fun* (1952). This was followed by the narrative *Alice in Wonderland* (1953) and *Homage to a Princess*, to a jazz score, on the occasion of the wedding of Prince Rainier and Grace Kelly.

In 1954, because the interest in August Bournonville's choreography aroused by the visit of the Royal Danish Ballet to London the previous year, Harald Lander was invited to mount the first British production of *divertissements* from *Napoli*. The next year he staged his own *Études*, and in 1956 Festival Ballet's first *Coppélia*.

The Fokine ballets were revived, often with the assistance of former members of Diaghilev's Ballets Russes. Tamara Karsavina assisted Dolin with the revival of *Le Spectre de la Rose*, in which John Gilpin danced the title role to great acclaim, partnering Anita Landa, Tatiana Riabouchinska, Moira Shearer, and Belinda Wright. For one season in the summer of 1953, Kovach and Rabovsky danced a version of this ballet choreographed by Ferenc Nádasi. In 1956 Serge Grigoriev and Lubov Tchernicheva served as *régisseurs* for the company and worked on *Petrouchka* and *Schéhérazade* in 1958 and *Prince Igor* in 1960.

Other works in the repertory during the 1950s included Frederick Ashton's *Vision of Marguerite* (1952), a reworking of his *Mephisto Valse* for a cast for four; Ruth Page's *Villa*, based on *The Merry Widow;* Beriozoff's *Esmeralda*, a muddled production that was soon cut to a one-act *divertissement* and a pas de deux; Jack Carter's *London Morning*, a romp set outside Buckingham Palace, the only ballet for which Noël Coward wrote the synopsis and score; and *Variations for Four*, created by Dolin to exhibit the talents of four male company members, John Gilpin, Flemming Flindt, Louis Godfrey, and André Prokovsky. Carter's *The Witch Boy* was added to the repertory in 1957 to show off Gilpin's ability as a dramatic performer.

After Dolin resigned as artistic director in 1960, Julian Braunsweg commissioned two full-evening ballets from Russian choreographers. *The Snow Maiden*, after Aleksandr Ostrovsky's play, was choreographed by Vladimir Burmeister to music by Tchaikovsky in 1961; Burmeister also gave London Festival Ballet the second act of his much praised *Swan Lake* to replace Dolin's production. Vaslav Orlikovsky choreographed Greig's *Peer Gynt*, the ballet being first performed in Monte Carlo in 1963; it was performed 181 times in three years. It included effective roles for the company's principals and guest artists, including Lucette Aldous, Irina Borowska, Marilyn Burr, Olga Ferri, John Gilpin, Karl Musil, and Irene Skorik. The production was televised in 1964. Orlikovsky also choreographed a version of Gounod's *Walpurgis Night* for the company's Christmas season at the Royal Albert Hall (1964), and he introduced Galina Samsova to the company.

The 1963/64 Christmas season at the Royal Albert Hall was a joint season with stars from the Bolshoi and Kirov companies. With the Royal Festival Hall closed for extensive renovation, the company did not perform again in central London until the following Christmas, when they appeared in a converted cinema, the New Victoria.

John Gilpin, one of the dancers who had left the company when Dolin did, returned a year later and from 1962 to 1965 served as artistic director. He made little impact on the policy or direction of London's Festival Ballet, and Braunsweg was increasingly responsible for artistic as well as administrative decisions. London's Festival Ballet had been a private enterprise mainly financed by Braunsweg, but in 1962 he was forced to put it into voluntary liquidation. A nonprofit organization, London's Festival Ballet Enterprises Limited, was set up, making the company eligible for financial aid; the London County Council came to the rescue with a grant of £30,000. The company, however, remained in a precarious financial position, and the new complete *Swan Lake* at the New Victoria brought disaster when it failed to attract an audience. The company was saved only by the intervention of the Arts Council's chairman, Lord Goodman. The new trust established to run the company insisted that Braunsweg resign.

In the mid-1960s, discussions concerning the future of British companies and means for funding them centered on London's Festival Ballet and Ballet Rambert, both under financial strain from continual touring. In April 1965 the Two Ballets' Trust was established with a view to placing the two companies under Donald Albery's direction; however, Albery was appointed director of London's Festival Ballet, and the following year Ballet Rambert reformed as a contemporary company, causing the trust to be disbanded in November 1966.

Donald Albery invited Norman McDowell of the recently disbanded London Dance Theatre to act as artistic director for a few months, and Jack Carter was appointed resident choreographer. Carter immediately revived his *Witch Boy* and mounted *The Four Seasons* (both designed by McDowell), but his main task was to overhaul the productions of the classics. Using existing designs, he choreographed new productions of *Swan Lake* and *The Nutcracker.* Carter also choreographed *Beatrix (La Jolie Fille de Gand)*, using the original nineteenth-century music and scenario by Adolphe Adam, and a production of *Coppélia.*

Albery acquired other major works for Festival Ballet, including Serge Lifar's *Noir et Blanc* and George Balanchine's *Night Shadow*, in which Margot Fonteyn appeared as guest artist in the role of the Sleepwalker. The most important and ambitious production at this time was *The Sleeping Beauty*, produced by Ben Stevenson, with designs by Norman McDowell and Beryl Grey as artistic adviser. The premiere at the Royal Festival Hall was danced by Noëlla Pontois and John Gilpin. They alternated in the leading roles with Galina Samsova and André Prokovsky, who were to lead the company over the next few years.

In 1968 Donald Albery resigned, and Beryl Grey was appointed the new artistic director. Between 1968 and 1984 London Festival Ballet was run by former principals of the Royal Ballet, John Field succeeding Beryl Grey in 1979. They both enriched the repertory with new ballets and developed young dancers, but because their vision was dominated by the model of the Royal Ballet, the company lost some of its individuality. Between 1970 and 1980 the company performed for approximately six months each year in Britain, dividing its time equally between London and the other regions of the country. Beginning in 1969, the London Coliseum was used for regular spring or summer seasons. The Coliseum is one of London's best large venues for dance; consequently the repertory had to be scaled up for its stage. The most lavish productions were Rudolf Nureyev's *The Sleeping Beauty*, staged to mark the company's twenty-fifth anniversary, and his *Romeo and Juliet*, created for the company in 1977. The repertory continued with a similar balance of nineteenth-century classics, works created for the Ballets Russes, major revivals, and new creations. Increasing numbers of full-evening ballets were presented. Among the revivals of nineteenth-century classics in this period were Witold Borkowski's *Don Quixote* (1970), Mary Skaeping's *Giselle* (1971), Nureyev's *The Sleeping Beauty* (1975), Ronald Hynd's *The Nutcracker* (1975), and two productions of *Swan Lake*—one, by Beryl Grey in 1972, and one by John Field, with new designs by Carl Toms, in 1982. The company's Bournonville repertory was revived and expanded, with Mona Vangsaae mounting a new version of *Bournonville Divertissement* (extracts from *Napoli* and the *Flower Festival* pas de deux) in 1971 and *Konservatoriet* in 1973. Vangsaae's son, Peter Schaufuss, a principal dancer in the company, was in the first cast of both these ballets. In 1979 Schaufuss mounted his first Bournonville ballet for London Festival Ballet, *La Sylphide*, which won both the Society of West End Theatres and the *Evening Standard* awards for ballet in 1979. In 1983 he staged another version of *Dances from Napoli*, and for the company's 1979 visit to New York, a complete *Napoli.*

ENGLISH NATIONAL BALLET. In 1979, Peter Schaufuss staged August Bournonville's *La Sylphide* for London Festival Ballet. Here, in a scene from act 1, are Patrick Armand as James, Josephine Jewkes as Effie, and Niels Bjørn Larsen as Madge, the witch. (Photograph by Catherine Ashmore; used by permission.)

The company's repertory of Fokine and Massine works was revived and expanded; special attention was given to accurate re-creation of the original designs. *Schéhérazade, Petrouchka,* and *Le Spectre de la Rose* were again revived by Beriozoff, who also added *The Golden Cockerel* to the repertory in 1976. Vasily Trunoff revived *Prince Igor* (1968), and Alicia Markova revived *Les Sylphides* (1976). Following Léonide Massine's acceptance of Beryl Grey's invitation to work with the company, four of his ballets were added it its repertory: *Le Beau Danube* (1971); *Le Tricorne* and *Gaîté Parisienne* (1973); and *Parade* (1974). Because of its rich early-Diaghilev repertory, London Festival Ballet was invited to appear as the Ballets Russes in the Herbert Ross film *Nijinsky*. Consequently, as the sets were available and the dancers had learned the choreography, the company was also able to perform *L'Après-midi d'un Faune* during its season with Nureyev at the Coliseum in 1979. Among other works acquired by the company were *Echoing of Trumpets* (1973) by Antony Tudor and *Onegin* (1983) by John Cranko. *Onegin* was performed annually until 1991 and provided an important vehicle for such guest artists as Marcia Haydée, Natalia Makarova, Ekaterina Maximova, Lynne Charles, Richard Cragun, Reid Anderson, and Ivan Liška.

Ronald Hynd began his association with London Festival Ballet in 1970, when he created *Dvořák Variations,* working for the first time with Peter Docherty, who has since designed most of Hynd's works. Together they created *The Sanguine Fan* (1976), a new version of *The Nutcracker* (1976), and *La Chatte* (1978). He also mounted *The Fairy's Kiss* (1974), *Rosalinda* (1979), and *The Seasons* (1983). In 1985 Hynd created a new production of *Coppélia* with designs by Desmond Heeley.

Following the success of his short ballets *Summer Solstice* (1972) and *In Nomine* (1973), Barry Moreland was appointed company choreographer. In 1974 he created his most popular ballet, *The Prodigal Son (in Ragtime),* a twentieth-century version of the biblical parable set to music by Scott Joplin; Paul Clarke, Patricia Ruanne, and Kenn Wells became associated with the principal roles.

ENGLISH NATIONAL BALLET. Members of the ensemble in a scene from act 1 of *Coppélia,* staged for the company in 1985 by Ronald Hynd. (Photograph © by Catherine Ashmore; used by permission.)

Moreland later choreographed *Dancing Space* (1976), after which his appointment as company choreographer ended, although he returned to create *Journey to Avalon* in 1980. During his tenure Moreland, who had previously worked with London Contemporary Dance Theatre, introduced a contemporary dance element into the company, as did Maina Gielgud, who danced Béjart's *Forme et Ligne* (1973), *Webern Op. 5* (1973), and *Rose Variations* (1974). Other contemporary works acquired were Glen Tetley's *Greening* (1978) and *Sphinx* (1979), and his creation of a new *Pulcinella* (1984).

While Beryl Grey headed the company, it continued to perform abroad, but the foreign tours changed from short seasons in a number of towns to longer seasons in major cities. In 1969 London Festival Ballet toured in Japan, Singapore, and Korea. During the late 1960s and early 1970s, the company made regular summer tours of Medterranean towns with a repertory of short ballets and divertissements, among which *Le Corsaire* pas de deux, and Balanchine's *Bourrée Fantasque* were frequently featured. The company also went on tours of Italian opera houses during the spring, sometimes dancing in operatic productions. By the end of the 1970s, the company's foreign tours featured ballets staged by Rudolf Nureyev, with Nureyev himself as guest artist. Nureyev's *The Sleeping Beauty* played seasons in Australia (1975) and Paris (1976), and his *Romeo and Juliet* was seen in Australia (1977), Paris (1978), New York (1978), and Washington (1978). The company also visited China in 1979, with a repertory made up of *Giselle, The Sanguine Fan, Greening,* and *Études.* Eva Evdokimova, Peter Schaufuss, Elisabetta Terabust, and Patrice Bart, all of whom had performed with the company throughout the 1970s, were guests for that tour. The trip to China left the company with a serious financial deficit, and there was much less touring under John Field's directorship. The company did, however, perform in Caracas, Venezuela, to mark the opening of the Teatro Teresa Carreño during the bicentenary of Simón Bolívar's birth.

Both Beryl Grey and John Field worked to develop dancers from within the company; among those who rose through the ranks to become principals were Alain Dubreuil, Dudley von Loggenburg, Andria Hall, Mary McKendry, and Janette Mulligan. The company had always had an international group of dancers, and particularly under John Field the number of dancers trained in Italy increased, including Lucia Truglia, Renata Calderini, and Maurizio Bellezza. One of Beryl Grey's most significant achievements was the establishment of a permanent home for the company. The Greater London Council and Arts Council of Great Britain gave financial assistance for the conversion of Queen Alexandra's house in London into rehearsal studios and company offices. Festival Ballet House (renamed Markova House in 1989) was opened in

ENGLISH NATIONAL BALLET. Peter Schaufuss and Katherine Healy in Frederick Ashton's lyrical *Romeo and Juliet,* c.1986. (Photograph by Leslie E. Spatt; from the Dance Collection, New York Public Library for the Performing Arts.)

1977. There were two important developments during John Field's directorship. One was the establishment of the Education and Community Programme, which helps people to understand and appreciate classical ballet through workshops, lecture-demonstrations, and informational publications. The other was the introduction of tours to small theaters by a group of dancers during the rehearsal periods; it was for one such group that André Prokovsky choreographed *The Storm* (later expanded for the full company) and *That Certain Feeling* to music by George Gershwin. This special touring group also gave company members the opportunity to choreograph, compose music, and design new ballets. Smaller-scale tours, often by two groups touring simultaneously, continued under successive artistic directors Peter Schaufuss, Iván Nagy, and Derek Deane but it was given a higher profile, sharing much of the repertory of one-act ballets also performed in larger venues. Operating with small units enables the company to visit two venues simultaneously and allows more overseas tours.

In 1984 Field resigned, and Schaufuss was appointed artistic director. Immediately standards improved, the repertory was broadened, more foreign tours were undertaken, and new dancers were invited to perform. Along with established stars, Schaufuss promoted very young dancers, including Katherine Healy, Trinidad Sevillano, Susan Hogard, and Patrick Armand. A school was established in 1988 to train dancers for the company. New one-act ballets were acquired from choreographers whose work was seen only occasionally in Britain but with whom Schaufuss had worked. Among them were Roland Petit's *L'Arlesienne* and *Carmen;* Maurice Béjart's *Song of a*

ENGLISH NATIONAL BALLET. Thomas Edur and Agnes Oaks were principal dancers of the company from 1991 to 1997. Here they are seen in Ben Stevenson's *Three Preludes*, set to the music of Sergei Rachmaninov. (Photograph © by Bill Cooper; used by permission.)

Wayfarer and *Boléro;* Balanchine's *Symphony in C* and *Apollo;* and Alvin Ailey's *Night Creature;* there were also creations from Kevin Haigen, Ulysses Dove, Niels Christie, Michael Clark, and Siobhan Davies. Natalia Makarova staged the Kingdom of the Shades scene from *La Bayadère* as a challenge for the corps de ballet.

Christopher Bruce was appointed associate choreographer in 1986, creating four new works and staging two existing ballets. The dramatic *Swansong* (1987), on the effects of torture, created for Koen Onzia, Matz Skoog, and Kevin Richmond, has proved to be one of the company's most successful creations. Bruce's productions helped to extend the range of the dancers' contemporary work, as did the acquisition of Paul Taylor's *Aureole* (1985) and José Limón's *The Moor's Pavane* (1989).

Classics continued to be important. Schaufuss created his own version of *The Nutcracker* (1986), with a scenario incorporating material from Tchaikovsky's biography, but the most important acquisition of Schaufuss's directorship was the reconstruction of Frederick Ashton's *Romeo and Juliet*. This initiated a period of cooperation between Ashton and the company. His *Apparitions* was reconstructed in 1987, and his additional choreography for

Swan Lake was incorporated into Makarova's 1988 production of the complete ballet.

On the eve of the company's fortieth anniversary, Schaufuss was dismissed, and Iván Nagy was appointed artistic director. Many dancers left, some to follow Schaufuss to the German Opera Ballet (Deutsche Oper) in Berlin, and dancers who had attracted attention in international competitions were recruited. Among them were José Manuel Carreño, who danced Petruchio to Maria Therese del Real's Katherine in Cranko's *The Taming of the Shrew* (1991) and the Estonians Agnes Oaks and Thomas Edur, who remained with the company for six seasons. Much of the repertory Nagy introduced was short-lived, including ballets performed by companies he had previously directed, such as Vicente Nebrada's *Our Waltzes* (1991) and Mauricio Wainrot's *Anne Frank* (1991). Nagy depended heavily on the choreography of Ben Stevenson, whose *Cinderella* (1973) and *Four Last Songs* (1983) returned to the repertory, and whose *Nutcracker* replaced Schaufuss's version in 1991. New commissions—such as Robert North's *A Stranger I Came* (1992), Kim Brandstrup's *White Nights* (1992), and Olga Roritz's *Seven Silences of Salome* (1993)—all rejected Nagy's orientation toward contemporary dance. His final contribution was to oversee Raisa Struchkova's mounting of the old Bolshoi's (Gorsky-Messerer) *Swan Lake* (1993).

Swan Lake was part of a long-term plan to restage the classics that continued under Derek Deane, who proposed to restrict productions to classical works and improve the quality of the company's dancing. Hynd produced *The Sleeping Beauty* (1993), Michael Corder, *Cinderella* (1996 restoring parts of the score cut from most British productions), and Nureyev's *Romeo and Juliet* was revived. Deane, himself, undertook a *Giselle* (1994), set circa 1920; *Alice in Wonderland* (1995), set as a full-evening family entertainment to a selection of music by Tchaikovsky; and an ambitious *Swan Lake* (1997), designed to be seen in the round at the Royal Albert Hall, London. Alongside these more obviously popular works, he introduced the Italian choreographer Maurio Bigonzetti to British audiences with *X.N.Tricities* (1994) and enlarged the company's Balanchine repertory with *Square Dance* (1994) and *Who Cares?* (1997). Deane has proved to be an outspoken director concerned generally with the standard of dance training in Britain and specifically with the excellence of his company. A popular repertory has been necessary to reduce the company's deficit, but in many ways it reaffirms the original policies of the company's founders. English National Ballet remains an international group of dancers touring and performing extensively throughout Britain and abroad and reaching out to new audiences with its lively program.

[*Many of the figures and works mentioned herein are the subjects of independent entries.*]

BIBLIOGRAPHY

Braunsweg, Julian. *Braunsweg's Ballet Scandals*. London, 1973.
Dolin, Anton. *Autobiography*. London, 1960.
Gillard, David. *Beryl Grey*. London, 1977.
Gilpin, John. *A Dance with Life*. London, 1982.
Hodgson, Moira. "London Festival Ballet: Looking at Its First Quarter Century, 1950–1975." *Dance Magazine* (November 1976): 51–61.
White, Joan W., ed. *Twentieth-Century Dance in Britain*. London, 1985.

JANE PRITCHARD

ENIGMA VARIATIONS. Ballet in one act. Choreography: Frederick Ashton. Music: Edward Elgar. Scenery and costumes: Julia Trevelyan Oman. First performance: 25 October 1968, Royal Opera House, Covent Garden, London, Royal Ballet. Principal dancers: Derek Rencher (Edward Elgar), Svetlana Beriosova (The Lady, Elgar's Wife), Anthony Dowell (Arthur Troyte Griffith), Desmond Doyle (A. J. Jaeger), Antoinette Sibley (Dora Penny, "Dora-

ENIGMA VARIATIONS. The original cast in the final tableau. Sir Edward Elgar (Derek Rencher) stands at the center; The Lady, His Wife (Svetlana Beriosova) is on his left. Their friends, who are "pictured within" the variations, are arranged about them. (Photograph by Houston Rogers; used by permission of the Board of Trustees of the Theatre Museum, London.)

bella"). Others in the cast: Stanley Holden (Hew David Steuart-Powell), Brian Shaw (Richard Baxter Townshend), Alexander Grant (William Meath Baker), Robert Mead (Richard P. Arnold), Vyvyan Lorrayne (Isabel Fitton), Georgina Parkinson (Winnifred Norbury), Wayne Sleep (George Robertson Sinclair), Deanne Bergsma (Lady Mary Lygon).

It amused the composer Elgar himself to imagine his score *Enigma Variations* being used for a ballet. Frank Staff created a version of it for Ballet Rambert in 1940, and in the 1950s Julia Oman, then a design student, submitted to the Royal Ballet a folder of designs for a ballet to this music. Only in 1966, however, did Ashton think seriously of choreographing to the score. Knowing Oman's theater and film designs, Ashton asked her to collaborate with him on the project.

Oman's use of intensely naturalistic detail was fitting for a ballet that used a degree of naturalistic movement unusual for a choreographer who had affirmed that "the subject of ballet is dancing." Elgar's subtitle for his score is *My Friends Pictured Within;* Ashton's overt theme is Elgar's social circle. Among the ballet's stage properties are a hammock, a Victorian tricycle and bicycle, and an earphone. The only apparent deviation from precisely au-

thentic Victorian costume is the use of pointe shoes for the women. This naturalism is prompted partly by Elgar's own intention to portray such realistic details in music as the fall of a character's bulldog into the river and the "engaging hesitation" in a character's speech.

One of the ballet's several ironies is that it concerns both the characters in Elgar's mind as he composed the score and the composer's later anxieties about the work's success. Ashton and Oman set the ballet at Elgar's Worcestershire home in 1889, in the period while Elgar waited to hear if the conductor Hans Richter would agree to conduct the premiere of the score. The ballet begins with a tableau, Elgar at its center, seen through a gauze. Possibly what follows, as the tableau breaks and the gauze lifts, is his memory or imaginings. Ashton used the score's original finale, during which the staged action features the arrival of Richter's telegram of acceptance, the congratulations of his friends, and a final ensemble pose for a celebratory photograph.

The ballet does contain much dancing, notably the variations of Troyte and Dorabella. But they are not central to the ballet. The use of naturalistic movement and mime, as in Chekhov, avoids expressionism and is part of the ballet's irony.

That which cannot be expressed is itself a theme of the work. The intimacy between the characters Isabel Fitton and Richard Arnold is in contrast to Elgar's own duets with several women. He partners both Dora Penny ("Dorabella"), a young girl who plainly adores him, and Lady Mary Lygon (her arms veiled, to indicate that she "was, at the time of composition, on a sea voyage"), who seems to be both muse and mistress. Elgar communicates most directly in the ballet's most subdued passages, with his wife and with A. J. Jaeger. In these scenes, both the value of friendship and its inability to meet all needs are shown. That *Enigma Variations* is at its most intense in feeling when at its most restrained in expression is part of its specifically English character.

BIBLIOGRAPHY

Croce, Arlene, et al. "A Conversation with Edwin Denby." *Ballet Review* 2.5 (1969): 3–19; 2.6 (1969): 32–45.

Croce, Arlene. "Loyal to the Royal." *New Yorker* (9 May 1983).

Goldner, Nancy. "Real Life Is Unrealistic." *Saturday Review* (July–August 1983).

Kirstein, Lincoln. *Movement and Metaphor: Four Centuries of Ballet.* New York, 1970.

Vaughan, David. *Frederick Ashton and His Ballets.* London, 1977.

FILM.   James Archibald, *Enigma Variations* (1969).

ALASTAIR MACAULAY

ENTERS, ANGNA (Anita Enters; born 18 April 1897 in Milwaukee, died 25 February 1989 in Tenafly, New Jersey), American dance-mime. Enters identified herself and her art as dance-mime, the result of her personal evolution from the ethnic and interpretive dance dominating the concert stage in the early 1920s. She went to New York City in 1919 to study fine arts at the Art Students League. While earning her living as a freelance illustrator, she began taking dancing lessons from Michio Ito. In addition, Enters studied eurythmics and traditional Japanese geisha dancing. In February 1921, Enters became Ito's professional dancing partner, performing a program of music interpretations and traditional Japanese dances.

Appearing on Broadway in the *Pin Wheel Revel* of 1922, Enters led a group dance, *Ecclesiastique,* and performed several solo dances of her own: *Le Petit Berger, Feline,* and *A Tribute to Gauguin.* In 1926, Angna Enters presented *Compositions in Dance Form,* an entire evening of solo performance, assisted only by pianist Madeleine Marshall. She took her solo program on tour across the United States and Europe for more than thirty years, until her retirement from performing in the mid-1960s.

In the late 1930s, Enters had reconceived her work as *The Theatre of Angna Enters,* which reflected her reliance on pantomimic movement rather than any single dance technique. Her repertory included more than 250 dance-mime compositions. For each character Enters designed a unique costume, arranged evocative music, and selected, where necessary, hand props and small set pieces.

Enters received her first Guggenheim Foundation Fellowship in 1934. With this award she studied ancient mime in Greece; with a second award in 1935, she studied dance in Egypt and the Near East. From this research she produced a large body of drawings and paintings, several new mime compositions based on religious themes, and a revival and revision of *Pagan Greece* (1933, rev. 1943), her only evening-length composition.

Enters had simultaneous careers as performer, artist, author, and, in her later years, as director and teacher. Her paintings and drawings were first exhibited in 1933. Beginning in the late 1920s, Enters contributed essays on the art of mime and dance to such magazines as *Drama, Dance Magazine, Twice a Year,* and *The New Masses.* Subsequently, she published six books: three volumes of autobiography, a play with music and set designs, a novel, and a journal of her first teaching experiences. In the early 1940s, Enters became a contract writer for the film studio Metro-Goldwyn-Mayer, a position she held through the early 1950s. She also created and staged the *commedia dell'arte* sequences for the film *Scaramouche* (MGM, 1952).

During the 1950s, Enters became associated with the Stella Adler Conservatory of Acting, teaching mime for actors. She directed major productions for the Houston Little Theatre and the Dallas Theatre Center, as well as for several universities in conjunction with teaching assignments as artist-in-residence. She taught last at Pennsylvania State University in 1970.

BIBLIOGRAPHY

Cocuzza, Ginnine. "Angna Enters: American Dance-Mime." *Drama Review* 24 (December 1980): 93–102.

Cocuzza, Ginnine. "First Person Plural: A Portfolio from the Theatre of Angna Enters." *Women and Performance* 1 (Spring–Summer 1983): 36–39.

Cohen-Stratyner, Barbara. *Biographical Dictionary of the Dance.* New York, 1982. Includes the most complete published listing of Enters's choreography.

Enters, Angna. *First Person Plural.* New York, 1937.

Enters, Angna. *Love Possessed Juana.* New York, 1939.

Enters, Angna. *Silly Girl.* Cambridge, Mass., 1944.

Enters, Angna. *Among the Daughters.* New York, 1955.

Enters, Angna. *Artist's Life.* New York, 1958.

Enters, Angna. *On Mime.* Middletown, Conn., 1965.

Mandel, Dorothy. *Uncommon Eloquence: A Biography of Angna Enters.* Denver, Colo., 1986.

GINNINE COCUZZA

ENTRECHATS. *See* Batterie.

ENTRÉE (It., *intrada, intrata;* Sp., *entrada;* Ger., *Aufzug, Eintritt;* Eng., entry). The term *entrée* signifies an entry, entrance, or beginning. Used in the vocabularies of music, ceremony, and dance, it also applies to the individual food course in a banquet and to the spectacle that accompanies the serving of it.

In music, an *entrée* is an instrumental piece accompanying the entrance of an important personage into a city or a performance space, signaling the beginning of a festive event, or opening a suite. *Entrées* are found in German music collections for the trumpet published around 1600 and in orchestral suites of the seventeenth century by Melchior Franck, Hermann Schein, Hans Leo Hassler, and others. In church services of the seventeenth century short organ pieces called *entrées* were used to give the correct pitch to the choir. A ceremonial *entrée* is the arrival and entry of a king or queen, an illustrious visitor, or a victorious war hero into a city. European history for centuries recorded such events, which were occasions of great pomp and circumstance involving the entire city. The citizens decorated streets and houses, put on theatrical spectacles at the stopping places of the entering cortège, and organized tournaments in city squares, ballet performances, and balls (see Saslow, 1996).

Within tournaments, equestrian *carroussels, courses à la barrière,* and similar quasi-military spectacles, an *entrée* is the group of floats, marching bands, orchestras, torchbearers, and so on that surrounds each of the protagonists during his or her approach to the event.

In dance, the term *intrata* or *intrada* first appears in Domenico da Piacenza's manual (c.1440), and the term is used consistently by Antonio Cornazano. It applies to the opening section of the *ballo,* usually in *saltarello* or *piva* meter, in which the dancers enter into the center of the performance space. The *incipit* of the *entrée,* four to seven notes as a rule, is repeated at the end, to accompany the exit of the dancers after completion of the figures, the main section of the *ballo* [*See* Ballo and Balletto.]

Michael Praetorius, in the third volume of his *Syntagma musicum,* defines *entrée* as the first of the three sections of ballets or dances performed at mummings and processions or entries "when the persons of the mumming first appear."

In the French *ballet de cour* an *entrée* is a group of dances representing various aspects of one theme performed by one or several dancers. While the *récits* separated the ballets into acts, the *entrées* of dances separate the acts into scenes. Each *entrée* was usually accompanied by its own group of costumed musicians.

Monsieur de Saint-Hubert (1641) stresses the importance of a novel and well-chosen subject for any ballet as a whole, of having *entrées* relevant to that subject, and of varying the style of the *entrées:* "Each must be pertinent. If there is a mixture of the serious and the grotesque, two grotesque *entrées* should not appear in succession; if they can be harmoniously mixed in with the serious, they will be much more diverting." The same diversity must be applied to the number of participating dancers; two *entrées* using the same number of dancers should not be too close together and *entrées* with just one or two protagonists should be kept to a minimum. "Those with three, four, five, six, seven, and eight dancers are the most attractive and make possible the most beautiful figures."

A "great" or "royal" ballet, according to Saint-Hubert, could have as many as thirty *entrées;* a "beau ballet" at least twenty; a small ballet from ten to twelve. Charles Compan (1787) states that each act of the five-act ballets could be composed of three, six, nine, or sometimes twelve *entrées.*

In the seventeenth century the thematic unity that characterized the earlier *ballets de cour* gave way to a structure in which each act treated a different subject, although all were related to the title of the whole work. This type of spectacle became known as the *ballet à entrées,* and was the forerunner of the *opéra-ballet,* in which each act is called an *entrée.* Within the genres of the *opéra-ballet* and the *tragédie lyrique,* the term *entrée* is also applied to the overture that is played at the beginning of a *divertissement,* which and accompanies the entrance of singers and dancers onto the stage. [*See* Opéra-Ballet and Tragédie Lyrique.]

All theater dances notated in Feuillet notation in the early eighteenth century are called *entrées.* Of these, the *entrée grave* was the most noble and majestic (Hilton, 1981). Usually in a slow musical meter (*sarabande, gigue lente*) it demanded the utmost in physical control and musical sensitivity of its male performers. Several such solo *entrées graves* are notated in Raoul-Auger Feuillet's *Recueil de dances* (1700), among them the "Entrée pour Apolon," composed to music from Jean-Baptiste Lully's *Le Triomphe de l'Amour* (1681). The same collection and also the ones by Guillaume-Louis Pecour (1704) and Michel Gaudrau (1714?) contain *entrée(s) seule(s)* for male and female soloists, and *entrée(s) à deux* for couples of mixed genders or of the same. In several instances the original performers of the *entrée* are mentioned by name (Mademoiselle Subligny, Mademoiselle Victoire, Mademoiselle Dangeville, Monsieur Balon, Monsieur Blondy, Monsieur Martel) and reference is made to the work, opera or ballet, to which the *entrée* belonged. In ballets since the eighteenth century the term *entrée* has often been used to designate the stage entrance of a dancer or a group of dancers and the section of the work performed by them.

BIBLIOGRAPHY

Anthony, James R. "Entrée." In *The New Grove Dictionary of Music and Musicians*. London, 1980.

Baron, John H. "Les Fées des forests de S. Germain ballet de cour, 1625." *Dance Perspectives*, no. 62 (1975): 3–15.

Christout, Marie-Françoise. *Le ballet de cour de Louis XIV, 1643–1672.* Paris, 1967.

Cohen, Selma Jeanne, ed. *Dance as a Theatre Art.* New York, 1974.

Compan, Charles. *Dictionnarie de danse.* Paris, 1787.

de Pure, Michel. *Idée des spectacles anciens et nouveaux.* Paris, 1668. Reprint (Geneva, 1972).

Ellis Little, Meredith, and Carol G. Marsh. *La Danse Noble: An Inventory of Dances and Sources.* Williamstown, Mass., 1992.

Fuller, David. "Intrada." In *The New Grove Dictionary of Music and Musicians.* London, 1980.

Hilton, Wendy. *Dance of Court and Theatre: The French Noble Style, 1690–1725.* Princeton, 1981.

Marsden, C. A. "Entrées et Fêtes Espagnoles au XVIe Siècle." *Les fêtes de la Renaissance* II (1960): 389–411.

Mattheson, Johann. *Der vollkommene Capellmeister, 1739.* Edited by Margarete Reimann. Kassel, 1954.

Praetorius, Michael. *Syntagma musicum.* Vol. 3. Wolfenbüttel, 1619.

Prunières, Henry. *Le ballet de cour en France avant Benserade et Lully.* Paris, 1914.

Reimann, Margarete. "Materialien zu einer Definition der Intrada." *Die Musikforschung* 10.3 (1957): 337–364.

Saint-Hubert, Monsieur de. *La manière de composer et de faire réussir les ballets* (1641). Edited by Marie-Françoise Christout. Geneva, 1993.

Saslow, James M. *The Medici Wedding of 1589: Florentine Festival as Theatrum Mundi.* New Haven, 1996.

Walther, Johann Gottfried. *Musikalisches Lexicon, oder, Musikalische Bibliothec.* Leipzig, 1732.

INGRID BRAINARD

ENTRÉE GRAVE is a French Baroque theater dance in quadruple meter (time); that is, a dance in which two *pas composés* or *temps* (step-units), instead of the usual one, are danced within a measure of music. The dance was apparently used only for the male technique.

The duple-meter music of the *entrée grave* is the most ceremonious in the Baroque dance repertory. With its majestic tempo, dotted rhythms, and lavish ornamentation, it is similar to the *grave* or *lent* section that begins the French overture developed by Jean-Baptiste Lully (1632–1687). Both seem to have grown out of instrumental *entrées* of late sixteenth-century *ballets de cour*, which were march-like pieces with dotted rhythms to which the dancers entered. The first example to have survived is from *Le Ballet de la Chienne* (1604). By 1640, pieces of this type had been considerably developed musically and were being called *ouvertures;* by 1658, Lully's *ballet de cour Alcidiane* had the first fully developed overture in the French style (Waterman, 1980).

It is as yet impossible to trace with certainty the development of the *entrée grave* because Lully does not so title his pieces, and the earliest known dances labeled *entrée grave* are those published when dance notation came into use in 1700. The earliest music to which a choreography has been identified as such is found in Lully's *Bellérophon* (1679), to which Raoul-Auger Feuillet (1650–c.1709) later choreographed a "ballet de neuf danseurs," which he published in 1700. The opening *entrée grave* of Feuillet's elaborate dance is for a male soloist and four other male dancers. A more famous use of the *entrée grave* was for the sun god Apollo in Lully's *Le Triomphe de l'Amour* (1681). Feuillet later choreographed a solo to the air originally designated an "Entrée pour Apolon et des Bergers Héroyques." A solo by Guillaume-Louis Pecour to this music was published by Feuillet in 1704.

In the more common duple-time dances, one step-unit is danced to one measure of music, providing one rhythmic stress on the downbeat. The dancer makes steps or springs on the half-note or the quarter-note level:

one step–unit

In the *entrée grave*, the measure is divided in half and viewed as two measures of duple time, the dancer moving on the quarter-note or the half-note level. The half notes are marked by the stress at the beginning of each step-unit:

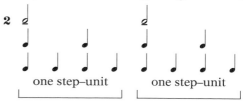

one step–unit   one step–unit

The extant dances, which are solos or duets for virtuosic male dancers, have swiftly moving choreography generously interspersed with *pas battus*. About half of the springing steps employed are *cabrioles, entrechats, jetés battus*, and other beaten steps. Pirouettes, with either *élevés* or *sautés*, are used frequently, often being combined with *battements*.

The *entrée grave* is usually bipartite, with the musical repeats A-A-B-B. A different dance figure is danced to each musical strain. The strains are of diverse lengths. For example, the "Entrée pour Apolon" has a strain of nine measures followed by one of nineteen measures. The *entrée grave* from *Bellérophon* has two strains of eleven measures.

The tempo of an *entrée grave* must be slow enough to accommodate the most active step-units, yet fast enough musically for the dotted rhythms to retain their tension. The dancer must preserve an air of majesty even during the performance of the most intricate and technically demanding step-units. The unusual structural relationship of music and dance require of the dancer an intellectual approach perhaps more than an instinctive rhythmic response.

[*See also* Ballet Technique, History of, *article on* French Court Dance.]

BIBLIOGRAPHY

Feuillet, Raoul-Auger. *Recueil de dances composées par M. Pécour.* Paris, 1700.

Feuillet, Raoul-Auger. "Traité de la cadence." In Feuillet's *Recueil de dances contenant un très grand nombres des meillieures entrées de ballet de M. Pécour.* Paris, 1704. Translated by John Weaver as *A Small Treatise of Time and Cadence in Dancing.* London, 1706.

Waterman, George G. "French Overture." In *The New Grove Dictionary of Music and Musicians.* London, 1980.

WENDY HILTON

EQUESTRIAN BALLET. *See* Horse Ballet. *See also* Circus.

ERDMAN, JEAN (born 1917? in Honolulu, Hawaii), American dancer, choreographer, teacher, theatrical director, and producer. Growing up in Hawaii, Erdman was exposed to native dances and to the Isadora Duncan technique. In 1938, after graduating from Sarah Lawrence College and taking a trip around the world, during which she saw the dances of Bali, Java, Cambodia, India, and Spain, she joined the Martha Graham Company.

In the five years that she danced with Graham, she was singled out for speaking roles in *Letter to the World*, as One Who Speaks at the New York premiere in January 1941, and as one of the Three Fates in *Punch and the Judy*, which premiered in August 1941 at the Bennington School of Dance. She began choreographing in 1941 and

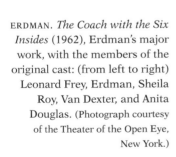

ERDMAN. *The Coach with the Six Insides* (1962), Erdman's major work, with the members of the original cast: (from left to right) Leonard Frey, Erdman, Sheila Roy, Van Dexter, and Anita Douglas. (Photograph courtesy of the Theater of the Open Eye, New York.)

the following year presented a concert of solos and duets with Merce Cunningham at Bennington and in New York City. Erdman left the Graham Company in 1943 and a year later founded the Jean Erdman Dance Group.

From the beginning Erdman focused on her belief that style belongs to the dance rather than to the dancer. "Each dance must have its unique image/idea, movement, vocabulary, dynamic rhythm, sounds and special world. This is the chief aesthetic rule for me," she wrote in a program note for a 1984 revival of some of her best-known solos. These included *The Transformations of Medusa* (1942), to music by Louis Horst; *Daughters of the Lonesome Isle* (1944), to music by John Cage; and *Changingwoman* (1951), to music by Henry Cowell. Erdman has carried the idea of "total theater" throughout her life's work.

Erdman worked and taught at the New Dance Group from 1943 to 1948, when she opened her own school. Always interested in ethnic forms, she returned to Hawaii in 1945 to study ceremonial dance and Japanese dance. She also attended the School of American Ballet and studied Spanish dance. In addition she taught at Columbia University Teachers College (1949–1951) and headed the dance departments at Bard College (1954–1957) and the School of the Arts at New York University (1967–1972), where she created the Professional Dance Training Program. During this time she choreographed and directed her productions and toured the United States, Europe, and the Far East.

Erdman's 1962 work *The Coach with the Six Insides*, based on James Joyce's *Finnegan's Wake*, with music by Teiji Ito, was fashioned as a multifaceted dance drama. *Coach* won great acclaim and has been revived many times since. Other poets, painters, and writers who have inspired Erdman include William Butler Yeats, Jean Cocteau, Jean-Paul Sartre, Paul Gauguin, William Saroyan, and Robinson Jeffers.

Erdman and her husband, the renowned mythologist and lecturer Joseph Campbell, created the Foundation for the Open Eye in 1972 as an expression of their combined interest in the drama of myth and poetry. The foundation supports the Theater of the Open Eye in New York City, which provides opportunities for playwrights, directors, and choreographers to develop new works through its New Stagings Lab and its dance festival and drama series.

BIBLIOGRAPHY
Current Biography. New York, 1971.
Sears, David. "A Coach Filled with Dance Drama." *New York Times* (21 February 1982).

VIDEOTAPE. "Dance and Myth: The World of Jean Erdman" (1994).

KITTY CUNNINGHAM

ESAMBAYEV, MAKHMUD (Makhmud Alisultan Esambaev; born 15 July 1924 in Stariya Atagi, Checheno-Ingush Autonomous Soviet Socialist Republic), dancer. Born in a Chechen village, Esambayev was obsessed by dancing in his youth and was often invited to give his fast and fiery renditions of the *lezghinka* and other folk dances at local weddings and celebrations. In 1938 he enrolled in the Grozny ballet school, but his studies were interrupted by World War II, for the duration of which he gained experience as a member of performing teams that toured the battlefronts to entertain the troops. From 1944 to 1956 Esambayev was a leading dancer of the ballet company in Frunze (now Bishkek), the capital of Kirghizia (now Kyrgyzstan), becoming especially noted as a character dancer. Among his roles were the Fairy Carabosse in *The Sleeping Beauty*, Rothbart in *Swan Lake*, the grasping, well-to-do peasant in Nurdin Tugelov's *Anar*, and the Cossack chieftain in Tugelov's *Cholpon*. Beginning in 1957, Esambayev appeared frequently on the concert stage with his program "Dances of Many Nations," featuring choreography by Mikhail Zaslavsky, Leonid Yakobson, Ivan Kovtunov, and others. In it he performed a wide variety of folk dances, lending authenticity to the specific features of each, which placed him in the top rank of Soviet dancers. The most popular dance sketches were *The Shepherd* (Checheno-Ingush), *The Golden God (bharata nāṭyam)*, *Bamboo* (Colombian), *Macumba* (Brazilian), *Negro Dance* (his own creation), and *The Poor Tailor* (Jewish).

The title of People's Artist of the USSR was conferred on him in 1974. The recognition he enjoyed among the public at large is illustrated by his repeated election to the Supreme Soviet of the USSR. He received the title of Hero of Socialist Labor in 1984. During the 1990s he has been on the faculty of the Academy of Science in Chechnya.

BIBLIOGRAPHY
Nashkhoev, Ruslan. *Charodei tantsa: Dokumentalnaia povest o M. Esambaeve*. 2d ed. Grozny, 1980.
Pozhidaev, Gennadii A. *Povest o tantse: Esambaeve*. Moscow, 1972.

YURI P. TYURIN
Translated from Russian

ESCUDERO, VICENTE (Vicente Escudero Uribe; born 27 October 1892, 1888, or 1885 in Valladolid, Spain, died 4 December 1980 in Barcelona), dancer, choreographer, and teacher of flamenco dance. Escudero may well have been a Gypsy, but he always refused to clarify this point. In his youth the family moved to Granada and settled in the Gypsy quarter of Sacro Monte, where he absorbed the local dances (and for which he would name his first company, formed in 1934).

By the early 1900s, Escudero was performing all over Spain in the popular *cafés cantantes* (cafés that featured singing). In Bilbao he met his mentor and only teacher of pure flamenco, Antonio el de Bilbao. Escudero then moved on to *fines de fiestas* (entr'acte performances in theaters). Toward the end of the 1910s he spent a year in Lisbon, where he met Carmita García, who became his longtime partner, and began to experiment with the structural traditions of flamenco. He particularly eschewed the *compás* (rhythmic phrases of twelve or four counts, rather than measured bars) used by all flamenco artists, but he did not tamper with the essential style of the dance.

In 1920, Escudero made his debut in Paris at the Olympia Theater and reaped immediate international renown. Influenced by his friendship with Pablo Picasso (who would later provide designs for Escudero's company) and by the surrealism then current in the Parisian art world, Escudero himself took up painting and design. His fame as a dancer was such that Anna Pavlova invited him to join her American tour. When her untimely death in 1931 brought it to a halt, Escudero carried on alone. Thereafter he toured the United States several times, always returning for appearances in Spain, where he was much in demand. La Argentina cast him in the principal role of her *El Amor Brujo* with Pastora Imperio in 1934 at the Teatro Español in Madrid. He performed with Argentina and her sister Pilar López in many programs. In 1940 he created the *seguiriyas* in dance for the first time.

By 1942, with World War II in progress and his appearances meeting a tepid reception, Escudero stopped performing and devoted himself to teaching, lecturing, and writing on flamenco. Moving to Paris in 1954, he opened a school and once again formed a company, which toured throughout Europe and the United States until 1961, when he retired definitively from performing. He spent his final years championing the cause of flamenco in his beloved Barcelona.

Escudero's innovations were many and wide-ranging. He danced to music previously reserved for flamenco singers, to multiple orchestras simultaneously playing different scores, and to no music at all—only the sounds of hand clapping, finger snapping, tongue clicking, and body slapping. (Tradition has it that he began this practice when he could not afford to pay a guitarist.) He applied contemporary art to his set and costume designs, and he railed against commercialism and academic schooling in flamenco performance. He is remembered today as an exponent of pure flamenco dance.

[*See also* Flamenco Dance.]

BIBLIOGRAPHY

Escudero, Vicente. *Mi baile.* Barcelona, 1947.
García Redondo, Francisca. *El círculo mágico en el centenario de Antonia Mercé, Vicente Escudero y Pastora Imperio.* Cáceres, 1988.
Krinkin, Alexandra V. "'Vicente, esto es.'" *Dance Magazine* (February 1955): 18–21.
Parker, Henry Taylor. *Motion Arrested: Dance Reviews of H. T. Parker.* Edited by Olive Holmes. Middletown, Conn., 1982.
Pohren, D. E. *Lives and Legends of Flamenco.* Madrid, 1964.
Wilson, G. B. L. *A Dictionary of Ballet.* Aylesbury Bucks, England, 1974.

MARINA GRUT

ESCUELA BOLERA is a genre of classical Spanish dance that derives its vocabulary from the early nineteenth-century bolero mixed in a theatrical context with versions of other Spanish dances, such as the *cachucha* and *tirana*, and with elements from French ballet. The synthesis took place in Seville during the Napoleonic era.

History. The French dancer Fernanda LeFebvre led a popular company of French and Spanish dancers who performed in Seville between 1800 and 1813. LeFebvre learned the bolero, which had developed in the late eighteenth century out of the Spanish *seguidillas*, and adapted it for the stage. Although her version was inauthentic, her talent pleased audiences. The Spanish composer Fernando Sor (1778–1839) decried LeFebvre's bolero as vulgar and ungraceful, but its wide popularity—especially among the French—led to its being incorporated in the foundations of the *escuela bolera*.

Other dancers who performed Spanish dances in Europe and England must also have contributed to the school. The great French dancer Armand Vestris debuted in London in 1809 dancing a bolero; he continued to present Spanish dances and created Spanish-style *divertissements*. Mademoiselle Mori performed such Spanish dances as the *guaracha* in London early in the nineteenth century. Maria Mercandotti first danced the *cachucha* in London in 1814. In 1816 the Spanish bolero dancers Luengo and Ramos performed at Covent Garden, London.

After the Napoleonic wars the theatrical bolero declined in Spain while it flourished in the theaters of Paris. The French writer Théophile Gautier, in *Voyage to Spain*, included a vivid and hilarious account of an "authentic" performance he witnessed, comparing the decrepit Spanish dancers with the stars who rendered the bolero on the stages of France.

The remnants of the great Spanish tradition were combined with the ballet-influenced French bolero by two Spanish duos, Dolores Serral and Mariano Camprubí of Madrid's Teatro Principe, and Francisco Font and Manuela Dubinon of Madrid's Teatro de la Cruz. They toured successfully, bringing the bolero and other dances to Paris, London, and other cities. The great choreographer August Bournonville encountered them in Copenhagen and later wrote that he had benefited from participating in a performance with them; his attempt was greeted with derision by the audience, but he put what he learned to good use in creating a Spanish ballet, *El Toreador*, which premiered in November 1840, with Bournonville dancing the *jaleo de Jerez* and a bolero.

A great ballerina who benefited from the Spanish school was Fanny Elssler; her "La Cachucha" solo was famous, and she also performed "La Cachucha de Cádiz." Other renowned ballerinas such as Fanny Cerrito, Marie Taglioni, and Lucile Grahn all included Spanish dances in their concert programs. Russian choreographer Marius Petipa made a trip to Spain to study its dances.

Native Spanish dancers also triumphed on the stages of mid-nineteenth century Europe, but critics accustomed to the idealized versions of ballet dancers sometimes misunderstood the authentic performances. The *cachucha* of La Nena (Manuela Perea) was compared unfavorably with that of Elssler, and Bournonville was scandalized by Pepita Oliva's *olé*.

Other dancers active within Spain at this time included Juan Camprubí, the son of Mariano, and his partner Manuela Garcia, who had studied flamenco in Granada. In 1847, they led twelve couples in a performance of *la rondeña* for the inauguration of the Gran Teatro del Liceo in Barcelona. Their repertory also included the *cachucha*, the *jaleo*, *seguidillas mollares*, *seguidillas manchegas*, *malagueñas*, *sevillanas*, *boleras robadas*, *jota aragonesa*, *ball plá*, and *ball rodó*.

A document surviving in Spain's National Archive of History, dated 11 March 1856, shows that the dancer and choreographer Antonio Ruiz filed a claim of ownership of certain theatrical Spanish dances "which, according to him, were previously only *bailes sueltos*." Ruiz was apparently trying to establish a kind of copyright on dances that had been passed down by imitation; his object was to codify these dances for the purpose of incorporating them in ballets. Ruiz was perhaps the first choreographer to create an entire ballet based on the vocabulary of Spanish dance.

Modern Status. Today the *escuela bolera* is an academic discipline taught in conservatories specializing in Spanish dance. These institutions also teach ballet, and this has resulted in a number of modifications in the arm carriage and footwork of bolero. In addition, the nationalist revival under the regime of Francisco Franco (ruled 1939–1975) included state sponsorship of Spanish culture societies, which had great social impact. Spanish dance, including a form of bolero less influenced by classical ballet, was taught in their programs.

Thus in the contemporary period, the *escuela bolera* has become a new combination of indigenous and imported dance traditions. Even elements from flamenco have been added. Today the *escuela bolera* has an uncertain admixture of Romantic European bolero, strictly Spanish versions, and modern compromises between the two.

The heart of the present *escuela bolera* is the Pericet family, the repository of traditional knowledge. Their patriarch was Angel Pericet Carmona (1877–1944), who at the end of the nineteenth century organized the first family dance academy in Seville to teach both *escuela bolera* and Spanish regional dances. In 1932, Angel Pericet moved his school to Madrid, leaving his brother Rafael (died 1956) to carry on in Seville. Rafael Pericet taught *barre* work and the steps of the *escuela bolera*, insisting that ballet shoes be worn. In 1942, Angel Pericet Carmona and his son Angel Pericet Jiménez (1899–1973) prepared a manual codifying the steps of bolero and how they were to be taught. In the 1990s, five of the younger Angel's children were still active: Amparo, Carmelita, and Angel as performers, and Eloy and Luisa as teachers.

The bolero performed by the Pericets is beautiful, but it is not the only remnant of the tradition that survives. Bournonville's choreographies are preserved in Copenhagen, and the bolero from act 2 of *Coppélia* is maintained in Cuba. There is a notated record of "La Cachucha" as danced by Elssler in 1887 in Leipzig. Neither can we discount the dances handed down by dancers who were less concerned with accurate preservation: Guillermina Martínez Cabreras (Mariemma), who was trained in Paris in classical ballet and by Francisco Miralles in *escuela bolera*; Elvira Lucena, who began with another teacher before studying with the Pericets; the students of Manuel and Antonio Otéro; or María de Ávila, a student of Luisa Pericet who had previously worked with Carlos Pérez Castillo (Maestro Coronas). There is in addition a Catalan tradition of *escuela bolera*, to which the dancer Roseta Mauri belongs. The traditions are many, as are the products of the present-day school. Even the members of the Pericet family display certain stylistic variations among themselves.

[*See also* Bolero *and the entry on the Pericet family.*]

BIBLIOGRAPHY

Aschengreen, Erik. "Pasión y fuego depurados hasta la belleza: Augusto Bournonville y la danza española." In *Encuentro internacional "La Escuela Bolera."* Madrid, 1992.

Bailar España 1990. Madrid, 1990.

Carrasco Benítez, Marta. "Las academias de baile en Sevilla: Los Pericet." In *Encuentro internacional "La Escuela Bolera."* Madrid, 1992.

Castellanos de Losada, Basilio Sebastián. *Memorias sobre baile.* Madrid, 1854.

Guest, Ivor. *The Romantic Ballet in England.* London, 1972.

Guest, Ivor. *The Romantic Ballet in Paris.* 2d rev. ed. London, 1980.

Matteo. "Woods That Dance." *Dance Perspectives*, no. 33 (Spring 1968).

Matteo. *The Language of Spanish Dances.* Norman, Okla., 1990.

Pericet Blanco, Eloy. "Influencia andaluza en la Escuela Bolera." In *Actas del II congreso de folclore Andaluz: Danza, música e indumentaria tradicional.* Seville, 1988.

Ruyter, Nancy Lee Chalfa. "La Escuela Bolera." *Dance Chronicle* 16.2 (1993): 249–257.

Suárez-Pajares, Javier, and Xoán M. Carreira. *The Origins of the Bolero School.* Studies in Dance History, vol. 4.1. Pennington, N.J., 1993.

Valdenebro, Pepa Guerra. *Así canta y baila Andalucía.* Malaga, 1987.

Zorn, Friedrich Albert. *Grammatik der Tanzkunst.* Leipzig, 1887. Translated by Benjamin P. Coates as *Grammar of the Art of Dancing* (Boston, 1905).

JAVIER SUÁREZ-PAJARES
with Estrella Casero García
Translated from Spanish

ESHKOL-WACHMAN MOVEMENT NOTATION.
See Notation.

ESMERALDA, LA. Ballet in two acts and five scenes. Choreography: Jules Perrot. Music: Cesare Pugni. Libretto: Jules Perrot, after Victor Hugo's novel *Notre-Dame de Paris*. Scenery: William Grieve. Costumes: Madame Copère. First performance: 9 March 1844, Her Majesty's Theatre, London. Principals: Carlotta Grisi (Esmeralda), Jules Perrot (Pierre Gringoire), Arthur Saint-Léon (Phoebus), Louis Gosselin (Claude Frollo), Antoine Louis Coulin (Quasimodo).

LA ESMERALDA. An artist's impression of the Feast of Fools scene in the original production. This woodblock engraving was printed in *The Illustrated London News*, 1844. (Courtesy of Madison U. Sowell and Debra H. Sowell, Brigham Young University, Provo, Utah.)

A poor and struggling poet, Pierre Gringoire, finds himself in the Cour de Miracles, the slums of medieval Paris inhabited by the worst rabble in the city. The Gypsy girl Esmeralda saves him by agreeing to marry him. She then falls in love with the noble Phoebus, who rescues her from her abductors, the lecherous priest Claude Frollo and Quasimodo, the bell-ringer of Notre-Dame. Esmeralda jilts Gringoire. At the wedding of Phoebus and Fleur de Lys, Esmeralda dances with the scarf presented to her by Phoebus. Fleur de Lys is shocked at her fiancé's treachery. Phoebus and Esmeralda leave together, but Claude Frollo catches up with them and stabs Phoebus. Esmeralda is accused of the murder and is condemned. But it turns out that Phoebus has survived after all. He proves Esmeralda's innocence, and Quasimodo kills Frollo.

The treatment of characters and the development of the dramatic action obeyed the principle of Romantic antithesis: the splendid nobleman, Phoebus, was a foil for

the poor but endearing poet, Gringoire; Esmeralda's exalted, poetic love contrasted with Claude Frollo's shocking cruelty. The stage was dominated by a motley crowd of beggars, cripples, soldiers, and townspeople dancing on the streets and squares of medieval Paris in the shadow of the somber bulk of Notre-Dame, the austere Gothic line of which symbolized the unchallenged and undivided power of the church. On the other hand, the ballet was full of elements of classical ballet with its well-defined forms and neat design. Building *La Esmeralda* as a dance play, Perrot tried to avoid inserted *divertissement* numbers, a new departure in the ballet of the mid-nineteenth century.

Four years after the ballet's London premiere it was staged by Perrot in Saint Petersburg at the Bolshoi Theater on 12 [24] December 1848. This version blunted the social edge of Hugo's novel. Esmeralda was not executed but saved by Phoebus. But even in this "prettified" form the problems raised by the ballet were new to the Russian stage. The ballet centered around the character of the heroine and her relationships with people from different classes of society. The creators of the Saint Petersburg revised version clearly sided with the "lower" classes, with Esmeralda, a "girl from the people" who symbolized and embodied the beautiful. Phoebus, Claude Frollo, Quasimodo, and Gringoire are all in love with her, each in his own way, and she is a magnet for the down-and-outs of the Cour des Miracles. At the Saint Petersburg premiere the role of Esmeralda was danced by Fanny Elssler, a pagan dancer *par excellence*—passionate, vivacious, and dynamic. Many fine Russian ballerinas were later seen in the role.

In Russian and Soviet ballet, *La Esmeralda* has been produced in different interpretations by different composers and choreographers. Marius Petipa revived the ballet twice for the Maryinsky Theater, in 1886 and in 1899. He left out some of the pantomime scenes and expanded and diversified the ballet's dancing palette. In particular, he added Esmeralda's dance at the ball given by Fleur de Lys—a dramatic danced prayer of the Gypsy girl who learns that her beloved has a fiancée. *La Esmeralda* was also produced in Moscow at the Bolshoi Theater by Perrot in 1850 and by José Mendes in 1890. In 1918 and 1933 the ballet was given in Petrograd based on Petipa's choreography.

The 1926 production of *La Esmeralda* by Vasily Tikhomirov at the Bolshoi Theater, Moscow, featured Ekaterina Geltser in the title role. The new version centered around not so much the personal drama of the characters as the cruel atmosphere of the Dark Ages. It also highlighted the theme of the people and the social implications of the message. Tikhomirov's version, however, was not without contradictions: the finale was again melodramatic in character, as in the first Saint Petersburg version; Esmeralda did not die, which contradicted

Hugo's novel. Geltser was noted for a vivid mime expressiveness, convincing impersonation, and a subtle penetration into the dramatic essence of the character.

A "new look" version of the ballet in three acts and nine scenes was staged by Agrippina Vaganova in 1935 in Leningrad at the Kirov Theater on 23 April 1935. Vaganova had sought to recreate the spirit of Perrot's original score and to purge *La Esmeralda*, as far as possible, of the various distortions that had built up over the nearly ninety-year stage history of the ballet. With this in view she emphasized the dramatic and logical structure of the action. The redesigned scenery created a romantic and picturesque period atmosphere of medieval Paris during the reign of Louis XI, at the turn of the Middle Ages to the Renaissance. Pursuing her goal of maximum realism Vaganova recomposed the dances of the Truands, the inhabitants of the Cour des Miracles. The passion and inner sensibility of Esmeralda contrasted with the emptiness of the affected Fleur de Lys, Phoebus's moral bankruptcy with the tender devotion of the deformed Quasimodo. Esmeralda, as interpreted by Tatiana Vecheslova, was full of a powerful tragic pathos. Far from being a graceful and frolicsome child of nature, Vecheslova's Esmeralda was a bold and proud heroine destined to die. Vaganova composed a delightful interlude for the ball scene at Fleur de Lys's—a virtuosic pas de deux of Diana and Actaeon, vaguely based on Greek mythology. This spectacular number served to set off Esmeralda's love. To this day the pas de deux is popular in the concert repertory. At the Leningrad premiere of Vaganova's version of *La Esmeralda* the pas de deux was brilliantly performed by the youthful Galina Ulanova and Vakhtang Chabukiani.

The year 1950 saw a new version of *La Esmeralda* presented by Moscow's Stanislavsky and Nemirovich-Danchenko Musical Theater. With choreography by Vladimir Burmeister, Violetta Bovt appeared as Esmeralda. Burmeister redesigned all the dances and made the characters resemble more closely those of Hugo's novel. As a result, Phoebus from a hero became a satirical negative character, and the moral superiority of the people, as represented by Esmeralda and Quasimodo, over the hypocritical and mendacious aristocracy was emphasized.

La Esmeralda in its various choreographic versions has been produced by leading ballet companies throughout Russia. A complete list of these productions through 1980 is in the *Soviet Encyclopedia of Ballet*, published in Moscow in 1981. One of the more popular evergreens of the classical repertory, the ballet has been produced by many leading ballet companies: London's Festival Ballet (Nicholas Beriozoff, 1954), Paris Opera Ballet (Roland Petit, 1965, called *Notre-Dame de Paris*), and the Australian Ballet (Bruce Wells, 1981, called *The Hunchback of Notre-Dame*) to name but a few.

BIBLIOGRAPHY
Beaumont, Cyril W. *Complete Book of Ballets*. London, 1937.
Guest, Ivor. *The Romantic Ballet in England*. London, 1972.
Guest, Ivor. *Jules Perrot*. London, 1984.
Roslavleva, Natalia. *Era of the Russian Ballet* (1966). New York, 1979.
Slonimsky, Yuri. *Mastera baleta*. Leningrad, 1937. See pages 87–131.
Slonimsky, Yuri. "Jules Perrot." Translated by Anatole Chujoy. *Dance Index* 4 (December 1945): 208–247.
Souritz, Elizabeth. *Soviet Choreographers in the 1920s*. Translated by Lynn Visson. Durham, N.C., 1990.
Swift, Mary Grace. *The Art of the Dance in the USSR*. South Bend, Indiana, 1969.

ELENA G. FEDORENKO
Translated from Russian

ESPINOSA FAMILY, dynasty of dancers of Spanish origin who eventually settled and did their most important work in England. Notable members included Léon Espinosa, his son Édouard, and his grandson Edward Kelland-Espinosa.

Léon Espinosa (born 1825 in The Hague, died 1903 in London), dancer. Léon Espinosa studied at the Paris Opera, made his debut in Paris in 1845, danced at the Théâtre de la Porte-Saint-Martin, and toured widely in the United States and Europe. He took a troupe down the Mississippi River, and family legend says he was captured by Indians. By 1865 he had reached Moscow, had been accepted for the Bolshoi Ballet, and had made his debut in *Le Roi Candaule* as a slave. He stayed for seven years, and because, at four feet, ten inches, he was so tiny—he was essentially a character dancer of prodigious technique—he was given the title *premier danseur de contraste*. By 1872 Espinosa had settled in London, where he opened a school. That same year, his son Édouard Henry was born. Espinosa staged an elaborate production of *Babil and Bijoux* at Covent Garden on 29 August 1872, dancing with Henriette Dor, who became Édouard's godmother (hence his middle name). *Babil and Bijoux* was lavishly backed by Lord Londesborough, and the whole enterprise is described by Osbert Sitwell, Londesborough's grandson, in his autobiography, *Left Hand, Right Hand* (1945).

In 1878 Espinosa and his wife, Matilda de Léon, and his two older sons, Léon and Marius (named after his godfather, Marius Petipa) went to Paris, where Édouard joined them the following year. Espinosa's dancing career was, however, ended by an injury.

Édouard Espinosa (Édouard Henry Espinosa; born 2 February 1872 in London, died 1950 in Worthing, England), dancer and teacher. Léon Espinosa was opposed to his son's pursuing a stage career but relented when the boy ran away from home. Édouard Espinosa began his studies in 1889 and later that year assisted his father in productions mounted by actor-manager Henry Irving at the Lyceum Theatre in London, an association that lasted for many years. An itinerant career followed. Espinosa was to create spectacular ballets and work in the commercial theater throughout the world, especially in South Africa, the United States, and Australia, but he made his greatest contributions to ballet as a teacher. In his introduction to Espinosa's *An Encyclopedia of the Ballet*, published in *The Dancing Times*, P. J. S. Richardson wrote, "He was the first in England and possibly the world to examine and analyse those traditional steps and movements which have been handed down to us from the great dancers and teachers of the past." Richardson also describes Espinosa (known as Espy) as an "analytical chemist" of the dance.

Espinosa devised a syllabus of ballet examinations at elementary, intermediate, and advanced standards, based on a progressive system of training that he used in his own school (where Ninette de Valois was a pupil) and that was to become the foundation for the syllabi of examining bodies today. He was also a passionate champion of the possibilities of a British national ballet. In 1920 he and Richardson founded what is today the Royal Academy of Dancing. In 1930 he left to found, with his wife Eve Kelland, a former dancer, the British Ballet Organisation.

Edward Kelland-Espinosa (born 1906 in London, died 13 October 1991 in London), dancer and producer. A pupil of his father, Édouard, and a brilliant tap dancer, Edward Kelland-Espinosa enjoyed a successful stage career together with his sister Yvette (born 1911 in London) and subsequently became a famous producer of pantomimes and summer shows. After 1950 he devoted all his time to running the British Ballet Organisation, of which he became chairman upon the death of his father. Since his own death in 1991, the British Ballet Organisation has continued under its administrative Board of Control, as Edward Kelland had secured its future by leaving a bequest and establishing a scholarship fund named after his father.

Other Family Members. Édouard's sisters were also famous teachers. Judith Espinosa (born 1876 in London, died 1949 in London) and Lea Espinosa (born 1883 in Paris, died in 1966 in Basingstoke, England) both worked in London. Ray Espinosa (born 1885 in Paris, died 1934 in Johannesburg) taught in South Africa under the name Madame Ravodna. Lea's son Geoffrey Espinosa (Geoffrey Hughes; born 1907 in London, died 1990 in London) was ballet master to Mona Inglesby's International Ballet for six years and then taught freelance. Lea's daughter Ray (born 1910 in London) taught near London until 1957. Geoffrey's wife, Bridget Espinosa (Bridget Kelly; born 1928 in Hampton, England, died 1989 in Jamaica), after a successful career as a dancer and teacher, opened her own London Studio Centre in 1978 under the patronage of Dame Ninette de Valois. Her son, Nicholas Espinosa (born 20 May 1956 in London), is now director.

BIBLIOGRAPHY

Ferguson, Rachel. *And Then He Danced: The Life of Espinosa by Himself.* London, c.1947.

Guest, Ivor. *Ballet in Leicester Square.* London, 1992.

Meisner, Nadine. "Professional Performers." *Dance,* no. 19 (Summer 1991): 20–21.

Moore, Lillian. "Léon Espinosa in America." *The Dancing Times* (March 1951): 333–335.

Richardson, Philip. "Classical Technique in England: Its Development under Foreign Teachers." *Ballet Annual* 2 (1948): 118–125.

Sitwell, Osbert. *Left Hand, Right Hand: An Autobiography,* vol. 1, *The Cruel Month.* London, 1945.

MARY CLARKE

ESPLANADE. Choreography: Paul Taylor. Music: Johann Sebastian Bach. Costumes: John Rawlings. Lighting: Jennifer Tipton. First performance: 1 March 1975, Lisner Auditorium, Washington D.C., Paul Taylor Dance Company. Dancers: Bettie de Jong, Carolyn Adams, Ruth Andrien, Eileen Cropley, Monica Morris, Lila York, Elie Chaib, Nicholas Gunn, Greg Reynolds.

Paul Taylor retired from performing in 1974 after being highly acclaimed for two decades as a dancer-choreographer. It was a milestone in his long, successful career: one which had an immediate impact on his repertory and, subsequently, on the development of his company. *Esplanade* was the first major work following Taylor's retirement. Previously, much of his choreography had been created on his own, powerful body and had featured him as the central male figure. With *Esplanade* and the series of important works that followed—*Runes* (1975), *Cloven Kingdom* and *Polaris* (both 1976), *Images* and *Dust* (both 1977) and *Airs* (1978)—Taylor began to explore the diverse talents of his dancers and, in shaping his work from the outside, discovered many new choreographic possibilities, particularly the complex structuring and spatial elements that became evident in his choreography from 1975 onwards.

The process of creating *Esplanade* recalled the period Taylor had spent in 1957 preparing for his *Seven New Dances* concert. As he had at that time, Taylor devoted weeks of rehearsals to experimenting with basic movement ideas. *Esplanade* even includes reference to his early studies of posture, gesture, and stillness, particularly in the second movement. In the later work, however, the focus is on locomotion and, most importantly, on its theatrical potential. Whereas *Seven New Dances* prompted negative criticism because of its seemingly nondance content, *Esplanade* confirmed Taylor's mature grasp of pedestrian movement on stage.

A girl running for a bus on Houston Street (a wide, busy highway close to Taylor's Broadway studio) was the starting point for *Esplanade*. This everyday occurrence inspired Taylor to set basic traveling actions to music by Bach and to use them as thematic ideas for the work's five sections. The first, third and fifth movements, featuring eight dancers (three men and five women), are based progressively on walking, running, and falling. They are characterized by quick changes of direction and clearly defined spatial patterns; and by follow-the-leader progressions and folk dance formations such as lines, circles, and square dances. There is an increase in speed and energy through the three sections; the even strides and occasional light runs of the first movement become fast sprints in double time (described by the dancers as "streaks") in the third movement, while the final movement is a nonstop display of off-balance *manèges*, baseball slides, and spiraling falls.

The first three movements are choreographed to Bach's Violin Concerto No. 2 in E Major; movements four and five are to the Largo and Allegro from his Concerto in D Minor for Two Violins. The second and fourth movements of *Esplanade*—the two adagio sections—are subtly linked by their contrasting themes of isolation and intimacy, the latter being composed essentially of contacting movements and male-female partnering. The second movement is the most enigmatic. It is led by a tall female dancer who does not appear elsewhere in the work, costumed, like the men, in leotard and trousers. (The other five women wear knee-length dresses with full circular skirts.) With its mysterious gestures and mournful emphasis, the second movement seems unrelated to the optimism and ensemble spirit of *Esplanade*'s other four sections. At a deeper level, however, the truncated arm gestures and still poses mirror the embraces and lifts of the fourth movement; and fleeting reference is made to several key moments in other sections—for example, two solos in the first and fifth movements include, respectively, a circular run and a back fall. When juxtaposed against the tense, reaching gestures of the female protagonist in the second movement, they are transformed from plotless, pure dance movements into a tableau of dysfunctional relationships—an underlying theme in many of Taylor's works.

Esplanade retains the simplicity of everyday movements yet, through rhythmic and spatial manipulation, they no longer belong to the street. Taylor has described the process as "transforming alchemy." He discovered it in early works such as *Junction* (1961) and *Aureole* (1962), but its full potency can be found in the rich stream of choreography from *Esplanade* onward. This was the period when many fine dancers replaced Taylor in the limelight as he realized new ideas (and also revisited previous themes) through their various responses. Significantly, a few weeks before the New York premiere of *Esplanade*, Taylor wrote a letter to his dancers about the crucial distinction between them and ordinary people: "Both walk, sure, but one is illumination, the other locomotion." His most ingenious achievement in *Esplanade* has been to turn pedestrian movement into dance phrases—dance that radiates from the stage and leaves a luminous afterglow.

BIBLIOGRAPHY
Baker, Robb. "All Kinds of Class." *Dance Magazine* (August 1975): 33.
Croce, Arlene. "Changes." *The New Yorker* (2 February 1976): 82–83. Reprinted in *Afterimages*. London, 1978.
Duncan, Kathy. "The Paul Taylor Dance Company." *Dance News* (October 1975): 11.
Hodgson, Moira. "Paul Taylor: Zunch is the Thing." *Dance News* (June 1975): 1, 3.
Kisselgoff, Anna. "Paul Taylor's Esplanade." *New York Times* (11 June 1975).

ANGELA KANE

ESSEX, JOHN (born c.1680, died February 1744), English dancer, writer, and dancing master. Nothing is known of Essex's early life and training, but in the early 1700s he was appearing as a dancer at the Theatre Royal, Drury Lane, and probably teaching dancing and music as well. In 1703 Christopher Rich, the owner of the Drury Lane, dropped him as a dancer after a dispute involving an appeal to the lord chamberlain. Essex then retired from the stage and concentrated on writing and establishing his fashionable practice as a dancing master.

Essex's work and publications followed the example of his colleague and friend John Weaver, with whom he was on good terms until his death. In 1710 he completed Weaver's campaign to make the use of Raoul-Auger Feuillet's system of dance notation current in England: his translation of Feuillet's *Recüeil de contredanses* (Paris, 1706) appeared as *For the Furthur* [sic] *Improvement of Dancing, a Treatis of Chorography* [sic] *or ye Art of Dancing Country Dances after a New Character*. Although he translated virtually all of Feuillet's introductory text, Essex added his own selection of country dances in simplified Feuillet notation. A second edition of the work appeared in about 1715, dedicated to the Princess of Wales (later Queen Caroline) and containing the *Princess's Passpied*, Essex's only dance to survive in notation. [*See* Feuillet Notation *and the entry on Weaver.*]

Essex distilled his experience as a genteel dancing master into a decorous treatise on social dance and comportment, *The Young Ladies Conduct: or, Rules for Education, under Several Heads; with Instructions upon Dances, both before and after Marriage* (1722). The work was influenced by the first chapter of Weaver's *An Essay towards an History of Dancing* (1712) and his *Anatomical and Mechanical Lectures upon Dancing* (1721) and belongs to the educational tradition of Thomas Caverley.

In 1728 Essex produced an English version of Pierre Rameau's *Le maître à danser* (Paris, 1725), one of the most important eighteenth-century dance manuals. His translation of the text, *The Dancing-Master: or, The Art of Dancing Explained*, included an important preface reflecting the state of dance in England. The translation was reissued several times, and in 1733 with new illustrations by the engraver George Bickham Junior.

During the 1724/25 season, both an Essex and an Essex Junior were billed as dancing at Drury Lane (the first time the name had appeared in the bills of any of the London theaters for more than twenty years). It is very unlikely that John Essex was either of the two, for he would probably have been at least in his mid-forties and had not appeared on the stage since 1703. Two of his sons, William and John, are recorded elsewhere as dancing masters, and perhaps they both made their debuts as dancers at this time. However, it is possible that John Essex himself appeared briefly this season before again retiring from the stage. The Essex who enjoyed a successful career as a dancer at Drury Lane from the mid-1720s until the mid-1730s was most likely his son.

Essex was married to Catherine Hawtayne and had several children. He lived on Fenchurch Street during the early part of his career, but in about 1730 moved to Great Broad Street; when he made his will, the year before he died, he was living on Gloucester Street, Holborn.

The artist William Hogarth is said to have represented Essex as the dancing master in the reception scene from *The Rake's Progress* (1735); this character also appears in the first plate of Hogarth's *Analysis of Beauty* (1735), correcting the posture of a classical statue. Nevertheless, no contemporary evidence exists to support this identification.

BIBLIOGRAPHY
Goff, Moira. "Dancing-Masters in Early Eighteenth-Century London." *Historical Dance* 3.3 (1994): 17–23.
Highfill, Philip H., Jr., et al., eds. *A Biographical Dictionary of Actors, Actresses, Musicians, Dancers, Managers, and Other Stage Personnel in London, 1660–1800*. Carbondale, Ill., 1973–.

RICHARD RALPH and MOIRA GOFF

ESTONIA. The territory of present-day Estonia, 17,400 square miles (45,000 square kilometers) on the Baltic Sea, has about 1.5 million people. It was conquered by the Danes in the thirteenth century, ruled by the Teutonic Knights from the fourteenth to the sixteenth century, and controlled by Sweden until 1721, when it passed to Russia. During the political upheavals of the Russian Revolution, it proclaimed independence in 1918 and subsequently became involved in the Baltic Wars of Independence, finally liberating itself from German and Russian control in 1920. Reannexed by the Soviet Union in 1940 as a constituent republic of the USSR, it once again became an independent country in 1991.

Folk Dance. The origins of Estonian ethnographic dance are rooted in the rituals and celebrations of Finno-

Ugric tribes that inhabited the region in ancient times. The oldest traditions, known only through rare scraps of information in historical documents, relate to the lyrical and epic songs sung by tribal peoples about a thousand years ago. It is recorded that these runic songs were accompanied by primitive dancelike movements. Thanks to the systematic collection and study of folk dances that have been carried out in Estonia since the turn of the century, survivals or echoes of such early traditions can be detected in dances of later origin and even in dances still performed today.

An example of the survival of primordial elements can be found in a folk dance from the island of Muhu: called the "Sage's Threshing Floor," it remains popular in the present day. It is suspected that this dance was first connected with the tradition of bawdy jokes performed at weddings, for it contains certain erotic and grotesque elements, but the dance movements also clearly imitate the actions of workers threshing grain. Today the dance is performed as an elegiac women's dance of a sacred character. The performers stand in a circle, holding hands, and execute steps almost on the full foot, with a strong accent on the first count of each step. After moving in a full circle, the dancers turn to face the center and bow, carrying their linked arms backward and upward. This figure is repeated to the other side, and the dancers turn to face outward.

Estonian folk dances can be typologically categorized as line and circle dances of ritual origin, imitative and acrobatic dances (specifically for male dancers), contradances, quadrilles, and duets (local variants of the waltz and the polka). The quadrilles and duets are associated with the development of European, particularly Scandinavian, social dances; they were, however, adapted to conform to local customs and to suit the Estonian national character. For centuries, dances of various types have been performed as part of the rituals, celebrations, and games of Estonian peoples, usually accompanied by singing and the playing of folk music on the bagpipe, the Estonian harp, and various rhythm instruments. Creative use of Estonian folk dance on professional theatrical stages began in the 1930s and has continued, albeit sporadically, to the present day.

There are many amateur dance circles and companies in Estonia, for the most part focusing on traditional dance, and festivals of folk music and dance, held regularly since 1869, attract thousands of participants and listeners. Touring companies that perform in traditional dance styles include Leigarid and Leegayus.

Theatrical Dance. Historical records reveal that dance companies from western and northern Europe toured Estonia as early as the seventeenth century, and it is well documented that in the eighteenth and nineteenth centuries dances of various kinds were regularly per-

formed in theaters playing to both Estonian-speaking and German-speaking audiences. Nevertheless, the rise of a self-consciously cosmopolitan and professional dance depended, ironically, on the Estonian national awakening of the late nineteenth century. In the 1870s, two national theaters were established, the first in Tartu, under the sponsorship of the Vanemuine Society, and the second in Tallinn, the capital city, under the Estonia Society. Dance on these stages was initially limited to discrete scenes in operas, operettas, and dramas.

Dance as a more autonomous form began to develop in the first decades of the twentieth century, under the influence of both Russian classical ballet and American and German modern dance. The sources of these two streams of influence were, respectively, Evgenia Litvinova, a Russian ballerina, and Gerd Neggo, a pupil of Rudolf Laban, the leader of the central European school of modern dance.

The foundation for classical ballet training in Estonia was laid when Litvinova, formerly of the Maryinsky Theater, Saint Petersburg, opened a studio in Tallinn in 1918. Her pupils Lillian Looring, Emmy Holz, Rahel Olbrei, and Robert Rood constituted the first generation of ballet dancers at the Estonia Theater, which became the center of development of an Estonian national ballet. All genres of theater art—operas, dramas, comedies, plays with songs and dances, and ballets—were performed here, although for many years evening-length ballets were only rarely presented. The first independent dance performance at the Estonia Theater, a ballet entitled *A Dream in a Sculptor's Studio*, was given in 1914; the second, a production of *Coppélia*, starring the Moscow ballerina Viktorina Kriger, was not presented until 1922.

For modern dance, the Tallinn studio of Gerd Neggo (1891–1974), opened in 1924, was very important both as a training ground and as a performance space. Neggo not only provided education and training for dancers and choreographers but offered an outlet for their arts by organizing concerts and performances. One of the first Estonian professional dancers, Ella Ilbak (born 1895), was a modernist much influenced by Isadora Duncan. Ilbak, like many talented Estonian dancers of the first decades of the century (including, for instance, Anna Ekston), found limited professional opportunities at home and performed mostly abroad.

In 1925 Rahel Olbrei (1898–1984) became the choreographer and manager of ballet performances at the Estonia Theater, and the next year she founded a permanent ballet company. Olbrei had studied both classical and modern dance (the latter with Émile Jaques-Dalcroze, Rudolf Laban, and Mary Wigman) and knew something of Asian dance traditions. In her choreography she strove for clear and expressive structure and for movement that conformed closely to the style and content of the music. Her

ESTONIA. Helmi Tohvelmann's production of *Kalevipoeg* (The Son of Kalev), set to the music of Eugen Kapp and mounted at the Vanemuine Theater in Tartu in 1947, was later transferred to the stage of the Estonia Theater in Tallinn, where this picture was taken. (Photograph from the Zentral Haus der DSF; reprinted from Koegler, *Ballett International*, Berlin, 1960, fig. 50.)

productions included original interpretations of *Giselle* in 1929, *The Nutcracker* in 1936, and *Swan Lake* in 1939. Before she emigrated in 1944, she was one of several Estonian choreographers to mount a production of *Kratt*, a ballet that was to become a national favorite.

Set to a score written in 1940 by Estonian composer Eduard Tubin, *Kratt* tells a Gothic, folkloric story reminiscent of both Goethe's *Faust* and Mary Shelley's *Frankenstein,* for Kratt is a being endowed with life by the Devil for the purpose of collecting treasures and gaining riches. In the libretto, a Greedy Master makes the figure of Kratt and calls forth the Devil through a secret magic ceremony. In exchange for three drops of the Master's blood, which symbolizes the selling of his soul, the Devil animates Kratt. The life of the owner of Kratt is in constant danger if he cannot bridle the forces called forth by him or if he

cannot protect Kratt from capture by strangers. The ballet ends with the death of the Greedy Master through Kratt's vindictiveness. A lyric line of action is carried through a subplot, centered on the love of the Master's daughter, and a servant of the Master's household who tries to discover the secret of Kratt's animation and bring it to an end.

Tubin's score, which combines folk motifs and contemporary orchestration, proved to be a boon for Estonian ballet, for it would be repeatedly reinterpreted by various choreographers in the postwar era. The first production of *Kratt*, mounted by Ida Urbel at the Vanemuine Theater in Tartu in 1943, included choreographic elements evocative of ancient pagan rituals, folk dances, and ceremonies of a witches' Sabbath; her dance language, strongly rustic in character, was a synthesis of ballet, modern dance, and pantomime. Subsequent productions of *Kratt* were mounted by Obrei in 1944; by Urbel, again, in 1961; by Enn Suve in 1966; and by Ulf Gadd, in Göteborg, Sweden, in 1984. Urbel's 1961 version was a more abstract and purely dance-oriented treatment than was her first production. In Olbrei's and Gadd's productions, the role of Kratt, usually danced by a ballerina, was performed by a male dancer; in Suve's production, the combination of pointe work from the vocabulary of classical ballet and the plastique of modern dance accentuated the role's fantastic character.

In the postwar period, the Vanemuine ballet company in Tartu was rejuvenated under the leadership of Ida Urbel. She produced classical ballets such as *The Nutcracker* and *Esmeralda* as well as works with implicit or explicit national themes such as *Tiina* (based on August Kitzberg's play), *Spring,* and *Kalevipoeg.* The first production of *Kalevipoeg* (The Son of Kalev), based on the national epic poem, was choreographed by Helmi Tohvelmann, who employed elements of folk dance to convey the hero's powerful, rustic character and to depict his mythic struggle against forces of darkness. Later efforts to treat the subject in the mode of Soviet-era classicism were not entirely successful.

Estonian ballet continued to develop mainly along the lines of choreographic drama. In the 1950s, the classic works of academic ballet as well as works of balletic "symphonism" were performed at the Estonia Theater. The 1954 production of *Swan Lake* by Vladimir Burmeister was a milestone event that also marked the debut of the outstanding lyrical ballerina Helmi Puur. In subsequent productions of other classic ballets, the company attempted to draw closer to its classical, academic heritage while at the same time embracing the broader view of the possibilities of ballet that arose with the appearance of such new works as *Tiina* and *Ballet Symphony.* The first production of *Tiina* was choreographed by Boris Fenster in Tallinn in 1955; later productions were mounted in Tartu by Ida Urbel in 1958 and Ülo Vilimaa in 1984. *Ballet*

Symphony, set to a score written in 1959 by Estonian composer Einó Tamberg, was choreographed by Udo Väljapts at the Vanemuine Theater in Tartu in 1960 and by Mai-Ester Murdmaa at the Estonia Theater in Tallinn in 1963. At both theaters the appearance of new choreographers in the early 1960s, such as Murdmaa, Vilimaa, and Suve, was of great significance, as they showed greater interest in abstract dance, new vocabularies of plastic movement, and intricate choreographic imagery.

In the repertory of the Estonia Theater, where a technically strong company works today, classical ballets are prominently featured. However, the distinctive character of this company has been shaped by the personal style and taste of its artistic director and principal choreographer, Mai-Ester Murdmaa (born 1938). Combining the vocabularies of ballet and modern dance, she has worked in a choreographic language that has grown increasingly intense as she has continued to make dramatically powerful comments on the human condition. Recurrent concerns are themes of personality, disturbed psychological states, and conflicts of value, as in *Medea* (1966), to music by Samuel Barber; *The Miraculous Mandarin* (1968), set to the Bartók score; *Joanna the Possessed* (1971), to an original score by Einó Tamberg; *The Prodigal Son* (1973), set to the Prokofiev score; and *Crime and Punishment* (1991), to music by Arvo Pärt. In other works she has dealt with the antagonism of the artist and society, as in *Prometheus* (1976), set to Beethoven's music, and *The Firebird* (1982), to the familiar Stravinsky score.

The repertory of the smaller and more heterogeneous company at the Vanemuine Theater has shown the influence especially of chief choreographer Ülo Vilimaa (born 1941). In addition to the story ballets traditionally presented on this stage, he has produced short, one-act ballets and abstract miniatures that are striking for their musicality and varied modes of expression. Compared to Murdmaa's passionate style, Vilimaa's is more harmonious and restrained. He has incorporated vocabularies from various dance schools and ethnic traditions, including Estonian folk dance, and has been particularly concerned with subjects from the national literature and folklore, as in *Kodalased* (Forefathers) and *Tiina.*

Since 1988, artistic exchange between Etonian dancers and their colleagues abroad has greatly accelerated. Classes in modern and jazz dance have been taught by American and Finnish teachers; ballets have been staged in the United States by Murdmaa and in Czechoslovakia by Vilimaa; Estonian companies have toured Europe. In 1989 a festival of modern choreography was held in Tallinn, with guest companies from East and West. In 1990 the first modern dance performance was staged at the Estonia Theater: *Turtle's Walk,* with choreography by Jeanne Yasko, from the United States, and Tiina Lindfors,

from Finland. The Nordic Star Dance Theater, an Estonian company dedicated to developing various styles of modern dance, was founded the same year, with Saima Kranig as artistic director. She has since built a repertory including works by Murdmaa and by a number of American modern dance choreographers brought to Tallinn especially to create works for the company.

[*See also the entry on Murdmaa.*]

BIBLIOGRAPHY
Aassalu, Heino. *Tiiu Randviir.* Tallinn, 1988.
Aumere, Helga. *Ida Urbel* (in Estonian). Tallinn, 1989.
"The Baltic Republics." *Ballett International* 13 (June–July 1990): 54–56.
Chernova, Natalia. "Anche in danze, autonomia." *Balletto Oggi* (August 1990): 41.
Kask, Karin, et al. *Estonskii teatr.* Moscow, 1978.
Mai Murdmaa. Tallinn, 1987. Text in Estonian, Russina, and English.
Paalma, Vilma, comp. *Estonia: Estonia State Academic Opera and Ballet Theatre.* Translated by Victoria Hain. Tallinn, 1978.
Põldmäe, Rudolf, and Herbert Tampere. *Valimik eesti rahvatantse.* Tartu, 1938.
Stein, Bonnie Sue. "Dance Struggles in the Baltics." *Dance Magazine* (September 1990): 20.
Swift, Mary Grace. *The Art of the Dance in the U.S.S.R.* Notre Dame, 1968.
Tormis, Lea. *Eesti balletist.* Tallinn, 1967.
Tormis, Lea. *Eesti ballett/Estonian Ballet.* Tallinn, 1984.
LEA TORMIS and DAVID SASSIAN

ETHIOPIA. A large arid country in northeastern Africa, Ethiopia has a rich and well-documented cultural heritage. Its thirty-two million inhabitants are predominantly Ethiopian Orthodox Christians and Muslims. The country's five major ethnic groups—Amhara, Gurage, Hamar, Tigré, and Oromo or Galla—have diverse traditions of both sacred and secular dance about which little is known outside Ethiopia.

A major attempt to introduce Ethiopian dance to a wider international audience and to document dances systematically was instigated in 1964 by the governments of Ethiopia and Hungary. Ethiopian experts taking part in the project included Tsegaye Debalke and Yoel Yohannes; Hungarian participants included György Martin and Bálint Sárosi. The Hungarian scholar Tibor Vadasy continued the work and produced several detailed studies of Ethiopian secular dance. The 1974 Ethiopian revolution and subsequent political turbulence limited outsiders' access to dance in the country.

Common Characteristics. The majority of dances are performed by both men and women as entertainment at wedding celebrations and other festivities for family and friends, or on national holidays, such as Mäsqäl (the celebration of the discovery of Jesus' cross by Saint Helena)

ETHIOPIA. Men and women from the Gondar region, in north-western Ethiopia, make articulate and vibrating motions with the shoulders, neck, head, and chest, in the famous *iskesta* (shoulder dance). Hand clapping, swaying, and jumping are also part of this dance. (Photograph courtesy of the Center for Ethiopian Arts and Culture, Washington, D.C.)

and Epiphany. Some dances have probably fulfilled other functions, such as courting, working, and preparing for battle. Dances are sometimes paired or performed in alternation with other dances; for example, the Tigré pair dance is performed with the Tigré circle dance.

The two-part division of the dances generally corresponds to the open, cyclical, binary musical form. Most dances appear to be in duple meter, except the Tigré dances, which are in triple. Dance is often accompanied by hand-clapping and drumming. The accompanying secular songs *(zäfän)* consist of solo statements and choral responses. Although part one is always shorter than part two, each can last from less than half a minute to several minutes before the cycle is repeated.

Part one functions as a warmup or rest period, sets the mood, and acts as a tension release after the climax in part two. Its basic foot motifs include stepping or stamping in place and walking in various rhythmic patterns.

The second, longer section contains the dance proper. Compared with part one, part two has an increased tempo, denser rhythmic patterns, a higher dynamic level, and a larger number of dance motifs, and it requires more energy to perform. These changes may occur gradually or quite abruptly.

The basic dance formation consists of a circle of about a dozen to more than a hundred dancers and singers. Within the circle, there are one to five solo dancers, soloists grouped in twos, threes, or fours, or solo dancers in multiple two- to four-line formation. Circle dances show a collective character in the first section and a collective solo character in the second section, in which the outer circle of performers encourages the soloists and provides the vocal and musical background. This duality is one of the characteristic features of the dance.

The principal characteristic of Ethiopian secular dance is *iskesta (əskəsta)*, which has been variously defined as a

ETHIOPIA. Wearing grass (sisal) costumes and monkey-skin headdresses, these dancers and musicians from the Kefa region, in western Ethiopia, celebrate the coffee harvest. Three men play the *hura,* a wind instrument made from wood, horn, or elephant tusk that sounds like a trumpet. This dance is characterized by jumping, stamping, fluid chest articulations, and mimetic gestures of picking coffee. (Photograph courtesy of the Center for Ethiopian Arts and Culture, Washington, D.C.)

dance genre, a specific dance, and a kind of dance in which the shoulders are shaken. Perhaps it is best defined as a dance technique with variations; the "shaking shoulder" serves as the focus of the technique itself. Movements involve direction (vertical, horizontal, and diagonal), manner of movement (jerking, shaking, and twisting), and the points between which shoulders are able to move.

There are, of course, gradients and varying combinations of direction and position, as in the "jerking *iskesta.*" When the technique is extended, it affects other body parts, such as the chest or even the entire body. *Iskesta* is always supported by different body and foot movements, such as bending, jumping, small springing actions, and knee flexions. *Iskesta* is favored by solo dancers to display their virtuosity, to stage a competition, and to create and perform new solo parts in combination with other dance techniques.

Characteristic Variations. Within part two of a particular dance, *iskesta* functions in three basic ways. First, it can be the most important component of a dance consisting solely of *iskesta,* although it is used in conjunction with foot movement, as in the Amhara dances in the province of Gojjam and in the Gondar region. Second, it can serve as accompaniment to another dance movement in which body or foot movements are equally or more important, as in some dances of the Gurage and Menjar regions. Third, it can serve as the finale, as in Tigré and Oromo dances.

In the Amhara dances, both partners or soloists perform different *iskesta* techniques simultaneously and change technique at will. In the province of Wallo, how-

ever, both partners perform the same *iskesta* techniques simultaneously and change technique only when given a signal by the dance leader.

The emphasis placed on *iskesta* ranges from very little, as when the basic movement of a dance does not require *iskesta* (for example, in the Gurage dances), to the primary importance it holds in the Amhara dances. Dancers from the Gondar region perform the greatest number of *iskesta* variations and are known for their great skill in executing them.

Dancers from the Menjar region prefer to use more foot motifs than do Gojjam and Gondar dancers. The Gurage people use the most foot motifs of all, and these foot motifs, rather than *iskesta,* define the character of Gurage dance.

Though the Gurage sing during the first part of a dance, the singing is replaced in the second part by a continuing, guttural breathing technique that corresponds rhythmically with the foot motifs. This breathing technique is another distinctive feature of Gurage dance performance.

Both the Gurage dances and the Oromo *ragada* dance are more energetic and violent in the second part, with angular jerking and kicking movements that affect the entire body. There are no pauses during this part, which lasts between ten and thirty seconds. In the Amhara and Tigré dances there are pauses, however, and the *iskesta,* which is performed with a more even level of energy, may last several minutes.

When Oromo dancers pause between the two parts of a dance, the solo partners make elastic bows toward each other. The head is bowed forward and sways left and right. This typical move is basic to the *šagové*, a couples' dance from Harar.

Some dances, such as the *hota* (an Amhara men's dance from Wallo), have no definite formation but simply consist of a close mass of men, who move and sing together in rhythm. Often, after the *iskesta*, the mass opens up and the men run away searching for another locale or "enemy." The running part of the dance occurs at both its beginning and end.

The Hamar *churra* takes place at night and appears to depict male and female courting. Two dozen male dancers form a semicircle; half the men step out of the semicircle and make high leaps, twisting and turning their bodies and moving their heads rhythmically in different directions. The men remaining in the semicircle clap independently; all the men then leap and clap in unison. This done, the women rush together toward the men, whose dance terminates at the very moment the women reach them. The women are chased away, and the entire sequence begins again. This dance is defined by the alternation of chaos and order; the destruction of order takes place at the instant it is achieved.

Ethiopian dances often require the use of special props, such as the drum, stick, sword, and *shamma* (the Ethiopian national costume). Drums play a decisive role in the Tigré circle dances. As leaders of the dance, two to five drummers give the basic rhythmic patterns and signal when to begin *iskesta* and when to repeat the dance sequence.

In the Wallo *hota* and Oromo men's war dances participants must have sticks, probably symbolic of weapons used in battle. In the Tigré sword dance *(siré)*, two to four men run forward out of a circle for sixty to ninety feet (20 to 30 meters), each holding a sword in one hand and its sheath in the other. Although they dance with sword in hand, it is never used to initiate an attack on a partner.

The Tigré pigeon dance *(awrus)* ostensibly depicts a duel between a pigeon and an eagle, but symbolically it represents the enticement of a man by a woman or two women. The shawl of the *shamma* is used by the woman as wings imitating a pigeon's flight and by the man as the eagle's outstretched wings.

Sacred Dance. The Ethiopian Orthodox Christian Church has four traditional branches of knowledge: *tergum*, the translation and interpretation of the canonical literature from Ge'ez into Amharic; *qene*, church poetry or versification; *qeddase*, the liturgical training given to priests; and *zema*, the songs of the liturgy, whose author is said to have been the sixth-century saint Yared, combined with sacred dance or *aquaquam*. At least some portion of the songs and the sacred dance must be mastered by lay theologians and church musicians.

The performance of the liturgy includes some undulations and other rhythmic movements of the body, sometimes accompanied by hand-clapping. It comes to an end with faster movements and the sacred dance that usually takes place only outside Mass.

[*See also* Central and East Africa.]

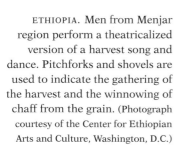

ETHIOPIA. Men from Menjar region perform a theatricalized version of a harvest song and dance. Pitchforks and shovels are used to indicate the gathering of the harvest and the winnowing of chaff from the grain. (Photograph courtesy of the Center for Ethiopian Arts and Culture, Washington, D.C.)

ETHIOPIA. (*top*) Adorned in headdresses fashioned from monkey manes and skins, these Oromo men, from central Ethiopia, prepare for a war dance. (*bottom*) The dances of the Dorze people, from southern Ethiopia, are characterized by clapping, jumping, and athletic stunts and are accompanied by vocal choirs. The stick held by the central figure is used to extend the expression of his body into space. (Photographs courtesy of the Center for Ethiopian Arts and Culture, Washington, D.C.)

BIBLIOGRAPHY
Courlander, Harold. "Notes from an Abyssinian Diary." *Musical Quarterly* 30 (July 1944): 345–355.
Heyer, Friedrich. "The Teaching of Tergum in the Ethiopian Orthodox Church." In *Proceedings of the Third International Conference of Ethiopian Studies.* Addis Ababa, 1969.
Lemma, Tesfaye. *Ethiopian Musical Instruments.* Addis Ababa, 1975.
Lepisa, Abba T. "The Three Modes and the Signs of the Songs in the Ethiopian Liturgy." In *Proceedings of the Third International Conference of Ethiopian Studies.* Addis Ababa, 1969.
Leslau, Wolf. *Concise Amharic Dictionary.* Wiesbaden, 1976.
Martin, György. "Dance Types in Ethiopia." *Journal of the International Folk Music Council* 19 (1967): 23–27.
Nelson, Harold D., and Irving Kaplan, eds. *Ethiopia: A Country Study.* 3d ed. Washington, D.C., 1981.
Powne, Michael. *Ethiopian Music.* London, 1968.
"Religious and Folk Dance." In *Patterns of Progress,* vol. 9, *Music, Dance, and Drama in Ethiopia.* Addis Ababa, 1968.
Sárosi, Bálint. "Melodic Patterns in the Folk Music of the Ethiopian Peoples." In *Proceedings of the Third International Conference of Ethiopian Studies.* Addis Ababa, 1969.
Suttner, Kurt. "Music in the Kingdom of the Lion of Juda." *World of Music* 9.4 (1967): 23–32.
Vadasy, Tibor. "Ethiopian Folk Dance I." *Journal of Ethiopian Studies* 8.2 (1970): 119–146.
Vadasy, Tibor. "Ethiopian Folk Dance II: Tegré and Guragé." *Journal of Ethiopian Studies* 9.2 (1971): 191–218.
Vadasy, Tibor. "Ethiopian Folk Dance III: Wällo and Galla." *Journal of Ethiopian Studies* 11.1 (1973): 213–231.

CYNTHIA TSE KIMBERLIN

ETHNIC DANCE. A series of terms have been used to denote what has often been viewed as a leftover category—dance that is not from a classical tradition such as ballet or the classical dance of India, not theatrical, not social, and not popular. Terms used to designate this troublesome category in the past include *primitive, tribal, peasant,* and *folk.* These terms apply to societies that have been considered either non-Western or nonindustrialized.

Applying the same logic, the phrase *ethnic dance* can be defined as dance done by ethnic groups. Ethnic dance is one of many symbols and behaviors used by ethnic groups to demonstrate their identity vis-à-vis other groups in a larger social context. A more complete definition of ethnic dance, then, is dance performed by members of an ethnic group to make a statement about their identity as members of that group.

It is futile and misguided to attempt to list the characteristics of ethnic dance in general. This approach was typical of some earlier studies of the arts, in which the focus was on the artistic product rather than on the artistic process or function. Ethnic dance can be defined more usefully in terms of function, context, and process. Some examples will demonstrate the implications of this definition.

Dance is a fundamental component of the identity of the Zapotec, an indigenous society of southern Mexico descended from one of the ancient Mesoamerican civilizations. They divide dance into two broad categories: *bailes* ("dances") include a number of contemporary social dances, such as the mambo or discotheque, and *sones* comprise what the Zapotec regard as Zapotec dance. If one analyzes the form of the *sones* in terms of characteristics that have been used to describe Mexican Indian dance, one would have to conclude that these do not belong to that form. The *son* is a combination of elements from the waltz and the fandango, although the *zapateado* (heel work) sections are similar to other Mexican Indian dances. The *son*, however, distinguishes the Zapotec both from other Mexican Indian groups and from the Mexican (Spanish) national culture. Variations in the performance of the *son* are even used to distinguish the Zapotec of Juchitán from those of Tehuantepec. The symbolism is effective because it is recognized by both Zapotec and non-Zapotec viewers.

The importance of the clarity and acceptance of symbols is demonstrated by another example of dance used to make a statement about identity. Native Americans have a complex dance repertory of contemporary social dances, pan-Indian dances, and dances associated with specific nations. If the context is one in which a Plains group wants to distinguish itself from a group from the Southwest, they are likely to perform Plains dances that are not in the repertory of the other group. If, however, the Plains group wants to make a statement about being Native Americans, as opposed to being acculturated North Americans, they are likely to do dances that reflect the perceptions of mainstream Canadian and American society about Native Americans. These may be Plains war dances—the pervasive symbol of Native Americans for the larger society—and this then exemplifies how double boundaries function. Those enclosed by a self-imposed inner boundary share a common cultural knowledge, so their interactions may be varied and complex, with a tolerance for ambiguity. The outer boundary, however, is imposed from without; in the process of interacting with others, the interactions become much more limited in scope, with a tendency to rely on stereotypes because of a lack of shared knowledge.

Dance has always been an effective symbol of identity. Because it is nonverbal, there is a directness of communication that occurs without analysis, description, or words.

Because it uses the human body to make patterns in time and space, dance elicits powerful responses. It can make a statement about identity by playing on the fundamental nature of movement and gestural styles peculiar to a group. Outsiders often see dancers portrayed as representatives of national or ethnic groups; witness the stereotypes of, among others, the Mexican hat dance, Argentine tango, Austrian ländler, Masai warrior dance, the Highland Fling, or Irish jig.

Ethnic dances are not unchanging and stable either in form or in function. If they are to be effective symbols of a group, they have to accommodate changes both in that group and in the larger societal context. Ethnic dance is as varied and mutable as the groups who use it to present an identity to the "other" with whom they must interact.

[*For related discussion, see* Methodologies in the Study of Dance, *article on* Ethnology.]

BIBLIOGRAPHY

Kealiinohomoku, Joann W. "An Anthropologist Looks at Ballet as a Form of Ethnic Dance." In *What Is Dance?*, edited by Roger Copeland and Marshall Cohen. New York, 1983.

Royce, Anya Peterson. *The Anthropology of Dance.* Bloomington, 1977.

ANYA PETERSON ROYCE

ETHNOGRAPHY AND DANCE. *See* Methodologies in the Study of Dance, *article on* Ethnology. *See also* European Traditional Dance; Film and Video, *article on* Ethnographic Studies.

ÉTUDES. Original title: *Étude.* Ballet in one act. Choreography: Harald Lander. Music: Karl Czerny, arranged by Knudåge Riisager. Scenery and costumes: Erik Nordgren. First performance: 15 January 1948, Royal Theater, Copenhagen. Principals: Margot Lander, Hans Brenaa, Svend Erik Jensen. Restaged and revised by Lander as *Études:* 19 November 1952, Paris Opera Ballet. Scenery: Moulene. Costumes: Fost. Principals: Micheline Bardin, Michel Renault, Alexandre Kalioujny.

The original version (1948) of *Études* was clearly modeled on a classical ballet class and owed several motifs to Bournonville: a "mirror" adagio recalled his *La Ventana*, the exercises in elevation his typical male solos, and the opening children's exercises his *Konservatoriet*. These were not, however, Lander's initial inspiration.

In the 1940s Lander experimented with nonnarrative symphonic ballet without great success. Riisager, bemused by a student rendering of Czerny piano études, approached Lander with the idea of creating a ballet and score based on the training of performers. The application of this formal theme gave Lander the matrix he needed to solve pure compositional problems. *Études* grew out of a close collaboration between the choreographer and the composer, who created from Czerny's piano studies a fully orchestrated symphonic fantasy. In 1951 Toni Pihl married Lander and took over the ballerina role (much of which was set on her as a student), performing with Erik Bruhn and Jensen.

The second version (1952), which is still performed, retained the sixteen sections of the first, rearranged for stronger theatrical impact. The scenario was clarified, and the balance between adagio and allegro was improved. Elements of Vaganova style were added—especially in the presentation of the ballerina and her partners—that counterposed Bournonville style. Aesthetically, the ballet represented belief in the human potential for collaboration and for mastery over the body.

Études was staged by Lander on European television and internationally, notably for London's Festival Ballet (1954), Het Nationale Ballet in Amsterdam (1957), American Ballet Theatre (1961), and in South America, Germany, Austria, and Scandinavia throughout the 1960s. It remains in current repertories.

BIBLIOGRAPHY

Beaumont, Cyril W. *Ballets Past and Present*. London, 1955.
Fridericia, Allan. *Harald Lander og hans balletter*. Copenhagen, 1951.
Lander, Harald. *Études*. Edited by Erik Aschengreen. Copenhagen, 1970.
Meinertz, Alexander. "*Études* and Danish Classicism." *Dance View* 12 (December 1995): 22–26.

VIDEOTAPE. *Études,* produced for television by Danmarks Radio (1968).

ALLAN FRIDERICIA

EUROPEAN DANCE TRADITIONS. *For discussion of theatrical, traditional, and folk dance traditions, see entries on individual countries.*

EUROPEAN TRADITIONAL DANCE. This overview addresses dance itself as well as the processes for the study and preservation of traditional dance. The dance of the ethnic groups that will be treated in this discussion was established in Europe prior to the twentieth century. Europe, in its standard geographic definition, extends from the Atlantic Ocean to the Ural Mountains. Trade and cultural exchange, both voluntary and involuntary, with neighboring areas (Islamic North Africa, the Middle East, and the Central Asian states, as well as certain polar peoples) has, however, contributed to European history and will be taken into account.

The European diaspora has not only extended European culture worldwide but has resulted in unique hybrid dance genres (some major examples being Latin American dances, North American square dance, and Israeli folk dance). This diaspora has also generated dance genres that have returned to Europe primarily as popular dance (such as the tango and tap dancing), some of which have been reabsorbed as folk dance.

Like the various entries on national dance, this overview was assembled at one point in the development of the scholarly study of traditional dance, and as such it can only reflect the current status of this field. Views of the uncharted territory tantalize with the range of topics still unstudied. For various reasons, also suggested in the course of this article, the scholarly study of traditional dance is one of the youngest, smallest, and least supported of academic fields—indeed, in many parts of Europe the study of dance is still not regarded as academic at all. This is not a complaint but a report of current status; indeed this is our challenge—compared with other well-established academic fields, dance ethnology remains excitingly open to future development. [*See* Methodologies in the Study of Dance, *article on* Ethnology.]

Geographic, Ethnographic, and Historical Background. In proportion to land area and population, Europe is a highly complex and heterogeneous human cultural area. Today the political map of Europe shows forty-seven states (more than 25 percent of the world total), several of which, in addition, are federations of states with distinct cultural differences. The term *nation*, often applied to countries—states and federations—is used more correctly to mean "a large, comprehensive ethnic group." (An example is Poland, which three times in its history ceased to exist as a state but had always retained its identity as a nation).

European states and cultural areas that are both among states or within states have each been most immediately identified by the following factors: ethnic identity, language, and religion (freedom to practice religion other than the official state religion was granted as late as the mid-nineteenth century in some states, e.g., Denmark).

Compared to the existing political structure, the current ethnographic makeup of Europe is far more complex. Many states include autonomous ethnic areas or recognized ethnic enclaves and groups; these ethnic groups frequently overlap political boundaries, producing both internal and external minorities (some of which number in millions of people).

Of the Indo-European language family, more than forty-three languages are spoken in Europe (in nine families—the three largest being Italic, Germanic, and Slavic). The distantly related languages are, for the most part, mutually incomprehensible (as different as Icelandic, Basque, Albanian, and Russian). In addition, more than ten non-Indo-European languages are present in Europe, as official state languages (Hungarian, Finnish), as official languages of autonomous regions, or as languages that have had historical effect on European languages (Arabic, Turkish, Hebrew). In addition to official languages, numerous dialects are spoken in Europe, often so different from their parent languages as to be effectively separate languages.

Europe may be divided broadly into three major cultural areas, generally corresponding to religion, with some language correlation. The clearest area, with parental origin in Greece, is that of the Eastern Orthodox church; this is predominantly a Slavic language area that uses the Cyrillic alphabet. This area is to the east of the central European area of Roman Catholicism; the border stretches from Lithuania in the north through Poland, Slovakia, Hungary, and Croatia. (The Roman Catholic Slavic areas are identified by their use of the Latin alphabet, in contrast to the Cryrillic of the Orthodox areas.) This religious/linguistic border cuts through the former state of Yugoslavia. Southern Europe is predominantly Roman Catholic, with languages of the Italic family. Northern Europe is predominantly Lutheran, with Germanic languages. The overlap of these two areas—including states with both Roman Catholic and Protestant religions, as well as Protestant religions other than Lutheran—is found within Germany, Switzerland, and Austria, and forms the national boundary between Belgium (Roman Catholic) and the Netherlands (Protestant). England and Ireland, as well as a number of peripheral or included nations, remain islands in this religious/linguistic mosaic.

A fourth major religion, Islam, has had a major influence on European traditional culture. Spain, Portugal, and some Mediterranean islands were occupied for seven centuries (711–1492) by the Moors,—Muslims of North Africa. Similarly, the Balkan region, occasionally as far north as Vienna, was occupied for centuries (fifteenth to twentieth) by the Ottoman Turks. Both occupations resulted in European areas having cultures differentiated from those of central Europe. This separation, ironically, resulted in the preservation of some aspects of traditional culture.

Europe's regional differences correlate in a number of ways, but not absolutely, with regional dance characteristics. The addition of the historical dimension increases any consideration of European ethnic and cultural complexity. Migrations and invasions have mixed peoples and resulted in various types of cultural interaction; these range from invading cultures introducing new dominant forms to outside cultures being absorbed quite completely into the existing culture. A primary task of European ethnography is this historical tracing of ethnic groups, their origins and interrelationships. (For an example of how the seeming clarity of "a nation" is actually compounded, see Iván Balassa and Gyula Ortutay, 1985). In

various parts of Europe, as well as within states, the rates of economic and social evolution have been quite different, resulting in marked differences in cultural evolution.

Since the first of the large kingdoms and the major migrations from the east of one millennium ago, the political borders of Europe have changed more than nine thousand times. A good historical atlas will show the complexity of these political changes. A long series of migrations, invasions, wars, and the political manipulation of peoples were carried out by ruling elites with virtually no regard for ordinary people (most European nations achieved democratic governments only in the nineteenth century and some only in the late twentieth). Whole populations, since the Roman Empire, have been forcibly and repeatedly moved, and areas have been colonized for political control. Political associations (empires, coalitions, etc.) have been formed primarily for economic or military purposes; these have often ignored, even suppressed, the underlying cultural differences in religion, language, and ethnic identity. Three empires often in conflict with one another—Prussia (northern Germany), the Habsburg (Austria-Hungary), and Russia (in effect extended through the Soviet Union)—effected major manipulations of ethnic cultures, leaving distinct cultural boundaries. Their manipulations have left many ethnically mixed areas for which no ethnographic borders can be drawn, so tensions remain unavoidable. Bitterness and mistrust, with centuries' deep origins, have become part of the consciousness of European nations.

Folklorism, Folklore, and Folkloristics. Both the current status of European traditional dance practice as well as the status of its academic study have been substantially determined by the broad political and ideological movement termed *folklorism*, defined here as "belief in the importance of folklore" (other definitions have been used). The term *folklore* means "the attitudes, beliefs, and mental abilities of people—revealed primarily in performance behavior, such as oral literature, customs, and performing arts, secondarily as revealed in physical artifacts." Folklore is or was maintained, with minimum reflection, by ordinary people outside the formal channels of education and the media, with minimal influence from the urban elite culture. The term *folkloristics* is understood as "the academic field established for the preservation and study of folklore." Folklorism emerged as one of two major European intellectual movements of the eighteenth and nineteenth centuries—democratic nationalism and romanticism.

Although most of Europe's states existed prior to the eighteenth century, these were predominantly ruled by aristocracies. The nationalism of the late eighteenth century was driven by populist, democratic revolutions based on those of the United States (1776) and France (1789). Before its democratization, European society was predominantly feudal; the differences in daily life between the aristocratic elite and the rural peasantry were great. In strict form, feudalism was a caste system that bordered on slavery; it was generally abolished only in the late eighteenth century but in some European countries as late as the mid-nineteenth century (e.g., Hungary). Democracy and public education came even later in Europe and, as with slavery, abolition did not result in overnight changes in the plight of rural people. Consequently, even today the contrast between the aristocracy and the group that, absorbing the peasantry, became the working class remains important in European consciousness.

Although the aristocracy held rural property, with serfs bound to it and working it, class distinctions actually correlated with town and country differences. In addition to housing the aristocracy, towns were also centers for merchants, craftsmen, and clergy—thus centers of skill and learning. Prior to the industrialization of transportation, the relative isolation of rural societies was maintained by the rigors of farming and the practical limits of transportation.

The culture of Europe's elite tended to be international, as reinforced by Christianity, which introduced a widespread uniformity not found in pre-Christian religions. It used universal languages, such as Latin, as languages of the elite. Since the churches also established educational institutions, this uniformity has been perpetuated in European education until today. This uniformity has allowed for the international transmission of standardized cultural products as well. Conversely, the rural peasantry was customarily uneducated, hence illiterate, had little access to travel or travelers, and therefore had minimal access to culture transmitted cross-culturally. This meant, however, that the peasantry produced its own localized culture with relatively minimal outside influence.

Folklorism, as a movement, was motivated by the populist desire to set the characteristics of each nation in clear distinction to others and to find local identity beneath international elite culture. The natural source of local identity was to be found in the longstanding rural cultures. This ideological motivation led to a still prevalent theory of cultural relativism—the belief that cultures differ so basically from one another that they not only can but must be studied as isolates, and that only persons born into a culture and raised in it can achieve full comprehension of that culture.

Related to the eighteenth- and nineteenth-century movement of folklorism was romanticism—an intellectual and emotional turning away from European formalism, in favor of nature and an assumed natural humanity. Romanticism received an impetus from the expeditions of discovery of "primitive" people, such as Pacific Islanders, who seemed to have a basic naturalness long lost to Euro-

peans. Romanticism, therefore, turned its focus in Europe back to a seemingly unreflective, pristine rural culture.

Folkloristics and folklorism, despite their focus, have been substantially urban intellectual movements. Their studies have been conducted, however, in a spirit of respect for original source persons, with a genuine desire to preserve and support traditional cultures.

Folklorism received increased urgency in the nineteenth century, during which industrialization and urbanization steadily reduced longstanding difference between rural and urban cultures. The continuous movement of the farming population away from rural areas, a rapidly expanding technology of mechanical transportation and electrical communications, and the extension of universal education to rural areas, all hastened a seemingly inevitable demise of traditional culture and its replacement by an elite-determined, commercial culture. Urban culture expanded rapidly, as middle-class culture; separated from its local roots, it soon imitated the elite, aristocratic culture (into the early twentieth century in western Europe but even later in eastern Europe).

While fieldwork in European folklore remains possible, very few of today's communities have been free from modern influences and most maintain little distinct local identity. Folkloristics, consequently tends to become more the study of artifacts in recorded collections than the study of living traditions. These changes have also gradually converted folklore from being the unreflecting culture of everyday life (called first existence folklore) into a deliberately cultivated alternative to modern technological culture (revival or second existence folklore). The revival movement seeks to maintain as much of the original functions of folklore as possible, often pursued with an ideology that masks inevitable change, which has proceeded in different regions at different paces yielding current conspicuous differences. In some regions culture very close to early forms still exists, in unbroken tradition with its original function, even alongside modern derivations (e.g., the Balkans, eastern Europe, Great Britain, and Norway); in other regions nearly all folklore exists mainly as revival activity (e.g., western and central Europe).

The scholarly study of folklore has broadened its attention from purely rural phenomena to incorporate any behavior reflective of self-generated local, nonelite culture—thus including urban folklore. Emphasis remains, however, on culture created by the people themselves, which resists the externally imposed, nearly uniform elite and commercial cultures.

During the twentieth century, the political use of folkloristic ideology reached some extreme points—in, for example, the fascist nationalist and communist systems—often suppressing genuine local cultures under a newly fabricated national culture (see Giurchescu, 1994). Such use has had the repercussive effect of degrading the social status of folklore to the point of an ideological avoidance of the term *folk*.

Terminology. Various terms have been applied to the dance at the focus of this article: *folk, traditional, vernacular,* and *national*. Closely related terms are *popular, social, ballroom,* and *recreational*. Given a worldwide view, additional terms could be included for comparison: *ethnic, tribal,* and *indigenous*. Related elite forms are customarily labeled *court, theatrical,* and *character*.

None of these terms, however, taken directly from a dictionary will be sufficiently precise. In addition, these terms are neither uniform among European languages nor used uniformly among writers on dance. A worldwide study would be far more complex. Here, a centralizing definition will be offered to which other definitions can be related.

The first four terms are tied directly to the folklorism movement: *folk*, being the democratic masses (initially and primarily rural), as opposed to the social elite (primarily urban); *traditional* (Lat., *trans*, "across" + *dictus*, "spoken"), being the transmission, orally or directly, without the mediation of technical communications or formal education; *vernacular*, belonging to specific localities; *national*, that which defines a nation, a large ethnic group.

The terms *ethnic* and *tribal* refer to a specific self-identified group of people. *Indigenous* corresponds to *vernacular*, a people belonging to a specific location.

Attempting an interrelationship of terms, dance in the perspective of folklorism and folkloristics would be the following:

1. Dance that can be identified as the cultural property of a distinctly identified group of people *(ethnic/folk)*, living in an identified local area *(vernacular/indigenous)*. Because different ethnic groups can live in the same area, however, the term *vernacular* is insufficient. (Also, the term *vernacular*, taken from linguistics, implies local deviation from a central standard language, which is not the case with dance—folk dance is not a deviation from or a vulgarization of, for example, ballet). The term *ethnic* remains the broadest specifier, whereas the term *folk* carries the distinction between rural nonelite and urban elite. (Many titles of traditional dances include ethnic and localizing identifiers; see Martin, 1985; Reynolds, 1992.)
2. Dance created by participants themselves from locally given materials; that is, dances and dance materials are regarded as unmediated group property and so individual creators are identified but rarely (dances are not considered choreographed).
3. Dance originally transmitted by direct learning *(tradi-tional* is analogous to *oral)*, hence necessarily limited to an ethnic group and geographic area; not mediated by formal educational institutions, by technical or recorded means (analogous to *illiterate)*. Seldom considered imported from outside groups. The term *traditional* also carries the core connotation of transmission proceeding continuously (at least from the preindustrial era, even from prehistory). That is, traditional cultural behavior is assumed to have old, relatively untraceable historical (or prehistoric) roots.
4. Dance functioning as an embedded part of human experience, with a locally determined social context and episodes. There are four general types of function—ritual, ceremonial, participatory, and presentational/competitive.
5. Dance that evolved in and was presumed to reflect preindustrial, rural societies (first existence); dance currently preserved and functioning but substantially mediated by research and revival movements (second existence).
6. Additional qualifiers, especially for Europe, are dance predominantly nonprofessional and dance predominantly nondramatic.

In the context of European folklorism, then, traditional dance and folk dance are virtually synonymous, either term showing a distinction from elite dance genres. With scholarship in other world cultures, however, all indigenous dance forms—including elite forms—are usually regarded as traditional dance.

The second set of terms discussed at the beginning of this section tends to be applied to the urban variations of rural-originated behavior. The term *popular*, like *folk*, implies belonging to the broad masses, but it does not rule out technical mediation (contemporary popular arts, such as pop music, are highly dependent on technology). Popular arts have also become nearly totally nonvernacular and nonethnic (that is virtually universally uniform). The terms *social* and *ballroom* are applied to dance genres often closely similar to folk genres but which are urban forms, uprooted from any local or ethnic identification. Social and ballroom dances are not dependent on transmission via tradition but rather are often diffused through printed books and nonlocal dance teachers. (An example is the Argentine tango in Poland—still popular but clearly recognized by participants as imported culture and not a part of Polish folk culture.) Recreational folk dance and revivals tend to be urban phenomena, dances uprooted from original ethnic and local occasions and functions; in following the ideology of folklorism, attempts are made to maintain as much authenticity as possible (including dance steps, musical accompaniment, costumes, etc.).

Participant dance corresponds closest with the terms

folk, popular, and *social,* and is done for the experience of dancing, both within oneself and in interaction with other dancers (recreational). Elite genres labeled court dance are also predominantly participant in function. Presentational and competitive dance, conversely, are motivated primarily by communication to an audience.

Folk, social/ballroom, and popular dance genres, while all of the participant type—hence having the same basic function and often similar structures—can be differentiated by the identity of the participants (folk dancing being originally rural and limited to local participants; social dancing being urban and not limited to locally identified individuals), by the degree of local identification of dance material (dance of an individual village versus those spread widely, to the extreme of international fads), and by tradition (degree of direct local learning, unmediated by teachers and texts, with deep-assumed roots).

Ritual and ceremonial dance still performed in scattered parts of Europe are the oldest historical forms, and their nature will be outlined below. Folk forms of presentational dance are rare; they tend to be men's virtuoso types. Since these occur usually in the context of participant folk dance events, they would not be classed as theatrical dance.

European traditional or folk dance, therefore, encompasses ritual and ceremonial dance as well as some presentational genres conducted for their original purposes in their original local contexts; it includes participant dance with specific local identity, performed in original context, with original function. Today's traditional dance includes dance performed within this original framework, as well as considerable revival performance that seeks to maintain the original traditional functions within an altered context.

History of European Traditional Dance. Compared to its closest relative in the performing arts—music—traditional dance in Europe has long been marginalized. Several factors have contributed to this marginalization. The first is the history of religion in Europe. In the first millennium of Christianity, dance played a role in liturgy, naturally reflecting its historical background from Judaism (see Backman, 1952; Oesterley, 1923). Beginning in the second millennium, however, Christianity turned against dance, with several centuries of proscriptions; the Reformation of the sixteenth century completed the elimination of dance from church-related activities. Ironically, some of the earliest European historical records of dance are found in church condemnations, and this suppression seems related to interactions with pagan religions as Christianity spread northward.

Prior to Christianity, European ethnic groups possessed a wide range of individually evolved and locally distinct religions. As Christianity encountered local religions and their rituals, attempts were made to absorb local forms gradually, done by overlaying Christian holidays and rituals on the existing ones. Since dance was a featured element of pre-Christian celebrations, it continued in the mixed environment. Gradually, however, the paganism of pre-Christian religions became unacceptable to the church; suppression replaced absorption. This process caused much ancient traditional culture to be lost as it led to an increasingly centralized and universal Christian culture.

The sovereignty of Christianity proceeded only gradually, over generations, and reached some parts of Europe (e.g., Lithuania) as late as the thirteenth century. The effect of the differences from the period of conversion to Christianity can be noted today as regional differences in traditional dance, with the areas of latest adoption showing the oldest retained traditions. Differences can also be marked among the three major Christian areas. Although it has the youngest of the Christian churches, the Protestant area shows the strongest effects of the prohibition, with virtually all ritual and ceremonial dance eliminated since the Reformation. In a number of Protestant subcultures, even participant dance remains forbidden (an example being the Danish Inner Mission). The Eastern Orthodox and the Roman Catholic churches, however, continued to take milder views of dance and allowed much traditional ritual and ceremony—at least outside liturgy itself—seen, for example, in the tradition of lush southern European processionals and in the rich dance tradition of southeastern Europe.

Music had been incorporated in Christian ritual from earliest times, first by the clerical elite and later by the broad mass of participants. Music was however more easily controlled and fit more intimately into the abstract emotionalism of religious service, thus it did not receive the prohibition of dance. Given status as good and acceptable, music flourished both in the church and in secular life, and great composers wrote for both the church and the nobility, receiving high social position. Dance, however, with no clerical support, could only function in secular society, and thus, if not branded as subversive behavior, it was reduced to the status of trivial diversion.

The marginalization of folk dance in Christian Europe was greatly enhanced by the growth of an urban elite and bourgeois culture, which held the "fine arts"—such as classical music and ballet—as models, and ignoring, even despising folk genres. Migrants to the cities, those uprooted from their local culture to mix with people from quite different localities had difficulty retaining their original cultures. Later expansions of popular culture only universalized the urban influence.

European regional differences are due mainly to distance from urban areas. Those regions farthest from cities—especially from the central European constellation of major cities—have preserved folk cultures that are older and more intact than those in the central areas.

Despite the ideology of folklorism, which is an urban phenomenon, the bulk of urban people continue to seek modernity. Today's rapidly increased communications, reaching a peak with satellite television, drastically reduces ethnic and local differences. For example, Music Television (MTV), broadcasting from New York City twenty-four hours daily, reaches even the small villages of eastern Europe, delivering its universally uniform commercial culture.

Marginalization of dance, indeed its prohibition by Christianity carried over into education, and until today dance has not been considered a suitable topic for Europe's schools. Even in countries with strong folk dance activism, folk dance is almost never included in official school curricula, and the cultivation of dance is left to private organizations. The reverse is true for music. Given longstanding support from both clerical and elite powers, music has always received considerable support in both private and public education and is part of the curriculum in all countries. Elite dance forms (especially ballet) do receive considerable state support, but training is conducted at the performance level through national theaters and conservatory-type institutions rather than at academic institutions.

Given the above two effects, Western dance literature, including that of the field called dance history, to this day focuses virtually exclusively on ballet and its modern offshoots. Books are still issued with titles such as *History of Dance* or *What Is Dance?* that deal only with ballet and modern dance—as if no other dance genres exist. A number of these books do begin with a short chapter on "primitive" and "folk dance," revealing the assumption that the European elite genres represent the supreme culmination of world dance evolution. In musicology, this dual imperialism—both elite and European—has been addressed and virtually eliminated, with non-Western musics accepted as respected cultural traditions.

Academic marginalization had emerged from the social marginalization of traditional dance. Only since the mid-twentieth century did the study of traditional dance begin to receive academic recognition. Programs of study have tended to depend on the presence of established individual scholars who profess an interest in dance. A generally accepted academic program has not yet been formalized, thus the existing programs have developed in isolation. A dance department is found only rarely in universities, so nearly all European dance ethnologists have received qualification within other academic areas, often in departments having little or no interest in or qualification for dance.

Despite such conspicuous historical marginalization, traditional dance has shown remarkable resiliency. Through the centuries, religious prohibition usually had only the minimal effect—that of removing dance from the liturgy; outside the church, dancing continued with little interference. If no longer a part of the life of the majority of modern Europeans, traditional dance remains firmly supported by a dedicated minority, both in Europe and in countries with large European immigrant communities. The model of living dance carried out as part of the everyday life of ordinary people has been preserved and remains available to future generations.

Historical Records. Although European traditional dance has a long history, marginalization has made its historical study difficult. There is a lack of historical sources. In the period when what we call folklore was the daily behavior pattern of ordinary people, a society evolved determined by urban elite clergy, aristocracy, and the bourgeoisie. Little motivation or reason existed for recording rural folk behavior. European cultural history has consequently long focused, almost exclusively, on its elite culture. Ironically, the bulk of useful early textual records of folk dance are the edicts against it, found either in church or city records. The later texts of travelers, along with occasional references in literature, include descriptions of dancing—but these are widely scattered, difficult to find, and in many of the more than fifty European languages. The known early documents tend to include only general descriptions of dance occasions and to be vague in describing actual dance movement. More seriously, written by nondance specialists, usually from outside the culture observed, these textual descriptions tend to be of questionable use. To be made useful, these sources require validation against contemporary sources.

The earliest evidence of actual dance movement is found iconographically. Images of dance exist from prehistoric times (often with considerable margin for interpretation; see figure 1). Reliable dance images emerge

EUROPEAN TRADITIONAL DANCE. Figure 1. A prehistoric cave drawing from Tunge, Sweden, showing a Germanic chain dance. (Reprinted from Oetke, 1982, plate 1.)

Hic pudor, hic morum probitas hic aulica suada,   Et lepor, & vitæ generosa modestia glifcit.   Quid mirum, divas ultro si dia fequantur

Quantum aula à Caula: tantum quoq, diftat agrefti   Aulicus: hoc præfens te laxa Chorea docebit   Sed bene. fic varia liqueant difcrimina vitæ

EUROPEAN TRADITIONAL DANCE. Figure 2. Court dance, possibly a pavane (above) and a peasant dance (below). Engraving by Theodore de Bry (1528–1598). (British Museum, London.)

much later, and in large numbers only after the invention of the printing press, which allowed wide duplication of realistic engravings. Such early printed sources reflect predominantly elite dance forms, but beginning in the fifteenth century rural, or folk, forms begin to appear more frequently; occasionally they are deliberately contrasted with elite parallels (figure 2). Although visual, and hence seemingly realistic, the effects of the creators' backgrounds as well as the limits to human perception require a critical approach for the validation of images, as with texts. The study of dance iconography, especially for traditional dance, ties into the well-developed field of iconography in general, but is only now in its beginning stages.

European notation that allows for the actual reproduction of dances dates from the mid-fifteenth century with one small book, the Cevera Manuscript of Spain. More than a century later, in 1588, Thoinot Arbeau's *Orchésographie* was published, the first model textbook of dancing, incorporating music notation and images with dance description. After nearly another century, the first edition of John Playford's collection of English dances was published in 1650, and this set the model for many later collections of figure type dances. Not too long after Playford there followed a series of books using the Feuillet system, the first seriously evolved abstract notation system. These books included some participant dances along with early theatrical genres. All these early works, were however, intended for elite/bourgeois users, and while they reflect folk origins they are not directly studies of folk dance. Nevertheless, with no parallel documents of folk dance, these sources remain important. [*See* Feuillet Notation; *and the entries on Arbeau and Playford.*]

Entering the era of folklorism, the nationalism inherent in folk dance studies, as well as the tendency to publish only in national languages, led to the predominant use of simple language descriptions of dance movement, coupled occasionally with track drawings. The first folkloristic collections of notated dance were made in the late nineteenth and early twentieth centuries, for example, the work of Cecil Sharp. This type of notation continues today as the predominant form, but the use of local languages strongly inhibits cross-cultural comparison. [*See the entry on Sharp.*]

Soon, attempting to escape the limits of language, a number of folk dance researchers developed their own dance notation systems, in each case claiming a special relationship to their national dance material. Thus numerous publications are available using notation systems comprehensible only with specific training, and this incompatibility is only a slight improvement over the use of a local language as notation. Some seventy-five dance notation systems now exist.

Fully evolved abstract notation capable of a sophisticated study of traditional dance, as well as rigorous comparative study, emerged only after the mid-twentieth century—the product of Rudolf Laban, called Labanotation (LN)—a millennium after the adoption of European music notation. Because of the ideology of nationalism and cultural relativism built into the study of traditional dance in Europe, this system has received little use; indeed in many national cases it has received outright rejection. The best example of major use is Hungary, where virtually all publications, since the 1950s both scholarly and practical, have used Labanotation as fluently as music notation.

This late development of a general, abstract dance notation was due primarily to the general low status to which dance had been relegated in Europe. Music had been a part of the Christian mass from the earliest period, and this led to the early development of music notation. The demise of dance from the liturgy, ending with total prohibition in some Christian sects, and the generally trivial use of dance in elite and bourgeois society, mitigated against the development of notation; coupled with this, is the complexity of human movement, which far exceeds the basic parameters of music. The later idealism of folklorism continued to mitigate against development of a general dance notation.

Because music had a much higher status than dance, and because music had a well-established notation system, much dance history including that of traditional dance can be done from notated collections of music. These collections, however, differ greatly in coverage among regions, with the greatest number found in the central European regions. (For an example of the combination of the use of printed dance music with documentary research, see Böhme, 1886.)

With the emergence and relative simplicity of late nineteenth-century sound-recording technology, and because the study of folk music received much greater emphasis than did folk dance, considerable dance music has been recorded in folk music collections. Unfortunately most of these recordings were carried out by music researchers, and they nearly always have no parallel dance documentation. They remain, nevertheless, valuable sources for dance history research.

Along with the music attached to particular dances, the titles of traditional dances, also transmitted through tradition with the dances, often provide information about the character and origins of the dances. Titles must be studied with very careful etymology, however, and backed up with proven dance data, since linguistic drift has frequently resulted in incomprehensible meanings, some even incorrectly interpreted. (For examples, see Emmerson, 1967; Martin, 1985; and Reynolds, 1990.)

Filming and videotaping the latest techniques for recording dance information, offer little historical depth, since motion picture photography only began in the 1890s. Again, because traditional dance was regarded as the ordinary behavior of nonelite classes, and because the expense and complexity of film far exceeded sound recording, films of historical value are exceptionally rare. The large-scale use of film began only in the 1950s, and then only in places with state support. This material now begins to assume historical status, and it can be used for longitudinal studies of change. Only in the 1970s did videotape come into use, seldom with professional equipment, leaving doubts about the durability of these recordings.

The amount of historical documentation differs very much among Europe's regions. The most peripheral regions maintained true traditional culture much longer (even to today) than the central areas; conversely, the central areas produced the earliest and largest amount of documentation. In some of the peripheral regions documentation is limited to the folkloristic period. Only for southern Europe is there documentation dating from the Greco-Roman classical era. In some regions much more historical research remains possible, but this is hampered by the general ahistorical ideology of folkloristics. Given the scarcity of data, the study of the history of traditional dance depends on an interrelated validity for all the above-listed sources coupled with sources of general cultural history.

The scarcity of information about European traditional dance is a major factor, but not the sole factor, limiting historical study.

Evolution and Diffusion. Traditional dance, like other cultural forms, changes with two main processes—evolution and diffusion.

Evolution takes place within an identified ethnic group; it is generated most basically by simple acts of personal creativity. Pronounced social changes can however have significant effect on dance function, which is further reflected in dance structure. For example, religious prohibition against ritual dance has often stimulated modifications into acceptable ceremonial or purely participant forms. Evolution can take place not only within individually identified dances but also within dance types and whole dialects or genres.

Diffusion is the process of absorbing influences from outside an identified group; it correlates with historical demography. A primary factor has been migration, which led to absorption or dominance by one culture over another. Trade, which includes the exchange of artisans, is a major factor in cultural contact, hence diffusion. Political interaction, such as royal ties, empire formation, and military intervention, as well as the church-related and study-related movement of individuals, lead to the diffusion of elite culture, which in turn has influenced folk culture. Itinerants, especially dance musicians, have contributed significantly to dance diffusion.

Prior to the industrialization of transportation, much demography was correlated with geographically imposed movement possibilities. For example, local trade usually extended only short distances, thus isolating peasant communities from much, but by no means all diffusion. Early trade routes along rivers, coasts, and across oceans and continents brought new culture traits to Europe's capitals before they were generally diffused to rural areas. Diffusion has increased in speed with the increase in the speed and range of general transportation and communications. This is seen especially in the outward diffusion of urban social dances into rural folk forms.

Although dance structure and function are interrelated,

evolution may take place in either factor alone or in both, in correlation. A gradual evolution of structure can proceed without change of function, or function can devolve, causing correlated changes in structure. Diffusion can also involve structure and function in various ways—for example, a dance having originally a ritual function can be diffused to another culture for purely participant use.

Interethnic or cross-cultural diffusion (horizontal). Diffusion among neighboring ethnic groups—those living in the same locality or those with commercial contact—is the most immediate form of diffusion. A characteristic example is in Transylvania, where the mixed population of Hungarians and Romanians has created dances quite different from corresponding nationals living in Hungary and Danubian Romania.

Cross-class diffusion (vertical). While the distinction between elite/urban versus rural cultures was far more pronounced in Europe before the eighteenth century, some cultural exchange between the two was inevitable. The nobility did maintain estates in the countryside to which they brought their urban and elite/bourgeois cultural forms—some of which were absorbed into folk usage. For example, the minuet is still danced today in Scandinavia as a folk dance, and the polonaise appears as both folk and social dances. Conversely, many elite forms are demonstrably derived from rural folk dance (a clear example is in Arbeau). This exchange of influence is seen predominantly with participant dances (see figure 2).

Results. Evolution and diffusion have proceeded with different processes and at different rates in the various European regions, nations, and local areas, thus yielding the complex historical layering of today's locally distinct dance cultures. Although some generalities of historical layering within Europe can be justified, each identifiable region, down to individual localities, will ultimately have its own scheme of historical layers.

Today's traditional dance is that collection of evolutionary and diffusionary layers present and recorded at the end of the nineteenth century and in the early twentieth century and preserved since then. This collection is a mixture of dances with different origins and quite different ages. Ironically, one of the effects of the folkloristic recording of dances is the stifling of evolution.

Rejection of diffusion. Because folklorism, as well as folkloristics, were driven by nationalistic motivation, diffusion is often not only ignored but rejected. Folklore is regarded as deep, old cultural property, and suggestions that it has merely been absorbed from neighboring states, especially those for which antipathy may exist harms cultural pride and raises an ethical issue for research (Reynolds, 1992). Rejecting diffusion also leads to the rejection of comparative studies.

The European diaspora and its return influence are *prima fascia* examples of diffusion; evolution in the diaspora often can be studied more directly and clearly than evolution in Europe itself. The lack of historical evidence for Europe's folk cultures, makes the study of both evolution and diffusion difficult. Only in areas with relatively dense documentation is such study possible.

Diffusion and natural evolution. European traditional dance shows very similar structures and function in widely scattered locations. This similarity, however, should not necessarily be taken to imply diffusion. Indeed similar dance structures and functions exist in cultures with no possible diffusionary contact with Europe. It can be argued that dance structure and function substantially emerge from genetically determined human structures and skills; thus it is natural for similar structures and functions to emerge spontaneously even in cultures having no contact (examples are standing in lines and circles, holding hands in various ways, use of implements in dance). This phenomenon in dance is parallel to a wide variety of genetically shared human behavior, such as hand grasping, tool making, and facial gesturing (for thorough studies, see Morris, 1977; 1985). This phenomenon is also parallel to structures of human myths, which bear striking similarities in cultures having no diffusionary contact. Such parallels and traits that evolve from them mean that diffusion must always be proved through the historical documentation of cultural demography (mainly economic and political), never merely assumed.

Preservation, Propagation, and Scholarship. Movements toward preservation, propagation, and scholarship of European traditional dance have emerged primarily from popular and individual initiative, often in response to folklorism and folkloristic interest in other behaviors, especially music. The primary motivation of these movements has been the folklorism ideal of seeking and maintaining local identity and individual creativity. (For an inside view of the origins and process of such movements, see the 1967 biography of Cecil Sharp by Maud Karpeles.)

Preservation, propagation and scholarship have evolved in close interaction, both in terms of individuals and institutions. Development and interaction have however proceeded quite differently in various countries and regions, yielding quite different organizational and institutional structures (for a model of a national survey covering the range of folk dance activities, see Martin, 1986). Movements for propagation have been organized under a variety of umbrella organizations, such as youth movements, sports associations, active folk museums, and teachers' continuing education. Ensembles meeting for personal recreation or preparation for presentations are locally organized, often with local town or sport association support. Most European scholars of traditional dance have emerged from this activist milieu, expanding personal interest and participation with academic qualification.

The scholarly study of traditional dance in Europe has been approached from a variety of backgrounds, ranging from standard folkloristics and ethnology/ethnography through classical mythology to zoology. Although often administratively separate, folkloristics and ethnology share much common theory and methodology. Folkloristics, however, tends to focus on materials within living memory (or recent recording) and thus does not function in the historical depth of ethnology. For this reason the broader specification "dance ethnology" has become the accepted descriptive term for the scholarly study of traditional dance in Europe, rather than "dance folkloristics." Anthropological approaches, reflecting a North American influence in dance ethnology, have had only recent influence in Europe; they are seen as theoretical additions to European ethnology rather than as revolutionary replacements.

Following the ideology of folklorism, European ethnology remains a virtually exclusive study by scholars of their own culture *(Volkskunde)*. This reduces, but by no means eliminates the methodological and theoretical issue behind etic-emic (outsider-insider; see Headland et al., 1990). The anthropological model of studying totally foreign cultures *(Völkerkunde)* has also long existed in Europe, but remains clearly separated from ethnology. Most European universities have two distinctly separate departments for these fields.

Even folkloristics, which should have recognized dance among the range of folklore, has been very late to recognize dance as a subject for serious study. For the following reasons dance was not a topic of interest for early folkloristics, and it was the last behavior to be included in its canon. (1) By the time folkloristics was established, dance, especially participant forms, did not seem to deeply embody ethnic identity nearly as much as language and its applications, such as folk song—thus dance could not be used to fulfill the ideology of folklorism. (2) The general anti-body mentality of Europe, especially that maintained during Victorian times and the development of folkloristics, placed dance lowest on the list of respected topics; this was compounded by a great deal of dance far too ribald for romantic intellectuals—thus justifying religious prohibition. (3) Elite Western dance forms tended to be dealt with solely as performing arts, with little theory and methodology for scholarly study on which the study of traditional dance could be built. Conversely, the development of ethnomusicology—the study of traditional world music systems—could proceed rapidly, simply by the modification and augmentation of classical musicology's existing sophisticated theory and methodology. Similarly, dance lacked the recording methods that paralleled music's, most importantly dance notation and practical mechanical recording. Only since the 1960s has dance ethnology begun to receive recognition as a field

with theoretical and methodological independence equivalent to that of ethnomusicology. Yet this has been achieved quite independent from elite dance forms. Integrated into general ethnology, in Europe dance ethnology benefits from its close interaction with ethnology in general.

Focused, formal programs for the academic study of traditional dance do not yet exist. In general, in Europe the arts are not subjects of university study but are reserved for conservatory focus. Academic training must therefore be carried out in a range of academic departments, virtually none specializing in dance. In many cases these departments have no adviser with specialization in dance, and no staff members, so young scholars are left to find their own ways of dealing with dance ethnology. Compared with other academic fields, this lack of common background training not only retards development but results in seeming conflicts of viewpoint.

In spite of academic limitations, the number of young scholars working to the master's or doctoral level has increased greatly from the 1960s. With most large-scale collection done, newer work tends to focus on increasingly specific topics. Lack of dance-specific theoretical bases, however, continues to retard development. (Publications dealing with European traditional dance are described in the bibliography.)

Institutions. In eastern Europe the practical propagation of traditional dance has been carried out largely by "houses of culture," institutions parallel to public education that foster all forms of amateur cultural activities. In western Europe support for its propagation falls to independent institutions (some dating from the earliest days of collecting), museums (offering courses in various folk arts), and occasionally institutions of higher education, as described above.

Institutions for research with archives and those for education and propagation exist only for certain European countries. In a number of countries they do not exist at all. Institutions for research often emerged from institutions for practical propagation, but in many cases the two functions remain merged. Much work is carried out by individuals, who are isolated within a range of quite different institutions. Because of language barriers, but perhaps more importantly because of the nationalist ideology of folklorism, no institution exists to deal with cross-cultural comparative study.

Because of the late development and recognition of dance ethnology as an academic field, the existing institutions for research and archives have been founded in several ways. In many cases they have been founded by a pioneering individual or by an activist revival group, based often on early personal collections of materials. Because of differing opportunities for support, the institutions are often found as departments of larger organizations. In eastern Europe most institutions for research and archives have been established (since the 1950s) formally under an Academy of Science, although located in various subinstitutions (such as music, folk art, ethnology, or archeology). In other countries, research institutions are parts of universities, museums, music conservatories, but in a few cases they exist as independent institutions. In a number of cases the functions of research and keeping archives and propagation and education are combined; in other cases (mainly in eastern Europe) they are separated, with research institutions requiring advanced academic status. Given the national differences, only careful tracing within each nation or state will reveal the specific structure and function of such institutions.

Only one major international organization in Europe focuses exclusively on research in dance ethnology—ICTM Study Group on Ethnochoreology. Founded in 1962 by the top scholars in eastern Europe, this group is now expanding to worldwide coverage and has a current membership of about one hundred. Meetings have so far all been in Europe, and the majority of members remain European. Meetings have made a wide range of ethnographic information available cross-culturally, and some cooperative theoretical discussion has been achieved; genuine comparative work, however, has been slow to develop (perhaps again reflecting folkloristic ideology).

In the area of propagation, two organizations are international: IOV (International Organization for Folk Art) and CIOFF (International Council of Folk Festivals). Both, however, are concerned mainly with organizing folk festivals, thus with propagation of stage presentational forms, as well as the teaching of dances. While both attempt to include research, this remains secondary to the performance interests of their members.

Effects and validity of early methodology. The ideology of folklorism coupled with the primary methodological models from folk music study led to certain biases early in dance study. These biases do not invalidate the data collected, but they do require that this data be amplified by additional data and an integrative methodology.

Following the pattern of folk song collecting, the early collectors of dance tended to assimilate a number of variants into single-model versions. In music, this had been practical, owing to the large number of variants, but it also carried the idealistic basis that the expert folklorist—nearly always with a background in elite Western music—was artistically qualified to produce a single, best version. Collectors thus became composers, producing a version based on various folk materials, and they usually assumed copyright ownership of their products (e.g., Cecil Sharp). Individual variations in folk performance were then regarded as mistakes or deviations from an assumed ideal version, equivalent to edited or poor performances of a classically composed work. The effects of this approach,

however, were to give an incomplete picture of the range of traditional differences and to suppress original individual creativity.

Similarly, since improvisation was not part of elite music tradition, it was not recognized in musicological theory. Thus it too became regarded as deviation in traditional dance and compressed into fixed models. The suppression of improvisation was first increased by the lack of longitudinal collecting and later by the use of film recording, both of which yield single performances rather than the richness of material that comes with improvisation. In sum, traditional dances were considered equivalent to single fixed works, as in elite culture, rather than as a flexible language with a large number of creators (Reynolds, 1990). As a result, once recorded and published, traditional dances assumed rigorously fixed forms that later generations rotely repeated from the publications, even after new research or practical dance mechanics spoke against the original versions.

Because of the absence of a sophisticated dance notation system based on an underlying developed movement analysis, the early verbal descriptions are often ambiguous, requiring complex critical review to achieve validity. Film can be an invaluable source for corroborating dance descriptions. In the absence of film, research must focus on living informants; if this is not possible, the remaining procedure is a complex interpretive process, one equivalent to interpreting historical notation systems.

Given the basic practical aim of the activist revival movements—making dances available for use in education and propagation—early collecting tended to focus on the dances themselves, with much less attention paid to their contexts and functions. In part, however, this occurred because the functional aspects remained generally known to most participants within each culture of use.

Because of an ideology focusing on a diffuse mass of people with no identifiable composers, as well as the reality of a detected range of differences in performance, the issue of any ownership by original source persons tended to be ignored. Original versions were regarded as material in the public domain, which could be used freely by anyone. Only later did the issue of the ownership of cultural property become an ethical issue. In some cases (an example being Norway), a strong sense of ownership has resulted in prohibiting outsiders from learning certain dances—even more rigorously, from the use of films or descriptions of particular local dances.

In larger collections, when dances were discovered to be identical or similar to those already published, they tended to be omitted in recording and publication—that is, research tended to focus on new, previously undiscovered dances. This led, however, to a distortion of regional distributions and differences. In some cases this reflected a convergent nationalism that sought to ignore regional differences, producing national dances rather than folk dances.

Similarly, the selection of dances worthy of recording was often influenced by the folkloristic ideal of ethnic tradition. Dances with deep tradition were promoted, whereas dances resulting from conspicuous recent diffusion were ignored. The result, however, was an incomplete picture of overall folk dance culture at a particular place and time. In addition, the small number of dedicated collectors, coupled with extremely weak support, meant that personal interest or choice often determined the focus of the collection.

From the point of view of young, academically trained scholars, early methodology is criticizable. This has led to occasional conflicts with established institutions and organizations. The results of all the early work, however, remain irreplaceable. The task today is to carry out supplementary cross validation using newly developed theory and methods, as well as newly collected data.

Factors against cross-cultural comparison. While a good number of publications exist on European folk dance, these are nearly all in local languages, and since these languages number over fifty, individual scholars obviously are highly limited in making comparative use of all publications.

The natural starting point for the reinforcement or reestablishment of nationalism—the first type of cultural behavior to receive attention—was language. Language thus became a model for the study of other behaviors, including dance. Languages, however, differ far more than do their underlying cultures, thus using language as a theoretical model tends to block comparison, artificially supporting the principle of cultural relativism. Various other types of behavior, such as dance, require their own unique comparable bases.

The lack of formal training in the field called traditional dance means that scholars have been trained in a wide variety of academic fields. Often, the underlying differences among these fields greatly interfere with comparative studies.

The difficulties of comparative work do not merely demonstrate an absence of overview concerning intercultural relationships. More seriously, an absence of comparison radically reduces the validity of data, methodology, and theory, thus retarding the development of dance ethnology in general.

Factors leading to an ahistorical view. Parallel with its acomparative view, research in European traditional dance also tends to be ahistorical. This occurs because of the scanty amount of historical data on dance in nonelite cultures. In addition, since the core motivation of folkloristics and ethnology has been the urgent need to find and preserve the rapidly vanishing remains of European folk culture, with few available scholars the historical work has been ignored. It is assumed that historical sources can be searched later, after the urgent collecting has been completed.

Both folkloristics and European anthropology tend to focus on collecting unrecorded oral or performance data (anthropology traditionally focused on societies having no written language or recorded history). Thus collections come only from living persons, with a focus on fieldwork and its methods. Since most people in living culture will likely be unaware of ethnographic historical processes, fieldwork methods do not adequately detect historical depth. Ethnology in Europe does however include the culture history and evolution of ethnic groups (ethnography), thereby reporting on both historical and archaeological methods.

Ethnography and folklore are too young as scholarly fields to have recorded much history within their own areas of collection. Longitudinal studies, which would show both evolution and diffusion, are rare, and (due to labor requirements) are all highly localized. Longitudinal comparative studies have not yet been attempted.

Here too, more deeply seated ideological attitudes likely underlie the above-mentioned limitations.

First, the ideology of folklorism focuses on the establishment of unique national (or ethnic) identity, and this radical cultural relativity leads to a rejection of cross-cultural comparison. This ideology also rejects the concept of diffusion, which necessarily suggests that at least some cultural property has been received from neighboring cultures. Carried one step further, since diffusion appears only in the historical dimension, cultural relativity also leads to rejection of the historical dimension.

Second, folklorism includes a hidden assumption that folk culture, as discovered by folklorists, has long been stable, is indeed archaic, and is now discovered intact (transmitted "unchanged" via tradition until the time of its detection by folklorists). This assumption of static development has removed the motivation to study in historical depth. The radical cultural relativity of anthropology, and to a lesser extent ethnology, leads to a rejection of the previous theories of diffusion and evolution, focusing on the current status as the only reality. While industrialization, urbanization, and technical communications have together generated a major break in human evolution, and while previous folk culture certainly had changed far more slowly than has modern culture, it is only reasonable to assume that some historical evolution and diffusion of traditional culture took place.

Dance Types and Functions: Structural Classification. European traditional dances can be classified most basically and unambiguously according to structure. As in any classification system, various factors are available on which to order the classification. The more factors that are included, the smaller the classes will be—thus only certain factors are selected as primary. Also, the order of classification can proceed in various ways, producing quite different classifications.

The most basic factor for dance classification is the starting configuration of the dancers, both in relationship to each other and to the dancing environment. This includes a number of subfactors: the shape of the group, the number of dancers, placement rules (gender, followed by age, social status [e.g., marital status]), leadership position, orientation of dancers in relation to the shape (hence to each other), and orientation to the dance environment (dance area, props, musicians, audience, etc.).

Gender is the major dimension of traditional dance; it cuts across both structural and functional analysis and classification. Gender effects in traditional dance are straightforward, having evolved from basic physical and social role differences. The configuration of a dance is further differentiated by the mode of the dancers contact—the dance "hold," the fastening. The fastening significantly limits subsequent movement, although it can change in the course of some dances. Physical contact can, in addition to body contacts, be mediated by props, implements (e.g., longswords, sticks).

Gender and the dance configuration, then, are the two factors at the core of function, social psychology, and gender effects in traditional dance. Classification may also include dynamic movement factors, primarily the paths of the group or individual dancers in the dance environment (which can include changes in formation and may necessarily be correlated with changes of fastening). Dances can also be classified according to the type of movement motifs incorporated, which are often correlated with musical meter (waltz, polka, etc.). Many motifs are structurally the same for men and women, but a significant number show conspicuous gender differences. Gender differences in motif vocabulary are highly genre specific, even within a single national collection. A final, detailed classification, differentiating structurally identical movements, may include levels of force or effort used. A common example would be identical movements performed with significantly different stress by men and by women (Kerr, 1991). Musical accompaniment, especially use of song and body percussion, may also be an important classifying factor.

Diachronic structure. Some dances are composed of major sections, even of quite different dances types, producing compound classification. Dances differ significantly in the degree of improvisation allowed. In European traditional dance this is nearly always a matter of diachronic rearrangement of known units, rather than totally free improvisation of movement. Improvisation may be a major classification factor and a major complication to analysis (Reynolds, 1994). All of the above factors ap-

pear in sophisticated dance notation, such as Labanotation, closely tying dance analysis and notation to dance classification.

Taken in all possible statistical permutations, the above factors would yield an extremely large number of possible dance types. In reality, however, only a very limited set of possibilities have been chosen. This selection reveals the processes of correlation between dance structure and deep psychological function. The dance structures have not been created, *ad hoc,* by individuals; they have evolved over centuries, indeed millennia, to meet the actual needs of ordinary people, which includes the historically ancient gender difference. Although seemingly simple, they thus incorporate basic, human organic functions that generate a comprehension of body experience with

EUROPEAN TRADITIONAL DANCE. *(top)* Figure 3. *Kolo* ("circle dance") from Dalmatia, Croatia, in the early 1950s. *(bottom)* Figure 4. A typical men's dance from southern Romania. Engraving after D. A. M. Raffet. (Figure 3 reprinted from Vinko Zganec and Nada Sremec, *Hrvatske Narodne Pjesme i Plesovi,* Zagreb, 1951, p. 43. Figure 4 reprinted from Grove, 1895, p. 13.)

EUROPEAN TRADITIONAL DANCE. Figure 5. "Singeing the Bride," a wedding ritual dance in which the bride is symbolically purified by jumping over a fire, Hungary, c.1937. Dances around large fires are still widely practiced in Europe on the evening of the summer solstice. (Photograph reprinted from Károly Viski, *Hungarian Dances*, London, 1937, after p. 120.)

environmental forces and structures, especially in interaction with other humans. If the interpretation of structure alone cannot fully support an explanation of the function or the meaning of dance, it is the foundation against which a higher level determination of meaning should be correlated and validated: fundamental meaning in dance must in some way be correlated with the unique bodily experience generated by dance. In other words, neither structure nor function can be dealt with in isolation from its counterpart—meaning.

In addition to correlation with function, then, structural classification serves as the basis for sorting out evolutionary and diffusional processes, as well as historical layering (Reynolds, 1992). Evolution and diffusion overlap in complex ways, yielding current regional, national, and local dance genres and dialects—and each shows its individual historical layering. As with other forms of generalized human behavior, the complexity of the distribution of dance types and dialects can only be dealt with statistically. (For the published model of dance classification, as well as the basic application of statistics, see Bucsan, 1971. For the core theory of dance dialects, plus additional examples of statistical application, see Bakka et al., 1995.)

Classification. European traditional dance can be classified into five major groups, each with some special case subdivisions.

1. Closed circle dances or chain-on-circular formation. Here, dancers are fastened by bodily contact, nearly entirely hand grasps of various sorts, ranging from very tight interwoven holds (figures 3 and 4) to the simple downward hold (figure 5). Group movement tends to be along the line of the formation, predominantly counterclockwise (rightward facing the sun). Both gestural and larger body movements are greatly limited by the tight fastening. Dancers in general face the center of circle but tend to turn partly in the direction of travel within the formation. These dances have no specific environmental orientation, except in cases in which a central object, potentially of ritual origin, is present or imagined (figures 6 and 7).

These dances allow for large numbers of participants; in some cases the number is limited only by available dance space.

The earliest of these dances tend to be for women only or men only, especially in areas of Islamic and Eastern Orthodox influence. Only rarely do traditional group dances freely allow the mixing of genders. Traditionally in many areas men and women are prohibited from any physical contact in public. In the Balkan area, line dances may join a group of men with women, but a kerchief is held to connect the groups (and the only couple dance deep in this area is of noncontact type, likely reflecting its eastern origin; see figure 15). More liberal mixing of genders is found in Roman Catholic and Protestant areas.

Motifs are usually simple and limited in number, thus focusing attention on dance experience rather than on display. Although the movement motifs for men and women are quite similar, each gender performs with char-

EUROPEAN TRADITIONAL DANCE. Figure 8. Young women dance and sing in this central Hungarian basket dance, 1955. (Photograph reprinted from György Martin, *A Magyar Körtanc és Európai Rokonsága*, Budapest, 1979, plate 45.)

EUROPEAN TRADITIONAL DANCE. *(above)* Figure 6. Clay sculpture from Cyprus, sixth century, showing people dancing around a tree. *(below)* Figure 7. An engraving by Theodore de Bry depicting a sixteenth-century egg dance. (Figure 6 Musée du Louvre; photograph used by permission. Figure 7 reprinted from Oetke, 1982, plate 41.)

acteristically different effort effects. One's social status traditionally prescribed the sequence in the line, and thus often correlated with costume distinctions (most commonly between married and unmarried women). Age is seldom a limitation, and older persons often show greater dance skills than younger ones.

Closed circle dances tend to have fixed structures, thus allowing little individual variation; they are seldom led. They tend to be for women only, often with singing as the sole accompaniment, emphasizing small-scale social structure (figure 8). Open circle dances tend to focus leadership on the end dancer, usually the right end, and in some cases this leader is responsible for improvisation, for the group or for himself (figure 9). These led dances tend somewhat to be for men only; women join traditionally by following at the end of the line of men or by dancing in a separate line.

There are three special case variations of circular dances. (1) Short line dances usually limit the number of dancers to six (approximately); they tend to be rigorous dances for men only. These further evolve into presentational forms facing an audience and restricted to lateral group movements. (2) Movement of chain dancers out of the basic circular formation yields serpentine formations, with unique group interaction and interlacing movements. (3) Certain circular dances are formed with fastening through implements rather than direct body contact. These are almost exclusively men's dances, examples being sword and hoop dances (figure 10).

Circular dances are the oldest of European traditional dances, as verified through both historical records and correlations with social evolutionary processes. They were preserved in greatest number in southeastern Eu-

rope, and they recede in prominence as we proceed toward western and northern Europe.

This configuration is frequently found in evidence of rituals, usually with the circle surrounding a ritual object, and it clearly establishes a strong sense of group unity as well as exclusion. Once found throughout Europe, in the central and western parts these have been largely superseded by later dances. The Balkan area, however, likely due to long Ottoman occupation, preserved these dances in largest concentrations. Special cases remain to be found in some isolated areas, such as Denmark's Faeroe Islands and in French Bretagne (Brittany).

2. Chain or closed circle dances with dancers not fastened bodily. For convenience, these are also labeled group solo dances. Orientation tends to be either toward the center or in the line of progression (walking forward). An absence of fastening allows for a true file configuration and, more importantly, use of the hands both for gestures and for manipulation of implements. These dances are usually highly energetic (figure 11). They are predominantly men's dances, usually of ritual or ceremonial function or origin, and they are limited to a moderate number (very approximately eight) of participants. They frequently focus around an object (*see* figure 12), occasionally of ritual function but also often a simple replacement (e.g., wine bottles). Leadership is usually pronounced and improvisation is often not only possible but highly valued. These dances are among the oldest in Europe and are found throughout the continent.

3. Couple dances. (This group includes special-case types of trios and two-couple quartets). The major group of couple dances have an obvious main focus function, in gender interaction, with clearly defined gender roles. Dancers are usually fastened in a variety of ways, allowing intense kinesthetic interaction (especially making use of centrifugal force) and male leadership (figures 13 and 14). An additional special-case form includes couple dances performed without contact. These noncontact forms are found almost exclusively in Europe's southern regions—those with Islamic influence—Spain, Portugal, Italy, and the Balkans (figure 15). Only outside these areas do contact couple dances with deep tradition appear. The other extreme is found in Lutheran areas, where not only do closed couple dances predominate but free mixing of partners is expected.

These dances could technically be performed by single couples alone, but they are nearly always danced by groups of couples. The grouping occurs in two major configurations, the first with couples randomly spaced and with little interaction among couples. These are primarily performed in place, with emphasis on centrifugal force, and with little path progression for individual couples. This subtype is the oldest of the couple dance types (figure 13). A second subtype has couples arranged on a circle with progression in the line of the circle (labeled round dances). Round dances appeared historically later than the first subtype and likely evolved from ceremonial processions of couples.

Both subtypes are specifically for the male and female couple, their functions closely associated with gender interaction and social role playing. Traditionally both subtypes are improvised, with the man taking responsibility for deciding structure and guiding the woman. Leading is done predominantly kinesthetically, with minimal visual support. The woman's role, perhaps actually more difficult than the man's, requires quick sensitivity to the leading kinesthetic signaling.

A few dances for male couples or for female couples exist, but they are of quite different function than the main type discussed above. Dances of this type for two men are nearly all combat simulations (figure 16). In most cases, implements have replaced weapons, with central European stick dances and broom dances being major examples. Dances for two women exist in the areas formerly influenced by Islamic occupation, and these likely reflect private interactions in Muslim society, which greatly restricted public expression by women.

4. Two straight lines opposing one another. Dancers in the starting configuration are usually not fastened, although a series of fastenings customarily takes place in the course of the dances. Dancers may be arranged either by rank or by file, with these positions often alternating in the course of the dances. A wide range of movements and

EUROPEAN TRADITIONAL DANCE. *(above)* Figure 11. Men performing the Bavarian *Schuplattler* ("shoeslapper"). Figure 12. *Verbunkos* (military recruiting dance), performed by men in the North Transdanubian Plain, western Hungary, in the 1950s. (Figure 11 reprinted from Wolfram, 1951, plate 31. Figure 12 photograph reprinted from Àgoston Lányi, György Martin, and Ernö Pesovár, *A Körverbunk*, Budapest, 1983.)

EUROPEAN TRADITIONAL DANCE. *(above)* Figure 13. A czardas-type wedding dance, Hungary. *(below)* Figure 14. *Négyes* (four-some), performed by men and women of a Hungarian minority group living in Szék, northeastern Romania, 1968. (Figure 13 photograph reprinted from Marián Réthei Prikkel, *A Magyarság Táncai*, Budapest, 1924. Figure 14 photograph by Péter Korniss; used by permission.)

paths are possible, either in relationship to dancers in the facing line or to dancers in one's own line. Lines are usually placed in relationship to an environmental factor, most commonly to musicians or to important members of the audience.

Opposing line dances are divided into two historically and socially disjunct types. The first group consists of dances for men only, deeply traditional ceremonial dances, in which the two opposing lines usually represent opponents and display combat, often with implements simulating weapons. A characteristic example is the group of Moorish dances, offered in various forms throughout southern and central Europe (figure 17). While the dancers usually include a leader, this role does not usually include dance improvisation. Great effort is expended.

The second subtype consists of dances for couples, called longways or contradances. These are likely derived from ceremonial procession; they are the most prominent of the current folk dances to show the influence of court and social dance (figure 18). These are among the later historical layers of dance genres. The lead couple is customarily placed closest to the most important social figure present (e.g., royalty). In most of these dances the couples begin arranged in lines facing each other (hence "contra"). These dances are usually led or at least introduced

EUROPEAN TRADITIONAL DANCE. *(left)* Figure 15. A couple performing a bolero, a Spanish dance style developed in the eighteenth century. Print after T. F. Lewis. *(below)* Figure 16. Two men in an Albanian sword dance, Koplik, Albania, 1959. (Figure 15 reprinted from Grove, 1895, after p. 322. Figure 16 photograph reprinted from Bertalan Andrásfalvy, et. al., *Magyar Néptánchagyományok*, Budapest, 1980, p. 115.)

by the head couple, but improvisation is traditionally not present. Step motifs tend to be very simple, but group patterns can be highly complex, reflecting hightened function of social interaction over individual movement experience. These dances have been recomposed with myriad combinations of basic motifs; the American forms are often improvised by a caller. Effort tends to be restrained.

The longways type of social dance is apparently the evolutionary source of the quadrille and the square dance, producing a genre that seemingly blends a circle dance with facing lines of couples. Most basically, quadrille dances are for four couples, although there are some other combinations. Dancers face inward, toward the couple opposite in the square. The possible number of sets of couples is restricted only by the dance space. Paths and fastenings, as with longways dances, have a large repertory. Traditionally these dance have fixed forms, but in the United States they evolved into the called square dance, with elaborate structures improvised by the caller (see Holden and Litman, 1961). [*See* Cotillon; Country Dance; Quadrille; *and* Square Dancing.]

5. *True solo dances.* These are the dances for a single dancer; they tend greatly to be for men only. Characteristic examples are crossed-sword dances performed over swords, or sticks replacing them, laid crosswise on the ground (figure 19), Irish/British step dances, and Hungarian men's dances. Military institutions generated a range solo men's dance with skilled weapon handling. These dances are scattered and rare today, so the historical layering is unresolved. (Closely related to these are dances

EUROPEAN TRADITIONAL DANCE. *(above)* Figure 17. A *moresca*-type stick dance performed in Ávila, Spain. This dance celebrates the end of the Moorish occupation of Spain. *(below)* Figure 18. Men and women square off in the "Dans à Dal," a line dance, near Léon in Brittany, France, in the early 1950s. (Figure 17 photograph reprinted from Curt Sachs, *Eine Weltgeschichte des Tanzes*, Berlin, 1933. Figure 18 photograph reprinted from Pierre Hélias, *Danses de Bretagne*, Châteaulin, 1955.)

for two men, all with functions of combat or physical contest.) [*See* Sword Dance.]

Whereas historical evidence shows the evolutionary appearance of dance structures to be roughly in the order of this presentation, it has not necessarily been a uniform or a linear progression, especially on the local level. Instead, dances of various types have evolved alongside others in the same culture; dances have diffused among cultures; and dances have been abandoned—all seemingly in unpredictable and in as yet unexplained ways.

Dance Types and Functions: Function Classification. The functions of dance, with their origins deep in the human subconscious, are integrated with deep-seated perceptual, cognitive, even metaphysical, aspects of the human mind. Dance movement structures, as presented above, have been chosen at particular points in human social evolution to meet not only the psychological needs of individual dancers but also to serve the social psychological functions of specific social occasions. The overall event structure, then, draws dance movement and dance structures into the overall meaning of social events.

Because function is psychological, not visible, it cannot be pictured or notated as a physical phenomenon. Function can only be inferred from dance movement and social event structure (based on a highly developed under-

EUROPEAN TRADITIONAL DANCE. Figure 19. A man performing a solo stick dance in central Hungary, 1961. (Photograph reprinted from Bertalan Andrásfalvy, et. al., *Magyar Néptánchagyományok*, Budapest, 1980, p. 149.)

standing of the human mind) interpreted from data achieved through participant interviewing and self-participation.

European traditional dance can be divided functionally into four major types: ritual, ceremonial, participant, and presentational/competitive. While not totally disjointed classes, certain major traits remain clear identifiers. A large number of factors would be included in a complete definition of dance function. For clarity, only key factors have been selected in the following discussion.

Ritual dances, now rare, are still found in scattered authentic forms:

1. The primary motivation for ritual dance is to achieve extraordinary experience or supernatural effect, thus achieving communion with supernatural forces, which in turn provides personal or social benefits, such as healing, protection, fertility, initiation, totemistic power, hunting power, resurrection, and so on.

2. The primary sensory systems in ritual dance are kinesthetic.
3. An audience is not required, indeed often prohibited.
4. Dances have specialized, esoteric, but not necessarily demanding technique.
5. Repertory is stable and usually highly limited. In order to maintain magical effects, individual creativity is extremely restricted.
6. Participation is especially restricted to initiated members, generating strong group bonding and social status.
7. Ritual dances may be integrated with drama, gesture, and pantomime, and implements and objects often play a central role.
8. Such dances are nearly always for men only.
9. Ritual dances are usually connected to highly specific occasions, tied to pre-Christian or Christian calendar events, often held only once yearly. An excellent and well-studied example is the Romanian *calus* (see Kligman, 1981). Many other examples are found in texts covering ritual dance (see below).

Ceremonial dances, now rare, serve secularized social functions:

1. The primary function is to display and solidify group identity and status, as well as individual rank.
2. Sensory systems are both kinesthetic and visual.
3. An audience is usually necessary to enhance primary functions.
4. Technique can range from simple to highly demanding.
5. Repertory can be highly limited, indeed to one dance.
6. Participation is also strictly limited to an identified social group.
7. Dances are mostly for men only, occasionally for structures of couples.
8. These dances appear in a wide variety of secularized social occasions. Examples are craftsmen's guild dances (such as the sword and hoop dances; see Alford, 1962), recruiting dances (such as the Hungarian *verbunkos*), house-raising festivities, many calendar customs, celebration of political events (such as the *morisca (moresca)*, celebrating liberation from Moorish occupation), processionals (such as the *polonaise* and the Helston Furry dance), and rites of passage (see Eliade, 1958). [*See* Moresca.]

Surveys and studies of ritual and ceremonial dances are found in Louis, 1963; Oetke, 1982, Wolfram, 1951, as well as in other sources listed below. Because of the apparent deep roots in European folklore and ethnology, ritual and ceremonial dance have received the most attention in academic studies, especially in the early period. The following two functional types were seen as too contemporary and too distant from deep folklore roots to warrant early academic study. Work with them, including large-scale collection, was initially left to amateur enthusiasts but has now been taken into more formal study.

Ritual and ceremonial dance cannot be taken out of the social context without the loss of genuine functions and meaning; they must be studied as deeply imbedded social behaviors. The remaining two types are less subject to this criterion.

Participant dance corresponds mainly with "folk," "popular," and "social" dance:

1. Primary motivation is the experience of dancing, both within oneself ("recreation") and in interaction with other dancers ("social").
2. The primary sensory systems are kinesthetic, focusing on experience and communication through kinesthetic channel.
3. An audience is not required; dance is performed predominantly for the dancers themselves. The closed circle and couple formations common in participant dance effectively separates grouped dancers from outside observers.
4. Technique is predominantly simple but with a complex range of possibilities. Technique is seldom taught separately from dance events.
5. Repertory can include a large number of dances, but local differences are large. Dance tend to be in fixed forms, with individual creators only rarely identified. Individual improvisation in dancing is traditional but degree allowed varies highly according to region.
6. Participation is generally restricted to an immediate group with shared dance lexicon and grammar, but participation by outsiders is rarely prohibited.
7. Some dances of this type are for men only, some for women only, but most are for groups or couples.
8. Participant dance forms are seldom tied to fixed occasions, but are often freely exchangeable among occasions. That is, they carry minimal specific kinetic ritual/ceremonial function.

Presentational/competitive dance is characterized by:

1. Primary motivation is communication to an audience, often as demonstration of special individual dance skill.
2. The primary sensory system is visual, often with some auditory correlation. Visual effects of dancers communicate to an audience through kinesthetic empathy with auditory reinforcement.
3. An audience is a required component of the overall event, and different types of audience enter into a classification of presentational events.

4. These tend to be solo or group-solo dances, allowing the greatest range of individual expression, creativity, and gestural expression.
5. Technique can be highly demanding; it can be taught separately from the dances themselves, in special training institutions. Movement focuses on physical skill, often with minimal specific social meaning.
6. Repertory is only minimally limited, but with clear genre limits. Emphasis on individual creativity and identification of new works is much greater than other functional types, but varies according to genre.
7. Dancers can be professional or semiprofessional.
8. Participation is strictly limited by the demands of the technique or performance unity (small number of performance elite).
9. Performance is on a specific dance area related to an audience.
10. Visual communication leads to association with drama, pantomime, and ordinary gestural communication, hence a tendency to textualization (storytelling through combined performing arts).
11. This dance type strongly tends to be for men only.
12. Men's forms especially serve as a demonstration of prowess (examples are the Norwegian *halling*, the German-Austrian *Schuplattler*, the Scottish crossed swords, and Irish/British step dancing).
13. Occasions—amateur public performance (e.g., street performance), competitions, festivals, tourist performance, professional and amateur folk dance theaters.

Ritual Dance and Functional Devolution. Both historical and ethnographic evidence strongly suggest that dance originated as a central part of ritual, and that later secularized forms of dance are, in various ways, reductions from this ancient human function. Sources demonstrating the ritual use of dance are found throughout European history—beginning with prehistory (in iconography) and continuing through biblical-era, Greek, and Roman documents (Oesterley, 1923). Usage in the early Christian church and in folk magic have similarly been documented (Grove, 1895; Backman, 1952). Folklore and mythology studies attempt to trace remnants of long-established ritual behavior with the goal of relating European forms to the rest of the world. A definition of dance at its ritual origins should be sufficiently inclusive, then, to serve as a framework for defining later devolved dance functions.

Seen from its ritual roots, dance would be defined as

• intentional, purposeful
• communally elaborated but biologically based (hence substantially universal), nonverbal, especially embodied human behavior
• perceived predominantly through the dynesthetic sensory systems (force detecting systems)

- functioning primarily not for the manipulation of the physical environment (work), for demonstration of achieved physical ability (sport), or for pragmatic intrahuman communication (gesture, drama, pantomime)
- but functioning personally and communally for transcendence into nonordinary processes of experiential knowledge (ecstasy, possession, trance)
- of the causative structures of the physical forces of the environment, of the human body, and of the bodies of other humans
- but more importantly by analogy and metaphor to experiential knowledge of causative psychic forces, including imagined anthropomorphic, animatic, and animistic forces
- and hence functioning fundamentally for communion with these forces, thus reinforcing and demonstrating human spiritual empowerment, especially the power to influence causative forces for human benefit.

Remnants and reductions. The functional classification provided in the above section is given in the order of historically demonstrable devolution; that is, these functional types represent identifiable historical layers

EUROPEAN TRADITIONAL DANCE. Figure 20. The Horn Dance of Abbots Bromley, central England, in the early 1960s. This ceremonial dance is still performed and has an unbroken tradition. (Photograph reprinted from Douglas Kennedy, *English Folk Dancing Today and Yesterday*, London, 1964.)

and show the process of a gradual reduction in the importance of dance in human society. Ritual dance, on loosing its spiritual function transforms into ceremonial functions; ceremonial dance, on loosing its socially embedded meaning transforms into participant functions; presentational/competitive dances are further yet from the deepest traditional functions.

This devolution can occur with minimal change in dance structure or even occasion. For example, ritual dance may be continued as ceremonial forms, done "because we have always done them," but questions of ritual meaning and origins cannot be answered by performers (an example is the Abbots Bromly Horn Dance, figure 20). By removal of even ceremonial context, dances can be reduced to purely recreational participant types, and even further, to children's games (examples of this process are the English sword dance and the Morris dance). In general, however, devolution of function results in significant changes in both structural and movement content (see Giurchescu, 1990; for a methodological model setting study of the effects of functional change on dance structure, see Nahachewsky, 1991).

When dance becomes solely presentational, major changes in function and structure seem inevitable. Nonpresentational dances function primarily through the kinesthetic sensory systems, with other senses—most importantly vision—functioning as secondary channels. With presentational forms, however, communication to

an audience through vision becomes predominant. In simple structural terms, stage presentation is predominantly frontal, thus diverging from the structures of the greatest part of traditional dance, which primarily emphasize a multidimensional orientation among the participants. More significantly, however, the transformation from presenting acts of personal experience to those of commanding attention and communicating to an audience has radical effect—most importantly pointing dance toward drama and spectacle. This leads to the adaptation of dance to storytelling and to greater emphasis on dramatic gesture and pantomime. As additional effects, the small number of specialist performers in relation to a larger audience tends to evolve some highly advanced skills, the addition of competitiveness, and increasingly dramatic presentation; this specialized skill tends to require and develop professionalism. Focus on external communication moves dance further away from its roots in deep personal experience. This was eloquently summed up by Curt Sachs:

> When in higher cultures dance becomes art in the narrower sense, when it becomes a spectacle, when it seeks to influence men rather than spirits, then its universal power is broken.
>
> (Sachs, 1937)

World History of the Dance. The transformation of European traditional dance forms to the theatrical stage is a phenomenon of the twentieth century. In many cases transformation was carried out under the influence of state ideological folklorism, with the main intention of emphasizing national identity. (For an insider study of political/nationalistic uses of traditional dance, see Giurchescu, 1994.) Especially in post–World War II Eastern Europe, large professional ensembles received state support, and the model set by state ensembles was followed through the state educational system. Young people were especially attracted to stage performance, so in rural communities two divergent dance groups are often found—one consisting of older people continuing the traditions of participant dance and another consisting of young people imitating the large state ensembles. Structure, movement content, and stage presentation were strongly influenced by elite urban forms; in many cases the large ensembles accepted only dancers with ballet training. The result was stage choreographies thoroughly beyond any original traditional meaning or structure. The most influential, indeed classic ensemble of the type has been the Moiseyev Dance Company. Because of basic functional differences from traditional forms, such theatrical transformations of European traditional dance are best discussed (both aesthetically and functionally) with other Western elite forms.

Conclusions and Future Directions. Given today's study of traditional dance, determined by the limitations discussed above, certain directions for future development emerge. Increased cross-cultural comparison remains open, requiring the overcoming of linguistic, methodological, and ideological barriers, especially the critical reevaluation of cultural relativism. This should yield increased, indeed revived, theoretical and pragmatic examination of diffusion and evolution. Comparison should lead to the increased validity of local approaches and, by avoiding duplication, release energy for focused advanced work.

Study in historical depth and the recognition of historical layers—as well as diffusion, which has been long ignored or even rejected—all need to return with new, critical approaches, including cross-fertilization with dance history. Dance iconography, now in its infancy, should grow productively. Historical methodology, however, will need to be added as a dimension perpendicular to fieldwork methodology.

Greater interdisciplinary work—necessarily beginning with increased interdisciplinary respect—should lead to genuinely new and fruitful comprehension of dance, including the reevaluation and respectful use of previous methodologies and data. Dance studies should be brought more fully into mainstream academia, interacting with such areas as history, philosophy (especially aesthetics and ethics), linguistics, and iconography. Greater integration of dance studies with the study of human behavior in general, particularly ethnology and psychology (specifically cross-cultural psychology), would be fruitful (for clear examples, see Morris, 1977 and 1985). Humanistic approaches should become willing to be tested against scientific approaches. The building of dance study as a discipline should lead to the development of a theory of dance—validly recognizing the unique characteristics of dance as both a biologically based human experience and a socially elaborated human behavior. This development will require recognition, again, of the limitations of the now-predominant folkloristic and anthropological approaches, and willingness to go beyond them. The predominant Western dance aesthetics, which focuses virtually exclusively on Western elite theatrical dance, should be augmented to include a humanly general aesthetics of dance (e.g., compare Copeland and Cohen, 1983, with Anderson, 1990).

In terms of the study of function, the period of urgent fieldwork collection, coupled with activist preservation movements, is reaching its limits. Folklore, either as maintained tradition or revival, has reached a stable state in modern societies. This means also that a necessary practical focus on structure, leading to collection and classification, can be softened. Function—often given less attention because "it was known by all," because it had been the focus of earlier research, or because it threatened the nationalist ideology of folklorism—can now receive renewed attention. With this development, fieldwork becomes not the only methodology, and interactions with other fields such as history, aesthetics, epistemology, and psychology become necessary.

In terms of aesthetics and ethics (etiquette), one characteristic of folklore is that these remain largely unreflected upon by its practitioners. Thus, traditional performing arts are not concerned with aesthetics or ethics. It does not mean, however, that neither exists, only that they are not customarily brought into conscious discussion. Relating dance to its context and function, aesthetics should accommodate ethics and etiquette (for a model of this approach, see Aldrich, 1991). As an approach to function, aesthetics remains open to increased research; traditional dance, with its roots in the naturally evolved deep human experience, should provide a rich source of natural aesthetics (see Anderson, 1990).

European traditional dance—with undeniable roots in prehistory and antiquity, providing both differentiating identity and unifying human experience—continues to devolve. Religious disdain, with a corresponding brainy/visual/verbal intellectual society, branded traditional dance as primitive, and in some strict religious communities succeeded in exterminating it. Minimally, dance has been trivialized as mere recreation or entertainment. Much dance has become the sole prerogative of elite professional performers, presenting it to a mass of passive consumers. Participant dance has evolved disco, a dance genre universal and undifferentiated, with absent gender, ethnic group, and historical identification: this results in a devaluation of the human experience. Allegra Fuller Snyder (1992) has profoundly compared this loss to the loss of genetic material in the continuing destruction of the physical environment, one which decreases the chances of human survival. Marginalized traditional dance deserves preservation, if only as a genetic time capsule, openable at some future time of return to humanized society, capable of contributing to revived respect for individual creativity, free from the dominance of supplied culture, as a revival of natural human aesthetics built on empowered bodily experience.

[*See also* Chain and Round Dances; Clogging; Hornpipe; Jig; Morris Dance; *and* Reel. *For historical discussion, see* Branle; Galliard; *and* Saltarello.]

BIBLIOGRAPHY. Most publications on the traditional dance of Europe are in one of the fifty or more local languages and deal with the dance of single nations or regions. Publications general to all of Europe or its regions are extremely rare, for reasons suggested in this article. Only publications cited in this article, or of special significance, will be cited here.

Given the seeming complexity of dance movement, coupled with the absence of a theory of dance movement, the earliest writings on traditional dance tend to focus solely on dance function, with little correlation with actual movement. While important as sources of information as well as stimulus for hypothesis formation, these publications can be frustrating because of the lack of hands-on viewing of dance itself. A second wave of publica-

tions consists of collections of descriptions, intended for archiving or propagation. These tend to include little description of function or context, apparently based on the assumption that anyone actively carrying out the dances would know functions and context. Publications making integrated use of notation/movement analysis with functional description are rare and are all from the most recent period of the rapid growth of academic dance ethnology.

Scholarly publication on traditional dance, which continued as a trickle from the early folkloristic period, has expanded rapidly since the 1970s. The bulk of master's and doctoral studies date from this period. Much of this valuable material, unfortunately, remains unpublished but is usually available through the authors.

No single textbook exists with an overview of the theory, methodology, and accumulated data of European traditional dance. No full bibliography covering all of Europe in historical depth is available. A summary of recent publications is found in the bibliography of members of the ICTM Study Group on Ethnochoreology (listed below).

Study of traditional dance has no international, topic-dedicated journal. Article-length publications appear predominantly in local language journals from a wide range of fields, making their location difficult. One journal, *Dance Studies*, edited by Roderyk Lange, has consistently included articles on traditional dance.

Compiled articles of research, predominantly on European cultures, have appeared regularly, but only since 1983, in proceedings of the ICTM Study Group on Ethnochoreology (listed separately below). Reviews and abstracts appear regularly in the *ICTM Dance Newsletter*.

Arbeau, Thoinot. *Orchesography* (1589). Translated by Mary Stewart Evans. New York, 1948. Reprinted with corrections, introduction, and notes by Julia Sutton, New York, 1967.

Aldrich, Elizabeth. *From the Ballroom to Hell: Grace and Folly in Nineteenth-Century Dance*. Evanston, Ill., 1991.

Alford, Violet. *Sword Dance and Drama*. London, 1962.

Anderson, Richard L. *Calliope's Sisters: A Comparative Study of Philosophies of Art*. Englewood Cliffs, N.J., 1990.

Backman, Eugène Louis. *Religious Dances in the Christian Church and in Popular Medicine*. Translated by E. Classen. London, 1952.

Bakka, Egil, et al. *Springar and Pols: Variation, Dialect, and Age*. Trondheim, Norway, 1995.

Balassa, Iván, and Gyula Ortutay. *Hungarian Ethnography and Folklore*. Budapest, 1985.

Böhme, Franz M. *Geschichte des Tanzes in Deutschland*. 2 vols. Leipzig, 1886.

Bucsan, Andrei. *Specificul dansului popular romanesc*. Bucharest, 1971.

Copeland, Roger, and Marshall Cohen, eds. *What Is Dance?* Oxford, 1983.

Dąbrowska, Grażyna, and Kurt Petermann, eds. *Analyse und Klassifikation von Volkstänzen*. Cracow, 1983. Proceedings of the tenth meeting of the ICTM Study Group on Folk Dance Terminology, 1976.

Dąbrowska, Grażyna, comp. *Dance, Ritual, and Music: Proceedings of the Eighteenth Symposium of the Study Group on Ethnochoreology*. Nowy Sacz, 1995.

Dunin, Elsie Ivancich, ed. *Dance Research Published or Publicly Presented by Members of the Study Group on Ethnochoreology*. Zagreb, 1995.

Eliade, Mircea. *Rites and Symbols of Initiation*. New York, 1958.

Emmerson, George S. *Scotland through Her Country Dances*. London, 1967.

Felföldi, László, ed. *Proceedings of the Sixteenth Symposium of the ICTM Study Group on Ethnochoreology*. Studia Musicologica Academiae Scientarum Hungaricae, 33. Budapest, 1991.

Frazer, James. *The Golden Bough*. Edited by Robert Fraser. New York, 1994.

Giurchescu, Anca. "Le Calus: Procès de transformation d'un rituel roumain." In *Tradition et histoire dans la culture populaire*, edited by Jean-Michel Guilcher. Grenoble, 1990.

Giurchescu, Anca. "The Power of the Dance Symbol and Its Socio-Political Use." In *Dance in Its Socio-Political Aspects/Dance and Costume: Proceedings of the Seventeenth Symposium of the Study Group on Ethnochoreology 1992*, edited by Irene Loutzaki. Nafplion, Greece, 1994.

Grove, Lilly M. *Dancing*. London, 1895.

Guest, Ann Hutchinson. *Choreo-Graphics: A Comparison of Dance Notation Systems from the Fifteenth Century to the Present*. New York, 1989.

Guilcher, Jean-Michel. *La contredanse et les renouvellements de la danse française*. Paris, 1969.

Headland, Thomas N., et al., eds. *Emics and Etics: The Insider/Outsider Debate*. Newbury Park, Calif., 1990.

Holden, Rickey, and Lloyd Litman. *Instant Hash: An Advanced Text on Modern Square Dance Figures*. Cleveland, 1961.

ICTM Dance Newsletter. Egtved, Denmark, 1988–.

Karpeles, Maud. *Cecil Sharp: His Life and Work*. Chicago, 1967.

Kerr, Kathleen A. "Differentiation of Ethnic Culture Regions Using Laban Movement Analysis: A Study of Bulgarian Dance." Ph.D. diss., Texas Woman's University, 1991.

Kligman, Gail. *Calus: Symbolic Transformation in Romanian Ritual*. Chicago, 1981.

Kurath, Gertrude Prokosch. "Panorama of Dance Ethnology." *Current Anthropology* 1 (1960):233–254.

Louis, Maurice L.-A. *Le folklore et la danse*. Paris, 1963.

Loutzaki, Irene, ed. *Dance in Its Socio-Political Aspects/Dance and Costume: Proceedings of the Seventeenth Symposium of the Study Group on Ethnochoreology 1992*. Nafplion, Greece, 1994.

Marcus, George, and Michael Fischer. *Anthropology as Cultural Critique*. Chicago, 1986.

Martin, György. "Ethnic and Social Strata in the Naming of Dances." *Hungarian Studies* 1.2 (1985): 179–190.

Martin, György, ed. *International Monograph on Folk Dance*, vol. 1, *Hungary, France*. Budapest, 1986.

Merriam, Alan P. *The Anthropology of Music*. Evanston, Ill., 1964.

Morris, Desmond. *Manwatching*. London, 1977.

Morris, Desmond. *Bodywatching: A Field Guide to the Human Species*. London, 1985.

Nahachewsky, Andriy. "The Kolomyika: Change and Diversity in Canadian Ukrainian Folk Dance." Ph.D. diss., University of Alberta, 1991.

Oesterley, W. O. E. *The Sacred Dance*. Cambridge, 1923.

Oetke, Herbert. *Der Deutsche Volkstanz*. 2 vols. Berlin, 1982.

Playford, John. *English Dancing Master, 1651*. Edited by Margaret Dean-Smith. London, 1957.

Reynolds, William C. "Film versus Notation for Dance: Basic Perceptual and Epistemological Differences." In *The Second International Congress on Movement Notation at the Fifth International Dance Conference*. Hong Kong, 1990.

Reynolds, William C. "Dänischer und deutscher Volkstanz: Einige verwandtschaftliche Beziehungen." In *Tanz und Tanzmusik in Überlieferung und Gegenwart*, edited by Marianne Bröcker. Bamberg, 1992.

Reynolds, William C. "Improvisation in Hungarian Folk Dance: Towards a Generative Grammar of European Folk Dance." *Acta Ethnographica Hungarica* 39 (1994). Festchrift for György Martin.

Sachs, Curt. *World History of the Dance*. Translated by Bessie Schönberg. New York, 1937.

Shanin, Teodor, ed. *Peasants and Peasant Society*. 2d ed. Oxford, 1987.

Sharp, Cecil, and Herbert C. Macilwaine. *The Morris Book*. 5 vols. London, 1909–1913. 2d ed. London, 1912–1924.

Sharp, Cecil. *The Sword Dances of Northern England*. 3 vols. London, 1912–1913. 2d ed. London, 1951.

Snyder, Allegra Fuller. "Past, Present, and Future." *UCLA Journal of Dance Ethnology* 16 (1992): 1–28.

Spence, Lewis. *Myth and Ritual in Dance, Game, and Rhyme*. London, 1947.

Torp, Lisbet, ed. *The Dance Event, a Complex Cultural Phenomenon: Proceedings of the Fifteenth Symposium of the Study Group on Ethnochoreology*. Copenhagen, 1988.

Urup, Henning, et al. *Gammaldans i Norden*. Trondheim, Norway, 1988.

Wolfram, Richard. *Die Volkstänze in Österreich und verwandte Tänze in Europa*. Salzburg, 1951.

FILMS.   The Institut für den Wissenschaftlichen Film, Göttingen, collects quality films and holds a number dealing with European ethnology, a few of which include dance. Although useful, the current collection is highly selective, hence not comprehensive.

WILLIAM C. REYNOLDS

EVDOKIMOVA, EVA (born 1 December 1948 in Geneva), ballet dancer. Born in Switzerland to an American mother and a Bulgarian father, Eva Evdokimova grew up in Munich, where she attended the children's ballet school of the Bavarian State Opera. She then studied at the Royal Ballet School in London and with Maria Fay, continuing in Copenhagen with Vera Volkova while dancing with the Royal Danish Ballet from 1966 to 1969. Appointed principal dancer at the West Berlin German Opera in 1969, she later became *prima ballerina*.

Evdokimova's international reputation grew rapidly after she won the only gold medal awarded in the senior section at the 1970 Varna International Ballet Competition. Thereafter she danced regularly with the London Festival Ballet, of which she became a regular principal dancer in the 1974/75 season. Though based in Berlin, she appeared as a guest artist with many other companies, including the Vienna and Munich state operas, and regularly appeared with Rudolf Nureyev in his various engagements.

Evdokimova danced all the ballerina roles of the traditional repertory (including August Bournonville's *La Sylphide* and Hilda in *A Folk Tale*), as well as modern roles in Birgit Cullberg's *Miss Julie* and in Glen Tetley's *Greening* and *The Sphinx*. Among the roles specially created for her are the Gardener's Daughter in Marcel Luipart's *Scarecrows* (Berlin, 1970), the title role in Valery Panov's *Cinderella* (Berlin, 1977), Nastasia in Panov's *The Idiot* (Berlin, 1979), and the leading role in Heinz Spoerli's *Verklärte Nacht* (Ludwigsburg, 1982).

With her exquisitely molded limbs and delicately chiseled features, Evdokimova became the prototype of the modern Romantic ballerina. Her Giselle, coached by Yvette Chauviré, and her Sylphide, directed by Peter Schaufuss, were roles to which her inner glow projected pure magic. The natural, easy flow of her line, the airiness of her jump, and the bounce of her *ballon,* with the soft ripples of her *port de bras,* combined with her innate musicality to lend her performances an unmistakable poetic refinement.

Evodokimova resigned as *prima ballerina* of the West Berlin German Opera at the end of the 1984/85 season. When her announced plans of founding a privately funded company under the name Ballet of America went unrealized, she continued to dance for a few more years as guest ballerina with various companies. In 1990 she gave memorable performances as Odette-Odile in Natalia Makarova's staging of *Swan Lake* for the English National Ballet. Since that time, she has quietly retired from the international dance scene.

BIBLIOGRAPHY

Barnes, Patricia. "All about Eva." *Ballet News* 4 (May 1983): 10–16.
Kleinert, Annemarie. *Portrait of an Artist: Eva Evdokimova.* London, 1982.

HORST KOEGLER

F

FABRE, JAN (born 14 December 1958 in Antwerp), Belgian choreographer, performance artist, visual artist, and theater director. Fabre studied at Antwerp's Royal Academy for Fine Arts and the Institute for Decorative Arts and Crafts. From 1976 to 1982, he created a series of twenty-nine solo performance artworks including *Money Performance* (1979, Ankerrui Theater, Antwerp); *After Art* (1980, Helfaer Theatre, Marquette University, Milwaukee, Wisconsin); and *It's Kill or Cure* (1982, Franklin Furnace, New York). Since 1980, Fabre has created more than seventeen ensemble and solo theater works, including three full-length ballets and two operas.

Das Glas im Kopf wird vom Glas: The Dance Sections, Fabre's first full-length ballet, set to Henryk Góreki's Symphony no. 3, Symphonie der Klagelieder, premiered at the Staatstheater Kassel in 1987 and was incorporated into the opera bearing the same name. In it, Fabre defies convention by presenting rudimentary movements of classical ballet in radically slow time. Dancers are costumed first in suits of armor, later in black bikinis. They define the performance space by their processions and positions in relation to large blue ballpoint pen drawings on silk.

The Sound of One Hand Clapping, created for the Frankfurt Ballet at the invitation of artistic director William Forsythe, is set to the music of Eugeniusz Knapik, Bernd Alois Zimmermann, and the Doors. First performed in 1990 at the Frankfurt Shauspielhaus by the Frankfurt Bal-

FABRE. Knights in shining armor and bikini-clad ballerinas in *Das Glas im Kopf wird vom Glas: The Dance Sections* (1987), Fabre's first full-length ballet. (Photograph by Flip Gils © 1987 by vzw Troubeleyn; used by permission.)

let with additional performers from Fabre's Antwerp-based Troubleyn group, this work was later incorporated into Fabre's 1992 opera, *Silent Screams, Difficult Dreams.* A third ballet, *Da un'altra faccia del tempo,* set to music by Eugeniusz Knapik and Sofia Gubaidulina, premiered at the Lunatheater, Brussels, in 1993.

Movement is central to Fabre's theater works. His interest in dance begins with movement rituals created for theater pieces such as *Het is theater zoals te verwuchten en te voorzien was* (This Is Theater Like It Was to Be Expected and Forseen, 1982), a "workday"-length episodic performance exploring nontheatrical human action and communication. The language of classical ballet first appears in 1984 in *De macht der theaterlijke dwaasheden* (The Power of Theatrical Madness), where a dancer repeats an adagio movement for thirteen minutes with her back to the audience, as an ode to ballet.

Fabre approaches dance in an experimental mode, neither classical, modern, nor postmodern. He pays homage to Marcel Duchamp and the Dadaists, but only as a reference point from which to forge his own way. Like the surrealists, he finds imagery in dreams. Fabre credits George Balanchine as a source of knowledge concerning space. Fabre's work is tightly constructed and physically and emotionally rigorous, often pushing performers to their limits.

Other examples of Fabre's choreography are found in the theater and opera works: *De macht der theaterlijke dwaasheden* (1984, Teatro Carlo Goldoni, Biennale di Venezia); *Het interview dat sterf . . .; Het paleis om vier uur's morgens . . . , A. G.,* and *De reïncarnatie van God* (1989, Theater Am Turm, Frankfurt); *Das Glas im Kopf wird vom Glas* (1990, De Vlaamse Opera, Antwerp); *Sweet Temptations* (1991, Vienna Festwochen); and *Silent Screams, Difficult Dreams* (1992, Staatstheater Kassel).

BIBLIOGRAPHY

Bousset, Sigrid, ed. *Jan Fabre: Texts on His Theatre-Work.* Brussels, 1993.

de Greef, Hugo, and Jan Hoet. *Jan Fabre: Im Gespräch mit Jan Hoet und Hugo de Greef.* Ostfildern, 1994.

Fabre, Jan, and Robert Mapplethorpe. *The Power of Theatrical Madness.* London, 1986.

Fabre, Jan. *Het interview dat sterft . . .; Het paleis om vier uur's morgens . . ., A. G.; De reïncarnatie van God.* Brussels, 1989.

Fabre, Jan, and Jean-Henri Fabre. *Fabre's Book of Insects.* Ghent, 1990.

Fabre, Jan, and Helmut Newton. *Das Glas im Kopf wird vom Glas: The Dance Sections.* Ghent, 1990.

Fabre, Jan. *Een familietragedie . . . , een theatertekst; Sweet Temptations.* Brussels, 1991.

Hrvatin, Emil. *Repetition, Madness, Discipline: Gesamt-Kunstwerk Jan Fabre.* Bagnolet, 1994.

Siegmund, Gerald, et al. *Jan Fabre: The Sound of One Hand Clapping.* Frankfurt, 1993.

Verschaffel, Bart, et al. *Jan Fabre: Texte zum Werke.* Hannover, 1992.

CURTIS L. CARTER

FADEYECHEV, NIKOLAI (Nikolai Borisovich Fadeechev; born 27 January 1933 in Moscow), Russian ballet dancer. After graduating in 1952 from the Moscow Ballet School, where he studied under Aleksandr Rudenko, Fadeyechev joined the Bolshoi Ballet as a soloist. His principal roles during his twenty-five-year career included Siegfried in *Swan Lake,* the Prince in *The Sleeping Beauty,* the Prince in *The Nutcracker,* Jean de Brienne in *Raymonda;* Albrecht in *Giselle,* the Poet in *Chopiniana,* Romeo in *Romeo and Juliet,* Vatslav in *The Fountain of Bakhchisarai,* Danila in *The Stone Flower,* Frondoso in *Laurencia,* Ilyas in *Asel,* Don José in *Carmen Suite,* and Karenin in *Anna Karenina.*

Fadeyechev was an excellent partner as well as a master of solo variations. He was the preferred cavalier of leading ballerinas such as Galina Ulanova and Maya Plisetskaya. In classical duets, apart from being a reliable and confident partner, Fadeyechev was able to convey poetically the beauty of love and the caring tenderness of a man in love. His dance had none of the pomposity, affectation, or strain of some other male dancers of his day, and it seemed that the dance was his element. The full-bodied quality of his movements, coupled with his soft gestures, was a natural prelude and barely noticeable transition to his soaring leaps, which were his forte. Fadeyechev was among those rare dancers whose technique is noted for light, seemingly slow-motion jumps, noiseless landings, and a smooth fluidity of movement. This and his noble but graceful *port de bras* created the impression that he could soar in the air.

Despite the exquisite elegance of his dance and his graphic if delicate acting style, Fadeyechev was essentially simple, straightforward, and manly. He seemed to radiate manly composure, calm friendliness, and restrained if casual warmth. He felt the musical continuity within the dance and was careful to maintain the smooth flow of every element of the dance and pantomime. Fadeyechev's romanticism was radiant and full of *joie de vivre,* with no suggestion of false exaltation or highstrung impetuosity. The dreamy quality of his heroes was a perfectly natural expression of lofty but simple aspirations.

Three roles stand out in Fadeyechev's long career. Appearing as Ilyas in Oleg Vinogradov's *Asel* (1967) Fadeyechev, for the first time in a career devoted to the romantic princes of the classical repertory, portrayed a contemporary man, a truck driver. He kept none of the romantic elegance, rounded arm positions, and graceful bearing of his princely roles, but seized the chance to display his range and flexibility by developing a special gait with a slight waddle, a sweeping breadth of movement, and good-humored, slightly angular mannerisms. He mastered with ease the complexity of this new kind of choreography, with its especially difficult lifts and supports. Equally challenging was the role of Don José in Al-

FADEYECHEV. A *premier danseur* of Moscow's Bolshoi Ballet, Fadeyechev was a favorite partner of Maya Plisetskaya and as a soloist was admired for his soaring leaps. (Photograph reprinted from a Bolshoi Ballet souvenir program, 1962.)

berto Alonso's *Carmen Suite* (1967). Whereas in *Asel* Fadeyechev had to find convincing character dance devices to convey features of modern everyday life, he now had to create a credible treatment of the ballet's tragic-grotesque content and message. Again he had to master a dance vocabulary that was far removed from the classical idiom; more a poignant pantomime stripped to the point of symbolism. José appeared as an obedient tool in the hands of the Corregidor. With his abrupt, clipped, march-like movements and turnabouts he seemed to be obeying inaudible commands. Fadeyechev created the image of a typical toy soldier, lifeless, inflexible, and yet infinitely lonely in his rigidly regimented existence. Appearing as Karenin in *Anna Karenina* (1972), choreographed by Maya Plisetskaya, Natalia Ryzhenko, and Vladimir Smirnov-Golovanov, Fadeyechev displayed great tact and a sense of measure, created by means of a straitened plastique, a correct, polite carelessness, and an inexorable, icy pomposity. Nevertheless, Fadeyechev's creations of Ilyas, José, and Karenin, however interesting, cannot eclipse his memorable achievements in the classical repertory.

Upon his retirement from the stage in 1977 Fadeyechev joined the Bolshoi faculty as a teacher and *répétiteur*. In 1993 he became associated with German Prybilov's new Renaissance Ballet company in Moscow. Fadeyechev was named a Merited Artist of the USSR in 1976.

BIBLIOGRAPHY

Gabovich, Mikhail. "Nikolai Fadeyechev." *Teatr*, no. 10 (1958).
Grishina, Elena. *Nikolai Fadeechev*. Moscow, 1990.
Hering, Doris. "And Still, the Chasm." *Dance Magazine* (November 1962):30–34.
Lvov-Anokhin, Boris. "Muzhestvenny lirizm." *Teatralnaia zhizn*, no. 2 (1965).
Moore, Lillian. "The Bolshoi Ballet Arrives on Film." *Dance Magazine* (January 1958):36–43.
Roslavleva, Natalia. *Era of the Russian Ballet* (1966). New York, 1979.

BORIS A. LVOV-ANOKHIN
Translated from Russian

FAEROE STEP. Also called Faroese step or *färöischer Schritt*, the Faeroe step is a three-measure, six-count step pattern common to chain dances of many European and Near Eastern cultures. Its basic form consists of three steps beginning on a given foot, followed by a pause, followed by one step with the other foot, followed by another pause.

Individual dances based on this pattern are defined by variations in such parameters as direction of progression, that is, left (clockwise) or right (counterclockwise); dynamics (low to high energy, accents); rhythm (the six counts may be of equal or unequal duration); tempo; and treatment of the pauses in counts four and six (action of nonsupporting foot or leg, possible hop on the supporting foot).

The term *Faeroe step* has been used among ethnic dance scholars since the 1908 publication of *Folkesangen på Færoerne* (The Folk Song in the Faeroe Islands) by Hjalmar Thuren. Thuren described the step pattern performed by the Faeroe Islanders in the chain dance accompanying their communal singing of old heroic ballads. He noted the similarity of this step to that of the *branle simple* and *branle gai* recorded by Thoinot Arbeau in 1588 and discussed possible historical connections.

Since Thuren, hundreds of dances from as far west as Brittany and as far east as Armenia and from Scandinavia to the Mediterranean Basin have been noted to be based on the Faeroe step pattern, suggesting the dances have a common origin. The step is particularly widespread among the peoples of the Balkan Peninsula, where it is the simplest of a complex family of three-measure dance patterns. Although there is no evidence of a genetic connection, the Faeroe step pattern is also the basis of standard versions of two American ballroom dances, the fox trot and the Lindy Hop.

BIBLIOGRAPHY

Allenby Jaffe, Nigel, and Margaret Allenby Jaffe. *Denmark*. Skipton, 1987.
Koudal, Jens Henrik. "Ethnomusicology and Folk Music Research in Denmark and the Faeroe Islands." *Yearbook for Traditional Dance* 24 (1993): 100–125.
Thuren, Hjalmar. *Folkesangen på Færoerne*. Copenhagen, 1908.
Torp, Lisbet, and Anca Giurchescu. "Folk Dance Collections and Folk Dance Research in Denmark and the Faeroe Islands." *Yearbook for Traditional Music* 24 (1993): 126–135.

Urup, Henning, et al. *Gammaldans i Norden*. Trondheim, Norway, 1988.

RICHARD CRUM

FAGAN, GARTH (born 3 May 1940 in Kingston, Jamaica), Jamaican dancer and choreographer. Fagan began dancing as a teenager in Jamaica with Ivy Baxter and the Jamaican National Dance Company. He studied with Pearl Primus and Lavinia Williams-Yarborough and later, in New York, with Martha Graham, José Limón, Mary Hinkson, and Alvin Ailey. At Wayne State University in Detroit, Michigan, he became director of the All-City Dance Company and a soloist with the Detroit Contemporary Dance Company and the Dance Theater of Detroit. In 1970 he was appointed to a professorship at the State University of New York at Brockport. He also taught at the university-affiliated Educational Opportunities Center in Rochester. There he formed a company of his own, originally called Bottom of the Bucket, BUT . . . Dance Theater, with dancers from the inner city trained by him. Among them were Steve Humphrey and A. Roger Smith, both of whom remained in his company for twenty years and more.

As the company gained recognition nationally and internationally, its title was changed first to Garth Fagan's Bucket Dance Theater, then to Garth Fagan Bucket Dance, and finally to Garth Fagan Dance. The company's choreography was by Fagan, in the technique that he developed, which includes elements of modern dance, Afro-Caribbean dance, and ballet, all subsumed into a personal language. The Fagan movement style is characterized by intricate polyrhythms, complex physical isolations, seemingly off-balance positions held motionless, and abrupt changes of direction and speed, sometimes taking place in the air. Although Fagan has continued to recruit dancers with no previous training, such as Valentina Alexander and Bit Knighton, his work has attracted dancers from various backgrounds, among them Norwood Pennewell, Natalie Rogers, and Christopher Morrison.

Fagan has choreographed some thirty-six works for his company, including the evening-length *Griot New York*, which was commissioned for the Brooklyn Academy of Music's Next Wave Festival and first given there in Decem-

FAGAN. Dancers from Garth Fagan's company in his *Easter Freeway Processional* (1983). (Photograph © 1984 by Jack Vartoogian; used by permission.)

ber 1991; it was made to music by Wynton Marsalis, with design by the sculptor Martin Puryear. The result was one of the most distinguished collaborations in contemporary dance. The West African word *griot* means "storyteller," but this is not a narrative dance; rather, it is a series of poetic images of life in the city, focusing now on individual men and women, now on the group. *Griot New York* was recorded for the Public Broadcasting Service (PBS) series *Dance in America* and was presented in 1995.

Other important works include *From Before* (1978), which encapsulates Fagan's dance heritage; the beautiful pantheistic trio *Oatka Trail* (1979); *Prelude* (1981/1983), a statement of his choreographic idiom; *Never Top 40* (1985); *Passion Distanced* (1987); *Time After Before Place* (1988); and *Telling a Story* (1989). Fagan has also choreographed dances for other companies, including Dance Theatre of Harlem (*Footprints Dressed in Red*, 1986), the Alvin Ailey American Dance Theater (*Jukebox for Alvin*, 1993), and the José Limón Company (*Never No Lament*, 1994). In 1986 he had staged the Duke Ellington musical *Queenie Pie*.

Fagan holds honorary doctorates from the Juilliard School, the University of Rochester, Nazareth College of Rochester, Hobart College, and William Smith College. He is a recipient of the Monarch Award from the National Council for Culture and Art, the Lillian Fairchild Award, and the Arts Achievement Award from Wayne State University, his alma mater.

BIBLIOGRAPHY

Emery, Lynne Fauley. *Black Dance from 1619 to Today*. 2d, rev. ed. Princeton, N.J., 1988.
Mason, Francis. "A Conversation with Garth Fagan." *Ballet Review* 23.1 (Spring 1995): 19–28.
Thorpe, Edward. *Black Dance*. Woodstock, N,Y., 1990.
Vaughan, David. "Garth Fagan Dance: Discipline Is Freedom." *Dance Magazine* (November 1990): 40–43.

DAVID VAUGHAN

FAIRY DOLL, THE. *See* Puppenfee, Die.

FALLA, MANUEL DE (Manuel María de Falla y Matheu; born 23 November 1876 in Cádiz, died 14 November 1946 in Alta Gracia, Argentina), Spanish composer. Falla was the foremost Spanish composer of his generation. The son of a merchant, he showed musical talent as a child, receiving piano lessons from his mother and other instruction in harmony and counterpoint. Later he traveled regularly to Madrid for advanced piano studies. When the family moved to Madrid in 1896, Falla completed the conservatory's usual seven-year course in two years.

Falla began to compose in adolescence and sought a reputation in the zarzuela, the distinctively Spanish form of romantic operetta and musical revue. He composed two in association with Amedeo Vives, a well-known *zarzuelista*, and three on his own, but only *Los Amores de la Inés* (1902) was produced, without receiving much success. His two-act opera *La Vida Breve* (Life Is Short) won first prize in a Madrid competition in 1905 but remained unperformed until 1913 at Nice, France.

Falla spent the years from 1907 to 1914 in Paris, where he became a friend of Claude Debussy, Paul Dukas, Maurice Ravel, and Igor Stravinsky, as well as of other Spanish expatriates such as Isaac Albéniz. While composing piano music and songs, he supported himself by giving piano lessons, accompanying singers at *soirées*, and doing translation work. He had started *Noches en los Jardines de España* (Nights in the Gardens of Spain) for piano and orchestra and had just finished *Siete Canciones Populares* (Seven Popular Songs) when the outbreak of World War I in 1914 impelled him to return home.

A request from Pastora Imperio, a celebrated Gypsy dancer and singer, brought about the composition of *El Amor Brujo* (Love, the Magician). In its first form as a *gitanería*, a Gypsy ballet with songs in two scenes with instrumental octet, it was performed in Madrid in 1915 by Pastora Imperio and her family. A revised version in one scene for voice and orchestra including piano was heard in concert in Madrid in 1916; it had a staged premiere in Paris in 1925, with new sets and choreography by the dancer Antonia Mercé, who was known as La Argentina.

El Amor Brujo, although derived from folk sources, had no actual folk melody used in the score. Falla nevertheless evokes the essential character of Andalusian Gypsy dance and song in its distinctive blend of tension and languor. He included the "Cádiz Tango" (in 7/8 meter), for the pantomime music, and the well-known "Ritual Fire Dance" (later transcribed for all kinds of probable and improbable instruments and used for all manner of equally unlikely dances). His was derived from a traditional Gypsy incantation intended to ward off evil spirits during the forging of pots and pans.

Falla's major dance achievement was *El Sombrero de Tres Picos* (The Three-Cornered Hat), based on a novel by Pedro de Alarcón. Falla composed it first as a mime play, which was produced by a Spanish company in Madrid in 1917 as *El Corregidor y la Molinera* (The Magistrate and the Miller's Wife). Serge Diaghilev liked it but asked for various changes to make the score suitable for a Ballets Russes production, which he entitled *Le Tricorne*.

The orchestra was enlarged, and to the Spanish dance forms (*fandango*, *seguidillas*, and *jota*), some quotations of folk melody were added—a *farruca* for the Miller's solo and a short prelude. Both were written in London immediately before the work's 1919 premiere. The prelude, for solo mezzo-soprano (accompanied only by castanets, handclapping, and stage shouts of "Olé!"), was added to give the audience time to admire Pablo Picasso's drop curtain. The music is Falla at his best, and combined with the work of Léonide Massine and Picasso it made an exemplary artistic achievement by Diaghilev's company. [*See* Tricorne, Le.*]

Falla then turned away from this colorful musical style to a more neoclassical idiom. With the poet Federico García Lorca, he experimented with puppet plays, which led to the puppet opera *El Retablo de Maese Pedro* (Master Peter's Puppet Show; 1923). An illness kept the composer housebound for four years. Then in 1939 he went to Argentina for a concert tour, and he remained there until his death in 1946. His body was later returned for burial in the crypt of Cádiz cathedral.

Most of his last creative efforts were given to setting an epic Catalan poem by Jacinto Verdaguer, in which the legend of the lost Atlantis is the starting point for a kind of masque of Spanish history. *Atlántida* was left unfinished, but after completion by Ernesto Halffter, it was first given in concert form in Barcelona in 1961 and staged the next year as a scenic cantata at the Teatro alla Scala, Milan, directed and choreographed by Margarete Wallmann.

Using few direct quotations from Spanish folk music, Falla penetrated the inherent qualities of Castilian as well as Andalusian character and made them integral to his own personality. This has been denied its fullest appreciation in relation to the adopted Spanishness of such composers as Claude Debussy, Emmanuel Chabrier, and Mikhail Glinka, although Falla is generous to them in his collected essays, *On Music and Musicians* (published in Spanish in 1948 and in English in 1979). His stylistic appreciation of his musical roots and his skill in cultivating his own art from them places his achievement at the crucial crossroads between Spanish nationalism and its sequel, which followed the disruptions caused by the 1936–1939 civil war in Spain and the wider European conflict that followed.

BIBLIOGRAPHY

Chase, Gilbert, and Andrew Budwig. *Manuel de Falla: A Bibliography and Research Guide*. New York, 1986.

Crichton, Ronald. *Manuel de Falla: A Descriptive Catalogue of His Works*. London, 1976.

Crichton, Ronald. *Falla*. London, 1982.

Falla, Manuel de. *On Music and Musicians* (1948). Translated by David Urman and J. M. Thomson. London, 1979.

Hoffelé, Jean-Charles. *Manuel de Falla*. Paris, 1992.

Pahissa, Jaime. *Manuel de Falla: His Life and Works*. London, 1954.

Persia, Jorge de. *Los últimos años de Manuel de Falla*. Madrid, 1993.

Pinamonti, Paolo, ed. *Manuel de Falla tra la Spagna e l'Europa: Atti del convegno internazionale di studi, Venezia, 15–17 maggio 1987*. Florence, 1989. Text in Italian and English.

Ruiz-Pipó, Antonio. *Catalogue de l'oeuvre de Manuel de Falla*. Paris, 1993.

Sopeña Ibáñez, Federico. *Vida y obra de Manuel de Falla*. Madrid, 1988.

NOËL GOODWIN

FANCY FREE. Ballet in one act. Choreography: Jerome Robbins. Music: Leonard Bernstein. Scenery: Oliver Smith. Costumes: Kermit Love. First performance: 18 April 1944, Metropolitan Opera House, New York, Ballet Theatre. Principals: John Kriza, Harold Lang, Jerome Robbins (Sailors), Muriel Bentley, Janet Reed, Shirley Eckl (Girls).

Fancy Free, a ballet as blithe and cheerful as its title, was an instant success, and its popularity led its creators to expand it into a musical comedy, *On the Town*. Although it depicts the escapades of three sailors on shore leave, *Fancy Free* exudes wholesomeness and an irrepressible optimism, avoiding any hint of the sordid, the tawdry, or the tragic.

The highlight of the Robbins-Bernstein ballet is a dance contest held by the three sailors to determine who will enjoy the company of two girls they have met. Each sailor's solo reflects his personality. The first, brash and assertive, shakes his linked hands overhead like a boxing champ. The long, lyrical phrases of the second sailor's dance reveal a more poetic nature. The third sways his hips sexily to a Latin beat. The girls are unable to decide, and a fight brews among the men; frightened, the girls flee. Discovering this, the sailors make peace and temporarily swear off women—very temporarily, for the entrance of a third temptress soon sends them after her in hot pursuit.

FANCY FREE. The original sailors: Harold Lang, John Kriza, and Jerome Robbins. (Photograph by Fred Fehl; used by permission.)

Robbins incorporated many everyday movements (chewing gum, adjusting a hat) into the ballet, giving it a highly convincing, naturalistic dimension. His sailors down their beer with more zest than elegance, and their interactions with the girls recall the boy next door rather than the ballet cavalier. Robbins succeeded here in couching his choreography in what might be termed an American vernacular movement style.

BIBLIOGRAPHY

Balanchine, George, with Francis Mason. *Balanchine's Complete Stories of the Great Ballets*. Rev. and enl. ed. Garden City, N.Y., 1977.

Goodwin, Noël. "Street Side Story." *Dance and Dancers* (November 1990): 12–13.

Kirstein, Lincoln. *Movement and Metaphor: Four Centuries of Ballet.* New York, 1970.

Robbins, Jerome. "Fancy Free." In *Dance as a Theatre Art*, edited by Selma Jeanne Cohen. New York, 1974.

SUSAN AU

FAN DANCING. Sally Rand (1904–1979), the celebrated American performer characterized by the New York *Herald Tribune* (24 February 1935) as "the girl who fanned a breeze into a tornado," attributed the invention of fan dancing to Cleopatra. Although Rand was a noted practitioner rather than scholar of her art form, she was correct in assigning an important place to fans in Egyptian society. Used to create a cool breeze and to whisk away flies, the fan had both practical and ceremonial purposes in Egypt, where the office of fan bearer denoted the highest honor; bestowed to reward valor, it was an actual occupation frequently shared with the ruler's sons. Fans made of feathers or wood painted to look like feathers were most prized. Two particularly fine examples were discovered in the tomb of King Tutankhamun (ruled c.1350 BCE). The significance of the fan and its bearer is displayed on the Ikhernofret stone (c.1868 BCE), considered to be the principal evidence of the Abydos Passion Play associated with the death and rebirth of Osiris. The stone's lower right corner shows an individual with a circular fan positioned in front of the person enthroned.

Ancient Assyrian representations of fans appear to reflect both rank and pleasure; the Tanagra figurines carry heart-shaped variations; and the feathered versions on Greek vases often are associated with Jupiter or are in the hands of dancers whose heads are turned backward, a convention for indicating rapid movement. The Romans were noted for making fans from peacock feathers. These may have been incorporated by the *pantomimi* into their wordless solo presentations that became popular during the reign of Augustus (27 BCE–14 CE) and were decried by Saint Augustine (354–430) as being more dangerous to morals than the circus. Biblical references (*Isaiah* 30.24

FAN DANCING. Fans have long been associated with Spanish dance. La Nena (Manuela Perea), a dancer at the Théâtre du Gymnase-Dramatique, Paris, was depicted posing with a fan in this lithograph, published c.1854. (Dance Collection, New York Public Library for the Performing Arts.)

and *Jeremiah* 15.7) articulate the use of fans in winnowing, a connection with harvest and fertility, and in removing flies. The *flabellum*, a long-handled ritual fan, was later used in the celebration of Mass to drive insects away from the Eucharist; the earliest extant example—housed in Florence's Bargello Museum—was made between 836 and 840.

Throughout Africa and the Pacific Islands, as well as among many Native American peoples, the fan specifically indicated the rank of chief. In medieval Japan, a war fan made of iron was used by the ruling samurai as both a military baton and a weapon of defense. Francis Parkman, in *The Discovery of the Great West: La Salle*, describes a ceremonial conference in 1682 when the French explorer was met by the white-robed chief of the Taensas Nation (in what is now Louisiana), who was preceded by

FAN DANCING. Petipa's *Don Quixote* contains a famous solo in which the ballerina, Kitri, dances flirtatiously with a fan. Kaleria Fedicheva was much admired for her performances as Kitri with the Kirov Ballet during the 1960s. (Photograph from the Dance Collection, New York Public Library for the Performing Arts.)

two men bearing white feather fans and a third carrying a burnished disk of copper. Eskimos in Tununak carefully distinguish the design of dancing fans according to gender, rather than rank. The masculine fan is a circle of wood with a few feathers, whereas the softer, female variety is a circle of felt, sealskin, or woven grass decorated with the white neck hairs of the caribou. Fans made of leaves, plaited fiber, feathers, cured skins, paper, and fabric continue to be fashioned throughout the world. As Lady Lilly Grove Frazer summarized in her 1895 treatise *Dancing*, "The fan has always been an adjunct of dance and is found at all times and everywhere, from China to Spain."

China and Japan have the longest continuous record of using fans, listed as one of the Eight Precious Things in Daoist symbolism, with a legendary origin placed be-

tween the third and second millennium BCE. Many traditional Chinese dances, characterized by a subtle interplay between fan and sleeve, are preserved in the repertory of the Beijing Opera in Taiwan, Hong Kong, and Singapore. Until the seventh century, fans were always rigid and were circular or semicircular in shape. A Japanese gentleman is credited with inventing the folding fan, based on observed mechanics of the wings of a bat, or *komori*, also the term for his innovation. No culture has a more varied tradition of performing with fans. On view in central Japan are examples of *shimotsuki kagura* that were related to some of the fan practices in the development of *nō* drama during the fourteenth century. Still performed in villages along the Sea of Japan are fan dances from the fifteenth century that predate the prototype *kabuki*, the popular national form that integrates music, language, spectacle, and dancing. Folk and presentational dances with fans, as well as those that are part of Shintō rituals, continue to be passed on from generation to generation.

Fans are part of classical dancing in India and its influences spread in the Hindu courts throughout Southeast Asia and the Indonesian Archipelago. The National Folk Ballet of Korea maintains several fan dances in repertory, especially *Puch'ae Chum*, which is sometimes performed by children. The Philippines also have a rich tradition in dancing with fans, which is sustained by research and presentations by the Bayanihan Philippine Dance Company. A highlight is the virtuosic *Kaganat sa Darangun*, a solo that incorporates six fans simultaneously.

Fans began to be imported from Asia to Europe during the sixteenth century, following Vasco da Gama's voyages in 1497 and 1502. Nancy Armstrong's informative *A Collector's History of Fans* credits Catherine de Médicis with introducing the folding fan to France upon her arrival as the bride of Henri II in 1549. In her portrait as the Grand Duchess of Tuscany, Christina of Lorraine is holding one of the new contraptions, called a *brisé*. The rigid flag-shaped fan is seen in Venetian paintings of the period; Antoine Caron shows a circular variant in his *Unidentified 'Course' in Fancy Dress;* Elizabethan ladies hung stiff feather fans from chains or ribbons at the waistline; and ostrich feather versions appear in the later paintings of Sir Anthony Van Dyck.

During the seventeenth century etiquette was developed for carrying a fan at court, and the making of fans contributed so substantially to the trade of England that a fan makers' grievance was presented in petition to Charles II to block the importation of these items from India. By the eighteenth century no well-dressed woman in Europe appeared in public without one. Writing in *The Spectator* (July 1711), Joseph Addison observed, "There is an infinite variety of motion to be made use of in the flutter of a fan." He also reported on the academy in London that trained young women exclusively in all appropriate conditions and exercises, because her handling of a fan was widely considered the distinguishing difference between a princess and a peasant. The six positions for holding a fan correctly were defined by the contemporary dancing and etiquette manuals and are reflected in eighteenth-century portraits. In Spain, where the watchful eyes of duennas had to be secretly avoided, an elaborate language of the fan developed. A closed fan resting over the right eye queried, "When can I see you?" Eyes hidden behind a widespread fan indicated, "I love you." Both Jean-Auguste Ingres and Jean-Baptiste Corot decorated fans, which seemed to change shape along with the fashion of women's skirts: expansive on the floors of Rococo ballrooms, very narrow in the silhouette dictated by the revolutionary Directoire, and generously broadened to match the width of Victorian petticoats.

The growing influence of dancing masters and tutors of deportment during the nineteenth century, along with the great popularity of cotillions, brought the fan into the ballroom in yet another guise, as one of the best known of the danced figures. Writing in his 1859 *Art of Dancing*, Edward Ferrero directed New Yorkers to place three chairs in the center of the floor. The first couple leads the waltz, then the gentleman seats the lady on one of the chairs and gives her a fan. He invites two additional men to join her. She selects one as her next partner and gives the fan to the other, who must follow the pair while fanning them and hopping on one leg. A description of the Italian dance "Bella della Ventola" (Opera Nazionale Dopolavoro, 1935) gives similar instructions, except that there are no chairs and the rejected partner is not required to hop.

Commemorative fans, in celebration of victories and treaties, were passed out by politicians and banks. Hosts of balls in nineteenth-century England presented each female guest with a fan that was printed with music for the dances of the evening. An earlier, especially beautiful example from the collection of the Russian dancer Evgenia Eduardova pictures Maria Medina and Salvatore Viganò in a scene entitled "Le Ballet de Genie."

FAN DANCING. *(above)* Japan has an extensive history of using fans in performance and is credited with inventing the folding fan, based on the mechanics of bat wings. *(left)* The use of fans in classical Indian dance spread to other dance genres throughout the Indonesian archipelago. The Balinese dancer I Made Bandem is seen here using a fan to make an expressive gesture. (Above photograph reprinted from Grove, 1895, p. 358. Left photograph by C. Kennard; used by permission of The Asia Society, New York.)

Actresses had long used fans in certain roles to add a graceful accent to gestures, but these devices were seldom seen on dancing stages outside of Spain and Asia until the middle of the nineteenth century. The phenomenon began at the ballet and spread through the spectacles and burlesques that evolved into the American musical comedy, in an era when audiences demanded legs, not artistry—though some productions boasted both. Publicity photos of Marie Bonfanti, the Italian ballerina who starred in the first (1866) and fourth (1879) New York productions of *The Black Crook*, show her posed with a feather fan. The statuesque Amazons, who followed the example of Lydia Thompson across popular stages clad in the infamous pink tights, or fleshings, carried mostly shields or spears, but there were exceptions. Long a symbol of decorum, fans provided a titillating contrast to the bold exposure of feminine flesh. The delectable Eliza Weathersby used a fan in one of her numbers in Edward N. Rice's *Evangeline*, which opened in 1874 and ran nearly as long and in as many incarnations as *The Black Crook*. One of the lavish extravaganzas imported from Italy, Luigi Manzotti's 1881 *Excelsior*, also incorporated a fan in at least one danced variation, photographed with Virginia Zucchi.

FAN DANCING. Korean folk ballet companies maintain fan dances in their repertories. This is the Children's Folk Ballet of Seoul in *Chunsa Chum* (Dance of the Angels). (Photograph © 1993 by Jack Vartoogian; used by permission.)

Both the number and variety of specialty dancers who performed in vaudeville in the last decade of the nineteenth century were remarkable; routines using every imaginable prop were created. Five of the most talented of the "specialty" artists—Loie Fuller, La Belle Otéro, Carmencita, Ruth St. Denis, and Isadora Duncan—all made dancing debuts between 1890 and 1893 and were widely copied. Carmencita, the imperious Spanish beauty, sometimes used a fan. Visitors to the World's Columbian Exposition in Chicago in 1893 were introduced to the *danse du ventre* of "Little Egypt" (actually a belly dancer from Damascus, Fahreda Mahzar), and stages across the United States filled with imitations, all with flying skirts and many with fans. Forty years later, also in Chicago, this development reached its pinnacle.

Revelation of the feminine form became increasingly prevalent in vaudeville. Part of the appeal of Fuller's *Serpentine Dance* was the fact that viewers could see her full silhouette through the shimmering transparencies that she swirled around herself. "Transformation dances," in which the artist removed a layer of costume to indicate the beginning of each new routine, were widely performed and provided the structure to St. Denis's *O-Mika*. St. Denis tantalizingly shed a cloak and five kimonos to reveal, in a blue chiffon garment, that she was not the perceived courtesan but an incarnation of the Japanese goddess of mercy. Sex mixed with exoticism became an ever-hotter ticket.

Beginning with the *Follies of 1907*, Florenz Ziegfeld and his initial director-choreographer, Julian Mitchell, refined the musical revue as the theatrical vehicle that perfectly reflected whatever was perceived to be the newest and most glamorous over the next two decades. With *Ziegfeld's Midnight Frolic*, which ran at the New Amsterdam Theater Roof in the period 1912–1929, the producer began to go beyond the short skirts of his chorines and show girls ultimately to present artfully veiled feminine nudity in symphonic montages, often designed by Ben Ali Hagen. When World War I formally concluded in 1919, American soldiers returned to find a changed landscape at home, where bobbed hair and short hemlines went hand-in-hand with a more open attitude toward the human body and sex.

The jazz age flirted with naughtiness, and nudes presented "aesthetically" became a racy style in photography and on the stage. In addition to Ziegfeld's lavish productions, the 1920s saw the emergence of a profusion of revues like *Greenwich Village Follies*, *Earl Carroll's Vanities*, *George White's Scandals*, *The Passing Show* of the Shuberts, *Grand Street Follies*, *Blackbirds*, London imports by Lew Leslie and Charles B. Cochran, and a host of lesser efforts, nearly all of which featured partly nude feminine forms. In 1923 Cleveland, Carrie Finnell, a modestly talented tap dancer, tried hopelessly to hold her audience's attention. Desperate to extend her vaudeville run, Finnell announced that she would take off an additional article of clothing each week during her tap number. By the end of fifty-two weeks she was performing completely in the nude, having played to sold-out houses for a year and in the process invented the art of striptease—later brought to such an acme of performance by Gypsy Rose Lee that H. L. Mencken described her as an "ecdysiast."

To pursue her study of ballet and to find work, Helen Gould Beck and her mother migrated from a farm in the Ozarks to Chicago during the Great Depression. A new life called for a new identity, so the young woman, naming herself after an atlas, became Sally Rand. She found a job as a dancer in a small club and went to a costume house to shop for an appropriately short dress. Instead she found two enormous fans made of white ostrich feathers and bought them on credit for $250. As a six-year-old, Rand had been inspired to dance by seeing Anna Pavlova perform in Kansas City. She later told Jane Everhart of the *Village Voice* (8 June 1972) that her wish since childhood had been to make choreography to evoke "the graceful flights of herons I'd seen over my grandfather's farm in Missouri." Rand created a dance to Debussy's "Clair de Lune" and to Chopin's Waltz in C-sharp Minor. She used very dim blue lights and the two seven-foot fans, underneath which she was nude except for body makeup.

Opening day in Chicago of the Century of Progress International Exposition in 1933 was preceded by Mrs. William Randolph Hearst's Milk Fund Ball. Rand, wearing nothing but her long blond tresses, crashed the ball on a white horse to announce her upcoming appearances at the fair. Crowds streamed in to see her *Fan Dance*, and many credit Rand's act with bringing financial solvency to the exposition. A second fan dancer, Faith Bacon, was added to the fair's attractions. Visiting Chicago in 1934, John Martin wrote in the *New York Times*,

> In spite of the ubiquity of the cult of fan dancers, which has spread its doctrine from the world's fair grounds into the "Loop" theatres and its propaganda over the billboards in remoter districts, there is a most encouraging outlook in Chicago for the dance in its less flamboyant aspects.

Rand performed her *Fan Dance* more than fourteen thousand times and never altered a single detail. Her filmed performance, which is quite beautiful, shares many qualities with the earlier work of Loie Fuller. During the depths of the Depression Rand earned more than $6,000 weekly and was paid $20,000 for a short movie of her solo. While she presented her original *Fan Dance* for more than forty years, the artist expanded her repertory and also formed her own company, which included half a dozen women who were over six feet tall. Known as "Her

FAN DANCING. Using two seven-foot fans, Sally Rand performed her *Fan Dance* for mesmerized audiences for more than forty years. (Photograph by Bloory; from the Dance Collection, New York Public Library for the Performing Arts.)

Sexellency," Rand varied her performance venues to include appearances with the Chicago Lyric Opera, the Metropolitan Opera Ballet, and the Ringling Brothers, Barnum and Bailey Circus and to take on a number of dramatic roles on the summer theater circuit. A generous supporter of young artists, she sponsored a modern dance concert by Kohana at the Guild Theater in 1935.

"I never stripped," Rand frequently told the press. In the *Fan Dance* she wore nothing at all, and in the *Bubble Dance*, she merely unhooked her short, transparent tunic at the end. Rand was so widely imitated that American dance archives from the 1930s abound with photographs of nameless dancers posed with fans in a vivid gamut of costumes. In the theater one broader consequence of her influence was the complete transformation of burlesque by the late 1940s, from the initial focus on satiric comedy to an exclusive preoccupation with bare female flesh. Always regarded as a "class" act, Rand was invited to perform for international dignitaries at the Fan Ball held in 1966 at the Waldorf Astoria; she danced at Madison Square Garden in 1972 as part of *The Big Show of 1936;*

and in 1979 she was honored by having an entire number created to salute her in the Broadway production of *Sugar Babies*.

The wealth that Sally Rand experienced was not shared by all in her sisterhood. Faith Bacon, who was named the most beautiful girl on Broadway in 1931 by Ziegfeld and Earl Carroll and who later gained star billing in the *Congress of Beauty* at the 1939–1940 New York World's Fair, committed suicide in 1956 by leaping from a hotel window in Chicago. Phyllis Dixey, Rand's British contemporary who also was inspired by Pavlova, left the theater to become a cook and domestic servant. Dixey did nude tableaux as well as artful stripteases and was well known for singing an introduction to her fan dance that announced, "Suddenly I discovered my talents were all covered, so I bought myself a little fan."

During the nineteenth and twentieth centuries, choreographers of concert dance and ballet used the fan sparingly. In rebellion against the past, modern dancers rarely incorporated fans. Ruth St. Denis employed them only to denote period authenticity, as in her role as the Duchess of Marlborough in the 1944 Paramount film *Kitty*. In Martha Graham's *Night Journey*, however, the chorus wields abstract fronds created by Isamu Noguchi, and the choreographer wove them brilliantly into both the visual and emotional context of the piece. As a symbol of emotional fervor, fans probably have never been exploited more expressively than by Alvin Ailey in his *Revelations*. Fans are no more prevalent in ballet, where they usually indicate rank and cultural habits or serve as props for comic relief: the six princesses in act 3 of Marius Petipa's *Swan Lake* emphasize the gracious majesty of their presence with fans; in August Bournonville's *La Ventana*, the heroine flourishes her Spanish heritage with a fan; Kitri's variation in *Don Quixote*; the female dancers in "Tea," from George Balanchine's *The Nutcracker*, snap fans to underscore their Chinese origin; and the Stepsisters in Frederick Ashton's *Cinderella* and the Hostess in Bronislava Nijinska's *Les Biches* accent frivolous behavior with fans. An exception is *The Sanguine Fan*, a score by Sir Edward Elgar that was inspired by one of the many fans painted by British artist Charles Conder. Elgar's manuscript, lost for more than fifty years, was discovered in 1973. Choreographed by Ronald Hynd for London Festival Ballet, the work was given its world premiere in Monte Carlo in 1976.

BIBLIOGRAPHY

Armstrong, Nancy J. *The Book of Fans*. New York, 1978.
Blondel, M.S. *History of Fans*. Paris, 1875.
Brinson, Peter, and Joan Wildeblood. *The Polite World*. London, 1965.
Everhart, Jane. "What Do You Say to a Naked 68-Year-Old Lady?" *The Village Voice* (8 June 1972).
Ferrero, Edward. *The Art of Dancing*. New York, 1859.
Grove, Lilly M. *Dancing*. London, 1895.
Lawler, Lillian B. *The Dance in Ancient Greece*. Middletown, Conn., 1964.
Opera Nazionale Dopolavoro. *Costumi, musica, danze et feste popolari italiane*. Rome, 1935.
Towle, Matthew. *The Young Gentleman and Lady's Private Tutor*. Oxford, 1770.
Uzanne, Octave. *The Fan*. London, 1884.

FILM.   *Danza Exotica* (Official Films, c.1942), featuring Sally Rand and Faith Bacon. Other selected films are held in the Asian Dance Project, Dance Collection, New York Public Library for the Performing Arts.

CAMILLE HARDY

FARBER, VIOLA (born 25 February 1931 in Heidelberg, Germany), American dancer, choreographer, and teacher. Farber came to the United States at the age of seven, and became a naturalized citizen in 1944. While studying dance with Katherine Litz and music with Lou Harrison in 1952 at Black Mountain College she met Merce Cunningham and John Cage, both of whom would prove profoundly influential in her artistic development.

Farber became a founding member of Cunningham's company the following year, and went on to create roles in a number of his most renowned early works, including *Crises*, *Paired* (a duet with the choreographer), *Rune*, and *Nocturne*. Always a passionate, quirky, and unpredictable performer, Farber made an indelible impression as one of the great individualists of Cunningham's early period. The fiercely intense focus and reckless, off-kilter aura of her stage persona contrasted strongly with the cool classicism of Cunningham's other leading dancer, Carolyn Brown; the two were sometimes called the fire and ice of Cunningham's company.

In addition to studying with Cunningham, Farber also took ballet classes from Margaret Craske and Alfredo Corvino in New York City, and modern from Erika Thimey in Washington, D.C. While dancing with Cunningham she also appeared with other choreographers, taking the role of a vampire in Litz's *Dracula*, dancing briefly with Paul Taylor's early group, and performing with Peter Saul in a collaboration with composers David Tudor, Gordon Mumma, and Cage, all of whom composed and performed with the Cunningham company. Farber was also the only female pianist in the famous premiere twenty-four-hour performance of Erik Satie's *Vexations* organized by Cage in 1963, playing the first and last of the work's 840 repetitions.

Farber left Cunningham in 1965, and formed her own company in 1968. She quickly developed a compelling style, challenging to both dancers and audiences, multifocal in movement material and in its use of space. Farber incorporated improvisation into her rehearsal process and in the performance of some of her first pieces. In dances such as *Poor Eddie* (1973) and *Willi I* (1974), the febrile atmosphere that defined much of her early work

FARBER. Viola Farber dancing in her solo *Legacy* (1968), set to an *étude* by Chopin, at Judson Memorial Church, New York City. The dancer's elegant line, the element of drama implied by the looming shadow, and the touch of antic humor suggested by the baseball glove she wears on her left hand, are all typical of Farber's early work. (Photograph by Theresa King; courtesy of Viola Farber.)

reached its highest pitch, a dark, violent intensity that some interpreted as sadomasochistic, despite moments of tenderness. Farber balanced such heavy works with humorous pieces such as *No Super, No Boiler* (1974) and *Lead Us Not into Penn Station* (1975). The early 1970s also saw quiet pieces like *Dune* and *Nightshade,* the latter choreographed to Beethoven's Sonata no. 14 ("Moonlight").

This use of classical music is exceptional for Farber, almost all of whose work has been either set to original music or danced in silence; composer Alvin Lucier was for many years her musical director. Other composers with whom she has worked include Jean-Pierre Drouet, Michel Portal, and Steve Lacy. Notable projects from the 1970s include *Brazos River,* a video collaboration with artist Robert Rauschenberg and composer David Tudor, commissioned by the Fort Worth Art Museum and KERA-TV. Funded by a grant from the National Endowment for the Arts in 1974, Farber made site-specific dances for such places as the Bronx Botanical Gardens and the Staten Island ferry waiting room. By the end of the decade Farber began to relax the characteristic intensity, though not the complexity, of her choreography, with such pieces as *Sunday Afternoon* (1976) and *Private Relations* (1979).

Farber began her teaching career at Adelphi University (1959–1967), the Cunningham Studio (1961–1969), and Bennington College (1967–1968). In the late 1960s and 1970s she taught extensively in Salt Lake City and Colum-

bus, Ohio; she has also served on the faculty of New York University, School of the Arts, and taught master classes throughout the United States and Europe. Her distinguished reputation as a pedagogue and choreographer led to her appointment by the French government as artistic director of the Centre National de Danse Contemporaine in Angers (1981–1983). There she expanded the training program and amalgamated it with a professional performance company of French and American dancers, for which she created nine works (for example, *Villa Nuage* and *Oiseaux-Pierres,* both 1982). Concurrently, Farber was responsible for developing a teacher training institute in Paris. She has frequently returned to Angers as a guest teacher, most recently in 1996. In 1984 she joined the faculty of the London School of Contemporary Dance, returning there again in 1986; she also taught in London at the National Theatre Studio in 1985. Since 1988 she has been the director of the dance program at Sarah Lawrence College in New York state.

Farber has often combined choreography with teaching, making pieces for students of the National Youth Dance Company (1986–1987) in London; and for the Groupe de Ballet of the Conservatoire National Supérieure de la Musique in Lyon (1989). She taught summer workshops at California State University/Long Beach in 1978, 1982, and 1983, choreographing on the students and performing with her long-time dancing partner (and former husband) Jeff Slayton. She has also choreographed and taught for professional repertory companies, including Ballet-Théâtre Contemporain of Angers (1977), Ballet-Théâtre Français de Nancy (1980), London's Extemporary Dance Company (1986–1987), the New Dance Ensemble of Minneapolis (as a McKnight fellow in 1988), and, under the auspices of the United States Information Agency, for the CE DE CE company of Lisbon (1996). She has made commissioned solos for Emilyn Claid (director of Extemporary), Pauline Daniels, and Ze'eva Cohen. In Amsterdam she has been a guest teacher for Dansproduktie (1993), and in Brussels for the company of Anne Teresa de Keersmaeker (1986). Farber has also taught technique and choreography at many international festivals, including the American Dance Festival (1987, 1996), the International Summer Dance Festival in Arles (1983, 1989), and the American Dance Festival in Seoul (1990); in 1988 she gave a five-day workshop for young choreographers at the West Berlin Festival entitled "Issues for the '90s." Farber maintains particularly close ties to France: in 1990 she taught subsidized daily classes at the Théâtre Contemporain de la Danse for unemployed professional dancers; and in 1992 she choreographed, with Mathilde Mounier, *Ainsi de Suite* for former members of her French company, a piece that was performed at the Avignon Festival, and in Paris and Brest. Farber continues to perform occasionally, and in 1995 appeared in a collaborative duet entitled *Three Step (Shipwreck)* with her former student, choreographer Ralph Lemon, in his company's final season, at the Joyce Theater in New York City.

BIBLIOGRAPHY

Bonis, Bernadette. "Viola Farber." *Danser* (January 1993: 42–47.
Farber, Viola. "La virtuousité." *Marsyas: Revue de pédagogie musicale et chorégraphique*, no. 21 (March, 1992).
Livet, Anne, ed. *Contemporary Dance*. New York, 1978.
McDonagh, Don, ed. *The Complete Guide to Modern Dance*. New York, 1976.

CHRISTOPHER CAINES

FARRELL, SUZANNE (Roberta Sue Ficker; born 16 August 1945 in Mount Healthy, Ohio), American ballet dancer. Suzanne Farrell has been called one of the great dancers of the latter half of the twentieth century. It has also been said that she was probably the most important dancer to have entered George Balanchine's life. She inspired some of his major works, and she danced virtually the entire spectrum of the Balanchine repertory—from his earliest extant ballet, *Apollo* (1928), to his very last creation, *Variations for Orchestra* (1982).

Reared in a suburb of Cincinnati, Roberta Sue Ficker, who was called Sue or Suzi, began ballet lessons at the age of eight at the Cincinnati College Conservatory of Music under Marian La Cour. When she was fourteen she was seen by Diana Adams, who was auditioning dancers for scholarships at the School of American Ballet under the auspices of the Ford Foundation. Adams recommended that the teenager go to New York to audition for Balanchine; upon doing so, she was awarded a scholarship to the school and given a grant to cover tuition at the Professional Children's School. She began her classes at the School of American Ballet in the autumn of 1960, and after slightly more than a year of study, she was invited to join the corps of the New York City Ballet.

Within another ten months, Suzi Ficker had changed her name to Suzanne Farrell and had danced her first leading role, the part of the Dark Angel in *Serenade*. After that, she continued to add one leading role after another. Although she formally passed through the rank of soloist, she danced only leading roles after her first year with the company. In 1963, partnered by Jacques d'Amboise, she created the principal parts in two new works by Balanchine: *Movements for Piano and Orchestra*, in which she substituted for an indisposed Diana Adams, and *Meditation*, a pas de deux made especially for her and d'Amboise. To celebrate her promotion to the rank of principal dancer in 1965, Balanchine composed an evening-length ballet for her, *Don Quxiote*, in which he danced opposite her in the role of the Don. [*See* Don Quixote, *article on* Balanchine Production.] In subsequent years, he created roles for her in *Brahms-Schoenberg Quartet* (1966), the *Diamonds* section of *Jewels* (1967), *Metastaseis & Pithoprakta*, *Slaughter on Tenth Avenue*, and *Requiem Canticles* (all, 1968).

By 1969, to many observers (including the public, company members, and company management), Farrell had become too prominent, too powerful. She had virtual ownership of leading roles in some three dozen ballets; there was never an understudy for a Farrell part. Her favored status within the company generated, not unnaturally, a good deal of resentment. Balanchine was clearly infatuated with her, and many people accused him of focusing his attention on her to the detriment of the company and other dancers. Thus, not everyone was unhappy when a personal crisis caused Farrell to leave New York City Ballet in the midst of the spring season of 1969.

While it is probably at least partly myth that Balanchine did not want his dancers to marry, it was, in fact, Farrell's marriage in February 1969 to Paul Mejia, also a dancer with New York City Ballet, that provided the pretext for her dismissal from the company. When Mejia was not cast in a coveted role at the Spring Gala Benefit the following May, Farrell delivered an ultimatum to the company management: if Mejia did not dance the role, both he and she would resign. To her dismay, their resignations were accepted.

FARRELL. George Balanchine and Farrell in *Don Quixote* (1965). (Photograph by Martha Swope © Time, Inc.; used by permission. Choreography by George Balanchine © by Suzanne Farrell.)

Subsequently, Farrell appeared as a guest artist with the National Ballet of Canada, dancing in *The Nutcracker, Swan Lake,* and *La Bayadère.* In the autumn of 1970 she and Mejia were invited to join Maurice Béjart's Ballet du XXᵉ Siècle, based in Brussels. The couple stayed with Béjart's company for a little more than four years, touring Europe, the Middle East, and North Africa. Eventually, the breach with Balanchine was healed, and Farrell rejoined New York City Ballet in the winter season of 1975. By then, she was a completely mature, finished artist. She immediately regained her former prominence, although without the former resentment, and she quickly became tacitly acknowledged as the company's *prima ballerina.* Mejia filled posts with several companies in various locales before settling down as associate artistic director and chief choreographer of the Chicago Lyric Ballet, directed by Maria Tallchief. Farrell often danced with this company as a guest artist.

By conventional ballet standards Farrell cannot be classified as having been either an allegro or an adagio dancer. Her first-rate musicianship and her formidable technique made her dancing as notable for its speed and clarity as for its heroic and elegaic qualities. During the latter part of her career with New York City Ballet, Balanchine made roles for her in *Tsigane* (1975), *Chaconne* (1976), *Vienna Waltzes* (1977), *Walpurgisnacht Ballet* and *Robert Schumann's "Davidsbündlertänze"* (both 1980), and *Mozartiana* (1981). Of her entire repertory of more than one hundred ballets, her roles in these ballets are among the most memorable.

The qualities of Farrell's dancing enchanted and excited audiences wherever she performed, whether with New York City Ballet or with other companies. Of many reviewers who attempted to describe her dancing, Lincoln Kirstein perhaps did as well as any, and better than most: "When she dances it is not only a body in motion but an apparatus analyzed and directed by operating intelligence. It is as if some sort of radium slumbers but is always present and ready in her corporal center; when ignited, it glows to white heat" (Kirstein, 1978).

After Balanchine's death in 1983, Farrell continued to be the principal interpreter of his works at New York City Ballet, although her repertory was much diminished. The new director of the company was Peter Martins, her most frequent partner for almost a decade. Just before he retired from the stage, in December 1983, he and Farrell

FARRELL. In April 1983 Farrell appeared as a guest artist with the Chicago City Ballet, in a role that Balanchine created for her in his 1975 ballet *Tzigane.* (Photograph by Steven Caras; from the archives at Jacob's Pillow, Becket, Massachusetts. Choreography by George Balanchine © by Suzanne Farrell.)

made their last official appearance together, as the Sugarplum Fairy and her cavalier in *The Nutcracker*. This was a memorable event, as it also marked the company's one-thousandth performance of Balanchine's Christmas classic. Although plagued by hip trouble, Farrell continued to dance in selected works for the next three years, until she could no longer perform. Following hip-replacement surgery in February 1987, she made a triumphant return to the stage in January 1988 in the "Rosenkavalier" section of *Vienna Waltzes*.

In the autumn of 1988 Farrell was invited by the Balanchine Trust to go to Leningrad to stage *Scotch Symphony* for the Kirov Ballet. At the instigation of Oleg Vinogradov, director of the Kirov, this work and *Theme and Variations*, which was to be set by Francia Russell, were to constitute "An Evening of Balanchine." When the program was presented in February 1989 it was the first authorized performance of Balanchine's choreography by a Soviet ballet company.

Farrell's farewell performance occurred later that year, on 26 November 1989. She danced for the last time with Peter Martins in a ballet he had made for her, *Sophisticated Lady*, set to the music of Duke Ellington, and in the solo role of the "Rosenkavalier" section of *Vienna Waltzes*. During curtain calls, she was showered with thousands of white roses. After her retirement, Farrell continued to act as a *répétiteur* for the Balanchine Trust, occasionally teaching and coaching roles at the New York City Ballet and guest teaching at the School of American Ballet.

In the course of her career, Farrell garnered a number of honors and awards. In 1965 she was given awards for merit by *Mademoiselle* magazine and the University of Cincinnati, and in 1976 she was the recipient of a *Dance Magazine* award. In 1980 she received the New York City Award of Honor for Arts and Culture and was the first dancer to receive the prestigious Brandeis University Award in the Creative Arts. In 1992 she was awarded an honorary doctoral degree by Middlebury College.

BIBLIOGRAPHY
Como, William. "Farrell on Farrell" (interview). *Dance Magazine* (April, May, June 1985).
Daniel, David. "Exits, Dancing." *Vanity Fair* (March 1987).
Daniel, David. "In Mr. B.'s Steps." *The New Yorker* (17 May 1993).
Farrell, Suzanne, with Toni Bentley. *Holding On to the Air: An Autobiography*. New York, 1990.
Kirstein, Lincoln. *Thirty Years: The New York City Ballet*. New York, 1978.
MacMahon, Deirdre. "The Constant Muse." *Dance Theatre Journal* 10 (Autumn 1992): 42–47.
McDonagh, Don. "Suzanne Farrell." *Ballet Review* 17 (Winter 1990): 62–68.

FILM AND VIDEOTAPE.   Farrell danced leading parts in three feature-length films: Balanchine's *A Midsummer Night's Dream* and Béjart's *Romeo and Juliet* and *I Trionfi di Petrarca*. She appears in a pas de deux in Herbert Ross's movie *The Turning Point* and in several episodes of "Choreography by Balanchine" on public television's *Dance in America* series. She can also be seen with Balanchine in a documentary film on Igor Stravinsky made by West German television in 1963.

DAVID DANIEL

FARRON, JULIA (Joyce Farron; born 22 July 1922 in London), British dancer and teacher. Farron began her ballet studies with Grace Cone, received a scholarship to the Vic-Wells Ballet School in 1935, and while still a student made her debut in *The Nutcracker* the same year. She was a full member of the company by 1936 and created her first role, Pépé (Julia's Dog) in *A Wedding Bouquet* in 1937. When the company staged *The Sleeping Princess* in 1939, her brilliant technique and speed were seen in her performances as both the Breadcrumb Fairy in the prologue and the Fairy Sapphire in act 3. Thirteen years later, employing the same qualities to dazzling effect, she would create Frederick Ashton's Neapolitan dance in *Swan Lake*, act 3.

The seeds of her future as a classical and *demi-caractère* dancer lay in those first few roles. A classicist of great charm and musicality, she was light and delicate in the White Couple pas de deux of *Les Patineurs* and the Valse in *Les Sylphides*, tart and witty in the Polka in *Façade*, and serenely composed as Dawn in *Coppélia*. Even more gifted as a *demi-caractère* dancer whose creations range from Belle Epine, the spiteful sister in *The Prince of the Pagodas* (1957), to the haughty Berta in *Ondine* (1958), she was splendid as Bathilde in *Giselle*, and particularly moving as the Betrayed Girl in *The Rake's Progress*. At the insistence of Ashton, when he became director of the Royal Ballet, she undertook the virtuoso ballerina role in George Balanchine's *Ballet Imperial*.

Farron retired in 1961. She returned to the Royal Ballet in 1964 as a guest artist and created one of her most vivid characterizations, Lady Capulet in *Romeo and Juliet*, the following year. For years the quintessence of majesty as the Queen in *Swan Lake*, in 1968 she became the first woman at the Royal Ballet to take the role of Carabosse in *The Sleeping Beauty*. In 1964 she also joined the staff of the Royal Ballet School where she remained, a valued and trusted teacher, until 1982, when she became assistant director of the Royal Academy of Dancing. In 1983, she was named artistic director of that organization and served it as director from 1986 to 1989.

BIBLIOGRAPHY
Anthony, Gordon. "Julia Farron." In Anthony's *A Camera at the Ballet: Pioneer Dancers of the Royal Ballet*. Newton Abbot, 1975.
Sorley Walker, Kathrine, and Sarah C. Woodcock. *The Royal Ballet: A Picture History*. Rev. ed. London, 1986.
Swinson, Cyril. *Six Dancers of Sadler's Wells*. London, 1956.

BARBARA NEWMAN

FAYER, YURI (Iurii Fedorovich Faier; born 17 January 1890 in Kiev, Ukraine, died 3 August 1971 in Moscow), conductor and violinist. Fayer studied music in Kiev, obtaining posts as violinist and orchestra leader in 1906 and becoming conductor at the Riga Opera, Latvia, for the 1909/10 season and at the Zimin Opera, Moscow, 1914/15. He continued to study violin at the Moscow Conservatory with Georgi Dulov, and after his graduation in 1919 he studied conducting further with A. F. Arends.

Meanwhile, he was appointed concert master and soloist of the Bolshoi Theater Orchestra in 1916, conductor in 1919, and chief conductor of the ballet in 1923. From then until his retirement in 1963, he conducted the majority of new productions staged by the company, winning the confidence, respect, and friendship of two generations of dancers, choreographers, and musicians. His achievement was the more remarkable for his having suffered since birth from retinitis pigmentosa, a condition of impaired eyesight that denied him all peripheral vision.

Fayer was nonetheless able to read music when held close, and early in his career he developed a facility for quickly and accurately committing scores to memory before conducting performances. This enabled him to work in close association with the stage and to give attention to matters of style, tempo, and phrasing carefully prepared in rehearsal. In this way, Fayer also acquired an expert knowledge of choreographic methods and content for classical to contemporary works. Many works were prepared in association with their composers, including Reinhold Glière, Aram Khachaturian, Sergei Prokofiev, and Dmitri Shostakovich.

The major productions Fayer conducted included *The Red Poppy* (1927), choreographed by Vasily Tikhomirov and Lev Laschilin to music by Glière, and a new version (1949), choreographed by Leonid Lavrovsky; the Bolshoi productions of *The Flames of Paris* (1933), choreographed by Vasily Vainonen to music by Boris Asafiev; *The Bright Stream* (1935), choreographed by Fedor Lopukhov to music by Shostakovich; *The Fountain of Bakhchisarai* (1936), choreographed by Rostislav Zakharov to music by Asafiev; a version of *The Prisoner of the Caucasus* (1938), choreographed by Zakharov to music by Asafiev; and *Raymonda* (1945), choreographed by Lavrovsky to music by Aleksandr Glazunov. Lavrovsky's first productions of Prokofiev's *Cinderella* (1945) and the posthumously staged *The Stone Flower* (1954) were conducted by Fayer, as were Lavrovsky's Moscow production of *Romeo and Juliet* (1946) and the Moiseyev version of Khachaturian's *Spartacus* (1958).

Fayer was also an outstanding conductor of the ballet classics, notably *Giselle, Swan Lake, The Sleeping Beauty, The Nutcracker, Coppélia,* and *Chopiniana,* to which Galina Ulanova, Maya Plisetskaya, and other leading Soviet dancers have paid tribute. During the 1950s, he con-

ducted most performances by the Bolshoi company on its first tours to western Europe and the United States. On these occasions audiences were frequently impressed by the orchestral playing, which complemented the dancing with emotional feeling and equivalent dramatic purpose; at the same time Fayer adjusted the tempo to show dancers to advantage without betraying the music's character.

His artistry in ballet conducting won him the Soviet Union's State Prize in 1941 and a designation as People's Artist of the Soviet Union ten years later. He remained in his Bolshoi Ballet appointment until poor health compelled his retirement in 1963.

BIBLIOGRAPHY

Fayer, Yuri. *O sebe, o muzyke, o balete.* 2d ed. Moscow, 1974.
Grigor'ev, Lev, and Iakov Platek. "Yu. F. Fayer." In *Sovremennye dirizhery.* Moscow, 1969.
Grigorovich, Yuri. *Balet: Entsiklopediya.* Moscow, 1981.
Obituary. *Dance Magazine* (October 1971): 17–18.
Plisetskaya, Maya. "Dirizhor Moskovskovo Baleta: K 75-letiyu Yu. F. Fayer." *Sovetskaia muzyka,* no. 1 (1965).
Slonimsky, Yuri, et al. *The Bolshoi Ballet Story* (in English). Moscow, 1959.

NOËL GOODWIN

FEDERAL DANCE PROJECT. A New Deal program, the Federal Dance Project (1936–1939) gave important support to American modern dance during its early development. In 1935, during the Great Depression, the U.S. Congress established the Works Progress Administration (WPA), and President Franklin D. Roosevelt, by executive order, added Federal I to provide productive employment for Americans engaged in the arts—including dancers within the Federal Theater Project (FTP).

In New York City, the American Dance Association (ADA), the New Dance League, and the Dance Guild organized to lobby for an independent Federal Dance Project (FDP). In January 1936, WPA chief Harry Hopkins asked Hallie V. Flanagan, head of FTP, to cooperate with ADA's executive committee (Helen Tamiris, Doris Humphrey, Felicia Sorel, Mura Dehn, Senia Gluck Sandor, and Roger Pryor Dodge) in establishing the Federal Dance Project. Don Oscar Becque, already supervisor of dance, was named New York director for the project.

Units were established in New York, Chicago, Los Angeles, Philadelphia, Tampa, Florida, and Portland, Oregon. Dancers were hired under four categories: ballet, modern dance, vaudeville, and teaching. Ballet was organized under the Zanfretti Ballet Company. In New York City, the modern dancers, because of their activity in initiating the FDP, dominated the project; few were transferred into other categories without protest. In cities other than New York, most participants were in the vaudeville category—which was active throughout the project—and many of

FEDERAL DANCE PROJECT. The fourth scene of Don Oscar Becque's *Young Tramps* (1936). Here, wandering Depression-era youths appeal to the Roosevelt administration's "Brain Trust" for aid. This production was the only new work commissioned by the Federal Dance Project in its first year. (Photograph from the Dance Collection, New York Public Library for the Performing Arts.)

these dancers were easily transferred to musicals or dance productions.

The goals—beyond economic relief—were to encourage a regional dance theater, to develop a common technique for including movements from all dance styles, and to broaden dances into full-length theater pieces that explored American themes, new choreography, varied accompaniments, and experimental sets.

In New York, with a budget of $150,000, Becque began work on a new piece, *Young Tramps*, and held auditions for 185 dancers, while the choreographers—Gluck Sandor and Felicia Sorel *(The Eternal Prodigal)*, Charles Weidman *(Candide)*, Humphrey *(Prelude, Parade, Celebration)*, and Tamiris *(Salut au Monde)* began restaging their dances for production. When Becque's auditions failed to fill the quota by April with dancers who fulfilled the requirement of being on relief, dancers from ADA picketed the FTP regional offices and were arrested. This kind of ADA political action became a model for many ensuing protests over auditions, transfers, and salary cuts and was encouraged or directed by the dancers' left-wing union, the City Projects Council (CPC). The CPC often helped bypass hiring requirements, by first shuttling dancers through their office and then the relief office just hours before audition times.

Embarrassed and threatened, Becque attempted to overcome what he saw as collusion between ADA and the CPC. He called for a mass reauditioning and requested the district WPA director to dismiss ADA's president, Helen Tamiris, from the project staff. In retaliation, a public meeting was held in November where Tamiris,

Humphrey, Nadia Chilkovsky, Fanya Geltman, Ruth Allerhand, and Paula Bass testified to Becque's incompetence and dictatorial attitude and decried compulsory ballet training for modern dancers. Becque was dismissed in December 1936. A series of temporary directors followed until reorganization in June 1937, when the Federal Dance Project was again within the FTP.

The FDP's first production opened 30 November 1936, with Gluck Sandor's *The Eternal Prodigal* (to Herbert Kingsley's music) at the Ritz Theater in New York. Despite his difficulties, Becque produced his *Young Tramps*, the project's only new work in 1936. Tamiris, the most dedicated and productive New York choreographer, restaged *How Long Brethren?* in 1937, produced a new dance in 1938, *Trojan Incident*, and in 1939, *Adalante*, which fulfilled Flanagan's ideal of a new dance drama. Humphrey restaged *With My Red Fires*, *The Race of Life*, and *To the Dance*.

FDP's Chicago unit, directed by choreographer-dancer Ruth Page, mixed classical and modern styles. In collaboration with Bentley Stone, Page choreographed *American Patterns* and *Frankie and Johnny* in 1938, and *Scrapbook* and *Guns and Castanets* in 1939. Other works produced included Berta Ochner's *Two Cautionary Tales* and *Midsummer Triptych* in 1938, and *Fantasy* in 1939; Grace and Kurt Graff's *Viennese Trilogy* and *Renaissance* in 1938; Katherine Dunham's *L'Ag'Ya* for the FDP's Chicago branch in 1938, based on her research in Martinique; and Eloise Moore's lecture-demonstration *Highlights in Dance History*. The Chicago unit also loaned dancers and choreographers for vaudeville and theater productions.

The Los Angeles unit, directed by choreographer-dancer Myra Kinch assisted by Bertha Wordell, used Flanagan's experimental concepts in American settings for *American Exodus, Bolero for a Bad Bull,* and *Gallop* in 1937, and *Introduction to Movement, American Holiday,* and *Let My People Go* in 1938.

The Tampa unit produced Spanish-style dances by Senia Salomonoff, Asa Thornton, and Josef Castle.

The Portland unit had Bess Whitcomb as director-choreographer. After attending FDP's Summer Theater at Vassar College in 1937, she produced theater-dance celebrations that included *Indian Celebration, Dance of the Flax Scutching Machines, American Negro Interlude* and *Bonneville,* and she performed throughout the Pacific Northwest.

The Philadelphia unit, under Malvina Fried with Carlton Moss (on loan from the New York Negro Project), produced *Prelude to Swing.* Exploring the development of American Negro music and featuring a Negro choral group and a swing orchestra, it included *Songs of the Plantation* and *Music of the City. Prelude to Swing* was acclaimed in June 1939, but it closed in two weeks since the project ended that year.

FEDERAL DANCE PROJECT. "Swing Low, Sweet Chariot" from *Prelude to Swing* (1939). This work, exploring African-American traditions in music, was produced by Malvina Fried and Carlton Moss for the Federal Dance Project in Philadelphia. (Photograph from the Dance Collection, New York Public Library for the Performing Arts.)

During the FDP's three-year history, hundreds of unemployed dancers got a chance to perform. Thousands of people got a chance to see some thirty dance productions, which charged nothing to $1.50 for admission.

Artistic and critical successes or failures were never considered in the decision to end the FDP. In this first partnership between the U.S. government and the arts, politics and bureaucracy too often interfered. Political opponents of President Roosevelt prevailed when they singled out parts of the WPA for budget cuts; within a few years, by 1942, all New Deal relief programs were ended. Martin Dies of the U.S. House Un-American Activities Committee had supported the House Budget Committee's choice of FTP for the first cuts, citing the project's radical left-wing image and accusing dancers of using art for communist propaganda. As World War II began, U.S. unemployment eased and the public welcomed the WPA cuts.

Despite its short life, the Federal Dance Project helped to promote modern dance in the United States and encouraged the move from short, disconnected concert pieces to full-length dances. Although a common technique was never imposed on the modern dancers of New York, tension between worker-dancer and artist-dancer sparked a new, nationalistic dance theater of left-wing radicalism and American populism that portrayed the New Deal mood. Unconcerned with the problem of technique, the other units mixed all types of dancers together to create full-length dance dramas about American life.

Inexpensive costumes and innovative set designs accompanied new music and the spoken word in FDP productions. By 1939, a Federal Arts Bureau and a National Dance Theatre became unrealistic goals.

[*For discussion of this topic in a larger context, see* United States of America, *historical overview.*]

BIBLIOGRAPHY

Skalski, Anna Lee. "Prelude to the Federal Dance Project: Political Organizing." Paper presented to the Society of Dance History Scholars, 17 February 1980.

ARCHIVES.   Dance Collection, New York Public Library for the Performing Arts. Library of Congress, Federal Theatre Project Production Bulletin Files and Correspondence Files. Research Center for the Federal Theatre Project, George Mason University.

ANNA LEE SKALSKI

FEDOROVA, SOFIA (Sof'ia Vasil'evna Fedorova; born 16 [28] September 1879 in Moscow, died 3 January 1963 in Neuilly, France), dancer. Upon graduation from the Moscow Theater School in 1899, Federova joined the Bolshoi Ballet. Between 1900 and 1909 her most important roles were in productions by Aleksandr Gorsky, including the Khan's Wife in *The Little Humpbacked Horse*, Esmeralda in *Gudule's Daughter*, Khita in *La Fille du Pharaon*, and Mercedes in *Don Quixote*. She also danced leading roles in the classical repertory, but these were not the type that stimulated her talent. She was an ideal interpreter of Gorsky's artistic conceptions. According to Vera Krasovskaya (1972), it was Fedorova's temperament and tragic passion, and "what is most important, her original and expressive acting that impressed the choreographer, who dreamed of sincere and strong characters in drama ballet." Of Fedorova's Khita, Krasovskaya writes, "The theme of savage slavery was depicted in tragic colors, expressing protest as well as a feeling of the hopelessness of this protest. Khita's dance showed a proud spirit that had been chained." The dancer was also praised for her interpretation of a possessed snake charmer in Gorsky's *Salammbô*. Fedorova appeared in Paris for the Ballets Russes 1909 season at the invitation of Serge Diaghilev. Immediately successful as the Polovtsian Girl in Michel Fokine's *Polovtsian Dances* from *Prince Igor*, she stayed on to dance in his *Cléopâtre* and *Schéhérazade* as well as other ballets before returning to Moscow in 1913. In 1922 she settled in Paris, where she taught and appeared in concerts. In the 1925/26 season she danced with the company of Anna Pavlova. Her last performances were with Diaghilev's company in 1928.

BIBLIOGRAPHY

Grigorov, S. *Baletnoe iskusstvo i S. V. Fedorova.* Moscow, 1914.

Krasovskaya, Vera. *Russkii baletnyi teatr nachala dvadtsatogo veka,* vol. 2, *Tantsovshchiki.* Leningrad, 1972.

Roslavleva, Natalia. *Era of the Russian Ballet* (1966). New York, 1979.

Smakov, Gennady. *The Great Russian Dancers.* New York, 1984.

Souritz, Elizabeth. *Soviet Choreographers in the 1920s.* Translated by Lynn Visson. Durham, N.C., 1990.

ELENA G. FEDORENKO
Translated from Russian

FEDOROVITCH, SOPHIE (Sof'ia Fedorovich; born 3 December 1893 in Minsk, died 25 January 1953 in London), Anglo-Russian scenery and costume designer. An elegant simplicity was the hallmark of Fedorovitch's stage and costume design. Frederick Ashton, for whom she designed eleven ballets, wrote, "Her method of designing seemed to be a process of elimination, clearing the stage of all unnecessary and irrelevant details." Although most closely associated with Ashton, she also designed for almost every British ballet company and for many major British choreographers, including Ninette de Valois and Andrée Howard. Two years before her death, Fedorovitch joined an advisory panel to the Sadler's Wells Ballet. She is considered one of the founders of twentieth-century British ballet.

Fedorovitch was born into a Polish family living in Russia (Belarus). She studied art in Kraków (then part of Austria) and returned to Russia, where she lived through the early years of the Russian Revolution. In 1920 she left for London and Paris, where she painted landscapes and portraits. Her works were exhibited in both cities and in 1928 she held her first solo show at the Beaux-Arts Gallery in London.

Her first design for a ballet was for *Les Nénuphars*, choreographed by Frances James in 1925; in 1926 she designed *A Tragedy of Fashion*, Ashton's first ballet. She did not, however, turn seriously to ballet design until 1932, when she stopped painting. At the same time she settled in London, where most of her stage works were produced. She became a British citizen in 1940.

Many of Fedorovitch's collaborators and critics have remarked on her economy of means. She used a limited palette and attempted to evoke an atmosphere rather than a detailed representation of a place or period. Ashton recalled that she attended rehearsals and was capable of changing her designs if the choreography took a new direction. He was particularly pleased with her designs for *Symphonic Variations* (1946), which he considered his "most flawless" ballet. The English critic Clive Barnes, however, noted her limitations: "She is not a designer of magnificence (imagine her tackling *The Sleeping Beauty*)," he wrote, and he faulted her for "a slight tendency towards the sentimental and pastel-coloured." He also felt that "nothing is wasted" in her designs.

As Cyril Beaumont has noted, Fedorovitch's sketches "were not wonderful drawings in themselves," but "more in the nature of notes, *aides-mémoires* to shapes and colours." The lack of detail in her sketches does not necessarily characterize the finished sets and costumes, which were more fully realized during construction.

Although most of Fedorovitch's work was done for ballet, she also designed plays and operas. Her most notable ballet designs include Ashton's *Horoscope* (1938), *Dante Sonata* (1940), and *Symphonic Variations* (1946); de Valois's *Orpheus and Eurydice* (1941); and Andrée Howard's *La Fête Étrange* (1940).

BIBLIOGRAPHY

Buckle, Richard. "Sophie Fedorovitch" (obituary). *Ballet Annual* 8 (1954): 59–61.

Fleet, Simon. "Sophie Fedorovitch as Ballet Designer." *Ballet Annual* 2 (1948): 73–79.

Fleet, Simon, comp. *Sophie Fedorovitch, Tributes and Attributes*. N.p., 1955.

Schouvaloff, Alexander. *Set and Costume Designs for Ballet and Theatre*. London, 1987.

Sophie Fedorovitch, 1893–1953: A Memorial Exhibition of Designs for Ballet, Opera, and Stage. London, 1955.

SUSAN AU

FEET. *For discussion of positions of the feet in ballet, see* Ballet Technique, *article on* Feet Positions.

FEIGL, EVA MARIA. *See* Violette, Eva Maria.

FELD, ELIOT (born 5 July 1942 in Brooklyn, New York), American dancer, choreographer, and artistic director. Feld grew up in Brooklyn and attended local dance classes from the age of six; later he studied at the School of American Ballet, appearing as the Prince in New York City Ballet's *The Nutcracker*. While at the High School of Performing Arts, he danced with the Pearl Lang and Donald McKayle companies and in *West Side Story*, eventually playing Baby John in the musical's stage and film versions. Later he studied with Richard Thomas.

At American Ballet Theatre (1963–1968), Feld was noted for his portrayals of character in *Billy the Kid* (title role), *Fancy Free* (First Sailor), and *Helen of Troy* (Hermes). The aspects of his dancing that have carried over into his choreography, however, are his athletic partnering ability and his emphasis on "real-life" energy rather than ballet convention and line. For American Ballet Theatre he choreographed his first ballets, *Harbinger* to music by Sergei Prokofiev and *At Midnight* to music by Gustav Mahler. These immediately earned him recognition as the most important new American choreographer since Jerome Robbins.

Feld resigned from American Ballet Theatre in order to have complete control of his work and organized his first group, the American Ballet Company. It made its debut at the Spoleto Festival in 1969 and became resident at the Brooklyn Academy of Music, with Barbara Fallis and Richard Thomas as advisers, Christopher Keene as music director, and nineteen to twenty-five young dancers of individuality and talent—such as Christine Sarry, who remained one of Feld's principal interpreters and partners for many years. The company relied primarily on Feld's own ballets, the most noteworthy exception being Herbert Ross's *The Maids*. Experiencing a fertile period, Feld was nevertheless unwilling to compromise on such matters as using live orchestras on tour, and in 1971 he had to disband the insolvent company.

Rejoining American Ballet Theatre for the 1971/72 season, along with some of his dancers, Feld choreographed the short-lived *Eccentrique* and his antiwar version of *A Soldier's Tale*, in which he danced the Pimp.

After a period of freelance work, Feld in 1974 formed the Eliot Feld Ballet (later called Feld Ballets/NY). For music he began relying primarily on chamber ensembles or recordings. The company's male dancers were typified by rugged individualism, but its women tended to display a stagy, doll-like quality, echoing the 1982 Feld title *Straw Hearts*. Besides occasionally appearing in large New York theaters, the company was at first a resident of the tiny Newman Theater of the New York Shakespeare Festival, and then for a time mainly toured outside New York. It made a State Department Bicentennial tour of Latin America in 1976 and its European debut in 1979. The year 1982 saw the completion of its own excellent Joyce Theater in New York. Feld and his then-executive director, Cora Cahan, showed great energy and resourcefulness in this venture and in the creation in 1978 of the New Ballet School, later called Ballet Tech, which selects and provides free classes for public-school children of professional potential; it graduated Darren Gibson as its first member of Feld's company in 1986. By 1996, Feld was placing major emphasis on feeding its graduates into the company. The company joined with American Ballet Theatre in 1986 to buy the Manhattan building housing their offices and studios, an important gain in the dance community's struggle against dwindling space.

Other than the works made for American Ballet Theatre, those that Feld has created outside his own companies have included *Meadowlark* for the Royal Winnipeg Ballet, *Winters Court* for the Royal Danish Ballet, *Jive* for

FELD. *Intermezzo, No. 2* (1984) was choreographed by Feld to the music of Johannes Brahms. From left to right, the dancers of Feld Ballets/NY are Cheryl Jones, David Lukcso, Megan Murphy, Timothy Cronin, Judith Denman, and Thomas Lemanski. (Photograph by Martha Swope © Time, Inc.; used by permission.)

the Joffrey Ballet, dances for the New York City Opera's *Song of Norway,* and an ice ballet, *Moon Skate,* for John Curry. Additional companies for which he has staged his ballets are the National Ballet of Canada, London's Festival Ballet, and the Royal Swedish Ballet.

Although the influence of George Balanchine, Antony Tudor, and Jerome Robbins was often clearly visible in Feld's early choreography, it had its own musical intelligence, contemporary feeling, and personal voice. Critics admired the dancers' natural demeanor and the use of classical technique and inventive lifts in the service of speed and a space-consuming flow of energy. "There is so much that is new in Eliot Feld's work," Marcia B. Siegel (1972) wrote, "that one forgets how classical he is. On the other hand, his company is so natural and honest, one doesn't notice how revolutionary he is either. . . . This type of aesthetic confusion accompanies every significant advance in art." Taking music rather than a story as his point of departure, Feld said, "My dance is always an expression of feelings. I think that's part of my talent. That's what makes the dance live" (Siegel, 1972).

Feld created a number of varied works that pass the test of innumerable viewings: *Harbinger,* a depiction of contemporary youth entirely through dance; *At Midnight,* with its yearning loner; the Brahms *Intermezzo,* with its romantic sweep; and *The Consort,* in which Renaissance courtiers turn peasants for a tormented bacchanale. Important pieces made early in his second company's existence include *Tzaddik* (music by Aaron Copland) and *Sephardic Song,* both drawing on Feld's Jewish heritage; the nervy and exhilarating *Mazurka,* to music by Frédéric Chopin; and a Fred Astaire and Ginger

Rogers tribute to music by George Gershwin, *The Real McCoy.*

The seeds of Feld's later, tightly controlled style were always present in his frank borrowings from other works, his tendency toward suite organization without development, and his ubiquitous lifts, in which the women were at first equal partners but later became subjects for manipulation. The use of highly stylized gestures of the whole body as choreographic motifs—witty in *A Footstep of Air,* emblematic in *A Soldier's Tale*—gradually replaced the early relaxed, natural arms and finally evolved into an often clichéed molding of static poses; Deborah Jowitt was "puzzled by the traces of puppet behavior that have entered his choreography on the arm of clarity and formality" ("Tighten Up, America," in *Village Voice,* 2 October 1978). While seeking a contemporary, unsentimental look in American (or Latin American) vernacular, usually with twentieth-century music, Feld's ballets became, in Siegel's words, "increasingly organized—the movement compressed into short, repetitive phrases, the floor patterns laid out in lines and small, carefully segregated areas, the group interacting on the simplest levels of unison or two-part canon" (Siegel, 1979). His extreme stylizations recall 1930s expressionism, but with its core of emotion replaced by sardonic detachment.

The elements of Feld's later work came together with a clear focus, however, in *Over the Pavement* (1982), set to music by Charles Ives. It uses only men. Feld again produces biting Americana and draws on the 1930s, an era that repeatedly engages his attention, but the depression-era workmen of this piece, warped by an assembly-line existence, seem to engage Feld's humanity, and they make a

FELD. Clay Jackson and members of Feld Ballets/NY in Feld's *Doo Dah Day* (1993), set to music by Stephen Foster. (Photograph © 1993 by Lois Greenfield; used by permission.)

fitting subject for expressionist treatment. His emblematic stylizations and repetition here produce apt and searing images.

Beginning with *The Grand Canon* (1984), Feld's output has included several works set to Steve Reich's music and influenced by postmodernism, using sneakers and ramps. In 1985 his company produced an important revival, the rarely seen Bronislava Nijinska ballet *Les Noces*. In 1997, Feld formed a new company under the name Ballet Tech. With the exception of Buffy Miller, Feld's longtime muse, the dancers are all graduates of his school.

BIBLIOGRAPHY

Emerson, Ken. "Feld's Foster." *Ballet Review* 22 (Fall 1994): 82–84.
Felciano, Rita. "Public-Private Partners in Ballet." *Dance Teacher Now* 14 (October 1992): 63–69.
France, Charles. "A Conversation with Eliot Feld." *Ballet Review* 3.6 (1971): 7–15.
Jowitt, Deborah. *The Dance in Mind: Profiles and Reviews, 1976–83.* Boston, 1985.
Reiter, Susan. "His Own Man." *Ballet News* 3 (June 1982): 10–14.
Siegel, Marcia B. *At the Vanishing Point.* New York, 1972.
Siegel, Marcia B. *Watching the Dance Go By.* Boston, 1977.
Siegel, Marcia B. "Early Feld." In Siegel's *The Shapes of Change.* New York, 1979.

FILM AND VIDEOTAPE. *The American Ballet Company* (Blackwood Productions, 1969). "The Feld Ballet," *Dance in America* (WNET-TV, New York, 1979).

MARILYN HUNT

FELDENKRAIS METHOD. *See* Body Therapies, *article on* Feldenkreis Method.

FEMINISM. *See* Methodologies in the Study of Dance, *article on* New Areas of Inquiry and Their Impact on Dance Research.

FENSTER, BORIS (Boris Aleksandrovich Fenster; born 17 [30] April 1916 in Petrograd, died 29 December 1960 in Leningrad), ballet dancer and choreographer. A 1936 graduate of the Leningrad Ballet School, Boris Fenster's teachers included Leonid Leontiev and Vladimir Ponomarev. As a student he assisted Leonid Lavrovsky in staging graduation productions. Fenster also served as soloist of the ballet company at Leningrad's Maly (now Modest Mussorgsky) Opera Theater, dancing the parts of Colin in Lavrovsky's version of *La Fille Mal Gardée*, Harlequin in Fedor Lopukhov's *Harlequinade*, René in Lavrovsky's *Fadette*, the Prince's Aide-de-camp in his *The Prisoner of the Caucasus*, and other character roles.

In 1940 Fenster completed the courses in choreography at the Leningrad Ballet School, where his teachers were Lopukhov and Lavrovsky. Under Lavrovsky's guidance, Fenster staged *Tom Sawyer* to music by Arseni Gladkovsky and *Bela* to music by Vladimir Deshevov. Even in these early works the choreographer displayed an interest in the literary themes that would characterize all his productions. Yuri Slonimsky (1967) reported that whenever they worked together on a libretto, Fenster "primarily assessed the elements of the dramatic structure in order to visualize the way his future production would be built."

Fenster's art was varied in genre and theme. He had a good sense of humor but was equally sensitive to tragedy. His most successful production in the comedy genre was *The False Bridegroom* (1946), based on Carlo Goldoni's play *The Servant of Two Masters;* he staged it at the Maly Opera Theater, where he led the ballet company from 1945 to 1956. Fenster's *Youth* (1949) was a significant Soviet ballet in the 1940s; in it the characters of Nikolai Ostrovsky's novel *How Steel Was Tempered* spoke in the expressive language of drama ballet. In the ballets *Doctor Oh-It-Hurts* (1948) and *The Twelve Months* (1954), the choreographer displayed his knowledge of child psychology. In *Taras Bulba* (1955), which he produced at the Kirov Opera and Ballet Theater, he created vivid national characters. That production ushered in a new phase in Fenster's artistic career. He evidently sensed that the expressive means of the drama ballet genre were nearly exhausted. Therefore, while retaining logically planned nar-

FENSTER. The climactic scene from Fenster's popular ballet *Taras Bulba* (1955), in which the Cossacks from the town of Sech break into a competitive dance, outdoing each other with feats of agility, strength, and daring. (Photograph reprinted from a Kirov Ballet souvenir program.)

rative, he allowed his characters, at moments of culmination, to reveal their inner world in extended solos and duets in which pure classical dance became abstraction. His untimely death in 1960—at the premiere of his last ballet, *Masquerade*, at the Kirov Theater—cut short his effort to intensify purely choreographic imagery.

Fenster was the chief choreographer of the Kirov Opera and Ballet Theater from 1956 to 1960. His awards included the State Prize of the USSR (1946 and 1949).

BIBLIOGRAPHY

Krasovskaya, Vera, and Boris Fenster. *Teatralnyi* 37 (1957).

Slonimsky, Yuri. *Sem baletnykh istorii.* Leningrad, 1967.

Swift, Mary Grace. *The Art of the Dance in the U.S.S.R.* Notre Dame, 1968.

NATALIA E. SHEREMETYEVSKAYA
Translated from Russian

FERNANDEZ, ROYES (born 15 July 1929 in New Orleans, died 3 March 1980 in New York), American dancer and teacher. Of French and Spanish parentage, Fernandez began studying ballet at the age of eight with the former Diaghilev dancer Lelia Haller in New Orleans. He made his professional debut in 1944 with the New Orleans Opera Ballet, and in the following year went to New York City for a few months to study with Alexandra Danilova. At the urging of Anton Dolin and Alicia Markova, he later returned to New York to take classes with Vincenzo Celli.

Fernandez joined de Basil's Original Ballet Russe in 1946 and from 1947 to 1954 also danced with the Markova-Dolin Ballet, Ballet Alicia Alonso, Le Grand Ballet du Marquis de Cuevas, Mia Slavenska Ballet, and Ballet Theatre (1951–1953). In 1954 he appeared with the Borovansky Ballet in Australia and led the company for two years as *premier danseur*. He rejoined the new American Ballet Theatre in December 1957 and soon became one of the company's most distinguished and popular dancers until he left in 1959. Guest engagements included a tour of the Middle East with the San Francisco Ballet in 1959, a season with the London Festival Ballet in 1962, and a world tour as the partner of Margot Fonteyn in 1963.

The handsome, dark-haired Fernandez shone in the nineteenth-century classics and also won critical and public acclaim in George Balanchine's *Apollo* and his *Theme and Variations*, and in Harald Lander's *Études*. His gift for drama was vividly displayed in Birgit Cullberg's *Lady from the Sea*, Antony Tudor's *Jardin aux Lilas*, José Limón's *The Moor's Pavane*, and Kenneth MacMillan's *Las Hermanas*, but Fernandez was noted primarily for his elegance, his bravura technique, and his exceptional qualities as a partner.

Fernandez retired from dancing in 1972 to devote himself to teaching. At the time of his death from cancer, he was professor of dance in the College of Arts at the State University of New York at Purchase, and he was on the faculty of American Ballet Theatre School.

BIBLIOGRAPHY

Goodman, Saul. *Dancers You Should Know: Twenty Biographies.* New York, 1964.

Obituary. *Dance Magazine* (May 1980): 12–13.

ARCHIVE. Dance Collection, New York Public Library for the Performing Arts, Louisiana State Historical Society.

PATRICIA BARNES

FERRARIS, AMALIA (born 1828 in Voghera, died 8 February 1904 in Florence), Italian ballet dancer. Having begun her dance studies under Claudio Chouchous at the ballet school of the Teatro Regio in Turin, Amalia Ferraris later became a pupil in the private school established by

Carlo Blasis and his wife Annunciata Ramaccini in Milan. Blasis considered her among his most successful students. In his writings, he spared no praise for the beauty of her bearing, the lightness of her dancing, and the precision and strength of her technique.

Ferraris made her debut as *prima ballerina di mezzo carattere* at the Teatro alla Scala in 1841, in Filippo Taglioni's *La Sylphide*, and in 1844 Blasis entrusted her with the part of Venus in his *"gran terzetto allegorico"* (great allegorical triptych) *Venere, Bacco e Amore*. She also danced in Genoa (1848–1849), Naples (1851–1852), and Venice (1855). She appeared in Rome (1854–1856) in several productions by Emanuele Viotti, among them *Ileria*, composed especially for her. She also performed in London at Her Majesty's Theatre in 1850, 1851, 1860, and 1863 and in Vienna in 1852, dancing in Jules Perrot's *Odetta*, reproduced by Domenico Ronzani.

From 1856 to 1863, Ferraris was a star of the Paris Opera, having made her debut on 11 August 1856 in the first performance of *Les Elfes*, choreographed by Joseph Mazilier. Her role as a stone statue that came to life allowed her to show off both her talents as a mime and the airiness of her dancing style. With Mazilier again as choreographer, she also appeared in the original cast of *Marco Spada*, along with Lucien Petipa, Louis Mérante, and Carolina Rosati, her rival on the stage, on 1 April 1857.

The culmination of Ferraris's success, however, came the following year, with her interpretation of the title role of *Sacountala*, conceived for her by Théophile Gautier and choreographed by Lucien Petipa. In *Le moniteur universel* (19 July 1868), Gautier wrote:

> Light as a dove's feather when she rises and firm as an arrow point on landing, she preserves the chaste and voluptous grace of Sacountala, her gentle resignation as a victim, and her quality of half flower, half woman. (Gautier, ed. Guest, 1986)

Later that year, Ferraris took leave from the Opera to go to Saint Petersburg, where she danced in Perrot's *Éoline, ou La Dryade* and in *Faust*, obtaining a triumphal success and securing a reputation equal to that of the great Romantic female dancers of the first generation.

In 1859, not long after Ferraris had returned to Paris, Rosati left the stage, and Ferraris became, indisputably, the queen of the Paris Opera. Her fame rose with her appearances in *Les Amours de Diane*, a *divertissement* choreographed by Lucien Petipa for the opera *Pierre de Médicis* (1860) by Józef Poniatowski. In 1861 she danced the leading role in two new ballets: Petipa's *Graziosa* and Pasquale Borri's *L'Étoile de Messine*. The latter work was a magnificent ballet that was a triumph for the choreographer as well as for Ferraris, who interpreted her role in a masterly and intense manner. Two years later, having left Paris, she appeared in London and Brussels. She eventually re-

turned to Italy, where she ended her career as a dancer, in 1868, at La Scala, performing in Paul Taglioni's *Leonilda* and in Hippolyte Monplaisir's *La Camargo*.

Ferraris later worked again in Paris, but as a teacher. She had settled in Florence with her husband, the poet Giuseppe Torre, who was at her side throughout her active life. Considered "a new Taglioni" for the grace and lightness of her dancing, she knew how to fuse harmoniously the characteristics of the Romantic style with the brilliance of the highly virtuosic technique prevailing in the second half of the century.

BIBLIOGRAPHY
Beaumont, Cyril W. *Complete Book of Ballets*. London, 1937.
Blasis, Carlo. *Notes upon Dancing, Historical and Practical*. Translated by R. Barton. London, 1847.
Blasis, Carlo. *Delle composizioni coreografiche e delle opere letterarie di Carlo Blasis*. Milan, 1854.
Gautier, Théophile. *Théâtre: Mystère, comédies et ballets*. New ed. Paris, 1882.
Gautier, Théophile. *Gautier on Dance*. Translated and edited by Ivor Guest. London, 1986.
Guest, Ivor. *The Ballet of the Second Empire*. London, 1974.
Guest, Ivor. *Le ballet de l'Opéra de Paris*. Paris, 1976.
Rossi, Luigi. Ferraris, Amalia." In *Dizionario del balletto*. Milan, 1994.
Vazem, Ekaterina. "Memoirs of a Ballerina of the St. Petersburg Bolshoi Theatre," part 2. Translated by Nina Dimitrievich. *Dance Research* 4.1 (Spring 1986): 3–28.

ARCHIVE. Walter Toscanini Collection of Research Materials in Dance, New York Public Library for the Performing Arts.

CLAUDIA CELI
Translated from Italian

FERRI, OLGA (Olga Ethel Ferri de Lommi; born 20 September 1928 in Buenos Aires), Argentinian dancer, choreographer, and ballet director. Ferri studied ballet in Argentina with Esmée Bulnes. She also trained in Paris with Victor Gsovsky and Nicholas Zvereff, and in the United States with Héctor Zaraspe and Alexander Minz. In 1959 she was a guest artist with Les Ballets de l'Étoile, Paris, of Milorad Miskovitch, and in the same year she also danced with the Berlin Opera Ballet and the Munich State Opera Ballet. She danced on occasion with London's Festival Ballet (1960–1963, 1966). Her repertory included *Giselle*, *Swan Lake*, *The Snow Maiden*, and other classics. In 1962 she starred in *The Life of Fanny Elssler*, produced for the Belgian Television Network by Jack Carter. In 1971 Rudolf Nureyev selected her for the South American premiere of *The Nutcracker* at the Teatro Colón in Buenos Aires. She also danced with him in Argentina and in Brazil in *Les Sylphides*, *Apollo*, and *Sleeping Beauty*. In 1973 she made her New York debut at a gala performance of the National Ballet, Washington, D.C.; she was subsequently invited to dance with the Eglevsky Ballet Company.

From 1973 to 1976 Ferri danced with various companies but returned to the Teatro Colón as guest *prima ballerina*, choreographer, and artistic director of the company (until 1977). She gave her farewell performance at a gala production of *Coppélia*.

Ferri's international premieres included leading roles in *Romeo and Juliet* (with José Neglia) and in George Skibine's *Cinderella;* Jack Carter's *The Sleeping Beauty* at the Teatro Colón; Carter's *Señor de Mañara* in Paris; Vaslav Orlikowsky's *Peer Gynt* for the Monte Carlo Opera; *The Idiot* by Tatiana Gsosvky, in Berlin; and the London premieres of Carter's *Grand Pas de Fiancées* and *Swan Lake*. She was the first Argentine to dance Pierre Lacotte's *La Sylphide*. Since 1980 she has been artistic adviser to the Argentine Classical Ballet Foundation.

International critics have called Olga Ferri one of the great Giselles. In 1979 she was awarded the grand prize of Argentina's National Fund for the Arts. For several years in succession she was named "Ballerina of the Year" by dance critics. The Argentine government named her a Knight of the Order of San Martín of Tours in 1985 and bestowed other honors on her in 1990, 1991, and 1992.

[*See also* Argentina, *article on* Ballet.]

BIBLIOGRAPHY

Anderson, Jack. "Concerning Miracles, Sylphs, and Buenos Aires." *Dance Magazine* (November 1974): 22–26.

Caamaño, Roberto. *La historia del Teatro Colón, 1908–1968.* 3 vols. Buenos Aires, 1969.

Fumagalli, Angel. *Olga Ferri: Formación y análisis de una bailarina argentina.* Buenos Aires, 1967.

JUAN UBALDO LAVANGA

FEUILLET NOTATION (also known as Beauchamps/Feuillet notation). With the invention of his dance notation system in the eighteenth century, Raoul-Auger Feuillet revolutionized the dance world. Published in 1700, his *Chorégraphie, ou L'art de décrire la dance par caractères et signes démonstratifs* was conceived as a self-teaching device, not a way of preserving dance. Yet owing to its immense popularity throughout Europe, even today a large body of theatrical and ballroom dances from that period in both printed and manuscript forms can still be found in most archives.

This ingenious system answered perfectly the demands of the times, as choreographer Jean-Georges Noverre pointed out:

> The tracks or figures of these dances were drawn, the steps were then indicated on the tracks by lines and conventional signs; the cadence or bar was marked by little transversel lines which divided the steps and fixed the time. The air to which the dance was composed was noted at the top of the page, so that eight bars of choreographic notation corresponded to eight bars of music. By means of this arrangement, one succeeded in spelling out the dance, provided that one took the precaution never to change the position of the book and to hold it always in the same direction.   (Noverre, 1803)

The "lines and conventional signs" to which Noverre referred indicated the placement of the feet in the five basic standing positions and the six basic leg movements of the body in action: *plié, relevé, sauté, cabriole, tombé,* and *glissé*. Ornaments (such as *ronds de jambe* and beats) and changes of direction initiated by turns—one-quarter, one-half, three-quarters, or full—could also be added on the shaft of the step symbol. Further signs indicated whether the foot was still in the air, rested on the heel, or on the point on the ground, as well as basic arm movements. Also included in *Chorégraphie* were a "Treatise on Cadence," examples of castanets notation, and tables of symbols that recorded various combinations of movements in standard pas. A modern reader would find it difficult to reconstruct the steps correctly without the help of a complementary text, such as Pierre Rameau's *Le maître à danser*. At the time of its publication, however, the system was thought remarkably simple and as easy to read as the musical notation to which it is often compared. As it was the custom to learn in advance the new dances choreographed each year by a leading choreographer, the system made it possible to study by oneself and to send the latest *menuet, rigaudon,* or *sarabande* to a friend in the provinces or abroad, a welcome commodity in an age that looked to France as the center of taste and fashion.

Chorégraphie was reprinted three times in thirteen years, translated into English by John Weaver in 1706, and appeared in various "improved" versions in France, Germany, Spain, and Portugal. Voltaire (1751) ranked the invention among the "achievements of his day" and Denis Diderot (1763) devoted ten pages to the subject in his *Encyclopédie*.

To this day, a mystery still surrounds the authorship of the notation. On 28 April 1704, four years after the publication of *Chorégraphie*, Feuillet was sued by Pierre Beauchamps, Louis XIV's court choreographer and dancing master. Beauchamps claimed to be the inventor of the notation system and produced five volumes of symbols to prove his case. A parchment dated 1687, but neither sealed nor signed by the chancellor and, therefore, of no legal validity, granted him the privilege to engrave dances in his own system. A law court deliberated in favor of Feuillet, however, which seems to indicate that the two systems might have been altogether different.

Feuillet left two wills that are as yet unpublished. The first one is dated 6 August 1706 and the second, dated 7 April 1710, was amended on 30 May, two weeks before his death. The names and various signatures appearing on the documents are consistently Raoul Anger Feuillet or Raoul Anger, sieur de Feuillet. Feuillet's sister, his resid-

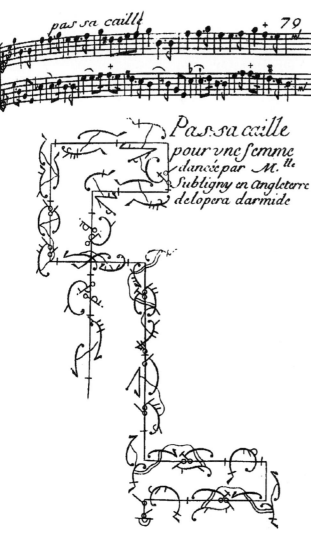

FEUILLET NOTATION. The first figure of "Passacaille pour une Femme," as published in Raoul-Auger Feuillet's *Chorégraphie* (1700). The dancer begins to follow the notation track at the bottom of the page and performs steps and spacial patterns as indicated. The sixteen bars of music correspond to the sixteen bars of the dance. (Dance Collection, New York Public Library for the Performing Arts.)

uary legatée, is simply called Perrine Anger. In these documents, Feuillet is said to be a widower taken care of by a governess during lengthy illnesses. The amendment of the second will concerns the publication *Chorégraphie*, which is left along with his violins and sword in the custody of Noël Dutot. Later, the name of Dutot is replaced by Étienne-Joseph Dezais, a man who subsequently bought Feuillet's business for a modest twelve-hundred livres.

[*See also* Ballet Technique, History of, *article on* French Court Dance; Notation; *and the entry on* Beauchamps. *For an additional example of Feuillet notation, see* Gavotte.]

PRIMARY SOURCES

Clément. *Principes de chorégraphie, ou L'art décrire et de lire la danse par caractères démonstratifs.* Paris, 1771.

Dupré, maître de danse. *Méthode pour apprendre de soi-même la chorégraphie, ou L'art de décrire et déchiffrer les danses par caractères, figures et signes démonstratifs.* Mans, 1757. Wholly inspired by Feuillet's method, although his name is never mentioned in the text.

Feldtenstein, C. J. *Erweiterung der Kunst nach der Chorographie zu tanzen.* Braunschweig, 1772.

Ferriol y Boxeraus, Bartolomé. *Reglas utiles para los aficionados a danzar.* Capua, 1745. Incorporates Feuillet's signs.

Feuillet, Raoul-Auger. *Chorégraphie, ou L'art de décrire la dance, par caractères, figures et signes démonstratifs, avec lesquels on apprend facilement de soy-même toutes sortes de dances.* Paris, 1700. 2d ed. Paris, 1701. 3d ed. Paris, 1709 (with J. E. Dezais).

Feuillet, Raoul-Auger. *Orchesography, or, The Art of Dancing by Characters and Demonstrative Figures.* Translated by John Weaver. London, 1706. 2d ed. London, 1710. 3d ed. London, c.1715.

Magny, Claude Marc. *Principes de chorégraphie, suivis d'un traité de la cadence.* Paris, 1765. Magny was a pupil of Feuillet, to whom he gives due credit.

Malpied. *Traité sur l'art de la danse dédié à M. Gardel l'Aîné, maître des ballets de l'Académie Royale le Musique.* Paris, c.1785. Feuillet's name does not appear in the text.

Peterson, Theodor Franz. *Praktische Einleitung in die Chorographie, oder Kunst einen Tanz durch Charaktere und Figuren.* Hamburg, 1769.

Peterson, Theodor Franz. *Praktische vollständige Einleitung in die Chorographie, oder Tanzzeichnungskunst, nach dem französischen Original.* Schleswig, 1797.

Rameau, Pierre. *Abbrégé de la nouvelle méthode, dans l'art d'écrire ou de tracer toutes sortes de danses de ville.* Paris, 1725. Rameau's "improved" version.

Siris, Paul. *The Art of Dancing, Demonstrated by Characters and Figures . . . Done from the French of Monsieur Feuillet, with Many Alterations in the Characters.* London, 1706. Siris's "altered" version.

Taubert, Gottfried. *Rechtschaffener Tantzmeister, oder Gründliche Erklärung der frantzösischen Tantz-Kunst.* Leipzig, 1717.

Tomlinson, Kellom. *The Art of Dancing Explained by Reading and Figures . . . Being the Original Work First Design'd in the Year 1724, and Now Published by Kellom Tomlinson, Dancing-Master.* 2 vols. London, 1735.

Tomlinson, Kellom. *A Work Book by Kellom Tomlinson: Commonplace Book of an Eighteenth-Century English Dancing Master* (c. 1708–1722). Edited by Jennifer Shennan. Stuyvesant, N.Y., 1992.

SECONDARY SOURCES

Dahms, Sibylle. "Historischer Tanz, Musikwissenschaft und Aufführungspraxis." *Österreichische Musikwissenschaft* 47 (October 1992): 581–587.

Derra de Moroda, Friderica. "Chorégraphie, the Dance Notation of the Eighteenth Century: Beauchamp or Feuillet?" *Book Collector* 16 (Winter 1967: 450–476.

Devero, Lisa C. "The Court Dance of Louis XIV as Exemplified by Feuillet's *Chorégraphie* (1700)." Ph.D. diss., New York University, 1991.

Diderot, Denis. "Chorégraphie, ou L'art décrire la danse." In *Encyclopédie,* vol. 3, *Recueil de planches sur les sciences, les arts libéraux, et les arts méchaniques.* Paris, 1763.

Garafola, Lynn. "Clio Meets Terpsichore." *Ballet Review* 14 (Summer 1986): 92–95.

Goff, Moira. "Court and Theatre Dances Published in England in the Early Eighteenth Century." *Factotum,* no. 33 (March 1991): 22–27.

Goff, Moira, and Jennifer Thorp. "Dance Notations Published in England, c. 1700-1740." *Dance Research* 9 (Autumn 1991): 32–50.

Harris-Warrick, Rebecca. "La Mariée: The History of a French Court Dance." In *Jean-Baptiste Lully and the Music of the French Baroque*, edited by John Heyer. New York, 1989.

Harris-Warrick, Rebecca. "Contexts for Choreographies." In *Jean-Baptiste Lully: Actes du colloque, Saint-Germain-en-Laye, Heidelberg, 1987*, edited by Jérôme de La Gorce and Herbert Schneider. Laaber, 1990.

Harris-Warrick, Rebecca. "Interpreting Pendulum Markings for French Baroque Dances." *Historical Performance* 6 (Spring 1993): 9–22.

Harris-Warrick, Rebecca, and Carol G. Marsh. *Musical Theatre at the Court of Louis XIV*. Cambridge, 1995.

Hilton, Wendy. *Dance of Court and Theatre: The French Noble Style, 1690–1725*. Princeton, 1981.

Lancelot, Francine. "Écriture de la danse: Le système Feuillet." *Revue de la Société d'Ethnographie Française* 1 (1971): 29–50.

Laurenti, Jean-Noël. "La pensée de Feuillet." In *Danses tracées*, edited by Laurence Louppe. Paris, 1991.

Little, Meredith Ellis, and Carol G. Marsh. *La Danse Noble: An Inventory of Dances and Sources*. Williamstown, Mass., 1992.

Noverre, Jean-Georges. *Lettres sur la danse, sur les ballets et les arts*. 4 vols. St. Petersburg, 1803–1804.

Rader, Patricia Weeks. "Harlequin and Hussar: Hester Santlow's Dancing Career in London, 1706–1733." Master's thesis, City University of New York, 1992.

Ritcheson, Shirley [Wynne]. "Feuillet's *Chorégraphie* and Its Implications in the Society of France and England." Ph.D. diss., Ohio State University, 1965.

Thorp, Jennifer. "P. Siris: An Early Eighteenth-Century Dancing-Master." *Dance Research* 10 (Autumn 1992): 71–92.

Voltaire. *Le siècle de Louis XIV*. Paris, 1751.

Wynne, Shirley S. "Reconstruction of a Dance from 1700." In *Conference on Research in Dance, 2d, Warrenton, Virginia, 1969*. New York, 1970.

RÉGINE ASTIER

FIELD, JOHN (John Greenfield; born 22 October 1921 in Doncaster, England, died 3 August 1991 in London), British dancer, teacher, and director. Field began to study ballet with Shelagh Elliott-Clarke at the age of fifteen, only, he said, "because I wanted to be in the theatre." As a performer, ballet producer, and company director, he more than realized his ambition. While dancing with the Liverpool Ballet Club, Field appeared in Ninette de Valois's *Haunted Ballroom*. He was seen by de Valois, who offered him a place at the Vic-Wells Ballet School. He joined the Vic-Wells Ballet in 1939 and advanced as far as soloist in such roles as the Blue Boy in *Les Patineurs*, the *Swan Lake* pas de trois, the jaunty Popular Song in *Façade*, and the Poet in *Les Sylphides*, before World War II and Royal Air Force service interrupted his progress. Upon his return to the company, Field stepped into principal roles, and he was officially appointed *premier danseur* in 1947.

The classical formality of *The Sleeping Beauty*, *Swan Lake*, *Giselle*, and *Ballet Imperial* suited him, as did characters more colorful than noble: the wicked huntsman, Orion, in *Sylvia*, for example, and Dorkon, a role he cre-

ated, in *Daphnis and Chloe*. A strong, reliable partner to all the company's ballerinas, he developed a real partnership with Beryl Grey, with whom he is best remembered in the classics and in the first cast of Frederick Ashton's coronation ballet, *Homage to the Queen* (1953). Field and Grey also danced together in an early stereoscopic film called *The Black Swan*.

Field gave up dancing early in 1956 to take on the administrative position of resident director of the Sadler's Wells Theatre Ballet; the following year he was appointed assistant director of the Royal Ballet in charge of the Touring Company, which flourished under his direction. His careful coaching gave the young dancers the full benefit of his experience, particularly in the classics, while young choreographers such as Kenneth MacMillan and John Cranko received repeated opportunities and constant encouragement.

In September 1970 the Touring Company was transformed into the New Group, and Field became co-director, with MacMillan, of the entire Royal Ballet. Differences about company policy, however, led to his resignation at the end of the year. After three years as director of the ballet at the Teatro alla Scala in Milan (1971–1974), Field returned to England and accepted the newly created post of artistic director of the Royal Academy of Dancing in 1975; a year later he was named director of the academy. From 1979 to 1984 he was the director of London Festival Ballet, where in 1980 he staged a new production of *Swan Lake*. In 1987 he was named director of the British Ballet Organisation.

[*See also* Royal Ballet.]

BIBLIOGRAPHY

Buckle, Richard. "John Field." *About the House* 3.7 (1970): 12–15.

Field, Anne Heaton, comp. *John Field, CBE: A Memorial Tribute*. London, 1992.

Field, John. "The Use of Benesh Notation in the Royal Ballet: John Field Talks to Fernau Hall." *The Dancing Times* (August 1968): 589.

Woodcock, Sarah C. *The Sadler's Wells Royal Ballet*. London, 1991.

BARBARA NEWMAN

FIGURE DANCES. Choreographies for the ballroom that are not processional dances, unadorned rounds, or dances performed by a couple hand in hand throughout are known as figure dances. A figure dance, whether it is called by that name or not, consists of a sequence of patterns, or figures, that the dancers—either individually or with partners—trace on the floor, using a variety of prescribed steps. Each figure is concordant with a segment of the accompanying music.

The earliest examples of figure dances are preserved in the Italian dance manuals of the fifteenth century. Certain *bassedanze* and most *balli* are figure dances, involving place changes and passing figures, S-curves, figure eights, heys, winding lines and circles, withdrawals and approaches. [See Ballo and Balletto; Bassedanse.] Many of the resulting patterns were purely ornamental; others were expressive of the theme of a given dance, such as the partner changes in Domenico da Piacenza's *ballo* "La Gelosia" (reconstruction in Brainard, 1981), the prowling circles of the "skirmish" in his "Verçeppe" (reconstruction in Brainard, 1981), or, even more pronounced, the figures of Domenico's *ballo* for ten, "La Tesara" (from *tessere*, "to weave"), in which four couples represent the shifting threads of the warp of a loom while two solo men glide forward and back through the formation like shuttles. Guglielmo Ebreo's *ballo* "Colonnese" is an early longways for six; the "Ballecto Chiamato Chirintana" for twelve (six couples) in the Siena version of Guglielmo's treatise, where it is ascribed to Domenico, is another. In both instances a set of figures is repeated progressively, bringing each couple into first place until at the end all are once again in their original positions within the formation. The English longways for six and for "as many as will" of the seventeenth century are constructed in exactly the same manner.

The same division of figure dances into ornamental and illustrative prevailed in the sixteenth century. The majority of the dances were for two to four dancers; those for six tended to go in a circle (for example, "Il Contrapasso Nuovo" in Fabritio Caroso's *Il ballarino* and "Barriera Nuova" in his *Della nobiltà di dame*). One of the rare longways is Caroso's "Chiaranzana" (in *Il ballarino*), whose figures included the ancient bridge and linear patterns up and down the set. Figures that were generated by the themes of dances include the tight coils, chains, and interlacings of Cesare Negri's "La Catena d'Amore" (in *Le gratie d'amore*) or the linear flight and pursuit figures in his "La Caccia d'Amore" (*Le gratie d'amore*). Two striking examples from France were given by Thoinot Arbeau: the weaving pattern of "Branle de la Haye" (in *Orchésographie*) represented the woven hedges found in the French countryside; "Les Bouffons" (*Orchésographie*), for four men, was an interpretation of hand-to-hand combat, with a square floor plan for the fighting passages, interrupted by neutralizing circular figures and ending in a Hey.

The concluding Hey, which was also present in many Italian figure dances (Caroso, Negri), in John Playford's country dances, and in theatrical choreographies (for example, Ben Jonson's masque *Pleasure Reconciled to Virtue*) was more than an ornamental configuration. For audiences and dancers alike, it had an ethical and cosmological significance (Miller, 1976, pp. 6ff.), representing the Great Chain of Being and the return of order and harmony after the diversities and dramatic conflicts of the preceding figures.

Starlike patterns that radiated from the center (as in Caroso's "Il Contrapasso Nuovo" and Playford's "Gather-

ing Peascods") were frequent in figure dances from the sixteenth century on. These were conceived from a spatial point of view and were meant to be seen from above, from the galleries and balconies that ran the length and width of halls and ballrooms.

A frequently recurring figure in Renaissance dances was a going around by the right hand followed by an outside curve left, then a going around by the left hand followed by an outside curve right. When followed by a two-hand revolution, this figure is the ancestor of one of the standard sets of figures of the *menuet* of the Baroque era: the presenting of right hands, presenting of left hands, presenting of both hands. The *passo e mezzo* "Ardente Sole" in Caroso's *Il ballarino* is a striking example of this famous configuration. The same dance also contains a rudimentary version of the other characteristic figure of the *menuet*, the reversed **S**, which during the first decades of the eighteenth century assumed a more angular **Z** shape. Guillaume-Louis Pecour has been credited with having effected this change, though it was by no means total.

While all the notated Baroque dances were figure dances, writers of the period applied the term especially to country dances and *contredanses*, which in turn led to the later *cotillons* and *quadrilles*. Edmund Pemberton's essay "For the further Improvement of Dancing: Being a Collection of Figure Dances / Of several Numbers, / Describ'd in Characters after / The newest Manner of Monsieur Feuillet" (London, 1711), which was designed for a girls' boarding school, contains several group minuets, a "Borée," a "Jigge," and country dances, all using an extraordinary variety of geometrical figures. Pemberton's dances, like the *contredanses* published by Raoul-Auger Feuillet in 1706, by Dezais in 1712, and by Gennaro Magri in 1779, included the classic figures of England's seventeenth-century country dances—Right- and Left-Hand Stars (called Moulinets in the nineteenth century), Single- and Two-Hand Turns, Dos-à-Dos, Heys, and progression patterns. With the help of the Feuillet notation it is possible to reconstruct the enigmatic "siding" figure of the English dance directions.

As the figures became more complex, the number of steps used in country dances and *contredanses* decreased to a basic few. Playford described only the double, the single, and the "Set and turne single" in his *Table* (1651). "Slips" (Playford's own term, probably for sideways chasing steps) occurred from time to time in the choreographies but not as frequently as Cecil Sharp's reconstructions suggest. Feuillet ("Avis sur les pas," in *Recueil de contredanses*, 1706) gave preference to *pas de gavote, pas de bourée, chassés de côté*, and *demys-contretemps; contredanses* in minuet meter used minuet steps; *pas de rigaudon* were preferred at the conclusion of figures, equivalent with cadence points in the music. Feuillet's linear tract of the figures is devoid of step symbols except in cases where a special effect was desired; musical measures are marked on the tract, as are the signs for taking and letting go of hands.

In country dances and *contredanses*, including eight-dancer "square dances" (the term was first used by Playford, 1651), the figures followed one another in a more or less predetermined sequence, as they did in many of the quadrilles of the nineteenth century, the immense variety of the figures notwithstanding (Wittman, 1981). Yet, even within the confines of a notated repertory, variation was possible. It was achieved by a method of construction called "to dance by the book" (Ger., *nach dem Buche tantzen*), which was used by, among others, the dancer, ballet master, and actor Joseph Lanz of Berlin in the late eighteenth century. Lanz put the designs of the 120 figures for his *anglaises* on individual cards numbered 1 through 6, placed them in a box (the *porte-feuille*), and provided a board with six compartments into which the dancing master, master of ceremonies, or leader of a ball could place the cards showing the figures of his choice to make up a new dance. All figures numbered 1 connected with all figures numbered 2, these with figures numbered 3, and so on, making sixty-four million different possible combinations for full-length or abbreviated four-figure *anglaises* (Taubert, 1983). [*See* Anglaise *and* Country Dance.]

The figure dances *par excellence* of the nineteenth century were the quadrilles, which were the subject of innumerable publications ("callbooks," "ballroom prompters") in Europe and the United States throughout the century. (For a brief survey of quadrilles, see Lamb, 1980.) Quadrilles usually consisted of five figures but could be expanded to six, as was the custom in Vienna; they were danced to music in clear eight- or sixteen-measure phrases, with as many internal repeats as the choreography required. The names of the most favored figures (Le Pantalon, L'Été, La Poule, La Pastourelle) were retained from earlier *contredanses;* La Trénis (The Trenise) was a figure named after the dancer Trenitz. One of the most famous quadrilles in five figures, "The Lancers," was danced in Ireland and Wales as early as 1817 and 1819, respectively, but was not seen in London until 1850.

In addition to the group figures such as the Grand Chain (or English Chain), the Ladies' Chain, rounds, crosses, and promenades, quadrilles frequently contained eight-bar solos that gave individual dancers an opportunity to shine. E. H. Conway's *Le Maître de Danse, or the Art of Dancing Cotillons* (New York, 1827) lists some fifteen different steps for quadrille solos. [*See* Quadrille.]

Figure dances are still performed today. Square dances are popular in both rural and urban areas of the United States; the heritage of the *contredanse* continues in the contras of New England, Kentucky, Louisiana, and French-speaking regions of Canada. The English Country Dance Society is devoted to the preservation of England's seventeenth-century figure dances; the Scottish Country Dance Society does the same for reels and the intricate figure dances of the Scottish highlands; sword dance and Morris dance teams flourish. Researchers and collectors of traditional figure dances, such as Douglas and Peter Kennedy, Sibyl Clark, and James Morrison, include in their collections new figure dances composed in the manner of the old by twentieth-century dance enthusiasts.

[*See also* Reel; Morris Dance; Square Dancing; *and* Sword Dance.]

BIBLIOGRAPHY
Brainard, Ingrid. *The Art of Courtly Dancing in the Early Renaissance.* West Newton, Mass., 1981.
Burford, Freda. "Contredanse." In *The New Grove Dictionary of Music and Musicians.* London, 1980.
Dick's Quadrille Call-Book, and Ball-Room Promptor. New York, 1878.
Feldmann, Fritz, and Karl Heinz Taubert. *Historische Tänze der musikalischen und choreographischen Weltliteratur: Von der Basse danse bis zum Menuett.* Die Tanzarchiv-Reihe, 15/16. 2d ed. Cologne, 1987.
Gerbes, Angelika. "Gottfried Taubert on Social and Theatrical Dance of the Early Eighteenth Century." Ph.D. diss., Ohio State University, 1972.
Guilcher, Jean-Michel. *La contredanse et les renouvellements de la danse française.* Paris, 1969.
Hilton, Wendy. *Dance of Court and Theatre: The French Noble Style, 1690–1725.* Princeton, 1981.
Lamb, Andrew. "Quadrille." In *The New Grove Dictionary of Music and Musicians.* London, 1980.
Little, Meredith Ellis. "Dance under Louis XIV and XV." *Early Music* 3 (October 1975): 331–340.
Little, Meredith Ellis. "Minuet." In *The New Grove Dictionary of Music and Musicians.* London, 1980.
Miller, James. "The Philosophical Background of Renaissance Dance." *York Dance Review*, no. 5 (Spring 1976): 3–15.
Morrison, James E., ed. *Twenty-Four Early American Country Dances, Cotillions, and Reels.* New York, 1976.
Porter, W.S., et al., eds. *The Apted Book of Country Dances.* London, 1966.
Richardson, Philip J.S. *The Social Dances of the Nineteenth Century in England.* London, 1960.
Sachs, Curt. *World History of the Dance.* Translated by Bessie Schönberg. New York, 1937.
Sweet, Ralph, and Kate Van Winkle Keller, eds. *A Choice Selection of American Country Dances of the Revolutionary Era, 1775–1795.* New York, 1976.
Sharp, Cecil J., et al. *The Country Dance Book.* 6 vols. London, 1909–1927.
Taubert, Karl Heinz. *Höfische Tänze: Ihre Geschichte und Choreographie.* Mainz, 1968.
Taubert, Karl Heinz. *Die Anglaise . . . mit dem Portefeuille Englischer Tänze von Joseph Lanz.* Zurich, 1983.
Van Cleef, Joy. "Rural Felicity: Social Dance in Eighteenth-Century Connecticut." *Dance Perspectives*, no. 65 (Spring 1976): 3–45.
Wilson, Thomas. *A Companion to the Ball Room.* London, 1816.
Wilson, Thomas. *The Quadrille and Cotillion Panorama.* London, 1819.
Wittman, Carl. "An Analysis of John Playford's 'English Dancing Master' (1651)." Master's thesis, Goddard College, 1981.

INGRID BRAINARD

FIJI. An independent nation of islands in the southern Pacific Ocean, approximately 1,500 miles (4,000 kilometers) northeast of Australia, Fiji shares Melanesian and Polynesian cultural elements, with stronger Melanesian influence in western Fiji and greater Polynesian influence in eastern Fiji (where close ties persist with the islands of Samoa and Tonga).

The *meke*, the principal Fijian performance genre, combines choreographed movement, vocal polyphony, and percussive accompaniment (in the form of bamboo stamping tubes, small wooden slit drums, and hand-clapping). *Meke* are composed by *dau ni vucu*, the trance-composition specialists, mediums who receive words, music, and movements from tutelary spirits. They rehearse the structured ensemble of singers who perform the words and provide some of the percussive accompaniment.

Early nineteenth-century Europeans and Americans in Fiji described a number of *meke* no longer performed today. There were dances imitating ocean waves and several varieties of animals, as well as whale's-tooth dances, dances celebrating the acquisition of goods, and dances accompanied by bamboo nose flutes. Today the *meke* most frequently performed include the *vakamalolo*, a sitting dance for men or women, and several standing dances: for men, the *meke wau*, a club dance; the *meke wesi*, or *meke moto*, a spear dance; and the *vakara ni iri*, a fan dance; and for women, the *seasea*, performed with or without fans, and the *meke iri*, a fan dance.

Most traditional Fijian dances employ linear patterns. Men's standing dances, which commonly depict historic or mythic battles in which dancers break formation and regroup to symbolize retreats and chases, are organized in ranks, with several central figures leading the action. Women's standing dances also involve linear patterns, which sometimes split to form mirrored or parallel formations.

Most individual dance movements in Fiji have no inherent lexical meaning. Instead, the small, finite core of dance movements used by the Fijian *dau ni vucu* illustrate and decorate the text by alluding to textual meaning. Both men's and women's dances emphasize arm, torso, and head movements. Men use broad, sharp, large movements, with elbows high, torso bent forward, knees flexed, and legs spread wide apart. Women's movements are smaller, subtler, more detailed, and more graceful; the torso is more erect, the elbows are lower, the arms not quite fully outstretched; there is more emphasis on wrist and finger articulation, head movements, and facial expressions.

European influence has increased since the 1950s. The English-derived term *danisi* refers to the movements and event structure of Euro-American popular dance. Young people enjoy dancing to Western rock and other forms of popular music, but the *taralala*, a post-missionary social round dance for couples, to guitar and vocal accompaniment, is popular with middle-aged and older Fijians.

[*See also* Polynesia.]

FIJI. A visual enhancement of sung poetry, most traditional Polynesian dances are based on complex arm movements performed, either sitting or standing, in rows facing an audience. Here, Fijian women perform a seated dance (*uakamoloto*). (Photograph by Charles H. Townsend; from the Department of Library Services, American Museum of Natural History, New York [no. 15019]; used by permission.)

BIBLIOGRAPHY

Quain, Buell. *Flight of the Chiefs.* New York, 1942.

Rougier, Emmanuel. "Danses et jeux aux Fijis." *Anthropos* 6 (1911): 466–484.

Thompson, Chris. "Fijian Music and Dance." *Transactions: Proceedings of the Fijian Society of Science and Industry* 11 (1966–1967): 14–21.

DOROTHY SARA-LOUISE LEE

FILLE MAL GARDÉE, LA. Choreography: Jean Dauberval. Music: popular songs and airs. First performance: 1 July 1789, Grand Théâtre, Bordeaux. Principals: Mademoiselle Théodore (Lise) and Eugène Hus (Colas).

With choreography by Jean Dauberval, Marius Petipa, Paul Taglioni, Bronislava Nijinska, Frederick Ashton, and scores of others and with music by Ferdinand Hérold, Peter Hertel, Léo Delibes, Léon Minkus, Cesare Pugni, and others, the ballets called *La Fille Mal Gardée* (The Poorly Guarded Daughter) form a dissimilar collection of works. Yet one thing draws all these badly guarded daughters together into a single family of, if not sisters, at least cousins—the story. It is a tribute to Dauberval's understanding of the balletic art that his *La Fille Mal Gardée* story has been and still is a popular favorite spanning some two hundred years and almost the entire globe. In fact, only one ballet is older—Vincenzo Galeotti's *The Whims of Cupid and the Ballet Master* (1786).

Dance historians have suggested two sources for the idea of *Fille*: Egidio Romualdo Duni's comic opera of the same name and an eighteenth-century print of a mother scolding her dishevelled child. Ivor Guest has cast doubt on the likelihood of the Duni connection, for Duni's music is not used in the ballet and Duni's story is different from Dauberval's. It is virtually impossible to determine what influence, if any, the print may have had.

Whatever the immediate source of inspiration, the basic outline of the plot upon which *Fille* was based was used endlessly for theatrical works of all kinds during Dauberval's day. Two young lovers are thwarted in their desires to marry by the girl's parent, who has another candidate in mind. A struggle of wits ensues at the end of which true love triumphs over authority and all are happy. The *Fille* characters too are drawn from a commonly used source, the *commedia dell'arte*—Lise and Colas are the young lovers; Alain, the clown or "zanny"; and Mother Simone, the "pantaloon."

Fille's common ancestry does not lessen the achievement of its creator, for he managed the difficult task of creating something fresh and original from old ingredients. And *Fille* represents a unique solution to the major problem faced by eighteenth-century *ballet d'action* choreographers such as Franz Hilverding, Jean-Baptiste de Hesse, and Jean-Georges Noverre. These men sought to make their ballets truly dramatic representations in which all parts contributed to the overall effect. Dancing, which was an essential part of ballet, did not readily lend itself to this purpose, for its abstract nature weakened its ability to present complex plots and detailed characterizations. The usual compromise was to introduce as little dance as possible. Dauberval's solution was special; he chose or created stories that lent themselves not only to nonverbal representation but to representation through dance. So successful was he at integrating dance into his action that to remove a dance sequence from one of his ballets was to render the whole work meaningless. It is this danceability of *Fille* that has led to its long success.

Synopsis. Act 1, scene 1—Mother Simone's house, a dairy. Lise enters seeking Colas, a young farmer; not finding him she leaves a ribbon on a tree and reenters her mother's house. Colas enters, finds the ribbon, and ties it to his stick. Lise enters, then Simone, and Colas is chased away. Female harvesters enter and are given work by Simone. She scolds Lise and puts her to work at the churn. Meanwhile Colas has slipped into the dairy behind her. When Simone departs, he enters kissing the ribbon, much to Lise's shy embarrassment. Colas pesters Lise for a kiss, but she is too shy. A noise sends Colas away. Simone returns and chides Lise for not doing enough work. Farmer Thomas and his son, Alain, enter and Lise is sent away while marriage arrangements are made. All leave for the harvest.

Act 1, scene 2—Fields and harvesters. Lunch is about to be taken. Thomas, Lise, Simone, and Alain enter. Dances begin and Simone takes part, giving Colas a chance to join Lise. Simone interrupts them, but the angry Thomas and his simpleton son leave. The harvesters perform a flute dance. A thunderstorm sends all fleeing for shelter.

Act 2—Inside Simone's house. Simone and Lise return from the harvest and sit down to spin. Simone has locked the door and drowses. Lise attempts to steal the door key, but Simone awakens and suggests that Lise should dance. She does so to the accompaniment of a tambourine. Colas is seen through the bars in the door. Harvesters enter and, after leaving a stack of sheaves, exit with Simone. Lise, left alone, sadly approaches the sheaves, only to be terrified as Colas, who had been hiding, leaps out. Simone returns, but not before Colas hides in her bedroom. Simone, suspecting that Lise has been speaking to Colas through the door, sends her up to the bedroom. Thomas, Alain, and the village notary arrive to finalize the marriage contract. Villagers arrive to celebrate. Alain goes to the bedroom to fetch Lise, but Colas leaps forward. The notary and villagers plead for the lovers and Simone gives in. General festivities follow.

This story, though rich in touching incidents, is simple and the characters are uncomplicated. There is sentiment and humor. Features such as the first-act ribbon add interest and help to explain the action. Although the characters can be well represented by the action alone, good opportunities help develop both Lise and Mother Simone in performance.

History. *La Fille Mal Gardée* (or *Le Ballet de la Paille, ou Il N'est Qu'un Pas du Mal au Bien,* as it was first called) premiered on 1 July 1789 at the Grand Théâtre in Bordeaux. Its success was opportune, for Dauberval was in need of reestablishing his popularity. His *Dorothée* (December 1788) had been a dismal failure; he was fighting with the theater management over money; and a power struggle involving the Chevalier Peicam was reaching its culmination. The row caused by Dauberval's refusal to employ the Bordeaux-born Peicam ended in the departure of the choreographer and his wife, Madame Théodore, from Bordeaux. They returned in April 1789, however, with a *lettre de cachet* signed by the king exiling Peicam from the city. Such was the prelude to the first performance of one of the most popular of ballets.

The year 1789 also marked the beginning of the French Revolution. The presence of everyday characters in *Fille* has prompted some writers to declare that the ballet represented Dauberval's statement of support for "the people." Yet no supporter of the common cause would have used the dreaded *lettre de cachet,* a symbol of royal tyranny. Furthermore, the story itself has no revolutionary message, and the characters are, in fact, formulated after aristocratic taste. It is true that during one performance, a revolutionary song was sung by one of the performers, but it had little to do with the ballet.

The musical score for *Fille* was, in keeping with common practice, an assortment of airs, arranged to support the ballet's dramatic action—for example, passages were borrowed from Franz Joseph Haydn. With no direct record of the first performance, the first Lise and Colas are not known, though it is likely that Lise was performed by Mademoiselle Théodore, and Colas by Eugène Hus. He was a principal dancer in Bordeaux at the time. A. Monsieur Brocard was the first Mother Simone (originally called Bagotte, a popular stage name).

Fille began its wanderings with a journey across the Channel on 30 April 1791 to the Pantheon Theatre in London, where it assumed the new title of *La Fille Mal Gardée;* Mademoiselle Théodore performed Lise and Charles-Louis Didelot was Colas. The London *Times* wrote on 2 May that "the ACTION throughout of DIDELOT and D'AUBERVAL renders totally unnecessary the descriptive word." On 16 May the same paper commented: "The Spinning Wheel and Tambourine scene may be deemed the perfection of Pantomime." In London, revivals and new productions carried the ballet well into the next century—the King's Theatre productions by James Harvey D'Egville (1799, 1800, 1802, and 1815); the Royalty Theatre production

LA FILLE MAL GARDÉE. One of the most successful versions of this two-hundred-year old ballet is Frederick Ashton's, created for the Royal Ballet in 1960. The National Ballet of Canada produced it in 1976 with Karen Kain as Lise and Frank Augustyn as Colas. There are seen here in the Ribbon pas de deux. (Photograph © 1977 by Jack Vartoogian; used by permission.)

(1802) entitled *Honi Soit qui Mal y Pense;* the Olympic Pavilion production (1808); the Surrey Theatre production (1825) by children under Jean-Baptiste Hullin; and the Adelphi Theatre production (1826).

It was not until 1803 that *Fille* made its way to Paris, in Eugène Hus's production at the Théâtre de la Porte-Saint-Martin. Here one of the great forgotten Lises, Madame Queriau, debuted. A Paris paper wrote of Queriau's performance:

> The girl is alone in her house, convinced that she is safe from all danger; suddenly her lover appears, the poor girl is struck motionless with astonishment and fright. This lover, who she had had such pleasure to see, is to her eyes a serpent ready to devour her: the efforts she makes to escape him, the struggles of fear and love, offer a new spectacle.

Although presented at various dancers' benefits for years, *Fille* did not receive its official Paris Opera premiere until 17 November 1828, when Jean-Louis Aumer produced it with a new score by Hérold. Marinette Launer

LA FILLE MAL GARDÉE. In 1981, more than one hundred and fifty years after its Paris premiere (1828), Heinz Spoerli was invited to mount a new production of *La Fille Mal Gardée* at the Paris Opera. He has since staged it in Basel, Helsinki, Düsseldorf, Oslo, Milan, and Hong Kong. This photograph was taken during a 1991 performance in Düsseldorf. (Photograph by Gundel Kilian; used by permission.)

danced Colas and Pauline Montessu was Lise. Marie Taglioni and August Bournonville also performed.

The ballet remained in the Paris Opera repertory until 1854; one of the most successful Lises was Fanny Elssler, who gave the role a deeply dramatic interpretation in 1837. In 1981 Heinz Spoerli produced a new version with music adapted by J.-M. Damase.

European productions of *Fille* proliferated—Salvatore Viganò in Venice, 1792; Lanchlin Duquesnay in Naples, 1797; Marseille and Lyon in the 1790s; and Guiseppe Salamoni in Moscow, 1800. It was in Russia that *Fille* found a well-guarded home; it has been produced there, relatively regularly, to the present day. In Saint Petersburg it was first presented on 2 December 1818 and revived by Dide-

lot in 1827. Fanny Elssler and Avdotia Istomina, favorites of Aleksandr Pushkin, helped maintain its popularity. Marias Petipa and Lev Ivanov collaborated on another Saint Petersburg production in 1885 using music that had been written by Hertel for an 1864 Berlin production by Paul Taglioni at the Royal Opera House. Alexandre Benois remembered the production and another famous Lise, Virginia Zucchi: "Zucchi gave a strikingly sincere and realistic performance. Here was a genuinely inexperienced girl who first felt the danger of temptation and then, moved by her passion for Colas, gave in to his tender entreaties without losing her charming shyness" (Guest, 1960, p. 50).

Russian productions and reproductions abound: Aleksandr Shiriaev, the Maryinsky Theatre with music by Hertel, Delibes, Minkus, Pugni, Anton Rubinstein, Riccardo Drigo; Aleksandr Gorsky, the Moscow Bolshoi, 1901; Sulamith Messerer and Igor Moiseyev in Moscow, 1930; Evgenia Dolinskaya in Moscow, 1932; Leonid Lavrosky at the Maly Opera Theater in Leningrad, 1937; Vladimir

Ponomarev in Kirov, 1943; the Leningrad Ballet School, 1959. Notable Lises have been Matilda Kshessinska, Olga Preobrajenska, Vera Trefilova, Tamara Karsavina, and Marina Semenova.

Most twentieth-century Western productions have followed one of the Russian traditions; Anna Pavlova in London, 15 July 1912; Alexandra Balashova in Paris, 1922; Mikhail Mordkin in Flint, Michigan, 13 October 1937; Nijinska at American Ballet Theatre, 1940; Fernand Nault at the American Ballet Centre Company, 1960. In the United States, *Fille* may have made its debut before 1800 in Philadelphia. The first certain performance was in New York in 1828.

Frederick Ashton's highly successful reworking for the Royal Ballet was first performed 28 January 1960 with Nadia Nerina as Lise and David Blair as Colas. "There exists in my imagination," wrote Ashton, "a life in the country of eternally late spring, a leafy pastorale of perpetual sunshine and the humming of bees—the suspended stillness of a Constable landscape of my beloved Suffolk, luminous and calm" (Guest, 1960, p. 9). It was this that Ashton tried to portray in his production, which he based closely upon the then-oldest-known libretto (Porte-Saint-Martin, 1803). The music was an arrangement by John Lanchbery based on the Hérold score discovered by ballet historian Ivor Guest. Designs were by Osbert Lancaster. Ashton's production has been staged by the Royal Danish Ballet (1964), the Australian Ballet (1967), PACT Ballet, Pretoria (1969), the Hungarian State Opera Ballet, Budapest (1971), the Bavarian State Opera Ballet, Munich (1971), the Royal Swedish Ballet (1972), the State Ballet of Turkey (1973), the National Ballet of Canada (1976), the San Francisco Ballet (1978), the Joffrey Ballet (1986), and the Houston Ballet (1992).

Ashton's tribute to Jean Dauberval sums up the old master's genius:

> But do not let us forget Dauberval: his is a masterly balletic conception, his characters are rounded and his action carries through to the end. The piece displays the most lively *sens du théâtre* in the clever arrangement of effective situations and charming tableaux. The interest is kept up to the end.
> (Guest, 1960, p. 11)

[*See also the entries on Dauberval and other choreographers mentioned herein.*]

BIBLIOGRAPHY

Brinson, Peter, and Clement Crisp. *The Pan Book of Ballet and Dance.* Rev. ed. London, 1981.
Chazin-Bennahum, Judith. *Dance in the Shadow of the Guillotine.* Carbondale, Ill., 1988.
Guest, Ivor. *La fille mal gardée.* London, 1960.
Guest, Ivor. "The Legacy of Dauberval." *Ballet Annual* 15 (1961): 104–108.
Guest, Ivor. "*La fille mal gardée:* New Light on the Original Production." *Dance Chronicle* 1.1 (1977): 3–7.
Guest, Ivor. *The Romantic Ballet in Paris.* 2d rev. ed. London, 1980.
Guest, Ivor. *Jules Perrot: Master of the Romantic Ballet.* London, 1984.
Kirstein, Lincoln. *Movement and Metaphor: Four Centuries of Ballet.* New York, 1970.
Lanchbery, John, and Ivor Guest. "The Scores of *La fille mal gardée*" (parts 1–3). *Theatre Research* 3.1–3.3 (1961).
Michel, Marcelle. "*La fille mal gardée,* ou La danse du tiers état." *Pour la Danse* (May 1989): 61–63.
Moore, Lillian. "'La fille mal gardée' in America." *Dance Magazine* (February 1961): 45–47, 64–65.
Percival, John. "The Well Guarded Daughter." *Dance and Dancers* (June 1992): 10–13.
Reynolds, Nancy, and Susan Reimer-Torn. *Dance Classics.* Pennington, N.J., 1991.

JOHN V. CHAPMAN

FILM AND VIDEO. [*To provide a historical survey of the use of the motion picture camera and its relation to dance, this entry comprises three articles.*
            Documenting Dance
            Ethnographic Studies
            Choreography for Camera
The first article explores the differences between an observer's viewing experience in a theater and watching the same dance on film or tape; the second focuses on the use of film and videotape in ethnographic documentation; the third considers use of the camera as part of the creative choreographic process. For discussion of related topics, see Film Musicals; Photography; *and* Television.]

Documenting Dance

One purpose for recording dance on film or videotape is to preserve the choreography by providing a visual supplement to, or a substitute for, the detail of written notation. Another is to attempt to translate the dance as a stage event to the screen, preserving and communicating, as far as possible, the values intended by the choreographer, expressed by the dancers, and experienced by the audience in the theater. This second purpose is a specific instance of the general form of film or video documentary.

The very first dance films were, in fact, simple records. The dance was shot in a single take, using a stationary camera and a fixed lens. Only the dancer moved; the camera and therefore the background were still. With no editing, time remained intact. Because dance is defined by movement in prescribed space over specific time, advances in film techniques that manipulate space and time by using moving cameras and editing, create problems when the two media interact. These problems have never really been solved because of the economic demands of performance and production.

Record films and tapes are still made for anthropological studies of dance as ritual, or as records of theatrical dance for restaging and study. Their intent is to record as clearly as possible, all the dancers, their steps, their entrances and exits, and the relationship of the movements to the total space. They must also show how music and choreography interact.

The purpose of documentary films, on the other hand, is to convey the *feeling* of the stage event, the choreographer's art, and the dancers' performance. The principles for such translations are extremely complex. The observer's experience in a theater differs profoundly from watching the same dance performance on film or tape. In watching a dance on film or tape, (1) the viewer does not himself make the bodily movements that change his field of view—the camera does; (2) the camera movement may unintentionally impose a sense of empathy with the choreographed movement; (3) the sensation of gravity is greatly diminished; and (4) it is very difficult to maintain the feeling of immediacy that a live theater audience experiences.

In live theater, the dancers move on the stage relative to the observer's fixed position. If the dancers are being watched from the balcony, their leaps are not as large in the field of view as they are when observed from below, nor are their legs as large relative to their heads and torsos. The viewer's own visual system assures him that these distortions are the consequences of his high-angle viewpoint. However, in a film or television performance it is the camera's movement and angle that provide the changing subjective viewpoint. The viewer's muscles provide no cues, neither correcting distortions of viewpoint nor explaining the shift in scene that has occurred.

Discrepancies in perception may also result from abrupt changes in view or cuts since it takes time to comprehend the content of an image when there is a cut from one shot to another. If the viewer is prepared to attend to motion that occurs in real time, as is required by the nature of dance, such differences in comprehension time are likely to affect the perceived rhythm of the dance in a way the choreographer may not have intended. Particularly disconcerting is the change from viewing the subject in close-up or in a medium shot full of crisp detail, to viewing the subject in a long shot, which has much less detail; while the viewer's eyes remain focused on the same plane (the screen), the change from detail to lack of clarity may then produce an unintentional beat even though no choreographic emphasis occurs, or an existing choreographic beat may be overemphasized. (The effect may be less acute in television because television has less resolution for detail.)

Camera movement also affects the viewer's empathy with the dancer. This may increase the viewer's attention to the film, but need not contribute at all to his perception of the choreography. In the waltz sequences from both Vincente Minnelli's *Madame Bovary* and Max Ophül's *Madame de . . .* the camera tracks with the main couple and holds them centered, stationary in the frame, against the whirling motion of the other dancers and of the background itself. The viewer sees this movement from the main couple's viewpoint. With a large screen or the viewer close to a smaller one, he will feel himself twirling, too, but without a hint of the choreography that produces the whirling visual field. When the choreography is important as an entity in itself, as opposed to being a component of a narrative film, a camera movement must not change it by investing some dance movement with more impact than the choreographer intended.

Another difference, from the viewer's perspective, between a live performance and a recorded one, is the diminished sense of the force of gravity in the latter. This loss is most noticeable when the quality of the movement is a primary distinguishing characteristic of the choreography—as in ballet, with its apparent ability to escape the ground, and in the stressed interaction between perceived weight and movement in modern dance.

The difficulty of translating tension and relaxation from stage to screen, as well as the loss of the sense of risk, result only in part from the diminished sense of gravity. In addition, the sense of immediacy experienced at a live performance is lost on the screen. The possibility always exists in film or tape that a fall or some other mistake has been eliminated, and that the multiple pirouettes have been constructed in editing, not through the effort and talent of the performer. A certain desire for perfection unattainable in live performance can be indulged in film. Another loss results when, in a filming session in which the performance is segmented into convenient units for camera setups, the dancers are prevented from expending the full energy they would in a straight run-through.

Further study is needed to determine what factors will make the audience perceive the effortfulness of dancers' performance. Perhaps fewer cuts will increase the sense of credibility, as Bazin suggests. Perhaps retaining small errors in performance will increase the viewers' sense of belief.

Broadcast television programs may still retain some of the immediacy inherent in the medium, but that is surely decreasing as viewers become habituated to post-production editing. In the case of live broadcasts, we may ask whether the viewers' knowledge that the dancing is occurring in real time compensates for the lack of post-production control during performance.

In the theater, the dancers not only respond to the other dancers but also project their personalities to the audience, while the members of the audience respond not only to the dancers but also to each other. In filmed and taped dance without an audience, the two communities are separated. On the other hand, in film and video the mobile camera has brought the image of the dancers much closer to the viewers. The danger here is that close-ups and medium shots may destroy the aesthetic distance necessary to maintain theatrical illusion. As Edwin Denby noted, dancers usually project to the back of the house, and their efforts seem exaggerated when the camera brings them close to the observer. Yet were they to accommodate their movements to such close-ups, they could not dance full out, and their performance, being attenuated, would lose power and energy. These difficulties in filming or taping dance are not insurmountable. Once they are aware of the main principles involved, filmmakers may enhance the documentary of performance while still preserving the choreographic intent.

Both film and dance are defined by change. Without it, the picture is a still and the dance is a frozen pose. Change in film may be produced by the subject's movement, by camera movement, or by cutting or dissolving from one camera view to another. Theoretically, an ideal rate of change that maintains the viewer's level of interest and involvement in the film is set by the complexity of the material in each shot, by whether the content of each shot is still or moving, and by the context in which that shot appears. Change in dance occurs through movement in fixed space and time. Spatially, the choreography determines the movement space within the performance area and the orientation and groupings of dancers to be perceived. Temporally, the choreography provides changes through movement that define its rhythm, emphasized by, or in counterpoint with, the beat of its accompaniment—music, drums, clapping, footsteps, and so on.

The various sources of visual change in film and dance interact with each other when the dance is being filmed. However, there are compensatory devices that can mitigate the differences in the experiences that are provided by live and recorded dance. A medium long-shot shows the full bodies of a couple or a soloist; it should provide enough movement on the screen to maintain the viewer's interest. Even in an adagio section where the actual movement is slow, filling the screen with only one or two figures results in a large area of motion on the screen at any one time. The movement may appear faster than normal when the figures are large, even though the dancing and its accompaniment remain synchronized.

The more rapid the cutting from shot to shot in a series of cuts, the faster the movement within the shots will seem. The smaller the screen space and the shorter the shot time, relatively speaking, the more quickly the movement passes through it, exaggerating the apparent change. In the case of a large group dance, or when the corps is dancing with the soloists, a wide shot is necessary to show everything. In such shots, the actual area on the screen covered by the movement of any one person will be very small. The filmmaker must intervene, so that the dance event being filmed remains visually alive: he must use a medium shot, the equivalent of opera glasses, to

maintain the interest of an audience whose expectations are at least the same as an audience viewing the performance live, and who are also affected by their expectations of standard film conventions. In addition, the documentary filmmaker must provide the extra dimension of performance value needed by professionals and scholars to supplement choreographic record films and written notation. A cut to a close-up of a repetition of steps by the corps would provide larger movement and greater change on the screen. However this solution creates two dangers. First, if choreographic repetition is filmed from different angles or in different sizes, the movement is not seen as repetition. Second, once the detail is shown, continuing the close-up will conflict with the urge to see the rest of the performance area: knowing that things are continuing offscreen produces an intellectual demand in the viewer for film change, even though the size of the movement provides adequate visual change on the screen. If a shot has enlarged the detail of one dancer among many, the audience will assume (or see) that other dancers are not standing still. If the director has earned its trust, the audience may feel safe in assuming that the other dancers are performing identical motions and that the overall pattern of their grouping (which is lost in the medium long-shot) is not the predominant feature of the choreography.

How does the director earn the audience's confidence? This would seem to be the fundamental question in filming dance. Its answer depends on who is watching the screen. Someone familiar with a particular piece may have different requirements than someone who is not.

At the start of a dance, it is probably necessary to show the whole corps when the dancers are moving. If there is a large corps as in *Swan Lake*, *Les Sylphides*, Marius Petipa's *La Bayadère*, and George Balanchine's *Symphony in C* and *Vienna Waltzes*, the need to see detail, and therefore to provide greater physical change on the screen, can be satisfied by cutting to a closer shot of several full-length figures from the center of the field. This technique is similar to the change in the level of attention that would take place if one were sitting in the theater watching the dancers, and follows traditional film-editing convention. The rate at which attention shifts from whole to detail and back to whole is a variable that is determined equally by the viewer's knowledge and by the amount and complexity of the movement. The visual questions that will occur to the educated viewer, and that the filmmaker should try to anticipate and answer as they arise, will be different from those of a novice in watching dance.

When there is only a small corps and one or two soloists the problem changes, and the choice of where to select details that will preserve the choreographic intent is far more critical. A cut to the detail of a solo or duet is appropriate when the corps leaves the stage or assumes a pose, or when representative movements of the group can be seen behind the main dancer. The return to a wider shot must be planned with care, taking into account not only the reappearance of the corps or the beginning of their movement but, equally important, the soloist's movement at that moment. The movement's value will be diminished because it will be much smaller in the return to the wider shot; moreover, any concurrent change in camera angle may be confounded with the movement itself. Movements in place, such as *promenades en arabesque*, pirouettes, and *fouettés*, will be least affected; they will appear tighter, if not actually faster, because they occur around an axis that remains the same. Another good choice for transition is within connecting sequences (what Merrill Brockway, original series producer/director of WNET's *Dance in America*, calls "traffic") rather than within movements in which progress is the distinguishing feature.

Once the wider view, now including the whole small group, has resumed, how long visual interest can be maintained again depends on the amount and complexity of the movement. If the steps and the spacing and the traveling of the dancers are all equally important, a shot including them all will probably provide enough change to maintain interest, assuming that it is visually comprehensible. Comprehensibility will be determined by such things as the angle from which the shot is taken, the background, and so on. An orderly, discernible progression of events is important to both film and dance, otherwise, as Rudolf Arnheim stresses ". . . there is no reason to remember past phrases of the spectacle, except perhaps to admire its variety." This is particularly true when film techniques obscure the inherent organization of the choreography, as in the RM Productions version of Balanchine's *Serenade:* many cuts were made from one small area of the field to another, or from one small area to the whole stage, motivated by the beat of the music, and not by the choreography's structure.

Not that music should be ignored. Music, or other accompaniment, provides another vital propellant for the progression of events. The influence of sound accompaniment is probably inversely proportional to the amount of purely visual change. In a wide shot, music may (for a time) compensate for the relatively small movements on the screen. In a full-figure medium shot, movement on the screen will normally maintain viewer interest, so the music's role will recede. If the choreography and music are complexly interrelated, careful analysis is needed to decide where cuts, and the beginning and ending of camera movement, may best be employed to serve the relationship of the musical and choreographic phrases. Visual changes should not be made when they will emphasize an unaccented beat of the music. Cutting on an accented beat may exaggerate the visual movement if the cut, the movement, and the climax of the musical phrase all occur at once. Alternatively, the impact of such a moment may be dissipated if the timing of the cut interrupts the completion of the movement. Used mindlessly, cutting on the beat may become a mechanical device, calling attention to itself, as in the aforementioned version of *Serenade.*

Other film techniques may conflict with the relationship between the dance and the music. Thus, a camera moving or zooming in on a pose at the end of a phrase disrupts the moment of rest in the choreography, unless the camera movement is clearly motivated by continuing music. Such a choice requires careful study. Rhythmic changes among different shots are particularly problematic. For example, if the dance movement has been divided so that the soloists are following the melody line while the corps is dancing to the pattern of the accompanying rhythm, a camera movement or a cutting rhythm based on the latter will upset the balance of the interaction of the two components.

It is clear that there are both desirable and undesirable interactions that define the craft of filming dance. The task of the filmmaker, in cooperation with the choreographer, is to discern and exploit those interactions in order to create for the film audience the satisfying experience of watching a live performance.

BIBLIOGRAPHY
Arnheim, Rudolf. *Film as Art.* Berkeley, 1957.
Bazin, André. *What Is Cinema?* Vol. 1. Translated by Hugh Gray. Berkeley, 1967.
Brooks, Virginia. "Conventions in the Documentary Recording of Dance: Research Needs." *Dance Research Journal* 19.2 (Winter 1987–1988): 15–26.
Brooks, Virginia. "Why Dance Films Do Not Look Right: A Study in the Nature of the Documentary of Movement as Visual Communication." *Studies in Visual Communication* 10.2 (1984): 44–66.
Denby, Edwin. *Looking at the Dance* (1949). New York, 1968.
Montague, Ivor. "Rhythm." In *The Movies as Medium*, edited by Lewis Jacobs. New York, 1970.

ARCHIVES.   Major collections of dance records and documentaries are held in the Dance Collection, New York Public Library for the Performing Arts; the Dansmuseet Archives, Stockholm; Deutsches Tanzfilminstitutes, Bremen; and the dance section of the Cinémathèque Française, Paris.

VIRGINIA LORING BROOKS

Ethnographic Studies

Ethnographic films are those that, according to anthropologist and filmmaker Karl G. Heider, reflect "ethnographic understanding." They are films about cultures and peoples that attempt to record their subject matter in an objective and truthful manner. Heider continues "film is the tool and ethnography is the goal." The unique qualities of the ethnographic film have been well summarized by Heider in his book *Ethnographic Film*. Jean Rouch, eminent French ethnographic filmmaker, emphasizes the process, suggesting that ethnographic film is a surrogate fieldwork experience resulting in a "shared anthropology."

Another descriptive term is used by John Collier, Jr., and Paul Hocking: "visual anthropology."

The ethnographic filmmaker struggles with the same problems as the dance filmmaker: how to capture truthfully and honestly a complex, dynamic three-dimensional time/space experience on a two-dimensional medium. As with a filmed performance of dance, to document that event

> uses techniques of filmmaking not to shape and change but to record the experience of seeing . . . [the filmmaker] does not add a new dimension of his own, but rather he puts back through his cinematic resources the dimension that was lost in the transfer [to film].   (Snyder, 1965)

The dynamic balance of emphasis between the subject and the medium is continually in question.

The history of ethnographic films is in fact the history of filmmaking as a whole. Some of the earliest Lumière and Edison motion picture footage attempted to document aspects of human culture and behavior. One of the more fascinating subjects for these filmmakers was dance. Perhaps the earliest ethnographic film concerned with dance may be Edison's film of the Hopi Snake Dance shot in 1889. Listings of these early films can be found in George Amberg's *A Catalogue of Dance Films* (1945). Examples of these early films still exist in the Library of Congress collection and the Human Studies Film Archive, Museum of Natural History, Smithsonian Institution, Washington, D.C., the latter being the major repository for ethnographic films in the United States. [*For the beginnings of motion picture photography, see* Photography.]

Jean Rouch considered Baldwin Spencer's footage of an Aboriginal Kangaroo Dance and rain ceremony, shot 4 April 1901, the beginning of ethnographic filmmaking. That dance, as the subject, points to the long relationship (which continues to exist) between ethnographic film and dance. Edward Curtis's work, shot in the field, includes important documentation of dance. Curtis, primarily a still photographer, filmed the Navajo Yeibechai Dance in 1906 and the Hopi Snake Dance 1912. In 1914 he made his more controversial and "staged" ethnography, *In the Land of the War Canoes,* which contained extensive dance sequences of the Kwakiutl of the Northwest Coast of North America. Another partially staged ethnography was Robert Flaherty's *Moana,* released to theater audiences in 1926, which also contains an excellent dance sequence. Flaherty's films were important in the development of the ethnographic film, but as Hollywood documentaries were not often regarded as ethnographic, because of his lack of anthropological training. Nevertheless, Flaherty's films served as models for later work in the field.

The 1930s included limited and varying efforts. Franz Boas's only film, *The Kwakiutl of British Columbia,* shot during the winter of 1930/31, included traditional Kwaki-

utl dances. *The Song of Ceylon,* made in 1934 by Basil Wright and John Grierson, contains a short but filmically brilliant sequence on the Kandyan Ves dancers. (John Grierson was often called the father of documentary film—documentary being the larger, generic term, of which ethnographic film is a subclass. Documentaries are generally broad in focus and filmic in approach.) In 1938, Gregory Bateson and Margaret Mead filmed *Trance and Dance in Bali.* Bateson's understanding of the significance of photography, both still and motion picture, as a new means of analyzing culture greatly added to the impact that it was to have on anthropological fieldwork and research.

The work of Maya Deren marked a significant turning point in experimental filmmaking and had an impact on the development of ethnographic filming. In 1943, her first film *Meshes of the Afternoon* heralded her as one of the leading experimental filmmakers. She was a pioneer in the use of the 16mm camera, and this, coupled with the professional quality of the image, opened doors to more realistic possibilities for taking the camera into the field. Deren's own approach to her films was highly cinematic, giving new insights into filmic time and space. In 1947, she was awarded a Guggenheim fellowship to go to Haiti to make a creative filmic essay on Vodun dance. From 1947 to 1951, she shot film on this subject but then realized that she was confronted with "a reality" that forced an abandonment of her "manipulations," as she states in her 1953 book, *Divine Horsemen: The Living Gods of Haiti.* Because she had not intended to make an ethnographic film and did not feel prepared to do so, she abandoned the project. Her film footage was edited posthumorously into the film *Divine Horsemen.* In that same period, *Dances of the Kwakiutl,* filmed by Robert Gardner and William Heich in Vancouver, British Columbia, marked perhaps the first effort to actually make an ethnographic study of a dance genre. Too short and choppy to be useful, its impact was minimal.

The first ethnographic film conference was held in 1948 at the Musée de l'Homme in Paris and might be said to mark the formal acknowledgment of the field. Organizations in Europe soon began to sponsor research and documentation of ethnographic subjects through film. These included the Centre National de Resources Scientifiques (CNRS) in Paris; the Centre Wallon de Films Ethnographiques, Brussels; and the Institut für den Wissenschaftlichen Film, Göttingen, with its *Encyclopaedia cinematographica.* These institutions remain major repositories for ethnographic films, and their collections contain many dance-related subjects. The Australian Institute of Aborginal Studies was also established to serve such a mission.

The Film Study Center of Harvard's Peabody Museum was established to collaborate on Bushman studies.

Filmed in the Kalahari Desert by John Marshall from 1951 to 1954, the first edited film that resulted from the work was *The Hunters*, finished in 1956 and released in 1958. The work of editing his footage was continued by Documentary Educational Resources, and the second film released was *N/um Tchai* (1966), about the medicine dance of the San people. Other films from this series, particularly *Bitter Melons* and *Melon Tossing*, contain dance-related materials.

Between 1961 and 1965, the Department of Anthropology at the University of California in Berkeley initiated an American Indian series. The project largely focused on the Pomo, a California Indian group. Films of this series include *Dances of the Kashia Pomo* (1964), *Kashia Men's Dances: Southwestern Pomo Indians* (1969), and *Sucking Doctor* (1963), a film that documents a shaman's curing dance. (A shorter version was titled *Pomo Shaman.*)

In the late 1960s, some African-based projects of note were made with support from the universities of Ife and Ibadan in Nigeria. *Studies in Nigerian Dance*, by Francis Speed and Peggy Harper, a trained dancer, choreographer, and ethnologist, were the first ethnographic films concerned with dance for which a dance-trained person was directly responsible. The three films *Tiv Women: The Tsough Dance; Miango Dance;* and *Kambari* were released between 1966 and 1970 and were followed in 1970 by *Gelede: A Yoruba Masquerade*. The supplementary written ethnography that accompanies each film also represents a first for the field of filmed ethnographic dance studies.

Ethnomusicologist Hugh Tracey and filmmaker Gei Zantzinger were responsible for four films made in southeastern Africa; *Zulu Country Dances* (1968), *Zulu Christian Dances* (1969), *Mgada Wa Mbanguzi* (1973), and *Mgodo Wa Mkandeni* (1973), the latter of Chopi dancers and musicians in southern Mozambique. All give thorough attention to dance and are accompanied by detailed ethnographic notes.

All of the above-mentioned films are cited in Heider's *Films for Ethnographic Teaching*. The availability of these films, and others, have had a marked effect on the development and teaching of dance ethnology. The University of California, Los Angeles, started offering the study of dance ethnology as a separate area of graduate studies in the early 1970s. Classes discussing and analyzing the function of dance in world cultures evolved because ethnographic films could bring these studies into the classroom.

Important ethnographic films of the early 1970s, such as the *Yanomamo Series* (1971), and *Ma Bugi* (1974), contained significant dance content. Hilary Harris, who had made *Nine Variations on a Dance Theme* (1967), worked with George Breidenbach and later Robert Gardner on the *Nuer* (1970). While sparse in dance materials, this film

is important to the dance analyst because of the kinesthetic approach to the study.

Allison Jablonko's *Maring in Motion* (1970) and the work of Stephanie Krebs (1970–1975), whose film *The Floating Lady* (1971) is a documentation of a Thai *khōn* dance drama, marked another step in the integration of ethnographic film and dance research. The ethnographic films they produced were tools for analysis rather than end products. Krebs used a "film elicitation technique" (Krebs, in Hockings, ed., 1995) to establish "conceptual categories of culture" (Krebs, 1975) while Jablonko (1963) developed a cinematographic micro-kinesic analysis of body movement style in order to analyze "the relationships between the movements of dance and the movements of daily activities" (Jablonko, 1968) among the Maring of New Guinea.

Both were influenced by nonverbal research, such as the work of Ray Birdwhistell (1970), and the Choreometric study initiated by Alan Lomax with the assistance of Irmgard Bartenieff and Forrestive Pauley (1968). The Choreometrics study produced its first film, *Dance and Human History* in 1976, *Palm Play* (1980), *Step Style* (1980), and *The Longest Trail* (1986). These studies were the first to use ethnographic footage for cross-cultural comparisons. Some films used in the study were commissioned by the Choreometrics project, which was sponsored by Columbia University and the National Institute of Mental Health; in addition they used existing footage from earlier ethnographic films. While broad in intent, one of the main criticisms of the work, was that the hypotheses and conclusions were drawn too early in the study before sufficient film samplings were available.

It was not until the late 1970s and early 1980s that videotaping began to be used in ethnographic documentation. This occurred because video technology had by that time produced a lightweight, compact, portable camera that was reliable in the field. The video camera had many important advantages; the first being the length of recording time. One could record continuously for up to an hour with the video camera, impossible with film technology. Instant playback was also available and synchronous sound was inherent to the technology. Ethnographic videotaping has had much more effect on research strategies than on shared ethnographic products. It allows for the careful and extensive coverage of an event without oppressive cost. Instant replay has encouraged the development of a new research technique, in which informants respond to the immediately viewed image. Robert Farris Thompson disclosed the significance of this approach in *African Art in Motion* (1974). Elsie Dunin of the University of California, Los Angeles, has done extensive work with south Slavs and south Slav immigrant communities in the United States and Chile. Her research, concerned with continuity and change in dance forms among immigrant populations, is grounded in this video technique.

Both storage and utilization are facilitated by the use of videotaping, which brings ethnographic tapes more readily into the library and classroom. Many universities and public libraries now have video viewing sections where one can select and study videotapes on a monitor with the same ease that one can take a book from the shelf. Videotaping has an advantage, because it is electronically recorded and transmitted, therefore it is easily disseminated. The future may see the sharing of ethnographic materials via satellite transmission from banks of research materials set up on a worldwide basis.

Because of constantly changing and improving technologies, it is hard to predict the next steps in the development of ethnographic research using film and videotape—and its impact on the research and understanding of dance in culture—but history seems to suggest that this alliance will continue and flourish.

BIBLIOGRAPHY

Amberg, George. "A Catalogue of Dance Films." *Dance Index* 4 (May 1945): 62–84.

Birdwhistell, Ray L. *Kinesics and Context.* Philadelphia, 1970.

Collier, John. *Visual Anthropology: Photography as a Research Method.* New York, 1967.

Deren, Maya. *Divine Horsemen: The Living Gods of Haiti.* New York, 1953.

Eaton, Mick. *Anthropology—Reality—Cinema: The Films of Jean Rouch.* London, 1979.

Heider, Karl G. *Ethnographic Film.* Austin, 1976.

Heider, Karl G., and Carol Hermer, ed. *Films for Anthropological Teaching.* 8th ed. Arlington, Va., 1983.

Hockings, Paul, ed. *Principles of Visual Anthropology.* 2d ed. New York, 1995.

Jablonko, Allison. "Dance and Daily Activities among the Maring People of New Guinea: A Cinematographic Analysis of Body Movement Style." Ph.D. diss., Columbia University, 1968.

Krebs, Stephanie. "Nonverbal Communication in Kohn Dance-Drama: Thai Society Onstage." Ph.D. diss., Harvard University, 1975.

Krebs, Stephanie. "The Film Elicitation Technique." In *Principles of Visual Anthropology,* 2d ed., edited by Paul Hockings. New York, 1995.

Lomax, Alan, ed. *Folk Song Style and Culture.* Washington, D.C., 1968.

Rouch, Jean. "The Camera and Man." *Studies in the Anthropology of Visual Communication* 1.1 (1974): 37–44.

Snyder, Allegra Fuller. "Three Kinds of Dance Film." *Dance Magazine* (September 1965).

Towers, Deidre, comp. *Dance Film and Video Guide.* Princeton, N.J., 1991.

ALLEGRA FULLER SNYDER

Choreography for Camera

The history of dance in experimental films begins with the work of Georges Méliès. Between 1896 and 1913, Méliès, often credited as the first avant-garde filmmaker, created approximately five hundred films.

In 1924, French painter Fernand Léger created *Ballet Mécanique* with the technical assistance of the American filmmaker Dudley Murphy. *Ballet Mécanique* has been described by film historian Arthur Knight as "a dance created out of the movement of levers, gears, pendulums, egg beaters, pots and pans—and incidentally, people." By not including theatrical dance in its subject matter, *Ballet Mécanique* suggested that dance for the camera might be defined in new ways.

The Dadaist ballet *Relâche* (1924) was probably the first live performance to include a film. *Relâche*, conceived by the painter Francis Picabia, was the final production of Les Ballets Suédois. The film, realized by René Clair, was shown between the ballet's two acts and has been shown separately under the title *Entr'acte*. Erik Satie composed the music for both the live and the filmed portions of *Relâche*. Although *Entr'acte* did not feature dancing, it did include amid its disparate images, frames, taken from below, of a ballerina who is gradually revealed to be a man. (It was in fact a woman wearing a beard.) Serge Diaghilev had turned down Picabia's proposal for his Ballets Russes company to work on *Relâche*. In 1928 the Ballets Russes did present Massine's *Ode*, with decor by Pavel Tchelitchev, which incorporated film projections by Pierre Charbonneau.

It was not until the 1940s that a filmmaker created a body of work that can be called film dances. Between 1943 and 1958, Maya Deren, an American, created six films. Deren was a poet who, before she began to make films, served as an assistant to the dancer/choreographer Katherine Dunham. Although only two of her films featured technically trained dancers, they all focused on human movement. Deren's own definition of dance was "the communication of meaning through the quality of movement."

Deren's first film, *Meshes of the Afternoon* (1943), a collaboration with her husband, filmmaker Alexander Hammid, uses the medium of film to convey a dreamlike experience that includes a mysterious figure, a key, a knife, and a house that rocks back and forth. In one sequence, as Deren (the protagonist) walks, each step lands her in a new environment: first on sand, then gravel, and, finally, concrete.

In *At Land* (1944), which also conveys a dreamlike experience, Deren is seen emerging from the sea, voyaging through life, and returning to the sea. Lengthy shots of static images and fast-paced montage sequences are used to emphasize the psychological dimensions of Deren's movements.

In *Choreography for the Camera* (1945) Deren filmed the Dunham dancer Talley Beatty performing a continuous solo dance amid changing environments: a leap that begins in a wood ends in a room; and a pirouette that starts in the same room is completed in the Metropolitan Museum of Art. The film ends with a leap filmed in reverse motion and sustained for longer than humanly possible, to communicate, in Deren's words, "the quality of release and ease with which a balloon mounts when it is suddenly freed." Throughout the film, the cinematic techniques of editing, reverse, slow and fast motion, panning, and the use of a wide-angle lens convey, as Deren put it, "the idea that in dancing one achieves a more magical relationship to space than one does in the course of ordinary walking."

A party sequence is central to Deren's *Ritual in Transfigured Time* (1946). In this film, scenes of initially spontaneous movements, expressions, and exchanges were repeated and manipulated in a variety of ways. It was Deren's intent to change "the quality of the scene from one of informality to that of a stylization akin to dance" and to transform a casual social encounter into an event that assumed "the solemnity and dimensions of ritual."

In Deren's *Meditation on Violence* (1948) a Chinese boxer executes three boxing techniques: *Wutang, Shaolin,* and *Shaolin* with sword. Each of these forms is a physical statement of metaphysical concepts, and Deren adapted her filming techniques to emphasize their unique properties. In *Wutang,* for example, the movement is flowing and is tied to a breath rhythm. Accordingly, the editing in this sequence was smooth and the camera movement emphasized the boxer's breathing pattern.

In 1958, Deren created *The Very Eye of Night,* a film that started with choreography originally designed for the stage. The credits list Antony Tudor, creator of the stage work, as "choreographic collaborator." Deren's intent in *The Very Eye of Night* (performed by students of the Metropolitan Opera Ballet School) was to convey the illusion of a dance in the sky. The film was printed as a negative, and horizon lines were eliminated to give the sense of free-floating figures.

Sarah Arledge and Sidney Peterson also experimented with film dances in the 1940s. Arledge's best-known film, *Introspection* (1947), used extreme distorting lenses and dancers dressed in leotards designed to draw attention to specific body shapes. The film focused on the rhythmic movement of these semiabstract forms. Peterson used multiple exposures in his film dances *Horror Dream* (1947) and *Clinic of Stumble* (1947), both of which were created in collaboration with the choreographer Marian Van Tuyl. *Horror Dream* depicts a dancer's anxiety before performance.

Shirley Clarke was a dancer before she became a filmmaker in the 1950s and, later, a videomaker. She had seen Deren's 1945 film, *Choreography for the Camera,* and her first film, *Dance in the Sun* (1953), reveals its influence. Clarke filmed Daniel Nagrin dancing a solo (originally choreographed for the stage) both at Jones Beach and indoors and then intercut the two versions. Clarke was dissatisfied with the results, but from this experiment she learned that "the dance had to be choreographed for the camera . . . and that dance in film was not only . . . pirouettes and *tours jetés,* but also someone walking down the street, or an eye looking up at you, or hair waving in the breeze. All this was the material of dance and . . . the very essence of film."

In *Bullfight* (1955) Clarke cut between a bullfighter and a dancer, and in *A Moment in Love* (1957), choreographed with Anna Sokolow, dancers Carmen Gutierrez and Paul Sanasardo portray lovers who see their reflections in water, fly through clouds, disappear, and reappear. While *A Moment in Love* was Clarke's last work with dancers, her films continued to be involved with rhythmic movement. In *Bridges Go Round* (1958), for example, she filmed and edited images of bridges to create a highly kinetic film.

Ed Emshwiller's multifaceted interest in film dances (and later video dances) evolved out of his work as an abstract expressionist painter. Starting in 1955, he used stop-motion cinematography to record the evolution of his paintings. In *Dance Chromatic* (1959), he shot images of Nancy Fenster dancing and then double-exposed the film with animated images of his abstract paintings.

In *Thanatopsis* (1962), Emshwiller left painting altogether; he contrasted fluttery, blurred images of dancer Becky Arnold with the immobile face of a man to create a mood of internal anguish. The soundtrack, which included heartbeats and sawing, contributed to the film's tension.

Emshwiller collaborated with choreographer Alwin Nikolais on several film and video works. *Totem* (1962–1963) was a film based on elements from Nikolais's stage work of the same name. *Fusion* (1967), a collaboration sponsored by the manufacturers of Springmaid towels, had two parts: a stage work and an independent film. In the stage work, dancers performed in front of a filmed backdrop in which images of dancers alternated with images of towel designs. In the independent film, images of dancers (sometimes wearing shape-transforming costumes) and images of towels were manipulated by means of the following cinematic techniques: superimpositions, zooms, pans, traveling mattes, inverted frames, and slowed and accelerated motion.

In the live piece *Bodyworks* (1965), Emshwiller performed and served as projectionist for his own film. Specifically, he moved about the performance space with a handheld projector and directed filmed images of the dancers onto the dancers themselves.

Two of the films that Hilary Harris made prior to his creation of *Nine Variations on a Dance Theme* (1967) exemplified his view that kinesthetic elements "are the guts of the medium, the material out of which film form is made." In both *Longhorns* (1951), whose subject matter was Texas longhorn steers, and *Highway* (1958), static objects were edited into highly dynamic imagery. In *Nine Variations*, Harris, who acknowledged his debt to Deren's *Choreography for the Camera*, explored a simple dance theme performed by Bettie de Jong. In each of the nine variations on this theme, Harris set himself specific guidelines. The first two variations were concerned with movement of the camera around the dancer and were filmed in a single take; later variations used zooms, camera angles, close-ups, and cuts.

Also in 1967, Canadian filmmaker Norman McLaren created *Pas de Deux* in conjunction with choreographer Ludmilla Chiriaeff and dancers Margaret Mercier and Vincent Warren. John Mueller has described the basic film technique as "the multiple superimposition of frames so that one sees not only where the dancer is now, but also where he or she was five, ten, or twenty frames ago." McLaren turned again to a pas de deux in his 1972 film, *Ballet Adagio*. In this study of a sequence choreographed by Asaf Messerer, McLaren filmed dancers David and Anna Marie Holmes in slow motion. In his 1983 film, *Narcissus*, McLaren experimented with multiple images and variable speeds to present dancers Jean-Louis Morin, Sylvie Kinal, and Sylvain LaFortune, in choreography by Fernand Nault.

In the 1960s, a number of artists associated with the Judson Dance Theater were involved in the creation of film dances or the incorporation of film into live performances. Among them were Trisha Brown, Beverly Schmidt, Elaine Summers, and Gene Friedman. As part of the suite *A String* (1966), Trisha Brown performed her solo *Homemade* with a film projector strapped to her back. As Brown moved, the projector haphazardly cast an image of her doing the same dance, without the projector, around the space. The result was a playful duet between choreographer in the flesh and celluloid alter ego. In 1963, Schmidt presented *Blossom*, a solo work that she later performed under the title *Duet for One*. In this piece she performed in front of slow motion black-and-white images of herself and also in front of colored slides. In 1964, Summers created *Fantastic Gardens*, a full-evening concert using film as an integral part of the choreography. Summers's *Walking Dance for Any Number*, first performed in 1965, was a work for two to ten dancers that incorporated four films projected simultaneously. From the early 1960s to the early 1980s, Summers created more than twenty-five films and videotapes, some presented with live performances, some intended to document live works, and some shown as simultaneous multiple-screen projections. Between 1964 and 1967 Gene Friedman created three film dances. In "Public," the first section of his *Three Dances* (1964), Gene Friedman filmed pedestrians from the rooftop of the Museum of Modern Art, showing

the subtlety of everyday gesture and spatial interaction. The third section, "Private," is a solo for dancer Judith Dunn, who is featured in Friedman's other two films of this period, *Index* (1964–1967) and *Official Doctrine* (1966).

In 1965, Stan VanDerBeek, an experimental filmmaker since the 1950s, created films that were projected onto three screens during a live performance of Merce Cunningham's *Variations V*. Distorted television images for this work were created by Nam June Paik. Also in 1965 VanDerBeek created a film for Robert Morris's live performance *Site* and *Pastoral: Et Al*, a live performance in which film dances were projected onto small screens carried by Elaine Summers and Burt Supree.

In 1966, a series of collaborations between artists and engineers, *Nine Evenings: Theatre and Engineering*, was held at the Sixty-ninth Regiment Armory in New York. The artists were Lucinda Childs, Alex Hay, Deborah Hay,

FILM AND VIDEO: Choreography for Camera. Trisha Brown in a 1989 revival of *Homemade* (1966). In this solo, Brown dances with a projector strapped to her back, which casts images of her performing the same dance without the projector. (Photograph © 1989 by Vincent Pereira; courtesy of the Trisha Brown Dance Company.)

Steve Paxton, Yvonne Rainer, Robert Rauschenberg, Oyvind Falstrom, David Tudor, and Robert Whitman.

Yvonne Rainer's piece for *Nine Evenings*, called *Carriage Discreteness*, incorporated film, live television, and slides. Rainer also incorporated the following films into later live performances: *Volleyball* (1967), *Hand Movie* (1968), *Trio Film* (1968), *Rhode Island Red* (1968), and *Lime* (1969).

Dancer/choreographer Don Redlich also experimented with the use of film in live performance. In *Dance for One Figure, Four Objects and Film Sequences* (1966), Redlich performed in front of a film of himself dancing down long corridors. In *Reacher* (1967) and in *Jibe* (1969), he again combined film with live performance; the films in these works were created by Jackson Tiffany.

In 1967, Robert Joffrey's *Astarte* combined spectacular multimedia effects from the sensor-laden environment of the 1960s discotheque (acid-rock music and strobe lighting) with a ballet performed by Trinette Singleton and Maximiliano Zomosa and a film created by Gardner Compton. Dance critic Marcia Siegel noted that "at a production cost of $60,000, it was probably the biggest mixed media dance ever done." Describing the form of the work as a whole, Compton stated: "*Astarte* sought to bridge the gap between the loose, unrefined area of the happening and . . . ballet." Speaking of the film in *Astarte*, he stated:

> What I filmed was Joffrey's choreography . . . However, I selected and chose for my camera . . . sometimes the movement would start with the live dancers and then be repeated and built through the film, although the dancers on stage were then doing something . . . different. At other times the film would initiate the theme, and the dancers would echo it.

Compton has other film dances to his credit, as well as many films that record staged works. In 1969, he directed *Seafall*, a film dance based on Edgar Allan Poe's poem "Annabel Lee." The film featured ballet dancers Lisa Bradley and Michael Uthoff as the young lovers who are parted by death. Filmed by the sea, *Seafall* evoked a romantic mood through superimpositions and alternating scenes of reality and fantasy.

In the middle and late 1960s, as a result of the introduction of low-cost videotaping equipment and the development of video synthesizers and colorizers by teams of artists and engineers (e.g., Nam June Paik and Shuya Abe, and Bill Etra and Steve Rutt), many experimental filmmakers started to work in video. Shirley Clarke and Ed Emshwiller were among these artists, as was Doris Chase.

In 1971, when Chase, a painter and sculptor, began to collaborate with choreographers who designed dances for the spaces defined by her sculptures, she became interested in documenting these works on film. This, in turn, led to experiments with video and dance. In *Moongates III* and *Tall Arches III* (both 1974), members of the Mary Staton Dance Ensemble interact with kinetic sculptures cre-

ated by Chase. Gus Solomons, Jr., dances a duet with a sculptural form created by the Rutt/Etra synthesizer in *Dance Nine* (1975), while in *Dance Seven* (1975), Marnee Morris of the New York City Ballet dances with video effects of feedback and debeaming. In *Dance Eleven* (1975), Cynthia Anderson of the Joffrey Ballet dances a duet with her own image reproduced electronically, and in *Dance Five* (1976), Kei Takei dances against a video-synthesized version of a kinetic sculpture.

Amy Greenfield is a dancer-choreographer and filmmaker whose work since the 1970s has been almost entirely for camera. By 1997 she had made thirty-four short films, videos, and holographs, as well as one feature-length film. Greenfield cites Deren, Emshwiller, Harris, and *cinéma vérité* filmmaker Ricky Leacock as important influences; Harris and Leacock have served as cameramen for some of her works. Greenfield serves as director, choreographer, performer, and editor for most of her works, many of which are solos or duets. Greenfield has often featured nudity in her works, betraying her visual fascination with the interaction of light, shadow, and other elements, such as sand or mud, on human skin. She typically uses close-up hand-held moving camera shots to create new ways for the viewer to experience movement. "Dance isn't steps to me," Greenfield says. "It's the total commitment of the human organism to a single-minded activity."

Element (1973) shows Greenfield repeatedly attempting to emerge from an expanse of thick black mud. In *Transport* (1971), the performers, on large, soft earthen hills, lift one another and move from place to place. In *Videotape for a Man and a Woman* (1979), Greenfield and Ben Dolphin, both nude, improvise together in scenes taped over a period of months, including a sequence in which the couple are seen on a beach, rolling into the surf. Some of Greenfield's work has been influenced by early modern dance: *4 Solos for 4 Women* (1980–1983), for example, relates to the expressionist solos of Mary Wigman; *Tides* (1981) relates to the writings of Isadora Duncan. In 1991, Greenfield presented her first feature-length film, *Antigone/Rites of Passion*, an interpretation of the Sophoclean tragedy. Featuring Greenfield as Antigone, Betram Ross as Oedipus/Creon, and Janet Eilber as Ismene, this work has been widely acclaimed.

Recently, Greenfield has begun to focus her interest on nudity as a theme, presenting in 1996 and 1997 *Raw-Edged Women*, an evolving program combining live performances with slides, film, and video projection. The program has included clips of Greenfield rolling in the surf, live and recorded erotic club dancing, a striptease, belly dancing, and notably a videotape of a Dadaist installation by Nam June Paik, in which a nude woman, wearing only a strand of pearls and high-heeled shoes, violently plays the piano with her body.

Film and videomaker Charles Atlas collaborated with choreographer Merce Cunningham on a number of projects, including film recordings of choreography, works created specifically for television, and more than a dozen experimental films and video dances. One of the central concerns of Atlas and Cunningham has been the problem of filming dancers effectively within film and video space, the space defined by the camera's triangular focal range. Typically, the Atlas-Cunningham collaborations have been choreographed for the camera and then modified for stage performance.

Several of the six sections of the Atlas-Cunningham video dance *Westbeth* (1974–1975) pay particular attention to the dramatic change in scale that occurs as dancers move toward and away from the camera. Although *Squaregame Video* (1976–1977) was performed on stage before it was taped, Cunningham choreographed it to take place only within a square portion of the proscenium stage, so that less drastic changes in the use of space would be required when the work was taped. In the video dance *Fractions* (1977–1978), up to four video monitors often share the screen space with the dancers. Images of dancers not seen in the central section of the screen or close-ups of those seen in full shots in the central section are shown on the monitors-within-the-screen.

The film dance *Locale* (1979–1980) was structured around the challenge of using moving cameras to film moving dancers; it was filmed with one stable camera and three kinds of moving cameras. In the film dance *Channels/Inserts* (1981–1982), Atlas and Cunningham divided the company's studio into sixteen possible areas for dancing. Atlas says that in editing this work he "used cross-cutting to indicate a simultaneity of dance events in different spaces: a presentation particularly well-suited to Cunningham's choreographic esthetic." In *Coast Zone* (1983), filmed at the Synod House of the Cathedral of Saint John the Divine, Atlas and Cunningham continued their experiments using moving cameras and composing shots of extreme depth of field.

In the mid-1980s, Atlas began collaborating with other choreographers, including former Cunningham dancers Douglas Dunn on *Secret of the Waterfall* (1983), shot at Martha's Vineyard, and Karole Armitage on *Parfango* (1983), *From an Island Summer* (1983–1984), and *Ex-Romance* (1987). Atlas also worked with the French choreographer Philippe DeCouflé on *Jump* (1984), an outlandish vision of a bar scene, and he directed two films with the English choreographer Michael Clark, *Hail the New Puritan* (1986) and *Because We Must* (1989).

Cunningham found another long-term collaborator in the film- and videomaker, and former painter, Elliot Caplan. The lighthearted *Deli Commedia* (1985) was the first work to come out of this partnership. Cunningham clearly has an affinity for screen choreography, in part because of his nonfrontal use of space. He has always exploited the camera's ablity to show dance from a variety of

FILM AND VIDEO: Choreography for Camera. Amy Greenfield with Henry Montes in Greenfield's feature-length film *Antigone/Rites of Passion* (1991). (Photograph by Robert A. Haller; used by permission.)

FILM AND VIDEO: Choreography for Camera. A photograph taken during the filming of *Coast Zone* (1983), shot at the Synod House of the Cathedral Church of Saint John the Divine, New York. This dance-film created by Merce Cunningham and Charles Atlas explores the use of extreme depth of field. (Photograph by Terry Stevenson; used by permission of Charles Atlas.)

vantage points. In a memorable, albeit fleeting, solo in *Points in Space* (1986), Cunningham appears framed by the negative spaces formed by his dancer's bodies. Commissioned by the British Broadcasting Corporation (BBC) and aired with a documentary about the process of its making, this Cunningham-Caplan videodance was later adapted for the stage and was set on the Paris Opera Ballet. In the video *Changing Steps* (1989), Caplan intercuts black-and-white footage of the original cast of Cunningham's 1973 stage work *Changing Steps,* comprised of solos for ten dancers, with scenes of newer company members performing the same work. *Beach Birds for Camera* (1991–1992) was conceived by Cunningham and Caplan simultaneously for stage and screen. *CRWDSPCR* (1996), their latest collaboration, was adapted from the stage production. Cunningham choreographed both these works with the aid of LifeForms, a computer-animation program developed at Simon Fraser University in Vancouver, Canada.

In the 1970s and 1980s, a number of former Cunningham dancers/choreographers as well as other postmodern choreographers incorporated film and videotape into their performances. Among them were Lucinda Childs, David Gordon, Kenneth King, and Trisha Brown.

Dance (1979) was a live collaboration for which Lucinda Childs created the choreography, visual artist Sol LeWitt directed the film, and composer Philip Glass composed and directed the recorded and live electronic score. In *Dance,* footage of dancers was projected onto a scrim behind which the live dancers performed essentially the same minimal movements. Lindley Hanlon refers to the relationship between the film and the performance as follows:

In the filmed images LeWitt uses a variety of angles, distances, multiple images, superimpositions, and tracking shots to spin off a variety of spatial experiences. A full range of the possible combinations of image and performance are utilized: dancers with or without film; film with or without dancers behind; one or two stories of filmed space; static or moving film images; various alignments and contrasts of actual and filmed figures.

David Gordon's 1982 performance, *TV Reel,* was built around references to the square-dance reels and the changing-partners' reality of contemporary romance. Throughout the work, images of the dancers appeared intermittently on two large video screens behind the live performers. The images on the screens typically augmented, rather than repeated, the dancers' movements. At times, the viewer's attention was drawn from one screen to the other and then back to the live performers. The video work for *TV Reel* was a collaboration between David Gordon and Dennis Diamond, who has also collaborated on video dances with Laura Dean, Senta Driver, Kenneth Rinker and Rosalind Newman, and who has produced numerous record tapes of dances.

In 1983, Kenneth King used live television in *Flextime;* in this piece, television monitors along the front of the performing area gave simultaneous camera's-eye views of the dancers. Also in 1983 Trisha Brown collaborated with composer/performer Laurie Anderson and visual artist Robert Rauschenberg in *Set and Reset.* Whereas, in an earlier collaboration, *Glacial Decoy* (1979), Brown and her company danced in front of Rauschenberg's slides as they were projected onto a series of screens lined up across the stage, in *Set and Reset* Rauschenberg's films were projected onto a structure (two pyramids and a cube made out of semitransparent fabric) that formed a ceiling over the dancers. In neither collaboration did Rauschenberg's images (houses, trees, buildings, etc.) have direct connection to the dancing.

The film and video dances created in the 1970s and 1980s were, like the live performances incorporating film and video, largely the creation of former Cunningham dancers/choreographers and other postmodern choreographers. By the 1990s, however, it had become common for choreographers to use video or film projections in their stage works. The film and video dances created before the 1960s were typically initiated by the filmmaker; in the 1960s, things began to turn around and, by the 1970s and 1980s, it was most often the dancer-choreographer rather than the filmmaker who was the work's *auteur*. The dancer-choreographer-composer Meredith Monk directed her original film *Ellis Island* (1982), in the ruins of the former immigration center before its restoration. Mixing color scenes of a contemporary guided tour with ghostly black-and-white images of long-ago travelers, Monk evoked an archetypal immigrant experience. Monk has created other films, including her seventy-four-minute *Book of Days* (1988).

Pooh Kaye, a visual artist turned dancer, began to make short films of herself in the 1970s. From the beginning of her work with film she was attracted to the use of pixelation (the basic unit or pictorial element), because it emphasized the comic, childlike, and frenetic quality of her movement. In 1983, she collaborated with filmmaker Elisabeth Ross on *Sticks on the Move*, described by Sally Banes as "a trick film in which outdoor light changes rapidly from day to night, people chase sticks and sticks chase people, and . . . humans and objects team up for uncanny feats of locomotion." In *The Painted Princess* (1993), Kaye combines live action and colorful animation to evoke images from Diego Veláquez's painting *Las Meninas* and Oscar Wilde's fairy tale *The Birthday of the Infanta*.

The film *Dune Dance* (1980) was directed by dancer-choreographer Carolyn Brown and filmed by James Klosty on the beach at Cape Cod, Massachusetts. Dressed in T-shirts and casual clothes, the dancers jump, roll, slide, and run to the accompaniment of excerpts from classical ballet scores.

David Woodberry's film *Invisible Dance* (1981) takes place in the midst of crowded New York City streets. Five dancers, dressed to blend in with pedestrians, alternate between their roles as pedestrians and as performers. Even when they suddenly start to perform highly stylized postmodern dance movements, the New York crowds appear unflappable. Woodberry made this film in collaboration with filmmaker Jody Weiner.

Johanna Boyce's *Waterbodies* (1981) was originally created as the backdrop for an evening-length work performed in a pool and was later shown independently. Boyce collaborated with filmmaker John Schabel on this work. *Waterbodies*, a two-projector, two-screen color work filmed in a pool, extended the definition of dance to cover swimming. In it, swimmers on one screen sometimes seem to relate directly to swimmers on the other screen.

Space City (1981–1982), a film created by Kenneth King and filmmakers Robyn Brentano and Andrew Horn, has three sections. The first takes place in an attic and evokes the past and the interior space of dreams. In the second section, which suggests the present, King moves in a confined area delineated by cartoonlike high-rise buildings. The last section takes place in an open abstract space with superimposed grids and suggests the future.

In 1983, a film-dance festival organized by Amy Greenfield and Elaine Summers was held at the Public Theatre in New York City. More than one hundred films covering the period 1890 to 1983 were shown, including many of those cited in this article. A catalog was produced in conjunction with the event.

The mid-1980s saw a boom of interest in dance projects related to video and film, both in mainstream culture and the avant-garde. With the advent of Music Television (MTV), music videos integrating dance segments helped establish the careers of pop stars like Michael Jackson, Madonna, Paula Abdul, and MC Hammer. On public television, the series *Alive from Off Center*, hosted by the offbeat pop star Laurie Anderson, provided a venue for less commercial experiments. Launched in 1985 with a $300,000 grant from the National Endowment for the Arts (NEA), this show became the most prominent venue for innovative dance films and videos in the United States. In its first seven years, *Alive from Off Center* showcased approximately forty new and existing dance works, including those of choreographers Trisha Brown, Twyla Tharp, Elizabeth Streb, Bill T. Jones, Susan Marshall, Marta Renzi, Karole Armitage, Michael Moschen, Bill Irwin, and Doug Elkins, in collaboration with directors such as James Byrne, Charles Atlas, Michael Schartz, and Mary Perillo.

Many of these artists used the camera to free the dancer from the studio or theater setting. The amusement area at Coney Island served as a backdrop for segments of Armitage and Atlas's *From an Island Summer*. In Elkins's *It Doesn't Wait* (1990), directed by Mark Openhaus, dancers weave through traffic and boogie at street corners. Other works presented on *Alive from Off Center* harnessed new video technologies to fabricate unreal landscapes. John Sanborn and Dean Winkler's *Luminaire* (1985), with choreography by Charles Moulton, presents a dancer drifting in a electronic web of shifting patterns. In *Landings* (1987), a short video directed by Schwartz, Streb's suspended body falls across the black void of the screen. In this apparent vacuum, gravity hurls her in unpredictable directions. At one point, electronically reproduced, multiple Strebs drip off the top of the screen like so many drops of water. Schwartz and Streb continued their fruitful collaboration with *Impact* (1990). In this video, camera angles evade gravity, making dancers bound off and crash into the edges of the monitor. Schwartz's use of techniques such as slow motion, amplifying the sounds the dancers make, and juxtaposing shots of sticks hitting the floor with shots of dancers doing the

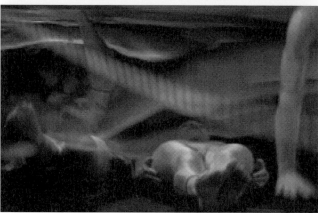

FILM AND VIDEO: Choreography for Camera. Stills from the videodance *Impact: Hurling Dervishes* (1990), directed and conceived by Michael Schwartz with choreography by Elizabeth Streb. (Courtesy of Mark Robison.)

same, heighten the sense of effort that Streb also strives to transmit in her stage work.

The lack of government funding and other institutional support in the United States has discouraged many resident artists from large-scale film or video projects. In 1993, the NEA eliminated the funding category of dance

video and film, previously allotted an annual budget of $200,000, which was awarded in ten to twenty separate grants. Although many artists still work in the field, there are few venues to show experimental films and videos in the United States. With the cancellation of *Alive from Off Center* from Public Television, cable television stations, including public-access stations, have helped fill the void. Since the early 1970s, the Dance Films Association in New York has run an annual competitive festival. In 1996, the American Dance Festival launched its first annual dance film and video competition. Three categories for submission included Choreography for Camera, Documentary, and Experimental. The combined factors of a lack of funding with the increasing accessibility and improved picture quality of video cameras and editing equipment have made video the medium of choice over film in the United States during the 1980s and 1990s. In Europe and Canada, however, where government support is more generous, more artists are working in film and creating larger scale projects with high production values.

Alive from Off Center aired some of these foreign productions, including excerpts of the Canadian film *Le Dortoir* (1991), directed by François Girard and choreographed by Danielle Tardif and Gilles Maheu. In this ambitious fifty-three-minute film, a large cast of men and women hurl themselves onto beds and against the dormitory walls. At times, angels float through the air, their presence calming the emotional turbulence below. Whereas *Le Dortoir* draws inspiration from French narrative cinema, Édouard Lock's *Human Sex* (1986), directed by Bernar Herbert as a Canadian project, features the fast cutting and driving athleticism of a music video. Lock has also integrated video projections into his multi-media performance spectacles for his company La La La Human Steps.

In the late 1980s and early 1990s a number of European festivals and competitions began that awarded prizes to dance films and videos in several categories. In 1988, the United Nations Educational, Scientific, and Cultural Organization (UNESCO) and the Vienna-based International Music Center (IMZ), cosponsored the first annual Grand Prix International de Video Danse. The IMZ split with the Grand Prix in 1990 to start a new competition called Dance Screen held in Frankfurt its first year. In 1994, the IMZ Dance Screen received more than 150 submissions, covering four award categories. Other European festivals in the field include the French festival Danse Visions and the Italian Coreografico Elettronico.

The first Grand Prix jury awarded Philippe DeCouflé's *Codex* (1988) a special prize for most original creation. A series of vignettes featuring fantastic costumes and scenery, *Codex* portrays the absurd goings of other worldly creatures. DeCouflé has since choreographed the festivities for the 1992 Olympics in France—the broadcast of which probably had a larger audience than any experimental dance film. DeCouflé's next film *Le P'tit Bal* (1993), a duet for the choreographer and Pascale Hubin, was awarded the IMZ Dance Screen award for best choreography.

Other winners of the Grand Prix for creative video/film dance collaborations include Anne Teresa De Keersmaeker and director Wolfgang Kolb, in 1989, for *Hoppla!;* Karine Saporta, in 1990, for *La Fiancée aux Yeux de Bois;* and Angelin Preljocaj, in 1992, for *Un Trait d'Union*, a humorous, at times surreal, depiction of an entangled relationship between two men. Kenneth Kvarnström's *Duo*, set in an aqueous cavern was honored in 1992, as was *Circumnavigation: Lisbonne-Vigo*, by the team N+N Corsino. The IMZ's Dance Screen festival has recognized some of these works and others including: *Scelsi Suites*, in 1990, choreographed and performed by Nicole Mossouz and Pascale Crochet, with direction by Dirk Greyspeirt; *Roseland*, in 1991, choreographed by Wim Vandekybus and directed by Walter Verdin; and *La Noces*, also in 1991, conceived by the French team Joëlle Bouvier and Régis Obadia. In this short film, a bride rolls along a long table and is tossed from guest to guest. The Bouvier-Obadia collaboration has produced several other stylish films, including the black-and-white *La Chambre* (1987), in which women perch on chairs affixed to a wall, and the combative duet *L'Etreinte* (1988). Other French notables in the field include choreographer Jean-Claude Gallotta and director Claude Mouriéras who collaborated on the film *Rei Dom.*

Whereas the Continental Europeans, particularly the French, have generally embraced a cinematic approach to film-dance, the British have tended to work more often with the small screen in mind. In broad terms, the French films tend to be more ethereal and imagistic, and the English more directly narrative. The BBC has sponsored much creative dance programming, including the *Dance House* series, which presents twelve five-minute films or videos per week by various choreographers; the shorts are scattered throughout the week, then seen together in a single one-hour program at week's end. British choreographer Lloyd Newson of the group DV8 and film director David Hinton have collaborated on two Grand Prix award-winning screen adaptations of stage choreography: *Dead Dreams of Monochrome Men* (1990) and *Strange Fish* (1993). An hour-long dance drama rife with religious imagery, *Strange Fish* follows a heroine through a series of tense relationships.

The BBC also commissioned Lea Anderson's thirty-minute program *Cross Channels* (1991), directed by Margaret Williams and produced by Ann Beresford. Through subtle, precise gestures, Anderson depicts the voyage across the English Channel of a group of men and women, while offering a witty gender critique. Williams and Beresford have worked on a number of other dance-related projects, including two films choreographed by Victoria Marks, an American who worked in England for many years. Created for the CanDoCo, a company of differently-abled dancers, their first film together *Outside In* (1994), has a recurring tango theme. Among other hon-

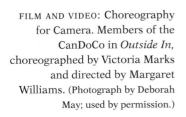

FILM AND VIDEO: Choreography for Camera. Members of the CanDoCo in *Outside In*, choreographed by Victoria Marks and directed by Margaret Williams. (Photograph by Deborah May; used by permission.)

ors, this film won the IMZ Dance Screen's Choreography Award. Their second collaboration, *Mothers and Daughters*, featuring real mother-and-daughter pairs, also won awards at Video Danse and IMZ Dance Screen.

With advances in digital-imaging it has become possible, in theory, to produce almost any conceivable image onscreen. The seamless juxtapositions that current technology allows has already changed the look of television advertisements and music videos, resulting in a new-style surrealism. The upcoming generation of dance-media artists has begun to take advantage of some possibilities the new technologies offer. Among others, William Forsythe of the Frankfurt Ballet has been experimenting with creating interactive dance CD-ROMs. In the mid-1990s, the Internet is emerging as an important venue for creative videodance and dance-animation works. Under the stewardship of Andrea Sferes, the pioneering web-site Dance-on-Line (formerly known as Dancing-on-a-Line), has begun posting video clips to accompany on-line text articles. The user can click on an icon and watch the "tape" roll. Eventually, Sferes hopes the site will become a destination for original videodance works.

The Internet has also been used as a vehicle for live performance. For example, the New York presenting organization called The Kitchen has used the Internet to transmit live video signals that link performers in various cities or countries in real-time. Some artists are envisioning the use of virtual reality to create cyber-space dance environments. A few of the many artists exploring the interactive performance possibilities offered by combining dance with video, animation, sound engineering, and Internet technologies include choreographer Dawn Stoppiello and composer Mark Coniglio under the rubric of their New York-based Troika Ranch; Amanda Steggel, creator of the performance/web-site "M@ggies Love Bytes"; and Susie Ramsay, an American based in Spain. Several symposiums and academic conferences on dance and technology have addressed the theoretical implications of the rapid advance of technology for the creative mind and body.

[*See also* Television.]

BIBLIOGRAPHY

Bozzini, Anne. "They Film as They Dance." *Ballett International* 14.1 (January 1991): 36–41.

Copeland, Roger. "New Dance/Film: Perspectives on Dance and Cinema." *Dance Magazine* 48(April 1974).

Dance Perspectives, no. 30 (Summer 1967). "Cine-Dance" issue.

Filmdance: 1890's–1983. New York, 1983. Filmdance Festival catalogue.

Grossman, Peter Z, and Jeffrey Bush. "Videodance." *Dance Scope* 9.2 (Spring/Summer 1975): 11–17.

Grossman, Peter Z. "Video and Dance: A Delicate Balance between Art and Technology." *Videography* (September 1977): 16–20.

Jessop, Douglas W. "Film and Dance: Interaction and Synthesis." Master's thesis, University of Colorado, 1975.

Lockyer, Bob. "Dance and Video: Some Random Thoughts." *Dance Theatre Journal* 1.4 (Fall 1983).

Lorber, Richard. "Toward an Aesthetics of Videodance." *Arts in Society* 13 (Summer–Fall 1976):242–253.

Maletic, Vera. "Videodance–Technology–Attitude Shift." *Dance Research Journal* 19.2 (Winter 1987–1988).

Millennium Film Journal 10–11 (Fall–Winter 1981–1982). Contains a section on "Dance/Movement."

Ramsay, Susie. "Bring Your Body: The Dance Community and New Technologies." On her website (http://art.net/~dtz/susie.html).

Schmidt, Jochen. "Exploitation or Symbiosis?: On the Contradictions between Dance and Video." *Ballett International* 14.1 (January 1991): 96–99.

Snyder, Allegra Fuller. *Dance Films: A Study of Choreo-Cinema*. Albany, N.Y., 1973.

FILM AND VIDEOTAPE.   See Dance Films Association, *Dance Film and Video Guide* (Princeton, 1991) for listings of dance films and videotapes available for rental or purchase. The newsletter of the Dance Films Association is *Dance on Camera News*.

ARCHIVES.   Dance Collection, New York Public Library for the Performing Arts. Dansmuseet Archives, Stockholm.

NANCY BECKER SCHWARTZ
Amended by Jody Sperling

FILM MUSICALS.

[*This entry comprises two articles focusing on the use of dance in film musicals. The first article is a description of musicals made in Hollywood; the second is a survey of Indian film musicals made by the Bombay film industry, known as Bollywood.*]

Hollywood Film Musicals

Although there was significant incidental use of dance in film before 1927 and the advent of sound, dance became an integral element only with the development during the 1930s and 1940s of the musical as a staple genre of Hollywood studio production. Dance directors, choreographers, and performers from Broadway turned to films, and the film musical became a primary expression of dance forms. Eccentric dancing and flash acts became as vital to the genre as ballet, modern, and tap dancing, and a symbiosis of dance styles became evident. Throughout the period of major studio production, dance contributed to the narrative cohesion of the musical, expressing character, and furthering plot. By the middle of the twentieth century, film musicals had become the primary means of popularizing almost every variety of dance. Later, when Hollywood reduced its output of musicals, television subsumed aspects of the genre but, while presenting dance to the largest audiences in history, has never made more than incidental contributions to the musical genre.

The musical has always been a stylistically innovative but thematically conservative genre espousing the values of popular entertainment and prevailing social norms. As a formal component of the films, dance often served to give new direction to a film's style while simultaneously demonstrating that the values reflected in the film were (or should be) the values of society. This link helps to categorize the genre in terms of set historical periods and within this chronology, by the systems of production of certain studios and by varying economic considerations. During the 1930s, RKO Pictures and Warner Brothers predominated in musical production; in the late 1940s and early 1950s, Metro-Goldwyn-Mayer (MGM) helped the genre reach its apex. As the studio contract system became moribund during the 1950s, however, fewer musicals were made, and as popular taste in music changed, the genre no longer enjoyed its earlier significance.

In the early years of sound, 1927 through 1930, Broadway stars, directors, choreographers, and song writers were imported wholesale into the film studios, and the forms of musical production that were then popular on the New York stage imbued the musicals being made in Hollywood. The *Ziegfeld Follies* and *George White's Scandals*, for example, had cinematic equivalents in *Show of Shows* (Warner Bros., 1929), *Fox Movietone Follies* (1929), *Paramount on Parade* (1930), and MGM's *Hollywood Revue of 1929*. The last film was representative of those revue films: starring most of MGM's contract performers, it was presented like a stage show, each number concluded by the drawing of a curtain. With certain exceptions, the camera never moved and shot the material as if it were a spectator in a theater. The dance routines, directed by Sammy Lee and Albertina Rasch, were evidence of the diversity of dance in such films. Lee, who had worked for Ziegfeld and in Earl Carroll's *Vanities*, staged specialty numbers and chorus line routines with some tap dancing (including toe tapping). Rasch, meanwhile, a trained ballet dancer, attempted to add an element of high art to the more popular show business aspect of the rest of the film. Indeed, during her several years in Hollywood she insisted on using her own dancers, trained by her and under contract to her, instead of those less competent performers seen in other numbers. Moreover, she also tried certain innovations in the camera-dance relationship: a flower-patterned routine, for example, was shot with an overhead camera in the way that Busby Berkeley subsequently made popular. These musical revue films were, in a sense, vaudeville shows, and even as production of such films decreased, some were still made occasionally, providing singers and dancers with the opportunity to perform material different from their norm. In *Ziegfeld Follies* (MGM, 1944), for instance, Gene Kelly and Fred Astaire danced together for the only time.

In the late 1920s, however, attempts were made to incorporate elements of traditional stage musicals into a new, primarily cinematic form. Musicals specifically designed for the screen displayed the same technical limitations as other films of the period but nevertheless became

FILM MUSICALS: Hollywood Film Musicals. A chorus line in a rehearsal scene from *Broadway Melody* (MGM, 1929). This early "talkie" was the first in a series of backstage musical films. (Photograph from the Film Stills Library, Museum of Modern Art, New York; used by permission.)

ancestors of a new tradition. *Broadway Melody* (MGM, 1929) combined elements of stage and screen to become the first in a line of films to depict backstage life in a musical setting. Most of the numbers in it are presented as part of the rehearsals or as a performance of the show within the film, and they feature such standard material as precision tap dancing for the chorus. "The Wedding of the Painted Doll," one of the film's major production numbers, combined ballet and acrobatics—cartwheels, somersaults, *chaîné* turns, and *fouetté pirouettes* all are part of the choreography—as did routines in other contemporary films. *Broadway Melody* showed that film editing was a crucial element of film dance. The chorus routines of the "Broadway Melody" number were shot in several takes, always in long shot, but when the soloist began to dance, multiple perspectives—close-up, medium shot—alternated during the dance. Little conscious arrangement of the camera for the choreography seems evident, but the filmmakers were in fact attempting a variety of approaches to the camera-subject relationship throughout the entire film. Two other 1929 films used dance in ways that musicals over the next twenty years would develop more fully. The dancing in *Hallelujah*, directed by King Vidor, suggests a relationship between sexuality and the characters' religious fervor. Moreover, by shooting asynchronously and postdubbing sound, Vidor used camera work that was more fluid than was the norm. In Ernst Lubitsch's *Love Parade*, the secondary characters were uninhibited dancers; in contrast, the aristocratic, major characters only sang. All three of these films reflected dance styles of the late 1920s and the ways in which early film musicals were hesitant steps toward presenting dance within a fledgling genre.

The Depression-ridden 1930s presented a great variety of film musicals. Dance directors, performers, and composers and writers all helped make the musical comedy particularly vital on the screen. The relationship between musicals on the stage and those on the screen would always be close, but from the 1930s through the 1950s the Hollywood musical had a life of its own, drawing on the resources of Broadway but developing a unique form of cinema. Among the first major figures from the stage to influence the film musical was Busby Berkeley, whose extravagant production numbers featuring many chorus dancers on elaborate sets, often shot with an overhead camera to emphasize the intricate patterns of movement, dominated musical production at Warner Brothers Studios. Although on occasion Berkeley's production rou-

tines included trained dancers, in general they emphasized patterns of movement characterized by parade drills, erotic motifs, and surreal imagery. Films such as *42nd Street* and the *Gold Diggers* series usually depicted backstage life, with the musical numbers serving as the culmination of the show for which the characters had been preparing since the opening scene. Generally viewed as escapist entertainment, these films nevertheless represented life in the 1930s. Dancers and singers striving against overwhelming odds in a financially difficult period had the spirit necessary to succeed, and the musical numbers embodied their success.

Instead of specializing in lavish production numbers featuring dozens of anonymous dancers, RKO and MGM musicals highlighted the talents of individual performers who were accomplished dancers, and they gave these studio films a wholly different quality. Indeed, Fred Astaire and Ginger Rogers were teamed for a series of intimate musicals that were the true beginnings of what has come to be called the integrated musical. In *Top Hat* (1935), *Swing Time* (1936), and other films, the dances, usually shot in long takes with the dancers seen full figure, served

FILM MUSICALS: Hollywood Film Musicals. Dick Powell takes Bebe Daniels's hand in a rehearsal scene from *42nd Street* (Warner Brothers, 1933). This popular film was to be adapted as a Broadway musical in 1980. (Photograph from the Film Stills Library, Museum of Modern Art, New York; used by permission.)

as courtship rituals in which the lead characters worked out their relationships, which ended, of course, in happiness and marriage. Eleanor Powell's virtuosic tap dancing made her the star of a series of MGM *Broadway Melody* films that continued the tradition of backstage stories of enterprising newcomers making it big on the stage. Powell, who combined formidable tap abilities with ballet and acrobatics, had a unique style that emphasized her as the dancing star. Except for one film with Fred Astaire *(Broadway Melody of 1941),* she usually co-starred with nonmusical actors, such as Robert Taylor and James Stewart, who would not detract from her dynamic routines. Her trademark movements, which included very rapid *chaîné* turns, high kicks, and tapping in and out of cartwheels and other acrobatic stunts, were part of almost every number she did. The characters she played were wholesome but imbued with energy and spirit, and they achieved success because of unmatched talent.

Although the musical stars achieved fame, the subordinate players often provided the greatest diversity of dance material. Eccentric and specialty dancers served as second leads or contributed isolated numbers in particular films. Lee Dixon, Buddy Ebsen, the DeMarcos, and the Nicholas Brothers, among others, appeared in many films throughout the 1930s and 1940s. Buddy Ebsen appeared in Eleanor Powell films as a boy next door whose gangly legs and undulating pelvis gave a comic idiosyncrasy to all his dancing. The Nicholas Brothers, whose flash act was highlighted by slides and jumps into splits, added enormous vitality to *Down Argentine Way* (1940), *The Great American Broadcast* (1941), and *Sun Valley Serenade* (1941), among others.

In addition to the Nicholas Brothers, the preeminent black dancer of the period was Bill ("Bojangles") Robinson, whose films with Shirley Temple at Twentieth Century–Fox demonstrated the tap dancing that had made him practically a stage legend. Because he was so popular with white audiences, Robinson made it possible for other black dancers to get roles at a time when their appearance in films was socially less acceptable. Their influence on later dancers and choreographers continued to imbue the musical with an energy that helped keep the genre popular for thirty years.

Musicals formed a substantial part of every studio's output from the 1930s through the 1950s, but dance did not always play a significant role. Because individual films were often dependent on the talents of a specific star, and because stars were under contract, certain studios became identified as producing particular kinds of films. At Universal, for example, Deanna Durbin's teenage singing persona prevailed in *100 Men and a Girl* (1936), *It's a Date* (1940), *Can't Help Singing* (1945), and about fifteen other films. Alice Faye, Betty Grable, and subsequently Marilyn Monroe were central to Twentieth Century–Fox's many

FILM MUSICALS: Hollywood Film Musicals. Ginger Rogers and Fred Astaire in *Shall We Dance?* (RKO, 1937), one of the ten films in which they starred together. (Photograph from the Film Stills Library, Museum of Modern Art, New York; used by permission.)

musicals, which emphasized singing but nevertheless did display dance in certain contexts, usually within a show the characters were preparing or as entertainment at some social event they attended. Dance was exhibition and spectacle in *Tin Pan Alley* (1940), *Moon over Miami* (1941), *Hello, Frisco, Hello* (1943), and *Billy Rose's Diamond Horseshoe* (1945). Faye was principally a singer, and in her films the dances were performed without the principals; Grable, however, did dance, and she performed pseudo-ethnic routines in *Down Argentine Way* and *Sweet Rosie O'Grady* (1943), for example. The dance directors for Fox's films (usually Seymour Felix, Nick Castle, or Hermes Pan) did not choreograph dances so much as stage routines, using the show to display costumes and movement as part of the overall spectacle. That tradition persisted at Fox, although in two Monroe films, *Gentlemen Prefer Blondes* (1953) and *There's No Business Like Show Business* (1954), Jack Cole did, within the spectacle, create dances that displayed something of his style of combining modern, jazz, and ethnic dance. The *Road* series starring Bing Crosby, Bob Hope, and Dorothy La-

FILM MUSICALS: Hollywood Film Musicals. Vera Zorina gazes at her reflection in the "Water Nymph Ballet" choreographed by George Balanchine in *The Goldwyn Follies* (MGM, 1938). (Photograph from the Film Stills Library, Museum of Modern Art, New York; used by permission.)

mour were Paramount's principal assays in the genre, whereas at Columbia, the films of Rita Hayworth gave dancing ability a preeminent position and allowed dancers and choreographers to explore new realms. Gene Kelly tried out experimental ideas in *Cover Girl* (1944), Fred Astaire worked with her in *You Were Never Lovelier* (1942), and Jack Cole prepared the dances for her in *Tonight and Every Night* (1944) and *Down to Earth* (1947).

During the 1940s, several factors contributed to the development of the integrated musical at MGM. The studio attracted people who had made important musicals at other studios and also, in turn, helped to energize the genre throughout Hollywood. Arthur Freed, a lyricist who produced many of MGM's major musicals in the 1940s and 1950s, oversaw the work of Gene Kelly, Judy Garland, Vincente Minnelli, Fred Astaire, Charles Walters, Stanley Donen, and many other performers and directors. Songwriters and musicians such as Betty Comden and Adolph Green, Ira Gershwin, John Green, André Previn, and Cole Porter; choreographers such as Robert Alton, Gene Kelly, Eugene Loring, Michael Kidd, and Jack Cole all worked for MGM. The fruits of their endeavors included *For Me*

and My Gal (1942), *Meet Me in St. Louis* (1944), *Easter Parade* (1948), *The Pirate* (1948), *On the Town* (1949), *An American in Paris* (1951), *Singin' in the Rain* (1952), and *The Band Wagon* (1953). In all of these films the songs and dances express character development, provide narrative explication, and achieve stylistic unity.

All of the dancers and choreographers working in film at this time had been trained in a variety of dance types, and they tried to combine different forms of dance in order to suit the purpose of a given film. Gene Kelly and Fred Astaire were the best known, but others also contributed substantially to the genre. Jack Cole and Eugene Loring, for example, were strongly committed to creating dance for the camera and to working with directors to ensure that musical numbers could flow naturally out of the story progression. Cole, who worked primarily at Columbia Pictures, even created the first dance company at a studio in order to have accomplished performers who could do the intricate choreography he devised. Loring provided a solid ballet base to the vernacular dance more common to Hollywood musicals. The integration of dance forms, however, emphasized the vitality of popular entertainment, an idea that recurs throughout the genre. Often pure ballet is portrayed as being effete, whereas tap dancing has energy, an idea exemplified by George Balanchine's Romeo and Juliet dance sequence in *The Goldwyn Follies* of 1938; in it, the elegant and reserved Capulets are ballet dancers, whereas the vibrant and earthy Montagues perform in a jazz idiom. In *The Band Wagon* the contrast between Cyd Charisse's ballet dancing and Fred Astaire's style becomes the crux of the film, and their show succeeds only when the pretensions of high art are abandoned for the democratic ideals of popular entertainment. Ballet and modern dance brought sophistication and technique to the movies, but filmmakers incorporated those forms with vernacular dance and used them for their own narrative purposes.

Musicals have always explained their characters' ability to sing and dance by making them professional dancers. Increasingly, however, the genre has tried to integrate the musical numbers into narratives by providing alternative motivations. The backstage musical naturally presented its characters as professional (or would-be) performers, but even musicals without the backstage theme honored that formula while adding to it. Throughout the 1930s Fred Astaire's characters were always dancers, and many of Gene Kelly's were as well, but that explanation for their dancing ability was subordinated to the film's narrative goals: The dances were not necessarily performed on the stage to entertain other characters or to cap a putting-on-the-show story; rather, the characters danced and sang as a natural means of expressing themselves. Joy, sorrow, love, despair—every emotion—became the source for a musical number and, as a result, a way to tell the story.

Professional performers gave way to more mundane characters, with the implication that at least in the genre—if not in real life—anyone could be a singer or a dancer and that feelings could be more fully expressed in song and dance. Gene Kelly's sailor in *On the Town*, his painter in *An American in Paris*, and Fred Astaire's photographer in *Funny Face* are all examples of characters whose ability to dance is assumed as a convention of the genre. The integrated musical, which attempted to use song and dance as an essential narrative element, was the culmination of all forms of the genre, and it became the ideal on Broadway as well as in film.

Unlike stage musicals, film musicals had a third element of exploration, the cinematic process itself, and dance became a prime impetus for the use of camera and editing in nontraditional ways. The camera-dance relationship had been a major concern of musical directors and performers since the late 1920s. Busby Berkeley had chosen bizarre angles to photograph many chorus dancers in patterns created by mechanical stage effects,

but the totality of the number was created by the editing. Fred Astaire, on the other hand, had eschewed such effects in order to highlight the unity of the dance, the camera allowing the dancers to present their material uninterrupted. At MGM, however, there was a conscious attempt at integration, with dances choreographed specifically for the camera. Although certain camera approaches dominated (shooting the dancers in full figure, for example), dance and film were partners. Matched-action editing on movement allowed the dance to be seen from multiple perspectives, and it provided dancers with different spatial opportunities. Not tied to the boundaries of a stage performance, choreographers became free to arrange their material in intricate ways for close viewing or, by contrast, in patterns for expanded spectacle. The title dance from *Singin' in the Rain* demonstrates the integra-

FILM MUSICALS: Hollywood Film Musicals. Jack Cole (center) and company in *Moon over Miami* (Twentieth Century–Fox, 1941). (Photograph from the Film Stills Library, Museum of Modern Art, New York; used by permission.)

FILM MUSICALS: Hollywood Film Musicals. Gene Kelly and Leslie Caron in *An American in Paris* (MGM, 1951). Directed by Vincente Minelli and choreographed by Kelly, this film integrated dance and narrative, especially in the final fantasy sequence. It was the first musical to win an Oscar as best picture of the year. (Photograph from the Film Stills Library, Museum of Modern Art, New York; used by permission.)

tion of dance and camera in this period. Elaborate camera movement is needed to follow Gene Kelly as he twirls his umbrella and himself through the water, but less complex shots allow the viewer to observe him more fully as he dances down the street. The lamppost, a fence, his umbrella, and the puddles are all sources of dance action. A sudden close-up of his face makes his joyous smile as much a choreographed element as his feet. At the end, the camera booms up as he casually ambles away. Continuity between the number and the narrative is achieved because the camera allows him to perform in identifiable space.

At its peak the MGM musical allowed stars and featured performers to contribute to a genre that used tradition to develop a new aesthetic form. Other studios followed suit, but the commitment to production of the genre was short-lived, for the studio contract system had become moribund. The production of musicals was inordinately dependent on that system; contract musicians, arrangers, and designers made it possible to produce musicals regularly. Arthur Freed, for example, produced approximately forty musicals in twenty-two years, and he was only one such producer at MGM. Each studio had the facilities and personnel to create several musicals a year. All this changed with the decline of the contract system, and as a result, musicals became more expensive to produce.

At the same time, moreover, the genre gradually became less popular. The relationship between the popular music of the 1930s and 1940s and music created for stage and screen had been strong. Irving Berlin, George Gershwin, and Jerome Kern, among many other leading songwriters, had regularly written material for the movies. Tastes in popular music changed radically in the 1950s, however, and rock-and-roll became the predominant music form. Although some rock musicals were made (Elvis Presley appeared in several), the genre did not in general adapt to the new music. The influence of television greatly altered movie-going habits as well, and film attendance plummeted. As a result, production companies, increasingly reluctant to gather the expensive forces necessary to create musicals, became dependent on successful Broadway shows for their sources.

Adaptations of stage musicals had always been important, but they did not predominate in Hollywood until original screen musicals could no longer be supported. Rodgers and Hammerstein's *Oklahoma!* (1955), *Carousel* (1956), and *The Sound of Music* (1965) stand out as major screen adaptations that varied little from their original Broadway versions. In the first two, Agnes de Mille's choreography was generally replicated. In *West Side Story* (1961), by contrast, Jerome Robbins adapted his original dances for the screen, recognizing the necessity of making camera placement and editing part of the process, and in *My Fair Lady* (1964), another important adaptation, Hermes Pan kept some of the recognizable Hanya Holm dance material, as in "The Ascot Gavotte" sequence. One filmmaker who made the musical his own during this period was Bob Fosse, whose *Sweet Charity* (1968) and

Cabaret (1972), though adaptations, were as cinematic as the original musicals he participated in at MGM early in his career. In *Cabaret,* particularly, Fosse made substantial modifications, and he used a fragmented film style to reveal his similarly fragmented choreographic style.

After 1951 and the establishment of nationwide television broadcasting, genre cinema in general began to be supplanted by genre television. Narrative musicals, however, did not attain the popularity of westerns, for example, as a television form, although occasional musical specials did maintain the tradition. (In 1957, for example, Rodgers and Hammerstein did a live, televised production of *Cinderella* starring Julie Andrews). In its own way though, television did revive an older form, the revue, with the creation of the musical-variety show. As early as 1948 the *Admiral Broadway Revue* and band leader Fred Waring in his own show were presenting individuals and groups in different musical contexts. Marge and Gower Champion appeared in the former along with other new performers who were just beginning their careers. During the 1950s Perry Como and Dinah Shore presided over

shows in which a chorus dance routine was standard. *The Ed Sullivan Show,* originally called *Toast of the Town,* was, from 1948 to 1971, a primary forum for musical numbers. Dancers appearing on Broadway or with ballet companies received nationwide exposure through what was essentially a vaudeville show. Such programs persisted into the 1960s, but individual musical specials eventually became the norm as the variety programs lost ratings and were canceled. Programs such as Bob Fosse's *Liza with a Z* in 1972 presented established stars in a revuelike format that did not create the demands of a film production but gave them the opportunity to perform in a different context. The Fosse show, for example, gave Liza Minnelli one of her prime chances to dance for the camera.

In the late 1970s film began to incorporate contemporary popular music, and the influence of television shooting and editing styles and the power of the record indus-

FILM MUSICALS: Hollywood Film Musicals. Gene Kelly, in the exuberant "Gotta Dance" number from *Singin' in the Rain* (MGM, 1952). (Photograph from the Film Stills Library, Museum of Modern Art, New York; used by permission.)

FILM MUSICALS: Hollywood Film Musicals. Joel Grey (center) as the Master of Ceremonies, with Kit-Kat Klub dancers in *Cabaret* (1972), choreographed by Bob Fosse. Set in the burlesque atmosphere of Berlin on the eve of World War II, *Cabaret* is the film version of John Kander and Fred Ebb's Broadway musical, an adaptation of John van Druten's play *I Am a Camera*, which was based on Christopher Isherwood's *Berlin Stories*. (Photograph from the Film Stills Library, Museum of Modern Art, New York; used by permission.)

try also began to show. *Saturday Night Fever* (1977), with its disco music soundtrack, gave John Travolta the opportunity to dance a rite of passage in which his character sheds his parochial background and gains a greater worldview. Musicals became increasingly dependent on the record industry as songs became identified with shows primarily through their exposure as recordings. *Flashdance* (1983), *Footloose* (1984), and *Dirty Dancing* (1987) are important examples, but the most obvious manifestation was in music video, films and tapes made solely to illustrate a recorded song. Michael Jackson's "Thriller," for example, presented a self-contained story—a horror musical, in fact—in an expanded version of his song. This was a new format in terms of presentation, but certainly it had antecedents in television programs such as *Your Hit Parade* and the extended numbers in many musicals. Although the musical has changed venue, the genre has survived in unexpected ways.

The musical has taken a variety of forms on film; the revue, the operetta, the backstage story, the integrated musical, all are common terms for aspects of the genre that have prevailed at different times. Similarly, within those different aspects of the genre, dance has played various roles. All dance types, however, have to some degree become homogenized into popular dance. Rarely are ballet or modern dance presented as pure forms; rather, they are used to expand the range of vernacular dance. By conven-

tion ballet movement has become associated with high art and dream sequences, but within the totality of a film all dance functions to promote the values of popular entertainment. The musical in all its forms is self-reflexive; it inquires into the nature of popular entertainment and concludes that its own purpose is to allow audiences to lose themselves in an artificial world in which everyone sings of love and dances for joy.

[*For related discussion, see the entries on Astaire, Berkeley, Bradley, Charisse, Cole, de Mille, Fosse, Holm, Kelly, Kidd, Loring, Nicholas Brothers, Powell, Rasch, Robbins, Robinson, Herbert Ross, Temple, and Ziegfeld. See also* Tap Dance *and* United States of America, *article on* Musical Theater.]

BIBLIOGRAPHY

Altman, Rick, ed. *Genre: The Musical*. London, 1981.

Altman, Rick. *The American Film Musical*. Bloomington, 1987.

Barrios, Richard. *A Song in the Dark: The Birth of the Hollywood Musical*. New York, 1995.

Butzel, Marcia. "Movement as Cinematic Narration: The Concept and Practice of Choreography in Film." Ph.D. diss., University of Iowa, 1985.

Cinéma 59 39 (August–September 1959).

Delamater, Jerome. *Dance in the Hollywood Musical*. Ann Arbor, 1981.

Dyer, Richard. "Social Values of Entertainment and Show Business." Ph.D. diss., University of Birmingham, 1972.

Feuer, Jane. *The Hollywood Musical*, 2d ed. Bloomington, 1993.

Mast, Gerald. *Can't Help Singin': The American Musical on Stage and Screen*. Woodstock, N.Y., 1987.

FILM. *That's Dancing!* (1985), directed by Jack Haley, Jr. *That's Entertainment!* (1974), directed by Jack Haley, Jr. *That's Entertainment, Part 2* (1976), directed by Gene Kelly. *That's Entertainment! III* (1994), directed by Bud Friedgen and Michael J. Sheridan.

JEROME DELAMATER

Bollywood Film Musicals

The Hindi feature film is a cinematic extravaganza designed to appeal to hundreds of millions of Indians through its inclusive presentation of story, (melo)drama, romance, comedy, tragedy, violence, music, and dance. Since its introduction in 1931, this form of mass entertainment has revolutionized Indian culture, leaving virtually no peoples or places untouched by its influence. Following the premiere of the world's first talking feature film, *The Jazz Singer,* in New York City on 6 October 1927, Indian silent filmmakers ordered sound equipment from the West, and joined the film-world frenzy in setting up soundproof studios, converting cinemas for sound, and producing the first Indian sound films. Despite the lack of resources, technical knowledge, government aid, trained actors and actresses, and involvement by the educated classes (who looked down on the new medium), India's early sound films drew enormous crowds. Two factors in particular aided this transition, and have continued to contribute significantly to the success and popularity of commercial Indian films. First, the use of vernacular languages (Hindi, Bengali, Tamil, Telugu, Marathi, and Gujarati within the first two years) had strong popular appeal, following a millennium of domination by foreign rulers whose languages, used at court, monopolized prestige and power. Second, all the early sound films included a profusion of songs, and most had dances. The dramatic tradition in India, from the Sanskrit dramas of the first centuries CE to the urban vernacular dramas of the nineteenth and twentieth centuries and to regional folk dramas, has continuously incorporated music, song, and dance, and sound film drew on these native forms of cultural expression, presenting them in a new technological medium.

The Hindi film experience, often two-and-a-half to three hours long, generally presents an escapist drama that

FILM MUSICALS: Bollywood Musicals. The drum dance from *Chandralekha* (1948). This hugely popular film, produced in Tamil by Gemini Studios of South India, Madras, was also dubbed in Hindi for a successful release in the North. (Photograph courtesy of Alison Arnold.)

combines traditional social customs and religious beliefs with elements of modern Western culture. Accepted film categories range from "social" to "mythological," "devotional," "historical," "legendary" (semi-historical), "biographical," "fantasy," and "costume." While the genres identified by these names are somewhat distinct, all Hindi film stories typically present a hero and a heroine, their chance meeting, a stumbling block to their future together, and their ultimate union with the triumph of good over evil. Furthermore, almost all Hindi films are musicals: each contains an average of six to ten songs approximately three to six minutes long, divided largely between the two main characters, as well as a few dances. Only a handful of Hindi feature films since the very first "All Talking, Singing, Dancing" production, *Alam Ara* (Beauty of the World), by Ardeshir Irani in 1931, have omitted songs and dances, and their failure at the box office only served to confirm audience preference for musical films (Barnouw and Krishnaswamy, 1980, p. 159; Rangoonwalla, 1975, pp. 99, 140).

The Indian film industry has the world's largest output of feature films, producing 795 films in 1995 compared with 420 released in the United States (Singh, 1996, p. 1; Matthews, 1996, p. 358). The Hindi film industry, known as "Bollywood"—a term that combines the name of the city that has been the industry's center since the 1950s, Bombay, with the name of its American counterpart, Hollywood—produced 156 Hindi feature films in 1995, representing 20 percent of India's total. Despite this low percentage, which has declined steadily since the 1950s, when Hindi productions represented approximately 40 percent of India's output, the Hindi film has held a dominant and influential position throughout its history. Unlike films in all other Indian languages, Hindi films have never been limited in their distribution to a small region of the country. Since virtually all Hindi films include songs and dances, film songs have represented a significant sector of India's popular music, which reaches the farthest corners of India via cinema, radio, television, cassette, and videocassette. Hindi film song and dance styles have clearly affected musical taste in India, in addition to influencing regional film music and non–film music traditions.

Song and Dance. Commercial Hindi cinema is unique in including songs and dances regardless of the type of film, whereas in Hollywood, as in European and other Asian cinemas, the "musical" was but one genre of many during the first decades of sound film. The universal use of song and dance in Indian films reflects at least two significant aspects of Indian culture: the integral nature of music in pre-industrial India, and the popular urban musical theater forms on which Hindi cinema drew inspiration in its earliest years. The first film producers and song composers (called music directors) used song to embellish and enhance the drama, and rarely to develop the story line as was common in American musicals. In the Prabhat Film Company's "mythological" film *Gopal Krishna* (1938), music director Master Krishnarao interspersed within the three-hour film fourteen songs that expressed Rādhā's relationship with Kṛṣṇa (Krishna), as he develops from childhood friend to devoted lover. Rai Chand Boral's thirteen songs in the devotional film *Vidyapati* (1937) include several that introduce different aspects of the poet-saint's character and role in the drama. The songs in early films were cast in a verse-and-refrain or through-composed melodic form, were accompanied by a small orchestra of Indian and Western instruments, usually had Hindustani lyrics (mixing Hindi and Urdu), and were sung by actor- or actress-singers who often had little musical training. They generally lasted two to three minutes, conforming to the length of a 78-rpm disc, on which the Gramophone company of India released most film songs by the late 1930s. Early sound-film music directors drew heavily on Indian light classical music and devotional song traditions, but soon began to experiment with musical style, structure, and orchestration.

Dances in early Hindi films were based on folk dances or on filmmakers' childhood memories of folk dances as well as on classical dance movements (Chatterjee, 1995, p. 199). Production companies did not employ professional choreographers at that time, and dance was relatively unimportant, again in contrast to Hollywood musicals, which frequently revolved around dance (for example, the films starring Fred Astaire and Ginger Rogers, or Gene Kelly). Even up to the early 1950s dance was not essential to a song "picturization" (film rendering), as it would become thirty years later. Producers nevertheless included in each production a few dances for their entertainment value. These cinematic spectacles, no longer than three minutes in length, included rural folklike dances with costumed dancers, and Indian and Western instrumental accompaniment (as in *Chandidas*, released by New Theatres in 1934, and *Roti*, by National Studios, in 1942), staged song-and-dance presentations (*Jhoola*, Bombay Talkies, 1941; *Sargam*, Filmistan, 1950), and pseudo-classical performances (*Vidyapati*, New Theatres, 1937). Occasionally the film story provided opportunities for more specialized song-and-dance scenes, such as a courtesan's performance for her clients (*Devdas*, New Theatres, 1937; *Aadmi*, Prabhat, 1939).

In the late 1940s and early 1950s the increasing percentage of "social" films with modern urban settings and romantic love stories saw the first Western dance bands on screen, and the use of Latin American–flavored dance music. Music director Naushad incorporated several such songs in *Andaaz* (High Society; Mehboob Productions, 1949), including a Western dance-band number and several songs featuring actor Dilip Kumar playing the piano

FILM MUSICALS: Bollywood Musicals. A *kathak*-style dance scene from the popular film *Jhanak Jhanak Payal Baje* (Jangle, Jangle, Sound the Bells; 1955), directed by V. Shantaram. Seen here are the hero and heroine, Gopi Krishna and Sandhya. This was one of the first Indian films shot in Technicolor. (Photograph courtesy of Alison Arnold.)

while the heroine, Nargis, danced. Music director C. Ramchandra also introduced samba and other syncopated Latin rhythms into his songs, notably in *Albela* (Dandy; Bhagwan Art Productions, 1951), which includes a small Latin American–style dance band on screen for the song "Diwānā Parwānā." Film dances, like film songs, were short and precomposed, to ensure that the dance movements would fit precisely with the fixed instrumental accompaniment recorded prior to shooting. Dance directors choreographed dance sequences creating their own hybrid mix of Indian and non-Indian styles.

In the period following India's independence from Britain in 1947, film distributors and exhibitors began to demand adherence to a production formula that proved enormously successful with Indian audiences: a few star actors and actresses, at least five songs, and some dances. With the breakup of 1930s and 1940s film studios (as in Hollywood), independent film producers were frequently dependent on distributors and moneylenders to complete their costly productions. They consequently focused their attention on elements of the Hindi film that appealed to distributors. Popular songs and dances not only helped draw full houses at theaters nationwide but could be exploited by the recording and broadcasting industries, bringing further fame and fortune for the films, and their song composers and singers. The 1950s became the "golden age of melody" in Hindi films, and music and dance directors as well as singers gained both greater recognition and higher fees.

Dance was not an integrated element of the Hindi film storyline except in rare instances. J. B. H. Wadia's 1941

production *Raj Nartaki* (Court Dancer) incorporated the Manipuri dance style into a tale of forbidden love starring the well-known dancer Sadhana Bose and her director husband, Madhu Bose. Columbia Pictures attempted to distribute the film, produced in three languages, in foreign markets also, but the second world war prevented the venture from succeeding. After the war, the world-famous dancer-choreographer Uday Shankar, elder brother of sitarist Ravi Shankar, released an independent production entitled *Kalpana* (Imagination). This 1948 film represented Shankar's attempt to reach a wider audience for his new dance idiom, through which he hoped to gain greater respect and appreciation for Indian classical dance. He drew on his expertise in *bharata nāṭyam*, *kathak*, and other classical dance styles to present a cinematic collage of dance sequences. This artistic film ran for twenty-six weeks in Calcutta, but it appealed largely to the upper classes and did not encourage other producers to attempt similar dance films. [*See the entry on Shankar.*] Two other productions that closely wove dance into the film narrative were *Jhanak Jhanak Payal Baje* (Jangle, Jangle, Sound the Bells; 1955) and *New Delhi* (1956). The former, an early Technicolor film by producer V. Shantaram, was a hugely successful formulaic love story that presented spectacular dances in *kathak* style together with simpler film-style dances. One of the film's songs, "Nain So Nain," sung by Hemant Kumar and Lata Mangeshkar, became the Binaca Gīt Mālā hit parade number-two song of 1956; the song accompanied a scene featuring the hero and heroine, played by Gopal Krishna and Sandhya, which concluded with a brilliantly colored costume

FILM MUSICALS: Bollywood Musicals. "Ramaiya Vastavaiya," a folk dance number from the film *Sri 420* (1955). Musical sequences in the film were directed by the Shankar-Jaikishen team. Raj Kapoor, the film's director, appears here (front, left) as its hero. (Photograph courtesy of Alison Arnold.)

dance. Mohan Sehgal's production *New Delhi* used the setting of a dance school run by the heroine, actress-dancer Vyjayantimala, to promote interregional marriage and national integration. The film integrates not only classical dance styles (*bharata nāṭyam, kathak,* etc.) but introduces possibly for the first time in Hindi film a *bhangra* performance. This lively Punjabi folk dance provided an alternative to the popular Western dance forms commonly employed in Hindi films, and its appeal among Indian audiences led to its incorporation in many subsequent films.

Film producers for the most part included dance numbers only as additional entertainment. This demand, created by financiers and distributors as well as the public, led to the cultivation of a peculiar variety of film actor- and actress-dancer, who generally played an insignificant role in the drama but achieved stardom though his or her indispensability. Such artists included Mumtaz Ali in the 1930s and 1940s, followed by Cuckoo and Helen. Producers often integrated film dancing with film song, and common formats would present the hero, heroine or other characters singing and dancing, various characters singing with non-acting dancers, or song scenes followed by dances. Typical choreographed dance situations in 1950s films include a pseudo–village group folk dance, wedding celebrations, performances at social parties, stage presentations, and fantasy or dream sequences.

Toward the end of the 1950s, film star Shammi Kapoor, younger brother of actor-producer Raj Kapoor, introduced a dance style reminiscent of the "bump-and-grind" movements of American rock-and-roll artists like Elvis

Presley, Little Richard, and Chuck Berry (Chatterjee, 1995, pp. 204–205). This dance style, featured in *Tumsa Nahin Dekha* (I've Never Seen Anyone Like You, 1957), gradually permeated Hindi cinema, as fast-paced rhythms, angular vocal lines, and catchy, repetitive refrains replaced lyrical song melodies over the next three decades. Song sequences from the 1960s on began to admit overtly sexual dance movements. Commercial Hindi film directors frequently focused such song-and-dance sequences on vamp characters. The film vamp, representing woman as lover and mistress, provided the predominantly male filmmakers with an excuse to incorporate racy, erotic songs and dances without disturbing the traditional, even mythological image of the perfect, submissive wife and mother, while allowing them to ignore the inadequacy of both stereotypes in reflecting women's changing roles in modern Indian society (Vasudev, 1983, pp. 98–99). Exceptional dancers such as Helen and Mumtaz played vamp roles from the 1950s to the 1970s. Their dances ranged from lively, flirtatious performances to fast, energetic, sensual displays.

A trend toward violent, action-packed thrillers with a minimum of songs and dances began in the 1970s and escalated in the mid 1980s into ever more violent dramas, incorporating token dance-songs along with scenes of murder, arson, and rape. The sexy new heroine, skilled in hand-to-hand combat and bent on vengeance, gyrated to the accompaniment of repetitive song melodies and trivial lyrics. In the late 1980s a parallel trend saw a return to melody-oriented songs with catchy, hummable tunes. While violence still pervaded Hindi films, melodic songs in *Qayamat Se Qayamat Tak* (From Crisis to Crisis), *Ram Lakhan, Tezaab* (Acid), and others became "super hits." As in the 1950s and 1960s the songs once again drew crowds to the theaters. In the screen rendering of the song "Ek Do Teen Char" (One Two Three Four) in *Tezaab*, composed by the duo Laxmikant-Pyarelal and sung by Alka Yagnik and chorus, the heroine Madhuri Dixit "slides, writhes, slithers, grimaces and shakes" (Chatterjee, 1995, p. 215). Such Hindi film dancing of the late 1980s was not always successful with audiences, but the song became a 1988 top-ten hit.

Song Creators. The Hindi film music director is responsible for creating and producing all the songs in a film. Typically the music director, together with the producer, director, lyricist, screenplay writer, and others, jointly decide on the optimal points in the story for songs and dances. From the 1940s to the 1960s filmmakers spaced their quota of songs more or less evenly throughout the film, inserting them in a variety of contexts. Most composers created each song's melody first, with or without the lyrics, then arranged the song for a studio orchestra. An identifiable film-song genre evolved through the 1930s and 1940s characterized by an alternating verse-and-refrain structure with instrumental interludes between the verses, melodies employing patterns derived from both Indian ragas and the Western major and minor scales, orchestral accompaniment with an occasional use of Western harmony (totally alien to Indian music), a thin, high-pitched (even stratospheric) vocal sound (among female singers), and expressive lyrics. Besides this mainstream form, composers also adapted traditional song genres by retaining their original structures but incorporating film-musical elements, resulting in the hybrid genres of film *qawwālī*, film *ghazal*, film *bhajan*, and others.

Until the 1960s Hindi film music directors were either singers or instrumentalists, or had received some Indian musical training before joining the film industry. The most famous and prolific among these include (in chronological order) Anil Biswas, Naushad Ali, Vasant Desai, C. Ramchandra, S. D. Burman, the Shankar-Jaikishen duo, O. P. Nayyar, Salil Chaudhury, Khayyam, Ravi, the Kalyanji–Anandji duo, R. D. Burman, and the Lakshmikant–Pyarelal duo. Some employed assistants to help with orchestration. In more recent years, music directors with little or no musical training have found employment in the industry, and rely heavily on music assistants and Western pop tunes for their film song creations.

Three other partners play integral roles in creating the film song prior to its editing by sound recording engineers: the lyricist, the singer, and the orchestral musicians. Their creativity is essential, but each has little control over the finished product. The lyricists of the first few decades were well-respected poets in their own right.

They composed emotionally expressive song texts using descriptive poetic language. Though not always credited in 1930s films, lyricists of this time period include Pandit Bhushan, Pandit Indra, Arzoo Lucknavi, Dinanath Madhok, Pyarelal Santoshi, Zia Sarhady, Sudarshan, and Narottam Vyas. Their numbers increased in the 1940s, encompassing well-known lyric writers Prem Dhavan, Indivar, Qamar Jalalabadi, Shams Lucknavi, Pradeep, and Narendra Sharma. In the 1950s and 1960s, lyricists Rajendra Krishan, Majruh Sultanpuri, and Shakeel Badayuni, among others, wrote more commonplace, less poetic song texts as they sought to appeal to an ever-broader mass audience. The trend has continued into the 1990s.

Film singers were initially the actors and actresses themselves, for the first sound-film cameras could only record sound and picture simultaneously. Many film actor- and actress-singers were former stage artists with singing experience, some were classically trained singers, while others had little or no vocal training. Early film singing thus varied according to the singer. The female vocal style was generally a forceful, husky, nasal tone, as in the voices of Shamshad Begum and Noorjahan. Males sang with an open-throated voice, but soon followed the lead of actor-singer Kundan Lal Saigal at New Theatres Film Company, Calcutta, who developed a quieter, crooning style. The advance in technology during the 1930s allowed separate audio and visual recording, which enabled music directors to prerecord the soundtrack prior to shooting. This led to the separation of film actors from the film singers whose voices they lip-synched. The latter became known as "playback singers," since their prerecorded voices were played back during shooting.

By 1950 talented singers had joined the industry, capable of whatever vocal skills music directors required. As invisible artists, however, the singers did not gain stardom equal to that of the actors and actresses for whom they sang. The number of popular singers was relatively small, considering the annual production output of approximately a thousand Hindi film songs. Male singers included Mohammad Rafi, Mukesh, Talat Mehmood, Manna Dey, and Kishore Kumar. Female singers Shamshad Begum, Geeta Dutt, and Suman Kalyanpur were well known, but the most prominent by far were Lata Mangeshkar and her sister Asha Bhosle. The encounter of the high-pitched voice of Lata with more advanced microphones resulted in a new "filmi" vocal style that has held sway to this day. The enormous popularity of Lata's voice, enhanced by the promotion and marketing of commercial cinema, radio, television, and the recording industry, has provoked a younger generation of singers to mirror her vocal style.

Bombay studio orchestras are now unionized groups of players comparable to film orchestras around the world. They include electronic keyboards and synthesizers, and

FILM MUSICALS: Bollywood Musicals. A choreographed folk-dance number typical of Hindi films, from *Madhumati* (1958), directed by Bimal Roy with musical direction by Salil Chaudhury. The film's heroine, Madhumati, is portrayed by Vyjayantimala, a well-known dancer in Hindi films. (Photograph courtesy of Alison Arnold.)

hire experienced, trained musicians able to read Western notation. From the first accompanying ensembles of harmonium, *tabla,* and violin or *sarangi,* orchestras quickly expanded in the 1930s to include a broader range of Western and Indian instruments: piano, clarinet, mandolin, *bansuri* flute, and *sitar.* Goan musicians from the neighboring state of Goa (a Portuguese colony until 1961) were prominent in Bombay and Pune film orchestras because of their ability to read staff notation and play Western music. The orchestra's role, like that of Indian light classical and stage music ensembles, was largely to provide melodic and rhythmic accompaniment. Bengali music directors experimented with harmonization in the late 1930s, and by the mid-1940s composers in Bombay and Madras were introducing Western chordal harmony. The size of the orchestra in the 1950s grew dramatically, ranging from fifty to a hundred players. Large string sections and many Western instruments became a status symbol

for music directors, who began composing film songs with long instrumental interludes. These nonvocal sections allowed more screen action during a song performance. The increased prominence of orchestral music by the 1970s led to the orchestra's dominance over the voice, as vocal melodies and lyrics came to play a secondary role.

Film Music and Dance in Indian Culture. Indian film songs were India's first mass-media popular music, and also the first such music to gain nationwide popularity. Transmitted via film, radio, television, recordings, and live performances, film music and dance presented Indians with a form of musical entertainment that was modern and yet Indian. Especially following the large-scale postindependence migrations of people from rural to urban areas, film song provided uprooted Indians with a music suited to their new urban way of life. For villagers who saw and heard films in traveling cinemas, film music and dance represented a window into a different world, linking village with city, tradition with modernity and westernization.

At least since the 1950s the mass distribution and consumption of film songs has exerted a counterinfluence on traditional Indian music genres and styles, on which the early Hindi film music directors drew heavily for their song compositions. Film song's effects have scarcely penetrated the world of Indian classical music, but the influence of film song in Indian folk music, theater, and light music is pervasive. This influence ranges widely from the incorporation of film song elements (the filmi vocal style, Western instruments, chordal harmony, etc.) into individual performances, to film music's replacement of traditional music genres. Scholars and writers have noted many instances—film song replacing folk songs in brass band repertory, village women composing lyrics to film tunes, popular film melodies invading *jatra* and *nautanki* urban theatrical forms, and *biraha* musicians introducing film songs into their repertory. The examples are numerous, and Bollywood's cultural influence undisputed.

Critics stress that marketing and media manipulation of this commercial product have forced film and its homogeneous film music on the Indian public, providing no other choice of popular musical entertainment. Advocates, on the other hand, claim that the overwhelming popularity of film song has made it India's modern urban folk music, since urban people sing it, dance to it, and even perform and record it. As it lives simultaneously in oral tradition and recorded format, they feel Indians have the choice of accepting or rejecting the film songs, the choice of attending or not attending films, and the power to bring success or failure to Hindi cinema and its music.

Indians both inside and outside the film industry have identified and recognized a singular achievement of Indian film song: in the words of music director Anil Biswas, "it has given the whole of India music consciousness and musical integration emotionally" (Arnold, 1991, p. 269). Composers like Biswas in the 1940s and 1950s sought to synthesize native and foreign musical traditions, and in raising people's consciousness of India's musical diversity, aimed to produce a modern, popular, identifiably Indian genre that could draw people together. Around the time of independence, film song not only gave Indians a common identity, but can be seen as part of the movement to forge a new national spirit, to put aside differences in support of the newly independent nation.

The popularity of Hindi film song and dance in Indian culture is a complex question; there are several possible reasons for its widespread acceptance. First, film song met with no native competition in the field of popular music until the 1970s. The Gramophone Company of India (GCI) held a vitual monopoly in the recording industry, and Hindi film song, with its wide linguistic market, dominated GCI record production output by the 1940s. Only in the 1970s did the introduction and spread of cassette technology enable the rise of small-scale producers and regional popular-music traditions, which has reduced film song's domination of the popular music market (Manuel, 1993). Second, film has had enormous appeal for Indians

as an inexpensive form of modern entertainment. Producers have aimed to attract the widest possible audience by presenting escapist film dramas with easily assimilated songs that have simple structures, catchy tunes, and straightforward lyrics, and with readily imitated dances. Third, Hindi film song has received broad musical exposure through aggressive and widespread distribution and exhibition of Hindi films. Such fast, nationwide circulation of music did not exist prior to sound cinema.

A further reason behind the popularity of Hindi film song may lie in its power to symbolize modern India, with its inherent conflicts of tradition and modernity, rural and urban, poor and rich, Hindu and Muslim, native and foreign. Film music directors have purposely sought to fuse musical and lyrical elements in order to encapsulate the diversity of modern Indian culture. Song composers have broadened their musical experience through travel or listening to foreign recordings, and their combined efforts have resulted in the eclecticism of Hindi film song.

FILM MUSICALS: Bollywood Musicals. Hema Malini, a classically trained dancer of *bharata nāṭyam* and the star of many films. Here, she appears in *Mrig Trishnaa* (1975), a film directed by Rajendranath Shukla, with musical direction by Shambu Sen. (Photograph courtesy of Alison Arnold.)

FILM MUSICALS: Bollywood Musicals. Fantasy song and dance scene from V. Shantaram's film *Jal Bin Machhli, Nritya Bin Bijli* (Water without Fish, Dance without Lightning; 1971). The Lakshmikant-Pyrarelal duo directed the musical numbers. (Photograph courtesy of Alison Arnold.)

Over their seven decades of existence, Hindi film song and dance have set many popular music trends among Indians. They have provided entertainment for young and old, and continue to appeal to Indians at home and abroad despite ever-increasing competition from native and foreign popular music. Hindi film songs are closely connected with their film productions and with cinema culture, yet they also live a separate existence as popular music. While Hindi films are undemocratically produced, and their songs and dances maintain a degree of stylistic homogeneity in contrast with the variety of Indian folk music, Bollywood film music is nevertheless music and dance of the Indian people, integrated into numerous native performance contexts, and enjoyed by hundreds of millions of Indians, in India and around the world.

[*See also the entries on Mallika Sarabhai and Sitara Devi.*]

BIBLIOGRAPHY

Arnold, Alison. "Popular Film Song in India: A Case of Mass-Market Musical Eclecticism." *Popular Music* 7.2 (1988): 177–188.

Arnold, Alison. "Hindi Filmi Git: On the History of Commercial Indian Popular Music." Ph.D. diss., University of Illinois at Urbana-Champaign, 1991.

Arnold, Alison. "Aspects of Production and Consumption in the Popular Hindi Film Industry." *Asian Music* 24.1 (1992–1993): 122–136.

Bannerjee, Shampa, and Anil Srivastava. *One Hundred Feature Films: An Annotated Filmography.* New York, 1988.

Barnouw, Erik, and S. Krishnaswamy. *Indian Film.* 2d ed. New York and Oxford, 1980.

Chatterjee, Partha. "A Bit of Song and Dance." In *Frames of Mind: Reflections on Indian Cinema*, edited by Aruna Vasudev, pp. 197–218. New Delhi, 1995.

Das Gupta, Chidananda. *The Painted Face: Studies in India's Popular Cinema.* New Delhi, 1991.

Manuel, Peter. *Cassette Culture: Popular Music and Technology in North India.* Chicago, 1993.

Matthews, Peter, ed. *The Guinness Book of Records 1996.* New York, 1996.

Ramachandran, T. M., ed. *Fifty Years of Indian Talkies (1931–1981): A Commemorative Volume.* Bombay, 1981.

Ranade, Ashok D. In *On Music and Musicians of Hindoostan.* New Delhi, 1984. See the chapter entitled "Indian Film Music: Changing Compulsions," pages 68–78.

Rangoonwalla, Firoze. *Indian Filmography: Silent & Hindi Films (1897–1969)*. Bombay, 1970.

Rangoonwalla, Firoze. *75 Years of Indian Cinema*. New Delhi, 1975.

"Rhythm Is Gonna Get You." *Stardust Annual '89* (International ed., 1989): 16–21.

Segal, Mohan. "Dance in Indian Cinema." In *70 Years of Indian Cinema (1913–1983)*, edited by T. M. Ramachandran, pp. 252–257. Bombay, 1985.

Singh, Har Mandir "Hamraz." "1995 se 795 fīcar films ka nirmān." *Listeners' Bulletin* 26.100 (April 1996): 1.

Vasudev, Aruna. "The Woman: Vamp or Victim." In *Indian Cinema Superbazaar*, edited by Aruna Vasudev and Philippe Lenglet, pp. 98–105. New Delhi, 1983.

Vasudev, Aruna., ed. *Frames of Mind: Reflections on Indian Cinema*. New Delhi, 1995.

ALISON ARNOLD

FILS PRODIGUE, LE. *See* Prodigal Son, The.

FINLAND. [*To survey dance in Finland, this entry comprises three articles. The first article focuses on traditional dance; the second explores the history of theatrical dance; the third provides a brief history of scholarship and writing.*]

Traditional Dance

Finnish folk dances combine features from cultures to the west, mainly Sweden, and from Russia to the east. Those identified as specifically Finnish today have been danced in the present Finnish state and in Karelia and Ingermanland, now part of Russia. It is usual to divide Finnish folk dances by region: those of the Swedish-speaking minority in western and southern Finland; those of Russian Orthodox Karelia; and those of the remainder of Finland. This classification, however, is somewhat misleading, because all these areas are heterogeneous and all have experienced varying influences from surrounding societies. Finnish folk dance is in fact a varied spectrum of dances from different regions, eras, and cultures.

Early Folk Dances. Little is known about Finnish folk dance before the nineteenth century, but dance is mentioned in a few early documents. In 1679 two men were accused in a court in Iisalmi of performing an indecent courting dance before noble spectators. Petrus Bång's chronicle of 1680 records that older people in Ruovesi and Savo sang while dancing. Surprisingly, the historian H. G. Porthan claimed in *De poesi fennica* (1778) that people of eastern Finland did not know how to dance, and that those in western Finland had learned dancing only recently from the Swedes. Nonetheless, a 1753 document from Lapua notes that some young people were punished for having danced so much on Sunday evening that they could not work on Monday.

Dancing in northern Europe was typically associated with agricultural and fertility rituals. There are few descriptions of such rituals from Finland proper, but many were preserved in Ingermanland into the nineteenth century. At a large festival, Vakkove, villagers gathered to drink beer, sing, and dance to guarantee a good harvest. The best-known agricultural ritual in western Finland is the Whitsun festival in the village of Ritvala, Sääksmäki; a procession of young girls moves across the fields, singing ancient songs. In Säkylä, southwestern Finland, a solo dance called *tarikko* was danced by older people in springtime; in Juva in the east, people danced the *vanhaa leipää* ("old bread") at the start of plowing. Fertility dances were also performed in many regions on Shrovetide and Christmas; Shrove Tuesday was known as Hyppästisstai (Dance Tuesday) in western Finland. On Boxing Day, young men might don masks and go from house to house performing songs and dances.

Dances connected with fertility rites often included movements imitating sexual intercourse, so collectors of folklore regarded them as indecent. The Finnish ethnographer Samuli Paulaharju wrote in 1905 that on the Karelian Isthmus, "drunken old men" danced the *pukkitantsu* ("goat dance"), in which they stood facing each other, singing and swinging their bellies. A similar dance from Sääminki was called the *tiiroo*. Many of these sexually colored dances were performed only by men, but a few were performed by both sexes. In Lehtimäki there was a dance called the *kaati-koopi* in which girls danced with their aprons pulled between their legs; both girls and boys performed birdlike jumps. In Nakkila, girls did a similar dance called the *krookeltussu*.

Song dances were performed all over Europe in the Middle Ages, usually in simple patterns such as circle or chain. In Scandinavia these dances were usually accompanied by long epic ballads, which in Finland came from the *Kalevala*, the Finnish national epic. These dances were performed as late as 1900 in the Karelian isthmus and Ingermanland, but for the most part, the medieval song-dance tradition had disappeared in Finland by end of the eighteenth century.

Song dances were sometimes performed by opposing lines of male and female dancers; each line danced and sang alternately. Such dances were known in eastern Karelia and among the Skolt-Lapps of northern Finland into the twentieth century. In southern Finland the tradition was preserved in the form of singing games, of which the best known is "Simosilla," which incorporates elements of medieval manor society. Even today, Finnish children know a similar singing game called "Kotini on Riia Raa" (My Home Is Riia Raa).

Instrumental music became common in dance events after the seventeenth century, but singing games were performed at dances as late as the 1950s. The *Kalevala* songs gradually disappeared, first in western Finland and later in the east, but new songs and singing games were introduced. At first only one couple at a time danced while the others watched, but later all the couples danced simultaneously. The choreography was usually very simple: a couple danced hand-in-hand, or couples moved in a circle using walking, running, or hopping steps.

Imported Social Dances. The first Finnish folk dances to use instrumental accompaniment were the *polska* and minuet. It is not known exactly when they were introduced, but they were danced in Sweden in the seventeenth century and probably entered Finland (then a Swedish possession) at that time. In the eighteenth century the *polska* became very popular in western and central Finland, and in some areas all social dances were known by that name. The steps were probably quite simple. Originally the *polska* was a couple dance with various handholds, but in the nineteenth century it was also danced in a circle, especially at weddings. Most Finnish *polskas* are in 3/4 time, but some are in 2/4 time.

The minuet was not so popular as the *polska*. It was danced mainly in western Finland, especially by Swedish-speaking people. It disappeared from most of the country in the nineteenth century, but it survived into the twentieth century in two areas on the western coast, particularly as a wedding dance. The Finnish minuet is performed by opposing lines of men and women and includes rather complex steps originating from the French tradition. Originally it was a slow, dignified dance, but its later form is almost as fast as the *polska*.

The folk dance tradition includes a number of solo and duo dances, which may be of ritual origin. One is known in Swedish-speaking regions as the *skinnkompass* (derived from French *gaillard* step *cinq pas*, "five steps") and by Finnish speakers as the *tikkuristi* ("cross of sticks") or *ristipuikko*. It was performed by one or two men who hopped over two crossed sticks or lines drawn on the ground. The similar *dansa på skarven* ("dance on the chink in the floor") and *dansa på strå* ("dance on the straw") were done in the Swedish-speaking region. In southern Finland two men danced holding a stick between them and kicking their legs over it; a similar dance is known in Estonia. There were a number of dances, usually performed by men, with names such as *Ryssaa* or *Rysk* ("Russian"), *pikku Ryssä* ("little Russian"), or *Kasakka* ("Cossack"); these were probably introduced in the nineteenth century when Finland was ruled by Russia. A group of dances called *Mustalainen* ("Gypsy") were done by a couple or a solo male dancer, with improvisation.

Country dances became popular in the eighteenth and nineteenth centuries. The oldest, called *Angleesi* or *Anke-liini* ("English"), were danced in longways sets; there were local variants such as the *lintunen* ("little bird") and *solavalssi* (longways waltz). Especially in the coastal regions, *Enkeliska* ("English dances"), which originated from Scottish reels, were danced in the nineteenth cen-

tury by sets of three to nine dancers. Other country dances were quadrilles and threesome dances. The quadrilles of western Finland usually consisted of eight to ten figures, but there were also smaller quadrilles of only one or two figures, especially in central Finland. Some quadrilles survived into the early twentieth century. They might include improvised figures in which the men performed the *trepak* and other skillful steps to impress the women.

The nineteenth century saw the introduction of large-scale ceremonial dances such as the *polonaise, purpuri* ("potpourri"), and *française*. The *polonaise* was especially popular at weddings and could also serve as the first figure of the *purpuri*. The *purpuri* often consisted of more than ten figures, including waltzes, mazurkas, quadrilles, and *polskas*, and could go on for hours. It was danced mainly in southern and western Finland but was known throughout the country. The *française* was danced in the late nineteenth century but never gained much popularity except around Helsinki, where it dominated dance events from 1860 to 1890.

Many new couple dances were introduced in the nineteenth century. The first was the waltz, introduced around 1800, which had become a folk dance by the 1840s. Gradually it replaced the *polska* and minuet as the first dance at weddings, a role it plays even today. There are several Finnish variations of the waltz; the most individual is the *silia valssi* or *slätvals* ("smooth waltz"), danced as part of the *purpuri* in parts of western Finland.

The polka was brought to Helsinki from Saint Petersburg in 1844 and became very popular by the beginning of the twentieth century. Its steps were also incorporated in complex dances such as quadrilles. Many variations of the polka developed.

The schottische and mazurka became popular in the late nineteenth century, the former under such names as *saksanpolkka, tyyskaa, tyska polka* ("German polka"), and *jenkka*. The mazurka was incorporated in some regional variants of the *purpuri* and was known as the polka-muzurka.

Most new dances in the twentieth century were imported from the Americas. The first were the one-step and two-step; the one-step became very popular under such names as *oonesteppi, pisto,* and *humppa*. The tango was introduced around World War I but did not become popular until the 1950s; Finns dance it in a unique manner, quite different from its original form. The fox trot has been danced since the 1920s. There have also been short-lived crazes for such imported dances as the rumba, conga, mambo, and cha-cha.

A new dancing style was introduced in the 1960s with the Twist, in which partners did not hold each other; this style is still used in popular dancing. Other social dances performed in Finland today include the waltz, tango, *humppa,* and (to a lesser extent) schottische. Older dances are done mainly by folk dance enthusiasts.

Research and Publication. The first researcher to collect Finnish folk dances was H. A. Reinholm in the 1840s. He wrote up the results of his field trips, but his book was never published. It was decades until another scholar undertook such work, when Viktor Allardt in the 1880s collected dances in his native region, Swedish-speaking southern Finland.

Systematic collection began in the early twentieth century. Collectors included Toivo Salonen, who traveled in western and central Finland; Hugo Dahl, in Swedish-speaking southern Finland; and Valdemar Lindbohm, in Rautalampi, central Finland. Dahl's and Lindbohm's collections were published in the first Finnish folk dance book, *Suomalainen kisapirtti* (1905), edited by Anni Collan; it contained instructions in both Finnish and Swedish. The first exclusively Swedish folk dance collection in Finland, *12 folkdanser,* was published two years later by Föreningen Brage.

The most important collectors in the Finnish-speaking regions were Anni Collan, Asko Pulkkinen, Emil Koskinen, and Otto Harju. Collan gathered many dances in central and southeastern Finland during the first decades of the twentieth century and published several books. Pulkkinen made many trips to eastern Finland to gather dances from 1907 to 1915, resulting in a number of books. Koskinen collected in southern Finland in 1916, and Harju in western and central Finland in the 1910s, but their work was not published until the 1970s.

In Swedish-speaking Finland, Yngvar Heikel made a monumental collection of dances, which he published in *Dansbeskrivningar* (1938). This book, issued by the Finlands Svenska Folkdansring (Swedish Folk Dance Circle in Finland), is still the most systematic and profound work on the subject.

Since these collections, only a little research and collection has been done. The noted Finnish ethnomusicologist Erkki Ala-Könni discussed folk dance in his doctoral dissertation, *Polska-tänze in Finnland* (1956). In recent decades Pirkko-Liisa Rausmaa has been the leading researcher, studying dances and editing books. The most notable scholars in the Swedish-speaking region are Ann-Mari Häggman and Gunnel Biskop.

Revival and Organizations. The first Finnish folk dance organization was founded in 1901 under the name Suomalaisen Kansantanssin Ystaavaat (Friends of Finnish Folk Dance). From the beginning it regarded collection as very important and gave stipends to many of the collectors mentioned above, as well as publishing many books. Today this organization has thousands of members in local clubs throughout Finland. However, the largest organization including folk dancing in its activities is Suomen Nuorisoseurojen Liitto (Union of Finnish Youth Associations); folk dancing has been an essential part of youth groups since the first decades of the twentieth century.

One of the first Swedish-speaking organizations to take an interest in folk dance was Föreningen Brage in Helsinki. It published the first Swedish-Finnish folk dance books, and Yngvar Heikel was involved in its activities. In 1931 a central organization, Finlands Svenska Folkdansring, was founded; today it has local clubs throughout the Swedish-speaking region.

Today there are tens of thousands of folk dance devotees in Finland. Since the 1970s amateur folk dance teachers have been trained at Varala College of Physical Education, and since 1991 professional folk dance teachers have been educated at the Conservatory of Oulu. In addition, the various folk dance associations have their own instructor-training programs.

[*For related discussion, see* European Traditional Dance.]

BIBLIOGRAPHY

Ala-Könni, Erkki. *Die polska-tänze in Finnland: Eine ethnomusikologische Untersuchung.* Suomen, 1956.

Allenby Jaffe, Nigel, and Margaret Allenby Jaffe. *Ten Dances from Finland.* Skipton, 1988.

Biskop, Gunnel. *Folkdans inom folkdansrörelsen: Folklig dans?* Helsingfors, 1990.

Heikel, Yngvar. *Dansbeskrivningar.* Finlands Svenska Folkdiktning, 6. Helsingfors, 1938.

Heikkilä, Sari. *Old Finnish Folk Dances.* Helsinki, 1988.

Högnäs, Per-Ove. *Lätar från Kökar.* Mariehamn, 1991.

Niemeläinen, Päivyt, ed. *Suomalainen kansantanssi.* Otava, 1983.

Rausmaa, Pirkko-Liisa, ed. *Tanhuvakka: Suuri suomalainen kansantanssikirja.* Porvoo, 1977.

Rausmaa, Pirkko-Liisa. *Ilokerä: Laulutansseja ja piirileikkejä.* Helsinki, 1984.

Rausmaa, Pirkko-Liisa. "Rituaalitanssit suomessa." *Musiikin suunta* 14.4 (1992).

PETRI HOPPU

Theatrical Dance

The earliest references to dance in Finland occur in the national epic, the *Kalevala,* and in a collection of songs, the *Kanteletar.* For the most part, however, the Christian Finns regarded dancing as sinful; Christianity had been introduced in the mid-twelfth century. In the Jagellonian court of the sixteenth century in Turku Castle, however, Duke Juhana and Duchess Katarina and their courtiers danced the chaconne, courante, gigue, and polonaise, which were so popular in other courts of Europe.

In the eighteenth century foreign teachers began to appear in the urban centers of Helsinki, Turku, and Viipuri, and wealthy citizens began to accept dancing as entertainment at their charity balls. Finland's first professional dancer was a Bavarian, Alina Frasa (1834–1899), who had studied with Italian and Russian masters.

The first notable native Finnish dancer was Maggie Gripenberg (1881–1976). Isadora Duncan visited Helsinki in 1908 and made a great impression on Gripenberg. After training with Anna Behle in Stockholm and with Émile Jaques-Dalcroze in Geneva, Gripenberg made her solo debut in Helsinki in 1911. Later she gave concerts in Europe and North America as well, winning first prize in a 1939 Brussels choreography competition and other prizes in Stockholm and Copenhagen. Noted for her musicality, Gripenberg taught for many years in Helsinki. Her pupils, however, did not equal her achievements, and her style did not continue to attract audiences in Finland. [*See the entry on Gripenberg.*] Another Finnish pioneer was Toivo Niskanen (1887–1961), who danced a classical pas de deux—the first Finn on record to do so—with Margit Lilius in 1917.

Ballet. The father of Finnish ballet was Edvard Fazer, who took over the direction of the Finnish Opera in 1919.

FINLAND: Theatrical Dance. Maggie Gripenberg, a pioneer of modern dance in Finland, performed her own choreography in *Aida* with the Finnish National Opera, c.1919. (Photograph courtesy of Saga Ambegaokar.)

Fazer had brought a group of Russian dancers, including Anna Pavlova, to western Europe in 1908 (a year before Serge Diaghilev did), and he believed that dance belonged in the opera house. Finnish interest in ballet was stirred by the visits of Pavlova and of Olga Preobrajenska.

From 1916 to 1924 ballet instruction was offered at the Helsinki College of Dance, founded by Rafael Penger. In addition to the Finnish staff, Russian teachers offered classes in classical technique, character dance, rhythm, plastic art, and mime. The schools of Elo Kuosmanen and Niskanen also provided dancers for the opera ballet, now called the Finnish National Ballet. Mary Paischeff was engaged as *prima ballerina* and George Gé as ballet master. Both Finns had studied in Russia. In 1922 Gé produced the first Finnish production of *Swan Lake*. He followed this successful premiere with other ballets from the Russian repertory, mostly fairy-tale works. The Helsinki ballet lost some of its best dancers, however, for lack of funds.

The second ballet master was Alexander Saxelin, who had studied in Leningrad and led the company from 1935 to 1954. During his tenure Helsinki's Lucia Nifontova won first prize as best classical dancer in the international choreography competition in Stockholm in 1945, and the company paid a successful visit to that city in 1946. Among the leading dancers of the time were Irja Koskinen, Klaus Salin, and Margaretha von Bahr.

Gé was ballet master again from 1955 to 1962, and Alfons Almi, director of the opera, worked to develop the ballet's international activities. During the 1950s and 1960s the company toured in Europe as well as in North and South America. At this time dancers attained a status equal to that of singers. Since 1956 the ballet school has been supported by the state, giving free instruction to pupils who pass the entrance examinations.

Although foreign choreographers provided much of the repertory in the 1950s and 1960s, the Finnish *prima ballerina* Elsa Sylvestersson created more than fifty ballets; some were original works based on Finnish music, but the majority were new versions of the classics. In the 1970s foreigners directed the company and contributed much of the repertory; among them were Birgit Cullberg from Sweden, Robert North from England, and Jiří Kylián from the Netherlands. Leading dancers were Marianna Rumjantseva, Seija Silfverberg, Maj-Lis Rajala, Seppo Koski, and Martti Valtonen.

For a long time the company did not look to native talent, but in 1983 the Finnish Theater Academy opened with a special dance department to train performers, teachers, and choreographers. The dance department concentrates on modern dance, and students start so late that most of them become teachers rather than performers. The ballet school of the Finnish National Opera provides professional dancers for its own company and for

FINLAND: Theatrical Dance. Scene from the Finnish National Ballet's production of *Romantic Rosette*. (Photograph from the Dance Collection, New York Public Library for the Performing Arts.)

others. This classical school is based on the Russian Vaganova system. In 1984 Doris Laine, formerly the company's *prima ballerina*, became director of the National Ballet of Finland, and in 1992 Jorma Uotinen became her successor. The company's leading dancers in the 1970s and 1980s were Arja Nieminen, Tarja Ranta, Matti Tikkanen, Ulrika Hallberg, Jarmo Rastas, Aku Ahjolinna, and Maija Hanninen; it also included Kirsi and Jukka Aromaa, who joined New York City Ballet for some time, Mikko Nissinen, who went to the San Francisco Ballet and came back, and Timo Kokkonen, to the Australian Ballet. Among the ballets in the varied, international repertory were *Concerto Barocco* by George Balanchine, *Le Loup* by Roland Petit, *The Swan of Tuonela* by Imre Eck, *Reflections* by Heikki Värtsi, and *Elective Affinities* by Tom Schilling. In the 1990s the leading dancers are Nina Hyvärinen, Jessica Kellgren, Minna Tervamäki, Kare Länsivuori, Juha Kirjonen, Anu Sistonen, Anatti Honkanen, Susanna Vironmäki, and Sempo Kivelä.

Modern Dance. The American modern dance influence was first felt in Finland in the early 1960s when Riitta Vainio, who had studied in Philadelphia, formed her own ensemble. The Praesens group, founded in 1961, also represented modern dance.

The first modern dance group to gain a firm foothold in Finland is the Raatikko Dance Theater of Vantaa, founded in 1972 as an alternative to institutionalized theater. The company strives to portray real life and bring new audiences to dance. The first leader of the group and one of its founders was Marjo Kuusela, whose choreography uses a number of techniques and styles but is always filled with vitality and expressiveness. Raatikko has lost its importance since Kuusela's era.

The Helsinki City Theater is the only theater in Finland with its own dance group, which provides dances for musical productions and also puts on independent programs. As artistic director of its dance company, Jorma Uotinen brought new audiences to dance. He studied with Serge Golovine and Carolyn Carlson; his individualistic style is close to total theater, combining movement, sound, lights, text, and music as equal elements. The directors after Uotinen have been Marjo Kuusela and Kenneth Kvarnström.

Other Dance Groups and Events. Other groups partly supported by the state are Hurjaruuth in Helsinki (for children), Ballet du Soleil (neoclassical) in Turku, Katrilli (the only professional folk dance group) in Helsinki, and Dance Theatre ERI (modern) in Turku. ERI was founded in 1989, is extremely versatile, and has toured Europe, Japan, and the United States.

A summer dance festival held each year in the city of

FINLAND: Theatrical Dance. *(left)* Ulrika Hallberg and Sakari Tiitinen in the Finnish National Ballet's production of *Wolf's Bride. (right)* Jarmo Rastas and Terttu Laurikainen of the Finnish National Ballet in Luc Bouy's duet *Your Eyes*, a dance performed without musical accompaniment. (Photographs courtesy of the Ministry for Foreign Affairs, Helsinki, Finland.)

Kuopio in eastern Finland includes performances by both native and visiting companies. Among the talented younger modern choreographers are Reijo Kela, Tommi Kitti, Tero Saarinen, and Tiina Lindfors.

BIBLIOGRAPHY

Arvelo, Ritva. *Tanssitaiteen vuosikymmenet*. Helsinki, 1987.
Dance Council of Finland. *Dancing in Finland*. Helsinki, 1991.
Garske, Rolf. "Dance Tradition, National Identity, International Exchanges." *Ballett International* 8 (February 1985): 6–11.
Garske, Rolf. "Say Goodbye to Old Things." *Ballett International* 12 (June 1989): 22–29.
Hirn, Sven. *Pelit ja leikit*. Helsinki, 1981.
Hirn, Sven. *Våra danspedagoger och dansnöjen: Om undervisning och evenemang före 1914*. Helsingfors, 1982.
Näslund, Erik. "Finsk Ballett på frammarsch." *Dans* (December 1975): 42–52.
Percival, John. "Crossroads in Finland." *Dance and Dancers* (November–December 1988): 34–37.
Räsänen, Auli. "Ballet and Dance: Protected and Promoted in the Security of the State." *Ballett International* 13 (January 1990): 131–135.
Reunamäki, Hannu, et al. *Celebration of Dance*. Kuopio, 1984.
Savolainen, Pentti. *Balladi Olavinlinnan oopperajuhlista*. Porvoo, 1995.
Suhonen, Tiina. "Finland's Free Dance." *Ballett International* 12 (June 1989): 30–31.
Suhonen, Tiina. "Dance and Nature." *Ballett International* 14 (June 1991): 19–23.
Talve, Ilmar. *Tanhuvakka*. Helsinki, 1977.
Talve, Ilmar. *Suomen Kansankulttuuri*. 3d ed. Helsinki, 1990.
Tolominen, Marjaana. "A Strong Generation." *Ballett International/ Tanz Aktuell* (May 1994): 12–13.
Vienola-Lindfors, Irma, and Raoul af Hällström. *Suomen Kansallisbaletti, 1922–1972*. Helsinki, 1981.
Wahl, Robert. "A New Era under Gradimir Pankov." *Ballett International* 6 (March 1983): 36–39.

IRMA VIENOLA-LINDFORS

Dance Research and Publication

Neither social dance nor theatrical dance in Finland has historically enjoyed the prestige that would have encouraged scientific research. In the 1970s, however, there was a rapid growth of interest in dance stimulating the creation of new forms of dance education and heralding a turn for the better in dance research.

Folk Dance and Social Dance. The notation of Finnish folk dances began around the turn of the twentieth century. Ample material on late nineteenth-century folk dance exists, but surprisingly little research has utilized it. The musicologist Erkki Ala-Könni's 1956 doctoral thesis, "Die Polska-Tänze in Finnland," is still one of the few investigations in the field of folk dance.

Since the 1970s, certain social dance phenomena have caught the interest of Finnish sociologists. In 1980, Elina Haavio-Mannila and Raija Snicker published a case study on *päivätanssit*, the afternoon ballroom dancing in restaurants. Pekka Sulkunen and his colleagues also discussed dancing at restaurants in their study *Lähiöravintola* (1985). The Working People's Music Institute published *Taistojen tiellä soiteltiin* (1983) by Vesa Kurkela, a study of working people's dance and theatrical traditions, and *Tanhuten valistukseen* (1986), also by Kurkela, on the role of folklore in the political education of young people; both of Kurkela's books examine aspects of social and folk dance. Although sociologists have included some studies of social or folk dance in their work, they have done so only because dance tends to reflect social change.

Theatrical Dance. In addition to sociological and musicological studies of dance, there have also been studies in departments of pedagogy, physical education, comparative religion, folklore, drama, philosophy, and cultural studies. There are about thirty master's theses on dance, with subjects ranging from professional dancers' educational backgrounds to the problems of teaching dance. Fewer than ten studies deal with theatrical dance. Aino Sarje's 1994 doctoral thesis "Theoretical Study of Conceptions of Art Dance in the 1980's in Finland" was the first on theatrical dance at the University of Helsinki.

The dance department set up in 1983 at the Theater Academy may be able to encourage dance research. At this institution it is possible to get a Ph.D. in dance, and the thesis examination may have either an artistic or a scientific character.

The history of theatrical dance in Finland has yet to be written, but some areas have already received tentative study. As a byproduct of the history of circus in Finland, Sven Hirn wrote *Våra danspedagoger och dansnöjen* (1982), a book on dance teachers and dance activities in Finland from the late eighteenth century to 1914. Irma Vienola-Lindfors and Raoul af Hällström have written a descriptive history of the National Ballet, *Suomen Kansallisbaletti, 1922–1972* (1981). In 1987, Ritva Arvelo and Auli Räsänen published *Tanssitaiteen vuosikymmenet*, a colorful survey for the fiftieth anniversary of the Finnish Dancers' Union.

Very little on dance in general has been published in Finland. Some recent topics, however, tell of the growing interest and the need for basic knowledge. The State Arts Council published *Tanssien tulevaisuuteen* (1989), a study by Riitta Repo on the legitimation of Finnish dance and the creation of the dance education system. In 1992, the Finnish Society of Research in Sport and Physical Education published Aino Sarje's study *Tanssin henki*, on aesthetic and philosophical theories of dance. In 1993, the Dance Council of Finland published the first biographical dictionary of Finnish dancers, dance teachers, and choreographers.

The Theater Academy's series of publications includes the first introduction in Finnish to traditional Asian theatre and dance by Jukka Miettinen (1987); an anthology of writings by twentieth-century choreographers and dance critics, collected and translated by Tiina Suhonen (1991); and a handbook on Cuban dance by Sanna Kuusisto and Risto Vuorimies (1991). The Continuing Education Center of the Theater Academy published a 1993 report by Johanna Laakkonen that investigates the career transitions of professional dancers and the possibilities of retraining. A major venture of the library of the Theater Academy was a bibliography of Finnish theatre and dance for 1975 to 1991, compiled by Leena Rantamäki (1993).

Very little dance research by Finnish writers has been published abroad. One example is Jukka Miettinen's monograph *Classical Dance and Theatre in South-East Asia* (1992).

Since the early 1980s the Helsinki Theater Museum has made a persistent effort to increase its dance collections and has organized a permanent exhibition on the early years of Finnish theatrical dance. Public discussion of dance themes has been encouraged by the dance review *Tanssi*, founded in 1981.

TIINA SUHONEN